Managerial Accounting

2010 Edition

John J. Wild
University of Wisconsin at Madison

Ken W. Shaw
University of Missouri at Columbia

McGraw-Hill Irwin

Boston Burr Ridge, IL Dubuque, IA New York
San Francisco St. Louis Bangkok Bogotá Caracas Kuala Lumpur
Lisbon London Madrid Mexico City Milan Montreal New Delhi
Santiago Seoul Singapore Sydney Taipei Toronto

To my wife **Gail** and children, **Kimberly, Jonathan, Stephanie,** and **Trevor.**

To my wife **Linda** and children, **Erin, Emily,** and **Jacob.**

MANAGERIAL ACCOUNTING: 2010 EDITION
Published by McGraw-Hill/Irwin, a business unit of The McGraw-Hill Companies, Inc., 1221 Avenue of the Americas, New York, NY, 10020.

This book is printed on acid-free paper.

3 4 5 6 7 8 9 0 DOW/DOW 0

ISBN 978-0-07-337958-6
MHID 0-07-337958-1

Vice president and editor-in-chief: *Brent Gordon*
Editorial director: *Stewart Mattson*
Publisher: *Tim Vertovec*
Executive editor: *Steve Schuetz*
Senior developmental editor: *Christina A. Sanders*
Executive marketing manager: *Sankha Basu*
Managing editor: *Lori Koetters*
Full service project manager: *Sharon Monday, Aptara®, Inc.*
Lead production supervisor: *Carol A. Bielski*
Lead designer: *Matthew Baldwin*
Senior photo research coordinator: *Lori Kramer*
Photo researcher: *Sarah Evertson*
Senior media project manager: *Jennifer Lohn*
Cover and interior design: *Matthew Baldwin*
Cover image: © *Getty Images*
Typeface: *10.5/12 Times Roman*
Compositor: *Aptara®, Inc.*
Printer: *R. R. Donnelley*

Library of Congress Cataloging-in-Publication Data

Wild, John J.
Managerial accounting / John J. Wild, Ken W. Shaw.—2010 ed.
p. cm.
Includes index.
ISBN-13: 978-0-07-337958-6 (alk. paper)
ISBN-10: 0-07-337958-1 (alk. paper)
1. Managerial accounting. I. Shaw, Ken W. II. Title.
HF5657.4.W523 2010
658.15′11—dc22

2008047781

www.mhhe.com

Dear Colleagues/Friends,

As we roll out the new edition of *Managerial Accounting*, we thank each of you who provided suggestions to enrich this textbook. As teachers, we know how important it is to select the right book for our course. This new edition reflects the advice and wisdom of many dedicated reviewers, focus group participants, students, and instructors. Our book consistently rates number one in customer loyalty because of you. Together, we have created the most readable, concise, current, and accurate managerial accounting book available today.

We are thrilled to welcome Ken Shaw to the *Managerial Accounting* team with this edition. Ken's teaching and work experience, along with his enthusiasm and dedication to students, fit nicely with our continuing commitment to develop cutting–edge classroom materials for instructors and students.

Throughout the writing process, we steered this book in the manner you directed. This path of development enhanced this book's technology and content, and guided its clear and concise writing.

Reviewers, instructors, and students say this book's enhanced technology caters to different learning styles and helps students better understand accounting. *McGraw-Hill Connect Accounting* offers new features to improve student learning and to assist instructor grading. Our *iPod* content lets students study on the go, while our *Algorithmic Test Bank* provides an infinite variety of exam problems. You and your students will find all these tools easy to apply.

We owe the success of this book to our colleagues who graciously took time to help us focus on the changing needs of today's instructors and students. We feel fortunate to have witnessed our profession's extraordinary devotion to teaching. Your feedback and suggestions are reflected in everything we write. Please accept our heartfelt thanks for your dedication in helping today's students understand and appreciate accounting.

With kindest regards,

John J. Wild Ken W. Shaw

Driving Student and Instructor Success

Managerial Accounting 2e

Help your students **steer towards success** by giving them the tools they need to accelerate in today's managerial accounting course.

This book helps **drive student success** by providing leading accounting content that engages students–with innovative technology.

One of the greatest challenges students confront in a managerial accounting course is seeing the relevance of materials. This book tackles this issue head on with **engaging content** and a **motivating style**. Students are motivated with reading materials that are **clear and relevant**. This book leads the pack in engaging students. Its chapter-opening vignettes showcase dynamic, successful, entrepreneurial individuals and companies guaranteed to **interest and excite readers**. This edition's featured companies (Best Buy, Circuit City, RadioShack, and Apple) engage students with their operations which are great vehicles for learning managerial accounting.

This book also delivers **innovative technology** to help drive student success. **McGraw-Hill Connect Accounting** provides students with instant grading feedback for assignments that are completed online. **Connect Plus** integrates an online version of the textbook with our Connect homework management system. An **algorithmic test bank** in Connect offers infinite variations of numerical test bank questions. This book also offers accounting students portable **iPod-ready content**.

We're confident you'll agree that Wild and Shaw's ***Managerial Accounting* (*MA*) will put your students in the driver's seat to success**.

John J. Wild is a distinguished professor of accounting at the University of Wisconsin at Madison. He previously held appointments at Michigan State University and the University of Manchester in England. He received his BBA, MS, and PhD from the University of Wisconsin.

Professor Wild teaches accounting courses at both the undergraduate and graduate levels. He has received numerous teaching honors, including the Mabel W. Chipman Excellence-in-Teaching Award, the departmental Excellence-in-Teaching Award, and the Teaching Excellence Award from the 2003 and 2005 business graduates at the University of Wisconsin. He also received the Beta Alpha Psi and Roland F. Salmonson Excellence-in-Teaching Award from Michigan State University. Professor Wild has received several research honors and is a past KPMG Peat Marwick National Fellow and is a recipient of fellowships from the American Accounting Association and the Ernst and Young Foundation.

Professor Wild is an active member of the American Accounting Association and its sections. He has served on several committees of these organizations, including the Outstanding Accounting Educator Award, Wildman Award, National Program Advisory, Publications, and Research Committees. Professor Wild is author of *Financial Accounting, Fundamental Accounting Principles, Financial and Managerial Accounting,* and *College Accounting*, each published by McGraw-Hill/Irwin. His research articles on accounting and analysis appear in The Accounting Review, Journal of Accounting Research, Journal of Accounting and Economics, Contemporary Accounting Research, Journal of Accounting, Auditing and Finance, Journal of Accounting and Public Policy, and other journals. He is past associate editor of Contemporary Accounting Research and has served on several editorial boards including The Accounting Review.

Professor Wild, his wife, and four children enjoy travel, music, sports, and community activities.

Ken W. Shaw is an associate professor of accounting and the CBIZ/MHM Scholar at the University of Missouri. He previously was on the faculty at the University of Maryland at College Park. He received an accounting degree from Bradley University and an MBA and PhD from the University of Wisconsin. He is a Certified Public Accountant with work experience in public accounting.

Professor Shaw teaches financial accounting at the undergraduate and graduate levels. He received the Williams Keepers LLC Teaching Excellence award in 2007, was voted the "Most Influential Professor" by the 2005 and 2006 School of Accountancy graduating classes, and is a two-time recipient of the O'Brien Excellence in Teaching Award. He is the advisor to his School's chapter of Beta Alpha Psi, a national accounting fraternity.

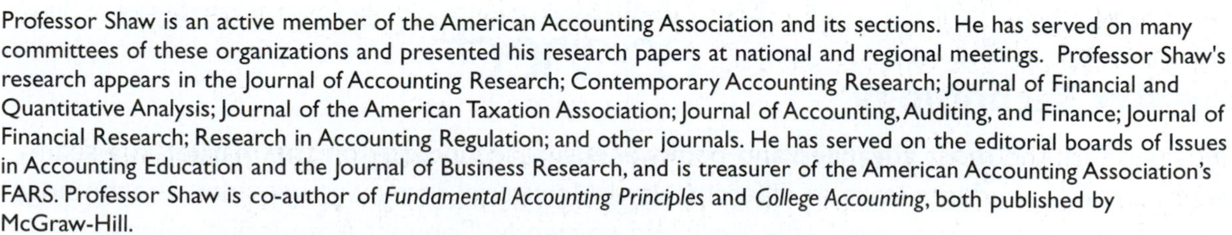

Professor Shaw is an active member of the American Accounting Association and its sections. He has served on many committees of these organizations and presented his research papers at national and regional meetings. Professor Shaw's research appears in the Journal of Accounting Research; Contemporary Accounting Research; Journal of Financial and Quantitative Analysis; Journal of the American Taxation Association; Journal of Accounting, Auditing, and Finance; Journal of Financial Research; Research in Accounting Regulation; and other journals. He has served on the editorial boards of Issues in Accounting Education and the Journal of Business Research, and is treasurer of the American Accounting Association's FARS. Professor Shaw is co-author of *Fundamental Accounting Principles* and *College Accounting*, both published by McGraw-Hill.

In his leisure time, Professor Shaw enjoys tennis, cycling, music, and coaching his children's sports teams.

Engaging Content

Managerial Accounting content continues to set the standard. This book describes key managerial accounting concepts clearly and concisely. For example, Chapter 1 sets the stage for student success by explaining cost classifications and the reporting of production activities. Also, take a look at Chapter 3, which presents a clear 4-step method for process costing involving analysis of (1) physical flow, (2) equivalent units, (3) cost per equivalent unit, and (4) cost assignment and reconciliation. And finally, overhead variances are shown in Chapter 8 with ample visual aids–see samples below. *Managerial Accounting* also motivates students with engaging chapter openers. Students identify with them and can even picture themselves as future entrepreneurs.

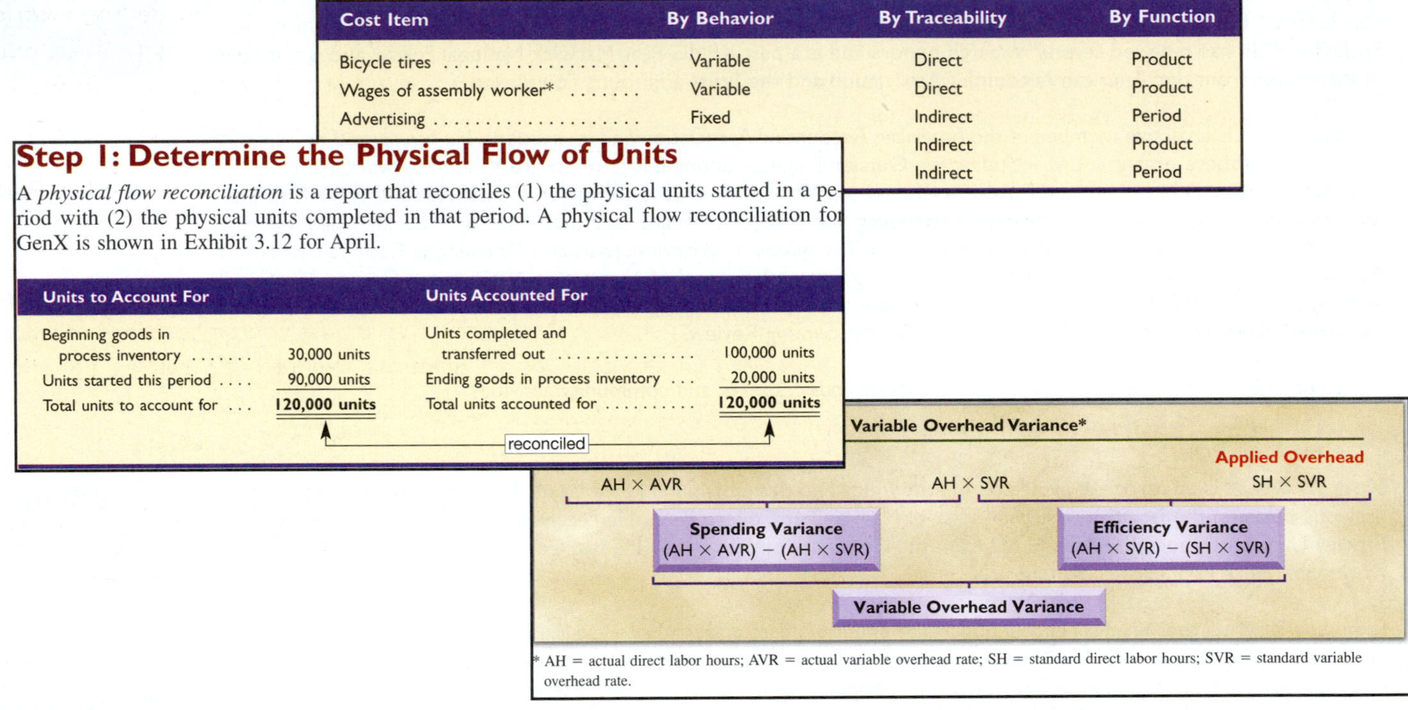

Cost Item	By Behavior	By Traceability	By Function
Bicycle tires	Variable	Direct	Product
Wages of assembly worker*	Variable	Direct	Product
Advertising	Fixed	Indirect	Period
		Indirect	Product
		Indirect	Period

Step 1: Determine the Physical Flow of Units

A *physical flow reconciliation* is a report that reconciles (1) the physical units started in a period with (2) the physical units completed in that period. A physical flow reconciliation for GenX is shown in Exhibit 3.12 for April.

Units to Account For		Units Accounted For	
Beginning goods in process inventory	30,000 units	Units completed and transferred out	100,000 units
Units started this period	90,000 units	Ending goods in process inventory	20,000 units
Total units to account for	**120,000 units**	Total units accounted for	**120,000 units**

* AH = actual direct labor hours; AVR = actual variable overhead rate; SH = standard direct labor hours; SVR = standard variable overhead rate.

State-of-the-Art Technology

Managerial Accounting offers the most advanced and comprehensive technology on the market in a seamless, easy-to-use platform. As students learn in different ways, *Managerial Accounting* provides a technology smorgasbord that helps students learn more effectively and efficiently. Connect Accounting, eBook options, and iPod content are some of the options. Connect Plus Accounting takes learning to another level by integrating an online version of the book with all the power of Connect Accounting. Technology offerings follow:

- Connect Accounting
- Connect Plus Accounting
- iPod content
- Algorithmic Test Bank
- Online Learning Center
- ALEKS for the Accounting Cycle

What Can McGraw-Hill Technology Offer You?

Whether you are just getting started with technology in your course, or you are ready to embrace the latest advances in electronic content delivery and course management, McGraw-Hill/Irwin has the technology you need, and provides training and support that will help you every step of the way.

Our most popular technologies, Connect Accounting and Connect Plus Accounting, are optional online homework management systems that allow you to assign problems and exercises from the text for your students to work out in an online format. Student results are automatically graded, and the students receive instant feedback on their work. Connect Plus adds an online version of the book.

Students can also use the Online Learning Center with this book to enhance their knowledge. Plus we offer iPod content for students who want to study on the go.

For instructors, we provide all of the crucial instructor supplements on one easy to use Instructor CD-ROM; we can help build a custom class Website for your course using PageOut; we can deliver an online course cartridge for you to use in Blackboard, WebCT, or eCollege; and we have a technical support team that will provide training and support for our key technology products.

How Can Students Study on the Go Using Their iPod?

iPod Content

Harness the power of one of the most popular technology tools students use today–the Apple iPod. Our innovative approach allows students to download audio and video presentations right into their iPod and take learning materials with them wherever they go. Students just need to visit the Online Learning Center at **www.mhhe.com/wildMA2e** to download our iPod content. For each chapter of the book they will be able to download audio narrated lecture presentations and videos for use on various versions of iPods. iPod Touch users can even access self-quizzes.

It makes review and study time as easy as putting in headphones.

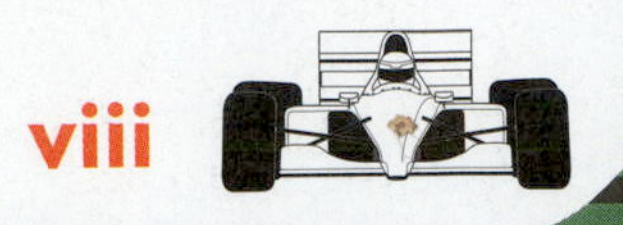

How Can My Students Use the Web to Complete Their Homework?

McGraw-Hill ***Connect Accounting*** is a web-based assignment and assessment platform that gives students the means to better connect with their coursework, with their instructors, and with the important concepts that they will need to know for success now and in the future.

With *Connect Accounting* instructors can deliver assignments, quizzes, and tests online. Nearly all the questions from the book are presented in an auto-gradable format and tied to the book's learning objectives. Instructors can edit existing questions and author entirely new problems. Track individual student performance—by question, assignment, or in relation to the class overall—with detailed grade reports. Integrate grade reports easily with Learning Management Systems (LMS) such as WebCT and Blackboard.

By choosing *Connect Accounting* instructors are providing their students with a powerful tool for improving academic performance and truly mastering course material. *Connect Accounting* allows students to practice important skills at their own pace and on their own schedule. Importantly, students' assessment results and instructors' feedback are all saved online—so students can continually review their progress and plot their course to success.

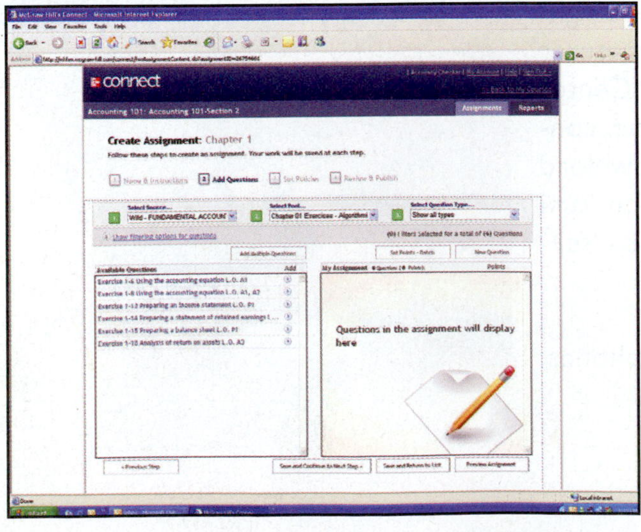

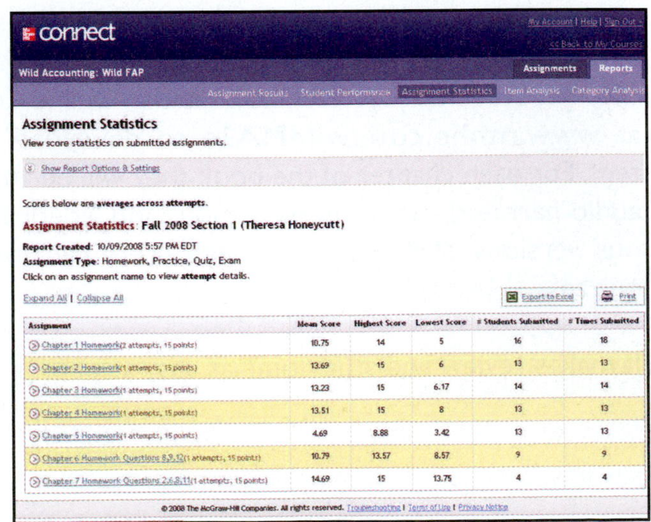

Assignment Statistics

View score statistics on submitted assignments.

Show Report Options & Settings

Scores below are **averages across attempts**.

Assignment Statistics: Fall 2008 Section 1 (Theresa Honeycutt)

Report Created: 10/09/2008 5:57 PM EDT

Assignment Type: Homework, Practice, Quiz, Exam

Click on an assignment name to view **attempt** details.

Expand All | Collapse All — Export to Excel — Print

Assignment	Mean Score	Highest Score	Lowest Score	# Students Submitted	# Times Submitted
Chapter 1 Homework (2 attempts, 15 points)	10.75	14	5	16	18
Chapter 2 Homework (1 attempts, 15 points)	13.69	15	6	13	13
Chapter 3 Homework (1 attempts, 15 points)	13.23	15	6.17	14	14
Chapter 4 Homework (1 attempts, 15 points)	13.51	15	8	13	13
Chapter 5 Homework (1 attempts, 15 points)	4.69	8.88	3.42	13	13
Chapter 6 Homework Questions 8,9,12 (1 attempts, 15 points)	10.79	13.57	8.57	9	9
Chapter 7 Homework Questions 2,6,8,11 (1 attempts, 15 points)	14.69	15	13.75	4	4

Some instructors may also choose ***Connect Plus Accounting*** for their students. Like *Connect Accounting*, *Connect Plus Accounting* provides students with online assignments and assessments, plus 24/7 online access to an eBook—an online edition of the text—to aid them in successfully completing their work, wherever and whenever they choose.

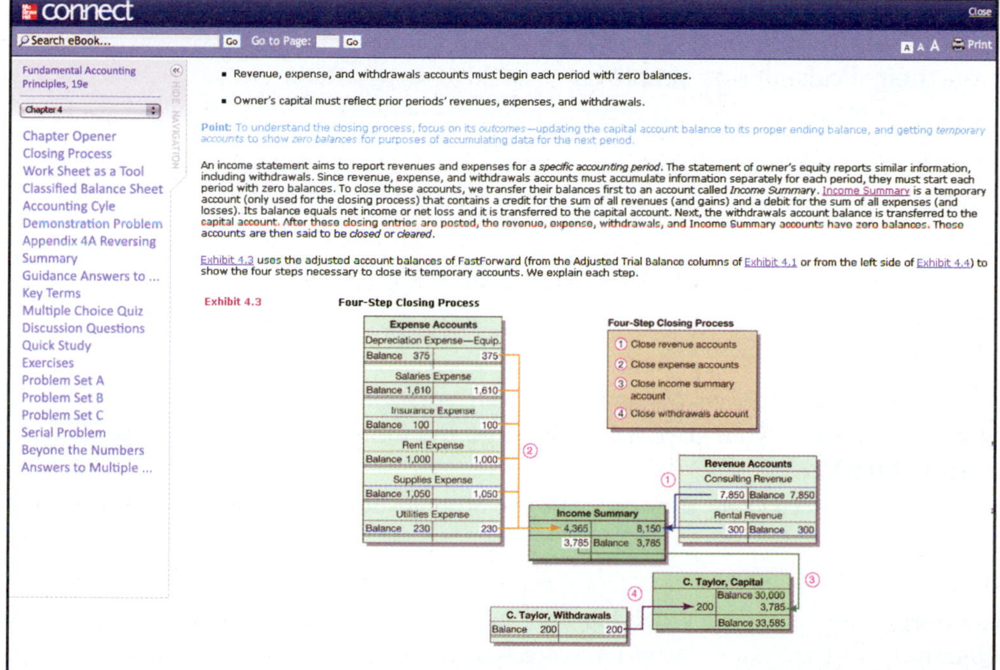

By simply clicking on the eBook button while in Connect, Connect Plus users will be linked directly to the relevant textbook materials without additional login requirements. This feature makes it quick and convenient to study and complete assignments online.

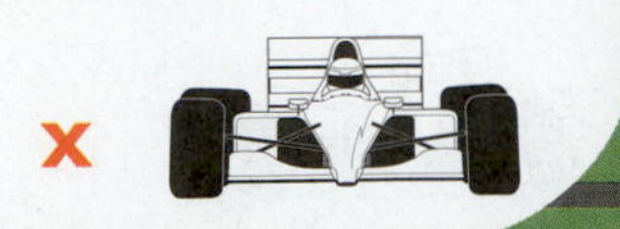

Use EZ Test Online with Apple iPod® iQuiz to help students succeed.

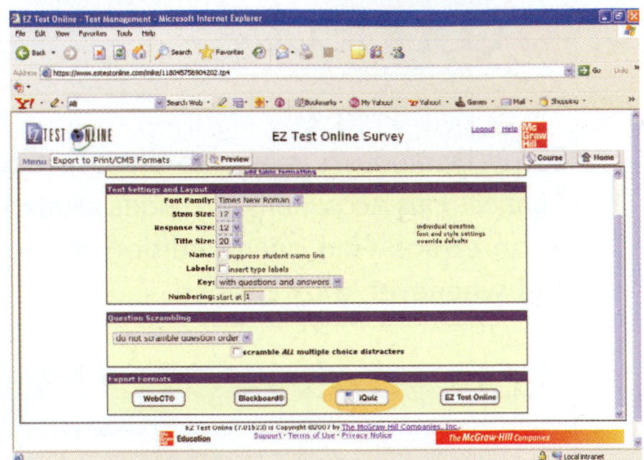

Using our EZ Test Online you can make test and quiz content available for a student's Apple iPod®.

Students must purchase the iQuiz game application from Apple for 99¢ to use the iQuiz content. It works on the iPod fifth generation iPods and better.

Instructors only need EZ Test Online to produce iQuiz-ready content. Instructors take their existing tests and quizzes and export them to a file that can then be made available to the student to take as a self-quiz on their iPods. It's as simple as that.

How Can Book-Related Web Resources Enhance My Course?

Online Learning Center (OLC)

We offer an Online Learning Center (OLC) that follows *Managerial Accounting* chapter by chapter.
It doesn't require any building or maintenance on your part. It's ready to go the moment you and your students type in the URL: **www.mhhe.com/wildMA2e**.
As students study and learn from *Managerial Accounting*, they can visit the Student Edition of the OLC Website to work with a multitude of helpful tools:

- Chapter Learning Objectives
- Interactive Chapter Quizzes
- PowerPoint® Presentations
- Narrated PowerPoint® Presentations
- Video Library
- Excel Template Assignments
- iPod Content

A secured Instructor Edition stores essential course materials to save you prep time before class. Everything you need to run a lively classroom and an efficient course is included. All resources available to students, plus . . .

- Instructor's Manual
- Solutions Manual
- Solutions to Excel Template Assignments
- Test Bank and Solutions

The OLC Website also serves as a doorway to other technology solutions, like course management systems.

Rick Barnhart, Grand Rapids Community College
"My overall impression (of the Website) is very favorable.... It is very user friendly and easy to navigate. The addition of the iPod content is great, because so many students have an MP3 player."

Save money. Go green. McGraw-Hill eBooks.

Green...it's on everybody's mind these days. It's not only about saving trees, it's also about saving money. At 55% of the bookstore price, McGraw-Hill eBooks are an eco-friendly and cost-saving alternative to the traditional printed textbook. So, do some good for the environment...and do some good for your wallet.

CourseSmart

CourseSmart is a new way to find and buy eTextbooks. CourseSmart has the largest selection of eTextbooks available anywhere, offering thousands of the most commonly adopted textbooks from a wide variety of higher education publishers. CourseSmart eTextbooks are available in one standard online reader with full text search, notes, and highlighting, and email tools for sharing between classmates. Visit **www.CourseSmart.com** for more information on ordering.

McGraw-Hill Connect Plus

If you use Connect in your course, your students can purchase McGraw-Hill Connect Plus for *MA* 2e. Connect Plus Accounting gives students direct access to an online edition of the book while working assignments within Connect Accounting. If you get stuck working a problem, simply click the "Hint" link and jump directly to relevant content in the online edition of the book.

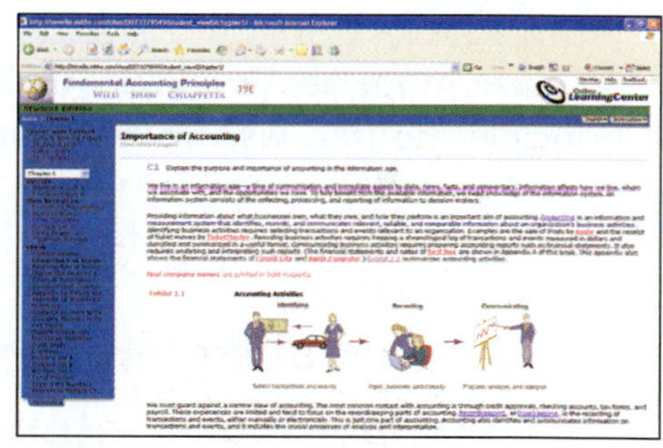

Visit the Online Learning Center at www.mhhe.com/wildMA2e to purchase McGraw-Hill's Connect Plus.

McGraw-Hill CARES

At McGraw-Hill, we understand that getting the most from new technology can be challenging. That's why our services don't stop after you purchase our book. You can e-mail our Product Specialists 24 hours a day, get product training online, or search our knowledge bank of Frequently Asked Questions on our support Website.

McGraw-Hill Customer Care Contact Information

For all Customer Support call **(800) 331-5094**
Email **be_support@mcgraw-hill.com**
Or visit **www.mhhe.com/support**
One of our Technical Support Analysts will assist you in a timely fashion.

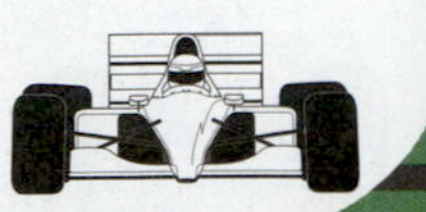

How Can McGraw-Hill Help Me Teach My Course Online?

ALEKS®

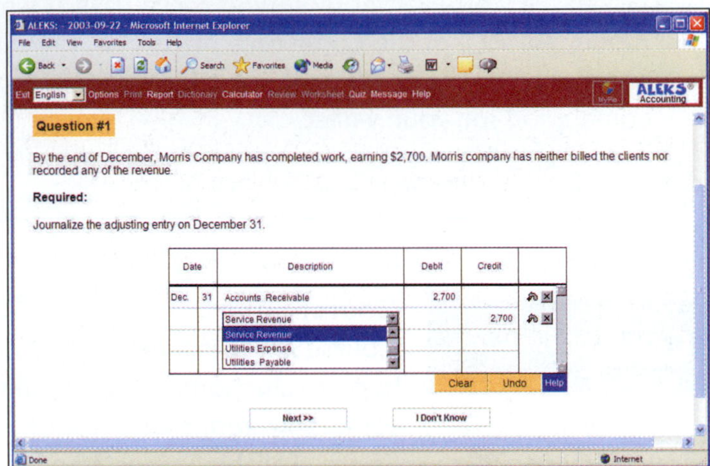

ALEKS® for the Accounting Cycle and ALEKS® for Financial Accounting

Available from McGraw-Hill over the World Wide Web, ALEKS (Assessment and LEarning in Knowledge Spaces) provides precise assessment and individualized instruction in the fundamental skills your students need to succeed in accounting.

ALEKS motivates your students because ALEKS can tell what a student knows, doesn't know, and is most ready to learn next. ALEKS does this using the ALEKS Assessment and Knowledge Space Theory as an artificial intelligence engine to exactly identify a student's knowledge of accounting. When students focus on precisely what they are ready to learn, they build the confidence and learning momentum that fuel success.

To learn more about adding ALEKS to your principles course, visit www.business.aleks.com.

Janice Stoudemire, Midlands Technical College
"The supplemental material that this accounting text provides is impressive: Homework Manager, the extensive online learning center, general ledger application software, as well as ALEKS."

How Can I Make My Classroom Discussions More Interactive?

CPS Classroom Performance System

This is a revolutionary system that brings ultimate interactivity to the classroom. CPS is a wireless response system that gives you immediate feedback from every student in the class. CPS units include easy-to-use software for creating and delivering questions and assessments to your class. With CPS you can ask subjective and objective questions. Then every student simply responds with their individual, wireless response pad, providing instant results. CPS is the perfect tool for engaging students while gathering important assessment data.

Liz Ott, Casper College
"I originally adopted the book because of the tools that accompanied it: Homework Manager, ALEKS, CPS."

Online Course Management

No matter what online course management system you use (WebCT, BlackBoard, or eCollege), we have a course content ePack available for *Managerial Accounting* 2e. Our new ePacks are specifically designed to make it easy for students to navigate and access content online. They are easier than ever to install on the latest version of the course management system.

Don't forget that you can count on the highest level of service from McGraw-Hill. Our online course management specialists are ready to assist you with your online course needs. They provide training and will answer any questions you have throughout the life of your adoption. So try our new ePack for *Managerial Accounting* 2e and make online course content delivery easy and fun.

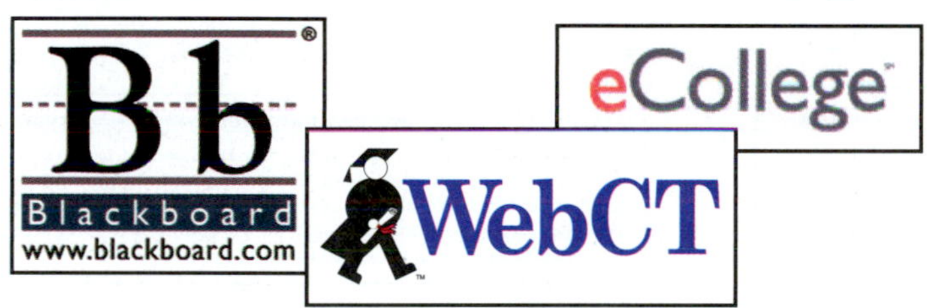

PageOut: McGraw-Hill's Course Management System

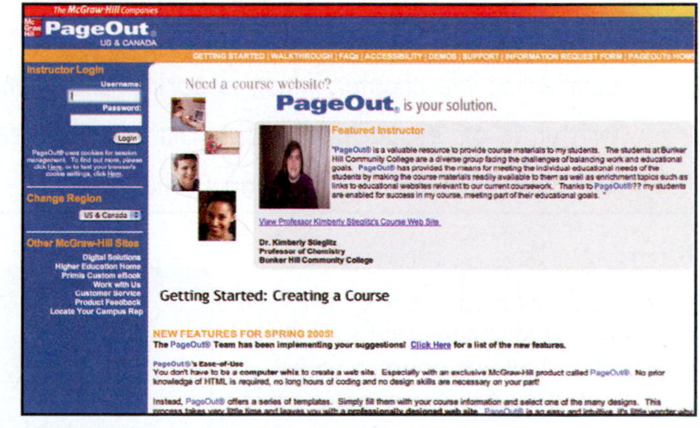

PageOut is the easiest way to create a Website for your course. There is no need for HTML coding, graphic design, or a thick how-to book. Just fill in a series of boxes with simple English and click on one of our professional designs. In no time, your course is online with a Website that contains your syllabus!

Should you need assistance in preparing your Website, we can help. Our team of product specialists is ready to take your course materials and build a custom Website to your specifications. You simply need to call a McGraw-Hill PageOut specialist to start the process. To learn more, please visit www.pageout.net and see "PageOut & Service" below.

Best of all, PageOut is free when you adopt *Managerial Accounting*!

PageOut Service

Our team of product specialists is happy to help you design your own course Website. Call 1-800-634-3963, press 0, and ask to speak with a PageOut specialist. You will be asked to send in your course materials and then participate in a brief telephone consultation. Once we have your information, we build your Website for you.

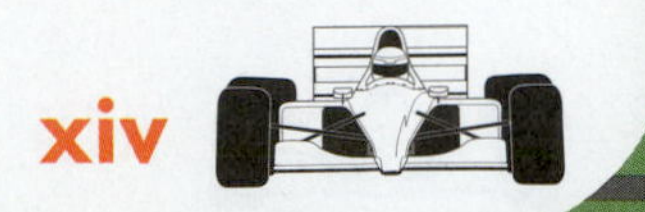

Decision Center

Whether we prepare, analyze, or apply accounting information, one skill remains essential: decision-making. To help develop good decision-making habits and to illustrate the relevance of accounting, *MA* 2e uses a unique pedagogical framework called the Decision Center. This framework is comprised of a variety of approaches and subject areas, giving students insight into every aspect of managerial decision-making. Answers to Decision Maker and Ethics boxes are at the end of each chapter.

Decision Insight

Eco-CVP Ford Escape, Toyota Prius, and Honda Insight are hybrids. Many promise to save owners $1,000 or more a year in fuel costs relative to comparables, and they generate fewer greenhouse gases. Are these models economically feasible? Analysts estimate that Ford can break even with its Escape when a $3,000 premium is paid over comparable gas-based models.

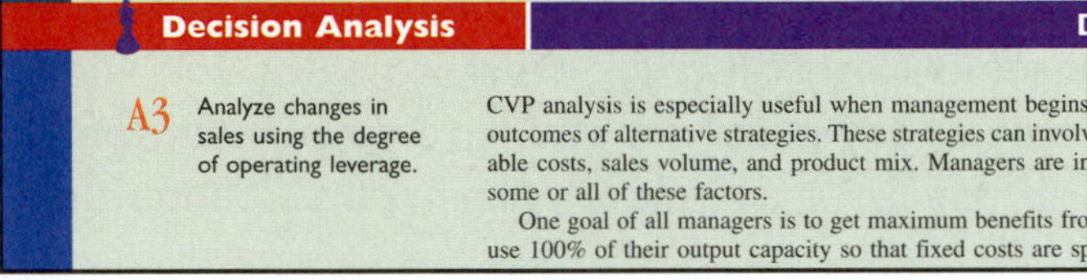

Decision Analysis

A3 Analyze changes in sales using the degree of operating leverage.

CVP analysis is especially useful when management begins outcomes of alternative strategies. These strategies can invol able costs, sales volume, and product mix. Managers are i some or all of these factors.

One goal of all managers is to get maximum benefits fro use 100% of their output capacity so that fixed costs are sp

Decision Ethics

Supervisor Your team is conducting a cost-volume-profit analysis for a new product. Different sales projections have different incomes. One member suggests picking numbers yielding favorable income because any estimate is "as good as any other." Another member points to a scatter diagram of 20 months' production on a comparable product and suggests dropping unfavorable data points for cost estimation. What do you do? [Answer—p. 187]

Decision Maker

Sales Manager You are evaluating orders from two customers but can accept only one of the orders because of your company's limited capacity. The first order is for 100 units of a product with a contribution margin ratio of 60% and a selling price of $1,000. The second order is for 500 units of a product with a contribution margin ratio of 20% and a selling price of $800. The incremental fixed costs are the same for both orders. Which order do you accept? [Answer—p. 187]

"This text has the best introductions of any text that I have reviewed or used. Some texts simply summarize the chapter, which is boring to students. Research indicates that material needs to be written in an 'engaging manner.' That's what these vignettes do—they get the students interested."
Clarice McCoy, Brookhaven College

CAP Model

The Conceptual/Analytical/Procedural (CAP) Model allows courses to be specially designed to meet your teaching needs or those of a diverse faculty. This model identifies learning objectives, textual materials, assignments, and test items by C, A, or P, allowing different instructors to teach from the same materials, yet easily customize their courses toward a conceptual, analytical, or procedural approach (or a combination thereof) based on personal preferences.

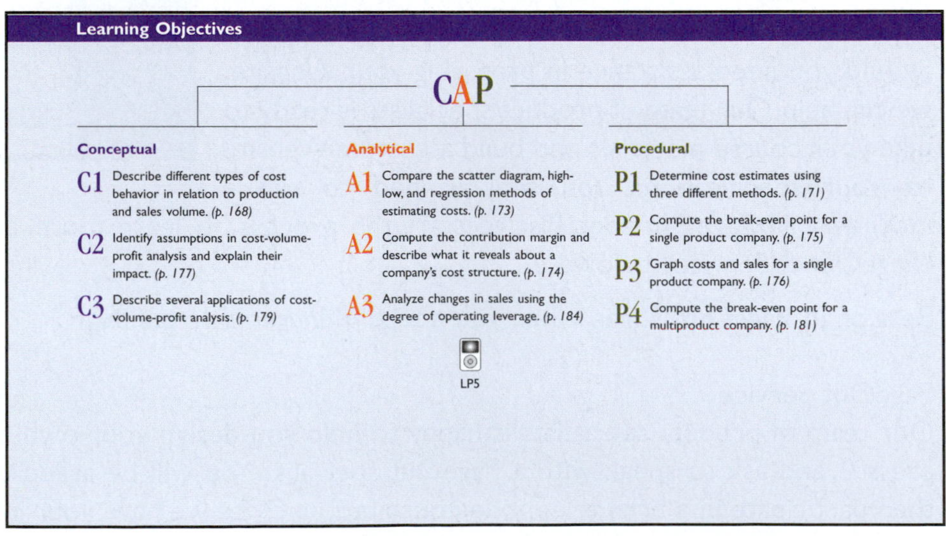

Learning Objectives

CAP

Conceptual

C1 Describe different types of cost behavior in relation to production and sales volume. *(p. 168)*

C2 Identify assumptions in cost-volume-profit analysis and explain their impact. *(p. 177)*

C3 Describe several applications of cost-volume-profit analysis. *(p. 179)*

Analytical

A1 Compare the scatter diagram, high-low, and regression methods of estimating costs. *(p. 173)*

A2 Compute the contribution margin and describe what it reveals about a company's cost structure. *(p. 174)*

A3 Analyze changes in sales using the degree of operating leverage. *(p. 184)*

LP5

Procedural

P1 Determine cost estimates using three different methods. *(p. 171)*

P2 Compute the break-even point for a single product company. *(p. 175)*

P3 Graph costs and sales for a single product company. *(p. 176)*

P4 Compute the break-even point for a multiproduct company. *(p. 181)*

Chapter Preview with Flow Chart

This feature provides a handy textual/visual guide at the start of every chapter. Students can now begin their reading with a clear understanding of what they will learn and when, allowing them to stay more focused and organized along the way.

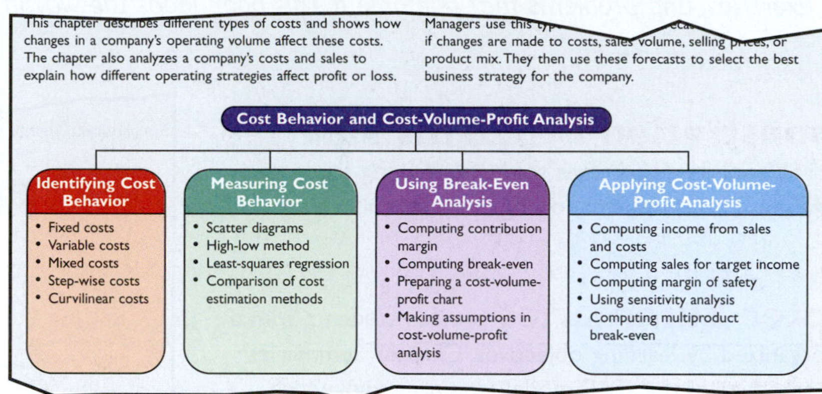

This chapter describes different types of costs and shows how changes in a company's operating volume affect these costs. The chapter also analyzes a company's costs and sales to explain how different operating strategies affect profit or loss.
if changes are made to costs, sales volume, selling prices, or product mix. They then use these forecasts to select the best business strategy for the company.
Cost Behavior and Cost-Volume-Profit Analysis
Identifying Cost Behavior
• Fixed costs
• Variable costs
• Mixed costs
• Step-wise costs
• Curvilinear costs
Measuring Cost Behavior
• Scatter diagrams
• High-low method
• Least-squares regression
• Comparison of cost estimation methods
Using Break-Even Analysis
• Computing contribution margin
• Computing break-even
• Preparing a cost-volume-profit chart
• Making assumptions in cost-volume-profit analysis
Applying Cost-Volume-Profit Analysis
• Computing income from sales and costs
• Computing sales for target income
• Computing margin of safety
• Using sensitivity analysis
• Computing multiproduct break-even

Quick Check

These short question/answer features reinforce the material immediately preceding them. They allow the reader to pause and reflect on the topics described, then receive immediate feedback before going on to new topics. Answers are provided at the end of each chapter.

Quick Check Answers—p. 188

4. Which of the following methods is likely to yield the most precise estimated line of cost behavior? (*a*) High-low, (*b*) least-squares regression, or (*c*) scatter diagram.
5. What is the primary weakness of the high-low method?
6. Using conventional CVP analysis, a mixed cost should be (*a*) disregarded, (*b*) treated as a fixed cost, or (*c*) separated into fixed and variable components.

Marginal Student Annotations

These annotations provide students with additional hints, tips, and examples to help them more fully understand the concepts and retain what they have learned. The annotations also include notes on global implications of accounting and further examples.

or $80,000 of monthly sales. units), we prepare a simpli- 0 revenue from sales of 800

Point: Even if a company operates at a level in excess of its break-even point, management may decide to stop operating because it is not earning a reasonable return on investment.

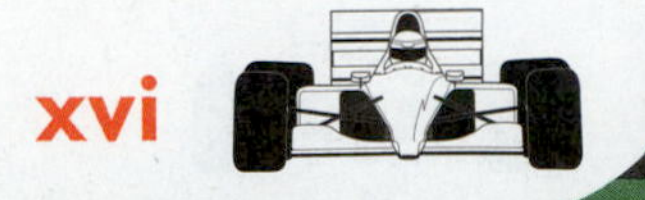

How are chapter concepts

Once a student has finished reading the chapter, how well he or she retains the material can depend greatly on the questions, exercises, and problems that reinforce it. This book leads the way in comprehensive, accurate assignments.

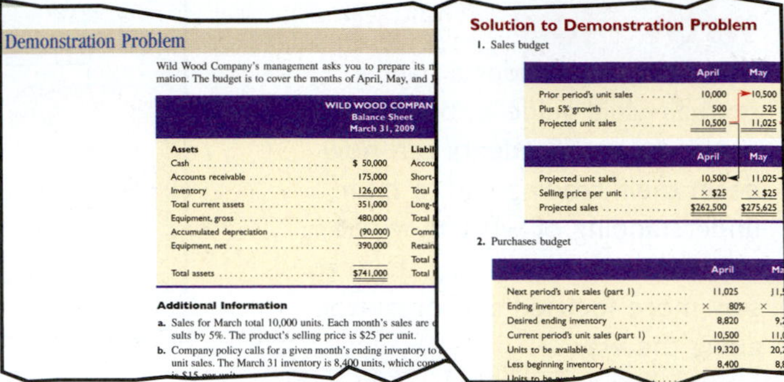

Demonstration Problem

Wild Wood Company's management asks you to prepare its m... mation. The budget is to cover the months of April, May, and J...

WILD WOOD COMPAN...
Balance Sheet
March 31, 2009

Assets	
Cash	$ 50,000
Accounts receivable	175,000
Inventory	126,000
Total current assets	351,000
Equipment, gross	480,000
Accumulated depreciation	(90,000)
Equipment, net	390,000
Total assets	$741,000

Additional Information

a. Sales for March total 10,000 units. Each month's sales are e... sults by 5%. The product's selling price is $25 per unit.

b. Company policy calls for a given month's ending inventory to... unit sales. The March 31 inventory is 8,400 units, which co...

Solution to Demonstration Problem

1. Sales budget

	April	May
Prior period's unit sales	10,000	10,500
Plus 5% growth	500	525
Projected unit sales	10,500	11,025

	April	May
Projected unit sales	10,500	11,025
Selling price per unit	× $25	× $25
Projected sales	$262,500	$275,625

2. Purchases budget

	April	Ma...
Next period's unit sales (part 1)	11,025	11,...
Ending inventory percent	× 80%	× ...
Desired ending inventory	8,820	9,...
Current period's unit sales (part 1)	10,500	11,...
Units to be available	19,320	20,...
Less beginning inventory	8,400	8,...

Demonstration Problems

Demonstration Problems present both a problem and a complete solution, allowing students to review the entire problem-solving process and achieve success.

Chapter Summaries

Chapter Summaries provide students with a review organized by learning objectives. Chapter Summaries are a component of the CAP model (see page xiv), which recaps each conceptual, analytical, and procedural objective.

Key Terms

Key Terms are bolded in the text and repeated at the end of the chapter with page numbers indicating their location. The book also includes a complete Glossary of Key Terms.

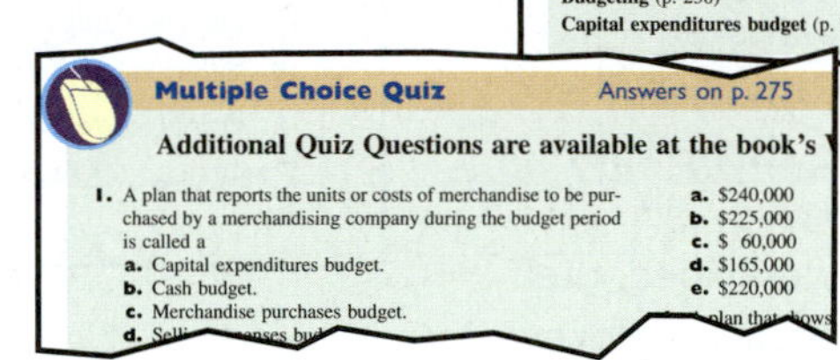

Key Terms

Key Terms are available at the book's Website for learning and testing in an onl...

Activity-based budgeting (ABB) (p. 251)
Budget (p. 238)
Budgeted balance sheet (p. 250)
Budgeted income statement (p. 250)
Budgeting (p. 238)
Capital expenditures budget (p. 247)
Cash budget (p. 248)
Continuous budgeting (p. 240)
General and administrative expense budget (p. 246)
Manufacturing budget (p. 257)
Master budget (p. 242)

Multiple Choice Questions

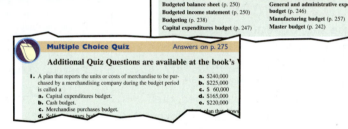

Multiple Choice Questions Multiple Choice Questions quickly test chapter knowledge before a student moves on to complete Quick Studies, Exercises, and Problems.

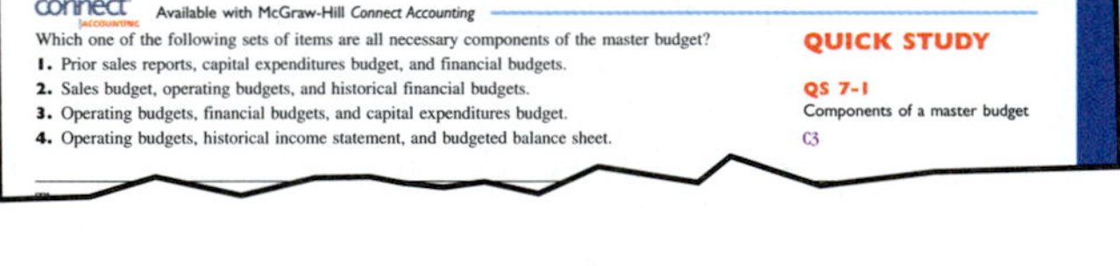

Multiple Choice Quiz — Answers on p. 275

Additional Quiz Questions are available at the book's W...

1. A plan that reports the units or costs of merchandise to be purchased by a merchandising company during the budget period is called a
   a. Capital expenditures budget.
   b. Cash budget.
   c. Merchandise purchases budget.

a. $240,000
b. $225,000
c. $ 60,000
d. $165,000
e. $220,000

Quick Study

Quick Study assignments are short exercises that often focus on one learning objective. All are included in Connect. There are usually 8-10 Quick Study assignments per chapter.

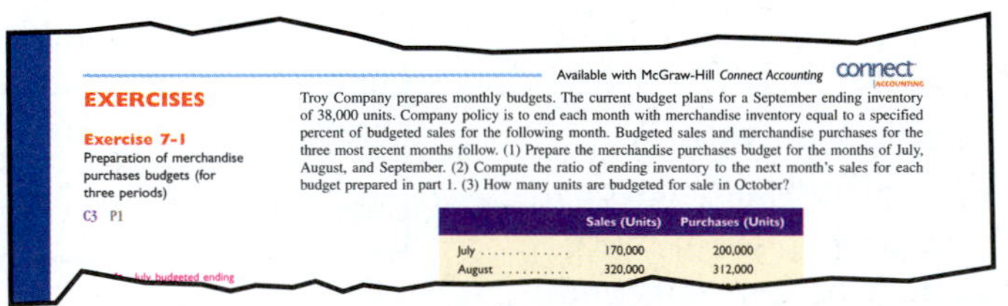

connect — Available with McGraw-Hill Connect Accounting

Which one of the following sets of items are all necessary components of the master budget?

1. Prior sales reports, capital expenditures budget, and financial budgets.
2. Sales budget, operating budgets, and historical financial budgets.
3. Operating budgets, financial budgets, and capital expenditures budget.
4. Operating budgets, historical income statement, and budgeted balance sheet.

QUICK STUDY

QS 7-1
Components of a master budget
C3

Exercises

Exercises are one of this book's many strengths and a competitive advantage. There are about 10-15 per chapter and all are included in Connect.

EXERCISES

Exercise 7-1
Preparation of merchandise purchases budgets (for three periods)
C3 P1

Available with McGraw-Hill Connect Accounting

Troy Company prepares monthly budgets. The current budget plans for a September ending inventory of 38,000 units. Company policy is to end each month with merchandise inventory equal to a specified percent of budgeted sales for the following month. Budgeted sales and merchandise purchases for the three most recent months follow. (1) Prepare the merchandise purchases budget for the months of July, August, and September. (2) Compute the ratio of ending inventory to the next month's sales for each budget prepared in part 1. (3) How many units are budgeted for sale in October?

	Sales (Units)	Purchases (Units)
July	170,000	200,000
August	320,000	312,000

Problem Sets A & B

Problem Sets A & B are proven problems that can be assigned as homework. All problems are coded according to the CAP model (see page xiv), and Set A is included in Connect.

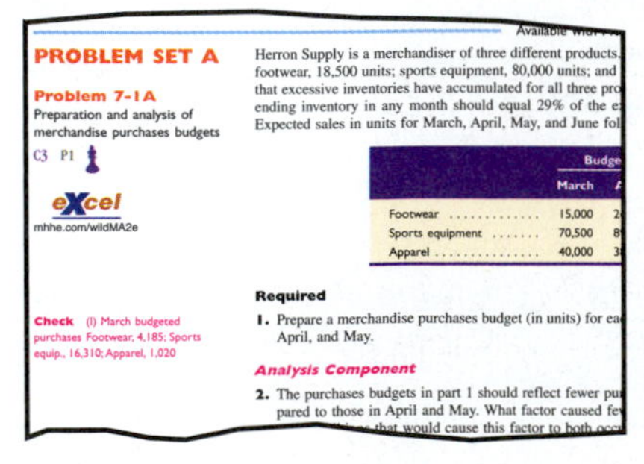

PROBLEM SET A

Problem 7-1A
Preparation and analysis of merchandise purchases budgets
C3 P1

eXcel
mhhe.com/wildMA2e

Herron Supply is a merchandiser of three different products... footwear, 18,500 units; sports equipment, 80,000 units; and... that excessive inventories have accumulated for all three pro... ending inventory in any month should equal 29% of the e... Expected sales in units for March, April, May, and June fol...

	March
Footwear	15,000
Sports equipment	70,500
Apparel	40,000

Required

1. Prepare a merchandise purchases budget (in units) for ea... April, and May.

Analysis Component

2. The purchases budgets in part 1 should reflect fewer pu... pared to those in April and May. What factor caused fe...

Check (1) March budgeted purchases Footwear, 4,185; Sports equip., 16,310; Apparel, 1,020

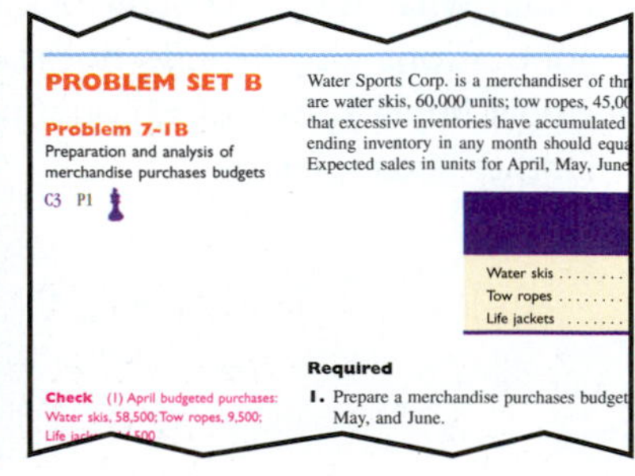

PROBLEM SET B

Problem 7-1B
Preparation and analysis of merchandise purchases budgets
C3 P1

Water Sports Corp. is a merchandiser of th... are water skis, 60,000 units; tow ropes, 45,0... that excessive inventories have accumulated... ending inventory in any month should equ... Expected sales in units for April, May, June...

Water skis
Tow ropes
Life jackets

Required

1. Prepare a merchandise purchases budget... May, and June.

Check (1) April budgeted purchases: Water skis, 58,500; Tow ropes, 9,500;

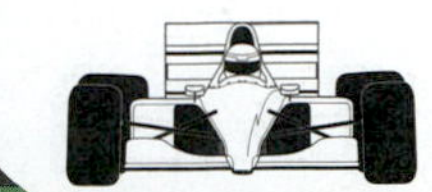

Beyond the Numbers exercises ask students to use accounting figures and understand their meaning. Students also learn how accounting applies to a variety of business situations. These creative and fun exercises are all new or updated, and are divided into sections:

- Reporting in Action
- Comparative Analysis
- Ethics Challenge
- Communicating in Practice
- Taking It To The Net
- Teamwork in Action
- Hitting the Road
- Entrepreneurial Decision
- Global Decision

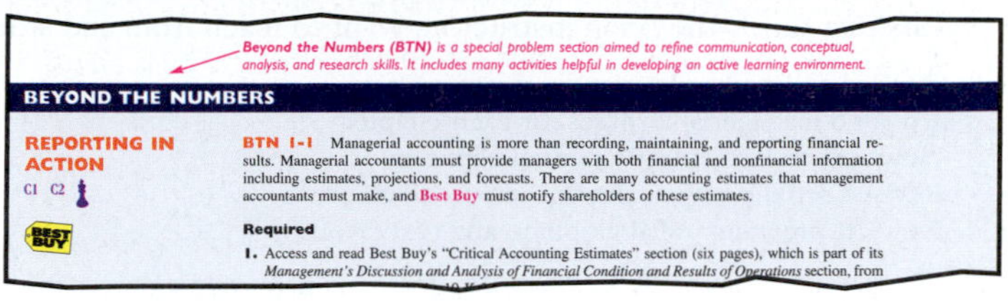

Serial Problem uses a continuous running case study to illustrate chapter concepts in a familiar context. The Serial Problem can be followed continuously from the first chapter or picked up at any later point in the book; enough information is provided to ensure students can get right to work.

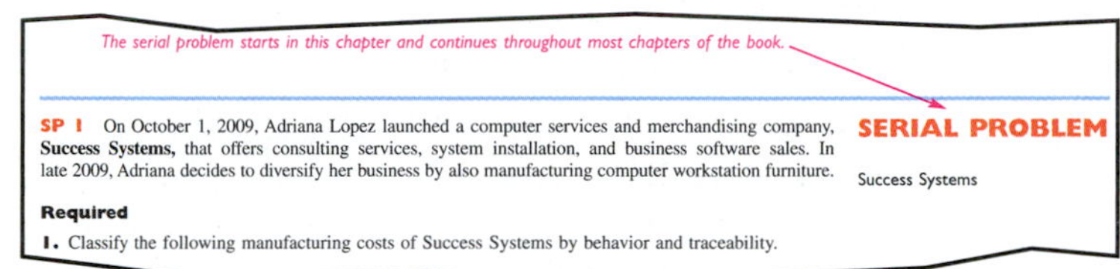

"The best feature of this book is the use of real (financial) information in the Beyond the Numbers section. This is something that I do on my own, which can be very time consuming. I also like the Entrepreneurial questions, which are not even addressed in most textbooks."

Cindy Navaroli, Chaffey Community College

The End of the Chapter Is Only the Beginning

Our valuable and proven assignments aren't just confined to the book. From problems that require technological solutions to materials found exclusively online, this book's end-of-chapter material is fully integrated with its technology package.

- Quick Studies, Exercises, and Problems available on Connect Accounting (see page viii) are marked with an icon.

- Online Learning Center (OLC) includes Interactive Quizzes, Excel template assignments, and more.

- Problems supported with Microsoft Excel template assignments are marked with an icon.

- Material that receives additional coverage (slide shows, videos, audio, etc.) available in iPod ready format are marked with an icon.

Put Away Your Red Pen

We pride ourselves on the accuracy of this book's assignment materials. Independent research reports that instructors and reviewers point to the accuracy of this book's assignment materials as one of its key competitive advantages.

The authors extend a special thanks to accuracy checkers Helen Roybark, Radford University; Beth Woods, CPA, Accuracy Counts; David Krug, Johnson County Community College; Yvonne Phang, Borough of Manhattan Community College; and Marilyn Sagrillo, University of Wisconsin - Green Bay. Also to Karen Wisneiwski, County College of Morris for creation of the online quizzes.

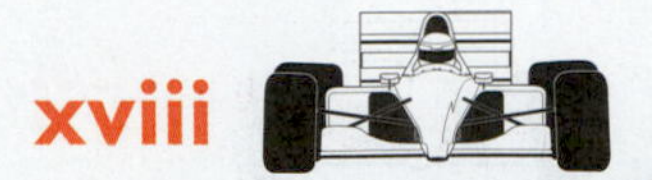

Enhancements for MA 2e

This edition's revisions are driven by feedback from instructors and students. Many of the revisions are summarized here. Feedback suggests that this is the book instructors want to teach from and students want to learn from. General revisions include:

- Revised and updated assignments throughout
- Updated managerial analyses for each chapter
- New and revised entrepreneurial elements
- Revised serial problem through nearly all chapters
- New art program, visual graphics, and text layout
- New Best Buy data with comparisons to Circuit City, RadioShack, Apple, and DSG (UK) with new assignments
- New graphics added to each chapter's analysis section
- New iPod content integrated and referenced in book

Chapter 1

Kernel Season's **NEW opener** with new entrepreneurial assignment

New section on fraud and the role of ethics in managerial accounting

Added discussion on Institute of Management Accountants and its road-map for resolving ethical dilemmas

Updated real-world examples including that for Apple

Added balance sheet to exhibits that show cost flows across accounting reports

New discussion on role of nonfinancial information

Chapter 2

Sprinturf **NEW opener** with new entrepreneurial assignment

New info on custom design involving Nike

Enhanced exhibit on job order production activities

Added discussion linking accurate overhead application for jobs to both product pricing and performance evaluation

Streamlined explanation of closing over- and underapplied overhead

New discussion of employee payroll fraud schemes

Chapter 3

Hood River Juice Company **NEW opener** with new entrepreneurial assignment

New discussion on impact of automation for quality control and overhead application

Added explanation for use of a process cost summary in product pricing

Chapter 4

Oregon Ice Cream Company **NEW opener** with new entrepreneurial assignment

Simplified the steps of activity-based costing (ABC) allocations

New discussion on using ABC to allocate selling and administrative costs

Enhanced presentation of, and enhanced graphics for, ABC procedures

Chapter 5

Moe's Southwest Grill **NEW opener** with new entrepreneurial assignment

New section on working with changes in estimates for CVP analysis

New graphics illustrating how changes in estimates impact break-even analysis

New discussion on weighted average contribution margin in multiple product CVP analysis

New Appendix 5A on using Excel to estimate least squares regression

New assignments on break-even and changes in estimates

Chapter 6

Bonobos **NEW opener** with new entrepreneurial assignment

Streamlined discussion of contribution margin income statements

Improved graphics comparing income reporting under absorption versus variable costing

Enhanced explanation of controllable vs. uncontrollable costs

Expanded the Demonstration Problem to be more comprehensive

Chapter 7

Jibbitz **NEW opener** with new entrepreneurial assignment

Enhanced discussion of master budgets

New assignments on preparing budgets and budgeted financial statement

Chapter 8

Martin Guitar **NEW opener** with new entrepreneurial assignment

Reorganized discussion of overhead variance analysis

Revised graphics on framework for understanding overhead variances

New discussion of increased automation for overhead application

Revised explanation of journal entries for standard costing

Simplified discussion of closing variance accounts

New assignments on variance analysis

Added journal entries to chapter demonstration problem

Chapter 9

RockBottomGolf.com **NEW opener** with new entrepreneurial assignment

Enhanced explanation of evaluating investment center performance with financial measures

New discussion of residual income

Added explanation of economic value added

New section on evaluating investment center performance with nonfinancial measures including balanced scorecard

New Appendix 9A on transfer pricing

Decision Analysis: new explanation of investment center profit margin and investment turnover with new assignments

Chapter 10

Prairie Sticks Bat Company **NEW opener** with new entrepreneurial assignment

Enhanced explanation of 'make or buy' decision

New discussion for 'segment elimination' decision

Enhanced presentation for managerial decision scenarios

Chapter 11

1-800-GOTJUNK **NEW opener** with new entrepreneurial assignment

New info graphic on cost of capital estimates across industries

Added discussion and example on use of profitability index to compare projects

New discussion on incorporating inflation in net present value calculations

Added explanation on conflicts between meeting analysts' forecasts and choosing profitable long-term projects

New Appendix 11A on using Excel to compute net present value and internal rate of return

New assignments on profitability index

Chapter 12

Jungle Jim's **NEW opener** with new entrepreneurial assignment

Updated graphics for operating, investing and financing cash flows

Enhanced steps 1 through 5 for preparing the statement of cash flows

Simplified summary Exhibit 12.12 for indirect adjustments

Updated real world examples and graphics including that for Harley, Starbucks, and Nike

New info on indirect vs direct method for U.S. GAAP vis-à-vis IFRSs

Chapter 13

The Motley Fool **UPDATED opener** with new entrepreneurial assignment

New Best Buy, Circuit City and RadioShack data throughout chapter, exhibits, and illustrations with comparative analysis

Enhanced presentation on comparative financial statements

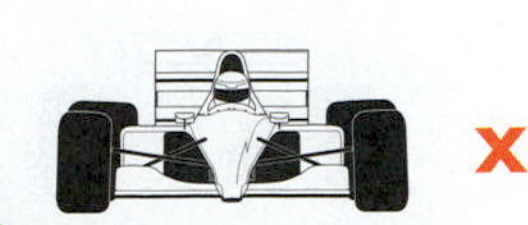

Assurance of Learning Ready

Assurance of learning is an important element of many accreditation standards. *Managerial Accounting* 2e is designed specifically to support your assurance of learning initiatives.

Each chapter in the book begins with a list of numbered learning objectives which appear throughout the chapter, as well as in the end-of-chapter problems and exercises. Every test bank question is also linked to one of these objectives, in addition to level of difficulty, AICPA skill area, and AACSB skill area. EZ Test, McGraw-Hill's easy-to-use test bank software, can search the test bank by these and other categories, providing an engine for targeted assurance of learning analysis and assessment.

AACSB Statement

The McGraw-Hill Companies is a proud corporate member of AACSB International. Understanding the importance and value of AACSB accreditation, *Managerial Accounting* 2e has sought to recognize the curricula guidelines detailed in the AACSB standards for business accreditation by connecting selected questions in the test bank to the general knowledge and skill guidelines found in the AACSB standards.

The statements contained in *Managerial Accounting* 2e are provided only as a guide for the users of this text. The AACSB leaves content coverage and assessment within the purview of individual schools, the mission of the school, and the faculty. While *Managerial Accounting* 2e and the teaching package make no claim of any specific AACSB qualification or evaluation, we have, within the *Managerial Accounting* 2e test bank labeled questions according to the six general knowledge and skills areas.

Instructor's Resource CD-ROM

ISBN13: 9780073360478
ISBN10: 0073360473

This is your all-in-one resource. It allows you to create custom presentations from your own materials or from the following book-specific materials provided in the CD's asset library:

- Instructor's Resource Manual
  Written by Christine Schalow, University of Wisconsin-Stevens Point.
  This manual contains (for each chapter) a Lecture Outline, a chart linking all assignment materials to Learning Objectives, a list of relevant active learning activities, and additional visuals with transparency masters.
- Solutions Manual
  Written by John J. Wild, Ken W. Shaw, and Marilyn Sagrillo.
- Test Bank, Computerized Test Bank
  Revised by Laurie Hays, Western Michigan University.
- PowerPoint® Presentations
  Prepared by Debra Schmidt, Cerritos College.
  Presentations allow for revision of lecture slides, and includes a viewer, allowing screens to be shown with or without the software.
- Link to PageOut

Algorithmic Test Bank

ISBN13: 9780073360447
ISBN10: 0073360449

Excel Working Papers CD

ISBN13: 9780073360454
ISBN10: 0073360457

Written by John J. Wild.

Working Papers delivered in Excel spreadsheets. These Excel Working Papers are available on CD-ROM; see your representative for information.

Study Guide

ISBN13: 9780073360538
ISBN10: 0073360538

Written by April Mohr, Jefferson Community and Technical College, SW.

Covers each chapter and appendix with reviews of the learning objectives, outlines of the chapters, summaries of chapter materials, and additional problems with solutions.

Contributing Author

The authors and book team wish to thank Marilyn Sagrillo for her excellent contributions.

Marilyn Sagrillo is an associate professor at the University of Wisconsin at Green Bay. She received her BA and MS from Northern Illinois University and her PhD from the University of Wisconsin at Madison. Her scholarly articles are published in *Accounting Enquiries*, *Journal of Accounting Case Research*, and the *Missouri Society of CPAs Casebook*. She is a member of the American Accounting Association and the Institute of Management Accountants. She previously received the UWGB Founder's Association Faculty Award for Excellence in Teaching. Professor Sagrillo is an active volunteer for the Midwest Renewable Energy Association. She also enjoys reading, traveling, and hiking.

Acknowledgments

John J. Wild, Ken W. Shaw, and McGraw-Hill would like to recognize the following instructors for their valuable feedback and involvement in the development of *Managerial Accounting* 2e. We are thankful for their suggestions, counsel, and encouragement.

Audrey Agnello, Niagara County Community College

Sylvia Allen, Los Angeles Valley College

Donna Altepeter, University of North Dakota

Juanita Ardavany, Los Angeles Valley College

Richard Barnhart, Grand Rapids Community College

Beverly Beatty, Anne Arundel Community College

Terry W. Bechtel, Northwestern State University of Louisiana

Gerard L. Berardino, Community College of Allegheny County-Boyce Campus

Patrick Borja, Citrus College

Phil Brown, Harding University

Chak-Tong Chau, University of Houston

Siu Chung, Los Angeles Valley College

Darlene Coarts, University of Northern Iowa

Ken Couvillion, Delta College

Walter DeAguero, Saddleback College

Mike Deschamps, Mira Costa College

Saturnino Gonzalez, El Paso Community College

Laurie Hays, Western Michigan University

Kathy Hill, Leeward Community College

Margaret Houston, Wright State University

Thomas Kam, Hawaii Pacific University

David Krug, Johnson County Community College

Tara Laken, Joliet Junior College

William Link, University of Missouri-St. Louis

Cathy Lumbattis, Southern Illinois University-Carbondale

James P. Makofske, Fresno City College

Stacie Mayes, Rose State College

April Mohr, Jefferson Community and Technical College, SW

Audrey S. Morrison, Pensacola Junior College

Susan Pallas, Southeast Community College

Ash Patel, Normandale Community College

Gary Pieroni, Diablo Valley College

Yvonne Phang, Borough of Manhattan Community College

James E. Racic, Lakeland Community College

Jenny Resnick, Santa Monica College

Helen Roybark, Radford University

Marilyn Sagrillo, University of Wisconsin Green Bay

Christine Schalow, University of Wisconsin Stevens Point

Debra Schmidt, Cerritos College

Randall Serrett, University of Houston-Downtown

Brad Smith, Des Moines Area Community College

Nancy Snow, University of Toledo

Gracelyn V. Stuart-Tuggle, Palm Beach Community College-South

Larry Swisher, Muskegon Community College

William Talbot, Montgomery College-Rockville

Diane Tanner, University of North Florida

Margaret Tanner, University of Arkansas

Scott Williams, County College of Morris

John Windler, University of Nebraska at Omaha

Karen Wisniewski, County College of Morris

Gloria Worthy, Southwest Tennessee Community College

Judith Zander, Grossmont College

In addition to the helpful and generous colleagues listed above, we thank the entire McGraw-Hill *Managerial Accounting* 2e team, including Stewart Mattson, Tim Vertovec, Steve Schuetz, Christina Sanders, Sharon Monday of Aptara, Lori Koetters, Matthew Baldwin, Carol Bielski, and Jennifer Lohn. We also thank the great marketing and sales support staff, including Krista Bettino, Sankha Basu, and Randy Sealy. Many talented educators and professionals worked hard to create the supplements for this book, and for their efforts we're grateful. Finally, many more people we either did not meet or whose efforts we did not personally witness nevertheless helped to make this book everything that it is, and we thank them all.

John J. Wild *Ken W. Shaw*

Brief Contents

* Appendixes C and D are available on the book's Website, mhhe.com/wildMA2e, and as print copy from a McGraw-Hill representative.

Contents

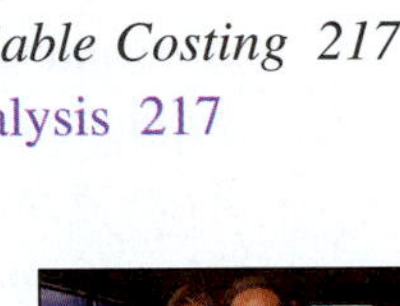

* Appendixes C & D are available on the book's Website, mhhe.com/wildMA2e, and as print copy from a McGraw-Hill representative.

Managerial Accounting

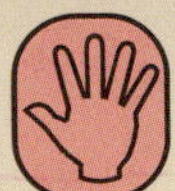

A Look at This Chapter

We begin our study of managerial accounting by explaining its purpose and describing its major characteristics. We also discuss cost concepts and describe how they help managers gather and organize information for making decisions. The reporting of manufacturing activities is also discussed.

A Look Ahead

The remaining chapters discuss the types of decisions managers must make and how managerial accounting helps with those decisions. The first of these chapters, Chapter 2, considers how we measure costs assigned to certain types of projects.

Chapter 1 Managerial Accounting Concepts and Principles

Learning Objectives

Learning Objectives *are classified as conceptual, analytical, or procedural.*

CAP

Conceptual

C1 Explain the purpose and nature of managerial accounting. *(p. 4)*

C2 Describe the lean business model. *(p. 7)*

C3 Describe fraud and the role of ethics in managerial accounting. *(p. 9)*

C4 Describe accounting concepts useful in classifying costs. *(p. 10)*

C5 Define product and period costs and explain how they impact financial statements. *(p. 11)*

C6 Explain how balance sheets and income statements for manufacturing and merchandising companies differ. *(p. 13)*

C7 Explain manufacturing activities and the flow of manufacturing costs. *(p. 17)*

Analytical

A1 Compute cycle time and cycle efficiency, and explain their importance to production management *(p. 20)*

Procedural

P1 Compute cost of goods sold for a manufacturer. *(p. 15)*

P2 Prepare a manufacturing statement and explain its purpose and links to financial statements. *(p. 18)*

LP1

Decision Feature

No Naked Popcorn

"Find a niche and stay focused"—Brian Taylor

*A **Decision Feature** launches each chapter showing the relevance of accounting for a real entrepreneur. An **Entrepreneurial Decision** problem at the end of the assignments returns to this feature with a mini-case.*

ELK GROVE VILLAGE, IL—As a hungry college student, Brian Taylor liked to eat popcorn. Lots of it. Bored with "naked popcorn," Brian began experimenting with seasonings such as nacho cheese, cajun, jalapeño, and apple cinnamon. After he shared his concoctions with friends, dorm mates, and others, the demand for Brian's seasonings ballooned. In less than two years, Brian had the number one shake-on popcorn seasoning in the market, **Kernel Season's** (**KernelSeasons.com**).

Brian launched Kernel Season's with $7,000 he earned from giving tennis lessons and selling knives. In the beginning, he gave away his popcorn seasonings to local theaters to build awareness. Just like his college friends, moviegoers loved the all-natural, low-calorie seasonings. Soon theaters across the country were asking for his seasonings, and Brian worked hard to meet demand. "I was the only employee," explains Brian. "I made sales and shipped orders. I was figuring it out as I went along."

Well, business is now popping. Fourteen varieties of Kernel Season's are available in over 14,000 movie theaters and 15,000 grocery stores. Annual sales now exceed $5 million, and Brian is on Inc.com's "30 under 30," a list of America's coolest young entrepreneurs.

Brian believes college is the best time to start a new business. "Risk is low, and banks understand young entrepreneurs are trying to get things going," explains Brian. But Brian emphasizes that understanding basic managerial principles, product and period costs, manufacturing statements, and cost flows is equally crucial. "[I was] dedicated to business classes," says Brian, including my "accounting class." Brian uses managerial accounting information from his production process to monitor and control costs and to assess new business opportunities, including Kernel Season's apparel. Brian further stresses that company success and growth require him to develop budgets, monitor product performance, and make quick decisions.

Brian believes entrepreneurs fill a void by creating a niche. However, financial success depends on monitoring and controlling operations to best meet customer needs. Brian cautions would-be entrepreneurs to "stay focused" because in the absence of applying managerial accounting principles and concepts, it's just naked popcorn.

[Sources: *Kernel Season's Website,* January 2009; *Lake County News Sun,* October 2003; *Female Entrepreneur,* July/August 2003; *Chicago Tonight* interview, August 2007; *StartupNation.com,* May 2007; *Inc.com Website,* May 2008]

Chapter Preview

*A **Preview** ope[illegible]ics covered.*

Managerial accounting, like financial accounting, [illegible] mation to help users make better decisions. H[illegible] rial accounting and financial accounting differ i[illegible] ways, which this chapter explains. This chapter [illegible] the accounting and reporting practices used by [illegible] and merchandising companies. A merchandising [illegible] products without changing their condition. A m[illegible] raw materials and turns them into finished [illegible]ale to customers. A third type of company earns [illegible]oviding services rather than products. The skills, [illegible]niques developed for measuring a manufacturing [illegible]vities apply to service companies as well. The [illegible]des by explaining the flow of manufacturing [illegible]reparing the manufacturing statement.

Managerial Accounting Concepts and Principles

Managerial Accounting Basics
- Purpose of managerial accounting
- Nature of managerial accounting
- Managerial decisions
- Managerial accounting in business
- Fraud and ethics in managerial accounting

Managerial Cost Concepts
- Types of cost classifications
- Identification of cost classifications
- Cost concepts for service companies

Reporting Manufacturing Activities
- Balance sheet
- Income statement
- Flow of activities
- Manufacturing statement

Managerial Accounting Basics

*Key **terms** are printed in bold and defined again in the end-of-book **glossary.***

Managerial accounting is an activity that provides financial and nonfinancial information to an organization's managers and other internal decision makers. This section explains the purpose of managerial accounting (also called *management accounting*) and compares it with financial accounting. The main purpose of the financial accounting system is to prepare general-purpose financial statements. That information is incomplete for internal decision makers who manage organizations.

Purpose of Managerial Accounting

C1 Explain the purpose and nature of managerial accounting.

The purpose of both managerial accounting and financial accounting is providing useful information to decision makers. They do this by collecting, managing, and reporting information in demand by their users. Both areas of accounting also share the common practice of reporting monetary information, although managerial accounting includes the reporting of nonmonetary information. They even report some of the same information. For instance, a company's financial statements contain information useful for both its managers (insiders) and other persons interested in the company (outsiders).

Point: Nonfinancial information, also called nonmonetary information, includes customer and employee satisfaction data, the percentage of on-time deliveries, and product defect rates.

The remainder of this book looks carefully at managerial accounting information, how to gather it, and how managers use it. We consider the concepts and procedures used to determine the costs of products and services as well as topics such as budgeting, break-even analysis, product costing, profit planning, and cost analysis. Information about the costs of products and services is important for many decisions that managers make. These decisions include predicting the future costs of a product or service. Predicted costs are used in product pricing, profitability analysis, and in deciding whether to make or buy a product or component. More generally, much of managerial accounting involves gathering information about costs for planning and control decisions.

Point: Costs are important to managers because they impact both the financial position and profitability of a business. Managerial accounting assists in analysis, planning, and control of costs.

Planning is the process of setting goals and making plans to achieve them. Companies formulate long-term strategic plans that usually span a 5- to 10-year horizon and then refine them with medium-term and short-term plans. Strategic plans usually set a firm's long-term direction by developing a road map based on opportunities such as new products, new markets, and capital investments. A strategic plan's goals and objectives are broadly defined given its long-term orientation. Medium- and short-term plans are more operational in nature. They translate the strategic plan into actions. These plans are more concrete and consist of better defined objectives and goals. A short-term plan often covers a one-year period that, when translated in monetary terms, is known as a budget.

Video1.1

Control is the process of monitoring planning decisions and evaluating an organization's activities and employees. It includes the measurement and evaluation of actions, processes, and outcomes. Feedback provided by the control function allows managers to revise their plans. Measurement of actions and processes also allows managers to take corrective actions to avoid undesirable outcomes. For example, managers periodically compare actual results with planned results. Exhibit 1.1 portrays the important management functions of planning and control.

EXHIBIT 1.1

Planning and Control

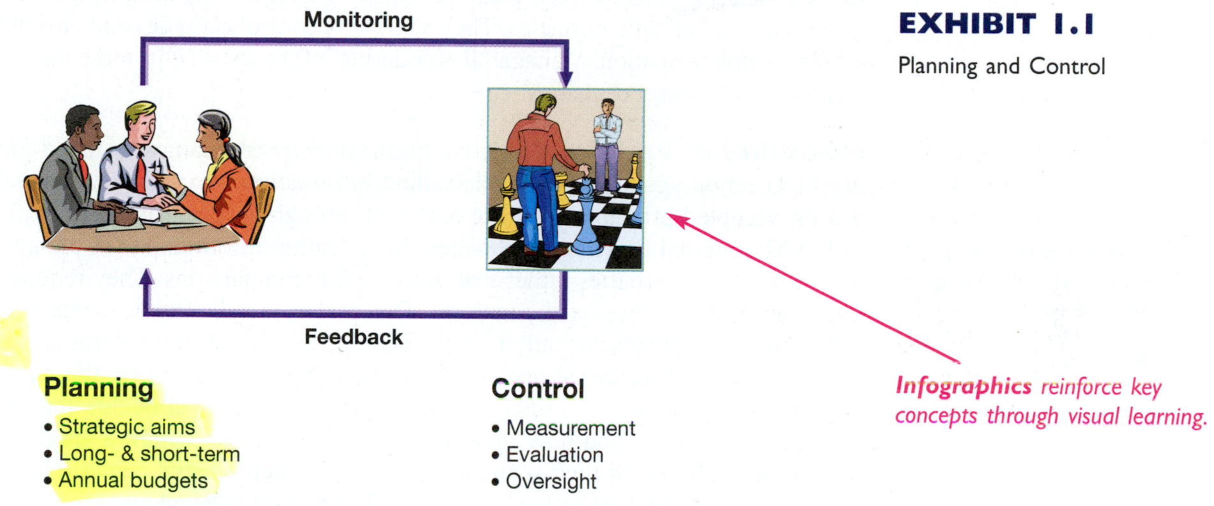
Monitoring
Feedback
Planning
• Strategic aims
• Long- & short-term
• Annual budgets
Control
• Measurement
• Evaluation
• Oversight

Infographics reinforce key concepts through visual learning.

Managers use information to plan and control business activities. In later chapters, we explain how managers also use this information to direct and improve business operations.

Nature of Managerial Accounting

Managerial accounting has its own special characteristics. To understand these characteristics, we compare managerial accounting to financial accounting; they differ in at least seven important ways. These differences are summarized in Exhibit 1.2. This section discusses each of these characteristics.

EXHIBIT 1.2

Key Differences between Managerial Accounting and Financial Accounting

"This company's outlook is good. I'll buy its shares."
"This department is doing well. We'll expand its product line."

	Financial Accounting	Managerial Accounting
1. Users and decision makers	Investors, creditors, and other users external to the organization	Managers, employees, and decision makers internal to the organization
2. Purpose of information	Assist external users in making investment, credit, and other decisions	Assist managers in making planning and control decisions
3. Flexibility of practice	Structured and often controlled by GAAP	Relatively flexible (no GAAP constraints)
4. Timeliness of information	Often available only after an audit is complete	Available quickly without the need to wait for an audit
5. Time dimension	Focus on historical information with some predictions	Many projections and estimates; historical information also presented
6. Focus of information	Emphasis on whole organization	Emphasis on an organization's projects, processes, and subdivisions
7. Nature of information	Monetary information	Mostly monetary; but also nonmonetary information

Point: It is desirable to accumulate information for management reports in a database separate from financial accounting records.

Users and Decision Makers Companies accumulate, process, and report financial accounting and managerial accounting information for different groups of decision makers. Financial accounting information is provided primarily to external users including investors, creditors, analysts, and regulators. External users rarely have a major role in managing a company's daily activities. Managerial accounting information is provided primarily to internal users who are responsible for making and implementing decisions about a company's business activities.

Purpose of Information Investors, creditors, and other external users of financial accounting information must often decide whether to invest in or lend to a company. If they have already done so, they must decide whether to continue owning the company or carrying the loan. Internal decision makers must plan a company's future. They seek to take advantage of opportunities or to overcome obstacles. They also try to control activities and ensure their effective and efficient implementation. Managerial accounting information helps these internal users make both planning and control decisions.

Point: The *Institute of Management Accountants* issues statements that govern the practice of managerial accounting. Accountants who pass a qualifying exam are awarded the CMA.

Flexibility of Practice External users compare companies by using financial reports and need protection against false or misleading information. Accordingly, financial accounting relies on accepted principles that are enforced through an extensive set of rules and guidelines, or GAAP. Internal users need managerial accounting information for planning and controlling their company's activities rather than for external comparisons. They require different types of information depending on the activity. This makes standardizing managerial accounting systems across companies difficult. Instead, managerial accounting systems are flexible. The design of a company's managerial accounting system depends largely on the nature of the business and the arrangement of its internal operations. Managers can decide for themselves what information they want and how they want it reported. Even within a single company, different managers often design their own systems to meet their special needs. The important question a manager must ask is whether the information being collected and reported is useful for planning, decision making, and control purposes.

Point: Financial statements are usually issued several weeks after the period-end. GAAP requires the reporting of important events that occur while the statements are being prepared. These events are called *subsequent events.*

Point: Independent auditors test the integrity of managerial accounting records when they are used in preparing financial statements.

Timeliness of Information Formal financial statements reporting past transactions and events are not immediately available to outside parties. Independent certified public accountants often must *audit* a company's financial statements before it provides them to external users. Thus, because audits often take several weeks to complete, financial reports to outsiders usually are not available until well after the period-end. However, managers can quickly obtain managerial accounting information. External auditors need not review it. Estimates and projections are acceptable. To get information quickly, managers often accept less precision in reports. As an example, an early internal report to management prepared right after the year-end could report net income for the year between $4.2 and $4.8 million. An audited income statement could later show net income for the year at $4.6 million. The internal report is not precise, but its information can be more useful because it is available earlier.

Internal auditing plays an important role in managerial accounting. Internal auditors evaluate the flow of information not only inside but also outside the company. Managers are responsible for preventing and detecting fraudulent activities in their companies.

Time Dimension To protect external users from false expectations, financial reports deal primarily with results of both past activities and current conditions. While some predictions such as service lives and salvage values of plant assets are necessary, financial accounting avoids predictions whenever possible. Managerial accounting regularly includes predictions of conditions and events. As an example, one important managerial accounting report is a budget, which predicts revenues, expenses, and other items. If managerial accounting reports were restricted to the past and present, managers would be less able to plan activities and less effective in managing and evaluating current activities.

EXHIBIT 1.3

Focus of External Reports

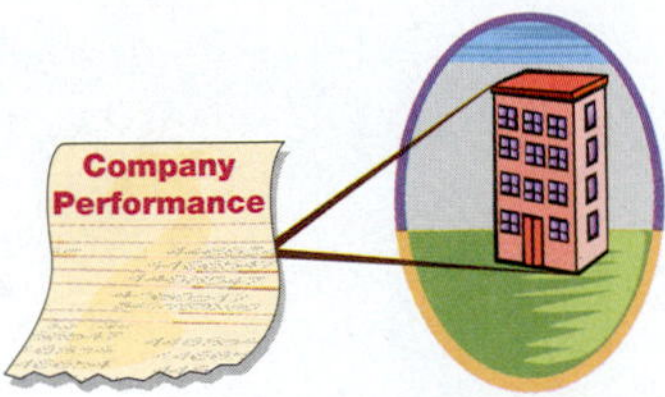

Focus of Information Companies often organize into divisions and departments, but investors rarely can buy shares in one division or department. Nor do creditors lend money to a company's single division or department. Instead, they own shares in or make loans to the entire company. Financial accounting focuses primarily on a company as a whole as depicted in Exhibit 1.3.

The focus of managerial accounting is different. While top-level managers are responsible for managing the whole company, most other managers are responsible for much smaller sets of activities. These middle-level and lower-level managers need managerial accounting reports dealing with specific activities, projects, and subdivisions for which they are responsible. For instance, division sales managers are directly responsible only for the results achieved in their divisions. Accordingly, division sales managers need information about results achieved in their own divisions to improve their performance. This information includes the level of success achieved by each individual, product, or department in each division as depicted in Exhibit 1.4.

EXHIBIT 1.4

Focus of Internal Reports

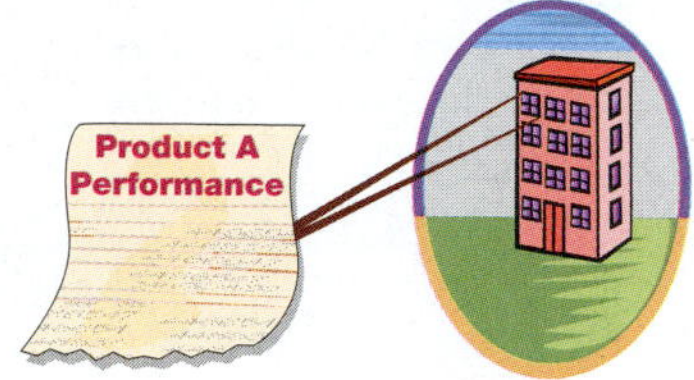

Nature of Information Both financial and managerial accounting systems report monetary information. Managerial accounting systems also report considerable nonmonetary information. Monetary information is an important part of managerial decisions, and nonmonetary information plays a crucial role, especially when monetary effects are difficult to measure. Common examples of nonmonetary information are the quality and delivery criteria of purchasing decisions.

***Decision Ethics** boxes are role-playing exercises that stress ethics in accounting and business.*

Decision Ethics

Production Manager You invite three friends to a restaurant. When the dinner check arrives, David, a self-employed entrepreneur, picks it up saying, "Here, let me pay. I'll deduct it as a business expense on my tax return." Denise, a salesperson, takes the check from David's hand and says, "I'll put this on my company's credit card. It won't cost us anything." Derek, a factory manager for a company, laughs and says, "Neither of you understands. I'll put this on my company's credit card and call it overhead on a cost-plus contract my company has with a client." (*A cost-plus contract means the company receives its costs plus a percent of those costs.*) Adds Derek, "That way, my company pays for dinner *and* makes a profit." Who should pay the bill? Why? [Answer—p. 26]

Managerial Decision Making

The previous section emphasized differences between financial and managerial accounting, but they are not entirely separate. Similar information is useful to both external and internal users. For instance, information about costs of manufacturing products is useful to all users in making decisions. Also, both financial and managerial accounting affect peoples' actions. For example, **Trek**'s design of a sales compensation plan affects the behavior of its salesforce. It also must estimate the dual effects of promotion and sales compensation plans on buying patterns of customers. These estimates impact the equipment purchase decisions for manufacturing and can affect the supplier selection criteria established by purchasing. Thus, financial and managerial accounting systems do more than measure; they also affect people's decisions and actions.

Managerial Accounting in Business

C2 Describe the lean business model.

We have explained the importance of managerial accounting for internal decision making. Although the analytical tools and techniques of managerial accounting have always been useful, their relevance and importance continue to increase. This is so because of changes in the business environment. This section describes some of these changes and their impact on managerial accounting.

Lean Business Model Two important factors have encouraged companies to be more effective and efficient in running their operations. First, there is an increased emphasis on *customers* as the most important constituent of a business. Customers expect to derive a certain value for the money they spend to buy products and services. Specifically, they expect that their suppliers will offer them the right service (or product) at the right time and the right price. This implies that companies accept the notion of **customer orientation,** which means that employees

understand the changing needs and wants of their customers and align their management and operating practices accordingly.

Second, our *global economy* expands competitive boundaries, thereby providing customers more choices. The global economy also produces changes in business activities. One notable case that reflects these changes in customer demand and global competition is auto manufacturing. The top three Japanese auto manufacturers (**Honda**, **Nissan**, and **Toyota**) once controlled more than 40% of the U.S. auto market. Customers perceived that Japanese auto manufacturers provided value not available from other manufacturers. Many European and North American auto manufacturers responded to this challenge and regained much of the lost market share.

Companies must be alert to these and other factors. Many companies have responded by adopting the **lean business model,** whose goal is to *eliminate waste* while "satisfying the customer" and "providing a positive return" to the company.

Lean Practices **Continuous improvement** rejects the notions of "good enough" or "acceptable" and challenges employees and managers to continuously experiment with new and improved business practices. This has led companies to adopt practices such as total quality management (TQM) and just-in-time (JIT) manufacturing. The philosophy underlying both practices is continuous improvement; the difference is in the focus.

Point: Goals of a TQM process include reduced waste, better inventory control, fewer defects, and continuous improvement. Just-in-time concepts have similar goals.

Total quality management focuses on quality improvement and applies this standard to all aspects of business activities. In doing so, managers and employees seek to uncover waste in business activities including accounting activities such as payroll and disbursements. To encourage an emphasis on quality, the U.S. Congress established the Malcolm Baldrige National Quality Award (MBQNA). Entrants must conduct a thorough analysis and evaluation of their business using guidelines from the Baldrige committee. **Ritz Carlton Hotel** is a recipient of the Baldrige award in the service category. The company applies a core set of values, collectively called *The Gold Standards,* to improve customer service.

Point: The time between buying raw materials and selling finished goods is called *throughput time.*

Just-in-time manufacturing is a system that acquires inventory and produces only when needed. An important aspect of JIT is that companies manufacture products only after they receive an order (a *demand-pull* system) and then deliver the customer's requirements on time. This means that processes must be aligned to eliminate any delays and inefficiencies including inferior inputs and outputs. Companies must also establish good relations and communications with their suppliers. On the downside, JIT is more susceptible to disruption than traditional systems. As one example, several **General Motors** plants were temporarily shut down due to a strike at an assembly division; the plants supplied components *just in time* to the assembly division.

Decision Insight boxes highlight relevant items from practice.

Decision Insight

Global Lean **Toyota Motor Corporation** pioneered lean manufacturing, and it has since spread to other manufacturers throughout the world. The goals include improvements in quality, reliability, inventory turnover, productivity, exports, and—above all—sales and income.

Implications for Managerial Accounting Adopting the lean business model can be challenging because to foster its implementation, all systems and procedures that a company follows must be realigned. Managerial accounting has an important role to play by providing accurate cost and performance information. Companies must understand the nature and sources of cost and must develop systems that capture costs accurately. Developing such a system is important to measuring the "value" provided to customers. The price that customers pay for

Video1.3

acquiring goods and services is an important determinant of value. In turn, the costs a company incurs are key determinants of price. All else being equal, the better a company is at controlling its costs, the better its performance.

Decision Insight

Balanced Scorecard The *balanced scorecard* aids continuous improvement by augmenting financial measures with information on the "drivers" (indicators) of future financial performance along four dimensions: (1) *financial*—profitability and risk, (2) *customer*—value creation and product and service differentiation, (3) *internal business processes*—business activities that create customer and owner satisfaction, and (4) *learning and growth*—organizational change, innovation, and growth.

Fraud and Ethics in Managerial Accounting

C3 Describe fraud and the role of ethics in managerial accounting.

Fraud, and the role of ethics in reducing fraud, are important factors in running business operations. Fraud involves the use of one's job for personal gain through the deliberate misuse of the employer's assets. Examples include theft of the employer's cash or other assets, overstating reimbursable expenses, payroll schemes, and financial statement fraud. Fraud affects all business and it is costly: A 2006 *Report to the Nation* from the Association of Certified Fraud Examiners estimates the average U.S. business loses 5% of its annual revenues to fraud.

The most common type of fraud, where employees steal or misuse the employer's resources, results in an average loss of $150,000 per occurrence. For example, in a billing fraud, an employee sets up a bogus supplier. The employee then prepares bills from the supplier and pays these bills from the employer's checking account. The employee cashes the checks sent to the bogus supplier and uses them for his or her own personal benefit.

Although there are many types of fraud schemes, all fraud

- Is done to provide direct or indirect benefit to the employee.
- Violates the employee's duties to his employer.
- Costs the employer money.
- Is secret.

Implications for Managerial Accounting Fraud increases a business's costs. Left undetected, these inflated costs can result in poor pricing decisions, an improper product mix, and faulty performance evaluations. Management can develop accounting systems to closely track costs and identify deviations from expected amounts. In addition, managers rely on an **internal control system** to monitor and control business activities. An internal control system is the policies and procedures managers use to

- Urge adherence to company policies.
- Promote efficient operations.
- Ensure reliable accounting.
- Protect assets.

Combating fraud and other dilemmas requires ethics in accounting. **Ethics** are beliefs that distinguish right from wrong. They are accepted standards of good and bad behavior. Identifying the ethical path can be difficult. The preferred path is a course of action that avoids casting doubt on one's decisions.

The **Institute of Management Accountants** (IMA), the professional association for management accountants, has issued a code of ethics to help accountants involved in solving ethical dilemmas. The IMA's Statement of Ethical Professional Practice requires that management accountants be competent, maintain confidentiality, act with integrity, and communicate information in a fair and credible manner.

The IMA provides a "road map" for resolving ethical conflicts. It suggests that an employee follow the company's policies on how to resolve such conflicts. If the conflict remains unresolved, an employee should contact the next level of management (such as the immediate supervisor) who is not involved in the ethical conflict.

Point: The IMA also issues the Certified Management Accountant (CMA) and the Certified Financial Manager (CFM) certifications. Employees with the CMA or CFM certifications typically earn higher salaries than those without.

Point: The **Sarbanes-Oxley Act** requires each issuer of securities to disclose whether it has adopted a code of ethics for its senior officers and the content of that code.

Quick Check is a chance to stop and reflect on key points.

Quick Check

Answers—p. 27

1. Managerial accounting produces information (*a*) to meet internal users' needs, (*b*) to meet a user's specific needs, (*c*) often focusing on the future, or (*d*) all of these.
2. What is the difference between the intended users of financial and managerial accounting?
3. Do generally accepted accounting principles (GAAP) control and dictate managerial accounting?
4. What is the basic objective for a company practicing total quality management?

Managerial Cost Concepts

C4 Describe accounting concepts useful in classifying costs.

An organization incurs many different types of costs that are classified differently, depending on management needs (different costs for different purposes). We can classify costs on the basis of their (1) behavior, (2) traceability, (3) controllability, (4) relevance, and (5) function. This section explains each concept for assigning costs to products and services.

Types of Cost Classifications

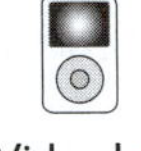

Video1.2

Classification by Behavior At a basic level, a cost can be classified as fixed or variable. A **fixed cost** does not change with changes in the volume of activity (within a range of activity known as an activity's *relevant range*). For example, straight-line depreciation on equipment is a fixed cost. A **variable cost** changes in proportion to changes in the volume of activity. Sales commissions computed as a percent of sales revenue are variable costs. Additional examples of fixed and variable costs for a bike manufacturer are provided in Exhibit 1.5. When cost items are combined, total cost can be fixed, variable, or mixed. *Mixed* refers to a combination of fixed and variable costs. Equipment rental often includes a fixed cost for some minimum amount and a variable cost based on amount of usage. Classification of costs by behavior is helpful in cost-volume-profit analyses and short-term decision making. We discuss these in Chapters 5 and 10.

EXHIBIT 1.5

Fixed and Variable Costs

Fixed Cost: Rent for Rocky Mountain Bikes' building is $22,000, and it doesn't change with the number of bikes produced.

Variable Cost: Cost of bicycle tires is variable with the number of bikes produced—this cost is $15 per pair.

Classification by Traceability A cost is often traced to a **cost object,** which is a product, process, department, or customer to which costs are assigned. **Direct costs** are those traceable to a single cost object. For example, if a product is a cost object, its material and labor costs are usually directly traceable. **Indirect costs** are those that cannot be easily and cost–beneficially traced to a single cost object. An example of an indirect cost is a maintenance plan that benefits two or more departments. Exhibit 1.6 identifies examples of both direct and indirect costs for the maintenance department in a manufacturing plant. Thus, salaries of Rocky Mountain Bikes' maintenance department employees are considered indirect if the cost object is bicycles and direct if the cost object is the maintenance department. Classification of costs by traceability is useful for cost allocation. This is discussed in Chapter 9.

Decision Maker

Entrepreneur You wish to trace as many of your assembly department's direct costs as possible. You can trace 90% of them in an economical manner. To trace the other 10%, you need sophisticated and costly accounting software. Do you purchase this software? [Answer—p. 26]

EXHIBIT 1.6

Direct and Indirect Costs of a Maintenance Department

Direct Costs

- Salaries of maintenance department employees
- Equipment purchased by maintenance department
- Materials purchased by maintenance department
- Maintenance department equipment depreciation

Indirect Costs

- Factory accounting
- Factory administration
- Factory rent
- Factory managers' salary
- Factory light and heat
- Factory internal audit
- Factory intranet
- Insurance on factory

Classification by Controllability A cost can be defined as **controllable** or **not controllable.** Whether a cost is controllable or not depends on the employee's responsibilities, as shown in Exhibit 1.7. This is referred to as *hierarchical levels* in management, or *pecking order.* For example, investments in machinery are controllable by upper-level managers but not lower-level managers. Many daily operating expenses such as overtime often are controllable by lower-level managers. Classification of costs by controllability is especially useful for assigning responsibility to and evaluating managers.

EXHIBIT 1.7

Controllability of Costs

Senior Manager
Controls costs of investments in land, buildings, and equipment.

Supervisor
Controls daily expenses such as supplies, maintenance, and overtime.

Classification by Relevance A cost can be classified by relevance by identifying it as either a sunk cost or an out-of-pocket cost. A **sunk cost** has already been incurred and cannot be avoided or changed. It is irrelevant to future decisions. One example is the cost of a company's office equipment previously purchased. An **out-of-pocket cost** requires a future outlay of cash and is relevant for decision making. Future purchases of equipment involve out-of-pocket costs. A discussion of relevant costs must also consider opportunity costs. An **opportunity cost** is the potential benefit lost by choosing a specific action from two or more alternatives. One example is a student giving up wages from a job to attend evening classes. Consideration of opportunity cost is important when, for example, an insurance company must decide whether to outsource its payroll function or maintain it internally. This is discussed in Chapter 10.

Point: Opportunity costs are not recorded by the accounting system.

Classification by Function Another cost classification (for manufacturers) is capitalization as inventory or to expense as incurred. Costs capitalized as inventory are called **product costs,** which refer to expenditures necessary and integral to finished products. They include direct materials, direct labor, and indirect manufacturing costs called *overhead costs.* Product costs pertain to activities carried out to manufacture the product. Costs expensed are called **period costs,** which refer to expenditures identified more with a time period than with finished products. They include selling and general administrative expenses. Period costs pertain to activities that are not part of the manufacturing process. A distinction between product and period costs is important because period costs are expensed in the income statement and product costs are assigned to inventory on the balance sheet until that inventory is sold. An ability to understand and identify product costs and period costs is crucial to using and interpreting a *manufacturing statement* described later in this chapter.

C5 Define product and period costs and explain how they impact financial statements.

Exhibit 1.8 shows the different effects of product and period costs. Period costs flow directly to the current income statement as expenses. They are not reported as assets. Product costs are first assigned to inventory. Their final treatment depends on when inventory is sold or disposed of. Product costs assigned to finished goods that are sold in year 2009 are reported on the 2009 income statement as part of cost of goods sold. Product costs assigned to unsold inventory are carried forward on the balance sheet at the end of year 2009. If this inventory is sold in year 2010, product costs assigned to it are reported as part of cost of goods sold in that year's income statement.

Point: Only costs of production and purchases are classed as product costs.

EXHIBIT 1.8

Period and Product Costs in Financial Statements

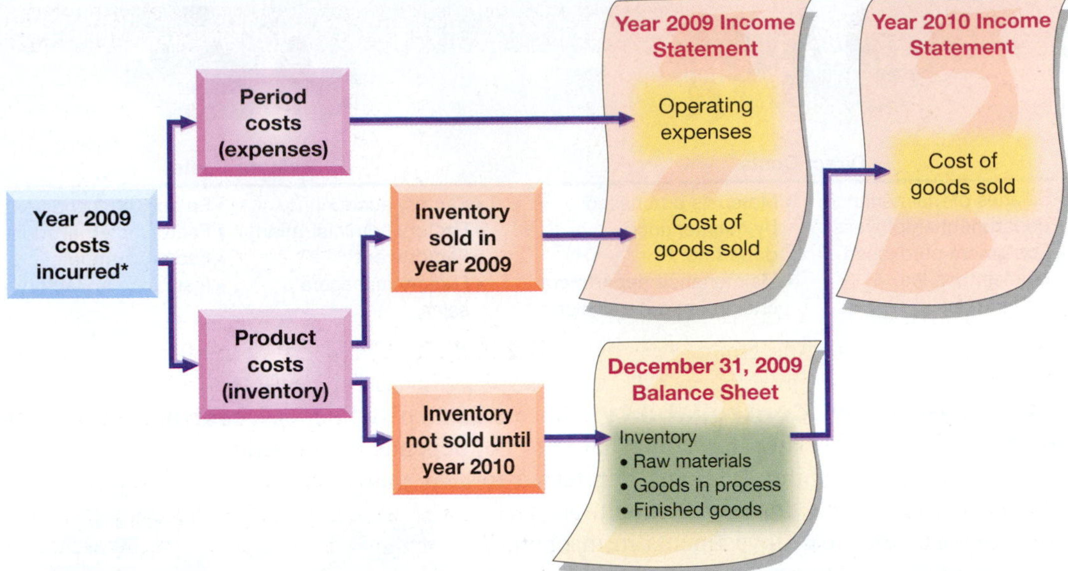

* This diagram excludes costs to acquire assets other than inventory.

Point: Product costs are either in the income statement as part of cost of goods sold or in the balance sheet as inventory. Period costs appear only on the income statement under operating expenses. See Exhibit 1.8.

Point: For a team approach to identifying period and product costs, see *Teamwork in Action* in the *Beyond the Numbers* section.

The difference between period and product costs explains why the year 2009 income statement does not report operating expenses related to either factory workers' wages or depreciation on factory buildings and equipment. Instead, both costs are combined with the cost of raw materials to compute the product cost of finished goods. A portion of these manufacturing costs (related to the goods sold) is reported in the year 2009 income statement as part of Cost of Goods Sold. The other portion is reported on the balance sheet at the end of that year as part of Inventory. The portion assigned to inventory could be included in any or all of raw materials, goods in process, or finished goods inventories.

Decision Maker boxes are role-playing exercises that stress the relevance of accounting.

Decision Maker

Purchase Manager You are evaluating two potential suppliers of seats for the manufacturing of motorcycles. One supplier (A) quotes a $145 price per seat and ensures 100% quality standards and on-time delivery. The second supplier (B) quotes a $115 price per seat but does not give any written assurances on quality or delivery. You decide to contract with the second supplier (B), saving $30 per seat. Does this decision have opportunity costs? [Answer—p. 27]

Identification of Cost Classifications

It is important to understand that a cost can be classified using any one (or combination) of the five different means described here. To do this we must understand costs and operations. Specifically, for the five classifications, we must be able to identify the *activity* for behavior, *cost object* for traceability, *management hierarchical level* for controllability, *opportunity cost* for relevance, and *benefit period* for function. Factory rent, for instance, can be classified as a product cost; it is fixed with respect to number of units produced, it is indirect with respect to the product, and it is not controllable by a production supervisor. Potential multiple classifications are shown in Exhibit 1.9 using different cost items incurred in manufacturing mountain bikes. The finished bike is the cost object. Proper allocation of these costs and the managerial decisions based on cost data depend on a correct cost classification.

Cost Concepts for Service Companies

Point: All expenses of service companies are period costs because these companies do not have inventory.

The cost concepts described are generally applicable to service organizations. For example, consider **Southwest Airlines**. Its cost of beverages for passengers is a variable cost based on number of passengers. The cost of leasing an aircraft is fixed with respect to number of passengers. We can also trace a flight crew's salary to a specific flight whereas we likely

EXHIBIT 1.9
Examples of Multiple Cost Classifications

Cost Item	By Behavior	By Traceability	By Function
Bicycle tires	Variable	Direct	Product
Wages of assembly worker*	Variable	Direct	Product
Advertising	Fixed	Indirect	Period
Production manager's salary	Fixed	Indirect	Product
Office depreciation	Fixed	Indirect	Period

* Although an assembly worker's wages are classified as variable costs, their actual behavior depends on how workers are paid and whether their wages are based on a union contract (such as piece rate or monthly wages).

cannot trace wages for the ground crew to a specific flight. Classification by function (such as product versus period costs) is not relevant to service companies because services are not inventoried. Instead, costs incurred by a service firm are expensed in the reporting period when incurred.

Managers in service companies must understand and apply cost concepts. They seek and rely on accurate cost estimates for many decisions. For example, an airline manager must often decide between canceling or rerouting flights. The manager must also be able to estimate costs saved by canceling a flight versus rerouting. Knowledge of fixed costs is equally important. We explain more about the cost requirements for these and other managerial decisions in Chapter 10.

Service Costs
- Beverages and snacks
- Cleaning fees
- Pilot and copilot salaries
- Attendant salaries
- Fuel and oil costs
- Travel agent fees
- Ground crew salaries

Quick Check Answers—p. 27

5. Which type of cost behavior increases total costs when volume of activity increases?
6. How could traceability of costs improve managerial decisions?

Reporting Manufacturing Activities

Companies with manufacturing activities differ from both merchandising and service companies. The main difference between merchandising and manufacturing companies is that merchandisers buy goods ready for sale while manufacturers produce goods from materials and labor. **Payless** is an example of a merchandising company. It buys and sells shoes without physically changing them. **Adidas** is primarily a manufacturer of shoes, apparel, and accessories. It purchases materials such as leather, cloth, dye, plastic, rubber, glue, and laces and then uses employees' labor to convert these materials to products. **Southwest Airlines** is a service company that transports people and items.

***Real company names** are printed in bold magenta.*

Manufacturing activities differ from both selling merchandise and providing services. Also, the financial statements for manufacturing companies differ slightly. This section considers some of these differences and compares them to accounting for a merchandising company.

Manufacturer's Balance Sheet

C6 Explain how balance sheets and income statements for manufacturing and merchandising companies differ.

Manufacturers carry several unique assets and usually have three inventories instead of the single inventory that merchandisers carry. Exhibit 1.10 shows three different inventories in the current asset section of the balance sheet for Rocky Mountain Bikes, a manufacturer. The three inventories are raw materials, goods in process, and finished goods.

Raw Materials Inventory **Raw materials inventory** refers to the goods a company acquires to use in making products. It uses raw materials in two ways: directly and indirectly. Most raw materials physically become part of a product and are identified with specific units or batches of a product. Raw materials used directly in a product are called *direct materials*. Other materials used to support production processes are sometimes not as clearly identified with specific units or batches of product. These materials are called **indirect materials** because they are not clearly identified with specific product units or batches. Items used as indirect materials often appear on a

Point: Reducing the size of inventories saves storage costs and frees money for other uses.

EXHIBIT 1.10

Balance Sheet for a Manufacturer

ROCKY MOUNTAIN BIKES
Balance Sheet
December 31, 2009

Assets		**Liabilities and Equity**	
Current assets		Current liabilities	
Cash	$ 11,000	Accounts payable	$ 14,000
Accounts receivable, net	30,150	Wages payable	540
Raw materials inventory	**9,000**	Interest payable	2,000
Goods in process inventory	**7,500**	Income taxes payable	32,600
Finished goods inventory	**10,300**	Total current liabilities	49,140
Factory supplies	350	Long-term liabilities	
Prepaid insurance	300	Long-term notes payable	50,000
Total current assets	68,600	Total liabilities	99,140
Plant assets			
Small tools, net	1,100	Stockholders' equity	
Delivery equipment, net	5,000	Common stock, $1.2 par	24,000
Office equipment, net	1,300	Paid-in capital	76,000
Factory machinery, net	65,500	Retained earnings	49,760
Factory building, net	86,700	Total stockholders' equity	149,760
Land	9,500	Total liabilities and equity	$248,900
Total plant assets, net	169,100		
Intangible assets (patents), net	11,200		
Total assets	$248,900		

balance sheet as factory supplies or are included in raw materials. Some direct materials are classified as indirect materials when their costs are low (insignificant). Examples include screws and nuts used in assembling mountain bikes and staples and glue used in manufacturing shoes. Using the *materiality principle,* individually tracing the costs of each of these materials and classifying them separately as direct materials does not make much economic sense. For instance, keeping detailed records of the amount of glue used to manufacture one shoe is not cost beneficial.

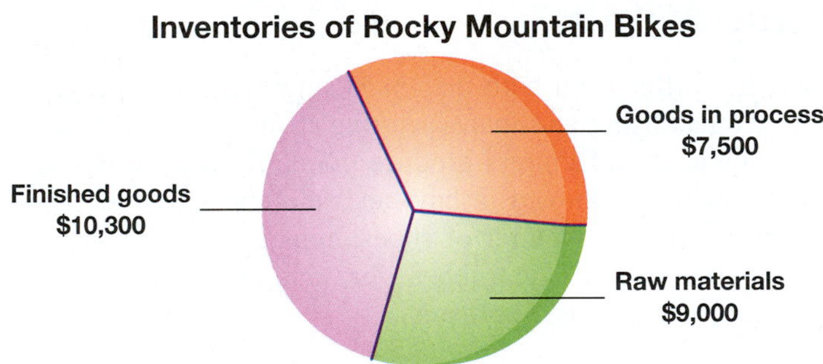

Goods in Process Inventory Another inventory held by manufacturers is **goods in process inventory,** also called *work in process inventory.* It consists of products in the process of being manufactured but not yet complete. The amount of goods in process inventory depends on the type of production process. If the time required to produce a unit of product is short, the goods in process inventory is likely small; but if weeks or months are needed to produce a unit, the goods in process inventory is usually larger.

Finished Goods Inventory A third inventory owned by a manufacturer is **finished goods inventory,** which consists of completed products ready for sale. This inventory is similar to merchandise inventory owned by a merchandising company. Manufacturers also often own unique plant assets such as small tools, factory buildings, factory equipment, and patents to manufacture products. The balance sheet in Exhibit 1.10 shows that Rocky Mountain Bikes owns all of these assets. Some manufacturers invest millions or even billions of dollars in production facilities and patents. Briggs & Stratton's recent balance sheet shows about $1 billion net investment in land, buildings, machinery and equipment, much of which involves production facilities. It manufactures more racing engines than any other company in the world.

Manufacturer's Income Statement

The main difference between the income statement of a manufacturer and that of a merchandiser involves the items making up cost of goods sold. Exhibit 1.11 compares the components of cost of goods sold for a manufacturer and a merchandiser. A merchandiser adds cost of goods purchased to beginning merchandise inventory and then subtracts ending merchandise inventory to get cost of goods sold. A manufacturer adds cost of goods manufactured to beginning finished goods inventory and then subtracts ending finished goods inventory to get cost of goods sold.

P1 Compute cost of goods sold for a manufacturer.

EXHIBIT 1.11

Cost of Goods Sold Computation

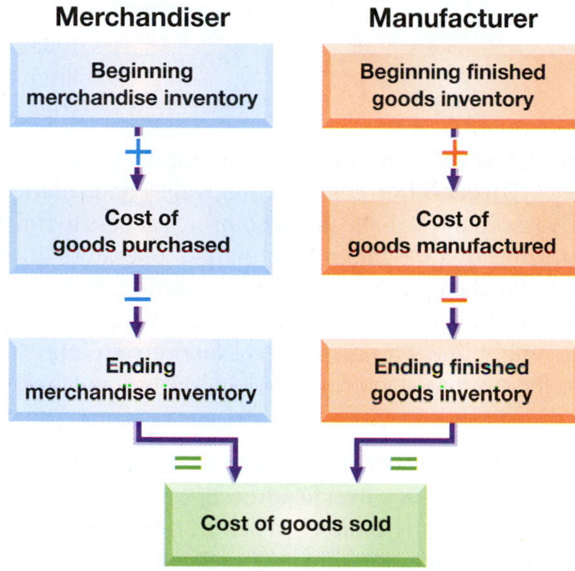

A merchandiser often uses the term *merchandise* inventory; a manufacturer often uses the term *finished goods* inventory. A manufacturer's inventories of raw materials and goods in process are not included in finished goods because they are not available for sale. A manufacturer also shows cost of goods *manufactured* instead of cost of goods *purchased.* This difference occurs because a manufacturer produces its goods instead of purchasing them ready for sale. We show later in this chapter how to derive cost of goods manufactured from the manufacturing statement.

The Cost of Goods Sold sections for both a merchandiser (Tele-Mart) and a manufacturer (Rocky Mountain Bikes) are shown in Exhibit 1.12 to highlight these differences. The remaining income statement sections are similar.

EXHIBIT 1.12

Cost of Goods Sold for a Merchandiser and Manufacturer

Merchandising (Tele-Mart) Company		Manufacturing (Rocky Mtn. Bikes) Company	
Cost of goods sold		Cost of goods sold	
Beginning *merchandise* inventory	$ 14,200	**Beginning *finished goods* inventory**	$ 11,200
Cost of merchandise *purchased*	234,150	**Cost of goods *manufactured****	170,500
Goods available for sale	248,350	Goods available for sale	181,700
Less ending *merchandise* inventory	12,100	**Less ending *finished goods* inventory**	10,300
Cost of goods sold	$236,250	Cost of goods sold	$171,400

* Cost of goods manufactured is reported in the income statement of Exhibit 1.14.

Although the cost of goods sold computations are similar, the numbers in these computations reflect different activities. A merchandiser's cost of goods purchased is the cost of buying products to be sold. A manufacturer's cost of goods manufactured is the sum of direct materials, direct labor, and factory overhead costs incurred in producing products. The remainder of this section further explains these three manufacturing costs and describes prime and conversion costs.

Direct Materials **Direct materials** are tangible components of a finished product. **Direct material costs** are the expenditures for direct materials that are separately and readily traced through the manufacturing process to finished goods. Examples of direct materials in manufacturing a mountain bike include its tires, seat, frame, pedals, brakes, cables, gears, and handlebars. The chart in the margin shows that direct materials generally make up about 45% of manufacturing costs in today's products, but this amount varies across industries and companies.

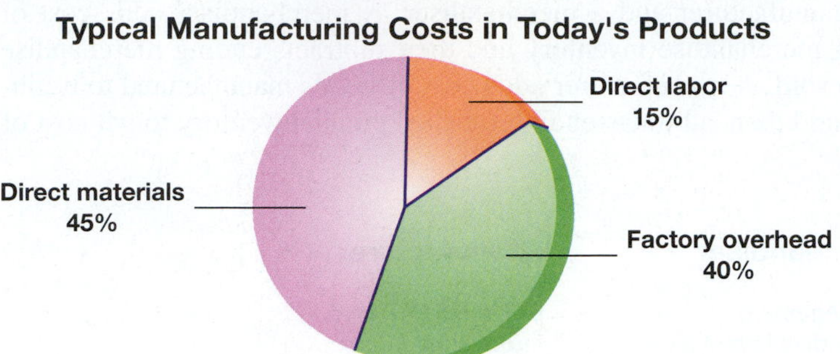

Direct Labor **Direct labor** refers to the efforts of employees who physically convert materials to finished product. **Direct labor costs** are the wages and salaries for direct labor that are separately and readily traced through the manufacturing process to finished goods. Examples of direct labor in manufacturing a mountain bike include operators directly involved in converting raw materials into finished products (welding, painting, forming) and assembly workers who attach materials such as tires, seats, pedals, and brakes to the bike frames. Costs of other workers on the assembly line who assist direct laborers are classified as **indirect labor costs. Indirect labor** refers to manufacturing workers' efforts not linked to specific units or batches of the product.

Point: Indirect labor costs are part of factory overhead.

Factory Overhead **Factory overhead** consists of all manufacturing costs that are not direct materials or direct labor. **Factory overhead costs** cannot be separately or readily traced to finished goods. These costs include indirect materials and indirect labor, costs not directly traceable to the product. Overtime paid to direct laborers is also included in overhead because overtime is due to delays, interruptions, or constraints not necessarily identifiable to a specific product or batches of product. Factory overhead costs also include maintenance of the mountain bike factory, supervision of its employees, repairing manufacturing equipment, factory utilities (water, gas, electricity), production manager's salary, factory rent, depreciation on factory buildings and equipment, factory insurance, property taxes on factory buildings and equipment, and factory accounting and legal services. Factory overhead does *not* include selling and administrative expenses because they are not incurred in manufacturing products. These expenses are called *period costs* and are recorded as expenses on the income statement when incurred.

Point: Factory overhead is also called *manufacturing overhead.*

EXHIBIT 1.13

Prime and Conversion Costs and Their Makeup

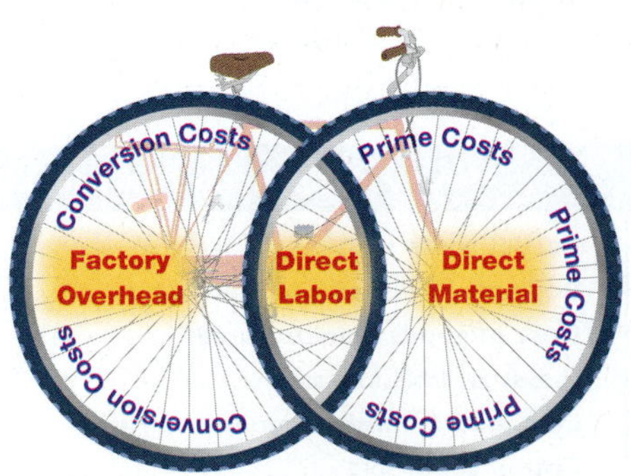

Point: Prime costs = Direct materials + Direct labor. Conversion costs = Direct labor + Factory overhead.

Prime and Conversion Costs Direct material costs and direct labor costs are also called **prime costs**—expenditures directly associated with the manufacture of finished goods. Direct labor costs and overhead costs are called **conversion costs**—expenditures incurred in the process of converting raw materials to finished goods. Direct labor costs are considered both prime costs and conversion costs. Exhibit 1.13 conveys the relation between prime and conversion costs and their components of direct material, direct labor, and factory overhead.

Reporting Performance Exhibit 1.14 shows the income statement for Rocky Mountain Bikes. Its operating expenses include sales salaries, office salaries, and depreciation of delivery and office equipment. Operating expenses do not include manufacturing costs such as factory workers' wages and depreciation of production equipment and the factory buildings. These manufacturing costs are reported as part of cost of goods manufactured and included in cost of goods sold. We explained why and how this is done in the section "Classification by Function."

Point: Manufacturers treat costs such as depreciation and rent as product costs if they are related to manufacturing.

EXHIBIT 1.14

Income Statement for a Manufacturer

ROCKY MOUNTAIN BIKES Income Statement For Year Ended December 31, 2009		
Sales		$310,000
Cost of goods sold		
Finished goods inventory, Dec. 31, 2008	$ 11,200	
Cost of goods manufactured	170,500	
Goods available for sale	181,700	
Less finished goods inventory, Dec. 31, 2009	10,300	
Cost of goods sold		171,400
Gross profit		138,600
Operating expenses		
Selling expenses		
Sales salaries expense	18,000	
Advertising expense	5,500	
Delivery wages expense	12,000	
Shipping supplies expense	250	
Insurance expense—Delivery equipment	300	
Depreciation expense—Delivery equipment	2,100	
Total selling expenses		38,150
General and administrative expenses		
Office salaries expense	15,700	
Miscellaneous expense	200	
Bad debts expense	1,550	
Office supplies expense	100	
Depreciation expense—Office equipment	200	
Interest expense	4,000	
Total general and administrative expenses		21,750
Total operating expenses		59,900
Income before income taxes		78,700
Income taxes expense		32,600
Net income		$ 46,100
Net income per common share (20,000 shares)		$ 2.31

Quick Check Answers—p. 27

7. What are the three types of inventory on a manufacturing company's balance sheet?
8. How does cost of goods sold differ for merchandising versus manufacturing companies?

Flow of Manufacturing Activities

C7 Explain manufacturing activities and the flow of manufacturing costs.

To understand manufacturing and its reports, we must first understand the flow of manufacturing activities and costs. Exhibit 1.15 shows the flow of manufacturing activities for a manufacturer. This exhibit has three important sections: *materials activity, production activity,* and *sales activity.* We explain each activity in this section.

Materials Activity The far left side of Exhibit 1.15 shows the flow of raw materials. Manufacturers usually start a period with some beginning raw materials inventory carried over from the previous period. The company then acquires additional raw materials in the current period. Adding these purchases to beginning inventory gives total raw materials available for use in production. These raw materials are then either used in production in the current period or remain in inventory at the end of the period for use in future periods.

Point: Knowledge of managerial accounting provides us a means of measuring manufacturing costs and is a sound foundation for studying advanced business topics.

Production Activity The middle section of Exhibit 1.15 describes production activity. Four factors come together in production: beginning goods in process inventory, direct materials,

EXHIBIT 1.15

Activities and Cost Flows in Manufacturing

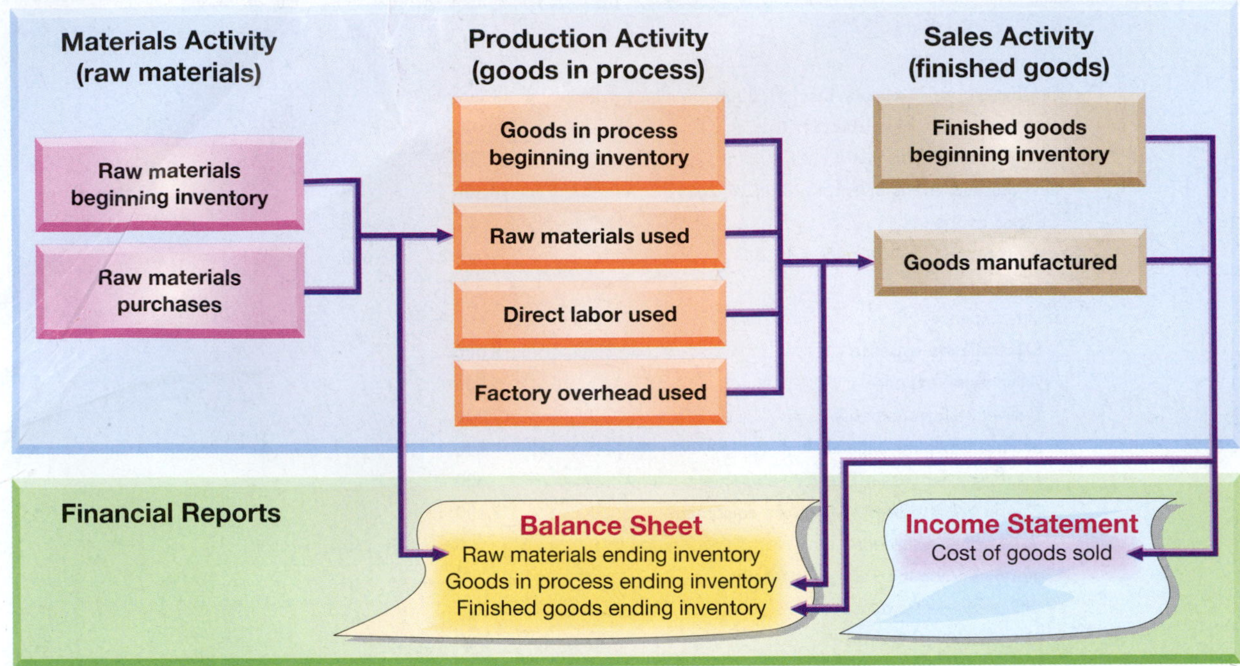

direct labor, and overhead. Beginning goods in process inventory consists of partly assembled products from the previous period. Production activity results in products that are either finished or remain unfinished. The cost of finished products makes up the cost of goods manufactured for the current period. Unfinished products are identified as ending goods in process inventory. The cost of unfinished products consists of direct materials, direct labor, and factory overhead, and is reported on the current period's balance sheet. The costs of both finished goods manufactured and goods in process are *product costs.*

Point: The series of activities that add value to a company's products or services is called a **value chain.**

Sales Activity The company's sales activity is portrayed in the far right side of Exhibit 1.15. Newly completed units are combined with beginning finished goods inventory to make up total finished goods available for sale in the current period. The cost of finished products sold is reported on the income statement as cost of goods sold. The cost of products not sold is reported on the current period's balance sheet as ending finished goods inventory.

Manufacturing Statement

P2 Prepare a manufacturing statement and explain its purpose and links to financial statements.

A company's manufacturing activities are described in a **manufacturing statement,** also called the *schedule of manufacturing activities* or the *schedule of cost of goods manufactured.* The manufacturing statement summarizes the types and amounts of costs incurred in a company's manufacturing process. Exhibit 1.16 shows the manufacturing statement for Rocky Mountain Bikes. The statement is divided into four parts: *direct materials, direct labor, overhead,* and *computation of cost of goods manufactured.* We describe each of these parts in this section.

① The manufacturing statement begins by computing direct materials used. We start by adding beginning raw materials inventory of $8,000 to the current period's purchases of $86,500. This yields $94,500 of total raw materials available for use. A physical count of inventory shows $9,000 of ending raw materials inventory. This implies a total cost of raw materials used during the period of $85,500 ($94,500 total raw materials available for use − $9,000 ending inventory). (*Note:* All raw materials are direct materials for Rocky Mountain Bikes.)

EXHIBIT 1.16
Manufacturing Statement

ROCKY MOUNTAIN BIKES Manufacturing Statement For Year Ended December 31, 2009			
①	**Direct materials**		
	Raw materials inventory, Dec. 31, 2008	$ 8,000	
	Raw materials purchases	86,500	
	Raw materials available for use	94,500	
	Less raw materials inventory, Dec. 31, 2009	9,000	
	Direct materials used		$ 85,500
②	**Direct labor**		60,000
③	**Factory overhead**		
	Indirect labor	9,000	
	Factory supervision	6,000	
	Factory utilities	2,600	
	Repairs—Factory equipment	2,500	
	Property taxes—Factory building	1,900	
	Factory supplies used	600	
	Factory insurance expired	1,100	
	Depreciation expense—Small tools	200	
	Depreciation expense—Factory equipment	3,500	
	Depreciation expense—Factory building	1,800	
	Amortization expense—Patents	800	
	Total factory overhead		30,000
④	Total manufacturing costs		175,500
	Add goods in process inventory, Dec. 31, 2008		2,500
	Total cost of goods in process		178,000
	Less goods in process inventory, Dec. 31, 2009		7,500
	Cost of goods manufactured		$170,500

② The second part of the manufacturing statement reports direct labor costs. Rocky Mountain Bikes had total direct labor costs of $60,000 for the period. This amount includes payroll taxes and fringe benefits.

③ The third part of the manufacturing statement reports overhead costs. The statement lists each important factory overhead item and its cost. Total factory overhead cost for the period is $30,000. Some companies report only *total* factory overhead on the manufacturing statement and attach a separate schedule listing individual overhead costs.

④ The final section of the manufacturing statement computes and reports the *cost of goods manufactured.* (Total manufacturing costs for the period are $175,500 [$85,500 + $60,000 + $30,000], the sum of direct materials used and direct labor and overhead costs incurred.) This amount is first added to beginning goods in process inventory. This gives the total goods in process inventory of $178,000 ($175,500 + $2,500). We then compute the current period's cost of goods manufactured of $170,500 by taking the $178,000 total goods in process and subtracting the $7,500 cost of ending goods in process inventory that consists of direct materials, direct labor, and factory overhead. The cost of goods manufactured amount is also called *net cost of goods manufactured* or *cost of goods completed*. Exhibit 1.14 shows that this item and amount are listed in the Cost of Goods Sold section of Rocky Mountain Bikes' income statement and the balance sheet.

Point: Direct material and direct labor costs increase with increases in production volume and are called *variable costs.* Overhead can be both variable and fixed. When overhead costs vary with production, they are called *variable overhead.* When overhead costs don't vary with production, they are called *fixed overhead.*

Point: Manufacturers sometimes report variable and fixed overhead separately in the manufacturing statement to provide more information to managers about cost behavior.

A managerial accounting system records costs and reports them in various reports that eventually determine financial statements. Exhibit 1.17 shows how overhead costs flow through the system: from an initial listing of specific costs, to a section of the manufacturing statement, to the reporting on the income statement and the balance sheet.

"My boss wants us to appeal to a younger and hipper crowd. So, I'd like to get a tattoo that says-- 'Accounting rules!'"

EXHIBIT 1.17

Overhead Cost Flows across Accounting Reports

Rocky Mountain Bikes
Factory Overhead Costs
For Year Ended December 31, 2009

Indirect labor	$ 9,000
Supervision	6,000
Other overhead items*	15,000
Total overhead	**$30,000**

*Overhead items are listed in Exhibit 1.16.

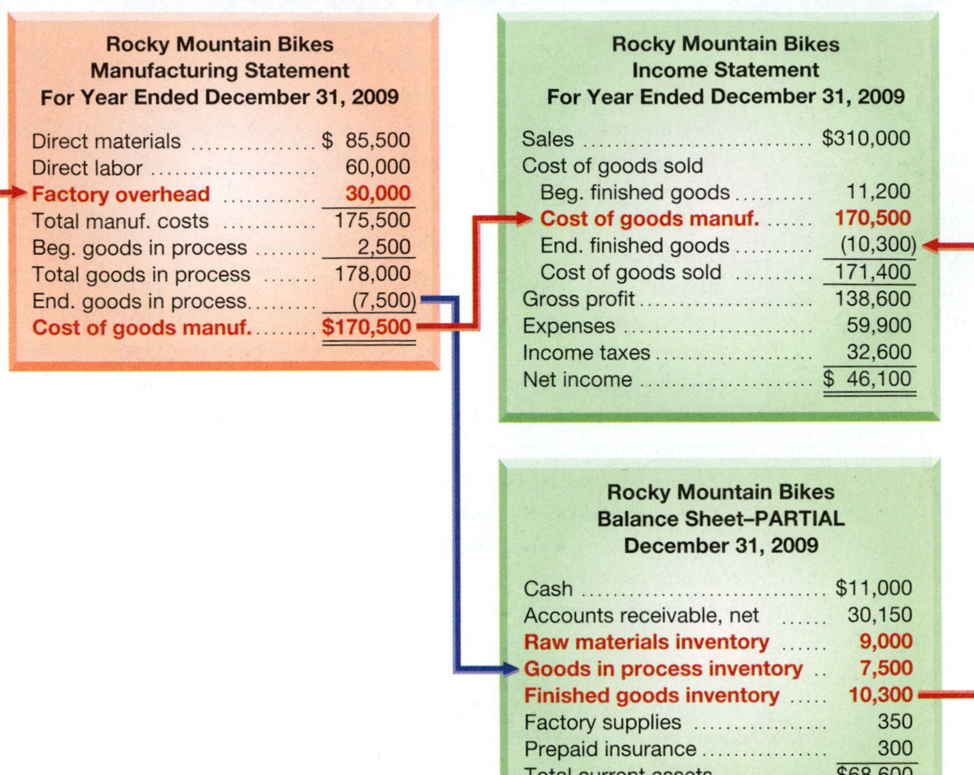

Rocky Mountain Bikes
Manufacturing Statement
For Year Ended December 31, 2009

Direct materials	$ 85,500
Direct labor	60,000
Factory overhead	**30,000**
Total manuf. costs	175,500
Beg. goods in process	2,500
Total goods in process	178,000
End. goods in process	(7,500)
Cost of goods manuf.	**$170,500**

Rocky Mountain Bikes
Income Statement
For Year Ended December 31, 2009

Sales	$310,000
Cost of goods sold	
Beg. finished goods	11,200
Cost of goods manuf.	**170,500**
End. finished goods	(10,300)
Cost of goods sold	171,400
Gross profit	138,600
Expenses	59,900
Income taxes	32,600
Net income	$ 46,100

Rocky Mountain Bikes
Balance Sheet–PARTIAL
December 31, 2009

Cash	$11,000
Accounts receivable, net	30,150
Raw materials inventory	**9,000**
Goods in process inventory	**7,500**
Finished goods inventory	**10,300**
Factory supplies	350
Prepaid insurance	300
Total current assets	$68,600

Management uses information in the manufacturing statement to plan and control the company's manufacturing activities. To provide timely information for decision making, the statement is often prepared monthly, weekly, or even daily. In anticipation of release of its much-hyped iPhone, **Apple** grew its inventory of Flash-based memory chips, a critical component, and its finished goods inventory. The manufacturing statement contains information useful to external users but is not a general-purpose financial statement. Companies rarely publish the manufacturing statement because managers view this information as proprietary and potentially harmful to them if released to competitors.

Quick Check

Answers—p. 27

9. A manufacturing statement (*a*) computes cost of goods manufactured for the period, (*b*) computes cost of goods sold for the period, or (*c*) reports operating expenses incurred for the period.

10. Are companies required to report a manufacturing statement?

11. How are both beginning and ending goods in process inventories reported on a manufacturing statement?

Decision Analysis *(a section at the end of each chapter) introduces and explains simple tools helpful in managerial decisions.*

Decision Analysis — Cycle Time and Cycle Efficiency

A1 Compute cycle time and cycle efficiency, and explain their importance to production management.

As lean manufacturing practices help companies move toward just-in-time manufacturing, it is important for these companies to reduce the time to manufacture their products and to improve manufacturing efficiency. One metric that measures that time element is **cycle time (CT).** A definition of cycle time is in Exhibit 1.18.

Cycle time = Process time + Inspection time + Move time + Wait time

EXHIBIT 1.18
Cycle Time

Process time is the time spent producing the product. *Inspection time* is the time spent inspecting (1) raw materials when received, (2) goods in process while in production, and (3) finished goods prior to shipment. *Move time* is the time spent moving (1) raw materials from storage to production and (2) goods in process from factory location to another factory location. *Wait time* is the time that an order or job sits with no production applied to it; this can be due to order delays, bottlenecks in production, and poor scheduling.

Process time is considered **value-added time** because it is the only activity in cycle time that adds value to the product from the customer's perspective. The other three time activities are considered **non-value-added time** because they add no value to the customer.

Companies strive to reduce non-value-added time to improve **cycle efficiency (CE).** Cycle efficiency is the ratio of value-added time to total cycle time—see Exhibit 1.19.

$$\textbf{Cycle efficiency} = \frac{\textbf{Value-added time}}{\textbf{Cycle time}}$$

EXHIBIT 1.19
Cycle Efficiency

To illustrate, assume that Rocky Mountain Bikes receives and produces an order for 500 Tracker® mountain bikes. Assume that the following times were measured during production of this order.

Process time... 1.8 days **Inspection time... 0.5 days** **Move time... 0.7 days** **Wait time... 3.0 days**

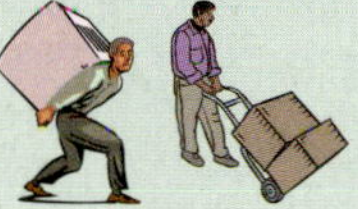

In this case, cycle time is 6.0 days, computed as 1.8 days + 0.5 days + 0.7 days + 3.0 days. Also, cycle efficiency is 0.3, or 30%, computed as 1.8 days divided by 6.0 days. This means that Rocky Mountain Bikes spends 30% of its time working on the product (value-added time). The other 70% is spent on non-value-added activities.

If a company has a CE of 1, it means that its time is spent entirely on value-added activities. If the CE is low, the company should evaluate its production process to see if it can identify ways to reduce non-value-added activities. The 30% CE for Rocky Mountain Bikes is low and its management should look for ways to reduce non-value-added activities.

*The **Demonstration Problem** is a review of key chapter content. The Planning the Solution offers strategies in solving the problem.*

Demonstration Problem 1: Cost Behavior and Classification

Understanding the classification and assignment of costs is important. Consider a company that manufactures computer chips. It incurs the following costs in manufacturing chips and in operating the company.

1. Plastic board used to mount the chip, $3.50 each.
2. Assembly worker pay of $15 per hour to attach chips to plastic board.
3. Salary for factory maintenance workers who maintain factory equipment.
4. Factory supervisor pay of $55,000 per year to supervise employees.
5. Real estate taxes paid on the factory, $14,500.
6. Real estate taxes paid on the company office, $6,000.
7. Depreciation costs on machinery used by workers, $30,000.
8. Salary paid to the chief financial officer, $95,000.
9. Advertising costs of $7,800 paid to promote products.
10. Salespersons' commissions of $0.50 for each assembled chip sold.
11. Management has the option to rent the manufacturing plant to six local hospitals to store medical records instead of producing and assembling chips.

Classify each cost in the following table according to the categories listed in the table header. A cost can be classified under more than one category. For example, the plastic board used to mount chips is classified as a direct material product cost and as a direct unit cost.

	Period Costs	Product Costs			Unit Cost Classification		Sunk Cost	Opportunity Cost
Cost	Selling and Administrative	Direct Material (Prime Cost)	Direct Labor (Prime and Conversion)	Factory Overhead (Conversion Cost)	Direct	Indirect		
1. Plastic board used to mount the chip, $3.50 each		✔			✔			

Solution to Demonstration Problem 1

	Period Costs	Product Costs			Unit Cost Classification		Sunk Cost	Opportunity Cost
Cost*	Selling and Administrative	Direct Material (Prime Cost)	Direct Labor (Prime and Conversion)	Factory Overhead (Conversion Cost)	Direct	Indirect		
1.		✔			✔			
2.			✔		✔			
3.				✔		✔		
4.				✔		✔		
5.				✔		✔		
6.	✔							
7.				✔		✔	✔	
8.	✔							
9.	✔							
10.	✔							
11.								✔

* Costs 1 through 11 refer to the 11 cost items described at the beginning of the problem.

Demonstration Problem 2: Reporting for Manufacturers

A manufacturing company's balance sheet and income statement differ from those for a merchandising or service company.

Required

1. Fill in the [BLANK] descriptors on the partial balance sheets for both the manufacturing company and the merchandising company. Explain why a different presentation is required.

Manufacturing Company

ADIDAS GROUP
Partial Balance Sheet
December 31, 2009

Current assets	
Cash	$10,000
[BLANK]	8,000
[BLANK]	5,000
[BLANK]	7,000
Supplies	500
Prepaid insurance	500
Total current assets	$31,000

Merchandising Company

PAYLESS SHOE OUTLET
Partial Balance Sheet
December 31, 2009

Current assets	
Cash	$ 5,000
[BLANK]	12,000
Supplies	500
Prepaid insurance	500
Total current assets	$18,000

2. Fill in the [BLANK] descriptors on the income statements for the manufacturing company and the merchandising company. Explain why a different presentation is required.

Manufacturing Company

ADIDAS GROUP
Partial Income Statement
For Year Ended December 31, 2009

Sales	$200,000
Cost of goods sold	
Finished goods inventory, Dec. 31, 2008	10,000
[BLANK]	120,000
Goods available for sale	130,000
Finished goods inventory, Dec. 31, 2009	(7,000)
Cost of goods sold	123,000
Gross profit	$ 77,000

Merchandising Company

PAYLESS SHOE OUTLET
Partial Income Statement
For Year Ended December 31, 2009

Sales	$190,000
Cost of goods sold	
Merchandise inventory, Dec. 31, 2008	8,000
[BLANK]	108,000
Goods available for sale	116,000
Merchandise inventory, Dec. 31, 2009	(12,000)
Cost of goods sold	104,000
Gross profit	$ 86,000

3. The manufacturer's cost of goods manufactured is the sum of (a) _______, (b) _______, and (c) _______ costs incurred in producing the product.

Solution to Demonstration Problem 2

1. Inventories for a manufacturer and for a merchandiser.

Manufacturing Company

ADIDAS GROUP
Partial Balance Sheet
December 31, 2009

Current assets	
Cash	$10,000
Raw materials inventory	8,000
Goods in process inventory	5,000
Finished goods inventory	7,000
Supplies	500
Prepaid insurance	500
Total current assets	$31,000

Merchandising Company

PAYLESS SHOE OUTLET
Partial Balance Sheet
December 31, 2009

Current assets	
Cash	$ 5,000
Merchandise inventory	12,000
Supplies	500
Prepaid insurance	500
Total current assets	$18,000

Explanation: A manufacturing company must control and measure three types of inventories: raw materials, goods in process, and finished goods. In the sequence of making a product, the raw materials move into production—called *goods in process inventory*—and then to finished goods. All raw materials and goods in process inventory at the end of each accounting period are considered current assets. All unsold finished inventory is considered a current asset at the end of each accounting period. The merchandising company must control and measure only one type of inventory, purchased goods.

2. Cost of goods sold for a manufacturer and for a merchandiser.

Manufacturing Company

ADIDAS GROUP
Partial Income Statement
For Year Ended December 31, 2009

Sales		$200,000
Cost of goods sold		
	Finished goods inventory, Dec. 31, 2008	10,000
	Cost of goods manufactured	120,000
	Goods available for sale	130,000
	Finished goods inventory, Dec. 31, 2009	(7,000)
	Cost of goods sold	123,000
Gross profit		$ 77,000

Merchandising Company

PAYLESS SHOE OUTLET
Partial Income Statement
For Year Ended December 31, 2009

Sales		$190,000
Cost of goods sold		
	Merchandise inventory, Dec. 31, 2008	8,000
	Cost of purchases	108,000
	Goods available for sale	116,000
	Merchandise inventory, Dec. 31, 2009	(12,000)
	Cost of goods sold	104,000
Gross profit		$ 86,000

Explanation: Manufacturing and merchandising companies use different reporting terms. In particular, the terms *finished goods* and *cost of goods manufactured* are used to reflect the production of goods, yet the concepts and techniques of reporting cost of goods sold for a manufacturing company and merchandising company are similar.

3. A manufacturer's cost of goods manufactured is the sum of (a) *direct material,* (b) *direct labor,* and (c) *factory overhead* costs incurred in producing the product.

Demonstration Problem 3: Manufacturing Statement

The following account balances and other information are from SUNN Corporation's accounting records for year-end December 31, 2009. Use this information to prepare (1) a table listing factory overhead costs, (2) a manufacturing statement (show only the total factory overhead cost), and (3) an income statement.

Advertising expense	$ 85,000	Goods in process inventory, Dec. 31, 2008	$ 8,000
Amortization expense—Factory patents	16,000	Goods in process inventory, Dec. 31, 2009	9,000
Bad debts expense	28,000	Income taxes	53,400
Depreciation expense—Office equipment	37,000	Indirect labor	26,000
Depreciation expense—Factory building	133,000	Interest expense	25,000
Depreciation expense—Factory equipment	78,000	Miscellaneous expense	55,000
Direct labor	250,000	Property taxes on factory equipment	14,000
Factory insurance expired	62,000	Raw materials inventory, Dec. 31, 2008	60,000
Factory supervision	74,000	Raw materials inventory, Dec. 31, 2009	78,000
Factory supplies used	21,000	Raw materials purchases	313,000
Factory utilities	115,000	Repairs expense—Factory equipment	31,000
Finished goods inventory, Dec. 31, 2008	15,000	Salaries expense	150,000
Finished goods inventory, Dec. 31, 2009	12,500	Sales	1,630,000

Planning the Solution

- Analyze the account balances and select those that are part of factory overhead costs.
- Arrange these costs in a table that lists factory overhead costs for the year.
- Analyze the remaining costs and select those related to production activity for the year; selected costs should include the materials and goods in process inventories and direct labor.

- Prepare a manufacturing statement for the year showing the calculation of the cost of materials used in production, the cost of direct labor, and the total factory overhead cost. When presenting overhead cost on this statement, report only total overhead cost from the table of overhead costs for the year. Show the costs of beginning and ending goods in process inventory to determine cost of goods manufactured.
- Organize the remaining revenue and expense items into the income statement for the year. Combine cost of goods manufactured from the manufacturing statement with the finished goods inventory amounts to compute cost of goods sold for the year.

Solution to Demonstration Problem 3

SUNN CORPORATION
Factory Overhead Costs
For Year Ended December 31, 2009

Amortization expense—Factory patents	$ 16,000
Depreciation expense—Factory building	133,000
Depreciation expense—Factory equipment	78,000
Factory insurance expired	62,000
Factory supervision	74,000
Factory supplies used	21,000
Factory utilities	115,000
Indirect labor	26,000
Property taxes on factory equipment	14,000
Repairs expense—Factory equipment	31,000
Total factory overhead	$570,000

SUNN CORPORATION
Manufacturing Statement
For Year Ended December 31, 2009

Direct materials	
Raw materials inventory, Dec. 31, 2008	$ 60,000
Raw materials purchase	313,000
Raw materials available for use	373,000
Less raw materials inventory, Dec. 31, 2009	78,000
Direct materials used	295,000
Direct labor	250,000
Factory overhead	570,000
Total manufacturing costs	1,115,000
Goods in process inventory, Dec. 31, 2008	8,000
Total cost of goods in process	1,123,000
Less goods in process inventory, Dec. 31, 2009	9,000
Cost of goods manufactured	$1,114,000

SUNN CORPORATION
Income Statement
For Year Ended December 31, 2009

Sales		$1,630,000
Cost of goods sold		
Finished goods inventory, Dec. 31, 2008	$ 15,000	
Cost of goods manufactured	1,114,000	
Goods available for sale	1,129,000	
Less finished goods inventory, Dec. 31, 2009	12,500	
Cost of goods sold		1,116,500
Gross profit		513,500
Operating expenses		
Advertising expense	85,000	
Bad debts expense	28,000	
Depreciation expense—Office equipment	37,000	
Interest expense	25,000	
Miscellaneous expense	55,000	
Salaries expense	150,000	
Total operating expenses		380,000
Income before income taxes		133,500
Income taxes		53,400
Net income		$ 80,100

*A **Summary** organized by learning objectives concludes each chapter.*

Summary

C1 Explain the purpose and nature of managerial accounting. The purpose of managerial accounting is to provide useful information to management and other internal decision makers. It does this by collecting, managing, and reporting both monetary and nonmonetary information in a manner useful to internal users. Major characteristics of managerial accounting include (1) focus on internal decision makers, (2) emphasis on planning and control, (3) flexibility, (4) timeliness, (5) reliance on forecasts and estimates, (6) focus on segments and projects, and (7) reporting both monetary and nonmonetary information.

C2 Describe the lean business model. The main purpose of the lean business model is the elimination of waste. Concepts such as total quality management and just-in-time production often aid in effective application of the model.

C3 Describe fraud and the role of ethics in managerial accounting. Fraud involves the use of one's job for personal gain through deliberate misuse of the employer's assets. All fraud is secret, violates the employee's job duties, provides financial benefits to the employee, and costs the employer money. A code of ethical beliefs can be used to resolve ethical conflicts.

C4 Describe accounting concepts useful in classifying costs. We can classify costs on the basis of their (1) behavior—fixed vs. variable, (2) traceability—direct vs. indirect, (3) controllability—controllable vs. uncontrollable, (4) relevance—sunk vs. out of pocket, and (5) function—product vs. period. A cost can be classified in more than one way, depending on the purpose for which the cost is being determined. These classifications help us understand cost patterns, analyze performance, and plan operations.

C5 Define product and period costs and explain how they impact financial statements. Costs that are capitalized because they are expected to have future value are called *product costs;* costs that are expensed are called *period costs.* This classification is important because it affects the amount of costs expensed in the income statement and the amount of costs assigned to inventory on the balance sheet. Product costs are commonly made up of direct materials, direct labor, and overhead. Period costs include selling and administrative expenses.

C6 Explain how balance sheets and income statements for manufacturing and merchandising companies differ. The main difference is that manufacturers usually carry three inventories on their balance sheets—raw materials, goods in process, and finished goods—instead of one inventory that merchandisers carry. The main difference between income statements of manufacturers and merchandisers is the items making up cost of goods sold. A merchandiser adds beginning merchandise inventory to cost of goods purchased and then subtracts ending merchandise inventory to get cost of goods sold. A manufacturer adds beginning finished goods inventory to cost of goods manufactured and then subtracts ending finished goods inventory to get cost of goods sold.

C7 Explain manufacturing activities and the flow of manufacturing costs. Manufacturing activities consist of materials, production, and sales activities. The materials activity consists of the purchase and issuance of materials to production. The production activity consists of converting materials into finished goods. At this stage in the process, the materials, labor, and overhead costs have been incurred and the manufacturing statement is prepared. The sales activity consists of selling some or all of finished goods available for sale. At this stage, the cost of goods sold is determined.

A1 Compute cycle time and cycle efficiency, and explain their importance to production management. It is important for companies to reduce the time to produce their products and to improve manufacturing efficiency. One measure of that time is cycle time (CT), defined as Process time + Inspection time + Move time + Wait time. Process time is value-added time; the others are non-value-added time. Cycle efficiency (CE) is the ratio of value-added time to total cycle time. If CE is low, management should evaluate its production process to see if it can reduce non-value-added activities.

P1 Compute cost of goods sold for a manufacturer. A manufacturer adds beginning finished goods inventory to cost of goods manufactured and then subtracts ending finished goods inventory to get cost of goods sold.

P2 Prepare a manufacturing statement and explain its purpose and links to financial statements. The manufacturing statement reports computation of cost of goods manufactured for the period. It begins by showing the period's costs for direct materials, direct labor, and overhead and then adjusts these numbers for the beginning and ending inventories of the goods in process to yield cost of goods manufactured.

Guidance Answers to **Decision Maker** and **Decision Ethics**

Production Manager It appears that all three friends want to pay the bill with someone else's money. David is using money belonging to the tax authorities, Denise is taking money from her company, and Derek is defrauding the client. To prevent such practices, companies have internal audit mechanisms. Many companies also adopt ethical codes of conduct to help guide employees. We must recognize that some entertainment expenses are justifiable and even encouraged. For example, the tax law allows certain deductions for entertainment that have a business purpose. Corporate policies also sometimes allow and encourage reimbursable spending for social activities, and contracts can include entertainment as allowable costs. Nevertheless, without further details, payment for this bill should be made from personal accounts.

Entrepreneur Tracing all costs directly to cost objects is always desirable, but you need to be able to do so in an economically feasible manner. In this case, you are able to trace 90% of the assembly department's direct costs. It may not be economical to spend more money on a new software to trace the final 10% of costs. You need to make a cost–benefit trade-off. If the software offers benefits beyond tracing the remaining 10% of the assembly department's costs, your decision should consider this.

Purchase Manager Opportunity costs relate to the potential quality and delivery benefits given up by not choosing supplier (A). Selecting supplier (B) might involve future costs of poor-quality seats (inspection, repairs, and returns). Also, potential delivery delays could interrupt work and increase manufacturing costs. Your company could also incur sales losses if the product quality of supplier (B) is low. As purchase manager, you are responsible for these costs and must consider them in making your decision.

Guidance Answers to **Quick Checks**

1. *d*
2. Financial accounting information is intended for users external to an organization such as investors, creditors, and government authorities. Managerial accounting focuses on providing information to managers, officers, and other decision makers within the organization.
3. No, GAAP do not control the practice of managerial accounting. Unlike external users, the internal users need managerial accounting information for planning and controlling business activities rather than for external comparison. Different types of information are required, depending on the activity. Therefore it is difficult to standardize managerial accounting.
4. Under TQM, all managers and employees should strive toward higher standards in their work and in the products and services they offer to customers.
5. Variable costs increase when volume of activity increases.
6. By being able to trace costs to cost objects (say, to products and departments), managers better understand the total costs associated with a cost object. This is useful when managers consider making changes to the cost object (such as when dropping the product or expanding the department).
7. Raw materials inventory, goods in process inventory, and finished goods inventory.
8. The cost of goods sold for merchandising companies includes all costs of acquiring the merchandise; the cost of goods sold for manufacturing companies includes the three costs of manufacturing: direct materials, direct labor, and overhead.
9. *a*
10. No; companies rarely report a manufacturing statement.
11. Beginning goods in process inventory is added to total manufacturing costs to yield total goods in process. Ending goods in process inventory is subtracted from total goods in process to yield cost of goods manufactured for the period.

A list of key terms with page references concludes each chapter (a complete glossary is at the end of the book and on the book's Website).

Key Terms mhhe.com/wildMA2e

Key Terms are available at the book's Website for learning and testing in an online Flashcard Format.

Continuous improvement (p. 8)
Control (p. 5)
Controllable or not controllable cost (p. 11)
Conversion costs (p. 16)
Cost object (p. 10)
Customer orientation (p. 7)
Cycle efficiency (CE) (p. 21)
Cycle time (CT) (p. 21)
Direct costs (p. 10)
Direct labor (p. 16)
Direct labor costs (p. 16)
Direct materials (p. 16)
Direct material costs (p. 16)
Ethics (p. 9)
Factory overhead (p. 16)
Factory overhead costs (p. 16)
Finished goods inventory (p. 14)
Fixed cost (p. 10)
Goods in process inventory (p. 14)
Indirect costs (p. 10)
Indirect labor (p. 16)
Indirect labor costs (p. 16)
Indirect materials (p. 13)
Institute of Management Accountants (IMA) (p. 9)
Internal control system (p. 9)
Just-in-time (JIT) manufacturing (p. 8)
Lean business model (p. 8)
Managerial accounting (p. 4)
Manufacturing statement (p. 18)
Non-value-added time (p. 21)
Opportunity cost (p. 11)
Out-of-pocket cost (p. 11)
Period costs (p. 11)
Planning (p. 4)
Prime costs (p. 16)
Product costs (p. 11)
Raw materials inventory (p. 13)
Sunk cost (p. 11)
Total quality management (TQM) (p. 8)
Value-added time (p. 21)
Value chain (p. 18)
Variable cost (p. 10)

Multiple Choice Quiz Answers on p. 45 mhhe.com/wildMA2e

Additional Quiz Questions are available at the book's Website.

Quiz1

1. Continuous improvement
   a. Is used to reduce inventory levels.
   b. Is applicable only in service businesses.
   c. Rejects the notion of "good enough."
   d. Is used to reduce ordering costs.
   e. Is applicable only in manufacturing businesses.

2. A direct cost is one that is
- **a.** Variable with respect to the cost object.
- **b.** Traceable to the cost object.
- **c.** Fixed with respect to the cost object.
- **d.** Allocated to the cost object.
- **e.** A period cost.

3. Costs that are incurred as part of the manufacturing process, but are not clearly traceable to the specific unit of product or batches of product, are called
- **a.** Period costs.
- **b.** Factory overhead.
- **c.** Sunk costs.
- **d.** Opportunity costs.
- **e.** Fixed costs.

4. The three major cost components of manufacturing a product are
- **a.** Direct materials, direct labor, and factory overhead.
- **b.** Period costs, product costs, and sunk costs.
- **c.** Indirect labor, indirect materials, and fixed expenses.
- **d.** Variable costs, fixed costs, and period costs.
- **e.** Opportunity costs, sunk costs, and direct costs.

5. A company reports the following for the current year.

Finished goods inventory, beginning year	$6,000
Finished goods inventory, ending year	3,200
Cost of goods sold	7,500

Its cost of goods manufactured for the current year is
- **a.** $1,500.
- **b.** $1,700.
- **c.** $7,500.
- **d.** $2,800.
- **e.** $4,700.

Discussion Questions

1. Describe the managerial accountant's role in business planning, control, and decision making.

2. Distinguish between managerial and financial accounting on
- **a.** Users and decision makers.
- **b.** Purpose of information.
- **c.** Flexibility of practice.
- **d.** Time dimension.
- **e.** Focus of information.
- **f.** Nature of information.

3. Identify the usual changes that a company must make when it adopts a customer orientation.

4. Distinguish between direct material and indirect material.

5. Distinguish between direct labor and indirect labor.

6. Distinguish between (*a*) factory overhead and (*b*) selling and administrative overhead.

7. What product cost is listed as both a prime cost and a conversion cost?

8. Assume that you tour **Apple**'s factory where it makes its products. List three direct costs and three indirect costs that you are likely to see.

9. Should we evaluate a manager's performance on the basis of controllable or noncontrollable costs? Why?

10. Explain why knowledge of cost behavior is useful in product performance evaluation.

11. Explain why product costs are capitalized but period costs are expensed in the current accounting period.

12. Explain how business activities and inventories for a manufacturing company, a merchandising company, and a service company differ.

13. Why does managerial accounting often involve working with numerous predictions and estimates?

14. How do an income statement and a balance sheet for a manufacturing company and a merchandising company differ?

15. Besides inventories, what other assets often appear on manufacturers' balance sheets but not on merchandisers' balance sheets?

16. Why does a manufacturing company require three different inventory categories?

17. Manufacturing activities of a company are described in the ______. This statement summarizes the types and amounts of costs incurred in its manufacturing ______.

18. What are the three categories of manufacturing costs?

19. List several examples of factory overhead.

20. List the four components of a manufacturing statement and provide specific examples of each for **Apple**.

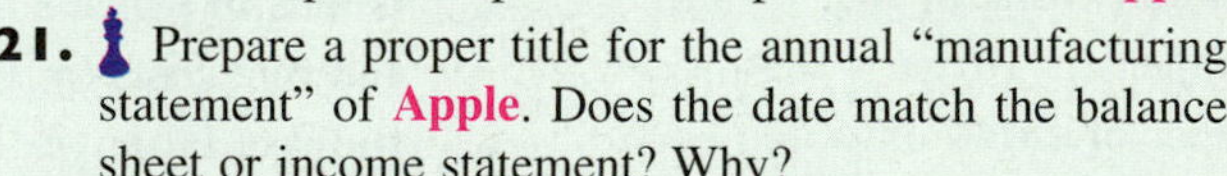

21. Prepare a proper title for the annual "manufacturing statement" of **Apple**. Does the date match the balance sheet or income statement? Why?

22. Describe the relations among the income statement, the manufacturing statement, and a detailed listing of factory overhead costs.

23. Define and describe *cycle time* and identify the components of cycle time.

24. Explain the difference between value-added time and non-value-added time.

25. Define and describe *cycle efficiency*.

26. Can management of a company such as **Best Buy** use cycle time and cycle efficiency as useful measures of performance? Explain.

27. Access **Anheuser-Busch**'s 2006 annual report (10-K) for the fiscal year ended December 31, 2006, at the SEC's EDGAR database (**SEC.gov**) or its Website (**Anheuser-Busch.com**). From its financial statement notes, identify the titles and amounts of its inventory components.

Denotes Discussion Questions that involve decision making.

Connect Accounting repeats assignments on the Connect Accounting. Website, which allows instructors to monitor, promote, and assess student learning. It can be used in practice, homework, or exam mode.

Quick Study exercises give readers a brief test of key elements.

connect *Most materials in this section are available in McGraw-Hill's Connect*

QUICK STUDY

QS 1-1
Managerial accounting defined
C1

Managerial accounting (choose one)

1. Provides information that is widely available to all interested parties.
2. Is directed at reporting aggregate data on the company as a whole.
3. Must follow generally accepted accounting principles.
4. Provides information to aid management in planning and controlling business activities.

QS 1-2
Managerial accounting versus financial accounting
C1

Identify whether each description most likely applies to managerial or financial accounting.

1. _______ It is directed at external users in making investment, credit, and other decisions.
2. _______ Its information is often available only after an audit is complete.
3. _______ Its primary focus is on the organization as a whole.
4. _______ Its principles and practices are very flexible.
5. _______ Its primary users are company managers.

QS 1-3
Lean business concepts
C2

Match each lean business concept with its best description by entering its letter in the blank.

1. _______ Just-in-time manufacturing
2. _______ Continuous improvements
3. _______ Customer orientation
4. _______ Total quality management

A. Every manager and employee constantly looks for ways to improve company operations.
B. Focuses on quality throughout the production process.
C. Inventory is acquired or produced only as needed.
D. Flexible product designs can be modified to accommodate customer choices.

QS 1-4
Fixed and variable costs
C4

Which of these statements is true regarding fixed and variable costs?

1. Fixed costs increase and variable costs decrease in total as activity volume decreases.
2. Both fixed and variable costs stay the same in total as activity volume increases.
3. Both fixed and variable costs increase as activity volume increases.
4. Fixed costs stay the same and variable costs increase in total as activity volume increases.

QS 1-5
Direct and indirect costs
C4

Crosby Company produces sporting equipment, including footballs. Identify each of the following costs as direct or indirect if the cost object is a football produced by Crosby.

1. Depreciation on equipment used to produce footballs.
2. Salary of manager who supervises the entire plant.
3. Labor used on the football production line.
4. Electricity used in the production plant.
5. Materials used to produce footballs.

QS 1-6
Product and period costs
C5

Which of these statements is true regarding product and period costs?

1. Factory maintenance is a product cost and sales commission is a period cost.
2. Sales commission is a product cost and factory rent is a period cost.
3. Factory wages are a product cost and direct material is a period cost.
4. Sales commission is a product cost and depreciation on factory equipment is a product cost.

QS 1-7
Inventory reporting for manufacturers
C6

Three inventory categories are reported on a manufacturing company's balance sheet: (*a*) raw materials, (*b*) goods in process, and (*c*) finished goods. Identify the usual order in which these inventory items are reported on the balance sheet.

1. (*b*)(*c*)(*a*) **2.** (*c*)(*b*)(*a*) **3.** (*a*)(*b*)(*c*) **4.** (*b*)(*a*)(*c*)

QS 1-8
Cost of goods sold P1

A company has year-end cost of goods manufactured of $8,000, beginning finished goods inventory of $1,000, and ending finished goods inventory of $1,500. Its cost of goods sold is

1. $8,500 **2.** $8,000 **3.** $7,500 **4.** $7,800

QS 1-9
Manufacturing flows identified
C7

Identify the usual sequence of manufacturing activities by filling in the blank (with 1, 2, or 3) corresponding to its order: _______ Production activities; _______ sales activities; _______ materials activities.

QS 1-10
Cost of goods manufactured
P2

Prepare the 2009 manufacturing statement for Biron Company using the following information.

Direct materials	$381,000
Direct labor	126,300
Factory overhead costs	48,000
Goods in process, Dec. 31, 2008	315,200
Goods in process, Dec. 31, 2009	285,500

QS 1-11
Manufacturing cycle time and efficiency
A1

Compute and interpret (*a*) manufacturing cycle time and (*b*) manufacturing cycle efficiency using the following information from a manufacturing company.

Process time	7.5 hours
Inspection time	1.0 hours
Move time	3.2 hours
Wait time	18.3 hours

QS 1-12
Cost of goods sold
P1

Compute cost of goods sold for year 2009 using the following information.

Finished goods inventory, Dec. 31, 2008	$ 690,000
Goods in process inventory, Dec. 31, 2008	167,000
Goods in process inventory, Dec. 31, 2009	144,600
Cost of goods manufactured, year 2009	1,837,400
Finished goods inventory, Dec. 31, 2009	567,200

Most materials in this section are available in McGraw-Hill's Connect connect

EXERCISES

Exercise 1-1
Sources of accounting information
C1 

This icon highlights assignments that enhance decision-making skills.

Both managerial accounting and financial accounting provide useful information to decision makers. Indicate in the following chart the most likely source of information for each business decision (a decision can require major input from both sources, in which case both can be marked).

	Primary Information Source	
Business Decision	Managerial	Financial
1. Determine amount of dividends to pay stockholders	____	____
2. Evaluate a purchasing department's performance	____	____
3. Report financial performance to board of directors	____	____
4. Estimate product cost for a new line of shoes	____	____
5. Plan the budget for next quarter	____	____
6. Measure profitability of all individual stores	____	____
7. Prepare financial reports according to GAAP	____	____
8. Determine location and size for a new plant	____	____

Exercise 1-2
Planning and control descriptions
C1

Complete the following statements by filling in the blanks.

1. _______ is the process of monitoring planning decisions and evaluating an organization's activities and employees.
2. _______ is the process of setting goals and making plans to achieve them.
3. _______ _______ usually covers a period of 5 to 10 years.
4. _______ _______ usually covers a period of one year.

Exercise 1-3
Characteristics of financial accounting and managerial accounting
C1

In the following chart, compare financial accounting and managerial accounting by describing how each differs for the items listed. Be specific in your responses.

	Financial Accounting	Managerial Accounting
1. Users and decision makers	_______	_______
2. Timeliness of information	_______	_______
3. Purpose of information	_______	_______
4. Nature of information	_______	_______
5. Flexibility of practice	_______	_______
6. Focus of information	_______	_______
7. Time dimension	_______	_______

Exercise 1-4
Customer orientation in practice
C2

Customer orientation means that a company's managers and employees respond to customers' changing wants and needs. A manufacturer of plastic fasteners has created a customer satisfaction survey that it asks each of its customers to complete. The survey asks about the following factors: (A) lead time; (B) delivery; (C) price; (D) product performance. Each factor is to be rated as unsatisfactory, marginal, average, satisfactory, or very satisfied.

a. Match the competitive forces 1 through 4 to the factors on the survey. A factor can be matched to more than one competitive force.

Survey Factor	Competitive Force
A. Lead time	_______ **1.** Cost
B. Delivery	_______ **2.** Time
C. Price	_______ **3.** Quality
D. Product performance	_______ **4.** Flexibility of service

b. How can managers of this company use the information from this customer satisfaction survey to better meet competitive forces and satisfy their customers?

Exercise 1-5
Management concepts
C2

Following are three separate events affecting the managerial accounting systems for different companies. Match the management concept(s) that the company is likely to adopt for the event identified. There is some overlap in the meaning of customer orientation and total quality management and, therefore, some responses can include more than one concept.

Event	Management Concept
_______ 1. The company starts reporting measures on customer complaints and product returns from customers.	a. Total quality management (TQM)
_______ 2. The company starts reporting measures such as the percent of defective products and the number of units scrapped.	b. Continuous improvement (CI)
_______ 3. The company starts measuring inventory turnover and discontinues elaborate inventory records. Its new focus is to pull inventory through the system.	c. Customer orientation (CO)
	d. Just-in-time (JIT) system

Exercise 1-6
Cost analysis and identification
C4 C5

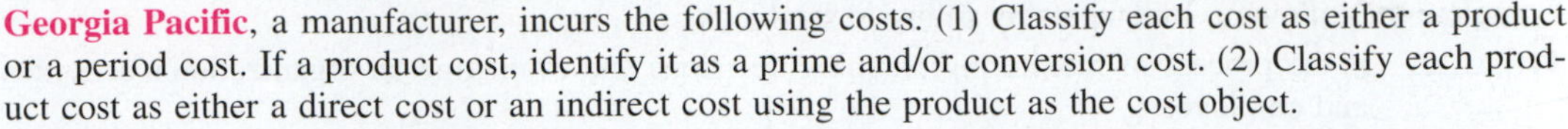

Georgia Pacific, a manufacturer, incurs the following costs. (1) Classify each cost as either a product or a period cost. If a product cost, identify it as a prime and/or conversion cost. (2) Classify each product cost as either a direct cost or an indirect cost using the product as the cost object.

Cost	Product Cost		Period Cost	Direct Cost	Indirect Cost
	Prime	Conversion			
1. Amortization of patents on factory machine	____	____	____	____	____
2. Payroll taxes for production supervisor	____	____	____	____	____
3. Accident insurance on factory workers	____	____	____	____	____
4. Depreciation—Factory building	____	____	____	____	____
5. State and federal income taxes	____	____	____	____	____
6. Wages to assembly workers	____	____	____	____	____
7. Direct materials used	____	____	____	____	____
8. Office supplies used	____	____	____	____	____
9. Bad debts expense	____	____	____	____	____
10. Small tools used	____	____	____	____	____
11. Factory utilities	____	____	____	____	____
12. Advertising	____	____	____	____	____

Exercise 1-7
Cost classifications C4

(1) Identify each of the five cost classifications discussed in the chapter. (2) List two purposes of identifying these separate cost classifications.

Exercise 1-8
Cost analysis and classification
C4

Listed here are product costs for the production of soccer balls. (1) Classify each cost (a) as either fixed or variable and (b) as either direct or indirect. (2) What pattern do you see regarding the relation between costs classified by behavior and costs classified by traceability?

Product Cost	Cost by Behavior		Cost by Traceability	
	Variable	Fixed	Direct	Indirect
1. Annual flat fee paid for office security	____	____	____	____
2. Leather covers for soccer balls	____	____	____	____
3. Lace to hold leather together	____	____	____	____
4. Wages of assembly workers	____	____	____	____
5. Coolants for machinery	____	____	____	____
6. Machinery depreciation	____	____	____	____
7. Taxes on factory	____	____	____	____

Exercise 1-9
Balance sheet identification and preparation
C6

Current assets for two different companies at calendar year-end 2009 are listed here. One is a manufacturer, Nordic Skis Mfg., and the other, Fresh Foods, is a grocery distribution company. (1) Identify which set of numbers relates to the manufacturer and which to the merchandiser. (2) Prepare the current asset section for each company from this information. Discuss why the current asset section for these two companies is different.

Account	Company 1	Company 2
Cash	$13,000	$11,000
Raw materials inventory	—	41,250
Merchandise inventory	44,250	—
Goods in process inventory	—	30,000
Finished goods inventory	—	50,000
Accounts receivable, net	62,000	81,000
Prepaid expenses	3,000	600

Exercise 1-10
Cost of goods sold computation
C6 P1

Compute cost of goods sold for each of these two companies for the year ended December 31, 2009.

		Computer Merchandising	Log Homes Manufacturing
1			
2			
3	Beginning inventory		
4	Merchandise	$301,000	
5	Finished goods		$602,000
6	Cost of purchases	580,000	
7	Cost of goods manufactured		790,000
8	Ending inventory		
9	Merchandise	201,000	
10	Finished goods		195,000

Check Computer Merchandising COGS, $680,000

Exercise 1-11
Cost of goods manufactured and cost of goods sold computation
P1 P2

Using the following data, compute (1) the cost of goods manufactured and (2) the cost of goods sold for both Jahmed Company and Kabiro Company.

	Jahmed Company	Kabiro Company
Beginning finished goods inventory	$15,000	$15,000
Beginning goods in process inventory	21,000	21,500
Beginning raw materials inventory	9,500	13,000
Rental cost on factory equipment	33,000	27,000
Direct labor	22,000	44,000
Ending finished goods inventory	19,500	12,000
Ending goods in process inventory	22,000	21,000
Ending raw materials inventory	10,500	9,400
Factory utilities	13,000	17,000
Factory supplies used	10,600	10,000
General and administrative expenses	22,000	54,000
Indirect labor	3,250	9,660
Repairs—Factory equipment	6,780	3,500
Raw materials purchases	24,000	47,000
Sales salaries	49,000	41,000

Check Jahmed COGS, $106,130

Exercise 1-12
Components of accounting reports
C7 P2

For each of the following account balances for a manufacturing company, place a ✔ in the appropriate column indicating that it appears on the balance sheet, the income statement, the manufacturing statement, and/or a detailed listing of factory overhead costs. Assume that the income statement shows the calculation of cost of goods sold and the manufacturing statement shows only the total amount of factory overhead. (An account balance can appear on more than one report.)

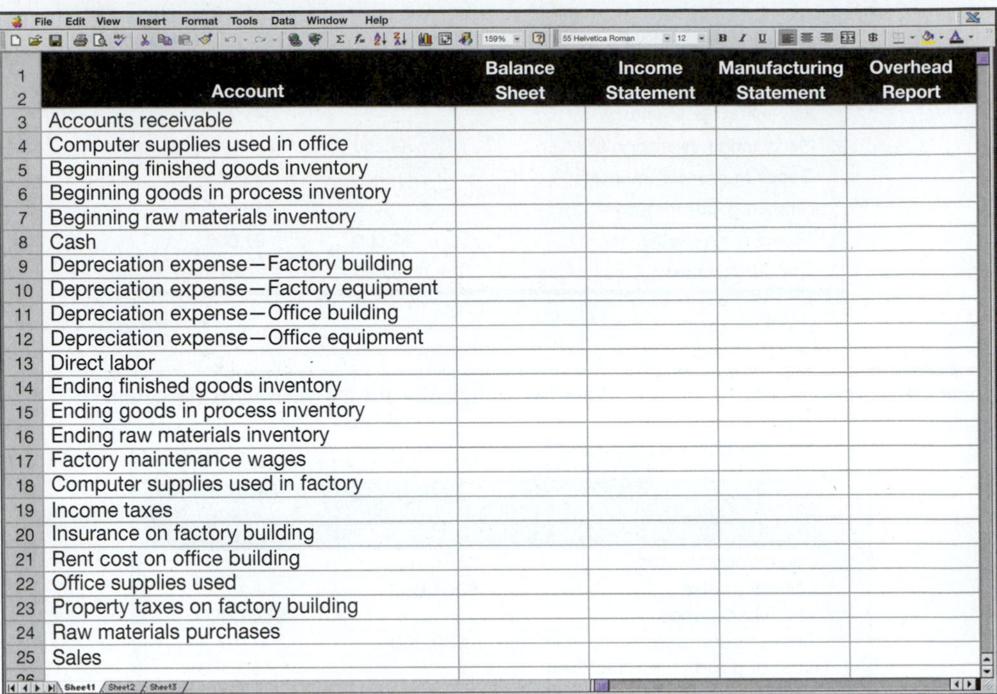

	Account	Balance Sheet	Income Statement	Manufacturing Statement	Overhead Report
3	Accounts receivable				
4	Computer supplies used in office				
5	Beginning finished goods inventory				
6	Beginning goods in process inventory				
7	Beginning raw materials inventory				
8	Cash				
9	Depreciation expense—Factory building				
10	Depreciation expense—Factory equipment				
11	Depreciation expense—Office building				
12	Depreciation expense—Office equipment				
13	Direct labor				
14	Ending finished goods inventory				
15	Ending goods in process inventory				
16	Ending raw materials inventory				
17	Factory maintenance wages				
18	Computer supplies used in factory				
19	Income taxes				
20	Insurance on factory building				
21	Rent cost on office building				
22	Office supplies used				
23	Property taxes on factory building				
24	Raw materials purchases				
25	Sales				

Exercise 1-13
Manufacturing statement preparation P2

Given the following selected account balances of Spalding Company, prepare its manufacturing statement for the year ended on December 31, 2009. Include a listing of the individual overhead account balances in this statement.

Sales	$1,363,000
Raw materials inventory, Dec. 31, 2008	40,000
Goods in process inventory, Dec. 31, 2008	53,600
Finished goods inventory, Dec. 31, 2008	60,400
Raw materials purchases	181,900
Direct labor	243,000
Factory computer supplies used	15,700
Indirect labor	54,000
Repairs—Factory equipment	7,250
Rent cost of factory building	56,000
Advertising expense	92,000
General and administrative expenses	140,000
Raw materials inventory, Dec. 31, 2009	44,000
Goods in process inventory, Dec. 31, 2009	41,200
Finished goods inventory, Dec. 31, 2009	66,200

Check Cost of goods manufactured, $566,250

Exercise 1-14
Income statement preparation P2

Use the information in Exercise 1-13 to prepare an income statement for Spalding Company (a manufacturer). Assume that its cost of goods manufactured is $566,250.

Exercise 1-15
Cost flows in manufacturing
C7 P2

The following chart shows how costs flow through a business as a product is manufactured. Some boxes in the flowchart show cost amounts. Compute the cost amounts for the boxes that contain question marks.

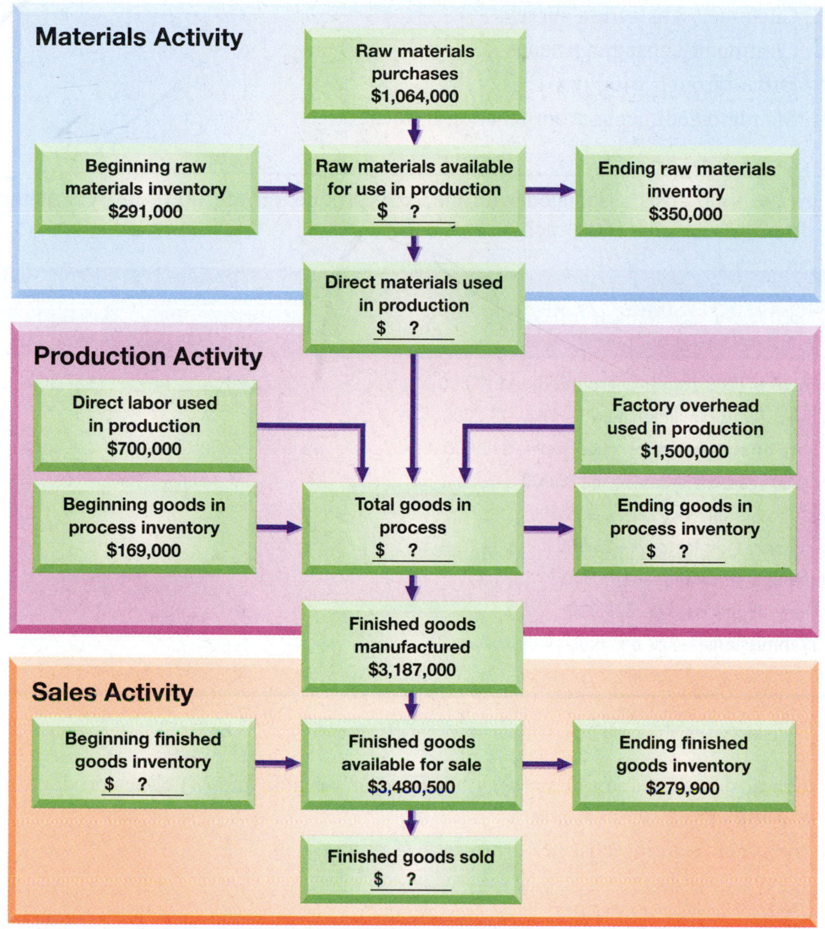

Exercise 1-16
C3

Fraud affects **Best Buy**. Refer to Best Buy's financial statements in Appendix A to answer the following:

1. Explain how inventory losses (such as theft) impact how Best Buy reports inventory on its balance sheet.

2. In what income statement account does Best Buy report inventory losses?

Problem Set B located at the end of Problem Set A is provided for each problem to reinforce the learning process.

connect *Most materials in this section are available in McGraw-Hill's Connect*

PROBLEM SET A

Problem 1-1A
Managerial accounting role
C1 C2

This chapter explained the purpose of managerial accounting in the context of the current business environment. Review the *automobile* section of your local newspaper; the Sunday paper is often best. Review advertisements of sport-utility vehicles and identify the manufacturers that offer these products and the factors on which they compete.

Required

Discuss the potential contributions and responsibilities of the managerial accounting professional in helping an automobile manufacturer succeed. (*Hint:* Think about information and estimates that a managerial accountant might provide new entrants into the sport-utility market.)

Problem 1-2A
Lean business concepts
C2 

Many fast-food restaurants compete on lean business concepts. Match each of the following activities at a fast-food restaurant with the lean business concept it strives to achieve. Some activities might relate to more than one lean business concept.

______ **1.** Courteous employees		**a.** Just-in-time (JIT)
______ **2.** Food produced to order		**b.** Continuous improvement (CI)
______ **3.** New product development		**c.** Total quality management (TQM)
______ **4.** Clean tables and floors		
______ **5.** Orders filled within three minutes		
______ **6.** Standardized food making processes		

[continued on next page]

_______ **7.** Customer satisfaction surveys

_______ **8.** Continually changing menus

_______ **9.** Drive-through windows

_______ **10.** Standardized menus from location to location

Problem 1-3A
Cost computation, classification, and analysis
C4

Listed here are the total costs associated with the 2009 production of 700 drum sets manufactured by Roland. The drum sets sell for $600 each.

Costs	Cost by Behavior		Cost by Function	
	Variable	Fixed	Product	Period
1. Drum stands (700 stands outsourced)—$17,500	$17,500		$17,500	
2. Annual flat fee for maintenance service—$7,000				
3. Rent cost of equipment for sales staff—$12,000				
4. Upper management salaries—$170,000				
5. Wages of assembly workers—$59,500				
6. Property taxes on factory—$3,500				
7. Accounting staff salaries—$42,000				
8. Machinery depreciation—$28,000				
9. Sales commissions—$20 per unit				
10. Plastic for casing—$12,600				

Required

Check (1) Total variable manufacturing cost, $89,600

1. Classify each cost and its amount as (*a*) either fixed or variable and (*b*) either product or period (the last cost is completed as an example).

2. Compute the manufacturing cost per drum set.

Analysis Component

3. Assume that 1,000 drum sets are produced in the next month. What do you predict will be the total cost of plastic for the casings and the per unit cost of the plastic for the casings? Explain.

4. Assume that 1,000 drum sets are produced in the next month. What do you predict will be the total cost of property taxes and the per unit cost of the property taxes? Explain.

Problem 1-4A
Cost classification and explanation
C4 C5

Assume that you must make a presentation to the marketing staff explaining the difference between product and period costs. Your supervisor tells you the marketing staff would also like clarification regarding prime and conversion costs and an explanation of how these terms fit with product and period cost. You are told that many on the staff are unable to classify costs in their merchandising activities.

Required

Prepare a one-page memorandum to your supervisor outlining your presentation to the marketing staff.

Problem 1-5A
Opportunity cost estimation and application
C1 C4 

Refer to *Decision Maker,* **Purchase Manager,** in this chapter. Assume that you are the motorcycle manufacturer's managerial accountant. The purchasing manager asks you about preparing an estimate of the related costs for buying motorcycle seats from supplier (B). She tells you this estimate is needed because unless dollar estimates are attached to nonfinancial factors, such as lost production time, her supervisor will not give it full attention. The manager also shows you the following information.

- Production output is 1,000 motorcycles per year based on 250 production days a year.
- Production time per day is 8 hours at a cost of $2,000 per hour to run the production line.
- Lost production time due to poor quality is 1%.
- Satisfied customers purchase, on average, three motorcycles during a lifetime.
- Satisfied customers recommend the product, on average, to five other people.
- Marketing predicts that using seat (B) will result in five lost customers per year from repeat business and referrals.
- Average contribution margin per motorcycle is $3,000.

Required

Estimate the costs (including opportunity costs) of buying motorcycle seats from supplier (B). This problem requires that you think creatively and make reasonable estimates; thus there could be more than one correct answer. (*Hint:* Reread the answer to *Decision Maker* and compare the cost savings for buying from supplier [B] to the sum of lost customer revenue from repeat business and referrals and the cost of lost production time.)

Check Estimated cost of lost production time, $40,000

Problem 1-6A
Ending inventory computation and evaluation
C2 C6

Laredo Boot Company makes specialty boots for the rodeo circuit. On December 31, 2008, the company had (*a*) 300 pairs of boots in finished goods inventory and (*b*) 1,400 heels at a cost of $16 each in raw materials inventory. During 2009, the company purchased 46,000 additional heels at $16 each and manufactured 16,800 pairs of boots.

Required

1. Determine the unit and dollar amounts of raw materials inventory in heels at December 31, 2009.

Check (1) Ending (heel) inventory, 13,800 units; $220, 800

Analysis Component

2. Write a one-half page memorandum to the production manager explaining why a just-in-time inventory system for heels should be considered. Include the amount of working capital that can be reduced at December 31, 2009, if the ending heel raw material inventory is cut by 75%.

Problem 1-7A
Inventory computation and reporting
C4 C6 P1

mhhe.com/wildMA2e

Shown here are annual financial data at December 31, 2009, taken from two different companies.

	Active Sports Retail	Sno-Board Manufacturing
Beginning inventory		
Merchandise	$145,000	
Finished goods		$340,000
Cost of purchases	240,000	
Cost of goods manufactured		582,000
Ending inventory		
Merchandise	110,000	
Finished goods		150,000

Required

1. Compute the cost of goods sold section of the income statement at December 31, 2009, for each company. Include the proper title and format in the solution.

Check (1) Sno-Board's cost of goods sold, $772,000

2. Write a half-page memorandum to your instructor (*a*) identifying the inventory accounts and (*b*) describing where each is reported on the income statement and balance sheet for both companies.

Problem 1-8A
Manufacturing and income statements; inventory analysis P2

The following calendar year-end information is taken from the December 31, 2009, adjusted trial balance and other records of Gucci Company.

Advertising expense	$ 26,600	Direct labor	$ 680,400
Depreciation expense—Office equipment	11,500	Income taxes expense	291,500
Depreciation expense—Selling equipment	10,800	Indirect labor	58,800
Depreciation expense—Factory equipment	38,200	Miscellaneous production costs	9,800
Factory supervision	105,700	Office salaries expense	74,000
Factory supplies used	7,800	Raw materials purchases	965,000
Factory utilities	34,000	Rent expense—Office space	23,000
Inventories		Rent expense—Selling space	25,200
Raw materials, December 31, 2008	165,900	Rent expense—Factory building	81,600
Raw materials, December 31, 2009	187,000	Maintenance expense—Factory equipment	37,100
Goods in process, December 31, 2008	18,100	Sales	4,630,000
Goods in process, December 31, 2009	24,600	Sales discounts	63,600
Finished goods, December 31, 2008	164,100	Sales salaries expense	398,400
Finished goods, December 31, 2009	135,900		

Required

Check (1) Cost of goods manufactured, $1,990,800

1. Prepare the company's 2009 manufacturing statement.
2. Prepare the company's 2009 income statement that reports separate categories for (*a*) selling expenses and (*b*) general and administrative expenses.

Analysis Component

3. Compute the (*a*) inventory turnover, defined as cost of goods sold divided by average inventory, and (*b*) days' sales in inventory, defined as 365 times ending inventory divided by cost of goods sold, for both its raw materials inventory and its finished goods inventory. (To compute turnover and days' sales in inventory for raw materials, use raw materials used rather than cost of goods sold.) Discuss some possible reasons for differences between these ratios for the two types of inventories.

Problem 1-9A
Manufacturing cycle time and efficiency

A1 

Mission Oak Company produces oak bookcases to customer order. It received an order from a customer to produce 5,000 bookcases. The following information is available for the production of the bookcases.

Process time	18.0 days
Inspection time	2.0 days
Move time	4.4 days
Wait time	20.6 days

Required

1. Compute the company's manufacturing cycle time.
2. Compute the company's manufacturing cycle efficiency. Interpret your answer.

Check (2) Manufacturing cycle efficiency, 0.40

Analysis Component

3. Assume that Mission Oak wishes to increase its manufacturing cycle efficiency to 0.75. What are some ways that it can accomplish this?

PROBLEM SET B

Problem 1-1B
Managerial accounting role

C1 C2

This chapter described the purpose of managerial accounting in the context of the current business environment. Review the *home electronics* section of your local newspaper; the Sunday paper is often best. Review advertisements of home electronics and identify the manufacturers that offer these products and the factors on which they compete.

Required

Discuss the potential contributions and responsibilities of the managerial accounting professional in helping a home electronics manufacturer succeed. (*Hint:* Think about information and estimates that a managerial accountant might provide new entrants into the home electronics market.)

Problem 1-2B
Lean business concepts

C2 

Eastman-Kodak manufactures digital cameras and must compete on lean manufacturing concepts. Match each of the following activities that it engages in with the lean manufacturing concept it strives to achieve. (Some activities might relate to more than one lean manufacturing concept.)

_______ 1. Lenses are received daily based on customer orders.

_______ 2. Customers receive a satisfaction survey with each camera purchased.

_______ 3. The manufacturing process is standardized and documented.

_______ 4. Cameras are produced in small lots, and only to customer order.

_______ 5. Manufacturing facilities are arranged to reduce move time and wait time.

_______ 6. Kodak conducts focus groups to determine new features that customers want in digital cameras.

a. Just-in-time (JIT)
b. Continuous improvement (CI)
c. Total quality management (TQM)

[continued on next page]

_______ **7.** Orders received are filled within two business days.

_______ **8.** Kodak works with suppliers to reduce inspection time of incoming materials.

_______ **9.** Kodak monitors the market to determine what features its competitors are offering on digital cameras.

_______ **10.** Kodak asks production workers for ideas to improve production.

Problem 1-3B

Cost computation, classification, and analysis

C4 

Listed here are the total costs associated with the production of 10,000 Blu-ray Discs (BDs) manufactured by New Age. The BDs sell for $15 each.

	Cost by Behavior		Cost by Function	
Costs	**Variable**	**Fixed**	**Product**	**Period**
1. Annual fixed fee for cleaning service—$3,000		$3,000		$3,000
2. Cost of office equipment rent—$700				
3. Upper management salaries—$100,000				
4. Labeling (10,000 outsourced)—$2,500				
5. Wages of assembly workers—$20,000				
6. Sales commissions—$0.50 per BD				
7. Machinery depreciation—$15,000				
8. Systems staff salaries—$10,000				
9. Cost of factory rent—$4,500				
10. Plastic for BDs—$1,000				

Required

1. Classify each cost and its amount as (*a*) either fixed or variable and (*b*) either product or period.

2. Compute the manufacturing cost per BD.

Check (2) Total variable manufacturing cost, $23,500

Analysis Component

3. Assume that 12,000 BDs are produced in the next month. What do you predict will be the total cost of plastic for the BDs and the per unit cost of the plastic for the BDs? Explain.

4. Assume that 12,000 BDs are produced in the next month. What do you predict will be the total cost of factory rent and the per unit cost of the factory rent? Explain.

Problem 1-4B

Cost classification and explanation

C4 C5

Assume that you must make a presentation to a client explaining the difference between prime and conversion costs. The client makes and sells 200,000 cookies per week. The client tells you that her sales staff also would like a clarification regarding product and period costs. She tells you that most of the staff lack training in managerial accounting.

Required

Prepare a one-page memorandum to your client outlining your planned presentation to her sales staff.

Problem 1-5B

Opportunity cost estimation and application

C1 C4 

Refer to *Decision Maker,* **Purchase Manager,** in this chapter. Assume that you are the motorcycle manufacturer's managerial accountant. The purchasing manager asks you about preparing an estimate of the related costs for buying motorcycle seats from supplier (B). She tells you this estimate is needed because unless dollar estimates are attached to nonfinancial factors such as lost production time, her supervisor will not give it full attention. The manager also shows you the following information.

- Production output is 1,000 motorcycles per year based on 250 production days a year.
- Production time per day is 8 hours at a cost of $500 per hour to run the production line.
- Lost production time due to poor quality is 1%.
- Satisfied customers purchase, on average, three motorcycles during a lifetime.
- Satisfied customers recommend the product, on average, to four other people.
- Marketing predicts that using seat (B) will result in four lost customers per year from repeat business and referrals.
- Average contribution margin per motorcycle is $4,000.

Required

Check Cost of lost customer revenue, $16,000

Estimate the costs (including opportunity costs) of buying motorcycle seats from supplier (B). This problem requires that you think creatively and make reasonable estimates; thus there could be more than one correct answer. (*Hint:* Reread the answer to *Decision Maker,* and compare the cost savings for buying from supplier [B] to the sum of lost customer revenue from repeat business and referrals and the cost of lost production time.)

Problem 1-6B
Ending inventory computation and evaluation
C2 C6 

CCMD Company makes specialty skates for the ice skating circuit. On December 31, 2008, the company had (*a*) 1,500 skates in finished goods inventory and (*b*) 2,500 blades at a cost of $15 each in raw materials inventory. During 2009, CCMD purchased 45,000 additional blades at $15 each and manufactured 20,000 pairs of skates.

Required

Check (1) Ending (blade) inventory, 7,500 units; $112,500

1. Determine the unit and dollar amounts of raw materials inventory in blades at December 31, 2009.

Analysis Component

2. Write a one-half page memorandum to the production manager explaining why a just-in-time inventory system for blades should be considered. Include the amount of working capital that can be reduced at December 31, 2009, if the ending blade raw material inventory is cut in half.

Problem 1-7B
Inventory computation and reporting
C4 C6 P1

Shown here are annual financial data at December 31, 2009, taken from two different companies.

	AAA Imports (Retail)	Marina Boats (Manufacturing)
Beginning inventory		
Merchandise	$ 50,000	
Finished goods		$200,000
Cost of purchases	350,000	
Cost of goods manufactured		686,000
Ending inventory		
Merchandise	25,000	
Finished goods		300,000

Required

Check (1) AAA Imports cost of goods sold, $375,000

1. Compute the cost of goods sold section of the income statement at December 31, 2009, for each company. Include the proper title and format in the solution.

2. Write a half-page memorandum to your instructor (*a*) identifying the inventory accounts and (*b*) identifying where each is reported on the income statement and balance sheet for both companies.

Problem 1-8B
Manufacturing and income statements; analysis of inventories
P2

The following calendar year-end information is taken from the December 31, 2009, adjusted trial balance and other records of Homestyle Furniture.

Advertising expense	$ 22,250	Direct labor	$ 564,500
Depreciation expense—Office equipment	10,440	Income taxes expense	138,700
Depreciation expense—Selling equipment	12,125	Indirect labor	61,000
Depreciation expense—Factory equipment	37,400	Miscellaneous production costs	10,440
Factory supervision	123,500	Office salaries expense	72,875
Factory supplies used	8,060	Raw materials purchases	896,375
Factory utilities	39,500	Rent expense—Office space	25,625
Inventories		Rent expense—Selling space	29,000
Raw materials, December 31, 2008	42,375	Rent expense—Factory building	95,500
Raw materials, December 31, 2009	72,430	Maintenance expense—Factory equipment	32,375
Goods in process, December 31, 2008	14,500	Sales	5,002,000
Goods in process, December 31, 2009	16,100	Sales discounts	59,375
Finished goods, December 31, 2008	179,200	Sales salaries expense	297,300
Finished goods, December 31, 2009	143,750		

Required

1. Prepare the company's 2009 manufacturing statement.
2. Prepare the company's 2009 income statement that reports separate categories for (*a*) selling expenses and (*b*) general and administrative expenses.

Check (1) Cost of goods manufactured, $1,836,995

Analysis Component

3. Compute the (*a*) inventory turnover, defined as cost of goods sold divided by average inventory, and (*b*) days' sales in inventory, defined as 365 times ending inventory divided by cost of goods sold, for both its raw materials inventory and its finished goods inventory. (To compute turnover and days' sales in inventory for raw materials, use raw materials used rather than cost of goods sold.) Discuss some possible reasons for differences between these ratios for the two types of inventories.

Problem 1-9B
Manufacturing cycle time and efficiency
A1 

Fast Ink produces ink-jet printers for personal computers. It received an order for 400 printers from a customer. The following information is available for this order.

Process time	8.0 hours
Inspection time	1.7 hours
Move time	4.5 hours
Wait time	10.8 hours

Required

1. Compute the company's manufacturing cycle time.
2. Compute the company's manufacturing cycle efficiency. Interpret your answer.

Analysis Component

3. Assume that Fast Ink wishes to increase its manufacturing cycle efficiency to 0.80. What are some ways that it can accomplish this?

The serial problem starts in this chapter and continues throughout most chapters of the book.

SERIAL PROBLEM

Success Systems

SP 1 On October 1, 2009, Adriana Lopez launched a computer services and merchandising company, **Success Systems,** that offers consulting services, system installation, and business software sales. In late 2009, Adriana decides to diversify her business by also manufacturing computer workstation furniture.

Required

1. Classify the following manufacturing costs of Success Systems by behavior and traceability.

Product Costs	Cost by Behavior		Cost by Traceability	
	Variable	Fixed	Direct	Indirect
1. Monthly flat fee to clean workshop	____	____	____	____
2. Laminate coverings for desktops	____	____	____	____
3. Taxes on assembly workshop	____	____	____	____
4. Glue to assemble workstation component parts	____	____	____	____
5. Wages of desk assembler	____	____	____	____
6. Electricity for workshop	____	____	____	____
7. Depreciation on tools	____	____	____	____

2. Prepare a manufacturing statement for Success Systems for the month ended January 31, 2010. Assume the following manufacturing costs:

Direct materials: $2,200

Factory overhead: $490

Direct labor: $900

Beginning goods in process: none (December 31, 2009)

Ending goods in process: $540 (January 31, 2010)

Beginning finished goods inventory: none (December 31, 2009)

Ending finished goods inventory: $350 (January 31, 2010)

Check (3) COGS, $2,700

3. Prepare the cost of goods sold section of a partial income statement for Success Systems for the month ended January 31, 2010.

Beyond the Numbers (BTN) *is a special problem section aimed to refine communication, conceptual, analysis, and research skills. It includes many activities helpful in developing an active learning environment.*

BEYOND THE NUMBERS

REPORTING IN ACTION

C1 C2 

BTN 1-1 Managerial accounting is more than recording, maintaining, and reporting financial results. Managerial accountants must provide managers with both financial and nonfinancial information including estimates, projections, and forecasts. There are many accounting estimates that management accountants must make, and **Best Buy** must notify shareholders of these estimates.

Required

1. Access and read Best Buy's "Critical Accounting Estimates" section (six pages), which is part of its *Management's Discussion and Analysis of Financial Condition and Results of Operations* section, from either its annual report or its 10-K for the year ended March 3, 2007 [BestBuy.com]. What are some of the accounting estimates that Best Buy made in preparing its financial statements? What are some of the effects if the actual results of Best Buy differ from its assumptions?
2. What is the management accountant's role in determining those estimates?

Fast Forward

3. Access **Best Buy**'s annual report for a fiscal year ending after March 3, 2007, from either its Website [BestBuy.com] or the SEC's EDGAR database [www.SEC.gov]. Answer the questions in parts (1) and (2) after reading the current MD&A section. Identify any major changes.

COMPARATIVE ANALYSIS

C1 C2 

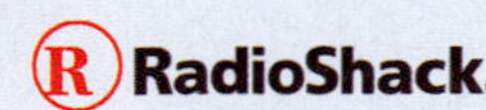

BTN 1-2 **Best Buy** and **RadioShack** are both merchandisers that rely on customer satisfaction. Access and read (1) Best Buy's "Business Strategy and Core Philosophies" section (one page) and (2) RadioShack's "Financial Impact of Turnaround Program" section (one page). Both sections are located in the respective company's *Management Discussion and Analysis of Financial Condition and Results of Operations* section from the annual report or 10-K. The Best Buy report is for the year ended March 3, 2007, and the RadioShack report is for the year ended December 31, 2006.

Required

1. Identify the strategic initiatives that each company put forward in its desire to better compete and succeed in the marketplace.
2. For each of these strategic initiatives for both companies, explain how it reflects (or does not reflect) a customer satisfaction focus.

ETHICS CHALLENGE

C3 C4 C5 

BTN 1-3 Assume that you are the managerial accountant at Infostore, a manufacturer of hard drives, CDs, and diskettes. Its reporting year-end is December 31. The chief financial officer is concerned about having enough cash to pay the expected income tax bill because of poor cash flow management. On November 15, the purchasing department purchased excess inventory of CD raw materials in anticipation of rapid growth of this product beginning in January. To decrease the company's tax liability, the chief financial officer tells you to record the purchase of this inventory as part of supplies and expense it in the current year; this would decrease the company's tax liability by increasing expenses.

Required

1. In which account should the purchase of CD raw materials be recorded?
2. How should you respond to this request by the chief financial officer?

COMMUNICATING IN PRACTICE

BTN 1-4 Write a one-page memorandum to a prospective college student about salary expectations for graduates in business. Compare and contrast the expected salaries for accounting (including different subfields such as public, corporate, tax, audit, and so forth), marketing, management, and finance majors. Prepare a graph showing average starting salaries (and those for experienced professionals in those fields if available). To get this information, stop by your school's career services office; libraries also have this information. The Website JobStar.org (click on *Salary Info*) also can get you started.

TAKING IT TO THE NET

C1 C3 

BTN 1-5 Managerial accounting professionals follow a code of ethics. As a member of the Institute of Management Accountants, the managerial accountant must comply with Standards of Ethical Conduct.

Required

1. Identify, print, and read the *Statement of Ethical Professional Practice* posted at www.IMAnet.org. (Search using "ethical professional practice.")
2. What four overarching ethical principles underlie the IMA's statement?
3. Describe the courses of action the IMA recommends in resolving ethical conflicts.

TEAMWORK IN ACTION

C7 P2

BTN 1-6 The following calendar-year information is taken from the December 31, 2009, adjusted trial balance and other records of Dahlia Company.

Advertising expense	$ 19,125	Direct labor	$ 650,750
Depreciation expense—Office equipment	8,750	Indirect labor	60,000
Depreciation expense—Selling equipment	10,000	Miscellaneous production costs	8,500
Depreciation expense—Factory equipment	32,500	Office salaries expense	100,875
Factory supervision	122,500	Raw materials purchases	872,500
Factory supplies used	15,750	Rent expense—Office space	21,125
Factory utilities	36,250	Rent expense—Selling space	25,750
Inventories		Rent expense—Factory building	79,750
Raw materials, December 31, 2008	177,500	Maintenance expense—Factory equipment	27,875
Raw materials, December 31, 2009	168,125	Sales	3,275,000
Goods in process, December 31, 2008	15,875	Sales discounts	57,500
Goods in process, December 31, 2009	14,000	Sales salaries expense	286,250
Finished goods, December 31, 2008	164,375		
Finished goods, December 31, 2009	129,000		

Required

1. *Each* team member is to be responsible for computing **one** of the following amounts. You are not to duplicate your teammates' work. Get any necessary amounts from teammates. Each member is to explain the computation to the team in preparation for reporting to class.

a. Materials used.
b. Factory overhead.
c. Total manufacturing costs.
d. Total cost of goods in process.
e. Cost of goods manufactured.

2. Check your cost of goods manufactured with the instructor. If it is correct, proceed to part (3).

3. *Each* team member is to be responsible for computing **one** of the following amounts. You are not to duplicate your teammates' work. Get any necessary amounts from teammates. Each member is to explain the computation to the team in preparation for reporting to class.

a. Net sales.
b. Cost of goods sold.
c. Gross profit.
d. Total operating expenses.
e. Net income or loss before taxes.

Point: Provide teams with transparencies and markers for presentation purposes.

ENTREPRENEURIAL DECISION

C1 C4 

BTN 1-7 Brian Taylor of Kernel Season's must understand his manufacturing costs to effectively operate and succeed as a profitable and efficient company.

Required

1. What are the three main categories of manufacturing costs that Brian must monitor and control? Provide examples of each.

2. How can Brian make the Kernel Season's manufacturing process more cost-effective? Provide examples of two useful managerial measures of time and efficiency.

3. What are four goals of a total quality management process? How can Kernel Season's use TQM to improve its business activities?

HITTING THE ROAD

C1 C5 

BTN 1-8 Visit your favorite fast-food restaurant. Observe its business operations.

Required

1. Describe all business activities from the time a customer arrives to the time that customer departs.

2. List all costs you can identify with the separate activities described in part 1.

3. Classify each cost from part 2 as fixed or variable, and explain your classification.

BTN 1-9 Access DSG's annual report for the year ended April 28, 2007 (www.DSGiplc.com). Read the section "Corporate Governance" dealing with the responsibilities of the board of directors.

GLOBAL DECISION

DSG

Required

1. Identify the responsibilities (see the "schedule of matters reserved for the board") of DSG's board of directors.

2. How would management accountants be involved in assisting the board of directors in carrying out their responsibilities? Explain.

ANSWERS TO MULTIPLE CHOICE QUIZ

1. c

2. b

3. b

4. a

5. Beginning finished goods + Cost of goods manufactured (COGM) − Ending finished goods = Cost of goods sold

$6,000 + COGM − $3,200 = $7,500

COGM = $4,700

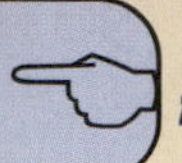

A Look Back

Chapter 1 introduced managerial accounting and explained basic cost concepts. We also described the lean business model and the reporting of manufacturing activities, including the manufacturing statement.

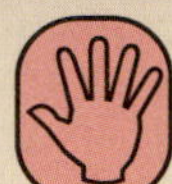

A Look at This Chapter

We begin this chapter by describing a cost accounting system. We then explain the procedures used to determine costs using a job order costing system. We conclude with a discussion of over- and underapplied overhead.

A Look Ahead

Chapter 3 focuses on measuring costs in process production companies. We explain process production, describe how to assign costs to processes, and compute and analyze cost per equivalent unit.

Chapter

Job Order Costing and Analysis

Learning Objectives

CAP

Conceptual

C1 Explain the cost accounting system. *(p. 48)*

C2 Describe important features of job order production. *(p. 48)*

C3 Explain job cost sheets and how they are used in job order cost accounting. *(p. 50)*

Analytical

A1 Apply job order costing in pricing services. *(p. 60)*

Procedural

P1 Describe and record the flow of materials costs in job order cost accounting. *(p. 51)*

P2 Describe and record the flow of labor costs in job order cost accounting. *(p. 53)*

P3 Describe and record the flow of overhead costs in job order cost accounting. *(p. 54)*

P4 Determine adjustments for overapplied and underapplied factory overhead. *(p. 59)*

LP2

Decision Feature

Working the Field

"Being successful is having a vision which you are excited to follow without the fear of failure"
—Hank Julicher

PHILADELPHIA, PA—One size fits all? Not when it comes to synthetic turf for athletic fields—this according to Hank Julicher, founder of **Sprinturf (Sprinturf.com).** "Not all fields are exactly alike, because no two owners have the same exact needs," insists Hank. "Many variables must be considered, including playing requirements, climate, and financial considerations." Designing, installing, and servicing synthetic turf systems are Sprinturf's mission.

"There is much more to a playing field than just the surface," explains Hank. "Many would argue that the base is the most important—it needs the strength to support athletes and vehicles, while still being able to drain over 20″ of rainfall per hour." For this, Sprinturf relies on its all-rubber infill system for its installations. Still, understanding customer needs is key. In extremely hot, arid climates, Sprinturf uses light-colored rubber infill to reduce the temperature of playing surfaces. In cold areas, Sprinturf offers solutions to reduce snow and ice buildup. Hank has put in fields from Utah State University to University of Montana to Long Beach City College. While a touchdown is worth 6 points on every Sprinturf field, each field is otherwise unique.

Manufacturers of custom products, such as that from Sprinturf, use state-of-the-art job order cost accounting to track costs. This includes tracking the cost of materials, labor and overhead, and managing those expenses. To help control costs and ensure product quality, Sprinturf does not outsource any part of the design or installation process. Controlling all aspects of the process enables it to better isolate costs and avoid the run-away costs often experienced by startups that fail to use costing techniques. Recruiting top-notch personnel and experienced supervisors also helps control labor costs. Reflecting the unique nature of each field, each installation is videotaped to ensure it is done exactly according to customer specifications.

Hank Julicher stresses cost control as vital to Sprinturf's success. "To take on two 800 pound gorillas in our industry, we had to be more creative, efficient, and cost-effective to win," explains Hank. "We just hung in there until the public recognized our quality and value." This winning formula has led to product growth that any team would envy.

[Sources: *Sprinturf Website*, January 2009; *Entrepreneur*, 2007; *PanStadia*, February and November 2005]

Chapter Preview

This chapter introduces a system for assigning costs to the flow of goods through a production process. We then describe the details of a *job order cost accounting system*. Job order costing is frequently used by manufacturers of custom products or providers of custom services. Manufacturers that use job order costing typically base it on a perpetual inventory system, which provides a continuous record of materials, goods in process, and finished goods inventories.

Job Order Costing and Analysis

Job Order Cost Accounting
- Cost accounting system
- Job order manufacturing
- Events in job order costing
- Job cost sheet

Job Order Cost Flows and Reports
- Materials cost flows and documents
- Labor cost flows and documents
- Overhead cost flows and documents
- Summary of cost flows

Adjustment of Overapplied or Underapplied Overhead
- Underapplied overhead
- Overapplied overhead

Job Order Cost Accounting

This section describes a cost accounting system and job order production and costing.

Cost Accounting System

C1 Explain the cost accounting system.

An ever-increasing number of companies use a cost accounting system to generate timely and accurate inventory information. A **cost accounting system** records manufacturing activities using a *perpetual* inventory system, which continuously updates records for costs of materials, goods in process, and finished goods inventories. A cost accounting system also provides timely information about inventories and manufacturing costs per unit of product. This is especially helpful for managers' efforts to control costs and determine selling prices. (A **general accounting system** records manufacturing activities using a *periodic* inventory system. Some companies still use a general accounting system, but its use is declining as competitive forces and customer demands have increased pressures on companies to better manage inventories.)

Point: Cost accounting systems accumulate costs and then assign them to products and services.

The two basic types of cost accounting systems are *job order cost accounting* and *process cost accounting*. We describe job order cost accounting in this chapter. Process cost accounting is explained in the next chapter.

Job Order Production

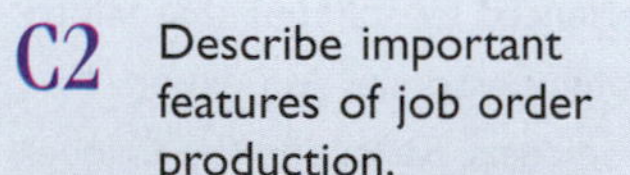

C2 Describe important features of job order production.

Many companies produce products individually designed to meet the needs of a specific customer. Each customized product is manufactured separately and its production is called **job order production,** or *job order manufacturing* (also called *customized production,* which is the production of products in response to special orders). Examples of such products include synthetic football fields, special-order machines, a factory building, custom jewelry, wedding invitations, and artwork.

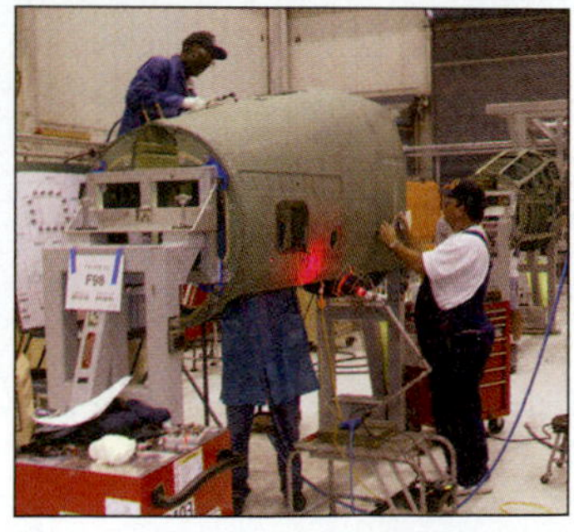

The production activities for a customized product represent a **job.** The principle of customization is equally applicable to both manufacturing *and* service companies. Most service companies meet customers' needs by performing a custom service for a specific customer. Examples of such services include an accountant auditing a client's financial statements, an interior designer remodeling an office, a wedding consultant planning and supervising a reception, and a lawyer defending a client. Whether the setting is manufacturing or services, job order operations involve meeting the needs of customers by producing or performing custom jobs.

Boeing's aerospace division is one example of a job order production system. Its primary business is twofold: (1) design, develop, and integrate space carriers and (2) provide systems engineering and integration of Department of Defense (DoD) systems. Many of its orders are customized and produced through job order operations.

When a job involves producing more than one unit of a custom product, it is often called a **job lot.** Products produced as job lots could include benches for a church, imprinted T-shirts for a 10K race or company picnic, or advertising signs for a chain of stores. Although these orders involve more than one unit, the volume of production is typically low, such as 50 benches, 200 T-shirts, or 100 signs. Another feature of job order production is the diversity, often called *heterogeneity,* of the products produced. Namely, each customer order is likely to differ from another in some important respect. These variations can be minor or major.

Point: Many professional examinations including the CPA and CMA exams require knowledge of job order and process cost accounting.

Decision Insight

Custom Design Managers once saw companies as the center of a solar system orbited by suppliers and customers. Now the customer has become the center of the business universe. **Nike** allows custom orders over the Internet, enabling customers to select materials, colors, and to personalize their shoes with letters and numbers. Soon consumers may be able to personalize almost any product, from cellular phones to appliances to furniture.

Events in Job Order Costing

The initial event in a normal job order operation is the receipt of a customer order for a custom product. This causes the company to begin work on a job. A less common case occurs when management decides to begin work on a job before it has a signed contract. This is referred to as *jobs produced on speculation.*

Video2.1

The first step in both cases is to predict the cost to complete the job. This cost depends on the product design prepared by either the customer or the producer. The second step is to negotiate a sales price and decide whether to pursue the job. Other than for government or other cost-plus contracts, the selling price is determined by market factors. Producers evaluate the market price, compare it to cost, and determine whether the profit on the job is reasonable. If the profit is not reasonable, the producer would determine a desired **target cost.** The third step is for the producer to schedule production of the job to meet the customer's needs and to fit within its own production constraints. Preparation of this work schedule should consider workplace facilities including equipment, personnel, and supplies. Once this schedule is complete, the producer can place orders for raw materials. Production occurs as materials and labor are applied to the job.

Point: Some jobs are priced on a *cost-plus basis:* The customer pays the manufacturer for costs incurred on the job plus a negotiated amount or rate of profit.

An overview of job order production activity is shown in Exhibit 2.1. This exhibit shows the March production activity of Road Warriors, which manufactures security-equipped cars and trucks. The company converts any vehicle by giving it a diversity of security items such as alarms, reinforced exterior, bulletproof glass, and bomb detectors. The company began by catering to high-profile celebrities, but it now caters to anyone who desires added security in a vehicle.

Job order production for Road Warriors requires materials, labor, and overhead costs. Recall that direct materials are goods used in manufacturing that are clearly identified with a particular job. Similarly, direct labor is effort devoted to a particular job. Overhead costs support production of more than one job. Common overhead items are depreciation on factory buildings and equipment, factory supplies, supervision, maintenance, cleaning, and utilities.

Exhibit 2.1 shows that materials, labor, and overhead are added to Jobs B15, B16, B17, B18, and B19, which were started during March. Road Warriors completed Jobs B15, B16, and B17 in March and delivered Jobs B15 and B16 to customers. At the end of March, Jobs B18 and B19 remain in goods in process inventory and Job B17 is in finished goods inventory. Both labor and materials costs are also separated into their direct and indirect components. Their indirect amounts are added to overhead. Total overhead cost is then allocated to the various jobs.

Decision Insight

Target Costing Many producers determine a target cost for their jobs. Target cost is determined as follows: Expected selling price − Desired profit = Target cost. If the projected target cost of the job as determined by job costing is too high, the producer can apply *value engineering,* which is a method of determining ways to reduce job cost until the target cost is met.

EXHIBIT 2.1

Job Order Production Activities

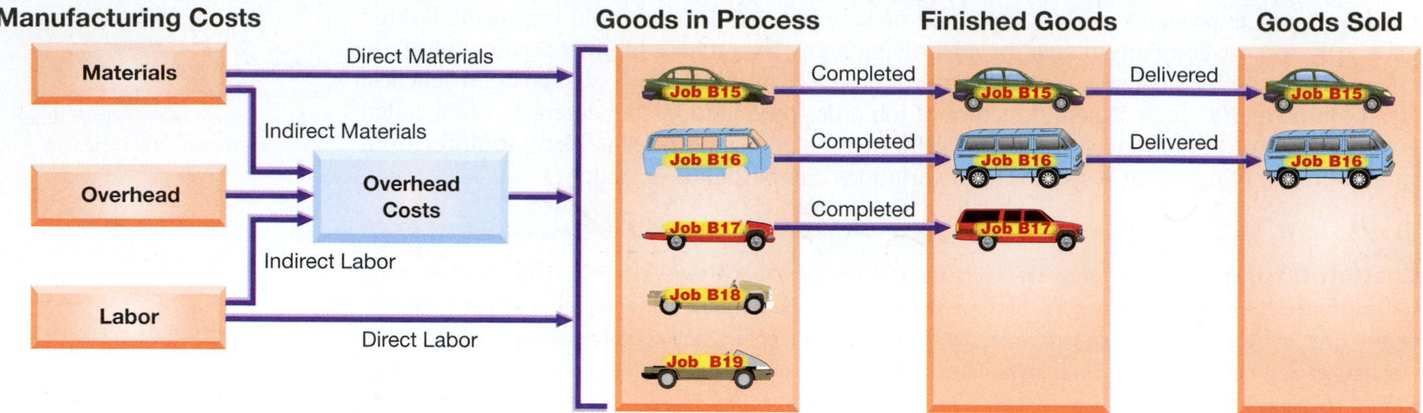

Job Cost Sheet

C3 Explain job cost sheets and how they are used in job order cost accounting.

General ledger accounts usually do not provide the accounting information that managers of job order cost operations need to plan and control production activities. This is so because the needed information often requires more detailed data. Such detailed data are usually stored in subsidiary records controlled by general ledger accounts. Subsidiary records store information about raw materials, overhead costs, jobs in process, finished goods, and other items. This section describes the use of these records.

A major aim of a **job order cost accounting system** is to determine the cost of producing each job or job lot. In the case of a job lot, the system also aims to compute the cost per unit. The accounting system must include separate records for each job to accomplish this, and it must capture information about costs incurred and charge these costs to each job.

A **job cost sheet** is a separate record maintained for each job. Exhibit 2.2 shows a job cost sheet for an alarm system that Road Warriors produced for a customer. This job cost sheet identifies the customer, the job number assigned, the product, and key dates. Costs incurred on the job are immediately recorded on this sheet. When each job is complete, the supervisor enters the date of completion, records any remarks, and signs the sheet. The job cost sheet in Exhibit 2.2 classifies costs as direct materials, direct labor, or overhead. It shows that a total of $600 in direct materials is added to Job B15 on four different dates. It also shows seven entries for direct labor costs that total $1,000. Road Warriors *allocates* (also termed *applies, assigns,* or *charges*) factory overhead costs of $1,600 to this job using an allocation rate of 160% of direct labor cost (160% × $1,000)—we discuss overhead allocation later in this chapter.

Point: Factory overhead consists of costs (other than direct materials and direct labor) that ensure the production activities are carried out.

While a job is being produced, its accumulated costs are kept in **Goods in Process Inventory.** The collection of job cost sheets for all jobs in process makes up a subsidiary ledger controlled by the Goods in Process Inventory account in the general ledger. Managers use job cost sheets to monitor costs incurred to date and to predict and control costs for each job.

Point: Documents (electronic and paper) are crucial in a job order system, and the job cost sheet is a cornerstone. Understanding it aids in grasping concepts of capitalizing product costs and product cost flow.

When a job is finished, its job cost sheet is completed and moved from the jobs in process file to the finished jobs file. This latter file acts as a subsidiary ledger controlled by the **Finished Goods Inventory** account. When a finished job is delivered to a customer, the job cost sheet is moved to a permanent file supporting the total cost of goods sold. This permanent file contains records from both current and prior periods.

Decision Maker

Management Consultant One of your tasks is to control and manage costs for a consulting company. At the end of a recent month, you find that three consulting jobs were completed and two are 60% complete. Each unfinished job is estimated to cost $10,000 and to earn a revenue of $12,000. You are unsure how to recognize goods in process inventory and record costs and revenues. Do you recognize any inventory? If so, how much? How much revenue is recorded for unfinished jobs this month? [Answer—p. 64]

EXHIBIT 2.2

Job Cost Sheet

Accounting System: Exhibit 2

File Edit Maintain Tasks Analysis Options Reports Window Help

Road Warriors, Los Angeles, California — **JOB COST SHEET**

Customer's Name	Carroll Connor	Job No.	B15
Address	1542 High Point Dr.	City & State	Portland, Oregon
Job Description	Level 1 Alarm System on Ford Expedition		

Date promised	Date started	Date completed
March 15	March 3	March 11

Direct Materials			Direct Labor			Overhead		
Date	Requisition	Cost	Date	Time Ticket	Cost	Date	Rate	Cost
3/3/2009	R-4698	100.00	3/3/2009	L-3393	120.00	3/11/2009	160% of Direct Labor Cost	1,600.00
3/7/2009	R-4705	225.00	3/4/2009	L-3422	150.00			
3/9/2009	R-4725	180.00	3/5/2009	L-3456	180.00			
3/10/2009	R-4777	95.00	3/8/2009	L-3479	60.00			
			3/9/2009	L-3501	90.00			
			3/10/2009	L-3535	240.00			
			3/11/2009	L-3559	160.00			
	Total	600.00		Total	1,000.00		Total	1,600.00

REMARKS: Completed job on March 11, and shipped to customer on March 15. Met all specifications and requirements.

Signed: *C. Luther, Supervisor*

SUMMARY:	
Materials	600.00
Labor	1,000.00
Overhead	1,600.00
Total cost	3,200.00

Quick Check

Answers—p. 65

1. Which of these products is likely to involve job order production? (*a*) inexpensive watches, (*b*) racing bikes, (*c*) bottled soft drinks, or (*d*) athletic socks.
2. What is the difference between a job and a job lot?
3. Which of these statements is correct? (*a*) The collection of job cost sheets for unfinished jobs makes up a subsidiary ledger controlled by the Goods in Process Inventory account, (*b*) Job cost sheets are financial statements provided to investors, or (*c*) A separate job cost sheet is maintained in the general ledger for each job in process.
4. What three costs are normally accumulated on job cost sheets?

Job Order Cost Flows and Reports

Materials Cost Flows and Documents

P1 Describe and record the flow of materials costs in job order cost accounting.

Materials

This section focuses on the flow of materials costs and the related documents in a job order cost accounting system. We begin analysis of the flow of materials costs by examining Exhibit 2.3. When materials are first received from suppliers, the employees count and inspect them and record the items' quantity and cost on a receiving report. The receiving report serves as the *source document* for recording materials received in both a materials ledger card and in the general ledger. In nearly all job order cost systems, **materials ledger cards** (or files) are perpetual records that are updated each time units are purchased and each time units are issued for use in production.

Point: Some companies certify certain suppliers based on the quality of their materials. Goods received from these suppliers are not always inspected by the purchaser to save costs.

To illustrate the purchase of materials, Road Warriors acquired $450 of wiring and related materials on March 4, 2009. This purchase is recorded as follows.

Mar. 4	Raw Materials Inventory—M-347	450	
	Accounts Payable		450
	To record purchase of materials for production.		

Assets = Liabilities + Equity
+450 +450

EXHIBIT 2.3
Materials Cost Flows through Subsidiary Records

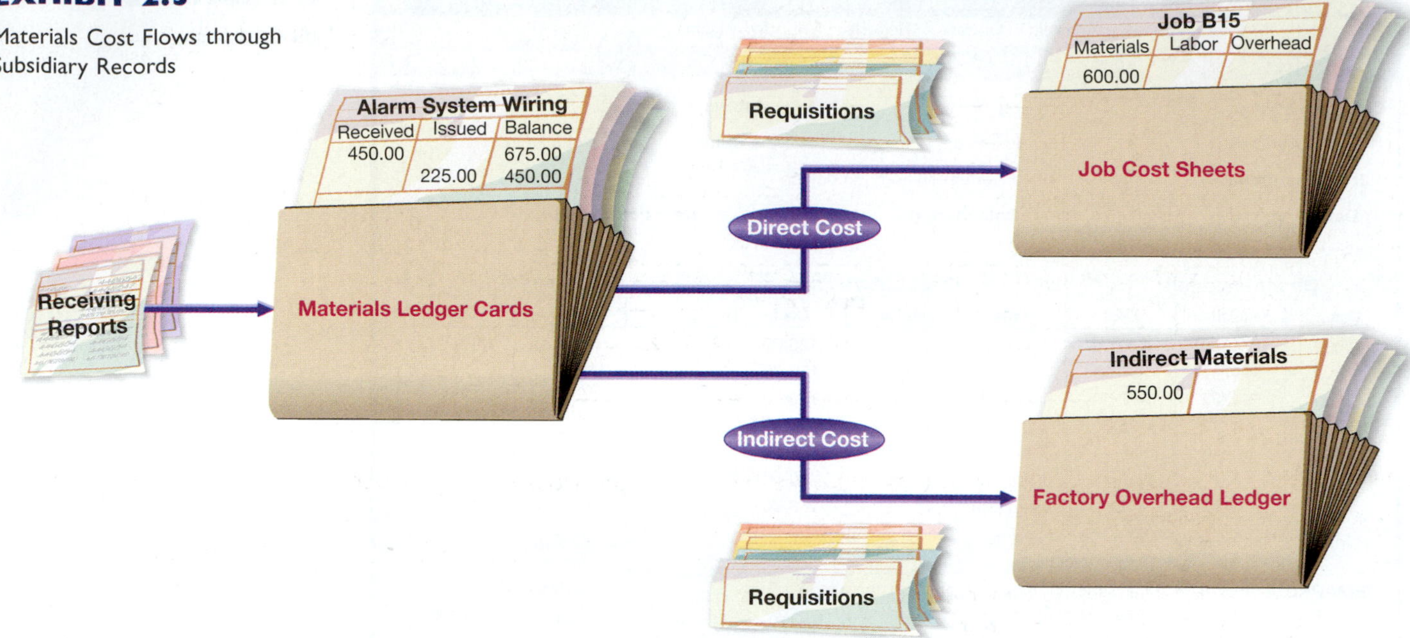

Exhibit 2.3 shows that materials can be requisitioned for use either on a specific job (direct materials) or as overhead (indirect materials). Cost of direct materials flows from the materials ledger card to the job cost sheet. The cost of indirect materials flows from the materials ledger card to the Indirect Materials account in the factory overhead ledger, which is a subsidiary ledger controlled by the Factory Overhead account in the general ledger.

Video2.1

Exhibit 2.4 shows a materials ledger card for material received and issued by Road Warriors. The card identifies the item as alarm system wiring and shows the item's stock number, its location in the storeroom, information about the maximum and minimum quantities that should be available, and the reorder quantity. For example, alarm system wiring is issued and recorded on March 7, 2009. The job cost sheet in Exhibit 2.2 showed that Job B15 used this wiring.

EXHIBIT 2.4
Materials Ledger Card

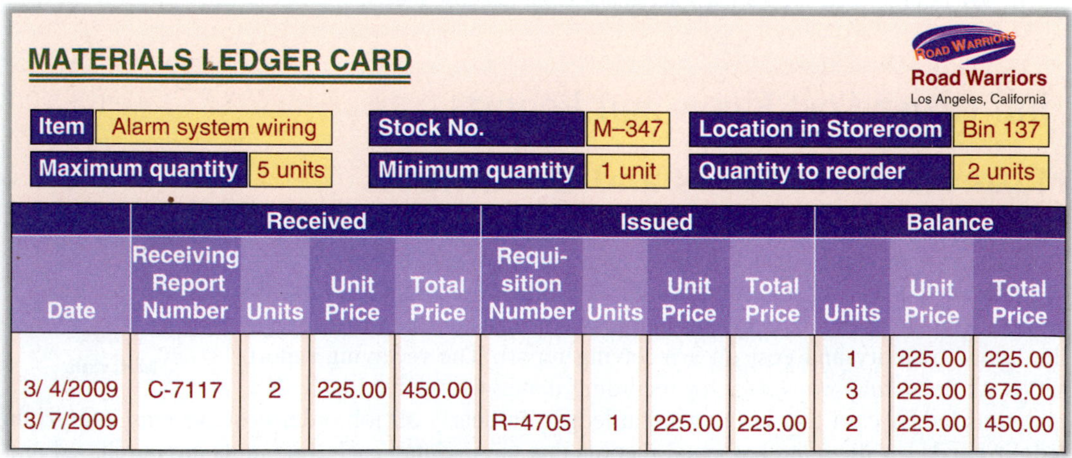

MATERIALS LEDGER CARD

Road Warriors
Los Angeles, California

Item	Alarm system wiring	Stock No.	M–347	Location in Storeroom	Bin 137
Maximum quantity	5 units	Minimum quantity	1 unit	Quantity to reorder	2 units

	Received				Issued				Balance		
Date	Receiving Report Number	Units	Unit Price	Total Price	Requi-sition Number	Units	Unit Price	Total Price	Units	Unit Price	Total Price
									1	225.00	225.00
3/ 4/2009	C-7117	2	225.00	450.00					3	225.00	675.00
3/ 7/2009					R–4705	1	225.00	225.00	2	225.00	450.00

When materials are needed in production, a production manager prepares a **materials requisition** and sends it to the materials manager. The requisition shows the job number, the type of material, the quantity needed, and the signature of the manager authorized to make the requisition. Exhibit 2.5 shows the materials requisition for alarm system wiring for Job B15. To see how this requisition ties to the flow of costs, compare the information on the requisition with the March 7, 2009, data in Exhibits 2.2 and 2.4.

Point: Requisitions are often accumulated and recorded in one entry. The frequency of entries depends on the job, the industry, and management procedures.

EXHIBIT 2.5

Materials Requisition

MATERIALS REQUISITION No. R–4705

Road Warriors
Los Angeles, California

Job No.	B15	Date	3/7/2009
Material Stock No.	M–347	Material Description	Alarm system wiring
Quantity Requested	1	Requested By	C. Luther
Quantity Provided	1	Date Provided	3/7/2009
Filled By	M. Bateman	Material Received By	C. Luther
Remarks			

The use of alarm system wiring on Job B15 yields the following entry (locate this cost item in the job cost sheet shown in Exhibit 2.2).

Mar. 7	Goods in Process Inventory—Job B15.	225	
	Raw Materials Inventory—M-347.		225
	To record use of material on Job B15.		

Assets = Liabilities + Equity
+225
−225

This entry is posted both to its general ledger accounts and to subsidiary records. Posting to subsidiary records includes a debit to a job cost sheet and a credit to a materials ledger card. (*Note:* An entry to record use of indirect materials is the same as that for direct materials *except* the debit is to Factory Overhead. In the subsidiary factory overhead ledger, this entry is posted to Indirect Materials.)

Labor Cost Flows and Documents

P2 Describe and record the flow of labor costs in job order cost accounting.

Exhibit 2.6 shows the flow of labor costs from clock cards and the Factory Payroll account to subsidiary records of the job order cost accounting system. Recall that costs in subsidiary records give detailed information needed to manage and control operations.

EXHIBIT 2.6

Labor Cost Flows through Subsidiary Records

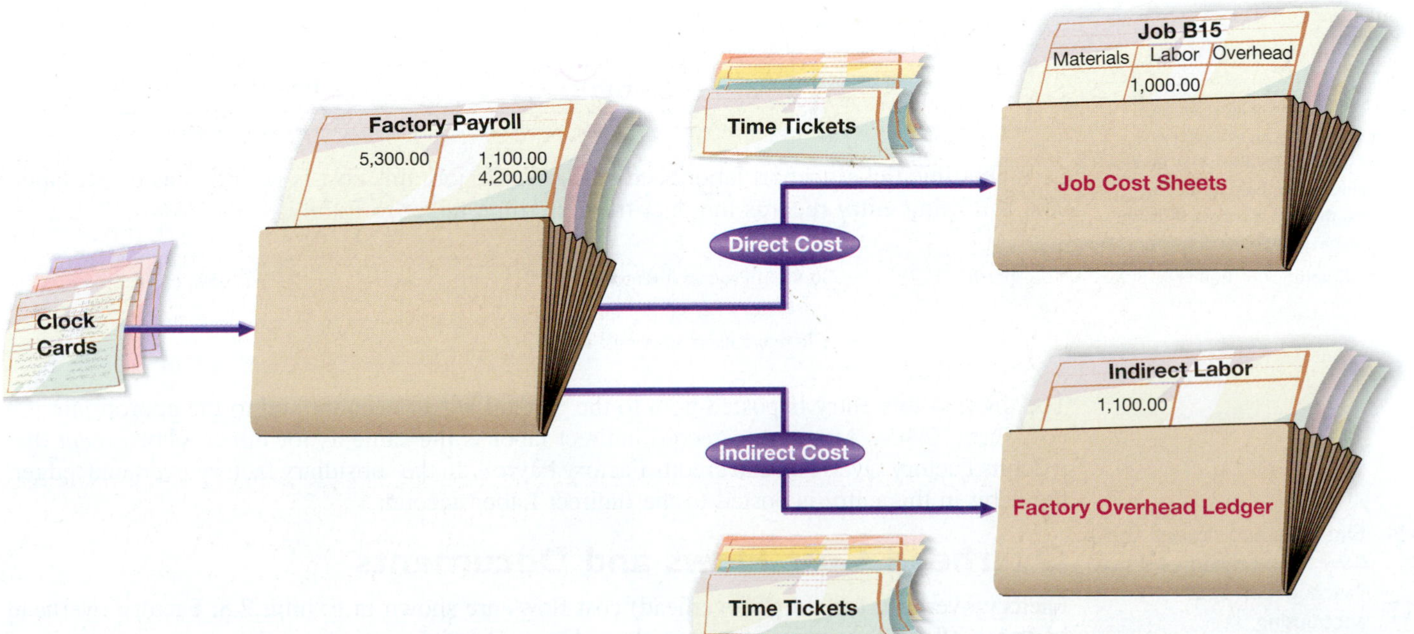

Point: Indirect materials are included in overhead on the job cost sheet. Assigning overhead costs to products is described in the next section.

Point: Many employee fraud schemes involve payroll, including overstated hours on clock cards.

The flow of costs in Exhibit 2.6 begins with **clock cards.** Employees commonly use these cards to record the number of hours worked, and they serve as source documents for entries to record labor costs. Clock card data on the number of hours worked is used at the end of each pay period to determine total labor cost. This amount is then debited to the Factory Payroll account, a temporary account containing the total payroll cost (both direct and indirect). Payroll cost is later allocated to both specific jobs and overhead.

According to clock card data, workers earned $1,500 for the week ended March 5. Illustrating the flow of labor costs, the accrual and payment of these wages are recorded as follows.

Assets = Liabilities + Equity
−1,500 −1,500

Mar. 6	Factory payroll	1,500	
	Cash		1,500
	To record the weekly payroll.		

"It's on Corporate Standard Time... It loses an hour of your pay every day."

To assign labor costs to specific jobs and to overhead, we must know how each employee's time is used and its costs. Source documents called **time tickets** usually capture these data. Employees regularly fill out time tickets to report how much time they spent on each job. An employee who works on several jobs during a day completes a separate time ticket for each job. Tickets are also prepared for time charged to overhead as indirect labor. A supervisor signs an employee's time ticket to confirm its accuracy.

Exhibit 2.7 shows a time ticket reporting the time a Road Warrior employee spent working on Job B15. The employee's supervisor signed the ticket to confirm its accuracy. The hourly rate and total labor cost are computed after the time ticket is turned in. To see the effect of this time ticket on the job cost sheet, look at the entry dated March 8, 2009, in Exhibit 2.2.

EXHIBIT 2.7

Time Ticket

ROAD WARRIORS

Road Warriors
Los Angeles, California

TIME TICKET

No. L–3479

Date March 8 20 09

Employee Name	Employee Number	Job No.
T. Zeller	3969	B15

TIME AND RATE INFORMATION:

Start Time	Finish Time	Elapsed Time	Hourly Rate
9:00	12:00	3.0	$20.00
Approved By C. Luther		Total Cost	$60.00

Remarks

When time tickets report labor used on a specific job, this cost is recorded as direct labor. The following entry records the data from the time ticket in Exhibit 2.7.

Point: In the accounting equation, we treat accounts such as Factory Overhead and Factory Payroll as temporary accounts, which hold various expenses until they are allocated to balance sheet or income statement accounts.

Assets = Liabilities + Equity
+60 +60

Mar. 8	Goods in Process Inventory—Job B15	60	
	Factory Payroll		60
	To record direct labor used on Job B15.		

The debit in this entry is posted both to the general ledger account and to the appropriate job cost sheet. (*Note:* An entry to record indirect labor is the same as for direct labor *except* that it debits Factory Overhead and credits Factory Payroll. In the subsidiary factory overhead ledger, the debit in this entry is posted to the Indirect Labor account.)

P3 Describe and record the flow of overhead costs in job order cost accounting.

Overhead Cost Flows and Documents

Factory overhead (or simply overhead) cost flows are shown in Exhibit 2.8. Factory overhead includes all production costs other than direct materials and direct labor. Two sources of

EXHIBIT 2.8

Overhead Cost Flows through Subsidiary Records

overhead costs are indirect materials and indirect labor. These costs are recorded from requisitions for indirect materials and time tickets for indirect labor. Two other sources of overhead are (1) vouchers authorizing payments for items such as supplies or utilities and (2) adjusting entries for costs such as depreciation on factory assets.

Overhead

Factory overhead usually includes many different costs and, thus, a separate account for each is often maintained in a subsidiary factory overhead ledger. This ledger is controlled by the Factory Overhead account in the general ledger. Factory Overhead is a temporary account that accumulates costs until they are allocated to jobs.

Recall that overhead costs are recorded with debits to the Factory Overhead account and with credits to other accounts such as Cash, Accounts Payable, and Accumulated Depreciation—Equipment. In the subsidiary factory overhead ledger, the debits are posted to their respective accounts such as Depreciation Expense—Equipment, Insurance Expense—Warehouse, or Amortization Expense—Patents.

To illustrate the recording of overhead, the following two entries reflect the depreciation of factory equipment and the accrual of utilities, respectively, for the week ended March 6.

Mar. 6	Factory Overhead	600	
	Accumulated Depreciation—Equipment		600
	To record depreciation on factory equipment.		
Mar. 6	Factory Overhead	250	
	Utilities Payable.		250
	To record the accrual of factory utilities.		

Assets = Liabilities + Equity
−600 −600

Assets = Liabilities + Equity
+250 −250

Exhibit 2.8 shows that overhead costs flow from the Factory Overhead account to job cost sheets. Because overhead is made up of costs not directly associated with specific jobs or job lots, we cannot determine the dollar amount incurred on a specific job. We know, however, that overhead costs represent a necessary part of business activities. If a job cost is to include all costs needed to complete the job, some amount of overhead must be included. Given the difficulty in determining the overhead amount for a specific job, however, we allocate overhead to individual jobs in some reasonable manner.

We generally allocate overhead by linking it to another factor used in production, such as direct labor or machine hours. The factor to which overhead costs are linked is known as the *allocation base.* A manager must think carefully about how many and which allocation bases to use. This managerial decision influences the accuracy with which overhead costs are allocated to individual jobs. In turn, the cost of individual jobs might impact a manager's decisions for pricing or performance evaluation. In Exhibit 2.2, overhead is expressed as 160% of direct labor. We then allocate overhead by multiplying 160% by the estimated amount of direct labor on the jobs.

We cannot wait until the end of a period to allocate overhead to jobs because perpetual inventory records are part of the job order costing system (demanding up-to-date costs). Instead, we

Point: The predetermined overhead rate is computed at the start of the period and is used throughout the period to allocate overhead to jobs.

Point: Predetermined overhead rates can be estimated using mathematical equations, statistical analysis, or professional experience.

must predict overhead in advance and assign it to jobs so that a job's total costs can be estimated prior to its completion. This estimated cost is useful for managers in many decisions including setting prices and identifying costs that are out of control. Being able to estimate overhead in advance requires a **predetermined overhead rate,** also called *predetermined overhead allocation* (or *application*) *rate.* This rate requires an estimate of total overhead cost and an allocation factor such as total direct labor cost before the start of the period. Exhibit 2.9 shows the usual formula for computing a predetermined overhead rate (estimates are commonly based on annual amounts). This rate is used during the period to allocate overhead to jobs. It is common for companies to use multiple activity (allocation) bases and multiple predetermined overhead rates for different types of products and services.

EXHIBIT 2.9

Predetermined Overhead Allocation Rate Formula

Predetermined overhead rate = Estimated overhead costs ÷ Estimated activity base

To illustrate, Road Warriors allocates overhead by linking it to direct labor. At the start of the current period, management predicts total direct labor costs of $125,000 and total overhead costs of $200,000. Using these estimates, management computes its predetermined overhead rate as 160% of direct labor cost ($200,000 ÷ $125,000). Specifically, reviewing the job order cost sheet in Exhibit 2.2, we see that $1,000 of direct labor went into Job B15. We then use the predetermined overhead rate of 160% to allocate $1,600 (equal to $1,000 × 1.60) of overhead to this job. The entry to record this allocation is

Example: If management predicts total direct labor costs of $100,000 and total overhead costs of $200,000, what is its predetermined overhead rate? *Answer:* 200% of direct labor cost.

Assets	= Liabilities	+ Equity
+1,600		+1,600

Mar. 11	Goods in Process Inventory—Job B15.	1,600	
	Factory Overhead		1,600
	To assign overhead to Job B15.		

Since the allocation rate for overhead is estimated at the start of a period, the total amount assigned to jobs during a period rarely equals the amount actually incurred. We explain how this difference is treated later in this chapter.

Decision Ethics

Web Consultant You are working on seven client engagements. Two clients reimburse your firm for actual costs plus a 10% markup. The other five pay a fixed fee for services. Your firm's costs include overhead allocated at $47 per labor hour. The managing partner of your firm instructs you to record as many labor hours as possible to the two markup engagements by transferring labor hours from the other five. What do you do? [Answer—p. 64]

Summary of Cost Flows

Point: Study the flow of manufacturing costs through general ledger accounts and job cost sheets. Use Exhibit 2.11 as reinforcement.

We showed journal entries for charging Goods in Process Inventory (Job B15) with the cost of (1) direct materials requisitions, (2) direct labor time tickets, and (3) factory overhead. We made separate entries for each of these costs, but they are usually recorded in one entry. Specifically, materials requisitions are often collected for a day or a week and recorded with a single entry summarizing them. The same is done with labor time tickets. When summary entries are made, supporting schedules of the jobs charged and the types of materials used provide the basis for postings to subsidiary records.

To show all production cost flows for a period and their related entries, we again look at Road Warriors' activities. Exhibit 2.10 shows costs linked to all of Road Warriors' production activities for March. Road Warriors did not have any jobs in process at the beginning of March, but it did apply materials, labor, and overhead costs to five new jobs in March. Jobs B15 and B16 are completed and delivered to customers in March, Job B17 is completed but not delivered, and Jobs B18 and B19 are still in process. Exhibit 2.10 also shows purchases of raw materials for $2,750, labor costs incurred for $5,300, and overhead costs of $6,720.

The upper part of Exhibit 2.11 shows the flow of these costs through general ledger accounts and the end-of-month balances in key subsidiary records. Arrow lines are numbered

EXHIBIT 2.10

Job Order Costs of All Production Activities

ROAD WARRIORS
Job Order Manufacturing Costs
For Month Ended March 31, 2009

Explanation	Materials	Labor	Overhead Incurred	Overhead Allocated	Goods in Process	Finished Goods	Cost of Goods Sold
Job B15	$ 600	$1,000		$1,600			$3,200
Job B16	300	800		1,280			2,380
Job B17	500	1,100		1,760		$3,360	
Job B18	150	700		1,120	$1,970		
Job B19	250	600		960	1,810		
Total job costs	1,800	4,200		$6,720	$3,780	$3,360	$5,580
Indirect materials	550		$ 550				
Indirect labor		1,100	1,100				
Other overhead			5,070				
Total costs used in production	2,350	$5,300	$6,720				
Ending materials inventory	1,400						
Materials available	3,750						
Less beginning materials inventory	(1,000)						
Materials purchased	$2,750						

EXHIBIT 2.11

Job Order Cost Flows and Ending Job Cost Sheets

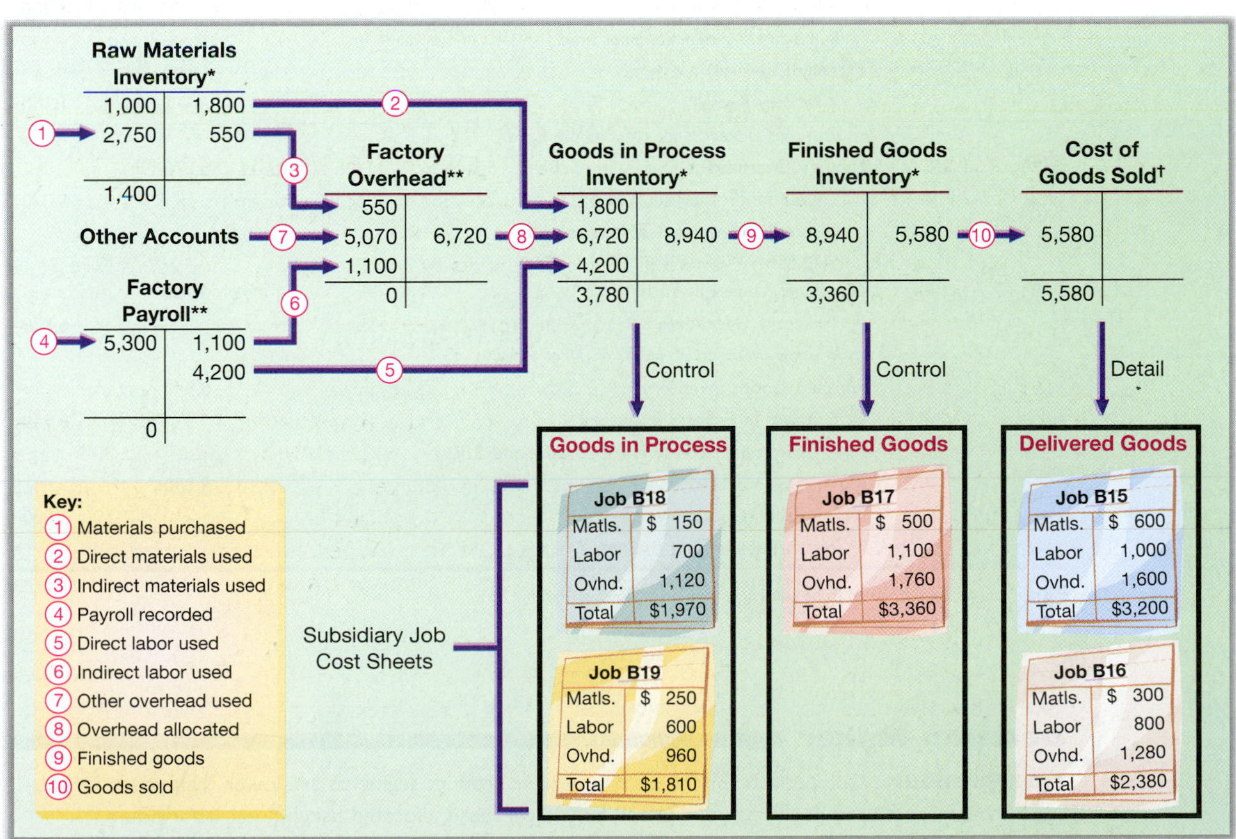

* The ending balances in the inventory accounts are carried to the balance sheet.

† The Cost of Goods Sold balance is carried to the income statement.

** Factory Payroll and Factory Overhead are considered temporary accounts; when these costs are allocated to jobs, the balances in these accounts are reduced.

to show the flows of costs for March. Each numbered cost flow reflects several entries made in March. The lower part of Exhibit 2.11 shows summarized job cost sheets and their status at the end of March. The sum of costs assigned to the jobs in process ($1,970 + $1,810) equals the $3,780 balance in Goods in Process Inventory shown in Exhibit 2.10. Also, costs assigned to Job B17 equal the $3,360 balance in Finished Goods Inventory. The sum of costs assigned to Jobs B15 and B16 ($3,200 + $2,380) equals the $5,580 balance in Cost of Goods Sold.

Exhibit 2.12 shows each cost flow with a single entry summarizing the actual individual entries made in March. Each entry is numbered to link with the arrow lines in Exhibit 2.11.

EXHIBIT 2.12

Entries for Job Order Production Costs*

①	Raw Materials Inventory	2,750	
	Accounts Payable		2,750
	Acquired materials on credit for factory use.		
②	Goods in Process Inventory	1,800	
	Raw Materials Inventory		1,800
	To assign costs of direct materials used.		
③	Factory Overhead	550	
	Raw Materials Inventory		550
	To record use of indirect materials.		
④	Factory Payroll	5,300	
	Cash (and other accounts)		5,300
	To record salaries and wages of factory workers (including various payroll liabilities).		
⑤	Goods in Process Inventory	4,200	
	Factory Payroll		4,200
	To assign costs of direct labor used.		
⑥	Factory Overhead	1,100	
	Factory Payroll		1,100
	To record indirect labor costs as overhead.		
⑦	Factory Overhead	5,070	
	Cash (and other accounts)		5,070
	To record factory overhead costs such as insurance, utilities, rent, and depreciation.		
⑧	Goods in Process Inventory	6,720	
	Factory Overhead		6,720
	To apply overhead at 160% of direct labor.		
⑨	Finished Goods Inventory	8,940	
	Goods in Process Inventory		8,940
	To record completion of Jobs B15, B16, and B17.		
⑩	Cost of Goods Sold	5,580	
	Finished Goods Inventory		5,580
	To record sale of Jobs B15 and B16.		

* Transactions are numbered to be consistent with arrow lines in Exhibit 2.11.

Point: *Actual* overhead is debited to Factory Overhead. *Allocated* overhead is credited to Factory Overhead.

Decision Maker

Entrepreneur Competitors' prices on one of your product segments are lower than yours. Of the total product cost used in setting your prices, 53% is overhead allocated using direct labor hours. You believe that product costs are distorted and wonder whether there is a better way to allocate overhead and to set product price. What do you suggest? [Answer—p. 65]

Quick Check Answers—p. 65

5. In job order cost accounting, which account is debited in recording a raw materials requisition? (*a*) Raw Materials Inventory, (*b*) Raw Materials Purchases, (*c*) Goods in Process Inventory if for a job, or (*d*) Goods in Process Inventory if they are indirect materials.
6. What are four sources of information for recording costs in the Factory Overhead account?
7. Why does job order cost accounting require a predetermined overhead rate?
8. What events result in a debit to Factory Payroll? What events result in a credit?

Adjustment of Overapplied or Underapplied Overhead

Refer to the debits in the Factory Overhead account in Exhibit 2.11 (or Exhibit 2.12). The total cost of factory overhead incurred during March is $6,720 ($550 + $5,070 + $1,100). The $6,720 exactly equals the amount assigned to goods in process inventory (see arrow line ⑧). Therefore, the overhead incurred equals the overhead applied in March. The amount of overhead incurred rarely equals the amount of overhead applied, however, because a job order cost accounting system uses a predetermined overhead rate in applying factory overhead costs to jobs. This rate is determined using estimated amounts before the period begins, and estimates rarely equal the exact amounts actually incurred. This section explains what we do when too much or too little overhead is applied to jobs.

Video2.1

Underapplied Overhead

P4 Determine adjustments for overapplied and underapplied factory overhead.

When less overhead is applied than is actually incurred, the remaining debit balance in the Factory Overhead account at the end of the period is called **underapplied overhead.** To illustrate, assume that Road Warriors actually incurred *other overhead costs* of $5,550 instead of the $5,070 shown in Exhibit 2.11. This yields an actual total overhead cost of $7,200 in March. Since the amount of overhead applied was only $6,720, the Factory Overhead account is left with a $480 debit balance as shown in the ledger account in Exhibit 2.13.

EXHIBIT 2.13

Underapplied Overhead in the Factory Overhead Ledger Account

Factory Overhead				Acct. No. 540
Date	**Explanation**	**Debit**	**Credit**	**Balance**
Mar. 31	Indirect materials cost	550		550 Dr.
31	Indirect labor cost	1,100		1,650 Dr.
31	Other overhead cost	5,550		7,200 Dr.
31	Overhead costs applied to jobs		6,720	480 Dr.

The $480 debit balance reflects manufacturing costs not assigned to jobs. This means that the balances in Goods in Process Inventory, Finished Goods Inventory, and Cost of Goods Sold do not include all production costs incurred. When the underapplied overhead amount is immaterial, it is allocated (closed) to the Cost of Goods Sold account with the following adjusting entry.

Example: If we do not adjust for underapplied overhead, will net income be overstated or understated? *Answer:* Overstated.

Mar. 31	Cost of Goods Sold	480	
	Factory Overhead		480
	To adjust for underapplied overhead costs.		

Assets = Liabilities + Equity
−480
+480

The $480 debit (increase) to Cost of Goods Sold reduces income by $480. (When the underapplied (or overapplied) overhead is material, the amount is normally allocated to the Cost of Goods Sold, Finished Goods Inventory, and Goods in Process Inventory accounts. This process is covered in advanced courses.)

Overapplied Overhead

When the overhead applied in a period exceeds the overhead incurred, the resulting credit balance in the Factory Overhead account is called **overapplied overhead.** We treat overapplied overhead at the end of the period in the same way we treat underapplied overhead, except that we debit Factory Overhead and credit Cost of Good Sold for the amount.

Decision Insight

Job Order Education Many companies invest in their employees, and the demand for executive education is strong. Annual spending on training and education exceeds $20 billion. Annual revenues for providers of executive education continue to rise, with about 40% of revenues coming from custom programs designed for one or a select group of companies.

Quick Check

Answers—p. 65

9. In a job order cost accounting system, why does the Factory Overhead account usually have an overapplied or underapplied balance at period-end?
10. When the Factory Overhead account has a debit balance at period-end, does this reflect overapplied or underapplied overhead?

Decision Analysis — Pricing for Services

A1 Apply job order costing in pricing services.

The chapter described job order costing mainly using a manufacturing setting. However, these concepts and procedures are applicable to a service setting. Consider AdWorld, an advertising agency that develops Web-based ads for small firms. Each of its customers has unique requirements, so costs for each individual job must be tracked separately.

AdWorld uses two types of labor: Web designers ($65 per hour) and computer staff ($50 per hour). It also incurs overhead costs that it assigns using two different predetermined overhead allocation rates: $125 per designer hour and $96 per staff hour. For each job, AdWorld must estimate the number of designer and staff hours needed. Then total costs pertaining to each job are determined using the procedures in the chapter. (*Note:* Most service firms have neither the category of materials cost nor inventory.)

To illustrate, a manufacturer of golf balls requested a quote from AdWorld for an advertising engagement. AdWorld estimates that the job will require 43 designer hours and 61 staff hours, with the following total estimated cost for this job.

Direct Labor		
Designers (43 hours × $65)	$ 2,795	
Staff (61 hours × $50)	3,050	
Total direct labor		$ 5,845
Overhead		
Designer related (43 hours × $125)	5,375	
Staff related (61 hours × $96)	5,856	
Total overhead		11,231
Total estimated job cost		$17,076

AdWorld can use this cost information to help determine the price quote for the job (see *Decision Maker,* **Sales Manager,** scenario in this chapter).

Another source of information that AdWorld must consider is the market, that is, how much competitors will quote for this job. Competitor information is often unavailable; therefore, AdWorld's managers must use estimates based on their assessment of the competitive environment.

Decision Maker

Sales Manager As AdWorld's sales manager, assume that you estimate costs pertaining to a proposed job as $17,076. Your normal pricing policy is to apply a markup of 18% from total costs. However, you learn that three other agencies are likely to bid for the same job, and that their quotes will range from $16,500 to $22,000. What price should you quote? What factors other than cost must you consider? [Answer—p. 65]

Demonstration Problem—Job Order Costing

The following information reflects Walczak Company's job order production activities for May.

Raw materials purchases	$16,000
Factory payroll cost	15,400
Overhead costs incurred	
Indirect materials	5,000
Indirect labor	3,500
Other factory overhead	9,500

Walczak's predetermined overhead rate is 150% of direct labor cost. Costs are allocated to the three jobs worked on during May as follows.

	Job 401	Job 402	Job 403
In-process balances on April 30			
Direct materials	$3,600		
Direct labor	1,700		
Applied overhead	2,550		
Costs during May			
Direct materials	3,550	$3,500	$1,400
Direct labor	5,100	6,000	800
Applied overhead	?	?	?
Status on May 31	**Finished (sold)**	**Finished (unsold)**	**In process**

Required

1. Determine the total cost of:
 a. The April 30 inventory of jobs in process.
 b. Materials used during May.
 c. Labor used during May.
 d. Factory overhead incurred and applied during May and the amount of any over- or underapplied overhead on May 31.
 e. Each job as of May 31, the May 31 inventories of both goods in process and finished goods, and the goods sold during May.

2. Prepare summarized journal entries for the month to record:
 a. Materials purchases (on credit), the factory payroll (paid with cash), indirect materials, indirect labor, and the other factory overhead (paid with cash).
 b. Assignment of direct materials, direct labor, and overhead costs to the Goods in Process Inventory account. (Use separate debit entries for each job.)
 c. Transfer of each completed job to the Finished Goods Inventory account.
 d. Cost of goods sold.
 e. Removal of any underapplied or overapplied overhead from the Factory Overhead account. (Assume the amount is not material.)

3. Prepare a manufacturing statement for May.

Planning the Solution

- Determine the cost of the April 30 goods in process inventory by totaling the materials, labor, and applied overhead costs for Job 401.

- Compute the cost of materials used and labor by totaling the amounts assigned to jobs and to overhead.
- Compute the total overhead incurred by summing the amounts for the three components. Compute the amount of applied overhead by multiplying the total direct labor cost by the predetermined overhead rate. Compute the underapplied or overapplied amount as the difference between the actual cost and the applied cost.
- Determine the total cost charged to each job by adding the costs incurred in April (if any) to the cost of materials, labor, and overhead applied during May.
- Group the costs of the jobs according to their completion status.
- Record the direct materials costs assigned to the three jobs, using a separate Goods in Process Inventory account for each job; do the same for the direct labor and the applied overhead.
- Transfer costs of Jobs 401 and 402 from Goods in Process Inventory to Finished Goods.
- Record the costs of Job 401 as cost of goods sold.
- Record the transfer of underapplied overhead from the Factory Overhead account to the Cost of Goods Sold account.
- On the manufacturing statement, remember to include the beginning and ending goods in process inventories and to deduct the underapplied overhead.

Solution to Demonstration Problem

1. Total cost of

a. April 30 inventory of jobs in process (Job 401).

Direct materials	$3,600
Direct labor	1,700
Applied overhead	2,550
Total cost	$7,850

b. Materials used during May.

Direct materials	
Job 401	$ 3,550
Job 402	3,500
Job 403	1,400
Total direct materials	8,450
Indirect materials	5,000
Total materials used	$13,450

c. Labor used during May.

Direct labor	
Job 401	$ 5,100
Job 402	6,000
Job 403	800
Total direct labor	11,900
Indirect labor	3,500
Total labor used	$15,400

d. Factory overhead incurred in May.

Actual overhead	
Indirect materials	$ 5,000
Indirect labor	3,500
Other factory overhead	9,500
Total actual overhead	18,000
Overhead applied (150% × $11,900)	17,850
Underapplied overhead	$ 150

e. Total cost of each job.

	401	402	403
In-process costs from April			
Direct materials	$ 3,600		
Direct labor	1,700		
Applied overhead*	2,550		
Cost incurred in May			
Direct materials	3,550	$ 3,500	$1,400
Direct labor	5,100	6,000	800
Applied overhead*	7,650	9,000	1,200
Total costs	$24,150	$18,500	$3,400

* Equals 150% of the direct labor cost.

Total cost of the May 31 inventory of goods in process (Job 403) = $3,400

Total cost of the May 31 inventory of finished goods (Job 402) = $18,500

Total cost of goods sold during May (Job 401) = $24,150

2. Journal entries.

a.

	Debit	Credit
Raw Materials Inventory	16,000	
Accounts Payable		16,000
To record materials purchases.		
Factory Payroll	15,400	
Cash		15,400
To record factory payroll.		
Factory Overhead	5,000	
Raw Materials Inventory		5,000
To record indirect materials.		
Factory Overhead	3,500	
Factory Payroll		3,500
To record indirect labor.		
Factory Overhead	9,500	
Cash		9,500
To record other factory overhead.		

b. Assignment of costs to Goods in Process Inventory.

	Debit	Credit
Goods in Process Inventory (Job 401)	3,550	
Goods in Process Inventory (Job 402)	3,500	
Goods in Process Inventory (Job 403)	1,400	
Raw Materials Inventory		8,450
To assign direct materials to jobs.		
Goods in Process Inventory (Job 401)	5,100	
Goods in Process Inventory (Job 402)	6,000	
Goods in Process Inventory (Job 403)	800	
Factory Payroll		11,900
To assign direct labor to jobs.		
Goods in Process Inventory (Job 401)	7,650	
Goods in Process Inventory (Job 402)	9,000	
Goods in Process Inventory (Job 403)	1,200	
Factory Overhead		17,850
To apply overhead to jobs.		

c. Transfer of completed jobs to Finished Goods Inventory.

	Debit	Credit
Finished Goods Inventory	42,650	
Goods in Process Inventory (Job 401)		24,150
Goods in Process Inventory (Job 402)		18,500
To record completion of jobs.		

d.

	Debit	Credit
Cost of Goods Sold	24,150	
Finished Goods Inventory		24,150
To record sale of Job 401.		

e.

	Debit	Credit
Cost of Goods Sold	150	
Factory Overhead		150
To assign underapplied overhead.		

3.

WALCZAK COMPANY Manufacturing Statement For Month Ended May 31		
Direct materials		$ 8,450
Direct labor		11,900
Factory overhead		
Indirect materials	$5,000	
Indirect labor	3,500	
Other factory overhead	9,500	18,000
Total production costs		38,350
Add goods in process, April 30		7,850
Total cost of goods in process		46,200
Less goods in process, May 31		3,400
Less underapplied overhead		150
Cost of goods manufactured		$42,650

See how underapplied overhead is reported. Overapplied overhead is similarly reported, but is added.

Summary

C1 Explain the cost accounting system. A cost accounting system records production activities using a perpetual inventory system, which continuously updates records for transactions and events that affect inventory costs.

C2 Describe important features of job order production. Certain companies called *job order manufacturers* produce custom-made products for customers. These customized products are produced in response to a customer's orders. A job order manufacturer produces products that usually are different and, typically, produced in low volumes. The production systems of job order companies are flexible and are not highly standardized.

C3 Explain job cost sheets and how they are used in job order cost accounting. In a job order cost accounting system, the costs of producing each job are accumulated on a separate job cost sheet. Costs of direct materials, direct labor, and overhead are accumulated separately on the job cost sheet and then added to determine the total cost of a job. Job cost sheets for jobs in process, finished jobs, and jobs sold make up subsidiary records controlled by general ledger accounts.

A1 Apply job order costing in pricing services. Job order costing can usefully be applied to a service setting. The resulting job cost estimate can then be used to help determine a price for services.

P1 Describe and record the flow of materials costs in job order cost accounting. Costs of materials flow from receiving reports to materials ledger cards and then to either job cost sheets or the Indirect Materials account in the factory overhead ledger.

P2 Describe and record the flow of labor costs in job order cost accounting. Costs of labor flow from clock cards to the Factory Payroll account and then to either job cost sheets or the Indirect Labor account in the factory overhead ledger.

P3 Describe and record the flow of overhead costs in job order cost accounting. Overhead costs are accumulated in the Factory Overhead account that controls the subsidiary factory overhead ledger. Then, using a predetermined overhead rate, overhead costs are charged to jobs.

P4 Determine adjustments for overapplied and underapplied factory overhead. At the end of each period, the Factory Overhead account usually has a residual debit (underapplied overhead) or credit (overapplied overhead) balance. If the balance is not material, it is transferred to Cost of Goods Sold, but if it is material, it is allocated to Goods in Process Inventory, Finished Goods Inventory, and Cost of Goods Sold.

Guidance Answers to Decision Maker and Decision Ethics

Management Consultant Service companies (such as this consulting firm) do not recognize goods in process inventory or finished goods inventory—an important difference between service and manufacturing companies. For the two jobs that are 60% complete, you could recognize revenues and costs at 60% of the total expected amounts. This means you could recognize revenue of $7,200 (0.60 × $12,000) and costs of $6,000 (0.60 × $10,000), yielding net income of $1,200 from each job.

Web Consultant The partner has a monetary incentive to *manage* the numbers and assign more costs to the two cost-plus engagements. This also would reduce costs on the fixed-price engagements. To act in such a manner is unethical. As a professional and an honest person, it is your responsibility to engage in ethical behavior. You must not comply with the partner's instructions. If the partner insists you act in an unethical manner, you should report the matter to a higher authority in the organization.

Entrepreneur An inadequate cost system can distort product costs. You should review overhead costs in detail. Once you know the different cost elements in overhead, you can classify them into groups such as material related, labor related, or machine related. Other groups can also be formed (we discuss this in Chapter 8). Once you have classified overhead items into groups, you can better establish overhead allocation bases and use them to compute predetermined overhead rates. These multiple rates and bases can then be used to assign overhead costs to products. This will likely improve product pricing.

Sales Manager The price based on AdWorld's normal pricing policy is $20,150 ($17,076 × 1.18), which is within the price range offered by competitors. One option is to apply normal pricing policy and quote a price of $20,150. On the other hand, assessing the competition, particularly in terms of their service quality and other benefits they might offer, would be useful. Although price is an input customers use to select suppliers, factors such as quality and timeliness (responsiveness) of suppliers are important. Accordingly, your price can reflect such factors.

Guidance Answers to **Quick Checks**

1. *b*
2. A job is a special order for a custom product. A job lot consists of a quantity of identical, special-order items.
3. *a*
4. Three costs normally accumulated on a job cost sheet are direct materials, direct labor, and factory overhead.
5. *c*
6. Four sources of factory overhead are materials requisitions, time tickets, vouchers, and adjusting entries.
7. Since a job order cost accounting system uses perpetual inventory records, overhead costs must be assigned to jobs before the end of a period. This requires the use of a predetermined overhead rate.
8. Debits are recorded when wages and salaries of factory employees are paid or accrued. Credits are recorded when direct labor costs are assigned to jobs and when indirect labor costs are transferred to the Factory Overhead account.
9. Overapplied or underapplied overhead usually exists at the end of a period because application of overhead is based on estimates of overhead and another variable such as direct labor. Estimates rarely equal actual amounts incurred.
10. A debit balance reflects underapplied factory overhead.

Key Terms

mhhe.com/wildMA2e

Key Terms are available at the book's Website for learning and testing in an online Flashcard Format.

Multiple Choice Quiz

Answers on p. •••

mhhe.com/wildMA2e

Additional Quiz Questions are available at the book's Website.

Quiz2

1. A company's predetermined overhead allocation rate is 150% of its direct labor costs. How much overhead is applied to a job that requires total direct labor costs of $30,000?
   - **a.** $15,000
   - **b.** $30,000
   - **c.** $45,000
   - **d.** $60,000
   - **e.** $75,000
2. A company's cost accounting system uses direct labor costs to apply overhead to goods in process and finished goods inventories. Its production costs for the period are: direct materials, $45,000; direct labor, $35,000; and overhead applied, $38,500. What is its predetermined overhead allocation rate?
   - **a.** 10%
   - **b.** 110%
   - **c.** 86%
   - **d.** 91%
   - **e.** 117%
3. A company's ending inventory of finished goods has a total cost of $10,000 and consists of 500 units. If the overhead applied to these goods is $4,000, and the predetermined

overhead rate is 80% of direct labor costs, how much direct materials cost was incurred in producing these 500 units?

a. $10,000
b. $ 6,000
c. $ 4,000
d. $ 5,000
e. $ 1,000

4. A company's Goods in Process Inventory T-account follows.

Goods in Process Inventory			
Beginning balance	9,000		
Direct materials	94,200		
Direct labor	59,200	?	Finished goods
Overhead applied	31,600		
Ending balance	17,800		

The cost of units transferred to Finished Goods inventory is

a. $193,000
b. $211,800
c. $185,000
d. $144,600
e. $176,200

5. At the end of its current year, a company learned that its overhead was underapplied by $1,500 and that this amount is not considered material. Based on this information, the company should

a. Close the $1,500 to Finished Goods Inventory.
b. Close the $1,500 to Cost of Goods Sold.
c. Carry the $1,500 to the next period.
d. Do nothing about the $1,500 because it is not material and it is likely that overhead will be overapplied by the same amount next year.
e. Carry the $1,500 to the Income Statement as "Other Expense."

Discussion Questions

1. Why must a company estimate the amount of factory overhead assigned to individual jobs or job lots?

2. The chapter used a percent of labor cost to assign factory overhead to jobs. Identify another factor (or base) a company might reasonably use to assign overhead costs.

3. What information is recorded on a job cost sheet? How do management and employees use job cost sheets?

4. In a job order cost accounting system, what records serve as a subsidiary ledger for Goods in Process Inventory? For Finished Goods Inventory?

5. What journal entry is recorded when a materials manager receives a materials requisition and then issues materials (both direct and indirect) for use in the factory?

6. How does the materials requisition help safeguard a company's assets?

7. What is the difference between a clock card and a time ticket?

8. What events cause debits to be recorded in the Factory Overhead account? What events cause credits to be recorded in the Factory Overhead account?

9. What account(s) is(are) used to eliminate overapplied or underapplied overhead from the Factory Overhead account, assuming the amount is not material?

10. Assume that **Apple** produces a batch of 1,000 iPods. Does it account for this as 1,000 individual jobs or as a job lot? Explain (consider costs and benefits).

11. Why must a company prepare a predetermined overhead rate when using job order cost accounting?

12. How would a hospital apply job order costing? Explain.

13. **Harley-Davidson** manufactures 30 custom-made luxury-model motorcycles. Does it account for these motorcycles as 30 individual jobs or as a job lot? Explain.

Harley-Davidson

14. **Best Buy**'s GeekSquad performs computer and home theater installation and service, for an upfront flat price. How can Best Buy use a job order costing system?

Denotes Discussion Questions that involve decision making.

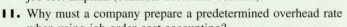

Most materials in this section are available in McGraw-Hill's Connect connect

QUICK STUDY

QS 2-1
Jobs and job lots
C2

Determine which products are most likely to be manufactured as a job and which as a job lot.

1. A custom-designed home.
2. Hats imprinted with company logo.
3. Little League trophies.
4. A hand-crafted table.
5. A 90-foot motor yacht.
6. Wedding dresses for a chain of stores.

QS 2-2
Job cost computation C3

The following information is from the materials requisitions and time tickets for Job 9-1005 completed by Franklin Boats. The requisitions are identified by code numbers starting with the letter Q and the time tickets start with W. At the start of the year, management estimated that overhead cost would equal 110% of direct labor cost for each job. Determine the total cost on the job cost sheet for Job 9-1005.

Date	Document	Amount
7/1/2009	Q-4698	$2,500
7/1/2009	W-3393	1,200
7/5/2009	Q-4725	2,000
7/5/2009	W-3479	900
7/10/2009	W-3559	600

QS 2-3
Direct materials journal entries P1

During the current month, a company that uses a job order cost accounting system purchases $25,000 in raw materials for cash. It then uses $6,000 of raw materials indirectly as factory supplies and uses $16,000 of raw materials as direct materials. Prepare entries to record these three transactions.

QS 2-4
Direct labor journal entries P2

During the current month, a company that uses a job order cost accounting system incurred a monthly factory payroll of $75,000, paid in cash. Of this amount, $29,000 is classified as indirect labor and the remainder as direct. Prepare entries to record these transactions.

QS 2-5
Factory overhead rates P3

A company incurred the following manufacturing costs this period: direct labor, $234,000; direct materials, $292,000; and factory overhead, $58,500. Compute its overhead cost as a percent of (1) direct labor and (2) direct materials.

QS 2-6
Factory overhead journal entries P3

During the current month, a company that uses a job order cost accounting system incurred a monthly factory payroll of $350,000, paid in cash. Of this amount, $90,000 is classified as indirect labor and the remainder as direct for the production of Job 65A. Factory overhead is applied at 90% of direct labor. Prepare the entry to apply factory overhead to this job lot.

QS 2-7
Entry for over- or underapplied overhead P4

A company allocates overhead at a rate of 150% of direct labor cost. Actual overhead cost for the current period is $475,000, and direct labor cost is $300,000. Prepare the entry to close over- or underapplied overhead to cost of goods sold.

connect *Most materials in this section are available in McGraw-Hill's Connect*

EXERCISES

Exercise 2-1
Documents in job order cost accounting
C2 C3 P1 P2 P3

The left column lists the titles of documents and accounts used in job order cost accounting. The right column presents short descriptions of the purposes of the documents. Match each document in the left column to its numbered description in the right column.

A. Voucher
B. Materials requisition
C. Factory Overhead account
D. Clock card
E. Factory Payroll account
F. Materials ledger card
G. Time ticket

_____ **1.** Shows amount of time an employee works on a job.
_____ **2.** Temporarily accumulates incurred labor costs until they are assigned to specific jobs or to overhead.
_____ **3.** Shows only total time an employee works each day.
_____ **4.** Perpetual inventory record of raw materials received, used, and available for use.
_____ **5.** Shows amount approved for payment of an overhead or other cost.
_____ **6.** Temporarily accumulates the cost of incurred overhead until the cost is assigned to specific jobs.
_____ **7.** Communicates the need for materials to complete a job.

Exercise 2-2
Analysis of cost flows
C2 P1 P2 P3 

As of the end of June, the job cost sheets at Tracer Wheels, Inc., show the following total costs accumulated on three custom jobs.

	Job 102	Job 103	Job 104
Direct materials	$25,000	$59,000	$56,000
Direct labor	14,000	26,700	40,000
Overhead	7,000	13,350	20,000

Job 102 was started in production in May and the following costs were assigned to it in May: direct materials, $13,000; direct labor, $3,600; and overhead, $1,600. Jobs 103 and 104 are started in June. Overhead cost is applied with a predetermined rate based on direct labor cost. Jobs 102 and 103 are finished in June, and Job 104 is expected to be finished in July. No raw materials are used indirectly in June. Using this information, answer the following questions. (Assume this company's predetermined overhead rate did not change across these months.)

1. What is the cost of the raw materials requisitioned in June for each of the three jobs?
2. How much direct labor cost is incurred during June for each of the three jobs?
3. What predetermined overhead rate is used during June?
4. How much total cost is transferred to finished goods during June?

Check (4) $145,050

Exercise 2-3
Overhead rate; costs assigned to jobs
P3

In December 2008, Matsushi Electronics' management establishes the year 2009 predetermined overhead rate based on direct labor cost. The information used in setting this rate includes estimates that the company will incur $750,000 of overhead costs and $500,000 of direct labor cost in year 2009. During March 2009, Matsushi began and completed Job No. 13-56.

1. What is the predetermined overhead rate for year 2009?
2. Use the information on the following job cost sheet to determine the total cost of the job.

Check (2) $23,450

JOB COST SHEET

Customer's Name: ESPN Co. Job No. 13-56

Job Description: 5 plasma monitors—150 inch

	Direct Materials		Direct Labor		Overhead Costs Applied	
Date	Requisition No.	Amount	Time-Ticket No.	Amount	Rate	Amount
Mar. 8	4-129	$4,000	T-306	$ 680		
Mar. 11	4-142	7,450	T-432	1,280		
Mar. 18	4-167	3,800	T-456	1,320		
Totals						

Exercise 2-4
Analysis of costs assigned to goods in process
P3

Wilson Company uses a job order cost accounting system that charges overhead to jobs on the basis of direct material cost. At year-end, the Goods in Process Inventory account shows the following.

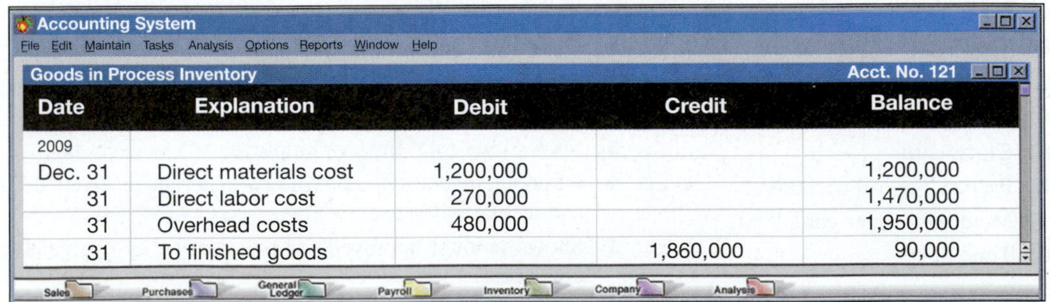

Date	Explanation	Debit	Credit	Balance
2009				
Dec. 31	Direct materials cost	1,200,000		1,200,000
31	Direct labor cost	270,000		1,470,000
31	Overhead costs	480,000		1,950,000
31	To finished goods		1,860,000	90,000

1. Determine the overhead rate used (based on direct material cost).
2. Only one job remained in the goods in process inventory at December 31, 2009. Its direct materials cost is $40,000. How much direct labor cost and overhead cost are assigned to it?

Check (2) Direct labor cost, $34,000

Exercise 2-5
Cost flows in a job order cost system
C3 P3

The following information is available for SafeLife Company, which produces special-order security products and uses a job order cost accounting system.

	April 30	May 31
Inventories		
Raw materials	$27,000	$ 41,000
Goods in process	9,000	20,600
Finished goods	70,000	33,000
Activities and information for May		
Raw materials purchases (paid with cash)		183,000
Factory payroll (paid with cash)		500,000
Factory overhead		
Indirect materials		6,000
Indirect labor		74,000
Other overhead costs		95,500
Sales (received in cash)		1,500,000
Predetermined overhead rate based on direct labor cost		55%

Compute the following amounts for the month of May.

1. Cost of direct materials used.
2. Cost of direct labor used.
3. Cost of goods manufactured.
4. Cost of goods sold.*
5. Gross profit.
6. Overapplied or underapplied overhead.

*Do not consider any underapplied or overapplied overhead.

Check (3) $811,700

Exercise 2-6
Journal entries for a job order cost accounting system
P1 P2 P3 P4

Use information in Exercise 2-5 to prepare journal entries for the following events in May.

1. Raw materials purchases for cash.
2. Direct materials usage.
3. Indirect materials usage.
4. Factory payroll costs in cash.
5. Direct labor usage.
6. Indirect labor usage.
7. Factory overhead excluding indirect materials and indirect labor (record credit to Other Accounts).
8. Application of overhead to goods in process.
9. Transfer of finished jobs to the finished goods inventory.
10. Sale and delivery of finished goods to customers for cash (record unadjusted cost of sales).
11. Allocation (closing) of overapplied or underapplied overhead to Cost of Goods Sold.

Exercise 2-7
Factory overhead computed, applied, and adjusted
P3 P4

In December 2008, Dreamvision established its predetermined overhead rate for movies produced during year 2009 by using the following cost predictions: overhead costs, $1,700,000, and direct labor costs, $500,000. At year end 2009, the company's records show that actual overhead costs for the year are $1,710,000. Actual direct labor cost had been assigned to jobs as follows.

Movies completed and released	$400,000
Movies still in production	90,000
Total actual direct labor cost	$490,000

1. Determine the predetermined overhead rate for year 2009.
2. Set up a T-account for overhead and enter the overhead costs incurred and the amounts applied to movies during the year using the predetermined overhead rate.
3. Determine whether overhead is overapplied or underapplied (and the amount) during the year.
4. Prepare the adjusting entry to allocate any over- or underapplied overhead to Cost of Goods Sold.

Check (3) $44,000 underapplied

Exercise 2-8
Factory overhead computed, applied, and adjusted
P3 P4

In December 2008, Jens Company established its predetermined overhead rate for jobs produced during year 2009 by using the following cost predictions: overhead costs, $1,500,000, and direct labor costs, $1,250,000. At year end 2009, the company's records show that actual overhead costs for the year are $1,660,000. Actual direct labor cost had been assigned to jobs as follows.

Jobs completed and sold	$1,027,500
Jobs in finished goods inventory	205,500
Jobs in goods in process inventory	137,000
Total actual direct labor cost	$1,370,000

1. Determine the predetermined overhead rate for year 2009.

2. Set up a T-account for Factory Overhead and enter the overhead costs incurred and the amounts applied to jobs during the year using the predetermined overhead rate.

3. Determine whether overhead is overapplied or underapplied (and the amount) during the year.

4. Prepare the adjusting entry to allocate any over- or underapplied overhead to Cost of Goods Sold.

Check (3) $16,000 underapplied

Exercise 2-9
Overhead rate calculation, allocation, and analysis P3

Campton Company applies factory overhead based on direct labor costs. The company incurred the following costs during 2009: direct materials costs, $635,500; direct labor costs, $2,000,000; and factory overhead costs applied, $1,200,000.

1. Determine the company's predetermined overhead rate for year 2009.

2. Assuming that the company's $54,000 ending Goods in Process Inventory account for year 2009 had $13,000 of direct labor costs, determine the inventory's direct materials costs.

3. Assuming that the company's $337,435 ending Finished Goods Inventory account for year 2009 had $137,435 of direct materials costs, determine the inventory's direct labor costs and its overhead costs.

Check (3) $75,000 overhead costs

Exercise 2-10
Costs allocated to ending inventories
P3

Santana Company's ending Goods in Process Inventory account consists of 10,000 units of partially completed product, and its Finished Goods Inventory account consists of 12,000 units of product. The factory manager determines that Goods in Process Inventory includes direct materials cost of $20 per unit and direct labor cost of $14 per unit. Finished goods are estimated to have $24 of direct materials cost per unit and $18 of direct labor cost per unit. The company established the predetermined overhead rate using the following predictions: estimated direct labor cost, $600,000, and estimated factory overhead, $750,000. The company allocates factory overhead to its goods in process and finished goods inventories based on direct labor cost. During the period, the company incurred these costs: direct materials, $1,070,000; direct labor, $580,000; and factory overhead applied, $725,000.

1. Determine the predetermined overhead rate.

2. Compute the total cost of the two ending inventories.

3. Compute cost of goods sold for the year (assume no beginning inventories and no underapplied or overapplied overhead).

Check (3) Cost of goods sold, $1,086,000

Exercise 2-11
Cost-based pricing
A1

Clemente Corporation has requested bids from several architects to design its new corporate headquarters. Troy Architects is one of the firms bidding on the job. Troy estimates that the job will require the following direct labor.

	Labor	Estimated Hours	Hourly Rate
1			
2	Architects	300	$400
3	Staff	300	65
4	Clerical	600	20

Troy applies overhead to jobs at 160% of direct labor cost. Troy would like to earn at least $90,000 profit on the architectural job. Based on past experience and market research, it estimates that the competition will bid between $450,000 and $550,000 for the job.

1. What is Troy's estimated cost of the architectural job?

2. What bid would you suggest that Troy submit?

Check (1) $393,900

connect *Most materials in this section are available in McGraw-Hill's Connect*

PROBLEM SET A

Problem 2-1A

Production costs computed and recorded; reports prepared

C3 P1 P2 P3 P4 

Lemmon Co.'s March 31 inventory of raw materials is $170,000. Raw materials purchases in April are $310,000, and factory payroll cost in April is $224,000. Overhead costs incurred in April are: indirect materials, $25,000; indirect labor, $19,000; factory rent, $25,000; factory utilities, $13,000; and factory equipment depreciation, $41,000. The predetermined overhead rate is 65% of direct labor cost. Job 306 is sold for $400,000 cash in April. Costs of the three jobs worked on in April follow.

	Job 306	Job 307	Job 308
Balances on March 31			
Direct materials	$ 9,000	$ 17,000	
Direct labor	19,000	5,000	
Applied overhead	12,350	3,250	
Costs during April			
Direct materials	75,000	160,000	$ 65,000
Direct labor	31,000	74,000	100,000
Applied overhead	?	?	?
Status on April 30	Finished (sold)	Finished (unsold)	In process

Required

1. Determine the total of each production cost incurred for April (direct labor, direct materials, and applied overhead), and the total cost assigned to each job (including the balances from March 31).

2. Prepare journal entries for the month of April to record the following.

a. Materials purchases (on credit), factory payroll (paid in cash), and actual overhead costs including indirect materials and indirect labor. (Factory rent and utilities are paid in cash.)

b. Assignment of direct materials, direct labor, and applied overhead costs to the Goods in Process Inventory.

c. Transfer of Jobs 306 and 307 to the Finished Goods Inventory.

d. Cost of goods sold for Job 306.

e. Revenue from the sale of Job 306.

f. Assignment of any underapplied or overapplied overhead to the Cost of Goods Sold account. (The amount is not material.)

Check (2f) $10,250 overapplied

3. Prepare a manufacturing statement for April (use a single line presentation for direct materials and show the details of overhead cost).

(3) Cost of goods manufactured, $473,850

4. Compute gross profit for April. Show how to present the inventories on the April 30 balance sheet.

Analysis Component

5. The over- or underapplied overhead is closed to Cost of Goods Sold. Discuss how this adjustment impacts business decision making regarding individual jobs or batches of jobs.

Problem 2-2A

Source documents, journal entries, overhead, and financial reports

P1 P2 P3 P4 

Mead Bay's computer system generated the following trial balance on December 31, 2009. The company's manager knows something is wrong with the trial balance because it does not show any balance for Goods in Process Inventory but does show balances for the Factory Payroll and Factory Overhead accounts.

	Debit	Credit
Cash	$ 40,000	
Accounts receivable	34,000	
Raw materials inventory	22,000	

[continued on next page]

[continued from previous page]

Goods in process inventory	0	
Finished goods inventory	12,000	
Prepaid rent	4,000	
Accounts payable		$ 8,500
Notes payable		11,500
Common stock		40,000
Retained earnings		84,000
Sales		178,000
Cost of goods sold	112,000	
Factory payroll	18,000	
Factory overhead	26,000	
Operating expenses	54,000	
Totals	$322,000	$322,000

After examining various files, the manager identifies the following six source documents that need to be processed to bring the accounting records up to date.

Materials requisition 21-3010:	$4,100 direct materials to Job 402
Materials requisition 21-3011:	$7,100 direct materials to Job 404
Materials requisition 21-3012:	$2,400 indirect materials
Labor time ticket 6052:	$2,000 direct labor to Job 402
Labor time ticket 6053:	$15,000 direct labor to Job 404
Labor time ticket 6054:	$1,000 indirect labor

Jobs 402 and 404 are the only units in process at year-end. The predetermined overhead rate is 150% of direct labor cost.

Required

1. Use information on the six source documents to prepare journal entries to assign the following costs.

a. Direct materials costs to Goods in Process Inventory.

b. Direct labor costs to Goods in Process Inventory.

c. Overhead costs to Goods in Process Inventory.

d. Indirect materials costs to the Factory Overhead account.

e. Indirect labor costs to the Factory Overhead account.

Check (2) $3,900 underapplied overhead

2. Determine the revised balance of the Factory Overhead account after making the entries in part 1. Determine whether there is any under- or overapplied overhead for the year. Prepare the adjusting entry to allocate any over- or underapplied overhead to Cost of Goods Sold, assuming the amount is not material.

(3) T. B. totals, $322,000

3. Prepare a revised trial balance.

(4) Net income, $8,100

4. Prepare an income statement for year 2009 and a balance sheet as of December 31, 2009.

Analysis Component

5. Assume that the $2,400 on materials requisition 21-3012 should have been direct materials charged to Job 404. Without providing specific calculations, describe the impact of this error on the income statement for 2009 and the balance sheet at December 31, 2009.

Problem 2-3A
Source documents, journal entries, and accounts in job order cost accounting
P1 P2 P3

Challenger Watercraft's predetermined overhead rate for year 2009 is 200% of direct labor. Information on the company's production activities during May 2009 follows.

a. Purchased raw materials on credit, $200,000.

b. Paid $130,000 cash for factory wages.

c. Paid $16,000 cash to a computer consultant to reprogram factory equipment.

d. Materials requisitions record use of the following materials for the month.

Job 136	$ 50,000
Job 137	33,000
Job 138	19,800
Job 139	22,600
Job 140	6,800
Total direct materials	132,200
Indirect materials	20,000
Total materials used	$152,200

e. Time tickets record use of the following labor for the month.

Job 136	$ 12,100
Job 137	10,800
Job 138	37,500
Job 139	39,400
Job 140	3,200
Total direct labor	103,000
Indirect labor	27,000
Total	$130,000

f. Applied overhead to Jobs 136, 138, and 139.

g. Transferred Jobs 136, 138, and 139 to Finished Goods.

h. Sold Jobs 136 and 138 on credit at a total price of $550,000.

i. The company incurred the following overhead costs during the month (credit Prepaid Insurance for expired factory insurance).

Depreciation of factory building	$68,500
Depreciation of factory equipment	37,500
Expired factory insurance	11,000
Accrued property taxes payable	35,000

j. Applied overhead at month-end to the Goods in Process (Jobs 137 and 140) using the predetermined overhead rate of 200% of direct labor cost.

Required

1. Prepare a job cost sheet for each job worked on during the month. Use the following simplified form.

Job No. ______	
Materials	$ ______
Labor	______
Overhead	______
Total cost	$ ______

2. Prepare journal entries to record the events and transactions *a* through *j*.

Check (2f) Cr. Factory Overhead, $178,000

3. Set up T-accounts for each of the following general ledger accounts, each of which started the month with a zero balance: Raw Materials Inventory; Goods in Process Inventory; Finished Goods Inventory; Factory Payroll; Factory Overhead; Cost of Goods Sold. Then post the journal entries to these T-accounts and determine the balance of each account.

Check (3) Finished Goods Inventory, $140,800

4. Prepare a report showing the total cost of each job in process and prove that the sum of their costs equals the Goods in Process Inventory account balance. Prepare similar reports for Finished Goods Inventory and Cost of Goods Sold.

Problem 2-4A
Overhead allocation and adjustment using a predetermined overhead rate
C3 P3 P4

mhhe.com/wildMA2e

In December 2008, Zander Company's manager estimated next year's total direct labor cost assuming 50 persons working an average of 2,000 hours each at an average wage rate of $30 per hour. The manager also estimated the following manufacturing overhead costs for year 2009.

Indirect labor	$ 339,200
Factory supervision	240,000
Rent on factory building	140,000
Factory utilities	318,000
Factory insurance expired	88,000
Depreciation—Factory equipment	480,000
Repairs expense—Factory equipment	60,000
Factory supplies used	88,800
Miscellaneous production costs	46,000
Total estimated overhead costs	$1,800,000

At the end of 2009, records show the company incurred $1,554,900 of actual overhead costs. It completed and sold five jobs with the following direct labor costs: Job 201, $604,000; Job 202, $573,000; Job 203, $318,000; Job 204, $726,000; and Job 205, $324,000. In addition, Job 206 is in process at the end of 2009 and had been charged $27,000 for direct labor. No jobs were in process at the end of 2008. The company's predetermined overhead rate is based on direct labor cost.

Required

1. Determine the following.
   a. Predetermined overhead rate for year 2009.
   b. Total overhead cost applied to each of the six jobs during year 2009.
   c. Over- or underapplied overhead at year-end 2009.

2. Assuming that any over- or underapplied overhead is not material, prepare the adjusting entry to allocate any over- or underapplied overhead to Cost of Goods Sold at the end of year 2009.

Check (1c) $11,700 underapplied
(2) Cr. Factory Overhead $11,700

Problem 2-5A
Production transactions; subsidiary records; and source documents
P1 P2 P3 P4

If the working papers that accompany this book are unavailable, do not attempt to solve this problem.
Morton Company manufactures variations of its product, a technopress, in response to custom orders from its customers. On May 1, the company had no inventories of goods in process or finished goods but held the following raw materials.

Material M	200 units @	$125 =	$25,000
Material R	95 units @	90 =	8,550
Paint	55 units @	40 =	2,200
Total cost			$35,750

On May 4, the company began working on two technopresses: Job 102 for Global Company and Job 103 for Kaddo Company.

Required

Follow the instructions in this list of activities and complete the sheets provided in the working papers.

a. Purchased raw materials on credit and recorded the following information from receiving reports and invoices.

Receiving Report No. 426, Material M, 250 units at $125 each.
Receiving Report No. 427, Material R, 90 units at $90 each.

Instructions: Record these purchases with a single journal entry and post it to general ledger T-accounts, using the transaction letter *a* to identify the entry. Enter the receiving report information on the materials ledger cards.

b. Requisitioned the following raw materials for production.

Requisition No. 35, for Job 102, 135 units of Material M.
Requisition No. 36, for Job 102, 72 units of Material R.
Requisition No. 37, for Job 103, 70 units of Material M.
Requisition No. 38, for Job 103, 38 units of Material R.
Requisition No. 39, for 15 units of paint.

Instructions: Enter amounts for direct materials requisitions on the materials ledger cards and the job cost sheets. Enter the indirect material amount on the materials ledger card and record a debit to the Indirect Materials account in the subsidiary factory overhead ledger. Do not record a journal entry at this time.

c. Received the following employee time tickets for work in May.

Time tickets Nos. 1 to 10 for direct labor on Job 102, $45,000.
Time tickets Nos. 11 to 30 for direct labor on Job 103, $32,500.
Time tickets Nos. 31 to 36 for equipment repairs, $9,625.

Instructions: Record direct labor from the time tickets on the job cost sheets and then debit indirect labor to the Indirect Labor account in the subsidiary factory overhead ledger. Do not record a journal entry at this time.

d. Paid cash for the following items during the month: factory payroll, $87,125, and miscellaneous overhead items, $51,000.

Instructions: Record these payments with journal entries and then post them to the general ledger accounts. Also record a debit in the Miscellaneous Overhead account in the subsidiary factory overhead ledger.

e. Finished Job 102 and transferred it to the warehouse. The company assigns overhead to each job with a predetermined overhead rate equal to 80% of direct labor cost.

Instructions: Enter the allocated overhead on the cost sheet for Job 102, fill in the cost summary section of the cost sheet, and then mark the cost sheet "Finished." Prepare a journal entry to record the job's completion and its transfer to Finished Goods and then post it to the general ledger accounts.

f. Delivered Job 102 and accepted the customer's promise to pay $200,000 within 30 days.

Instructions: Prepare journal entries to record the sale of Job 102 and the cost of goods sold. Post them to the general ledger accounts.

g. Applied overhead to Job 103 based on the job's direct labor to date.

Instructions: Enter overhead on the job cost sheet but do not make a journal entry at this time.

h. Recorded the total direct and indirect materials costs as reported on all the requisitions for the month.

Instructions: Prepare a journal entry to record these costs and post it to general ledger accounts.

Check (h) Dr. Goods in Process Inventory, $35,525

i. Recorded the total direct and indirect labor costs as reported on all time tickets for the month.

Instructions: Prepare a journal entry to record these costs and post it to general ledger accounts.

j. Recorded the total overhead costs applied to jobs.

Instructions: Prepare a journal entry to record the allocation of these overhead costs and post it to general ledger accounts.

Check Balance in Factory Overhead, $775 Cr., overapplied

PROBLEM SET B

Problem 2-1B

Production costs computed and recorded; reports prepared

C3 P1 P2 P3 P4 

Grant Co.'s August 31 inventory of raw materials is $75,000. Raw materials purchases in September are $200,000, and factory payroll cost in September is $110,000. Overhead costs incurred in September are: indirect materials, $15,000; indirect labor, $7,000; factory rent, $10,000; factory utilities, $6,000; and factory equipment depreciation, $15,000. The predetermined overhead rate is 50% of direct labor cost. Job 114 is sold for $190,000 cash in September. Costs for the three jobs worked on in September follow.

	Job 114	Job 115	Job 116
Balances on August 31			
Direct materials	$ 7,000	$ 9,000	
Direct labor	9,000	8,000	
Applied overhead	4,500	4,000	

[continued on next page]

[continued from previous page]

Costs during September			
Direct materials	50,000	85,000	$40,000
Direct labor	15,000	34,000	60,000
Applied overhead	?	?	?
Status on September 30	Finished (sold)	Finished (unsold)	In process

Required

1. Determine the total of each production cost incurred for September (direct labor, direct materials, and applied overhead), and the total cost assigned to each job (including the balances from August 31).

2. Prepare journal entries for the month of September to record the following.

a. Materials purchases (on credit), factory payroll (paid in cash), and actual overhead costs including indirect materials and indirect labor. (Factory rent and utilities are paid in cash.)

b. Assignment of direct materials, direct labor, and applied overhead costs to Goods in Process Inventory.

c. Transfer of Jobs 114 and 115 to the Finished Goods Inventory.

d. Cost of Job 114 in the Cost of Goods Sold account.

e. Revenue from the sale of Job 114.

f. Assignment of any underapplied or overapplied overhead to the Cost of Goods Sold account. (The amount is not material.)

Check (2f) $1,500 overapplied

(3) Cost of goods manufactured, $250,000

3. Prepare a manufacturing statement for September (use a single line presentation for direct materials and show the details of overhead cost).

4. Compute gross profit for September. Show how to present the inventories on the September 30 balance sheet.

Analysis Component

5. The over- or underapplied overhead adjustment is closed to Cost of Goods Sold. Discuss how this adjustment impacts business decision making regarding individual jobs or batches of jobs.

Problem 2-2B

Source documents, journal entries, overhead, and financial reports

P1 P2 P3 P4 

Coleman Company's computer system generated the following trial balance on December 31, 2009. The company's manager knows that the trial balance is wrong because it does not show any balance for Goods in Process Inventory but does show balances for the Factory Payroll and Factory Overhead accounts.

	Debit	Credit
Cash	$ 96,000	
Accounts receivable	84,000	
Raw materials inventory	52,000	
Goods in process inventory	0	
Finished goods inventory	18,000	
Prepaid rent	6,000	
Accounts payable		$ 21,000
Notes payable		27,000
Common stock		60,000
Retained earnings		174,000
Sales		360,000
Cost of goods sold	210,000	
Factory payroll	32,000	
Factory overhead	54,000	
Operating expenses	90,000	
Totals	$642,000	$642,000

After examining various files, the manager identifies the following six source documents that need to be processed to bring the accounting records up to date.

Materials requisition 94-231:	$9,200 direct materials to Job 603
Materials requisition 94-232:	$15,200 direct materials to Job 604
Materials requisition 94-233:	$4,200 indirect materials
Labor time ticket 765:	$10,000 direct labor to Job 603
Labor time ticket 766:	$16,000 direct labor to Job 604
Labor time ticket 777:	$6,000 indirect labor

Jobs 603 and 604 are the only units in process at year-end. The predetermined overhead rate is 200% of direct labor cost.

Required

1. Use information on the six source documents to prepare journal entries to assign the following costs.

   a. Direct materials costs to Goods in Process Inventory.

   b. Direct labor costs to Goods in Process Inventory.

   c. Overhead costs to Goods in Process Inventory.

   d. Indirect materials costs to the Factory Overhead account.

   e. Indirect labor costs to the Factory Overhead account.

2. Determine the revised balance of the Factory Overhead account after making the entries in part 1. Determine whether there is under- or overapplied overhead for the year. Prepare the adjusting entry to allocate any over- or underapplied overhead to Cost of Goods Sold, assuming the amount is not material.

3. Prepare a revised trial balance.

4. Prepare an income statement for year 2009 and a balance sheet as of December 31, 2009.

Check (2) $12,200 underapplied overhead

(3) T. B. totals, $642,000

(4) Net income, $47,800

Analysis Component

5. Assume that the $4,200 indirect materials on materials requisition 94-233 should have been direct materials charged to Job 604. Without providing specific calculations, describe the impact of this error on the income statement for 2009 and the balance sheet at December 31, 2009.

Problem 2-3B

Source documents, journal entries, and accounts in job order cost accounting

P1 P2 P3

Bradley Company's predetermined overhead rate is 200% of direct labor. Information on the company's production activities during September 2009 follows.

a. Purchased raw materials on credit, $250,000.

b. Paid $168,000 cash for factory wages.

c. Paid $22,000 cash for miscellaneous factory overhead costs.

d. Materials requisitions record use of the following materials for the month.

Job 487	$ 60,000
Job 488	40,000
Job 489	24,000
Job 490	28,000
Job 491	8,000
Total direct materials	160,000
Indirect materials	24,000
Total materials used	$184,000

e. Time tickets record use of the following labor for the month.

Job 487	$ 16,000
Job 488	14,000
Job 489	50,000
Job 490	52,000
Job 491	4,000
Total direct labor	136,000
Indirect labor	32,000
Total	$168,000

f. Allocated overhead to Jobs 487, 489, and 490.

g. Transferred Jobs 487, 489, and 490 to Finished Goods.

h. Sold Jobs 487 and 489 on credit for a total price of $680,000.

i. The company incurred the following overhead costs during the month (credit Prepaid Insurance for expired factory insurance).

Depreciation of factory building	$74,000
Depreciation of factory equipment	42,000
Expired factory insurance	14,000
Accrued property taxes payable	62,000

j. Applied overhead at month-end to the Goods in Process (Jobs 488 and 491) using the predetermined overhead rate of 200% of direct labor cost.

Required

1. Prepare a job cost sheet for each job worked on in the month. Use the following simplified form.

Job No. ______	
Materials	$ ______
Labor	______
Overhead	______
Total cost	$ ______

Check (2f) Cr. Factory Overhead, $236,000

(3) Finished Goods Inventory, $184,000

2. Prepare journal entries to record the events and transactions *a* through *j*.

3. Set up T-accounts for each of the following general ledger accounts, each of which started the month with a zero balance: Raw Materials Inventory, Goods in Process Inventory, Finished Goods Inventory, Factory Payroll, Factory Overhead, Cost of Goods Sold. Then post the journal entries to these T-accounts and determine the balance of each account.

4. Prepare a report showing the total cost of each job in process and prove that the sum of their costs equals the Goods in Process Inventory account balance. Prepare similar reports for Finished Goods Inventory and Cost of Goods Sold.

Problem 2-4B

Overhead allocation and adjustment using a predetermined overhead rate

C3 P3 P4

In December 2008, Bigby Company's manager estimated next year's total direct labor cost assuming 100 persons working an average of 2,000 hours each at an average wage rate of $15 per hour. The manager also estimated the following manufacturing overhead costs for year 2009.

Indirect labor	$ 319,200
Factory supervision	240,000
Rent on factory building	140,000
Factory utilities	88,000
Factory insurance expired	68,000
Depreciation—Factory equipment	480,000
Repairs expense—Factory equipment	60,000
Factory supplies used	68,800
Miscellaneous production costs	36,000
Total estimated overhead costs	$1,500,000

At the end of 2009, records show the company incurred $1,450,000 of actual overhead costs. It completed and sold five jobs with the following direct labor costs: Job 625, $708,000; Job 626, $660,000; Job 627, $350,000; Job 628, $840,000; and Job 629, $368,000. In addition, Job 630 is in process at the end of 2009 and had been charged $20,000 for direct labor. No jobs were in process at the end of 2008. The company's predetermined overhead rate is based on direct labor cost.

Required

1. Determine the following.

a. Predetermined overhead rate for year 2009.

b. Total overhead cost applied to each of the six jobs during year 2009.

c. Over- or underapplied overhead at year-end 2009.

2. Assuming that any over- or underapplied overhead is not material, prepare the adjusting entry to allocate any over- or underapplied overhead to Cost of Goods Sold at the end of year 2009.

Check (1c) $23,000 overapplied

(2) Dr. Factory Overhead, $23,000

Problem 2-5B
Production transactions; subsidiary records; and source documents

P1 P2 P3 P4

If the working papers that accompany this book are unavailable, do not attempt to solve this problem. Parador Company produces variations of its product, a megatron, in response to custom orders from its customers. On June 1, the company had no inventories of goods in process or finished goods but held the following raw materials.

Material M	120 units @ $400 =	$48,000
Material R	80 units @ 320 =	25,600
Paint	44 units @ 144 =	6,336
Total cost		$79,936

On June 3, the company began working on two megatrons: Job 450 for Doso Company and Job 451 for Border, Inc.

Required

Follow instructions in this list of activities and complete the sheets provided in the working papers.

a. Purchased raw materials on credit and recorded the following information from receiving reports and invoices.

Receiving Report No. 20, Material M, 150 units at $400 each.
Receiving Report No. 21, Material R, 70 units at $320 each.

Instructions: Record these purchases with a single journal entry and post it to general ledger T-accounts, using the transaction letter *a* to identify the entry. Enter the receiving report information on the materials ledger cards.

b. Requisitioned the following raw materials for production.

Requisition No. 223, for Job 450, 80 units of Material M.
Requisition No. 224, for Job 450, 60 units of Material R.
Requisition No. 225, for Job 451, 40 units of Material M.
Requisition No. 226, for Job 451, 30 units of Material R.
Requisition No. 227, for 12 units of paint.

Instructions: Enter amounts for direct materials requisitions on the materials ledger cards and the job cost sheets. Enter the indirect material amount on the materials ledger card and record a debit to the Indirect Materials account in the subsidiary factory overhead ledger. Do not record a journal entry at this time.

c. Received the following employee time tickets for work in June.

Time tickets Nos. 1 to 10 for direct labor on Job 450, $80,000.
Time tickets Nos. 11 to 20 for direct labor on Job 451, $64,000.
Time tickets Nos. 21 to 24 for equipment repairs, $24,000.

Instructions: Record direct labor from the time tickets on the job cost sheets and then debit indirect labor to the Indirect Labor account in the subsidiary factory overhead ledger. Do not record a journal entry at this time.

d. Paid cash for the following items during the month: factory payroll, $168,000, and miscellaneous overhead items, $73,600.

Instructions: Record these payments with journal entries and post them to the general ledger accounts. Also record a debit in the Miscellaneous Overhead account in the subsidiary factory overhead ledger.

e. Finished Job 450 and transferred it to the warehouse. The company assigns overhead to each job with a predetermined overhead rate equal to 70% of direct labor cost.

Instructions: Enter the allocated overhead on the cost sheet for Job 450, fill in the cost summary section of the cost sheet, and then mark the cost sheet "Finished." Prepare a journal entry to record the job's completion and its transfer to Finished Goods and then post it to the general ledger accounts.

f. Delivered Job 450 and accepted the customer's promise to pay $580,000 within 30 days.

Instructions: Prepare journal entries to record the sale of Job 450 and the cost of goods sold. Post them to the general ledger accounts.

g. Applied overhead cost to Job 451 based on the job's direct labor used to date.

Instructions: Enter overhead on the job cost sheet but do not make a journal entry at this time.

Check (h) Dr. Goods in Process Inventory, $76,800

h. Recorded the total direct and indirect materials costs as reported on all the requisitions for the month.

Instructions: Prepare a journal entry to record these costs and post it to general ledger accounts.

i. Recorded the total direct and indirect labor costs as reported on all time tickets for the month.

Instructions: Prepare a journal entry to record these costs and post it to general ledger accounts.

j. Recorded the total overhead costs applied to jobs.

Check Balance in Factory Overhead, $1,472 Cr., overapplied

Instructions: Prepare a journal entry to record the allocation of these overhead costs and post it to general ledger accounts.

SERIAL PROBLEM

Success Systems

(This serial problem began in Chapter 1 and continues through most of the book. If previous chapter segments were not completed, the serial problem can begin at this point. It is helpful, but not necessary, to use the Working Papers that accompany the book.)

SP 2 The computer workstation furniture manufacturing that Adriana Lopez started in January is progressing well. As of the end of June, Success Systems' job cost sheets show the following total costs accumulated on three furniture jobs.

	Job 6.02	Job 6.03	Job 6.04
Direct materials	$1,500	$3,300	$2,700
Direct labor	800	1,420	2,100
Overhead	400	710	1,050

Job 6.02 was started in production in May, and these costs were assigned to it in May: direct materials, $600; direct labor, $180; and overhead, $90. Jobs 6.03 and 6.04 were started in June. Overhead cost is applied with a predetermined rate based on direct labor costs. Jobs 6.02 and 6.03 are finished in June, and Job 6.04 is expected to be finished in July. No raw materials are used indirectly in June. (Assume this company's predetermined overhead rate did not change across these months.)

Required

Check (1) Total materials, $6,900

(3) 50%

1. What is the cost of the raw materials used in June for each of the three jobs and in total?

2. How much total direct labor cost is incurred in June?

3. What predetermined overhead rate is used in June?

4. How much cost is transferred to finished goods inventory in June?

BEYOND THE NUMBERS

REPORTING IN ACTION

C2  

BTN 2-1 **Best Buy**'s financial statements and notes in Appendix A provide evidence of growth potential in its domestic sales.

Required

1. Identify at least two types of costs that will predictably increase as a percent of sales with growth in domestic sales.

2. Explain why you believe the types of costs identified for part 1 will increase, and describe how you might assess Best Buy's success with these costs. (*Hint:* You might consider the gross margin ratio.)

Fast Forward

3. Access Best Buy's annual report for a fiscal year ending after March 3, 2007, from its Website [BestBuy.com] or the SEC's EDGAR database [www.SEC.gov]. Review and report its growth in sales along with its cost and income levels (including its gross margin ratio).

COMPARATIVE ANALYSIS

C1 

BTN 2-2 Retailers as well as manufacturers can apply just-in-time (JIT) to their inventory management. Both Best Buy and Circuit City want to know the impact of a JIT inventory system for their operating cash flows. Review each company's statement of cash flows in Appendix A to answer the following.

Required

1. Identify the impact on operating cash flows (increase or decrease) for changes in inventory levels (increase or decrease) for both companies for each of the three most recent years.
2. What impact would a JIT inventory system have on both Best Buy's and Circuit City's operating income? Link the answer to your response for part 1.
3. Would the move to a JIT system have a one-time or recurring impact on operating cash flow?

ETHICS CHALLENGE

P3

BTN 2-3 An accounting professional requires at least two skill sets. The first is to be technically competent. Knowing how to capture, manage, and report information is a necessary skill. Second, the ability to assess manager and employee actions and biases for accounting analysis is another skill. For instance, knowing how a person is compensated helps anticipate information biases. Draw on these skills and write a one-half page memo to the financial officer on the following practice of allocating overhead.

Background: Assume that your company sells portable housing to both general contractors and the government. It sells jobs to contractors on a bid basis. A contractor asks for three bids from different manufacturers. The combination of low bid and high quality wins the job. However, jobs sold to the government are bid on a cost-plus basis. This means price is determined by adding all costs plus a profit based on cost at a specified percent, such as 10%. You observe that the amount of overhead allocated to government jobs is higher than that allocated to contract jobs. These allocations concern you and motivate your memo.

Point: Students could compare responses and discuss differences in concerns with allocating overhead.

COMMUNICATING IN PRACTICE

C2 C3 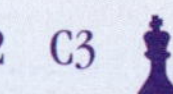

BTN 2-4 Assume that you are preparing for a second interview with a manufacturing company. The company is impressed with your credentials but has indicated that it has several qualified applicants. You anticipate that in this second interview, you must show what you offer over other candidates. You learn the company currently uses a periodic inventory system and is not satisfied with the timeliness of its information and its inventory management. The company manufactures custom-order holiday decorations and display items. To show your abilities, you plan to recommend that it use a cost accounting system.

Required

In preparation for the interview, prepare notes outlining the following:

1. Your cost accounting system recommendation and why it is suitable for this company.
2. A general description of the documents that the proposed cost accounting system requires.
3. How the documents in part 2 facilitate the operation of the cost accounting system.

Point: Have students present a mock interview, one assuming the role of the president of the company and the other the applicant.

TAKING IT TO THE NET

C2  

BTN 2-5 Many contractors work on custom jobs that require a job order costing system.

Required

Access the Website AMSI.com and click on *Construction Management Software,* and then on STARBUILDER. Prepare a one-page memorandum for the CEO of a construction company providing information about the job order costing software this company offers. Would you recommend that the company purchase this software?

TEAMWORK IN ACTION

C2 

BTN 2-6 Consider the activities undertaken by a medical clinic in your area.

Required

1. Do you consider a job order cost accounting system appropriate for the clinic?
2. Identify as many factors as possible to lead you to conclude that it uses a job order system.

ENTREPRENEURIAL DECISION

C2 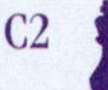 

BTN 2-7 Refer to the chapter opener regarding Hank Julicher and his company, Sprinturf. All successful businesses track their costs, and it is especially important for startup businesses to monitor and control costs.

Required

1. Assume that Sprinturf uses a job order costing system. For the three basic cost categories of direct materials, direct labor, and overhead, identify at least two typical costs that would fall into each category for Sprinturf.
2. Assume a local high school expresses an interest in purchasing a synthetic field installation from Sprinturf. The high school's budget will allow them to pay no more than $600,000 for the field. How can Sprinturf use job cost information to assess whether to pursue this opportunity?

HITTING THE ROAD

C3 P2 P3 P4 

BTN 2-8 Job order cost accounting is frequently used by home builders.

Required

1. You (or your team) are to prepare a job cost sheet for a single-family home under construction. List four items of both direct materials and direct labor. Explain how you think overhead should be applied.
2. Contact a builder and compare your job cost sheet to this builder's job cost sheet. If possible, speak to that company's accountant. Write your findings in a short report.

GLOBAL DECISION

C1 

BTN 2-9 DSG, Circuit City, and Best Buy are competitors in the global marketplace. Access DSG's annual report (www.DSGiplc.com) for the year ended April 28, 2007. The following information is available for DSG.

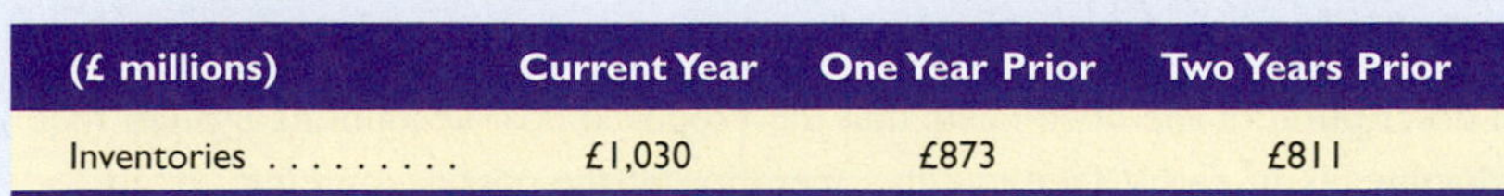

(£ millions)	Current Year	One Year Prior	Two Years Prior
Inventories	£1,030	£873	£811

Required

1. Determine the change in DSG's inventories for the last two years. Then identify the impact on net resources generated by operating activities (increase or decrease) for changes in inventory levels (increase or decrease) for DSG for the last two years.
2. Would a move to a JIT system likely impact DSG more than it would Best Buy or Circuit City? Explain.

ANSWERS TO MULTIPLE CHOICE QUIZ

1. c; \$30,000 × 150% = \$45,000
2. b; \$38,500/\$35,000 = 110%
3. e; Direct materials + Direct labor + Overhead = Total cost;
   Direct materials + (\$4,000/.80) + \$4,000 = \$10,000
   Direct materials = \$1,000
4. e; \$9,000 + \$94,200 + \$59,200 + \$31,600 − Finished goods = \$17,800
   Thus, finished goods = \$176,200
5. b

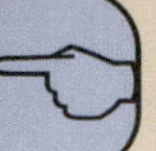

A Look Back

Chapter 2 introduced managerial accounting and described cost concepts and the reporting of manufacturing activities. Chapter 2 explained job order costing—an important cost accounting system for customized products and services.

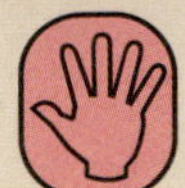

A Look at This Chapter

This chapter focuses on how to measure and account for costs in process operations. We explain process production, describe how to assign costs to processes, and compute cost per equivalent unit for a process.

A Look Ahead

Chapter 4 introduces the activity-based costing (ABC) system, which provides managers with strategic cost information that is not readily available from other costing methods.

Chapter 3 Process Costing and Analysis

Learning Objectives

CAP

Conceptual

C1 Explain process operations and the way they differ from job order operations. *(p. 86)*

C2 Define equivalent units and explain their use in process cost accounting. *(p. 93)*

C3 Explain the four steps in accounting for production activity in a period. *(p. 94)*

C4 Define a process cost summary and describe its purposes. *(p. 98)*

C5 *Appendix 3A*—Explain and illustrate the four steps in accounting for production activity using FIFO. *(p. 105)*

Analytical

A1 Compare process cost accounting and job order cost accounting. *(p. 87)*

A2 Explain and illustrate a hybrid costing system. *(p. 101)*

Procedural

P1 Record the flow of direct materials costs in process cost accounting. *(p. 90)*

P2 Record the flow of direct labor costs in process cost accounting. *(p. 91)*

P3 Record the flow of factory overhead costs in process cost accounting. *(p. 91)*

P4 Compute equivalent units produced in a period. *(p. 93)*

P5 Prepare a process cost summary. *(p. 98)*

P6 Record the transfer of completed goods to Finished Goods Inventory and Cost of Goods Sold. *(p. 99)*

LP3

Decision Feature

The Big Apple

"If we are willing to eat it, we're willing to squeeze it"
—David Ryan

HOOD RIVER, OR—After a few years of working in the family business of growing apples and making cider, David Ryan launched his own company, **Hood River Juice Company** [HRJCO.com], to focus on the processing stage of apple juice and cider. Like many entrepreneurs, David sought guidance from experienced mentors, in his case the Small Business Development Center located in the local community college. These mentors explained managerial accounting and the financial aspects of successful manufacturing.

Today, before an apple enters David's production process, it is inspected by his drivers when the apples are loaded from the field. A foreman then inspects the apples again when unloading them at his factory. David's factory employees then wash and hand select the best apples from those that survive the previous two inspections.

Apple quality is paramount. Explains David, "If we are willing to eat it, we're willing to squeeze it." From cutting apples into small pieces and squeezing those pieces into juice, through filtering the juice and packaging the finished product, David's production process is monitored and accounting reports are produced.

Entrepreneurs such as David are aided by process cost summaries that help them monitor and control the costs of material, labor, and overhead applied to production processes. For example, David tries to maintain regular full-time employees to better manage costs. Thus, he purchases and processes apples year-round as opposed to only seasonal production. David estimates this year-round process reduces his overhead costs by 40%. "Needless to say, every company has their own overhead they have to deal with," explains David. "If your total throughput is down by 35%, you must look elsewhere to get the margin to be sustainable. The only way to do that is to cut your overhead." Managerial accounting information aids in his decisions.

David's focus on cost management minimizes the risk of bad decisions, and his passion for quality control enables him to improve process operations. His overriding goal is customer satisfaction. That focus has led him to produce bulk apple juice for use in protein shakes and smoothies, and it has allowed his customers to select from over 50 varieties of apples for a custom-blended juice. Juice drinkers seem happy: From an initial investment of $36,000 in 2000, David's annual sales now exceed $14 million. Those are juicy numbers.

[Sources: *Hood River Juice Company Website*, January 2009; *Yakima-Herald.com*, March 2008; *Hood River News*, February 2006; *Entrepreneur*, April 2008]

Chapter Preview

The type of product or service a company offers determines its cost accounting system. Job order costing is used to account for custom products and services that meet the demands of a particular customer. Not all products are manufactured in this way; many carry standard designs so that one unit is no different than any other unit. Such a system often produces large numbers of units on a continuous basis, all of which pass through similar processes. This chapter describes how to use a process cost accounting system to account for these types of products. It also explains how costs are accumulated for each process and then assigned to units passing through those processes. This information helps us understand and estimate the cost of each process as well as find ways to reduce costs and improve processes.

Process Costing and Analysis

Process Operations
- Comparing job order and process operations
- Organization of process operations
- GenX Company—an illustration

Process Cost Accounting
- Direct and indirect costs
- Accounting for materials costs
- Accounting for labor costs
- Accounting for factory overhead

Equivalent Units of Production (EUP)
- Accounting for goods in process
- Differences between EUP for materials, labor, and overhead

Process Costing Illustration
- Physical flow of units
- EUP
- Cost per EUP
- Cost reconciliation
- Process cost summary
- Transfers to finished goods and to cost of goods sold

Process Operations

C1 Explain process operations and the way they differ from job order operations.

Process operations, also called *process manufacturing* or *process production,* is the mass production of products in a continuous flow of steps. This means that products pass through a series of sequential processes. Petroleum refining is a common example of process operations. Crude oil passes through a series of steps before it is processed into different grades of petroleum. **Exxon Mobil**'s oil activities reflect a process operation. An important characteristic of process operations is the high level of standardization necessary if the system is to produce large volumes of products. Process operations also extend to services. Examples include mail sorting in large post offices and order processing in large mail-order firms such as **L.L. Bean**. The common feature in these service organizations is that operations are performed in a sequential manner using a series of standardized processes. Other companies using process operations include **Kellogg** (cereals), **Pfizer** (drugs), **Procter & Gamble** (household products), **Xerox** (copiers), **Coca-Cola** (soft drinks), **Heinz** (ketchup), **Penn** (tennis balls), and **Hershey** (chocolate). For a virtual tour of tennis ball manufacturing, see pennracquet.com/factory.html.

Each of these examples of products and services involves operations having a series of *processes,* or steps. Each process involves a different set of activities. A production operation that processes chemicals, for instance, might include the four steps shown in Exhibit 3.1. Understanding such processes for companies with process operations is crucial for measuring their costs. Increasingly, process operations use machines and automation to control product quality and reduce manufacturing costs.

EXHIBIT 3.1

Process Operations: Chemicals

Comparing Job Order and Process Operations

Job order and process operations can be considered as two ends of a continuum. Important features of both systems are shown in Exhibit 3.2. We often describe job order and process operations with manufacturing examples, but both also apply to service companies. In a job order costing system, the measurement focus is on the individual job or batch. In a process costing system, the measurement focus is on the process itself and the standardized units produced.

A1 Compare process cost accounting and job order cost accounting.

EXHIBIT 3.2

Comparing Job Order and Process Operations

Job Order Operations	Process Operations
• Custom orders	• Repetitive procedures
• Heterogeneous products and services	• Homogeneous products and services
• Low production volume	• High production volume
• High product flexibility	• Low product flexibility
• Low to medium standardization	• High standardization

Organization of Process Operations

In a process operation, each process is identified as a separate *production department, workstation,* or *work center.* With the exception of the first process or department, each receives the output from the prior department as a partially processed product. Depending on the nature of the process, a company applies direct labor, overhead, and, perhaps, additional direct materials to move the product toward completion. Only the final process or department in the series produces finished goods ready for sale to customers.

Tracking costs for several related departments can seem complex. Yet because process costing procedures are applied to the activity of each department or process separately, we need to consider only one process at a time. This simplifies the procedures.

When the output of one department becomes an input to another department, as is the case in sequential processing, we simply transfer the costs associated with those units from the first department into the next. We repeat these steps from department to department until the final process is complete. At that point the accumulated costs are transferred with the product from Goods in Process Inventory to Finished Goods Inventory. The next section illustrates a company with a single process, but the methods illustrated apply to a multiprocess scenario as each department's costs are handled separately for each department.

Decision Insight

Accounting for Health Many service companies use process departments to perform specific tasks for consumers. Hospitals, for instance, have radiology and physical therapy facilities with special equipment and trained employees. When patients need services, they are processed through departments to receive prescribed care. Service companies need process cost accounting information as much as manufacturers to estimate costs of services, to plan future operations, to control costs, and to determine customer charges.

GenX Company— An Illustration

The GenX Company illustrates process operations. It produces Profen®, an over-the-counter pain reliever for athletes. GenX sells Profen to wholesale distributors, who in turn sell it to retailers. Profen is produced by mixing its active ingredient, Profelene, with flavorings and preservatives, molding it into Profen tablets, and packaging the tablets. Exhibit 3.3 shows a summary floor plan of the GenX factory, which has five areas.

1. *Storeroom*—materials are received and then distributed when requisitioned.
2. *Production support offices*—used by administrative and maintenance employees who support manufacturing operations.
3. *Locker rooms*—workers change from street clothes into sanitized uniforms before working in the factory.
4. *Production floor*—area where the powder is processed into tablets.
5. *Warehouse*—finished products are stored before being shipped to wholesalers.

Point: Electronic monitoring of operations is common in factories.

EXHIBIT 3.3

Floor Plan of GenX's Factory

The first step in process manufacturing is to decide when to produce a product. Management determines the types and quantities of materials and labor needed and then schedules the work. Unlike a job order process, where production often begins only after receipt of a custom order, managers of companies with process operations often forecast the demand expected for their products. Based on these plans, production begins. The flowchart in Exhibit 3.4 shows the production steps for GenX. The following sections explain how GenX uses a process cost accounting system to compute these costs. Many of the explanations refer to this exhibit and its numbered cost flows ① through ⑩. (*Hint:* The amounts for the numbered cost flows in Exhibit 3.4 are summarized in Exhibit 3.21. Those amounts are explained in the following pages, but it can help to refer to Exhibit 3.21 as we proceed through the explanations.)

EXHIBIT 3.4

Process Operations and Costs: GenX

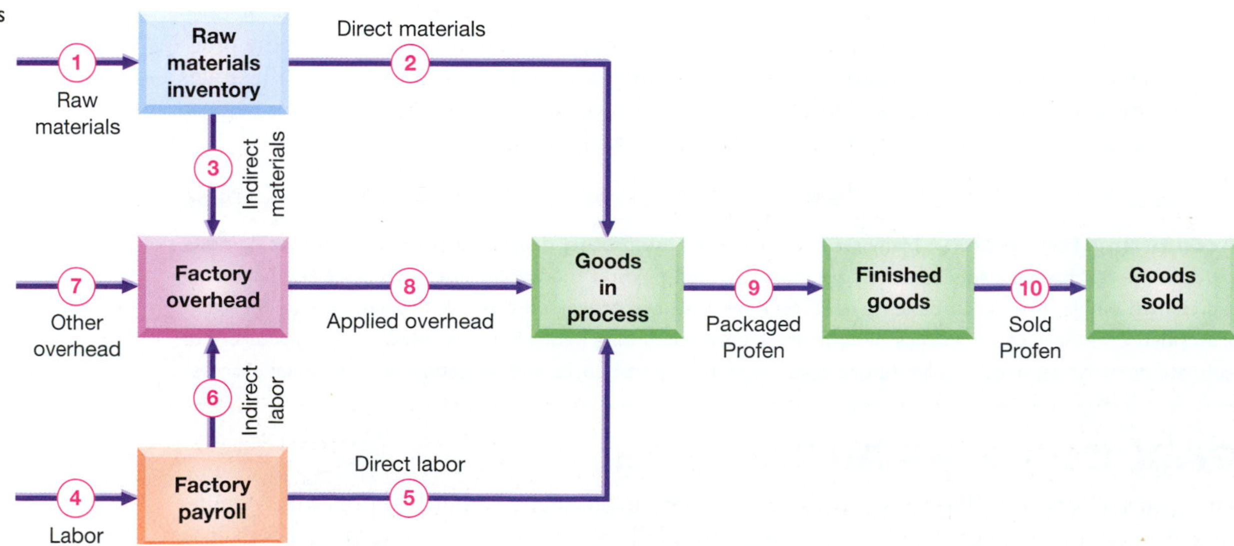

Process Cost Accounting

Video3.1

Process and job order operations are similar in that both combine materials, labor, and overhead in the process of producing products. They differ in how they are organized and managed. The measurement focus in a job order costing system is on the individual job or batch, whereas in a process costing system, it is on the individual process. Regardless of the measurement focus, we are ultimately interested in determining the cost per unit of product (or service) resulting from either system.

Specifically, the **job order cost accounting system** assigns direct materials, direct labor, and overhead to jobs. The total job cost is then divided by the number of units to compute a cost per unit for that job. The **process cost accounting system** assigns direct materials, direct labor, and overhead to specific processes (or departments). The total costs associated with each process are then divided by the number of units passing through that process to determine the cost per equivalent unit (defined later in the chapter) for that process. Differences in the way these two systems apply materials, labor, and overhead costs are highlighted in Exhibit 3.5.

#1 Class Notes

Point: The cost object in a job order system is the specific job; the cost object in a process costing system is the process.

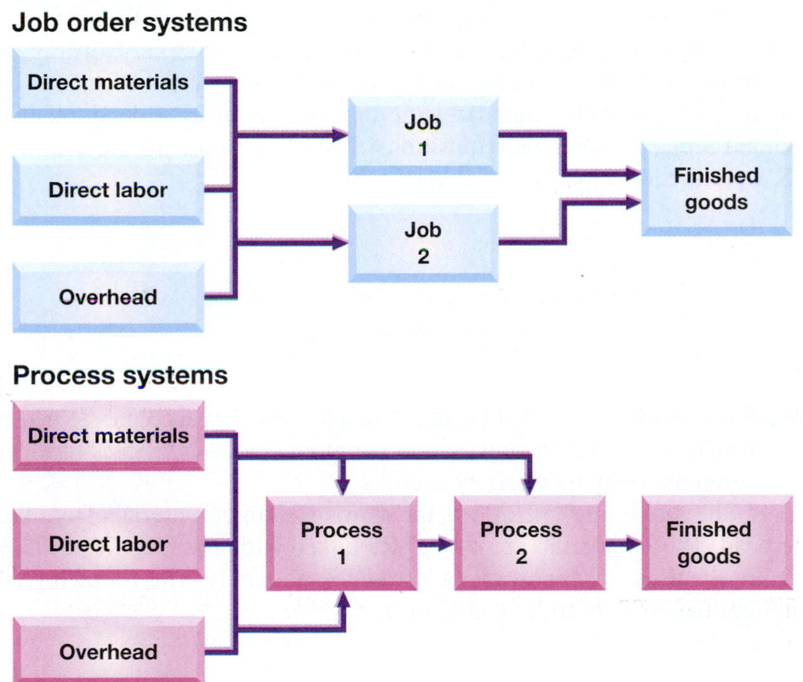

EXHIBIT 3.5

Comparing Job Order and Process Cost Accounting Systems

Direct and Indirect Costs

Like job order operations, process cost accounting systems use the concepts of direct and indirect costs. Materials and labor that can be traced to specific processes are assigned to those processes as direct costs. Materials and labor that cannot be traced to a specific process are indirect costs and are assigned to overhead. Some costs classified as overhead in a job order system may be classified as direct costs in process cost accounting. For example, depreciation of a machine used entirely by one process is a direct cost of that process.

Point: If a cost can be traced to the cost object, it is direct; if it cannot, it is indirect.

Decision Insight

JIT Boon to Process Operations Companies that adopt JIT manufacturing often organize their production system as a series of sequential processes. One survey found 60% of companies that converted to JIT used process operations; this compares to only 20% before converting to JIT.

P1 Record the flow of direct materials costs in process cost accounting.

Accounting for Materials Costs

In Exhibit 3.4, arrow line ① reflects the arrival of materials at GenX's factory. These materials include Profelene, flavorings, preservatives, and packaging. They also include supplies for the production support office. GenX uses a perpetual inventory system and makes all purchases on credit. The summary entry for receipts of raw materials in April follows (dates in journal entries numbered ① through ⑩ are omitted because they are summary entries, often reflecting two or more transactions or events).

Assets = Liabilities + Equity
+11,095 +11,095

		Debit	Credit
①	Raw Materials Inventory	11,095	
	Accounts Payable		11,095
	Acquired materials on credit for factory use.		

Arrow line ② in Exhibit 3.4 reflects the flow of direct materials to production, where they are used to produce Profen. Most direct materials are physically combined into the finished product; the remaining direct materials include those used and clearly linked with a specific process. The manager of a process usually obtains materials by submitting a *materials requisition* to the materials storeroom manager. In some situations, materials move continuously from raw materials inventory through the manufacturing process. **Pepsi Bottling**, for instance, uses a process in which inventory moves continuously through the system. In these cases, a **materials consumption report** summarizes the materials used by a department during a reporting period and replaces materials requisitions. The entry to record the use of direct materials by GenX's production department in April follows.

Assets = Liabilities + Equity
+9,900
−9,900

		Debit	Credit
②	Goods in Process Inventory	9,900	
	Raw Materials Inventory		9,900
	To assign costs of direct materials used in production.		

This entry transfers costs from one asset account to another asset account. (When two or more production departments exist, a company uses two or more Goods in Process Inventory accounts to separately accumulate costs incurred by each.)

Example: What types of materials might the flow of arrow line ③ in Exhibit 3.4 reflect? *Answer:* Goggles, gloves, protective clothing, recordkeeping supplies, and cleaning supplies.

In Exhibit 3.4, the arrow line ③ reflects the flow of indirect materials from the storeroom to factory overhead. These materials are not clearly linked with any specific production process or department but are used to support overall production activity. The following entry records the cost of indirect materials used by GenX in April.

Assets = Liabilities + Equity
−1,195 −1,195

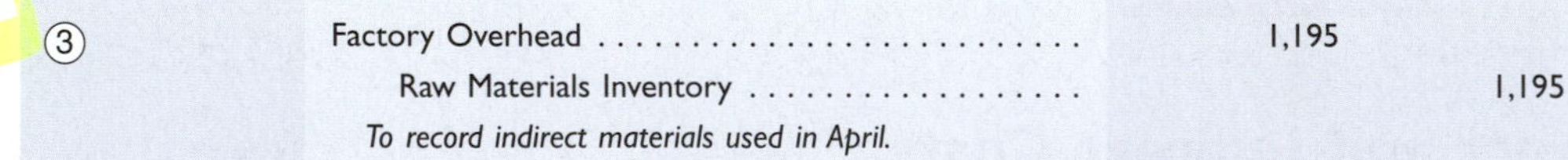

		Debit	Credit
③	Factory Overhead	1,195	
	Raw Materials Inventory		1,195
	To record indirect materials used in April.		

After the entries for both direct and indirect materials are posted, the Raw Materials Inventory account appears as shown in Exhibit 3.6. The April 30 balance sheet reports the $4,000 Raw Materials Inventory account as a current asset.

EXHIBIT 3.6

Raw Materials Inventory

Raw Materials Inventory					Acct. No. 132
Date		**Explanation**	**Debit**	**Credit**	**Balance**
Mar.	31	Balance			4,000
Apr.	30	Materials purchases	11,095		15,095
	30	Direct materials usage		9,900	5,195
	30	Indirect materials usage		1,195	4,000

Accounting for Labor Costs

P2 Record the flow of direct labor costs in process cost accounting.

Exhibit 3.4 shows GenX factory payroll costs as reflected in arrow line ④. Total labor costs of $8,920 are paid in cash and are recorded in the Factory Payroll account.

		Debit	Credit
④	Factory Payroll	8,920	
	Cash		8,920
	To record factory wages for April.		

Assets = Liabilities + Equity
−8,920 −8,920

Time reports from the production department and the production support office triggered this entry. (For simplicity, we do not separately identify withholdings and additional payroll taxes for employees.) In a process operation, the direct labor of a production department includes all labor used exclusively by that department. This is the case even if the labor is not applied to the product itself. If a production department in a process operation, for instance, has a full-time manager and a full-time maintenance worker, their salaries are direct labor costs of that process and are not factory overhead.

Arrow line ⑤ in Exhibit 3.4 shows GenX's use of direct labor in the production department. The following entry transfers April's direct labor costs from the Factory Payroll account to the Goods in Process Inventory account.

		Debit	Credit
⑤	Goods in Process Inventory	5,700	
	Factory Payroll		5,700
	To assign costs of direct labor used in production.		

Assets = Liabilities + Equity
+5,700 +5,700

Arrow line ⑥ in Exhibit 3.4 reflects GenX's indirect labor costs. These employees provide clerical, maintenance, and other services that help produce Profen efficiently. For example, they order materials, deliver them to the factory floor, repair equipment, operate and program computers used in production, keep payroll and other production records, clean up, and move the finished goods to the warehouse. The following entry charges these indirect labor costs to factory overhead.

Point: A department's indirect labor cost might include an allocated portion of the salary of a manager who supervises two or more departments. Allocation of costs between departments is discussed in a later chapter.

		Debit	Credit
⑥	Factory Overhead	3,220	
	Factory Payroll		3,220
	To record indirect labor as overhead.		

Assets = Liabilities + Equity
−3,220
+3,220

After these entries for both direct and indirect labor are posted, the Factory Payroll account appears as shown in Exhibit 3.7. The temporary Factory Payroll account is now closed to another temporary account, Factory Overhead, and is ready to receive entries for May. Next we show how to apply overhead to production and close the temporary Factory Overhead account.

EXHIBIT 3.7

Factory Payroll

Factory Payroll					Acct. No. 530
Date		**Explanation**	**Debit**	**Credit**	**Balance**
Mar.	31	Balance			0
Apr.	30	Total payroll for April	8,920		8,920
	30	Direct labor costs		5,700	3,220
	30	Indirect labor costs		3,220	0

Accounting for Factory Overhead

P3 Record the flow of factory overhead costs in process cost accounting.

Overhead costs other than indirect materials and indirect labor are reflected by arrow line ⑦ in Exhibit 3.4. These overhead items include the costs of insuring production assets, renting the factory building, using factory utilities, and depreciating equipment not directly related to a specific process. The following entry records overhead costs for April.

Assets	= Liabilities	+ Equity
−180	+645	−2,425
−750		
−850		

		Debit	Credit
⑦	Factory Overhead	2,425	
	Prepaid Insurance		180
	Utilities Payable		645
	Cash		750
	Accumulated Depreciation—Factory Equipment . .		850
	To record overhead items incurred in April.		

After this entry is posted, the Factory Overhead account balance is $6,840, comprising indirect materials of $1,195, indirect labor of $3,220, and $2,425 of other overhead.

Arrow line ⑧ in Exhibit 3.4 reflects the application of factory overhead to production. Factory overhead is applied to processes by relating overhead cost to another variable such as direct labor hours or machine hours used. With increasing automation, companies with process operations are more likely to use machine hours to allocate overhead. In some situations, a single allocation basis such as direct labor hours (or a single rate for the entire plant) fails to provide useful allocations. As a result, management can use different rates for different production departments. Based on an analysis of its operations, GenX applies its April overhead at a rate of 120% of direct labor cost, as shown in Exhibit 3.8.

Point: The time it takes to process (cycle) products through a process is sometimes used to allocate costs.

EXHIBIT 3.8

Applying Factory Overhead

	Direct Labor Cost	Predetermined Rate	Overhead Applied
Production Department	$5,700	120%	$6,840

GenX records its applied overhead with the following entry.

Assets	= Liabilities	+ Equity
+6,840		+6,840

		Debit	Credit
⑧	Goods in Process Inventory	6,840	
	Factory Overhead.		6,840
	Allocated overhead costs to production at 120% of direct labor cost.		

After posting this entry, the Factory Overhead account appears as shown in Exhibit 3.9. For GenX, the amount of overhead applied equals the actual overhead incurred during April. In most cases, using a predetermined overhead rate leaves an overapplied or underapplied balance in the Factory Overhead account. At the end of the period, this overapplied or underapplied balance should be closed to the Cost of Goods Sold account, as described in the job order costing chapter.

EXHIBIT 3.9

Factory Overhead

Example: If applied overhead results in a $6,940 credit to the factory overhead account, does it yield an over- or underapplied overhead amount? *Answer:* $100 overapplied overhead

Factory Overhead					Acct. No. 540
Date		Explanation	Debit	Credit	Balance
Mar.	31	Balance			0
Apr.	30	Indirect materials usage	1,195		1,195
	30	Indirect labor costs	3,220		4,415
	30	Other overhead costs	2,425		6,840
	30	Applied to production departments		6,840	0

Decision Ethics

Budget Officer You are working to identify the direct and indirect costs of a new processing department that has several machines. This department's manager instructs you to classify a majority of the costs as indirect to take advantage of the direct labor-based overhead allocation method so it will be charged a lower amount of overhead (because of its small direct labor cost). This would penalize other departments with higher allocations. It also will cause the performance ratings of managers in these other departments to suffer. What action do you take? [Answer—p. 110]

Quick Check

Answers—p. 111

1. A process operation (*a*) is another name for a job order operation, (*b*) does not use the concepts of direct materials or direct labor, or (*c*) typically produces large quantities of homogeneous products or services.
2. Under what conditions is a process cost accounting system more suitable for measuring production costs than a job order cost accounting system?
3. When direct materials are assigned and used in production, the entry to record their use includes (*a*) a credit to Goods in Process Inventory, (*b*) a debit to Goods in Process Inventory, or (*c*) a debit to Raw Materials Inventory.
4. What are the three cost categories incurred by both job order and process operations?
5. How many Goods in Process Inventory accounts are needed in a process cost system?

Equivalent Units of Production

We explained how materials, labor, and overhead costs for a period are accumulated in the Goods in Process Inventory account, but we have not explained the arrow lines labeled ⑨ and ⑩ in Exhibit 3.4. These lines reflect the transfer of products from the production department to finished goods inventory, and from finished goods inventory to cost of goods sold. To determine the costs recorded for these flows, we must first determine the cost per unit of product and then apply this result to the number of units transferred.

C2 Define equivalent units and explain their use in process cost accounting.

Accounting for Goods in Process

If a process has *no beginning and no ending goods in process inventory,* the unit cost of goods transferred out of a process is computed as follows.

Video3.1

$$\frac{\textbf{Total cost assigned to the process (direct materials, direct labor, and overhead)}}{\textbf{Total number of units started and finished in the period}}$$

If a process has a beginning or ending inventory of partially processed units (or both), then the total cost assigned to the process must be allocated to all completed and incomplete units worked on during the period. Therefore, the denominator must measure the entire production activity of the process for the period, called **equivalent units of production** (or **EUP**), a phrase that refers to the number of units that could have been started *and* completed given the cost incurred during a period. This measure is then used to compute the cost per equivalent unit and to assign costs to finished goods and goods in process inventory.

To illustrate, assume that GenX adds (or introduces) 100 units into its process during a period. Suppose at the end of that period, the production supervisor determines that those 100 units are 60% of the way through the process. Therefore, equivalent units of production for that period total 60 EUP (100 units × 60%). This means that with the resources used to put 100 units 60% of the way through the process, GenX could have started and completed 60 whole units.

Point: For GenX, "units" might refer to individual Profen tablets. For a juice maker, units might refer to gallons.

Differences in Equivalent Units for Materials, Labor, and Overhead

In many processes, the equivalent units of production for direct materials are not the same with respect to direct labor and overhead. To illustrate, consider a five-step process operation shown in Exhibit 3.10.

P4 Compute equivalent units produced in a period.

EXHIBIT 3.10

An Illustrative Five-Step Process Operation

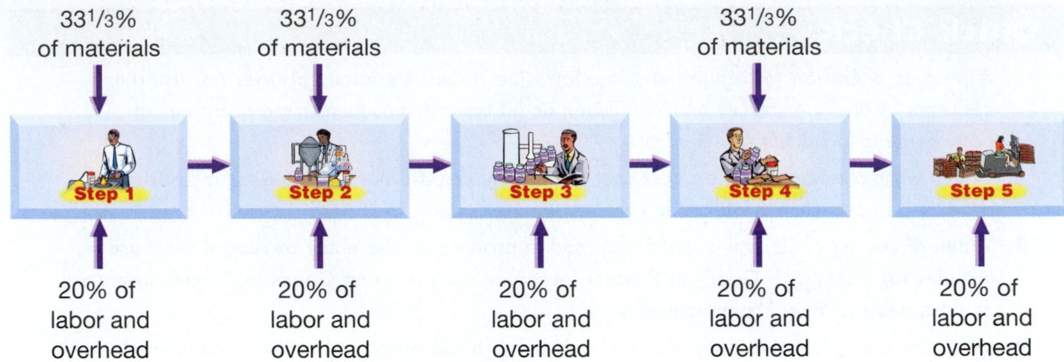

This exhibit shows that one-third of the direct material cost is added at each of three steps: 1, 2, and 4. One-fifth of the direct labor cost is added at each of the five steps. One-fifth of the overhead also is added at each step because overhead is applied as a percent of direct labor for this company.

When units finish step 1, they are one-third complete with respect to direct materials but only one-fifth complete with respect to direct labor and overhead. When they finish step 2, they are two-thirds complete with respect to direct materials but only two-fifths complete with respect to direct labor and overhead. When they finish step 3, they remain two-thirds complete with respect to materials but are now three-fifths complete with respect to labor and overhead. When they finish step 4, they are 100% complete with respect to materials (all direct materials have been added) but only four-fifths complete with respect to labor and overhead.

For example, if 300 units of product are started and processed through step 1 of Exhibit 3.10, they are said to be one-third complete *with respect to materials*. Expressed in terms of equivalent finished units, the processing of these 300 units is equal to finishing 100 EUP with respect to materials (300 units × 33⅓%). However, only one-fifth of direct labor and overhead has been applied to the 300 units at the end of step 1. This means that the equivalent units of production *with respect to labor and overhead* total 60 EUP (300 units × 20%).

Decision Insight

Process Services Customer interaction software is a hot item in customer service processes. Whether in insurance, delivery, or technology services, companies are finding that this software can turn their customer service process into an asset. How does it work? For starters, it cuts time spent on service calls because a customer describes a problem only once. It also yields a database of customer questions and complaints that gives insights into needed improvements. It recognizes incoming phone numbers and accesses previous dealings.

Process Costing Illustration

C3 Explain the four steps in accounting for production activity in a period.

This section applies process costing concepts and procedures to GenX. **This illustration uses the weighted-average method for inventory costs. The FIFO method is illustrated in Appendix 3A.** (Assume a weighted-average cost flow for all computations and assignments in this chapter unless explicitly stated differently. When using a just-in-time inventory system, different inventory methods yield similar results because inventories are immaterial.)

Exhibit 3.11 shows selected information from the production department for the month of April. Accounting for a department's activity for a period includes four steps involving analysis of (1) physical flow, (2) equivalent units, (3) cost per equivalent unit, and (4) cost assignment and reconciliation. The next sections describe each step.

EXHIBIT 3.11

Production Data

Beginning goods in process inventory (March 31)	
Units of product	30,000
Percentage of completion—Direct materials	100%
Percentage of completion—Direct labor	65%
Direct materials costs	$ 3,300
Direct labor costs	$ 600
Factory overhead costs applied (120% of direct labor)	$ 720
Activities during the current period (April)	
Units started this period	90,000
Units transferred out (completed)	100,000
Direct materials costs	$ 9,900
Direct labor costs	$ 5,700
Factory overhead costs applied (120% of direct labor)	$ 6,840
Ending goods in process inventory (April 30)	
Units of product	20,000
Percentage of completion—Direct materials	100%
Percentage of completion—Direct labor	25%

Step 1: Determine the Physical Flow of Units

Video3.1

A *physical flow reconciliation* is a report that reconciles (1) the physical units started in a period with (2) the physical units completed in that period. A physical flow reconciliation for GenX is shown in Exhibit 3.12 for April.

EXHIBIT 3.12

Physical Flow Reconciliation

Units to Account For		Units Accounted For	
Beginning goods in process inventory	30,000 units	Units completed and transferred out	100,000 units
Units started this period	90,000 units	Ending goods in process inventory	20,000 units
Total units to account for	**120,000 units**	Total units accounted for	**120,000 units**

reconciled

The weighted-average method does not require us to separately track the units in beginning work in process from those units started this period. Instead, the units are treated as part of a large pool with an average cost per unit.

Step 2: Compute Equivalent Units of Production

The second step is to compute *equivalent units of production* for direct materials, direct labor, and factory overhead for April. Overhead is applied using direct labor as the allocation base for GenX. This also implies that equivalent units are the same for both labor and overhead.

GenX used its direct materials, direct labor, and overhead to make finished units of Profen and to begin processing some units that are not yet complete. We must convert the physical units measure to equivalent units based on how each input has been used. Equivalent units are computed by multiplying the number of physical units by the percentage of completion for each input—see Exhibit 3.13.

EXHIBIT 3.13

Equivalent Units of Production—Weighted Average

Equivalent Units of Production	Direct Materials	Direct Labor	Factory Overhead
Equivalent units completed and transferred out (100,000 × 100%)	100,000 EUP	100,000 EUP	100,000 EUP
Equivalent units for ending goods in process			
Direct materials (20,000 × 100%)	20,000		
Direct labor (20,000 × 25%)		5,000	
Factory overhead (20,000 × 25%)			5,000
Equivalent units of production	120,000 EUP	105,000 EUP	105,000 EUP

The first row of Exhibit 3.13 reflects units transferred out in April. The production department entirely completed its work on the 100,000 units transferred out. These units have 100% of the materials, labor, and overhead required, or 100,000 equivalent units of each input (100,000 × 100%).

The second row references the ending goods in process, and rows three, four, and five break it down by materials, labor, and overhead. For direct materials, the units in ending goods in process inventory (20,000 physical units) include all materials required, so there are 20,000 equivalent units (20,000 × 100%) of materials in the unfinished physical units. Regarding labor, the units in ending goods in process inventory include 25% of the labor required, which implies 5,000 equivalent units of labor (20,000 × 25%). These units are only 25% complete and labor is used uniformly through the process. Overhead is applied on the basis of direct labor for GenX, so equivalent units for overhead are computed identically to labor (20,000 × 25%).

The final row reflects the whole units of product that could have been manufactured with the amount of inputs used to create some complete and some incomplete units. For GenX, the amount of inputs used to produce 100,000 complete units and to start 20,000 additional units is equivalent to the amount of direct materials in 120,000 whole units, the amount of direct labor in 105,000 whole units, and the amount of overhead in 105,000 whole units.

Step 3: Compute the Cost per Equivalent Unit

Equivalent units of production for each product (from step 2) is used to compute the average cost per equivalent unit. Under the **weighted-average method,** the computation of EUP does not separate the units in beginning inventory from those started this period; similarly, this method combines the costs of beginning goods in process inventory with the costs incurred in the current period. This process is illustrated in Exhibit 3.14.

EXHIBIT 3.14

Cost per Equivalent Unit of Production—Weighted Average

Cost per Equivalent Unit of Production	Direct Materials	Direct Labor	Factory Overhead
Costs of beginning goods in process inventory	$ 3,300	$ 600	$ 720
Costs incurred this period	9,900	5,700	6,840
Total costs	$13,200	$6,300	$7,560
÷ Equivalent units of production (from Step 2)	120,000 EUP	105,000 EUP	105,000 EUP
= Cost per equivalent unit of production	$0.11 per EUP*	$0.06 per EUP†	$0.072 per EUP‡

*$13,200 ÷ 120,000 EUP †$6,300 ÷ 105,000 EUP ‡$7,560 ÷ 105,000 EUP

For direct materials, the cost averages $0.11 per EUP, computed as the sum of direct materials cost from beginning goods in process inventory ($3,300) and the direct materials cost incurred in April ($9,900), and this sum ($13,200) is then divided by the 120,000 EUP for materials (from step 2). The costs per equivalent unit for labor and overhead are similarly computed. Specifically, direct labor cost averages $0.06 per EUP, computed as the sum of labor cost in beginning goods in process inventory ($600) and the labor costs incurred in April ($5,700), and this sum ($6,300) divided by 105,000 EUP for labor. Overhead costs averages $0.072 per EUP, computed as the sum of overhead cost in the beginning goods in process inventory ($720) and the overhead costs applied in April ($6,840), and this sum ($7,560) divided by 105,000 EUP for overhead.

Step 4: Assign and Reconcile Costs

The EUP from step 2 and the cost per EUP from step 3 are used in step 4 to assign costs to (a) units that production completed and transferred to finished goods and (b) units that remain in process. This is illustrated in Exhibit 3.15.

EXHIBIT 3.15

Report of Costs Accounted For—Weighted Average

Cost of units completed and transferred out		
Direct materials (100,000 EUP × $0.11 per EUP)	$11,000	
Direct labor (100,000 EUP × $0.06 per EUP)	6,000	
Factory overhead (100,000 EUP × $0.072 per EUP)	7,200	
Cost of units completed this period		$ 24,200
Cost of ending goods in process inventory		
Direct materials (20,000 EUP × $0.11 per EUP)	2,200	
Direct labor (5,000 EUP × $0.06 per EUP)	300	
Factory overhead (5,000 EUP × $0.072 per EUP)	360	
Cost of ending goods in process inventory		2,860
Total costs accounted for		**$27,060**

Cost of Units Completed and Transferred The 100,000 units completed and transferred to finished goods inventory required 100,000 EUP of direct materials. Thus, we assign $11,000 (100,000 EUP × $0.11 per EUP) of direct materials cost to those units. Similarly, those units had received 100,000 EUP of direct labor and 100,000 EUP of factory overhead (recall Exhibit 3.13). Thus, we assign $6,000 (100,000 EUP × $0.06 per EUP) of direct labor and $7,200 (100,000 EUP × $0.072 per EUP) of overhead to those units. The total cost of the 100,000 completed and transferred units is $24,200 ($11,000 + $6,000 + $7,200) and their average cost per unit is $0.242 ($24,200 ÷ 100,000 units).

Cost of Units for Ending Goods in Process There are 20,000 incomplete units in goods in process inventory at period-end. For direct materials, those units have 20,000 EUP of material (from step 2) at a cost of $0.11 per EUP (from step 3), which yields the materials cost of goods in process inventory of $2,200 (20,000 EUP × $0.11 per EUP). For direct labor, the in-process units have 25% of the required labor, or 5,000 EUP (from step 2). Using the $0.06 labor cost per EUP (from step 3) we obtain the labor cost of goods in process inventory of $300 (5,000 EUP × $0.06 per EUP). For overhead, the in-process units reflect 5,000 EUP (from step 2). Using the $0.072 overhead cost per EUP (from step 3) we obtain overhead costs with in-process inventory of $360 (5,000 EUP × $0.072 per EUP). Total cost of goods in process inventory at period-end is $2,860 ($2,200 + $300 + $360).

As a check, management verifies that total costs assigned to those units completed and transferred plus the costs of those in process (from Exhibit 3.15) equal the costs incurred by production. Exhibit 3.16 shows the costs incurred by production this period. We then reconcile the *costs accounted for* in Exhibit 3.15 with the *costs to account for* in Exhibit 3.16.

EXHIBIT 3.16

Report of Costs to Account For—Weighted Average

Cost of beginning goods in process inventory		
Direct materials	$3,300	
Direct labor	600	
Factory overhead	720	$ 4,620
Cost incurred this period		
Direct materials	9,900	
Direct labor	5,700	
Factory overhead	6,840	22,440
Total costs to account for		**$27,060**

At GenX, the production department manager is responsible for $27,060 in costs: $4,620 that is assigned to the goods in process at the start of the period plus $22,440 of materials, labor, and overhead incurred in the period. At period-end, that manager must show where these costs are assigned. The manager for GenX reports that $2,860 are assigned to units in process and $24,200 are assigned to units completed (per Exhibit 3.15). The sum of these amounts equals $27,060. Thus, the total *costs to account for* equal the total *costs accounted for* (minor differences can sometimes occur from rounding).

C4 Define a process cost summary and describe its purposes.

Point: Managers can examine changes in monthly costs per equivalent unit to help control the production process. When prices are set in a competitive market, managers can use process cost summary information to determine which costs should be cut to achieve a profit.

Process Cost Summary An important managerial accounting report for a process cost accounting system is the **process cost summary** (also called *production report*), which is prepared separately for each process or production department. Three reasons for the summary are to (1) help department managers control and monitor their departments, (2) help factory managers evaluate department managers' performances, and (3) provide cost information for financial statements. A process cost summary achieves these purposes by describing the costs charged to each department, reporting the equivalent units of production achieved by each department, and determining the costs assigned to each department's output. For our purposes, it is prepared using a combination of Exhibits 3.13, 3.14, 3.15, and 3.16.

P5 Prepare a process cost summary.

The process cost summary for GenX is shown in Exhibit 3.17. The report is divided into three sections. Section ① lists the total costs charged to the department, including direct materials, direct labor, and overhead costs incurred, as well as the cost of the beginning goods in process inventory. Section ② describes the equivalent units of production for the department. Equivalent units for materials, labor, and overhead are in separate columns. It also reports direct

EXHIBIT 3.17

Process Cost Summary

GenX COMPANY
Process Cost Summary
For Month Ended April 30, 2009

①

Costs Charged to Production		
Costs of beginning goods in process		
Direct materials	$3,300	
Direct labor	600	
Factory overhead	720	$ 4,620
Costs incurred this period		
Direct materials	9,900	
Direct labor	5,700	
Factory overhead	6,840	22,440
Total costs to account for		**$27,060**

②

Unit Cost Information

Units to account for:		Units accounted for:	
Beginning goods in process	30,000	Completed and transferred out	100,000
Units started this period	90,000	Ending goods in process	20,000
Total units to account for	120,000	Total units accounted for	120,000

Equivalent Units of Production (EUP)	**Direct Materials**	**Direct Labor**	**Factory Overhead**
Units completed and transferred out	100,000 EUP	100,000 EUP	100,000 EUP
Units of ending goods in process			
Direct materials (20,000 × 100%)	20,000		
Direct labor (20,000 × 25%)		5,000	
Factory overhead (20,000 × 25%)			5,000
Equivalent units of production	120,000 EUP	105,000 EUP	105,000 EUP

Cost per EUP	**Direct Materials**	**Direct Labor**	**Factory Overhead**
Costs of beginning goods in process	$ 3,300	$ 600	$ 720
Costs incurred this period	9,900	5,700	6,840
Total costs	$13,200	$6,300	$7,560
÷EUP	120,000 EUP	105,000 EUP	105,000 EUP
Cost per EUP	$0.11 per EUP	$0.06 per EUP	$0.072 per EUP

③

Cost Assignment and Reconciliation		
Costs transferred out (cost of goods manufactured)		
Direct materials (100,000 EUP × $0.11 per EUP)	$11,000	
Direct labor (100,000 EUP × $0.06 per EUP)	6,000	
Factory overhead (100,000 EUP × $0.072 per EUP)	7,200	$ 24,200
Costs of ending goods in process		
Direct materials (20,000 EUP × $0.11 per EUP)	2,200	
Direct labor (5,000 EUP × $0.06 per EUP)	300	
Factory overhead (5,000 EUP × $0.072 per EUP)	360	2,860
Total costs accounted for		**$27,060**

reconciled

materials, direct labor, and overhead costs per equivalent unit. Section ③ allocates total costs among units worked on in the period. The $24,200 is the total cost of goods transferred out of the department, and the $2,860 is the cost of partially processed ending inventory units. The assigned costs are then added to show that the total $27,060 cost charged to the department in section ① is now assigned to the units in section ③.

Quick Check Answers—p. 111

6. Equivalent units are (*a*) a measure of a production department's productivity in using direct materials, direct labor, or overhead; (*b*) units of a product produced by a foreign competitor that are similar to units produced by a domestic company; or (*c*) generic units of a product similar to brand name units of a product.
7. Interpret the meaning of a department's equivalent units with respect to direct labor.
8. A department began the period with 8,000 units that were one-fourth complete with respect to direct labor. It completed 58,000 units, and ended with 6,000 units that were one-third complete with respect to direct labor. What were its direct labor equivalent units for the period using the weighted-average method?
9. A process cost summary for a department has three sections. What information is presented in each of them?

Transfers to Finished Goods Inventory and Cost of Goods Sold

P6 Record the transfer of completed goods to Finished Goods Inventory and Cost of Goods Sold.

Arrow line ⑨ in Exhibit 3.4 reflects the transfer of completed products from production to finished goods inventory. The process cost summary shows that the 100,000 units of finished Profen are assigned a cost of $24,200. The entry to record this transfer follows.

⑨	Finished Goods Inventory	24,200	
	Goods in Process Inventory		24,200
	To record transfer of completed units.		

Assets = Liabilities + Equity
+24,200
−24,200

The credit to Goods in Process Inventory reduces that asset balance to reflect that 100,000 units are no longer in production. The cost of these units has been transferred to Finished Goods Inventory, which is recognized as a $24,200 increase in this asset. After this entry is posted, there remains a balance of $2,860 in the Goods in Process Inventory account, which is the amount computed in Step 4 previously. The cost of units transferred from Goods in Process Inventory to Finished Goods Inventory is called the **cost of goods manufactured.** Exhibit 3.18 reveals the activities in the Goods in Process Inventory account for this period. The ending balance of this account equals the cost assigned to the partially completed units in section ③ of Exhibit 3.17.

EXHIBIT 3.18
Goods in Process Inventory

Goods in Process Inventory					Acct. No. 134
Date		Explanation	Debit	Credit	Balance
Mar.	31	Balance			4,620
Apr.	30	Direct materials usage	9,900		14,520
	30	Direct labor costs incurred	5,700		20,220
	30	Factory overhead applied	6,840		27,060
	30	Transfer completed product to warehouse		24,200	2,860

Arrow line ⑩ in Exhibit 3.4 reflects the sale of finished goods. Assume that GenX sold 106,000 units of Profen this period, and that its beginning inventory of finished goods consisted of 26,000 units with a cost of $6,292. Also assume that its ending finished goods inventory consists of 20,000 units at a cost of $4,840. Using this information, we can compute its cost of goods sold for April as shown in Exhibit 3.19.

Point: We omit the journal entry for sales, but it totals the number of units sold times price per unit.

EXHIBIT 3.19
Cost of Goods Sold

Beginning finished goods inventory	$ 6,292
+ Cost of goods manufactured this period	24,200
= Cost of goods available for sale	$30,492
− Ending finished goods inventory	4,840
= Cost of goods sold	$25,652

The summary entry to record cost of goods sold for this period follows.

Assets = Liabilities + Equity
−25,652 −25,652

(10)	Cost of Goods Sold	25,652	
	Finished Goods Inventory		25,652
	To record cost of goods sold for April.		

The Finished Goods Inventory account now appears as shown in Exhibit 3.20.

EXHIBIT 3.20
Finished Goods Inventory

Finished Goods Inventory					Acct. No. 135
Date		Explanation	Debit	Credit	Balance
Mar.	31	Balance			6,292
Apr.	30	Transfer in cost of goods manufactured	24,200		30,492
	30	Cost of goods sold		25,652	4,840

Summary of Cost Flows Exhibit 3.21 shows GenX's manufacturing cost flows for April. Each of these cost flows and the entries to record them have been explained. The flow of costs through the accounts reflects the flow of production activities and products.

EXHIBIT 3.21*
Cost Flows through GenX

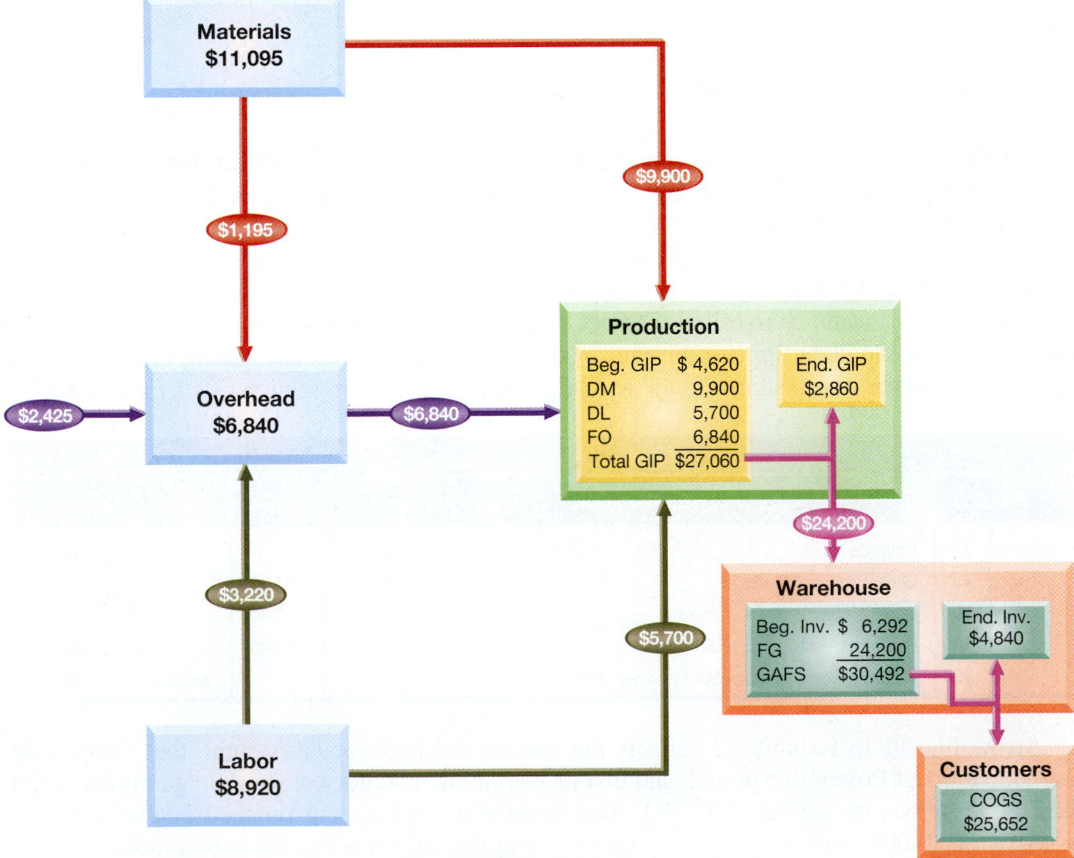

*Abbreviations: GIP (goods in process); DM (direct materials); DL (direct labor); FO (factory overhead); FG (finished goods); GAFS (goods available for sale); COGS (cost of goods sold).

Decision Insight

Best of Both Customer orientation demands both flexibility and standardization. Flexibility allows companies to supply products or services to a customer's specifications as in a job order setting, and standardization helps achieve efficiencies and lower costs as in a process operation.

Effect of the Lean Business Model on Process Operations

Adopting lean business practices often yields changes in process operations. Management concerns with throughput and just-in-time manufacturing, for instance, cause boundary lines between departments to blur. In some cases, higher quality and better efficiency are obtained by entirely reorganizing production processes. For example, instead of producing different types of computers in a series of departments, a separate work center for each computer can be established in one department. When such a rearrangement occurs, the process cost accounting system is changed to account for each work center's costs.

To illustrate, when a company adopts a just-in-time inventory system, its inventories can be minimal. If raw materials are not ordered or received until needed, a Raw Materials Inventory account may be unnecessary. Instead, materials cost is immediately debited to the Goods in Process Inventory account. Similarly, a Finished Goods Inventory account may not be needed. Instead, cost of finished goods may be immediately debited to the Cost of Goods Sold account.

Decision Insight

Lean Machine Attention to customer orientation has led to improved processes for companies. A manufacturer of control devices improved quality and reduced production time by forming teams to study processes and suggest improvements. Another company set up project groups to evaluate its production processes.

Hybrid Costing System

Decision Analysis

A2 Explain and illustrate a hybrid costing system.

This chapter explained the process costing system and contrasted it with the job order costing system. Many organizations use a *hybrid system* that contains features of both process and job order operations. A recent survey of manufacturers revealed that a majority use hybrid systems.

To illustrate, consider a car manufacturer's assembly line. On one hand, the line resembles a process operation in that the assembly steps for each car are nearly identical. On the other hand, the specifications of most cars have several important differences. At the **Ford** Mustang plant, each car assembled on a given day can be different from the previous car and the next car. This means that the costs of materials (subassemblies or components) for each car can differ. Accordingly, while the conversion costs (direct labor and overhead) can be accounted for using a process costing system, the component costs (direct materials) are accounted for using a job order system (separately for each car or type of car).

A hybrid system of processes requires a *hybrid costing system* to properly cost products or services. In the Ford plant, the assembly costs per car are readily determined using process costing. The costs of additional components can then be added to the assembly costs to determine each car's total cost (as in job order costing). To illustrate, consider the following information for a daily assembly process at Ford.

Assembly process costs	
Direct materials	$10,600,000
Direct labor	$5,800,000
Factory overhead	$6,200,000
Number of cars assembled	1,000
Costs of three different types of steering wheels	$240, $330, $480
Costs of three different types of seats	$620, $840, $1,360

The assembly process costs $22,600 per car. Depending on the type of steering wheel and seats the customer requests, the cost of a car can range from $23,460 to $24,440 (a $980 difference).

Today companies are increasingly trying to standardize processes while attempting to meet individual customer needs. To the extent that differences among individual customers' requests are large, understanding the costs to satisfy those requests is important. Thus, monitoring and controlling both process and job order costs are important.

Decision Ethics

Entrepreneur You operate a process production company making similar products for three different customers. One customer demands 100% quality inspection of products at your location before shipping. The added costs of that inspection are spread across all customers, not just the one demanding it. If you charge the added costs to that customer, you could lose that customer and experience a loss. Moreover, your other two customers have agreed to pay 110% of full costs. What actions (if any) do you take?

[Answer—pp. 110–111]

Demonstration Problem

Pennsylvania Company produces a product that passes through a single production process. Then completed products are transferred to finished goods in its warehouse. Information related to its manufacturing activities for July follows.

Raw Materials	
Beginning inventory	$100,000
Raw materials purchased on credit	211,400
Direct materials used	(190,000)
Indirect materials used	(51,400)
Ending inventory	$ 70,000
Factory Payroll	
Direct labor incurred	$ 55,500
Indirect labor incurred	50,625
Total payroll (paid in cash)	$106,125
Factory Overhead	
Indirect materials used	$ 51,400
Indirect labor used	50,625
Other overhead costs	71,725
Total factory overhead incurred	$173,750
Factory Overhead Applied	
Overhead applied (200% of direct labor)	$111,000

Production Department	
Beginning goods in process inventory (units)	5,000
Percentage completed—Materials	100%
Percentage completed—Labor and overhead	60%
Beginning goods in process inventory (costs)	
Direct materials used	$ 20,000
Direct labor incurred	9,600
Overhead applied (200% of direct labor)	19,200
Total costs of beginning goods in process	$ 48,800
Units started this period	20,000
Units completed this period	17,000
Ending goods in process inventory (units)	8,000
Percentage completed—Materials	100%
Percentage completed—Labor and overhead	20%
Finished Goods Inventory	
Beginning finished goods inventory	$ 96,400
Cost transferred in from production	321,300
Cost of goods sold	(345,050)
Ending finished goods inventory	$ 72,650

Required

1. Prepare a physical flow reconciliation for July as illustrated in Exhibit 3.12.
2. Compute the equivalent units of production in July for direct materials, direct labor, and factory overhead.
3. Compute the costs per equivalent units of production in July for direct materials, direct labor, and factory overhead.
4. Prepare a report of costs accounted for and a report of costs to account for.

5. Prepare summary journal entries to record the transactions and events of July for (a) raw materials purchases, (b) direct materials usage, (c) indirect materials usage, (d) factory payroll costs, (e) direct labor usage, (f) indirect labor usage, (g) other overhead costs (credit Other Accounts), (h) application of overhead to production, (i) transfer of finished goods from production, and (j) the cost of goods sold.

Planning the Solution

- Track the physical flow to determine the number of units completed in July.
- Compute the equivalent unit of production for direct materials, direct labor, and factory overhead.
- Compute the costs per equivalent unit of production with respect to direct materials, direct labor, and overhead; and determine the cost per unit for each.
- Compute the total cost of the goods transferred to production by using the equivalent units and unit costs. Determine (a) the cost of the beginning in-process inventory, (b) the materials, labor, and overhead costs added to the beginning in-process inventory, and (c) the materials, labor, and overhead costs added to the units started and completed in the month.
- Determine the cost of goods sold using balances in finished goods and cost of units completed this period.
- Use the information to record the summary journal entries for July.

Solution to Demonstration Problem

1. Physical flow reconciliation.

Units to Account For		Units Accounted For	
Beginning goods in process inventory	5,000 units	Units completed and transferred out	17,000 units
Units started this period	20,000 units	Ending goods in process inventory	8,000 units
Total units to account for	**25,000 units**	Total units accounted for	**25,000 units**

reconciled

2. Equivalent units of production.

Equivalent Units of Production	Direct Materials	Direct Labor	Factory Overhead
Equivalent units completed and transferred out	17,000 EUP	17,000 EUP	17,000 EUP
Equivalent units in ending goods in process			
Direct materials (8,000 × 100%)	8,000		
Direct labor (8,000 × 20%)		1,600	
Factory overhead (8,000 × 20%)			1,600
Equivalent units of production	25,000 EUP	18,600 EUP	18,600 EUP

3. Costs per equivalent unit of production.

Costs per Equivalent Unit of Production	Direct Materials	Direct Labor	Factory Overhead
Costs of beginning goods in process	$ 20,000	$ 9,600	$ 19,200
Costs incurred this period	190,000	55,500	111,000**
Total costs	$210,000	$65,100	$130,200
÷ Equivalent units of production (from part 2)	25,000 EUP	18,600 EUP	18,600 EUP
= Costs per equivalent unit of production	$8.40 per EUP	$3.50 per EUP	$7.00 per EUP

**Factory overhead applied

4. Reports of costs accounted for and of costs to account for.

Report of Costs Accounted For		
Cost of units transferred out (cost of goods manufactured)		
Direct materials ($8.40 per EUP × 17,000 EUP)	$142,800	
Direct labor ($3.50 per EUP × 17,000 EUP)	59,500	
Factory overhead ($7.00 per EUP × 17,000 EUP)	119,000	
Cost of units completed this period		$ 321,300
Cost of ending goods in process inventory		
Direct materials ($8.40 per EUP × 8,000 EUP)	67,200	
Direct labor ($3.50 per EUP × 1,600 EUP)	5,600	
Factory overhead ($7.00 per EUP × 1,600 EUP)	11,200	
Cost of ending goods in process inventory		84,000
Total costs accounted for		**$405,300**

Report of Costs to Account For		
Cost of beginning goods in process inventory		
Direct materials	$ 20,000	
Direct labor	9,600	
Factory overhead	19,200	$ 48,800
Cost incurred this period		
Direct materials	190,000	
Direct labor	55,500	
Factory overhead	111,000	356,500
Total costs to account for		**$405,300**

reconciled

5. Summary journal entries for the transactions and events in July.

a.	Raw Materials Inventory	211,400	
	Accounts Payable		211,400
	To record raw materials purchases.		
b.	Goods in Process Inventory	190,000	
	Raw Materials Inventory		190,000
	To record direct materials usage.		
c.	Factory Overhead	51,400	
	Raw Materials Inventory		51,400
	To record indirect materials usage.		
d.	Factory Payroll	106,125	
	Cash		106,125
	To record factory payroll costs.		
e.	Goods in Process Inventory	55,500	
	Factory Payroll		55,500
	To record direct labor usage.		
f.	Factory Overhead	50,625	
	Factory Payroll		50,625
	To record indirect labor usage.		
g.	Factory Overhead	71,725	
	Other Accounts		71,725
	To record other overhead costs.		

[continued on next page]

[continued from previous page]

h.	Goods in Process Inventory	111,000	
	Factory Overhead		111,000
	To record application of overhead.		
i.	Finished Goods Inventory	321,300	
	Goods in Process Inventory		321,300
	To record transfer of finished goods from production.		
j.	Cost of Goods Sold	345,050	
	Finished Goods Inventory		345,050
	To record cost of goods sold.		

APPENDIX

FIFO Method of Process Costing

3A

C5 Explain and illustrate the four steps in accounting for production activity using FIFO.

The **FIFO method** of process costing assigns costs to units assuming a first-in, first-out flow of product. The objectives, concepts, and journal entries (not amounts) are the same as for the weighted-average method, but computation of equivalent units of production and cost assignment are slightly different.

Exhibit 3A.1 shows selected information from GenX's production department for the month of April. Accounting for a department's activity for a period includes four steps: (1) determine physical flow, (2) compute equivalent units, (3) compute cost per equivalent unit, and (4) determine cost assignment and reconciliation. This appendix describes each of these steps using the FIFO method for process costing.

EXHIBIT 3A.1

Production Data

Beginning goods in process inventory (March 31)	
Units of product	30,000
Percentage of completion—Direct materials	100%
Percentage of completion—Direct labor	65%
Direct materials costs	$ 3,300
Direct labor costs	$ 600
Factory overhead costs applied (120% of direct labor)	$ 720
Activities during the current period (April)	
Units started this period	90,000
Units transferred out (completed)	100,000
Direct materials costs	$ 9,900
Direct labor costs	$ 5,700
Factory overhead costs applied (120% of direct labor)	$ 6,840
Ending goods in process inventory (April 30)	
Units of product	20,000
Percentage of completion—Direct materials	100%
Percentage of completion—Direct labor	25%

Step 1: Determine Physical Flow of Units

A *physical flow reconciliation* is a report that reconciles (1) the physical units started in a period with (2) the physical units completed in that period. The physical flow reconciliation for GenX is shown in Exhibit 3A.2 for April.

EXHIBIT 3A.2

Physical Flow Reconciliation

Units to Account For		Units Accounted For	
Beginning goods in process inventory	30,000 units	Units completed and transferred out	100,000 units
Units started this period	90,000 units	Ending goods in process inventory ...	20,000 units
Total units to account for ...	**120,000 units**	Total units accounted for	**120,000 units**

reconciled

FIFO assumes that the 100,000 units transferred to finished goods during April include the 30,000 units from the beginning goods in process inventory. The remaining 70,000 units transferred out are from units started in April. Of the total 90,000 units started in April, 70,000 were completed, leaving 20,000 units unfinished at period-end.

Step 2: Compute Equivalent Units of Production—FIFO

GenX used its direct materials, direct labor, and overhead both to make complete units of Profen and to start some units that are not yet complete. We need to convert the physical measure of units to equivalent units based on how much of each input has been used. We do this by multiplying the number of physical units by the percentage of processing applied to those units in the current period; this is done for each input (materials, labor, and overhead). The FIFO method accounts for cost flow in a sequential manner—earliest costs are the first to flow out. (This is different from the weighted-average method, which combines prior period costs—those in beginning Goods in Process Inventory—with costs incurred in the current period.)

Three distinct groups of units must be considered in determining the equivalent units of production under the FIFO method: (a) units in beginning Goods in Process Inventory that were completed this period, (b) units started *and* completed this period, and (c) units in ending Goods in Process Inventory. We must determine how much material, labor, and overhead are used for each of these unit groups. These computations are shown in Exhibit 3A.3. The remainder of this section explains these computations.

EXHIBIT 3A.3

Equivalent Units of Production—FIFO

Equivalent Units of Production	Direct Materials	Direct Labor	Factory Overhead
(a) Equivalent units to complete beginning goods in process			
Direct materials (30,000 × 0%)	0 EUP		
Direct labor (30,000 × 35%)		10,500 EUP	
Factory overhead (30,000 × 35%)			10,500 EUP
(b) Equivalent units started and completed*	70,000	70,000	70,000
(c) Equivalent units in ending goods in process			
Direct materials (20,000 × 100%)	20,000		
Direct labor (20,000 × 25%)		5,000	
Factory overhead (20,000 × 25%)			5,000
Equivalent units of production	90,000 EUP	85,500 EUP	85,500 EUP

*Units completed this period	100,000 units
Less units in beginning goods in process	30,000
Units started and completed this period	70,000 units

(a) Beginning Goods in Process Under FIFO, we assume that production first completes any units started in the prior period. There were 30,000 physical units in beginning goods in process inventory. Those units were 100% complete with respect to direct materials as of the end of the prior period. This means that no materials (0%) are needed in April to complete those 30,000 units. So the equivalent units of *materials* to complete beginning goods in process are zero (30,000 × 0%)—see first row under row "(a)" in Exhibit 3A.3. The units in process as of April 1 had already been through 65% of production prior to this period and need only go through the remaining 35% of production. The equivalent units of *labor* to complete the beginning goods in process are 10,500 (30,000 × 35%)—

see the second row under row "(a)." This implies that the amount of labor required this period to complete the 30,000 units started in the prior period is the amount of labor needed to make 10,500 units, start-to-finish. Finally, overhead is applied based on direct labor costs, so GenX computes equivalent units for overhead as it would for direct labor.

(b) Units Started and Completed This Period After completing any beginning goods in process, FIFO assumes that production begins on newly started units. GenX began work on 90,000 new units this period. Of those units, 20,000 remain incomplete at period-end. This means that 70,000 of the units started in April were completed in April. These complete units have received 100% of materials, labor, and overhead. Exhibit 3A.3 reflects this by including 70,000 equivalent units (70,000 × 100%) of materials, labor, and overhead in its equivalent units of production—see row "(b)."

(c) Ending Goods in Process The 20,000 units started in April that GenX was not able to complete by period-end consumed materials, labor, and overhead. Specifically, those 20,000 units received 100% of materials and, therefore, the equivalent units of materials in ending goods in process inventory are 20,000 (20,000 × 100%)—see the first row under row "(c)." For labor and overhead, the units in ending goods in process were 25% complete in production. This means the equivalent units of labor and overhead for those units are 5,000 (20,000 × 25%) as GenX incurs labor and overhead costs uniformly throughout its production process. Finally, for each input (direct materials, direct labor, and factory overhead), the equivalent units for each of the unit groups (a), (b), and (c) are added to determine the total equivalent units of production with respect to each—see the final row in Exhibit 3A.3.

Step 3: Compute Cost per Equivalent Unit—FIFO

To compute cost per equivalent unit, we take the product costs (for each of direct materials, direct labor, and factory overhead from Exhibit 3A.1) added in April and divide by the equivalent units of production from step 2. Exhibit 3A.4 illustrates these computations.

EXHIBIT 3A.4

Cost per Equivalent Unit of Production—FIFO

Cost per Equivalent Unit of Production	Direct Materials	Direct Labor	Factory Overhead
Costs incurred this period	$9,900	$5,700	$6,840
÷ Equivalent units of production (from Step 2)	90,000 EUP	85,500 EUP	85,500 EUP
Cost per equivalent unit of production	$0.11 per EUP	$0.067 per EUP	$0.08 per EUP

It is essential to compute costs per equivalent unit for *each* input because production inputs are added at different times in the process. The FIFO method computes the cost per equivalent unit based solely on this period's EUP and costs (unlike the weighted-average method, which adds in the costs of the beginning goods in process inventory).

Step 4: Assign and Reconcile Costs

The equivalent units determined in step 2 and the cost per equivalent unit computed in step 3 are both used to assign costs (1) to units that the production department completed and transferred to finished goods and (2) to units that remain in process at period-end.

In Exhibit 3A.5, under the section for cost of units transferred out, we see that the cost of units completed in April includes the $4,620 cost carried over from March for work already applied to the 30,000 units that make up beginning Goods in Process Inventory, plus the $1,544 incurred in April to complete those units. This section also includes the $17,990 of cost assigned to the 70,000 units started and completed this period. Thus, the total cost of goods manufactured in April is $24,154 ($4,620 + $1,544 + $17,990). The average cost per unit for goods completed in April is $0.242 ($24,154 ÷ 100,000 completed units).

The computation for cost of ending goods in process inventory is in the lower part of Exhibit 3A.5. The cost of units in process includes materials, labor, and overhead costs corresponding to the percentage of these resources applied to those incomplete units in April. That cost of $2,935 ($2,200 + $335 + $400) also is the ending balance for the Goods in Process Inventory account.

EXHIBIT 3A.5

Report of Costs Accounted For—FIFO

Cost of units transferred out (cost of goods manufactured)		
Cost of beginning goods in process inventory		$ 4,620
Cost to complete beginning goods in process		
Direct materials ($0.11 per EUP × 0 EUP)	$ 0	
Direct labor ($0.067 per EUP × 10,500 EUP)	704	
Factory overhead ($0.08 per EUP × 10,500 EUP)	840	1,544
Cost of units started and completed this period		
Direct materials ($0.11 per EUP × 70,000 EUP)	7,700	
Direct labor ($0.067 per EUP × 70,000 EUP)	4,690	
Factory overhead ($0.08 per EUP × 70,000 EUP)	5,600	17,990
Total cost of units finished this period		24,154
Cost of ending goods in process inventory		
Direct materials ($0.11 per EUP × 20,000 EUP)	2,200	
Direct labor ($0.067 per EUP × 5,000 EUP)	335	
Factory overhead ($0.08 per EUP × 5,000 EUP)	400	
Total cost of ending goods in process inventory		2,935
Total costs accounted for		**$27,089**

Management verifies that the total costs assigned to units transferred out and units still in process equal the total costs incurred by production. We reconcile the costs accounted for (in Exhibit 3A.5) to the costs that production was charged for as shown in Exhibit 3A.6.

EXHIBIT 13A.6

Report of Costs to Account For—FIFO

Cost of beginning goods in process inventory		
Direct materials	$3,300	
Direct labor	600	
Factory overhead	720	$ 4,620
Costs incurred this period		
Direct materials	9,900	
Direct labor	5,700	
Factory overhead	6,840	22,440
Total costs to account for		**$27,060**

The production manager is responsible for $27,060 in costs: $4,620 that had been assigned to the department's Goods in Process Inventory as of April 1 plus $22,440 of materials, labor, and overhead costs the department incurred in April. At period-end, the manager must identify where those costs were assigned. The production manager can report that $24,154 of cost was assigned to units completed in April and $2,935 was assigned to units still in process at period-end. The sum of these amounts is $29 different from the $27,060 total costs incurred by production due to rounding in step 3—rounding errors are common and not a concern.

The final report is the process cost summary, which summarizes key information from Exhibits 3A.3, 3A.4, 3A.5, and 3A.6. Reasons for the summary are to (1) help managers control and monitor costs, (2) help upper management assess department manager performance, and (3) provide cost information for financial reporting. The process cost summary, using FIFO, for GenX is in Exhibit 3A.7. Section ① lists the total costs charged to the department, including direct materials, direct labor, and overhead costs incurred, as well as the cost of the beginning goods in process inventory. Section ② describes the equivalent units of production for the department. Equivalent units for materials, labor, and overhead are in separate columns. It also reports direct materials, direct labor, and overhead costs per equivalent unit. Section ③ allocates total costs among units worked on in the period.

Decision Maker

Cost Manager As cost manager for an electronics manufacturer, you apply a process costing system using FIFO. Your company plans to adopt a just-in-time system and eliminate inventories. What is the impact of the use of FIFO (versus the weighted-average method) given these plans? [Answer—p. 111]

EXHIBIT 3A.7
Process Cost Summary

GenX COMPANY
Process Cost Summary
For Month Ended April 30, 2009

①	**Costs charged to production**			
	Costs of beginning goods in process inventory			
	Direct materials		$3,300	
	Direct labor		600	
	Factory overhead		720	$ 4,620
	Costs incurred this period			
	Direct materials		9,900	
	Direct labor		5,700	
	Factory overhead		6,840	22,440
	Total costs to account for			$27,060

Unit cost information ②

Units to account for		Units accounted for	
Beginning goods in process	30,000	Transferred out	100,000
Units started this period	90,000	Ending goods in process	20,000
Total units to account for	120,000	Total units accounted for	120,000

Equivalent units of production	**Direct Materials**	**Direct Labor**	**Factory Overhead**
Equivalent units to complete beginning goods in process			
Direct materials (30,000 × 0%)	0 EUP		
Direct labor (30,000 × 35%)		10,500 EUP	
Factory overhead (30,000 × 35%)			10,500 EUP
Equivalent units started and completed	70,000	70,000	70,000
Equivalent units in ending goods in process			
Direct materials (20,000 × 100%)	20,000		
Direct labor (20,000 × 25%)		5,000	
Factory overhead (20,000 × 25%)			5000
Equivalent units of production	90,000 EUP	85,500 EUP	85,500 EUP

Cost per equivalent unit of production	**Direct Materials**	**Direct Labor**	**Factory Overhead**
Costs incurred this period	$9,900	$5,700	$6,840
÷ Equivalent units of production	90,000 EUP	85,500 EUP	85,500 EUP
Cost per equivalent unit of production	$0.11 per EUP	$0.067 per EUP	$0.08 per EUP

③	**Cost assignment and reconciliation**		
	(cost of units completed and transferred out)		
	Cost of beginning goods in process		$ 4,620
	Cost to complete beginning goods in process		
	Direct materials ($0.11 per EUP × 0 EUP)	$ 0	
	Direct labor ($0.067 per EUP × 10,500 EUP)	704	
	Factory overhead ($0.08 per EUP × 10,500 EUP)	840	1,544
	Cost of units started and completed this period		
	Direct materials ($0.11 per EUP × 70,000 EUP)	7,700	
	Direct labor ($0.067 per EUP × 70,000 EUP)	4,690	
	Factory overhead ($0.08 per EUP × 70,000 EUP)	5,600	17,990
	Total cost of units finished this period		24,154
	Cost of ending goods in process		
	Direct materials ($0.11 per EUP × 20,000 EUP)	2,200	
	Direct labor ($0.067 per EUP × 5,000 EUP)	335	
	Factory overhead ($0.08 per EUP × 5,000 EUP)	400	
	Total cost of ending goods in process		2,935
	Total costs accounted for		$27,089*

(Total costs to account for and total costs accounted for: reconciled)

*$29 difference due to rounding

Summary

C1 Explain process operations and the way they differ from job order operations. Process operations produce large quantities of similar products or services by passing them through a series of processes, or steps, in production. Like job order operations, they combine direct materials, direct labor, and overhead in the operations. Unlike job order operations that assign the responsibility for each job to a manager, process operations assign the responsibility for each *process* to a manager.

C2 Define equivalent units and explain their use in process cost accounting. Equivalent units of production measure the activity of a process as the number of units that would be completed in a period if all effort had been applied to units that were started and finished. This measure of production activity is used to compute the cost per equivalent unit and to assign costs to finished goods and goods in process inventory.

C3 Explain the four steps in accounting for production activity in a period. The four steps involved in accounting for production activity in a period are (1) recording the physical flow of units, (2) computing the equivalent units of production, (3) computing the cost per equivalent unit of production, and (4) reconciling costs. The last step involves assigning costs to finished goods and goods in process inventory for the period.

C4 Define a process cost summary and describe its purposes. A process cost summary reports on the activities of a production process or department for a period. It describes the costs charged to the department, the equivalent units of production for the department, and the costs assigned to the output. The report aims to (1) help managers control their departments, (2) help factory managers evaluate department managers' performances, and (3) provide cost information for financial statements.

C5 Explain and illustrate the four steps in accounting for production activity using FIFO. The FIFO method for process costing is applied and illustrated to (1) report the physical flow of units, (2) compute the equivalent units of production, (3) compute the cost per equivalent unit of production, and (4) assign and reconcile costs.

A1 Compare process cost accounting and job order cost accounting. Process and job order manufacturing operations are similar in that both combine materials, labor, and factory overhead to produce products or services. They differ in the way they are organized and managed. In job order operations, the job order cost accounting system assigns materials, labor, and overhead to specific jobs. In process operations, the process cost accounting system assigns materials, labor, and overhead to specific processes. The total costs associated with each process are then divided by the number of units passing through that process to get cost per equivalent unit. The costs per equivalent unit for all processes are added to determine the total cost per unit of a product or service.

A2 Explain and illustrate a hybrid costing system. A hybrid costing system contains features of both job order and process costing systems. Generally, certain direct materials are accounted for by individual products as in job order costing, but direct labor and overhead costs are accounted for similar to process costing.

P1 Record the flow of direct materials costs in process cost accounting. Materials purchased are debited to a Raw Materials Inventory account. As direct materials are issued to processes, they are separately accumulated in a Goods in Process Inventory account for that process.

P2 Record the flow of direct labor costs in process cost accounting. Direct labor costs are initially debited to the Factory Payroll account. The total amount in it is then assigned to the Goods in Process Inventory account pertaining to each process.

P3 Record the flow of factory overhead costs in process cost accounting. The different factory overhead items are first accumulated in the Factory Overhead account and are then allocated, using a predetermined overhead rate, to the different processes. The allocated amount is debited to the Goods in Process Inventory account pertaining to each process.

P4 Compute equivalent units produced in a period. To compute equivalent units, determine the number of units that would have been finished if all materials (or labor or overhead) had been used to produce units that were started and completed during the period. The costs incurred by a process are divided by its equivalent units to yield cost per unit.

P5 Prepare a process cost summary. A process cost summary includes the physical flow of units, equivalent units of production, costs per equivalent unit, and a cost reconciliation. It reports the units and costs to account for during the period and how they were accounted for during the period. In terms of units, the summary includes the beginning goods in process inventory and the units started during the month. These units are accounted for in terms of the goods completed and transferred out, and the ending goods in process inventory. With respect to costs, the summary includes materials, labor, and overhead costs assigned to the process during the period. It shows how these costs are assigned to goods completed and transferred out, and to ending goods in process inventory.

P6 Record the transfer of completed goods to Finished Goods Inventory and Cost of Goods Sold. As units complete the final process and are eventually sold, their accumulated cost is transferred to Finished Goods Inventory and finally to Cost of Goods Sold.

Guidance Answers to Decision Maker and Decision Ethics

Budget Officer By instructing you to classify a majority of costs as indirect, the manager is passing some of his department's costs to a common overhead pool that other departments will partially absorb. Since overhead costs are allocated on the basis of direct labor for this company and the new department has a relatively low direct labor cost, the new department will be assigned less overhead. Such action suggests unethical behavior by this manager. You must object to such reclassification. If this manager refuses to comply, you must inform someone in a more senior position.

Entrepreneur By spreading the added quality-related costs across three customers, the entrepreneur is probably trying to remain competitive with respect to the customer that demands the 100% quality inspection. Moreover, the entrepreneur is partly covering the added costs by recovering two-thirds of them from the other two customers who are paying 110% of total costs. This act likely breaches the trust placed by the two customers in this entrepreneur's application of its costing system. The costing system should be changed, and the entrepreneur should consider renegotiating the pricing and/or quality test agreement with this one customer (at the risk of losing this currently loss-producing customer).

Cost Manager Differences between the FIFO and weighted-average methods are greatest when large work in process inventories exist and when costs fluctuate. The method used if inventories are eliminated does not matter; both produce identical costs.

Guidance Answers to **Quick Checks**

1. *c*

2. When a company produces large quantities of similar products/services, a process cost system is often more suitable.

3. *b*

4. The costs are direct materials, direct labor, and overhead.

5. A goods in process inventory account is needed for *each* production department.

6. *a*

7. Equivalent units with respect to direct labor are the number of units that would have been produced if all labor had been used on units that were started and finished during the period.

8.

Units completed and transferred out	58,000 EUP
Units of ending goods in process	
Direct labor (6,000 × 1/3)	2,000 EUP
Units of production	60,000 EUP

9. The first section shows the costs charged to the department. The second section describes the equivalent units produced by the department. The third section shows the assignment of total costs to units worked on during the period.

Key Terms mhhe.com/wildMA2e

Key Terms are available at the book's Website for learning and testing in an online Flashcard Format.

Cost of goods manufactured (p. 99)
Equivalent units of production (EUP) (p. 93)
FIFO method (p. 105)
Job order cost accounting system (p. 89)
Materials consumption report (p. 90)
Process cost accounting system (p. 89)
Process cost summary (p. 98)
Process operations (p. 86)
Weighted-average method (p. 96)

Multiple Choice Quiz Answers on p. 127 mhhe.com/wildMA2e

Additional Quiz Questions are available at the book's Website.

Quiz3

1. Equivalent units of production are equal to
- **a.** Physical units that were completed this period from all effort being applied to them.
- **b.** The number of units introduced into the process this period.
- **c.** The number of finished units actually completed this period.
- **d.** The number of units that could have been started and completed given the cost incurred.
- **e.** The number of units in the process at the end of the period.

2. Recording the cost of raw materials purchased for use in a process costing system includes a
- **a.** Credit to Raw Materials Inventory.
- **b.** Debit to Goods in Process Inventory.
- **c.** Debit to Factory Overhead.
- **d.** Credit to Factory Overhead.
- **e.** Debit to Raw Materials Inventory.

3. The production department started the month with a beginning goods in process inventory of $20,000. During the month, it was assigned the following costs: direct materials, $152,000; direct labor, $45,000; overhead applied at the rate of 40% of direct labor cost. Inventory with a cost of $218,000 was transferred to finished goods. The ending balance of goods in process inventory is
- **a.** $330,000.
- **b.** $ 17,000.
- **c.** $220,000.
- **d.** $112,000.
- **e.** $118,000.

4. A company's beginning work in process inventory consists of 10,000 units that are 20% complete with respect to direct labor costs. A total of 40,000 units are completed this period. There are 15,000 units in goods in process, one-third complete for direct labor, at period-end. The equivalent units of production (EUP) with respect to direct labor at period-end, assuming the weighted average method, are

a. 45,000 EUP.
b. 40,000 EUP.
c. 5,000 EUP.
d. 37,000 EUP.
e. 43,000 EUP.

5. Assume the same information as in question 4. Also assume that beginning work in process had $6,000 in direct labor cost and that $84,000 in direct labor is added during this period. What is the cost per EUP for labor?

a. $0.50 per EUP
b. $1.87 per EUP
c. $2.00 per EUP
d. $2.10 per EUP
e. $2.25 per EUP

Assume the weighted-average inventory method is used for all assignments unless stated differently. Superscript letter A denotes assignments based on Appendix 3A.

Discussion Questions

1. Can services be delivered by means of process operations? Support your answer with an example.
2. What is the main factor for a company in choosing between the job order costing and process costing accounting systems? Give two likely applications of each system.
3. Identify the control document for materials flow when a materials requisition slip is not used.
4. The focus in a job order costing system is the job or batch. Identify the main focus in process costing.
5. Are the journal entries that match cost flows to product flows in process costing primarily the same or much different than those in job order costing? Explain.
6. Explain in simple terms the notion of equivalent units of production (EUP). Why is it necessary to use EUP in process costing?
7. What are the two main inventory methods used in process costing? What are the differences between these methods?
8. Why is it possible for direct labor in process operations to include the labor of employees who do not work directly on products or services?
9. Assume that a company produces a single product by processing it first through a single production department. Direct labor costs flow through what accounts in this company's process cost system?
10. After all labor costs for a period are allocated, what balance should remain in the Factory Payroll account?
11. Is it possible to have under- or overapplied overhead costs in a process cost accounting system? Explain.
12. Explain why equivalent units of production for both direct labor and overhead can be the same as, and why they can be different from, equivalent units for direct materials.
13. List the four steps in accounting for production activity in a reporting period (for process operations).
14. What purposes does a process cost summary serve?
15. Are there situations where **Best Buy** can use process costing? Identify at least one and explain it.

16. **Apple** produces iMacs with a multiple production line. Identify and list some of its production processing steps and departments.

Denotes Discussion Questions that involve decision making.

Most materials in this section are available in McGraw-Hill's Connect connect

QUICK STUDY

QS 3-1
Matching of product to cost accounting system
C1

For each of the following products and services, indicate whether it is most likely produced in a process operation or in a job order operation.

1. Door hinges
2. Cut flower arrangements
3. House paints
4. Concrete swimming pools
5. Custom tailored suits
6. Grand pianos
7. Wall clocks
8. Sport shirts
9. Bolts and nuts
10. Folding chairs
11. Headphones
12. Designed boathouse

QS 3-2
Recording costs of direct materials
P1

Industrial Boxes makes cardboard shipping cartons in a single operation. This period, Industrial purchased $124,000 in raw materials. Its production department requisitioned $100,000 of those materials for use in producing cartons. Prepare journal entries to record its (1) purchase of raw materials and (2) requisition of direct materials.

QS 3-3
Recording costs of direct labor
P2

Refer to the information in QS 3-2. Industrial Boxes incurred $270,000 in factory payroll costs, of which $250,000 was direct labor. Prepare journal entries to record its (1) total factory payroll incurred and (2) direct labor used in production.

QS 3-4
Recording costs of factory overhead
P3

Refer to the information in QS 3-2 and QS 3-3. Industrial Boxes requisitioned $18,000 of indirect materials from its raw materials and used $20,000 of indirect labor in its production of boxes. Also, it incurred $312,000 of other factory overhead costs. It applies factory overhead at the rate of 135% of direct labor costs. Prepare journal entries to record its (1) indirect materials requisitioned, (2) indirect labor used in production, (3) other factory overhead costs incurred, and (4) application of overhead to production.

QS 3-5
Recording transfer of costs to finished goods P6

Refer to the information in QS 3-2, QS 3-3, and QS 3-4. Industrial Boxes completed 40,000 boxes costing $550,000 and transferred them to finished goods. Prepare its journal entry to record the transfer of the boxes from production to finished goods inventory.

QS 3-6
Computing equivalent units of production
P4

The following refers to units processed in Sunflower Printing's binding department in March. Compute the total equivalent units of production with respect to labor for March using the weighted-average inventory method.

	Units of Product	Percent of Labor Added
Beginning goods in process	75,000	85%
Goods started	155,000	100
Goods completed	170,000	100
Ending goods in process	60,000	25

QS 3-7
Computing EUP cost C4 P5

The cost of beginning inventory plus the costs added during the period should equal the cost of units ____________________ plus the cost of ____________________.

QS 3-8
Hybrid costing system A2

Explain a hybrid costing system. Identify a product or service operation that might well fit a hybrid costing system.

QS 3-9[A]
Computing equivalent units—FIFO C2 C5 P4

Refer to QS 3-6 and compute the total equivalent units of production with respect to labor for March using the FIFO inventory method.

connect *Most materials in this section are available in McGraw-Hill's Connect*

EXERCISES

Exercise 3-1
Terminology in process cost accounting
C1 A1 P1 P2 P3

Match each of the following items A through G with the best numbered description of its purpose.

A. Raw Materials Inventory account
B. Materials requisition
C. Finished Goods Inventory account
D. Factory Overhead account
E. Process cost summary
F. Equivalent units of production
G. Goods in Process Inventory

_______ **1.** Notifies the materials manager to send materials to a production department.
_______ **2.** Holds costs of indirect materials, indirect labor, and similar costs until assigned to production.
_______ **3.** Holds costs of direct materials, direct labor, and applied overhead until products are transferred from production to finished goods (or another department).
_______ **4.** Standardizes partially completed units into equivalent completed units.
_______ **5.** Holds costs of finished products until sold to customers.
_______ **6.** Describes the activity and output of a production department for a period.
_______ **7.** Holds costs of materials until they are used in production or as factory overhead.

Exercise 3-2
Journal entries in process cost accounting
P1 P2 P3

Festive Toy Company manufactures toy trucks. Prepare journal entries to record its following production activities for January.

1. Purchased $40,000 of raw materials on credit.
2. Used $17,000 of direct materials in production.
3. Used $20,500 of indirect materials.

4. Incurred total labor cost of $77,000, which is paid in cash.
5. Used $58,000 of direct labor in production.
6. Used $19,000 of indirect labor.
7. Incurred overhead costs of $22,000 (paid in cash).
8. Applied overhead at 90% of direct labor costs.
9. Transferred completed products with a cost of $137,000 to finished goods inventory.
10. Sold $450,000 of products on credit. Their cost is $150,000.

Check (8) Cr. Factory Overhead, $52,200

Exercise 3-3

Recording cost flows in a process cost system

P1 P2 P3 P6

Seattle Lumber produces bagged bark for use in landscaping. Production involves packaging bark chips in plastic bags in a bagging department. The following information describes production operations for October.

	Bagging Department
Direct materials used	$ 460,000
Direct labor used	$ 76,000
Predetermined overhead rate (based on direct labor)	180%
Goods transferred from bagging to finished goods	$(407,000)

The company's revenue for the month totaled $900,000 from credit sales, and its cost of goods sold for the month is $500,000. Prepare summary journal entries dated October 31 to record its October production activities for (1) direct material usage, (2) direct labor usage, (3) overhead allocation, (4) goods transfer from production to finished goods, and (5) sales.

Check (3) Cr. Factory Overhead, $136,800

Exercise 3-4

Interpretation of journal entries in process cost accounting

P1 P2 P3 P6

The following journal entries are recorded in Lewis Co.'s process cost accounting system. Lewis produces apparel and accessories. Overhead is applied to production based on direct labor cost for the period. Prepare a brief explanation (including any overhead rates applied) for each journal entry *a* through *j*.

a.	Raw Materials Inventory	52,000	
	Accounts Payable		52,000
b.	Goods in Process Inventory	42,000	
	Raw Materials Inventory		42,000
c.	Goods in Process Inventory	26,000	
	Factory Payroll		26,000
d.	Factory Payroll	32,000	
	Cash		32,000
e.	Factory Overhead	10,000	
	Cash		10,000
f.	Factory Overhead	10,000	
	Raw Materials Inventory		10,000
g.	Factory Overhead	6,000	
	Factory Payroll		6,000
h.	Goods in Process Inventory	32,500	
	Factory Overhead		32,500
i.	Finished Goods Inventory	88,000	
	Goods in Process Inventory		88,000
j.	Accounts Receivable	250,000	
	Sales		250,000
	Cost of Goods Sold	100,000	
	Finished Goods Inventory		100,000

Exercise 3-5
Computing equivalent units of production—weighted average
C2 P4

During April, the production department of a process manufacturing system completed a number of units of a product and transferred them to finished goods. Of these transferred units, 30,000 were in process in the production department at the beginning of April and 120,000 were started and completed in April. April's beginning inventory units were 60% complete with respect to materials and 40% complete with respect to labor. At the end of April, 41,000 additional units were in process in the production department and were 80% complete with respect to materials and 30% complete with respect to labor.

1. Compute the number of units transferred to finished goods.
2. Compute the number of equivalent units with respect to both materials used and labor used in the production department for April using the weighted-average method.

Check (2) EUP for materials, 182,800

Exercise 3-6
Costs assigned to output and inventories—weighted average
C3 P4 P5 

The production department described in Exercise 3-5 had $425,184 of direct materials and $326,151 of direct labor cost charged to it during April. Also, its beginning inventory included $59,236 of direct materials cost and $22,794 of direct labor.

1. Compute the direct materials cost and the direct labor cost per equivalent unit for the department.
2. Using the weighted-average method, assign April's costs to the department's output—specifically, its units transferred to finished goods and its ending goods in process inventory.

Check (2) Costs accounted for, $833,365

Exercise 3-7[A]
Computing equivalent units of production—FIFO
C5 P4

Refer to the information in Exercise 3-5 to compute the number of equivalent units with respect to both materials used and labor used in the production department for April using the FIFO method.

Exercise 3-8[A]
Costs assigned to output—FIFO
C5 P4 P5

Refer to the information in Exercise 3-6 and complete its parts (1) and (2) using the FIFO method.

Exercise 3-9
Equivalent units computed—weighted average
C2 P4 P5 

The production department in a process manufacturing system completed 383,000 units of product and transferred them to finished goods during a recent period. Of these units, 63,000 were in process at the beginning of the period. The other 320,000 units were started and completed during the period. At period-end, 59,000 units were in process. Compute the department's equivalent units of production with respect to direct materials under each of three separate assumptions:

1. All direct materials are added to products when processing begins.
2. Direct materials are added to products evenly throughout the process. Beginning goods in process inventory was 40% complete, and ending goods in process inventory was 75% complete.
3. One-half of direct materials is added to products when the process begins and the other half is added when the process is 75% complete as to direct labor. Beginning goods in process inventory is 40% complete as to direct labor, and ending goods in process inventory is 60% complete as to direct labor.

Check (3) EUP for materials, 412,500

Exercise 3-10[A]
Equivalent units computed—FIFO
C5 P4

Refer to the information in Exercise 3-9 and complete it for each of the three separate assumptions using the FIFO method for process costing.

Check (3) EUP for materials, 381,000

Exercise 3-11
Flowchart of costs for a process operation P1 P2 P3 P6

The following flowchart shows the August production activity of the Jez Company. Use the amounts shown on the flowchart to compute the missing four numbers identified by blanks.

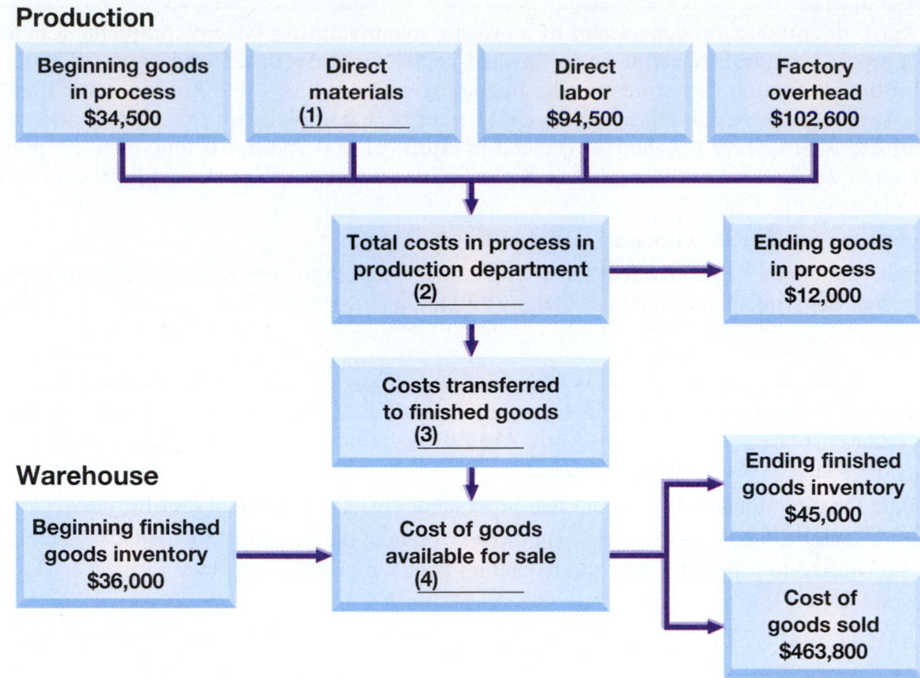

Exercise 3-12
Completing a process cost summary
P5

The following partially completed process cost summary describes the July production activities of Anton Company. Its production output is sent to its warehouse for shipping. Prepare its process cost summary using the weighted-average method.

Equivalent Units of Production	Direct Materials	Direct Labor	Factory Overhead
Units transferred out	64,000	64,000	64,000
Units of ending goods in process	5,000	3,000	3,000
Equivalent units of production	69,000	67,000	67,000
Costs per EUP	**Direct Materials**	**Direct Labor**	**Factory Overhead**
Costs of beginning goods in process	$ 37,100	$ 1,520	$ 3,040
Costs incurred this period	715,000	125,780	251,560
Total costs	$752,100	$127,300	$254,600
Units in beginning goods in process			4,000
Units started this period			65,000
Units completed and transferred out			64,000
Units in ending goods in process			5,000

Exercise 3-13
Process costing—weighted average
P1 P2 P6

Nu-Test Company uses the weighted-average method of process costing to assign production costs to its products. Information for September follows. Assume that all materials are added at the beginning of its production process, and that direct labor and factory overhead are added uniformly throughout the process.

Goods in process inventory, September 1 (4,000 units, 100% complete with respect to direct materials, 80% complete with respect to direct labor and overhead; includes $90,000 of direct material cost, $51,200 in direct labor cost, $61,440 overhead cost)	$202,640
Units started in September	56,000
Units completed and transferred to finished goods inventory	46,000
Goods in process inventory, September 30 (? units, 100% complete with respect to direct materials, 40% complete with respect to direct labor and overhead)	?

[continued on next page]

[continued from previous page]

Costs incurred in September	
Direct materials	$750,000
Direct labor	$310,000
Overhead applied at 120% of direct labor cost	?

Required

Fill in the blanks labeled *a* through *uu* in the following process cost summary.

NU-TEST COMPANY
Process Cost Summary
For Month Ended September 30

Costs Charged to Production

Costs of beginning goods in process		
Direct materials	$ 90,000	
Direct labor	51,200	
Factory overhead	61,440	$202,640
Costs incurred this period		
Direct materials	$750,000	
Direct labor	310,000	
Factory overhead	(a)____	(b)____
Total costs to account for		(c)____

Check (c) $1,634,640

Unit Cost Information

Units to account for		Units accounted for	
Beginning goods in process	4,000	Completed and transferred out	46,000
Units started this period	56,000	Ending goods in process	(d)____
Total units to account for	(e)____	Total units accounted for	(f)____

Equivalent Units of Production (EUP)				**Direct Materials**	**Direct Labor**	**Factory Overhead**
Units completed and transferred out				(g)____EUP	(h)____EUP	(i)____EUP
Units of ending goods in process						
Materials	(j)____	×	100%	(k)____EUP		
Direct labor	(l)____	×	40%		(m)____EUP	
Factory overhead	(n)____	×	40%			(o)____EUP
Equivalent units of production (EUP)				(p)____EUP	(q)____EUP	(r)____EUP

Cost per EUP	**Direct Materials**	**Direct Labor**	**Factory Overhead**
Costs of beginning goods in process	$ 90,000	$ 51,200	$61,440
Costs incurred this period	750,000	310,000	(s)____
Total costs	$840,000	$361,200	(t)____
÷ EUP	(u)____	(v)____	(w)____
Cost per EUP	(x)____	(y)____	(z)____

(z) $8.40 per EUP

Cost Assignment and Reconciliation

	Cost/EUP	×	EUP		
Costs transferred out					
Direct materials	(aa)____	×	(bb)____	(cc)____	
Direct labor	(dd)____	×	(ee)____	(ff)____	
Factory overhead	(gg)____	×	(hh)____	(ii)____	
Costs of goods completed and transferred out					(jj)____
Costs of ending goods in process					
Direct materials	(kk)____	×	(ll)____	(mm)____	
Direct labor	(nn)____	×	(oo)____	(pp)____	
Factory overhead	(qq)____	×	(rr)____	(ss)____	
Costs of ending goods in process					(tt)____
Total costs accounted for					(uu)____

Most materials in this section are available in McGraw-Hill's Connect connect

PROBLEM SET A

Problem 3-1A

Production cost flow and measurement; journal entries

P1 P2 P3 P6

Harvey Company manufactures woven blankets and accounts for product costs using process costing. The following information is available regarding its May inventories.

	Beginning Inventory	Ending Inventory
Raw materials inventory	$ 30,000	$ 51,000
Goods in process inventory	441,500	504,000
Finished goods inventory	638,000	554,000

The following additional information describes the company's production activities for May.

Raw materials purchases (on credit)	$ 270,000
Factory payroll cost (paid in cash)	1,583,000
Other overhead cost (Other Accounts credited)	86,000
Materials used	
Direct	$ 187,000
Indirect	62,000
Labor used	
Direct	$ 704,000
Indirect	879,000
Overhead rate as a percent of direct labor	110%
Sales (on credit)	$3,000,000

Required

Check (1b) Cost of goods sold $1,686,900

1. Compute the cost of (a) products transferred from production to finished goods, and (b) goods sold.

2. Prepare summary journal entries dated May 31 to record the following production activities during May: (a) raw materials purchases, (b) direct materials usage, (c) indirect materials usage, (d) payroll costs, (e) direct labor costs, (f) indirect labor costs, (g) other overhead costs, (h) overhead applied, (i) goods transferred from production to finished goods, and (j) sale of finished goods.

Problem 3-2A

Cost per equivalent unit; costs assigned to products

P4 P5

mhhe.com/wildMA2e

Carmen Company uses weighted-average process costing to account for its production costs. Direct labor is added evenly throughout the process. Direct materials are added at the beginning of the process. During November, the company transferred 735,000 units of product to finished goods. At the end of November, the goods in process inventory consists of 207,000 units that are 90% complete with respect to labor. Beginning inventory had $244,920 of direct materials and $69,098 of direct labor cost. The direct labor cost added in November is $1,312,852, and the direct materials cost added is $1,639,080.

Required

1. Determine the equivalent units of production with respect to (a) direct labor and (b) direct materials.

Check (2) Direct labor cost per equivalent unit, $1.50

(3b) $693,450

2. Compute both the direct labor cost and the direct materials cost per equivalent unit.

3. Compute both direct labor cost and direct materials cost assigned to (a) units completed and transferred out, and (b) ending goods in process inventory.

Analysis Component

4. The company sells and ships all units to customers as soon as they are completed. Assume that an error is made in determining the percentage of completion for units in ending inventory. Instead of being 90% complete with respect to labor, they are actually 75% complete. Write a one-page memo to the plant manager describing how this error affects its November financial statements.

Problem 3-3A
Journalizing in process costing; equivalent units and costs

P1 P2 P3 P4 P6

Crystal Company produces large quantities of a standardized product. The following information is available for its production activities for March.

Raw materials		**Factory overhead incurred**	
Beginning inventory	$ 26,000	Indirect materials used	$ 81,500
Raw materials purchased (on credit)	255,000	Indirect labor used	50,000
Direct materials used	(172,000)	Other overhead costs	159,308
Indirect materials used	(81,500)	Total factory overhead incurred	$290,808
Ending inventory	$ 27,500		
Factory payroll		**Factory overhead applied (140% of direct labor cost)**	
Direct labor used	$207,720	Total factory overhead applied	$290,808
Indirect labor used	50,000		
Total payroll cost (paid in cash)	$257,720		

Additional information about units and costs of production activities follows.

Units		**Costs**		
Beginning goods in process inventory	2,200	Beginning goods in process inventory		
Started	30,000	Direct materials	$3,500	
Ending goods in process inventory	5,900	Direct labor	3,225	
		Factory overhead	4,515	$ 11,240
Status of ending goods in process inventory		Direct materials added		172,000
Materials—Percent complete	50%	Direct labor added		207,720
Labor and overhead—Percent complete	65%	Overhead applied (140% of direct labor)		290,808
		Total costs		$681,768
		Ending goods in process inventory		$ 82,128

During March, 25,000 units of finished goods are sold for $85 cash each. Cost information regarding finished goods follows.

Beginning finished goods inventory	$155,000
Cost transferred in	599,640
Cost of goods sold	(612,500)
Ending finished goods inventory	$142,140

Required

1. Prepare journal entries dated March 31 to record the following March activities: (a) purchase of raw materials, (b) direct materials usage, (c) indirect materials usage, (d) factory payroll costs, (e) direct labor costs used in production, (f) indirect labor costs, (g) other overhead costs—credit Other Accounts, (h) overhead applied, (i) goods transferred to finished goods, and (j) sale of finished goods.

2. Prepare a process cost summary report for this company, showing costs charged to production, units cost information, equivalent units of production, cost per EUP, and its cost assignment and reconciliation.

Check (2) Cost per equivalent unit: materials, $6.00; labor, $7.00; overhead, $9.80

Analysis Component

3. The company provides incentives to its department managers by paying monthly bonuses based on their success in controlling costs per equivalent unit of production. Assume that the production department underestimates the percentage of completion for units in ending inventory with the result that its equivalent units of production in ending inventory for March are understated. What impact does this error have on the March bonuses paid to the production managers? What impact, if any, does this error have on April bonuses?

Problem 3-4A
Process cost summary; equivalent units
P4 P5 P6

mhhe.com/wildMA2e

King Co. produces its product through a single processing department. Direct materials are added at the start of production, and direct labor and overhead are added evenly throughout the process. The company uses monthly reporting periods for its weighted-average process cost accounting system. Its Goods in Process Inventory account follows after entries for direct materials, direct labor, and overhead costs for October.

Goods in Process Inventory					Acct. No. 133
Date		Explanation	Debit	Credit	Balance
Oct.	1	Balance			348,638
	31	Direct materials	104,090		452,728
	31	Direct labor	416,360		869,088
	31	Applied overhead	244,920		1,114,008

Its beginning goods in process consisted of $60,830 of direct materials, $176,820 of direct labor, and $110,988 of factory overhead. During October, the company started 140,000 units and transferred 153,000 units to finished goods. At the end of the month, the goods in process inventory consisted of 20,600 units that were 80% complete with respect to direct labor and factory overhead.

Required

Check (1) Costs transferred to finished goods, $1,002,150

1. Prepare the company's process cost summary for October using the weighted-average method.
2. Prepare the journal entry dated October 31 to transfer the cost of the completed units to finished goods inventory.

Problem 3-5A
Process cost summary; equivalent units; cost estimates
P4 P5 

Cisneros Co. manufactures a single product in one department. All direct materials are added at the beginning of the manufacturing process. Direct labor and overhead are added evenly throughout the process. The company uses monthly reporting periods for its weighted-average process cost accounting. During May, the company completed and transferred 11,100 units of product to finished goods inventory. Its 1,500 units of beginning goods in process consisted of $9,900 of direct materials, $61,650 of direct labor, and $49,320 of factory overhead. It has 1,200 units (100% complete with respect to direct materials and 80% complete with respect to direct labor and overhead) in process at month-end. After entries to record direct materials, direct labor, and overhead for May, the company's Goods in Process Inventory account follows.

Goods in Process Inventory					Acct. No. 133
Date		Explanation	Debit	Credit	Balance
May	1	Balance			120,870
	31	Direct materials	248,400		369,270
	31	Direct labor	601,650		970,920
	31	Applied overhead	481,320		1,452,240

Required

Check (1) EUP for labor and overhead, 12,060 EUP

(2) Cost transferred to finished goods, $1,332,000

1. Prepare the company's process cost summary for May.
2. Prepare the journal entry dated May 31 to transfer the cost of completed units to finished goods inventory.

Analysis Components

3. The cost accounting process depends on numerous estimates.
  a. Identify two major estimates that determine the cost per equivalent unit.
  b. In what direction might you anticipate a bias from management for each estimate in part 3a (assume that management compensation is based on maintaining low inventory amounts)? Explain your answer.

Problem 3-6A[A]
Process cost summary; equivalent units; cost estimates—FIFO
C5 P5 P6

Refer to the data in Problem 3-5A. Assume that Cisneros uses the FIFO method to account for its process costing system. The following additional information is available:

- Beginning goods in process consisted of 1,500 units that were 100% complete with respect to direct materials and 40% complete with respect to direct labor and overhead.
- Of the 11,100 units completed, 1,500 were from beginning goods in process. The remaining 9,600 were units started and completed during May.

Required

1. Prepare the company's process cost summary for May using FIFO.
2. Prepare the journal entry dated May 31 to transfer the cost of completed units to finished goods inventory.

Check (1) EUP for labor and overhead, 11,460 EUP

(2) Cost transferred to finished goods, $1,333,920

PROBLEM SET B

Problem 3-1B
Production cost flow and measurement; journal entries

P1 P2 P3 P6

Select Toys Company manufactures video game consoles and accounts for product costs using process costing. The following information is available regarding its June inventories.

	Beginning Inventory	Ending Inventory
Raw materials inventory	$36,000	$ 55,000
Goods in process inventory	78,000	125,000
Finished goods inventory	80,000	99,000

The following additional information describes the company's production activities for June.

Raw materials purchases (on credit)	$100,000
Factory payroll cost (paid in cash)	200,000
Other overhead cost (Other Accounts credited)	85,250
Materials used	
Direct	$ 60,000
Indirect	21,000
Labor used	
Direct	$175,000
Indirect	25,000
Overhead rate as a percent of direct labor	75%
Sales (on credit)	$500,000

Required

1. Compute the cost of (a) products transferred from production to finished goods, and (b) goods sold.
2. Prepare journal entries dated June 30 to record the following production activities during June: (a) raw materials purchases, (b) direct materials usage, (c) indirect materials usage, (d) payroll costs, (e) direct labor costs, (f) indirect labor costs, (g) other overhead costs, (h) overhead applied, (i) goods transferred from production to finished goods, and (j) sale of finished goods.

Check (1b) Cost of goods sold, $300,250

Problem 3-2B
Cost per equivalent unit; costs assigned to products

P4 P5

Maximus Company uses process costing to account for its production costs. Direct labor is added evenly throughout the process. Direct materials are added at the beginning of the process. During September, the production department transferred 40,000 units of product to finished goods. Beginning goods in process had $116,000 of direct materials and $172,800 of direct labor cost. At the end of September, the goods in process inventory consists of 4,000 units that are 25% complete with respect to labor. The direct materials cost added in September is $1,424,000, and direct labor cost added is $3,960,000.

Required

1. Determine the equivalent units of production with respect to (a) direct labor and (b) direct materials.
2. Compute both the direct labor cost and the direct materials cost per equivalent unit.
3. Compute both direct labor cost and direct materials cost assigned to (a) units completed and transferred out, and (b) ending goods in process inventory.

Check (2) Direct labor cost per equivalent unit, $100.80

(3b) $240,800

Analysis Component

4. The company sells and ships all units to customers as soon as they are completed. Assume that an error is made in determining the percentage of completion for units in ending inventory. Instead of being 25% complete with respect to labor, they are actually 75% complete. Write a one-page memo to the plant manager describing how this error affects its September financial statements.

Problem 3-3B

Journalizing in process costing; equivalent units and costs

P1 P2 P3 P4 P6 

Fantasia Company produces large quantities of a standardized product. The following information is available for its production activities for May.

Raw materials		**Factory overhead incurred**	
Beginning inventory	$ 16,000	Indirect materials used	$20,280
Raw materials purchased (on credit)	110,560	Indirect labor used	18,160
Direct materials used	(98,560)	Other overhead costs	17,216
Indirect materials used	(20,280)	Total factory overhead incurred	$55,656
Ending inventory	$ 7,720	**Factory overhead applied (90% of direct labor cost)**	
Factory payroll		Total factory overhead applied	$55,656
Direct labor used	$ 61,840		
Indirect labor used	18,160		
Total payroll cost (paid in cash)	$ 80,000		

Additional information about units and costs of production activities follows.

Units		**Costs**		
Beginning goods in process inventory	8,000	Beginning goods in process inventory		
Started	24,000	Direct materials	$2,240	
Ending goods in process inventory	6,000	Direct labor	1,410	
		Factory overhead	1,269	$ 4,919
Status of ending goods in process inventory		Direct materials added		98,560
Materials—Percent complete	100%	Direct labor added		61,840
Labor and overhead—Percent complete	25%	Overhead applied (90% of direct labor)		55,656
		Total costs		$220,975
		Ending goods in process inventory		$ 25,455

During May, 30,000 units of finished goods are sold for $30 cash each. Cost information regarding finished goods follows.

Beginning finished goods inventory	$ 74,200
Cost transferred in from production	195,520
Cost of goods sold	(225,000)
Ending finished goods inventory	$ 44,720

Required

1. Prepare journal entries dated May 31 to record the following May activities: (a) purchase of raw materials, (b) direct materials usage, (c) indirect materials usage, (d) factory payroll costs, (e) direct labor costs used in production, (f) indirect labor costs, (g) other overhead costs—credit Other Accounts, (h) overhead applied, (i) goods transferred to finished goods, and (j) sale of finished goods.

2. Prepare a process cost summary report for this company, showing costs charged to production, unit cost information, equivalent units of production, cost per EUP, and its cost assignment and reconciliation.

Check (2) Cost per equivalent unit: materials, $3.15; labor, $2.30; overhead, $2.07

Analysis Component

3. This company provides incentives to its department managers by paying monthly bonuses based on their success in controlling costs per equivalent unit of production. Assume that production overestimates the percentage of completion for units in ending inventory with the result that its equivalent units of production in ending inventory for May are overstated. What impact does this error have on bonuses paid to the managers of the production department? What impact, if any, does this error have on these managers' June bonuses?

Problem 3-4B
Process cost summary; equivalent units
P4 P5 P6

Paloma Company produces its product through a single processing department. Direct materials are added at the beginning of the process. Direct labor and overhead are added to the product evenly throughout the process. The company uses monthly reporting periods for its weighted-average process cost accounting. Its Goods in Process Inventory account follows after entries for direct materials, direct labor, and overhead costs for November.

Goods in Process Inventory					Acct. No. 133
Date		Explanation	Debit	Credit	Balance
Nov.	1	Balance			10,650
	30	Direct materials	58,200		68,850
	30	Direct labor	213,400		282,250
	30	Applied overhead	320,100		602,350

The 3,750 units of beginning goods in process consisted of $3,400 of direct materials, $2,900 of direct labor, and $4,350 of factory overhead. During November, the company finished and transferred 50,000 units of its product to finished goods. At the end of the month, the goods in process inventory consisted of 6,000 units that were 100% complete with respect to direct materials and 25% complete with respect to direct labor and factory overhead.

Required

1. Prepare the company's process cost summary for November using the weighted-average method.
2. Prepare the journal entry dated November 30 to transfer the cost of the completed units to finished goods inventory.

Check (1) Cost transferred to finished goods, $580,000

Problem 3-5B
Process cost summary; equivalent units; cost estimates
P4 P5 

Foster Co. manufactures a single product in one department. Direct labor and overhead are added evenly throughout the process. Direct materials are added as needed. The company uses monthly reporting periods for its weighted-average process cost accounting. During January, Foster completed and transferred 220,000 units of product to finished goods inventory. Its 10,000 units of beginning goods in process consisted of $8,400 of direct materials, $13,960 of direct labor, and $34,900 of factory overhead. 40,000 units (50% complete with respect to direct materials and 30% complete with respect to direct labor and overhead) are in process at month-end. After entries for direct materials, direct labor, and overhead for January, the company's Goods in Process Inventory account follows.

Goods in Process Inventory					Acct. No. 133
Date		Explanation	Debit	Credit	Balance
Jan.	1	Balance			57,260
	31	Direct materials	111,600		168,860
	31	Direct labor	176,280		345,140
	31	Applied overhead	440,700		785,840

Required

1. Prepare the company's process cost summary for January.
2. Prepare the journal entry dated January 31 to transfer the cost of completed units to finished goods inventory.

Check (1) EUP for labor and overhead, 232,000
(2) Cost transferred to finished goods, $741,400

Analysis Components

3. The cost accounting process depends on several estimates.
   a. Identify two major estimates that affect the cost per equivalent unit.
   b. In what direction might you anticipate a bias from management for each estimate in part 3a (assume that management compensation is based on maintaining low inventory amounts)? Explain your answer.

Problem 3-6B[A]
Process cost summary; equivalent units; cost estimates—FIFO
C5 P5 P6

Refer to the information in Problem 3-5B. Assume that Foster uses the FIFO method to account for its process costing system. The following additional information is available.

- Beginning goods in process consists of 10,000 units that were 75% complete with respect to direct materials and 60% complete with respect to direct labor and overhead.
- Of the 220,000 units completed, 10,000 were from beginning goods in process; the remaining 210,000 were units started and completed during January.

Required

1. Prepare the company's process cost summary for January using FIFO. Round cost per EUP to one-tenth of a cent.
2. Prepare the journal entry dated January 31 to transfer the cost of completed units to finished goods inventory.

Check (1) Labor and overhead EUP, 226,000
(2) Cost transferred, $743,480

SERIAL PROBLEM

Success Systems
C1 A1

(This serial problem began in Chapter 1 and continues through most of the book. If previous chapter segments were not completed, the serial problem can begin at this point.)

SP 3 The computer workstation furniture manufacturing that Adriana Lopez started is progressing well. At this point, Adriana is using a job order costing system to account for the production costs of this product line. Adriana has heard about process costing and is wondering whether process costing might be a better method for her to keep track of and monitor her production costs.

Required

1. What are the features that distinguish job order costing from process costing?
2. Do you believe that Adriana should continue to use job order costing or switch to process costing for her workstation furniture manufacturing? Explain.

COMPREHENSIVE PROBLEM

Major League Bat Company
(Review of Chapters 1, 3)

CP 3 Major League Bat Company manufactures baseball bats. In addition to its goods in process inventories, the company maintains inventories of raw materials and finished goods. It uses raw materials as direct materials in production and as indirect materials. Its factory payroll costs include direct labor for production and indirect labor. All materials are added at the beginning of the process, and direct labor and factory overhead are applied uniformly throughout the production process.

Required

You are to maintain records and produce measures of inventories to reflect the July events of this company. Set up the following general ledger accounts and enter the June 30 balances: Raw Materials Inventory, $25,000; Goods in Process Inventory, $8,135 ($2,660 of direct materials, $3,650 of direct labor, and $1,825 of overhead); Finished Goods Inventory, $110,000; Sales, $0; Cost of Goods Sold, $0; Factory Payroll, $0; and Factory Overhead, $0.

1. Prepare journal entries to record the following July transactions and events.
   - **a.** Purchased raw materials for $125,000 cash (the company uses a perpetual inventory system).
   - **b.** Used raw materials as follows: direct materials, $52,440; and indirect materials, $10,000.
   - **c.** Incurred factory payroll cost of $227,250 paid in cash (ignore taxes).
   - **d.** Assigned factory payroll costs as follows: direct labor, $202,250; and indirect labor, $25,000.
   - **e.** Incurred additional factory overhead costs of $80,000 paid in cash.
   - **f.** Allocated factory overhead to production at 50% of direct labor costs.
2. Information about the July inventories follows. Use this information with that from part 1 to prepare a process cost summary, assuming the weighted-average method is used.

Check (1f) Cr. Factory Overhead, $101,125

Check (2) EUP for overhead, 14,200

Units	
Beginning inventory	5,000 units
Started	14,000 units
Ending inventory	8,000 units
Beginning inventory	
Materials—Percent complete	100%
Labor and overhead—Percent complete	75%
Ending inventory	
Materials—Percent complete	100%
Labor and overhead—Percent complete	40%

3. Using the results from part 2 and the available information, make computations and prepare journal entries to record the following:
   a. Total costs transferred to finished goods for July (label this entry g). (3a) $271,150
   b. Sale of finished goods costing $265,700 for $625,000 in cash (label this entry h).
4. Post entries from parts 1 and 3 to the ledger accounts set up at the beginning of the problem.
5. Compute the amount of gross profit from the sales in July. (*Note:* Add any underapplied overhead to, or deduct any overapplied overhead from, the cost of goods sold. Ignore the corresponding journal entry.)

BEYOND THE NUMBERS

REPORTING IN ACTION

C2 

BTN 3-1 Best Buy reports in notes to its financial statements that, in addition to its merchandise sold, it includes the following costs (among others) in cost of goods sold: freight expenses associated with moving inventories from vendors to distribution centers, costs of services provided, customer shipping and handling expenses, costs associated with operating its distribution network, and freight expenses associated with moving merchandise from distribution centers to retail stores.

Required

1. Why do you believe Best Buy includes these costs in its cost of goods sold?
2. What effect does this cost accounting policy for its cost of goods sold have on Best Buy's financial statements and any analysis of these statements? Explain.

Fast Forward

3. Access Best Buy's financial statements for the fiscal years after March 3, 2007, from its Website (BestBuy.com) or the SEC's EDGAR Website (sec.gov). Review its footnote relating to Cost of Goods Sold and Selling, General, and Administrative Expense. Has Best Buy changed its policy with respect to what costs are included in the cost of goods sold? Explain.

COMPARATIVE ANALYSIS

C1

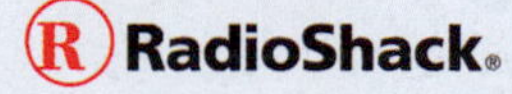

BTN 3-2 Retailers such as Best Buy, Circuit City, and RadioShack usually work to maintain a high-quality and low-cost operation. One ratio routinely computed for this assessment is the cost of goods sold divided by total expenses. A decline in this ratio can mean that the company is spending too much on selling and administrative activities. An increase in this ratio beyond a reasonable level can mean that the company is not spending enough on selling activities. (Assume for this analysis that total expenses equal the cost of goods sold plus selling, general, and administrative expenses.)

Required

1. For Best Buy, Circuit City, and RadioShack refer to Appendix A and compute the ratios of cost of goods sold to total expenses for their two most recent fiscal years.
2. Comment on the similarities or differences in the ratio results across both years among the companies.

ETHICS CHALLENGE

C1 C3

BTN 3-3 Many accounting and accounting-related professionals are skilled in financial analysis, but most are not skilled in manufacturing. This is especially the case for process manufacturing environments (for example, a bottling plant or chemical factory). To provide professional accounting and financial services, one must understand the industry, product, and processes. We have an ethical responsibility to develop this understanding before offering services to clients in these areas.

Required

Write a one-page action plan, in memorandum format, discussing how you would obtain an understanding of key business processes of a company that hires you to provide financial services. The memorandum should specify an industry, a product, and one selected process and should draw on at least one reference, such as a professional journal or industry magazine.

COMMUNICATING IN PRACTICE

A1 C1 P1 P2

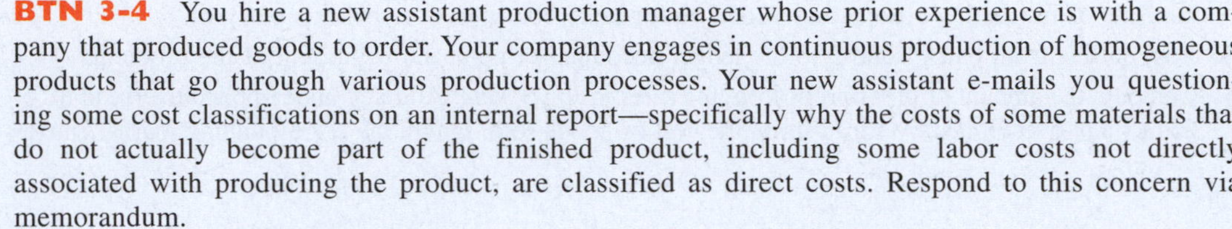

BTN 3-4 You hire a new assistant production manager whose prior experience is with a company that produced goods to order. Your company engages in continuous production of homogeneous products that go through various production processes. Your new assistant e-mails you questioning some cost classifications on an internal report—specifically why the costs of some materials that do not actually become part of the finished product, including some labor costs not directly associated with producing the product, are classified as direct costs. Respond to this concern via memorandum.

TAKING IT TO THE NET

C1 C3

BTN 3-5 Many companies acquire software to help them monitor and control their costs and as an aid to their accounting systems. One company that supplies such software is proDacapo (prodacapo.com). There are many other such vendors. Access proDacapo's Website, click on "Business Process Management," and review the information displayed.

Required

How is process management software helpful to businesses? Explain with reference to costs, efficiency, and examples, if possible.

TEAMWORK IN ACTION

C1 P1 P2 P3 P6

BTN 3-6 The purpose of this team activity is to ensure that each team member understands process operations and the related accounting entries. Find the activities and flows identified in Exhibit 3.4 with numbers ①–⑩. Pick a member of the team to start by describing activity number ① in this exhibit, then verbalizing the related journal entry, and describing how the amounts in the entry are computed. The other members of the team are to agree or disagree; discussion is to continue until all members express understanding. Rotate to the next numbered activity and next team member until all activities and entries have been discussed. If at any point a team member is uncertain about an answer, the team member may pass and get back in the rotation when he or she can contribute to the team's discussion.

ENTREPRENEURIAL DECISION

C4 A2

BTN 3-7 Read the chapter opener about Hood River Juice Company. David Ryan explained that purchasing apples year-round and processing them immediately reduces costs, and that his company blends juices to fit customer needs.

Required

1. How does not holding raw materials inventories (apples) reduce costs? If the items are not used in production, how can they affect profits? Explain.
2. Explain why Hood River Juice Company might use a hybrid costing system.

BTN 3-8 In process costing, the process is analyzed first and then a unit measure is computed in the form of equivalent units for direct materials, direct labor, overhead, and all three combined. The same analysis applies to both manufacturing and service processes.

HITTING THE ROAD

C3 

Point: The class can compare and discuss the different processes studied and the answers provided.

Required

Visit your local **U.S. Mail** center. Look into the back room, and you will see several ongoing processes. Select one process, such as sorting, and list the costs associated with this process. Your list should include materials, labor, and overhead; be specific. Classify each cost as fixed or variable. At the bottom of your list, outline how overhead should be assigned to your identified process. The following format (with an example) is suggested.

Cost Description	Direct Material	Direct Labor	Overhead	Variable Cost	Fixed Cost
Manual sorting		X		X	
⋮					
Overhead allocation suggestions:					

BTN 3-9 DSG international plc, Best Buy, Circuit City, and RadioShack are competitors in the global marketplace. Selected data for DSG follow.

GLOBAL DECISION

C1 

(millions of pounds)	Current Year	Prior Year
Cost of goods sold	£7,285	£6,369
General, selling, and administrative expenses	381	339
Total expenses	£7,666	£6,708

Required

1. Review the discussion of the importance of the cost of goods sold divided by total expenses ratio in BTN 3-2. Compute the cost of goods sold to total expenses ratio for DSG for the two years of data provided.

2. Comment on the similarities or differences in the ratio results calculated in part 1 and in BTN 3-2 across years and companies.

ANSWERS TO MULTIPLE CHOICE QUIZ

1. d

2. e

3. b; $20,000 + $152,000 + $45,000 + $18,000 − $218,000 = $17,000

4. a; 40,000 + (15,000 × 1/3) = 45,000 EUP

5. c; ($6,000 + $84,000) ÷ 45,000 EUP = $2 per EUP

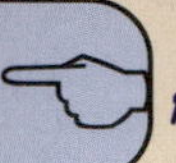

A Look Back

Chapters 2 and 3 described costing systems used by companies to accumulate product costing information for the reporting of inventories and cost of goods sold.

A Look at This Chapter

This chapter introduces the activity-based costing (ABC) system with the potential for greater accuracy of cost allocations. ABC provides managers with cost information for strategic decisions that is not readily available with other costing methods.

A Look Ahead

Chapter 5 discusses the importance of information on both costs and sales behavior for managers in performing cost-volume-profit (CVP) analysis, which is a valuable managerial tool.

Chapter 4

Activity-Based Costing and Analysis

Learning Objectives

CAP

Conceptual

C1 Distinguish between the plantwide overhead rate method, the departmental overhead rate method, and the activity-based costing method. *(p. 130)*

C2 Explain cost flows for the plantwide overhead rate method. *(p. 131)*

C3 Explain cost flows for the departmental overhead rate method. *(p. 133)*

C4 Explain cost flows for activity-based costing. *(p. 135)*

Analytical

A1 Identify and assess advantages and disadvantages of the plantwide overhead rate method. *(p. 132)*

A2 Identify and assess advantages and disadvantages of the departmental overhead rate method. *(p. 134)*

A3 Identify and assess advantages and disadvantages of activity-based costing. *(p. 142)*

Procedural

P1 Allocate overhead costs to products using the plantwide overhead rate method. *(p. 131)*

P2 Allocate overhead costs to products using the departmental overhead rate method. *(p. 133)*

P3 Allocate overhead costs to products using activity-based costing. *(p. 136)*

Decision Feature

Creaming Success

"We're ice cream guys ... we can be successful!"
—Tom Gleason

EUGENE, OR—Shortly after taking over a small ice cream company, owner Tom Gleason was distressed to keep finding a competitor's ice cream in his refrigerator. His wife, Julie, wanted something different. Julie asked Tom to make ice cream "pure, from the best ingredients, no preservatives, no pesticides, child friendly, and . . . indulgent." From that directive, began a new path for his **Oregon Ice Cream Company (OregonIceCream.com)**.

Tom's company now offers many exotic temptations: Espresso Explosion, Huckleberry Heaven, Mt. St. Helen's Mud Pie, and Extreme Moose Tracks, to name just a few. However, product quality, innovation, and production efficiency are key ingredients in its success. And, a special line, labeled *Julie's Organic Ice Cream,* uses certified organic cream and organically grown fresh fruit and sugar. To make it all happen, Tom uses a state-of-the-art information system to monitor and regulate its production machinery. In the spirit of continuous improvement, Tom explains that they "developed an extrusion process that produces an [ice cream] texture that is better than molded alternatives."

With its new, extensive line of products, the managers must be adept at interpreting product cost summaries. As Brian Cobb, director of production puts it, "I'm all about dollars, gallons, and time." Tom insists that without good cost and production process controls, his income would quickly evaporate. Activity-based costing (ABC) procedures help his managers monitor and control costs and ensure product quality. ABC is especially useful in companies such as Tom's, where different products require different processes and varying levels of overhead. For example, *Julie's Organic* is made in small batches, while chocolate and vanilla are made in large production runs. Further, ice cream sandwiches and dessert bars require different machine and labor activities, and ABC helps in allocating overhead costs, such as research and development, plant maintenance and clean-up crew costs, to the different products.

The Oregon Ice Cream Company recipe is working. Each week, cream, sugar, skim milk, powder and wafers arrive at the company's ice cream assembly plant. There, the company runs two production shifts per day, six days per week, all year long, to meet increasing customer demand. Sales of *Julie's Organic Ice Cream* have increased ten-fold in recent years, making Oregon Ice Cream Company the top ice cream producer in the Northwest and the number one organic ice cream maker in the country. Importantly, Tom no longer finds competitors' ice cream in his freezer. "[But] we are just getting started," proclaims Tom. "Our goal is to be the predominant super-premium organic ice cream."

[Sources: *Oregon Ice Cream Company Website*, January 2009; *The Register-Guard*, December 2007; *Mail Tribune*, September 2004; *Dairyfoods.com*, January 2008]

Chapter Preview

Prior chapters described costing systems used to assign costs to product units. This discussion emphasized the valuation of inventory and the cost of goods sold. Although the information from these prior costing systems conform to generally accepted accounting principles (GAAP) for external reporting, it has limitations. This chapter introduces the activity-based costing (ABC) system, which is used by managers who desire more accurate product cost information.

Activity-Based Costing and Analysis

Assigning Overhead Costs
- Single plantwide overhead rate method
- Multiple departmental overhead rate method
- Activity-based costing rates and method

Applying Activity-Based Costing
- Step 1 Identify activities and cost pools
- Step 2 Trace overhead costs to cost pools
- Step 3 Determine activity rate
- Step 4 Assign overhead costs to cost objects

Assessing Activity-Based Costing
- Advantages of activity-based costing
- Disadvantages of activity-based costing

Assigning Overhead Costs

C1 Distinguish between the plantwide overhead rate method, the departmental overhead rate method, and the activity-based costing method.

Managerial activities such as product pricing, product mix decisions, and cost control depend on accurate product cost information. Distorted product cost information can result in poor decisions. Knowing accurate costs for producing, delivering, and servicing products helps managers set a price to cover product costs and yield a profit.

In competitive markets, price is established through the forces of supply and demand. In these situations, managers must understand product costs to assess whether the market price is high enough to justify the cost of entering the market. Disparities between market prices and producer costs give managers insight into their efficiency relative to competitors.

Product costs consist of direct materials, direct labor, and overhead (indirect costs). Since the physical components of a product (direct materials) and the work of making a product (direct labor) can be traced to units of output, the assignment of costs of these factors is usually straightforward. Overhead costs, however, are not directly related to production volume, and therefore cannot be traced to units of product in the same way that direct materials and direct labor can.

For example, we can trace the cost of putting tires on a car because we know there is a logical relation between the number of cars produced and the number of tires needed for each car. The cost to heat an automobile manufacturing factory, however, is not readily linked with the number of cars made. Consequently, we must use an allocation system to assign overhead costs such as utilities and factory maintenance. This chapter introduces three methods of overhead allocation: (1) the single plantwide overhead rate method, (2) the departmental overhead rate method, and (3) the activity-based costing method. It then explains the activity-based system in detail.

The *plantwide overhead rate method* uses a single rate for allocating overhead costs to products. This rate is a volume-based measure such as direct labor hours, direct labor dollars, or machine hours. The *departmental overhead rate method* uses multiple volume-based measures to allocate overhead costs to products. This method arguably improves on the single rate allocations of the plantwide method. *Activity-based costing* focuses on activities and the costs of carrying out activities (organized into cost pools). Rates based on these activities are then used to assign overhead to products in proportion to the amount of activity required to produce them.

Plantwide Overhead Rate Method

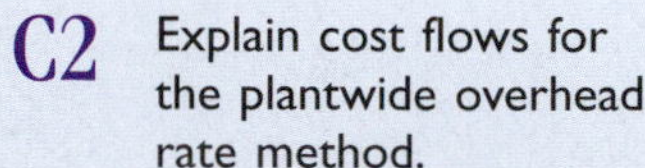

C2
Explain cost flows for the plantwide overhead rate method.

Cost Flows under Plantwide Overhead Rate Method The first method is known as the *single plantwide overhead rate method,* or simply the *plantwide overhead rate method,* for allocating overhead costs to products. For this method, the target of the cost assignment, or **cost object,** is the unit of product—see Exhibit 4.1. The rate is determined using volume-related measures such as direct labor hours, direct labor cost dollars, or machine hours, which are readily available in most manufacturing settings. In some industries, overhead costs are closely related to these volume-related measures. In such cases it is logical to use this method as a basis for assigning indirect manufacturing costs to products.

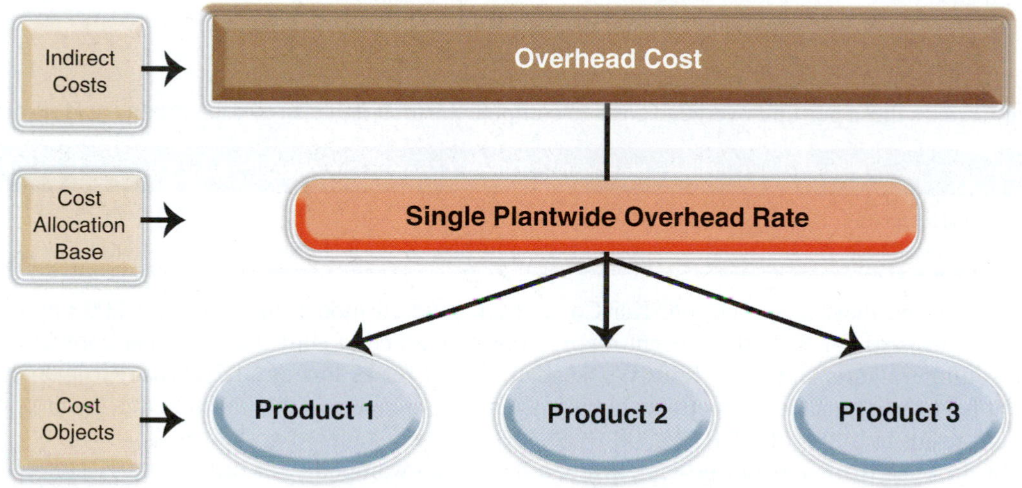

EXHIBIT 4.1

Plantwide Overhead Rate Method

P1 Allocate overhead costs to products using the plantwide overhead rate method.

Applying the Plantwide Overhead Rate Method Under the single plantwide overhead rate method, total budgeted overhead costs are combined into one overhead cost pool. This cost pool is then divided by the chosen allocation base, such as total direct labor hours, to arrive at a single plantwide overhead rate. This rate then is applied to assign costs to all products based on the allocation base such as direct labor hours required to manufacture each product.

To illustrate, consider data from KartCo, a go-kart manufacturer that produces both standard and custom go-karts for amusement parks. The standard go-kart is a basic model sold primarily to amusement parks that service county and state fairs. Custom go-karts are produced for theme parks who want unique go-karts that coordinate with their respective themes.

Assume that KartCo applies the plantwide overhead rate method and uses direct labor hours (DLH) as its overhead allocation base. KartCo's DLH information is in Exhibit 4.2.

EXHIBIT 4.2

KartCo's Budgeted Direct Labor Hours

	Number of Units	Direct Labor Hours per Unit	Total Direct Labor Hours
Standard go-kart . . .	5,000	15	75,000
Custom go-kart . . .	1,000	25	25,000
Total			100,000

KartCo's overhead cost information is in Exhibit 4.3. Its overhead cost consists of indirect labor and factory utilities.

EXHIBIT 4.3

KartCo's Budgeted Overhead Cost

Indirect labor cost	$4,000,000
Factory utilities	800,000
Total overhead cost	$4,800,000

The single plantwide overhead rate for KartCo is computed as follows.

Plantwide overhead rate	=	Total budgeted overhead cost	÷	Total budgeted direct labor hours
	=	$4,800,000	÷	100,000 DLH
	=	$48 per DLH		

This plantwide overhead rate is then used to allocate overhead cost to products based on the number of direct labor hours required to produce each unit as follows.

Overhead allocated to each product unit = Plantwide overhead rate × DLH per unit

For KartCo, overhead cost is allocated to its two products as follows (on a per-unit basis).

Standard go-kart:	$48 per DLH × 15 DLH = $ 720
Custom go-kart:	$48 per DLH × 25 DLH = $1,200

KartCo uses these per-unit overhead costs to compute the total unit cost of each product as follows.

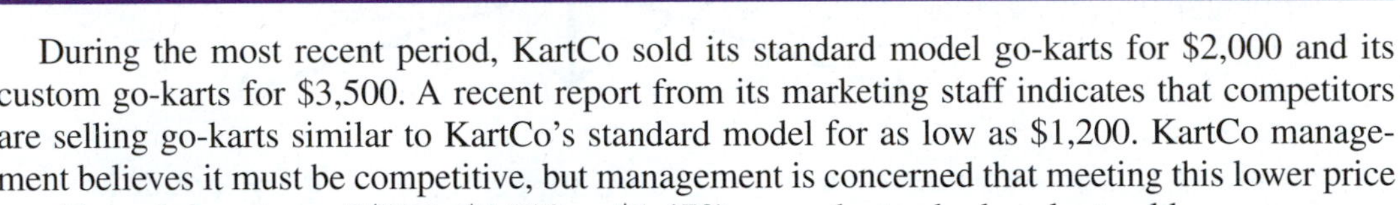

	Direct Materials	Direct Labor	Overhead	Total Cost per Unit
Standard go-kart	$400	$350	$ 720	$1,470
Custom go-kart	600	500	1,200	2,300

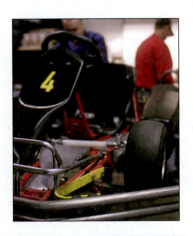

During the most recent period, KartCo sold its standard model go-karts for $2,000 and its custom go-karts for $3,500. A recent report from its marketing staff indicates that competitors are selling go-karts similar to KartCo's standard model for as low as $1,200. KartCo management believes it must be competitive, but management is concerned that meeting this lower price would result in a loss of $270 ($1,200 − $1,470) on each standard go-kart sold.

In the case of its custom go-kart, KartCo has been swamped with orders and is unable to meet demand. Accordingly, management is considering a change in strategy. Some discussion has ensued about dropping its standard model and concentrating on its custom model. Yet management recognizes that its pricing and cost decisions are influenced by its cost assignments. Thus, before making any strategic marketing decisions, management has directed its cost analysts to further review production costs for both the standard and custom go-kart models. To pursue this analysis, we need additional knowledge about this method's advantages and disadvantages, and some insights into alternative cost allocation methods.

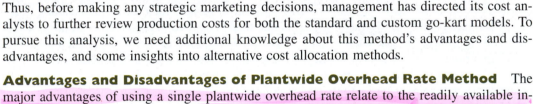

A1 Identify and assess advantages and disadvantages of the plantwide overhead rate method.

Advantages and Disadvantages of Plantwide Overhead Rate Method The major advantages of using a single plantwide overhead rate relate to the readily available information needed to implement this method and its ease of implementation. Also, the plantwide overhead rate method is often sufficient to meet external financial reporting needs.

The usefulness of overhead allocations based on a single plantwide overhead rate for managerial decisions depends on two crucial assumptions: (1) overhead costs correlate (change) with the allocation base such as direct labor hours; and (2) all products use overhead costs in the same proportions.

The reasonableness of these assumptions varies. For companies that manufacture few products or whose operations are labor intensive, overhead allocations based on a single plantwide overhead rate can yield reasonably useful information for managerial decisions. However, for many other companies, such as those with many different products or those with products that use resources in very different ways, the assumptions are dubious. There is also evidence that over the past few decades overhead costs have steadily increased while direct labor costs have decreased as a percentage of total manufacturing cost, which places greater importance on accurate cost allocations.

When overhead costs, such as machinery depreciation, bear little if any relation to direct labor hours used, allocating overhead cost using a single plantwide overhead rate based on direct labor hours can distort product cost and lead to poor managerial decisions. Despite such shortcomings, some companies continue to allocate overhead cost using a single plantwide overhead rate, largely because of its simplicity. Good management decisions often require a more refined allocation method.

Departmental Overhead Rate Method

C3 Explain cost flows for the departmental overhead rate method.

Cost Flows under Departmental Overhead Rate Method Many companies have several departments that produce various products and consume overhead resources in substantially different ways. Under such circumstances, use of a single plantwide overhead rate can produce cost assignments that fail to accurately reflect the cost to manufacture a specific product. In these cases, use of multiple overhead rates can result in better overhead cost allocations and improve management decisions.

The *departmental overhead rate method* uses a different overhead rate for each production department. This is usually done through a two-stage assignment process, each with its different cost objects (target of cost assignment). In the first stage the departments are the cost objects and in the second stage the products are the cost objects (see Exhibit 4.4).

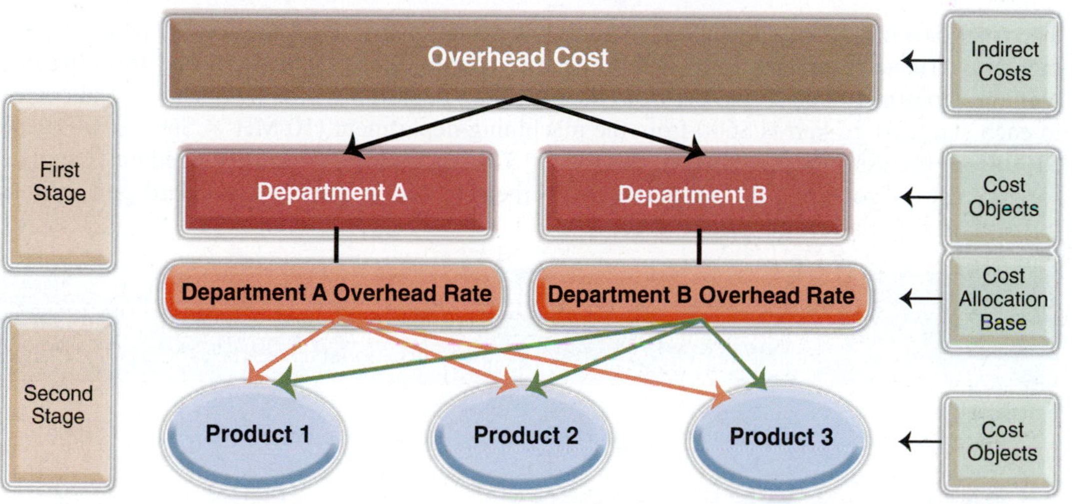

EXHIBIT 4.4
Departmental Overhead Rate Method

Exhibit 4.4 shows that under the departmental overhead rate method, overhead costs are first determined separately for each production department. Next, an overhead rate is computed for each production department to allocate the overhead costs of each department to products passing through that department. The departmental overhead rate method allows each department to have its own overhead rate and its own allocation base. For example, an assembly department can use direct labor hours to allocate its overhead cost while the machining department can use machine hours as its base.

P2 Allocate overhead costs to products using the departmental overhead rate method.

Applying the Departmental Overhead Rate Method To illustrate the departmental overhead rate method, let's return to KartCo. KartCo has two production departments, the machining department and the assembly department. The first stage requires that KartCo assign its $4,800,000 overhead cost to its two production departments. KartCo determines from an analysis of its indirect labor and factory utilities that $4,200,000 of overhead costs are traceable to its machining department and the remaining $600,000 are traceable to its assembly department. In some cases it is difficult for companies to trace overhead costs to distinct departments as some overhead costs can be common to several departments. In these cases, companies must allocate overhead to departments applying reasonable allocation bases.

The second stage demands that after overhead costs are assigned to departments, each department determines an allocation base for its operations. For KartCo, the machining department uses machine hours (MH) as a base for allocating its overhead and the assembly department uses direct labor hours (DLH) as the base for allocating its overhead. For this stage, the relevant information for the machining and assembly departments is in Exhibit 4.5.

EXHIBIT 4.5
Allocation Information for Machining and Assembly Departments

	Number of Units	Machining Department		Assembly Department	
		Hours per Unit	Total Hours	Hours per Unit	Total Hours
Standard go-kart	5,000	10 MH per unit	50,000 MH	5 DLH per unit	25,000 DLH
Custom go-kart	1,000	20 MH per unit	20,000 MH	5 DLH per unit	5,000 DLH
Totals			70,000 MH		30,000 DLH

Each department computes its own overhead rate using the following formula.

$$\textbf{Departmental overhead rate} = \frac{\textbf{Total departmental overhead cost}}{\textbf{Total units in departmental allocation base}}$$

For KartCo, its departmental overhead rates are computed as follows.

$$\text{Machining department overhead rate} = \frac{\$4{,}200{,}000}{70{,}000 \text{ MH}} = \$60 \text{ per MH}$$

$$\text{Assembly department overhead rate} = \frac{\$600{,}000}{30{,}000 \text{ DLH}} = \$20 \text{ per DLH}$$

The final part of the second stage is to apply overhead costs to each product based on departmental overhead rates. For KartCo, since each standard go-kart requires 10 MH from the machining department and five DLH from the assembly department, the overhead cost allocated to each standard go-kart is $600 from the machining department (10 MH × $60 per MH) and $100 from the assembly department (5 DLH × $20 per DLH). The same procedure is applied for its custom go-kart. The allocation of overhead costs to KartCo's standard and custom go-karts is summarized in Exhibit 4.6.

EXHIBIT 4.6

Overhead Allocation Using Departmental Overhead Rates

		Standard Go-Kart		Custom Go-Kart	
	Departmental Overhead Rate	Hours per Unit	Overhead Allocated	Hours per Unit	Overhead Allocated
Machining department	$60 per MH	10 MH per unit	$600	20 MH per unit	$1,200
Assembly department	$20 per DLH	5 DLH per unit	100	5 DLH per unit	100
Totals			$700		$1,300

A2 Identify and assess advantages and disadvantages of the departmental overhead rate method.

Advantages and Disadvantages of Departmental Overhead Rate Method

Allocated overhead costs vary depending upon the allocation methods used. Exhibit 4.7 summarizes and compares the allocated overhead costs for standard and custom go-karts under the single plantwide overhead rate and the departmental overhead rate methods. The overhead cost allocated to each standard go-kart decreased from $720 under the plantwide overhead rate method to $700 under the departmental overhead rate method, whereas overhead cost allocated to each custom go-kart increased from $1,200 to $1,300. These differences occur because the custom go-kart requires more hours in the machining department (20 MH) than the standard go-kart requires (10 MH).

EXHIBIT 4.7

Comparison of Plantwide Overhead Rate and Departmental Overhead Rate Methods

	Standard Go-Kart	Custom Go-Kart
Overhead under plantwide overhead rate method	$720	$1,200
Overhead under departmental overhead rate method	$700	$1,300

Compared to the plantwide overhead rate method, the departmental overhead rate method usually results in more accurate overhead allocations. When cost analysts are able to logically trace costs to cost objects, costing accuracy is improved. For KartCo, costs are traced to departments and then assigned to units based on how long they spend in each department. The single plantwide overhead rate of $48 per hour is a combination of the $60 per hour machining department rate and the $20 per hour assembly department rate.

While the departmental overhead rate method is more refined than the plantwide overhead rate method, it has limitations that can distort product costs. Even though the departmental overhead rate method allows each department to have its own overhead rate, it relies on the premise that different products are similar in volume, complexity, and batch size, and that departmental overhead costs are directly proportional to the department allocation base (such as direct labor hours and machine hours for KartCo). When products differ in batch size and complexity, they usually consume different amounts of overhead resources in terms of machine setup costs, engineering modification costs, and other overhead costs. This is likely the situation for KartCo with its high-volume standard model with basic features vis-à-vis its low-volume custom model built to customer specifications.

More generally, overhead costs are often affected by many issues and are frequently too complex to be explained by one factor like direct labor hours or machine hours. Technological advances also affect direct labor costs, often lowering them as a percentage of total costs. (In some companies, direct labor cost is such a small part of total cost that it is treated as overhead.) Computing multiple overhead rates is an improvement over a single allocation rate based on direct labor. However, because departmental overhead costs are still allocated based on measures closely related to production volume (such as labor hours or machine hours), they too fail to accurately assign many overhead costs that are not driven by production volume such as machine depreciation or utility costs. When the number of jobs, products, and departments increases, the possibility of improperly assigning overhead costs also increases. This can lead to poor managerial decisions and a company's eventual failure.

For KartCo, using the multiple departmental overhead rate method yields the following total costs for its products.

	Direct Materials	Direct Labor	Overhead Total	Cost per Unit
Standard go-kart	$400	$350	$ 700	$1,450
Custom go-kart	600	500	1,300	2,400

These costs per unit under the departmental overhead rate method are different from those under the plantwide overhead rate method. Further, this information suggests that KartCo management seriously review future production for its standard go-kart product. Specifically, these cost data imply that KartCo cannot make a profit on its standard go-kart if it meets competitors' $1,200 price.

Decision Ethics

Department Manager Three department managers jointly decide to hire a consulting firm for advice on increasing departmental effectiveness and efficiency. The consulting firm spends 50% of its efforts on department "A" and 25% on each of the other two departments. The manager for department "A" suggests that the three departments equally share the consulting fee. As a manager of one of the other two departments, do you believe equal sharing is fair? [Answer—p. 147]

Activity-Based Costing Rates and Method

C4 Explain cost flows for activity-based costing.

Cost Flows under Activity-Based Costing Method **Activity-based costing (ABC)** attempts to more accurately assign overhead costs to the users of overhead by focusing on *activities*. The premise of ABC is that it takes activities to make products and provide services. These activities drive costs. For instance, costs are incurred when we perform actions; cutting raw materials, inspecting parts, and processing invoices all cause resources to be used.

There are two basic stages to ABC as shown in Exhibit 4.8. The first stage of ABC cost assignment is to identify the activities (cost objects) involved in manufacturing products and match those activities with the costs they cause (drive). To reduce the total number of activities that must be assigned costs, the homogeneous activities (those caused by the same factor such as cutting metal) are grouped into activity cost *pools*. The second stage of ABC is to compute an activity rate for each cost pool and then use this rate to allocate overhead costs to products, which are the cost objects of this second stage.

Point: Homogeneous means similar.

The basic principle underlying activity-based costing is that an **activity,** which is a task, operation, or procedure, is what causes costs to be incurred. For example, warehousing products consumes resources (costs) such as employee time for driving a forklift, the electricity to power the forklift, and the wear and tear on a forklift. Also, training employees drives costs such as fees or salaries paid to trainers and the training supplies required. Generally, all activities of an organization can be linked to use of resources. An **activity cost pool** is a collection of costs that are related to the same or similar activity. Pooling costs to determine an **activity overhead (pool) rate** for all costs incurred by the same activity reduces the number of cost assignments required.

EXHIBIT 4.8
Activity-Based Costing Method

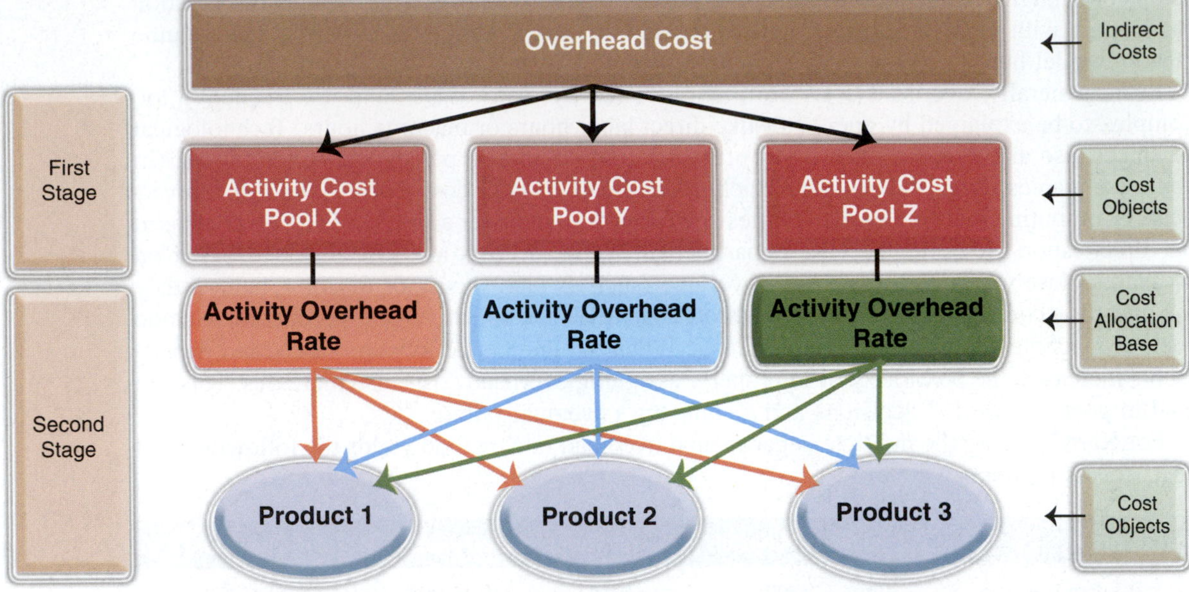

Differences between ABC and Multiple Departmental Rates Using ABC differs from using multiple departmental rates in how overhead cost pools are identified and in how overhead cost in each pool is allocated. When using multiple departmental rates, each department is a cost pool, and overhead cost allocated to each department is assigned to products using a volume-based factor (such as direct labor hours or machine hours). This assumes that overhead costs in each department are directly proportional to the volume-based factor. ABC, on the other hand, recognizes that overhead costs are more complex. For example, purchasing costs might make up one activity cost pool (spanning more than one department) that would include activities such as the number of invoices. ABC emphasizes activities and costs of carrying out these activities. Under ABC, only costs related to the same activity are grouped into a cost pool. Therefore, ABC arguably better reflects the complex nature of overhead costs and how these costs are used in making products.

Quick Check Answers—p. 148

1. Which method of cost assignment requires more than one overhead rate? (a) Plantwide overhead rate method (b) Departmental overhead rate method (c) ABC (d) Both *b* and *c*.
2. Which method of overhead costing is the most accurate when products differ in level of complexity? (a) ABC (b) Plantwide overhead rate method (c) Departmental overhead rate method.
3. ABC assumes that costs are incurred because of what? (a) Management decisions (b) Activities (c) Financial transactions.

Applying Activity-Based Costing

Activity-based costing accumulates overhead costs into activity cost pools and then uses activity rates to allocate those costs to products. This involves four steps: (1) identify activities and the costs they cause; (2) group similar activities into activity cost pools; (3) determine an activity rate for each activity cost pool; and (4) allocate overhead costs to products using those activity rates. To illustrate, let's return to KartCo and apply steps 1 through 4.

Step 1: Identify Activities and Cost Pools

P3 Allocate overhead costs to products using activity-based costing.

Step 1 in applying ABC is to identify activities. This is commonly done through discussions with employees in production departments and through reviews of production activities. The more activities that ABC tracks, the more accurately overhead costs are assigned. However, tracking too many activities makes the system cumbersome and costly to maintain. Consequently, we try to reach a balance where it is often necessary to reduce the number of activities tracked by

combining similar activities. An activity can also involve several related tasks. The aim of this first step is to understand actions performed in the organization that drive costs.

Activities causing overhead cost can be separated into four levels of types of activities: (1) **unit level activities,** (2) **batch level activities,** (3) **product level activities,** and (4) **facility level activities.** These four activities are described as follows.

Activity Levels

Unit level activities are performed on each product unit. For example, the machining department needs electricity to power the machinery to produce each unit of product. Unit level costs tend to change with the number of units produced.

Batch level activities are performed only on each batch or group of units. For example, machine setup is needed only for each batch regardless of the units in that batch, and customer order processing must be performed for each order regardless of the number of units ordered. Batch level costs do not vary with the number of units, but instead with the number of batches.

Product level activities are performed on each product line and are not affected by either the numbers of units or batches. For example, product design is needed only for each product line. Product level costs do not vary with the number of units or batches produced.

Facility level activities are performed to sustain facility capacity as a whole and are not caused by any specific product. For example, rent and factory maintenance costs are incurred no matter what is being produced. Facility level costs do not vary with what is manufactured, how many batches are produced, or the output quantity.

Additional examples of activities commonly found within each of the four activity levels are shown in the following table. This is not a complete list, but reviewing it can help in understanding this hierarchy of production activities. This list also includes common measures used to reflect the specific activity identified. Knowing this hierarchy can help us simplify and understand activity-based costing.

Activity Level	Examples of Activity	Activity Driver (Measure)
Unit level	Cutting parts	Machine hours
	Assembling components	Direct labor hours
	Printing checks	Number of checks
Batch level	Calibrating machines	Number of batches
	Receiving shipments	Number of orders
	Sampling product quality	Number of lots produced
Product level	Designing modifications	Change requests
	Organizing production	Engineering hours
	Controlling inventory	Parts per product
Facility level	Cleaning workplace	Square feet of floors*
	Providing electricity	Kilowatt hours*
	Providing personnel support	Number of employees*

* Facility level costs are not traceable to individual product lines, batches, or units. They are normally assigned to units using a unit-level driver such as direct labor hours or machine hours even though they are caused by another activity.

Once activities are identified, a company sets up activity cost pools. It is crucial that activities in each cost pool be similar and reflect a similar activity level. After a review of its overhead activities, KartCo set up the following four activity cost pools.

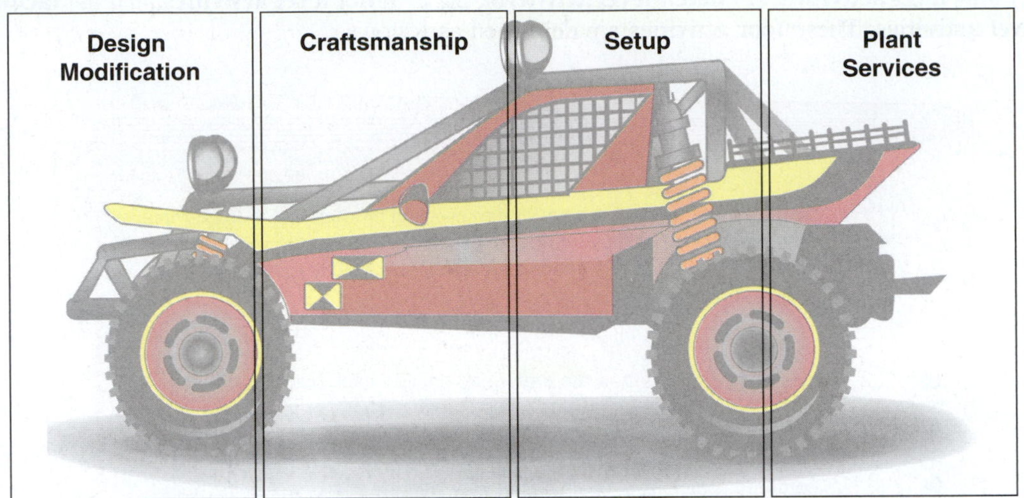

Decision Maker

Cost Analyst Your employer is exploring the possibility of implementing an activity-based costing system in the plant where you are newly assigned as a cost analyst. Your responsibilities are to identify manufacturing activities and link them to the costs they drive. You have never worked in this type of manufacturing operation and you are unsure about what activities are performed and their costs. What steps should you pursue to yield a quality report? [Answer—p. 147]

Step 2: Trace Overhead Costs to Cost Pools

Step 2 in applying ABC is to assign overhead costs to cost pools. Overhead costs are commonly accumulated by each department in a traditional accounting system. Some of these overhead costs are traced directly to a specific activity cost pool. At KartCo, for example, the assembly department supervisor's salary is assigned to its design modification cost pool and its machine repair costs are traced to its setup cost pool. Companies try to trace as many overhead costs to specific activity cost pools as possible to improve costing accuracy.

Recall that a premise of ABC is that operations are a series of activities that cause costs to be incurred. Instead of combining costs from different activities into one plantwide pool or multiple departmental pools, ABC focuses on activities as the cost object in the first step of cost assignment. We are then able to *trace* costs to a cost object and then combine activities that are used by products in similar ways to reduce the number of cost allocations.

KartCo has total overhead cost of $4,800,000 consisting of $4,000,000 indirect labor costs and $800,000 factory utilities costs. Details gathered by KartCo about its overhead costs are shown in Exhibit 4.9. Column totals for indirect labor and factory utilities correspond to amounts in Exhibit 4.3. Activity-based costing provides more detail about the activities and the costs they cause than is provided from traditional costing methods.

EXHIBIT 4.9

KartCo Overhead Cost Details

Activity	Indirect Labor	Factory Utilities	Total Overhead
Replacing tools	$ 700,000	—	$ 700,000
Machine repair	1,300,000	—	1,300,000
Factory maintenance	800,000	—	800,000
Engineer salaries	1,200,000	—	1,200,000
Assembly line power	—	$600,000	600,000
Heating and lighting	—	200,000	200,000
Totals	$4,000,000	$800,000	$4,800,000

After a review and analysis of its activities, KartCo management assigns its overhead costs into its four activity cost pools as shown in Exhibit 4.10. To assign costs to pools, management looks for costs that are caused by the activities of that pool and activity level. For KartCo there is only one activity driver within each activity level, but that is not always the case. It is common to see several different activity drivers within each activity level. We pool only those costs that are related to the same driver.

EXHIBIT 4.10

Assigning Overhead to Activity Cost Pools

Activity Pools	Activity Cost	Pool Cost	Activity Driver
Craftsmanship			30,000 direct labor hours
Assembly line power	$ 600,000	$ 600,000	
Setup			200 batches
Replacing tools	700,000		
Machine repair	1,300,000	2,000,000	
Design modification			10 designs
Engineer salaries	1,200,000	1,200,000	
Plant services			
Factory maintenance	800,000		20,000 square feet
Heating and lighting	200,000	1,000,000	
Total overhead cost		$4,800,000	

Exhibit 4.10 shows that $600,000 of overhead costs are assigned to the craftsmanship cost pool; $2,000,000 to the setup cost pool; $1,200,000 to the design-modification cost pool; and $1,000,000 to the plant services cost pool. This reduces the potential number of overhead rates from six (one for each of its six activities) to four (one for each pool). For KartCo, the craftsmanship pool reflects unit level costs, the setup pool reflects batch level costs, the design-modification pool reflects product level costs, and plant services reflect facility level costs.

Decision Insight

Measuring Health Activity-based costing is used in many settings. Its only requirements are existence of costs and demand for reliable cost information. A study found that activity-based costing improves health care costing accuracy, enabling improved profitability analysis and decision making. Identifying cost drivers in a health care setting is challenging and fraught with ethical concerns.

Step 3: Determine Activity Rate

Step 3 is to compute activity rates used to assign overhead costs to final cost objects such as products. Proper determination of activity rates depends on (1) proper identification of the factor that drives the cost in each activity cost pool and (2) proper measures of activities.

Identifying the factor that drives cost, the **activity cost driver,** is that activity causing costs in the pool to be incurred. For KartCo's overhead, craftsmanship costs are mainly driven (caused) by assembling products, setup costs are driven by system repairs and retooling, design-modification costs are driven by new features, and plant service costs are driven by building occupancy. The activity cost driver, a measure of activity level, serves as the allocation base. KartCo uses direct labor hours as the activity driver for the craftsmanship cost pool, the number of batches as the activity driver for its setup cost pool, the number of products devised or modified for its design-modification cost pool, and the number of square feet occupied for its plant services cost pool.

To compute the activity rate, total cost in an activity cost pool is divided by the measure of the activity. For KartCo, recall that overhead costs allocated to setup and craftsmanship cost pools were $2,000,000 and $600,000, respectively (see Exhibit 4.10). Also, total direct labor hours of craftsmanship equal 30,000, and 200 batches of go-karts were produced during the period. Thus, activity rates for those two cost pools are computed as follows.

Craftsmanship cost pool activity rate	**= $600,000 ÷ 30,000 DLH = $20 per DLH**
Setup cost pool activity rate	**= $2,000,000 ÷ 200 batches = $10,000 per batch**

To compute its activity rate for the design-modification cost pool, KartCo estimates the number of design modifications to be 10 for the period. For its plant services cost pool, KartCo plans to use 20,000 square feet of floor space. Recall that overhead costs allocated to design modification and to the plant services cost pools were $1,200,000 and $1,000,000, respectively. Activity rates for those two cost pools are computed as follows.

Design modification
cost pool activity rate = $1,200,000 ÷ 10 designs = $120,000 per design

Plant services
cost pool activity rate = $1,000,000 ÷ 20,000 square feet = $50 per sq. ft.

The activity rate computations for KartCo are summarized in Exhibit 4.11.

EXHIBIT 4.11

Activity Rates for KartCo

Activity Cost Pools	Overhead Costs Assigned to Pool	Activity Measure Chosen	Number of Activities	Activity Rate
Craftsmanship	$ 600,000	DLH	30,000 DLH	$20 per DLH
Setup	2,000,000	Batches	200 batches	$10,000 per batch
Design modification	1,200,000	Number of designs	10 designs	$120,000 per design
Plant services	1,000,000	Square feet	20,000 sq. ft.	$50 per sq. ft.

Step 4: Assign Overhead Costs to Cost Objects

Step 4 is to assign overhead costs in each activity cost pool to final cost objects using activity rates. (This is referred to as the *second-stage assignment;* where steps 1 through 3 make up the *first-stage assignment.*) To accomplish this, overhead costs in each activity cost pool are allocated to product lines based on the level of activity for each product line. After costs in all cost pools are allocated, the costs for each product line are totaled and then divided by the number of units of that product line to arrive at overhead cost per product unit.

For KartCo, overhead costs in each pool are allocated to the standard go-karts and the custom go-karts using the activity rates from Exhibit 4.11. The activities used by each product line and the overhead costs allocated to standard and custom go-karts under ABC for KartCo are summarized in Exhibit 4.12. To illustrate, the $500,000 of overhead costs in the craftsmanship cost pool is allocated to standard go-karts as follows.

Overhead allocated to
standard go-kart = Activities consumed × Activity rate
= 25,000 DLH × $20 = $500,000

We know that standard go-karts require 25,000 direct labor hours and the activity rate for craftsmanship is $20 per direct labor hour. Multiplying the number of direct labor hours by the activity rate yields the craftsmanship costs assigned to standard go-karts. Custom go-karts consumed 5,000 direct labor hours, so we assign $100,000 (5,000 DLH × $20 per DLH) to that product line. We similarly allocate overhead to setup, design modification, and plant services pools for each type of go-kart.

EXHIBIT 4.12

Overhead Allocated to Go-Karts for KartCo

	Standard Go-Karts			Custom Go-Karts		
	Activities Consumed	Activity Rate	Activity Cost Allocated	Activities Consumed	Activity Rate	Activity Cost Allocated
Craftsmanship	25,000 DLH	$20 per DLH	$ 500,000	5,000 DLH	$20 per DLH	$ 100,000
Setup	40 batches	$10,000 per batch	400,000	160 batches	$10,000 per batch	1,600,000
Design modification	0 designs	$120,000 per design	0	10 designs	$120,000 per design	1,200,000
Plant services	12,000 sq. ft.	$50 per sq. ft.	600,000	8,000 sq. ft.	$50 per sq. ft.	400,000
Total cost			$1,500,000			$3,300,000

In assigning overhead costs to products, KartCo assigned no design modification costs to standard go-karts because standard go-karts are sold as "off-the-shelf" items.

Overhead cost per unit is computed by dividing total overhead cost allocated to each product line by the number of product units. KartCo's overhead cost per unit for its standard and custom go-karts is computed and shown in Exhibit 4.13.

EXHIBIT 4.13

Overhead Cost per Unit for Go-Karts Using ABC

	(A) Total Overhead Cost Allocated	(B) Budgeted Units of Production	(A ÷ B) Overhead Cost perUnit
Standard go-kart	$1,500,000	5,000 units	$ 300 per unit
Custom go-kart	3,300,000	1,000 units	$3,300 per unit

Total cost per unit for KartCo using ABC for its two products follows.

	Direct Materials	Direct Labor	Overhead	Total Cost per Unit
Standard go-kart ...	$400	$350	$ 300	$1,050
Custom go-kart ...	600	500	3,300	4,400

Assuming that ABC more accurately assigns costs, we now are able to help KartCo's management understand how its competitors can sell their standard models at $1,200 and why KartCo is flooded with orders for custom go-karts. Specifically, if the cost to produce a standard go-kart is $1,050, as shown above (and not $1,470 as computed using the plantwide rate), a profit of $150 ($1,200 − $1,050) occurs on each standard unit sold at the competitive $1,200 market price. Further, selling its custom go-kart at $3,500 is a mistake by KartCo management because it is losing $900 ($3,500 − $4,400) on each custom go-kart sold. That is, KartCo has underpriced its custom go-kart relative to its production costs and competitors' prices, which explains why the company has more custom orders than it can supply.

Point: Accurately assigning costs to products is key to setting many product prices. If product costs are inaccurate and result in prices that are too low, the company loses money on each item sold. Likewise, if product prices are improperly set too high, the company loses business to competitors. ABC can be used to more accurately set prices.

Overhead allocation per go-kart under the single plantwide rate method, multiple departmental rate method, and ABC is summarized in Exhibit 4.14. Overhead cost allocated to standard go-karts is much less under ABC than under either of the volume-based costing methods. One reason for this difference is the large design modification costs that were spread over all go-karts under both the plantwide rate and the departmental rate methods even though standard go-karts require no engineering modification. When ABC is used, overhead costs commonly shift from standardized, large-volume products to low-volume, customized specialty products that consume disproportionate resources.

EXHIBIT 4.14

Comparison of Overhead Allocations by Method

	Overhead Cost per Go-Kart	
Allocation Method	**Standard Go-Kart**	**Custom Go-Kart**
Plantwide overhead rate method	$720	$1,200
Departmental overhead rate method	700	1,300
ABC overhead rate method	300	3,300

Decision Insight

ABCs of Banking First Tennessee National Corporation, a bank, applied ABC to reveal that 30% of its CD customers provided nearly 90% of its profits from CDs. Further, another 30% of its CD customers were actually losing money for the bank. Management used ABC to correct this problem.

Quick Check

Answers—p. 148

4. What is a cost driver? Provide an example of a typical cost driver.
5. What is an activity driver? Provide an example of a typical activity driver.
6. Traditional volume-based costing methods tend to: (a) overstate the cost of low-volume products, (b) overstate the cost of high-volume products, or (c) both a and b.

Assessing Activity-Based Costing

A3 Identify and assess advantages and disadvantages of activity-based costing.

While activity-based costing improves the accuracy of overhead cost allocations to products, it too has limitations. This section describes the major advantages and disadvantages of activity-based costing.

Advantages of Activity-Based Costing

More Accurate Overhead Cost Allocation Companies have typically used either a plantwide overhead rate or multiple departmental overhead rates because these methods are more straightforward than ABC and are acceptable under GAAP for external reporting. Under these traditional systems, overhead costs are pooled in a few large pools and are spread uniformly across high- and low-volume products. With ABC, overhead costs are grouped into activity pools. There are usually more activity pools under ABC than cost pools under traditional costing, which usually increases costing accuracy. More important is that overhead costs in each ABC pool are caused by a single activity. This means that overhead costs in each activity pool are allocated to products based on the cost of resources consumed by a product (input) rather than on how many units are produced (output). In sum, overhead cost allocation under ABC is more accurate because (1) there are more cost pools, (2) costs in each pool are more similar, and (3) allocation is based on activities that cause overhead costs.

Point: ABC can allocate the selling and administrative costs expensed by GAAP to activities; such costs can include marketing costs, costs to process orders, and costs to process customer returns.

More Effective Overhead Cost Control In traditional costing, overhead costs are usually allocated to products based on either direct labor hours or machine hours. Such allocation typically leads management to focus attention on direct labor cost or machine hours. Yet, direct labor or machine hours are often not the cause of overhead costs and often not even linked with these volume-related measures. As we saw with KartCo, design modifications markedly affect its overhead costs. Consequently, a plantwide overhead rate or departmental overhead rate based on direct labor or machine hours can mislead managers, preventing effective control of overhead costs and leading to product mispricing. ABC, on the other hand, can be used to identify activities that can benefit from process improvement. ABC can also help managers effectively control overhead cost by focusing on processes or activities such as batching setups, order processing, and design modifications instead of focusing only on direct labor or machine hours. For KartCo, identification of large design-modification costs would allow managers to work on initiatives to improve this process. Besides controlling overhead costs, KartCo's better assignment of overhead costs (particularly design-modification costs) for its go-karts helps its managers make better production and pricing decisions.

Focus on Relevant Factors Basing cost assignment on activities is not limited to determining product costs, as illustrated by KartCo. ABC can be used to assign costs to any cost object that is of management interest. For instance, a marketing manager often wants to determine the profitability of various market segments. Activity-based costing can be used to accurately assign costs of shipping, advertising, order-taking, and customer service that are unrelated to sales and costs of products sold. Such an activity-based analysis can reveal to the marketing department some customers that are better left to the competition if they consume a larger amount of marketing resources than the gross profit generated by sales to those customers. Generally, ABC provides better customer profitability information by including all resources consumed to serve a customer. This allows managers to make better pricing decisions on custom orders and to better manage customers by focusing on those that are most profitable.

Point: The *Demonstration Problem* illustrates how ABC is applied for a services company.

Better Management of Activities Being competitive requires that managers be able to use resources efficiently. Understanding how costs are incurred is a first step toward controlling costs. One important contribution of ABC is helping managers identify the causes of costs, that is, the activities driving them. ***Activity-based management (ABM)*** is an outgrowth of ABC that draws on the link between activities and cost incurrence for better management. The way to control a cost requires changing how much of an activity is performed.

Decision Maker

Entrepreneur You are the entrepreneur of a startup pharmaceutical company. You are assigning overhead to product units based on machine hours in the packaging area. Profits are slim due to increased competition. One of your larger overhead costs is $10,000 for cleaning and sterilization that occurs each time the packaging system is converted from one product to another. These overhead costs average $0.10 per product unit. Can you reduce cleaning and sterilizing costs by reducing the number of units produced? If not, what should you do to control these overhead costs? [Answer—p. 147]

Disadvantages of Activity-Based Costing

Costs to Implement and Maintain ABC Designing and implementing an activity-based costing system requires management commitment and financial resources. For ABC to be effective, a thorough analysis of cost activities must be performed and appropriate cost pools must be determined. Collecting and analyzing cost data are expensive and so is maintaining an ABC system. While technology, such as bar coding, has made it possible for many companies to use ABC, it is still too costly for some. Managers must weigh the cost of implementing and maintaining an ABC system against the potential benefits of ABC in light of company circumstances.

Uncertainty with Decisions Remains As with all cost information, managers must interpret ABC data with caution in making managerial decisions. In the KartCo case, given the huge design-modification costs for custom go-karts determined under the ABC system, a manager might be tempted to decline some custom go-kart orders to save overhead costs. However, in the short run, some or all of the design-modification costs cannot be saved even if some custom go-kart orders are rejected. Managers must examine carefully the controllability of costs before making decisions.

Quick Check

Answers—p. 148

7. What are three advantages of ABC over traditional volume-based allocation methods?
8. What is the main advantage of traditional volume-based allocation methods compared to activity-based costing? How should a manager decide which method to use?

Customer Profitability

Decision Analysis

Are all customers equal? To help answer this, let's return to the KartCo case and assume that costs of providing customer support (such as delivery, installation, and warranty work) are related to the distance a technician must travel to provide services. If the annual cost of customer services is expected to be $250,000 and the distance traveled by technicians is 100,000 miles annually, KartCo would want to link the cost of customer services with individual customers to make efficient marketing decisions.

Using these data, an activity rate of $2.50 per mile ($250,000/100,000 miles) is computed for assigning customer service costs to individual customers. For KartCo, it would compute a typical customer profitability report for one of its customers, Six Flags, as follows.

Customer Profitability Report—Six Flags

Sales (10 standard go-karts × $1,200)		$12,000
Less: Product costs		
Direct materials (10 go-karts × $400 per go-kart)	$4,000	
Direct labor (10 go-karts × $350 per go-kart)	3,500	
Overhead (10 go-karts × $300 per go-kart, Exhibit 4.13)	3,000	10,500
Product profit margin		1,500
Less: Customer service costs (200 miles × $2.50 per mile)		500
Customer profit margin		$ 1,000

Analysis indicates that a total profit margin of $1,000 is generated from this customer. The management of KartCo can see that if this customer requires service technicians to travel more than 600 miles ($1,500 ÷ $2.50 per mile), the sale of 10 standard go-karts to this customer would be unprofitable. ABC encourages management to consider all resources consumed to serve a customer, not just manufacturing costs that are the focus of traditional costing methods.

Demonstration Problem

Silver Law Firm provides litigation and mediation services to a variety of clients. Attorneys keep track of the time they spend on each case, which is used to charge fees to clients at a rate of $300 per hour. A management advisor commented that activity-based costing might prove useful in evaluating the costs of its legal services, and the firm has decided to evaluate its fee structure by comparing ABC to its alternative cost allocations. The following data relate to a typical month at the firm. During a typical month the firm handles seven mediation cases and three litigation cases.

	Activity Driver	Total Amount	Consumption By Service Type: Litigation	Consumption By Service Type: Mediation	Activity Cost
Providing legal advice	Billable hours	200	75	125	$30,000
Overhead costs					
Internal support departments					
Preparing documents	Documents	30	16	14	$ 4,000
Occupying office space	Billable hours	200	75	125	1,200
Heating and lighting of office	Billable hours	200	75	125	350
External support departments					
Registering court documents	Documents	30	16	14	1,250
Retaining consultants (investigators, psychiatrists)	Court dates	6	5	1	10,000
Using contract services (couriers, security guards)	Court dates	6	5	1	5,000
Total overhead costs					$21,800

Required

1. Determine the cost of providing legal services to each type of case using activity-based costing (ABC).
2. Determine the cost of each type of case using a single plantwide rate for nonattorney costs based on billable hours.
3. Determine the cost of each type of case using multiple departmental overhead rates for the internal support department (based on number of documents) and external support department (based on billable hours).
4. Compare and discuss the costs assigned under each method for management decisions.

Planning the Solution

- Compute pool rates and assign costs to cases using ABC.
- Compute costs for the cases using the volume-based methods and discuss differences between these costs and the costs computed using ABC.

Solution to Demonstration Problem

1. We need to set up activity pools and compute pool rates for ABC. All activities except "occupying office space" and "heating and lighting" are unit level (meaning they are traceable to the individual cases handled by the law firm). "Preparing documents" and "registering documents" are both driven by the number of documents associated with each case. We can therefore combine these activities and their costs into a single pool, which we call "clerical support." Similarly, "retaining consultants" and "using services" are related to the number of times the attorneys must go to court (court dates).

We combine these activities and their costs into another activity cost pool labeled "litigation support." The costs associated with occupying office space and the heating and lighting are facility level activities and are not traceable to individual cases. Yet they are costs that must be covered by fees charged to clients. We assign these costs using a convenient base—in this example we use the number of billable hours, which attorneys record for each client. Providing legal advice is the direct labor for a law firm.

Activity Pool	Activity Cost	Pool Cost	Activity Driver	Pool Rate (Pool Cost ÷ Activity Driver)
Providing legal advice	$30,000	$30,000	200 billable hours	$150 per billable hour
Clerical support				
Preparing documents	4,000			
Registering documents	1,250	5,250	30 documents	$175 per document
Litigation support				
Retaining consultants	10,000			
Using services	5,000	15,000	6 court dates	$2,500 per court date
Facility costs				
Occupying office space	1,200			
Heating and lighting	350	1,550	200 billable hours	$7.75 per billable hour

We next determine the cost of providing each type of legal service as shown in the following table. Specifically, the pool rates from above are used to assign costs to each type of service provided by the law firm. Since litigation consumed 75 billable hours of attorney time, we assign $11,250 (75 billable hours × $150 per billable hour) of the cost of providing legal advice to this type of case. Mediation required 125 hours of attorney time, so $18,750 (125 billable hours × $150 per billable hour) of the cost to provide legal advice is assigned to mediation cases. Clerical support cost $175 per document, so the costs associated with activities in this cost pool are assigned to litigation cases (16 documents × $175 per document = $2,800) and mediation cases (14 documents × $175 per document = $2,450). The costs of activities in the litigation support and the facility cost pools are similarly assigned to the two case types.

We compute the total cost of litigation ($27,131.25) and mediation ($24,668.75) and divide these totals by the number of cases of each type to determine the average cost of each case type: $9,044 for litigation and $3,524 for mediation. This analysis shows that charging clients $300 per billable hour without regard to the type of case results in litigation clients being charged less than the cost to provide that service ($7,500 versus $9,044).

	Pool Rate	Litigation		Mediation	
Providing legal advice	$150 per billable hour	75 hours	$11,250.00	125 hours	$18,750.00
Clerical support	$175 per document	16 docs	2,800.00	14 docs	2,450.00
Litigation support	$2,500 per court date	5 court dates	12,500.00	1 court date	2,500.00
Facility costs	$7.75 per billable hour	75 hours	581.25	125 hours	968.75
Total cost			$27,131.25		$24,668.75
÷ Number of cases			3 cases		7 cases
Average cost per case			**$9,044**		**$3,524**
Average fee per case			**$7,500***		**$5,357**[†]

* (75 billable hours × $300 per hour) ÷ 3 cases

[†] (125 billable hours × $300 per hour) ÷ 7 cases

2. The cost of each type of case using a single plantwide rate for nonattorney costs (that is, all costs except for those related to providing legal advice) based on billable hours is as follows.

Total overhead cost/ Total billable hours = $21,800/200 billable hours = $109 per hour

We then determine the cost of providing each type of legal service as follows.

		Litigation		Mediation	
Providing legal advice	$150 per billable hour	75 hours	$11,250	125 hours	$18,750
Overhead (from part 2)	$109 per billable hour	75 hours	8,175	125 hours	13,625
Total cost			$19,425		$32,375
÷ Number of cases			3 cases		7 cases
Average cost per case			**$6,475**		**$4,625**
Average fee per case . . . . (from part 1)			**$7,500**		**$5,357**

3. The cost of each type of case using multiple departmental overhead rates for the internal support department (based on number of documents) and external support department (based on billable hours) is determined as follows.

		Departmental Cost	Base	Departmental Rate (Departmental Cost ÷ Base)
Internal support departments				
Preparing documents	$ 4,000			
Occupying office space	1,200			
Heating and lighting of office	350	$ 5,550	30 documents	$185 per document
External support departments				
Registering documents	1,250			
Retaining consultants	10,000			
Using contract services	5,000	16,250	200 billable hours	$81.25 per hour

The departmental overhead rates computed above are used to assign overhead costs to the two types of legal services. For the internal support department we use the overhead rate of $185 per document to assign $2,960 ($185 × 16 documents) to litigation and $2,590 ($185 × 14 documents) to mediation. For the external support department we use the overhead rate of $81.25 per hour to assign $6,093.75 ($81.25 × 75 hours) to litigation and $10,156.25 ($81.25 × 125 hours) to mediation. As shown below, the resulting average costs of litigation cases and mediation cases are $6,768 and $4,499, respectively. Using this method of cost assignment, it *appears* that the fee of $300 per billable hour is adequate to cover costs associated with each case.

		Litigation		Mediation	
Attorney fees	$150 per billable hour	75 hours	$11,250.00	125 hours	$18,750.00
Internal support	$185 per document	16 documents	2,960.00	14 documents	2,590.00
External support	$81.25 per hour	75 hours	6,093.75	125 hours	10,156.25
Total cost			$20,303.75		$31,496.25
÷ Number of cases			3 cases		7 cases
Average cost per case			**$6,768**		**$4,499**
Average fee per case . . . . . (from part 1)			**$7,500**		**$5,357**

4. A comparison and discussion of the costs assigned under each method follows.

	Method of Assigning Overhead Costs		
Average Cost per Case	Activity-Based Costing	Plantwide Overhead Rate	Departmental Overhead Rates
Litigation cases	$9,044	$6,475	$6,768
Mediation cases	3,524	4,625	4,499

The departmental and plantwide overhead rate methods assign overhead on the basis of volume-related measures (billable hours and document filings). Litigation costs *appear* profitable under these methods, because the average costs are below the average revenue of $7,500. ABC, however, focuses attention on activities that drive costs. A large part of overhead costs was for consultants and contract services, which were unrelated to the number of cases, but related to the type of cases consuming those resources. Using ABC, the costs shift from the high-volume cases (mediation) to the low-volume cases (litigation). When the firm considers the consumption of resources for these cases using ABC, it finds that the fees charged to litigate cases is insufficient (average revenue of $7,500 versus average cost of $9,044). The law firm is charging too little for the complex cases that require litigation.

Summary

C1 **Distinguish between the plantwide overhead rate method, the departmental overhead rate method, and the activity-based costing method.** Overhead costs can be assigned to cost objects using a plantwide rate that combines all overhead costs into a single rate, usually based on direct labor hours, machine hours, or direct labor cost. Multiple departmental overhead rates that include overhead costs traceable to departments are used to allocate overhead based on departmental functions. ABC links overhead costs to activities and assigns overhead based on how much of each activity is required for a product.

C2 **Explain cost flows for the plantwide overhead rate method.** All overhead costs are combined in the plantwide overhead rate to form a single rate that is then used to assign overhead to each product. It is a one-step allocation.

C3 **Explain cost flows for the departmental overhead rate method.** When using departmental overhead rates, overhead costs are first traced to specific departments where various costs are incurred. Overhead rates for each department are then used to assign overhead to products that pass through each department.

C4 **Explain cost flows for activity-based costing.** With ABC, overhead costs are first traced to the activities that cause them, and then cost pools are formed combining costs caused by the same activity. Overhead rates based on these activities are then used to assign overhead to products in proportion to the amount of activity required to produce them.

A1 **Identify and assess advantages and disadvantages of the plantwide overhead rate method.** A single plantwide overhead rate is a simple way to assign overhead cost. A disadvantage is that it can inaccurately assign costs when costs are caused by multiple factors and when different products consume different amounts of inputs.

A2 **Identify and assess advantages and disadvantages of the departmental overhead rate method.** Overhead costing accuracy is improved by use of multiple departmental rates because differences across departmental functions can be linked to costs incurred in departments. Yet, accuracy of cost assignment with departmental rates suffers from the same problems associated with plantwide rates because activities required for each product are not identified with costs of providing those activities.

A3 **Identify and assess advantages and disadvantages of activity-based costing.** ABC improves product costing accuracy and draws management attention to relevant factors to control. The cost of constructing and maintaining an ABC system can sometimes outweigh its value.

P1 **Allocate overhead costs to products using the plantwide overhead rate method.** The plantwide overhead rate equals total budgeted overhead divided by budgeted plant volume, the latter often measured in direct labor hours or machine hours. This rate multiplied by the number of direct labor hours (or machine hours) required for each product provides the overhead assigned to each product.

P2 **Allocate overhead costs to products using the departmental overhead rate method.** When using multiple departmental rates, overhead cost must first be traced to each department and then divided by the measure of output for that department to yield the departmental overhead rate. Overhead is applied to products using this rate as products pass through each department.

P3 **Allocate overhead costs to products using activity-based costing.** With ABC, overhead costs are matched to activities that cause them. If there is more than one cost with the same activity, these costs are combined into pools. An overhead rate for each pool is determined by dividing total cost for that pool by its activity measure. Overhead costs are assigned to products by multiplying the ABC pool rate by the amount of the activity required for each product.

Guidance Answers to Decision Maker and Decision Ethics

Department Manager When dividing a bill, common sense suggests fairness. That is, if one department consumes more services than another, we attempt to share the bill in proportion to consumption. Equally dividing the bill among the number of departments is fair if each consumed equal services. This same notion applies in assigning costs to products and services. For example, dividing overhead costs by the number of units is fair if all products consumed overhead in equal proportion.

Cost Analyst Before the accounting system can report information, relevant and accurate data must be collected. One step is to ask questions—it is a good way to leverage others' experience and knowledge to quickly learn operations. A cost analyst must also understand the manufacturing operation to itemize activities for ABC. Thus, step two might be to tour the manufacturing facility, observing manufacturing operations, asking probing questions, and requesting recommendations from the people who work in those operations. We must remember that these employees are the experts who can provide the data we need to implement an activity-based costing system.

Entrepreneur Cleaning and sterilizing costs are not directly related to the volume of product manufactured. Thus, changing the number of units produced does not necessarily reduce these costs. Further, expressing costs of cleaning and sterilizing on a per unit basis is often misleading for the person responsible for controlling costs. Costs of cleaning and sterilizing are related to changing from one product line to another. Consequently, the way to control those costs is to control the number of times the packing system has to be changed for a different product line. Thus, efficient product scheduling would help reduce those overhead costs and improve profitability.

Guidance Answers to **Quick Checks**

1. d
2. a
3. b
4. A cost driver is an activity that causes costs to be incurred. Setup costs, design modifications, and plant services such as maintenance and utilities are examples of typical cost drivers.
5. An activity driver is the measurement used for cost drivers. An example is machine hours.
6. b
7. Three advantages of ABC over traditional methods are: (a) more accurate product costing; (b) more effective cost control; and (c) focus on relevant factors for decision making.
8. Traditional volume-based methods are easier and less costly to implement and maintain. The choice of accounting method should be made by comparing the costs of alternatives with their benefits.

Key Terms

mhhe.com/wildMA2e

Key Terms are available at the book's Website for learning and testing in an online Flashcard Format.

Activity (p. 135)
Activity-based costing (ABC) (p. 135)
Activity-based management (p. 142)
Activity cost driver (p. 139)
Activity cost pool (p. 135)
Activity driver (p. 139)
Activity overhead (pool) rate (p. 135)
Batch level activities (p. 137)
Cost driver (p. 139)
Cost object (p. 131)
Facility level activities (p. 137)
Product level activities (p. 137)
Unit level activities (p. 137)

Multiple Choice Quiz

Answers on p. 165

mhhe.com/wildMA2e

Additional Quiz Questions are available at the book's Website.

1. In comparison to a traditional cost system, and when there are batch level or product level costs, an activity-based costing system usually:
   a. Shifts costs from low-volume to high-volume products.
   b. Shifts costs from high-volume to low-volume products.
   c. Shifts costs from standardized to specialized products.
   d. Shifts costs from specialized to standardized products.
2. Which of the following statements is (are) true?
   a. An activity-based costing system is generally easier to implement and maintain than a traditional costing system.
   b. One of the goals of activity-based management is the elimination of waste by allocating costs to products that waste resources.
   c. Activity-based costing uses a number of activity cost pools, each of which is allocated to products on the basis of direct labor hours.
   d. Activity rates in activity-based costing are computed by dividing costs from the first-stage allocations by the activity measure for each activity cost pool.
3. All of the following are examples of batch level activities except:
   a. Purchase order processing.
   b. Setting up equipment.
   c. Clerical activity associated with processing purchase orders to produce an order for a standard product.
   d. Employee recreational facilities.
4. A company has two products: A and B. It uses activity-based costing and prepares the following analysis showing budgeted cost and activity for each of its three activity cost pools.

Activity Cost Pool	Budgeted Overhead Cost	Budgeted Activity		
		Product A	Product B	Total
Activity 1	$ 80,000	200	800	1,000
Activity 2	58,400	1,000	500	1,500
Activity 3	360,000	600	5,400	6,000

Annual production and sales level of Product A is 18,188 units, and the annual production and sales level of Product B is 31,652 units. The approximate overhead cost per unit of Product B under activity-based costing is:

a. $2.02
b. $5.00
c. $12.87
d. $22.40

5. A company uses activity-based costing to determine the costs of its two products: A and B. The budgeted cost and activity for each of the company's three activity cost pools follow.

Activity Cost Pool	Budgeted Cost	Budgeted Activity		
		Product A	Product B	Total
Activity 1	$19,800	800	300	1,100
Activity 2	16,000	2,200	1,800	4,000
Activity 3	14,000	400	300	700

The activity rate under the activity-based costing method for Activity 3 is approximately:

a. $4.00
b. $8.59
c. $18.00
d. $20.00

Discussion Questions

1. Why are overhead costs allocated to products and not traced to products as direct materials and direct labor are?
2. What are three common methods of assigning overhead costs to a product?
3. What is a cost object?
4. Why are direct labor hours and machine hours commonly used as the bases for overhead allocation?
5. What are the advantages of using a single plantwide overhead rate?
6. The usefulness of a single plantwide overhead rate is based on two assumptions. What are those assumptions?
7. Explain why a single plantwide overhead rate can distort the cost of a particular product.
8. If plantwide overhead rates are allowed for reporting costs to external users, why might a company choose to use a more complicated and more expensive method for assigning overhead costs to products?
9. Why are multiple departmental overhead rates more accurate for product costing than a single plantwide overhead rate?
10. In what way are departmental overhead rates similar to a single plantwide overhead rate? How are they different?
11. What is the first step in applying activity-based costing?
12. What is a cost driver?
13. What is an activity driver?
14. What are the four activity levels associated with activity-based costing? Define each.
15. Activity-based costing is generally considered more accurate than other methods of assigning overhead. If this is so, why do all manufacturing companies not use it?
16. "Activity-based costing is only useful for manufacturing companies." Is this a true statement? Explain.

Denotes Discussion Questions that involve decision making.

connect *Most materials in this section are available in McGraw-Hill's Connect*

QUICK STUDY

QS 4-1
Costing terminology
C1

In the blank next to the following terms, place the letter *A* through *G* corresponding to the best description of that term.

1. ______ unit level activity
2. ______ activity driver
3. ______ batch level activity
4. ______ cost object
5. ______ plantwide overhead rate
6. ______ cost pool

A. A task that must be performed for each unit produced.
B. A group of costs that have the same activity drivers.
C. Anything to which costs will be assigned.
D. Tasks that are performed for each group of units such as a production run or lot.
E. An activity that causes a cost to be incurred.
F. Measurement associated with an activity.
G. A single factor used to apply indirect manufacturing costs in all departments.

QS 4-2
Identify activity control levels
C4

Identify each of the following activities as unit level (U), batch level (B), product level (P), or facility level (F) to indicate the way each is incurred with respect to production.

1. ______ Sampling cookies to determine quality.
2. ______ Paying real estate taxes on the factory building.
3. ______ Attaching labels to collars of shirts.
4. ______ Mixing of bread dough in a commercial bakery.
5. ______ Polishing of gold wedding rings.
6. ______ Cleaning the assembly department.
7. ______ Redesigning a bicycle seat in response to customer feedback.

QS 4-3
Compute and apply plantwide and departmental overhead rates
P1 P2

Fortel Manufacturing identified the following data in its two production departments.

	Assembly	Finishing
Manufacturing overhead costs	$600,000	$1,200,000
Direct labor hours worked	12,000 DLH	20,000 DLH
Machine hours used	6,000 MH	16,000 MH

Required

1. What is the company's single plantwide overhead rate based on direct labor hours?
2. What are the company's departmental overhead rates if the assembly department assigns overhead based on direct labor hours and the finishing department assigns overhead based on machine hours?

QS 4-4
Comparing plantwide overhead rate to ABC
P3

Chen Company identified the following activities, costs, and activity drivers.

Activity	Expected Costs	Expected Activity
Handling materials	$625,000	100,000 parts in stock
Inspecting product	900,000	1,500 batches
Processing purchase orders	105,000	700 orders
Paying suppliers	175,000	500 invoices
Insuring the factory	300,000	40,000 square feet
Designing packaging	375,000	10 models

Required

1. Compute the activity rate for each activity.
2. Compute a single plantwide overhead rate assuming that the company assigns overhead based on 100,000 budgeted direct labor hours.

QS 4-5
Assigning costs using ABC
P1 P3

Refer to the data in QS4-4. Assume that the following information is available for the company's two products.

	Fast Model	Standard Model
Production volume	10,000 units	30,000 units
Parts required	20,000 parts	30,000 parts
Batches made	250 batches	100 batches
Purchase orders	50 orders	20 orders
Invoices	50 invoices	10 invoices
Space occupied	10,000 sq. ft.	7,000 sq. ft.
Models	1 model	1 model

Required

1. Assign overhead costs to each product model using activity-based costing (ABC). What is the cost per unit of each model?
2. Assign overhead costs to each product model using the single plantwide overhead rate assuming the fast model requires 25,000 direct labor hours and the standard model requires 60,000 direct labor hours. What is the overhead cost per unit for each model?

QS 4-6
Assigning costs using ABC
P3

Qinto Company sells two types of products, Basic and Deluxe. The company provides technical support for users of its products, at an expected cost of $250,000 per year. The company expects to process 10,000 customer service calls per year.

Required

1. Determine the company's cost of technical support per service call.
2. During the month of January, Qinto received 650 calls for customer service on its Deluxe model, and 150 calls for customer service on its Basic model. Assign technical support costs to each model using ABC.

connect *Most materials in this section are available in McGraw-Hill's Connect*

EXERCISES

Exercise 4-1
Activity classification
C4

Following are activities in providing medical services at Healthcare Clinic.

A. Ordering medical equipment
B. Heating the clinic
C. Filling prescriptions
D. Providing security services
E. Registering patients
F. Cleaning beds
G. Washing linens
H. Stocking examination rooms

Required

1. Classify each activity as unit level (U), batch level (B), product level (P), or facility level (F).
2. Identify an activity driver that might be used to measure these activities at the clinic.

Exercise 4-2
Comparing costs under ABC to traditional plantwide overhead rate
P1 P3 A1 A3

Teradyne Crystal makes fine tableware in its Ireland factory. The following data are taken from its production plans for 2009.

Direct labor costs	€5,870,000
Setup costs	630,000

	Wine Glasses	Commemorative Vases
Expected production	211,000 units	17,000 units
Direct labor hours required	254,000 DLH	16,400 DLH
Machine setups required	200 setups	800 setups

Required

1. Determine the setup cost per unit for the wine glasses and for the commemorative vases if setup costs are assigned using a single plantwide overhead rate based on direct labor hours.
2. Determine setup costs per unit for the wine glasses and for the commemorative vases if the setup costs are assigned based on the number of setups.
3. Which method is better for assigning costs to each product? Explain.

Check (2) Vases, €29.65 per unit

Exercise 4-3
Comparing plantwide overhead rate to departmental overhead rates
P1 P2 A1 A2

Supertronic Plastics produces parts for a variety of small machine manufacturers. Most products go through two operations, molding and trimming, before they are ready for packaging. Expected costs and activities for the molding department and for the trimming department for 2009 follow.

	Molding	Trimming
Direct labor hours	52,000 DLH	48,000 DLH
Machine hours	30,500 MH	3,600 MH
Overhead costs	$730,000	$590,000

Data for two special order parts to be manufactured by the company in 2009 follow:

	Part A27C	Part X82B
Number of units	9,800 units	54,500 units
Machine hours		
Molding	5,100 MH	1,020 MH
Trimming	2,600 MH	650 MH
Direct labor hours		
Molding	5,500 DLH	2,150 DLH
Trimming	700 DLH	3,500 DLH

Required

1. Compute the plantwide overhead rate using direct labor hours as the base.
2. Determine the overhead cost assigned to each product line using the plantwide rate computed in requirement 1.
3. Compute a departmental overhead rate for the molding department based on machine hours and a department overhead rate for the trimming department based on direct labor hours.
4. Determine the total overhead cost assigned to each product line using the departmental overhead rates from requirement 3.
5. Determine the overhead cost per unit for each product line using the plantwide rate. Compare these costs to the cost per unit if departmental rates were used.

Exercise 4-4
Multiple choice overhead questions
C4 A3

1. With ABC, overhead costs should be traced to which cost object first?
   a. Units of product
   b. Activities
   c. Departments
   d. Product lines
2. When using departmental overhead rates, which of the following cost objects is the first in the cost assignment process?
   a. Activities
   b. Units of product
   c. Departments
   d. Product lines
3. Which costing method tends to overstate the cost of high-volume products?
   a. Traditional volume-based costing
   b. Activity-based costing
   c. Job order costing
   d. Differential costing
4. If management wants the most accurate product cost, which of the following costing methods should be used?
   a. Volume-based costing using departmental overhead rates
   b. Volume-based costing using a plantwide overhead rate
   c. Normal costing using a plantwide overhead rate
   d. Activity-based costing

Exercise 4-5
Assigning overhead costs using the plantwide rate and departmental rates
P1 P2

Rayol produces lamps and home lighting fixtures. Its most popular product is a brushed aluminum desk lamp. This lamp is made from components shaped in the fabricating department and assembled in its implementation department. Information related to the 35,000 desk lamps produced annually follow.

Direct materials	$280,000
Direct labor	
Fabricating department (7,000 DLH × $20 per DLH)	$140,000
Implementation department (16,000 DLH × $29 per DLH)	$464,000
Machine hours	
Fabricating department	15,040 MH
Implementation department	21,000 MH

Expected overhead cost and related data for the two production departments follow.

	Fabricating	Implementation
Direct labor hours	75,000 DLH	125,000 DLH
Machine hours	80,000 MH	62,500 MH
Overhead cost	$300,000	$200,000

Required

1. Determine the plantwide overhead rate for Rayol using direct labor hours as a base.
2. Determine the total manufacturing cost per unit for the aluminum desk lamp using the plantwide overhead rate.
3. Compute departmental overhead rates based on machine hours in the fabricating department and direct labor hours in the implementation department.
4. Use departmental overhead rates from requirement 3 to determine the total manufacturing cost per unit for the aluminum desk lamps.

Check (2) $26.90 per unit

Check (4) $27.60 per unit

Exercise 4-6
Using the plantwide overhead rate to assess prices
C2 A1 P1

Real Cool produces two different models of air conditioners. The company produces the mechanical systems in their components department. The mechanical systems are combined with the housing assembly in its finishing department. The activities, costs, and drivers associated with these two manufacturing processes and the production support process follow.

Process	Activity	Overhead Cost	Driver	Quantity
Components	Changeover	$ 500,000	Number of batches	800
	Machining	279,000	Machine hours	6,000
	Setups	225,000	Number of setups	120
		$1,004,000		
Finishing	Welding	$ 180,300	Welding hours	3,000
	Inspecting	210,000	Number of inspections	700
	Rework	75,000	Rework orders	300
		$ 465,300		
Support	Purchasing	$ 135,000	Purchase orders	450
	Providing space	32,000	Number of units	5,000
	Providing utilities	65,000	Number of units	5,000
		$ 232,000		

Additional production information concerning its two product lines follows.

	Model 145	Model 212
Units produced	1,500	3,500
Welding hours	800	2,200
Batches	400	400
Number of inspections	400	300
Machine hours	1,800	4,200
Setups	60	60
Rework orders	160	140
Purchase orders	300	150

Required

1. Using a plantwide overhead rate based on machine hours, compute the overhead cost per unit for each product line.

2. Determine the total cost per unit for each product line if the direct labor and direct materials costs per unit are $250 for Model 145 and $180 for Model 212.

Check (3) Model 212, $(50.26) per unit loss

3. If the market price for Model 145 is $800 and the market price for Model 212 is $470, determine the profit or loss per unit for each model. Comment on the results.

Exercise 4-7

Using departmental overhead rates to assess prices

C3 A2 P2

Refer to the information in Exercise 4-6 to answer the following requirements.

Required

1. Determine departmental overhead rates and compute the overhead cost per unit for each product line. Base your overhead assignment for the components department on machine hours. Use welding hours to assign overhead costs to the finishing department. Assign costs to the support department based on number of purchase orders.

2. Determine the total cost per unit for each product line if the direct labor and direct materials costs per unit are $250 for Model 145 and $180 for Model 212.

Check (3) Model 212, $(30.38) per unit loss

3. If the market price for Model 145 is $800 and the market price for Model 212 is $470, determine the profit or loss per unit for each model. Comment on the results.

Exercise 4-8

Using ABC to assess prices

C4 A3 P3

Refer to the information in Exercise 4-6 to answer the following requirements.

Required

1. Using ABC, compute the overhead cost per unit for each product line.

2. Determine the total cost per unit for each product line if the direct labor and direct materials costs per unit are $200 for Model 145 and $180 for Model 212.

Check (3) Model 212, $24.88 per unit profit

3. If the market price for Model 145 is $800 and the market price for Model 212 is $470, determine the profit or loss per unit for each model. Comment on the results.

Exercise 4-9

Using ABC for strategic decisions

P1 P3

Consider the following data for two products of Rowena Manufacturing.

	Overhead Cost	Product A	Product B
Number of units produced		10,000 units	2,000 units
Direct labor cost (@ $24 per DLH)		0.20 DLH per unit	0.25 DLH per unit
Direct materials cost		$2 per unit	$3 per unit
Activity			
Machine setup	$121,000		
Materials handling	48,000		
Quality control	80,000		
	$249,000		

Required

1. Using direct labor hours as the basis for assigning overhead costs, determine the total production cost per unit for each product line.
2. If the market price for Product A is $20 and the market price for Product B is $60, determine the profit or loss per unit for each product. Comment on the results.
3. Consider the following additional information about these two product lines. If ABC is used for assigning overhead costs to products, what is the cost per unit for Product A and for Product B?

Check (2) Product B, $26.10 per unit profit

	Product A	Product B
Number of setups required for production	10 setups	12 setups
Number of parts required	1 part/unit	3 parts/unit
Inspection hours required	40 hours	210 hours

4. Determine the profit or loss per unit for each product. Should this information influence company strategy? Explain.

(4) Product B, ($24.60) per unit loss

Exercise 4-10
Using ABC in a service company
P3

Kumar & Knight is an architectural firm that provides services for residential construction projects. The following data pertain to a recent reporting period.

	Activities	Costs
Design department		
Client consultation	1,500 contact hours	$270,000
Drawings	2,000 design hours	115,000
Modeling	40,000 square feet	30,000
Project management department		
Supervision	600 days	$120,000
Billings	8 jobs	10,000
Collections	8 jobs	12,000

Required

1. Using ABC, compute the firm's activity overhead rates. Form activity cost pools where appropriate.
2. Assign costs to a 9,200 square foot job that requires 450 contact hours, 340 design hours, and 200 days to complete.

Check (2) $150,200

connect *Most materials in this section are available in McGraw-Hill's Connect*

PROBLEM SET A

Problem 4-1A
Evaluating product line costs and prices using ABC
P3

Health Drinks Company produces two beverages, PowerPunch and SlimLife. Data about these products follow.

	PowerPunch	SlimLife
Production volume	12,500 bottles	180,000 bottles
Liquid materials	1,400 gallons	37,000 gallons
Dry materials	620 pounds	12,000 pounds
Bottles	12,500 bottles	180,000 bottles
Labels	3 labels per bottle	1 label per bottle
Machine setups	500 setups	300 setups
Machine hours	200 MH	3,750 MH

Additional data from its two production departments follow.

Department	Driver	Cost
Mixing department		
Liquid materials	Gallons	$ 2,304
Dry materials	Pounds	6,941
Utilities	Machine hours	1,422
Bottling department		
Bottles	Units	$77,000
Labeling	Labels per bottle	6,525
Machine setup	Setups	20,000

Required

1. Determine the cost of each product line using ABC.

2. What is the cost per bottle for PowerPunch? What is the cost per bottle of SlimLife? (*Hint:* Your answer should draw on the total cost for each product line computed in requirement 1.)

Check (3) $2.22 profit per bottle

3. If PowerPunch sells for $3.75 per bottle, how much profit does the company earn per bottle of PowerPunch that it sells?

4. What is the minimum price that the company should set per bottle of SlimLife? Explain.

Problem 4-2A

Applying activity-based costing

C1 C4 A1 A3 P3

Crafton Manufacturing produces machine tools for the construction industry. The following details about overhead costs were taken from its company records.

Production Activity	Indirect Labor	Indirect Materials	Other Overhead
Grinding	$320,000		
Polishing		$135,000	
Product modification	600,000		
Providing power			$255,000
System calibration	500,000		

Additional information on the drivers for its production activities follows.

Grinding	13,000 machine hours
Polishing	13,000 machine hours
Product modification	1,500 engineering hours
Providing power	17,000 direct labor hours
System calibration	400 batches

Required

1. Classify each activity as unit level, batch level, product level, or facility level.

2. Compute the activity overhead rates using ABC. Form cost pools as appropriate.

3. Determine overhead costs to assign to the following jobs using ABC.

	Job 3175	Job 4286
Number of units	200 units	2,500 units
Machine hours	550 MH	5,500 MH
Engineering hours	26 eng. hours	32 eng. hours
Batches	30 batches	90 batches
Direct labor hours	500 DLH	4,375 DLH

4. What is the overhead cost per unit for Job 3175? What is the overhead cost per unit for Job 4286?

5. If the company used a plantwide overhead rate based on direct labor hours, what is the overhead cost for each unit of Job 3175? Of Job 4286?

6. Compare the overhead costs per unit computed in requirements 4 and 5 for each job. Which method more accurately assigns overhead costs?

Check (4) Job 3175, $373.25 per unit

Problem 4-3A
Assessing impacts of using a plantwide overhead rate versus ABC
A1 A2 A3

Maxlon Company manufactures custom-made furniture for its local market and produces a line of home furnishings sold in retail stores across the country. The company uses traditional volume-based methods of assigning direct materials and direct labor to its product lines. Overhead has always been assigned by using a plantwide overhead rate based on direct labor hours. In the past few years, management has seen its line of retail products continue to sell at high volumes, but competition has forced it to lower prices on these items. The prices are declining to a level close to its cost of production.

Meanwhile, its custom-made furniture is in high demand and customers have commented on its favorable (lower) prices compared to its competitors. Management is considering dropping its line of retail products and devoting all of its resources to custom-made furniture.

Required

1. What reasons could explain why competitors are forcing the company to lower prices on its high-volume retail products?

2. Why do you believe the company charges less for custom-order products than its competitors?

3. Does a company's costing method have any effect on its pricing decisions? Explain.

4. Aside from the differences in volume of output, what production differences do you believe exist between making custom-order furniture and mass-market furnishings?

5. What information might the company obtain from using ABC that it might not obtain using volume-based costing methods?

Problem 4-4A
Comparing costs using ABC with the plantwide overhead rate
C1 P1 P3 A1 A3

The following data are for the two products produced by Aplan Company.

	Product A	Product B
Direct materials	$15 per unit	$24 per unit
Direct labor hours	0.3 DLH per unit	1.6 DLH per unit
Machine hours	0.1 MH per unit	1.2 MH per unit
Batches	125 batches	225 batches
Volume	10,000 units	2,000 units
Engineering modifications	12 modifications	58 modifications
Number of customers	500 customers	400 customers
Market price	$30 per unit	$120 per unit

The company's direct labor rate is $20 per direct labor hour (DLH). Additional information follows.

	Costs	Driver
Indirect manufacturing		
Engineering support	$24,500	Engineering modifications
Electricity	34,000	Machine hours
Setup costs	52,500	Batches
Nonmanufacturing		
Customer service	81,000	Number of customers

Required

1. Compute the manufacturing cost per unit using the plantwide overhead rate based on direct labor hours. What is the gross profit per unit?

Check (1) Product A, $26.37 per unit cost

2. How much gross profit is generated by each customer of Product A using the plantwide overhead rate? How much gross profit is generated by each customer of Product B using the plantwide overhead rate? What is the cost of providing customer service to each customer? What information is provided by this comparison?

(3) Product A, $24.30 per unit cost

3. Determine the manufacturing cost per unit of each product line using ABC. What is the gross profit per unit?

4. How much gross profit is generated by each customer of Product A using ABC? How much gross profit is generated by each customer of Product B using ABC? Is the gross profit per customer adequate?

5. Which method of product costing gives better information to managers of this company? Explain why.

Problem 4-5A

Pricing analysis with ABC and a plantwide overhead rate

A1 A2 P1

Camper-Craft Corporation produces two lines of tents sold to outdoor enthusiasts. The tents are cut to specifications in department A. In department B the tents are sewn and folded. The activities, costs, and drivers associated with these two manufacturing processes and its production support activities follow.

Process	Activity	Overhead Cost	Driver	Quantity
Department A	Pattern alignment	$ 64,400	Batches	560
	Cutting	50,430	Machine hours	12,300
	Moving product	100,800	Moves	2,400
		$215,630		
Department B	Sewing	$327,600	Direct labor hours	4,200
	Inspecting	24,000	Inspections	600
	Folding	47,880	Units	22,800
		$399,480		
Support	Design	$280,000	Modification orders	280
	Providing space	51,600	Square feet	8,600
	Materials handling	184,000	Square yards	920,000
		$515,600		

Additional production information on the two lines of tents follows.

	Pup Tent	Pop-Up Tent
Units produced	15,200 units	7,600 units
Moves	800 moves	1,600 moves
Batches	140 batches	420 batches
Number of inspections	240 inspections	360 inspections
Machine hours	7,000 MH	5,300 MH
Direct labor hours	2,600 DLH	1,600 DLH
Modification orders	70 modification orders	210 modification orders
Space occupied	4,300 square feet	4,300 square feet
Material required	450,000 square yards	470,000 square yards

Required

1. Using a plantwide overhead rate based on direct labor hours, compute the overhead cost that is assigned to each pup tent and each pop-up tent.

2. Using the plantwide overhead rate, determine the total cost per unit for the two products if the direct materials and direct labor cost is $25 per pup tent and $32 per pop-up tent.

3. If the market price of the pup tent is $65 and the market price of the pop-up tent is $200, determine the gross profit per unit for each tent. What might management conclude about the pup tent?

Check (4) Pup tent, $58.46 per unit cost

4. Using ABC, compute the total cost per unit for each tent if the direct labor and direct materials cost is $25 per pup tent and $32 per pop-up tent.

5. If the market price is $65 per pup tent and $200 per pop-up tent, determine the gross profit per unit for each tent. Comment on the results.

6. Would your pricing analysis be improved if the company used, instead of ABC, departmental rates determined using machine hours in Department A and direct labor hours in Department B? Explain.

connect ACCOUNTING Available with McGraw-Hill *Connect Accounting*

PROBLEM SET B

Problem 4-1B
Evaluating product line costs and prices using ABC
P3

Mathtime Educational Products produces two electronic, handheld educational games: *Fun with Fractions* and *Count Calculus*. Data on these products follow.

	Fun with Fractions	Count Calculus
Production volume	150,000 units	10,000 units
Components	450,000 parts	100,000 parts
Direct labor hours	15,000 DLH	2,000 DLH
Packaging materials	150,000 boxes	10,000 boxes
Shipping cartons	100 units per carton	25 units per carton
Machine setups	52 setups	52 setups
Machine hours	5,000 MH	2,000 MH

Additional data from its two production departments follow.

Department	Driver	Cost
Assembly department		
Component cost	Parts	$495,000
Assembly labor	Direct labor hours	244,800
Maintenance	Machine hours	100,800
Wrapping department		
Packaging materials	Boxes	$460,800
Shipping	Cartons	27,360
Machine setup	Setups	187,200

Required

1. Using ABC, determine the cost of each product line.
2. What is the cost per unit for Fun with Fractions? What is the cost per unit of Count Calculus?
3. If Count Calculus sells for $59.95 per unit, how much profit does the company earn per unit of Count Calculus sold?
4. What is the minimum price that the company should set per unit of Fun with Fractions? Explain.

Check (3) $32.37 profit per unit

Problem 4-2B
Applying activity-based costing
C1 C4 A1 A3 P3

Fancy Foods produces gourmet gift baskets that it distributes online as well as from its small retail store. The following details about overhead costs are taken from its records.

Production Activity	Indirect Labor	Indirect Materials	Other Overhead
Wrapping	$300,000	$200,000	
Assembling	400,000		
Product design	180,000		
Obtaining business licenses			$100,000
Cooking	150,000	120,000	

Additional information on the drivers for its production activities follows.

Wrapping	100,000 units
Assembling	20,000 direct labor hours
Product design	3,000 design hours
Obtaining business licenses	20,000 direct labor hours
Cooking	1,000 batches

Required

1. Classify each activity as unit level, batch level, product level, or facility level.
2. Compute the activity overhead rates using ABC. Form cost pools as appropriate.
3. Determine the overhead cost to assign to the following jobs using ABC.

	Holiday Basket	Executive Basket
Number of units	8,000 units	1,000 units
Direct labor hours	2,000 DLH	500 DLH
Design hours	40 design hours	40 design hours
Batches	80 batches	200 batches

Check (4) Holiday Basket, $14.25 per unit

(5) Holiday Basket, $18.13 per unit

4. What is the cost per unit for the Holiday Basket? What is the cost per unit for the Executive Basket?
5. If the company used a plantwide overhead rate based on direct labor hours, what is the overhead cost for each Holiday Basket unit? What would be the overhead cost for each Executive Basket unit if a single plantwide overhead rate is used?
6. Compare the costs per unit computed in requirements 4 and 5 for each job. Which cost assignment method provides the most accurate cost? Explain.

Problem 4-3B

Assessing impacts of using a plantwide overhead rate versus ABC

A1 A2 A3

Lakeside Paper produces cardboard boxes. The boxes require designing, cutting, and printing. (The boxes are shipped flat and customers fold them as necessary.) Lakeside has a reputation for providing high-quality products and excellent service to customers, who are major U.S. manufacturers. Costs are assigned to products based on the number of machine hours required to produce them.

Three years ago, a new marketing executive was hired. She suggested the company offer custom design and manufacturing services to small specialty manufacturers. These customers required boxes for their products and were eager to have Lakeside as a supplier. Within one year Lakeside found that it was so busy with orders from small customers, that it had trouble supplying boxes to all its customers on a timely basis. Large, long-time customers began to complain about slow service and several took their business elsewhere. Within another 18 months, Lakeside was in financial distress with a backlog of orders to be filled.

Required

1. What do you believe are the major costs of making its boxes? How are those costs related to the volume of boxes produced?
2. How did Lakeside's new customers differ from its previous customers?
3. Would the unit cost to produce a box for new customers be different from the unit cost to produce a box for its previous customers? Explain.
4. Could Lakeside's fate have been different if it had used ABC for determining the cost of its boxes?
5. What information would have been available with ABC that might have been overlooked using a traditional volume-based costing method?

Problem 4-4B

Comparing costs using ABC with the plantwide overhead rate

C1 A1 A3 P1 P3

Davis Company makes two distinct products with the following information available for each.

	Standard	Deluxe
Direct materials	$4 per unit	$8 per unit
Direct labor hours	4 DLH per unit	5 DLH per unit
Machine hours	3 MH per unit	3 MH per unit
Batches	175 batches	75 batches
Volume	40,000 units	10,000 units
Engineering modifications	50 modifications	25 modifications
Number of customers	1,000 customers	1,000 customers
Market price	$92 per unit	$125 per unit

The company's direct labor rate is $20 per direct labor hour (DLH). Additional information follows.

	Costs	Driver
Indirect manufacturing		
Engineering support	$ 56,250	Engineering modifications
Electricity	112,500	Machine hours
Setup costs	41,250	Batches
Nonmanufacturing		
Customer service	250,000	Number of customers

Required

1. Compute the manufacturing cost per unit using the plantwide overhead rate based on machine hours. What is the gross profit per unit?

2. How much gross profit is generated by each customer of the standard product using the plantwide overhead rate? How much gross profit is generated by each customer of the deluxe product using the plantwide overhead rate? What is the cost of providing customer service to each customer? What information is provided by this comparison?

3. Determine the manufacturing cost per unit of each product line using ABC. What is the gross profit per unit?

4. How much gross profit is generated by each customer of the standard product using ABC? How much gross profit is generated by each customer of the deluxe product using ABC? Is the gross profit per customer adequate?

5. Which method of product costing gives better information to managers of this company? Explain.

Check (1) Gross profit per unit: Standard, $3.80; Deluxe, $12.80

(3) Gross profit per unit: Standard, $4.09; Deluxe, $11.64

Problem 4-5B
Pricing analysis with ABC and a plantwide overhead rate
A1 A2 P1

Spicy Salsa Company produces its condiments in two types: Extra Fine for restaurant customers and Family Style for home use. Salsa is prepared in department 1 and packaged in department 2. The activities, overhead costs, and drivers associated with these two manufacturing processes and its production support activities follow.

Process	Activity	Overhead Cost	Driver	Quantity
Department 1	Mixing	$ 4,500	Machine hours	1,500
	Cooking	11,250	Machine hours	1,500
	Product testing	112,500	Batches	600
		$128,250		
Department 2	Machine calibration	$250,000	Production runs	400
	Labeling	12,000	Cases of output	120,000
	Defects	6,000	Cases of output	120,000
		$268,000		
Support	Recipe formulation	$ 90,000	Focus groups	45
	Heat, lights, and water	27,000	Machine hours	1,500
	Materials handling	65,000	Container types	8
		$182,000		

Additional production information about its two product lines follows.

	Extra Fine	Family Style
Units produced	20,000 cases	100,000 cases
Batches	200 batches	400 batches
Machine hours	500 MH	1,000 MH
Focus groups	30 groups	15 groups
Container types	5 containers	3 containers
Production runs	200 runs	200 runs

Required

1. Using a plantwide overhead rate based on cases, compute the overhead cost that is assigned to each case of Extra Fine Salsa and each case of Family Style Salsa.

2. Using the plantwide overhead rate, determine the total cost per unit for the two products if the direct materials and direct labor cost is $6 per case of Extra Fine and $5 per case of Family Style.

Check (2) Cost per case: Extra Fine, $10.82; Family Style, $9.82

3. If the market price of Extra Fine Salsa is $18 per case and the market price of Family Style Salsa is $9 per case, determine the gross profit per case for each product. What might management conclude about each product line?

4. Using ABC, compute the total cost per case for each product type if the direct labor and direct materials cost is $6 per case of Extra Fine and $5 per case of Family Style.

(4) Cost per case: Extra Fine, $20.02; Family Style, $7.98

5. If the market price is $18 per case of Extra Fine and $9 per case of Family Style, determine the gross profit per case for each product. How should management interpret the market prices given your computations?

6. Would your pricing analysis be improved if the company used departmental rates based on machine hours in department 1 and number of cases in department 2, instead of ABC? Explain.

SERIAL PROBLEM

(This serial problem began in Chapter 1 and continues through most of the book. If previous chapter segments were not completed, the serial problem can begin at this point. It is helpful, but not necessary, to use the Working Papers that accompany the book.)

SP 4 After reading an article about activity-based costing in a trade journal for the furniture industry, Adriana Lopez wondered if it was time to critically analyze overhead costs at Success Systems. In a recent month, Lopez found that setup costs, inspection costs, and utility costs made up most of its overhead. Additional information about overhead follows.

Activity	Cost	Driver
Setting up machines	$20,000	25 batches
Inspecting components	$ 7,500	5,000 parts
Providing utilities	$10,000	5,000 machine hours

Overhead has been applied to output at a rate of 50% of direct labor costs. The following data pertain to Job 6.15.

Direct materials	$2,500
Direct labor	$3,500
Batches	2 batches
Number of parts	400 parts
Machine hours	600 machine hours

Required

1. Classify each of its three overhead activities as unit level, batch level, product level, or facility level.

2. What is the total cost of Job 6.15 if Success Systems applies overhead at 50% of direct labor cost?

3. What is the total cost of Job 6.15 if Success Systems uses activity-based costing?

4. Which approach to assigning overhead gives a better representation of the costs incurred to produce Job 6.15? Explain.

BEYOND THE NUMBERS

REPORTING IN ACTION

C1 A3

BTN 4-1 Refer to financial statements of Best Buy (BestBuy.com) and Circuit City (CircuitCity.com) to answer the following.

Required

1. Identify at least two activities at Best Buy and at Circuit City that cause costs to be incurred. Do you believe these companies should be concerned about controlling costs of the activities you identified? Explain.

2. Would you classify Best Buy and Circuit City as service, merchandising, or manufacturing companies? Explain.
3. Is activity-based costing useful for companies such as Best Buy and Circuit City? Explain.

BTN 4-2 Best Buy and Circuit City are competitors, and both sell products through their Websites and in retail stores. Compare these companies' income statements and answer the following.

COMPARATIVE ANALYSIS

C4 A3

Required

1. Which company has a higher ratio of costs to revenues? Show your analysis.
2. How might the use of activity-based costing help the less competitive company become *more* competitive?
3. Which company has more retail stores? What are the activities associated with opening a new retail store?

BTN 4-3 In conducting interviews and observing factory operations to implement an activity-based costing system, you determine that several activities are unnecessary or redundant. For example, warehouse personnel were inspecting purchased components as they were received at the loading dock. Later that day, the components were inspected again on the shop floor before being installed in the final product. Both of these activities caused costs to be incurred but were not adding value to the product. If you include this observation in your report, one or more employees who perform inspections will likely lose their jobs.

ETHICS CHALLENGE

A3

Required

1. As a plant employee, what is your responsibility to report your findings to superiors?
2. Should you attempt to determine if the redundancy is justified? Explain.
3. What is your responsibility to the employees whose jobs will likely be lost by your report?
4. What facts should you consider before making your decision to report or not?

BTN 4-4 The chief executive officer (CEO) of your company recently returned from a luncheon meeting where activity-based costing was presented and discussed. Though her background is not in accounting, she has worked for the company for 15 years and is thoroughly familiar with its operations. Her impression of the presentation about ABC was that it was just another way of dividing up total overhead cost and that the total would still be the same "no matter how you sliced it."

COMMUNICATING IN PRACTICE

C1 C4

Required

Write a memorandum to the CEO, no more than one page, explaining how ABC is different from traditional volume-based costing methods. Also, identify its advantages and disadvantages vis-à-vis traditional methods. Be sure it is written to be understandable to someone who is not an accountant.

BTN 4-5 Accounting professionals that work for private companies often obtain the Certified Management Accountant (CMA) designation to indicate their proficiency in several business areas in addition to managerial accounting. The CMA examination is administered by the Institute of Management Accountants (IMA).

TAKING IT TO THE NET

C1

Required

Go to the IMA Website (IMAnet.org) and determine which parts of the CMA exam cover activity-based costing. A person planning to become a CMA should take what college course work?

TEAMWORK IN ACTION

C4 A3 P3

BTN 4-6 Observe the operations at your favorite fast-food restaurant.

Required

1. How many people does it take to fill a typical order of sandwich, beverage, and one side-order?
2. Describe the activities involved in its food service process.
3. What costs are related to each activity identified in requirement 2?

ENTREPRENEURIAL DECISION

C4 A3

BTN 4-7 **Oregon Ice Cream Company** has expanded its product offerings from basic chocolate and vanilla type flavors to nearly 100 flavors of ice creams, yogurts, and sorbets, and more than 500 different frozen dairy treats. Tom Gleason's managers for Oregon Ice Cream Company realize that financial success depends on cost control as well as revenue generation.

Required

1. If Oregon Ice Cream Company wanted to expand its product line to include yogurt smoothies, what activities would it need to perform that are not required for its current product lines?
2. Related to part 1, should the additional overhead costs related to new product lines be shared by existing product lines? Explain your reasoning.

HITTING THE ROAD

C4 A3 P3

BTN 4-8 Visit and observe the processes of three different fast-food restaurants—these visits can be done as individuals or as teams. The objective of activity based costing is to accurately assign costs to products and to improve operational efficiency.

Required

1. Individuals (or teams) can be assigned to each of three different fast-food establishments. Make a list of the activities required to process an order of a sandwich, beverage, and one side-order at each restaurant. Record the time required for each process, from placing the order to receiving the completed order.
2. What activities do the three establishments have in common? What activities are different across the establishments?
3. Is the number of activities related to the time required to process an order? Is the number of activities related to the price charged to customers? Explain both.
4. Make recommendations for improving the processes you observe. Would your recommendations increase or decrease the cost of operations?

GLOBAL DECISION

C4 A3

BTN 4-9 Visit the Websites and review the financial statements for **DSG international** (DSGiplc.com), **Best Buy** (BestBuy.com), and **Circuit City** (CircuitCity.com). Each of these companies is a retailer of electronics with extensive online markets.

Required

1. In what country(ies) are DSG's Electricals division stores located?
2. In what country(ies) are the retail stores for Best Buy and Circuit City located?
3. How would customer service activities be different for DSG than for Best Buy or Circuit City? How would these differences affect their costs?

ANSWERS TO MULTIPLE CHOICE QUIZ

1. b; Under traditional costing methods, overhead costs are allocated to products on the basis of some measure of volume such as direct labor hours or machine hours. This results in much of the overhead cost being allocated to high-volume products. In contrast, under activity-based costing, some overhead costs are allocated on the basis of batch level or product level activities. This change in allocation bases results in shifting overhead costs from high-volume products to low-volume products.

2. d; Generally, an activity-based costing system is more difficult to implement and maintain than a traditional costing system (thus statement A is false). Instead of eliminating waste by allocating costs to products that waste resources, activity-based management is a management approach that focuses on managing activities as a means of eliminating waste and reducing delays and defects (thus statement B is false). Instead of using a single allocation base (such as direct labor hours), activity-based costing uses a number of allocation bases for assigning costs to products (thus statement C is false). Statement D is true.

3. d; Batch level activities are activities that are performed each time a batch of goods is handled or processed, regardless of how many units are in a batch. Further, the amount of resources consumed depends on the number of batches rather than on the number of units in the batch. Worker recreational facilities relate to the organization as a whole rather than to specific batches and, as such, are not considered to be batch level. On the other hand, purchase order processing, setting up equipment, and the clerical activities described are activities that are performed each time a batch of goods is handled or processed, and, as such, are batch level activities.

4. c;

	(A) Activity Rate (Budgeted overhead cost ÷ Budgeted activity)	(B) Actual Activity	(A × B) Overhead Cost Applied to Production
Activity 1 . . .	($80,000 ÷ 1,000) = $80.00	800	$ 64,000
Activity 2 . . .	($58,400 ÷ 1,500) = $38.93*	500	19,465
Activity 3 . . .	($360,000 ÷ 6,000) = $60.00	5,400	324,000
Total overhead cost per unit for Product B . . .			$407,465
Divided by number of units produced . . .			÷ 31,652
Overhead cost per unit of Product B . . .			$ 12.87

* rounded

5. d; The activity rate for Activity 3 is determined as follows:

Budgeted cost	÷	Budgeted activity	=	Activity rate
$14,000	÷	700	=	$20

A Look Back

Chapter 4 introduced the activity-based costing (ABC) system with the potential for greater accuracy of cost allocations, ABC provides managers with cost information for strategic decisions.

A Look at This Chapter

This chapter shows how information on both costs and sales behavior is useful to managers in performing cost-volume-profit analysis. This analysis is an important part of successful management and sound business decisions.

A Look Ahead

Chapter 6 compares reports prepared under variable costing with those under absorption costing, and it explains how variable costing can improve managerial decisions.

Chapter

Cost Behavior and Cost-Volume-Profit Analysis

Learning Objectives

CAP

Conceptual

C1 Describe different types of cost behavior in relation to production and sales volume. *(p. 168)*

C2 Identify assumptions in cost-volume-profit analysis and explain their impact. *(p. 177)*

C3 Describe several applications of cost-volume-profit analysis. *(p. 179)*

Analytical

A1 Compare the scatter diagram, high-low, and regression methods of estimating costs. *(p. 173)*

A2 Compute the contribution margin and describe what it reveals about a company's cost structure. *(p. 174)*

A3 Analyze changes in sales using the degree of operating leverage. *(p. 184)*

Procedural

P1 Determine cost estimates using three different methods. *(p. 171)*

P2 Compute the break-even point for a single product company. *(p. 175)*

P3 Graph costs and sales for a single product company. *(p. 176)*

P4 Compute the break-even point for a multiproduct company. *(p. 181)*

LP5

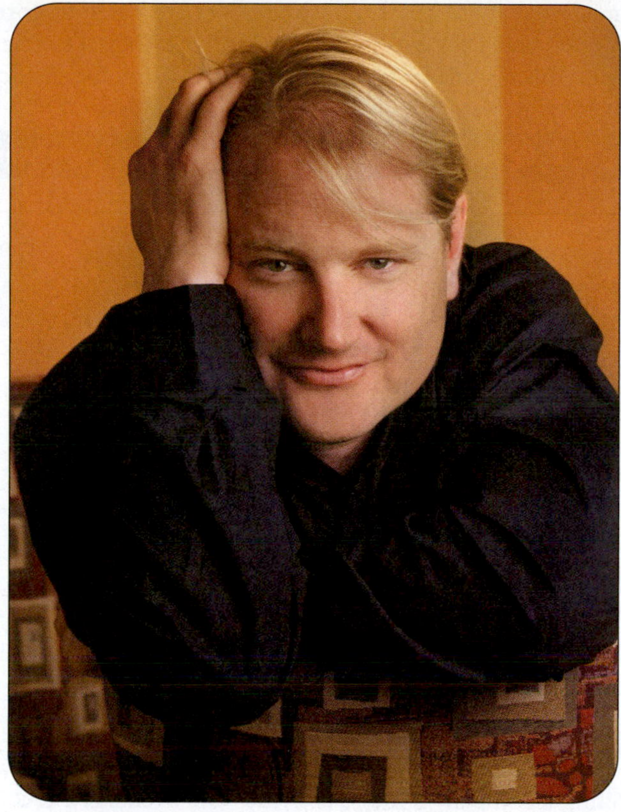

Decision Feature

Recipe for Growth

"Don't sit on the sidelines talking about your dream . . . get out and make it happen"—Martin Sprock

"Welcome to Moe's"! A chorus of welcomes greets each customer at **Moe's Southwest Grill (Moes.com),** a chain of quirky Tex-Mex restaurants, which is part of Raving Brands. The zaniness continues with menu items such as Art Vandalay, Joey Bag of Donuts, the Close Talker, and the Billy Barou. They play music from "dead rock stars" like the Beatles, Elvis Presley, and Jimi Hendrix because "Moe wanted to pay tribute to his heroes who have passed on and would never have a chance to taste his food."

Moe's founder Martin Sprock explains, "We make a point of having the happiest associates. You feel good visiting our stores, and that means something to me. I'd go so far as to say I'd actually be willing to take a date to them."

But there is more to Moe's than fun. Moe's features burritos, tacos, quesadillas, and salads. To appeal to health-conscious diners, Moe's does not use frozen ingredients or microwaves or cook with fat. This recipe has resulted in Moe's being one of the fastest-growing "fast casual" restaurants.

With such rapid growth, an understanding of cost behavior is critical. Identifying fixed and variable costs is key to understanding break-even points and maintaining the right mix of menu choices. Each Moe's manager earns a degree from "Moe's Training School," where the finer points of cost management are taught. Moe's online ordering and payment system is linked with its cash registers to enable managers to better determine which menu items are in demand. An understanding of how costs relate to sales volume and profits helps drive the menu options.

Martin Sprock's vision is to run a chain of restaurants that treats employees as well as they treat owners. This family-first mentality and service-oriented approach have spurred Moe's growth. Sprock, a former ski bum, encourages potential entrepreneurs to get out and make it happen. "I had no money when I started trying to fulfill my ambitions . . . I just did it."

[Sources: *Moe's Southwest Grill Website*, January 2009; *Go AirTran Airways* Magazine, 2005; *Atlanta Business Chronicle*, May 2008; *Pittsburgh Business Times*, March 2008.

Chapter Preview

This chapter describes different types of costs and shows how changes in a company's operating volume affect these costs. The chapter also analyzes a company's costs and sales to explain how different operating strategies affect profit or loss. Managers use this type of analysis to forecast what will happen if changes are made to costs, sales volume, selling prices, or product mix. They then use these forecasts to select the best business strategy for the company.

Cost Behavior and Cost-Volume-Profit Analysis

Identifying Cost Behavior
- Fixed costs
- Variable costs
- Mixed costs
- Step-wise costs
- Curvilinear costs

Measuring Cost Behavior
- Scatter diagrams
- High-low method
- Least-squares regression
- Comparison of cost estimation methods

Using Break-Even Analysis
- Computing contribution margin
- Computing break-even
- Preparing a cost-volume-profit chart
- Making assumptions in cost-volume-profit analysis

Applying Cost-Volume-Profit Analysis
- Computing income from sales and costs
- Computing sales for target income
- Computing margin of safety
- Using sensitivity analysis
- Computing multiproduct break-even

Identifying Cost Behavior

Video5.1

Planning a company's future activities and events is a crucial phase in successful management. One of the first steps in planning is to predict the volume of activity, the costs to be incurred, sales to be made, and profit to be received. An important tool to help managers carry out this step is **cost-volume-profit (CVP) analysis,** which helps them predict how changes in costs and sales levels affect income. In its basic form, CVP analysis involves computing the sales level at which a company neither earns an income nor incurs a loss, called the *break-even point.* For this reason, this basic form of cost-volume-profit analysis is often called *break-even analysis.* Managers use variations of CVP analysis to answer questions such as these:

Point: *Profit* is another term for *income.*

- What sales volume is needed to earn a target income?
- What is the change in income if selling prices decline and sales volume increases?
- How much does income increase if we install a new machine to reduce labor costs?
- What is the income effect if we change the sales mix of our products or services?

Consequently, cost-volume-profit analysis is useful in a wide range of business decisions.

Conventional cost-volume-profit analysis requires management to classify all costs as either *fixed* or *variable* with respect to production or sales volume. The remainder of this section discusses the concepts of fixed and variable cost behavior as they relate to CVP analysis.

Decision Insight

No Free Lunch Hardly a week goes by without a company advertising a free product with the purchase of another. Examples are a free printer with a digital camera purchase or a free monitor with a computer purchase. Can these companies break even, let alone earn profits? We are reminded of the *no-free-lunch* adage, meaning that companies expect profits from the companion or add-on purchase to make up for the free product.

C1 Describe different types of cost behavior in relation to production and sales volume.

Fixed Costs

A *fixed cost* remains unchanged in amount when the volume of activity varies from period to period within a relevant range. For example, $5,000 in monthly rent paid for a factory building remains the same whether the factory operates with a single eight-hour shift or around the clock with three shifts. This means that rent cost is the same each month at any level of output from zero to the plant's full productive capacity. Notice that while *total* fixed cost does not change as the level of production changes, the fixed cost *per unit* of output decreases as volume increases. For instance, if 20 units are produced when monthly rent is \$5,000, the average rent cost per unit is \$250 (computed as \$5,000/20 units). When production increases to 100 units per month, the average cost per unit decreases to \$50 (computed as \$5,000/100 units). The average cost decreases to \$10 per unit if production increases to 500 units per month. Common examples of fixed costs include depreciation, property taxes, office salaries, and many service department costs.

Point: Fixed costs do not change when volume changes, but the per unit cost declines as volume increases.

When production volume and costs are graphed, units of product are usually plotted on the *horizontal axis* and dollars of cost are plotted on the *vertical axis.* Fixed costs then are represented as a horizontal line because they remain constant at all levels of production. To illustrate, the graph in Exhibit 5.1 shows that fixed costs remain at \$32,000 at all production levels up to the company's monthly capacity of 2,000 units of output. The *relevant range* for fixed costs in Exhibit 5.1 is 0 to 2,000 units. If the relevant range changes (that is, production capacity extends beyond this range), the amount of fixed costs will likely change.

Example: If the fixed cost line in Exhibit 5.1 is shifted upward, does the total cost line shift up, down, or remain in the same place? *Answer:* It shifts up by the same amount.

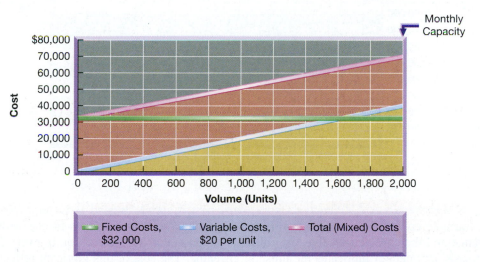

EXHIBIT 5.1

Relations of Fixed and Variable Costs to Volume

Monthly Capacity

Cost: \$80,000; 70,000; 60,000; 50,000; 40,000; 30,000; 20,000; 10,000; 0

Volume (Units): 0; 200; 400; 600; 800; 1,000; 1,200; 1,400; 1,600; 1,800; 2,000

Fixed Costs, \$32,000 — Variable Costs, \$20 per unit — Total (Mixed) Costs

Example: If the level of fixed costs in Exhibit 5.1 changes, does the slope of the total cost line change? *Answer:* No, the slope doesn't change. The total cost line is simply shifted upward or downward.

Variable Costs

A *variable cost* changes in proportion to changes in volume of activity. The direct materials cost of a product is one example of a variable cost. If one unit of product requires materials costing \$20, total materials costs are \$200 when 10 units of product are manufactured, \$400 for 20 units, \$600 for 30 units, and so on. Notice that variable cost *per unit* remains constant but the *total* amount of variable cost changes with the level of production. In addition to direct materials, common variable costs include direct labor (if employees are paid per unit), sales commissions, shipping costs, and some overhead costs.

Point: Fixed costs are constant in total but vary (decline) per unit as more units are produced. Variable costs vary in total but are fixed per unit.

When variable costs are plotted on a graph of cost and volume, they appear as a straight line starting at the zero cost level. This straight line is upward (positive) sloping. The line rises as volume of activity increases. A variable cost line using a \$20 per unit cost is graphed in Exhibit 5.1.

Mixed Costs

A **mixed cost** includes both fixed and variable cost components. For example, compensation for sales representatives often includes a fixed monthly salary and a variable commission based on sales. The total cost line in Exhibit 5.1 is a mixed cost. Like a fixed cost, it is greater than zero when volume is zero; but unlike a fixed cost, it increases steadily in proportion to increases in volume. The mixed cost line in Exhibit 5.1 starts on the vertical axis at the \$32,000 fixed cost point. Thus, at the zero volume level, total cost equals the fixed costs. As the activity level increases, the mixed cost line increases at an amount equal to the variable cost per unit. This line is highest when volume of activity is at 2,000 units (the end point of the relevant range). In CVP analysis, mixed costs are often separated into fixed and variable components. The fixed component is added to other fixed costs, and the variable component is added to other variable costs.

Step-Wise Costs

A **step-wise cost** reflects a step pattern in costs. Salaries of production supervisors often behave in a step-wise manner in that their salaries are fixed within a *relevant range* of the current production volume. However, if production volume expands significantly (for example, with the addition of another shift), additional supervisors must be hired. This means that the total cost for supervisory salaries goes up by a lump-sum amount. Similarly, if volume takes another significant step up, supervisory salaries will increase by another lump sum. This behavior reflects a step-wise cost, also known as a *stair-step cost,* which is graphed in Exhibit 5.2. See how the step-wise cost line is flat within ranges (steps). Then, when volume significantly changes, it shifts to another level for that range (step).

EXHIBIT 5.2

Step-Wise and Curvilinear Costs

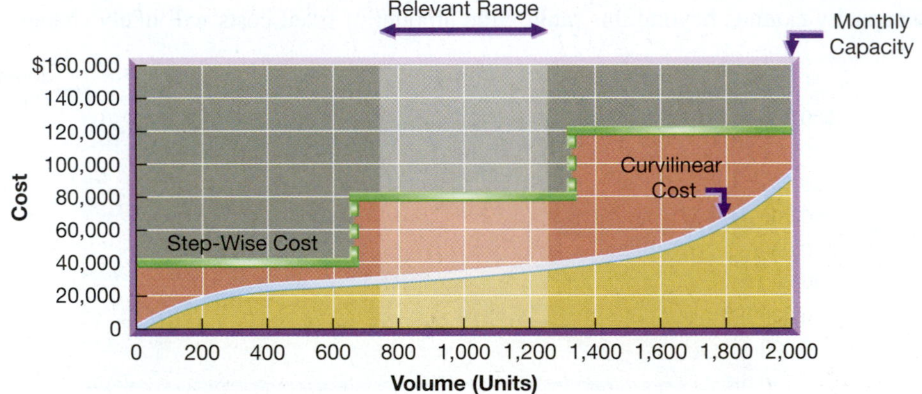

In a conventional CVP analysis, a step-wise cost is usually treated as either a fixed cost or a variable cost. This treatment involves manager judgment and depends on the width of the range and the expected volume. To illustrate, suppose after the production of every 25 snowboards, an operator lubricates the finishing machine. The cost of this lubricant reflects a step-wise pattern. Also, suppose that after the production of every 1,000 units, the snowboard cutting tool is replaced. Again, this is a step-wise cost. Note that the range of 25 snowboards is much narrower than the range of 1,000 snowboards. Some managers might treat the lubricant cost as a variable cost and the cutting tool cost as a fixed cost.

Point: Computer spreadsheets are important and effective tools for CVP analysis and for analyzing alternative "what-if" strategies.

Curvilinear Costs

A variable cost, as explained, is a *linear* cost; that is, it increases at a constant rate as volume of activity increases. A **curvilinear cost,** also called a *nonlinear cost,* increases at a nonconstant rate as volume increases. When graphed, curvilinear costs appear as a curved line. Exhibit 5.2 shows a curvilinear cost beginning at zero when production is zero and then increasing at different rates.

An example of a curvilinear cost is total direct labor cost when workers are paid by the hour. At low to medium levels of production, adding more employees allows each of them to specialize by doing certain tasks repeatedly instead of doing several different tasks. This often yields additional units of output at lower costs. A point is eventually reached at which adding more employees creates inefficiencies. For instance, a large crew demands more time and effort in communicating and coordinating their efforts. While adding employees in this case increases output, the labor cost per unit increases, and the total labor cost goes up at a steeper slope. This pattern is seen in Exhibit 5.2 where the curvilinear cost curve starts at zero, rises, flattens out, and then increases at a faster rate as output nears the maximum.

Point: Cost-volume-profit analysis helped Rod Canion, Jim Harris, and Bill Murto raise start-up capital of $20 million to launch **Compaq Computer.** They showed that break-even volumes were attainable within the first year.

Quick Check Answers—p. 188

1. Which of the following statements is typically true? (*a*) Variable cost per unit increases as volume increases, (*b*) fixed cost per unit decreases as volume increases, or (*c*) a curvilinear cost includes both fixed and variable elements.
2. Describe the behavior of a fixed cost.
3. If cost per unit of activity remains constant (fixed), why is it called a variable cost?

Measuring Cost Behavior

P1 Determine cost estimates using three different methods.

Identifying and measuring cost behavior requires careful analysis and judgment. An important part of this process is to identify costs that can be classified as either fixed or variable, which often requires analysis of past cost behavior. Three methods are commonly used to analyze past costs: scatter diagrams, high-low method, and least-squares regression. Each method is discussed in this section using the unit and cost data shown in Exhibit 5.3, which are taken from a start-up company that uses units produced as the activity base in estimating cost behavior.

EXHIBIT 5.3
Data for Estimating Cost Behavior

Month	Units Produced	Total Cost
January	17,500	$20,500
February	27,500	21,500
March	25,000	25,000
April	35,000	21,500
May	47,500	25,500
June	22,500	18,500
July	30,000	23,500
August	52,500	28,500
September	37,500	26,000
October	57,500	26,000
November	62,500	31,000
December	67,500	29,000

Scatter Diagrams

Scatter diagrams display past cost and unit data in graphical form. In preparing a scatter diagram, units are plotted on the horizontal axis and cost is plotted on the vertical axis. Each individual point on a scatter diagram reflects the cost and number of units for a prior period. In Exhibit 5.4, the prior 12 months' costs and numbers of units are graphed. Each point reflects total costs incurred and units produced for one of those months. For instance, the point labeled March had units produced of 25,000 and costs of $25,000.

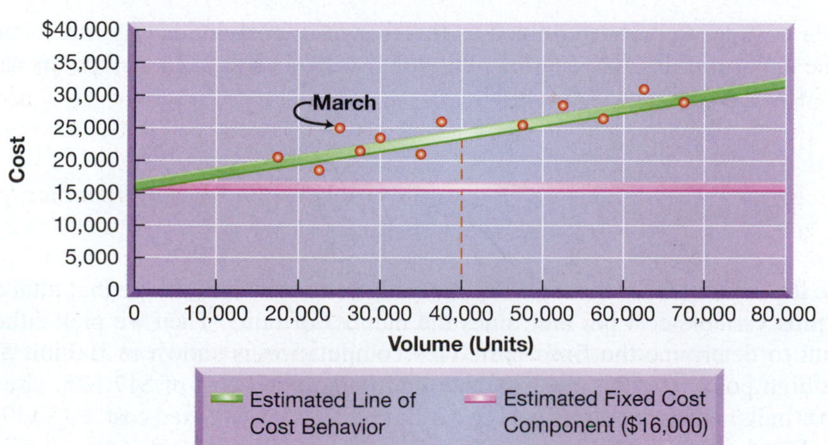

EXHIBIT 5.4
Scatter Diagram

The **estimated line of cost behavior** is drawn on a scatter diagram to reflect the relation between cost and unit volume. This line best visually "fits" the points in a scatter diagram. Fitting this line demands judgment. The line drawn in Exhibit 5.4 intersects the vertical axis at approximately $16,000, which reflects fixed cost. To compute variable cost per unit, or the slope, we perform three steps. First, we select any two points on the horizontal axis (units), say 0 and 40,000. Second, we draw a vertical line from each of these points to intersect the estimated line of cost behavior. The point on the vertical axis (cost) corresponding to the 40,000 units point that intersects the estimated line is roughly $24,000. Similarly, the cost corresponding to zero units is $16,000 (the fixed cost point). Third, we compute the slope of the line, or variable cost, as the change in cost divided by the change in units. Exhibit 5.5 shows this computation.

EXHIBIT 5.5

Variable Cost per Unit (Scatter Diagram)

$$\frac{\textbf{Change in cost}}{\textbf{Change in units}} = \frac{\$24{,}000 - \$16{,}000}{40{,}000 - 0} = \frac{\$8{,}000}{40{,}000} = \$0.20 \text{ per unit}$$

Example: In Exhibits 5.4 and 5.5, if units are projected at 30,000, what is the predicted cost? *Answer:* Approximately $22,000.

Variable cost is $0.20 per unit. Thus, the cost equation that management will use to estimate costs for different unit levels is **$16,000 plus $0.20 per unit**.

High-Low Method

The **high-low method** is a way to estimate the cost equation by graphically connecting the two cost amounts at the highest and lowest unit volumes. In our case, the lowest number of units is 17,500, and the highest is 67,500. The costs corresponding to these unit volumes are $20,500 and $29,000, respectively (see the data in Exhibit 5.3). The estimated line of cost behavior for the high-low method is then drawn by connecting these two points on the scatter diagram corresponding to the lowest and highest unit volumes as follows.

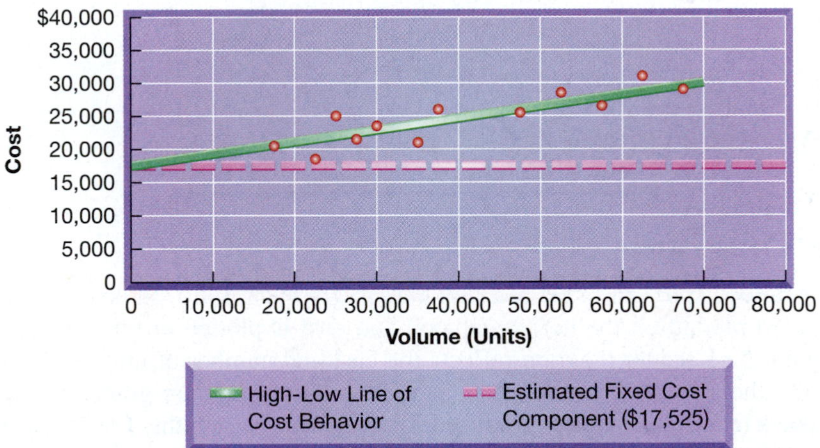

Point: Note that the high-low method identifies the high and low points of the volume (activity) base, and the costs linked with those extremes—which may not be the highest and lowest costs.

The variable cost per unit is determined as the change in cost divided by the change in units and uses the data from the high and low unit volumes. This results in a slope, or variable cost per unit, of $0.17 as computed in Exhibit 5.6.

EXHIBIT 5.6

Variable Cost per Unit (High-Low Method)

$$\frac{\textbf{Change in cost}}{\textbf{Change in units}} = \frac{\$29{,}000 - \$20{,}500}{67{,}500 - 17{,}500} = \frac{\$8{,}500}{50{,}000} = \$0.17 \text{ per unit}$$

To estimate the fixed cost for the high-low method, we use the knowledge that total cost equals fixed cost plus variable cost per unit times the number of units. Then we pick either the high or low point to determine the fixed cost. This computation is shown in Exhibit 5.7—where we use the high point (67,500 units) in determining the fixed cost of $17,525. Use of the low point (17,500 units) yields the same fixed cost estimate: $20,500 = Fixed cost + ($0.17 per unit × 17,500), or Fixed cost = $17,525.

EXHIBIT 5.7

Fixed Cost (High-Low Method)

Total cost = Fixed cost + (Variable cost × Units)	
\$29,000 = Fixed cost + (\$0.17 per unit × 67,500 units)	
Then, Fixed cost = \$17,525	

Thus, the cost equation used to estimate costs at different units is **\$17,525 plus \$0.17 per unit**. This cost equation differs slightly from that determined from the scatter diagram method. A deficiency of the high-low method is that it ignores all cost points except the highest and lowest. The result is less precision because the high-low method uses the most extreme points rather than the more usual conditions likely to recur.

Least-Squares Regression

Least-squares regression is a statistical method for identifying cost behavior. For our purposes, we use the cost equation estimated from this method but leave the computational details for more advanced courses. Such computations for least-squares regression are readily done using most spreadsheet programs or calculators. We illustrate this using Excel® in Appendix 5A.

The regression cost equation for the data presented in Exhibit 5.3 is **\$16,947 plus \$0.19 per unit**; that is, the fixed cost is estimated as \$16,947 and the variable cost at \$0.19 per unit. Both costs are reflected in the following graph.

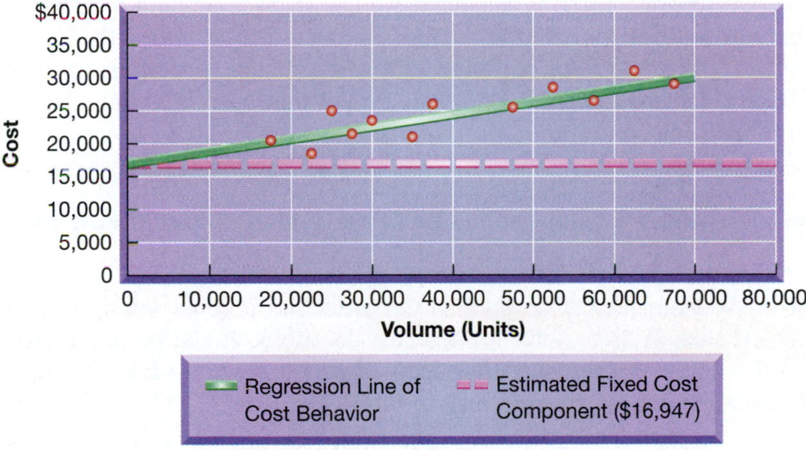

Comparison of Cost Estimation Methods

A1 Compare the scatter diagram, high-low, and regression methods of estimating costs.

The three cost estimation methods result in slightly different estimates of fixed and variable costs as summarized in Exhibit 5.8. Estimates from the scatter diagram are based on a visual fit of the cost line and are subject to interpretation. Estimates from the high-low method use only two sets of values corresponding to the lowest and highest unit volumes. Estimates from least-squares regression use a statistical technique and all available data points.

EXHIBIT 5.8

Comparison of Cost Estimation Methods

Estimation Method	Fixed Cost	Variable Cost
Scatter diagram	\$16,000	\$0.20 per unit
High-low method	17,525	0.17 per unit
Least-squares regression	16,947	0.19 per unit

We must remember that all three methods use *past data.* Thus, cost estimates resulting from these methods are only as good as the data used for estimation. Managers must establish that the data are reliable in deriving cost estimates for the future.

Quick Check Answers—p. 188

4. Which of the following methods is likely to yield the most precise estimated line of cost behavior? (*a*) High-low, (*b*) least-squares regression, or (*c*) scatter diagram.
5. What is the primary weakness of the high-low method?
6. Using conventional CVP analysis, a mixed cost should be (*a*) disregarded, (*b*) treated as a fixed cost, or (*c*) separated into fixed and variable components.

Using Break-Even Analysis

Video5.2

Break-even analysis is a special case of cost-volume-profit analysis. This section describes break-even analysis by computing the break-even point and preparing a CVP (or break-even) chart.

Contribution Margin and Its Measures

A2 Compute the contribution margin and describe what it reveals about a company's cost structure.

We explained how managers classify costs by behavior. This often refers to classifying costs as being fixed or variable with respect to volume of activity. In manufacturing companies, volume of activity usually refers to the number of units produced. We then classify a cost as either fixed or variable, depending on whether total cost changes as the number of units produced changes. Once we separate costs by behavior, we can then compute a product's contribution margin. **Contribution margin per unit,** or *unit contribution margin,* is the amount by which a product's unit selling price exceeds its total unit variable cost. This excess amount contributes to covering fixed costs and generating profits on a per unit basis. Exhibit 5.9 shows the contribution margin per unit formula.

EXHIBIT 5.9
Contribution Margin per Unit

$$\textbf{Contribution margin per unit} = \textbf{Sales price per unit} - \textbf{Total variable cost per unit}$$

The **contribution margin ratio,** which is the percent of a unit's selling price that exceeds total unit variable cost, is also useful for business decisions. It can be interpreted as the percent of each sales dollar that remains after deducting the total unit variable cost. Exhibit 5.10 shows the formula for the contribution margin ratio.

EXHIBIT 5.10
Contribution Margin Ratio

$$\textbf{Contribution margin ratio} = \frac{\textbf{Contribution margin per unit}}{\textbf{Sales price per unit}}$$

To illustrate the use of contribution margin, let's consider **Rydell**, which sells footballs for \$100 per unit and incurs variable costs of \$70 per unit sold. Its fixed costs are \$24,000 per month with monthly capacity of 1,800 units (footballs). Rydell's contribution margin per unit is \$30, which is computed as follows.

Selling price per unit	\$100
Variable cost per unit	70
Contribution margin per unit	\$ 30

Its contribution margin ratio is 30%, computed as \$30/\$100. This reveals that for each unit sold, Rydell has \$30 that contributes to covering fixed cost and profit. If we consider sales in dollars, a contribution margin of 30% implies that for each \$1 in sales, Rydell has \$0.30 that contributes to fixed cost and profit.

Decision Maker

Sales Manager You are evaluating orders from two customers but can accept only one of the orders because of your company's limited capacity. The first order is for 100 units of a product with a contribution margin ratio of 60% and a selling price of $1,000. The second order is for 500 units of a product with a contribution margin ratio of 20% and a selling price of $800. The incremental fixed costs are the same for both orders. Which order do you accept? [Answer—p. 187]

Computing the Break-Even Point

P2 Compute the break-even point for a single product company.

The **break-even point** is the sales level at which a company neither earns a profit nor incurs a loss. The concept of break-even is applicable to nearly all organizations, activities, and events. One of the most important items of information when launching a project is whether it will break even—that is, whether sales will at least cover total costs. The break-even point can be expressed in either units or dollars of sales.

To illustrate the computation of break-even analysis, let's again look at Rydell, which sells footballs for $100 per unit and incurs $70 of variable costs per unit sold. Its fixed costs are $24,000 per month. Rydell breaks even for the month when it sells 800 footballs (sales volume of $80,000). We compute this break-even point using the formula in Exhibit 5.11. This formula uses the contribution margin per unit, which for Rydell is $30 ($100 − $70). From this we can compute the break-even sales volume as $24,000/$30, or 800 units per month.

$$\textbf{Break-even point in units} = \frac{\textbf{Fixed costs}}{\textbf{Contribution margin per unit}}$$

EXHIBIT 5.11

Formula for Computing Break-Even Sales (in Units)

At a price of $100 per unit, monthly sales of 800 units yield sales dollars of $80,000 (called *break-even sales dollars*). This $80,000 break-even sales can be computed directly using the formula in Exhibit 5.12.

Point: The break-even point is where total expenses equal total sales and the profit is zero.

$$\textbf{Break-even point in dollars} = \frac{\textbf{Fixed costs}}{\textbf{Contribution margin ratio}}$$

EXHIBIT 5.12

Formula for Computing Break-Even Sales (in Dollars)

Rydell's break-even point in dollars is computed as $24,000/0.30, or $80,000 of monthly sales. To verify that Rydell's break-even point equals $80,000 (or 800 units), we prepare a simplified income statement in Exhibit 5.13. It shows that the $80,000 revenue from sales of 800 units exactly equals the sum of variable and fixed costs.

Point: Even if a company operates at a level in excess of its break-even point, management may decide to stop operating because it is not earning a reasonable return on investment.

RYDELL COMPANY
Contribution Margin Income Statement (at Break-Even)
For Month Ended January 31, 2009

Sales (800 units at $100 each)	$80,000
Variable costs (800 units at $70 each)	56,000
Contribution margin	24,000
Fixed costs	24,000
Net income	$ 0

EXHIBIT 5.13

Contribution Margin Income Statement for Break-Even Sales

Point: A contribution margin income statement is also referred to as a ***variable costing income statement.*** This differs from the traditional ***absorption costing*** approach where all product costs are assigned to units sold and to units in ending inventory. Recall that variable costing expenses all fixed product costs. Thus, income for the two approaches differs depending on the level of finished goods inventory; the lower inventory is, the more similar the two approaches are.

The statement in Exhibit 5.13 is called a *contribution margin income statement.* It differs in format from a conventional income statement in two ways. First, it separately classifies costs and expenses as variable or fixed. Second, it reports contribution margin (Sales − Variable costs). The contribution margin income statement format is used in this chapter's assignment materials because of its usefulness in CVP analysis.

Preparing a Cost-Volume-Profit Chart

P3 Graph costs and sales for a single product company.

Exhibit 5.14 is a graph of Rydell's cost-volume-profit relations. This graph is called a **cost-volume-profit (CVP) chart,** or a *break-even chart* or *break-even graph.* The horizontal axis is the number of units produced and sold and the vertical axis is dollars of sales and costs. The lines in the chart depict both sales and costs at different output levels.

EXHIBIT 5.14

Cost-Volume-Profit Chart

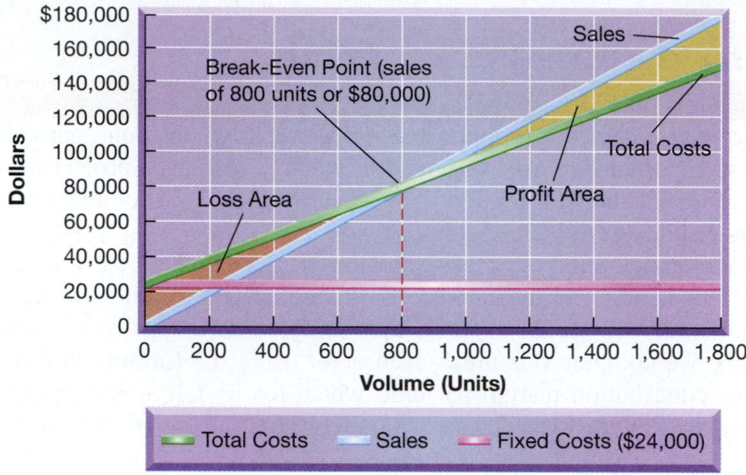

We follow three steps to prepare a CVP chart, which can also be drawn with computer programs that convert numeric data to graphs:

1. Plot fixed costs on the vertical axis ($24,000 for Rydell). Draw a horizontal line at this level to show that fixed costs remain unchanged regardless of output volume (drawing this fixed cost line is not essential to the chart).
2. Draw the total (variable plus fixed) costs line for a relevant range of volume levels. This line starts at the fixed costs level on the vertical axis because total costs equal fixed costs at zero volume. The slope of the total cost line equals the variable cost per unit ($70). To draw the line, compute the total costs for any volume level, and connect this point with the vertical axis intercept ($24,000). Do not draw this line beyond the productive capacity for the planning period (1,800 units for Rydell).
3. Draw the sales line. Start at the origin (zero units and zero dollars of sales) and make the slope of this line equal to the selling price per unit ($100). To sketch the line, compute dollar sales for any volume level and connect this point with the origin. Do not extend this line beyond the productive capacity. Total sales will be at the highest level at maximum capacity.

Example: In Exhibit 5.14, the sales line intersects the total cost line at 800 units. At what point would the two lines intersect if selling price is increased by 20% to $120 per unit? *Answer:* $24,000/($120 − $70) = 480 units

The total costs line and the sales line intersect at 800 units in Exhibit 5.14, which is the break-even point—the point where total dollar sales of $80,000 equals the sum of both fixed and variable costs ($80,000).

On either side of the break-even point, the vertical distance between the sales line and the total costs line at any specific volume reflects the profit or loss expected at that point. At volume levels to the left of the break-even point, this vertical distance is the amount of the expected loss because the total costs line is above the total sales line. At volume levels to the right of the break-even point, the vertical distance represents the expected profit because the total sales line is above the total costs line.

Decision Maker

Operations Manager As a start-up manufacturer, you wish to identify the behavior of manufacturing costs to develop a production cost budget. You know three methods can be used to identify cost behavior from past data, but past data are unavailable because this is a start-up. What do you do? [Answer—p. 187]

Making Assumptions in Cost-Volume-Profit Analysis

C2 Identify assumptions in cost-volume-profit analysis and explain their impact.

Cost-volume-profit analysis assumes that relations can normally be expressed as simple lines similar to those in Exhibits 5.4 and 5.14. Such assumptions allow users to answer several important questions, but the usefulness of the answers depends on the validity of three assumptions: (1) constant selling price per unit, (2) constant variable costs per unit, and (3) constant total fixed costs. These assumptions are not always realistic, but they do not necessarily limit the usefulness of CVP analysis as a way to better understand costs and sales. This section discusses these assumptions and other issues for CVP analysis.

Working with Assumptions The behavior of individual costs and sales often is not perfectly consistent with CVP assumptions. If the expected costs and sales behavior differ from the assumptions, the results of CVP analysis can be limited. Still, we can perform useful analyses in spite of limitations with these assumptions for several reasons.

Summing costs can offset individual deviations. Deviations from assumptions with individual costs are often minor when these costs are summed. That is, individual variable cost items may not be perfectly variable, but when we sum these variable costs, their individual deviations can offset each other. This means the assumption of variable cost behavior can be proper for total variable costs. Similarly, an assumption that total fixed costs are constant can be proper even when individual fixed cost items are not exactly constant.

Point: CVP analysis can be very useful for business decision making even when its assumptions are not strictly met.

CVP is applied to a relevant range of operations. Sales, variable costs, and fixed costs often are reasonably reflected in straight lines on a graph when the assumptions are applied over a relevant range. The **relevant range of operations** is the normal operating range for a business. Except for unusually difficult or prosperous times, management typically plans for operations within a range of volume neither close to zero nor at maximum capacity. The relevant range excludes extremely high and low operating levels that are unlikely to occur. The validity of assuming that a specific cost is fixed or variable is more acceptable when operations are within the relevant range. As shown in Exhibit 5.2, a curvilinear cost can be treated as variable and linear if the relevant range covers volumes where it has a nearly constant slope. If the normal range of activity changes, some costs might need reclassification.

Video5.2

CVP analysis yields estimates. CVP analysis yields approximate answers to questions about costs, volumes, and profits. These answers do not have to be precise because the analysis makes rough estimates about the future. As long as managers understand that CVP analysis gives estimates, it can be a useful tool for starting the planning process. Other qualitative factors also must be considered.

Working with Output Measures CVP analysis usually describes the level of activity in terms of *sales volume,* which can be expressed in terms of either units sold or dollar sales. However, other measures of output exist. For instance, a manufacturer can use the number of units produced as a measure of output. Also, to simplify analysis, we sometimes assume that the production level is the same as the sales level. That is, inventory levels do not change. This often is justified by arguing that CVP analysis provides only approximations.

Example: If the selling price declines, what happens to the break-even point? *Answer:* It increases.

Quick Check

Answers—p. 188

7. Fixed cost divided by the contribution margin ratio yields the (*a*) break-even point in dollars, (*b*) contribution margin per unit, or (*c*) break-even point in units.
8. A company sells a product for $90 per unit with variable costs of $54 per unit. What is the contribution margin ratio?
9. Refer to Quick Check (8). If fixed costs for the period are $90,000, what is the break-even point in dollars?
10. What three basic assumptions are used in CVP analysis?

Working with Changes in Estimates Because CVP analysis uses estimates, knowing how changes in those estimates impact break-even is useful. For example, a manager might form three estimates for each of the components of breakeven: optimistic, most likely, and pessimistic. Then ranges of break-even points in units can be computed using the formula in Exhibit 5.11.

To illustrate, assume Rydell's managers provide the set of estimates in Exhibit 5.15.

EXHIBIT 5.15

Alternative Estimates for Break-Even Analysis

	Selling Price per Unit	Variable Cost per Unit	Total Fixed Costs
Optimistic	$105	$68	$21,000
Most likely	100	70	24,000
Pessimistic	95	72	27,000

If, for example, Rydell's managers believe they can raise the selling price of a football to $105, without any change in variable or fixed costs, then the revised contribution margin per football is $35, and the revised break-even in units follows in Exhibit 5.16.

EXHIBIT 5.16

Revised Break-Even in Units

$$\text{Revised break-even point in units} = \frac{\$24{,}000}{\$35} = 686 \text{ units}$$

EXHIBIT 5.17

Scatter Diagrams—Break-Even Points for Alternative Estimates

Repeating this calculation using each of the other eight separate estimates above, and graphing the results, yields the three scatter diagrams in Exhibit 5.17.

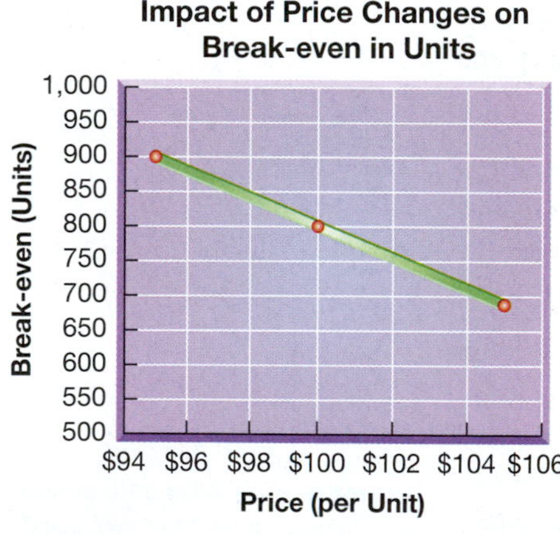

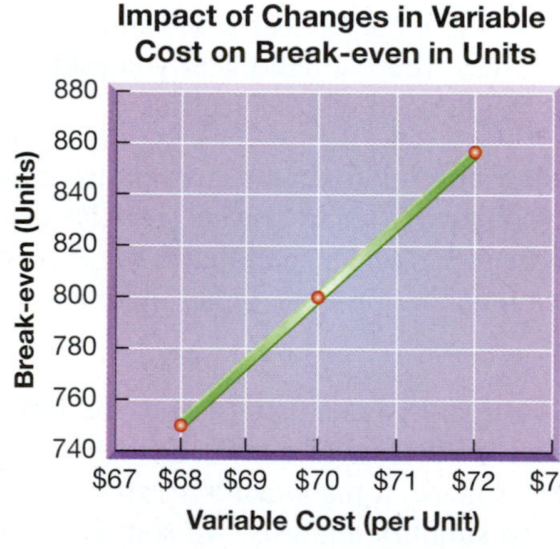

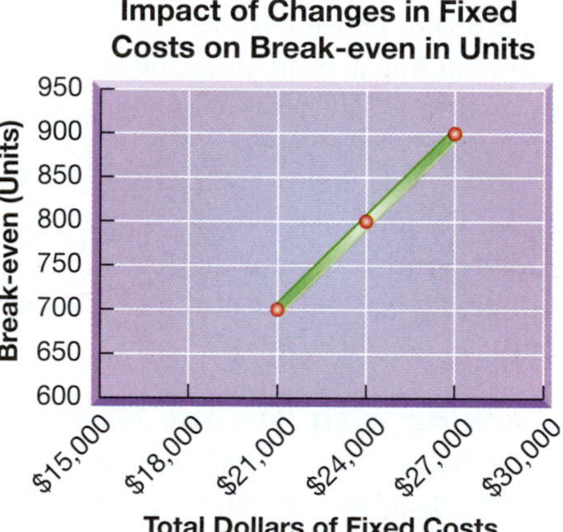

These scatter diagrams show how changes in selling prices, variable costs, and fixed costs impact break-even. When selling prices can be increased without impacting costs, break-even decreases. When competition drives selling prices down, and the company cannot reduce costs, break-even increases. Increases in either variable or fixed costs, if they cannot be passed on to customers via higher selling prices, will increase break-even. If costs can be reduced and selling prices held constant, the break-even decreases.

Point: This analysis changed only one estimate at a time; managers can examine how combinations of changes in estimates will impact break-even.

Applying Cost-Volume-Profit Analysis

Managers consider a variety of strategies in planning business operations. Cost-volume-profit analysis is useful in helping managers evaluate the likely effects of these strategies, which is the focus of this section.

Computing Income from Sales and Costs

C3 Describe several applications of cost-volume-profit analysis.

An important question managers often need an answer to is "What is the predicted income from a predicted level of sales?" To answer this, we look at four variables in CVP analysis. These variables and their relations to income (pretax) are shown in Exhibit 5.18. We use these relations to compute expected income from predicted sales and cost levels.

EXHIBIT 5.18

Income Relations in CVP Analysis

Sales
− Variable costs
Contribution margin
− Fixed costs
Income (pretax)

To illustrate, let's assume that Rydell's management expects to sell 1,500 units in January 2009. What is the amount of income if this sales level is achieved? Following Exhibit 5.18, we compute Rydell's expected income in Exhibit 5.19.

EXHIBIT 5.19

Computing Expected Pretax Income from Expected Sales

RYDELL COMPANY
Contribution Margin Income Statement
For Month Ended January 31, 2009

Sales (1,500 units at $100 each)	$150,000
Variable costs (1,500 units at $70 each)	105,000
Contribution margin	45,000
Fixed costs	24,000
Income (pretax)	$ 21,000

The $21,000 income is pretax. To find the amount of *after-tax* income from selling 1,500 units, management must apply the proper tax rate. Assume that the tax rate is 25%. Then we can prepare the after-tax income statement shown in Exhibit 5.20. We can also compute pretax income as after-tax income divided by (1 − tax rate); for Rydell, this is $15,750/(1 − 0.25), or $21,000.

EXHIBIT 5.20

Computing Expected After-Tax Income from Expected Sales

RYDELL COMPANY
Contribution Margin Income Statement
For Month Ended January 31, 2009

Sales (1,500 units at $100 each)	$150,000
Variable costs (1,500 units at $70 each)	105,000
Contribution margin	45,000
Fixed costs	24,000
Pretax income	21,000
Income taxes (25%)	5,250
Net income (after tax)	$ 15,750

Management then assesses whether this income is an adequate return on assets invested. Management should also consider whether sales and income can be increased by raising or lowering prices. CVP analysis is a good tool for addressing these kinds of "what-if" questions.

"How many units must I sell to earn $50,000?"

Computing Sales for a Target Income

Many companies' annual plans are based on certain income targets (sometimes called *budgets*). Rydell's income target for this year is to increase income by 10% over the prior year. When prior year income is known, Rydell easily computes its target income. CVP analysis helps to determine the sales level needed to achieve the target income. Computing this sales level is important because planning for the year is then based on this level. We use the formula shown in Exhibit 5.21 to compute sales for a target *after-tax* income.

EXHIBIT 5.21

Computing Sales (Dollars) for a Target After-Tax Income

$$\textbf{Dollar sales at target after-tax income} = \frac{\textbf{Fixed costs} + \textbf{Target pretax income}}{\textbf{Contribution margin ratio}}$$

To illustrate, Rydell has monthly fixed costs of $24,000 and a 30% contribution margin ratio. Assume that it sets a target monthly after-tax income of $9,000 when the tax rate is 25%. This means the pretax income is targeted at $12,000 [$9,000/(1 − 0.25)] with a tax expense of $3,000. Using the formula in Exhibit 5.21, we find that $120,000 of sales are needed to produce a $9,000 after-tax income as shown in Exhibit 5.22.

EXHIBIT 5.22

Rydell's Dollar Sales for a Target Income

$$\text{Dollar sales at target after-tax income} = \frac{\$24{,}000 + \$12{,}000}{30\%} = \$120{,}000$$

Point: Break-even is a special case of the formulas in Exhibits 5.21 and 5.23; simply set target pretax income to $0 and the formulas reduce to those in Exhibits 5.11 and 5.12.

We can alternatively compute *unit sales* instead of dollar sales. To do this, we substitute *contribution margin per unit* for the contribution margin ratio in the denominator. This gives the number of units to sell to reach the target after-tax income. Exhibit 5.23 illustrates this for Rydell. The two computations in Exhibits 5.22 and 5.23 are equivalent because sales of 1,200 units at $100 per unit equal $120,000 of sales.

EXHIBIT 5.23

Computing Sales (Units) for a Target After-Tax Income

$$\textbf{Unit sales at target after-tax income} = \frac{\textbf{Fixed costs} + \textbf{Target pretax income}}{\textbf{Contribution margin per unit}}$$

$$= \frac{\$24{,}000 + \$12{,}000}{\$30} = 1{,}200 \text{ units}$$

Computing the Margin of Safety

All companies wish to sell more than the break-even number of units. The excess of expected sales over the break-even sales level is called a company's **margin of safety,** the amount that sales can drop before the company incurs a loss. It can be expressed in units, dollars, or even as a percent of the predicted level of sales. To illustrate, if Rydell's expected sales are $100,000, the margin of safety is $20,000 above break-even sales of $80,000. As a percent, the margin of safety is 20% of expected sales as shown in Exhibit 5.24.

EXHIBIT 5.24

Computing Margin of Safety (in Percent)

$$\textbf{Margin of safety (in percent)} = \frac{\textbf{Expected sales} - \textbf{Break-even sales}}{\textbf{Expected sales}}$$

$$= \frac{\$100{,}000 - \$80{,}000}{\$100{,}000} = 20\%$$

Management must assess whether the margin of safety is adequate in light of factors such as sales variability, competition, consumer tastes, and economic conditions.

Decision Ethics

Supervisor Your team is conducting a cost-volume-profit analysis for a new product. Different sales projections have different incomes. One member suggests picking numbers yielding favorable income because any estimate is "as good as any other." Another member points to a scatter diagram of 20 months' production on a comparable product and suggests dropping unfavorable data points for cost estimation. What do you do? [Answer—p. 187]

Using Sensitivity Analysis

Earlier we showed how changing one of the estimates in a CVP analysis impacts breakeven. We can also examine strategies that impact several estimates in the CVP analysis. For instance, we might want to know what happens to income if we automate a currently manual process. We can use CVP analysis to predict income if we can describe how these changes affect a company's fixed costs, variable costs, selling price, and volume.

To illustrate, assume that Rydell Company is looking into buying a new machine that would increase monthly fixed costs from $24,000 to $30,000 but decrease variable costs from $70 per unit to $60 per unit. The machine is used to produce output whose selling price will remain unchanged at $100. This results in increases in both the unit contribution margin and the contribution margin ratio. The revised contribution margin per unit is $40 ($100 − $60), and the revised contribution margin ratio is 40% of selling price ($40/$100). Using CVP analysis, Rydell's revised break-even point in dollars would be $75,000 as computed in Exhibit 5.25.

Example: If fixed costs decline, what happens to the break-even point? *Answer:* It decreases.

EXHIBIT 5.25

Revising Break-Even When Changes Occur

$$\textbf{Revised break-even point in dollars} = \frac{\textbf{Revised fixed costs}}{\textbf{Revised contribution margin ratio}} = \frac{\$30{,}000}{40\%} = \$75{,}000$$

The revised fixed costs and the revised contribution margin ratio can be used to address other issues including computation of (1) expected income for a given sales level and (2) the sales level needed to earn a target income. Once again, we can use sensitivity analysis to generate different sets of revenue and cost estimates that are *optimistic, pessimistic,* and *most likely.* Different CVP analyses based on these estimates provide different scenarios that management can analyze and use in planning business strategy.

Point: Price competition led paging companies to give business to resellers—companies that lease services at a discount and then resell to subscribers. **Paging Network** charged some resellers under $1 per month, less than a third of what was needed to break even. Its CEO now admits the low-price strategy was flawed.

Decision Insight

Eco-CVP Ford Escape, Toyota Prius, and Honda Insight are hybrids. Many promise to save owners $1,000 or more a year in fuel costs relative to comparables, and they generate fewer greenhouse gases. Are these models economically feasible? Analysts estimate that **Ford** can break even with its Escape when a $3,000 premium is paid over comparable gas-based models.

Quick Check

Answers—p. 188

11. A company has fixed costs of $50,000 and a 25% contribution margin ratio. What dollar sales are necessary to achieve an after-tax net income of $120,000 if the tax rate is 20%? (*a*) $800,000, (*b*) $680,000, or (*c*) $600,000.
12. If a company's contribution margin ratio decreases from 50% to 25%, what can be said about the unit sales needed to achieve the same target income level?
13. What is a company's margin of safety?

Computing a Multiproduct Break-Even Point

P4 Compute the break-even point for a multiproduct company.

To this point, we have looked only at cases where the company sells a single product or service. This was to keep the basic CVP analysis simple. However, many companies sell multiple products or services, and we can modify the CVP analysis for use in these cases. An important assumption in a multiproduct setting is that the sales mix of different products is known and remains constant during the planning period. **Sales mix** is the ratio (proportion) of the sales volumes for the various products. For instance, if a company normally sells 10,000 footballs, 5,000 softballs, and 4,000 basketballs per month, its sales mix can be expressed as 10:5:4 for footballs, softballs, and basketballs.

To apply multiproduct CVP analysis, we can estimate the break-even point by using a **composite unit,** which consists of a specific number of units of each product in proportion to their expected sales mix. Multiproduct CVP analysis treats this composite unit as a single product. To illustrate, let's look at **Hair-Today**, a styling salon that offers three cuts: basic, ultra, and budget in the ratio of 4 basic units to 2 ultra units to 1 budget unit (expressed as 4:2:1). Management wants to estimate its break-even point for next year. Unit selling prices for these three cuts are basic, $20; ultra, $32; and budget, $16. Using the 4:2:1 sales mix, the selling price of a composite unit of the three products is computed as follows.

4 units of basic @ $20 per unit	$ 80
2 units of ultra @ $32 per unit	64
1 unit of budget @ $16 per unit	16
Selling price of a composite unit	$160

Point: Selling prices and variable costs are usually expressed in per unit amounts. Fixed costs are usually expressed in total amounts.

Hair-Today's fixed costs are $192,000 per year, and its variable costs of the three products are basic, $13; ultra, $18.00; and budget, $8.00. Variable costs for a composite unit of these products follow.

4 units of basic @ $13 per unit	$52
2 units of ultra @ $18 per unit	36
1 unit of budget @ $8 per unit	8
Variable costs of a composite unit	$96

Hair-Today's $64 contribution margin for a composite unit is computed by subtracting the variable costs of a composite unit ($96) from its selling price ($160). We then use the contribution margin to determine Hair-Today's break-even point in composite units in Exhibit 5.26.

EXHIBIT 5.26

Break-Even Point in Composite Units

$$\textbf{Break-even point in composite units} = \frac{\textbf{Fixed costs}}{\textbf{Contribution margin per composite unit}}$$

$$= \frac{\$192{,}000}{\$64} = 3{,}000 \text{ composite units}$$

Point: The break-even point in dollars for Exhibit 5.26 is $192,000/($64/$160) = $480,000.

This computation implies that Hair-Today breaks even when it sells 3,000 composite units. To determine how many units of each product it must sell to break even, we multiply the number of units of each product in the composite by 3,000 as follows.

Basic:	4 × 3,000	12,000 units
Ultra:	2 × 3,000	6,000 units
Budget:	1 × 3,000	3,000 units

Instead of computing contribution margin per composite unit, a company can compute a **weighted-average contribution margin.** Given the 4:2:1 product mix, basic cuts comprise 57.14% (computed as 4/7) of the company's haircuts, ultra makes up 14.29% of its business, and budget cuts comprise 28.57%. The weighted-average contribution margin follows in Exhibit 5.27.

EXHIBIT 5.27

Weighted-Average Contribution Margin

	Unit contribution margin	×	Percentage of sales mix	=	Weighted unit contribution margin
Basic	$ 7		57.14%		$4.000
Ultra	14		28.57		4.000
Budget	8		14.29		1.143
Weighted-average contribution margin					$9.143

The company's break-even point in units is computed as follows:

EXHIBIT 5.28

Break-Even in Units Using Weighted-Average Contribution Margin

$$\textbf{Break-even point in units} = \frac{\textbf{Fixed costs}}{\textbf{Weighted-average contribution margin}}$$

$$= \frac{\$192{,}000}{\$9.143} = 21{,}000 \text{ units}$$

We see that the weighted-average contribution margin method yields 21,000 whole units as the break-even amount, the same total as the composite unit approach.

Exhibit 5.29 verifies the results for composite units by showing Hair-Today's sales and costs at this break-even point using a contribution margin income statement.

EXHIBIT 5.29

Multiproduct Break-Even Income Statement

HAIR-TODAY
Forecasted Contribution Margin Income Statement (at Breakeven)

	Basic	Ultra	Budget	Totals
Sales				
Basic (12,000 @ $20)	$240,000			
Ultra (6,000 @ $32)		$192,000		
Budget (3,000 @ $16)			$48,000	
Total sales				$480,000
Variable costs				
Basic (12,000 @ $13)	156,000			
Ultra (6,000 @ $18)		108,000		
Budget (3,000 @ $8)			24,000	
Total variable costs				288,000
Contribution margin	$ 84,000	$ 84,000	$24,000	192,000
Fixed costs				192,000
Net income				$ 0

A CVP analysis using composite units can be used to answer a variety of planning questions. Once a product mix is set, all answers are based on the assumption that the mix remains constant at all relevant sales levels as other factors in the analysis do. We also can vary the sales mix to see what happens under alternative strategies.

Decision Maker

Entrepreneur A CVP analysis indicates that your start-up, which markets electronic products, will break even with the current sales mix and price levels. You have a target income in mind. What analysis might you perform to assess the likelihood of achieving this income? [Answer—p. 187]

Quick Check

Answers—p. 188

14. The sales mix of a company's two products, X and Y, is 2:1. Unit variable costs for both products are $2, and unit sales prices are $5 for X and $4 for Y. What is the contribution margin per composite unit? (*a*) $5, (*b*) $10, or (*c*) $8.

15. What additional assumption about sales mix must be made in doing a conventional CVP analysis for a company that produces and sells more than one product?

Decision Analysis — Degree of Operating Leverage

A3 Analyze changes in sales using the degree of operating leverage.

CVP analysis is especially useful when management begins the planning process and wishes to predict outcomes of alternative strategies. These strategies can involve changes in selling prices, fixed costs, variable costs, sales volume, and product mix. Managers are interested in seeing the effects of changes in some or all of these factors.

One goal of all managers is to get maximum benefits from their fixed costs. Managers would like to use 100% of their output capacity so that fixed costs are spread over the largest number of units. This would decrease fixed cost per unit and increase income. The extent, or relative size, of fixed costs in the total cost structure is known as **operating leverage.** Companies having a higher proportion of fixed costs in their total cost structure are said to have higher operating leverage. An example of this is a company that chooses to automate its processes instead of using direct labor, increasing its fixed costs and lowering its variable costs. A useful managerial measure to help assess the effect of changes in the level of sales on income is the **degree of operating leverage (DOL)** defined in Exhibit 5.30.

EXHIBIT 5.30
Degree of Operating Leverage

DOL = Total contribution margin (in dollars)/Pretax income

To illustrate, let's return to Rydell Company. At a sales level of 1,200 units, Rydell's total contribution margin is $36,000 (1,200 units × $30 contribution margin per unit). Its pretax income, after subtracting fixed costs of $24,000, is $12,000 ($36,000 − $24,000). Rydell's degree of operating leverage at this sales level is 3.0, computed as contribution margin divided by pretax income ($36,000/$12,000). We then use DOL to measure the effect of changes in the level of sales on pretax income. For instance, suppose Rydell expects sales to increase by 10%. If this increase is within the relevant range of operations, we can expect this 10% increase in sales to result in a 30% increase in pretax income computed as DOL multiplied by the increase in sales (3.0 × 10%). Similar analyses can be done for expected decreases in sales.

Demonstration Problem

Sport Caps Co. manufactures and sells caps for different sporting events. The fixed costs of operating the company are $150,000 per month, and the variable costs for caps are $5 per unit. The caps are sold for $8 per unit. The fixed costs provide a production capacity of up to 100,000 caps per month.

Required

1. Use the formulas in the chapter to compute the following:
   a. Contribution margin per cap.
   b. Break-even point in terms of the number of caps produced and sold.
   c. Amount of net income at 30,000 caps sold per month (ignore taxes).
   d. Amount of net income at 85,000 caps sold per month (ignore taxes).
   e. Number of caps to be produced and sold to provide $45,000 of after-tax income, assuming an income tax rate of 25%.
2. Draw a CVP chart for the company, showing cap output on the horizontal axis. Identify (*a*) the break-even point and (*b*) the amount of pretax income when the level of cap production is 70,000. (Omit the fixed cost line.)
3. Use the formulas in the chapter to compute the
   a. Contribution margin ratio.
   b. Break-even point in terms of sales dollars.
   c. Amount of net income at $250,000 of sales per month (ignore taxes).
   d. Amount of net income at $600,000 of sales per month (ignore taxes).
   e. Dollars of sales needed to provide $45,000 of after-tax income, assuming an income tax rate of 25%.

Planning the Solution

- Identify the formulas in the chapter for the required items expressed in units and solve them using the data given in the problem.

- Draw a CVP chart that reflects the facts in the problem. The horizontal axis should plot the volume in units up to 100,000, and the vertical axis should plot the total dollars up to $800,000. Plot the total cost line as upward sloping, starting at the fixed cost level ($150,000) on the vertical axis and increasing until it reaches $650,000 at the maximum volume of 100,000 units. Verify that the break-even point (where the two lines cross) equals the amount you computed in part 1.
- Identify the formulas in the chapter for the required items expressed in dollars and solve them using the data given in the problem.

Solution to Demonstration Problem

1. a. Contribution margin per cap = Selling price per unit − Variable cost per unit
= $8 − $5 = $3

b. Break-even point in caps $= \dfrac{\text{Fixed costs}}{\text{Contribution margin per cap}} = \dfrac{\$150{,}000}{\$3} = \underline{\underline{50{,}000 \text{ caps}}}$

c. Net income at 30,000 caps sold = (Units × Contribution margin per unit) − Fixed costs
= (30,000 × $3) − $150,000 = $(60,000) loss

d. Net income at 85,000 caps sold = (Units × Contribution margin per unit) − Fixed costs
= (85,000 × $3) − $150,000 = $105,000 profit

e. Pretax income = $45,000/(1 − 0.25) = $60,000
Income taxes = $60,000 × 25% = $15,000

Units needed for $45,000 income $= \dfrac{\text{Fixed costs} + \text{Target pretax income}}{\text{Contribution margin per cap}}$

$= \dfrac{\$150{,}000 + \$60{,}000}{\$3} = \underline{\underline{70{,}000 \text{ caps}}}$

2. CVP chart.

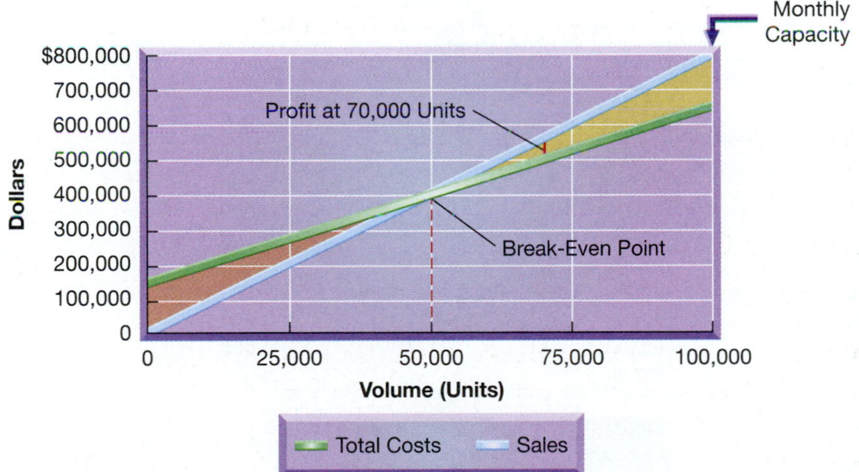

3. a. Contribution margin ratio $= \dfrac{\text{Contribution margin per unit}}{\text{Selling price per unit}} = \dfrac{\$3}{\$8} = \underline{\underline{0.375}}, \text{ or } \underline{\underline{37.5\%}}$

b. Break-even point in dollars $= \dfrac{\text{Fixed costs}}{\text{Contribution margin ratio}} = \dfrac{\$150{,}000}{37.5\%} = \underline{\underline{\$400{,}000}}$

c. Net income at sales of $250,000 = (Sales × Contribution margin ratio) − Fixed costs
= ($250,000 × 37.5%) − $150,000 = $(56,250) loss

d. Net income at sales of $600,000 = (Sales × Contribution margin ratio) − Fixed costs
= ($600,000 × 37.5%) − $150,000 = $75,000 income

e. Dollars of sales to yield $45,000 after-tax income $= \dfrac{\text{Fixed costs} + \text{Target pretax income}}{\text{Contribution margin ratio}}$

$= \dfrac{\$150{,}000 + \$60{,}000}{37.5\%} = \underline{\underline{\$560{,}000}}$

APPENDIX

5A Using Excel to Estimate Least-Squares Regression

Microsoft Excel® 2007 and other spreadsheet software can be used to perform least-squares regressions to identify cost behavior. In Excel®, the INTERCEPT and SLOPE functions are used. The following screen shot reports the data from Exhibit 5.3 in cells Al through C13 and shows the cell contents to find the intercept (cell B16) and slope (cell B17). Cell B16 uses Excel® to find the intercept from a least-squares regression of total cost (shown as C2:C13 in cell B16) on units produced (shown as B2:B13 in cell B16). Spreadsheet software is useful in understanding cost behavior when many data points (such as monthly total costs and units produced) are available.

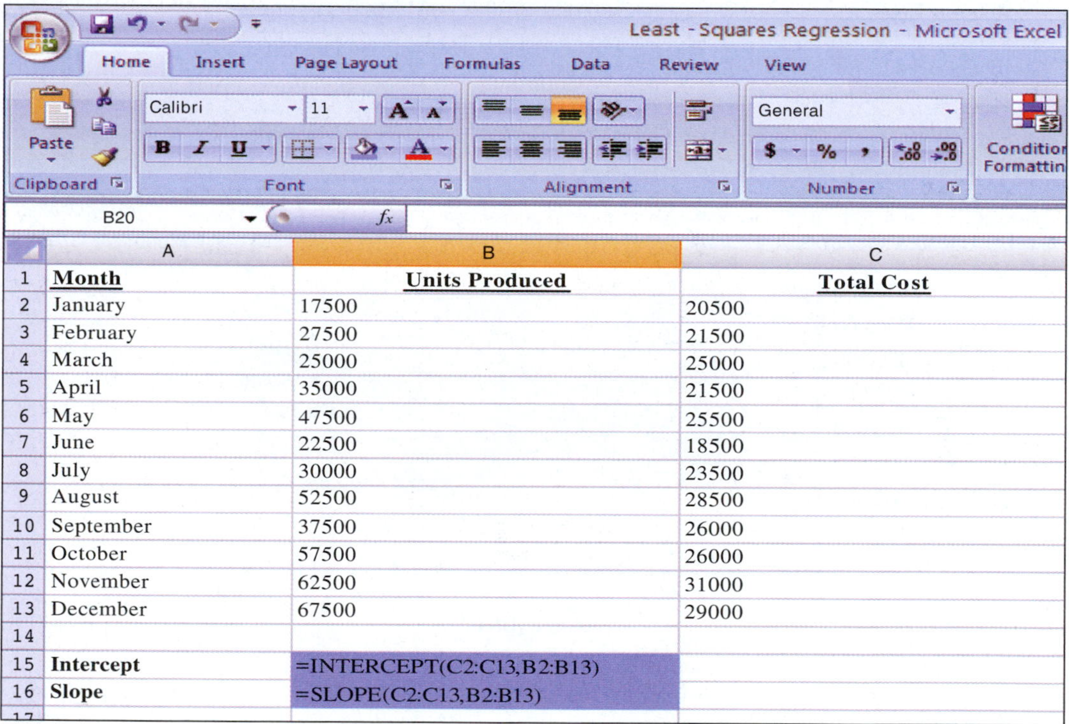

	A	B	C
1	**Month**	**Units Produced**	**Total Cost**
2	January	17500	20500
3	February	27500	21500
4	March	25000	25000
5	April	35000	21500
6	May	47500	25500
7	June	22500	18500
8	July	30000	23500
9	August	52500	28500
10	September	37500	26000
11	October	57500	26000
12	November	62500	31000
13	December	67500	29000
14			
15	**Intercept**	=INTERCEPT(C2:C13,B2:B13)	
16	**Slope**	=SLOPE(C2:C13,B2:B13)	

Excel® can also be used to create scatter diagrams such as that in Exhibit 5.4. In contrast to visually drawing a line that "fits" the data, Excel® more precisely fits the regression line. To draw a scatter diagram with a line of fit, follow these steps:

1. Highlight the data cells you wish to diagram; in this example, start from cell C13 and highlight through cell B2.
2. Then select "Insert" and "Scatter" from the drop-down menus. Selecting the chart type in the upper left corner of the choices under Scatter will produce a diagram that looks like that in Exhibit 5.4, without a line of fit.
3. To add a line of fit (also called trend line), select "Layout" and "Trendline" from the drop-down menus. Selecting "Linear Trendline" will produce a diagram that looks like that in Exhibit 5.4, including the line of fit.

Summary

C1 Describe different types of cost behavior in relation to production and sales volume. Cost behavior is described in terms of how its amount changes in relation to changes in volume of activity within a relevant range. Fixed costs remain constant to changes in volume. Total variable costs change in direct proportion to volume changes. Mixed costs display the effects of both fixed and variable components. Step-wise costs remain constant over a small volume range, then change by a lump sum and remain constant over another volume range, and so on. Curvilinear costs change in a nonlinear relation to volume changes.

C2 Identify assumptions in cost-volume-profit analysis and explain their impact. Conventional cost-volume-profit analysis is based on assumptions that the product's selling price remains constant and that variable and fixed costs behave in a manner consistent with their variable and fixed classifications.

C3 Describe several applications of cost-volume-profit analysis. Cost-volume-profit analysis can be used to predict what can happen under alternative strategies concerning sales volume, selling prices, variable costs, or fixed costs. Applications include "what-if" analysis, computing sales for a target income, and break-even analysis.

A1 Compare the scatter diagram, high-low, and regression methods of estimating costs. Cost estimates from a scatter diagram are based on a visual fit of the cost line. Estimates from the high-low method are based only on costs corresponding to the lowest and highest sales. The least-squares regression method is a statistical technique and uses all data points.

A2 Compute the contribution margin and describe what it reveals about a company's cost structure. Contribution margin per unit is a product's sales price less its total variable costs. Contribution margin ratio is a product's contribution margin per unit divided by its sales price. Unit contribution margin is the amount received from each sale that contributes to fixed costs and income. The contribution margin ratio reveals what portion of each sales dollar is available as contribution to fixed costs and income.

A3 Analyze changes in sales using the degree of operating leverage. The extent, or relative size, of fixed costs in a company's total cost structure is known as *operating leverage*. One tool useful in assessing the effect of changes in sales on income is the degree of operating leverage, or DOL. DOL is the ratio of the contribution margin divided by pretax income. This ratio can be used to determine the expected percent change in income given a percent change in sales.

P1 Determine cost estimates using three different methods. Three different methods used to estimate costs are the scatter diagram, the high-low method, and least-squares regression. All three methods use past data to estimate costs.

P2 Compute the break-even point for a single product company. A company's break-even point for a period is the sales volume at which total revenues equal total costs. To compute a break-even point in terms of sales units, we divide total fixed costs by the contribution margin per unit. To compute a break-even point in terms of sales dollars, divide total fixed costs by the contribution margin ratio.

P3 Graph costs and sales for a single product company. The costs and sales for a company can be graphically illustrated using a CVP chart. In this chart, the horizontal axis represents the number of units sold and the vertical axis represents dollars of sales or costs. Straight lines are used to depict both costs and sales on the CVP chart.

P4 Compute the break-even point for a multiproduct company. CVP analysis can be applied to a multiproduct company by expressing sales volume in terms of composite units. A composite unit consists of a specific number of units of each product in proportion to their expected sales mix. Multiproduct CVP analysis treats this composite unit as a single product.

Guidance Answers to **Decision Maker** and **Decision Ethics**

Sales Manager The contribution margin per unit for the first order is $600 (60% of $1,000); the contribution margin per unit for the second order is $160 (20% of $800). You are likely tempted to accept the first order based on its high contribution margin per unit, but you must compute the total contribution margin based on the number of units sold for each order. Total contribution margin is $60,000 ($600 per unit × 100 units) and $80,000 ($160 per unit × 500 units) for the two orders, respectively. The second order provides the largest return in absolute dollars and is the order you would accept. Another factor to consider in your selection is the potential for a long-term relationship with these customers including repeat sales and growth.

Operations Manager Without the availability of past data, none of the three methods described in the chapter can be used to measure cost behavior. Instead, the manager must investigate whether data from similar manufacturers can be accessed. This is likely difficult due to the sensitive nature of such data. In the absence of data, the manager should develop a list of the different production inputs and identify input-output relations. This provides guidance to the manager in measuring cost behavior. After several months, actual cost data will be available for analysis.

Supervisor Your dilemma is whether to go along with the suggestions to "manage" the numbers to make the project look like it will achieve sufficient profits. You should not succumb to these suggestions. Many people will likely be affected negatively if you manage the predicted numbers and the project eventually is unprofitable. Moreover, if it does fail, an investigation would likely reveal that data in the proposal were "fixed" to make it look good. Probably the only benefit from managing the numbers is the short-term payoff of pleasing those who proposed the product. One way to deal with this dilemma is to prepare several analyses showing results under different assumptions and then let senior management make the decision.

Entrepreneur You must first compute the level of sales required to achieve the desired net income. Then you must conduct sensitivity analysis by varying the price, sales mix, and cost estimates. Results from the sensitivity analysis provide information you can use to assess the possibility of reaching the target sales level. For instance, you might have to pursue aggressive marketing strategies to push the high-margin products, or you might have to cut prices to increase sales and profits, or another strategy might emerge.

Guidance Answers to **Quick Checks**

1. *b*

2. A fixed cost remains unchanged in total amount regardless of output levels. However, fixed *cost per unit* declines with increased output.

3. Such a cost is considered variable because the *total* cost changes in proportion to volume changes.

4. *b*

5. The high-low method ignores all costs and sales (activity base) volume data points except the costs corresponding to the highest and lowest (most extreme) sales (activity base) volume.

6. *c*

7. *a*

8. ($90 − $54)/$90 = 40%

9. $90,000/40% = $225,000

10. Three basic CVP assumptions are that (1) selling price per unit is constant, (2) variable costs per unit are constant, and (3) total fixed costs are constant.

11. a; Two steps are required for explanation:
(1) Pretax income = $120,000/(1 − 0.20) = $150,000
(2) $\frac{\$50{,}000 + \$150{,}000}{25\%} = \$800{,}000$

12. If the contribution margin ratio decreases from 50% to 25%, unit sales would have to double.

13. A company's margin of safety is the excess of the predicted sales level over its break-even sales level.

14. *c*; Selling price of a composite unit:

2 units of X @ $5 per unit	$10
1 unit of Y @ $4 per unit	4
Selling price of a composite unit	$14

Variable costs of a composite unit:

2 units of X @ $2 per unit	$4
1 unit of Y @ $2 per unit	2
Variable costs of a composite unit	$6

Therefore, the contribution margin per composite unit is $8.

15. It must be assumed that the sales mix remains unchanged at all sales levels in the relevant range.

Key Terms

mhhe.com/wildMA2e

Key Terms are available at the book's Website for learning and testing in an online Flashcard Format.

Break-even point (p. 175)
Composite unit (p. 182)
Contribution margin per unit (p. 174)
Contribution margin ratio (p. 174)
Cost-volume-profit (CVP) analysis (p. 168)
Cost-volume-profit (CVP) chart (p. 176)
Curvilinear cost (p. 170)
Degree of operating leverage (DOL) (p. 184)
Estimated line of cost behavior (p. 172)
High-low method (p. 172)
Least-squares regression (p. 173)
Margin of safety (p. 180)
Mixed cost (p. 169)
Operating leverage (p. 184)
Relevant range of operations (p. 177)
Sales mix (p. 181)
Scatter diagram (p. 171)
Step-wise cost (p. 170)
Weighted-average contribution margin (p. 182)

Multiple Choice Quiz

Answers on p. 203

mhhe.com/wildMA2e

Additional Quiz Questions are available at the book's Website.

Quiz5

1. A company's only product sells for $150 per unit. Its variable costs per unit are $100, and its fixed costs total $75,000. What is its contribution margin per unit?
a. $50
b. $250
c. $100
d. $150
e. $25

2. Using information from question 1, what is the company's contribution margin ratio?
a. 66⅔%
b. 100%
c. 50%
d. 0%
e. 33⅓%

3. Using information from question 1, what is the company's break-even point in units?
a. 500 units
b. 750 units
c. 1,500 units
d. 3,000 units
e. 1,000 units

4. A company's forecasted sales are $300,000 and its sales at break-even are $180,000. Its margin of safety in dollars is
a. $180,000.
b. $120,000.

c. $480,000.
d. $60,000.
e. $300,000.

5. A product sells for $400 per unit and its variable costs per unit are $260. The company's fixed costs are $840,000. If the company desires $70,000 pretax income, what is the required dollar sales?

a. $2,400,000
b. $200,000
c. $2,600,000
d. $2,275,000
e. $1,400,000

Superscript letter A denotes assignments based on Appendix 5A.

Discussion Questions

1. How is cost-volume-profit analysis useful?
2. What is a variable cost? Identify two variable costs.
3. When output volume increases, do variable costs per unit increase, decrease, or stay the same within the relevant range of activity? Explain.
4. When output volume increases, do fixed costs per unit increase, decrease, or stay the same within the relevant range of activity? Explain.
5. How do step-wise costs and curvilinear costs differ?
6. Define and describe *contribution margin* per unit.
7. Define and explain the *contribution margin ratio.*
8. Describe the contribution margin ratio in layperson's terms.
9. In performing CVP analysis for a manufacturing company, what simplifying assumption is usually made about the volume of production and the volume of sales?
10. What two arguments tend to justify classifying all costs as either fixed or variable even though individual costs might not behave exactly as classified?
11. How does assuming that operating activity occurs within a relevant range affect cost-volume-profit analysis?
12. List three methods to measure cost behavior.
13. How is a scatter diagram used to identify and measure the behavior of a company's costs?
14. In cost-volume-profit analysis, what is the estimated profit at the break-even point?
15. Assume that a straight line on a CVP chart intersects the vertical axis at the level of fixed costs and has a positive slope that rises with each additional unit of volume by the amount of the variable costs per unit. What does this line represent?
16. Why are fixed costs depicted as a horizontal line on a CVP chart?
17. Each of two similar companies has sales of $20,000 and total costs of $15,000 for a month. Company A's total costs include $10,000 of variable costs and $5,000 of fixed costs. If Company B's total costs include $4,000 of variable costs and $11,000 of fixed costs, which company will enjoy more profit if sales double?
18. ______ of ______ reflects expected sales in excess of the level of break-even sales.
19. **Apple** produces iPods for sale. Identify some of the variable and fixed product costs associated with that production. [*Hint:* Limit costs to product costs.]
20. Should **Best Buy** use single product or multi-product break-even analysis? Explain.

21. **Apple** is thinking of expanding sales of its most popular Macintosh model by 65%. Do you expect its variable and fixed costs for this model to stay within the relevant range? Explain.

Denotes Discussion Questions that involve decision making.

connect *Most materials in this section are available in McGraw-Hill's Connect*

QUICK STUDY

QS 5-1
Cost behavior identification
C1

Determine whether each of the following is best described as a fixed, variable, or mixed cost with respect to product units.

1. Packaging expense.
2. Factory supervisor's salary.
3. Taxes on factory building.
4. Depreciation expense of warehouse.
5. Rubber used to manufacture athletic shoes.
6. Maintenance of factory machinery.
7. Wages of an assembly-line worker paid on the basis of acceptable units produced.

QS 5-2
Cost behavior identification
C1

Listed here are four series of separate costs measured at various volume levels. Examine each series and identify whether it is best described as a fixed, variable, step-wise, or curvilinear cost. (It can help to graph the cost series.)

Volume (Units)	Series 1	Series 2	Series 3	Series 4
0	$450	$ 0	$ 800	$100
100	450	800	800	105
200	450	1,600	800	120
300	450	2,400	1,600	145
400	450	3,200	1,600	190
500	450	4,000	2,400	250
600	450	4,800	2,400	320

QS 5-3
Cost behavior estimation
C1 P1

This scatter diagram reflects past maintenance hours and their corresponding maintenance costs.

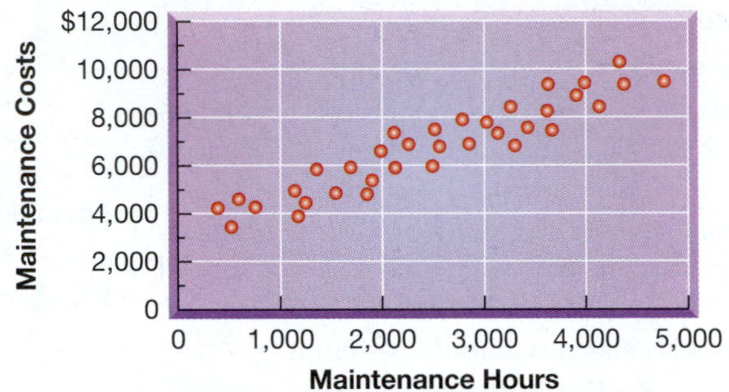

1. Draw an estimated line of cost behavior.
2. Estimate the fixed and variable components of maintenance costs.

QS 5-4
Cost behavior estimation—high-low method
C1 P1

The following information is available for a company's maintenance cost over the last seven months. Using the high-low method, estimate both the fixed and variable components of its maintenance cost.

Month	Maintenance Hours	Maintenance Cost
June	18	$5,450
July	36	6,900
August	24	5,100
September	30	6,000
October	42	6,900
November	48	8,100
December	12	3,600

QS 5-5
Contribution margin ratio
A2 

Compute and interpret the contribution margin ratio using the following data: sales, $100,000; total variable cost, $60,000.

QS 5-6
Contribution margin per unit and break-even units
A2 P2

BSD Phone Company sells its cordless phone for $150 per unit. Fixed costs total $270,000, and variable costs are $60 per unit. Determine the (1) contribution margin per unit and (2) break-even point in units.

QS 5-7
Assumptions in CVP analysis
C2

Refer to the information from QS 5-6. How will the break-even point in units change in response to each of the following independent changes in selling price per unit, variable cost per unit, or total fixed costs? Use I for increase and D for decrease. (It is not necessary to compute new break-even points.)

Change	Breakeven in Units Will
1. Variable cost to $50 per unit	________
2. Total fixed cost to $272,000	________
3. Selling price per unit to $145	________
4. Total fixed cost to $260,000	________
5. Variable cost to $67 per unit	________
6. Selling price per unit to $160	________

QS 5-8
Contribution margin ratio and break-even dollars
P2

Refer to QS 5-6. Determine the (1) contribution margin ratio and (2) break-even point in dollars.

QS 5-9
CVP analysis and target income
C3 P2

Refer to QS 5-6. Assume that BSD Phone Co. is subject to a 30% income tax rate. Compute the units of product that must be sold to earn after-tax income of $252,000.

QS 5-10
CVP assumptions
C2

Which one of the following is an assumption that underlies cost-volume-profit analysis?

1. For costs classified as variable, the costs per unit of output must change constantly.
2. For costs classified as fixed, the costs per unit of output must remain constant.
3. All costs have approximately the same relevant range.
4. The selling price per unit must change in proportion to the number of units sold.

QS 5-11
Operating leverage analysis
A3

A high proportion of Company A's total costs are variable with respect to units sold; a high proportion of Company B's total costs are fixed with respect to units sold. Which company is likely to have a higher degree of operating leverage (DOL)? Explain.

QS 5-12
Multiproduct break-even
P4

Call Me Company manufactures and sells two products, green beepers and gold beepers, in the ratio of 5:3. Fixed costs are $66,500, and the contribution margin per composite unit is $95. What number of both green and gold beepers is sold at the break-even point?

connect *Most materials in this section are available in McGraw-Hill's Connect*

EXERCISES

Exercise 5-1
Measurement of cost behavior using a scatter diagram
P1

A company reports the following information about its sales and its cost of sales. Each unit of its product sells for $1,000. Use these data to prepare a scatter diagram. Draw an estimated line of cost behavior and determine whether the cost appears to be variable, fixed, or mixed.

Period	Sales	Cost of Sales
1	$45,000	$30,300
2	34,500	22,500
3	31,500	21,000
4	22,500	16,500
5	27,000	18,000
6	37,500	28,500

Exercise 5-2
Cost behavior in graphs
C1 

Following are five graphs representing various cost behaviors. (1) Identify whether the cost behavior in each graph is mixed, step-wise, fixed, variable, or curvilinear. (2) Identify the graph (by number) that best illustrates each cost behavior: (a) Factory policy requires one supervisor for every 30 factory workers; (b) real estate taxes on factory; (c) electricity charge that includes the standard monthly charge plus a charge for each kilowatt hour; (d) commissions to salespersons; and (e) costs of hourly paid workers

[continued on next page]

that provide substantial gains in efficiency when a few workers are added but gradually smaller gains in efficiency when more workers are added.

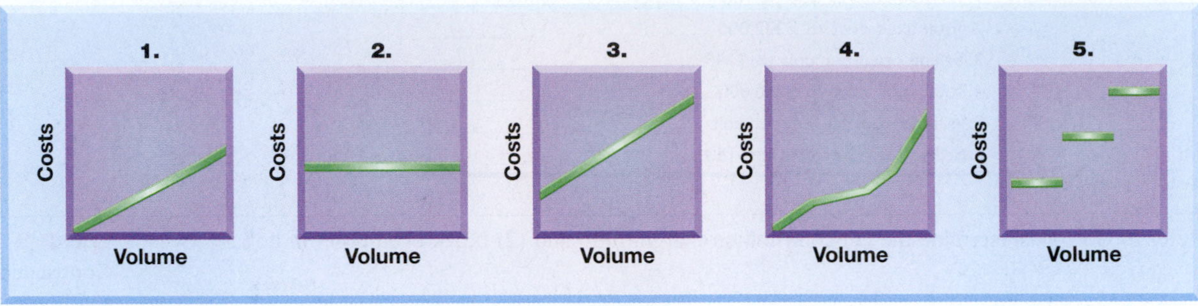

Exercise 5-3
Cost behavior defined
C1

The left column lists several cost classifications. The right column presents short definitions of those costs. In the blank space beside each of the numbers in the right column, write the letter of the cost best described by the definition.

A. Total cost
B. Variable cost
C. Fixed cost
D. Mixed cost
E. Curvilinear cost
F. Step-wise cost

______ **1.** This cost is the combined amount of all the other costs.

______ **2.** This cost remains constant over a limited range of volume; when it reaches the end of its limited range, it changes by a lump sum and remains at that level until it exceeds another limited range.

______ **3.** This cost has a component that remains the same over all volume levels and another component that increases in direct proportion to increases in volume.

______ **4.** This cost increases when volume increases, but the increase is not constant for each unit produced.

______ **5.** This cost remains constant over all volume levels within the productive capacity for the planning period.

______ **6.** This cost increases in direct proportion to increases in volume; its amount is constant for each unit produced.

Exercise 5-4
Cost behavior identification
C1 

Following are five series of costs *A* through *E* measured at various volume levels. Examine each series and identify which is fixed, variable, mixed, step-wise, or curvilinear.

	Volume (Units)	Series A	Series B	Series C	Series D	Series E
1	0	$5,000	$ 0	$1,000	$2,500	$ 0
2	400	5,000	3,600	1,000	3,100	6,000
3	800	5,000	7,200	2,000	3,700	6,600
4	1,200	5,000	10,800	2,000	4,300	7,200
5	1,600	5,000	14,400	3,000	4,900	8,200
6	2,000	5,000	18,000	3,000	5,500	9,600
7	2,400	5,000	21,600	4,000	6,100	13,500

Exercise 5-5
Predicting sales and variable costs using contribution margin
C3

Stewart Company management predicts that it will incur fixed costs of $230,000 and earn pretax income of $350,000 in the next period. Its expected contribution margin ratio is 25%. Use this information to compute the amounts of (1) total dollar sales and (2) total variable costs.

Exercise 5-6
Scatter diagram and measurement of cost behavior
P1 

Use the following information about sales and costs to prepare a scatter diagram. Draw a cost line that reflects the behavior displayed by this cost. Determine whether the cost is variable, step-wise, fixed, mixed, or curvilinear.

Period	Sales	Costs	Period	Sales	Costs
1	$1,520	$1,180	9	$1,160	$ 780
2	1,600	1,120	10	640	480
3	400	460	11	480	460
4	800	800	12	1,440	1,100
5	960	780	13	560	520
6	1,240	1,100	14	880	820
7	1,360	1,180	15	760	520
8	1,080	860			

Exercise 5-7
Cost behavior estimation—scatter diagram and high-low
P1

A company reports the following information about its sales and cost of sales. Draw an estimated line of cost behavior using a scatter diagram, and compute fixed costs and variable costs per unit sold. Then use the high-low method to estimate the fixed and variable components of the cost of sales.

Period	Units Sold	Cost of Sales	Period	Units Sold	Cost of Sales
1	0	$2,500	6	2,000	5,500
2	400	3,100	7	2,400	6,100
3	800	3,700	8	2,800	6,700
4	1,200	4,300	9	3,200	7,300
5	1,600	4,900	10	3,600	7,900

Exercise 5-8[A]
Measurement of cost behavior using regression
P1

Refer to the information from Exercise 5-7. Use spreadsheet software to use ordinary least-squares regression to estimate the cost equation, including fixed and variable cost amounts.

Exercise 5-9
Contribution margin, break-even, and CVP chart
P2 P3 A2

Seton Company manufactures a single product that sells for $360 per unit and whose total variable costs are $270 per unit. The company's annual fixed costs are $1,125,000. (1) Use this information to compute the company's (a) contribution margin, (b) contribution margin ratio, (c) break-even point in units, and (d) break-even point in dollars of sales. (2) Draw a CVP chart for the company.

Exercise 5-10
Income reporting and break-even analysis
C3

Refer to Exercise 5-9. (1) Prepare a contribution margin income statement for Seton Company showing sales, variable costs, and fixed costs at the break-even point. (2) If the company's fixed costs increase by $270,000, what amount of sales (in dollars) is needed to break even? Explain.

Exercise 5-11
Computing sales to achieve target income
C3

Seton Company management (in Exercise 5-9) targets an annual after-tax income of $1,620,000. The company is subject to a 20% income tax rate. Assume that fixed costs remain at $1,125,000. Compute the (1) unit sales to earn the target after-tax net income and (2) dollar sales to earn the target after-tax net income.

Exercise 5-12
Forecasted income statement
C3

Seton Company sales manager (in Exercise 5-9) predicts that annual sales of the company's product will soon reach 80,000 units and its price will increase to $400 per unit. According to the production manager, the variable costs are expected to increase to $280 per unit but fixed costs will remain at $1,125,000. The income tax rate is 20%. What amounts of pretax and after-tax income can the company expect to earn from these predicted changes? (*Hint:* Prepare a forecasted contribution margin income statement as in Exhibit 5.20.)

Check Forecasted income, $6,780,000

Exercise 5-13
Predicting unit and dollar sales
C3

Maya Company management predicts $600,000 of variable costs, $700,000 of fixed costs, and a pretax income of $110,000 in the next period. Management also predicts that the contribution margin per unit will be $9. Use this information to compute the (1) total expected dollar sales for next period and (2) number of units expected to be sold next period.

Exercise 5-14
Computation of variable and fixed costs; CVP chart
P3

Corveau Company expects to sell 400,000 units of its product next year, which would generate total sales of $34 million. Management predicts that pretax net income for next year will be $2,500,000 and that the contribution margin per unit will be $50. (1) Use this information to compute next year's total expected (a) variable costs and (b) fixed costs. (2) Prepare a CVP chart from this information.

Exercise 5-15
CVP analysis using composite units P4

Check (3) 1,500 units

Modern Home sells windows and doors in the ratio of 9:1 (windows:doors). The selling price of each window is $90 and of each door is $250. The variable cost of a window is $60 and of a door is $220. Fixed costs are $450,000. Use this information to determine the (1) selling price per composite unit, (2) variable costs per composite unit, (3) break-even point in composite units, and (4) number of units of each product that will be sold at the break-even point.

Exercise 5-16
CVP analysis using weighted-average contribution margin
P4

Refer to the information from Exercise 5-15. Use the information to determine the (1) weighted-average contribution margin, (2) break-even point in units, and (3) number of units of each product that will be sold at the break-even point.

Exercise 5-17
CVP analysis using composite units
P4

Precision Tax Service offers tax and consulting services to individuals and small businesses. Data for fees and costs of three types of tax returns follow. Precision provides services in the ratio of 5:3:2 (easy, moderate, business). Fixed costs total $18,000 for the tax season. Use this information to determine the (1) selling price per composite unit, (2) variable costs per composite unit, (3) break-even point in composite units, and (4) number of units of each product that will be sold at the break-even point.

Type of Return	Fee Charged	Variable Cost per Return
Easy (form 1040EZ)	$ 50	$ 30
Moderate (form 1040)	125	75
Business	275	100

Exercise 5-18
CVP analysis using weighted-average contribution margin
P4

Refer to the information from Exercise 5-17. Use the information to determine the (1) weighted-average contribution margin, (2) break-even point in units, and (3) number of units of each product that will be sold at the break-even point.

Exercise 5-19
Operating leverage computed and applied
A3 

Company A is a manufacturer with current sales of $1,500,000 and a 60% contribution margin. Its fixed costs equal $650,000. Company B is a consulting firm with current service revenues of $1,500,000 and a 25% contribution margin. Its fixed costs equal $125,000. Compute the degree of operating leverage (DOL) for each company. Identify which company benefits more from a 20% increase in sales and explain why.

connect *Most materials in this section are available in McGraw-Hill's Connect*

PROBLEM SET A

Problem 5-1A
Contribution margin income statement and contribution margin ratio
A2

The following costs result from the production and sale of 2,000 drum sets manufactured by Harris Drum Company for the year ended December 31, 2009. The drum sets sell for $500 each. The company has a 25% income tax rate.

Variable production costs	
Plastic for casing	$ 34,000
Wages of assembly workers	164,000
Drum stands	52,000
Variable selling costs	
Sales commissions	30,000
Fixed manufacturing costs	
Taxes on factory	10,000
Factory maintenance	20,000
Factory machinery depreciation	80,000
Fixed selling and administrative costs	
Lease of equipment for sales staff	20,000
Accounting staff salaries	70,000
Administrative management salaries	250,000

Check (1) Net income, $202,500

Required

1. Prepare a contribution margin income statement for the company.
2. Compute its contribution margin per unit and its contribution margin ratio.

Analysis Component

3. Interpret the contribution margin and contribution margin ratio from part 2.

Problem 5-2A
CVP analysis and charting
P2 P3

mhhe.com/wildMA2e

Extreme Equipment Co. manufactures and markets a number of rope products. Management is considering the future of Product HG, a special rope for hang gliding, that has not been as profitable as planned. Since Product HG is manufactured and marketed independently of the other products, its total costs can be precisely measured. Next year's plans call for a $200 selling price per 100 yards of HG rope. Its fixed costs for the year are expected to be $330,000, up to a maximum capacity of 20,000,000 yards of rope. Forecasted variable costs are $170 per 100 yards of HG rope.

Required

1. Estimate Product HG's break-even point in terms of (a) sales units and (b) sales dollars.
2. Prepare a CVP chart for Product HG like that in Exhibit 5.14. Use 20,000,000 yards as the maximum number of sales units on the horizontal axis of the graph, and $4,000,000 as the maximum dollar amount on the vertical axis.
3. Prepare a contribution margin income statement showing sales, variable costs, and fixed costs for Product HG at the break-even point.

Check (1) Break-even sales, 11,000 units or $2,200,000

Problem 5-3A
Scatter diagram and cost behavior estimation
P1

Alden Co.'s monthly sales and cost data for its operating activities of the past year follow. Management wants to use these data to predict future fixed and variable costs.

Period	Sales	Total Cost	Period	Sales	Total Cost
1	$325,000	$162,500	7	$355,000	$242,000
2	170,000	106,250	8	275,000	156,750
3	270,000	210,600	9	75,000	60,000
4	210,000	105,000	10	155,000	135,625
5	295,000	206,500	11	99,000	99,000
6	195,000	117,000	12	105,000	76,650

Required

1. Prepare a scatter diagram for these data with sales volume (in $) plotted on the horizontal axis and total cost plotted on the vertical axis.
2. Estimate both the variable costs per sales dollar and the total monthly fixed costs using the high-low method. Draw the total costs line on the scatter diagram in part 1.
3. Use the estimated line of cost behavior and results from part 2 to predict future total costs when sales volume is (a) $210,000 and (b) $300,000.

Check (2) Variable costs, $0.65 per sales dollar; fixed costs, $11,250

Problem 5-4A

Break-even analysis; income targeting and forecasting

C3 P2

Teller Co. sold 20,000 units of its only product and incurred a $70,000 loss (ignoring taxes) for the current year as shown here. During a planning session for year 2010's activities, the production manager notes that variable costs can be reduced 50% by installing a machine that automates several operations. To obtain these savings, the company must increase its annual fixed costs by $210,000. The maximum output capacity of the company is 40,000 units per year.

TELLER COMPANY
Contribution Margin Income Statement
For Year Ended December 31, 2009

Sales	$1,000,000
Variable costs	800,000
Contribution margin	200,000
Fixed costs	270,000
Net loss	$ (70,000)

Required

1. Compute the break-even point in dollar sales for year 2009.
2. Compute the predicted break-even point in dollar sales for year 2010 assuming the machine is installed and there is no change in the unit sales price.
3. Prepare a forecasted contribution margin income statement for 2010 that shows the expected results with the machine installed. Assume that the unit sales price and the number of units sold will not change, and no income taxes will be due.
4. Compute the sales level required in both dollars and units to earn $210,000 of after-tax income in 2010 with the machine installed and no change in the unit sales price. Assume that the income tax rate is 30%. (*Hint:* Use the procedures in Exhibits 5.21 and 5.23.)
5. Prepare a forecasted contribution margin income statement that shows the results at the sales level computed in part 4. Assume an income tax rate of 30%.

Check (3) Net income, $120,000

(4) Required sales, $1,300,000 or 26,000 units

(5) Net income, $210,000

Problem 5-5A

Break-even analysis, different cost structures, and income calculations

C3 

Shol Co. produces and sells two products, T and O. It manufactures these products in separate factories and markets them through different channels. They have no shared costs. This year, the company sold 51,000 units of each product. Sales and costs for each product follow.

	Product T	Product O
Sales	$2,040,000	$2,040,000
Variable costs	1,632,000	255,000
Contribution margin	408,000	1,785,000
Fixed costs	127,500	1,504,500
Income before taxes	280,500	280,500
Income taxes (34% rate)	95,370	95,370
Net income	$ 185,130	$ 185,130

Required

1. Compute the break-even point in dollar sales for each product.
2. Assume that the company expects sales of each product to decline to 40,000 units next year with no change in unit sales price. Prepare forecasted financial results for next year following the format of the contribution margin income statement as just shown with columns for each of the two products (assume a 34% tax rate). Also, assume that any loss before taxes yields a 34% tax savings.
3. Assume that the company expects sales of each product to increase to 65,000 units next year with no change in unit sales price. Prepare forecasted financial results for next year following the format of the contribution margin income statement shown with columns for each of the two products (assume a 34% tax rate).

Check (2) After-tax income: T, $127,050; O, $(68,970)

(3) After-tax income: T, $259,050; O, $508,530

Analysis Component

4. If sales greatly decrease, which product would experience a greater loss? Explain.
5. Describe some factors that might have created the different cost structures for these two products.

Problem 5-6A
Analysis of price, cost, and volume changes for contribution margin and net income

C3 P2

mhhe.com/wildMA2e

This year Calypso Company sold 60,000 units of its only product for $20 per unit. Manufacturing and selling the product required $97,500 of fixed manufacturing costs and $157,500 of fixed selling and administrative costs. Its per unit variable costs follow.

Material	$8.00
Direct labor (paid on the basis of completed units)	5.00
Variable overhead costs	1.60
Variable selling and administrative costs	0.40

Next year the company will use new material, which will reduce material costs by 50% and direct labor costs by 60% and will not affect product quality or marketability. Management is considering an increase in the unit sales price to reduce the number of units sold because the factory's output is nearing its annual output capacity of 65,000 units. Two plans are being considered. Under plan 1, the company will keep the price at the current level and sell the same volume as last year. This plan will increase income because of the reduced costs from using the new material. Under plan 2, the company will increase price by 25%. This plan will decrease unit sales volume by 15%. Under both plans 1 and 2, the total fixed costs and the variable costs per unit for overhead and for selling and administrative costs will remain the same.

Required

1. Compute the break-even point in dollar sales for both (a) plan 1 and (b) plan 2.
2. Prepare a forecasted contribution margin income statement with two columns showing the expected results of plan 1 and plan 2. The statements should report sales, total variable costs, contribution margin, total fixed costs, income before taxes, income taxes (30% rate), and net income.

Check (1) Breakeven: Plan 1, $425,000; Plan 2, $375,000

(2) Net income: Plan 1, $325,500; Plan 2, $428,400

Problem 5-7A
Break-even analysis with composite units

P4 C3

Patriot Co. manufactures and sells three products: red, white, and blue. Their unit sales prices are red, $74; white, $108; and blue, $99. The per unit variable costs to manufacture and sell these products are red, $48; white, $75; and blue, $90. Their sales mix is reflected in a ratio of 5:4:2 (red:white:blue). Annual fixed costs shared by all three products are $179,200. One type of raw material has been used to manufacture all three products. The company has developed a new material of equal quality for less cost. The new material would reduce variable costs per unit as follows: red, by $10; white, by $16; and blue, by $13. However, the new material requires new equipment, which will increase annual fixed costs by $22,400. (Round answers to whole composite units.)

Required

1. If the company continues to use the old material, determine its break-even point in both sales units and sales dollars of each individual product.
2. If the company uses the new material, determine its new break-even point in both sales units and sales dollars of each individual product.

Check (1) Old plan breakeven, 640 composite units

(2) New plan breakeven, 480 composite units

Analysis Component

3. What insight does this analysis offer management for long-term planning?

PROBLEM SET B

Problem 5-1B
Contribution margin income statement and contribution margin ratio

A2

The following costs result from the production and sale of 240,000 CD sets manufactured by Jawan Company for the year ended December 31, 2009. The CD sets sell for $9 each. The company has a 25% income tax rate.

Variable manufacturing costs	
Plastic for CD sets	$ 21,600
Wages of assembly workers	300,000
Labeling	43,200
Variable selling costs	
Sales commissions	24,000
Fixed manufacturing costs	
Rent on factory	100,000
Factory cleaning service	75,000
Factory machinery depreciation	125,000
Fixed selling and administrative costs	
Lease of office equipment	120,000
Systems staff salaries	600,000
Administrative management salaries	300,000

Required

Check (1) Net income, $338,400

1. Prepare a contribution margin income statement for the company.

2. Compute its contribution margin per unit and its contribution margin ratio.

Analysis Component

3. Interpret the contribution margin and contribution margin ratio from part 2.

Problem 5-2B
CVP analysis and charting

P2 P3

Tip-Top Co. manufactures and markets several products. Management is considering the future of one product, electronic keyboards, that has not been as profitable as planned. Since this product is manufactured and marketed independently of the other products, its total costs can be precisely measured. Next year's plans call for a $175 selling price per unit. The fixed costs for the year are expected to be $420,000, up to a maximum capacity of 10,000 units. Forecasted variable costs are $105 per unit.

Required

Check (1) Break-even sales, 6,000 units or $1,050,000

1. Estimate the keyboards' break-even point in terms of (a) sales units and (b) sales dollars.

2. Prepare a CVP chart for keyboards like that in Exhibit 5.14. Use 10,000 keyboards as the maximum number of sales units on the horizontal axis of the graph, and $1,600,000 as the maximum dollar amount on the vertical axis.

3. Prepare a contribution margin income statement showing sales, variable costs, and fixed costs for keyboards at the break-even point.

Problem 5-3B
Scatter diagram and cost behavior estimation

P1

Merdam Co.'s monthly sales and costs data for its operating activities of the past year follow. Management wants to use these data to predict future fixed and variable costs.

Period	Sales	Total Cost	Period	Sales	Total Cost
1	$390	$194	7	$290	$186
2	250	174	8	370	210
3	210	146	9	270	170
4	310	178	10	170	116
5	190	162	11	350	190
6	430	220	12	230	158

Required

1. Prepare a scatter diagram for these data with sales volume (in $) plotted on the horizontal axis and total costs plotted on the vertical axis.

2. Estimate both the variable costs per sales dollar and the total monthly fixed costs using the high-low method. Draw the total costs line on the scatter diagram in part 1.

Check (2) Variable costs, $0.40 per sales dollar; fixed costs, $48

3. Use the estimated line of cost behavior and results from part 2 to predict future total costs when sales volume is (a) $200 and (b) $340.

Problem 5-4B
Break-even analysis; income targeting and forecasting

C3 P2

Noru Co. sold 30,000 units of its only product and incurred a $75,000 loss (ignoring taxes) for the current year as shown here. During a planning session for year 2010's activities, the production manager notes that variable costs can be reduced 40% by installing a machine that automates several operations. To obtain these savings, the company must increase its annual fixed costs by $220,000. The maximum output capacity of the company is 50,000 units per year.

NORU COMPANY
Contribution Margin Income Statement
For Year Ended December 31, 2009

Sales	$1,125,000
Variable costs	900,000
Contribution margin	225,000
Fixed costs	300,000
Net loss	$ (75,000)

Required

1. Compute the break-even point in dollar sales for year 2009.

2. Compute the predicted break-even point in dollar sales for year 2010 assuming the machine is installed and no change occurs in the unit sales price. (Round the change in variable costs to a whole number.)

3. Prepare a forecasted contribution margin income statement for 2010 that shows the expected results with the machine installed. Assume that the unit sales price and the number of units sold will not change, and no income taxes will be due.

Check (3) Net income, $65,000

4. Compute the sales level required in both dollars and units to earn $104,000 of after-tax income in 2010 with the machine installed and no change in the unit sales price. Assume that the income tax rate is 20%. (*Hint:* Use the procedures in Exhibits 5.21 and 5.23.)

(4) Required sales, $1,250,000 or 33,334 units

5. Prepare a forecasted contribution margin income statement that shows the results at the sales level computed in part 4. Assume an income tax rate of 20%.

(5) Net income, $104,000 (rounded)

Problem 5-5B
Break-even analysis, different cost structures, and income calculations

C3 

Best Co. produces and sells two products, BB and TT. It manufactures these products in separate factories and markets them through different channels. They have no shared costs. This year, the company sold 100,000 units of each product. Sales and costs for each product follow.

	Product BB	Product TT
Sales	$1,600,000	$1,600,000
Variable costs	1,120,000	200,000
Contribution margin	480,000	1,400,000
Fixed costs	200,000	1,120,000
Income before taxes	280,000	280,000
Income taxes (32% rate)	89,600	89,600
Net income	$ 190,400	$ 190,400

Required

1. Compute the break-even point in dollar sales for each product.

2. Assume that the company expects sales of each product to decline to 67,000 units next year with no change in the unit sales price. Prepare forecasted financial results for next year following the format of the contribution margin income statement as shown here with columns for each of the two products (assume a 32% tax rate, and that any loss before taxes yields a 32% tax savings).

Check (2) After-tax income: BB, $82,688; TT, $(123,760)

3. Assume that the company expects sales of each product to increase to 125,000 units next year with no change in the unit sales prices. Prepare forecasted financial results for next year following the format of the contribution margin income statement as shown here with columns for each of the two products (assume a 32% tax rate).

(3) After-tax income: BB, $272,000; TT, $428,400

Analysis Component

4. If sales greatly increase, which product would experience a greater increase in profit? Explain.
5. Describe some factors that might have created the different cost structures for these two products.

Problem 5-6B
Analysis of price, cost, and volume changes for contribution margin and net income
C3 P2

This year Blanko Company earned a disappointing 3.85% after-tax return on sales (Net income/Sales) from marketing 50,000 units of its only product. The company buys its product in bulk and repackages it for resale at the price of $20 per unit. Blanko incurred the following costs this year.

Total variable unit costs	$400,000
Total variable packaging costs	50,000
Fixed costs	$495,000
Income tax rate	30%

The marketing manager claims that next year's results will be the same as this year's unless some changes are made. The manager predicts the company can increase the number of units sold by 60% if it reduces the selling price by 20% and upgrades the packaging. This change would increase variable packaging costs by 20%. Increased sales would allow the company to take advantage of a 25% quantity purchase discount on the cost of the bulk product. Neither the packaging change nor the volume discount would affect fixed costs, which provide an annual output capacity of 100,000 units.

Required

Check (1) Breakeven for new strategy, $900,000

(2) Net income: Existing strategy, $38,500; new strategy, $146,300

1. Compute the break-even point in dollar sales under the (a) existing business strategy and (b) new strategy that alters both unit sales price and variable costs.
2. Prepare a forecasted contribution margin income statement with two columns showing the expected results of (a) the existing strategy and (b) changing to the new strategy. The statements should report sales, total variable costs (unit and packaging), contribution margin, fixed costs, income before taxes, income taxes, and net income. Also determine the after-tax return on sales for these two strategies.

Problem 5-7B
Break-even analysis with composite units
P4 C3 

Milagro Co. manufactures and sells three products: product 1, product 2, and product 3. Their unit sales prices are product 1, $200; product 2, $150; and product 3, $100. The per unit variable costs to manufacture and sell these products are product 1, $150; product 2, $75; and product 3, $40. Their sales mix is reflected in a ratio of 6:4:2. Annual fixed costs shared by all three products are $5,400,000. One type of raw material has been used to manufacture products 1 and 2. The company has developed a new material of equal quality for less cost. The new material would reduce variable costs per unit as follows: product 1 by $50, and product 2, by $25. However, the new material requires new equipment, which will increase annual fixed costs by $200,000.

Required

Check (1) Old plan breakeven, 7,500 composite units

(2) New plan breakeven, 5,000 composite units

1. If the company continues to use the old material, determine its break-even point in both sales units and sales dollars of each individual product.
2. If the company uses the new material, determine its new break-even point in both sales units and sales dollars of each individual product.

Analysis Component

3. What insight does this analysis offer management for long-term planning?

SERIAL PROBLEM

Success Systems

(This serial problem began in Chapter 1 and continues through most of the book. If previous chapter segments were not completed, the serial problem can begin at this point. It is helpful, but not necessary, to use the working papers that accompany the book.)

SP 5 Success Systems sells upscale modular desk units and office chairs in the ratio of 3:2 (desk unit:chair). The selling prices are $1,250 per desk unit and $500 per chair. The variable costs are $750 per desk unit and $250 per chair. Fixed costs are $120,000.

Required

1. Compute the selling price per composite unit.
2. Compute the variable costs per composite unit.
3. Compute the break-even point in composite units.
4. Compute the number of units of each product that would be sold at the break-even point.

Check (3) 60 composite units

BEYOND THE NUMBERS

REPORTING IN ACTION

C1 

BTN 5-1 Best Buy offers services to customers that help them use products they purchase from Best Buy. One of these services is its Geek Squad, which is Best Buy's 24-hour computer support task force. As you complete the following requirements, assume that the Geek Squad uses many of Best Buy's existing resources such as its purchasing department and its buildings and equipment.

Required

1. Identify several of the variable, mixed, and fixed costs that the Geek Squad is likely to incur in carrying out its services.
2. Assume that Geek Squad revenues are expected to grow by 25% in the next year. How do you expect the costs identified in part 1 to change, if at all?
3. How is your answer to part 2 different from many of the examples discussed in the chapter? (*Hint:* Consider how the contribution margin ratio changes as volume—sales or customers served—increases.)

COMPARATIVE ANALYSIS

P2 C3 A2 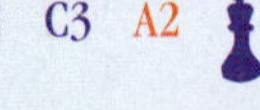

BTN 5-2 Both Best Buy and Circuit City sell numerous consumer products, and each of these companies has a different product mix.

Required

1. Assume the following data are available for both companies. Compute each company's break-even point in unit sales. (Each company sells many products at many different selling prices, and each has its own variable costs. This assignment assumes an *average* selling price per unit and an *average* cost per item.)

	Best Buy	Circuit City
Average selling price per item sold	$90	$40
Average variable cost per item sold	$64	$30
Total fixed costs	$5,980 million	$2,570 million

2. If unit sales were to decline, which company would experience the larger decline in operating profit? Explain.

ETHICS CHALLENGE

C1 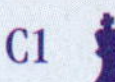

BTN 5-3 Labor costs of an auto repair mechanic are seldom based on actual hours worked. Instead, the amount paid a mechanic is based on an industry average of time estimated to complete a repair job. The repair shop bills the customer for the industry average amount of time at the repair center's billable cost per hour. This means a customer can pay, for example, $120 for two hours of work on a car when the actual time worked was only one hour. Many experienced mechanics can complete repair jobs faster than the industry average. The average data are compiled by engineering studies and surveys conducted in the auto repair business. Assume that you are asked to complete such a survey for a repair center. The survey calls for objective input, and many questions require detailed cost data and analysis. The mechanics and owners know you have the survey and encourage you to complete it in a way that increases the average billable hours for repair work.

Required

Write a one-page memorandum to the mechanics and owners that describes the direct labor analysis you will undertake in completing this survey.

COMMUNICATING IN PRACTICE

C2

BTN 5-4 Several important assumptions underlie CVP analysis. Assumptions often help simplify and focus our analysis of sales and costs. A common application of CVP analysis is as a tool to forecast sales, costs, and income.

Required

Assume that you are actively searching for a job. Prepare a one-half page report identifying (1) three assumptions relating to your expected revenue (salary) and (2) three assumptions relating to your expected costs for the first year of your new job. Be prepared to discuss your assumptions in class.

TAKING IT TO THE NET

C1 C3 

BTN 5-5 Access and review the entrepreneurial information at Business Owner's Toolkit [Toolkit.cch.com]. Access and review its *New Business Cash Needs Estimate* under the Business Tools/Business Finance menu bar or similar worksheets related to controls of cash and costs.

Required

Write a one-half page report that describes the information and resources available at the Business Owner's Toolkit to help the owner of a start-up business to control and monitor its costs.

TEAMWORK IN ACTION

C2

BTN 5-6 A local movie theater owner explains to you that ticket sales on weekends and evenings are strong, but attendance during the weekdays, Monday through Thursday, is poor. The owner proposes to offer a contract to the local grade school to show educational materials at the theater for a set charge per student during school hours. The owner asks your help to prepare a CVP analysis listing the cost and sales projections for the proposal. The owner must propose to the school's administration a charge per child. At a minimum, the charge per child needs to be sufficient for the theater to break even.

Required

Your team is to prepare two separate lists of questions that enable you to complete a reliable CVP analysis of this situation. One list is to be answered by the school's administration, the other by the owner of the movie theater.

ENTREPRENEURIAL DECISION

C1  

BTN 5-7 Martin Sprock is a diligent businessman. He continually searches for new menu items to further increase the profitability of Moe's Southwest Grill.

Required

1. What information should Sprock search for to help him decide whether to add new menu items or other products to existing Moe's product lines?
2. What managerial tools are available to Sprock to help make the decisions in part 1?

HITTING THE ROAD

P4 

BTN 5-8 Multiproduct break-even analysis is often viewed differently when actually applied in practice. You are to visit a local fast-food restaurant and count the number of items on the menu. To apply multiproduct break-even analysis to the restaurant, similar menu items must often be fit into groups. A reasonable approach is to classify menu items into approximately five groups. We then estimate average selling price and average variable cost to compute average contribution margin. (*Hint:* For fast-food restaurants, the highest contribution margin is with its beverages, at about 90%.)

Required

1. Prepare a one-year multiproduct break-even analysis for the restaurant you visit. Begin by establishing groups. Next, estimate each group's volume and contribution margin. These estimates are necessary to compute each group's contribution margin. Assume that annual fixed costs in total are $500,000 per year. (*Hint:* You must develop your own estimates on volume and contribution margin for each group to obtain the break-even point and sales.)
2. Prepare a one-page report on the results of your analysis. Comment on the volume of sales necessary to break even at a fast-food restaurant.

BTN 5-9 Access and review DSG's Website (www.DSGiplc.com) to answer the following questions.

GLOBAL DECISION

C3 

DSG

1. Do you believe that DSG's managers use single product CVP analysis or multiproduct break-even point analysis? Explain.
2. How does the addition of a new product line affect DSG's CVP analysis?
3. How does the addition of a new store affect DSG's CVP analysis?

ANSWERS TO MULTIPLE CHOICE QUIZ

1. a; $150 − $100 = $50
2. e; ($150 − $100)/$150 = 33⅓%
3. c; $75,000/$50 CM per unit = 1,500 units
4. b; $300,000 − $180,000 = $120,000
5. c; Contribution margin ratio = ($400 − $260)/$400 = 0.35
   Targeted sales = ($840,000 + $70,000)/0.35 = $2,600,000

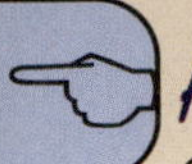

A Look Back

Chapter 5 looked at cost behavior and its use by managers in performing cost-volume-profit analysis. It also illustrated the application of cost-volume-profit analysis.

A Look at This Chapter

This chapter describes managerial accounting reports that reflect variable costing. It also compares reports prepared under variable costing with those under absorption costing, and it explains how variable costing can improve business decisions.

A Look Ahead

Chapter 7 introduces and describes the budgeting process and its importance to management. It also explains the master budget and its usefulness to the planning of future company activities.

Chapter

Variable Costing and Performance Reporting

Learning Objectives

CAP

Conceptual

C1 Distinguish between absorption costing and variable costing. *(p. 206)*

C2 Describe how absorption costing can result in over-production. *(p. 213)*

C3 Explain the role of variable costing in pricing special orders. *(p. 215)*

Analytical

A1 Analyze income reporting for both absorption and variable costing. *(p. 208)*

A2 Compute and interpret break-even volume in units. *(p. 217)*

Procedural

P1 Compute unit cost under both absorption and variable costing. *(p. 207)*

P2 Prepare an income statement using absorption costing and using variable costing. *(p. 209)*

P3 Prepare a contribution margin report. *(p. 209)*

P4 Convert income under variable costing to the absorption cost basis. *(p. 213)*

Decision Feature

Fancy Pants

"We want guys to wear pants that not everyone in the world will have"—Andy Dunn

NEW YORK—Brian Spaly didn't like his pants. High-end pants were too expensive, the fit was too tight, and he felt that mass market pants were boring. So, Brian borrowed a sewing machine, learned how to sew, and began designing his own pants. "I had no idea what I was doing," admits Brian. "But it turns out it's not that complicated." Brian's business college classmates took note of his new pants and asked if he could make some for them. After a 'small production run' and a few samples, the word got out and Brian's company, **Bonobos** **(Bonobos.com)** was born—the company name comes from the bonobo chimpanzee, known for its peaceful and friendly nature.

Brian soon teamed with a buddy, Andy Dunn, and their focus became "fashionable pants for real guys." Their strategy was multi-faceted: pants that fit; pants in unconventional colors such as hunter orange and mountain turquoise; pants with funky names such as *Orange Crush, Spider Fighters*, and *Tequila.* A one-day sale from their apartment yielded sales of 47 pairs, suggesting their new venture had legs. "The real question became: 'Can I design and make better pants?' Because the market needs it," insists Brian. "There is no one else doing it, so I gotta do it."

Bonobos' business model is unique: All Bonobos pants are handmade, and now sold only online. Further, monitoring and controlling costs are crucial to its success. Instead of trying to drive material costs down by buying in bulk, Bonobos prefers to spend whatever it takes to achieve a high level of quality and style. Bonobos often makes fifty or a hundred pairs of a certain style of pants, and then never makes that style again—adding to its distinctiveness. Selling prices are set to cover the variable fabric costs of each style of pants and to yield an adequate contribution margin.

Bonobos avoids fixed costs and strives to keep costs other than materials to a minimum. Operating only online avoids the overhead costs of having retail facilities that its competitors pass on to customers. The company shuns advertising. "Our most successful marketers are guys who love our pants," explains Andy. One exception was for a line of "Cubbie" blue pants where Andy purchased a $63 self-service ad on Facebook to target Chicago Cubs fans. Within days, Bonobos sold out of the special edition pants at $120 per pair. In addition, Bonobos uses customers and friends as models to further slash costs. In essence, the variable fabric costs are what drive its decisions regarding product lines and product pricing. Accordingly, its costing system, with reports on variable costs, contribution margins, and break-even points, is key.

With a keen eye for style and a focus on quality and cost control, Bonobos continues to grow. In its first six months of operations, it sold over 2,000 pairs of pants. "We're energized and trying to make as many shorts and pants as we can," says Brian. Although the founders are having fun (such as naming their company after a chimp and with waistbands featuring tequila bottles), their goals are high. Admits Andy, "We've set out to become the go-to brand for men's pants."

[Sources: *Bonobos Website,* January 2009; *The Wall Street Journal,* May 2008; *Chicago Tribune,* June 2008; *Los Angeles Times,* May 2008; *San Francisco Chronicle,* March 2008; *Fabulmag.com,* June 2008]

Chapter Preview

Product-costing information is crucial for most business decisions. This chapter explains and illustrates the concept of variable costing. We then compare variable costing to that of absorption costing commonly used for financial reporting. We show that income is different when computed under variable or absorption costing whenever the number of units produced is different from units sold. We also show how absorption costing can be misleading (though not wrong) and how variable costing can result in better production and pricing decisions.

Variable Costing and Performance Reporting

Variable Costing and Absorption Costing
- Absorption costing
- Variable costing
- Computing unit costs

Performance Reporting (Income) Implications
- When production equals sales
- When production exceeds sales
- When production is less than sales
- Income reporting
- Converting variable cost reports to absorption cost

Comparing Variable Costing and Absorption Costing
- Planning production
- Setting prices
- Controlling costs
- Limitations of variable costing

Introducing Variable Costing and Absorption Costing

C1 Distinguish between absorption costing and variable costing.

Product costs consist of direct materials, direct labor, and overhead. Direct materials and direct labor costs are those that can be identified and traced to the product(s). Overhead, which consists of costs such as electricity, equipment depreciation, and supervisor salaries, is not traceable to the product. Overhead costs must be allocated to products.

There are a variety of costing methods for identifying and allocating overhead costs to products. A prior chapter focused on *how* to allocate overhead costs to products. This chapter focuses on *what* overhead costs are included in product costs.

Under the traditional costing approach, *all* manufacturing costs are assigned to products. Those costs consist of direct materials, direct labor, variable overhead, and fixed overhead. This traditional approach is referred to as **absorption costing** (also called *full costing*), which assumes that products *absorb* all costs incurred to produce them. While widely used for financial reporting (GAAP), this costing method can result in misleading product cost information for managers' business decisions.

Under **variable costing,** only costs that change in total with changes in production level are included in product costs. Those consist of direct materials, direct labor, and variable overhead. The overhead cost that does not change with changes in production is fixed overhead—and, thus, is excluded from product costs. Instead, fixed overhead is treated as a period cost; meaning it is expensed in the period when it is incurred.

Absorption Costing

Product cost generally consists of direct materials, direct labor, and overhead. Costs of both direct materials and direct labor usually are easily traced to specific products. Overhead costs, however, must be allocated to products because they cannot be traced to product units. Under absorption costing, *all* overhead costs, both fixed and variable, are allocated to products as the following diagram shows.

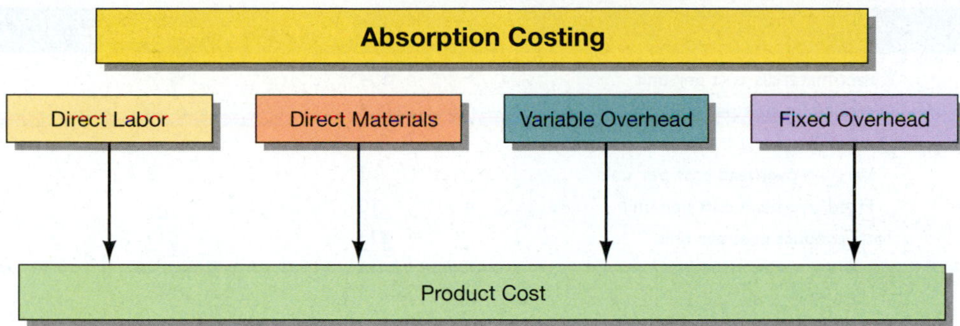

Variable Costing

Under variable costing, the costs of direct materials and direct labor are traced to products, and only variable overhead costs (not fixed overhead) are allocated to products. Fixed overhead costs are treated as period costs and are reported as expense in the period when incurred.

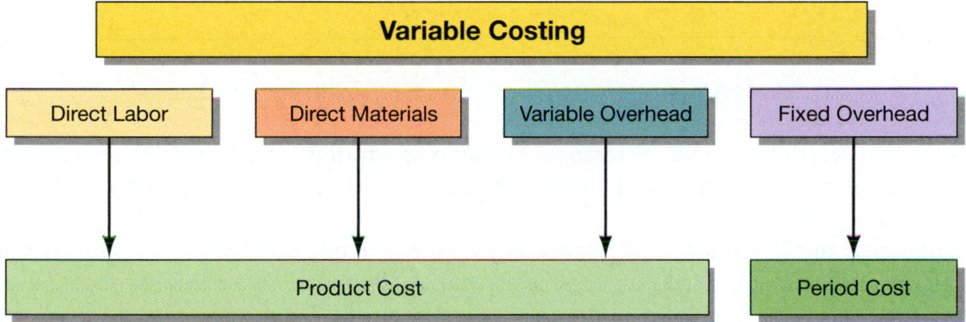

Computing Unit Cost

P1 Compute unit cost under both absorption and variable costing.

To illustrate the difference between absorption costing and variable costing, let's consider the product cost data in Exhibit 6.1 from IceAge, a skate manufacturer.

EXHIBIT 6.1

Summary Product Cost Data

Direct materials cost	$4 per unit
Direct labor cost	8 per unit
Overhead cost	
Variable overhead cost	$ 180,000
Fixed overhead cost	600,000
Total overhead cost	$ 780,000
Expected units produced	60,000 units

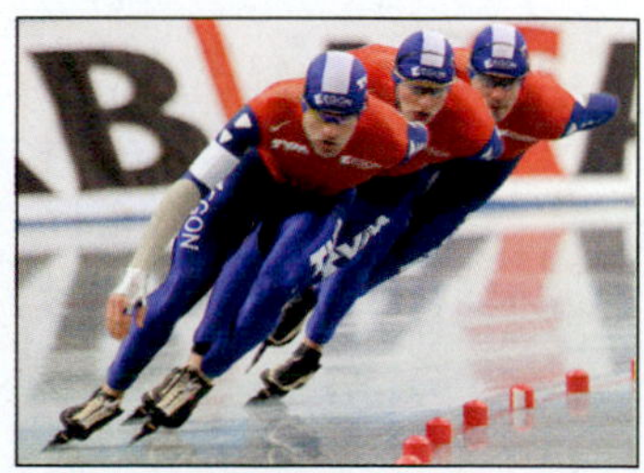

Drawing on the product cost data, Exhibit 6.2 shows the product unit cost computations for both absorption and variable costing. For absorption costing, the product unit cost is $25, which consists of $4 in direct materials, $8 in direct labor, $3 in variable overhead ($180,000/60,000 units), and $10 in fixed overhead ($600,000/60,000 units).

For variable costing, the product unit cost is $15, which consists of $4 in direct materials, $8 in direct labor, and $3 in variable overhead. Fixed overhead costs of $600,000 are treated as a period cost and are recorded as expense in the period incurred. The difference between the two costing methods is the exclusion of fixed overhead from product costs for variable costing.

EXHIBIT 6.2

Unit Cost Computation

	Absorption Costing	Variable Costing
Direct materials cost per unit	$ 4	$ 4
Direct labor cost per unit	8	8
Overhead cost		
Variable overhead cost per unit	3	3
Fixed overhead cost per unit	10	—
Total product cost per unit	$25	$15

Quick Check Answers—p. 221

1. Which of the following cost elements are included when computing unit cost under absorption costing?
   a. Direct materials b. Direct labor c. Variable overhead d. Fixed overhead
2. Which of the following cost elements are included when computing unit cost under variable costing?
   a. Direct materials b. Direct labor c. Variable overhead d. Fixed overhead

Performance Reporting (Income) Implications

A1 Analyze income reporting for both absorption and variable costing.

The prior section illustrated the differences between absorption costing and variable costing in computing unit cost. This section shows the implications of those differences for performance (income) reporting.

To illustrate the reporting implications, we return to IceAge Company. Exhibit 6.3 summarizes the production cost data for IceAge as well as additional data on nonproduction costs. Assume that IceAge's variable costs per unit are constant and that its annual fixed costs remain unchanged during the three-year period 2007 through 2009.

EXHIBIT 6.3

Summary Cost Information for 2007–2009

Production Costs		Nonproduction Costs	
Direct materials cost	$4 per unit	Variable selling and administrative expenses	$2 per unit
Direct labor cost	$8 per unit	Fixed selling and administrative expenses	$200,000 per year
Variable overhead cost	$3 per unit		
Fixed overhead cost	$600,000 per year		

The reported sales and production information for IceAge follows. Its sales price was a constant $40 per unit over this time period. We see that the units produced equal those sold for 2007, but exceed those sold for 2008, and are less than those sold for 2009.

	Units Produced	Units Sold	Units in Ending Inventory
2007	60,000	60,000	0
2008	60,000	40,000	20,000
2009	60,000	80,000	0

Drawing on the information above, we next prepare the income statement for IceAge both under absorption costing and under variable costing. Our purpose is to highlight differences between these two costing methods under three different cases: when units produced are equal to, exceed, or are less than units sold.

Units Produced Equal Units Sold

Exhibit 6.4 presents the 2007 income statement for both costing methods (2008 and 2009 statements will follow). The income statement under variable costing (on the right) is referred to as the **contribution margin income statement.** Contribution margin is the excess of sales over variable costs. This amount contributes to covering all fixed costs and earning income. Under variable costing, the expenses are grouped according to cost behavior—variable or fixed, and production or nonproduction. Under the traditional format of absorption costing, expenses are grouped according to function.

P2 Prepare an income statement using absorption costing and using variable costing.

EXHIBIT 6.4

Income for 2007—Quantity Produced Equals Quantity Sold*

ICEAGE COMPANY Income Statement (Absorption Costing) For Year Ended December 31, 2007	
Sales[†] (60,000 × $40)	$2,400,000
Cost of goods sold (60,000 × $25)	1,500,000
Gross margin	900,000
Selling and administrative expenses [$200,000 + (60,000 × $2)]	320,000
Net income	$ 580,000

* See Exhibit 6.2 for unit cost computation under absorption and under variable costing.

[†] Units produced equal 60,000; units sold equal 60,000.

ICEAGE COMPANY Income Statement (Variable Costing) For Year Ended December 31, 2007		
Sales[†] (60,000 × $40)		$2,400,000
Variable expenses		
Variable production costs (60,000 × $15)	$900,000	
Variable selling and administrative expenses (60,000 × $2) . . .	120,000	1,020,000
Contribution margin		1,380,000
Fixed expenses		
Fixed overhead	600,000	
Fixed selling and administrative expense . .	200,000	800,000
Net income		$ 580,000

A performance report that excludes fixed expenses and net income is a contribution margin report.

Point: Contribution margin income statements prepared under variable costing are useful in performing cost-volume-profit analyses.

Exhibit 6.4 reveals that *reported income is identical under absorption costing and variable costing when the units produced equal the units sold.*

Contribution Margin Report A performance report that excludes fixed expenses and net income is known as a **contribution margin report.** Looking at the variable costing income statement in Exhibit 6.4, a contribution margin report would end with the contribution margin of $1,380,000. However, a *contribution margin income statement* includes fixed expenses and net income as shown in Exhibit 6.4.

P3 Prepare a contribution margin report.

Point: Contribution margin (Sales − Variable expenses) is different from gross margin (Sales − Cost of sales).

Exhibit 6.4A reorganizes the information from Exhibit 6.4 to show the assignment of costs to different expenses and assets under both absorption costing and variable costing. When quantity produced equals quantity sold there is no difference in total costs assigned. Yet, there is a difference in what categories receive those costs. Absorption costing assigns $1,500,000 to cost of goods sold compared to $900,000 for variable costing. The $600,000 difference is a period cost for variable costing.

EXHIBIT 6.4A

Production Cost Assignment for 2007

	Cost of Goods Sold (Expense)		Ending Inventory (Asset)		Period Cost (Expense)	2007 Expense
Absorption Costing						
Direct materials	60,000 × $4	$ 240,000	0 × $4	$ 0		$ 240,000
Direct labor	60,000 × $8	480,000	0 × $8	0		480,000
Variable overhead . . .	60,000 × $3	180,000	0 × $3	0		180,000
Fixed overhead	60,000 × $10	600,000	0 × $10	0		600,000
Total costs		$1,500,000		$ 0		**$1,500,000**
Variable Costing						
Direct materials	60,000 × $4	$ 240,000	0 × $4	$ 0		$ 240,000
Direct labor	60,000 × $8	480,000	0 × $8	0		480,000
Variable overhead . . .	60,000 × $3	180,000	0 × $3	0		180,000
Fixed overhead					$600,000	600,000
Total costs		$ 900,000		$ 0	$600,000	**$1,500,000**
Cost difference . . .						**$ 0**

Decision Insight

Manufacturing Margin Some managers compute *manufacturing margin* (also called *production margin*), which is sales less variable production costs. Some managers also require that internal income statements show this amount to highlight variable product costs on income. The contribution margin section of IceAge's statement would appear as follows (compare this to Exhibit 6.4).

Sales	$2,400,000
Variable production costs	900,000
Manufacturing margin	1,500,000
Variable selling & admin. exp.	120,000
Contribution margin	$1,380,000

Units Produced Exceed Units Sold

Exhibit 6.5 shows absorption costing and variable costing income statements for 2008. In 2008, 60,000 units were produced, which is the same as in 2007. However, only 40,000 units were sold.

The income statements reveal that for 2008, income is $320,000 under absorption costing. Under variable costing, income is $120,000, which is $200,000 less than under absorption costing. The cause of this $200,000 difference rests with the different treatment of fixed overhead under the two costing methods.

EXHIBIT 6.5

Income for 2008—Quantity Produced Exceeds Quantity Sold*

ICEAGE COMPANY
Income Statement (Absorption Costing)
For Year Ended December 31, 2008

Sales† (40,000 × $40)	$1,600,000
Cost of goods sold (40,000 × $25)	1,000,000
Gross margin	600,000
Selling and administrative expenses [$200,000 + (40,000 × $2)]	280,000
Net income	$ 320,000

* See Exhibit 6.2 for unit cost computation under absorption and under variable costing.

† Units produced equal 60,000; units sold equal 40,000.

ICEAGE COMPANY
Income Statement (Variable Costing)
For Year Ended December 31, 2008

Sales† (40,000 × $40)		$1,600,000
Variable expenses		
Variable production costs (40,000 × $15)	$600,000	
Variable selling and administrative expenses (40,000 × $2)	80,000	680,000
Contribution margin		920,000
Fixed expenses		
Fixed overhead	600,000	
Fixed selling and administrative expense	200,000	800,000
Net income		$ 120,000

Under variable costing, the entire $600,000 fixed overhead cost is treated as an expense in computing 2008 income. Under absorption costing, the fixed overhead cost is allocated to each unit of product at the rate of $10 per unit (from Exhibit 6.2). When production exceeds sales by 20,000 units (60,000 versus 40,000), the $200,000 ($10 × 20,000 units) of fixed overhead cost allocated to these 20,000 units is carried as part of the cost of ending inventory (see Exhibit 6.5A). This means that $200,000 of fixed overhead cost incurred in 2008 is not expensed until future periods when it is reported in cost of goods sold as those products are sold. Consequently, income for 2008 under absorption costing is $200,000 higher than income under variable costing.

Exhibit 6.5A reorganizes the information from Exhibit 6.5 to show the assignment of costs to different expenses and assets under both absorption costing and variable costing. When quantity produced exceeds quantity sold there is a difference in total costs assigned. As a result, income under absorption costing is greater than under variable costing because of the greater fixed overhead cost allocated to ending inventory (asset) under absorption costing. Those cost differences extend to cost of goods sold, ending inventory, and period costs.

EXHIBIT 6.5A

Production Cost Assignment for 2008

		Cost of Goods Sold (Expense)		Ending Inventory (Asset)	Period Cost (Expense)	2008 Expense
Absorption Costing						
Direct materials	40,000 × $4	$ 160,000	20,000 × $4	$ 80,000		$ 160,000
Direct labor	40,000 × $8	320,000	20,000 × $8	160,000		320,000
Variable overhead . .	40,000 × $3	120,000	20,000 × $3	60,000		120,000
Fixed overhead	40,000 × $10	400,000	20,000 × $10	200,000		400,000
Total costs		$1,000,000		$500,000		**$1,000,000**
Variable Costing						
Direct materials	40,000 × $4	$ 160,000	20,000 × $4	$ 80,000		$ 160,000
Direct labor	40,000 × $8	320,000	20,000 × $8	160,000		320,000
Variable overhead . .	40,000 × $3	120,000	20,000 × $3	60,000		120,000
Fixed overhead					$600,000	600,000
Total costs		$ 600,000		$300,000	$600,000	**$1,200,000**
Cost difference . . .						**$ (200,000)**

Units Produced Are Less Than Units Sold

Exhibit 6.6 shows absorption costing and variable costing income statements for 2009. In 2009, IceAge produced 20,000 fewer units than it sold. Production equaled 60,000 units, but units sold were 80,000. IceAge's income statements reveal that income is $840,000 under absorption costing, but it is $1,040,000 under variable costing.

Point: IceAge can sell more units than it produced in 2009 because of inventory carried over from 2008.

The cause of this $200,000 difference lies with the treatment of fixed overhead. Beginning inventory in 2009 under absorption costing included $200,000 of fixed overhead cost incurred in 2008, which is assigned to cost of goods sold in 2009 under absorption costing.

EXHIBIT 6.6

Income for 2009—Quantity Produced Is Less Than Quantity Sold*

ICEAGE COMPANY
Income Statement (Absorption Costing)
For Year Ended December 31, 2009

Sales† (80,000 × $40)	$3,200,000
Cost of goods sold (80,000 × $25) . . .	2,000,000
Gross margin	1,200,000
Selling and administrative expenses [$200,000 + (80,000 × $2)]	360,000
Net income	$ 840,000

* See Exhibit 6.2 for unit cost computation under absorption and under variable costing.

† Units produced equal 60,000; units sold equal 80,000.

ICEAGE COMPANY
Income Statement (Variable Costing)
For Year Ended December 31, 2009

Sales† (80,000 × $40)		$3,200,000
Variable expenses		
Variable production costs (80,000 × $15)	$1,200,000	
Variable selling and administrative expenses (80,000 × $2)	160,000	1,360,000
Contribution margin		1,840,000
Fixed expenses		
Fixed overhead	600,000	
Fixed selling and administrative expense	200,000	800,000
Net income		$1,040,000

Exhibit 6.6A reorganizes the information from Exhibit 6.6 to show the assignment of costs to different expenses and assets under both absorption costing and variable costing. When quantity produced is less than quantity sold there is a difference in total costs assigned.

Specifically, ending inventory in 2008 under absorption costing was $500,000 (20,000 units × $25) whereas it was only $300,000 (20,000 units × $15) under variable costing—see Exhibit 6.5A. Consequently, when that inventory is sold in 2009, the 2009 income under absorption costing is $200,000 less than the income under variable costing. That inventory cost difference flows through cost of goods sold and then to income.

EXHIBIT 6.6A

Production Cost Assignment for 2009

	Cost of Goods Sold (Expense)		Ending Inventory (Asset)		Period Cost (Expense)	2009 Expense
Absorption Costing						
Direct materials	80,000 × $4	$ 320,000	0 × $4	$ 0		$ 320,000
Direct labor	80,000 × $8	640,000	0 × $8	0		640,000
Variable overhead ...	80,000 × $3	240,000	0 × $3	0		240,000
Fixed overhead	80,000 × $10	800,000	0 × $10	0		800,000
Total costs		$2,000,000		$ 0		**$2,000,000**
Variable Costing						
Direct materials	80,000 × $4	$ 320,000	0 × $4	$ 0		$ 320,000
Direct labor	80,000 × $8	640,000	0 × $8	0		640,000
Variable overhead ...	80,000 × $3	240,000	0 × $3	0		240,000
Fixed overhead					$600,000	600,000
Total costs		$1,200,000		$ 0	$600,000	**$1,800,000**
Cost difference ...						**$ 200,000**

Summarizing Income Reporting

Income reported under both variable costing and absorption costing for the period 2007 through 2009 for IceAge is summarized in Exhibit 6.7. We see that the differences in income are due to timing as total income is $1,740,000 for this time period for *both* methods. Further, income under absorption costing and that under variable costing will be different whenever the quantity produced and the quantity sold are different. Specifically, *income under absorption costing is higher when more units are produced relative to units sold and is lower when fewer units are produced than are sold.*

EXHIBIT 6.7

Summary of Income Reporting

	Units Produced	Units Sold	Income Under Absorption Costing	Income Under Variable Costing	Differences
2007	60,000	60,000	$ 580,000	$ 580,000	$ 0
2008	60,000	40,000	320,000	120,000	200,000
2009	60,000	80,000	840,000	1,040,000	(200,000)
Totals	180,000	180,000	$1,740,000	$1,740,000	$ 0

Point: As companies adopt lean practices, including just-in-time manufacturing, inventory levels fall. Lower inventory levels reduce differences between absorption and variable costing income.

Our illustration using IceAge had the total number of units produced over 2007–2009 exactly equal to the number of units sold over that period. This meant that the difference between absorption costing income and variable costing income for the *total* three-year period is zero. In reality, it is unusual for production and sales quantities to exactly equal each other over such a short period of time. This means that we normally continue to see differences in income for these two methods extending over several years.

Quick Check Answers—p. 221

3. Which of the following statements is true when units produced exceed units sold?
   a. Variable costing income exceeds absorption costing income.
   b. Variable costing income equals absorption costing income.
   c. Variable costing income is less than absorption costing income.
4. Which of the following statements is true when units produced are less than units sold?
   a. Variable costing income exceeds absorption costing income.
   b. Variable costing income equals absorption costing income.
   c. Variable costing income is less than absorption costing income.

Converting Reports under Variable Costing to Absorption Costing

P4 Convert income under variable costing to the absorption cost basis.

Companies commonly use variable costing for internal reporting and business decisions, and use absorption costing for external reporting and tax reporting. For companies concerned about the cost of maintaining two costing systems, it is comforting to know that we can readily convert reports under variable costing to that using absorption costing.

Income under variable costing is restated to that under absorption costing by adding the fixed production cost in ending inventory and subtracting the fixed production cost in beginning inventory.

Using IceAge's data, in 2008, absorption costing income was $200,000 higher than variable costing income. The $200,000 difference was because the fixed overhead cost incurred in 2008 was allocated to the 20,000 units of ending inventory under absorption costing (and not expensed in 2008 under absorption costing). On the other hand, the $200,000 fixed overhead costs (along with all other fixed costs) were expensed in 2008 under variable costing.

Exhibit 6.8 shows the computations for restating income under the two costing methods. To restate variable costing income to absorption costing income for 2008, we must add back the **fixed overhead cost deferred in** (ending) **inventory.** Similarly, to restate variable costing income to absorption costing income for 2009, we must deduct the **fixed overhead cost recognized from** (beginning) **inventory,** which was incurred in 2008, but expensed in the 2009 cost of goods sold when the inventory was sold.

EXHIBIT 6.8

Converting Variable Costing Income to Absorption Costing Income

	2007	2008	2009
Variable costing income	$580,000	$120,000	$1,040,000
Add: Fixed overhead cost deferred in ending inventory (20,000 × $10)	0	200,000	0
Less: Fixed overhead cost recognized from beginning inventory (20,000 × $10)	0	0	(200,000)
Absorption costing income	$580,000	$320,000	$ 840,000

Comparing Variable Costing and Absorption Costing

This section discusses how absorption costing can lead to undesirable production and pricing decisions and how variable costing can result in better business decisions.

Planning Production

C2 Describe how absorption costing can result in over-production.

Production planning is an important managerial function. Producing too much leads to excess inventory, which in turn leads to higher storage and financing costs, and to greater risk of product obsolescence. On the other hand, producing too little can lead to lost sales and customer dissatisfaction.

Production levels should be based on reliable sales forecasts. However over-production and inventory buildup can occur because of how managers are evaluated and rewarded. For instance, many companies link manager bonuses to income computed under absorption costing because this is how income is reported to shareholders (per GAAP).

To illustrate how a reward system can lead to over-production under absorption costing, let's use IceAge's 2007 data with one change: assume that its manager decides to produce 100,000 units instead of 60,000. Since only 60,000 units are sold, the 40,000 units of excess production will be stored in inventory.

The left side of Exhibit 6.9 shows the unit cost when 60,000 units are produced (same as Exhibit 6.2). The right side shows unit cost when 100,000 units are produced. The exhibit is prepared under absorption costing for 2007.

EXHIBIT 6.9

Unit Cost Under Absorption Costing for Different Production Levels

When 60,000 Units Are Produced		When 100,000 Units Are Produced	
Direct materials cost	$ 4 per unit	Direct materials cost	$ 4 per unit
Direct labor cost	8 per unit	Direct labor cost	8 per unit
Variable overhead cost	3 per unit	Variable overhead cost	3 per unit
Total variable cost	15 per unit	Total variable cost	15 per unit
Fixed overhead ($600,000/60,000 units)	10 per unit	Fixed overhead ($600,000/100,000 units)	6 per unit
Total product cost	$25 per unit	Total product cost	$21 per unit

Total production cost *per unit* is $4 less when 100,000 units are produced. Specifically, cost per unit is $21 when 100,000 units are produced versus $25 per unit at 60,000 units. The reason for this difference is because the company is spreading the $600,000 fixed overhead cost over more units when 100,000 units are produced than when 60,000 are produced.

The difference in cost per unit impacts performance reporting. Exhibit 6.10 presents the income statement under absorption costing for the two alternative production levels.

EXHIBIT 6.10

Income Under Absorption Costing for Different Production Levels

ICEAGE COMPANY Income Statement (Absorption Costing) For Year Ended December 31, 2007 [60,000 Units Produced; 60,000 Units Sold]		
Sales (60,000 × $40)		$2,400,000
Cost of goods sold (60,000 × $25)		1,500,000
Gross margin		900,000
Selling and administrative expenses		
Variable (60,000 × $2)	$120,000	
Fixed	200,000	320,000
Net income		$ 580,000

ICEAGE COMPANY Income Statement (Absorption Costing) For Year Ended December 31, 2007 [100,000 Units Produced; 60,000 Units Sold]		
Sales (60,000 × $40)		$2,400,000
Cost of goods sold (60,000 × $21)		1,260,000
Gross margin		1,140,000
Selling and administrative expenses		
Variable (60,000 × $2)	$120,000	
Fixed	200,000	320,000
Net income		$ 820,000

Point: The 41% income increase is computed as:
$$\frac{\$820{,}000 - \$580{,}000}{\$580{,}000} = 0.41$$

Common sense suggests that because the company's variable cost per unit, total fixed costs, and sales are identical in both cases, merely producing more units and creating excess ending inventory should not increase income. Yet, as we see in Exhibit 6.10, income under absorption costing is 41% greater if management produces 40,000 more units than necessary and builds up ending inventory. The reason is that $240,000 of fixed overhead (40,000 units × $6) is assigned to ending inventory instead of being expensed as cost of goods sold in 2007. This shows that a manager can report increased income merely by producing more and disregarding whether the excess units can be sold or not.

Manager bonuses are tied to income computed under absorption costing for many companies. Accordingly, these managers may be enticed to increase production that increases income and their bonuses. This incentive problem encourages inventory buildup, which leads to increased costs in storage, financing, and obsolescence. If the excess inventory is never sold, it will be disposed of at a loss.

The manager incentive problem can be avoided when income is measured using variable costing. To illustrate, Exhibit 6.11 reports income under variable costing for the same production levels used in Exhibit 6.10. This demonstrates that managers cannot increase income under variable costing by merely increasing production without increasing sales.

Why is income under absorption costing affected by the production level when that for variable costing is not? The answer lies in the different treatment of fixed overhead costs for the two methods. Under absorption costing, fixed overhead *per unit* is lower when 100,000 units are produced than when 60,000 units are produced, and then fixed overhead cost is allocated to more units—recall Exhibit 6.9. If those excess units produced are not sold, the fixed overhead cost allocated to those units is not expensed until a future period when those units are sold.

EXHIBIT 6.11

Income Under Variable Costing for Different Production Levels

ICEAGE COMPANY Income Statement (Variable Costing) For Year Ended December 31, 2007 [60,000 Units Produced; 60,000 Units Sold]		
Sales (60,000 × $40)		$2,400,000
Variable expenses		
Variable production costs (60,000 × $15)	$900,000	
Variable selling and administrative expenses (60,000 × $2)	120,000	1,020,000
Contribution margin		1,380,000
Fixed expenses		
Fixed overhead	600,000	
Fixed selling and administrative expense	200,000	800,000
Net income		$ 580,000

ICEAGE COMPANY Income Statement (Variable Costing) For Year Ended December 31, 2007 [100,000 Units Produced; 60,000 Units Sold]		
Sales (60,000 × $40) . . .		$2,400,000
Variable expenses		
Variable production costs (60,000 × $15) . . .	$900,000	
Variable selling and administrative expenses (60,000 × $2)	120,000	1,020,000
Contribution margin . .		1,380,000
Fixed expenses		
Fixed overhead	600,000	
Fixed selling and administrative expense	200,000	800,000
Net income		$ 580,000

Reported income under variable costing, on the other hand, is not affected by production level changes because *all* fixed production costs are expensed in the year when incurred. Under variable costing, companies increase reported income by selling more units—it is not possible to increase income just by producing more units and creating excess inventory.

Point: A per unit cost that is constant at all production levels is a *variable cost per unit.*

Decision Ethics

Production Manager Your company produces and sells MP3 players. Due to competition, your company projects sales to be 35% less than last year. In a recent meeting, the CEO expressed concern that top executives may not receive bonuses because of the expected sales decrease. The controller suggests that if the company continues to produce as many units as last year, reported income might achieve the level for bonuses to be paid. Should your company produce excess inventory to maintain income? What ethical issues arise? [Answer—p. 221]

Setting Prices

C3 Explain the role of variable costing in pricing special orders.

Setting prices for products and services is one of the more complex and important managerial decisions. Although many factors impact pricing, cost is a crucial factor. Cost information from both absorption costing and variable costing can aid managers in pricing.

Over the long run, price must be high enough to cover all costs, including variable costs and fixed costs, and still provide an acceptable return to owners. For this purpose, absorption cost information is useful because it reflects the full costs that sales must exceed for the company to be profitable.

Over the short run, however, fixed production costs such as the cost to maintain plant capacity does not change with changes in production levels. With excess capacity, increases in production level would increase variable production costs, but not fixed costs. This implies that while managers try to maintain the long-run price on existing orders, which covers all production costs, managers should accept special orders *provided the special order price exceeds variable cost.*

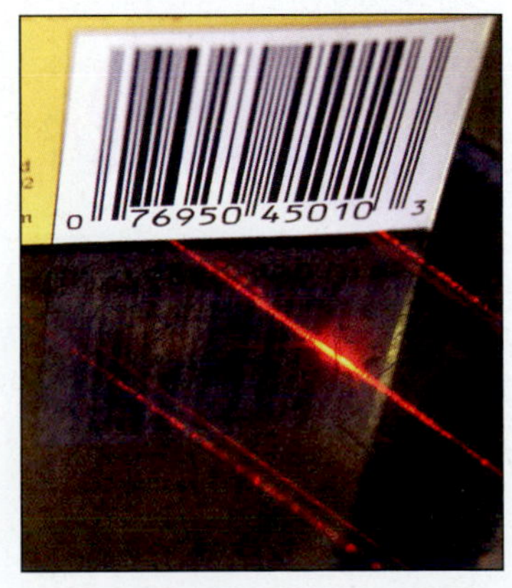

To illustrate, let's return to the data of IceAge Company. Recall that its variable production cost per unit is $15 and its total production cost per unit is $25 (at production level of 60,000 units). Assume that it receives a special order for 1,000 pairs of skates at an offer price of $22 per pair from a foreign skating school. This special order will not affect IceAge's regular sales and its plant has excess capacity to fill the order.

Drawing on absorption costing information, we observe that cost is $25 per unit and that the special order price is $22 per unit. These data would suggest that management reject the order as it would lose $3,000, computed as 1,000 units at $3 loss per pair ($22 − $25).

However, closer analysis suggests that this order should be accepted. This is because the $22 order price exceeds the $15 variable cost of the product. Specifically, Exhibit 6.12 reveals that the incremental revenue from accepting the order is $22,000 (1,000 units at $22 per unit), whereas the incremental production cost of the order is $15,000 (1,000 units at $15 per unit) and the incremental variable selling and administrative cost is $2,000 (1,000 units at $2 per unit). Thus, both its contribution margin and net income would increase by $5,000 from accepting the order. We see that variable costing reveals this opportunity while absorption costing obscures it.

Point: Use of relevant costs in special order and other managerial decisions is covered more extensively in a later chapter.

EXHIBIT 6.12

Computing Incremental Income for a Special Order

Rejecting Special Order		Accepting Special Order	
Incremental sales	$ 0	Incremental sales (1,000 × $22)	$22,000
Incremental costs	0	Incremental costs	
		Variable production cost (1,000 × $15)	15,000
		Variable selling and admin. expense (1,000 × $2)	2,000
Incremental income	$ 0	Incremental income	$ 5,000

The reason for increased income from accepting the special order lies in the different behavior of variable and fixed production costs. We see that if the order is rejected, only variable costs are saved. Fixed costs, on the other hand, do not change in the short run regardless of rejecting or accepting this order. Since incremental revenue from the order exceeds incremental costs (only variable cost in this case), accepting the special order increases company income.

Point: Fixed overhead costs won't increase when these additional units are sold because the company already has the capacity.

Decision Insight

Costing for Services Most of this chapter's illustrations use data from a manufacturer. Yet, variable costing also applies to service companies. A "special order" example is pricing for airlines when they sell tickets a day or so before a flight at deeply discounted prices. Provided the discounted price exceeds variable costs, such sales increase contribution margin and net income.

Controlling Costs

Every company strives to control costs to be competitive. An effective cost control practice is to hold managers responsible only for their **controllable costs.** A cost is controllable if a manager has the power to determine or at least markedly affect the amount incurred. **Uncontrollable costs** are not within the manager's control or influence. For example, direct materials cost is controllable by a production supervisor. On the other hand, costs related to production capacity are not controllable by that supervisor as that supervisor does not have authority to change factory size or add new machinery. Generally, variable production costs and fixed production costs are controlled at different levels of management. Similarly, variable selling and administrative costs are usually controlled at a level of management different from that which controls fixed selling and administrative costs.

Under absorption costing, both variable production costs and fixed production costs are included in product cost. This makes it difficult to evaluate the effectiveness of cost control by different levels of managers. Variable costing separates the variable costs from fixed costs and, therefore, makes it easier to identify and assign control over costs.

Decisions to change a company's fixed costs are usually assigned to higher-level managers. This is different from most variable costs that are assigned to lower-level managers and supervisors. When we separately report variable and fixed cost elements, as is done with an income statement in the **contribution format,** it highlights the impact of each cost element for income. This makes it easier for us to identify problem areas and to take cost control measures by appropriate levels of management. This approach is also useful in evaluating the performance of managers of different segments within a company.

Decision Maker

Internal Auditor Your company uses absorption costing for preparing its GAAP-based income statement and balance sheet. Management is disappointed because its external auditors are requiring it to write off an inventory amount because it exceeds what the company could reasonably sell in the foreseeable future. Why would management produce more than it sells? Why would management be disappointed about the write-off? [Answer—p. 221]

Limitations of Reports Using Variable Costing

An important generally accepted accounting principle is that of matching. Most managers interpret the matching principle as expensing all manufacturing costs, both variable and fixed, in the period when the related product is sold rather than when incurred. Consequently, absorption costing is almost exclusively used for external reporting. For income tax purposes, absorption costing is the only acceptable basis for filings with the Internal Revenue Service (IRS) under the Tax Reform Act of 1986.

Thus, and despite the many useful applications and insights provided by variable cost reports, *absorption costing is the only acceptable basis for both external reporting and tax reporting*. Also, as we discussed, top executives are often awarded bonuses based on income computed using absorption costing. These realities contribute to the widespread use of absorption costing by companies.

Quick Check

Answers—p. 221

5. Why is information under variable costing useful in making short-run pricing decisions when idle capacity exits?
6. Discuss the usefulness of absorption costing versus variable costing in controlling costs.
7. What are the limitations of variable costing?

Break-Even Analysis

Decision Analysis

A2 Compute and interpret break-even volume in units.

The previous chapter discussed cost-volume-profit (CVP) analysis for making managerial decisions. However, if the income statement is prepared under absorption costing, the data needed for CVP analysis are not readily available. Accordingly, substantial effort is required to go back to the accounting records and reclassify the cost data to obtain information necessary for conducting CVP analysis.

On the other hand, if the income statement is prepared using the contribution format, the data needed for CVP analysis are readily available. To illustrate, we can draw on IceAge's contribution margin income statement from Exhibit 6.4 (reproduced below) to readily compute its contribution margin per unit and its break-even volume in units.

ICEAGE COMPANY
Income Statement (Variable Costing)
For Year Ended December 31, 2007

	Dollars		Per Unit	
Sales (60,000 × $40)		$2,400,000		$40
Variable expenses				
Variable production costs (60,000 × $15)	$900,000		$15	
Variable selling and administrative expenses (60,000 × $2)	120,000	1,020,000	2	17
Contribution margin		1,380,000		$23
Fixed expenses				
Fixed overhead	600,000			
Fixed selling and administrative expense	200,000	800,000		
Net income		$ 580,000		

We compute and report the company's contribution margin per unit and its components in the far right columns of the exhibit above. Recall that contribution margin per unit is defined as follows.

$$\begin{aligned}\text{Contribution margin per unit} &= \text{Sales price per unit} - \text{Variable cost per unit}\\ &= \$40 - \$17 = \$23\end{aligned}$$

The above report shows that its variable cost per unit consists of \$15 in variable production costs and \$2 in variable selling and administrative costs.

We also see that the company's total fixed costs of \$800,000 is the sum of \$600,000 in fixed overhead cost and \$200,000 in fixed selling and administrative cost. From this information we can compute the company's break-even volume in units as follows.

$$\text{Break-even volume in units} = \frac{\text{Total fixed costs}}{\text{Contribution margin per unit}} = \frac{\$800{,}000}{\$23} = 34{,}783 \text{ units}$$

This finding implies that the company must produce and sell 34,783 units to break-even (zero income). Sales less than that amount would yield a net loss and sales above that amount would yield net income.

Demonstration Problem

Navaroli Company began operations on January 5, 2008. Cost and sales information for its first two calendar years of operations are summarized below.

Manufacturing costs	
Direct materials	$80 per unit
Direct labor	$120 per unit
Factory overhead costs for the year	
Variable overhead	$30 per unit
Fixed overhead	$14,000,000
Nonmanufacturing costs	
Variable selling and administrative	$10 per unit
Fixed selling and administrative	$ 8,000,000
Production and sales data	
Units produced, 2008	200,000 units
Units sold, 2008	140,000 units
Units in ending inventory, 2008	60,000 units
Units produced, 2009	80,000 units
Units sold, 2009	140,000 units
Units in ending inventory, 2009	0 units
Sales price per unit	$600 per unit

Required

1. Prepare an income statement for the company for 2008 under absorption costing.
2. Prepare an income statement for the company for 2008 under variable costing.
3. Explain the source(s) of the difference in reported income for 2008 under the two costing methods.
4. Prepare an income statement for the company for 2009 under absorption costing.
5. Prepare an income statement for the company for 2009 under variable costing.
6. Prepare a schedule to convert variable costing income to absorption costing income for the years 2008 and 2009. Use the format in Exhibit 6.8.

Planning the Solution

- Set up a table to compute the unit cost under the two costing methods (refer to Exhibit 6.2).
- Prepare an income statement under both of the two costing methods (refer to Exhibit 6.5).
- Consider differences in the treatment of fixed production costs for the income statement to answer requirements 3 and 6.

Solution to Demonstration Problem

Before the income statement for 2008 is prepared, unit costs for 2008 are computed under the two costing methods as follows.

	Absorption Costing	Variable Costing
Direct materials per unit	$ 80	$ 80
Direct labor per unit	120	120
Overhead per unit		
Variable overhead per unit	30	30
Fixed overhead per unit*	70	—
Total production cost per unit	$300	$230

* Fixed overhead per unit = $14,000,000 ÷ 200,000 units = $70 per unit.

1. Absorption costing income statement for 2008.

NAVAROLI COMPANY
Income Statement
For Year Ended December 31, 2008

Sales (140,000 × $600)	$84,000,000
Cost of goods sold (140,000 × $300)	42,000,000
Gross margin	42,000,000
Selling and administrative expenses ($1,400,000 + $8,000,000)	9,400,000
Net income	$32,600,000

2. Variable costing income statement for 2008.

NAVAROLI COMPANY
Income Statement (Contribution Format)
For Year Ended December 31, 2008

Sales (140,000 × $600)		$84,000,000
Variable expenses		
Variable production costs (140,000 × $230)	$32,200,000	
Variable selling and administrative costs	1,400,000	33,600,000
Contribution margin		50,400,000
Fixed expenses		
Fixed overhead	14,000,000	
Fixed selling and administrative	8,000,000	22,000,000
Net income		$28,400,000

3. Income under absorption costing is $4,200,000 more than that under variable costing even though sales are identical for each. This difference is due to the different treatment of fixed overhead cost. Under variable costing, the entire $14,000,000 of fixed overhead is expensed on the 2008 income statement. However, under absorption costing, $70 of fixed overhead cost is allocated to each of the 200,000 units produced. Since there were 60,000 units unsold at year-end, $4,200,000 (60,000 units × $70 per unit) of fixed overhead cost allocated to these units will be carried on its balance sheet in ending inventory. Consequently, reported income under absorption costing is $4,200,000 higher than variable costing income for the current period.

Before the income statement for 2009 is prepared, unit costs are computed under the two costing methods as follows.

	Absorption Costing	Variable Costing
Direct materials per unit	$ 80	$ 80
Direct labor per unit	120	120
Overhead per unit		
Variable overhead per unit	30	30
Fixed overhead per unit*	175	—
Total production cost per unit	$405	$230

* Fixed overhead per unit = $14,000,000/80,000 units = $175 per unit.

4. Absorption costing income statement for 2009.

NAVAROLI COMPANY Income Statement For Year Ended December 31, 2009		
Sales (140,000 × $600)		$84,000,000
Cost of goods sold		
From beginning inventory (60,000 × $300)	$18,000,000	
Produced during the year (80,000 × $405)	32,400,000	50,400,000
Gross margin		33,600,000
Selling and administrative expenses ($1,400,000 + $8,000,000)		9,400,000
Net income		$24,200,000

5. Variable costing income statement for 2009.

NAVAROLI COMPANY Income Statement (Contribution Format) For Year Ended December 31, 2009		
Sales (140,000 × $600)		$84,000,000
Variable expenses		
Variable production costs (140,000 × $230)	$32,200,000	
Variable selling and administrative costs	1,400,000	33,600,000
Contribution margin		50,400,000
Fixed expenses		
Fixed overhead	14,000,000	
Fixed selling and administrative	8,000,000	22,000,000
Net income		$28,400,000

6. Conversion of variable costing income to absorption costing income.

	2008	2009
Variable costing income	$28,400,000	$28,400,000
Add: Fixed overhead cost deferred in ending inventory (60,000 × $70)	4,200,000	0
Less: Fixed overhead cost recognized from beginning inventory (60,000 × $70)	0	(4,200,000)
Absorption costing income	$32,600,000	$24,200,000

Summary

C1 Distinguish between absorption costing and variable costing. Product cost consists of direct materials, direct labor, and overhead. Absorption costing and variable costing methods differ on what overhead costs are allocated to products. Under absorption costing, all overhead costs, both fixed and variable, are allocated to products. Under variable costing, only variable overhead costs are allocated to products; the fixed overhead costs are treated as a period cost and are charged as an expense in the period when incurred.

C2 Describe how absorption costing can result in over-production. Under absorption costing, fixed overhead costs are allocated to all units including both units sold and units in ending inventory. Consequently, expenses associated with the fixed overhead allocated to ending inventory are deferred to a future period. As a result, the larger ending inventory is, the more overhead cost is deferred to the future, and the greater current period income is.

C3 Explain the role of variable costing in pricing special orders. Over the short run, fixed production costs such as cost of maintaining plant capacity do not change with changes in production levels. When there is excess capacity, increases in production levels would only increase variable costs. Thus, managers should accept special orders as long as the order price is greater than the variable cost. This is because accepting the special order would increase only variable costs.

A1 Analyze income reporting for both absorption and variable costing. Under absorption costing, some fixed overhead cost is allocated to ending inventory and is carried on the balance sheet to the next period. However, all fixed costs are expensed in the period incurred under variable costing. Consequently, absorption costing income is generally greater than variable costing income if units produced exceed units sold, and conversely.

A2 Compute and interpret break-even volume in units. Break-even volume in units is defined as total fixed costs divided by contribution margin per unit. The result gives managers a unit goal to achieve breakeven; if the goal is surpassed, the company earns income.

P1 Compute unit cost under both absorption and variable costing. Absorption cost per unit includes direct materials, direct labor, and *all* overhead, whereas variable cost per unit includes direct materials, direct labor, and only *variable* overhead.

P2 Prepare an income statement using absorption costing and using variable costing. The variable costing income statement differs from the absorption costing income statement in that it classifies expenses based on cost behavior rather than function. Instead of gross margin, the variable costing income statement shows contribution margin. This contribution margin format focuses attention on the relation between costs and sales that is not evident from the absorption costing format.

P3 Prepare a contribution margin report. Under variable costing, the total variable costs are first deducted from sales to arrive at contribution margin. Variable costs and contribution margin are also shown as ratios (after dividing by dollar sales).

P4 Convert income under variable costing to the absorption cost basis. Variable costing income can be adjusted to absorption costing income by adding the fixed cost allocated to ending inventory and subtracting the fixed cost previously allocated to beginning inventory.

Guidance Answers to Decision Maker and Decision Ethics

Production Manager Under absorption costing, fixed production costs are spread over all units produced. Thus, fixed cost for each unit would be lower if more units are produced because the fixed cost is spread over more units. This means the company can increase income by producing excess units even if sales remain constant. With sales lagging, producing excess inventory leads to increased financing cost and inventory obsolescence. Also, producing excess inventory to meet income levels for bonuses harms company owners and is unethical. You must discuss this with the appropriate managers.

Internal Auditor If manager bonuses are tied to income, they would have incentives to increase income for personal gain. If absorption costing is used to determine income, management can reduce current period expenses (and raise income) with over-production, which shifts fixed production costs to future periods. This decision fails to consider whether there is a viable market for all units that are produced. If there is not, an auditor can conclude that the inventory does not have "future economic value" and pressure management to write it off. Such a write-off reduces income by the cost of the excess inventory.

Guidance Answers to Quick Checks

1. a, b, c, and d; Direct materials, direct labor, variable overhead, and fixed overhead.
2. a, b, and c; Direct materials, direct labor, and variable overhead.
3. c; see Exhibit 6.5
4. a; see Exhibit 6.6
5. This is because only the variable cost will be avoided if a special order is rejected, as fixed cost does not change with changes to short-run sales. This means a company is better off taking an order provided the order price exceeds variable cost.
6. Variable costs and fixed costs are typically influenced by decisions at different managerial levels. Since reports under variable costing separate variable costs from fixed costs, variable costing makes it easier to identify and control these cost elements.
7. Variable costing is not accepted for external reporting and income tax purposes—only absorption costing is acceptable for those purposes.

Key Terms

mhhe.com/wildMA2e

Key Terms are available at the book's Website for learning and testing in an online Flashcard Format.

Absorption costing (also called full costing) (p. 206)
Contribution format (p. 216)
Contribution margin income statement (p. 209)
Contribution margin report (p. 209)
Controllable costs (p. 216)
Fixed overhead cost deferred in inventory (p. 213)
Fixed overhead cost recognized from inventory (p. 213)
Uncontrollable costs (p. 216)
Variable costing (also called direct or marginal costing) (p. 206)

Multiple Choice Quiz

Answers on p. 235

mhhe.com/wildMA2e

Additional Quiz Questions are available at the book's Website.

Answer questions 1 and 2 using the following company data.

Units produced	1,000
Variable costs	
Direct materials	$3 per unit
Direct labor	$5 per unit
Variable overhead	$3 per unit
Variable selling and administrative	$1 per unit
Fixed overhead	$3,000
Fixed selling and administrative	$1,000

1. Product cost per unit under absorption costing is:
a. $11
b. $12
c. $14
d. $15
e. $16

2. Product cost per unit under variable costing is:
a. $11
b. $12
c. $14
d. $15
e. $16

3. Under variable costing, which costs are included in product cost?
a. All variable product costs, including direct materials, direct labor, and variable overhead.
b. All variable and fixed allocations of product costs, including direct materials, direct labor, and both variable and fixed overhead.
c. All variable product costs except for variable overhead.
d. All variable and fixed allocations of product costs, except for both variable and fixed overhead.

4. The difference between unit product cost under absorption costing as compared to that under variable costing is:
a. Direct materials and direct labor.
b. Fixed and variable portions of overhead.
c. Fixed overhead only.
d. Variable overhead only.

5. When production exceeds sales, which of the following is true?
a. No change occurs to inventories for either absorption costing or variable costing methods.
b. Use of absorption costing produces a higher net income than the use of variable costing.
c. Use of absorption costing produces a lower net income than the use of variable costing.
d. Use of absorption costing causes inventory value to decrease more than it would through the use of variable costing.

Discussion Questions

1. What costs are normally included as part of product costs under the method of absorption costing?

2. What costs are normally included as part of product costs under the method of variable costing?

3. Describe how the following items are computed: *a.* Gross margin, and *b.* Contribution margin

4. When units produced exceed units sold for a reporting period, would income under variable costing be greater than, equal to, or less than income under absorption costing? Explain.

5. Describe how use of absorption costing in determining income can lead to over-production and a buildup of inventory. Explain how variable costing can avoid this same problem.

6. How can absorption costing lead to incorrect short-run pricing decisions?

7. What conditions must exist to achieve accurate short-run pricing decisions using variable costing?

8. Describe the usefulness of variable costing for controlling company costs.

9. Explain how contribution margin analysis is useful for managerial decisions and performance evaluations.

10. What are the major limitations of variable costing?

11. How can variable costing income statements be converted to absorption costing?

12. How can variable costing reports prepared using the contribution margin format help managers in computing break-even volume in units?

13. How can **Best Buy** use variable costing to help better understand its operations and to make better pricing decisions?

14. Assume that **Apple** has received a special order from a retailer for 1,000 specially outfitted iMacs. This is a one-time order, which will not require any additional capacity or fixed costs. What should Apple consider when determining a selling price for these iMacs?

Denotes Discussion Questions that involve decision making.

connect *Most materials in this section are available in McGraw-Hill's Connect*

QUICK STUDY

QS 6-1
Computing unit cost under absorption costing
C1 P1

Jordyn Company reports the following information regarding its production costs. Compute its production cost per unit under absorption costing.

Direct materials	$20 per unit
Direct labor	$30 per unit
Overhead costs for the year	
Variable overhead	$ 10 per unit
Fixed overhead	$160,000
Units produced	20,000 units

QS 6-2
Computing unit cost under variable costing C1 P1

Refer to Jordyn Company's data in QS 6-1. Compute its production cost per unit under variable costing.

QS 6-3
Computing manufacturing margin P2

Leila Company sold 10,000 units of its product at a price of $80 per unit. Total variable cost is $50 per unit, consisting of $40 in variable production cost and $10 in variable selling and administrative cost. Compute the manufacturing (production) margin for the company under variable costing.

QS 6-4
Computing contribution margin
P3

Refer to the information for Leila Company in QS 6-3. Compute the contribution margin for this company.

QS 6-5
Production level, absorption costing, and gross margin
P3 A1 

Martol Company reports the following cost data for its single product. The company regularly sells 20,000 units of its product at a price of $80 per unit. If Martol doubles its production to 40,000 units while sales remain at the current 20,000 unit level, by how much would the company's gross margin increase or decrease under absorption costing?

Direct materials	$10 per unit
Direct labor	$12 per unit
Overhead costs for the year	
Variable overhead	$3 per unit
Fixed overhead per year	$40,000
Normal production level (in units)	20,000 units

QS 6-6
Production level, variable costing, gross margin P2 P3

Refer to the information about Martol Company in QS 6-5. Would the answer to the question in QS 6-5 change if the company uses variable costing? Explain.

QS 6-7
Break-even volume in units
A2

Lor Company's single product sells at a price of $108 per unit. Cost data for its single product follows. Compute this company's break-even volume in units.

Direct materials	$20 per unit
Direct labor	$28 per unit
Overhead costs	
Variable overhead	$ 6 per unit
Fixed overhead per year	$80,000 per year
Selling and administrative expenses	
Variable	$ 18 per unit
Fixed	$100,000 per year

QS 6-8
Special order pricing
C3

Sheyla Company produces a product that sells for $84 per unit. A customer contacts Sheyla and offers to purchase 2,000 units of its product at a price of $76 per unit. Variable production costs with this order would be $30 per unit, and variable selling expenses would be $18 per unit. Assuming that this special order would not require any additional fixed costs, and that Sheyla has sufficient capacity to produce the product without affecting regular sales, explain to Sheyla's management why it might be a good decision to accept this special order.

QS 6-9
Converting variable costing income to absorption costing
P4

Aivars Company reports the following variable costing income statement for its single product. This company's sales totaled 50,000 units, but its production was 80,000 units. It had no beginning finished goods inventory for the current period.

AIVARS COMPANY Income Statement (Variable Costing)	
Sales (50,000 units × $60 per unit)	$3,000,000
Variable expenses	
Variable manufacturing expense (50,000 units × $28 per unit)	1,400,000
Variable selling and admin. expense (50,000 units × $5 per unit)	250,000
Total variable expenses	1,650,000
Contribution margin	1,350,000
Fixed expenses	
Fixed overhead	320,000
Fixed selling and administrative expense	160,000
Total fixed expenses	480,000
Net income	$ 870,000

1. Convert this company's variable costing income statement to an absorption costing income statement.
2. Explain the difference in income between the variable costing and absorption costing income statement.

Most materials in this section are available in McGraw-Hill's Connect connect

EXERCISES

Exercise 6-1
Computing unit and inventory costs under absorption costing and variable costing
P1

Duo Company reports the following information for the current year, which is its first year of operations.

Direct materials	$15 per unit
Direct labor	$16 per unit
Overhead costs for the year	
Variable overhead	$ 80,000 per year
Fixed overhead	$160,000 per year
Units produced this year	20,000 units
Units sold this year	14,000 units
Ending finished goods inventory in units	6,000 units

1. Compute the cost per unit of finished goods using absorption costing.
2. Compute the cost per unit of finished goods using variable costing.
3. Determine the cost of ending finished goods inventory using absorption costing.
4. Determine the cost of ending finished goods inventory using variable costing.

Check (1) Absorption cost per unit, $43; (2) Variable cost per unit, $35

Exercise 6-2
Income reporting under absorption costing and variable costing
P2 A1 

Adams Company, a manufacturer of in-home decorative fountains, began operations on September 1 of the current year. Its cost and sales information for this year follows.

Production costs	
Direct materials	$40 per unit
Direct labor	$60 per unit
Overhead costs for the year	
Variable overhead	$3,000,000
Fixed overhead	$7,000,000
Nonproduction costs for the year	
Variable selling and administrative	$ 770,000
Fixed selling and administrative	$4,250,000
Production and sales for the year	
Units produced	100,000 units
Units sold	70,000 units
Sales price per unit	$350 per unit

1. Prepare an income statement for the company using absorption costing.
2. Prepare an income statement for the company using variable costing.
3. Under what circumstance(s) is reported income identical under both absorption costing and variable costing?

Check (1) Absorption costing income, $5,480,000; (2) Variable costing income, $3,380,000

Exercise 6-3
Income reporting under absorption costing and variable costing
P2 A1 

Norwood Company, a producer of solid oak tables, reports the following data from its current year operations, which is its second year of business.

Sales price per unit	$320 per unit
Units produced this year	115,000 units
Units sold this year	118,000 units
Units in beginning-year inventory	3,000 units
Beginning inventory costs	
Variable (3,000 units × $135)	$405,000
Fixed (3,000 units × $80)	240,000
Total	$645,000
Production costs this year	
Direct materials	$40 per unit
Direct labor	$62 per unit
Overhead costs this year	
Variable overhead	$3,220,000
Fixed overhead	$7,400,000
Nonproduction costs this year	
Variable selling and administrative	$1,416,000
Fixed selling and administrative	4,600,000

1. Prepare the current year income statement for the company using absorption costing.
2. Prepare the current year income statement for the company using variable costing.
3. Explain any difference between the two income numbers under the two costing methods in parts 1 and 2.

Check (1) Absorption costing income, $8,749,000; (2) Variable costing income, $8,989,000

Exercise 6-4

Converting absorption costing income to variable costing income

P2 P4 

Kenai Kayaking, a manufacturer of kayaks, began operations this year. During this first year, the company produced 1,050 kayaks and sold 800. At the current year-end, the company reported the following income statement information using absorption costing.

Sales (800 × $1,050)	$840,000
Cost of goods sold (800 × $500)	400,000
Gross margin	440,000
Selling and administrative expenses	230,000
Net income	$210,000

Additional Information

a. Production cost per kayak totals $500, which consists of $400 in variable production cost and $100 in fixed production cost—the latter amount is based on $105,000 of fixed production costs allocated to the 1,050 kayaks produced.

b. The $230,000 in selling and administrative expense consists of $75,000 that is variable and $155,000 that is fixed.

Check (1) Variable costing income, $185,000

1. Prepare an income statement for the current year of Kenai Kayaking under variable costing.

2. Explain the difference in income between the variable costing and absorption costing income statement.

Exercise 6-5

Converting variable costing income to absorption costing income

P2 P4

Lyon Furnaces prepares the income statement under variable costing for its managerial reports, and it prepares the income statement under absorption costing for external reporting. For its first month of operations, this company prepares the following income statement information under variable costing.

Sales (225 × $1,600)	$360,000
Variable production cost (225 × $625)	140,625
Variable selling and administrative expenses (225 × $65)	14,625
Contribution margin	204,750
Fixed overhead cost	56,250
Fixed selling and administrative expense	75,000
Net income	$ 73,500

Additional Information

During this first month of operations, 375 furnaces were produced and 225 were sold; this left 150 furnaces in ending inventory.

Check (1) Absorption costing income, $96,000

1. Prepare this company's income statement for its first month of operations under absorption costing.

2. Explain the difference in income between the variable costing and absorption costing income statement.

Exercise 6-6

Unit costs and income statement under absorption costing and variable costing

P1 P2 P4

Blue Sky Company reports the following costing data on its product for its first year of operations. During this first year, the company produced 44,000 units and sold 36,000 units at a price of $140 per unit.

Production costs	
Direct materials per unit	$60
Direct labor per unit	$22
Variable overhead per unit	$8
Fixed overhead for the year	$528,000
Selling and administrative cost	
Variable selling and administrative cost per unit	$11
Fixed selling and administrative cost per year	$105,000

1. Assume that this company uses absorption costing.

Check (1a) Absorption cost per unit, $102

a. Determine its unit product cost.

b. Prepare its income statement for the year under absorption costing.

2. Assume that this company uses variable costing.

(2a) Variable cost per unit, $90

a. Determine its unit product cost.

b. Prepare its income statement for the year under variable costing.

Exercise 6-7
Variable costing for services
C3 

Midsouth Airlines provides charter airplane services. In October this year, the company was operating at 60% of its capacity when it received a bid from the local community college. The college was organizing a Washington, D.C., trip for its international student group. The college only budgeted $30,000 for roundtrip airfare. Midsouth Airlines normally charges between $50,000 and $60,000 for such service given the number of travelers. Midsouth determined its cost for the roundtrip flight to Washington to be $44,000, which consists of the following:

Variable cost	$15,000
Fixed cost	29,000
Total cost	$44,000

Although the manager at Midsouth supports the college's educational efforts, she could not justify accepting the $30,000 bid for the trip given the projected $14,000 loss. Still, she decides to consult with you, an independent financial consultant. Do you believe the airline should accept the bid from the college? Prepare a memorandum, with supporting computations, explaining why or why not.

Exercise 6-8
Variable costing and contribution margin income statement
P3 A1

Down Jackets has three types of costs: jacket cost, factory rent cost, and utilities cost. This company sells its jackets for $16.50 each. Management has prepared the following estimated cost information for next month under two different sales levels.

	At 10,000 Jackets	At 12,000 Jackets
Jacket cost	$80,000	$96,000
Rent cost	6,000	6,000
Utilities cost	8,400	9,900

Required

1. Compute what the company should expect for total variable cost if 11,000 jackets are sold next month. (*Hint:* Use the high-low method to separate jacket and utilities costs into their variable and fixed components.)

2. Prepare its contribution format income statement for a monthly sales volume of 12,000 jackets.

Check (2) Income, $86,100

Exercise 6-9
Contribution margin format income statement
P3 A1

Polarix is a retailer of ATVs (all terrain vehicles) and accessories. An income statement for its Consumer ATV Department for the current year follows. ATVs sell, on average, for $3,800. Variable selling expenses are $270 each. The remaining selling expenses are fixed. Administrative expenses are 40% variable and 60% fixed. The company does not manufacture its own ATVs; it purchases them from a supplier for $1,830 each.

POLARIX Income Statement—Consumer ATV Department For Year Ended December 21, 2009		
Sales		$646,000
Cost of goods sold		311,100
Gross margin		334,900
Operating expenses		
Selling expenses	$135,000	
Administrative expenses	59,500	194,500
Net income		$140,400

Required

1. Prepare an income statement for this current year using the contribution margin format.

2. For each ATV sold during this year, what is the contribution toward covering fixed expenses and that toward earning income?

Check (2) $1,560

Most materials in this section are available in McGraw-Hill's Connect connect

PROBLEM SET A

Problem 6-1A

Converting an absorption costing income statement to a variable costing income statement

P1 P2 P4 A1

Torres Company began operations this year. During this first year, the company produced 100,000 units and sold 80,000 units. The absorption costing income statement for its first year of operations follows.

Sales (80,000 units × $50 per unit)		$4,000,000
Cost of goods sold		
Beginning inventory	$ 0	
Cost of goods manufactured (100,000 units × $30 per unit)	3,000,000	
Cost of good available for sale	3,000,000	
Ending inventory (20,000 × $30)	600,000	
Cost of goods sold		2,400,000
Gross margin		1,600,000
Selling and administrative expenses		530,000
Net income		$1,070,000

Additional Information

a. Selling and administrative expenses consist of $350,000 in annual fixed expenses and $2.25 per unit in variable selling and administrative expenses.

b. The company's product cost of $30 per unit is computed as follows.

Direct materials	$5 per unit
Direct labor	$14 per unit
Variable overhead	$2 per unit
Fixed overhead ($900,000/100,000 units)	$9 per unit

Required

Check (1) Variable costing income, $890,000

1. Prepare an income statement for the company under variable costing.

2. Explain any difference between the income under variable costing (from part 1) and the income reported above.

Problem 6-2A

Converting an absorption costing income statement to a variable costing income statement (two consecutive years)

P2 P4 A1

Powell Company produces a single product. Its income statement under absorption costing for its first two years of operation follow.

	2008	2009
Sales ($46 per unit)	$920,000	$1,840,000
Cost of goods sold ($31 per unit)	620,000	1,240,000
Gross margin	300,000	600,000
Selling and administrative expenses	290,000	340,000
Net income	$ 10,000	$ 260,000

Additional Information

a. Sales and production data for these first two years follow.

	2008	2009
Units produced	30,000	30,000
Units sold	20,000	40,000

b. Variable cost per unit and total fixed costs are unchanged during 2008 and 2009. The company's $31 per unit product cost consists of the following.

Direct materials	$ 5
Direct labor	9
Variable overhead	7
Fixed overhead ($300,000/30,000 units)	10
Total product cost per unit	$31

c. Selling and administrative expenses consist of the following.

	2008	2009
Variable selling and administrative ($2.5 per unit)	$ 50,000	$100,000
Fixed selling and administrative	240,000	240,000
Total selling and administrative	$290,000	$340,000

Required

1. Prepare income statements for the company for each of its first two years under variable costing.

2. Explain any difference between the absorption costing income and the variable costing income for these two years.

Check (1) 2008 net loss, $(90,000)

Problem 6-3A
CVP analysis, absorption costing, and variable costing
A1 A2

Refer to information about Powell Company in Problem 6-2A. In the company's planning documents, Kyra Powell, the company's president, reports that the break-even volume (in units) for the company is 21,739 units. This break-even point is computed as follows.

$$\text{Break-even volume} = \frac{\text{Total fixed cost}}{\text{Contribution margin per unit}} = \frac{\$540{,}000}{\$22.50} = 24{,}000 \text{ units}$$

Total fixed cost consists of $300,000 in fixed production cost and $240,000 in fixed selling and administrative expenses. The contribution margin per unit of $22.50 is computed by deducting the $23.50 variable cost per unit (which consists of $21 in variable production cost and $2.50 in variable selling and administrative cost) from the $46 sales price per unit. In 2008, the company sold 20,000 units, which was below break-even, and Kyra was concerned that the company's income statement would show a net loss. To her surprise, the company's 2008 income statement revealed a net income of $10,000 as shown in Problem 6-2A.

Required

Prepare a one-half-page memorandum to the president explaining how the company could report net income when it sold less than its break-even volume in units.

Problem 6-4A
Variable cost analysis for a services company
C3

Winter Garden is a luxury hotel with 150 suites. Its regular suite rate is $250 per night per suite. The hotel's cost per night is $140 per suite and consists of the following.

Variable direct labor and materials cost	$ 30
Fixed cost [($6,022,500/150 suites) ÷ 365 days]	110
Total cost per night per suite	$140

The hotel manager received an offer to hold the local Rotary Club annual meeting at the hotel in March, which is the hotel's low season with an occupancy rate of under 50%. The Rotary Club would reserve 50 suites for three nights if the hotel could offer a 50% discount, or a rate of $125 per night. The hotel manager is inclined to reject the offer because the cost per suite per night is $140. The manager believes that if 50 suites are offered at the rate of $125 per night for three nights, the hotel would lose $2,250, computed as ($125 − $140) × 50 suites × 3 nights.

Required

Prepare an analysis of this offer for the hotel manager. Explain (with supporting computations) whether the offer from the Rotary Club should be accepted or rejected.

Check $14,250 contribution margin

Problem 6-5A
Income reporting, absorption costing, and managerial ethics
C2 P2 A1 

Safety Chemical produces and sells an ice-melting granular used on roadways and sidewalks in winter. It annually produces and sells about 100 tons of its granular. In its nine-year history, the company has never reported a net loss. However, because of this year's unusually mild winter, projected demand for its product is only 60 tons. Based on its predicted production and sales of 60 tons, the company projects the following income statement (under absorption costing).

Sales (60 tons at $21,000 per ton)	$1,260,000
Cost of goods sold (60 tons at $16,000 per ton)	960,000
Gross margin	300,000
Selling and administrative expenses	318,600
Net loss	$ (18,600)

Its product cost information follows and consists mainly of fixed cost because of its automated production process requiring expensive equipment.

Variable direct labor and material costs per ton	$ 3,500
Fixed cost per ton ($750,000 ÷ 60 tons)	12,500
Total product cost per ton	$16,000

Selling and administrative expenses consist of variable selling and administrative expenses of $310 per ton and fixed selling and administrative expenses of $300,000 per year. The company's president is concerned about the adverse reaction from its creditors and shareholders if the projected net loss is reported. The operations manager mentions that since the company has large storage capacity, it can report a net income by keeping its production at the usual 100-ton level even though it expects to sell only 60 tons. The president was puzzled by the suggestion that the company can report income by producing more without increasing sales.

Required

Check (1) $281,400 absorption costing income

1. Can the company report a net income by increasing production to 100 tons and storing the excess production in inventory? Your explanation should include an income statement (using absorption costing) based on production of 100 tons and sales of 60 tons.

2. Should the company produce 100 tons given that projected demand is 60 tons? Explain, and also refer to any ethical implications of such a managerial decision.

PROBLEM SET B

Problem 6-1B

Converting an absorption costing income statement to a variable costing income statement

P1 P2 P4 A1

Mitchell Company began operations this year. During this first year, the company produced 300,000 units and sold 250,000 units. Its income statement under absorption costing for its first year of operations follows.

Sales (250,000 units × $18 per unit)		$4,500,000
Cost of goods sold		
Beginning inventory	$ 0	
Cost of goods manufactured (300,000 units × $7.50 per unit)	2,250,000	
Cost of good available for sale	2,250,000	
Ending inventory (50,000 × $7.50)	375,000	
Cost of goods sold		1,875,000
Gross margin		2,625,000
Selling and administrative expenses		2,200,000
Net income		$ 425,000

Additional Information

a. Selling and administrative expenses consist of $1,200,000 in annual fixed expenses and $4 per unit in variable selling and administrative expenses.

b. The company's product cost of $7.50 per unit is computed as follows.

Direct materials	$2.00 per unit
Direct labor	$2.40 per unit
Variable overhead	$1.60 per unit
Fixed overhead ($450,000/300,000 units)	$1.50 per unit

Required

1. Prepare the company's income statement under variable costing.

2. Explain any difference between the company's income under variable costing (from part 1) and the income reported above.

Check (1) Variable costing income, $350,000

Problem 6-2B
Converting an absorption costing income statement to a variable costing income statement (two consecutive years)
P2 P4 A1

Flores Company produces a single product. Its income statement under absorption costing for its first two years of operation follow.

	2008	2009
Sales ($35 per unit)	$1,925,000	$2,275,000
Cost of goods sold ($26 per unit)	1,430,000	1,690,000
Gross margin	495,000	585,000
Selling and administrative expenses	465,000	495,000
Net income	$ 30,000	$ 90,000

Additional Information

a. Sales and production data for these first two years follow.

	2008	2009
Units produced	60,000	60,000
Units sold	55,000	65,000

b. Its variable cost per unit and total fixed costs are unchanged during 2008 and 2009. Its $26 per unit product cost consists of the following.

Direct materials	$ 4
Direct labor	6
Variable overhead	8
Fixed overhead ($480,000/60,000 units)	8
Total product cost per unit	$26

c. Its selling and administrative expenses consist of the following.

	2008	2009
Variable selling and administrative ($3 per unit)	$165,000	$195,000
Fixed selling and administrative	300,000	300,000
Total selling and administrative	$465,000	$495,000

Required

1. Prepare this company's income statements under variable costing for each of its first two years.

2. Explain any difference between the absorption costing income and the variable costing income for these two years.

Check (1) 2008 net loss, $(10,000)

Problem 6-3B
CVP analysis, absorption costing, and variable costing
A1 A2

Refer to information about Flores Company in Problem 6-2B. In the company's planning documents, Roberto Flores, the company president, reports that the company's break-even volume in unit sales is 55,715 units. This break-even point is computed as follows.

$$\text{Break-even volume} = \frac{\text{Total fixed cost}}{\text{Contribution margin per unit}} = \frac{\$780{,}000}{\$14} = 55{,}715 \text{ units}$$

Total fixed cost consists of $480,000 in fixed production cost and $300,000 in fixed selling and administrative expenses. The contribution margin per unit of $14 is computed by deducting the $21 variable cost per unit (which consists of $18 in variable production cost and $2 in variable selling and administrative cost) from the $35 sales price per unit. In 2008, it sold 55,000 units, which was below break-even, and Roberto Flores was concerned that the company's income statement would show a net loss. To his surprise, the company's 2008 income statement revealed a net income of $30,000 as shown in Problem 6-2B.

Required

Prepare a one-half-page memorandum to the president explaining how the company could report net income when it sold less than its break-even volume in units.

Problem 6-4B

Variable cost analysis for a services company

C3

Elegant Plaza Hotel is a luxury hotel with 400 rooms. Its regular room rate is $300 per night per room. The hotel's cost is $120 per night per room and consists of the following.

Variable direct labor and materials cost	$ 40
Fixed cost ([$18,250,000/400 rooms] ÷ 365 days)	125
Total cost per night per room	$165

The hotel manager received an offer to hold the Junior States of America (JSA) convention at the hotel in February, which is the hotel's low season with an occupancy rate of under 45%. JSA would reserve 100 rooms for four nights if the hotel could offer a 50% discount, or a rate of $150 per night. The hotel manager is inclined to reject the offer because the cost per room per night is $165. The manager believes that if 100 rooms are offered at the rate of $150 per night for four nights, the hotel would lose $6,000, computed as ($150 − $165) × 100 rooms × 4 nights.

Required

Check Contribution margin, $44,000

Prepare an analysis of this offer for the hotel manager. Explain (with supporting computations) whether the offer from JSA should be accepted or rejected.

Problem 6-5B

Income reporting, absorption costing, and managerial ethics

C2 P2 A1 

Proto Chemical produces and sells an ice-melting granular used on roadways and sidewalks in winter. The company annually produces and sells about 300,000 lbs of its granular. In its ten-year history, the company has never reported a net loss. Because of this year's unusually mild winter, projected demand for its product is only 250,000 lbs. Based on its predicted production and sales of 250,000 lbs, the company projects the following income statement under absorption costing.

Sales (250,000 lbs at $8 per lb.)	$2,000,000
Cost of goods sold (250,000 lbs at $6.80 per lb.)	1,700,000
Gross margin	300,000
Selling and administrative expenses	450,000
Net loss	$ (150,000)

Its product cost information follows and consists mainly of fixed production cost because of its automated production process requiring expensive equipment.

Variable direct labor and materials costs per lb.	$2.00
Fixed production cost per lb ($1,200,000/250,000 lbs.)	4.80
Total product cost per lb.	$6.80

The company's selling and administrative expenses are all fixed. The president is concerned about the adverse reaction from its creditors and shareholders if the projected net loss is reported. The controller suggests that since the company has large storage capacity, it can report a net income by keeping its production at the usual 300,000 lbs level even though it expects to sell only 250,000 lbs. The president was puzzled by the suggestion that the company can report a profit by producing more without increasing sales.

Required

1. Can the company report a net income by increasing production to 300,000 lbs and storing the excess production in inventory? Your explanation should include an income statement (using absorption costing) based on production of 300,000 lbs and sales of 250,000 lbs.

2. Should the company produce 300,000 lbs given that projected demand is 250,000 lbs? Explain, and also refer to any ethical implications of such a managerial decision.

Check (1) $50,000 absorption income

SERIAL PROBLEM

(This serial problem began in Chapter 1 and continues through most of the book. If previous chapter segments were not completed, the serial problem can begin at this point. It is helpful, but not necessary, to use the Working Papers that accompany the book.)

SP 6 Adriana Lopez expected sales of her line of computer workstation furniture to equal 300 workstations (at a sales price of $3,000) for 2010. The workstations' manufacturing costs include the following.

Direct materials.	$800 per unit
Direct labor	$400 per unit
Variable overhead	$100 per unit
Fixed overhead	$24,000 per year

The selling expenses related to these workstations follow.

Variable selling expenses	$50 per unit
Fixed selling expenses	$4,000 per year

Adriana is considering how many workstations to produce in 2010. She is confident that she will be able to sell any workstations in her 2010 ending inventory during 2011. However, Adriana does not want to overproduce as she does not have sufficient storage space for many more workstations.

Required

1. Compute Success Systems' absorption costing income assuming
   a. 300 workstations are produced.
   b. 320 workstations are produced.

2. Compute Success Systems' variable costing income assuming
   a. 300 workstations are produced.
   b. 320 workstations are produced.

3. Explain to Adriana any differences in the income figures determined in parts 1 and 2. How should Adriana use the information from parts 1 and 2 to help make production decisions?

BEYOND THE NUMBERS

REPORTING IN ACTION

BTN 6-1 One of many services Best Buy offers is its Geek Squad (GeekSquad.com), who "are ready to take the hassle out of your technology woes." The Geek Squad offers a wide variety of services, including repairing crashed hard drives, containing virus outbreaks, removing spyware, and helping protect and back up important data.

Required

For Best Buy to determine what services and products to offer through its Geek Squad, would variable or absorption costing be a better approach to analyze those new services or products? Explain.

COMPARATIVE ANALYSIS

BTN 6-2 To compete with **Best Buy's Geek Squad** (**GeekSquad.com**), **Circuit City** recently began a similar service named **firedog** (**firedog.com**). Firedog offers in-home, in-store, and online services for computer repair, installation and support, and home theater product installation.

Required

1. What are some of the costs that Circuit City had to consider when deciding whether to offer the firedog service? Are those costs different from what Best Buy must consider when offering additional new Geek Squad products or services? Explain.
2. Would variable or absorption costing be more useful to Circuit City in analyzing whether firedog is profitable? Explain.

ETHICS CHALLENGE

C2 P2 A1 

BTN 6-3 FDP Company produces a variety of home security products. Gary Price, the company's president, is concerned with the fourth quarter market demand for the company's products. Unless something is done in the last two months of the year, the company is likely to miss its earnings expectation of Wall Street analysts. Price still remembers when FDP's earnings were below analysts' expectation by two cents a share three years ago, and the company's share price fell 19% the day earnings were announced. In a recent meeting, Price told his top management that something must be done quickly. One proposal by the marketing vice president was to give a deep discount to the company's major customers to increase the company's sales in the fourth quarter. The company controller pointed out that while the discount could increase sales, it may not help the bottom line; to the contrary, it could lower income. The controller said, "Since we have enough storage capacity, we might simply increase our production in the fourth quarter to increase our reported profit."

Required

1. Gary Price is not sure how the increase in production without a corresponding increase in sales could help boost the company's income. Explain to Price how reported income varies with respect to production level.
2. Is there an ethical concern in this situation? If so, which parties are affected? Explain.

COMMUNICATING IN PRACTICE

C2

BTN 6-4 Mertz Chemical has three divisions. Its consumer product division faces strong competition from companies overseas. During its recent teleconference, Ryan Peterson, the consumer product division manager, reported that his division's sales for the current year were below its break-even point. However, when the division's annual reports were received, Billie Mertz, the company president, was surprised that the consumer product division actually reported a profit of $264,000. How could this be possible?

Required

Assume that you work in the corporate controller's office. Write a one-half-page memorandum to the president explaining how the division can report income even if its sales are below the break-even point.

TAKING IT TO THE NET

C1

BTN 6-5 This chapter discussed the variable costing method and how to use variable costing information to make various business decisions. We also can find several Websites on variable costing and its business applications.

Required

1. Review the Website of **Value Based Management** at ValueBasedManagement.net. Identify and print the site page on the topic of variable costing (ValueBasedManagement.net/Methods_Variable_Costing.html).
2. What other phrases are used in practice for *variable costing*?
3. According to this Website, what are the consequences of variable costing for profit calculation?

BTN 6-6 This chapter identified many decision contexts in which variable costing information is more relevant than absorption costing. However, absorption costing is still used by many companies and remains the only acceptable basis for external (and tax) reporting.

TEAMWORK IN ACTION

C1 C5

Required

Break into teams and identify at least one specific decision context in which absorption costing information is more relevant than variable costing. Be prepared to discuss your answers in class.

BTN 6-7 Bonobos, which was launched by entrepreneurial friends Brian Spaly and Andy Dunn, produces high-quality pants in unique styles and limited quantities. Selling prices for a pair of Bonobos pants typically range from $110 per pair to $350 per pair.

ENTREPRENEURIAL DECISION

C1

Required

1. Based on information in this chapter's opener, identify at least four examples of the types of costs that likely explain the wide range of selling prices for Bonobos' pants.
2. The founders of Bonobos use variable costing in their business decisions. If Bonobos used absorption costing, would you expect the company's income to be more, less than, or about the same as its income measured under variable costing? Explain.

BTN 6-8 Visit a local hotel and observe its daily operating activities. The costs associated with some of its activities are variable while others are fixed with respect to occupancy levels.

HITTING THE ROAD

C3

Required

1. List cost items that are likely variable for the hotel.
2. List cost items that are likely fixed for the hotel.
3. Compare the fixed cost items with variable cost items. Rank costs within each category based on your perception of which ones you believe are the larger.
4. Based on your observations and the answers to parts 1 through 3, explain why many hotels offer discounts as high as 50% or more during their low occupancy season.

BTN 6-9 Assume that DSG international (DSGiplc.com) is considering offering a service similar to Best Buy's Geek Squad. However, instead of developing the group internally, they are considering buying a company that already offers such services.

GLOBAL DECISION

C1 A1

Required

Would absorption or variable costing be most useful to DSG in evaluating whether to acquire an existing business that provides services similar to the Geek Squad? Explain.

ANSWERS TO MULTIPLE CHOICE QUIZ

1. c; $14, computed as $3 + $5 + $3 + ($3,000/1,000 units).
2. a; $11, computed as $3 + $5 + $3 (consisting of all variable product costs).
3. a
4. c
5. b

A Look Back

Chapter 6 compared reports prepared under variable costing with those under absorption costing, and it explained how variable costing can improve managerial decisions.

A Look at This Chapter

This chapter explains the importance of budgeting and describes the master budget and its preparation. It also discusses the value of the master budget to the planning of future business activities.

A Look Ahead

Chapter 8 focuses on flexible budgets, standard costs, and variance reporting. It explains the usefulness of these procedures and reports for business decisions.

Chapter 7 Master Budgets and Performance Planning

Learning Objectives

CAP

Conceptual

C1 Describe the importance and benefits of budgeting. *(p. 238)*

C2 Explain the process of budget administration. *(p. 240)*

C3 Describe a master budget and the process of preparing it. *(p. 242)*

Analytical

A1 Analyze expense planning using activity-based budgeting. *(p. 251)*

LP7

Procedural

P1 Prepare each component of a master budget and link each to the budgeting process. *(p. 244)*

P2 Link both operating and capital expenditures budgets to budgeted financial statements. *(p. 248)*

P3 *Appendix 7A*—Prepare production and manufacturing budgets. *(p. 257)*

Decision Feature

Lucky Charms

"The Number One thing is you have got to take the chance"—Rich Schmelzer

BOULDER, CO—Each pair of **Crocs (Crocs.com)** shoes includes ventilation holes for breathability and to filter water out. Sheri Schmelzer and her kids thought it more fun to use clay and rhinestones to decorate the holes with fun charms. Sheri's husband Rich, an entrepreneur, immediately saw the profit potential—within 48 hours the Schmelzer's had filed patents for the design of **Jibbitz (Jibbitz.com),** which are small accessories made to fit in the holes of Crocs. Today, Jibbitz accessories come in various shapes and sizes, and include more than 1100 designs such as peace signs, flowers, musical notes, sports gear, and letters to spell out words.

Jibbitz started small, with an assembly line in the family's basement and a Website to process orders. Like many new businesses, Jibbitz began with few formal budgets or plans. "We didn't write a business plan" admits Sheri. Rich explains "We recalibrated our business every week depending on what we sold. We were very nimble." Soon, Jibbitz was processing hundreds of orders per day. "It turned from a very simple business to a very complex business," says Rich.

As business grew, master budgets and the budgeting process became more important. Budgets helped formalize business plans and goals, and helped direct employees—a team of staff designers and warehouse personnel in Boulder, and a manufacturing group in Asia. Realizing that a too-rapid sales growth could strain its capacity to meet customer expectations, Jibbitz avoids advertising and has turned down some large retailers' bids to carry its products. An understanding of sales budgets and their link to expense budgets was vital in making these decisions. Likewise, production and manufacturing budgets helped plan for use of materials, labor, and overhead.

Eventually, Rich and Sheri teamed up with Crocs. Now operating as a division within Crocs, budgeting remains important. If Jibbitz meets certain sales and income targets, Rich and Sheri will receive an additional payment from Crocs. Linking their budgeted data to budgeted income statements, and using that information to control costs, is key to that future payment. Still, both Sheri and Rich stress the importance of having fun and a passion for what they do as keys to success. "I'm having a blast," explains Sheri. "I don't want it to stop."

[Sources: *Jibbitz Website,* January 2009; *Crocs Website,* January 2009; *Crocs 2007 10-K report; Rocky Mountain News,* September 2007; *Ladies Who Launch Magazine,* March 2008; *Business 2.0,* November 2006; *Boulder Daily Camera,* August 2006; *Denverpost.com,* October 2006]

Chapter Preview

Management seeks to turn its strategies into action plans. These action plans include financial details that are compiled in a master budget. The budgeting process serves several purposes, including motivating employees and communicating with them. The budget process also helps coordinate a company's activities toward common goals and is useful in evaluating results and management performance. This chapter explains how to prepare a master budget and use it as a formal plan of a company's future activities. The ability to prepare this type of plan is of enormous help in starting and operating a company. Such planning gives managers a glimpse into the future, and it can help translate ideas into actions.

Master Budgets and Performance Planning

Budget Process
- Strategic budgeting
- Benchmarking budgets
- Budgeting and human behavior
- Budgeting as a management tool
- Budgeting communication

Budget Administration
- Budget committee
- Budget reporting
- Budget timing

Master Budget
- Master budget components
- Operating budgets
- Capital expenditures budget
- Financial budgets

Budget Process

Strategic Budgeting

C1 Describe the importance and benefits of budgeting.

Most companies prepare long-term strategic plans spanning 5 to 10 years. They then fine-tune them in preparing medium-term and short-term plans. Strategic plans usually set a company's long-term direction. They provide a road map for the future about potential opportunities such as new products, markets, and investments. The strategic plan can be inexact, given its long-term focus. Medium- and short-term plans are more operational and translate strategic plans into actions. These action plans are fairly concrete and consist of defined objectives and goals.

Short-term financial plans are called *budgets* and typically cover a one-year period. A **budget** is a formal statement of a company's future plans. It is usually expressed in monetary terms because the economic or financial aspects of the business are the primary factors driving management's decisions. All managers should be involved in **budgeting,** the process of planning future business actions and expressing them as formal plans. Managers who plan carefully and formalize plans in a budgeting process increase the likelihood of both personal and company success. (Although most firms prepare annual budgets, it is not unusual for organizations to prepare three-year and five-year budgets that are revised at least annually.)

Companies Performing Annual Budgeting

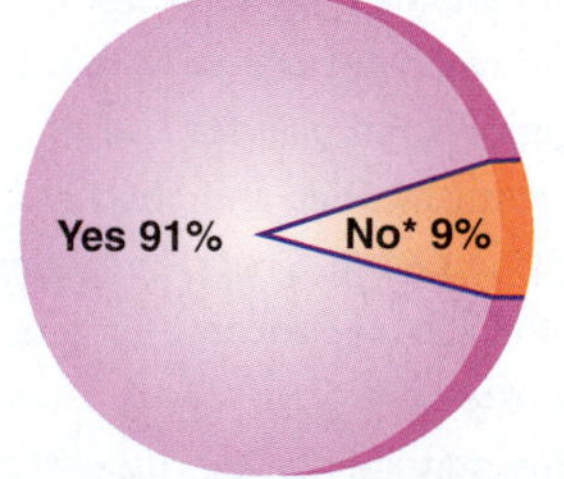

*Most of the 9% have eliminated annual budgeting in favor of rolling or continual budgeting.

The relevant focus of a budgetary analysis is the future. Management must focus on future transactions and events and the opportunities available. A focus on the future is important because the pressures of daily operating problems often divert management's attention and take precedence over planning. A good budgeting system counteracts this tendency by formalizing the planning process and demanding relevant input. Budgeting makes planning an explicit management responsibility.

Benchmarking Budgets

The control function requires management to evaluate (benchmark) business operations against some norm. Evaluation involves comparing actual results against one of two usual alternatives: (1) past performance or (2) expected performance.

An evaluation assists management in identifying problems and taking corrective actions if necessary. Evaluation using expected, or budgeted, performance is potentially superior to using past performance to decide whether actual results trigger a need for corrective actions. This is so because past performance fails to consider several changes that can affect current and future activities. Changes in economic conditions, shifts in competitive advantages within the industry, new product developments, increased or decreased advertising, and other factors reduce the usefulness of comparisons with past results. In hi-tech industries, for instance, increasing competition, technological advances, and other innovations often reduce the usefulness of performance comparisons across years.

Video7.1

Budgeted performance is computed after careful analysis and research that attempts to anticipate and adjust for changes in important company, industry, and economic factors. Therefore, budgets usually provide management an effective control and monitoring system.

Point: Managers can evaluate performance by preparing reports that compare actual results to budgeted plans.

Budgeting and Human Behavior

Budgeting provides standards for evaluating performance and can affect the attitudes of employees evaluated by them. It can be used to create a positive effect on employees' attitudes, but it can also create negative effects if not properly applied. Budgeted levels of performance, for instance, must be realistic to avoid discouraging employees. Personnel who will be evaluated should be consulted and involved in preparing the budget to increase their commitment to meeting it. Performance evaluations must allow the affected employees to explain the reasons for apparent performance deficiencies.

The budgeting process has three important guidelines: (1) Employees affected by a budget should be consulted when it is prepared (*participatory budgeting*), (2) goals reflected in a budget should be attainable, and (3) evaluations should be made carefully with opportunities to explain any failures. Budgeting can be a positive motivating force when these guidelines are followed. Budgeted performance levels can provide goals for employees to attain or even exceed as they carry out their responsibilities. This is especially important in organizations that consider the annual budget a "sacred" document.

Point: The practice of involving employees in the budgeting process is known as *participatory budgeting*.

Decision Insight

Budgets Exposed When companies go public and trade their securities on an organized exchange, management usually develops specific future plans and budgets. For this purpose, companies often develop detailed six- to twelve-month budgets and less-detailed budgets spanning 2 to 5 years.

Budgeting as a Management Tool

An important management objective in large companies is to ensure that activities of all departments contribute to meeting the company's overall goals. This requires coordination. Budgeting provides a way to achieve this coordination.

We describe later in this chapter that a company's budget, or operating plan, is based on its objectives. This operating plan starts with the sales budget, which drives all other budgets including production, materials, labor, and overhead. The budgeting process coordinates the activities of these various departments to meet the company's overall goals.

Budgeting Communication

Managers of small companies can adequately explain business plans directly to employees through conversations and other informal communications. However, conversations can create uncertainty and confusion if not supported by clear documentation of the plans. A written budget is preferred and can inform employees in all types of organizations about management's plans. The budget can also communicate management's specific action plans for the employees in the budget period.

Decision Ethics

Budget Staffer Your company's earnings for the current period will be far below the budgeted amount reported in the press. One of your superiors, who is aware of the upcoming earnings shortfall, has accepted a management position with a competitor. This superior is selling her shares of the company. What are your ethical concerns, if any? [Answer—p. 259]

Budget Administration

Budget Committee

C2 Explain the process of budget administration.

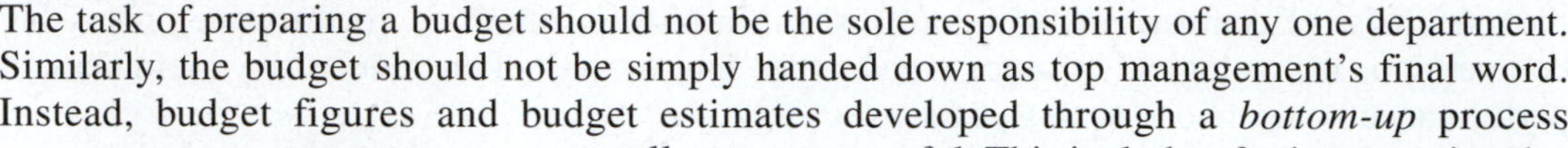

The task of preparing a budget should not be the sole responsibility of any one department. Similarly, the budget should not be simply handed down as top management's final word. Instead, budget figures and budget estimates developed through a *bottom-up* process usually are more useful. This includes, for instance, involving the sales department in preparing sales estimates. Likewise, the production department should have initial responsibility for preparing its own expense budget. Without active employee involvement in preparing budget figures, there is a risk these employees will feel that the numbers fail to reflect their special problems and needs.

Most budgets should be developed by a bottom-up process, but the budgeting system requires central guidance. This guidance is supplied by a budget committee of department heads and other executives responsible for seeing that budgeted amounts are realistic and coordinated. If a department submits initial budget figures not reflecting efficient performance, the budget committee should return them with explanatory comments on how to improve them. Then the originating department must either adjust its proposals or explain why they are acceptable. Communication between the originating department and the budget committee should continue as needed to ensure that both parties accept the budget as reasonable, attainable, and desirable.

Point: In a large company, developing a budget through a bottom-up process can involve hundreds of employees and take several weeks to finalize.

The concept of continuous improvement applies to budgeting as well as production. **BP**, one of the world's largest energy companies, streamlined its monthly budget report from a one-inch-thick stack of monthly control reports to a tidy, two-page flash report on monthly earnings and key production statistics. The key to this efficiency gain was the integration of new budgeting and cost allocation processes with its strategic planning process. BP's controller explained the new role of the finance department with respect to the budgetary control process as follows: "there's less of an attitude that finance's job is to control. People really have come to see that our job is to help attain business objectives."

Budget Reporting

The budget period usually coincides with the accounting period. Most companies prepare at least an annual budget, which reflects the objectives for the next year. To provide specific guidance, the annual budget usually is separated into quarterly or monthly budgets. These short-term budgets allow management to periodically evaluate performance and take needed corrective action.

Managers can compare actual results to budgeted amounts in a report such as that shown in Exhibit 7.1. This report shows actual amounts, budgeted amounts, and their differences. A difference is called a *variance*. Management examines variances to identify areas for improvement and corrective action.

Budget Timing

The time period required for the annual budgeting process can vary considerably. For example, budgeting for 2010 can begin as early as January 2009 or as late as December 2009. Large, complex organizations usually require a longer time to prepare their budgets than do smaller organizations. This is so because considerable effort is required to coordinate the different units (departments) within large organizations.

Companies Using Rolling Budgets

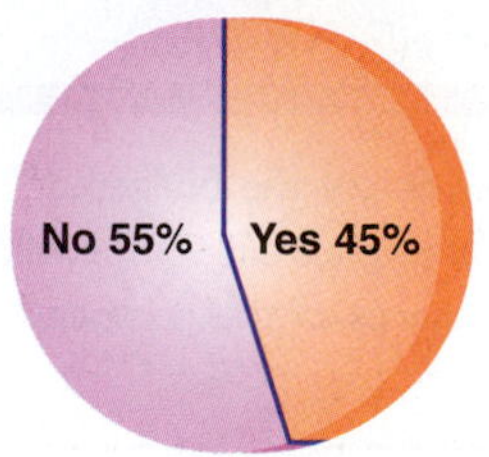

Many companies apply **continuous budgeting** by preparing **rolling budgets.** As each monthly or quarterly budget period goes by, these companies revise their entire set of budgets for the months or quarters remaining and add new monthly or quarterly budgets to replace the ones that have lapsed. At any point in time, monthly or quarterly budgets are available for the next

EXHIBIT 7.1

Comparing Actual Performance with Budgeted Performance

ECCENTRIC MUSIC Income Statement with Variations from Budget For Month Ended April 30, 2009	Actual	Budget	Variance
Net sales	$60,500	$57,150	$+3,350
Cost of goods sold	41,350	39,100	+2,250
Gross profit	19,150	18,050	+1,100
Operating expenses			
Selling expenses			
Sales salaries	6,250	6,000	+250
Advertising	900	800	+100
Store supplies	550	500	+50
Depreciation—Store equipment	1,600	1,600	
Total selling expenses	9,300	8,900	+400
General and administrative expenses			
Office salaries	2,000	2,000	
Office supplies used	165	150	+15
Rent	1,100	1,100	
Insurance	200	200	
Depreciation—Office equipment	100	100	
Total general and administrative expenses	3,565	3,550	+15
Total operating expenses	12,865	12,450	+415
Net income	$ 6,285	$ 5,600	$ +685

Example: Assume that you must explain variances to top management. Which variances in Exhibit 7.1 would you research and why? *Answer:* Sales and cost of goods sold—due to their large variances.

12 months or four quarters. Exhibit 7.2 shows rolling budgets prepared at the end of five consecutive periods. The first set (at top) is prepared in December 2008 and covers the four calendar quarters of 2009. In March 2009, the company prepares another rolling budget for the next four quarters through March 2010. This same process is repeated every three months. As a result, management is continuously planning ahead.

EXHIBIT 7.2

Rolling Budgets

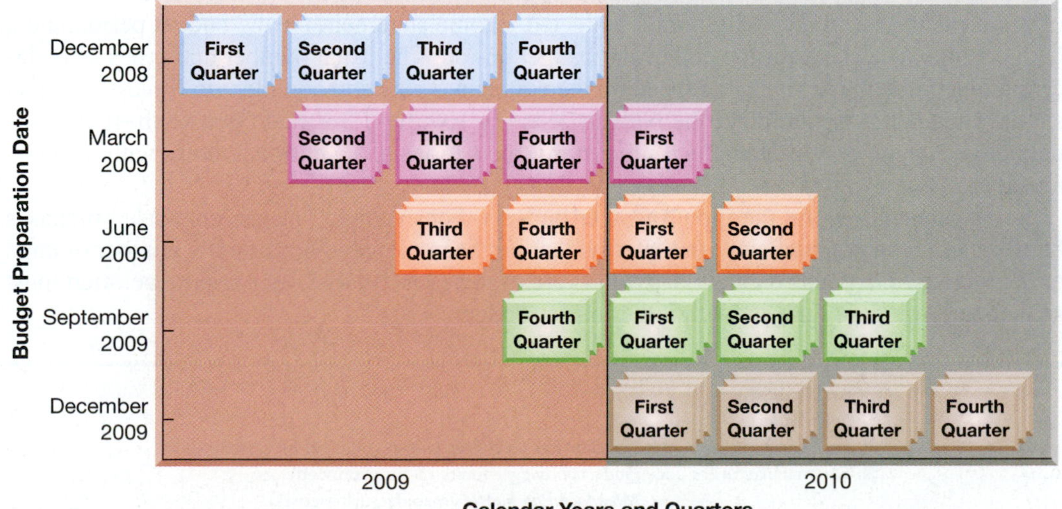

Exhibit 7.2 reflects an annual budget composed of four quarters prepared four times per year using the most recent information available. For example, the budget for the fourth quarter of 2009 is prepared in December 2008 and revised in March, June, and September of 2009. When continuous budgeting is not used, the fourth-quarter budget is nine months old and perhaps out of date when applied.

Decision Insight

Budget Calendar Many companies use long-range operating budgets. For large companies, three groups usually determine or influence the budgets: creditors, directors, and management. All three are interested in the companies' future cash flows and earnings. The annual budget process often begins six months or more before the budget is due to the board of directors. A typical budget calendar, shown here, provides insight into the budget process during a typical calendar year.

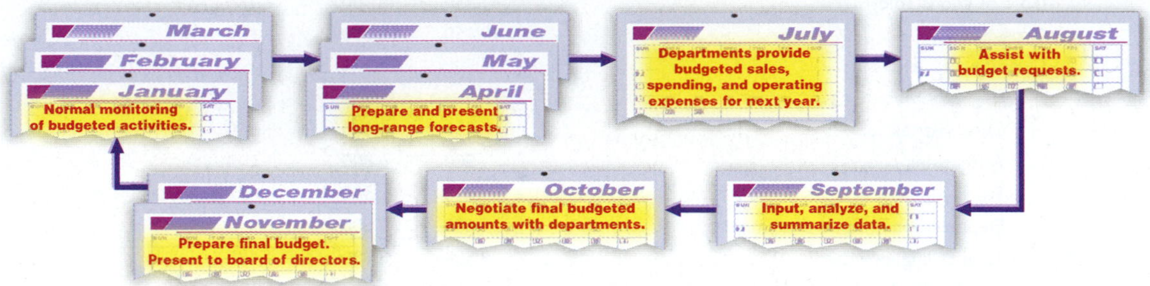

Quick Check

Answers—p. 259

1. What are the major benefits of budgeting?
2. What is the main responsibility of the budget committee?
3. What is the usual time period covered by a budget?
4. What are rolling budgets?

Master Budget

C3 Describe a master budget and the process of preparing it.

A **master budget** is a formal, comprehensive plan for a company's future. It contains several individual budgets that are linked with each other to form a coordinated plan.

Master Budget Components

The master budget typically includes individual budgets for sales, purchases, production, various expenses, capital expenditures, and cash. Managers often express the expected financial results of these planned activities with both a budgeted income statement for the budget period and a budgeted balance sheet for the end of the budget period. The usual number and types of budgets included in a master budget depend on the company's size and complexity. A master budget should include, at a minimum, the budgets listed in Exhibit 7.3. In addition to these individual budgets, managers often include supporting calculations and additional tables with the master budget.

Some budgets require the input of other budgets. For example, the merchandise purchases budget cannot be prepared until the sales budget has been prepared because the number of units to be purchased depends on how many units are expected to be sold. As a result, we often must sequentially prepare budgets within the master budget.

EXHIBIT 7.3

Basic Components of a Master Budget

Operating budgets
- *Sales budget*
- For merchandisers add: *Merchandise purchases budget* (units to be purchased)
- For manufacturers add: *Production budget* (units to be produced)
Manufacturing budget (manufacturing costs)
- *Selling expense budget*
- *General and administrative expense budget*

Capital expenditures budget (expenditures for plant assets)

Financial budgets
- *Cash budget* (cash receipts and disbursements)
- *Budgeted income statement*
- *Budgeted balance sheet*

Decision Insight

Budgeting Targets Budgeting is a crucial part of any acquisition. Analysis begins by projecting annual sales volume and prices. It then estimates cost of sales, expenses, and income for the next several years. Using the present value of this projected income stream, buyers determine an offer price.

Video7.1

A typical sequence for a quarterly budget consists of the five steps in Exhibit 7.4. Any stage in this budgeting process might reveal undesirable outcomes, so changes often must be made to prior budgets by repeating the previous steps. For instance, an early version of the cash budget could show an insufficient amount of cash unless cash outlays are reduced. This could yield a reduction in planned equipment purchases. A preliminary budgeted balance sheet could also reveal too much debt from an ambitious capital expenditures budget. Findings such as these often result in revised plans and budgets.

EXHIBIT 7.4

Master Budget Sequence

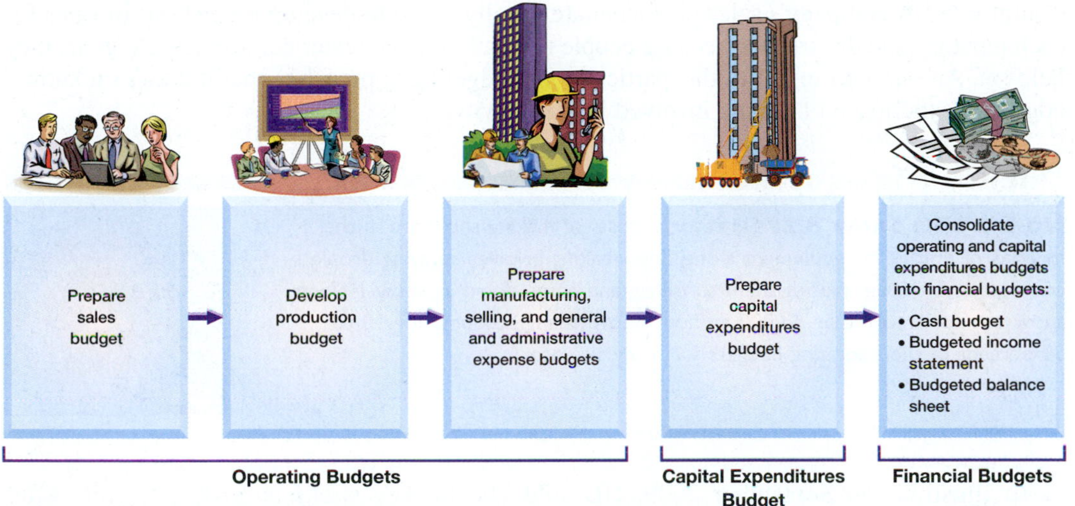

The remainder of this section explains how Hockey Den (HD), a retailer of youth hockey sticks, prepares its master budget. Its master budget includes operating, capital expenditures, and cash budgets for each month in each quarter. It also includes a budgeted income statement for each quarter and a budgeted balance sheet as of the last day of each quarter. We show how HD prepares budgets for October, November, and December 2009. Exhibit 7.5 presents HD's balance sheet at the start of this budgeting period, which we often refer to as we prepare the component budgets.

EXHIBIT 7.5

Balance Sheet Prior to the Budgeting Periods

HOCKEY DEN
Balance Sheet
September 30, 2009

Assets		
Cash		$ 20,000
Accounts receivable		42,000
Inventory (900 units @ $60)		54,000
Equipment*	$200,000	
Less accumulated depreciation	36,000	164,000
Total assets		$280,000
Liabilities and Equity		
Liabilities		
Accounts payable	$ 58,200	
Income taxes payable (due 10/31/2009)	20,000	
Note payable to bank	10,000	$ 88,200
Stockholders' equity		
Common stock	150,000	
Retained earnings	41,800	191,800
Total liabilities and equity		$280,000

* Equipment is depreciated on a straight-line basis over 10 years (salvage value is $20,000).

Operating Budgets

P1 Prepare each component of a master budget and link each to the budgeting process.

This section explains HD's preparation of operating budgets. Its operating budgets consist of the sales budget, merchandise purchases budget, selling expense budget, and general and administrative expense budget. HD does not prepare production and manufacturing budgets because it is a merchandiser. (The preparation of production budgets and manufacturing budgets is described in Appendix 7A.)

Sales Budget The first step in preparing the master budget is planning the **sales budget,** which shows the planned sales units and the expected dollars from these sales. The sales budget is the starting point in the budgeting process because plans for most departments are linked to sales.

The sales budget should emerge from a careful analysis of forecasted economic and market conditions, business capacity, proposed selling expenses (such as advertising), and predictions of unit sales. A company's sales personnel are usually asked to develop predictions of sales for each territory and department because people normally feel a greater commitment to goals they help set. Another advantage to this participatory budgeting approach is that it draws on knowledge and experience of people involved in the activity.

Decision Insight

No Biz Like Snow Biz Ski resorts' costs of making snow are in the millions of dollars for equipment alone. Snowmaking involves spraying droplets of water into the air, causing them to freeze and come down as snow. Making snow can cost more than $2,000 an hour. Snowmaking accounts for 40 to 50 percent of the operating budgets for many ski resorts.

Example: Assume a company's sales force receives a bonus when sales exceed the budgeted amount. How would this arrangement affect the bottom-up process of sales forecasts? *Answer:* Sales reps may understate their budgeted sales.

To illustrate, in September 2009, HD sold 700 hockey sticks at $100 per unit. After considering sales predictions and market conditions, HD prepares its sales budget for the next quarter (three months) plus one extra month (see Exhibit 7.6). The sales budget includes January 2010 because the purchasing department relies on estimated January sales to decide on December 2009 inventory purchases. The sales budget in Exhibit 7.6 includes forecasts of both unit sales and unit prices. Some sales budgets are expressed only in total sales dollars, but most are more detailed. Management finds it useful to know budgeted units and unit prices for many different products, regions, departments, and sales representatives.

EXHIBIT 7.6

Sales Budget for Planned Unit and Dollar Sales

HOCKEY DEN
Monthly Sales Budget
October 2009–January 2010

	Budgeted Unit Sales	Budgeted Unit Price	Budgeted Total Sales
September 2009 (actual)	700	$100	$ 70,000
October 2009	1,000	$100	$100,000
November 2009	800	100	80,000
December 2009	1,400	100	140,000
Totals for the quarter	3,200	100	$320,000
January 2010	900	100	$ 90,000

Decision Maker

Entrepreneur You run a start-up that manufactures designer clothes. Business is seasonal, and fashions and designs quickly change. How do you prepare reliable annual sales budgets? [Answer—p. 259]

Merchandise Purchases Budget Companies use various methods to help managers make inventory purchasing decisions. These methods recognize that the number of units added to inventory depends on budgeted sales volume. Whether a company manufactures or purchases the product it sells, budgeted future sales volume is the primary factor in most inventory management decisions. A company must also consider its inventory system and other factors that we discuss next.

Just-in-time inventory systems. Managers of *just-in-time* (JIT) inventory systems use sales budgets for short periods (often as few as one or two days) to order just enough merchandise or materials to satisfy the immediate sales demand. This keeps the amount of inventory to a minimum (or zero in an ideal situation). A JIT system minimizes the costs of maintaining inventory, but it is practical only if customers are content to order in advance or if managers can accurately determine short-term sales demand. Suppliers also must be able and willing to ship small quantities regularly and promptly.

Point: Accurate estimates of future sales are crucial in a JIT system.

Safety stock inventory systems. Market conditions and manufacturing processes for some products do not allow use of a just-in-time system. Companies in these cases maintain sufficient inventory to reduce the risk and cost of running short. This practice requires enough purchases to satisfy the budgeted sales amounts and to maintain a **safety stock,** a quantity of inventory that provides protection against lost sales caused by unfulfilled demands from customers or delays in shipments from suppliers.

Merchandise purchases budget preparation. A merchandiser usually expresses a **merchandise purchases budget** in both units and dollars. Exhibit 7.7 shows the general layout for this budget in equation form. If this formula is expressed in units and only one product is involved, we can compute the number of dollars of inventory to be purchased for the budget by multiplying the units to be purchased by the cost per unit.

EXHIBIT 7.7

General Formula for a Merchandise Purchases Budget

To illustrate, after assessing the cost of keeping inventory along with the risk and cost of inventory shortages, HD decided that the number of units in its inventory at each month-end should equal 90% of next month's predicted sales. For example, inventory at the end of October should equal 90% of budgeted November sales, and the November ending inventory should equal 90% of budgeted December sales, and so on. Also, HD's suppliers expect the September 2009 per unit cost of $60 to remain unchanged through January 2010. This information along with knowledge of 900 units in inventory at September 30 (see Exhibit 7.5) allows the company to prepare the merchandise purchases budget shown in Exhibit 7.8.

Example: Assume Hockey Den adopts a JIT system in purchasing merchandise. How will its sales budget differ from its merchandise purchases budget? *Answer:* The two budgets will be similar because future inventory should be near zero.

EXHIBIT 7.8

Merchandise Purchases Budget

HOCKEY DEN
Merchandise Purchases Budget
October 2009–December 2009

	October	November	December
Next month's budgeted sales (units)	800	1,400	900
Ratio of inventory to future sales	× 90%	× 90%	× 90%
Budgeted ending inventory (units)	720	1,260	810
Add budgeted sales (units)	1,000	800	1,400
Required units of available merchandise	1,720	2,060	2,210
Deduct beginning inventory (units)	900	720	1,260
Units to be purchased	820	1,340	950
Budgeted cost per unit	$ 60	$ 60	$ 60
Budgeted cost of merchandise purchases	$49,200	$80,400	$57,000

Example: If ending inventory in Exhibit 7.8 is required to equal 80% of next month's predicted sales, how many units must be purchased each month? *Answer:* Budgeted ending inventory: Oct. = 640 units; Nov. = 1,120 units; Dec. = 720 units. Required purchases: Oct. = 740 units; Nov. = 1,280 units; Dec. = 1,000 units.

The first three lines of HD's merchandise purchases budget determine the required ending inventories (in units). Budgeted unit sales are then added to the desired ending inventory to give the required units of available merchandise. We then subtract beginning inventory to determine the budgeted number of units to be purchased. The last line is the budgeted cost of the purchases, computed by multiplying the number of units to be purchased by the predicted cost per unit.

We already indicated that some budgeting systems describe only the total dollars of budgeted sales. Likewise, a system can express a merchandise purchases budget only in terms of the total cost of merchandise to be purchased, omitting the number of units to be purchased. This method assumes a constant relation between sales and cost of goods sold. HD, for instance, might assume the expected cost of goods sold to be 60% of sales, computed from the budgeted unit cost of $60 and the budgeted sales price of $100. However, it still must consider the effects of changes in beginning and ending inventories in determining the amounts to be purchased.

Selling Expense Budget The **selling expense budget** is a plan listing the types and amounts of selling expenses expected during the budget period. Its initial responsibility usually rests with the vice president of marketing or an equivalent sales manager. The selling expense budget is normally created to provide sufficient selling expenses to meet sales goals reflected in the sales budget. Predicted selling expenses are based on both the sales budget and the experience of previous periods. After some or all of the master budget is prepared, management might decide that projected sales volume is inadequate. If so, subsequent adjustments in the sales budget can require corresponding adjustments in the selling expense budget.

Example: If sales commissions in Exhibit 7.9 are increased, which budgets are affected? *Answer:* Selling expenses budget, cash budget, and budgeted income statement.

To illustrate, HD's selling expense budget is in Exhibit 7.9. The firm's selling expenses consist of commissions paid to sales personnel and a $2,000 monthly salary paid to the sales manager. Sales commissions equal 10% of total sales and are paid in the month sales occur. Sales commissions are variable with respect to sales volume, but the sales manager's salary is fixed. No advertising expenses are budgeted for this particular quarter.

EXHIBIT 7.9

Selling Expense Budget

HOCKEY DEN
Selling Expense Budget
October 2009–December 2009

	October	November	December	Totals
Budgeted sales	$100,000	$80,000	$140,000	$320,000
Sales commission percent	× 10%	× 10%	× 10%	× 10%
Sales commissions	10,000	8,000	14,000	32,000
Salary for sales manager	2,000	2,000	2,000	6,000
Total selling expenses	$ 12,000	$10,000	$ 16,000	$ 38,000

General and Administrative Expense Budget The **general and administrative expense budget** plans the predicted operating expenses not included in the selling expenses budget. General and administrative expenses can be either variable or fixed with respect to sales volume. The office manager responsible for general administration often is responsible for preparing the initial general and administrative expense budget.

Interest expense and income tax expense are often classified as general and administrative expenses in published income statements, but normally cannot be planned at this stage of the budgeting process. The prediction of interest expense follows the preparation of the cash budget and the decisions regarding debt. The predicted income tax expense depends on the budgeted amount of pretax income. Both interest and income taxes are usually beyond the control of the office manager. As a result, they are not used in comparison to the budget to evaluate that person's performance.

Exhibit 7.10 shows HD's general and administrative expense budget. It includes salaries of $54,000 per year, or $4,500 per month (paid each month when they are earned). Using information in Exhibit 7.5, the depreciation on equipment is computed as $18,000 per year [($200,000 − $20,000)/10 years], or $1,500 per month ($18,000/12 months).

EXHIBIT 7.10

General and Administrative Expense Budget

HOCKEY DEN General and Administrative Expense Budget October 2009–December 2009	October	November	December	Totals
Administrative salaries	$4,500	$4,500	$4,500	$13,500
Depreciation of equipment	1,500	1,500	1,500	4,500
Total general and administrative expenses	$6,000	$6,000	$6,000	$18,000

Example: In Exhibit 7.10, how would a rental agreement of $5,000 per month plus 1% of sales affect the general and administrative expense budget? (Budgeted sales are in Exhibit 7.6.)
Answer: Rent expense: Oct. = $6,000; Nov. = $5,800; Dec. = $6,400; Total = $18,200; *Revised total general and administrative expenses:* Oct. = $12,000; Nov. = $11,800; Dec. = $12,400; Total = $36,200.

Quick Check

Answers—p. 259

5. What is a master budget?
6. A master budget (*a*) always includes a manufacturing budget specifying the units to be produced; (*b*) is prepared with a process starting with the operating budgets and continues with the capital expenditures budget and then financial budgets; or (*c*) is prepared with a process ending with the sales budget.
7. What are the three primary categories of budgets in the master budget?
8. In preparing monthly budgets for the third quarter, a company budgeted sales of 120 units for July and 140 units for August. Management wants each month's ending inventory to be 60% of next month's sales. The June 30 inventory consists of 50 units. How many units of product for July acquisition should the merchandise purchases budget specify for the third quarter? (*a*) 84, (*b*) 120, (*c*) 154, or (*d*) 204.
9. How do the operating budgets for merchandisers and manufacturers differ?
10. How does a just-in-time inventory system differ from a safety stock system?

Capital Expenditures Budget

The **capital expenditures budget** lists dollar amounts to be both received from plant asset disposals and spent to purchase additional plant assets to carry out the budgeted business activities. It is usually prepared after the operating budgets. Since a company's plant assets determine its productive capacity, this budget is usually affected by long-range plans for the business. Yet the process of preparing a sales or purchases budget can reveal that the company requires more (or less) capacity, which implies more (or less) plant assets.

Capital budgeting is the process of evaluating and planning for capital (plant asset) expenditures. This is an important management task because these expenditures often involve long-run commitments of large amounts, affect predicted cash flows, and impact future debt and equity financing. This means that the capital expenditures budget is often linked with management's evaluation of the company's ability to take on more debt. We describe capital budgeting in Chapter 11.

Hockey Den does not anticipate disposal of any plant assets through December 2009, but it does plan to acquire additional equipment for $25,000 cash near the end of December 2009. This is the only budgeted capital expenditure from October 2009 through January 2010. Thus, no separate budget is shown. The cash budget in Exhibit 7.11 reflects this $25,000 planned expenditure.

Financial Budgets

After preparing its operating and capital expenditures budgets, a company uses information from these budgets to prepare at least three financial budgets: the cash budget, budgeted income statement, and budgeted balance sheet.

EXHIBIT 7.11
Cash Budget

HOCKEY DEN Cash Budget October 2009–December 2009	October	November	December
Beginning cash balance	$ 20,000	$ 20,000	$ 22,272
Cash receipts from customers (Exhibit 7.12)	82,000	92,000	104,000
Total cash available	102,000	112,000	126,272
Cash disbursements			
Payments for merchandise (Exhibit 7.13)	58,200	49,200	80,400
Sales commissions (Exhibit 7.9)	10,000	8,000	14,000
Salaries			
Sales (Exhibit 7.9)	2,000	2,000	2,000
Administrative (Exhibit 7.10)	4,500	4,500	4,500
Income taxes payable (Exhibit 7.5)	20,000		
Dividends ($150,000 × 2%)		3,000	
Interest on bank loan			
October ($10,000 × 1%)	100		
November ($22,800 × 1%)		228	
Purchase of equipment			25,000
Total cash disbursements	94,800	66,928	125,900
Preliminary cash balance	$ 7,200	$ 45,072	$ 372
Additional loan from bank	12,800		19,628
Repayment of loan to bank		22,800	
Ending cash balance	$ 20,000	$ 22,272	$ 20,000
Loan balance, end of month	$ 22,800	$ 0	$ 19,628

Example: If the minimum ending cash balance in Exhibit 7.11 is changed to $25,000 for each month, what is the projected loan balance at Dec. 31, 2009?
Answer:

Loan balance, Oct. 31	$27,800
November interest	278
November payment	25,022
Loan balance, Nov. 30	2,778
December interest	28
Additional loan in Dec.	21,928
Loan balance, Dec. 31	$24,706

P2 Link both operating and capital expenditures budgets to budgeted financial statements.

Cash Budget After developing budgets for sales, merchandise purchases, expenses, and capital expenditures, the next step is to prepare the **cash budget,** which shows expected cash inflows and outflows during the budget period. It is especially important to maintain a cash balance necessary to meet ongoing obligations. By preparing a cash budget, management can prearrange loans to cover anticipated cash shortages before they are needed. A cash budget also helps management avoid a cash balance that is too large. Too much cash is undesirable because it earns a relatively low (if any) return.

When preparing a cash budget, we add expected cash receipts to the beginning cash balance and deduct expected cash disbursements. If the expected ending cash balance is inadequate, additional cash requirements appear in the budget as planned increases from short-term loans. If the expected ending cash balance exceeds the desired balance, the excess is used to repay loans or to acquire short-term investments. Information for preparing the cash budget is mainly taken from the operating and capital expenditures budgets.

To illustrate, Exhibit 7.11 presents HD's cash budget. The beginning cash balance for October is taken from the September 30, 2009, balance sheet in Exhibit 7.5. The remainder of this section describes the computations in the cash budget.

We begin with reference to HD's budgeted sales (Exhibit 7.6). Analysis of past sales indicates that 40% of the firm's sales are for cash. The remaining 60% are credit sales; these customers are expected to pay in full in the month following the sales. We now can compute the budgeted cash receipts from customers as shown in Exhibit 7.12. October's budgeted cash receipts consist of $40,000 from expected cash sales ($100,000 × 40%) plus the anticipated collection of $42,000 of accounts receivable from the end of September. Each month's cash receipts from customers are transferred to the second line of Exhibit 7.11.

Next, we see that HD's merchandise purchases are entirely on account. It makes full payment during the month following its purchases. Therefore, cash disbursements for

	September	October	November	December
Sales	$70,000	$100,000	$80,000	$140,000
Less ending accounts receivable (60%)	42,000	60,000	48,000	84,000
Cash receipts from				
Cash sales (40% of sales)		40,000	32,000	56,000
Collections of prior month's receivables		42,000	60,000	48,000
Total cash receipts		$ 82,000	$92,000	$104,000

EXHIBIT 7.12

Computing Budgeted Cash Receipts

purchases can be computed from the September 30, 2009, balance sheet (Exhibit 7.5) and the merchandise purchases budget (Exhibit 7.8). This computation is shown in Exhibit 7.13.

October payments (September 30 balance)	$58,200
November payments (October purchases)	49,200
December payments (November purchases)	80,400

EXHIBIT 7.13

Computing Cash Disbursements for Purchases

The monthly budgeted cash disbursements for sales commissions and salaries are taken from the selling expense budget (Exhibit 7.9) and the general and administrative expense budget (Exhibit 7.10). The cash budget is unaffected by depreciation as reported in the general and administrative expenses budget.

Income taxes are due and payable in October as shown in the September 30, 2009, balance sheet (Exhibit 7.5). The cash budget in Exhibit 7.11 shows this $20,000 expected payment in October. Predicted income tax expense for the quarter ending December 31 is 40% of net income and is due in January 2010. It is therefore not reported in the October–December 2009 cash budget but in the budgeted income statement as income tax expense and on the budgeted balance sheet as income tax liability.

Hockey Den also pays a cash dividend equal to 2% of the par value of common stock in the second month of each quarter. The cash budget in Exhibit 7.11 shows a November payment of $3,000 for this purpose (2% of $150,000; see Exhibit 7.5).

Hockey Den has an agreement with its bank that promises additional loans at each month-end, if necessary, to keep a minimum cash balance of $20,000. If the cash balance exceeds $20,000 at a month-end, HD uses the excess to repay loans. Interest is paid at each month-end at the rate of 1% of the beginning balance of these loans. For October, this payment is 1% of the $10,000 amount reported in the balance sheet of Exhibit 7.5. For November, HD expects to pay interest of $228, computed as 1% of the $22,800 expected loan balance at October 31. No interest is budgeted for December because the company expects to repay the loans in full at the end of November. Exhibit 7.11 shows that the October 31 cash balance declines to $7,200 (before any loan-related activity). This amount is less than the $20,000 minimum. Hockey Den will bring this balance up to the minimum by borrowing $12,800 with a short-term note. At the end of November, the budget shows an expected cash balance of $45,072 before any loan activity. This means that HD expects to repay $22,800 of debt. The equipment purchase budgeted for December reduces the expected cash balance to $372, far below the $20,000 minimum. The company expects to borrow $19,628 in that month to reach the minimum desired ending balance.

Example: Give one reason for maintaining a minimum cash balance when the budget shows extra cash is not needed. *Answer:* For unexpected events.

Decision Insight

Netting Cash The **Hockey Company**—whose brands include CCM, JOFA, and KOHO—reported net cash outflows for investing activities of $32 million. Much of this amount was a prepayment to the **NHL** for a 10-year license agreement.

Budgeted Income Statement One of the final steps in preparing the master budget is to summarize the income effects. The **budgeted income statement** is a managerial accounting report showing predicted amounts of sales and expenses for the budget period. Information needed for preparing a budgeted income statement is primarily taken from already prepared budgets. The volume of information summarized in the budgeted income statement is so large for some companies that they often use spreadsheets to accumulate the budgeted transactions and classify them by their effects on income. We condense HD's budgeted income statement and show it in Exhibit 7.14. All information in this exhibit is taken from earlier budgets. Also, we now can predict the amount of income tax expense for the quarter, computed as 40% of the budgeted pretax income. This amount is included in the cash budget and/or the budgeted balance sheet as necessary.

EXHIBIT 7.14

Budgeted Income Statement

HOCKEY DEN Budgeted Income Statement For Three Months Ended December 31, 2009		
Sales (Exhibit 7.6, 3,200 units @ $100)		$320,000
Cost of goods sold (3,200 units @ $60)		192,000
Gross profit		128,000
Operating expenses		
Sales commissions (Exhibit 7.9)	$32,000	
Sales salaries (Exhibit 7.9)	6,000	
Administrative salaries (Exhibit 7.10)	13,500	
Depreciation on equipment (Exhibit 7.10)	4,500	
Interest expense (Exhibit 7.11)	328	56,328
Income before income taxes		71,672
Income tax expense ($71,672 × 40%)		28,669
Net income		$ 43,003

Point: Lending institutions often require potential borrowers to provide cash budgets, budgeted income statements, and budgeted balance sheets, as well as data on past performance.

Budgeted Balance Sheet The final step in preparing the master budget is summarizing the company's financial position. The **budgeted balance sheet** shows predicted amounts for the company's assets, liabilities, and equity as of the end of the budget period. HD's budgeted balance sheet in Exhibit 7.15 is prepared using information from the other budgets. The sources of amounts are reported in the notes to the budgeted balance sheet.[1]

Decision Insight

Plan Ahead Most companies allocate dollars based on budgets submitted by department managers. These managers verify the numbers and monitor the budget. Managers must remember, however, that a budget is judged by its success in helping achieve the company's mission. One analogy is that a hiker must know the route to properly plan a hike and monitor hiking progress.

[1] An eight-column spreadsheet, or work sheet, can be used to prepare a budgeted balance sheet (and income statement). The first two columns show the ending balance sheet amounts from the period prior to the budget period. The budgeted transactions and adjustments are entered in the third and fourth columns in the same manner as adjustments are entered on an ordinary work sheet. After all budgeted transactions and adjustments have been entered, the amounts in the first two columns are combined with the budget amounts in the third and fourth columns and sorted to the proper Income Statement (fifth and sixth columns) and Balance Sheet columns (seventh and eighth columns). Amounts in these columns are used to prepare the budgeted income statement and balance sheet.

EXHIBIT 7.15

Budgeted Balance Sheet

HOCKEY DEN Budgeted Balance Sheet December 31, 2009		
Assets		
Cash[a]		$ 20,000
Accounts receivable[b]		84,000
Inventory[c]		48,600
Equipment[d]	$225,000	
Less accumulated depreciation[e]	40,500	184,500
Total assets		$337,100
Liabilities and Equity		
Liabilities		
Accounts payable[f]	$ 57,000	
Income taxes payable[g]	28,669	
Bank loan payable[h]	19,628	$105,297
Stockholders' equity		
Common stock[i]	150,000	
Retained earnings[j]	81,803	231,803
Total liabilities and equity		$337,100

[a] Ending balance for December from the cash budget in Exhibit 7.11.
[b] 60% of $140,000 sales budgeted for December from the sales budget in Exhibit 7.6.
[c] 810 units in budgeted December ending inventory at the budgeted cost of $60 per unit (from the purchases budget in Exhibit 7.8).
[d] September 30 balance of $200,000 from the beginning balance sheet in Exhibit 7.5 plus $25,000 cost of new equipment from the cash budget in Exhibit 7.11.
[e] September 30 balance of $36,000 from the beginning balance sheet in Exhibit 7.5 plus $4,500 expense from the general and administrative expense budget in Exhibit 7.10.
[f] Budgeted cost of purchases for December from the purchases budget in Exhibit 7.8.
[g] Income tax expense from the budgeted income statement for the fourth quarter in Exhibit 7.14.
[h] Budgeted December 31 balance from the cash budget in Exhibit 7.11.
[i] Unchanged from the beginning balance sheet in Exhibit 7.5.
[j] September 30 balance of $41,800 from the beginning balance sheet in Exhibit 7.5 plus budgeted net income of $43,003 from the budgeted income statement in Exhibit 7.14 minus budgeted cash dividends of $3,000 from the cash budget in Exhibit 7.11.

Quick Check

Answers—p. 259

11. In preparing a budgeted balance sheet, (*a*) plant assets are determined by analyzing the capital expenditures budget and the balance sheet from the beginning of the budget period, (*b*) liabilities are determined by analyzing the general and administrative expense budget, or (*c*) retained earnings are determined from information contained in the cash budget and the balance sheet from the beginning of the budget period.

12. What sequence is followed in preparing the budgets that constitute the master budget?

Activity-Based Budgeting

Decision Analysis

A1 Analyze expense planning using activity-based budgeting.

Activity-based budgeting (ABB) is a budget system based on expected activities. Knowledge of expected activities and their levels for the budget period enables management to plan for resources required to perform the activities. To illustrate, we consider the budget of a company's accounting department. Traditional budgeting systems list items such as salaries, supplies, equipment, and utilities. Such an itemized budget informs management of the use of the funds budgeted (for example, salaries), but management cannot assess the basis for increases or decreases in budgeted amounts as compared to prior periods. Accordingly, management often makes across-the-board cuts or increases. In contrast, ABB requires management to list activities performed by, say, the accounting department such as auditing, tax reporting, financial reporting, and cost accounting. Exhibit 7.16 contrasts a traditional budget with an activity-based budget for a company's accounting department. An understanding of the resources required to perform the activities, the costs associated with these resources,

EXHIBIT 7.16

Activity-Based Budgeting versus Traditional Budgeting (for an accounting department)

Activity-Based Budget		Traditional Budget	
Auditing	$ 58,000	Salaries	$152,000
Tax reporting	71,000	Supplies	22,000
Financial reporting	63,000	Depreciation	36,000
Cost accounting	32,000	Utilities	14,000
Total	$224,000	Total	$224,000

and the way resource use changes with changes in activity levels allows management to better assess how expenses will change to accommodate changes in activity levels. Moreover, by knowing the relation between activities and costs, management can attempt to reduce costs by eliminating nonvalue-added activities.

Decision Maker

Environmental Manager You hold the new position of environmental control manager for a chemical company. You are asked to develop a budget for your job and identify job responsibilities. How do you proceed? [Answer—p. 259]

Demonstration Problem

Wild Wood Company's management asks you to prepare its master budget using the following information. The budget is to cover the months of April, May, and June of 2009.

WILD WOOD COMPANY
Balance Sheet
March 31, 2009

Assets		Liabilities and Equity	
Cash	$ 50,000	Accounts payable	$156,000
Accounts receivable	175,000	Short-term notes payable	12,000
Inventory	126,000	Total current liabilities	168,000
Total current assets	351,000	Long-term note payable	200,000
Equipment, gross	480,000	Total liabilities	368,000
Accumulated depreciation	(90,000)	Common stock	235,000
Equipment, net	390,000	Retained earnings	138,000
		Total stockholders' equity	373,000
Total assets	$741,000	Total liabilities and equity	$741,000

Additional Information

a. Sales for March total 10,000 units. Each month's sales are expected to exceed the prior month's results by 5%. The product's selling price is $25 per unit.

b. Company policy calls for a given month's ending inventory to equal 80% of the next month's expected unit sales. The March 31 inventory is 8,400 units, which complies with the policy. The purchase price is $15 per unit.

c. Sales representatives' commissions are 12.5% of sales and are paid in the month of the sales. The sales manager's monthly salary will be $3,500 in April and $4,000 per month thereafter.

d. Monthly general and administrative expenses include $8,000 administrative salaries, $5,000 depreciation, and 0.9% monthly interest on the long-term note payable.

e. The company expects 30% of sales to be for cash and the remaining 70% on credit. Receivables are collected in full in the month following the sale (none is collected in the month of the sale).

f. All merchandise purchases are on credit, and no payables arise from any other transactions. One month's purchases are fully paid in the next month.

g. The minimum ending cash balance for all months is $50,000. If necessary, the company borrows enough cash using a short-term note to reach the minimum. Short-term notes require an interest payment of 1% at each month-end (before any repayment). If the ending cash balance exceeds the minimum, the excess will be applied to repaying the short-term notes payable balance.

h. Dividends of $100,000 are to be declared and paid in May.

i. No cash payments for income taxes are to be made during the second calendar quarter. Income taxes will be assessed at 35% in the quarter.

j. Equipment purchases of $55,000 are scheduled for June.

Required

Prepare the following budgets and other financial information as required:

1. Sales budget, including budgeted sales for July.
2. Purchases budget, the budgeted cost of goods sold for each month and quarter, and the cost of the June 30 budgeted inventory.
3. Selling expense budget.
4. General and administrative expense budget.
5. Expected cash receipts from customers and the expected June 30 balance of accounts receivable.
6. Expected cash payments for purchases and the expected June 30 balance of accounts payable.
7. Cash budget.
8. Budgeted income statement.
9. Budgeted statement of retained earnings.
10. Budgeted balance sheet.

Planning the Solution

- The sales budget shows expected sales for each month in the quarter. Start by multiplying March sales by 105% and then do the same for the remaining months. July's sales are needed for the purchases budget. To complete the budget, multiply the expected unit sales by the selling price of $25 per unit.
- Use these results and the 80% inventory policy to budget the size of ending inventory for April, May, and June. Add the budgeted sales to these numbers and subtract the actual or expected beginning inventory for each month. The result is the number of units to be purchased each month. Multiply these numbers by the per unit cost of $15. Find the budgeted cost of goods sold by multiplying the unit sales in each month by the $15 cost per unit. Compute the cost of the June 30 ending inventory by multiplying the expected units available at that date by the $15 cost per unit.
- The selling expense budget has only two items. Find the amount of the sales representatives' commissions by multiplying the expected dollar sales in each month by the 12.5% commission rate. Then include the sales manager's salary of $3,500 in April and $4,000 in May and June.
- The general and administrative expense budget should show three items. Administrative salaries are fixed at $8,000 per month, and depreciation is $5,000 per month. Budget the monthly interest expense on the long-term note by multiplying its $200,000 balance by the 0.9% monthly interest rate.
- Determine the amounts of cash sales in each month by multiplying the budgeted sales by 30%. Add to this amount the credit sales of the prior month (computed as 70% of prior month's sales). April's cash receipts from collecting receivables equals the March 31 balance of $175,000. The expected June 30 accounts receivable balance equals 70% of June's total budgeted sales.
- Determine expected cash payments on accounts payable for each month by making them equal to the merchandise purchases in the prior month. The payments for April equal the March 31 balance of accounts payable shown on the beginning balance sheet. The June 30 balance of accounts payable equals merchandise purchases for June.
- Prepare the cash budget by combining the given information and the amounts of cash receipts and cash payments on account that you computed. Complete the cash budget for each month by either borrowing enough to raise the preliminary balance to the minimum or paying off short-term debt as much as the balance allows without falling below the minimum. Show the ending balance of the short-term note in the budget.
- Prepare the budgeted income statement by combining the budgeted items for all three months. Determine the income before income taxes and multiply it by the 35% rate to find the quarter's income tax expense.
- The budgeted statement of retained earnings should show the March 31 balance plus the quarter's net income minus the quarter's dividends.

- The budgeted balance sheet includes updated balances for all items that appear in the beginning balance sheet and an additional liability for unpaid income taxes. Amounts for all asset, liability, and equity accounts can be found either in the budgets, other calculations, or by adding amounts found there to the beginning balances.

Solution to Demonstration Problem

1. Sales budget

	April	May	June	July
Prior period's unit sales	10,000	10,500	11,025	11,576
Plus 5% growth	500	525	551	579
Projected unit sales	10,500	11,025	11,576	12,155

	April	May	June	Quarter
Projected unit sales	10,500	11,025	11,576	
Selling price per unit	× $25	× $25	× $25	
Projected sales	$262,500	$275,625	$289,400	$827,525

2. Purchases budget

	April	May	June	Quarter
Next period's unit sales (part 1)	11,025	11,576	12,155	
Ending inventory percent	× 80%	× 80%	× 80%	
Desired ending inventory	8,820	9,261	9,724	
Current period's unit sales (part 1)	10,500	11,025	11,576	
Units to be available	19,320	20,286	21,300	
Less beginning inventory	8,400	8,820	9,261	
Units to be purchased	10,920	11,466	12,039	
Budgeted cost per unit	× $15	× $15	× $15	
Projected purchases	$163,800	$171,990	$180,585	$516,375

Budgeted cost of goods sold

	April	May	June	Quarter
This period's unit sales (part 1)	10,500	11,025	11,576	
Budgeted cost per unit	× $15	× $15	× $15	
Projected cost of goods sold	$157,500	$165,375	$173,640	$496,515

Budgeted inventory for June 30

Units (part 2)	9,724
Cost per unit	× $15
Total	$145,860

3. Selling expense budget

	April	May	June	Quarter
Budgeted sales (part 1)	$262,500	$275,625	$289,400	$827,525
Commission percent	× 12.5%	× 12.5%	× 12.5%	× 12.5%
Sales commissions	32,813	34,453	36,175	103,441
Manager's salary	3,500	4,000	4,000	11,500
Projected selling expenses	$ 36,313	$ 38,453	$ 40,175	$114,941

4. General and administrative expense budget

	April	May	June	Quarter
Administrative salaries	$ 8,000	$ 8,000	$ 8,000	$24,000
Depreciation	5,000	5,000	5,000	15,000
Interest on long-term note payable (0.9% × $200,000)	1,800	1,800	1,800	5,400
Projected expenses	$14,800	$14,800	$14,800	$44,400

5. Expected cash receipts from customers

	April	May	June	Quarter
Budgeted sales (part 1)	$262,500	$275,625	$289,400	
Ending accounts receivable (70%)	$183,750	$192,938	$202,580	
Cash receipts				
Cash sales (30%)	$ 78,750	$ 82,687	$ 86,820	$248,257
Collections of prior period's receivables	175,000	183,750	192,938	551,688
Total cash to be collected	$253,750	$266,437	$279,758	$799,945

6. Expected cash payments to suppliers

	April	May	June	Quarter
Cash payments (equal to prior period's purchases)	$156,000	$163,800	$171,990	$491,790
Expected June 30 balance of accounts payable (June purchases)			$180,585	

7. Cash budget

	April	May	June
Beginning cash balance	$ 50,000	$ 89,517	$ 50,000
Cash receipts (part 5)	253,750	266,437	279,758
Total cash available	303,750	355,954	329,758
Cash payments			
Payments for merchandise (part 6)	156,000	163,800	171,990
Sales commissions (part 3)	32,813	34,453	36,175
Salaries			
Sales (part 3)	3,500	4,000	4,000
Administrative (part 4)	8,000	8,000	8,000
Interest on long-term note (part 4)	1,800	1,800	1,800
Dividends		100,000	
Equipment purchase			55,000
Interest on short-term notes			
April ($12,000 × 1.0%)	120		
June ($6,099 × 1.0%)			61
Total cash payments	202,233	312,053	277,026
Preliminary balance	101,517	43,901	52,732
Additional loan		6,099	
Loan repayment	(12,000)		(2,732)
Ending cash balance	$ 89,517	$ 50,000	$ 50,000
Ending short-term notes	$ 0	$ 6,099	$ 3,367

8.

WILD WOOD COMPANY Budgeted Income Statement For Quarter Ended June 30, 2009		
Sales (part 1)		$ 827,525
Cost of goods sold (part 2)		496,515
Gross profit		331,010
Operating expenses		
Sales commissions (part 3)	$103,441	
Sales salaries (part 3)	11,500	
Administrative salaries (part 4)	24,000	
Depreciation (part 4)	15,000	
Interest on long-term note (part 4)	5,400	
Interest on short-term notes (part 7)	181	
Total operating expenses		159,522
Income before income taxes		171,488
Income taxes (35%)		60,021
Net income		$ 111,467

9.

WILD WOOD COMPANY Budgeted Statement of Retained Earnings For Quarter Ended June 30, 2009	
Beginning retained earnings (given)	$138,000
Net income (part 8)	111,467
	249,467
Less cash dividends (given)	100,000
Ending retained earnings	$149,467

10.

WILD WOOD COMPANY Budgeted Balance Sheet June 30, 2009		
Assets		
Cash (part 7)		$ 50,000
Accounts receivable (part 5)		202,580
Inventory (part 2)		145,860
Total current assets		398,440
Equipment (given plus purchase)	$535,000	
Less accumulated depreciation (given plus expense)	105,000	430,000
Total assets		$828,440
Liabilities and Equity		
Accounts payable (part 6)		$180,585
Short-term notes payable (part 7)		3,367
Income taxes payable (part 8)		60,021
Total current liabilities		243,973
Long-term note payable (given)		200,000
Total liabilities		443,973
Common stock (given)		235,000
Retained earnings (part 9)		149,467
Total stockholders' equity		384,467
Total liabilities and equity		$828,440

APPENDIX

Production and Manufacturing Budgets

7A

Unlike a merchandising company, a manufacturer must prepare a **production budget** instead of a merchandise purchases budget. A production budget, which shows the number of units to be produced each month, is similar to merchandise purchases budgets except that the number of units to be purchased each month (as shown in Exhibit 7.8) is replaced by the number of units to be manufactured each month. A production budget does not show costs; it is *always expressed in units of product*. Exhibit 7A.1 shows the production budget for **Toronto Sticks Company (TSC)**, a manufacturer of hockey sticks. TSC is an exclusive supplier of hockey sticks to Hockey Den, meaning that TSC uses HD's budgeted sales figures (Exhibit 7.6) to determine its production and manufacturing budgets.

P3 Prepare production and manufacturing budgets.

EXHIBIT 7A.1

Production Budget

TSC
Production Budget
October 2009–December 2009

	October	November	December
Next period's budgeted sales (units)	800	1,400	900
Ratio of inventory to future sales	× 90%	× 90%	× 90%
Budgeted ending inventory (units)	720	1,260	810
Add budgeted sales for the period (units)	1,000	800	1,400
Required units of available production	1,720	2,060	2,210
Deduct beginning inventory (units)	(900)	(720)	(1,260)
Units to be produced	820	1,340	950

A **manufacturing budget** shows the budgeted costs for direct materials, direct labor, and overhead. It is based on the budgeted production volume from the production budget. The manufacturing budget for most companies consists of three individual budgets: direct materials budget, direct labor budget, and overhead budget. Exhibits 7A.2–7A.4 show these three manufacturing budgets for TSC. These budgets yield the total expected cost of goods to be manufactured in the budget period.

The *direct materials budget* is driven by the budgeted materials needed to satisfy each month's production requirement. To this we must add the desired ending inventory requirements. The desired ending inventory of direct materials as shown in Exhibit 7A.2 is 50% of next month's budgeted materials requirements of wood. For instance, in October 2009, an ending inventory of 335 units of material is desired (50% of November's 670 units). The desired ending inventory for December 2009 is 225 units,

EXHIBIT 7A.2

Direct Materials Budget

TSC
Direct Materials Budget
October 2009–December 2009

	October	November	December
Budget production (units)	820	1,340	950
Materials requirements per unit	× 0.5	× 0.5	× 0.5
Materials needed for production (units)	410	670	475
Add budgeted ending inventory (units)	335	237.5	225
Total materials requirements (units)	745	907.5	700
Deduct beginning inventory (units)	(205)	(335)	(237.5)
Materials to be purchased (units)	540	572.5	462.5
Material price per unit	$ 20	$ 20	$ 20
Total cost of direct materials purchases	$10,800	$11,450	$9,250

computed from the direct material requirement of 450 units for a production level of 900 units in January 2010. The total materials requirements are computed by adding the desired ending inventory figures to that month's budgeted production material requirements. For October 2009, the total materials requirement is 745 units (335 + 410). From the total materials requirement, we then subtract the units of materials available in beginning inventory. For October 2009, the materials available from September 2009 are computed as 50% of October's materials requirements to satisfy production, or 205 units (50% of 410). Therefore, direct materials purchases in October 2009 are budgeted at 540 units (745 − 205). See Exhibit 7A.2.

TSC's *direct labor budget* is shown in Exhibit 7A.3. About 15 minutes of labor time is required to produce one unit. Labor is paid at the rate of $12 per hour. Budgeted labor hours are computed by multiplying the budgeted production level for each month by one-quarter (0.25) of an hour. Direct labor cost is then computed by multiplying budgeted labor hours by the labor rate of $12 per hour.

EXHIBIT 7A.3

Direct Labor Budget

TSC
Direct Labor Budget
October 2009–December 2009

	October	November	December
Budgeted production (units)	820	1,340	950
Labor requirements per unit (hours)	× 0.25	× 0.25	× 0.25
Total labor hours needed	205	335	237.5
Labor rate (per hour)	$ 12	$ 12	$ 12
Labor dollars	$2,460	$4,020	$2,850

TSC's *factory overhead budget* is shown in Exhibit 7A.4. The variable portion of overhead is assigned at the rate of $2.50 per unit of production. The fixed portion stays constant at $1,500 per month. The budget in Exhibit 7A.4 is in condensed form; most overhead budgets are more detailed, listing each overhead cost item.

EXHIBIT 7A.4

Factory Overhead Budget

TSC
Factory Overhead Budget
October 2009–December 2009

	October	November	December
Budgeted production (units)	820	1,340	950
Variable factory overhead rate	× $2.50	× $2.50	× $2.50
Budgeted variable overhead	2,050	3,350	2,375
Budgeted fixed overhead	1,500	1,500	1,500
Budgeted total overhead	$3,550	$4,850	$3,875

Summary

C1 Describe the importance and benefits of budgeting. Planning is a management responsibility of critical importance to business success. Budgeting is the process management uses to formalize its plans. Budgeting promotes management analysis and focuses its attention on the future. Budgeting also provides a basis for evaluating performance, serves as a source of motivation, is a means of coordinating activities, and communicates management's plans and instructions to employees.

C2 Explain the process of budget administration. Budgeting is a detailed activity that requires administration. At least three aspects are important: budget committee, budget reporting, and budget timing. A budget committee oversees the budget preparation. The budget period pertains to the time period for which the budget is prepared such as a year or month.

C3 Describe a master budget and the process of preparing it. A master budget is a formal overall plan for a company. It consists of plans for business operations and capital expenditures, plus the financial results of those activities. The budgeting process begins with a sales budget. Based on expected sales volume, companies can budget purchases, selling expenses, and administrative expenses. Next, the capital expenditures budget is prepared, followed by the cash budget and budgeted financial statements. Manufacturers also must budget production quantities, materials purchases, labor costs, and overhead.

A1 Analyze expense planning using activity-based budgeting. Activity-based budgeting requires management to identify activities performed by departments, plan necessary activity levels, identify resources required to perform these activities, and budget the resources.

P1 Prepare each component of a master budget and link each to the budgeting process. The term *master budget* refers to a collection of individual component budgets. Each component budget is designed to guide persons responsible for activities covered by that component. A master budget must reflect the components of a company and their interaction in pursuit of company goals.

P2 Link both operating and capital expenditures budgets to budgeted financial statements. The operating budgets, capital expenditures budget, and cash budget contain much of the information to prepare a budgeted income statement for the budget period and a budgeted balance sheet at the end of the budget period. Budgeted financial statements show the expected financial consequences of the planned activities described in the budgets.

P3 Prepare production and manufacturing budgets. A manufacturer must prepare a *production budget* instead of a purchases budget. A *manufacturing budget* shows the budgeted production costs for direct materials, direct labor, and overhead.

Guidance Answers to **Decision Maker** and **Decision Ethics**

Budget Staffer Your superior's actions appear unethical because she is using private information for personal gain. As a budget staffer, you are low in the company's hierarchical structure and probably unable to confront this superior directly. You should inform an individual with a position of authority within the organization about your concerns.

Entrepreneur You must deal with two issues. First, because fashions and designs frequently change, you cannot heavily rely on previous budgets. As a result, you must carefully analyze the market to understand what designs are in vogue. This will help you plan the product mix and estimate demand. The second issue is the budgeting period. An annual sales budget may be unreliable because tastes can quickly change. Your best bet might be to prepare monthly and quarterly sales budgets that you continuously monitor and revise.

Environmental Manager You are unlikely to have data on this new position to use in preparing your budget. In this situation, you can use activity-based budgeting. This requires developing a list of activities to conduct, the resources required to perform these activities, and the expenses associated with these resources. You should challenge yourself to be absolutely certain that the listed activities are necessary and that the listed resources are required.

Guidance Answers to **Quick Checks**

1. Major benefits include promoting a focus on the future; providing a basis for evaluating performance; providing a source of motivation; coordinating the departments of a business; and communicating plans and instructions.
2. The budget committee's responsibility is to provide guidance to ensure that budget figures are realistic and coordinated.
3. Budget periods usually coincide with accounting periods and therefore cover a month, quarter, or a year. Budgets can also be prepared for longer time periods, such as five years.
4. Rolling budgets are budgets that are periodically revised in the ongoing process of continuous budgeting.
5. A master budget is a comprehensive or overall plan for the company that is generally expressed in monetary terms.
6. *b*
7. The master budget includes operating budgets, the capital expenditures budget, and financial budgets.
8. *c*; Computed as $(60\% \times 140) + 120 - 50 = 154$.
9. Merchandisers prepare merchandise purchases budgets; manufacturers prepare production and manufacturing budgets.
10. A just-in-time system keeps the level of inventory to a minimum and orders merchandise or materials to meet immediate sales demand. A safety stock system maintains an inventory that is large enough to meet sales demands plus an amount to satisfy unexpected sales demands and an amount to cover delayed shipments from suppliers.
11. *a*
12. (a) Operating budgets (such as sales, selling expense, and administrative budgets), (b) capital expenditures budget, (c) financial budgets: cash budget, budgeted income statement, and budgeted balance sheet.

Key Terms

mhhe.com/wildMA2e

Key Terms are available at the book's Website for learning and testing in an online Flashcard Format.

Activity-based budgeting (ABB) (p. 251)
Budget (p. 238)
Budgeted balance sheet (p. 250)
Budgeted income statement (p. 250)
Budgeting (p. 238)
Capital expenditures budget (p. 247)
Cash budget (p. 248)
Continuous budgeting (p. 240)
General and administrative expense budget (p. 246)
Manufacturing budget (p. 257)
Master budget (p. 242)
Merchandise purchases budget (p. 245)
Production budget (p. 257)
Rolling budgets (p. 240)
Safety stock (p. 245)
Sales budget (p. 244)
Selling expense budget (p. 246)

Multiple Choice Quiz

Answers on p. 275 mhhe.com/wildMA2e

Additional Quiz Questions are available at the book's Website.

Quiz7

1. A plan that reports the units or costs of merchandise to be purchased by a merchandising company during the budget period is called a
- **a.** Capital expenditures budget.
- **b.** Cash budget.
- **c.** Merchandise purchases budget.
- **d.** Selling expenses budget.
- **e.** Sales budget.

2. A hardware store has budgeted sales of $36,000 for its power tool department in July. Management wants to have $7,000 in power tool inventory at the end of July. Its beginning inventory of power tools is expected to be $6,000. What is the budgeted dollar amount of merchandise purchases?
- **a.** $36,000
- **b.** $43,000
- **c.** $42,000
- **d.** $35,000
- **e.** $37,000

3. A store has the following budgeted sales for the next five months.

May	$210,000
June	186,000
July	180,000
August	220,000
September	240,000

Cash sales are 25% of total sales and all credit sales are expected to be collected in the month following the sale. The total amount of cash expected to be received from customers in September is
- **a.** $240,000
- **b.** $225,000
- **c.** $ 60,000
- **d.** $165,000
- **e.** $220,000

4. A plan that shows the expected cash inflows and cash outflows during the budget period, including receipts from loans needed to maintain a minimum cash balance and repayments of such loans, is called
- **a.** A rolling budget.
- **b.** An income statement.
- **c.** A balance sheet.
- **d.** A cash budget.
- **e.** An operating budget.

5.[A] The following sales are predicted for a company's next four months.

	September	October	November	December
Unit sales . .	480	560	600	480

Each month's ending inventory of finished goods should be 30% of the next month's sales. At September 1, the finished goods inventory is 140 units. The budgeted production of units for October is
- **a.** 572 units.
- **b.** 560 units.
- **c.** 548 units.
- **d.** 600 units.
- **e.** 180 units.

Superscript letter [A] denotes assignments based on Appendix 7A.

Discussion Questions

1. Identify at least three roles that budgeting plays in helping managers control and monitor a business.

2. What two common benchmarks can be used to evaluate actual performance? Which of the two is generally more useful?

3. What is the benefit of continuous budgeting?

4. Identify three usual time horizons for short-term planning and budgets.

5. Why should each department participate in preparing its own budget?

6. How does budgeting help management coordinate and plan business activities?

7. Why is the sales budget so important to the budgeting process?

8. What is a selling expense budget? What is a capital expenditures budget?

9. Budgeting promotes good decision making by requiring managers to conduct ______ and by focusing their attention on the ______.

10. What is a cash budget? Why must operating budgets and the capital expenditures budget be prepared before the cash budget?

11.[A] What is the difference between a production budget and a manufacturing budget?

12. Would a manager of a **Best Buy** retail store participate more in budgeting than a manager at the corporate offices? Explain.

BEST BUY

13. Does the manager of a local **Circuit City** retail store participate in long-term budgeting? Explain.

14. Assume that **Apple**'s iMac division is charged with preparing a master budget. Identify the participants—for example, the sales manager for the sales budget—and describe the information each person provides in preparing the master budget.

Denotes Discussion Questions that involve decision making.

connect Most materials in this section are available in McGraw-Hill's Connect

QUICK STUDY

QS 7-1
Components of a master budget C3

Which one of the following sets of items are all necessary components of the master budget?

1. Prior sales reports, capital expenditures budget, and financial budgets.
2. Sales budget, operating budgets, and historical financial budgets.
3. Operating budgets, financial budgets, and capital expenditures budget.
4. Operating budgets, historical income statement, and budgeted balance sheet.

QS 7-2
Budget motivation C1

The motivation of employees is one goal of budgeting. Identify three guidelines that organizations should follow if budgeting is to serve effectively as a source of motivation for employees.

QS 7-3
Purchases budget P1

Brill Company's July sales budget calls for sales of $800,000. The store expects to begin July with $30,000 of inventory and to end the month with $35,000 of inventory. Gross margin is typically 40% of sales. Determine the budgeted cost of merchandise purchases for July.

QS 7-4
Budgeting process C2 

Good management includes good budgeting. (1) Explain why the bottom-up approach to budgeting is considered a more successful management technique than a top-down approach. (2) Provide an example of implementation of the bottom-up approach to budgeting.

QS 7-5
Computing budgeted accounts receivable
P2

RedTop Company anticipates total sales for June and July of $540,000 and $472,000, respectively. Cash sales are normally 30% of total sales. Of the credit sales, 25% are collected in the same month as the sale, 70% are collected during the first month after the sale, and the remaining 5% are collected in the second month. Determine the amount of accounts receivable reported on the company's budgeted balance sheet as of July 31.

QS 7-6
Cash budget
P1 P2

Use the following information to prepare a cash budget for the month ended on March 31 for Grant Company. The budget should show expected cash receipts and cash disbursements for the month of March and the balance expected on March 31.

a. Beginning cash balance on March 1, $75,000.
b. Cash receipts from sales, $315,000.
c. Budgeted cash disbursements for purchases, $204,000.
d. Budgeted cash disbursements for salaries, $90,000.
e. Other budgeted cash expenses, $30,000.
f. Cash repayment of bank loan, $25,000.

QS 7-7
Activity-based budgeting
A1 

Activity-based budgeting is a budget system based on *expected activities.* (1) Describe activity-based budgeting, and explain its preparation of budgets. (2) How does activity-based budgeting differ from traditional budgeting?

QS 7-8[A]
Production budget
P3

Luna Company manufactures watches and has a JIT policy that ending inventory must equal 8% of the next month's sales. It estimates that October's actual ending inventory will consist of 24,000 watches. November and December sales are estimated to be 300,000 and 250,000 watches, respectively. Compute the number of watches to be produced that would appear on the company's production budget for the month of November.

QS 7-9[A]
Factory overhead budget P3

Refer to information from QS 7-8[A]. Luna Company assigns variable overhead at the rate of $1.75 per unit of production. Fixed overhead equals $5,000,000 per month. Prepare a factory overhead budget for November.

QS 7-10
Sales budget P1

Tech-Cam sells miniature digital cameras for $800 each. 450 units were sold in May, and it forecasts 2% growth in unit sales each month. Determine (a) the number of camera sales and (b) the dollar amount of camera sales for the month of June.

QS 7-11
Selling expense budget P1

Refer to information from QS 7-10. Tech-Cam pays a sales manager a monthly salary of $3,000 and a commission of 7.5% of camera sales (in dollars). Prepare a selling expense budget for the month of June.

QS 7-12
Cash budget P1

Refer to information from QS 7-10. Assume 30% of Tech-Cam's sales are for cash. The remaining 70% are credit sales; these customers pay in the month following the sale. Compute the budgeted cash receipts for June.

QS 7-13
Budgeted financial statements P2

Following are selected accounts for a company. For each account, indicate whether it will appear on a budgeted income statement (BIS) or a budgeted balance sheet (BBS). If an item will not appear on either budgeted financial statement, label it NA.

Sales	______
Administrative salaries paid	______
Accumulated depreciation	______
Depreciation expense	______
Interest paid on bank loan	______
Cash dividends paid	______
Bank loan owed	______

Most materials in this section are available in McGraw-Hill's Connect connect

EXERCISES

Exercise 7-1
Preparation of merchandise purchases budgets (for three periods)
C3 P1

Troy Company prepares monthly budgets. The current budget plans for a September ending inventory of 38,000 units. Company policy is to end each month with merchandise inventory equal to a specified percent of budgeted sales for the following month. Budgeted sales and merchandise purchases for the three most recent months follow. (1) Prepare the merchandise purchases budget for the months of July, August, and September. (2) Compute the ratio of ending inventory to the next month's sales for each budget prepared in part 1. (3) How many units are budgeted for sale in October?

	Sales (Units)	Purchases (Units)
July	170,000	200,000
August	320,000	312,000
September	280,000	262,000

Check July budgeted ending inventory, 64,000

Exercise 7-2
Preparation of cash budgets (for three periods)
C3 P2

Franke Co. budgeted the following cash receipts and cash disbursements for the first three months of next year.

	Cash Receipts	Cash Disbursements
January	$525,000	$484,000
February	411,000	350,000
March	456,000	520,000

According to a credit agreement with the company's bank, Franke promises to have a minimum cash balance of $20,000 at each month-end. In return, the bank has agreed that the company can borrow up to $160,000 at an annual interest rate of 12%, paid on the last day of each month. The interest is computed based on the beginning balance of the loan for the month. The company has a cash balance of $20,000 and a loan balance of $40,000 at January 1. Prepare monthly cash budgets for each of the first three months of next year.

Check January ending cash balance, $20,600

Exercise 7-3
Preparation of a cash budget
C3 P2

Use the following information to prepare the July cash budget for Anker Co. It should show expected cash receipts and cash disbursements for the month and the cash balance expected on July 31.

a. Beginning cash balance on July 1: $63,000.

b. Cash receipts from sales: 30% is collected in the month of sale, 50% in the next month, and 20% in the second month after sale (uncollectible accounts are negligible and can be ignored). Sales amounts are: May (actual), $1,700,000; June (actual), $1,200,000; and July (budgeted), $1,400,000.

c. Payments on merchandise purchases: 90% in the month of purchase and 10% in the month following purchase. Purchases amounts are: June (actual), $620,000; and July (budgeted), $790,000.
d. Budgeted cash disbursements for salaries in July: $220,000.
e. Budgeted depreciation expense for July: $11,000.
f. Other cash expenses budgeted for July: $230,000.
g. Accrued income taxes due in July: $50,000.
h. Bank loan interest due in July: $7,000.

Check Ending cash balance, $143,000

Exercise 7-4
Preparing a budgeted income statement and balance sheet
C3 P2

Use the information in Exercise 7-3 and the following additional information to prepare a budgeted income statement for the month of July and a budgeted balance sheet for July 31.

a. Cost of goods sold is 60% of sales.
b. Inventory at the end of June is $80,000 and at the end of July is $30,000.
c. Salaries payable on June 30 are $50,000 and are expected to be $60,000 on July 31.
d. The equipment account balance is $1,600,000 on July 31. On June 30, the accumulated depreciation on equipment is $280,000.
e. The $7,000 cash payment of interest represents the 1% monthly expense on a bank loan of $700,000.
f. Income taxes payable on July 31 are $24,600, and the income tax rate applicable to the company is 30%.
g. The only other balance sheet accounts are: Common Stock, with a balance of $850,000 on June 30; and Retained Earnings, with a balance of $931,000 on June 30.

Check Net income, $57,400; Total assets, $2,702,000

Exercise 7-5
Computing budgeted cash payments for purchases
C3 P2

DeVon Company's cost of goods sold is consistently $30 per unit. The company plans to carry ending merchandise inventory for each month equal to 20% of the next month's budgeted unit sales; August beginning inventory is 2,000 units. All merchandise is purchased on credit, and 40% of the purchases made during a month is paid for in that month. Another 25% is paid for during the first month after purchase, and the remaining 35% is paid for during the second month after purchase. Expected unit sales are: August (actual), 10,000; September (actual), 9,500; October (estimated), 8,750; November (estimated), 8,250. Use this information to determine October's expected cash payments for purchases. (*Hint:* Use the layout of Exhibit 7.8, but revised for the facts given here.)

Check Budgeted purchases: August, $297,000; October, $259,500

Exercise 7-6
Computing budgeted purchases and costs of goods sold
C3 P1 P2

Dollar Value Company purchases all merchandise on credit. It recently budgeted the following month-end accounts payable balances and merchandise inventory balances. Cash payments on accounts payable during each month are expected to be: May, $1,500,000; June, $1,530,000; July, $1,350,000; and August, $1,495,000. Use the available information to compute the budgeted amounts of (1) merchandise purchases for June, July, and August, and (2) cost of goods sold for June, July, and August.

	Accounts Payable	Merchandise Inventory
May 31	$120,000	$250,000
June 30	170,000	200,000
July 31	300,000	250,000
August 31	150,000	350,000

Check June purchases, $1,580,000; June cost of goods sold, $1,630,000

Exercise 7-7
Computing budgeted accounts payable and purchases—sales forecast in dollars
P1 P2

E-Sound, a merchandising company specializing in home computer speakers, budgets its monthly cost of goods sold to equal 50% of sales. Its inventory policy calls for ending inventory in each month to equal 40% of the next month's budgeted cost of goods sold. All purchases are on credit, and 40% of the purchases in a month is paid for in the same month. Another 40% is paid for during the first month after purchase, and the remaining 20% is paid for in the second month after purchase. The following sales budgets are set: July, $200,000; August, $140,000; September, $170,000; October, $125,000; and

November, $115,000. Compute the following: (1) budgeted merchandise purchases for July, August, September, and October; (2) budgeted payments on accounts payable for September and October; and (3) budgeted ending balances of accounts payable for September and October. (*Hint:* For part 1, refer to Exhibits 7.7 and 7.8 for guidance, but note that budgeted sales are in dollars for this assignment.)

Check July purchases, $88,000; Sept. payments on accts. pay., $78,400

Exercise 7-8^A

Preparing production budgets (for two periods) P3

Electro Company manufactures an innovative automobile transmission for electric cars. Management predicts that ending inventory for the first quarter will be 38,500 units. The following unit sales of the transmissions are expected during the rest of the year: second quarter, 221,000 units; third quarter, 497,000 units; and fourth quarter, 243,500 units. Company policy calls for the ending inventory of a quarter to equal 40% of the next quarter's budgeted sales. Prepare a production budget for both the second and third quarters that shows the number of transmissions to manufacture.

Check Second quarter production, 381,300 units

Exercise 7-9^A

Direct materials budget P3

Refer to information from Exercise 7-8^A. Electro Company reports direct materials requirements of 0.60 per unit. It also aims to end each quarter with an ending inventory of direct materials equal to 40% of next quarter's budgeted materials requirements. Direct materials cost $175 per unit. Prepare a direct materials budget for the second quarter.

Exercise 7-10^A

Direct labor budget P3

Refer to information from Exercise 7-8^A. Each transmission requires 2 direct labor hours, at a cost of $18 per hour. Prepare a direct labor budget for the second quarter.

Most materials in this section are available in McGraw-Hill's Connect connect

PROBLEM SET A

Problem 7-1A

Preparation and analysis of merchandise purchases budgets

C3 P1

mhhe.com/wildMA2e

Herron Supply is a merchandiser of three different products. The company's February 28 inventories are footwear, 18,500 units; sports equipment, 80,000 units; and apparel, 50,000 units. Management believes that excessive inventories have accumulated for all three products. As a result, a new policy dictates that ending inventory in any month should equal 29% of the expected unit sales for the following month. Expected sales in units for March, April, May, and June follow.

	Budgeted Sales in Units			
	March	April	May	June
Footwear	15,000	26,500	31,500	35,000
Sports equipment	70,500	89,000	96,000	89,500
Apparel	40,000	38,000	34,000	23,000

Required

1. Prepare a merchandise purchases budget (in units) for each product for each of the months of March, April, and May.

Check (1) March budgeted purchases Footwear, 4,185; Sports equip., 16,310; Apparel, 1,020

Analysis Component

2. The purchases budgets in part 1 should reflect fewer purchases of all three products in March compared to those in April and May. What factor caused fewer purchases to be planned? Suggest business conditions that would cause this factor to both occur and impact the company in this way.

Problem 7-2A

Preparation of cash budgets (for three periods) C3 P2

mhhe.com/wildMA2e

During the last week of August, Muir Company's owner approaches the bank for a $100,000 loan to be made on September 2 and repaid on November 30 with annual interest of 12%, for an interest cost of $3,000. The owner plans to increase the store's inventory by $80,000 during September and needs the loan to pay for inventory acquisitions. The bank's loan officer needs more information about Muir's ability to repay the loan and asks the owner to forecast the store's November 30 cash position. On September 1, Muir is expected to have a $4,000 cash balance, $152,000 of accounts receivable, and $115,000 of accounts payable. Its budgeted sales, merchandise purchases, and various cash disbursements for the next three months follow.

Budgeted Figures*	September	October	November
Sales	$350,000	$400,000	$425,000
Merchandise purchases	275,000	185,000	180,000
Cash disbursements			
Payroll	25,000	30,000	35,000
Rent	12,000	12,000	12,000
Other cash expenses	38,000	29,000	24,500
Repayment of bank loan			100,000
Interest on the bank loan			3,000

* Operations began in August; August sales were $200,000 and purchases were $115,000.

The budgeted September merchandise purchases include the inventory increase. All sales are on account. The company predicts that 24% of credit sales is collected in the month of the sale, 44% in the month following the sale, 21% in the second month, 8% in the third, and the remainder is uncollectible. Applying these percents to the August credit sales, for example, shows that $88,000 of the $200,000 will be collected in September, $42,000 in October, and $16,000 in November. All merchandise is purchased on credit; 85% of the balance is paid in the month following a purchase, and the remaining 15% is paid in the second month. For example, of the $115,000 August purchases, $97,750 will be paid in September and $17,250 in October.

Required

Prepare a cash budget for September, October, and November for Muir Company. Show supporting calculations as needed.

Check Budgeted cash balance: September, $103,250; October, $73,250; November, $67,750

Problem 7-3A

Preparation and analysis of cash budgets with supporting inventory and purchases budgets

C3 P2 

Culver Company sells its product for $165 per unit. Its actual and projected sales follow.

	Units	Dollars
April (actual)	4,000	$ 660,000
May (actual)	2,200	363,000
June (budgeted)	5,000	825,000
July (budgeted)	6,500	1,072,500
August (budgeted)	3,700	610,500

All sales are on credit. Recent experience shows that 28% of credit sales is collected in the month of the sale, 42% in the month after the sale, 25% in the second month after the sale, and 5% proves to be uncollectible. The product's purchase price is $110 per unit. All purchases are payable within 10 days. Thus, 60% of purchases made in a month is paid in that month and the other 40% is paid in the next month. The company has a policy to maintain an ending monthly inventory of 19% of the next month's unit sales plus a safety stock of 135 units. The April 30 and May 31 actual inventory levels are consistent with this policy. Selling and administrative expenses for the year are $1,140,000 and are paid evenly throughout the year in cash. The company's minimum cash balance at month-end is $60,000. This minimum is maintained, if necessary, by borrowing cash from the bank. If the balance exceeds $60,000, the company repays as much of the loan as it can without going below the minimum. This type of loan carries an annual 12% interest rate. On May 31, the loan balance is $39,000, and the company's cash balance is $60,000.

Required

1. Prepare a table that shows the computation of cash collections of its credit sales (accounts receivable) in each of the months of June and July.
2. Prepare a table that shows the computation of budgeted ending inventories (in units) for April, May, June, and July.
3. Prepare the merchandise purchases budget for May, June, and July. Report calculations in units and then show the dollar amount of purchases for each month.

Check (1) Cash collections: June, $548,460; July, $737,550

(3) Budgeted purchases: May, $300,520; June, $581,350

(5) Budgeted ending loan balance: June, $54,948; July, $39,375

4. Prepare a table showing the computation of cash payments on product purchases for June and July.
5. Prepare a cash budget for June and July, including any loan activity and interest expense. Compute the loan balance at the end of each month.

Analysis Component

6. Refer to your answer to part 5. Culver's cash budget indicates the company will need to borrow more than $15,000 in June and will be able to pay most of it back in July. Suggest some reasons that knowing this information in May would be helpful to management.

Problem 7-4A
Preparation and analysis of budgeted income statements
C3 P2 

Poole, a one-product mail-order firm, buys its product for $75 per unit and sells it for $140 per unit. The sales staff receives a 10% commission on the sale of each unit. Its December income statement follows.

POOLE COMPANY Income Statement For Month Ended December 31, 2009	
Sales	$1,400,000
Cost of goods sold	750,000
Gross profit	650,000
Expenses	
Sales commissions (10%)	140,000
Advertising	215,000
Store rent	26,000
Administrative salaries	42,000
Depreciation	52,000
Other expenses	13,000
Total expenses	488,000
Net income	$ 162,000

Management expects December's results to be repeated in January, February, and March of 2010 without any changes in strategy. Management, however, has an alternative plan. It believes that unit sales will increase at a rate of 10% *each* month for the next three months (beginning with January) if the item's selling price is reduced to $125 per unit and advertising expenses are increased by 15% and remain at that level for all three months. The cost of its product will remain at $75 per unit, the sales staff will continue to earn a 10% commission, and the remaining expenses will stay the same.

Required

Check (1) Budgeted net income: January, $32,250; February, $73,500; March, $118,875

1. Prepare budgeted income statements for each of the months of January, February, and March that show the expected results from implementing the proposed changes. Use a three-column format, with one column for each month.

Analysis Component

2. Use the budgeted income statements from part 1 to recommend whether management should implement the proposed changes. Explain.

Problem 7-5A
Preparation of a complete master budget
C2 C3 P1 P2

Near the end of 2009, the management of Nygaard Sports Co., a merchandising company, prepared the following estimated balance sheet for December 31, 2009.

NYGAARD SPORTS COMPANY Estimated Balance Sheet December 31, 2009		
Assets		
Cash		$ 35,000
Accounts receivable		520,000
Inventory		142,500
Total current assets		697,500
Equipment	$540,000	
Less accumulated depreciation	67,500	472,500
Total assets		$1,170,000

[continued on next page]

[continued from previous page]

Liabilities and Equity		
Accounts payable	$345,000	
Bank loan payable	14,000	
Taxes payable (due 3/15/2010)	91,000	
Total liabilities		$ 450,000
Common stock	473,000	
Retained earnings	247,000	
Total stockholders' equity		720,000
Total liabilities and equity		$1,170,000

To prepare a master budget for January, February, and March of 2010, management gathers the following information.

a. Nygaard Sports' single product is purchased for $30 per unit and resold for $53 per unit. The expected inventory level of 4,750 units on December 31, 2009, is more than management's desired level for 2010, which is 20% of the next month's expected sales (in units). Expected sales are: January, 7,500 units; February, 9,250 units; March, 10,750 units; and April, 10,500 units.

b. Cash sales and credit sales represent 20% and 80%, respectively, of total sales. Of the credit sales, 57% is collected in the first month after the month of sale and 43% in the second month after the month of sale. For the December 31, 2009, accounts receivable balance, $130,000 is collected in January and the remaining $390,000 is collected in February.

c. Merchandise purchases are paid for as follows: 20% in the first month after the month of purchase and 80% in the second month after the month of purchase. For the December 31, 2009, accounts payable balance, $70,000 is paid in January and the remaining $275,000 is paid in February.

d. Sales commissions equal to 20% of sales are paid each month. Sales salaries (excluding commissions) are $72,000 per year.

e. General and administrative salaries are $156,000 per year. Maintenance expense equals $2,100 per month and is paid in cash.

f. Equipment reported in the December 31, 2009, balance sheet was purchased in January 2009. It is being depreciated over eight years under the straight-line method with no salvage value. The following amounts for new equipment purchases are planned in the coming quarter: January, $36,000; February, $96,000; and March, $28,800. This equipment will be depreciated under the straight-line method over eight years with no salvage value. A full month's depreciation is taken for the month in which equipment is purchased.

g. The company plans to acquire land at the end of March at a cost of $155,000, which will be paid with cash on the last day of the month.

h. Nygaard Sports has a working arrangement with its bank to obtain additional loans as needed. The interest rate is 12% per year, and interest is paid at each month-end based on the beginning balance. Partial or full payments on these loans can be made on the last day of the month. The company has agreed to maintain a minimum ending cash balance of $25,000 in each month.

i. The income tax rate for the company is 43%. Income taxes on the first quarter's income will not be paid until April 15.

Required

Prepare a master budget for each of the first three months of 2010; include the following component budgets (show supporting calculations as needed, and round amounts to the nearest dollar):

1. Monthly sales budgets (showing both budgeted unit sales and dollar sales).

2. Monthly merchandise purchases budgets.

3. Monthly selling expense budgets.

4. Monthly general and administrative expense budgets.

5. Monthly capital expenditures budgets.

6. Monthly cash budgets.

7. Budgeted income statement for the entire first quarter (not for each month).

8. Budgeted balance sheet as of March 31, 2010.

Check (2) Budgeted purchases: January, $138,000; February, $286,500
(3) Budgeted selling expenses: January, $85,500; February, $104,050
(6) Ending cash bal.: January, $25,000; February, $175,308
(8) Budgeted total assets at March 31, $1,527,448

Problem 7-6A[A]
Preparing production and direct materials budgets
C3 P3

Black Diamond Company produces snow skis. Each ski requires 2 pounds of carbon fiber. The company's management predicts that 4,800 skis and 6,100 pounds of carbon fiber will be in inventory on June 30 of the current year and that 152,000 skis will be sold during the next (third) quarter. Management wants to end the third quarter with 3,700 skis and 4,200 pounds of carbon fiber in inventory. Carbon fiber can be purchased for $15 per pound.

Required

1. Prepare the third-quarter production budget for skis.
2. Prepare the third-quarter direct materials (carbon fiber) budget; include the dollar cost of purchases.

Check (1) Units manuf., 150,900; (2) Cost of carbon fiber purchases, $4,498,500

PROBLEM SET B

Problem 7-1B
Preparation and analysis of merchandise purchases budgets
C3 P1 

Water Sports Corp. is a merchandiser of three different products. The company's March 31 inventories are water skis, 60,000 units; tow ropes, 45,000 units; and life jackets, 75,000 units. Management believes that excessive inventories have accumulated for all three products. As a result, a new policy dictates that ending inventory in any month should equal 10% of the expected unit sales for the following month. Expected sales in units for April, May, June, and July follow.

	Budgeted Sales in Units			
	April	May	June	July
Water skis	105,000	135,000	195,000	150,000
Tow ropes	50,000	45,000	55,000	50,000
Life jackets	80,000	95,000	100,000	60,000

Required

1. Prepare a merchandise purchases budget (in units) for each product for each of the months of April, May, and June.

Check (1) April budgeted purchases: Water skis, 58,500; Tow ropes, 9,500; Life jackets, 14,500

Analysis Component

2. The purchases budgets in part 1 should reflect fewer purchases of all three products in April compared to those in May and June. What factor caused fewer purchases to be planned? Suggest business conditions that would cause this factor to both occur and affect the company as it has.

Problem 7-2B
Preparation of cash budgets (for three periods)
C3 P2

During the last week of March, Harlan Stereo's owner approaches the bank for an $80,000 loan to be made on April 1 and repaid on June 30 with annual interest of 12%, for an interest cost of $2,400. The owner plans to increase the store's inventory by $120,000 in April and needs the loan to pay for inventory acquisitions. The bank's loan officer needs more information about Harlan Stereo's ability to repay the loan and asks the owner to forecast the store's June 30 cash position. On April 1, Harlan Stereo is expected to have a $6,000 cash balance, $270,000 of accounts receivable, and $200,000 of accounts payable. Its budgeted sales, merchandise purchases, and various cash disbursements for the next three months follow.

	Budgeted Figures*	April	May	June
2	Sales	$440,000	$600,000	$760,000
3	Merchandise purchases	420,000	360,000	440,000
4	Cash disbursements			
5	Payroll	32,000	34,000	36,000
6	Rent	12,000	12,000	12,000
7	Other cash expenses	128,000	16,000	14,000
8	Repayment of bank loan			80,000
9	Interest on the bank loan.........			2,400

* Operations began in March; March sales were $360,000 and purchases were $200,000.

The budgeted April merchandise purchases include the inventory increase. All sales are on account. The company predicts that 25% of credit sales is collected in the month of the sale, 45% in the month following the sale, 20% in the second month, 9% in the third, and the remainder is uncollectible. Applying these percents to the March credit sales, for example, shows that $162,000 of the $360,000 will be collected in April, $72,000 in May, and $32,400 in June. All merchandise is purchased on credit; 80% of the balance is paid in the month following a purchase and the remaining 20% is paid in the second month. For example, of the $200,000 March purchases, $160,000 will be paid in April and $40,000 in May.

Required

Prepare a cash budget for April, May, and June for Harlan Stereo. Show supporting calculations as needed.

Check Budgeted cash balance: April, $26,000; May, $8,000; June, $72,000

Problem 7-3B

Preparation and analysis of cash budgets with supporting inventory and purchases budgets

C3 P2

Parador Company sells its product for $22 per unit. Its actual and projected sales follow.

	Units	Dollars
January (actual)	9,000	$198,000
February (actual)	11,250	247,500
March (budgeted)	9,500	209,000
April (budgeted)	9,375	206,250
May (budgeted)	10,500	231,000

All sales are on credit. Recent experience shows that 40% of credit sales is collected in the month of the sale, 35% in the month after the sale, 23% in the second month after the sale, and 2% proves to be uncollectible. The product's purchase price is $12 per unit. All purchases are payable within 21 days. Thus, 30% of purchases made in a month is paid in that month and the other 70% is paid in the next month. The company has a policy to maintain an ending monthly inventory of 20% of the next month's unit sales plus a safety stock of 100 units. The January 31 and February 28 actual inventory levels are consistent with this policy. Selling and administrative expenses for the year are $960,000 and are paid evenly throughout the year in cash. The company's minimum cash balance for month-end is $25,000. This minimum is maintained, if necessary, by borrowing cash from the bank. If the balance exceeds $25,000, the company repays as much of the loan as it can without going below the minimum. This type of loan carries an annual 12% interest rate. At February 28, the loan balance is $20,000, and the company's cash balance is $25,000.

Required

1. Prepare a table that shows the computation of cash collections of its credit sales (accounts receivable) in each of the months of March and April.
2. Prepare a table showing the computations of budgeted ending inventories (units) for January, February, March, and April.
3. Prepare the merchandise purchases budget for February, March, and April. Report calculations in units and then show the dollar amount of purchases for each month.
4. Prepare a table showing the computation of cash payments on product purchases for March and April.
5. Prepare a cash budget for March and April, including any loan activity and interest expense. Compute the loan balance at the end of each month.

Check (1) Cash collections: March, $215,765; April, $212,575

(3) Budgeted purchases: February, $130,800; March, $113,700

(5) Ending cash balance: March, $25,000, April, $33,219

Analysis Component

6. Refer to your answer to part 5. Parador's cash budget indicates whether the company must borrow additional funds at the end of March. Suggest some reasons that knowing the loan needs in advance would be helpful to management.

Problem 7-4B

Preparation and analysis of budgeted income statements

C3 P2

Tech-Media buys its product for $90 and sells it for $200 per unit. The sales staff receives a 12% commission on the sale of each unit. Its June income statement follows.

TECH-MEDIA COMPANY Income Statement For Month Ended June 30, 2009	
Sales	$2,000,000
Cost of goods sold	900,000
Gross profit	1,100,000
Expenses	
Sales commissions (12%)	240,000
Advertising	225,000
Store rent	32,000
Administrative salaries	75,000
Depreciation	80,000
Other expenses	25,000
Total expenses	677,000
Net income	$ 423,000

Management expects June's results to be repeated in July, August, and September without any changes in strategy. Management, however, has another plan. It believes that unit sales will increase at a rate of 10% *each* month for the next three months (beginning with July) if the item's selling price is reduced to $180 per unit and advertising expenses are increased by 20% and remain at that level for all three months. The cost of its product will remain at $90 per unit, the sales staff will continue to earn a 12% commission, and the remaining expenses will stay the same.

Required

Check Budgeted net income: July, $270,400; August, $345,640; September, $428,404

1. Prepare budgeted income statements for each of the months of July, August, and September that show the expected results from implementing the proposed changes. Use a three-column format, with one column for each month.

Analysis Component

2. Use the budgeted income statements from part 1 to recommend whether management should implement the proposed plan. Explain.

Problem 7-5B
Preparation of a complete master budget
C2 C3 P1 P2

Near the end of 2009, the management of Pak Corp., a merchandising company, prepared the following estimated balance sheet for December 31, 2009.

PAK CORPORATION Estimated Balance Sheet December 31, 2009		
Assets		
Cash		$ 36,000
Accounts receivable		470,000
Inventory		300,000
Total current assets		806,000
Equipment	$1,080,000	
Less accumulated depreciation	135,000	945,000
Total assets		$1,751,000
Liabilities and Equity		
Accounts payable	$ 395,000	
Bank loan payable	25,000	
Taxes payable (due 3/15/2010)	20,000	
Total liabilities		$ 440,000
Common stock	550,000	
Retained earnings	761,000	
Total stockholders' equity		1,311,000
Total liabilities and equity		$1,751,000

To prepare a master budget for January, February, and March of 2010, management gathers the following information.

a. Pak Corp.'s single product is purchased for $30 per unit and resold for $45 per unit. The expected inventory level of 10,000 units on December 31, 2009, is more than management's desired level for 2010, which is 25% of the next month's expected sales (in units). Expected sales are: January, 12,000 units; February, 16,000 units; March, 20,000 units; and April, 18,000 units.

b. Cash sales and credit sales represent 25% and 75%, respectively, of total sales. Of the credit sales, 60% is collected in the first month after the month of sale and 40% in the second month after the month of sale. For the $470,000 accounts receivable balance at December 31, 2009, $330,000 is collected in January 2010 and the remaining $140,000 is collected in February 2010.

c. Merchandise purchases are paid for as follows: 20% in the first month after the month of purchase and 80% in the second month after the month of purchase. For the $395,000 accounts payable balance at December 31, 2009, $207,000 is paid in January 2010 and the remaining $188,000 is paid in February 2010.

d. Sales commissions equal to 20% of sales are paid each month. Sales salaries (excluding commissions) are $180,000 per year.

e. General and administrative salaries are $540,000 per year. Maintenance expense equals $6,000 per month and is paid in cash.

f. Equipment reported in the December 31, 2009, balance sheet was purchased in January 2009. It is being depreciated over 8 years under the straight-line method with no salvage value. The following amounts for new equipment purchases are planned in the coming quarter: January, $72,000; February, $96,000; and March, $28,800. This equipment will be depreciated using the straight-line method over 8 years with no salvage value. A full month's depreciation is taken for the month in which equipment is purchased.

g. The company plans to acquire land at the end of March at a cost of $150,000, which will be paid with cash on the last day of the month.

h. Pak Corp. has a working arrangement with its bank to obtain additional loans as needed. The interest rate is 12% per year, and interest is paid at each month-end based on the beginning balance. Partial or full payments on these loans can be made on the last day of the month. Pak has agreed to maintain a minimum ending cash balance of $36,000 in each month.

i. The income tax rate for the company is 30%. Income taxes on the first quarter's income will not be paid until April 15.

Required

Prepare a master budget for each of the first three months of 2010; include the following component budgets (show supporting calculations as needed, and round amounts to the nearest dollar):

1. Monthly sales budgets (showing both budgeted unit sales and dollar sales).

2. Monthly merchandise purchases budgets.

3. Monthly selling expense budgets.

4. Monthly general and administrative expense budgets.

5. Monthly capital expenditures budgets.

6. Monthly cash budgets.

7. Budgeted income statement for the entire first quarter (not for each month).

8. Budgeted balance sheet as of March 31, 2010.

Check (2) Budgeted purchases: January, $180,000; February, $510,000; (3) Budgeted selling expenses: January, $123,000; February, $159,000

(6) Ending cash bal.: January, $36,000; February, $55,617

(8) Budgeted total assets at March 31, $2,355,317

Problem 7-6B^A
Preparing production and direct materials budgets
C3 P3

Thorpe Company produces baseball bats. Each bat requires 3 pounds of aluminum alloy. Management predicts that 4,000 bats and 7,500 pounds of aluminum alloy will be in inventory on March 31 of the current year and that 125,000 bats will be sold during this year's second quarter. Management wants to end the second quarter with 3,000 finished bats and 6,000 pounds of aluminum alloy in inventory. Aluminum alloy can be purchased for $4 per pound.

Required

1. Prepare the second-quarter production budget for bats.

2. Prepare the second-quarter direct materials (aluminum alloy) budget; include the dollar cost of purchases.

Check (1) Units manuf., 124,000; (2) Cost of aluminum purchases, $1,482,000

SERIAL PROBLEM

Success Systems

(This serial problem began in Chapter 1 and continues through most of the book. If previous chapter segments were not completed, the serial problem can begin at this point. It is helpful, but not necessary, to use the Working Papers that accompany the book.)

SP 7 Adriana Lopez expects second quarter 2010 sales of her new line of computer furniture to be the same as the first quarter's sales (reported below) without any changes in strategy. Monthly sales averaged 40 desk units (sales price of $1,250) and 20 chairs (sales price of $500).

SUCCESS SYSTEMS Segment Income Statement* For Quarter Ended March 31, 2010	
Sales†	$180,000
Cost of goods sold‡	115,000
Gross profit	65,000
Expenses	
Sales commissions (10%)	18,000
Advertising expenses	9,000
Other fixed expenses	18,000
Total expenses	45,000
Net income	$ 20,000

* Reflects revenue and expense activity only related to the computer furniture segment.

† Revenue: (120 desks × $1,250) + (60 chairs × $500) = $150,000 + $30,000 = $180,000

‡ Cost of goods sold: (120 desks × $750) + (60 chairs × $250) + $10,000 = $115,000

Lopez believes that sales will increase each month for the next three months (April, 48 desks, 32 chairs; May, 52 desks, 35 chairs; June, 56 desks, 38 chairs) *if* selling prices are reduced to $1,150 for desks and $450 for chairs, and advertising expenses are increased by 10% and remain at that level for all three months. The products' variable cost will remain at $750 for desks and $250 for chairs. The sales staff will continue to earn a 10% commission, the fixed manufacturing costs per month will remain at $10,000 and other fixed expenses will remain at $6,000 per month.

Required

Check (1) Budgeted income (loss): April, $(660); May, $945

1. Prepare budgeted income statements for each of the months of April, May, and June that show the expected results from implementing the proposed changes. Use a three-column format, with one column for each month.
2. Use the budgeted income statements from part 1 to recommend whether Lopez should implement the proposed changes. Explain.

BEYOND THE NUMBERS

REPORTING IN ACTION

P2 C2 C3 

BTN 7-1 Financial statements often serve as a starting point in formulating budgets. You are assigned to review Best Buy's financial statements to determine its cash paid for dividends in the current year and the budgeted cash needed to pay its next year's dividend.

Required

1. Which financial statement(s) reports the amount of (a) cash dividends paid and (b) annual cash dividends declared? Explain where on the statement(s) this information is reported.
2. Indicate the amount of cash dividends (a) paid in the year ended March 3, 2007, and (b) to be paid (budgeted for) next year under the assumption that annual cash dividends equal 20% of the prior year's net income.

Fast Forward

3. Access Best Buy's financial statements for a fiscal year ending after March 3, 2007, from either its Website [BestBuy.com] or the SEC's EDGAR database [www.SEC.gov]. Compare your answer for part 2 with actual cash dividends paid for that fiscal year. Compute the error, if any, in your estimate. Speculate as to why dividends were higher or lower than budgeted.

COMPARATIVE ANALYSIS

P2 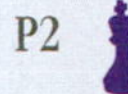

BTN 7-2 One source of cash savings for a company is improved management of inventory. To illustrate, assume that **Best Buy** and **Circuit City** both have $300,000 per month in sales in the Virginia area, and both forecast this level of sales per month for the next 24 months. Also assume that both Best Buy and Circuit City have a 20% contribution margin and equal fixed costs, and that cost of goods sold is the only variable cost. Assume that the main difference between Best Buy and Circuit City is the distribution system. Best Buy uses a just-in-time system and requires ending inventory of only 10% of next month's sales in inventory at each month-end. However, Circuit City is building an improved distribution system and currently requires 40% of next month's sales in inventory at each month-end.

Required

1. Compute the amount by which Circuit City can reduce its inventory level if it can match Best Buy's system of maintaining an inventory equal to 10% of next month's sales. (*Hint:* Focus on the facts given and only on the Virginia area.)

2. Explain how the analysis in part 1 that shows ending inventory levels for both the 40% and 10% required inventory policies can help justify a just-in-time inventory system. You can assume a 15% interest cost for resources that are tied up in ending inventory.

ETHICS CHALLENGE

C1 C2

BTN 7-3 Both the budget process and budgets themselves can impact management actions, both positively and negatively. For instance, a common practice among not-for-profit organizations and government agencies is for management to spend any amounts remaining in a budget at the end of the budget period, a practice often called "use it or lose it." The view is that if a department manager does not spend the budgeted amount, top management will reduce next year's budget by the amount not spent. To avoid losing budget dollars, department managers often spend all budgeted amounts regardless of the value added to products or services. All of us pay for the costs associated with this budget system.

Required

Write a one-half page report to a local not-for-profit organization or government agency offering a solution to the "use it or lose it" budgeting problem.

COMMUNICATING IN PRACTICE

P1

BTN 7-4 The sales budget is usually the first and most crucial of the component budgets in a master budget because all other budgets usually rely on it for planning purposes.

Required

Assume that your company's sales staff provides information on expected sales and selling prices for items making up the sales budget. Prepare a one-page memorandum to your supervisor outlining concerns with the sales staff's input in the sales budget when its compensation is at least partly tied to these budgets. More generally, explain the importance of assessing any potential bias in information provided to the budget process.

TAKING IT TO THE NET

C2 P1 P2

BTN 7-5 Access information on e-budgets through The Manage Mentor:
http://www.themanagementor.com/kuniverse/kmailers_universe/finance_kmailers/cfa/budgeting2.htm
Read the information provided at this website and complete the following requirements.

Required

1. Assume the role of a senior manager in a large, multidivision company. What are the benefits of using e-budgets?
2. As a senior manager, what concerns do you have with the concept and application of e-budgets?

TEAMWORK IN ACTION

A1

BTN 7-6 Your team is to prepare a budget report outlining the costs of attending college (full-time) for the next two semesters (30 hours) or three quarters (45 hours). This budget's focus is solely on attending college; do not include personal items in the team's budget. Your budget must include tuition, books, supplies, club fees, food, housing, and all costs associated with travel to and from college. This budgeting exercise is similar to the initial phase in activity-based budgeting. Include a list of any assumptions you use in completing the budget. Be prepared to present your budget in class.

ENTREPRENEURIAL DECISION

C1

BTN 7-7 Jibbitz produces charms to fit in the holes of Crocs shoes. Assume Jibbitz is considering expanding its product line to include necklaces that hold the charms. They plan on meeting with a financial institution for potential funding and have asked by its loan officers for their business plan.

Required

1. What should Jibbitz's business plan include?
2. How can budgeting help the owners efficiently develop and operate their business?

HITTING THE ROAD

C3 P1

BTN 7-8 To help understand the factors impacting a sales budget, you are to visit three businesses with the same ownership or franchise membership. Record the selling prices of two identical products at each location, such as regular and premium gas sold at Chevron stations. You are likely to find a difference in prices for at least one of the three locations you visit.

Required

1. Identify at least three external factors that must be considered when setting the sales budget. (*Note:* There is a difference between internal and external factors that impact the sales budget.)
2. What factors might explain any differences identified in the prices of the businesses you visited?

GLOBAL DECISION

BTN 7-9 Access DSG's income statement (www.DSGiplc.com) for the year ended April 28, 2007.

Required

1. Is DSG's administrative expense budget likely to be an important budget in its master budgeting process? Explain. (*Hint:* Review its Note 3.)
2. Identify three types of expenses that would be reported as administrative expenses on DSG's income statement.
3. Who likely has the initial responsibility for DSG's administrative expense budget? Explain.

ANSWERS TO MULTIPLE CHOICE QUIZ

1. c
2. e; Budgeted purchases = \$36,000 + \$7,000 − \$6,000 = \$37,000
3. b; Cash collected = 25% of September sales + 75% of August sales = (0.25 × \$240,000) + (0.75 × \$220,000) = \$225,000
4. d
5. a; 560 units + (0.30 × 600 units) − (0.30 × 560 units) = 572 units

A Look Back

Chapter 7 explained the master budget and its component budgets as well as their usefulness for planning and monitoring company activities.

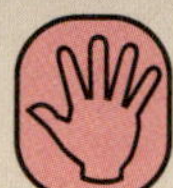

A Look at This Chapter

This chapter describes flexible budgets, variance analysis, and standard costs. It explains how each is used for purposes of better controlling and monitoring business activities.

A Look Ahead

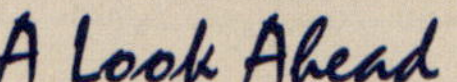

Chapter 9 introduces responsibility accounting and managerial control. It also describes useful measures of departmental performance.

Chapter 8 Flexible Budgets and Standard Costing

Learning Objectives

CAP

Conceptual

C1 Define *standard costs* and explain their computation and uses. *(p. 283)*

C2 Describe variances and what they reveal about performance. *(p. 284)*

C3 Explain how standard cost information is useful for management by exception. *(p. 294)*

Analytical

A1 Compare fixed and flexible budgets. *(p. 280)*

A2 Analyze changes in sales from expected amounts. *(p. 296)*

LP8

Procedural

P1 Prepare a flexible budget and interpret a flexible budget performance report. *(p. 280)*

P2 Compute materials and labor variances. *(p. 286)*

P3 Compute overhead variances. *(p. 290)*

P4 Prepare journal entries for standard costs and account for price and quantity variances. *(p. 294)*

Decision Feature

Good Vibrations

"Look at each part of the process and improve it"
—Chris Martin

NAZARETH, PA—Eric Clapton. Paul McCartney. Johnny Cash. Jimi Hendrix. What do these musical legends have in common? All played guitars manufactured by the **Martin Guitar Company** (**MartinGuitar.com**). Martin manufactures high-quality guitars and recently sold its millionth. This family-owned company, headed by Christian (Chris) F. Martin, has prospered by hurdling challenges facing all manufacturers—materials quality, product design, quality control, manufacturing methods, and new investment.

Chris' entrepreneurial spirit stimulated innovative product design and growth while adhering closely to product quality. Understanding cost analysis and variances, flexible and fixed budgets, and standard costs helps his company control its production process. Martin's "X" bracing system is a key part of the distinctive Martin guitar tone. The company also embraces continuous improvement. Recently it began a lean manufacturing project to improve production efficiency, work flow, and cycle time in one of its plants.

Martin Guitar adheres to tight standards variances. Vince Gentilcore, Martin's director of quality, classifies production problems into three types: materials, process, and employee. Developing managerial accounting systems to evaluate its performance on each of these dimensions is key. "[Defects] in wood affect yield, productivity, and costs of quality," explains Vince. "We have exacting specifications and controls in place to detect problems; we don't allow material to go into a guitar that doesn't satisfy our requirements." As for process, he closely monitors the company's computer-controlled machines to ensure excessive tool wear does not impair product quality. Another key to process control, explains Vince, is "the moisture content of the wood, which we track on a regular basis." Regarding employee costs, Chris Martin explains that "we have work quotas; we know how much labor costs and how long it takes."

Achieving high standards is the goal at Martin Guitar. "We're trying to make the best," proclaims Chris. "We are doing so much more volume today, even with all those competitors. [Our workers] hold the company to an extraordinarily high standard." With standards like these, Chris' company produces a pretty tune.

[Sources: *Martin Guitar Website,* January 2009; *Quality Digest,* November 2007; *Modern Guitars Magazine,* December and March 2005; For a virtual tour of Martin Guitars see MartinGuitar.com/visit/vtour.php]

Chapter Preview

Budgeting helps organize and formalize management's planning activities. This chapter extends the study of budgeting to look more closely at the use of budgets to evaluate performance. Evaluations are important for controlling and monitoring business activities. This chapter also describes and illustrates the use of standard costs and variance analyses. These managerial tools are useful for both evaluating and controlling organizations and for the planning of future activities.

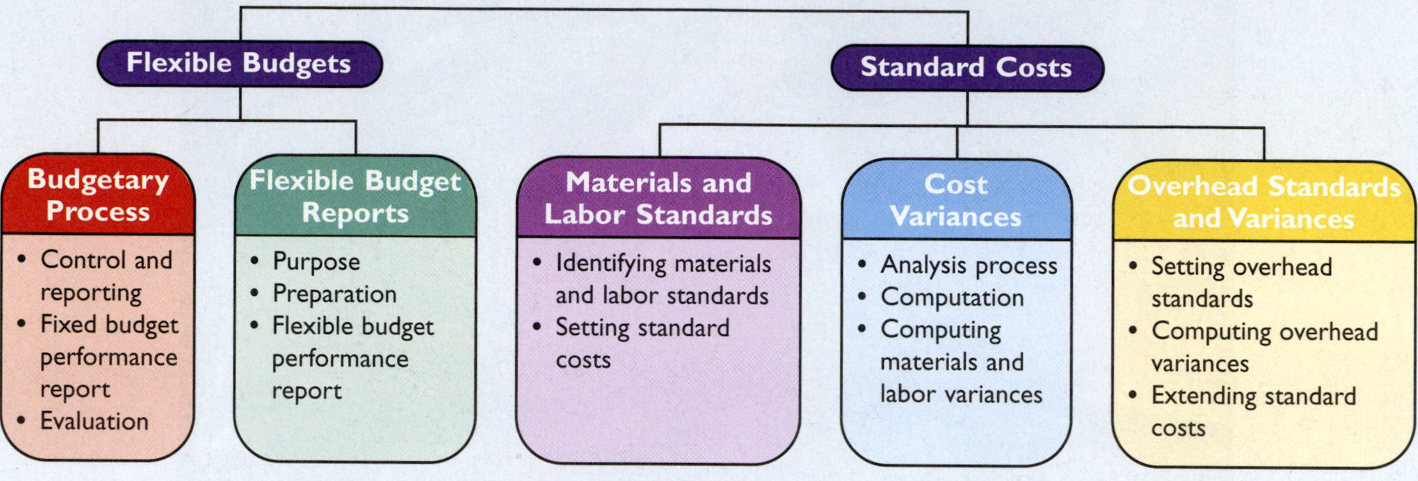

Section 1—Flexible Budgets

This section introduces fixed budgets and fixed budget performance reports. It then introduces flexible budgets and flexible budget performance reports and illustrates their advantages.

Budgetary Process

Video8.2

A master budget reflects management's planned objectives for a future period. The preparation of a master budget is based on a predicted level of activity such as sales volume for the budget period. This section discusses the effects on the usefulness of budget reports when the actual level of activity differs from the predicted level.

Budgetary Control and Reporting

Budgetary control refers to management's use of budgets to monitor and control a company's operations. This includes using budgets to see that planned objectives are met. **Budget reports** contain relevant information that compares actual results to planned activities. This comparison is motivated by a need to both monitor performance and control activities. Budget reports are sometimes viewed as progress reports, or *report cards,* on management's performance in achieving planned objectives. These reports can be prepared at any time and for any period. Three common periods for a budget report are a month, quarter, and year.

Point: Budget reports are often used as a base to determine bonuses of managers.

The budgetary control process involves at least four steps: (1) develop the budget from planned objectives, (2) compare actual results to budgeted amounts and analyze any differences, (3) take corrective and strategic actions, and (4) establish new planned objectives and prepare a new budget. Exhibit 8.1 shows this continual process of budgetary control. Budget

EXHIBIT 8.1

Process of Budgetary Control

reports and related documents are effective tools for managers to obtain the greatest benefits from this budgetary process.

Fixed Budget Performance Report

In a fixed budgetary control system, the master budget is based on a single prediction for sales volume or other activity level. The budgeted amount for each cost essentially assumes that a specific (or *fixed*) amount of sales will occur. A **fixed budget,** also called a *static budget,* is based on a single predicted amount of sales or other measure of activity.

One benefit of a budget is its usefulness in comparing actual results with planned activities. Information useful for analysis is often presented for comparison in a performance report. As shown in Exhibit 8.2, a **fixed budget performance report** for Optel compares actual results for January 2009 with the results expected under its fixed budget that predicted 10,000 (composite) units of sales. Optel manufactures inexpensive eyeglasses, frames, contact lens, and related supplies. For this report, its production volume equals sales volume (its inventory level did not change).

EXHIBIT 8.2
Fixed Budget Performance Report

OPTEL
Fixed Budget Performance Report
For Month Ended January 31, 2009

	Fixed Budget	Actual Results	Variances*
Sales (in units)	10,000	12,000	
Sales (in dollars)	$100,000	$125,000	$25,000 F
Cost of goods sold			
Direct materials	10,000	13,000	3,000 U
Direct labor	15,000	20,000	5,000 U
Overhead			
Factory supplies	2,000	2,100	100 U
Utilities	3,000	4,000	1,000 U
Depreciation—machinery	8,000	8,000	0
Supervisory salaries	11,000	11,000	0
Selling expenses			
Sales commissions	9,000	10,800	1,800 U
Shipping expenses	4,000	4,300	300 U
General and administrative expenses			
Office supplies	5,000	5,200	200 U
Insurance expenses	1,000	1,200	200 U
Depreciation—office equipment	7,000	7,000	0
Administrative salaries	13,000	13,000	0
Total expenses	88,000	99,600	11,600 U
Income from operations	$ 12,000	$ 25,400	$13,400 F

* F = Favorable variance; U = Unfavorable variance.

This type of performance report designates differences between budgeted and actual results as variances. We see the letters *F* and *U* located beside the numbers in the third number column of this report. Their meanings are as follows:

F = **Favorable variance** When compared to budget, the actual cost or revenue contributes to a *higher* income. That is, actual revenue is higher than budgeted revenue, or actual cost is lower than budgeted cost.

U = **Unfavorable variance** When compared to budget, the actual cost or revenue contributes to a *lower* income; actual revenue is lower than budgeted revenue, or actual cost is higher than budgeted cost.

This convention is common in practice and is used throughout this chapter.

Example: How is it that the favorable sales variance in Exhibit 8.2 is linked with so many unfavorable cost and expense variances? *Answer:* Costs have increased with the increase in sales.

Budget Reports for Evaluation

A primary use of budget reports is as a tool for management to monitor and control operations. Evaluation by Optel management is likely to focus on a variety of questions that might include these:

- Why is actual income from operations $13,400 higher than budgeted?
- Are amounts paid for each expense item too high?
- Is manufacturing using too much direct material?
- Is manufacturing using too much direct labor?

The performance report in Exhibit 8.2 provides little help in answering these questions because actual sales volume is 2,000 units higher than budgeted. A manager does not know if this higher level of sales activity is the cause of variations in total dollar sales and expenses or if other factors have influenced these amounts. This inability of fixed budget reports to adjust for changes in activity levels is a major limitation of a fixed budget performance report. That is, it fails to show whether actual costs are out of line due to a change in actual sales volume or some other factor.

Decision Insight

Green Budget Budget reporting and evaluation are used at the **Environmental Protection Agency (EPA)**. It regularly prepares performance plans and budget requests that describe performance goals, measure outcomes, and analyze variances.

Flexible Budget Reports

Purpose of Flexible Budgets

A1 Compare fixed and flexible budgets.

To help address limitations with the fixed budget performance report, particularly from the effects of changes in sales volume, management can use a flexible budget. A **flexible budget,** also called a *variable budget,* is a report based on predicted amounts of revenues and expenses corresponding to the actual level of output. Flexible budgets are useful both before and after the period's activities are complete.

Video8.2

A flexible budget prepared before the period is often based on several levels of activity. Budgets for those different levels can provide a "what-if" look at operations. The different levels often include both a best case and worst case scenario. This allows management to make adjustments to avoid or lessen the effects of the worst case scenario.

A flexible budget prepared after the period helps management evaluate past performance. It is especially useful for such an evaluation because it reflects budgeted revenues and costs based on the actual level of activity. Thus, comparisons of actual results with budgeted performance are more likely to identify the causes of any differences. This can help managers focus attention on real problem areas and implement corrective actions. This is in contrast to a fixed budget, whose primary purpose is to assist managers in planning future activities and whose numbers are based on a single predicted amount of budgeted sales or production.

Preparation of Flexible Budgets

P1 Prepare a flexible budget and interpret a flexible budget performance report.

A flexible budget is designed to reveal the effects of volume of activity on revenues and costs. To prepare a flexible budget, management relies on the distinctions between fixed and variable costs. Recall that the cost per unit of activity remains constant for variable costs so that the total amount of a variable cost changes in direct proportion to a change in activity level. The total amount of fixed cost remains unchanged regardless of changes in the level of activity within a relevant (normal) operating range. (Assume that costs can be reasonably classified as variable or fixed within a relevant range.)

When we create the numbers constituting a flexible budget, we express each variable cost as either a constant amount per unit of sales or as a percent of a sales dollar. In the case of a fixed cost, we express its budgeted amount as the total amount expected to occur at any sales volume within the relevant range.

Exhibit 8.3 shows a set of flexible budgets for Optel in January 2009. Seven of its expenses are classified as variable costs. Its remaining five expenses are fixed costs. These classifications result from management's investigation of each expense. Variable and fixed expense categories are *not* the same for every company, and we must avoid drawing conclusions from specific cases. For example, depending on the nature of a company's operations, office supplies expense can be either fixed or variable with respect to sales.

Point: The usefulness of a flexible budget depends on valid classification of variable and fixed costs. Some costs are mixed and must be analyzed to determine their variable and fixed portions.

EXHIBIT 8.3

Flexible Budgets

OPTEL
Flexible Budgets
For Month Ended January 31, 2009

	Flexible Budget				
	Variable Amount per Unit	Total Fixed Cost	Flexible Budget for Unit Sales of 10,000	Flexible Budget for Unit Sales of 12,000	Flexible Budget for Unit Sales of 14,000
Sales	$10.00		$100,000	$120,000	$140,000
Variable costs					
Direct materials	1.00		10,000	12,000	14,000
Direct labor	1.50		15,000	18,000	21,000
Factory supplies	0.20		2,000	2,400	2,800
Utilities	0.30		3,000	3,600	4,200
Sales commissions	0.90		9,000	10,800	12,600
Shipping expenses	0.40		4,000	4,800	5,600
Office supplies	0.50		5,000	6,000	7,000
Total variable costs	4.80		48,000	57,600	67,200
Contribution margin	$ 5.20		$ 52,000	$ 62,400	$ 72,800
Fixed costs					
Depreciation—machinery		$ 8,000	8,000	8,000	8,000
Supervisory salaries		11,000	11,000	11,000	11,000
Insurance expense		1,000	1,000	1,000	1,000
Depreciation—office equipment		7,000	7,000	7,000	7,000
Administrative salaries		13,000	13,000	13,000	13,000
Total fixed costs		$40,000	40,000	40,000	40,000
Income from operations			$ 12,000	$ 22,400	$ 32,800

The layout for the flexible budgets in Exhibit 8.3 follows a *contribution margin format*—beginning with sales followed by variable costs and then fixed costs. Both the expected individual and total variable costs are reported and then subtracted from sales. The difference between sales and variable costs equals contribution margin. The expected amounts of fixed costs are listed next, followed by the expected income from operations before taxes.

Example: Using Exhibit 8.3, what is the budgeted income from operations for unit sales of (a) 11,000 and (b) 13,000? *Answers:* $17,200 for unit sales of 11,000; $27,600 for unit sales of 13,000.

The first and second number columns of Exhibit 8.3 show the flexible budget amounts for variable costs per unit and each fixed cost for any volume of sales in the relevant range. The third, fourth, and fifth columns show the flexible budget amounts computed for three different sales volumes. For instance, the third column's flexible budget is based on 10,000 units. These numbers are the same as those in the fixed budget of Exhibit 8.2 because the expected volumes are the same for these two budgets.

Recall that Optel's actual sales volume for January is 12,000 units. This sales volume is 2,000 units more than the 10,000 units originally predicted in the master budget. When differences between actual and predicted volume arise, the usefulness of a flexible budget is apparent. For instance, compare the flexible budget for 10,000 units in the third column (which is the same as the fixed budget in Exhibit 8.2) with the flexible budget for 12,000 units in the

Point: Flexible budgeting allows a budget to be prepared at the *actual* output level. Performance reports are then prepared comparing the flexible budget to actual revenues and costs.

Point: A flexible budget yields an "apples to apples" comparison because budgeted activity levels are the same as the actual.

fourth column. The higher levels for both sales and variable costs reflect nothing more than the increase in sales activity. Any budget analysis comparing actual with planned results that ignores this information is less useful to management.

To illustrate, when we evaluate Optel's performance, we need to prepare a flexible budget showing actual and budgeted values at 12,000 units. As part of a complete profitability analysis, managers could compare the actual income of $25,400 (from Exhibit 8.2) with the $22,400 income expected at the actual sales volume of 12,000 units (from Exhibit 8.3). This results in a total favorable income variance of $3,000 to be explained and interpreted. This variance is markedly lower from the $13,400 favorable variance identified in Exhibit 8.2 using a fixed budget, but still suggests good performance. After receiving the flexible budget based on January's actual volume, management must determine what caused this $3,000 difference. The next section describes a flexible budget performance report that provides guidance in this analysis.

Decision Maker

Entrepreneur The heads of both the strategic consulting and tax consulting divisions of your financial services firm complain to you about the unfavorable variances on their performance reports. "We worked on more consulting assignments than planned. It's not surprising our costs are higher than expected. To top it off, this report characterizes our work as *poor!*" How do you respond? [Answer—p. 302]

Flexible Budget Performance Report

A **flexible budget performance report** lists differences between actual performance and budgeted performance based on actual sales volume or other activity level. This report helps direct management's attention to those costs or revenues that differ substantially from budgeted amounts. Exhibit 8.4 shows Optel's flexible budget performance report for January. We prepare this report after the actual volume is known to be 12,000 units. This report shows a $5,000 favorable variance in total dollar sales. Because actual and budgeted volumes are both 12,000 units, the $5,000 sales variance must have resulted from a higher than expected selling price. Further analysis of the facts surrounding this $5,000 sales variance reveals a favorable sales variance per unit of nearly $0.42 as shown here:

Actual average price per unit (rounded to cents)	$125,000/12,000 =	$10.42
Budgeted price per unit	$120,000/12,000 =	10.00
Favorable sales variance per unit	$5,000/12,000 =	$ 0.42

The other variances in Exhibit 8.4 also direct management's attention to areas where corrective actions can help control Optel's operations. Each expense variance is analyzed as the sales variance was. We can think of each expense as the joint result of using a given number of units of input and paying a specific price per unit of input. Optel's expense variances total $2,000 unfavorable, suggesting poor control of some costs, particularly direct materials and direct labor.

Each variance in Exhibit 8.4 is due in part to a difference between *actual price* per unit of input and *budgeted price* per unit of input. This is a **price variance.** Each variance also can be due in part to a difference between *actual quantity* of input used and *budgeted quantity* of input. This is a **quantity variance.** We explain more about this breakdown, known as **variance analysis,** later in the standard costs section.

Quick Check

Answers—p. 302

1. A flexible budget (*a*) shows fixed costs as constant amounts of cost per unit of activity, (*b*) shows variable costs as constant amounts of cost per unit of activity, or (*c*) is prepared based on one expected amount of budgeted sales or production.
2. What is the initial step in preparing a flexible budget?
3. What is the main difference between a fixed and a flexible budget?
4. What is the contribution margin?

EXHIBIT 8.4

Flexible Budget Performance Report

OPTEL Flexible Budget Performance Report For Month Ended January 31, 2009	Flexible Budget	Actual Results	Variances*
Sales (12,000 units)	$120,000	$125,000	$5,000 F
Variable costs			
Direct materials	12,000	13,000	1,000 U
Direct labor	18,000	20,000	2,000 U
Factory supplies	2,400	2,100	300 F
Utilities	3,600	4,000	400 U
Sales commissions	10,800	10,800	0
Shipping expenses	4,800	4,300	500 F
Office supplies	6,000	5,200	800 F
Total variable costs	57,600	59,400	1,800 U
Contribution margin	62,400	65,600	3,200 F
Fixed costs			
Depreciation—machinery	8,000	8,000	0
Supervisory salaries	11,000	11,000	0
Insurance expense	1,000	1,200	200 U
Depreciation—office equipment	7,000	7,000	0
Administrative salaries	13,000	13,000	0
Total fixed costs	40,000	40,200	200 U
Income from operations	$ 22,400	$ 25,400	$3,000 F

* F = Favorable variance; U = Unfavorable variance.

Section 2—Standard Costs

Standard costs are preset costs for delivering a product or service under normal conditions. These costs are established by personnel, engineering, and accounting studies using past experiences and data. Management uses these costs to assess the reasonableness of actual costs incurred for producing the product or service. When actual costs vary from standard costs, management follows up to identify potential problems and take corrective actions.

Standard costs are often used in preparing budgets because they are the anticipated costs incurred under normal conditions. Terms such as *standard materials cost, standard labor cost,* and *standard overhead cost* are often used to refer to amounts budgeted for direct materials, direct labor, and overhead.

C1 Define *standard costs* and explain their computation and uses.

Point: Since standard costs are often budgeted costs, they can be used to prepare both fixed budgets and flexible budgets.

Materials and Labor Standards

This section explains how to set materials and labor standards and how to prepare a standard cost card.

Video8.1

Identifying Standard Costs

Managerial accountants, engineers, personnel administrators, and other managers combine their efforts to set standard costs. To identify standards for direct labor costs, we can conduct time and motion studies for each labor operation in the process of providing a product or service. From these studies, management can learn the best way to perform the operation and then set the standard labor time required for the operation under normal conditions. Similarly, standards for materials are set by studying the quantity, grade, and cost of each material used. Standards for overhead costs are explained later in the chapter.

Point: Business practice often uses the word *budget* when speaking of total amounts and *standard* when discussing per unit amounts.

Regardless of the care used in setting standard costs and in revising them as conditions change, actual costs frequently differ from standard costs, often as a result of one or more factors. For instance, the actual quantity of material used can differ from the standard, or the price paid per unit of material can differ from the standard. Quantity and price differences from

Example: What factors might be considered when deciding whether to revise standard costs? *Answer:* Changes in the processes and/or resources needed to carry out the processes.

standard amounts can also occur for labor. That is, the actual labor time and actual labor rate can vary from what was expected. The same analysis applies to overhead costs.

Decision Insight

Cruis'n Standards The **Corvette** consists of hundreds of parts for which engineers set standards. Various types of labor are also involved in its production, including machining, assembly, painting, and welding, and standards are set for each. Actual results are periodically compared with standards to assess performance.

Setting Standard Costs

To illustrate the setting of a standard cost, we consider a professional league baseball bat manufactured by **ProBat**. Its engineers have determined that manufacturing one bat requires 0.90 kg. of high-grade wood. They also expect some loss of material as part of the process because of inefficiencies and waste. This results in adding an *allowance* of 0.10 kg., making the standard requirement 1.0 kg. of wood for each bat.

Point: Companies promoting continuous improvement strive to achieve ideal standards by eliminating inefficiencies and waste.

The 0.90 kg. portion is called an *ideal standard;* it is the quantity of material required if the process is 100% efficient without any loss or waste. Reality suggests that some loss of material usually occurs with any process. The standard of 1.0 kg. is known as the *practical standard,* the quantity of material required under normal application of the process.

High-grade wood can be purchased at a standard price of $25 per kg. The purchasing department sets this price as the expected price for the budget period. To determine this price, the purchasing department considers factors such as the quality of materials, future economic conditions, supply factors (shortages and excesses), and any available discounts. The engineers also decide that two hours of labor time (after including allowances) are required to manufacture a bat. The wage rate is $20 per hour (better than average skilled labor is required). ProBat assigns all overhead at the rate of $10 per labor hour. The standard costs of direct materials, direct labor, and overhead for one bat are shown in Exhibit 8.5 in what is called a *standard cost card.* These cost amounts are then used to prepare manufacturing budgets for a budgeted level of production.

EXHIBIT 8.5

Standard Cost Card

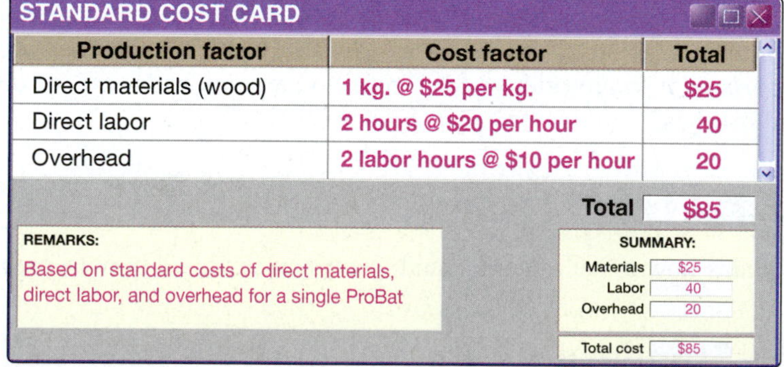

STANDARD COST CARD

Production factor	Cost factor	Total
Direct materials (wood)	1 kg. @ $25 per kg.	$25
Direct labor	2 hours @ $20 per hour	40
Overhead	2 labor hours @ $10 per hour	20
	Total	$85

REMARKS:
Based on standard costs of direct materials, direct labor, and overhead for a single ProBat

SUMMARY:

Materials	$25
Labor	40
Overhead	20
Total cost	$85

Cost Variances

C2 Describe variances and what they reveal about performance.

A **cost variance,** also simply called a *variance,* is the difference between actual and standard costs. A cost variance can be favorable or unfavorable. A variance from standard cost is considered favorable if actual cost is less than standard cost. It is considered unfavorable if actual cost is more than standard cost.[1] This section discusses variance analysis.

[1] Short-term favorable variances can sometimes lead to long-term unfavorable variances. For instance, if management spends less than the budgeted amount on maintenance or insurance, the performance report would show a favorable variance. Cutting these expenses can lead to major losses in the long run if machinery wears out prematurely or insurance coverage proves inadequate.

Cost Variance Analysis

Video8.1

Variances are usually identified in performance reports. When a variance occurs, management wants to determine the factors causing it. This often involves analysis, evaluation, and explanation. The results of these efforts should enable management to assign responsibility for the variance and then to take actions to correct the situation.

To illustrate, ProBat's standard materials cost for producing 500 bats is $12,500. Assume that its actual materials cost for those 500 bats proved to be $13,000. The $500 unfavorable variance raises questions that call for answers that, in turn, can lead to changes to correct the situation and eliminate this variance in the next period. A performance report often identifies the existence of a problem, but we must follow up with further investigation to see what can be done to improve future performance.

Exhibit 8.6 shows the flow of events in the effective management of variance analysis. It shows four steps: (1) preparing a standard cost performance report, (2) computing and analyzing variances, (3) identifying questions and their explanations, and (4) taking corrective and strategic actions. These variance analysis steps are interrelated and are frequently applied in good organizations.

EXHIBIT 8.6
Variance Analysis

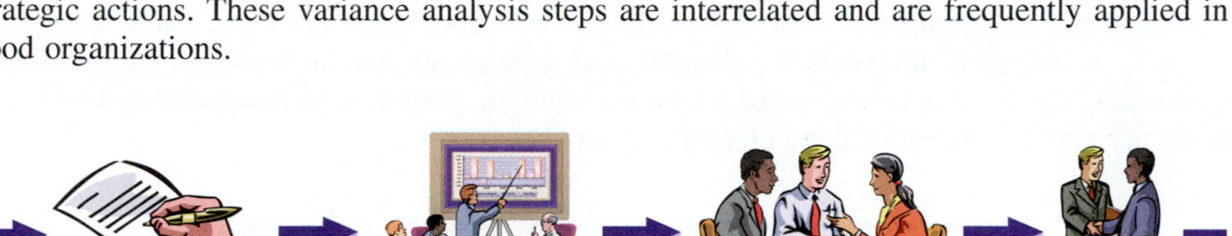

Cost Variance Computation

Management needs information about the factors causing a cost variance, but first it must properly compute the variance. In its most simple form, a cost variance (CV) is computed as the difference between actual cost (AC) and standard cost (SC) as shown in Exhibit 8.7.

EXHIBIT 8.7
Cost Variance Formulas

Cost Variance (CV) = **Actual Cost** (AC) − **Standard Cost** (SC)

where:

Actual Cost (AC) = **Actual Quantity** (AQ) × **Actual Price** (AP)

Standard Cost (SC) = **Standard Quantity** (SQ) × **Standard Price** (SP)

A cost variance is further defined by its components. Actual quantity (AQ) is the input (material or labor) used to manufacture the quantity of output. Standard quantity (SQ) is the expected input for the quantity of output. Actual price (AP) is the amount paid to acquire the input (material or labor), and standard price (SP) is the expected price.

Two main factors cause a cost variance: (1) the difference between actual price and standard price results in a *price* (or rate) *variance* and (2) the difference between actual quantity and standard quantity results in a *quantity* (or usage or efficiency) *variance*. To assess the impacts of these two factors in a cost variance, we use the formulas in Exhibit 8.8.

Point: Price and quantity variances for direct labor are nearly always referred to as *rate* and *efficiency variances*, respectively.

EXHIBIT 8.8
Price Variance and Quantity Variance Formulas

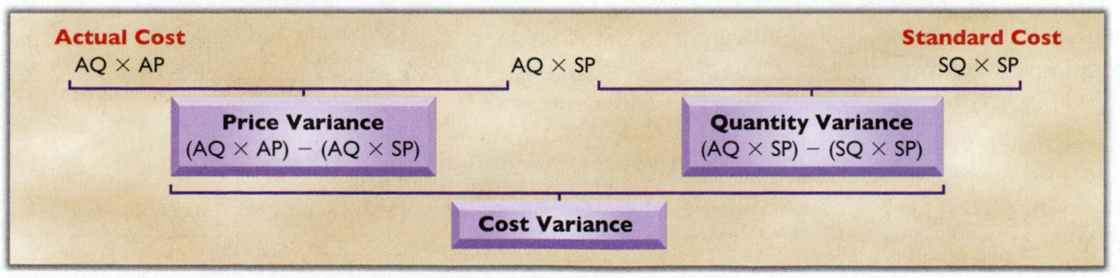

In computing a price variance, the quantity (actual) is held constant. In computing a quantity variance, the price (standard) is held constant. The cost variance, or total variance, is the sum of the price and quantity variances. These formulas identify the sources of the cost variance. Managers sometimes find it useful to apply an alternative (but equivalent) computation for the price and quantity variances as shown in Exhibit 8.9.

EXHIBIT 8.9

Alternative Price Variance and Quantity Variance Formulas

Price Variance (PV) = [**Actual Price** (AP) − **Standard Price** (SP)] × **Actual Quantity** (AQ)

Quantity Variance (QV) = [**Actual Quantity** (AQ) − **Standard Quantity** (SQ)] × **Standard Price** (SP)

The results from applying the formulas in Exhibits 8.8 and 8.9 are identical.

Computing Materials and Labor Variances

P2 Compute materials and labor variances.

We illustrate the computation of the materials and labor cost variances using data from G-Max, a company that makes specialty golf equipment and accessories for individual customers. This company has set the following standard quantities and costs for materials and labor per unit for one of its hand-crafted golf clubheads:

Direct materials (1 lb. per unit at $1 per lb.)	$1.00
Direct labor (1 hr. per unit at $8 per hr.)	8.00
Total standard direct cost per unit	$9.00

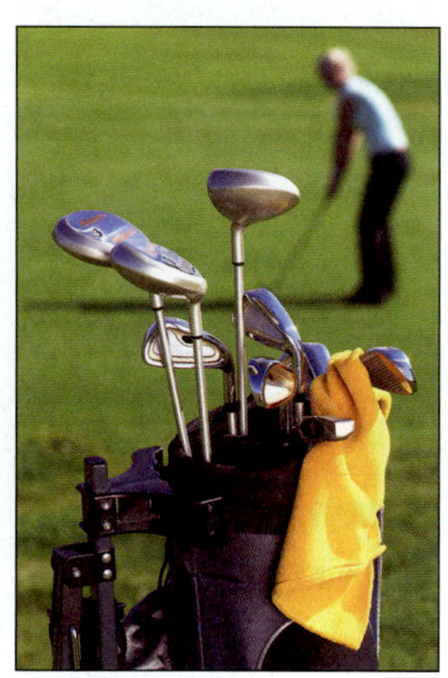

Materials Cost Variances During May 2009, G-Max budgeted to produce 4,000 clubheads (units). It actually produced only 3,500 units. It used 3,600 pounds of direct materials (titanium) costing $1.05 per pound, meaning its total materials cost was $3,780. This information allows us to compute both actual and standard direct materials costs for G-Max's 3,500 units and its direct materials cost variance as follows:

Actual cost	3,600 lbs. @ $1.05 per lb.	= $3,780
Standard cost	3,500 lbs. @ $1.00 per lb.	= 3,500
Direct materials cost variance (unfavorable)		= $ 280

To better isolate the causes of this $280 unfavorable total direct materials cost variance, the materials price and quantity variances for these G-Max clubheads are computed and shown in Exhibit 8.10.

EXHIBIT 8.10

Materials Price and Quantity Variances

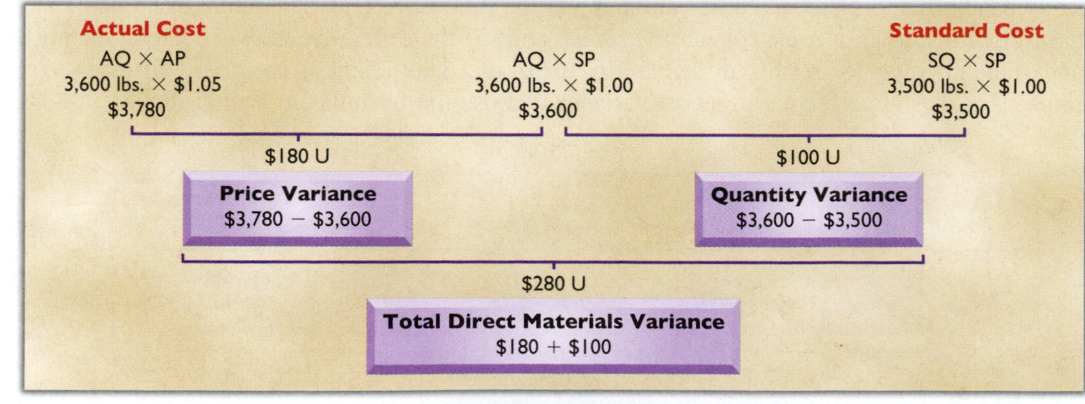

The $180 unfavorable price variance results from paying 5 cents more per unit than the standard price, computed as 3,600 lbs. × $0.05. The $100 unfavorable quantity variance is due to using 100 lbs. more materials than the standard quantity, computed as 100 lbs. × $1. The total direct materials variance is $280 and it is unfavorable. This information allows management to ask the responsible individuals for explanations and corrective actions.

Example: Identify at least two factors that might have caused the $100 unfavorable quantity variance and the $180 unfavorable price variance in Exhibit 8.10. *Answer:* Poor quality materials or untrained workers for the former; poor price negotiation or higher-quality materials for the latter.

The purchasing department is usually responsible for the price paid for materials. Responsibility for explaining the price variance in this case rests with the purchasing manager if a price higher than standard caused the variance. The production department is usually responsible for the amount of material used and in this case is responsible for explaining why the process used more than the standard amount of materials.

Variance analysis presents challenges. For instance, the production department could have used more than the standard amount of material because its quality did not meet specifications and led to excessive waste. In this case, the purchasing manager is responsible for explaining why inferior materials were acquired. However, the production manager is responsible for explaining what happened if analysis shows that waste was due to inefficiencies, not poor quality material.

In evaluating price variances, managers must recognize that a favorable price variance can indicate a problem with poor product quality. **Redhook Ale**, a micro brewery in the Pacific Northwest, can probably save 10% to 15% in material prices by buying six-row barley malt instead of the better two-row from Washington's Yakima valley. Attention to quality, however, has helped Redhook Ale become the first craft brewer to be kosher certified. Redhook's purchasing activities are judged on both the quality of the materials and the purchase price variance.

Labor Cost Variances Labor cost for a specific product or service depends on the number of hours worked (quantity) and the wage rate paid to employees (price). When actual amounts for a task differ from standard, the labor cost variance can be divided into a rate (price) variance and an efficiency (quantity) variance.

To illustrate, G-Max's direct labor standard for 3,500 units of its hand-crafted clubheads is one hour per unit, or 3,500 hours at $8 per hour. Since only 3,400 hours at $8.30 per hour were actually used to complete the units, the actual and standard labor costs are

Actual cost	3,400 hrs. @ $8.30 per hr.	= $28,220
Standard cost	3,500 hrs. @ $8.00 per hr.	= 28,000
Direct labor cost variance (unfavorable)		= $ 220

This analysis shows that actual cost is merely $220 over the standard and suggests no immediate concern. Computing both the labor rate and efficiency variances reveals a different picture, however, as shown in Exhibit 8.11.

EXHIBIT 8.11
Labor Rate and Efficiency Variances*

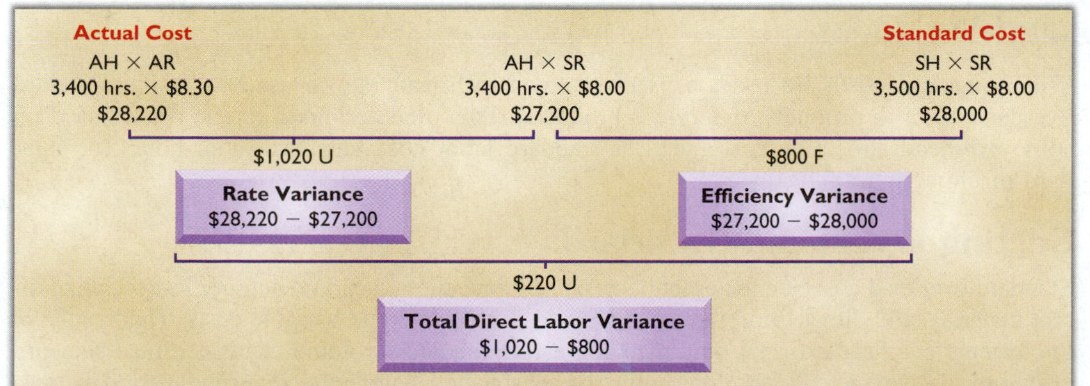

* AH is actual direct labor hours: AR is actual wage rate; SH is standard direct labor hours allowed for actual output; SR is standard wage rate.

Example: Compute the rate variance and the efficiency variance for Exhibit 8.11 if 3,700 actual hours are used at an actual price of $7.50 per hour. *Answer:* $1,850 favorable labor rate variance and $1,600 unfavorable labor efficiency variance.

The analysis in Exhibit 8.11 shows that an $800 favorable efficiency variance results from using 100 fewer direct labor hours than standard for the units produced, but this favorable variance is more than offset by a wage rate that is $0.30 per hour higher than standard. The personnel administrator or the production manager needs to explain why the wage rate is higher than expected. The production manager should also explain how the labor hours were reduced. If this experience can be repeated and transferred to other departments, more savings are possible.

One possible explanation of these labor rate and efficiency variances is the use of workers with different skill levels. If this is the reason, senior management must discuss the implications with the production manager who has the responsibility to assign workers to tasks with the appropriate skill level. In this case, an investigation might show that higher-skilled workers were used to produce 3,500 units of hand-crafted clubheads. As a result, fewer labor hours might be required for the work, but the wage rate paid these workers is higher than standard because of their greater skills. The effect of this strategy is a higher than standard total cost, which would require actions to remedy the situation or adjust the standard.

Decision Maker

Human Resource Manager You receive the manufacturing variance report for June and discover a large unfavorable labor efficiency (quantity) variance. What factors do you investigate to identify its possible causes? [Answer—p. 302]

Quick Check

Answers—pp. 302–303

5. A standard cost (*a*) changes in direct proportion to changes in the level of activity, (*b*) is an amount incurred at the actual level of production for the period, or (*c*) is an amount incurred under normal conditions to provide a product or service.
6. What is a cost variance?
7. The following information is available for York Company.

Actual direct labor hours per unit	2.5 hours
Standard direct labor hours per unit	2.0 hours
Actual production (units)	2,500 units
Budgeted production (units)	3,000 units
Actual rate per hour	$3.10
Standard rate per hour	$3.00

The labor efficiency variance is (*a*) $3,750 U, (*b*) $3,750 F, or (*c*) $3,875 U.

8. Refer to Quick Check 7; the labor rate variance is (*a*) $625 F or (*b*) $625 U.
9. If a materials quantity variance is favorable and a materials price variance is unfavorable, can the total materials cost variance be favorable?

Overhead Standards and Variances

Video8.1&8.3

When standard costs are used, a predetermined overhead rate is used to assign standard overhead costs to products or services produced. This predetermined rate is often based on some overhead allocation base (such as standard labor cost, standard labor hours, or standard machine hours).

Setting Overhead Standards

Standard overhead costs are the amounts expected to occur at a certain activity level. Unlike direct materials and direct labor, overhead includes fixed costs and variable costs. This results in the average overhead cost per unit changing as the predicted volume changes. Since standard costs are also budgeted costs, they must be established before the reporting period begins. Standard overhead costs are therefore average per unit costs based on the predicted activity level.

To establish the standard overhead cost rate, management uses the same cost structure it used to construct a flexible budget at the end of a period. This cost structure identifies the different overhead cost components and classifies them as variable or fixed. To get the standard overhead rate, management selects a level of activity (volume) and predicts total overhead cost. It then divides this total by the allocation base to get the standard rate. Standard direct labor hours expected to be used to produce the predicted volume is a common allocation base and is used in this section.

To illustrate, Exhibit 8.12 shows the overhead cost structure used to develop G-Max's flexible overhead budgets for May 2009. The predetermined standard overhead rate for May is set before the month begins. The first two number columns list the per unit amounts of variable costs and the monthly amounts of fixed costs. The four right-most columns show the costs expected to occur at four different levels of production activity. The predetermined overhead rate per labor hour is smaller as volume of activity increases because total fixed costs remain constant.

G-Max managers predicted an 80% activity level for May, or a production volume of 4,000 clubheads. At this volume, they budget $8,000 as the May total overhead. This choice implies a $2 per unit (labor hour) average overhead cost ($8,000/4,000 units). Since G-Max has a standard of one direct labor hour per unit, the predetermined standard overhead rate for May is $2 per standard direct labor hour. The variable overhead rate remains constant at $1 per direct labor hour regardless of the budgeted production level. The fixed overhead rate changes according to the budgeted production volume. For instance, for the predicted level of 4,000 units of production, the fixed rate is $1 per hour ($4,000 fixed costs/4,000 units). For a production level of 5,000 units, however, the fixed rate is $0.80 per hour ($4,000 fixed costs/5,000 units).

When choosing the predicted activity level, management considers many factors. The level can be set as high as 100% of capacity, but this is rare. Factors causing the activity level to

Point: Managers consider the types of overhead costs when choosing the basis for assigning overhead costs to products.

Point: With increased automation, machine hours are frequently used in applying overhead instead of labor hours.

Point: Variable costs per unit remain constant, but fixed costs per unit decline with increases in volume. This means the average total overhead cost per unit declines with increases in volume.

EXHIBIT 8.12

Flexible Overhead Budgets

G-MAX
Flexible Overhead Budgets
For Month Ended May 31, 2009

	Flexible Budget: Variable Amount per Unit	Flexible Budget: Total Fixed Cost	Flexible Budget at 70% Capacity	Flexible Budget at 80% Capacity	Flexible Budget at 90% Capacity	Flexible Budget at 100% Capacity
Production (in units)	1 unit		3,500	**4,000**	4,500	5,000
Factory overhead						
Variable costs						
Indirect labor	$0.40/unit		$1,400	**$1,600**	$1,800	$2,000
Indirect materials	0.30/unit		1,050	**1,200**	1,350	1,500
Power and lights	0.20/unit		700	**800**	900	1,000
Maintenance	0.10/unit		350	**400**	450	500
Total variable overhead costs	$1.00/unit		3,500	**4,000**	4,500	5,000
Fixed costs (per month)						
Building rent		$1,000	1,000	**1,000**	1,000	1,000
Depreciation—machinery		1,200	1,200	**1,200**	1,200	1,200
Supervisory salaries		1,800	1,800	**1,800**	1,800	1,800
Total fixed overhead costs		$4,000	4,000	**4,000**	4,000	4,000
Total factory overhead			$7,500	**$8,000**	$8,500	$9,000
Standard direct labor hours 1 hr./unit			3,500 hrs.	**4,000 hrs.**	4,500 hrs.	5,000 hrs.
Predetermined overhead rate per standard direct labor hour			$ 2.14	**$ 2.00**	$ 1.89	$ 1.80

be less than full capacity include difficulties in scheduling work, equipment under repair or maintenance, and insufficient product demand. Good long-run management practices often call for some plant capacity in excess of current operating needs to allow for special opportunities and demand changes.

Decision Insight

Measuring Up In the spirit of continuous improvement, competitors compare their processes and performance standards against benchmarks established by industry leaders. Those that use **benchmarking** include Precision Lube, Jiffy Lube, All Tune and Lube, and Speedee Oil Change and Tune-Up.

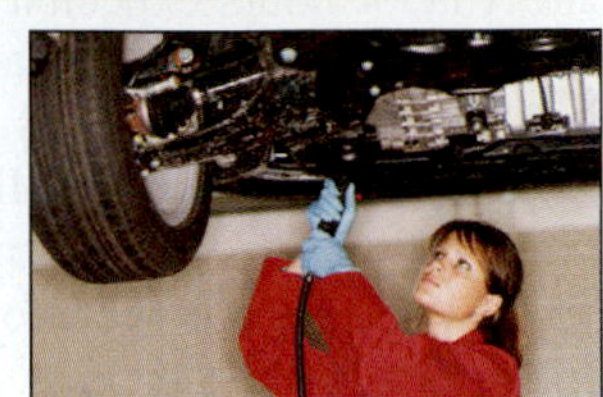

Computing Overhead Cost Variances

When standard costs are used, the cost accounting system applies overhead to the good units produced using the predetermined standard overhead rate. At period-end, the difference between the total overhead cost applied to products and the total overhead cost actually incurred is called an **overhead cost variance** (total overhead variance), which is defined in Exhibit 8.13.

EXHIBIT 8.13
Overhead Cost Variance

Overhead cost variance (OCV) = Actual overhead incurred (AOI) − Standard overhead applied (SOA)

EXHIBIT 8.14
Framework for Total Overhead Variance

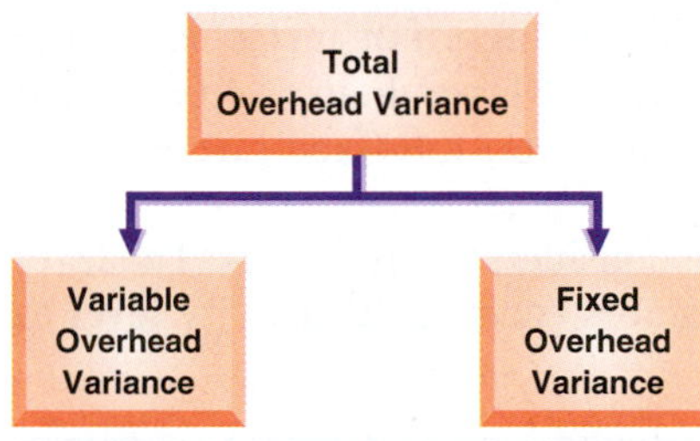

To help identify factors causing the overhead cost variance, managers analyze this variance separately for variable and fixed overhead, as illustrated in Exhibit 8.14. The results provide information useful for taking strategic actions to improve company performance.

P3 Compute overhead variances.

Computing Variable and Fixed Overhead Cost Variances To illustrate the computation of overhead cost variances, we return to the G-Max data. We know that G-Max produced 3,500 units when 4,000 units were budgeted. Additional data from cost reports show that the actual overhead cost incurred is $7,650 (the variable portion of $3,650 and the fixed portion of $4,000). Recall from Exhibit 8.12 that each unit requires 1 hour of direct labor, that variable overhead is applied at a rate of $1.00 per direct labor hour, and that the predetermined fixed overhead rate is $1.00 per direct labor hour. Using this information, we can compute overhead variances for both variable and fixed overhead as follows:

Actual variable overhead (given)	$3,650
Applied variable overhead (3,500 × $1.00)	3,500
Unfavorable variable overhead variance	$ 150

Actual fixed overhead (given)	$4,000
Applied fixed overhead (3,500 × $1.00)	3,500
Unfavorable fixed overhead variance	$ 500

"Well, according to the books, you've got too much overhead."

Management should seek to determine the causes of these unfavorable variances and take corrective action. To help better isolate the causes of these variances, more detailed overhead variances can be used, as shown in the next section.

Computing Controllable Overhead Variances and Volume Variances The total overhead variance for G-Max is $650 unfavorable, consisting of $150 unfavorable variable overhead variance and $500 unfavorable fixed overhead variance.

Similar to analysis of direct materials and direct labor, both the variable and fixed overhead variances can be separately analyzed. Exhibit 8.15 shows an expanded framework for understanding these component overhead variances. A **spending variance** occurs when management pays an amount different than the standard price to acquire an item. For instance, the actual wage rate paid to indirect labor might be higher than the standard rate. Similarly, actual supervisory salaries might be different than expected. Spending variances such as these cause management to investigate the reasons that the amount paid differs from the standard. Both variable and fixed overhead costs can yield their own spending variances. Analyzing variable overhead includes computing an **efficiency variance,** which occurs when standard direct labor hours (the allocation base) expected for actual production differ from the actual direct labor hours used. This efficiency variance reflects on the cost-effectiveness in using the overhead allocation base (such as direct labor).

EXHIBIT 8.15

Expanded Framework for Total Overhead Variance

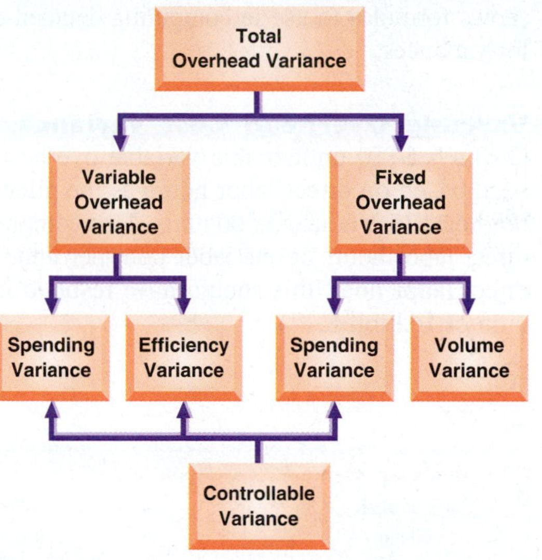

A **volume variance** occurs when a difference occurs between the actual volume of production and the standard volume of production. The budgeted fixed overhead amount is the same regardless of the volume of production (within the relevant range). This budgeted amount is computed based on the standard direct labor hours that the budgeted production volume allows. The applied overhead is based, however, on the standard direct labor hours allowed for the actual volume of production. A difference between budgeted and actual production volumes results in a difference in the standard direct labor hours allowed for these two production levels. This situation yields a volume variance different from zero.

Example: Does an unfavorable volume variance indicate poor management performance? *Answer:* No, it only indicates production volume was less than expected. This can be due to many factors, such as falling demand for company products, that are usually viewed outside a manager's control.

We can combine the variable overhead spending variance, the fixed overhead spending variance, and the variable overhead efficiency variance to get **controllable variance.** The controllable variance is so named because it refers to activities usually under management control. Exhibit 8.16

EXHIBIT 8.16

Variable and Fixed Overhead Variances

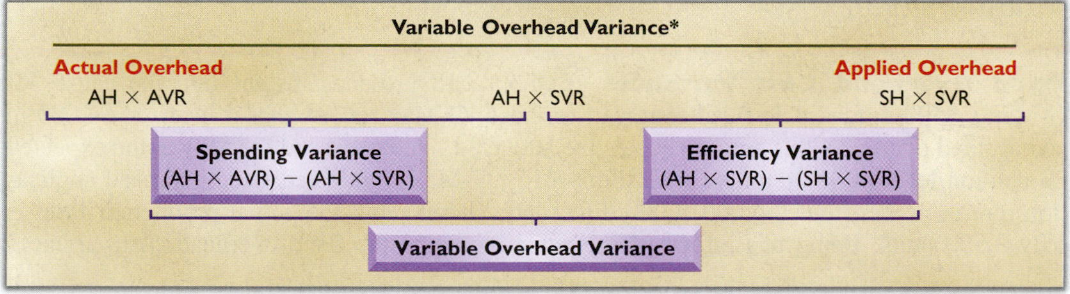

* AH = actual direct labor hours; AVR = actual variable overhead rate; SH = standard direct labor hours; SVR = standard variable overhead rate.

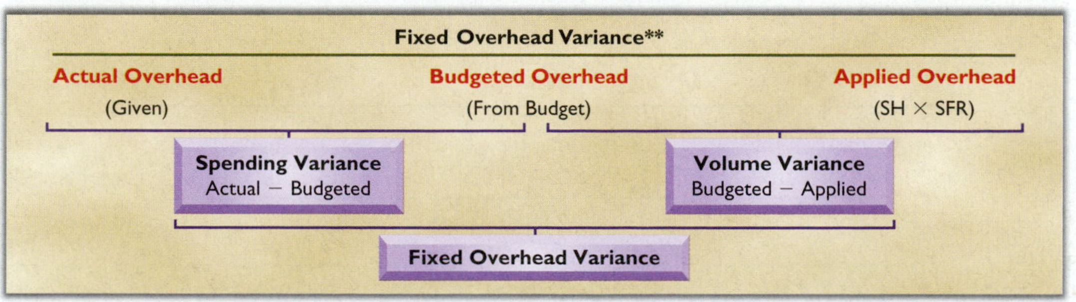

** SH = standard direct labor hours; SFR = standard fixed overhead rate.

shows formulas to use in computing detailed overhead variances that can better identify reasons for variances.

Variable Overhead Cost Variances Exhibit 8.17 offers insight into the causes of G-Max's $150 unfavorable variable overhead cost variance. Recall that G-Max applies overhead based on direct labor hours as the allocation base. We know that it used 3,400 direct labor hours to produce 3,500 units. This compares favorably to the standard requirement of 3,500 direct labor hours at one labor hour per unit. At a standard variable overhead rate of $1.00 per direct labor hour, this should have resulted in variable overhead costs of $3,400 (middle column of Exhibit 8.17).

EXHIBIT 8.17

Computing Variable Overhead Cost Variances

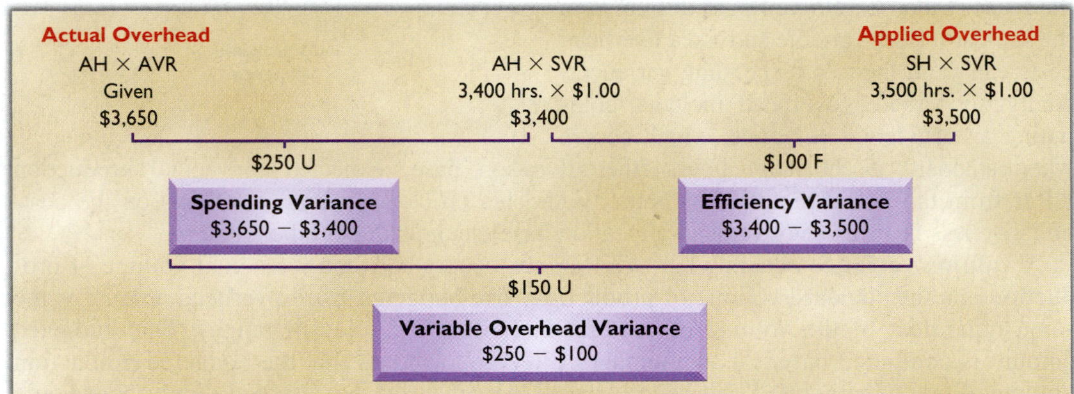

G-Max's cost records, however, report actual variable overhead of $3,650, or $250 higher than expected. This means G-Max has an unfavorable variable overhead spending variance of $250 ($3,650 − $3,400). On the other hand, G-Max used 100 fewer labor hours than expected to make 3,500 units, and its actual variable overhead is lower than its applied variable overhead. Thus, G-Max has a favorable variable overhead efficiency variance of $100 ($3,400 − $3,500).

Fixed Overhead Cost Variances Exhibit 8.18 provides insight into the causes of G-Max's $500 unfavorable fixed overhead variance. G-Max reports that it incurred $4,000 in actual fixed overhead; this amount equals the budgeted fixed overhead for May at the expected production level of 4,000 units (see Exhibit 8.12). G-Max's budgeted fixed overhead application rate is $1 per hour ($4,000/4,000 direct labor hours), but the actual production level is only 3,500 units. Using this information, we can compute the fixed overhead cost variances

EXHIBIT 8.18

Computing Fixed Overhead Cost Variances

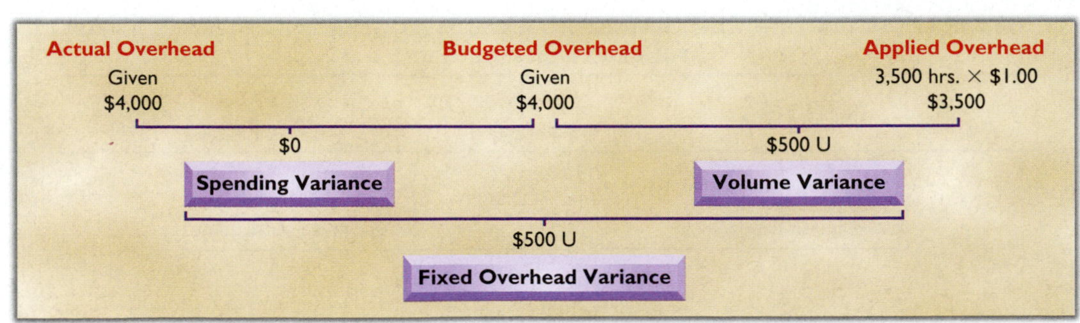

shown in Exhibit 8.18. The applied fixed overhead is computed by multiplying 3,500 standard hours allowed for the actual production by the $1 fixed overhead allocation rate. Exhibit 8.18 reveals that the fixed overhead spending variance is zero, suggesting good control of fixed overhead costs. The volume variance of $500 occurs because 500 fewer units are produced than budgeted; namely, 80% of the manufacturing capacity is budgeted but only 70% is used.

An unfavorable volume variance implies that the company did not reach its predicted operating level. Management needs to know why the actual level of performance differs from the expected level. The main purpose of the volume variance is to identify what portion of the total variance is caused by failing to meet the expected volume level. This information permits management to focus on the controllable variance.

Overhead Variance Reports Using the information from Exhibits 8.17 and 8.18, we compute the total controllable overhead variance as $150 unfavorable ($250 U + $100 F + $0). To help management isolate the reasons for this controllable variance, an *overhead variance report* can be prepared.

A complete overhead variance report provides managers information about specific overhead costs and how they differ from budgeted amounts. Exhibit 8.19 shows G-Max's overhead variance report for May. It reveals that (1) fixed costs and maintenance cost were incurred as expected, (2) costs for indirect labor and power and lights were higher than expected, and (3) indirect materials cost was less than expected.

The total controllable variance amount is also readily available from Exhibit 8.19. The overhead variance report shows the total volume variance as $500 unfavorable (shown at the top) and the $150 unfavorable controllable variance (reported at the bottom right). The sum of the controllable variance and the volume variance equals the total (fixed and variable) overhead variance of $650 unfavorable.

EXHIBIT 8.19

Overhead Variance Report

G-MAX
Overhead Variance Report
For Month Ended May 31, 2009

Volume Variance			
Expected production level	80% of capacity		
Production level achieved	70% of capacity		
Volume variance	**$500 (unfavorable)**		

Controllable Variance	**Flexible Budget**	**Actual Results**	**Variances***
Variable overhead costs			
Indirect labor	$1,400	$1,525	$125 U
Indirect materials	1,050	1,025	25 F
Power and lights	700	750	50 U
Maintenance	350	350	0
Total variable overhead costs	3,500	3,650	150 U†
Fixed overhead costs			
Building rent	1,000	1,000	0
Depreciation—machinery	1,200	1,200	0
Supervisory salaries	1,800	1,800	0
Total fixed overhead costs	4,000	4,000	0‡
Total overhead costs	$7,500	$7,650	$150 U

* F = Favorable variance; U = Unfavorable variance.

† Total variable overhead (spending and efficiency) variance.

‡ Fixed overhead spending variance.

Extensions of Standard Costs

This section extends the application of standard costs for control purposes, for service companies, and for accounting systems.

Standard Costs for Control

C3 Explain how standard cost information is useful for management by exception.

To control business activities, top management must be able to affect the actions of lower-level managers responsible for the company's revenues and costs. After preparing a budget and establishing standard costs, management should take actions to gain control when actual costs differ from standard or budgeted amounts.

Reports such as the ones illustrated in this chapter call management's attention to variances from business plans and other standards. When managers use these reports to focus on problem areas, the budgeting process contributes to the control function. In using budgeted performance reports, practice of management by exception is often useful. **Management by exception** means that managers focus attention on the most significant variances and give less attention to areas where performance is reasonably close to the standard. This practice leads management to concentrate on the exceptional or irregular situations. Management by exception is especially useful when directed at controllable items.

Decision Ethics

Internal Auditor You discover a manager who always spends exactly what is budgeted. About 30% of her budget is spent just before the period-end. She admits to spending what is budgeted, whether or not it is needed. She offers three reasons: (1) she doesn't want her budget cut, (2) "management by exception" focuses on budget deviations; and (3) she believes the money is budgeted to be spent. What action do you take? [Answer—p. 302]

Standard Costs for Services

Many managers use standard costs and variance analysis to investigate manufacturing costs. Many managers also recognize that standard costs and variances can help them control *nonmanufacturing* costs. Companies providing services instead of products can benefit from the use of standard costs. Application of standard costs and variances can be readily adapted to nonmanufacturing situations. To illustrate, many service providers use standard costs to help control expenses. First, they use standard costs as a basis for budgeting all services. Second, they use periodic performance reports to compare actual results to standards. Third, they use these reports to identify significant variances within specific areas of responsibility. Fourth, they implement the appropriate control procedures.

Decision Insight

Health Budget Medical professionals continue to struggle with business realities. Quality medical service is paramount, but efficiency in providing that service also is important. The use of budgeting and standard costing is touted as an effective means to control and monitor medical costs, especially overhead.

Standard Cost Accounting System

P4 Prepare journal entries for standard costs and account for price and quantity variances.

We have shown how companies use standard costs in management reports. Most standard cost systems also record these costs and variances in accounts. This practice simplifies recordkeeping and helps in preparing reports. Although we do not need knowledge of standard cost accounting practices to understand standard costs and their use, we must know how to interpret the accounts in which standard costs and variances are recorded. The entries in this section briefly illustrate the important aspects of this process for G-Max's standard costs and variances for May.

The first of these entries records standard materials cost incurred in May in the Goods in Process Inventory account. This part of the entry is similar to the usual accounting entry, but the amount of the debit equals the standard cost ($3,500) instead of the actual cost ($3,780).

This entry credits Raw Materials Inventory for actual cost. The difference between standard and actual direct materials costs is recorded with debits to two separate materials variance accounts (recall Exhibit 8.10). Both the materials price and quantity variances are recorded as debits because they reflect additional costs higher than the standard cost (if actual costs were less than the standard, they are recorded as credits). This treatment (debit) reflects their unfavorable effect because they represent higher costs and lower income.

May 31	Goods in Process Inventory	3,500	
	Direct Materials Price Variance*	**180**	
	Direct Materials Quantity Variance	**100**	
	Raw Materials Inventory		3,780
	To charge production for standard quantity of materials used (3,500 lbs.) at the standard price ($1 per lb.), and to record material price and material quantity variances.		

Assets = Liabilities + Equity
+3,500 −100
−3,780 −180

* Many companies record the materials price variance when materials are purchased. For simplicity, we record both the materials price and quantity variances when materials are issued to production.

The second entry debits Goods in Process Inventory for the standard labor cost of the goods manufactured during May ($28,000). Actual labor cost ($28,220) is recorded with a credit to the Factory Payroll account. The difference between standard and actual labor costs is explained by two variances (see Exhibit 8.11). The direct labor rate variance is unfavorable and is debited to that account. The direct labor efficiency variance is favorable and that account is credited. The direct labor efficiency variance is favorable because it represents a lower cost and a higher net income.

May 31	Goods in Process Inventory	28,000	
	Direct Labor Rate Variance	**1,020**	
	Direct Labor Efficiency Variance		**800**
	Factory Payroll		28,220
	To charge production with 3,500 standard hours of direct labor at the standard $8 per hour rate, and to record the labor rate and efficiency variances.		

Assets = Liabilities + Equity
+28,000 +28,220
− 1,020
+ 800

The entry to assign standard predetermined overhead to the cost of goods manufactured must debit the $7,000 predetermined amount to the Goods in Process Inventory account. Actual overhead costs of $7,650 were debited to Factory Overhead during the period (entries not shown here). Thus, when Factory Overhead is applied to Goods in Process Inventory, the actual amount is credited to the Factory Overhead account. To account for the difference between actual and standard overhead costs, the entry includes a $250 debit to the Variable Overhead Spending Variance, a $100 credit to the Variable Overhead Efficiency Variance, and a $500 debit to the Volume Variance (recall Exhibits 8.17 and 8.18). An alternative (simpler) approach is to record the difference with a $150 debit to the Controllable Variance account and a $500 debit to the Volume Variance account (recall from Exhibit 8.15 that controllable variance is the sum of both variable overhead variances and the fixed overhead spending variance).

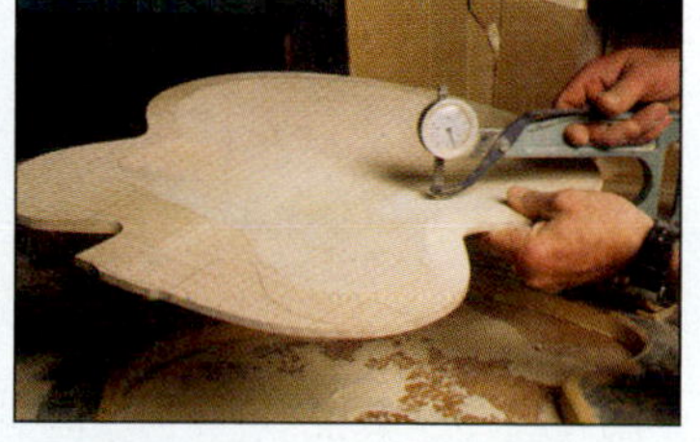

May 31	Goods in Process Inventory	7,000	
	Volume Variance	**500**	
	Variable Overhead Spending Variance	**250**	
	Variable Overhead Efficiency Variance		**100**
	Factory Overhead		7,650
	To apply overhead at the standard rate of $2 per standard direct labor hour (3,500 hours), and to record overhead variances.		

Assets = Liabilities + Equity
+7,000 +7,650
− 250
− 500
+ 100

The balances of these different variance accounts accumulate until the end of the accounting period. As a result, the unfavorable variances of some months can offset the favorable variances of other months.

These ending variance account balances, which reflect results of the period's various transactions and events, are closed at period-end. If the amounts are *immaterial,* they are added to or subtracted from the balance of the Cost of Goods Sold account. This process is similar to that shown in the job order costing chapter for eliminating an underapplied or overapplied balance in the Factory Overhead account. (*Note:* These variance balances, which represent differences between actual and standard costs, must be added to or subtracted from the materials, labor, and overhead costs recorded. In this way, the recorded costs equal the actual costs incurred in the period; a company must use actual costs in external financial statements prepared in accordance with generally accepted accounting principles.)

Point: If variances are material they can be allocated between Goods in Process Inventory, Finished Goods Inventory, and Cost of Goods Sold. This closing process is explained in advanced courses.

Quick Check

Answers—p. 302

10. Under what conditions is an overhead volume variance considered favorable?

11. To use management by exception with standard costs, a company (*a*) must record standard costs in its accounting, (*b*) should compute variances from flexible budget amounts to allow management to focus its attention on significant differences between actual and budgeted results, or (*c*) should analyze only variances for direct materials and direct labor.

12. A company uses a standard cost accounting system. Prepare the journal entry to record these direct materials variances:

Direct materials cost actually incurred	$73,200
Direct materials quantity variance (favorable)	3,800
Direct materials price variance (unfavorable)	1,300

13. If standard costs are recorded in the manufacturing accounts, how are recorded variances treated at the end of an accounting period?

Decision Analysis

Sales Variances

A2 Analyze changes in sales from expected amounts.

This chapter explained the computation and analysis of cost variances. A similar variance analysis can be applied to sales. To illustrate, consider the following sales data from G-Max for two of its golf products, Excel golf balls and Big Bert® drivers.

	Budgeted	Actual
Sales of Excel golf balls (units)	1,000 units	1,100 units
Sales price per Excel golf ball	$10	$10.50
Sales of Big Bert® drivers (units)	150 units	140 units
Sales price per Big Bert® driver	$200	$190

Using this information, we compute both the *sales price variance* and the *sales volume variance* as shown in Exhibit 8.20. The total sales price variance is $850 unfavorable, and the total sales volume variance is $1,000 unfavorable. Neither variance implies anything positive about these two products. However, further analysis of these total sales variances reveals that both the sales price and sales volume variances for Excel golf balls are favorable, meaning that both the unfavorable total sales price variance and the unfavorable total sales volume variance are due to the Big Bert driver.

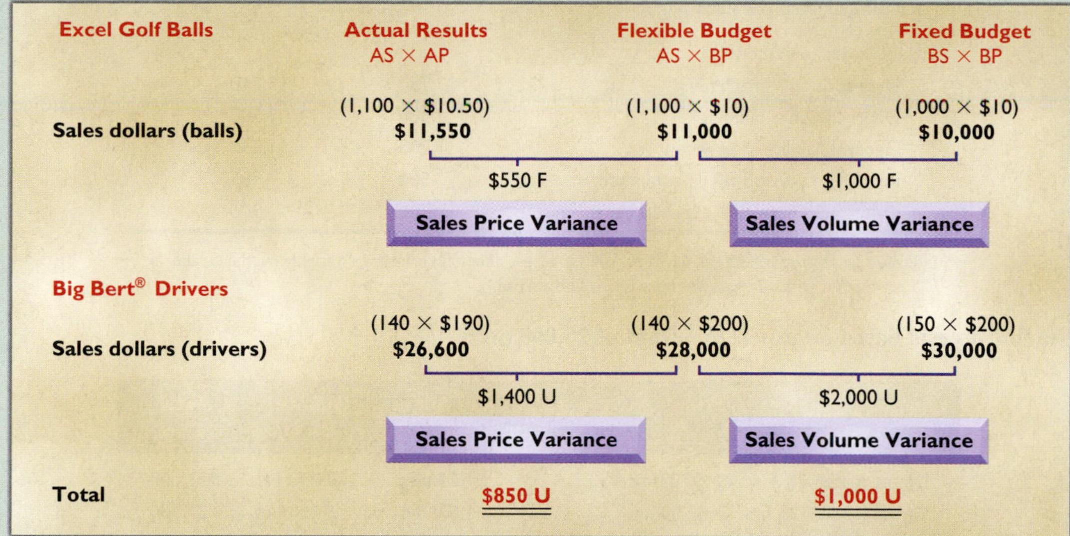

EXHIBIT 8.20

Computing Sales Variances*

* AS = actual sales units; AP = actual sales price; BP = budgeted sales price; BS = budgeted sales units (fixed budget).

Managers use sales variances for planning and control purposes. The sales variance information is used to plan future actions to avoid unfavorable variances. G-Max sold 90 total combined units (both balls and drivers) more than planned, but these 90 units were not sold in the proportion budgeted. G-Max sold fewer than the budgeted quantity of the higher-priced driver, which contributed to the unfavorable total sales variances. Managers use such detail to question what caused the company to sell more golf balls and fewer drivers. Managers also use this information to evaluate and even reward their salespeople. Extra compensation is paid to salespeople who contribute to a higher profit margin. Finally, with multiple products, the sales volume variance can be separated into a *sales mix variance* and a *sales quantity variance*. The sales mix variance is the difference between the actual and budgeted sales mix of the products. The sales quantity variance is the difference between the total actual and total budgeted quantity of units sold.

Decision Maker

Sales Manager The current performance report reveals a large favorable sales volume variance but an unfavorable sales price variance. You did not expect to see a large increase in sales volume. What steps do you take to analyze this situation? [Answer—p. 302]

Demonstration Problem

Pacific Company provides the following information about its budgeted and actual results for June 2009. Although the expected June volume was 25,000 units produced and sold, the company actually produced and sold 27,000 units as detailed here:

	Budget (25,000 units)	Actual (27,000 units)
Selling price	$5.00 per unit	$5.23 per unit
Variable costs (per unit)		
Direct materials	1.24 per unit	1.12 per unit
Direct labor	1.50 per unit	1.40 per unit
Factory supplies*	0.25 per unit	0.37 per unit
Utilities*	0.50 per unit	0.60 per unit
Selling costs	0.40 per unit	0.34 per unit

[continued on next page]

[continued from previous page]

Fixed costs (per month)		
Depreciation—machinery*	$3,750	$3,710
Depreciation—building*	2,500	2,500
General liability insurance	1,200	1,250
Property taxes on office equipment	500	485
Other administrative expense	750	900

* Indicates factory overhead item; $0.75 per unit or $3 per direct labor hour for variable overhead, and $0.25 per unit or $1 per direct labor hour for fixed overhead.

Standard costs based on expected output of 25,000 units

	Per Unit of Output	Quantity to Be Used	Total Cost
Direct materials, 4 oz. @ $0.31/oz.	$1.24/unit	100,000 oz.	$31,000
Direct labor, 0.25 hrs. @ $6.00/hr.	1.50/unit	6,250 hrs.	37,500
Overhead	1.00/unit		25,000

Actual costs incurred to produce 27,000 units

	Per Unit of Output	Quantity Used	Total Cost
Direct materials, 4 oz. @ $0.28/oz.	$1.12/unit	108,000 oz.	$30,240
Direct labor, 0.20 hrs. @ $7.00/hr.	1.40/unit	5,400 hrs.	37,800
Overhead	1.20/unit		32,400

Standard costs based on expected output of 27,000 units

	Per Unit of Output	Quantity to Be Used	Total Cost
Direct materials, 4 oz. @ $0.31/oz.	$1.24/unit	108,000 oz.	$33,480
Direct labor, 0.25 hrs. @ $6.00/hr.	1.50/unit	6,750 hrs.	40,500
Overhead			26,500

Required

1. Prepare June flexible budgets showing expected sales, costs, and net income assuming 20,000, 25,000, and 30,000 units of output produced and sold.
2. Prepare a flexible budget performance report that compares actual results with the amounts budgeted if the actual volume had been expected.
3. Apply variance analysis for direct materials, for direct labor, and for overhead.
4. Prepare journal entries to record standard costs, and price and quantity variances, for: (*a*) direct materials, (*b*) direct labor, and (*c*) factory overhead.

Planning the Solution

- Prepare a table showing the expected results at the three specified levels of output. Compute the variable costs by multiplying the per unit variable costs by the expected volumes. Include fixed costs at the given amounts. Combine the amounts in the table to show total variable costs, contribution margin, total fixed costs, and income from operations.
- Prepare a table showing the actual results and the amounts that should be incurred at 27,000 units. Show any differences in the third column and label them with an *F* for favorable if they increase income or a *U* for unfavorable if they decrease income.
- Using the chapter's format, compute these total variances and the individual variances requested:
  - Total materials variance (including the direct materials quantity variance and the direct materials price variance).

- Total direct labor variance (including the direct labor efficiency variance and rate variance).
- Total overhead variance (including both variable and fixed overhead variances and their component variances).

Solution to Demonstration Problem

1.

PACIFIC COMPANY
Flexible Budgets
For Month Ended June 30, 2009

	Flexible Budget		Flexible Budget for Unit Sales of 20,000	Flexible Budget for Unit Sales of 25,000	Flexible Budget for Unit Sales of 30,000
	Variable Amount per Unit	Total Fixed Cost			
Sales	$5.00		$100,000	$125,000	$150,000
Variable costs					
Direct materials	1.24		24,800	31,000	37,200
Direct labor	1.50		30,000	37,500	45,000
Factory supplies	0.25		5,000	6,250	7,500
Utilities	0.50		10,000	12,500	15,000
Selling costs	0.40		8,000	10,000	12,000
Total variable costs	3.89		77,800	97,250	116,700
Contribution margin	$1.11		22,200	27,750	33,300
Fixed costs					
Depreciation—machinery		$3,750	3,750	3,750	3,750
Depreciation—building		2,500	2,500	2,500	2,500
General liability insurance		1,200	1,200	1,200	1,200
Property taxes on office equipment		500	500	500	500
Other administrative expense		750	750	750	750
Total fixed costs		$8,700	8,700	8,700	8,700
Income from operations			$ 13,500	$ 19,050	$ 24,600

2.

PACIFIC COMPANY
Flexible Budget Performance Report
For Month Ended June 30, 2009

	Flexible Budget	Actual Results	Variance*
Sales (27,000 units)	$135,000	$141,210	**$6,210 F**
Variable costs			
Direct materials	33,480	30,240	**3,240 F**
Direct labor	40,500	37,800	**2,700 F**
Factory supplies	6,750	9,990	**3,240 U**
Utilities	13,500	16,200	**2,700 U**
Selling costs	10,800	9,180	**1,620 F**
Total variable costs	105,030	103,410	**1,620 F**
Contribution margin	29,970	37,800	**7,830 F**
Fixed costs			
Depreciation—machinery	3,750	3,710	**40 F**
Depreciation—building	2,500	2,500	**0**
General liability insurance	1,200	1,250	**50 U**
Property taxes on office equipment	500	485	**15 F**
Other administrative expense	750	900	**150 U**
Total fixed costs	8,700	8,845	**145 U**
Income from operations	$ 21,270	$ 28,955	**$7,685 F**

* F = Favorable variance; U = Unfavorable variance.

3. Variance analysis of materials, labor, and overhead costs.

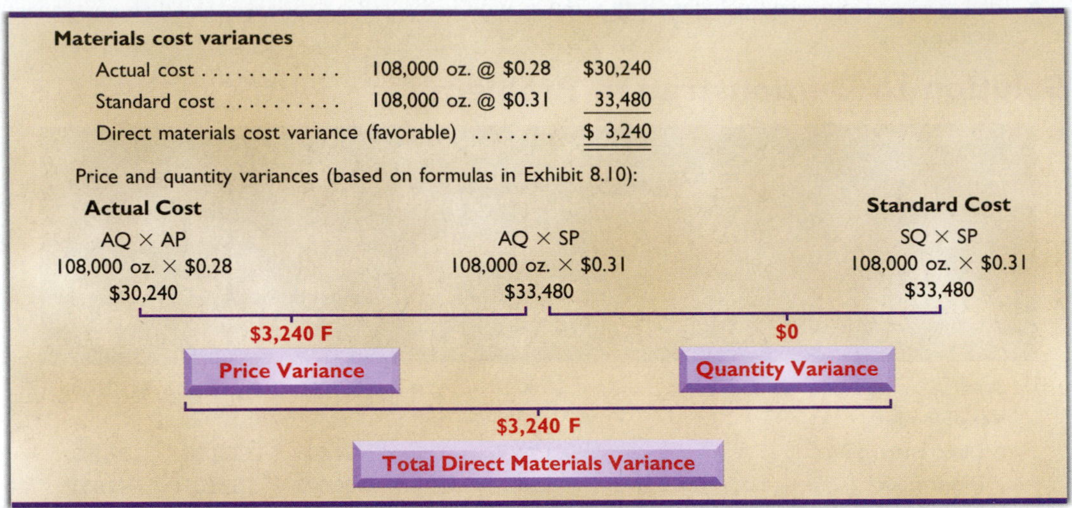
Materials cost variances

Actual cost	108,000 oz. @ $0.28	$30,240
Standard cost	108,000 oz. @ $0.31	33,480
Direct materials cost variance (favorable)		$ 3,240

Price and quantity variances (based on formulas in Exhibit 8.10):

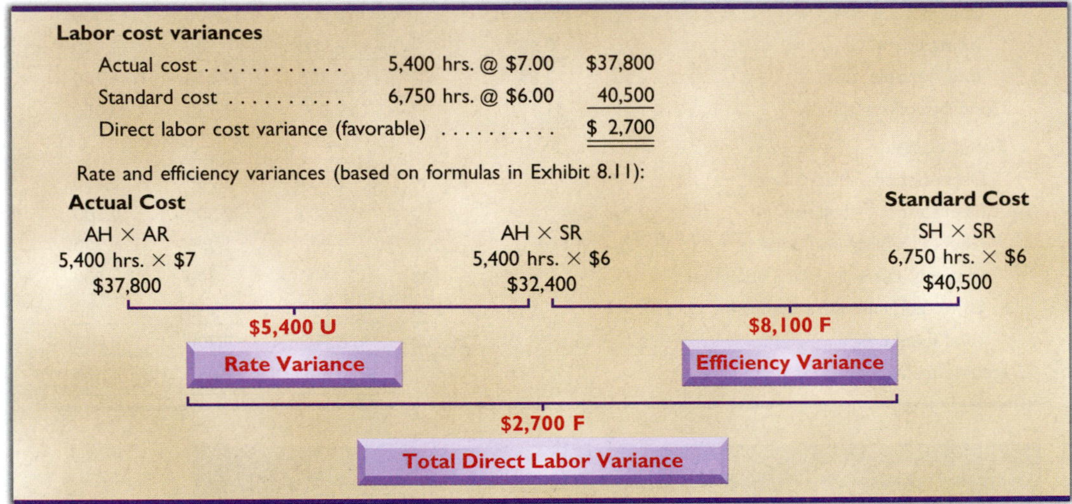
Labor cost variances

Actual cost	5,400 hrs. @ $7.00	$37,800
Standard cost	6,750 hrs. @ $6.00	40,500
Direct labor cost variance (favorable)		$ 2,700

Rate and efficiency variances (based on formulas in Exhibit 8.11):

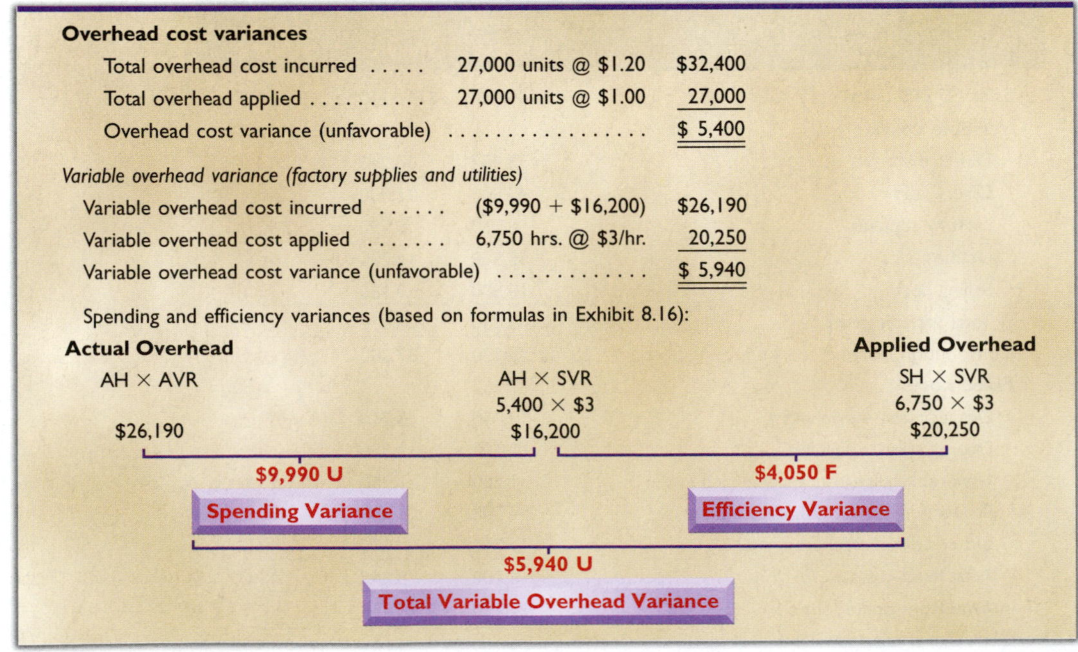
Overhead cost variances

Total overhead cost incurred	27,000 units @ $1.20	$32,400
Total overhead applied	27,000 units @ $1.00	27,000
Overhead cost variance (unfavorable)		$ 5,400

Variable overhead variance (factory supplies and utilities)

Variable overhead cost incurred	($9,990 + $16,200)	$26,190
Variable overhead cost applied	6,750 hrs. @ $3/hr.	20,250
Variable overhead cost variance (unfavorable)		$ 5,940

Spending and efficiency variances (based on formulas in Exhibit 8.16):

[continued on next page]

[continued from previous page]

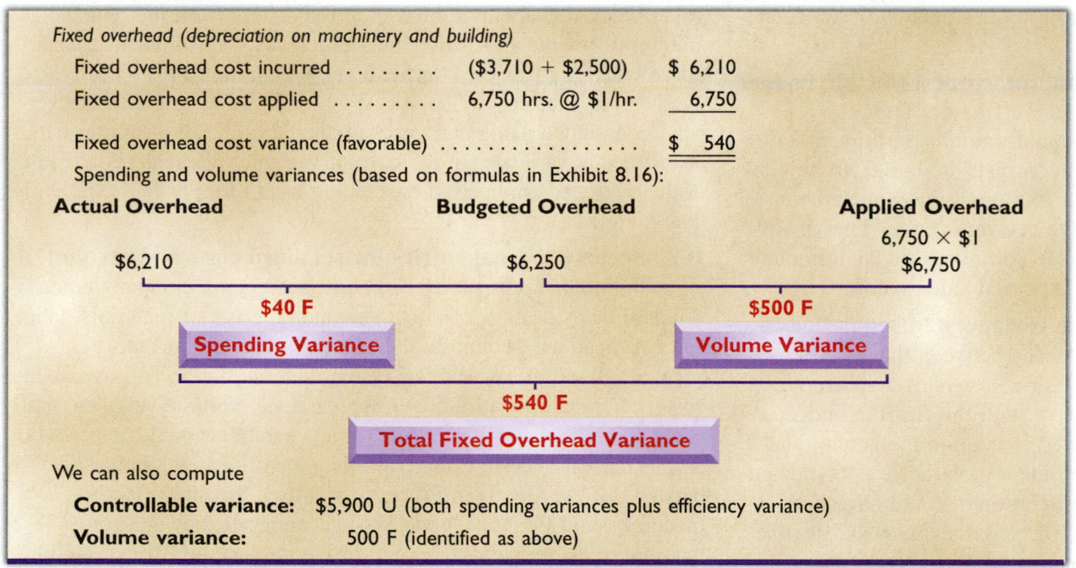

Fixed overhead (depreciation on machinery and building)

Fixed overhead cost incurred	($3,710 + $2,500)	$ 6,210
Fixed overhead cost applied	6,750 hrs. @ $1/hr.	6,750
Fixed overhead cost variance (favorable)		$ 540

Spending and volume variances (based on formulas in Exhibit 8.16):

We can also compute

Controllable variance: $5,900 U (both spending variances plus efficiency variance)

Volume variance: 500 F (identified as above)

4.

		Dr.	Cr.
a.	Goods in Process Inventory	33,480	
	Direct Materials Price Variance		3,240
	Raw Materials Inventory		30,240
b.	Goods in Process Inventory	40,500	
	Direct Labor Rate Variance	5,400	
	Direct Labor Efficiency Variance		8,100
	Factory Payroll		37,800
c.	Goods in Process Inventory*	27,000	
	Variable Overhead Spending Variance	9,990	
	Variable Overhead Efficiency Variance		4,050
	Fixed Overhead Spending Variance		40
	Fixed Overhead Volume Variance		500
	Factory Overhead**		32,400

* $20,250 + $6,750 **$26,190 + $6,210

Summary

C1 Define *standard costs* and explain their computation and uses. Standard costs are the normal costs that should be incurred to produce a product or perform a service. They should be based on a careful examination of the processes used to produce a product or perform a service as well as the quantities and prices that should be incurred in carrying out those processes. On a performance report, standard costs (which are flexible budget amounts) are compared to actual costs, and the differences are presented as variances.

C2 Describe variances and what they reveal about performance. Management can use variances to monitor and control activities. Total cost variances can be broken into price and quantity variances to direct management's attention to those responsible for quantities used and prices paid.

C3 Explain how standard cost information is useful for management by exception. Standard cost accounting provides management information about costs that differ from budgeted (expected) amounts. Performance reports disclose the costs or areas of operations that have significant variances from budgeted amounts. This allows managers to focus attention on the exceptions and less attention on areas proceeding normally.

A1 Compare fixed and flexible budgets. A fixed budget shows the revenues and costs expected to occur at a specified volume level. If actual volume is at some other level, the amounts in the fixed budget do not provide a reasonable basis for evaluating actual performance. A flexible budget expresses variable costs in per unit terms so that it can be used to develop budgeted amounts for any volume level within the relevant range. Thus, managers compute budgeted amounts for evaluation after a period for the volume that actually occurred.

A2 Analyze changes in sales from expected amounts. Actual sales can differ from budgeted sales, and managers can investigate this difference by computing both the sales price and sales volume variances. The *sales price variance* refers to that portion of total variance resulting from a difference between actual and budgeted selling prices. The *sales volume variance* refers to that portion of total variance resulting from a difference between actual and budgeted sales quantities.

P1 **Prepare a flexible budget and interpret a flexible budget performance report.** To prepare a flexible budget, we express each variable cost as a constant amount per unit of sales (or as a percent of sales dollars). In contrast, the budgeted amount of each fixed cost is expressed as a total amount expected to occur at any sales volume within the relevant range. The flexible budget is then determined using these computations and amounts for fixed and variable costs at the expected sales volume.

P2 **Compute materials and labor variances.** Materials and labor variances are due to differences between the actual costs incurred and the budgeted costs. The price (or rate) variance is computed by comparing the actual cost with the flexible budget amount that should have been incurred to acquire the actual quantity of resources. The quantity (or efficiency) variance is computed by comparing the flexible budget amount that should have been incurred to acquire the actual quantity of resources with the flexible budget amount that should have been incurred to acquire the standard quantity of resources.

P3 **Compute overhead variances.** Overhead variances are due to differences between the actual overhead costs incurred and the overhead applied to production. An overhead spending variance arises when the actual amount incurred differs from the budgeted amount of overhead. An overhead efficiency (or volume) variance arises when the flexible overhead budget amount differs from the overhead applied to production. It is important to realize that overhead is assigned using an overhead allocation base, meaning that an efficiency variance (in the case of variable overhead) is a result of the overhead application base being used more or less efficiently than planned.

P4 **Prepare journal entries for standard costs and account for price and quantity variances.** When a company records standard costs in its accounts, the standard costs of materials, labor, and overhead are debited to the Goods in Process Inventory account. Based on an analysis of the material, labor, and overhead costs, each quantity variance, price variance, volume variance, and controllable variance is recorded in a separate account. At period-end, if the variances are material, they are allocated among the balances of the Goods in Process Inventory, Finished Goods Inventory, and Cost of Goods Sold accounts. If they are not material, they are simply debited or credited to the Cost of Goods Sold account.

Guidance Answers to **Decision Maker** and **Decision Ethics**

Entrepreneur From the complaints, this performance report appears to compare actual results with a fixed budget. This comparison is useful in determining whether the amount of work actually performed was more or less than planned, but it is not useful in determining whether the divisions were more or less efficient than planned. If the two consulting divisions worked on more assignments than expected, some costs will certainly increase. Therefore, you should prepare a flexible budget using the actual number of consulting assignments and then compare actual performance to the flexible budget.

Human Resource Manager As HR manager, you should investigate the causes for any labor-related variances although you may not be responsible for them. An unfavorable labor efficiency variance occurs because more labor hours than standard were used during the period. There are at least three possible reasons for this: (1) materials quality could be poor, resulting in more labor consumption due to rework; (2) unplanned interruptions (strike, breakdowns, accidents) could have occurred during the period; and (3) the production manager could have used a different labor mix to expedite orders. This new labor mix could have consisted of a larger proportion of untrained labor, which resulted in more labor hours.

Internal Auditor Although the manager's actions might not be unethical, this action is undesirable. The internal auditor should report this behavior, possibly recommending that for the purchase of such discretionary items, the manager must provide budgetary requests using an activity-based budgeting process. The internal auditor would then be given full authority to verify this budget request.

Sales Manager The unfavorable sales price variance suggests that actual prices were lower than budgeted prices. As the sales manager, you want to know the reasons for a lower than expected price. Perhaps your salespeople lowered the price of certain products by offering quantity discounts. You then might want to know what prompted them to offer the quantity discounts (perhaps competitors were offering discounts). You want to break the sales volume variance into both the sales mix and sales quantity variances. You could find that although the sales quantity variance is favorable, the sales mix variance is not. Then you need to investigate why the actual sales mix differs from the budgeted sales mix.

Guidance Answers to **Quick Checks**

1. *b*
2. The first step is classifying each cost as variable or fixed.
3. A fixed budget is prepared using an expected volume of sales or production. A flexible budget is prepared using the actual volume of activity.
4. The contribution margin equals sales less variable costs.
5. *c*
6. It is the difference between actual cost and standard cost.

7. *a*; Total actual hours: 2,500 × 2.5 = 6,250
   Total standard hours: 2,500 × 2.0 = 5,000
   Efficiency variance = (6,250 − 5,000) × $3.00
   = $3,750 U
8. *b*; Rate variance = ($3.10 − $3.00) × 6,250 = $625 U
9. Yes, this will occur when the materials quantity variance is more than the materials price variance.
10. The overhead volume variance is favorable when the actual operating level is higher than the expected level.
11. *b*
12.

Goods in Process Inventory	75,700	
Direct Materials Price Variance	1,300	
Direct Materials Quantity Variance		3,800
Raw Materials Inventory		73,200

13. If the variances are material, they should be prorated among the Goods in Process Inventory, Finished Goods Inventory, and Cost of Goods Sold accounts. If they are not material, they can be closed to Cost of Goods Sold.

Key Terms

mhhe.com/wildMA2e

Key Terms are available at the book's Website for learning and testing in an online Flashcard Format.

Budget report (p. 278)
Budgetary control (p. 278)
Controllable variance (p. 291)
Cost variance (p. 284)
Efficiency variance (p. 291)
Favorable variance (p. 279)
Fixed budget (p. 279)
Fixed budget performance report (p. 279)
Flexible budget (p. 280)
Flexible budget performance report (p. 282)
Management by exception (p. 294)
Overhead cost variance (p. 290)
Price variance (p. 282)
Quantity variance (p. 282)
Spending variance (p. 291)
Standard costs (p. 283)
Unfavorable variance (p. 279)
Variance analysis (p. 282)
Volume variance (p. 291)

Multiple Choice Quiz

Answers on p. 319

mhhe.com/wildMA2e

Additional Quiz Questions are available at the book's Website.

Quiz8

1. A company predicts its production and sales will be 24,000 units. At that level of activity, its fixed costs are budgeted at $300,000, and its variable costs are budgeted at $246,000. If its activity level declines to 20,000 units, what will be its fixed costs and its variable costs?
   a. Fixed, $300,000; variable, $246,000
   b. Fixed, $250,000; variable, $205,000
   c. Fixed, $300,000; variable, $205,000
   d. Fixed, $250,000; variable, $246,000
   e. Fixed, $300,000; variable, $300,000
2. Using the following information about a single product company, compute its total actual cost of direct materials used.
   - Direct materials standard cost: 5 lbs. × $2 per lb. = $10.
   - Total direct materials cost variance: $15,000 unfavorable.
   - Actual direct materials used: 300,000 lbs.
   - Actual units produced: 60,000 units.

   a. $585,000
   b. $600,000
   c. $300,000
   d. $315,000
   e. $615,000
3. A company uses four hours of direct labor to produce a product unit. The standard direct labor cost is $20 per hour. This period the company produced 20,000 units and used 84,160 hours of direct labor at a total cost of $1,599,040. What is its labor rate variance for the period?
   a. $83,200 F
   b. $84,160 U
   c. $84,160 F
   d. $83,200 U
   e. $ 960 F
4. A company's standard for a unit of its single product is $6 per unit in variable overhead (4 hours × $1.50 per hour). Actual data for the period show variable overhead costs of $150,000 and production of 24,000 units. Its total variable overhead cost variance is
   a. $ 6,000 F.
   b. $ 6,000 U.
   c. $114,000 U.
   d. $114,000 F.
   e. $ 0.
5. A company's standard for a unit of its single product is $4 per unit in fixed overhead ($24,000 total/6,000 units budgeted). Actual data for the period show total actual fixed overhead of $24,100 and production of 4,800 units. Its volume variance is
   a. $4,800 U.
   b. $4,800 F.
   c. $ 100 U.
   d. $ 100 F.
   e. $4,900 U.

Discussion Questions

1. What limits the usefulness to managers of fixed budget performance reports?
2. Identify the main purpose of a flexible budget for managers.
3. Prepare a flexible budget performance report title (in proper form) for Spalding Company for the calendar year 2009. Why is a proper title important for this or any report?
4. What type of analysis does a flexible budget performance report help management perform?
5. In what sense can a variable cost be considered constant?
6. What department is usually responsible for a direct labor rate variance? What department is usually responsible for a direct labor efficiency variance? Explain.
7. What is a price variance? What is a quantity variance?
8. What is the purpose of using standard costs?
9. In an analysis of fixed overhead cost variances, what is the volume variance?
10. What is the predetermined standard overhead rate? How is it computed?
11. In general, variance analysis is said to provide information about ________ and ________ variances.
12. In an analysis of overhead cost variances, what is the controllable variance and what causes it?
13. What are the relations among standard costs, flexible budgets, variance analysis, and management by exception?
14. How can the manager of a music department of a **Best Buy** retail store use flexible budgets to enhance performance?

15. Is it possible for a retail store such as **Circuit City** to use variances in analyzing its operating performance? Explain.

16. Assume that **Apple** is budgeted to operate at 80% of capacity but actually operates at 75% of capacity. What effect will the 5% deviation have on its controllable variance? Its volume variance?

Denotes Discussion Questions that involve decision making.

Most materials in this section are available in McGraw-Hill's Connect connect

QUICK STUDY

QS 8-1
Flexible budget performance report
P1

Quail Company reports the following selected financial results for May. For the level of production achieved in May, the budgeted amounts would be sales, $650,000; variable costs, $375,000; and fixed costs, $150,000. Prepare a flexible budget performance report for May.

Sales (100,000 units)	$637,500
Variable costs	356,250
Fixed costs	150,000

QS 8-2
Labor cost variances
C2 P2

Martin Company's output for the current period results in a $10,000 unfavorable direct labor rate variance and a $5,000 unfavorable direct labor efficiency variance. Production for the current period was assigned a $200,000 standard direct labor cost. What is the actual total direct labor cost for the current period?

QS 8-3
Materials cost variances
C2 P2

Blanda Company's output for the current period was assigned a $300,000 standard direct materials cost. The direct materials variances included a $24,000 favorable price variance and a $4,000 favorable quantity variance. What is the actual total direct materials cost for the current period?

QS 8-4
Materials cost variances
C2 P2

For the current period, Roja Company's manufacturing operations yield an $8,000 unfavorable price variance on its direct materials usage. The actual price per pound of material is $156; the standard price is $154. How many pounds of material are used in the current period?

QS 8-5
Management by exception
C3 

Managers use *management by exception* for control purposes. (1) Describe the concept of management by exception. (2) Explain how standard costs help managers apply this concept to monitor and control costs.

QS 8-6
Overhead cost variances P3

Gohan Company's output for the current period yields a $12,000 favorable overhead volume variance and a $21,500 unfavorable overhead controllable variance. Standard overhead charged to production for the period is $410,000. What is the actual total overhead cost incurred for the period?

QS 8-7
Preparing overhead entries P4

Refer to the information in QS 8-6. Gohan records standard costs in its accounts. Prepare the journal entry to charge overhead costs to the Goods in Process Inventory account and to record any variances.

QS 8-8
Computing sales price and volume variances
A2

Wills Company specializes in selling used trucks. During the first six months of 2009, the dealership sold 50 trucks at an average price of $18,000 each. The budget for the first six months of 2009 was to sell 45 trucks at an average price of $19,000 each. Compute the dealership's sales price variance and sales volume variance for the first six months of 2009.

QS 8-9
Overhead cost variances
P3

Harp Company applies overhead using machine hours and reports the following information. Compute the total variable overhead cost variance.

Actual machine hours used	4,950 hours
Standard machine hours	5,000 hours
Actual variable overhead rate per hour	$2.10
Standard variable overhead rate per hour	$2.00

QS 8-10
Overhead spending and efficiency variances P3

Refer to the information from QS 8-9. Compute the variable overhead spending variance and the variable overhead efficiency variance.

connect *Most materials in this section are available in McGraw-Hill's Connect*

EXERCISES

Exercise 8-1
Preparation of flexible budgets
P1

Tryon Company's fixed budget for the first quarter of calendar year 2009 reveals the following. Prepare flexible budgets following the format of Exhibit 8.3 that show variable costs per unit, fixed costs, and three different flexible budgets for sales volumes of 14,500, 15,000, and 15,500 units.

Sales (15,000 units)		$3,030,000
Cost of goods sold		
Direct materials	$345,000	
Direct labor	705,000	
Production supplies	405,000	
Plant manager salary	90,000	1,545,000
Gross profit		1,485,000
Selling expenses		
Sales commissions	150,000	
Packaging	240,000	
Advertising	100,000	490,000
Administrative expenses		
Administrative salaries	110,000	
Depreciation—office equip.	60,000	
Insurance	48,000	
Office rent	54,000	272,000
Income from operations		$ 723,000

Check Income (at 14,500 units), $683,500

Exercise 8-2
Classification of costs as fixed or variable
P1 

RTEX Company manufactures and sells mountain bikes. It normally operates eight hours a day, five days a week. Using this information, classify each of the following costs as fixed or variable. If additional information would affect your decision, describe the information.

a. Management salaries
b. Incoming shipping expenses
c. Office supplies
d. Taxes on property
e. Gas used for heating
f. Direct labor
g. Repair expense for tools
h. Depreciation on tools
i. Pension cost
j. Bike frames
k. Screws for assembly

Exercise 8-3
Preparation of a flexible budget performance report

A1

Hall Company's fixed budget performance report for June follows. The $660,000 budgeted expenses include $450,000 variable expenses and $210,000 fixed expenses. Actual expenses include $200,000 fixed expenses. Prepare a flexible budget performance report that shows any variances between budgeted results and actual results. List fixed and variable expenses separately.

	Fixed Budget	Actual Results	Variances
Sales (in units)	9,000	7,900	
Sales (in dollars)	$720,000	$647,800	$72,200 U
Total expenses	660,000	606,850	53,150 F
Income from operations	$ 60,000	$ 40,950	$19,050 U

Check Income variance, $13,950 F

Exercise 8-4
Preparation of a flexible budget performance report

A1

Burton Company's fixed budget performance report for July follows. The $675,000 budgeted expenses include $634,500 variable expenses and $40,500 fixed expenses. Actual expenses include $52,500 fixed expenses. Prepare a flexible budget performance report showing any variances between budgeted and actual results. List fixed and variable expenses separately.

	Fixed Budget	Actual Results	Variances
Sales (in units)	9,000	11,400	
Sales (in dollars)	$900,000	$1,140,000	$240,000 F
Total expenses	675,000	810,000	135,000 U
Income from operations	$225,000	$ 330,000	$105,000 F

Check Income variance, $34,200 F

Exercise 8-5
Computation and interpretation of labor variances C2 P2

Check October rate variance, $14,880 F

After evaluating Pima Company's manufacturing process, management decides to establish standards of 1.4 hours of direct labor per unit of product and $15 per hour for the labor rate. During October, the company uses 3,720 hours of direct labor at a $40,920 total cost to produce 4,000 units of product. In November, the company uses 4,560 hours of direct labor at a $54,720 total cost to produce 3,500 units of product. (1) Compute the rate variance, the efficiency variance, and the total direct labor cost variance for each of these two months. (2) Interpret the October direct labor variances.

Exercise 8-6
Computation and interpretation of total variable and fixed overhead variances

C2 P3

Venture Company set the following standard costs for one unit of its product for 2009.

Direct material (20 lbs. @ $5.00 per lb.)	$100.00
Direct labor (10 hrs. @ $16.00 per hr.)	160.00
Factory variable overhead (10 hrs. @ $8.00 per hr.)	80.00
Factory fixed overhead (10 hrs. @ $3.20 per hr.)	32.00
Standard cost	$372.00

The $11.20 ($8.00 + $3.20) total overhead rate per direct labor hour is based on an expected operating level equal to 75% of the factory's capacity of 50,000 units per month. The following monthly flexible budget information is also available.

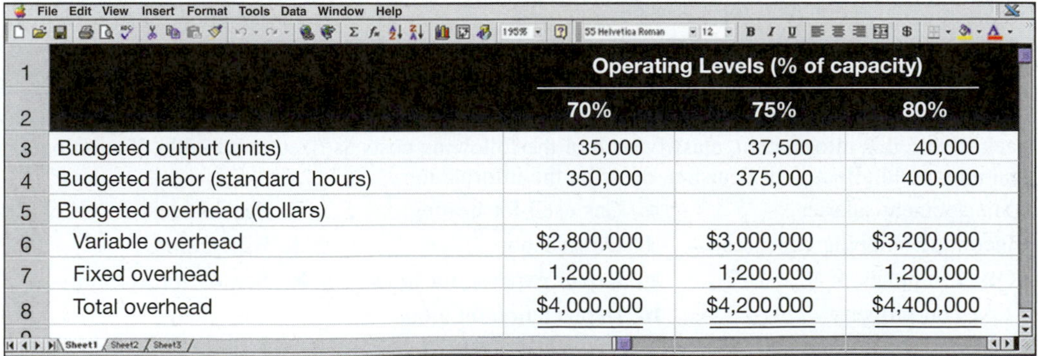

		Operating Levels (% of capacity)		
		70%	75%	80%
3	Budgeted output (units)	35,000	37,500	40,000
4	Budgeted labor (standard hours)	350,000	375,000	400,000
5	Budgeted overhead (dollars)			
6	Variable overhead	$2,800,000	$3,000,000	$3,200,000
7	Fixed overhead	1,200,000	1,200,000	1,200,000
8	Total overhead	$4,000,000	$4,200,000	$4,400,000

During the current month, the company operated at 70% of capacity, employees worked 340,000 hours, and the following actual overhead costs were incurred.

Variable overhead costs	$2,750,000
Fixed overhead costs	1,257,200
Total overhead costs	$4,007,200

(1) Show how the company computed its predetermined overhead application rate per hour for total overhead, variable overhead, and fixed overhead. (2) Compute the variable and fixed overhead variances.

Check (2) Variable overhead cost variance, $50,000 F

Exercise 8-7
Computation and interpretation of overhead spending, efficiency, and volume variances P3

Refer to the information from Exercise 8-6. Compute and interpret the following.

1. Variable overhead spending and efficiency variances.

2. Fixed overhead spending and volume variances.

3. Controllable variance.

Check (2) Variable overhead: Spending, $30,000 U; efficiency, $80,000 F

Exercise 8-8
Computation and interpretation of materials variances
C2 P2 

Listor Company made 3,800 bookshelves using 23,200 board feet of wood costing $290,000. The company's direct materials standards for one bookshelf are 8 board feet of wood at $12 per board foot. (1) Compute the direct materials variances incurred in manufacturing these bookshelves. (2) Interpret the direct materials variances.

Check Price variance, $11,600 U

Exercise 8-9
Materials variances recorded and closed
C3 P4

Refer to Exercise 8-8. Listor Company records standard costs in its accounts and its material variances in separate accounts when it assigns materials costs to the Goods in Process Inventory account. (1) Show the journal entry that both charges the direct materials costs to the Goods in Process Inventory account and records the materials variances in their proper accounts. (2) Assume that Listor's material variances are the only variances accumulated in the accounting period and that they are immaterial. Prepare the adjusting journal entry to close the variance accounts at period-end. (3) Identify the variance that should be investigated according to the management by exception concept. Explain.

Check (2) Cr. to cost of goods sold, $74,800

Exercise 8-10
Computation of total variable and fixed overhead variances
P3

Integra Company expects to operate at 80% of its productive capacity of 52,000 units per month. At this planned level, the company expects to use 26,000 standard hours of direct labor. Overhead is allocated to products using a predetermined standard rate based on direct labor hours. At the 80% capacity level, the total budgeted cost includes $57,200 fixed overhead cost and $280,800 variable overhead cost. In the current month, the company incurred $320,000 actual overhead and 23,000 actual labor hours while producing 37,000 units. (1) Compute its overhead application rate for total overhead, variable overhead, and fixed overhead. (2) Compute its total overhead variance.

Check (1) Variable overhead rate, $10.80 per hour

Exercise 8-11
Computation of volume and controllable overhead variances P3

Refer to the information from Exercise 8-10. Compute the (1) overhead volume variance and (2) overhead controllable variance.

Check (2) $13,050 U

Exercise 8-12
Computing and interpreting sales variances A2

Wiz Electronics sells computers. During May 2009, it sold 500 computers at a $1,000 average price each. The May 2009 fixed budget included sales of 550 computers at an average price of $950 each. (1) Compute the sales price variance and the sales volume variance for May 2009. (2) Interpret the findings.

connect *Most materials in this section are available in McGraw-Hill's Connect*

PROBLEM SET A

Problem 8-1A
Computation of materials, labor, and overhead variances
C2 P2 P3

Beck Company set the following standard unit costs for its single product.

Direct materials (26 lbs. @ $4 per lb.)	$104.00
Direct labor (8 hrs. @ $8 per hr.)	64.00
Factory overhead—variable (8 hrs. @ $5 per hr.)	40.00
Factory overhead—fixed (8 hrs. @ $7 per hr.)	56.00
Total standard cost	$264.00

mhhe.com/wildMA2e

The predetermined overhead rate is based on a planned operating volume of 70% of the productive capacity of 50,000 units per quarter. The following flexible budget information is available.

	Operating Levels		
	60%	70%	80%
Production in units	30,000	35,000	40,000
Standard direct labor hours	240,000	280,000	320,000
Budgeted overhead			
Fixed factory overhead	$1,960,000	$1,960,000	$1,960,000
Variable factory overhead	$1,200,000	$1,400,000	$1,600,000

During the current quarter, the company operated at 80% of capacity and produced 40,000 units of product; actual direct labor totaled 178,600 hours. Units produced were assigned the following standard costs:

Direct materials (1,040,000 lbs. @ $4 per lb.)	$ 4,160,000
Direct labor (320,000 hrs. @ $8 per hr.)	2,560,000
Factory overhead (320,000 hrs. @ $12 per hr.)	3,840,000
Total standard cost	$10,560,000

Actual costs incurred during the current quarter follow:

Direct materials (1,035,000 lbs. @ $4.10)	$ 4,243,500
Direct labor (327,000 hrs. @ $7.75)	2,534,250
Fixed factory overhead costs	1,875,000
Variable factory overhead costs	1,482,717
Total actual costs	$10,135,467

Required

Check (1) Materials variances: Price, $103,500 U; quantity, $20,000 F. (2) Labor variances: Rate, $81,750 F; efficiency, $56,000 U

1. Compute the direct materials cost variance, including its price and quantity variances.
2. Compute the direct labor variance, including its rate and efficiency variances.
3. Compute the total variable overhead and total fixed overhead variances.
4. Compute these variances: (a) variable overhead spending and efficiency, (b) fixed overhead spending and volume, and (c) total overhead controllable.

Problem 8-2A
Preparation and analysis of a flexible budget
P1 A1

Major Company's 2009 master budget included the following fixed budget report. It is based on an expected production and sales volume of 15,000 units.

MAJOR COMPANY Fixed Budget Report For Year Ended December 31, 2009		
Sales		$3,300,000
Cost of goods sold		
Direct materials	$960,000	
Direct labor	240,000	
Machinery repairs (variable cost)	60,000	
Depreciation—plant equipment	300,000	
Utilities ($60,000 is variable)	180,000	
Plant management salaries	210,000	1,950,000
Gross profit		1,350,000
Selling expenses		
Packaging	75,000	
Shipping	105,000	
Sales salary (fixed annual amount)	235,000	415,000
General and administrative expenses		
Advertising expense	100,000	
Salaries	241,000	
Entertainment expense	85,000	426,000
Income from operations		$ 509,000

Required

1. Classify all items listed in the fixed budget as variable or fixed. Also determine their amounts per unit or their amounts for the year, as appropriate.

2. Prepare flexible budgets (see Exhibit 8.3) for the company at sales volumes of 14,000 and 16,000 units.

3. The company's business conditions are improving. One possible result is a sales volume of approximately 18,000 units. The company president is confident that this volume is within the relevant range of existing capacity. How much would operating income increase over the 2009 budgeted amount of $509,000 if this level is reached without increasing capacity?

4. An unfavorable change in business is remotely possible; in this case, production and sales volume for 2009 could fall to 12,000 units. How much income (or loss) from operations would occur if sales volume falls to this level?

Check (2) Budgeted income at 16,000 units, $629,000

(4) Potential operating income, $149,000

Problem 8-3A
Preparation and analysis of a flexible budget performance report

P1 A2

mhhe.com/wildMA2e

Refer to the information in Problem 8-2A. Major Company's actual income statement for 2009 follows.

MAJOR COMPANY Statement of Income from Operations For Year Ended December 31, 2009		
Sales (18,000 units)		$3,948,000
Cost of goods sold		
Direct materials	$1,160,000	
Direct labor	293,000	
Machinery repairs (variable cost)	63,000	
Depreciation—plant equipment	300,000	
Utilities (fixed cost is $147,500)	215,500	
Plant management salaries	220,000	2,251,500
Gross profit		1,696,500
Selling expenses		
Packaging	87,500	
Shipping	118,500	
Sales salary (annual)	253,000	459,000
General and administrative expenses		
Advertising expense	107,000	
Salaries	241,000	
Entertainment expense	88,500	436,500
Income from operations		$ 801,000

Required

1. Prepare a flexible budget performance report for 2009.

Check (1) Variances: Fixed costs, $66,000 U; income, $68,000 U

Analysis Component

2. Analyze and interpret both the (a) sales variance and (b) direct materials variance.

Problem 8-4A
Flexible budget preparation; computation of materials, labor, and overhead variances; and overhead variance report

P1 P2 P3 C2

Silver Company set the following standard costs for one unit of its product.

Direct materials (5 lbs. @ $6 per lb.)	$30.00
Direct labor (2 hrs. @ $12 per hr.)	24.00
Overhead (2 hrs. @ $16.65 per hr.)	33.30
Total standard cost	$87.30

The predetermined overhead rate ($16.65 per direct labor hour) is based on an expected volume of 75% of the factory's capacity of 20,000 units per month. Following are the company's budgeted overhead costs per month at the 75% level.

Overhead Budget (75% Capacity)		
Variable overhead costs		
Indirect materials	$ 21,000	
Indirect labor	96,000	
Power	22,500	
Repairs and maintenance	57,000	
Total variable overhead costs		$196,500
Fixed overhead costs		
Depreciation—building	23,000	
Depreciation—machinery	71,000	
Taxes and insurance	18,000	
Supervision	191,000	
Total fixed overhead costs		303,000
Total overhead costs		$499,500

The company incurred the following actual costs when it operated at 75% of capacity in October.

Direct materials (75,500 lbs. @ $6.10 per lb.)		$ 460,550
Direct labor (29,000 hrs. @ $12.20 per hr.)		353,800
Overhead costs		
Indirect materials	$ 22,500	
Indirect labor	88,800	
Power	21,500	
Repairs and maintenance	60,250	
Depreciation—building	23,000	
Depreciation—machinery	65,000	
Taxes and insurance	18,100	
Supervision	185,000	484,150
Total costs		$1,298,500

Required

1. Examine the monthly overhead budget to (a) determine the costs per unit for each variable overhead item and its total per unit costs, and (b) identify the total fixed costs per month.

2. Prepare flexible overhead budgets (as in Exhibit 8.12) for October showing the amounts of each variable and fixed cost at the 65%, 75%, and 85% capacity levels.

3. Compute the direct materials cost variance, including its price and quantity variances.

4. Compute the direct labor cost variance, including its rate and efficiency variances.

5. Compute the (a) variable overhead spending and efficiency variances, (b) fixed overhead spending and volume variances, and (c) total overhead controllable variance.

6. Prepare a detailed overhead variance report (as in Exhibit 8.19) that shows the variances for individual items of overhead.

Check (2) Budgeted total overhead at 13,000 units, $473,300.

(3) Materials variances: Price, $7,550 U; quantity, $3,000 U

(4) Labor variances: Rate, $5,800 U; efficiency, $12,000 F

Problem 8-5A
Materials, labor, and overhead variances; and overhead variance report
C2 P2 P3

Green Company has set the following standard costs per unit for the product it manufactures.

Direct materials (15 lbs. @ $3.90 per lb.)	$ 58.50
Direct labor (4 hrs. @ $18 per hr.)	72.00
Overhead (4 hrs. @ $4.20 per hr.)	16.80
Total standard cost	$147.30

The predetermined overhead rate is based on a planned operating volume of 80% of the productive capacity of 10,000 units per month. The following flexible budget information is available.

	Operating Levels		
	70%	80%	90%
Production in units	7,000	8,000	9,000
Standard direct labor hours	28,000	32,000	36,000
Budgeted overhead			
Variable overhead costs			
Indirect materials	$ 14,000	$ 16,000	$ 18,000
Indirect labor	20,300	23,200	26,100
Power	5,600	6,400	7,200
Maintenance	38,500	44,000	49,500
Total variable costs	78,400	89,600	100,800
Fixed overhead costs			
Rent of factory building	15,000	15,000	15,000
Depreciation—machinery	10,000	10,000	10,000
Supervisory salaries	19,800	19,800	19,800
Total fixed costs	44,800	44,800	44,800
Total overhead costs	$123,200	$134,400	$145,600

During May, the company operated at 90% of capacity and produced 9,000 units, incurring the following actual costs.

Direct materials (139,000 lbs. @ $3.80 per lb.)		$ 528,200
Direct labor (33,000 hrs. @ $18.50 per hr.)		610,500
Overhead costs		
Indirect materials	$16,000	
Indirect labor	27,500	
Power	7,200	
Maintenance	42,000	
Rent of factory building	15,000	
Depreciation—machinery	10,000	
Supervisory salaries	24,000	141,700
Total costs		$1,280,400

Required

1. Compute the direct materials variance, including its price and quantity variances.

2. Compute the direct labor variance, including its rate and efficiency variances.

3. Compute these variances: (a) variable overhead spending and efficiency, (b) fixed overhead spending and volume, and (c) total overhead controllable.

4. Prepare a detailed overhead variance report (as in Exhibit 8.19) that shows the variances for individual items of overhead.

Check (1) Materials variances: Price, $13,900 F; quantity, $15,600 U (2) Labor variances: Rate, $16,500 U; efficiency, $54,000 F

Problem 8-6A
Materials, labor, and overhead variances recorded and analyzed
C3 P4 

Brose Company's standard cost accounting system recorded this information from its December operations.

Standard direct materials cost	$104,000
Direct materials quantity variance (unfavorable)	3,000
Direct materials price variance (favorable)	550
Actual direct labor cost	90,000
Direct labor efficiency variance (favorable)	6,850
Direct labor rate variance (unfavorable)	1,200
Actual overhead cost	375,000
Volume variance (unfavorable)	13,000
Controllable variance (unfavorable)	9,000

Check (1) Dr. Goods in Process Inventory (for overhead), $353,000

Required

1. Prepare December 31 journal entries to record the company's costs and variances for the month. (Do not prepare the journal entry to close the variances.)

Analysis Component

2. Identify the areas that would attract the attention of a manager who uses management by exception. Explain what action(s) the manager should consider.

PROBLEM SET B

Problem 8-1B
Computation of materials, labor, and overhead variances
C2 P2 P3

Krug Company set the following standard unit costs for its single product.

Direct materials (5 lbs. @ $2 per lb.)	$10.00
Direct labor (0.3 hrs. @ $15 per hr.)	4.50
Factory overhead—variable (0.3 hrs. @ $10 per hr.)	3.00
Factory overhead—fixed (0.3 hrs. @ $14 per hr.)	4.20
Total standard cost	$21.70

The predetermined overhead rate is based on a planned operating volume of 80% of the productive capacity of 600,000 units per quarter. The following flexible budget information is available.

	Operating Levels		
	70%	80%	90%
Production in units	420,000	480,000	540,000
Standard direct labor hours	126,000	144,000	162,000
Budgeted overhead			
Fixed factory overhead	$2,016,000	$2,016,000	$2,016,000
Variable factory overhead	1,260,000	1,440,000	1,620,000

During the current quarter, the company operated at 70% of capacity and produced 420,000 units of product; direct labor hours worked were 125,000. Units produced were assigned the following standard costs:

Direct materials (2,100,000 lbs. @ $2 per lb.)	$4,200,000
Direct labor (126,000 hrs. @ $15 per hr.)	1,890,000
Factory overhead (126,000 hrs. @ $24 per hr.)	3,024,000
Total standard cost	$9,114,000

Actual costs incurred during the current quarter follow:

Direct materials (2,000,000 lbs. @ $2.15)	$4,300,000
Direct labor (125,000 hrs. @ $15.50)	1,937,500
Fixed factory overhead costs	1,960,000
Variable factory overhead costs	1,200,000
Total actual costs	$9,397,500

Required

Check (1) Materials variances: Price, $300,000 U; quantity, $200,000 F (2) Labor variances: Rate, $62,500 U; efficiency, $15,000 F

1. Compute the direct materials cost variance, including its price and quantity variances.
2. Compute the direct labor variance, including its rate and efficiency variances.
3. Compute the total variable overhead and total fixed overhead variances.
4. Compute these variances: (a) variable overhead spending and efficiency, (b) fixed overhead spending and volume, and (c) total overhead controllable.

Problem 8-2B
Preparation and analysis of a flexible budget P1 A1

Toronto Company's 2009 master budget included the following fixed budget report. It is based on an expected production and sales volume of 10,000 units.

TORONTO COMPANY Fixed Budget Report For Year Ended December 31, 2009		
Sales		$1,500,000
Cost of goods sold		
Direct materials	$600,000	
Direct labor	130,000	
Machinery repairs (variable cost)	28,500	
Depreciation—machinery	125,000	
Utilities (25% is variable cost)	100,000	
Plant manager salaries	70,000	1,053,500
Gross profit		446,500
Selling expenses		
Packaging	40,000	
Shipping	58,000	
Sales salary (fixed annual amount)	80,000	178,000
General and administrative expenses		
Advertising	40,500	
Salaries	120,500	
Entertainment expense	45,000	206,000
Income from operations		$ 62,500

Required

1. Classify all items listed in the fixed budget as variable or fixed. Also determine their amounts per unit or their amounts for the year, as appropriate.

2. Prepare flexible budgets (see Exhibit 8.3) for the company at sales volumes of 9,500 and 10,500 units.

Check (2) Budgeted income at 10,500 units, $93,425

3. The company's business conditions are improving. One possible result is a sales volume of approximately 12,000 units. The company president is confident that this volume is within the relevant range of existing capacity. How much would operating income increase over the 2009 budgeted amount of $62,500 if this level is reached without increasing capacity?

4. An unfavorable change in business is remotely possible; in this case, production and sales volume for 2009 could fall to 8,000 units. How much income (or loss) from operations would occur if sales volume falls to this level?

(4) Potential operating loss, $(61,200)

Problem 8-3B

Preparation and analysis of a flexible budget performance report

P1 A2

Refer to the information in Problem 8-2B. Toronto Company's actual income statement for 2009 follows.

TORONTO COMPANY Statement of Income from Operations For Year Ended December 31, 2009		
Sales (10,500 units)		$1,596,000
Cost of goods sold		
Direct materials	$612,500	
Direct labor	157,500	
Machinery repairs (variable cost)	26,250	
Depreciation—machinery	125,000	
Utilities (variable cost, $28,000)	105,000	
Plant manager salaries	77,500	1,103,750
Gross profit		492,250
Selling expenses		
Packaging	39,375	
Shipping	54,250	
Sales salary (annual)	81,000	174,625
General and administrative expenses		
Advertising expense	52,000	
Salaries	116,000	
Entertainment expense	50,000	218,000
Income from operations		$ 99,625

Required

Check (1) Variances: Fixed costs, $22,500 U; income, $6,200 F

1. Prepare a flexible budget performance report for 2009.

Analysis Component

2. Analyze and interpret both the (a) sales variance and (b) direct materials variance.

Problem 8-4B

Flexible budget preparation; computation of materials, labor, and overhead variances; and overhead variance report

P1 P2 P3 C2

Stevens Company set the following standard costs for one unit of its product.

Direct materials (9 lb. @ $6 per lb.)	$ 54.00
Direct labor (3 hrs. @ $16 per hr.)	48.00
Overhead (3 hrs. @ $11.75 per hr.)	35.25
Total standard cost	$137.25

The predetermined overhead rate ($11.75 per direct labor hour) is based on an expected volume of 75% of the factory's capacity of 20,000 units per month. Following are the company's budgeted overhead costs per month at the 75% level.

Overhead Budget (75% Capacity)		
Variable overhead costs		
Indirect materials	$ 33,750	
Indirect labor	135,000	
Power	22,500	
Repairs and maintenance	67,500	
Total variable overhead costs		$258,750
Fixed overhead costs		
Depreciation—building	36,000	
Depreciation—machinery	108,000	
Taxes and insurance	27,000	
Supervision	99,000	
Total fixed overhead costs		270,000
Total overhead costs		$528,750

The company incurred the following actual costs when it operated at 75% of capacity in December.

Direct materials (139,000 lbs. @ $6.10)		$ 847,900
Direct labor (43,500 hrs. @ $16.30)		709,050
Overhead costs		
Indirect materials	$ 31,600	
Indirect labor	133,400	
Power	23,500	
Repairs and maintenance	69,700	
Depreciation—building	36,000	
Depreciation—machinery	110,000	
Taxes and insurance	24,500	
Supervision	99,000	527,700
Total costs		$2,084,650

Required

1. Examine the monthly overhead budget to (a) determine the costs per unit for each variable overhead item and its total per unit costs, and (b) identify the total fixed costs per month.

Check (2) Budgeted total overhead at 17,000 units, $563,250

2. Prepare flexible overhead budgets (as in Exhibit 8.12) for December showing the amounts of each variable and fixed cost at the 65%, 75%, and 85% capacity levels.

(3) Materials variances: Price, $13,900 U; quantity, $24,000 U

3. Compute the direct materials cost variance, including its price and quantity variances.

4. Compute the direct labor cost variance, including its rate and efficiency variances.

5. Compute the (a) variable overhead spending and efficiency variances, (b) fixed overhead spending and volume variances, and (c) total overhead controllable variance.

6. Prepare a detailed overhead variance report (as in Exhibit 8.19) that shows the variances for individual items of overhead.

(4) Labor variances: Rate, $13,050 U; efficiency, $24,000 F

Problem 8-5B
Materials, labor, and overhead variances; and overhead variance report
C2 P2 P3

Harris Company has set the following standard costs per unit for the product it manufactures.

Direct materials (5 lbs. @ $3.00 per lb.)	$15
Direct labor (2 hr. @ $20 per hr.)	40
Overhead (2 hr. @ $10 per hr.)	20
Total standard cost	$75

The predetermined overhead rate is based on a planned operating volume of 80% of the productive capacity of 10,000 units per month. The following flexible budget information is available.

	Operating Levels		
	70%	80%	90%
Production in units	7,000	8,000	9,000
Standard direct labor hours	14,000	16,000	18,000
Budgeted overhead			
Variable overhead costs			
Indirect materials	$ 17,500	$ 20,000	$22,500
Indirect labor	28,000	32,000	36,000
Power	7,000	8,000	9,000
Maintenance	3,500	4,000	4,500
Total variable costs	56,000	64,000	72,000
Fixed overhead costs			
Rent of factory building	24,000	24,000	24,000
Depreciation—machinery	40,000	40,000	40,000
Taxes and insurance	4,800	4,800	4,800
Supervisory salaries	27,200	27,200	27,200
Total fixed costs	96,000	96,000	96,000
Total overhead costs	$152,000	$160,000	$168,000

During March, the company operated at 90% of capacity and produced 9,000 units, incurring the following actual costs.

Direct materials (46,000 lbs. @ $2.95 per lb.)		$ 135,700
Direct labor (18,800 hrs. @ $20.10 per hr.)		377,880
Overhead costs		
Indirect materials	$22,000	
Indirect labor	32,000	
Power	9,600	
Maintenance	4,750	
Rent of factory building	24,000	
Depreciation—machinery	39,400	
Taxes and insurance	5,200	
Supervisory salaries	28,000	164,950
Total costs		$678,530

Required

Check (1) Materials variances: Price, $2,300 F; quantity, $3,000 U
(2) Labor variances: Rate, $1,880 U; efficiency, $16,000 U

1. Compute the direct materials cost variance, including its price and quantity variances.
2. Compute the direct labor variance, including its rate and efficiency variances.
3. Compute these variances: (a) variable overhead spending and efficiency, (b) fixed overhead spending and volume, and (c) total overhead controllable.
4. Prepare a detailed overhead variance report (as in Exhibit 8.19) that shows the variances for individual items of overhead.

Problem 8-6B
Materials, labor, and overhead variances recorded and analyzed
C3 P4 

Del Company's standard cost accounting system recorded this information from its June operations.

Standard direct materials cost	$260,000
Direct materials quantity variance (favorable)	10,000
Direct materials price variance (favorable)	3,000
Actual direct labor cost	130,000
Direct labor efficiency variance (favorable)	6,000
Direct labor rate variance (unfavorable)	1,000
Actual overhead cost	500,000
Volume variance (unfavorable)	24,000
Controllable variance (unfavorable)	16,000

Required

Check (1) Dr. Goods in Process Inventory (for overhead), $460,000

1. Prepare journal entries dated June 30 to record the company's costs and variances for the month. (Do not prepare the journal entry to close the variances.)

Analysis Component

2. Identify the areas that would attract the attention of a manager who uses management by exception. Describe what action(s) the manager should consider.

SERIAL PROBLEM

Success Systems

(This serial problem began in Chapter 1 and continues through most of the book. If previous chapter segments were not completed, the serial problem can begin at this point. It is helpful, but not necessary, to use the working papers that accompany the book.)

SP 8 Success Systems' second quarter 2010 fixed budget performance report for its computer furniture operations follows. The $156,000 budgeted expenses include $108,000 in variable expenses for desks and $18,000 in variable expenses for chairs, as well as $30,000 fixed expenses. The actual expenses include $31,000 fixed expenses. Prepare a flexible budget performance report that shows any variances between budgeted results and actual results. List fixed and variable expenses separately.

	Fixed Budget	Actual Results	Variances
Desk sales (in units)	144	150	
Chair sales (in units)	72	80	
Desk sales (in dollars)	$180,000	$186,000	$6,000 F
Chair sales (in dollars)	$ 36,000	$ 41,200	$5,200 F
Total expenses	$156,000	$163,880	$7,880 U
Income from operations	$ 60,000	$ 63,320	$3,320 F

Check Variances: Fixed expenses, $1,000 U

BEYOND THE NUMBERS

REPORTING IN ACTION

C1 

BTN 8-1 Analysis of flexible budgets and standard costs emphasizes the importance of a similar unit of measure for meaningful comparisons and evaluations. When **Best Buy** compiles its financial reports in compliance with GAAP, it applies the same unit of measurement, U.S. dollars, for most measures of business operations. One issue for Best Buy is how best to adjust account values for its subsidiaries that compile financial reports in currencies other than the U.S. dollar.

Required

1. Read Best Buy's Note 1 in Appendix A and identify the financial statement where it reports the annual adjustment for foreign currency translation.
2. Record the annual amount of its foreign currency translation adjustment for the fiscal years 2005 through 2007.

Fast Forward

3. Access Best Buy's financial statements for a fiscal year ending after March 3, 2007, from either its Website [BestBuy.com] or the SEC's EDGAR database [www.SEC.gov]. (a) Identify its foreign currency translation adjustment. (b) Does this adjustment increase or decrease net income? Explain.

COMPARATIVE ANALYSIS

A2

BTN 8-2 The usefulness of budgets, variances, and related analyses often depends on the accuracy of management's estimates of future sales activity.

Required

1. Identify and record the prior three years' sales (in dollars) for both Best Buy, Circuit City, and RadioShack using their financial statements in Appendix A.
2. Using the data in part 1, predict all three companies' sales activity for the next two to three years. (If possible, compare your predictions to actual sales figures for these years.)

ETHICS CHALLENGE

C1

BTN 8-3 Setting materials, labor, and overhead standards is challenging. If standards are set too low, companies might purchase inferior products and employees might not work to their full potential. If standards are set too high, companies could be unable to offer a quality product at a profitable rate and employees could be overworked. The ethical challenge is to set a high but reasonable standard. Assume that as a manager, you are asked to set the standard materials price and quantity for the new 1,000 CKB Mega-Max chip, a technically advanced product. To properly set the price and quantity standards, you assemble a team of specialists to provide input.

Required

Identify four types of specialists that you would assemble to provide information to help set the materials price and quantity standards. Briefly explain why you chose each individual.

COMMUNICATING IN PRACTICE

P4 C2

BTN 8-4 The reason we use the words *favorable* and *unfavorable* when evaluating variances is made clear when we look at the closing of accounts. To see this, consider that (1) all variance accounts are closed at the end of each period (temporary accounts), (2) a favorable variance is always a credit balance, and (3) an unfavorable variance is always a debit balance. Write a one-half page memorandum to your instructor with three parts that answer the three following requirements. (Assume that variance accounts are closed to Cost of Goods Sold.)

Required

1. Does Cost of Goods Sold increase or decrease when closing a favorable variance? Does gross margin increase or decrease when a favorable variance is closed to Cost of Goods Sold? Explain.
2. Does Cost of Goods Sold increase or decrease when closing an unfavorable variance? Does gross margin increase or decrease when an unfavorable variance is closed to Cost of Goods Sold? Explain.
3. Explain the meaning of a favorable variance and an unfavorable variance.

TAKING IT TO THE NET

C1 

BTN 8-5 Access iSixSigma's Website (iSixSigma.com) to search for and read information about *benchmarking* to complete the following requirements.

Required

1. Write a one-paragraph explanation (in layperson's terms) of benchmarking.
2. How does standard costing relate to benchmarking?

TEAMWORK IN ACTION

BTN 8-6 Many service industries link labor rate and time (quantity) standards with their processes. One example is the standard time to board an aircraft. The reason time plays such an important role in the service industry is that it is viewed as a competitive advantage: best service in the shortest amount of time. Although the labor rate component is difficult to observe, the time component of a service delivery standard is often readily apparent—for example, "Lunch will be served in less than five minutes, or it is free."

Required

Break into teams and select two service industries for your analysis. Identify and describe all the time elements each industry uses to create a competitive advantage.

ENTREPRENEURIAL DECISION

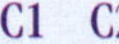  

BTN 8-7 Entrepreneur Chris Martin of Martin Guitar (see Chapter opener) uses a costing system with standard costs for direct materials, direct labor, and overhead costs. Two comments frequently are mentioned in relation to standard costing and variance analysis: "Variances are not explanations" and "Management's goal is not to minimize variances."

Required

Write Chris Martin a short memo (no more than 1 page) interpreting these two comments.

HITTING THE ROAD

BTN 8-8 Training employees to use standard amounts of materials in production is common. Typically large companies invest in this training but small organizations do not. One can observe these different practices in a trip to two different pizza businesses. Visit both a local pizza business and a national pizza chain business and then complete the following.

Required

1. Observe and record the number of raw material items used to make a typical cheese pizza. Also observe how the person making the pizza applies each item when preparing the pizza.
2. Record any differences in how items are applied between the two businesses.
3. Estimate which business is more profitable from your observations. Explain.

GLOBAL DECISION

BTN 8-9 Access the annual report of DSG (at www.DSGiplc.com) for the year ended April 28, 2007. The usefulness of its budgets, variances, and related analyses depends on the accuracy of management's estimates of future sales activity.

Required

1. Identify and record the prior two years' sales (in pounds) for DSG from its income statement.
2. Using the data in part 1, predict sales activity for DSG for the next two years. Explain your prediction process.

ANSWERS TO MULTIPLE CHOICE QUIZ

1. c; Fixed costs remain at \$300,000; Variable costs = (\$246,000/24,000 units) × 20,000 units = \$205,000.
2. e; Budgeted direct materials + Unfavorable variance = Actual cost of direct materials used; or, 60,000 units × \$10 per unit = \$600,000 + \$15,000 U = \$615,000.
3. c; (AH × AR) − (AH × SR) = \$1,599,040 – (84,160 hours × \$20 per hour) = \$84,160 F.
4. b; Actual variable overhead − Variable overhead applied to production = Variable overhead cost variance; or \$150,000 − (96,000 hours × \$1.50 per hour) = \$6,000 U.
5. a; Budgeted fixed overhead − Fixed overhead applied to production = Volume variance; or \$24,000 − (4,800 units × \$4 per unit) = \$4,800 U.

A Look Back

Chapter 8 discussed flexible budgets, variance analysis, and standard costs. It explained how management uses each to control and monitor business activities.

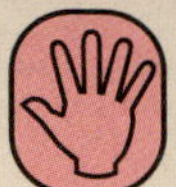

A Look at This Chapter

This chapter describes responsibility accounting, measuring departmental performance, transfer pricing, and allocating common costs across departments. It also identifies managerial reports useful in directing a company's activities.

A Look Ahead

Chapter 10 explains several tools and procedures used in making and evaluating short-term managerial decisions.

Chapter

Decentralization and Performance Evaluation

Learning Objectives

CAP

Conceptual

C1 Explain departmentalization and the role of departmental accounting. *(p. 322)*

C2 Distinguish between direct and indirect expenses. *(p. 324)*

C3 Identify bases for allocating indirect expenses to departments. *(p. 324)*

C4 Explain controllable costs and responsibility accounting. *(p. 333)*

C5 *Appendix 9A*—Explain transfer pricing and methods to set transfer prices. *(p. 339)*

C6 *Appendix 9B*—Describe allocation of joint costs across products. *(p. 341)*

Analytical

A1 Analyze investment centers using return on assets, residual income, and balanced scorecard. *(p. 331)*

A2 Analyze investment centers using profit margin and investment turnover. *(p. 336)*

Procedural

P1 Prepare departmental income statements. *(p. 326)*

P2 Prepare departmental contribution reports. *(p. 329)*

LP9

Decision Feature

On The Green

"The more clicks we can get, the better our future"
—Todd Rath

ROCHESTER, NY—Brothers Tom and Todd Rath paid their college tuition by diving for lost golf balls and then reselling them. Today, their company **RockBottomGolf.com** applies a similar strategy of buying leftover products and reselling them. "Some of our critics refer to us as the 'graveyard of golf,'" explains Tom. "Oftentimes, we may be selling the last 3,000 drivers a manufacturer has ever made. If anyone can find a home for it, we can." The company boasts over 500,000 customers, affectionately referred to as "Rock Heads."

RockBottom's warehouse sports signs with "Scratch," the company's cartoonish, red-bearded caveman mascot. Scratch is surrounded with slogans such as: "A Clean Cave Is a Happy Cave" and "A Happy Rock Head Stays a Rock Head." Though Scratch is goofy, the company is all business. Offering a wide inventory of well-known brands of golf clubs, bags, balls, apparel, and accessories, the company buys in large lots and strives to keep overhead low. For example, they located their distribution center in Virginia—enabling them to ship to over 60% of the U.S. population within two days. Also, they pack items in small, uniformly sized boxes to lower costs and offer free shipping on certain orders.

Many other cost management procedures are applied. For example, they analyze "checkout flow," providing details on the point at which potential customers drop out of the checkout process and how many drop out. "If I had a 50% checkout success rate one day and 23% the next day, this lets me see that," explains Todd. This mix of financial and nonfinancial information helps Todd steer more customers through the checkout process. He also tracks customer approval ratings, currently above 99%, as a performance measure.

The diversity of its product offerings requires additional cost management. Company managers monitor direct, indirect, and controllable costs, and allocate them to departments and products. Understanding how the company's product lines—such as clubs, bags, apparel—are performing and their contribution margins helps them plan for expansion. As Todd emphasizes, "We use tools to measure our ROI (return on investment). We will only expand as long as there are customers to win."

Their expansion plans do not stop with golf. RockBottomGolf wants to become RockBottomSports, with many other sporting goods products available. This increased departmentalization will require them to monitor contribution margins, return on investment, checkout flow, and customer approval. With its fast-paced growth and position as the top golf retailer on the Internet, RockBottomGolf is "on the green."

[Sources: *RockBottomGolf.com Website,* January 2009; *Internet Retailer,* July 2007; *Inside Business-Hampton Roads,* October 2006.]

Chapter Preview

This chapter describes how to allocate costs shared by more than one product across those different products and how to allocate indirect costs of shared items such as utilities, advertising, and rent. This knowledge helps managers better understand how to assign costs and assess company performance. The chapter also introduces additional managerial accounting reports useful in managing a company's activities and explains how and why management divides companies into departments.

Decentralization and Performance Evaluation

Departmental Accounting
- Motivation for departmentalization
- Departmental evaluation
- Departmental reporting and analysis

Departmental Expense Allocation
- Direct and indirect expenses
- Allocation of indirect expenses
- Departmental income statements
- Departmental contribution to overhead

Investment Centers
- Financial measures of performance
- Nonfinancial measures of performance
- Balanced scorecard

Responsibility Accounting
- Controllable versus direct costs
- Responsibility accounting system
- Transfer pricing

This chapter describes and illustrates allocation of costs for performance evaluation. We begin with departmental accounting and expense allocations and conclude with responsibility accounting.

Departmental Accounting

Video9.1

Companies are divided into *departments,* also called *subunits,* when they are too large to be managed effectively as a single unit. Managerial accounting for departments has two main goals. The first is to set up a **departmental accounting system** to provide information for managers to evaluate the profitability or cost effectiveness of each department's activities. The second goal is to set up a **responsibility accounting system** to control costs and expenses and evaluate managers' performances by assigning costs and expenses to the managers responsible for controlling them. Departmental and responsibility accounting systems are related and share much information.

Motivation for Departmentalization

C1 Explain departmentalization and the role of departmental accounting.

Many companies are so large and complex that they are broken into separate divisions for efficiency and/or effectiveness purposes. Divisions then are usually organized into separate departments. When a company is departmentalized, each department is often placed under the direction of a manager. As a company grows, management often divides departments into new departments so that responsibilities for a department's activities do not overwhelm the manager's ability to oversee and control them. A company also creates departments to take advantage of the skills of individual managers. Departments are broadly classified as either operating or service departments.

Departmental Evaluation

Point: To improve profitability, **Sears, Roebuck & Co.** eliminated several departments, including its catalog division.

When a company is divided into departments, managers need to know how each department is performing. The accounting system must supply information about resources used and outputs achieved by each department. This requires a system to measure and accumulate revenue and expense information for each department whenever possible.

Departmental information is rarely distributed publicly because of its potential usefulness to competitors. Information about departments is prepared for internal managers to help control operations, appraise performance, allocate resources, and plan strategy. If a department is highly profitable, management may decide to expand its operations, or if a department is performing poorly, information about revenues or expenses can suggest useful changes.

More companies are emphasizing customer satisfaction as a main responsibility of many departments. This has led to changes in the measures reported. Increasingly, financial measurements are being supplemented with quality and customer satisfaction indexes. **Motorola**, for instance, uses two key measures: the number of defective parts per million parts produced and the percent of orders delivered on time to customers. (Note that some departments have only "internal customers.")

Financial information used to evaluate a department depends on whether it is evaluated as a profit center, cost center, or investment center. A **profit center** incurs costs and generates revenues; selling departments are often evaluated as profit centers. A **cost center** incurs costs without directly generating revenues. An **investment center** incurs costs and generates revenues, and is responsible for effectively using center assets. The manufacturing departments of a manufacturer and its service departments such as accounting, advertising, and purchasing, are all cost centers.

Evaluating managers' performance depends on whether they are responsible for profit centers, cost centers, or investment centers. Profit center managers are judged on their abilities to generate revenues in excess of the department's costs. They are assumed to influence both revenue generation and cost incurrence. Cost center managers are judged on their abilities to control costs by keeping them within a satisfactory range under an assumption that only they influence costs. Investment center managers are evaluated on their use of center assets to generate income.

Point: Selling departments are often treated as *revenue centers;* their managers are responsible for maximizing sales revenues.

Decision Insight

Nonfinancial Measures A majority of companies now report nonfinancial performance measures to management. Common measures are cycle time, defect rate, on-time deliveries, inventory turnover, customer satisfaction, and safety. When nonfinancial measures are used with financial measures, the performance measurement system resembles a ***balanced scorecard.*** Many of these companies also use activity-based management as part of their performance measurement system.

Departmental Reporting and Analysis

Companies use various measures (financial and nonfinancial) and reporting formats to evaluate their departments. The type and form of information depend on management's focus and philosophy. **Hewlett-Packard**'s statement of corporate objectives, for instance, indicates that its goal is to satisfy customer needs. Its challenge is to set up managerial accounting systems to provide relevant feedback for evaluating performance in terms of its stated objectives. Also, the means used to obtain information about departments depend on how extensively a company uses computer and information technology.

When accounts are not maintained separately in the general ledger by department, a company can create departmental information by using a *departmental spreadsheet analysis*. For example, after recording sales in its usual manner, a company can compute daily total sales by department and enter these totals on a sales spreadsheet. At period-end, column totals of the spreadsheet show sales by department. The combined total of all columns equals the balance of the Sales account. A merchandiser that uses a spreadsheet analysis of department sales often uses separate spreadsheets to accumulate sales, sales returns, purchases, and purchases returns by department. If each department keeps a count of its inventory, it can also compute its gross profit (assuming it's a profit center).

Point: Many retailers use a point-of-sales system capturing sales data and creating requests to release inventory from the warehouse and order more merchandise. **Walmart**'s sales system not only collects data for internal use but also is used by **Procter & Gamble** to plan its production and product deliveries to **Walmart.**

Point: Link Wood Products, a manufacturer of lawn and garden products, records each sale by department on a spreadsheet. Daily totals are accumulated in another spreadsheet to obtain monthly totals by department.

Quick Check

Answers—p. 343

1. What is the difference between a departmental accounting system and a responsibility accounting system?
2. Service departments (*a*) manufacture products, (*b*) make sales directly to customers, (c) produce revenues, (*d*) assist operating departments.
3. Explain the difference between a cost center and a profit center. Cite an example of each.

Departmental Expense Allocation

When a company computes departmental profits, it confronts some accounting challenges that involve allocating its expenses across its operating departments.

Direct and Indirect Expenses

C2 Distinguish between direct and indirect expenses.

Direct expenses are costs readily traced to a department because they are incurred for that department's sole benefit. They require no allocation across departments. For example, the salary of an employee who works in only one department is a direct expense of that one department.

Indirect expenses are costs that are incurred for the joint benefit of more than one department and cannot be readily traced to only one department. For example, if two or more departments share a single building, all enjoy the benefits of the expenses for rent, heat, and light. Indirect expenses are allocated across departments benefiting from them when we need information about departmental profits. Ideally, we allocate indirect expenses by using a cause-effect relation. When we cannot identify cause-effect relations, we allocate each indirect expense on a basis approximating the relative benefit each department receives. Measuring the benefit for each department from an indirect expense can be difficult.

Point: Utility expense has elements of both direct and indirect expenses.

Illustration of Indirect Expense Allocation To illustrate how to allocate an indirect expense, we consider a retail store that purchases janitorial services from an outside company. Management allocates this cost across the store's three departments according to the floor space each occupies. Costs of janitorial services for a recent month are $300. Exhibit 9.1 shows the square feet of floor space each department occupies. The store computes the percent of total square feet allotted to each department and uses it to allocate the $300 cost.

EXHIBIT 9.1

Indirect Expense Allocation

Department	Square Feet	Percent of Total	Allocated Cost
Jewelry	2,400	60%	$180
Watch repair	600	15	45
China and silver	1,000	25	75
Totals	4,000	100%	$300

Specifically, because the jewelry department occupies 60% of the floor space, 60% of the total $300 cost is assigned to it. The same procedure is applied to the other departments. When the allocation process is complete, these and other allocated costs are deducted from the gross profit for each department to determine net income for each. One consideration in allocating costs is to motivate managers and employees to behave as desired. As a result, a cost incurred in one department might be best allocated to other departments when one of the other departments caused the cost.

Allocation of Indirect Expenses

C3 Identify bases for allocating indirect expenses to departments.

This section describes how to identify the bases used to allocate indirect expenses across departments. No standard rule identifies the best basis because expense allocation involves several factors, and the relative importance of these factors varies across departments and organizations. Judgment is required, and people do not always agree. In our discussion, note the parallels between activity-based costing and the departmental expense allocation procedures described here.

Point: Expense allocations cannot always avoid some arbitrariness.

Wages and Salaries Employee wages and salaries can be either direct or indirect expenses. If their time is spent entirely in one department, their wages are direct expenses of that department. However, if employees work for the benefit of more than one department, their wages are indirect expenses and must be allocated across the departments benefited. An employee's contribution to a department usually depends on the number of hours worked in contributing to that department. Thus, a reasonable basis for allocating employee wages and salaries is the *relative amount of time spent in each department.* In the case of a supervisor who manages more than one department, recording the time spent in each department may not always be practical. Instead, a company can allocate the supervisor's salary to departments on the basis of the number of employees in each department—a reasonable basis if a supervisor's main task is managing people. Another basis of allocation is on sales across departments, also a reasonable basis if a supervisor's job reflects on departmental sales.

Point: Some companies ask supervisors to estimate time spent supervising specific departments for purposes of expense allocation.

Rent and Related Expenses Rent expense for a building is reasonably allocated to a department on the basis of floor space it occupies. Location can often make some floor space more valuable than other space. Thus, the allocation method can charge departments that occupy more valuable space a higher expense per square foot. Ground floor retail space, for instance, is often more valuable than basement or upper-floor space because all customers pass departments near the entrance but fewer go beyond the first floor. When no precise measures of floor space values exist, basing allocations on data such as customer traffic and real estate assessments is helpful. When a company owns its building, its expenses for depreciation, taxes, insurance, and other related building expenses are allocated like rent expense.

Advertising Expenses Effective advertising of a department's products increases its sales and customer traffic. Moreover, advertising products for some departments usually helps other departments' sales because customers also often buy unadvertised products. Thus, many stores treat advertising as an indirect expense allocated on the basis of each department's proportion of total sales. For example, a department with 10% of a store's total sales is assigned 10% of advertising expense. Another method is to analyze each advertisement to compute the Web/newspaper space or TV/radio time devoted to the products of a department and charge that department for the proportional costs of advertisements. Management must consider whether this more detailed and costly method is justified.

Equipment and Machinery Depreciation Depreciation on equipment and machinery used only in one department is a direct expense of that department. Depreciation on equipment and machinery used by more than one department is an indirect expense to be allocated across departments. Accounting for each department's depreciation expense requires a company to keep records showing which departments use specific assets. The number of hours that a department uses equipment and machinery is a reasonable basis for allocating depreciation.

Point: Employee morale suffers when allocations are perceived as unfair. Thus, it is important to carefully design and explain the allocation of service department costs.

Utilities Expenses Utilities expenses such as heating and lighting are usually allocated on the basis of floor space occupied by departments. This practice assumes their use is uniform across departments. When this is not so, a more involved allocation can be necessary, although there is often a trade-off between the usefulness of more precise allocations and the effort to compute them.

Point: Manufacturers often allocate electricity cost to departments on the basis of the horsepower of equipment located in each department.

Service Department Expenses To generate revenues, operating departments require support services provided by departments such as personnel, payroll, advertising, and purchasing. Such service departments are typically evaluated as cost centers because they do not produce revenues. (Evaluating them as profit centers requires the use of a system that "charges" user departments a price that then serves as the "revenue" generated by service departments.) A departmental accounting system can accumulate and report costs incurred directly by each service department for this purpose. The system then allocates a service department's expenses to operating departments benefiting from them. This is often done, for example, using traditional two-stage cost allocation (see Chapter 4). Exhibit 9.2 shows some commonly used bases for allocating service department expenses to operating departments.

Point: When a service department "charges" its user departments within a company, a *transfer pricing system* must be set up to determine the "revenue" from its services provided.

EXHIBIT 9.2

Bases for Allocating Service Department Expenses

Service Department	Common Allocation Bases
Office expenses	Number of employees or sales in each department
Personnel expenses	Number of employees in each department
Payroll expenses	Number of employees in each department
Advertising expenses	Sales or amount of advertising charged directly to each department
Purchasing costs	Dollar amounts of purchases or number of purchase orders processed
Cleaning expenses	Square feet of floor space occupied
Maintenance expenses	Square feet of floor space occupied

P1 Prepare departmental income statements.

Departmental Income Statements

An income statement can be prepared for each operating department once expenses have been assigned to it. Its expenses include both direct expenses and its share of indirect expenses. For this purpose, compiling all expenses incurred in service departments before assigning them to operating departments is useful. We illustrate the steps to prepare departmental income statements using **A-1 Hardware** and its five departments. Two of them (office and purchasing) are service departments and the other three (hardware, housewares, and appliances) are operating (selling) departments. Allocating costs to operating departments and preparing departmental income statements involves four steps. (1) Accumulating direct expenses by department. (2) Allocating indirect expenses across departments. (3) Allocating service department expenses to operating department. (4) Preparing departmental income statements.

Step 1 Step 1 accumulates direct expenses for each service and operating department as shown in Exhibit 9.3. Direct expenses include salaries, wages, and other expenses that each department incurs but does not share with any other department. This information is accumulated in departmental expense accounts.

EXHIBIT 9.3

Step 1: Direct Expense Accumulation

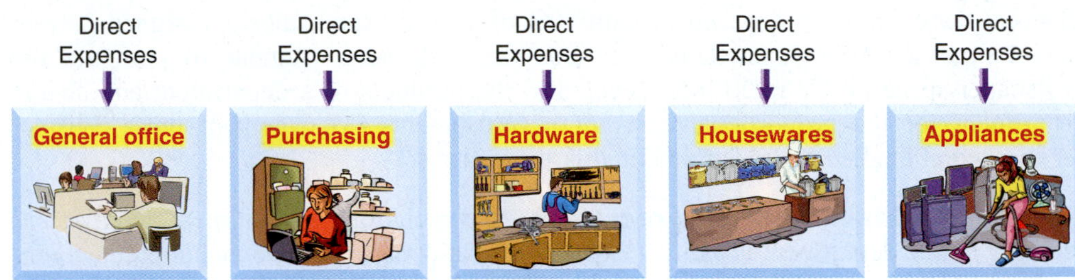

Point: We sometimes allocate service department costs across other service departments before allocating them to operating departments. This "step-wise" process is in advanced courses.

Step 2 Step 2 allocates indirect expenses across all departments as shown in Exhibit 9.4. Indirect expenses can include items such as depreciation, rent, advertising, and any other expenses that cannot be directly assigned to a department. Indirect expenses are recorded in company expense accounts, an allocation base is identified for each expense, and costs are allocated using a *departmental expense allocation spreadsheet* described in step 3.

EXHIBIT 9.4

Step 2: Indirect Expense Allocation

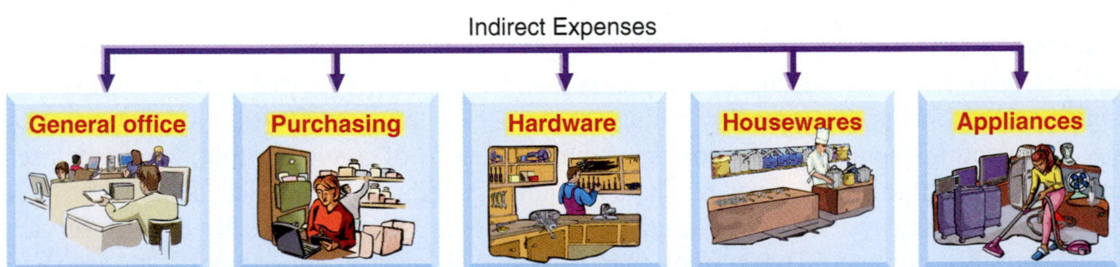

Step 3 Step 3 allocates expenses of the service departments (office and purchasing) to the operating departments. Service department costs are not allocated to other service departments. Exhibit 9.5 reflects the allocation of service department expenses using the allocation base(s). All of the direct and indirect expenses of service departments are allocated to operating departments.[1]

[1] In some cases we allocate a service department's expenses to other service departments when they use its services. For example, expenses of a payroll office benefit all service and operating departments and can be assigned to all departments. Nearly all examples and assignment materials in this book allocate service expenses only to operating departments for simplicity.

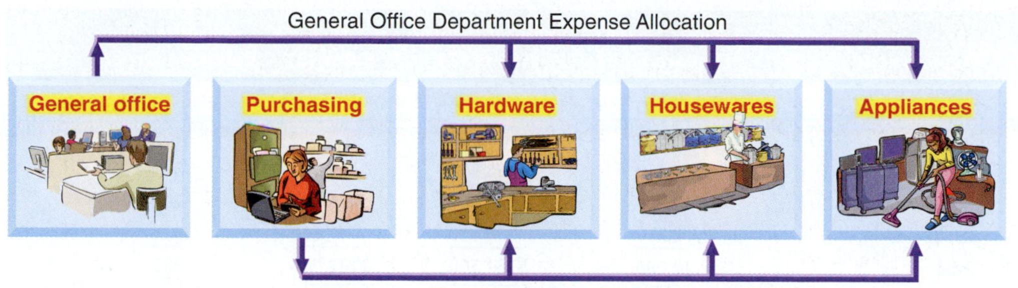

EXHIBIT 9.5

Step 3: Service Department Expense Allocation to Operating Departments

Computations for both steps 2 and 3 are commonly made using a departmental expense allocation spreadsheet as shown in Exhibit 9.6. The first two sections of this spreadsheet list direct expenses and indirect expenses by department. The third section lists the service department expenses and their allocations to operating departments. The allocation bases are identified in the second column, and total expense amounts are reported in the third column.

EXHIBIT 9.6

Departmental Expense Allocation Spreadsheet

A-1 HARDWARE
Departmental Expense Allocations
For Year Ended December 31, 2009

	Allocation Base	Expense Account Balance	Allocation of Expenses to Departments: General Office Dept.	Purchasing Dept.	Hardware Dept.	Housewares Dept.	Appliances Dept.
Direct expenses							
Salaries expense	Payroll records	$51,900	$13,300	$8,200	$15,600	$ 7,000	$ 7,800
Depreciation—Equipment	Depreciation records	1,500	500	300	400	100	200
Supplies expense	Requisitions	900	200	100	300	200	100
Indirect expenses							
Rent expense	Amount and value of space	12,000	600	600	4,860	3,240	2,700
Utilities expense	Floor space	2,400	300	300	810	540	450
Advertising expense	Sales	1,000			500	300	200
Insurance expense	Value of insured assets	2,500	400	200	900	600	400
Total department expenses		72,200	15,300	9,700	23,370	11,980	11,850
Service department expenses							
General office department	Sales		(15,300)		7,650	4,590	3,060
Purchasing department	Purchase orders			(9,700)	3,880	2,630	3,190
Total expenses allocated to operating departments		$72,200	$ 0	$ 0	$34,900	$19,200	$18,100

The departmental expense allocation spreadsheet is useful in implementing the first three steps. To illustrate, first (step 1) the three direct expenses of salaries, depreciation, and supplies are accumulated in each of the five departments.

Second (step 2), the four indirect expenses of rent, utilities, advertising, and insurance are allocated to all departments using the allocation bases identified. For example, consider rent allocation. Exhibit 9.7 lists the five departments' square footage of space occupied. The two service departments (office and purchasing) occupy 25% of the total space (3,000 sq. feet/12,000 sq. feet). However, they are located near the back of the building, which is of lower value than space near the front that is occupied by operating departments. Management estimates that space near the back accounts for $1,200 of the total rent expense of $12,000. Exhibit 9.8 shows how we allocate the $1,200 rent expense between these two service departments in proportion to their square footage. Exhibit 9.8 shows a simple rule for cost allocations: Allocated cost = Percentage of allocation base × Total cost. We then allocate the remaining $10,800 of rent expense to the three operating departments

EXHIBIT 9.7

Departments' Allocation Bases

Department	Floor Space (Square Feet)	Value of Insured Assets ($)	Sales ($)	Number of Purchase Orders
General office	1,500	$ 38,000		—
Purchasing	1,500	19,000		—*
Hardware	4,050	85,500	$119,500	394
Housewares	2,700	57,000	71,700	267
Appliances	2,250	38,000	47,800	324
Total	12,000	$237,500	$239,000	985

* Purchasing department tracks purchase orders by department.

EXHIBIT 9.8

Allocating Indirect (Rent) Expense to Service Departments

Department	Square Feet	Percent of Total	Allocated Cost
General office	1,500	50.0%	$ 600
Purchasing	1,500	50.0	600
Totals	3,000	100.0%	$1,200

as shown in Exhibit 9.9. We continue step 2 by allocating the $2,400 of utilities expense to all departments based on the square footage occupied as shown in Exhibit 9.10.

EXHIBIT 9.9

Allocating Indirect (Rent) Expense to Operating Departments

Department	Square Feet	Percent of Total	Allocated Cost
Hardware	4,050	45.0%	$ 4,860
Housewares	2,700	30.0	3,240
Appliances	2,250	25.0	2,700
Totals	9,000	100.0%	$10,800

EXHIBIT 9.10

Allocating Indirect (Utilities) Expense to All Departments

Department	Square Feet	Percent of Total	Allocated Cost
General office	1,500	12.50%	$ 300
Purchasing	1,500	12.50	300
Hardware	4,050	33.75	810
Housewares	2,700	22.50	540
Appliances	2,250	18.75	450
Totals	12,000	100.00%	$2,400

Exhibit 9.11 shows the allocation of $1,000 of advertising expense to the three operating departments on the basis of sales dollars. We exclude service departments from this allocation because they do not generate sales.

EXHIBIT 9.11

Allocating Indirect (Advertising) Expense to Operating Departments

Department	Sales	Percent of Total	Allocated Cost
Hardware	$119,500	50.0%	$ 500
Housewares	71,700	30.0	300
Appliances	47,800	20.0	200
Totals	$239,000	100.0%	$1,000

To complete step 2 we allocate insurance expense to each service and operating department as shown in Exhibit 9.12.

EXHIBIT 9.12

Allocating Indirect (Insurance) Expense to All Departments

Department	Value of Insured Assets	Percent of Total	Allocated Cost
General Office	$ 38,000	16.0%	$ 400
Purchasing	19,000	8.0	200
Hardware	85,500	36.0	900
Housewares	57,000	24.0	600
Appliances	38,000	16.0	400
Total	$237,500	100.0%	$2,500

Third (step 3), total expenses of the two service departments are allocated to the three operating departments as shown in Exhibits 9.13 and 9.14.

EXHIBIT 9.13

Allocating Service Department (General Office) Expenses to Operating Departments

Department	Sales	Percent of Total	Allocated Cost
Hardware	$119,500	50.0%	$ 7,650
Housewares	71,700	30.0	4,590
Appliances	47,800	20.0	3,060
Total	$239,000	100.0%	$15,300

EXHIBIT 9.14

Allocating Service Department (Purchasing) Expenses to Operating Departments

Department	Number of Purchase Orders	Percent of Total	Allocated Cost
Hardware	394	40.00%	$3,880
Housewares	267	27.11	2,630
Appliances	324	32.89	3,190
Total	985	100.00%	$9,700

Step 4 The departmental expense allocation spreadsheet can now be used to prepare performance reports for the company's service and operating departments. The general office and purchasing departments are cost centers, and their managers will be evaluated on their control of costs. Actual amounts of service department expenses can be compared to budgeted amounts to help assess cost center manager performance.

Amounts in the operating department columns are used to prepare departmental income statements as shown in Exhibit 9.15. This exhibit uses the spreadsheet for its operating expenses; information on sales and cost of goods sold comes from departmental records.

Example: If the $15,300 general office expenses in Exhibit 9.6 are allocated equally across departments, what is net income for the hardware department and for the combined company? *Answer:* Hardware income, $13,350; combined income, $19,000.

Departmental Contribution to Overhead

P2 Prepare departmental contribution reports.

Data from departmental income statements are not always best for evaluating each profit center's performance, especially when indirect expenses are a large portion of total expenses and when weaknesses in assumptions and decisions in allocating indirect expenses can markedly affect net income. In these and other cases, we might better evaluate profit center performance using the **departmental contribution to overhead,** which is a report of the amount of sales less *direct* expenses.[2] We can also examine cost center performance by focusing on control of direct expenses.

The upper half of Exhibit 9.16 shows a departmental (profit center) contribution to overhead as part of an expanded income statement. This format is common when reporting departmental contributions to overhead. Using the information in Exhibits 9.15 and 9.16, we can evaluate the profitability of the three profit centers. For instance, let's compare the

Point: Net income is the same in Exhibits 9.15 and 9.16. The method of reporting indirect expenses in Exhibit 9.16 does not change total net income but does identify each department's contribution to overhead and net income.

[2] A department's contribution is said to be "to overhead" because of the practice of considering all indirect expenses as overhead. Thus, the excess of a department's sales over direct expenses is a contribution toward at least a portion of its total overhead.

EXHIBIT 9.15

Departmental Income Statements

A-1 HARDWARE Departmental Income Statements For Year Ended December 31, 2009	Hardware Department	Housewares Department	Appliances Department	Combined
Sales	$119,500	$71,700	$47,800	$239,000
Cost of goods sold	73,800	43,800	30,200	147,800
Gross profit	45,700	27,900	17,600	91,200
Operating expenses				
Salaries expense	15,600	7,000	7,800	30,400
Depreciation expense—Equipment	400	100	200	700
Supplies expense	300	200	100	600
Rent expense	4,860	3,240	2,700	10,800
Utilities expense	810	540	450	1,800
Advertising expense	500	300	200	1,000
Insurance expense	900	600	400	1,900
Share of general office expenses	7,650	4,590	3,060	15,300
Share of purchasing expenses	3,880	2,630	3,190	9,700
Total operating expenses	34,900	19,200	18,100	72,200
Net income (loss)	**$ 10,800**	**$ 8,700**	**$ (500)**	**$ 19,000**

performance of the appliances department as described in these two exhibits. Exhibit 9.15 shows a $500 net loss resulting from this department's operations, but Exhibit 9.16 shows a $9,500 positive contribution to overhead, which is 19.9% of the appliance department's sales. The contribution of the appliances department is not as large as that of the other selling departments, but a $9,500 contribution to overhead is better than a $500 loss. This tells us that the appliances department is not a money loser. On the contrary, it is contributing $9,500 toward defraying total indirect expenses of $40,500.

EXHIBIT 9.16

Departmental Contribution to Overhead

A-1 HARDWARE Income Statement Showing Departmental Contribution to Overhead For Year Ended December 31, 2009	Hardware Department	Housewares Department	Appliances Department	Combined
Sales	$119,500	$ 71,700	$47,800	$239,000
Cost of goods sold	73,800	43,800	30,200	147,800
Gross profit	45,700	27,900	17,600	91,200
Direct expenses				
Salaries expense	15,600	7,000	7,800	30,400
Depreciation expense—Equipment	400	100	200	700
Supplies expense	300	200	100	600
Total direct expenses	16,300	7,300	8,100	31,700
Departmental contributions to overhead	**$ 29,400**	**$20,600**	**$ 9,500**	**$ 59,500**
Indirect expenses				
Rent expense				10,800
Utilities expense				1,800
Advertising expense				1,000
Insurance expense				1,900
General office department expense				15,300
Purchasing department expense				9,700
Total indirect expenses				40,500
Net income				**$ 19,000**
Contribution as percent of sales	24.6%	28.7%	19.9%	24.9%

Quick Check Answers—p. 343

4. If a company has two operating (selling) departments (shoes and hats) and two service departments (payroll and advertising), which of the following statements is correct? (*a*) Wages incurred in the payroll department are direct expenses of the shoe department, (*b*) Wages incurred in the payroll department are indirect expenses of the operating departments, or (*c*) Advertising department expenses are allocated to the other three departments.
5. Which of the following bases can be used to allocate supervisors' salaries across operating departments? (*a*) Hours spent in each department, (*b*) number of employees in each department, (*c*) sales achieved in each department, or (*d*) any of the above, depending on which information is most relevant and accessible.
6. What three steps are used to allocate expenses to operating departments?
7. An income statement showing departmental contribution to overhead, (*a*) subtracts indirect expenses from each department's revenues, (*b*) subtracts only direct expenses from each department's revenues, or (*c*) shows net income for each department.

Investment Centers

This section introduces both financial and nonfinancial measures of investment center performance.

Financial Performance Evaluation Measures

A1 Analyze investment centers using return on assets, residual income, and balanced scorecard.

Investment center managers are typically evaluated using performance measures that combine income and assets. Consider the following data for ZTel, a company which operates two divisions: LCD and S-Phone. The LCD division manufactures liquid crystal display (LCD) touch-screen monitors and sells them for use in computers, cellular phones, and other products. The S-Phone division sells smartphones, mobile phones that also function as personal computers, MP3 players, cameras, and global positioning satellite (GPS) systems. Exhibit 9.17 shows current year income and assets for those divisions.

EXHIBIT 9.17

Investment Center Income and Assets

	LCD	S-Phone
Net income	$ 526,500	$ 417,600
Average invested assets	2,500,000	1,850,000

Investment Center Return on Total Assets One measure to evaluate division performance is the **investment center return on total assets,** also called *return on investment* (ROI). This measure is computed as follows

$$\textbf{Return on investment} = \frac{\textbf{Investment center net income}}{\textbf{Investment center average invested assets}}$$

The return on investment for the LCD division is 21% (rounded), computed as $526,500/$2,500,000. The S-Phone division's return on investment is 23% (rounded), computed as $417,600/$1,850,000. Though the LCD division earned more dollars of net income, it was less efficient in using its assets to generate income compared to the S-Phone division.

Investment Center Residual Income Another way to evaluate division performance is to compute **investment center residual income,** which is computed as follows

$$\textbf{Residual income} = \begin{matrix}\textbf{Investment center}\\\textbf{net income}\end{matrix} - \begin{matrix}\textbf{Target investment center}\\\textbf{net income}\end{matrix}$$

Assume ZTel's top management sets target net income at 8% of divisional assets. For an investment center, this **hurdle rate** is typically the cost of obtaining financing. Applying this hurdle rate using the data from Exhibit 9.17 yields the residual income for ZTel's divisions in Exhibit 9.18:

EXHIBIT 9.18

Investment Center Residual Income

	LCD	S-Phone
Net income	$526,500	$417,600
Less: Target net income		
$2,500,000 × 8%	200,000	
$1,850,000 × 8%		148,000
Investment center residual income	$326,500	$269,600

Unlike return on assets, residual income is expressed in dollars. The LCD division outperformed the S-Phone division on the basis of residual income. However, this result is due in part to the LCD division having a larger asset base than the S-Phone division.

Using residual income to evaluate division performance encourages division managers to accept all opportunities that return more than the target net income, thus increasing company value. For example, the S-Phone division might not want to accept a new customer that will provide a 15% return on investment, since that will reduce the S-Phone division's overall return on investment (23% as shown above). However, the S-Phone division should accept this opportunity because the new customer would increase residual income by providing net income above the target net income.

Point: Residual income is also called *economic value added* (EVA).

Nonfinancial Performance Evaluation Measures

Evaluating performance solely on financial measures such as return on investment or residual income has limitations. For example, some investment center managers might forgo profitable opportunities to keep their return on investment high. Also, residual income is less useful when comparing investment centers of different size. And, both return on investment and residual income can encourage managers to focus too heavily on short-term financial goals.

In response to these limitations, companies consider nonfinancial measures. For example, a delivery company such as **FedEx** might track the percentage of on-time deliveries. The percentage of defective tennis balls manufactured can be used to assess performance of **Penn**'s production managers. **Walmart**'s credit card screens commonly ask customers at check-out whether the cashier was friendly or the store was clean. This kind of information can help division managers run their divisions and help top management evaluate division manager performance.

Balanced Scorecard

The **balanced scorecard** is a system of performance measures, including nonfinancial measures, used to assess company and division manager performance. The balanced scorecard requires managers to think of their company from four perspectives:

1. *Customer:* What do customers think of us?
2. *Internal processes:* Which of our operations are critical to meeting customer needs?
3. *Innovation and learning:* How can we improve?
4. *Financial:* What do our owners think of us?

Point: One survey indicates that nearly 60% of global companies use some form of balanced scorecard.

The balanced scorecard collects information on several key performance indicators within each of the four perspectives. These key indicators vary across companies. Exhibit 9.19 lists common performance measures.

After selecting key performance indicators, companies collect data on each indicator and compare actual amounts to expected amounts to assess performance. For example, a company might have a goal of filling 98% of customer orders within two hours. Balanced scorecard reports are often presented in graphs or tables that can be updated frequently. Such timely information aids division managers in their decisions, and can be used by top management to evaluate division manager performance.

EXHIBIT 9.19

Balanced Scorecard Performance Indicators

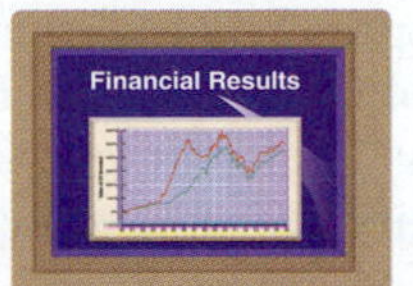

Customer	Internal Process	Innovation/Learning	Financial
• Customer satisfaction rating • # of new customers acquired • % of on-time deliveries • % of sales from new products • Time to fill orders % of sales returned	• Defect rates • Cycle time • Product costs • Labor hours per order • Production days without an accident	• Employee satisfaction • Employee turnover • $ spent on training • # of new products • # of patents • $ spent on research	• Net income • ROI • Sales growth • Cash flow • Residual income • Stock price

Exhibit 9.20 is an example of balanced scorecard reporting on the customer perspective for an Internet retailer. This scorecard reports for example that the retailer is getting 62% of its potential customers successfully through the checkout process, and that 2.2% of all orders are returned. The *color* of the arrows in the right-most column reveals whether the company is exceeding its goal (green), barely meeting the goal (yellow), or not meeting the goal (red). The *direction* of the arrows reveals any trend in performance: an upward arrow indicates improvement, a downward arrow indicates declining performance, and an arrow pointing sideways indicates no change. A review of these arrows' color and direction suggests the retailer is meeting or exceeding its goals on checkout success, orders returned, and customer satisfaction. Further, checkout success and customer satisfaction are improving. The red arrow shows the company has received more customer complaints than was hoped for; however, the number of customer complaints is declining. A manager would combine this information with similar information on the internal process, innovation and learning, and financial perspectives to get an overall view of division performance.

EXHIBIT 9.20

Balanced Scorecard Reporting: Internet Retailer

Customer Perspective	Actual	Goal
Checkout success	62%	↑ (green)
Orders returned	2.20%	↔ (yellow)
Customer satisfaction rating	9.5	↑ (green)
Number of customer complaints	142	↓ (red)

Decision Maker

Center Manager Your center's usual return on total assets is 19%. You are considering two new investments for your center. The first requires a $250,000 average investment and is expected to yield annual net income of $50,000. The second requires a $1 million average investment with an expected annual net income of $175,000. Do you pursue either? [Answer—p. 343]

Responsibility Accounting

C4 Explain controllable costs and responsibility accounting.

Departmental accounting reports often provide data used to evaluate a department's performance, but are they useful in assessing how well a department *manager* performs? Neither departmental income nor its contribution to overhead may be useful because many expenses can be outside a manager's control. Instead, we often evaluate a manager's performance using responsibility accounting reports that describe a department's activities in terms of **controllable costs.**[3] A cost is controllable if a manager has the power to determine or at least significantly affect the amount incurred. **Uncontrollable costs** are not within the manager's control or influence.

Controllable versus Direct Costs

Controllable costs are not always the same as direct costs. Direct costs are readily traced to a department, but the department manager might or might not control their amounts. For example, department managers often have little or no control over depreciation expense because they cannot affect the amount of equipment assigned to their departments. Also, department managers rarely control their own salaries. However, they can control or influence items such as the cost of supplies used in their department. When evaluating managers' performances, we should use data reflecting their departments' outputs along with their controllable costs and expenses.

Distinguishing between controllable and uncontrollable costs depends on the particular manager and time period under analysis. For example, the cost of property insurance is usually not controllable at the department manager's level but by the executive responsible for obtaining the company's insurance coverage. Likewise, this executive might not control costs resulting from insurance policies already in force. However, when a policy expires, this executive can renegotiate a replacement policy and then controls these costs. Therefore, all costs are controllable at some management level if the time period is sufficiently long. We must use good judgment in identifying controllable costs.

Responsibility Accounting System

A *responsibility accounting system* uses the concept of controllable costs to assign managers the responsibility for costs and expenses under their control. Prior to each reporting period, a company prepares plans that identify costs and expenses under each manager's control. These plans are called **responsibility accounting budgets.** To ensure the cooperation of managers and the reasonableness of budgets, managers should be involved in preparing their budgets.

A responsibility accounting system also involves performance reports. A **responsibility accounting performance report** accumulates and reports costs and expenses that a manager is responsible for and their budgeted amounts. Management's analysis of differences between budgeted amounts and actual costs and expenses often results in corrective or strategic managerial actions. Upper-level management uses performance reports to evaluate the effectiveness of lower-level managers in controlling costs and expenses and keeping them within budgeted amounts.

A responsibility accounting system recognizes that control over costs and expenses belongs to several levels of management. We illustrate this by considering the organization chart in Exhibit 9.21. The lines in this chart connecting the managerial positions reflect channels of authority. For example, the four department managers of this consulting firm (benchmarking, cost management, outsourcing, and service) are responsible for controllable costs and expenses incurred in their

EXHIBIT 9.21

Organizational Responsibility Chart

[3] The terms *cost* and *expense* are often used interchangeably in managerial accounting, but they are not necessarily the same. *Cost* often refers to the monetary outlay to acquire some resource that can have present and future benefit. *Expense* usually refers to an expired cost. That is, as the benefit of a resource expires, a portion of its cost is written off as an expense.

departments, but these same costs are subject to the overall control of the vice president (VP) for operational consulting. Similarly, this VP's costs are subject to the control of the executive vice president (EVP) for operations, the president, and, ultimately, the board of directors.

At lower levels, managers have limited responsibility and relatively little control over costs and expenses. Performance reports for low-level management typically cover few controllable costs. Responsibility and control broaden for higher-level managers; therefore, their reports span a wider range of costs. However, reports to higher-level managers seldom contain the details reported to their subordinates but are summarized for two reasons: (1) lower-level managers are often responsible for these detailed costs and (2) detailed reports can obscure broader, more important issues facing a company.

Point: Responsibility accounting does not place blame. Instead, responsibility accounting is used to identify opportunities for improving performance.

Exhibit 9.22 shows summarized performance reports for the three management levels identified in Exhibit 9.21. Exhibit 9.22 shows that costs under the control of the benchmarking department manager are totaled and included among controllable costs of the VP for operational consulting. Also, costs under the control of the VP are totaled and included among controllable costs of the EVP for operations. In this way, a responsibility accounting system provides relevant information for each management level.

EXHIBIT 9.22

Responsibility Accounting Performance Reports

Executive Vice President, Operations	**For July**		
Controllable Costs	**Budgeted Amount**	**Actual Amount**	**Over (Under) Budget**
Salaries, VPs	$ 80,000	$ 80,000	$ 0
Quality control costs	21,000	22,400	1,400
Office costs	29,500	28,800	(700)
Operational consulting	**276,700**	**279,500**	**2,800**
Strategic consulting	390,000	380,600	(9,400)
Totals	$ 797,200	$ 791,300	$ (5,900)

Vice President, Operational Consulting	**For July**		
Controllable Costs	**Budgeted Amount**	**Actual Amount**	**Over (Under) Budget**
Salaries, department managers	$ 75,000	$ 78,000	$ 3,000
Depreciation	10,600	10,600	0
Insurance	6,800	6,300	(500)
Benchmarking department	**79,600**	**79,900**	**300**
Cost management department	61,500	60,200	(1,300)
Outsourcing department	24,300	24,700	400
Service department	18,900	19,800	900
Totals	**$276,700**	**$279,500**	**$2,800**

Manager, Benchmarking Department	**For July**		
Controllable Costs	**Budgeted Amount**	**Actual Amount**	**Over (Under) Budget**
Salaries	$ 51,600	$ 52,500	$ 900
Supplies	8,000	7,800	(200)
Other controllable costs	20,000	19,600	(400)
Totals	**$ 79,600**	**$ 79,900**	**$ 300**

Technological advances increase our ability to produce vast amounts of information that often exceed our ability to use it. Good managers select relevant data for planning and controlling the areas under their responsibility. A good responsibility accounting system makes every effort to provide relevant information to the right person (the one who controls the cost) at the right time (before a cost is out of control).

Point: Responsibility accounting usually divides a company into subunits, or *responsibility centers.* A center manager is evaluated on how well the center performs, as reported in responsibility accounting reports.

Quick Check

Answers—p. 343

8. Are the reports of departmental net income and the departmental contribution to overhead useful in assessing a department manager's performance? Explain.
9. Performance reports to evaluate managers should (*a*) include data about controllable expenses, (*b*) compare actual results with budgeted levels, or (*c*) both (*a*) and (*b*).

Decision Analysis — Investment Center Profit Margin and Investment Turnover

A2 Analyze investment centers using profit margin and investment turnover.

We can further examine investment center (division) performance by splitting return on investment into **profit margin** and **investment turnover** as follows

Return on investment = Profit margin × Investment turnover

$$\frac{\textbf{Investment center net income}}{\textbf{Investment center average assets}} = \frac{\textbf{Investment center net income}}{\textbf{Investment center sales}} \times \frac{\textbf{Investment center sales}}{\textbf{Investment center average assets}}$$

Profit margin measures the income earned per dollar of sales. **Investment turnover** measures how efficiently an investment center generates sales from its invested assets. Higher profit margin and higher investment turnover indicate better performance. To illustrate, consider **Best Buy** which reports in Exhibit 9.23 results for two divisions (segments): Domestic and International.

EXHIBIT 9.23

Best Buy Division Sales, Income, and Assets

($ millions)	Domestic	International
Sales	$24,616	$2,817
Net income	1,393	49
Average invested assets	8,372	1,922

Profit margin and investment turnover for its Domestic and International divisions are computed and shown in Exhibit 9.24:

EXHIBIT 9.24

Best Buy Division Profit Margin and Investment Turnover

($ millions)	Domestic	International
Profit Margin		
$1,393/$24,616	5.66%	
$49/$2,817		1.74%
Investment Turnover		
$24,616/$8,372	2.94	
$2,817/$1,922		1.47

Best Buy's Domestic division generates 5.66 cents of profit per $1 of sales, while its International division generates only 1.74 cents of profit per dollar of sales. Its Domestic division also uses its assets more efficiently; its investment turnover of 2.94 is twice that of its International division's 1.47. Top management can use profit margin and investment turnover to evaluate the performance of division managers. The measures can also aid management when considering further investment in its divisions.

Decision Maker

Division Manager You manage a division in a highly competitive industry. You will receive a cash bonus if your division achieves an ROI above 12%. Your division's profit margin is 7%, equal to the industry average, and your division's investment turnover is 1.5. What actions can you take to increase your chance of receiving the bonus? [Answer—p. 343]

Demonstration Problem

Management requests departmental income statements for Hacker's Haven, a computer store that has five departments. Three are operating departments (hardware, software, and repairs) and two are service departments (general office and purchasing).

	General Office	Purchasing	Hardware	Software	Repairs
Sales	—	—	$960,000	$600,000	$840,000
Cost of goods sold	—	—	500,000	300,000	200,000
Direct expenses					
Payroll	$60,000	$45,000	80,000	25,000	325,000
Depreciation	6,000	7,200	33,000	4,200	9,600
Supplies	15,000	10,000	10,000	2,000	25,000

The departments incur several indirect expenses. To prepare departmental income statements, the indirect expenses must be allocated across the five departments. Then the expenses of the two service departments must be allocated to the three operating departments. Total cost amounts and the allocation bases for each indirect expense follow.

Indirect Expense	Total Cost	Allocation Basis
Rent	$150,000	Square footage occupied
Utilities	50,000	Square footage occupied
Advertising	125,000	Dollars of sales
Insurance	30,000	Value of assets insured
Service departments		
General office	?	Number of employees
Purchasing	?	Dollars of cost of goods sold

The following additional information is needed for indirect expense allocations.

Department	Square Feet	Sales	Insured Assets	Employees	Cost of Goods Sold
General office	500		$ 60,000		
Purchasing	500		72,000		
Hardware	4,000	$ 960,000	330,000	5	$ 500,000
Software	3,000	600,000	42,000	5	300,000
Repairs	2,000	840,000	96,000	10	200,000
Totals	10,000	$2,400,000	$600,000	20	$1,000,000

Required

1. Prepare a departmental expense allocation spreadsheet for Hacker's Haven.
2. Prepare a departmental income statement reporting net income for each operating department and for all operating departments combined.

Planning the Solution

- Set up and complete four tables to allocate the indirect expenses—one each for rent, utilities, advertising, and insurance.
- Allocate the departments' indirect expenses using a spreadsheet like the one in Exhibit 9.6. Enter the given amounts of the direct expenses for each department. Then enter the allocated amounts of the indirect expenses that you computed.
- Complete two tables for allocating the general office and purchasing department costs to the three operating departments. Enter these amounts on the spreadsheet and determine the total expenses allocated to the three operating departments.
- Prepare departmental income statements like the one in Exhibit 9.15. Show sales, cost of goods sold, gross profit, individual expenses, and net income for each of the three operating departments and for the combined company.

Solution to Demonstration Problem

Allocations of the four indirect expenses across the five departments.

Rent	Square Feet	Percent of Total	Allocated Cost
General office	500	5.0%	$ 7,500
Purchasing	500	5.0	7,500
Hardware	4,000	40.0	60,000
Software	3,000	30.0	45,000
Repairs	2,000	20.0	30,000
Totals	10,000	100.0%	$150,000

Utilities	Square Feet	Percent of Total	Allocated Cost
General office	500	5.0%	$ 2,500
Purchasing	500	5.0	2,500
Hardware	4,000	40.0	20,000
Software	3,000	30.0	15,000
Repairs	2,000	20.0	10,000
Totals	10,000	100.0%	$50,000

Advertising	Sales Dollars	Percent of Total	Allocated Cost
Hardware	$ 960,000	40.0%	$ 50,000
Software	600,000	25.0	31,250
Repairs	840,000	35.0	43,750
Totals	$2,400,000	100.0%	$125,000

Insurance	Assets Insured	Percent of Total	Allocated Cost
General office	$ 60,000	10.0%	$ 3,000
Purchasing	72,000	12.0	3,600
Hardware	330,000	55.0	16,500
Software	42,000	7.0	2,100
Repairs	96,000	16.0	4,800
Totals	$600,000	100.0%	$30,000

1. Allocations of service department expenses to the three operating departments.

General Office Allocations to	Employees	Percent of Total	Allocated Cost
Hardware	5	25.0%	$23,500
Software	5	25.0	23,500
Repairs	10	50.0	47,000
Totals	20	100.0%	$94,000

Purchasing Allocations to	Cost of Goods Sold	Percent of Total	Allocated Cost
Hardware	$ 500,000	50.0%	$37,900
Software	300,000	30.0	22,740
Repairs	200,000	20.0	15,160
Totals	$1,000,000	100.0%	$75,800

HACKER'S HAVEN
Departmental Expense Allocations
For Year Ended December 31, 2009

	Allocation Base	Expense Account Balance	General Office Dept.	Purchasing Dept.	Hardware Dept.	Software Dept.	Repairs Dept.
Direct Expenses							
Payroll		$ 535,000	$ 60,000	$ 45,000	$ 80,000	$ 25,000	$ 325,000
Depreciation		60,000	6,000	7,200	33,000	4,200	9,600
Supplies		62,000	15,000	10,000	10,000	2,000	25,000
Indirect Expenses							
Rent	Square ft.	150,000	7,500	7,500	60,000	45,000	30,000
Utilities	Square ft.	50,000	2,500	2,500	20,000	15,000	10,000
Advertising	Sales	125,000	—	—	50,000	31,250	43,750
Insurance	Assets	30,000	3,000	3,600	16,500	2,100	4,800
Total expenses		1,012,000	94,000	75,800	269,500	124,550	448,150
Service Department Expenses							
General office	Employees		(94,000)		23,500	23,500	47,000
Purchasing	Goods sold			(75,800)	37,900	22,740	15,160
Total expenses allocated to operating departments		$1,012,000	$ 0	$ 0	$330,900	$170,790	$510,310

2. Departmental income statements for Hacker's Haven.

HACKER'S HAVEN Departmental Income Statements For Year Ended December 31, 2009	Hardware	Software	Repairs	Combined
Sales	$ 960,000	$ 600,000	$ 840,000	$2,400,000
Cost of goods sold	500,000	300,000	200,000	1,000,000
Gross profit	460,000	300,000	640,000	1,400,000
Expenses				
Payroll	80,000	25,000	325,000	430,000
Depreciation	33,000	4,200	9,600	46,800
Supplies	10,000	2,000	25,000	37,000
Rent	60,000	45,000	30,000	135,000
Utilities	20,000	15,000	10,000	45,000
Advertising	50,000	31,250	43,750	125,000
Insurance	16,500	2,100	4,800	23,400
Share of general office	23,500	23,500	47,000	94,000
Share of purchasing	37,900	22,740	15,160	75,800
Total expenses	330,900	170,790	510,310	1,012,000
Net income	**$129,100**	**$129,210**	**$129,690**	**$ 388,000**

APPENDIX

Transfer Pricing 9A

C5 Explain transfer pricing and methods to set transfer prices.

Divisions in decentralized companies sometimes do business with one another. For example, a separate division of **Harley-Davidson** manufactures its plastic and fiberglass parts used in the company's motorcycles. **Anheuser-Busch**'s metal container division makes cans and lids used in its brewing operations, and also sells cans and lids to soft-drink companies. A division of **Prince** produces strings used in tennis rackets made by **Prince** and other manufacturers.

Determining the price that should be used to record transfers between divisions in the same company is the focus of this appendix. Because these transactions are transfers within the same company, the price to record them is called the **transfer price.** In decentralized organizations, division managers have input on or decide those prices. Transfer prices can be used in cost, profit, and investment centers. Since these transfers are not with customers outside the company, the transfer price has no direct impact on the company's overall profits. However, transfer prices can impact performance evaluations and, if set incorrectly, lead to bad decisions.

Point: Transfer pricing can impact company profits when divisions are located in countries with different tax rates; this is covered in advanced courses.

Alternative Transfer Prices

Exhibit 9A.1 reports data on the LCD division of ZTel. LCD manufactures liquid crystal display (LCD) touch-screen monitors for use in ZTel's S-Phone division's smartphones, which sell for $400 each. The monitors can also be used in other products. So, LCD can sell its monitors to buyers other than S-Phone. Likewise, the S-Phone division can purchase monitors from suppliers other than LCD.

Exhibit 9A.1 reveals the range of transfer prices for transfers of monitors from LCD to S-Phone. The manager of LCD wants to report a division profit; thus, this manager will not accept a transfer price less than $40 (variable manufacturing cost per unit) because doing so would cause the division to lose

EXHIBIT 9A.1

LCD Division Manufacturing Information—Monitors

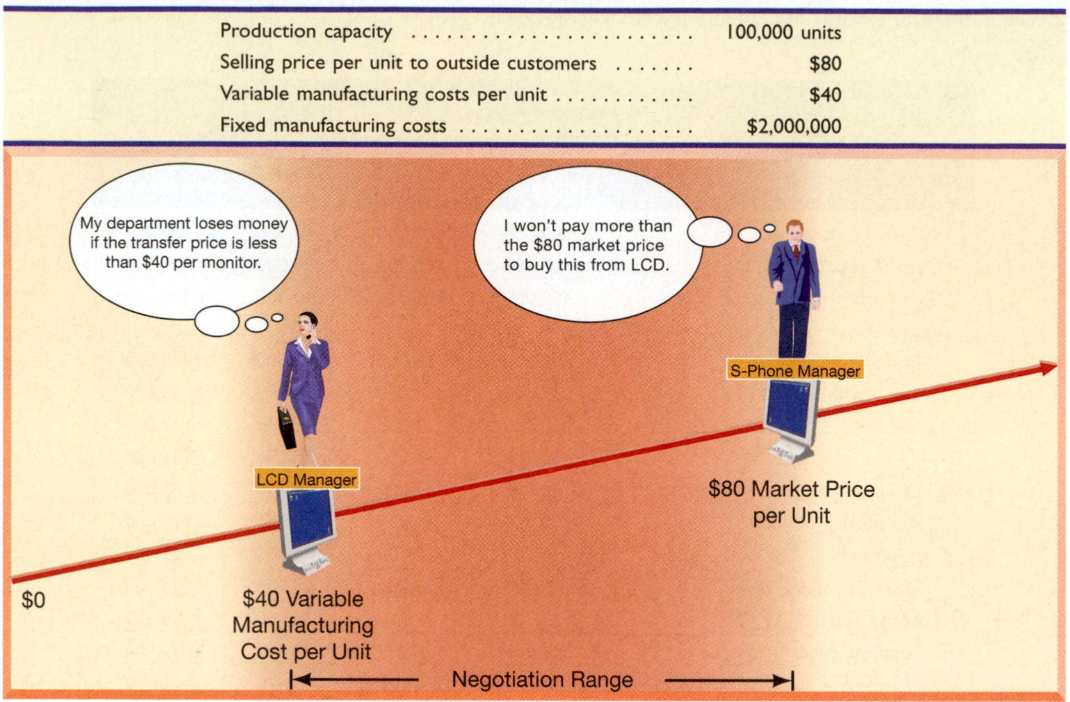

Production capacity	100,000 units
Selling price per unit to outside customers	$80
Variable manufacturing costs per unit	$40
Fixed manufacturing costs	$2,000,000

money on each monitor transferred. The LCD manager will only consider transfer prices of $40 or more. On the other hand, the S-Phone division manager also wants to report a division profit. Thus, this manager will not pay more than $80 per monitor because similar monitors can be bought from outside suppliers at that price. The S-Phone manager will only consider transfer prices of $80 or less. As any transfer price between $40 and $80 per monitor is possible, how does ZTel determine the transfer price? The answer depends in part on whether the LCD division has excess capacity to manufacture monitors.

No Excess Capacity Assume the LCD division can sell every monitor it produces, and thus is producing 100,000 units. In that case, a **market-based transfer price** of $80 per monitor is preferred. At that price, the LCD division manager is willing to either transfer monitors to S-Phone or sell to outside customers. The S-Phone manager cannot buy monitors for less than $80 from outside suppliers, so the $80 price is acceptable. Further, with a transfer price of $80 per monitor, top management of ZTel is indifferent to S-Phone buying from LCD or buying similar-quality monitors from outside suppliers.

With no excess capacity, the LCD manager will not accept a transfer price less than $80 per monitor. For example, suppose the S-Phone manager suggests a transfer price of $70 per monitor. At that price the LCD manager incurs an unnecessary *opportunity cost* of $10 per monitor (computed as $80 market price minus $70 transfer price). This would lower the LCD division's income and hurt its performance evaluation.

Excess Capacity Assume that the LCD division has excess capacity. For example, the LCD division might currently be producing only 80,000 units. Because LCD has $2,000,000 of fixed manufacturing costs, both LCD and the top management of ZTel prefer that S-Phone purchases its monitors from LCD. For example, if S-Phone purchases its monitors from an outside supplier at the market price of $80 each, LCD manufactures no units. Then, LCD reports a division loss equal to its fixed costs, and ZTel overall reports a lower net income as its costs are higher. Consequently, with excess capacity, LCD should accept any transfer price of $40 per unit or greater and S-Phone should purchase monitors from LCD. This will allow LCD to recover some (or all) of its fixed costs and increase ZTel's overall profits. For example, if a transfer price of $50 per monitor is used, the S-Phone manager is pleased to buy from LCD, since that price is below the market price of $80. For each monitor transferred from LCD to S-Phone at $50, the LCD division receives a *contribution margin* of $10 (computed as $50 transfer price less $40 variable cost) to contribute towards recovering its fixed costs. This form of transfer pricing is called **cost-based transfer pricing.** Under this approach the transfer price might be based on variable costs, total costs, or variable costs plus a markup. Determining the transfer price under excess capacity is complex and is covered in advanced courses.

Additional Issues in Transfer Pricing Several additional issues arise in determining transfer prices which include the following:

- **No market price exists.** Sometimes there is no market price for the product being transferred. The product might be a key component that requires additional conversion costs at the next stage and is not easily replicated by an outside company. For example, there is no market for a console for a Nissan Maxima and there is no substitute console Nissan can use in assembling a Maxima. In this case a market-based transfer price cannot be used.
- **Cost control.** To provide incentives for cost control, transfer prices might be based on standard, rather than actual costs. For example, if a transfer price of actual variable costs plus a markup of $20 per unit is used in the case above, LCD has no incentive to control its costs.
- **Division managers' negotiation.** With excess capacity, division managers will often negotiate a transfer price that lies between the variable cost per unit and the market price per unit. In this case, the **negotiated transfer price** and resulting departmental performance reports reflect, in part, the negotiating skills of the respective division managers. This might not be best for overall company performance.
- **Nonfinancial factors.** Factors such as quality control, reduced lead times, and impact on employee morale can be important factors in determining transfer prices.

Transfer Pricing Approaches Used by Companies

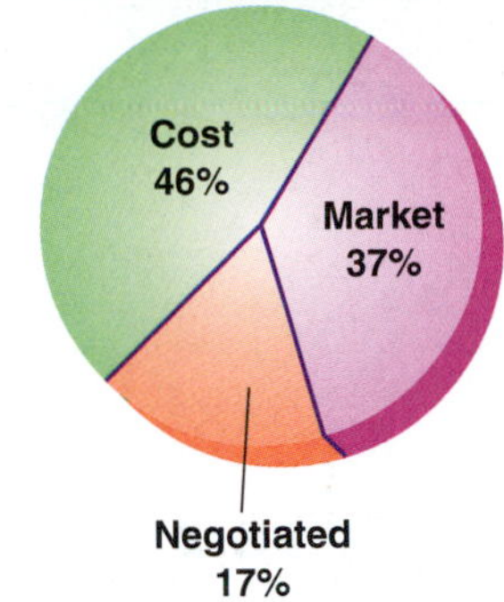

APPENDIX

Joint Costs and Their Allocation 9B

C6 Describe allocation of joint costs across products.

Most manufacturing processes involve **joint costs,** which refer to costs incurred to produce or purchase two or more products at the same time. A joint cost is like an indirect expense in the sense that more than one cost object share it. For example, a sawmill company incurs a joint cost when it buys logs that it cuts into lumber as shown in Exhibit 9B.1. The joint cost includes the logs (raw material) and its cutting (conversion) into boards classified as Clear, Select, No. 1 Common, No. 2 Common, No. 3 Common, and other types of lumber and by-products.

EXHIBIT 9B.1

Joint Products from Logs

Joint Cost: Cutting of Logs → Split-off Point → Joint Products: Clear; Select; No. 1 Common; No. 2 Common; No. 3 Common

When a joint cost is incurred, a question arises as to whether to allocate it to different products resulting from it. The answer is that when management wishes to estimate the costs of individual products, joint costs are included and must be allocated to these joint products. However, when management needs information to help decide whether to sell a product at a certain point in the production process or to process it further, the joint costs are ignored.

Financial statements prepared according to GAAP must assign joint costs to products. To do this, management must decide how to allocate joint costs across products benefiting from these costs. If some products are sold and others remain in inventory, allocating joint costs involves assigning costs to both cost of goods sold and ending inventory.

The two usual methods to allocate joint costs are the (1) *physical basis* and (2) the *value basis.* The physical basis typically involves allocating joint cost using physical characteristics such as the ratio of pounds, cubic feet, or gallons of each joint product to the total pounds, cubic feet, or gallons of all joint products flowing from the cost. This method is not preferred because the resulting cost allocations do not reflect the relative market values the joint cost generates. The preferred approach is the value basis, which allocates joint cost in proportion to the sales value of the output produced by the process at the "split-off point"; see Exhibit 9B.1.

Physical Basis Allocation of Joint Cost To illustrate the physical basis of allocating a joint cost, we consider a sawmill that bought logs for $30,000. When cut, these logs produce 100,000 board feet of lumber in the grades and amounts shown in Exhibit 9B.2. The logs produce 20,000 board feet of No. 3 Common lumber, which is 20% of the total. With physical allocation, the No. 3 Common lumber is assigned 20% of the $30,000 cost of the logs, or $6,000 ($30,000 × 20%). Because this low-grade lumber sells for $4,000, this allocation gives a $2,000 loss from its production and sale. The physical basis for allocating joint costs does not reflect the extra value flowing into some products or the inferior value flowing into others. That is, the portion of a log that produces Clear and Select grade lumber is worth more than the portion used to produce the three grades of common lumber, but the physical basis fails to reflect this.

EXHIBIT 9B.2

Allocating Joint Costs on a Physical Basis

Grade of Lumber	Board Feet Produced	Percent of Total	Allocated Cost	Sales Value	Gross Profit
Clear and Select	10,000	10.0%	$ 3,000	$12,000	$ 9,000
No. 1 Common	30,000	30.0	9,000	18,000	9,000
No. 2 Common	40,000	40.0	12,000	16,000	4,000
No. 3 Common	20,000	20.0	6,000	4,000	(2,000)
Totals	100,000	100.0%	$30,000	$50,000	$20,000

Value Basis Allocation of Joint Cost Exhibit 9B.3 illustrates the value basis method of allocation. It determines the percents of the total costs allocated to each grade by the ratio of each grade's sales value to the total sales value of $50,000 (sales value is the unit selling price multiplied by the number of units produced). The Clear and Select lumber grades receive 24% of the total cost ($12,000/$50,000) instead of the 10% portion using a physical basis. The No. 3 Common lumber receives only 8% of the total cost, or $2,400, which is much less than the $6,000 assigned to it using the physical basis.

EXHIBIT 9B.3

Allocating Joint Costs on a Value Basis

Grade of Lumber	Sales Value	Percent of Total	Allocated Cost	Gross Profit
Clear and Select	$12,000	24.0%	$ 7,200	$ 4,800
No. 1 Common	18,000	36.0	10,800	7,200
No. 2 Common	16,000	32.0	9,600	6,400
No. 3 Common	4,000	8.0	2,400	1,600
Totals	$50,000	100.0%	$30,000	$20,000

Example: Refer to Exhibit 9B.3. If the sales value of Clear and Select lumber is changed to $10,000, what is the revised ratio of the market value of No. 1 Common to the total? *Answer:* $18,000/$48,000 = 37.5%

An outcome of value basis allocation is that *each* grade produces exactly the same 40% gross profit at the split-off point. This 40% rate equals the gross profit rate from selling all the lumber made from the $30,000 logs for a combined price of $50,000.

Quick Check

Answers—p. 343

10. A company produces three products, B1, B2, and B3. The joint cost incurred for the current month for these products is $180,000. The following data relate to this month's production:

Product	Units Produced	Unit Sales Value
B1	96,000	$3.00
B2	64,000	6.00
B3	32,000	9.00

The amount of joint cost allocated to product B3 using the value basis allocation is (*a*) $30,000, (*b*) $54,000, or (*c*) $90,000.

Summary

C1 Explain departmentalization and the role of departmental accounting. Companies are divided into departments when they are too large to be effectively managed as a single unit. Operating departments carry out an organization's main functions. Service departments support the activities of operating departments. Departmental accounting systems provide information for evaluating departmental performance.

C2 Distinguish between direct and indirect expenses. Direct expenses are traced to a specific department and are incurred for the sole benefit of that department. Indirect expenses benefit more than one department. Indirect expenses are allocated to departments when computing departmental net income.

C3 Identify bases for allocating indirect expenses to departments. Ideally, we allocate indirect expenses by using a cause-effect relation for the allocation base. When a cause-effect relation is not identifiable, each indirect expense is allocated on a basis reflecting the relative benefit received by each department.

C4 Explain controllable costs and responsibility accounting. A controllable cost is one that is influenced by a specific management level. The total expenses of operating a department often include some items a department manager does not control. Responsibility accounting systems provide information for evaluating the performance of department managers. A responsibility accounting system's performance reports for evaluating department managers should include only the expenses (and revenues) that each manager controls.

C5 Explain transfer pricing and methods to set transfer prices. Transfer prices are used to record transfers of items between divisions of the same company. Transfer prices can be based on costs or market prices, or can be negotiated by division managers.

C6 Describe allocation of joint costs across products. A joint cost refers to costs incurred to produce or purchase two or more products at the same time. When income statements are prepared, joint costs are usually allocated to the resulting joint products using either a physical or value basis.

A1 Analyze investment centers using return on assets, residual income, and balanced scorecard. A financial measure often used to evaluate an investment center manager is the *investment center return on total assets,* also called *return on investment.* This measure is computed as the center's net income divided by the center's average total assets. Residual income, computed as investment center net income minus a target net income is an alternative financial measure of investment center performance. A balanced scorecard uses a combination of financial and non-financial measures to evaluate performance.

A2 Analyze investment centers using profit margin and investment turnover. Return on investment can also be computed as profit margin times investment turnover. Profit margin (equal to net income/sales) measures the income earned per dollar of sales and investment turnover (equal to sales/assets) measures how efficiently a division uses its assets.

P1 Prepare departmental income statements. Each profit center (department) is assigned its expenses to yield its own income statement. These costs include its direct expenses and its share of indirect expenses. The departmental income statement lists its revenues and costs of goods sold to determine gross profit. Its operating expenses (direct expenses and its indirect expenses allocated to the department) are deducted from gross profit to yield departmental net income.

P2 Prepare departmental contribution reports. The departmental contribution report is similar to the departmental income statement in terms of computing the gross profit for each department. Then the direct operating expenses for each department are deducted from gross profit to determine the contribution generated by each department. Indirect operating expenses are deducted *in total* from the company's combined contribution.

Guidance Answers to **Decision Maker** and **Decision Ethics**

Center Manager We must first realize that the two investment opportunities are not comparable on the basis of absolute dollars of income or on assets. For instance, the second investment provides a higher income in absolute dollars but requires a higher investment. Accordingly, we need to compute return on total assets for each alternative: (1) \$50,000 ÷ \$250,000 = 20%, and (2) \$175,000 ÷ \$1 million = 17.5%. Alternative 1 has the higher return and is preferred over alternative 2. Do you pursue one, both, or neither? Because alternative 1's return is higher than the center's usual return of 19%, it should be pursued, assuming its risks are acceptable. Also, since alternative 1 requires a small investment, top management is likely to be more agreeable to pursuing it. Alternative 2's return is lower than the usual 19% and is not likely to be acceptable.

Division Manager Your division's ROI without further action is 10.5% (equal to 7% × 1.5). In a highly competitive industry, it is difficult to increase profit margins by raising prices. Your division might be better able to control its costs to increase its profit margin. In addition, you might engage in a marketing program to increase sales without increasing your division's invested assets. Investment turnover and thus ROI will increase if the marketing campaign attracts customers.

Guidance Answers to **Quick Checks**

1. A departmental accounting system provides information used to evaluate the performance of *departments.* A responsibility accounting system provides information used to evaluate the performance of *department managers.*
2. *d*
3. A cost center, such as a service department, incurs costs without directly generating revenues. A profit center, such as a product division, incurs costs but also generates revenues.

4. *b*
5. *d*
6. (1) Assign the direct expenses to each department. (2) Allocate indirect expenses to all departments. (3) Allocate the service department expenses to the operating departments.
7. *b*
8. No, because many expenses that enter into these calculations are beyond the manager's control, and managers should not be evaluated using costs they do not control.
9. *c*
10. *b*; $180,000 × ([32,000 × $9]/[96,000 × $3 + 64,000 × $6 + 32,000 × $9]) = $54,000.

Key Terms

mhhe.com/wildMA2e

Key Terms are available at the book's Website for learning and testing in an online Flashcard Format.

Multiple Choice Quiz

Answers on p. 361

mhhe.com/wildMA2e

Additional Quiz Questions are available at the book's Website.

Quiz9

1. A retailer has three departments—housewares, appliances, and clothing—and buys advertising that benefits all departments. Advertising expense is $150,000 for the year, and departmental sales for the year follow: housewares, $356,250; appliances, $641,250; clothing, $427,500. How much advertising expense is allocated to appliances if allocation is based on departmental sales?
a. $37,500
b. $67,500
c. $45,000
d. $150,000
e. $641,250

2. Expenses that are easily traced and assigned to a specific department because they are incurred for the sole benefit of that department are called
a. Uncontrollable expenses
b. Fixed expenses
c. Direct expenses
d. Controllable expenses
e. Indirect expenses

3. A difficult challenge in computing the total expenses of a department is
a. Determining the direct expenses of the department.
b. Determining the amount of sales of the department.
c. Determining the gross profit ratio.
d. Assigning indirect expenses to the department.
e. Assigning direct expenses to the department.

4. A company operates three retail departments as profit centers, and the following information is available for each. Which department has the largest dollar amount of departmental contribution to overhead and what is the dollar amount contributed?

Department	Sales	Cost of Goods Sold	Direct Expenses	Allocated Indirect Expenses
X	$500,000	$350,000	$50,000	$40,000
Y	200,000	75,000	20,000	50,000
Z	350,000	150,000	75,000	10,000

a. Department Y, $ 55,000
b. Department Z, $125,000
c. Department X, $500,000
d. Department Z, $200,000
e. Department X, $ 60,000

5. Using the data in question 4, Department X's contribution to overhead as a percentage of sales is
a. 20%
b. 30%
c. 12%
d. 48%
e. 32%

Superscript letter A(B) denotes assignments based on Appendix 9A (9B).

Discussion Questions

1. Why are many companies divided into departments?
2. What is the difference between operating departments and service departments?
3. What are two main goals in managerial accounting for reporting on and analyzing departments?
4. Is it possible to evaluate a cost center's profitability? Explain.
5. What is the difference between direct and indirect expenses?
6. Suggest a reasonable basis for allocating each of the following indirect expenses to departments: (a) salary of a supervisor who manages several departments, (b) rent, (c) heat, (d) electricity for lighting, (e) janitorial services, (f) advertising, (g) expired insurance on equipment, and (h) property taxes on equipment.
7. How is a department's contribution to overhead measured?
8. What are controllable costs?
9. Controllable and uncontrollable costs must be identified with a particular _____ and a definite _____ period.
10. Why should managers be closely involved in preparing their responsibility accounting budgets?
11. In responsibility accounting, who receives timely cost reports and specific cost information? Explain.
12.[A] What is a transfer price? Under what conditions is a market-based transfer price most likely to be used?
13.[B] What is a joint cost? How are joint costs usually allocated among the products produced from them?
14.[B] Give two examples of products with joint costs.
15. Each retail store of **Best Buy** has several departments. Why is it useful for its management to (a) collect accounting information about each department and (b) treat each department as a profit center?
16. **Apple** delivers its products to locations around the world. List three controllable and three uncontrollable costs for its delivery department.

Denotes Discussion Questions that involve decision making.

connect *Most materials in this section are available in McGraw-Hill's Connect*

QUICK STUDY

QS 9-1
Allocation and measurement terms
C1 C2 C3 C4 A1

In each blank next to the following terms, place the identifying letter of its best description.

1. _______ Cost center
2. _______ Investment center
3. _______ Departmental accounting system
4. _______ Operating department
5. _______ Profit center
6. _______ Responsibility accounting system
7. _______ Service department

A. Engages directly in manufacturing or in making sales directly to customers.
B. Does not directly manufacture products but contributes to profitability of the entire company.
C. Incurs costs and also generates revenues.
D. Provides information used to evaluate the performance of a department.
E. Incurs costs without directly yielding revenues.
F. Provides information used to evaluate the performance of a department manager.
G. Holds manager responsible for revenues, costs, and investments.

QS 9-2
Basis for cost allocation
C3 

For each of the following types of indirect expenses and service department expenses, identify one allocation basis that could be used to distribute it to the departments indicated.

1. Computer service expenses of production scheduling for operating departments.
2. General office department expenses of the operating departments.
3. Maintenance department expenses of the operating departments.
4. Electric utility expenses of all departments.

QS 9-3
Allocating costs to departments
P1

Macee Department Store has three departments, and it conducts advertising campaigns that benefit all departments. Advertising costs are $100,000 this year, and departmental sales for this year follows. How much advertising cost is allocated to each department if the allocation is based on departmental sales?

Department	Sales
Department 1	$220,000
Department 2	400,000
Department 3	180,000

QS 9-4
Allocating costs to departments
P1

Mervon Company has two operating departments: Mixing and Bottling. Mixing has 300 employees and occupies 22,000 square feet. Bottling has 200 employees and occupies 18,000 square feet. Indirect factory costs for the current period follow: Administrative, $160,000; and Maintenance, $200,000. Administrative costs are allocated to operating departments based on the number of workers. Determine the administrative cost allocated to each operating department.

QS 9-5
Allocating costs to departments
P1

Refer to the information in QS 9-4. If the maintenance costs are allocated to operating departments based on square footage, determine the amount of maintenance costs allocated to each operating department.

QS 9-6
Departmental contribution to overhead
P2

Use the information in the following table to compute each department's contribution to overhead (both in dollars and as a percent). Which department contributes the largest dollar amount to total overhead? Which contributes the highest percent (as a percent of sales)?

	Dept. A	Dept. B	Dept. C
Sales	$106,000	$360,000	$168,000
Cost of goods sold	68,370	207,400	99,120
Gross profit	37,630	152,600	68,880
Total direct expenses	6,890	74,120	15,120
Contribution to overhead	$____	$____	$____
Contribution percent	____%	____%	____%

QS 9-7
Investment center analysis
A1 

Compute return on assets for each of these **Best Buy** divisions (each is an investment center). Comment on the relative performance of each investment center.

Investment Center	Net Income	Average Assets	Return on Assets
Cameras and camcorders	$4,500,000	$20,000,000	____
Phones and communications	1,500,000	12,500,000	____
Computers and accessories	800,000	10,000,000	____

QS 9-8
Computing residual income
A1

Refer to information in QS 9-7. Assume a target income of 12% of average invested assets. Compute residual income for each of Best Buy's divisions.

QS 9-9
Computing performance measures
A1 A2

A company's shipping division (an investment center) has sales of $2,700,000, net income of $216,000, and average invested assets of $2,000,000. Compute the division's return on invested assets, profit margin, and investment turnover.

QS 9-10 Performance measures A1 A2

Fill in the blanks in the schedule below for two separate investment centers A and B.

	Investment Center	
	A	B
Sales	$____	$3,200,000
Net income	$126,000	$____
Average invested assets	$700,000	____
Profit margin	6%	____%
Investment turnover	____	1.6
Return on assets	____%	10%

QS 9-11 Performance measures—balanced scorecard A1

Classify each of the performance measures below into the most likely balanced scorecard perspective it relates to. Label your answers using C (customer), P (internal process), I (innovation and growth), or F (financial).

1. Change in market share ____
2. Employee training sessions attended ____
3. Number of days of employee absences ____
4. Customer wait time ____
5. Number of new products introduced ____
6. Length of time raw materials are in inventory ____
7. Profit margin ____
8. Customer satisfaction index ____

QS 9-12 Performance measures—balanced scorecard A1

Walt Disney reports the following information for its two Parks and Resorts divisions.

	East Coast		West Coast	
	Current year	Prior year	Current year	Prior year
Hotel occupancy rates	89%	86%	92%	93%

Assume Walt Disney uses a balanced scorecard and sets a target of 90% occupancy in its resorts. Using Exhibit 9.20 as a guide, show how the company's performance on hotel occupancy would appear on a balanced scorecard report.

QS 9-13[A] Determining transfer prices without excess capacity C5

The Windshield division of Chee Cycles makes windshields for use in Chee's Assembly division. The Windshield division incurs variable costs of $175 per windshield and has capacity to make 50,000 windshields per year. The market price is $300 per windshield. The Windshield division incurs total fixed costs of $1,500,000 per year. If the Windshield division is operating at full capacity, what transfer price should be used on transfers between the Windshield and Assembly divisions? Explain.

QS 9-14[A] Determining transfer prices with excess capacity C5

Refer to information in QS 9-13. If the Windshield division has excess capacity, what is the range of possible transfer prices that could be used on transfers between the Windshield and Assembly divisions? Explain.

QS 9-15[B] Joint cost allocation C6

A company purchases a 10,020 square foot commercial building for $500,000 and spends an additional $50,000 to divide the space into two separate rental units and prepare it for rent. Unit A, which has the desirable location on the corner and contains 3,340 square feet, will be rented for $2.00 per square foot. Unit B contains 6,680 square feet and will be rented for $1.50 per square foot. How much of the joint cost should be assigned to Unit B using the value basis of allocation?

Most materials in this section are available in McGraw-Hill's Connect connect

EXERCISES

Exercise 9-1
Departmental expense allocations
C3

Firefly Co. has four departments: materials, personnel, manufacturing, and packaging. In a recent month, the four departments incurred three shared indirect expenses. The amounts of these indirect expenses and the bases used to allocate them follow.

Indirect Expense	Cost	Allocation Base
Supervision	$ 80,000	Number of employees
Utilities	61,000	Square feet occupied
Insurance	16,700	Value of assets in use
Total	$157,700	

Departmental data for the company's recent reporting period follow.

Department	Employees	Square Feet	Asset Values
Materials	40	27,000	$ 60,000
Personnel	22	5,000	1,200
Manufacturing	104	45,000	42,000
Packaging	34	23,000	16,800
Total	200	100,000	$120,000

Check (2) Total of $40,820 assigned to Materials Dept.

(1) Use this information to allocate each of the three indirect expenses across the four departments. (2) Prepare a summary table that reports the indirect expenses assigned to each of the four departments.

Exercise 9-2
Rent expense allocated to departments
C3

Expert Garage pays $128,000 rent each year for its two-story building. The space in this building is occupied by five departments as specified here.

Paint department	1,200 square feet of first-floor space
Engine department	3,600 square feet of first-floor space
Window department	1,920 square feet of second-floor space
Electrical department	1,056 square feet of second-floor space
Accessory department	1,824 square feet of second-floor space

Check Allocated to Paint Dept., $20,800

The company allocates 65% of total rent expense to the first floor and 35% to the second floor, and then allocates rent expense for each floor to the departments occupying that floor on the basis of space occupied. Determine the rent expense to be allocated to each department. (Round percents to the nearest one-tenth and dollar amounts to the nearest whole dollar.)

Exercise 9-3
Departmental expense allocation spreadsheet
C3

Off-Road Cycle Shop has two service departments (advertising and administration) and two operating departments (cycles and clothing). During 2009, the departments had the following direct expenses and occupied the following amount of floor space.

Department	Direct Expenses	Square Feet
Advertising	$ 21,000	1,820
Administrative	15,000	1,540
Cycles	102,000	6,440
Clothing	12,000	4,200

The advertising department developed and distributed 100 advertisements during the year. Of these, 72 promoted cycles and 28 promoted clothing. The store sold $300,000 of merchandise during the year. Of this amount, $228,000 is from the cycles department, and $72,000 is from the clothing department. The utilities expense of $65,000 is an indirect expense to all departments. Prepare a departmental expense allocation spreadsheet for Off-Road Cycle Shop. The spreadsheet should assign (1) direct expenses to each of the four departments, (2) the $65,000 of utilities expense to the four departments on the basis of floor space occupied, (3) the advertising department's expenses to the two operating departments on the basis of the number of ads placed that promoted a department's products, and (4) the administrative department's expenses to the two operating departments based on the amount of sales. Provide supporting computations for the expense allocations.

Check Total expenses allocated to Cycles Dept., $169,938

Exercise 9-4
Service department expenses allocated to operating departments

P1

The following is a partially completed lower section of a departmental expense allocation spreadsheet for Haston Bookstore. It reports the total amounts of direct and indirect expenses allocated to its five departments. Complete the spreadsheet by allocating the expenses of the two service departments (advertising and purchasing) to the three operating departments.

				Allocation of Expenses to Departments				
		Allocation Base	Expense Account Balance	Advertising Dept.	Purchasing Dept.	Books Dept.	Magazines Dept.	Newspapers Dept.
5	Total department expenses..........		$653,000	$23,000	$30,000	$426,000	$85,000	$89,000
6	**Service department expenses**							
7	Advertising department.............	Sales		?		?	?	?
8	Purchasing department.............	Purch. orders			?	?	?	?
9	Total expenses allocated to							
10	operating departments.............		?	$ 0	$ 0	?	?	?

Advertising and purchasing department expenses are allocated to operating departments on the basis of dollar sales and purchase orders, respectively. Information about the allocation bases for the three operating departments follows.

Department	Sales	Purchase Orders
Books	$440,000	400
Magazines	160,000	250
Newspapers	200,000	350
Total	$800,000	1,000

Check Total expenses allocated to Books Dept., $450,650

Exercise 9-5
Indirect payroll expense allocated to departments

C3

Jaria Stevens works in both the jewelry department and the hosiery department of a retail store. Stevens assists customers in both departments and arranges and stocks merchandise in both departments. The store allocates Stevens' $35,000 annual wages between the two departments based on a sample of the time worked in the two departments. The sample is obtained from a diary of hours worked that Stevens kept in a randomly chosen two-week period. The diary showed the following hours and activities spent in the two departments. Allocate Stevens' annual wages between the two departments.

Selling in jewelry department	41 hours
Arranging and stocking merchandise in jewelry department	4 hours
Selling in hosiery department	24 hours
Arranging and stocking merchandise in hosiery department	6 hours
Idle time spent waiting for a customer to enter one of the selling departments	5 hours

Check Assign $14,000 to Hosiery

Exercise 9-6
Managerial performance evaluation
C4 

Rex Stanton manages an auto dealership's service department. The recent month's income statement for his department follows. (1) Analyze the items on the income statement and identify those that definitely should be included on a performance report used to evaluate Stanton's performance. List them and explain why you chose them. (2) List and explain the items that should definitely be excluded. (3) List the items that are not definitely included or excluded and explain why they fall into that category.

Revenues		
Sales of parts	$ 72,000	
Sales of services	105,000	$177,000
Costs and expenses		
Cost of parts sold	30,000	
Building depreciation	9,300	
Income taxes allocated to department	8,700	
Interest on long-term debt	7,500	
Manager's salary	12,000	
Payroll taxes	8,100	
Supplies	15,900	
Utilities	4,400	
Wages (hourly)	16,000	
Total costs and expenses		111,900
Departmental net income		$ 65,100

Exercise 9-7
Investment center analysis
A1 

You must prepare a return on investment analysis for the regional manager of Veggie Burgers. This growing chain is trying to decide which outlet of two alternatives to open. The first location (A) requires a $500,000 investment and is expected to yield annual net income of $85,000. The second location (B) requires a $200,000 investment and is expected to yield annual net income of $42,000. Compute the return on investment for each Veggie Burgers alternative and then make your recommendation in a one-half page memorandum to the regional manager. (The chain currently generates an 18% return on total assets.)

Exercise 9-8
Computing performance measures
A1

ZMart, a retailer of consumer goods, provides the following information on two of its departments (each considered an investment center).

Investment Center	Sales	Net Income	Average Invested Assets
Electronics	$10,000,000	$750,000	$3,750,000
Sporting goods	8,000,000	800,000	5,000,000

(1) Compute return on investment for each department. Using return on investment, which department is most efficient at using assets to generate returns for the company? (2) Assume a target income level of 12% of average invested assets. Compute residual income for each department. Which department generated the most residual income for the company? (3) Assume the Electronics department is presented with a new investment opportunity that will yield a 15% return on assets. Should the new investment opportunity be accepted? Explain.

Exercise 9-9
Computing performance measures
A2

Refer to information in Exercise 9-8. Compute profit margin and investment turnover for each department. Which department generates the most net income per dollar of sales? Which department is most efficient at generating sales from average invested assets?

Exercise 9-10
Performance measures—balanced scorecard
A1

MidCoast Airlines uses the following performance measures. Classify each of the performance measures below into the most likely balanced scorecard perspective it relates to. Label your answers using C (customer), P (internal process), I (innovation and growth), or F (financial).

1. Percentage of ground crew trained ________
2. On-time flight percentage ________
3. Percentage of on-time departures ________
4. Market value ________
5. Flight attendant training sessions attended ________
6. Revenue per seat ________
7. Customer complaints ________
8. Time airplane is on ground between flights ________
9. Number of reports of mishandled or lost baggage ________
10. Cash flow from operations ________
11. Accidents or safety incidents per mile flown ________
12. Airplane miles per gallon of fuel ________
13. Return on investment ________
14. Cost of leasing airplanes ________

Exercise 9-11[A]
Determining transfer prices
C5

The Trailer department of Sprint Bicycles makes bike trailers that attach to bicycles and can carry children or cargo. The trailers have a retail price of $100 each. Each trailer incurs $40 of variable manufacturing costs. The Trailer department has capacity for 20,000 trailers per year, and incurs fixed costs of $500,000 per year.

Required

1. Assume the Assembly division of Sprint Bicycles wants to buy 5,000 trailers per year from the Trailer division. If the Trailer division can sell all of the trailers it manufactures to outside customers, what price should be used on transfers between Sprint Bicycle's divisions? Explain.
2. Assume the Trailer division currently only sells 10,000 trailers to outside customers, and the Assembly division wants to buy 5,000 trailers per year from the Trailer division. What is the range of acceptable prices that could be used on transfers between Sprint Bicycle's divisions? Explain.
3. Assume transfer prices of either $40 per trailer or $70 per trailer are being considered. Comment on the preferred transfer prices from the perspectives of the Trailer division manager, the Assembly division manager, and the top management of Sprint Bicycles.

Exercise 9-12[B]
Joint real estate costs assigned
C6

Mountain Home Properties is developing a subdivision that includes 300 home lots. The 225 lots in the Canyon section are below a ridge and do not have views of the neighboring canyons and hills; the 75 lots in the Hilltop section offer unobstructed views. The expected selling price for each Canyon lot is $50,000 and for each Hilltop lot is $100,000. The developer acquired the land for $2,500,000 and spent another $2,000,000 on street and utilities improvements. Assign the joint land and improvement costs to the lots using the value basis of allocation and determine the average cost per lot.

Check Total Canyon cost, $2,700,000

Exercise 9-13[B]
Joint product costs assigned
C6

Ocean Seafood Company purchases lobsters and processes them into tails and flakes. It sells the lobster tails for $20 per pound and the flakes for $15 per pound. On average, 100 pounds of lobster are processed into 57 pounds of tails and 24 pounds of flakes, with 19 pounds of waste. Assume that the company purchased 3,000 pounds of lobster for $6.00 per pound and processed the lobsters with an additional labor cost of $1,800. No materials or labor costs are assigned to the waste. If 1,570 pounds of tails and 640 pounds of flakes are sold, what is (1) the allocated cost of the sold items and (2) the allocated cost of the ending inventory? The company allocates joint costs on a value basis.

Check (2) Inventory cost, $1,760

Most materials in this section are available in McGraw-Hill's Connect connect

PROBLEM SET A

Problem 9-1A
Allocation of building occupancy costs to departments

C3 

mhhe.com/wildMA2e

Citizens Bank has several departments that occupy both floors of a two-story building. The departmental accounting system has a single account, Building Occupancy Cost, in its ledger. The types and amounts of occupancy costs recorded in this account for the current period follow.

Depreciation—Building	$ 31,500
Interest—Building mortgage	47,000
Taxes—Building and land	14,000
Gas (heating) expense	4,425
Lighting expense	5,250
Maintenance expense	9,625
Total occupancy cost	$111,800

The building has 5,000 square feet on each floor. In prior periods, the accounting manager merely divided the $111,800 occupancy cost by 10,000 square feet to find an average cost of $11.18 per square foot and then charged each department a building occupancy cost equal to this rate times the number of square feet that it occupied.

Helen Lanya manages a first-floor department that occupies 1,000 square feet, and Jose Jimez manages a second-floor department that occupies 1,700 square feet of floor space. In discussing the departmental reports, the second-floor manager questions whether using the same rate per square foot for all departments makes sense because the first-floor space is more valuable. This manager also references a recent real estate study of average local rental costs for similar space that shows first-floor space worth $40 per square foot and second-floor space worth $10 per square foot (excluding costs for heating, lighting, and maintenance).

Required

Check (1) Total allocated to Lanya and Jimez, $30,186 (2) Total occupancy cost to Lanya, $16,730

1. Allocate occupancy costs to the Lanya and Jimez departments using the current allocation method.

2. Allocate the depreciation, interest, and taxes occupancy costs to the Lanya and Jimez departments in proportion to the relative market values of the floor space. Allocate the heating, lighting, and maintenance costs to the Lanya and Jimez departments in proportion to the square feet occupied (ignoring floor space market values).

Analysis Component

3. Which allocation method would you prefer if you were a manager of a second-floor department? Explain.

Problem 9-2A
Departmental contribution to income

P2  

Vortex Company operates a retail store with two departments. Information about those departments follows.

	Department A	Department B
Sales	$800,000	$450,000
Cost of goods sold	497,000	291,000
Direct expenses		
Salaries	125,000	88,000
Insurance	20,000	10,000
Utilities	24,000	14,000
Depreciation	21,000	12,000
Maintenance	7,000	5,000

The company also incurred the following indirect costs.

Salaries	$36,000
Insurance	6,000
Depreciation	15,000
Office expenses	50,000

Indirect costs are allocated as follows: salaries on the basis of sales; insurance and depreciation on the basis of square footage; and office expenses on the basis of number of employees. Additional information about the departments follows.

Department	Square footage	Number of employees
A	28,000	75
B	12,000	50

Required

1. For each department, determine the departmental contribution to overhead and the departmental net income.

2. Should Department B be eliminated? Explain.

Check (1) Dept. A net income, $38,260

Problem 9-3A
Departmental income statements; forecasts
P1 

mhhe.com/wildMA2e

Warton Company began operations in January 2009 with two operating (selling) departments and one service (office) department. Its departmental income statements follow.

WARTON COMPANY Departmental Income Statements For Year Ended December 31, 2009	Clock	Mirror	Combined
Sales	$170,000	$95,000	$265,000
Cost of goods sold	83,300	58,900	142,200
Gross profit	86,700	36,100	122,800
Direct expenses			
Sales salaries	21,000	7,100	28,100
Advertising	2,100	700	2,800
Store supplies used	550	350	900
Depreciation—Equipment	2,300	900	3,200
Total direct expenses	25,950	9,050	35,000
Allocated expenses			
Rent expense	7,040	3,780	10,820
Utilities expense	2,800	1,600	4,400
Share of office department expenses	13,500	6,500	20,000
Total allocated expenses	23,340	11,880	35,220
Total expenses	49,290	20,930	70,220
Net income	$ 37,410	$15,170	$ 52,580

Warton plans to open a third department in January 2010 that will sell paintings. Management predicts that the new department will generate $50,000 in sales with a 45% gross profit margin and will require the following direct expenses: sales salaries, $8,500; advertising, $1,100; store supplies, $400; and equipment depreciation, $1,000. It will fit the new department into the current rented space by taking some square footage from the other two departments. When opened the new painting department will fill one-fifth of the space presently used by the clock department and one-fourth used by the mirror department. Management does not predict any increase in utilities costs, which are allocated to the departments in proportion to occupied space (or rent expense). The company allocates office department expenses to the operating departments in proportion to their sales. It expects the painting department to increase total office department expenses by $8,000. Since the painting department will bring new customers into the store, management expects sales in both the clock and mirror departments to increase by 8%. No changes for those departments' gross profit percents or their direct expenses are expected except for store supplies used, which will increase in proportion to sales.

Required

Prepare departmental income statements that show the company's predicted results of operations for calendar year 2010 for the three operating (selling) departments and their combined totals. (Round percents to the nearest one-tenth and dollar amounts to the nearest whole dollar.)

Check 2010 forecasted combined net income (sales), $65,832 ($336,200)

Problem 9-4A
Responsibility accounting performance reports; controllable and budgeted costs
C4 P2

Billie Whitehorse, the plant manager of Travel Free's Ohio plant, is responsible for all of that plant's costs other than her own salary. The plant has two operating departments and one service department. The camper and trailer operating departments manufacture different products and have their own managers. The office department, which Whitehorse also manages, provides services equally to the two operating departments. A budget is prepared for each operating department and the office department. The company's responsibility accounting system must assemble information to present budgeted and actual costs in performance reports for each operating department manager and the plant manager. Each performance report includes only those costs that a particular operating department manager can control: raw materials, wages, supplies used, and equipment depreciation. The plant manager is responsible for the department managers' salaries, utilities, building rent, office salaries other than her own, and other office costs plus all costs controlled by the two operating department managers. The annual departmental budgets and actual costs for the two operating departments follow.

	Budget			Actual		
	Campers	Trailers	Combined	Campers	Trailers	Combined
Raw materials	$195,900	$276,200	$ 472,100	$194,800	$273,600	$ 468,400
Employee wages	104,200	205,200	309,400	107,200	208,000	315,200
Dept. manager salary	44,000	53,000	97,000	44,800	53,900	98,700
Supplies used	34,000	92,200	126,200	32,900	91,300	124,200
Depreciation—Equip.	63,000	127,000	190,000	63,000	127,000	190,000
Utilities	3,600	5,200	8,800	4,500	4,700	9,200
Building rent	5,700	10,000	15,700	6,200	9,300	15,500
Office department costs	67,750	67,750	135,500	68,550	68,550	137,100
Totals	$518,150	$836,550	$1,354,700	$521,950	$836,350	$1,358,300

The office department's annual budget and its actual costs follow.

	Budget	Actual
Plant manager salary	$100,000	$ 84,000
Other office salaries	46,500	30,100
Other office costs	22,000	21,000
Totals	$168,500	$135,100

Required

1. Prepare responsibility accounting performance reports like those in Exhibit 9.22 that list costs controlled by the following:

a. Manager of the camper department.

b. Manager of the trailer department.

c. Manager of the Ohio plant.

In each report, include the budgeted and actual costs and show the amount that each actual cost is over or under the budgeted amount.

Check (1a) $800 total over budget

(1c) Ohio plant controllable costs, $15,400 total under budget

Analysis Component

2. Did the plant manager or the operating department managers better manage costs? Explain.

Problem 9-5A[B]
Allocation of joint costs
C6

Florida Orchards produced a good crop of peaches this year. After preparing the following income statement, the company believes it should have given its No. 3 peaches to charity and saved its efforts.

FLORIDA ORCHARDS Income Statement For Year Ended December 31, 2009	No. 1	No. 2	No. 3	Combined
Sales (by grade)				
No. 1: 300,000 lbs. @ $1.50/lb	$450,000			
No. 2: 250,000 lbs. @ $0.75/lb		$187,500		
No. 3: 600,000 lbs. @ $0.50/lb			$300,000	
Total sales				$937,500
Costs				
Tree pruning and care @ $0.40/lb	120,000	100,000	240,000	460,000
Picking, sorting, and grading @ $0.10/lb	30,000	25,000	60,000	115,000
Delivery costs	15,000	15,000	37,500	67,500
Total costs	165,000	140,000	337,500	642,500
Net income (loss)	$285,000	$ 47,500	$ (37,500)	$295,000

In preparing this statement, the company allocated joint costs among the grades on a physical basis as an equal amount per pound. The company's delivery cost records show that $30,000 of the $67,500 relates to crating the No. 1 and No. 2 peaches and hauling them to the buyer. The remaining $37,500 of delivery costs is for crating the No. 3 peaches and hauling them to the cannery.

Required

1. Prepare reports showing cost allocations on a sales value basis to the three grades of peaches. Separate the delivery costs into the amounts directly identifiable with each grade. Then allocate any shared delivery costs on the basis of the relative sales value of each grade.

Check (1) $147,200 tree pruning and care costs allocated to No. 3

2. Using your answers to part 1, prepare an income statement using the joint costs allocated on a sales value basis.

(2) Net income from No. 1 & No. 2 peaches, $152,820 & $63,680

Analysis Component

3. Do you think delivery costs fit the definition of a joint cost? Explain.

PROBLEM SET B

Problem 9-1B
Allocation of building occupancy costs to departments
C3 

Marshall's has several departments that occupy all floors of a two-story building that includes a basement floor. Marshall rented this building under a long-term lease negotiated when rental rates were low. The departmental accounting system has a single account, Building Occupancy Cost, in its ledger. The types and amounts of occupancy costs recorded in this account for the current period follow.

Building rent	$320,000
Lighting expense	20,000
Cleaning expense	32,000
Total occupancy cost	$372,000

The building has 7,500 square feet on each of the upper two floors but only 5,000 square feet in the basement. In prior periods, the accounting manager merely divided the $372,000 occupancy cost by 20,000 square feet to find an average cost of $18.60 per square foot and then charged each department a building occupancy cost equal to this rate times the number of square feet that it occupies.

Riley Miller manages a department that occupies 2,000 square feet of basement floor space. In discussing the departmental reports with other managers, she questions whether using the same rate per square foot for all departments makes sense because different floor space has different values. Miller checked a recent real estate report of average local rental costs for similar space that shows first-floor space worth $48 per square foot, second-floor space worth $24 per square foot, and basement space worth $12 per square foot (excluding costs for lighting and cleaning).

Required

Check Total costs allocated to Miller's Dept., (1) $37,200; (2) $18,000

1. Allocate occupancy costs to Miller's department using the current allocation method.
2. Allocate the building rent cost to Miller's department in proportion to the relative market value of the floor space. Allocate to Miller's department the lighting and heating costs in proportion to the square feet occupied (ignoring floor space market values). Then, compute the total occupancy cost allocated to Miller's department.

Analysis Component

3. Which allocation method would you prefer if you were a manager of a basement department?

Problem 9-2B

Departmental contribution to income

P2 

Sadar Company operates a store with two departments: videos and music. Information about those departments follows.

	Videos Department	Music Department
Sales	$370,500	$279,500
Cost of goods sold	320,000	175,000
Direct expenses		
Salaries	35,000	25,000
Maintenance	12,000	10,000
Utilities	5,000	4,500
Insurance	4,200	3,700

The company also incurred the following indirect costs.

Advertising	$15,000
Salaries	27,000
Office expenses	3,200

Indirect costs are allocated as follows: advertising on the basis of sales; salaries on the basis of number of employees; and office expenses on the basis of square footage. Additional information about the departments follows.

Department	Square footage	Number of employees
Videos	5,000	3
Music	3,000	2

Required

Check (1) Music dept. net income, $42,850

1. For each department, determine the departmental contribution to overhead and the departmental net income.
2. Should the video department be eliminated? Explain.

Problem 9-3B

Departmental income statements; forecasts

P1 

Collosal Entertainment began operations in January 2009 with two operating (selling) departments and one service (office) department. Its departmental income statements follow.

COLLOSAL ENTERTAINMENT Departmental Income Statements For Year Ended December 31, 2009	Movies	Video Games	Combined
Sales	$900,000	$300,000	$1,200,000
Cost of goods sold	630,000	231,000	861,000
Gross profit	270,000	69,000	339,000
Direct expenses			
Sales salaries	55,500	22,500	78,000
Advertising	18,750	9,000	27,750
Store supplies used	6,000	1,500	7,500
Depreciation—Equipment	6,750	4,500	11,250
Total direct expenses	87,000	37,500	124,500

[continued on next page]

[continued from previous page]

Allocated expenses			
Rent expense	61,500	13,500	75,000
Utilities expense	11,070	2,430	13,500
Share of office department expenses	84,375	28,125	112,500
Total allocated expenses	156,945	44,055	201,000
Total expenses	243,945	81,555	325,500
Net income (loss)	$ 26,055	$ (12,555)	$ 13,500

The company plans to open a third department in January 2010 that will sell compact discs. Management predicts that the new department will generate $450,000 in sales with a 35% gross profit margin and will require the following direct expenses: sales salaries, $27,000; advertising, $15,000; store supplies, $3,000; and equipment depreciation, $1,800. The company will fit the new department into the current rented space by taking some square footage from the other two departments. When opened, the new compact disc department will fill one-fourth of the space presently used by the movie department and one-third of the space used by the video game department. Management does not predict any increase in utilities costs, which are allocated to the departments in proportion to occupied space (or rent expense). The company allocates office department expenses to the operating departments in proportion to their sales. It expects the compact disc department to increase total office department expenses by $15,000. Since the compact disc department will bring new customers into the store, management expects sales in both the movie and video game departments to increase by 8%. No changes for those departments' gross profit percents or for their direct expenses are expected, except for store supplies used, which will increase in proportion to sales.

Required

Prepare departmental income statements that show the company's predicted results of operations for calendar year 2010 for the three operating (selling) departments and their combined totals. (Round percents to the nearest one-tenth and dollar amounts to the nearest whole dollar.)

Check 2010 forecasted movies net income (sales), $78,674 ($972,000)

Problem 9-4B
Responsibility accounting performance reports; controllable and budgeted costs
C4 P2

Warren Brown, the plant manager of LMN Co.'s San Diego plant, is responsible for all of that plant's costs other than his own salary. The plant has two operating departments and one service department. The refrigerator and dishwasher operating departments manufacture different products and have their own managers. The office department, which Brown also manages, provides services equally to the two operating departments. A monthly budget is prepared for each operating department and the office department. The company's responsibility accounting system must assemble information to present budgeted and actual costs in performance reports for each operating department manager and the plant manager. Each performance report includes only those costs that a particular operating department manager can control: raw materials, wages, supplies used, and equipment depreciation. The plant manager is responsible for the department managers' salaries, utilities, building rent, office salaries other than his own, and other office costs plus all costs controlled by the two operating department managers. The April departmental budgets and actual costs for the two operating departments follow.

	Budget			Actual		
	Refrigerators	Dishwashers	Combined	Refrigerators	Dishwashers	Combined
Raw materials	$ 480,000	$240,000	$ 720,000	$ 462,000	$242,400	$ 704,400
Employee wages	204,000	96,000	300,000	209,640	97,800	307,440
Dept. manager salary	66,000	58,800	124,800	66,000	55,800	121,800
Supplies used	18,000	10,800	28,800	16,800	11,640	28,440
Depreciation—Equip.	63,600	44,400	108,000	63,600	44,400	108,000
Utilities	36,000	21,600	57,600	41,400	24,840	66,240
Building rent	75,600	20,400	96,000	78,960	19,800	98,760
Office department costs	84,600	84,600	169,200	90,000	90,000	180,000
Totals	$1,027,800	$576,600	$1,604,400	$1,028,400	$586,680	$1,615,080

The office department's budget and its actual costs for April follow.

	Budget	Actual
Plant manager salary	$ 96,000	$102,000
Other office salaries	48,000	42,240
Other office costs	25,200	35,760
Totals	$169,200	$180,000

Required

1. Prepare responsibility accounting performance reports like those in Exhibit 9.22 that list costs controlled by the following:

a. Manager of the refrigerator department.

b. Manager of the dishwasher department.

c. Manager of the San Diego plant.

In each report, include the budgeted and actual costs for the month and show the amount by which each actual cost is over or under the budgeted amount.

Check (1a) $13,560 total under budget

(1c) San Diego plant controllable costs, $4,680 total over budget

Analysis Component

2. Did the plant manager or the operating department managers better manage costs? Explain.

Problem 9-5B[B]

Allocation of joint costs

C6

Rita and Rick Redding own and operate a tomato grove. After preparing the following income statement, Rita believes they should have offered the No. 3 tomatoes to the public for free and saved themselves time and money.

RITA AND RICK REDDING
Income Statement
For Year Ended December 31, 2009

	No. 1	No. 2	No. 3	Combined
Sales (by grade)				
No. 1: 600,000 lbs. @ $1.80/lb	$1,080,000			
No. 2: 480,000 lbs. @ $1.25/lb		$600,000		
No. 3: 120,000 lbs. @ $0.40/lb			$ 48,000	
Total sales				$1,728,000
Costs				
Land preparation, seeding, and cultivating @ $0.70/lb	420,000	336,000	84,000	840,000
Harvesting, sorting, and grading @ $0.04/lb	24,000	19,200	4,800	48,000
Delivery costs	20,000	14,000	6,000	40,000
Total costs	464,000	369,200	94,800	928,000
Net income (loss)	$ 616,000	$230,800	$(46,800)	$ 800,000

In preparing this statement, Rita and Rick allocated joint costs among the grades on a physical basis as an equal amount per pound. Also, their delivery cost records show that $34,000 of the $40,000 relates to crating the No. 1 and No. 2 tomatoes and hauling them to the buyer. The remaining $6,000 of delivery costs is for crating the No. 3 tomatoes and hauling them to the cannery.

Required

Check (1) $1,344 harvesting, sorting and grading costs allocated to No. 3

1. Prepare reports showing cost allocations on a sales value basis to the three grades of tomatoes. Separate the delivery costs into the amounts directly identifiable with each grade. Then allocate any shared delivery costs on the basis of the relative sales value of each grade. (Round percents to the nearest one-tenth and dollar amounts to the nearest whole dollar.)

2. Using your answers to part 1, prepare an income statement using the joint costs allocated on a sales value basis.

(2) Net income from No. 1 & No. 2 tomatoes, $503,138 & $279,726

Analysis Component

3. Do you think delivery costs fit the definition of a joint cost? Explain.

BEYOND THE NUMBERS

REPORTING IN ACTION

C4

BTN 9-1 Review Best Buy's income statement in Appendix A and identify its revenues for the years ended March 3, 2007, February 25, 2006, and February 26, 2005. For the year ended March 3, 2007, Best Buy reports the following product revenue mix. (Assume that its product revenue mix is the same for each of the three years reported when answering the requirements.)

Home Office	Entertainment Software	Consumer Electronics	Appliances
33%	12%	45%	10%

Required

1. Compute the amount of revenue from each of its product lines for the years ended March 3, 2007, February 25, 2006, and February 26, 2005.
2. If Best Buy wishes to evaluate each of its product lines, how can it allocate its operating expenses to each of them to determine each product line's profitability?

Fast Forward

3. Access Best Buy's annual report for a fiscal year ending after March 3, 2007, from its Website (BestBuy.com) or the SEC's EDGAR database (sec.gov). Compute its revenues for its product lines for the most recent year(s). Compare those results to those from part 1. How has its product mix changed?

COMPARATIVE ANALYSIS

P1

RadioShack.

BTN 9-2 Best Buy, Circuit City, and RadioShack compete across the country in several markets. The most common competitive markets for these companies are by location.

Required

1. Design a three-tier responsibility accounting organizational chart assuming that you have available internal information for all three companies. Use Exhibit 9.21 as an example. The goal of this assignment is to design a reporting framework for the companies; numbers are not required. Limit your reporting framework to sales activity only.
2. Explain why it is important to have similar performance reports when comparing performance within a company (and across different companies). Be specific in your response.

ETHICS CHALLENGE

P1

BTN 9-3 Senior Security Co. offers a range of security services for senior citizens. Each type of service is considered within a separate department. Mary Pincus, the overall manager, is compensated partly on the basis of departmental performance by staying within the quarterly cost budget. She often revises operations to make sure departments stay within budget. Says Pincus, "I will not go over budget even if it means slightly compromising the level and quality of service. These are minor compromises that don't significantly affect my clients, at least in the short term."

Required

1. Is there an ethical concern in this situation? If so, which parties are affected? Explain.
2. Can Mary Pincus take action to eliminate or reduce any ethical concerns? Explain.
3. What is Senior Security's ethical responsibility in offering professional services?

COMMUNICATING IN PRACTICE

C4 C5 P1 

BTN 9-4 Home Station is a national home improvement chain with more than 100 stores throughout the country. The manager of each store receives a salary plus a bonus equal to a percent of the store's net income for the reporting period. The following net income calculation is on the Denver store manager's performance report for the recent monthly period.

Sales	$2,500,000
Cost of goods sold	800,000
Wages expense	500,000
Utilities expense	200,000
Home office expense	75,000
Net income	$925,000
Manager's bonus (0.5%)	$ 4,625

In previous periods, the bonus had also been 0.5% of net income, but the performance report had not included any charges for the home office expense, which is now assigned to each store as a percent of its sales.

Required

Assume that you are the national office manager. Write a one-half page memorandum to your store managers explaining why home office expense is in the new performance report.

TAKING IT TO THE NET

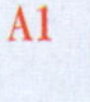 

BTN 9-5 This chapter described and used spreadsheets to prepare various managerial reports (see Exhibit 9-6). You can download from Websites various tutorials showing how spreadsheets are used in managerial accounting and other business applications.

Required

1. Link to the Website Lacher.com. Scroll down past "Microsoft Excel Examples" and select "Business Solutions." Identify and list three tutorials for review.
2. Describe in a one-half page memorandum to your instructor how the applications described in each tutorial are helpful in business and managerial decision making.

TEAMWORK IN ACTION

C1 C2 

BTN 9-6 Refer to Problem 9-1A involving the allocation of building occupancy costs to departments to answer the following requirements.

Required

1. Separate the class into 3-person teams. Each member of the 3-person team is assigned to complete one of the following tasks individually: (i) Allocate occupancy costs to the Lanya and Jimez departments using the current allocation method. (ii) Allocate the depreciation, interest, and taxes occupancy costs to the Lanya and Jimez departments in proportion to the relative market values of floor space. (iii) Allocate the heating, lighting, and maintenance costs to the Lanya and Jimez departments in proportion to the square feet occupied (ignoring floor space market values). Confirm your answers with the instructor.
2. The two people assigned to task *ii* and task *iii* from part 1 are to meet and determine the total occupancy costs allocated to the Lanya and Jimez departments. The person assigned to task *i* is to help with this determination.
3. Using answers for parts 1 and 2, the 3-person team is to discuss and explain which allocation method a manager of a second-floor department would prefer. Each team should be prepared to present their solutions to the class.

ENTREPRENEURIAL DECISION

P1  

BTN 9-7 RockBottomGolf is an Internet retailer and the focus of this chapter's opener. It sells discounted golf merchandise through departments such as clubs, bags, apparel, and accessories. The company plans to expand to include many other types of sporting goods.

Required

1. How can RockBottomGolf use departmental income statements to assist in understanding and controlling operations?

2. Are departmental income statements always the best measure of a department's performance? Explain.
3. Provide examples of nonfinancial performace indicators RockBottomGolf might use as part of a balanced scorecard system of performance evaluation.

BTN 9-8 Visit a local movie theater and check out both its concession area and its showing areas. The manager of a theater must confront questions such as:

- How much return do we earn on concessions?
- What types of movies generate the greatest sales?
- What types of movies generate the greatest net income?

HITTING THE ROAD

P1

Required

Assume that you are the new accounting manager for a 16-screen movie theater. You are to set up a responsibility accounting reporting framework for the theater.

1. Recommend how to segment the different departments of a movie theater for responsibility reporting.
2. Propose an expense allocation system for heat, rent, insurance, and maintenance costs of the theater.

BTN 9-9 Selected product data from DSG international plc (www.DSGiplc.com) follow.

GLOBAL DECISION

DSG

Product Segment for Year Ended (£ millions)	Net Sales		Operating Income	
	April 28, 2007	April 29, 2006	April 28, 2007	April 29, 2006
Computing	£2,198	£2,040	£97	£107
Electrical	5,281	4,912	193	198
e-commerce	451	26	1	0

Required

1. Compute the percentage growth in net sales for each product line from fiscal year 2006 to 2007.
2. Which product line's net sales grew the fastest?
3. Which segment was the most profitable?
4. How can DSG's managers use this information?

ANSWERS TO MULTIPLE CHOICE QUIZ

1. b; [$641,250/($356,250 + $641,250 + $427,500)] × $150,000 = $67,500
2. c
3. d
4. b;

	Department X	Department Y	Department Z
Sales	$500,000	$200,000	$350,000
Cost of goods sold	350,000	75,000	150,000
Gross profit	150,000	125,000	200,000
Direct expenses	50,000	20,000	75,000
Departmental contribution	$100,000	$105,000	$125,000

5. a; $100,000/$500,000 = 20%

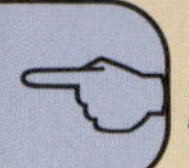

A Look Back

Chapter 9 focused on cost allocation and performance measurement. We identified several reports useful in measuring and analyzing the activities of a company, its departments, and its managers.

A Look at This Chapter

This chapter explains several tools and procedures useful for making and evaluating short-term managerial decisions. It also describes how to assess the consequences of such decisions.

A Look Ahead

Chapter 11 focuses on capital budgeting decisions. It explains and illustrates several methods that help identify projects with the higher return on investment.

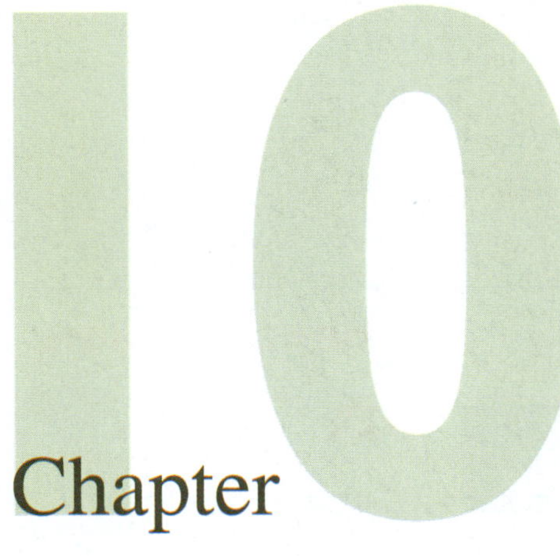

Chapter 10 Relevant Costing for Managerial Decisions

Learning Objectives

CAP

Conceptual

C1 Describe the importance of relevant costs for short-term decisions. *(p. 364)*

Analytical

A1 Evaluate short-term managerial decisions using relevant costs. *(p. 365)*

A2 Determine product selling price based on total costs. *(p. 372)*

Procedural

P1 Identify relevant costs and apply them to managerial decisions. *(p. 366)*

LP10

Decision Feature

Batter Up

"Now batting, a 34-ounce Prairie Sticks double-dipped black maple bat!" —PA Announcer

RED DEER, CANADA—Jared Greenberg, of the Red Deer Riggers, and Dan Zinger of the Red Deer Stags, dream to make it to the major leagues . . . not as players, but as makers of baseball bats. Their start-up company, **Prairie Sticks Bat Company (PrairieSticks.com),** started in Jared's workshop with a hand lathe and a piece of wood when local amateur players had trouble getting maple bats from manufacturers. Jared says he began producing bats for his teammates and friends "just like you would do in your middle school shop class."

Prairie Sticks' bats are made from four different types of wood, each with different prices (the company also makes fungo bats and training bats). Jared and Dan use product contribution margins in determining their best sales mix. This is especially important given their constraints on machine hours and labor—they have only one hydraulic tracing lathe and no other employees that make bats.

This past year they sold 1,500 bats. With production growth comes new business questions. Do we take a one-time deal with a buyer? Do we scrap or rework unacceptable inventory? Do we make or buy certain raw materials? These questions need answers. Jared and Dan focus on relevant costs and incremental revenues for insight into answering those questions. If a customer wants a bat in a color Prairie Sticks does not stock, the company charges a higher price to cover the incremental cost of the new color. The company makes novelty bats, unusable for play but fine for gifts and awards, out of inferior wood. These novelty bats sell at reduced prices, but enable the company to avoid costly rework and processing costs. They also sell apparel and hats, made by outside manufacturers.

Prairie Sticks now makes bats for big leaguers. It uses the same wood as the major batmakers; and $100,000 worth of equipment, including the hydraulic lathe, can turn out an unfinished bat in less than two minutes. Soon, they hope to step to the plate to accept additional business.

A recent news release reported that a minor league player had been traded for "10 Prairie Sticks double-dipped maple bats, black," which led to major publicity and a surge in orders. "It's been crazy," says Jared. "[Since] this story has broken . . . we're on the verge of picking up our Major League vendor's license," explains Dan. That would be a tape-measure home run.

[Sources: *Prairie Sticks Bat Company Website,* January 2009; *AlbertaLocalNews.com,* May 2008; *Fox Sports on MSN.com,* May 2008; *Edmonton CityTV.com* interview, May 2008]

Chapter Preview

Making business decisions involves choosing between alternative courses of action. Many factors affect business decisions, yet analysis typically focuses on finding the alternative that offers the highest return on investment or the greatest reduction in costs. In all situations, managers can reach a sounder decision if they identify the consequences of alternative choices in financial terms. This chapter explains several methods of analysis that can help managers make short-term business decisions.

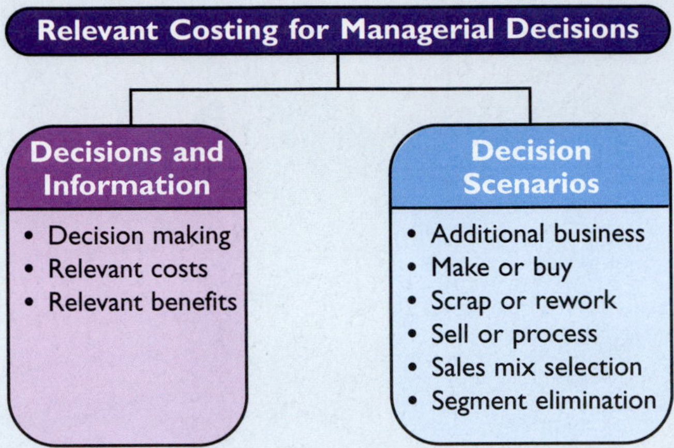

Relevant Costing for Managerial Decisions
Decisions and Information
• Decision making
• Relevant costs
• Relevant benefits
Decision Scenarios
• Additional business
• Make or buy
• Scrap or rework
• Sell or process
• Sales mix selection
• Segment elimination

This chapter focuses on methods that use accounting information to make important managerial decisions. Most of these scenarios involve short-term decisions. This differs from methods used for longer-term managerial decisions that are described in the next chapter and in several other chapters of this book.

Decisions and Information

Video10.1

This section explains how managers make decisions and the information relevant to those decisions.

Decision Making

Managerial decision making involves five steps: (1) define the decision task, (2) identify alternative courses of action, (3) collect relevant information and evaluate each alternative, (4) select the preferred course of action, and (5) analyze and assess decisions made. These five steps are illustrated in Exhibit 10.1.

EXHIBIT 10.1

Managerial Decision Making

Both managerial and financial accounting information play an important role in most management decisions. The accounting system is expected to provide primarily *financial* information such as performance reports and budget analyses for decision making. *Nonfinancial* information is also relevant, however; it includes information on environmental effects, political sensitivities, and social responsibility.

Relevant Costs

C1 Describe the importance of relevant costs for short-term decisions.

Most financial measures of revenues and costs from accounting systems are based on historical costs. Although historical costs are important and useful for many tasks such as product pricing and the control and monitoring of business activities, we sometimes find that an analysis of *relevant costs,* or *avoidable costs,* is especially useful. Three types of costs are pertinent to our discussion of relevant costs: sunk costs, out-of-pocket costs, and opportunity costs.

A *sunk cost* arises from a past decision and cannot be avoided or changed; it is irrelevant to future decisions. An example is the cost of computer equipment previously purchased by a company. Most of a company's allocated costs, including fixed overhead items such as depreciation and administrative expenses, are sunk costs.

An *out-of-pocket cost* requires a future outlay of cash and is relevant for current and future decision making. These costs are usually the direct result of management's decisions. For instance, future purchases of computer equipment involve out-of-pocket costs.

Example: Depreciation and amortization are allocations of the original cost of plant and intangible assets. Are they out-of-pocket costs? *Answer:* No; they are sunk costs.

An *opportunity cost* is the potential benefit lost by taking a specific action when two or more alternative choices are available. An example is a student giving up wages from a job to attend summer school. Companies continually must choose from alternative courses of action. For instance, a company making standardized products might be approached by a customer to supply a special (nonstandard) product. A decision to accept or reject the special order must consider not only the profit to be made from the special order but also the profit given up by devoting time and resources to this order instead of pursuing an alternative project. The profit given up is an opportunity cost. Consideration of opportunity costs is important. The implications extend to internal resource allocation decisions. For instance, a computer manufacturer must decide between internally manufacturing a chip versus buying it externally. In another case, management of a multidivisional company must decide whether to continue operating or close a particular division.

Point: Opportunity costs are not entered in accounting records. This does not reduce their relevance for managerial decisions.

Besides relevant costs, management must also consider the relevant benefits associated with a decision. **Relevant benefits** refer to the additional or *incremental* revenue generated by selecting a particular course of action over another. For instance, a student must decide the relevant benefits of taking one course over another. In sum, both relevant costs and relevant benefits are crucial to managerial decision making.

Managerial Decision Scenarios

Managers experience many different scenarios that require analyzing alternative actions and making a decision. We describe several different types of decision scenarios in this section. We set these tasks in the context of FasTrac, an exercise supplies and equipment manufacturer introduced earlier. *We treat each of these decision tasks as separate from each other.*

A1 Evaluate short-term managerial decisions using relevant costs.

Additional Business

FasTrac is operating at its normal level of 80% of full capacity. At this level, it produces and sells approximately 100,000 units of product annually. Its per unit and annual total costs are shown in Exhibit 10.2.

Video10.1

EXHIBIT 10.2

Selected Operating Income Data

	Per Unit	Annual Total
Sales (100,000 units)	$10.00	$1,000,000
Direct materials	(3.50)	(350,000)
Direct labor	(2.20)	(220,000)
Overhead	(1.10)	(110,000)
Selling expenses	(1.40)	(140,000)
Administrative expenses	(0.80)	(80,000)
Total costs and expenses	(9.00)	(900,000)
Operating income	$ 1.00	$ 100,000

A current buyer of FasTrac's products wants to purchase additional units of its product and export them to another country. This buyer offers to buy 10,000 units of the product at $8.50 per unit, or $1.50 less than the current price. The offer price is low, but FasTrac is considering the proposal because this sale would be several times larger than any single previous sale and it would use idle capacity. Also, the units will be exported, so this new business will not affect current sales.

P1 Identify relevant costs and apply them to managerial decisions.

To determine whether to accept or reject this order, management needs to know whether accepting the offer will increase net income. The analysis in Exhibit 10.3 shows that if management relies on per unit historical costs, it would reject the sale because it yields a loss. However, historical costs are *not* relevant to this decision. Instead, the relevant costs are the additional costs, called **incremental costs.** These costs, also called *differential costs,* are the additional costs incurred if a company pursues a certain course of action. FasTrac's incremental costs are those related to the added volume that this new order would bring.

EXHIBIT 10.3

Analysis of Additional Business Using Historical Costs

	Per Unit	Total
Sales (10,000 additional units)	$ 8.50	$ 85,000
Direct materials	(3.50)	(35,000)
Direct labor	(2.20)	(22,000)
Overhead	(1.10)	(11,000)
Selling expenses	(1.40)	(14,000)
Administrative expenses	(0.80)	(8,000)
Total costs and expenses	(9.00)	(90,000)
Operating loss	$(0.50)	$ (5,000)

To make its decision, FasTrac must analyze the costs of this new business in a different manner. The following information regarding the order is available:

- Manufacturing 10,000 additional units requires direct materials of $3.50 per unit and direct labor of $2.20 per unit (same as for all other units).
- Manufacturing 10,000 additional units adds $5,000 of incremental overhead costs for power, packaging, and indirect labor (all variable costs).
- Incremental commissions and selling expenses from this sale of 10,000 additional units would be $2,000 (all variable costs).
- Incremental administrative expenses of $1,000 for clerical efforts are needed (all fixed costs) with the sale of 10,000 additional units.

We use this information, as shown in Exhibit 10.4, to assess how accepting this new business will affect FasTrac's income.

EXHIBIT 10.4

Analysis of Additional Business Using Relevant Costs

	Current Business	Additional Business	Combined
Sales	$1,000,000	$ 85,000	$1,085,000
Direct materials	(350,000)	(35,000)	(385,000)
Direct labor	(220,000)	(22,000)	(242,000)
Overhead	(110,000)	(5,000)	(115,000)
Selling expenses	(140,000)	(2,000)	(142,000)
Administrative expense	(80,000)	(1,000)	(81,000)
Total costs and expenses	(900,000)	(65,000)	(965,000)
Operating income	$ 100,000	$ 20,000	$ 120,000

The analysis of relevant costs in Exhibit 10.4 suggests that the additional business be accepted. It would provide $85,000 of added revenue while incurring only $65,000 of added costs. This would yield $20,000 of additional pretax income, or a pretax profit margin of 23.5%. More generally, FasTrac would increase its income with any price that exceeded $6.50 per unit ($65,000 incremental cost/10,000 additional units).

An analysis of the incremental costs pertaining to the additional volume is always relevant for this type of decision. We must proceed cautiously, however, when the additional volume approaches or exceeds the factory's existing available capacity. If the additional volume requires the company to expand its capacity by obtaining more equipment, more space, or more personnel, the incremental costs could quickly exceed the incremental revenue. Another cautionary note is the effect on existing sales. All new units of the extra business will be sold outside FasTrac's normal domestic sales channels. If accepting additional business would cause existing sales to decline, this information must be included in our analysis. The contribution margin lost from a decline in sales is an opportunity cost. If future cash flows over several time periods are affected, their net present value also must be computed and used in this analysis.

The key point is that *management must not blindly use historical costs, especially allocated overhead costs.* Instead, the accounting system needs to provide information about the incremental costs to be incurred if the additional business is accepted.

Example: Exhibit 10.4 uses quantitative information. Suggest some qualitative factors to be considered when deciding whether to accept this project. *Answer:* (1) Impact on relationships with other customers and (2) Improved relationship with customer buying additional units.

Decision Maker

Partner You are a partner in a small accounting firm that specializes in keeping the books and preparing taxes for clients. A local restaurant is interested in obtaining these services from your firm. Identify factors that are relevant in deciding whether to accept the engagement. [Answer—p. 375]

Make or Buy

The managerial decision to make or buy a component for one of its current products is commonplace and depends on incremental costs. To illustrate, FasTrac has excess productive capacity it can use to manufacture Part 417, a component of the main product it sells. The part is currently purchased and delivered to the plant at a cost of $1.20 per unit. FasTrac estimates that making Part 417 would cost $0.45 for direct materials, $0.50 for direct labor, and an undetermined amount for overhead. The task is to determine how much overhead to add to these costs so we can decide whether to make or buy Part 417. If FasTrac's normal predetermined overhead application rate is 100% of direct labor cost, we might be tempted to conclude that overhead cost is $0.50 per unit, computed as 100% of the $0.50 direct labor cost. We would then mistakenly conclude that total cost is $1.45 ($0.45 of materials + $0.50 of labor + $0.50 of overhead). A wrong decision in this case would be to conclude that the company is better off buying the part at $1.20 each than making it for $1.45 each.

Instead, as we explained earlier, only incremental overhead costs are relevant in this situation. Thus, we must compute an *incremental overhead rate.* Incremental overhead costs might include, for example, additional power for operating machines, extra supplies, added cleanup costs, materials handling, and quality control. We can prepare a per unit analysis in this case as shown in Exhibit 10.5.

EXHIBIT 10.5

Make or Buy Analysis

	Make	Buy
Direct materials	$0.45	—
Direct labor	0.50	—
Overhead costs	**[?]**	**—**
Purchase price	—	$ 1.20
Total incremental costs	**$0.95 + [?]**	**$1.20**

We can see that if incremental overhead costs are less than $0.25 per unit, the total cost of making the component is less than the purchase price of $1.20 and FasTrac should make the part. FasTrac's decision rule in this case is that any amount of overhead less than $0.25 per unit yields a total cost for Part 417 that is less than the $1.20 purchase price. FasTrac must consider several nonfinancial factors in the make or buy decision, including product quality, timeliness of delivery (especially in a just-in-time setting), reactions of customers and suppliers, and other intangibles such as employee morale and workload. It must also consider whether making the part requires incremental fixed costs to expand plant capacity. When these added factors are considered, small cost differences may not matter.

Point: Managers must consider nonfinancial factors when making decisions.

Decision Insight

Make or Buy Services Companies apply make or buy decisions to their services. Many now outsource their payroll activities to a payroll service provider. It is argued that the prices paid for such services are close to what it costs them to do it, and without the headaches.

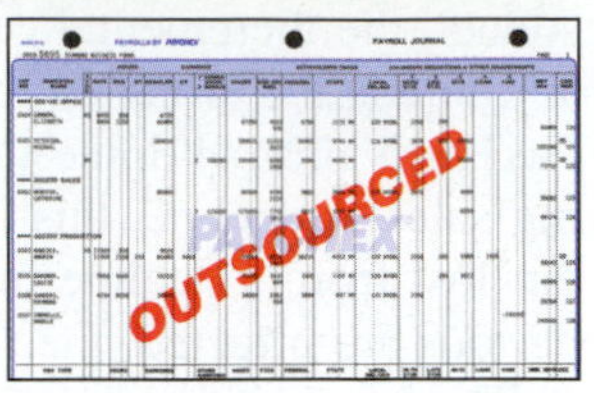

Scrap or Rework

Managers often must make a decision on whether to scrap or rework products in process. Remember that costs already incurred in manufacturing the units of a product that do not meet quality standards are sunk costs that have been incurred and cannot be changed. Sunk costs are irrelevant in any decision on whether to sell the substandard units as scrap or to rework them to meet quality standards.

To illustrate, assume that FasTrac has 10,000 defective units of a product that have already cost $1 per unit to manufacture. These units can be sold as is (as scrap) for $0.40 each, or they can be reworked for $0.80 per unit and then sold for their full price of $1.50 each. Should FasTrac sell the units as scrap or rework them?

To make this decision, management must recognize that the already incurred manufacturing costs of $1 per unit are sunk (unavoidable). These costs are *entirely irrelevant* to the decision. In addition, we must be certain that all costs of reworking defects, including interfering with normal operations, are accounted for in our analysis. For instance, reworking the defects means that FasTrac is unable to manufacture 10,000 *new* units with an incremental cost of $1 per unit and a selling price of $1.50 per unit, meaning it incurs an opportunity cost equal to the lost $5,000 net return from making and selling 10,000 new units. This opportunity cost is the difference between the $15,000 revenue (10,000 units × $1.50) from selling these new units and their $10,000 manufacturing costs (10,000 units × $1). Our analysis is reflected in Exhibit 10.6.

EXHIBIT 10.6

Scrap or Rework Analysis

	Scrap	Rework
Sale of scrapped/reworked units	$ 4,000	$ 15,000
Less costs to rework defects		(8,000)
Less opportunity cost of not making new units		**(5,000)**
Incremental net income	**$4,000**	**$ 2,000**

The analysis yields a $2,000 difference in favor of scrapping the defects, yielding a total incremental net income of $4,000. If we had failed to include the opportunity costs of $5,000, the rework option would have shown an income of $7,000 instead of $2,000, mistakenly making the reworking appear more favorable than scrapping.

Quick Check

Answers—p. 376

1. A company receives a special order for 200 units that requires stamping the buyer's name on each unit, yielding an additional fixed cost of $400 to its normal costs. Without the order, the company is operating at 75% of capacity and produces 7,500 units of product at the following costs:

Direct materials	$37,500
Direct labor	60,000
Overhead (30% variable)	20,000
Selling expenses (60% variable)	25,000

The special order will not affect normal unit sales and will not increase fixed overhead and selling expenses. Variable selling expenses on the special order are reduced to one-half the normal amount. The price per unit necessary to earn $1,000 on this order is (*a*) $14.80, (*b*) $15.80, (*c*) $19.80, (*d*) $20.80, or (*e*) $21.80.

2. What are the incremental costs of accepting additional business?

Sell or Process

The managerial decision to sell partially completed products as is or to process them further for sale depends significantly on relevant costs. To illustrate, suppose that FasTrac has 40,000 units of partially finished Product Q. It has already spent $0.75 per unit to manufacture these 40,000 units at a $30,000 total cost. FasTrac can sell the 40,000 units to another manufacturer as raw material for $50,000. Alternatively, it can process them further and produce finished products X, Y, and Z at an incremental cost of $2 per unit. The added processing yields the products and revenues shown in Exhibit 10.7. FasTrac must decide whether the added revenues from selling finished products X, Y, and Z exceed the costs of finishing them.

EXHIBIT 10.7

Revenues from Processing Further

Product	Price	Units	Revenues
Product X	$4.00	10,000	$ 40,000
Product Y	6.00	22,000	132,000
Product Z	8.00	6,000	48,000
Spoilage	—	2,000	0
Totals		40,000	$220,000

Exhibit 10.8 shows the two-step analysis for this decision. First, FasTrac computes its incremental revenue from further processing Q into products X, Y, and Z. This amount is the difference between the $220,000 revenue from the further processed products and the $50,000 FasTrac will give up by not selling Q as is (a $50,000 opportunity cost). Second, FasTrac computes its incremental costs from further processing Q into X, Y, and Z. This amount is $80,000 (40,000 units × $2 incremental cost). The analysis shows that FasTrac can earn incremental net income of $90,000 from a decision to further process Q. (Notice that the earlier incurred $30,000 manufacturing cost for the 40,000 units of Product Q does not appear in Exhibit 10.8 because it is a sunk cost and as such is irrelevant to the decision.)

Example: Does the decision change if incremental costs in Exhibit 10.8 increase to $4 per unit and the opportunity cost increases to $95,000? *Answer:* Yes. There is now an incremental net loss of $35,000.

EXHIBIT 10.8

Sell or Process Analysis

Revenue if processed	$220,000
Revenue if sold as is	(50,000)
Incremental revenue	170,000
Cost to process	(80,000)
Incremental net income	**$ 90,000**

Quick Check

Answers—p. 376

3. A company has already incurred a $1,000 cost in partially producing its four products. Their selling prices when partially and fully processed follow with additional costs necessary to finish these partially processed units:

Product	Unfinished Selling Price	Finished Selling Price	Further Processing Costs
Alpha	$300	$600	$150
Beta	450	900	300
Gamma	275	425	125
Delta	150	210	75

Which product(s) should *not* be processed further, (*a*) Alpha, (*b*) Beta, (*c*) Gamma, or (*d*) Delta?

4. Under what conditions is a sunk cost relevant to decision making?

Sales Mix Selection

When a company sells a mix of products, some are likely to be more profitable than others. Management is often wise to concentrate sales efforts on more profitable products. If

Point: A method called *linear programming* is useful for finding the optimal sales mix for several products subject to many market and production constraints. This method is described in advanced courses.

production facilities or other factors are limited, an increase in the production and sale of one product usually requires reducing the production and sale of others. In this case, management must identify the most profitable combination, or *sales mix* of products. To identify the best sales mix, management must know the contribution margin of each product, the facilities required to produce each product, any constraints on these facilities, and its markets.

To illustrate, assume that FasTrac makes and sells two products, A and B. The same machines are used to produce both products. A and B have the following selling prices and variable costs per unit:

	Product A	Product B
Selling price per unit	$5.00	$7.50
Variable costs per unit	3.50	5.50
Contribution margin per unit	$1.50	$2.00

The variable costs are included in the analysis because they are the incremental costs of producing these products within the existing capacity of 100,000 machine hours per month. We consider three separate cases.

Case 1: Assume that (1) each product requires 1 machine hour per unit for production and (2) the markets for these products are unlimited. Under these conditions, FasTrac should produce as much of Product B as it can because of its larger contribution margin of $2 per unit. At full capacity, FasTrac would produce $200,000 of total contribution margin per month, computed as $2 per unit times 100,000 machine hours.

Case 2: Assume that (1) Product A requires 1 machine hour per unit, (2) Product B requires 2 machine hours per unit, and (3) the markets for these products are unlimited. Under these conditions, FasTrac should produce as much of Product A as it can because it has a contribution margin of $1.50 per machine hour compared with only $1 per machine hour for Product B. Exhibit 10.9 shows the relevant analysis.

EXHIBIT 10.9

Sales Mix Analysis

	Product A	Product B
Selling price per unit	$ 5.00	$ 7.50
Variable costs per unit	3.50	5.50
Contribution margin per unit	$ 1.50	$ 2.00
Machine hours per unit	1.0	2.0
Contribution margin per machine hour	**$1.50**	**$1.00**

Example: For Case 2, if Product B's variable costs per unit increase to $6, Product A's variable costs per unit decrease to $3, and the same machine hours per unit are used, which product should FasTrac produce? *Answer:* Product A. Its contribution margin of $2 per machine hour is higher than B's $.75 per machine hour.

At its full capacity of 100,000 machine hours, FasTrac would produce 100,000 units of Product A, yielding $150,000 of total contribution margin per month. In contrast, if it uses all 100,000 hours to produce Product B, only 50,000 units would be produced yielding a contribution margin of $100,000. These results suggest that when a company faces excess demand and limited capacity, only the most profitable product per input should be manufactured.

Case 3: The need for a mix of different products arises when market demand is not sufficient to allow a company to sell all that it produces. For instance, assume that (1) Product A requires 1 machine hour per unit, (2) Product B requires 2 machine hours per unit, and (3) the market for Product A is limited to 80,000 units. Under these conditions, FasTrac should produce no more than 80,000 units of Product A. This would leave another 20,000 machine hours of capacity for making Product B. FasTrac should use this spare capacity to produce 10,000 units of Product B. This sales mix would maximize FasTrac's total contribution margin per month at an amount of $140,000.

Point: FasTrac might consider buying another machine to reduce the constraint on production. A strategy designed to reduce the impact of constraints or bottlenecks, on production, is called the *theory of constraints*.

Decision Insight

Companies such as **Gap, Abercrombie & Fitch,** and **American Eagle** must continuously monitor and manage the sales mix of their product lists. Selling their products in hundreds of countries and territories further complicates their decision process. The contribution margin of each product is crucial to their product mix strategies.

Segment Elimination

When a segment such as a department or division is performing poorly, management must consider eliminating it. Segment information on either net income (loss) or its contribution to overhead is not sufficient for this decision. Instead, we must look at the segment's avoidable expenses and unavoidable expenses. **Avoidable expenses,** also called *escapable expenses,* are amounts the company would not incur if it eliminated the segment. **Unavoidable expenses,** also called *inescapable expenses,* are amounts that would continue even if the segment is eliminated.

To illustrate, FasTrac considers eliminating its treadmill division because its $48,300 total expenses are higher than its $47,800 sales. Classification of this division's operating expenses into avoidable or unavoidable expenses is shown in Exhibit 10.10.

EXHIBIT 10.10

Classification of Segment Operating Expenses for Analysis

	Total	Avoidable Expenses	Unavoidable Expenses
Cost of goods sold	$ 30,000	$ 30,000	—
Direct expenses			
Salaries expense	7,900	7,900	—
Depreciation expense—Equipment	200	—	$ 200
Indirect expenses			
Rent and utilities expense	3,150	—	3,150
Advertising expense	400	400	—
Insurance expense	400	300	100
Service department costs			
Share of office department expenses	3,060	2,200	860
Share of purchasing expenses	3,190	1,000	2,190
Total	**$48,300**	**$41,800**	**$6,500**

FasTrac's analysis shows that it can avoid $41,800 expenses if it eliminates the treadmill division. Because this division's sales are $47,800, eliminating it will cause FasTrac to lose $6,000 of income. *Our decision rule is that a segment is a candidate for elimination if its revenues are less than its avoidable expenses.* Avoidable expenses can be viewed as the costs to generate this segment's revenues.

Example: How can insurance be classified as either avoidable or unavoidable? *Answer:* Depends on whether the assets insured can be removed and the premiums canceled.

When considering elimination of a segment, we must assess its impact on other segments. A segment could be unprofitable on its own, but it might still contribute to other segments' revenues and profits. It is possible then to continue a segment even when its revenues are less than its avoidable expenses. Similarly, a profitable segment might be discontinued if its space, assets, or staff can be more profitably used by expanding existing segments or by creating new ones. Our decision to keep or eliminate a segment requires a more complex analysis than simply looking at a segment's performance report. Such reports provide useful information, but they do not provide all the information necessary for this decision.

Example: Give an example of a segment that a company might profitably use to attract customers even though it might incur a loss. *Answer:* Warranty and post-sales services.

Qualitative Decision Factors

Managers must consider qualitative factors in making managerial decisions. Consider a decision on whether to buy a component from an outside supplier or continue to make it. Several qualitative decision factors must be considered. For example, the quality, delivery, and reputation of the proposed supplier are important. The effects from deciding not to make the component can include potential layoffs and impaired worker morale. Consider another situation in which a company is considering a one-time sale to a new customer at a special low price. Qualitative factors to consider in this situation include the effects of a low price on the company's image and the threat that regular customers might demand a similar price. The company must also consider whether this customer is really a one-time customer. If not, can it continue to offer this low price in the long run? Clearly, management cannot rely solely on financial data to make such decisions.

Quick Check

Answers—p. 376

5. What is the difference between avoidable and unavoidable expenses?
6. A segment is a candidate for elimination if (*a*) its revenues are less than its avoidable expenses, (*b*) it has a net loss, (*c*) its unavoidable expenses are higher than its revenues.

Decision Analysis — Setting Product Price

A2 Determine product selling price based on total costs.

Relevant costs are useful to management in determining prices for special short-term decisions. But longer run pricing decisions of management need to cover both variable and fixed costs, and yield a profit.

There are several methods to help management in setting prices. The *cost-plus* methods are probably the most common, where management adds a **markup** to cost to reach a target price. We will describe the **total cost method,** where management sets price equal to the product's total costs plus a desired profit on the product. This is a four-step process:

1. Determine total costs.

Total costs = Production (direct materials, direct labor, and overhead) + Nonproduction (selling and administrative) costs

2. Determine total cost per unit.

Total cost per unit = Total costs ÷ Total units expected to be produced and sold

3. Determine the dollar markup per unit.

Markup per unit = Total cost per unit × Markup percentage

where Markup percentage = Desired profit/Total costs

4. Determine selling price per unit.

Selling price per unit = Total cost per unit + Markup per unit

To illustrate, consider a company that produces MP3 players. The company desires a 20% return on its assets of $1,000,000, and it expects to produce and sell 10,000 players. The following additional company information is available:

Variable costs (per unit)	
Production costs	$44
Nonproduction costs	6
Fixed costs (in dollars)	
Overhead	$140,000
Nonproduction	60,000

We apply our four-step process to determine price.

1. Total costs = Production costs + Nonproduction costs
   = [($44 × 10,000 units) + $140,000] + [($6 × 10,000 units) + $60,000]
   = $700,000
2. Total cost per unit = Total costs/Total units expected to be produced and sold
   = $700,000/10,000
   = $70
3. Markup per unit = Total cost per unit × (Desired profit/Total costs)
   = $70 × [(20% × $1,000,000)/$700,000]
   = $20
4. Selling price per unit = Total cost per unit + Markup per unit
   = $70 + $20
   = $90

To verify that our price yields the $200,000 desired profit (20% × $1,000,000), we compute the following simplified income statement using the information above.

Sales ($90 × 10,000)	$900,000
Expenses	
Variable ($50 × 10,000)	500,000
Fixed ($140,000 + $60,000)	200,000
Income	$200,000

Companies use cost-plus pricing as a starting point for determining selling prices. Many factors determine price, including consumer preferences and competition.

Demonstration Problem

Determine the appropriate action in each of the following managerial decision situations.

1. Packer Company is operating at 80% of its manufacturing capacity of 100,000 product units per year. A chain store has offered to buy an additional 10,000 units at $22 each and sell them to customers so as not to compete with Packer Company. The following data are available.

Costs at 80% Capacity	Per Unit	Total
Direct materials	$ 8.00	$ 640,000
Direct labor	7.00	560,000
Overhead (fixed and variable)	12.50	1,000,000
Totals	$27.50	$2,200,000

In producing 10,000 additional units, fixed overhead costs would remain at their current level but incremental variable overhead costs of $3 per unit would be incurred. Should the company accept or reject this order?

2. Green Company uses Part JR3 in manufacturing its products. It has always purchased this part from a supplier for $40 each. It recently upgraded its own manufacturing capabilities and has enough excess capacity (including trained workers) to begin manufacturing Part JR3 instead of buying it. The company prepares the following cost projections of making the part, assuming that overhead is allocated to the part at the normal predetermined rate of 200% of direct labor cost.

Direct materials	$11
Direct labor	15
Overhead (fixed and variable) (200% of direct labor)	30
Total	$56

The required volume of output to produce the part will not require any incremental fixed overhead. Incremental variable overhead cost will be $17 per unit. Should the company make or buy this part?

3. Gold Company's manufacturing process causes a relatively large number of defective parts to be produced. The defective parts can be (a) sold for scrap, (b) melted to recover the recycled metal for reuse, or (c) reworked to be good units. Reworking defective parts reduces the output of other good units because no excess capacity exists. Each unit reworked means that one new unit cannot be produced. The following information reflects 500 defective parts currently available.

Proceeds of selling as scrap	$2,500
Additional cost of melting down defective parts	400
Cost of purchases avoided by using recycled metal from defects	4,800
Cost to rework 500 defective parts	
Direct materials	0
Direct labor	1,500
Incremental overhead	1,750
Cost to produce 500 new parts	
Direct materials	6,000
Direct labor	5,000
Incremental overhead	3,200
Selling price per good unit	40

Should the company melt the parts, sell them as scrap, or rework them?

Planning the Solution

- Determine whether Packer Company should accept the additional business by finding the incremental costs of materials, labor, and overhead that will be incurred if the order is accepted. Omit fixed costs that the order will not increase. If the incremental revenue exceeds the incremental cost, accept the order.
- Determine whether Green Company should make or buy the component by finding the incremental cost of making each unit. If the incremental cost exceeds the purchase price, the component should be purchased. If the incremental cost is less than the purchase price, make the component.
- Determine whether Gold Company should sell the defective parts, melt them down and recycle the metal, or rework them. To compare the three choices, examine all costs incurred and benefits received from the alternatives in working with the 500 defective units versus the production of 500 new units. For the scrapping alternative, include the costs of producing 500 new units and subtract the $2,500 proceeds from selling the old ones. For the melting alternative, include the costs of melting the defective units, add the net cost of new materials in excess over those obtained from recycling, and add the direct labor and overhead costs. For the reworking alternative, add the costs of direct labor and incremental overhead. Select the alternative that has the lowest cost. The cost assigned to the 500 defective units is sunk and not relevant in choosing among the three alternatives.

Solution to Demonstration Problem

1. This decision involves accepting additional business. Since current unit costs are $27.50, it appears initially as if the offer to sell for $22 should be rejected, but the $27.50 cost includes fixed costs. When the analysis includes only *incremental* costs, the per unit cost is as shown in the following table. The offer should be accepted because it will produce $4 of additional profit per unit (computed as $22 price less $18 incremental cost), which yields a total profit of $40,000 for the 10,000 additional units.

Direct materials	$ 8.00
Direct labor	7.00
Variable overhead (given)	3.00
Total incremental cost	$18.00

2. For this make or buy decision, the analysis must not include the $13 nonincremental overhead per unit ($30 − $17). When only the $17 incremental overhead is included, the relevant unit cost of

manufacturing the part is shown in the following table. It would be better to continue buying the part for $40 instead of making it for $43.

Direct materials	$11.00
Direct labor	15.00
Variable overhead	17.00
Total incremental cost	$43.00

3. The goal of this scrap or rework decision is to identify the alternative that produces the greatest net benefit to the company. To compare the alternatives, we determine the net cost of obtaining 500 marketable units as follows:

Incremental Cost to Produce 500 Marketable Units	Sell as Is	Melt and Recycle	Rework Units
Direct materials			
New materials	$ 6,000	$6,000	
Recycled metal materials		(4,800)	
Net materials cost		1,200	
Melting costs		400	
Total direct materials cost	6,000	1,600	
Direct labor	5,000	5,000	$1,500
Incremental overhead	3,200	3,200	1,750
Cost to produce 500 marketable units	14,200	9,800	3,250
Less proceeds of selling defects as scrap	(2,500)		
Opportunity costs*			5,800
Net cost	$11,700	$9,800	$9,050

* The $5,800 opportunity cost is the lost contribution margin from not being able to produce and sell 500 units because of reworking, computed as ($40 − [$14,200/500 units]) × 500 units.

The incremental cost of 500 marketable parts is smallest if the defects are reworked.

Summary

C1 Describe the importance of relevant costs for short-term decisions. A company must rely on relevant costs pertaining to alternative courses of action rather than historical costs. Out-of-pocket expenses and opportunity costs are relevant because these are avoidable; sunk costs are irrelevant because they result from past decisions and are therefore unavoidable. Managers must also consider the relevant benefits associated with alternative decisions.

A1 Evaluate short-term managerial decisions using relevant costs. Relevant costs are useful in making decisions such as to accept additional business, make or buy, and sell as is or process further. For example, the relevant factors in deciding whether to produce and sell additional units of product are incremental costs and incremental revenues from the additional volume.

A2 Determine product selling price based on total costs. Product selling price is estimated using total production and nonproduction costs plus a markup. Price is set to yield management's desired profit for the company.

P1 Identify relevant costs and apply them to managerial decisions. Several illustrations apply relevant costs to managerial decisions, such as whether to accept additional business; make or buy; scrap or rework products; sell products or process them further; or eliminate a segment and how to select the best sales mix.

Guidance Answers to Decision Maker and Decision Ethics

Partner You should identify the differences between existing clients and this potential client. A key difference is that the restaurant business has additional inventory components (groceries, vegetables, meats, etc.) and is likely to have a higher proportion of depreciable assets. These differences imply that the partner must spend more hours auditing the records and understanding the business, regulations, and standards that pertain to the restaurant business. Such differences suggest that the partner must use a different "formula" for quoting a price to this potential client vis-à-vis current clients.

Guidance Answers to **Quick Checks**

1. *e*; Variable costs per unit for this order of 200 units follow:

Direct materials ($37,500/7,500)	$ 5.00
Direct labor ($60,000/7,500)	8.00
Variable overhead [(0.30 × $20,000)/7,500]	0.80
Variable selling expenses [(0.60 × $25,000 × 0.5)/7,500]	1.00
Total variable costs per unit	$14.80

Cost to produce special order: (200 × $14.80) + $400 = $3,360.

Price per unit to earn $1,000: ($3,360 + $1,000)/200 = 21.80.

2. They are the additional (new) costs of accepting new business.

3. *d*;

	Incremental benefits		Incremental costs
Alpha	$300 ($600 − $300)	>	$150 (given)
Beta	$450 ($900 − $450)	>	$300 (given)
Gamma	$150 ($425 − $275)	>	$125 (given)
Delta	$ 60 ($210 − $150)	<	$ 75 (given)

4. A sunk cost is *never* relevant because it results from a past decision and is already incurred.

5. Avoidable expenses are ones a company will not incur by eliminating a segment; unavoidable expenses will continue even after a segment is eliminated.

6. *a*

Key Terms

mhhe.com/wildMA2e

Key Terms are available at the book's Website for learning and testing in an online Flashcard Format.

Avoidable expense (p. 371)
Incremental cost (p. 366)
Markup (p. 372)
Relevant benefits (p. 365)
Unavoidable expense (p. 371)
total cost method (p. 372)

Multiple Choice Quiz

Answers on p. 389

mhhe.com/wildMA2e

Additional Quiz Questions are available at the book's Website.

Quiz10

1. A company inadvertently produced 3,000 defective MP3 players. The players cost $12 each to produce. A recycler offers to purchase the defective players as they are for $8 each. The production manager reports that the defects can be corrected for $10 each, enabling them to be sold at their regular market price of $19 each. The company should:
   a. Correct the defect and sell them at the regular price.
   b. Sell the players to the recycler for $8 each.
   c. Sell 2,000 to the recycler and repair the rest.
   d. Sell 1,000 to the recycler and repair the rest.
   e. Throw the players away.

2. A company's productive capacity is limited to 480,000 machine hours. Product X requires 10 machine hours to produce; and Product Y requires 2 machine hours to produce. Product X sells for $32 per unit and has variable costs of $12 per unit; Product Y sells for $24 per unit and has variable costs of $10 per unit. Assuming that the company can sell as many of either product as it produces, it should:
   a. Produce X and Y in the ratio of 57% and 43%.
   b. Produce X and Y in the ratio of 83% X and 17% Y.
   c. Produce equal amounts of Product X and Product Y.
   d. Produce only Product X.
   e. Produce only Product Y.

3. A company receives a special one-time order for 3,000 units of its product at $15 per unit. The company has excess capacity and it currently produces and sells the units at $20 each to its regular customers. Production costs are $13.50 per unit, which includes $9 of variable costs. To produce the special order, the company must incur additional fixed costs of $5,000. Should the company accept the special order?
   a. Yes, because incremental revenue exceeds incremental costs.
   b. No, because incremental costs exceed incremental revenue.
   c. No, because the units are being sold for $5 less than the regular price.
   d. Yes, because incremental costs exceed incremental revenue.
   e. No, because incremental cost exceeds $15 per unit when total costs are considered.

4. A cost that cannot be changed because it arises from a past decision and is irrelevant to future decisions is
   a. An uncontrollable cost.
   b. An out-of-pocket cost.
   c. A sunk cost.
   d. An opportunity cost.
   e. An incremental cost.

5. The potential benefit of one alternative that is lost by choosing another is known as
   a. An alternative cost.
   b. A sunk cost.
   c. A differential cost.
   d. An opportunity cost.
   e. An out-of-pocket cost.

Discussion Questions

1. Identify the five steps involved in the managerial decision-making process.
2. Is nonfinancial information ever useful in managerial decision making?
3. What is a relevant cost? Identify the two types of relevant costs.
4. Why are sunk costs irrelevant in deciding whether to sell a product in its present condition or to make it into a new product through additional processing?
5. What is an out-of-pocket cost? Are out-of-pocket costs recorded in the accounting records?
6. What is an opportunity cost? Are opportunity costs recorded in the accounting records?
7. Identify some qualitative factors that should be considered when making managerial decisions.
8. Identify the incremental costs incurred by **Best Buy** for shipping one additional iPod from a warehouse to a retail store along with the store's normal order of 75 iPods.

9. **Circuit City** is considering eliminating one of its stores in a large U.S. city. What are some factors that Circuit City should consider in making this decision?

10. Assume that **Apple** manufactures and sells 500,000 units of a product at $30 per unit in domestic markets. It costs $20 per unit to manufacture ($13 variable cost per unit, $7 fixed cost per unit). Can you describe a situation under which the company is willing to sell an additional 25,000 units of the product in an international market at $15 per unit?

Denotes Discussion Questions that involve decision making.

connect *Most materials in this section are available in McGraw-Hill's Connect*

QUICK STUDY

QS 10-1
Identification of relevant costs
P1

Helix Company has been approached by a new customer to provide 2,000 units of its regular product at a special price of $6 per unit. The regular selling price of the product is $8 per unit. Helix is operating at 75% of its capacity of 10,000 units. Identify whether the following costs are relevant to Helix's decision as to whether to accept the order at the special selling price. No additional fixed manufacturing overhead will be incurred because of this order. The only additional selling expense on this order will be a $0.50 per unit shipping cost. There will be no additional administrative expenses because of this order. Place an X in the appropriate column to identify whether the cost is relevant or irrelevant to accepting this order.

Item	Relevant	Not relevant
a. Selling price of $6.00 per unit	______	______
b. Direct materials cost of $1.00 per unit	______	______
c. Direct labor of $2.00 per unit	______	______
d. Variable manufacturing overhead of $1.50 per unit	______	______
e. Fixed manufacturing overhead of $0.75 per unit	______	______
f. Regular selling expenses of $1.25 per unit	______	______
g. Additional selling expenses of $0.50 per unit	______	______
h. Administrative expenses of $0.60 per unit	______	______

QS 10-2
Analysis of relevant costs
A1

Refer to the data in QS 10-1. Based on financial considerations alone, should Helix accept this order at the special price? Explain.

QS 10-3
Identification of relevant nonfinancial factors
C1 A1

Refer to QS 10-1 and QS 10-2. What nonfinancial factors should Helix consider before accepting this order? Explain.

QS 10-4
Sell or process
C1 A1

Marathon Company has 10,000 units of its product that were produced last year at a total cost of $150,000. The units were damaged in a rain storm because the warehouse where they were stored developed a leak in the roof. Marathon can sell the units as is for $2 each or it can repair the units at a total cost of $18,000 and then sell them for $5 each. Should Marathon sell the units as is or repair them and then sell them? Explain.

QS 10-5
Selection of sales mix
C1 A1

Flash Memory Company can sell all units of computer memory X and Y that it can produce, but it has limited production capacity. It can produce four units of X per hour *or* six units of Y per hour, and it has 16,000 production hours available. Contribution margin is $10 for Product X and $8 for Product Y. What is the most profitable sales mix for this company?

QS 10-6
Analysis of incremental costs
C1 A1 

Falcon Company incurs a $18 per unit cost for Product A, which it currently manufactures and sells for $27 per unit. Instead of manufacturing and selling this product, the company can purchase Product B for $10 per unit and sell it for $24 per unit. If it does so, unit sales would remain unchanged and $10 of the $18 per unit costs assigned to Product A would be eliminated. Should the company continue to manufacture Product A or purchase Product B for resale?

Most materials in this section are available in McGraw-Hill's Connect connect

EXERCISES

Exercise 10-1
Decision to accept additional business or not
C1 A1 

Harlan Co. expects to sell 300,000 units of its product in the next period with the following results.

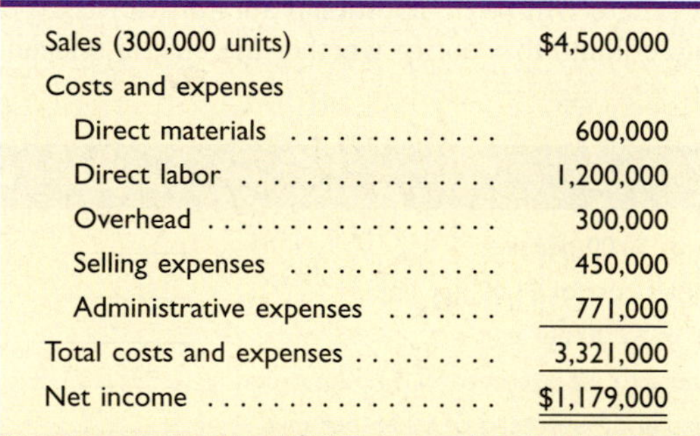

Sales (300,000 units)	$4,500,000
Costs and expenses	
Direct materials	600,000
Direct labor	1,200,000
Overhead	300,000
Selling expenses	450,000
Administrative expenses	771,000
Total costs and expenses	3,321,000
Net income	$1,179,000

The company has an opportunity to sell 30,000 additional units at $13 per unit. The additional sales would not affect its current expected sales. Direct materials and labor costs per unit would be the same for the additional units as they are for the regular units. However, the additional volume would create the following incremental costs: (1) total overhead would increase by 16% and (2) administrative expenses would increase by $129,000. Prepare an analysis to determine whether the company should accept or reject the offer to sell additional units at the reduced price of $13 per unit.

Check Income increase, $33,000

Exercise 10-2
Decision to accept new business or not
C1 A1

Goshford Company produces a single product and has capacity to produce 100,000 units per month. Costs to produce its current sales of 80,000 units follow. The regular selling price of the product is $100 per unit. Management is approached by a new customer who wants to purchase 20,000 units of the product for $75. If the order is accepted, there will be no additional fixed manufacturing overhead, and no additional fixed selling and administrative expenses. The customer is not in the company's regular selling territory, so there will be a $5 per unit shipping expense in addition to the regular variable selling and administrative expenses.

	Per Unit	Costs at 80,000 Units
Direct materials	$12.50	$1,000,000
Direct labor	15.00	1,200,000
Variable manufacturing overhead	10.00	800,000
Fixed manufacturing overhead	17.50	1,400,000
Variable selling and administrative expenses	14.00	1,120,000
Fixed selling and administrative expenses	13.00	1,040,000
Totals	$82.00	$6,560,000

Required

1. Determine whether management should accept or reject the new business.

2. What nonfinancial factors should management consider when deciding whether to take this order?

Check (1) Additional volume effect on net income, $370,000

Exercise 10-3
Make or buy decision
C1 A1

Simons Company currently manufactures one of its crucial parts at a cost of $2.72 per unit. This cost is based on a normal production rate of 40,000 units per year. Variable costs are $1.20 per unit, fixed costs related to making this part are $40,000 per year, and allocated fixed costs are $50,000 per year. Allocated fixed costs are unavoidable whether the company makes or buys the part. Simons is considering buying the part from a supplier for a quoted price of $2.16 per unit guaranteed for a three-year period. Should the company continue to manufacture the part, or should it buy the part from the outside supplier? Support your answer with analyses.

Check $1,600 increased costs to make

Exercise 10-4
Make or buy decision C1 A1

Gelb Company currently manufactures 40,000 units of a key component for its manufacturing process at a cost of $4.45 per unit. Variable costs are $1.95 per unit, fixed costs related to making this component are $65,000 per year, and allocated fixed costs are $58,500 per year. The allocated fixed costs are unavoidable whether the company makes or buys this component. The company is considering buying this component from a supplier for $3.50 per unit. Should it continue to manufacture the component, or should it buy this component from the outside supplier? Support your decision with analysis of the data provided.

Check Increased cost to make, $3,000

Exercise 10-5
Sell or process decision
C1 A1 

Starr Company has already manufactured 50,000 units of Product A at a cost of $50 per unit. The 50,000 units can be sold at this stage for $1,250,000. Alternatively, it can be further processed at a $750,000 total additional cost and be converted into 10,000 units of Product B and 20,000 units of Product C. Per unit selling price for Product B is $75 and for Product C is $50. Prepare an analysis that shows whether the 50,000 units of Product A should be processed further or not.

Exercise 10-6
Sell or rework decision
C1 A1

Varto Company has 7,000 units of its sole product in inventory that it produced last year at a cost of $22 each. This year's model is superior to last year's and the 7,000 units cannot be sold at last year's regular selling price of $35 each. Varto has two alternatives for these items: (1) they can be sold to a wholesaler for $8 each, or (2) they can be reworked at a cost of $125,000 and then sold for $25 each. Prepare an analysis to determine whether Varto should sell the products as is or rework them and then sell them.

Check Incremental net income of reworking, $(6,000)

Exercise 10-7
Analysis of income effects from eliminating departments
C1 A1 

Johns Co. expects its five departments to yield the following income for next year.

		Dept. M	Dept. N	Dept. O	Dept. P	Dept. T
2	Sales	$34,000	$23,500	$33,000	$27,500	$ 10,500
3	Expenses					
4	Avoidable	4,700	18,900	15,800	8,000	14,900
5	Unavoidable	20,000	5,100	2,900	15,000	5,900
6	Total expenses	24,700	24,000	18,700	23,000	20,800
7	Net income (loss)	$ 9,300	$ (500)	$14,300	$ 4,500	$(10,300)

Recompute and prepare the departmental income statements (including a combined total column) for the company under each of the following separate scenarios: Management (1) does not eliminate any department, (2) eliminates departments with expected net losses, and (3) eliminates departments with sales dollars that are less than avoidable expenses. Explain your answers to parts 2 and 3.

Check Total income (2) $17,100, (3) $21,700

Exercise 10-8
Income analysis of eliminating departments
C1 A1

Marinette Company makes several products, including canoes. The company has been experiencing losses from its canoe segment and is considering dropping that product line. The following information is available regarding its canoe segment. Should management discontinue the manufacturing of canoes? Support your decision.

MARINETTE COMPANY Income Statement—Canoe Segment		
Sales		$2,000,000
Variable costs		
Direct materials	$450,000	
Direct labor	500,000	
Variable overhead	300,000	
Variable selling and administrative	200,000	
Total variable costs		1,450,000
Contribution margin		550,000
Fixed costs		
Direct	375,000	
Indirect	300,000	
Total fixed costs		675,000
Net income		$ (125,000)

Check Income impact if canoe segment dropped, $(175,000)

Exercise 10-9
Sales mix determination and analysis
C1 A1

Jersey Company owns a machine that can produce two specialized products. Production time for Product TLX is two units per hour and for Product MTV is five units per hour. The machine's capacity is 2,200 hours per year. Both products are sold to a single customer who has agreed to buy all of the company's output up to a maximum of 3,740 units of Product TLX and 2,090 units of Product MTV. Selling prices and variable costs per unit to produce the products follow. Determine (1) the company's most profitable sales mix and (2) the contribution margin that results from that sales mix.

	Product TLX	Product MTV
Selling price per unit	$11.50	$6.90
Variable costs per unit	3.45	4.14

Check (2) $34,661

Exercise 10-10
Sales mix
C1 A1

Childress Company produces three products, K1, S5, and G9. Each product uses the same type of direct material. K1 uses 4 pounds of the material, S5 uses 3 pounds of the material, and G9 uses 6 pounds of the material. Demand for all products is strong, but only 50,000 pounds of material are available. Information about the selling price per unit and variable cost per unit of each product follows. Orders for which product should be produced and filled first, then second, and then third? Support your answer.

	K1	S5	G9
Selling price	$160	$112	$210
Variable costs	96	85	144

Check K1 contribution margin per pound, $16

Most materials in this section are available in McGraw-Hill's Connect connect

PROBLEM SET A

Problem 10-1A
Analysis of income effects of additional business
C1 A1

mhhe.com/wildMA2e

Ingraham Products manufactures and sells to wholesalers approximately 200,000 packages per year of underwater markers at $4 per package. Annual costs for the production and sale of this quantity are shown in the table.

Direct materials	$256,000
Direct labor	64,000
Overhead	192,000
Selling expenses	80,000
Administrative expenses	53,000
Total costs and expenses	$645,000

A new wholesaler has offered to buy 33,000 packages for $3.44 each. These markers would be marketed under the wholesaler's name and would not affect Ingraham Products' sales through its normal channels. A study of the costs of this additional business reveals the following:

- Direct materials costs are 100% variable.
- Per unit direct labor costs for the additional units would be 50% higher than normal because their production would require overtime pay at one-and-one-half times the usual labor rate.
- 35% of the normal annual overhead costs are fixed at any production level from 150,000 to 300,000 units. The remaining 65% of the annual overhead cost is variable with volume.
- Accepting the new business would involve no additional selling expenses.
- Accepting the new business would increase administrative expenses by a $5,000 fixed amount.

Required

Prepare a three-column comparative income statement that shows the following:

1. Annual operating income without the special order (column 1).
2. Annual operating income received from the new business only (column 2).
3. Combined annual operating income from normal business and the new business (column 3).

Check Operating income: (1) $155,000, (2) $29,848

Problem 10-2A
Analysis of income effects of additional business

C1 A1

Calla Company produces skateboards that sell for $50 per unit. The company currently has the capacity to produce 90,000 skateboards per year, but is selling 80,000 skateboards per year. Annual costs for 80,000 skateboards follow.

Direct materials	$ 800,000
Direct labor	640,000
Overhead	960,000
Selling expenses	560,000
Administrative expenses	480,000
Total costs and expenses	$3,440,000

A new retail store has offered to buy 10,000 of its skateboards for $45 per unit. The store is in a different market from Calla's regular customers and it would not affect regular sales. A study of its costs in anticipation of this additional business reveals the following:

- Direct materials and direct labor are 100% variable.
- Thirty percent of overhead is fixed at any production level from 80,000 units to 90,000 units; the remaining 70% of annual overhead costs are variable with respect to volume.
- Selling expenses are 60% variable with respect to number of units sold, and the other 40% of selling expenses are fixed.
- There will be an additional $2 per unit selling expense for this order.
- Administrative expenses would increase by a $1,000 fixed amount.

Required

1. Prepare a three-column comparative income statement that reports the following:
   a. Annual income without the special order.
   b. Annual income from the special order.
   c. Combined annual income from normal business and the new business.
2. Should Calla accept this order? What nonfinancial factors should Calla consider? Explain.

Check (1b) Added income from order, $123,000

Analysis Component

3. Assume that the new customer wants to buy 15,000 units instead of 10,000 units—it will only buy 15,000 units or none and will not take a partial order. Without any computations, how does this change your answer for part 2?

Problem 10-3A
Make or buy
C1 A1

Haver Company currently produces component RX5 for its sole product. The equipment that is used to produce RX5 must be replaced, and management must decide whether to replace the equipment or buy RX5 from an outside supplier. The current cost per unit to manufacture the required 50,000 units of RX5 follows.

Direct materials	$ 5.00
Direct labor	8.00
Overhead	9.00
Total cost per unit	$22.00

Direct materials and direct labor are 100% variable. Overhead is 80% fixed, and the current fixed overhead includes $0.50 per unit depreciation on the old equipment. If management buys the new equipment, it will incur depreciation of $1.12 per unit. An outside supplier has offered to supply the 50,000 units of RX5 for $18.00 per unit.

Required

1. Determine whether the company should make or buy the RX5.
2. What factors beside cost must management consider when deciding whether to make or buy RX5?

Check (1) Incremental cost to make RX5, $771,000

Problem 10-4A
Sell or process
C1 A1

Harold Manufacturing produces denim clothing. This year, it produced 5,000 denim jackets at a manufacturing cost of $45 each. These jackets were damaged in the warehouse during storage. Management investigated the matter and identified three alternatives for these jackets.

1. Jackets can be sold to a second-hand clothing shop for $6 each.
2. Jackets can be disassembled at a cost of $32,000 and sold to a recycler for $12 each.
3. Jackets can be reworked and turned into good jackets. However, with the damage, management estimates it will be able to assemble the good parts of the 5,000 jackets into only 3,000 jackets. The remaining pieces of fabric will be discarded. The cost of reworking the jackets will be $102,000, but the jackets can then be sold for their regular price of $45 each.

Required

Which alternative should Harold choose? Show analysis for each alternative.

Check Incremental income for alternative 2, $28,000

Problem 10-5A
Analysis of sales mix strategies
C1 A1 

Virginia Company is able to produce two products, G and B, with the same machine in its factory. The following information is available.

	Product G	Product B
Selling price per unit	$280	$240
Variable costs per unit	130	60
Contribution margin per unit	$150	$180
Machine hours to produce 1 unit	0.2 hours	2.0 hours
Maximum unit sales per month	1,200 units	200 units

The company presently operates the machine for a single eight-hour shift for 22 working days each month. Management is thinking about operating the machine for two shifts, which will increase its productivity by another eight hours per day for 22 days per month. This change would require $63,000 additional fixed costs per month.

Required

1. Determine the contribution margin per machine hour that each product generates.
2. How many units of Product G and Product B should the company produce if it continues to operate with only one shift? How much total contribution margin does this mix produce each month?
3. If the company adds another shift, how many units of Product G and Product B should it produce? How much total contribution margin would this mix produce each month? Should the company add the new shift? Explain.
4. Suppose that the company determines that it can increase Product G's maximum sales to 1,400 units per month by spending $24,000 per month in marketing efforts. Should the company pursue this strategy and the double shift? Explain.

Check Units of Product G: (2) 880, (3) 1,200, (4) 1,400

Problem 10-6A
Analysis of possible elimination of a department

C1 A1 

Eclectic Decor Company's management is trying to decide whether to eliminate Department 200, which has produced losses or low profits for several years. The company's 2009 departmental income statement shows the following.

ECLECTIC DECOR COMPANY
Departmental Income Statements
For Year Ended December 31, 2009

	Dept. 100	Dept. 200	Combined
Sales	$437,000	$280,000	$717,000
Cost of goods sold	263,000	207,000	470,000
Gross profit	174,000	73,000	247,000
Operating expenses			
Direct expenses			
Advertising	17,500	13,500	31,000
Store supplies used	5,000	4,600	9,600
Depreciation—Store equipment	4,200	3,000	7,200
Total direct expenses	26,700	21,100	47,800
Allocated expenses			
Sales salaries	52,000	31,200	83,200
Rent expense	9,500	4,750	14,250
Bad debts expense	9,500	7,400	16,900
Office salary	15,600	10,400	26,000
Insurance expense	1,900	1,000	2,900
Miscellaneous office expenses	2,500	1,700	4,200
Total allocated expenses	91,000	56,450	147,450
Total expenses	117,700	77,550	195,250
Net income (loss)	$ 56,300	$ (4,550)	$ 51,750

In analyzing whether to eliminate Department 200, management considers the following:

a. The company has one office worker who earns $500 per week, or $26,000 per year, and four salesclerks who each earn $400 per week, or $20,800 per year.

b. The full salaries of two salesclerks are charged to Department 100. The full salary of one sales clerk is charged to Department 200. The salary of the fourth clerk, who works half-time in both departments, is divided evenly between the two departments.

c. Eliminating Department 200 would avoid the sales salaries and the office salary currently allocated to it. However, management prefers another plan. Two salesclerks have indicated that they will be quitting soon. Management believes that their work can be done by the other two clerks if the one office worker works in sales half-time. Eliminating Department 200 will allow this shift of duties. If this change is implemented, half the office worker's salary would be reported as sales salaries and half would be reported as office salary.

d. The store building is rented under a long-term lease that cannot be changed. Therefore, Department 100 will use the space and equipment currently used by Department 200.

e. Closing Department 200 will eliminate its expenses for advertising, bad debts, and store supplies; 70% of the insurance expense allocated to it to cover its merchandise inventory; and 25% of the miscellaneous office expenses presently allocated to it.

Required

1. Prepare a three-column report that lists items and amounts for (a) the company's total expenses (including cost of goods sold)—in column 1, (b) the expenses that would be eliminated by closing Department 200—in column 2, and (c) the expenses that will continue—in column 3.

Check (1) Total expenses: (a) $665,250, (b) $275,225

2. Prepare a forecasted annual income statement for the company reflecting the elimination of Department 200 assuming that it will not affect Department 100's sales and gross profit. The statement should reflect the reassignment of the office worker to one-half time as a salesclerk.

(2) Forecasted net income without Department 200, $46,975

Analysis Component

3. Reconcile the company's combined net income with the forecasted net income assuming that Department 200 is eliminated (list both items and amounts). Analyze the reconciliation and explain why you think the department should or should not be eliminated.

PROBLEM SET B

Problem 10-1B
Analysis of income effects of additional business

C1 A1

Wyn Company manufactures and sells to local wholesalers approximately 150,000 units per month at a sales price of $4 per unit. Monthly costs for the production and sale of this quantity follow.

Direct materials	$192,000
Direct labor	48,000
Overhead	144,000
Selling expenses	60,000
Administrative expenses	40,000
Total costs and expenses	$484,000

A new out-of-state distributor has offered to buy 25,000 units next month for $3.44 each. These units would be marketed in other states and would not affect Wyn's sales through its normal channels. A study of the costs of this new business reveals the following:

- Direct materials costs are 100% variable.
- Per unit direct labor costs for the additional units would be 50% higher than normal because their production would require time-and-a-half overtime pay to meet the distributor's deadline.
- Twenty-five percent of the normal annual overhead costs are fixed at any production level from 125,000 to 200,000 units. The remaining 75% is variable with volume.
- Accepting the new business would involve no additional selling expenses.
- Accepting the new business would increase administrative expenses by a $2,000 fixed amount.

Required

Prepare a three-column comparative income statement that shows the following:

Check Operating income: (1) $116,000, (2) $22,000

1. Monthly operating income without the special order (column 1).
2. Monthly operating income received from the new business only (column 2).
3. Combined monthly operating income from normal business and the new business (column 3).

Problem 10-2B
Analysis of income effects of additional business

C1 A1

Mervin Company produces circuit boards that sell for $8 per unit. It currently has capacity to produce 600,000 circuit boards per year, but is selling 550,000 boards per year. Annual costs for the 550,000 circuit boards follow.

Direct materials	$ 825,000
Direct labor	1,100,000
Overhead	1,375,000
Selling expenses	275,000
Administrative expenses	550,000
Total costs and expenses	$4,125,000

An overseas customer has offered to buy 50,000 circuit boards for $6 per unit. The customer is in a different market from its regular customers and would not affect regular sales. A study of its costs in anticipation of this additional business reveals the following:

- Direct materials and direct labor are 100% variable.
- Twenty percent of overhead is fixed at any production level from 550,000 units to 600,000 units; the remaining 80% of annual overhead costs are variable with respect to volume.
- Selling expenses are 40% variable with respect to number of units sold, and the other 60% of selling expenses are fixed.
- There will be an additional $0.20 per unit selling expense for this order.
- Administrative expenses would increase by a $700 fixed amount.

Required

1. Prepare a three-column comparative income statement that reports the following:
   a. Annual income without the special order.
   b. Annual income from the special order.
   c. Combined annual income from normal business and the new business.
2. Should management accept the order? What nonfinancial factors should Mervin consider? Explain.

Check (1b) Additional income from order, $4,300

Analysis Component

3. Assume that the new customer wants to buy 100,000 units instead of 50,000 units—it will only buy 100,000 units or none and will not take a partial order. Without any computations, how does this change your answer in part 2?

Problem 10-3B
Make or buy
C1 A1

Alto Company currently produces component TH1 for its sole product. The equipment that it uses to produce TH1 must be replaced, and management must decide whether to replace the equipment or buy TH1 from an outside supplier. The current cost per unit to manufacture its required 400,000 units of TH1 follows.

Direct materials	$1.20
Direct labor	1.50
Overhead	6.00
Total cost per unit	$8.70

Direct materials and direct labor are 100% variable. Overhead is 75% fixed, and the current fixed overhead includes $1 per unit depreciation on the old equipment. If management buys the new equipment, it will incur depreciation of $1.50 per unit. An outside supplier has offered to supply the 400,000 units of TH1 for $4 per unit.

Required

1. Determine whether management should make or buy the TH1.

2. What factors besides cost must management consider when deciding whether to make or buy TH1?

Check (1) Incremental cost to make TH1, $1,880,000

Problem 10-4B
Sell or process
C1 A1

Micron Manufacturing produces electronic equipment. This year, it produced 7,500 oscilloscopes at a manufacturing cost of $300 each. These oscilloscopes were damaged in the warehouse during storage and, while usable, cannot be sold at their regular selling price of $500 each. Management has investigated the matter and has identified three alternatives for these oscilloscopes.

1. They can be sold to a wholesaler for $75 each.

2. They can be disassembled at a cost of $400,000 and the parts sold to a recycler for $130 each.

3. They can be reworked and turned into good units. The cost of reworking the units will be $3,200,000, after which the units can be sold at their regular price of $500 each.

Required

Which alternative should management pursue? Show analysis for each alternative.

Check Incremental income for alternative 2, $575,000

Problem 10-5B
Analysis of sales mix strategies
C1 A1 

Verto Company is able to produce two products, R and T, with the same machine in its factory. The following information is available.

	Product R	Product T
Selling price per unit	$ 120	$160
Variable costs per unit	65	90
Contribution margin per unit	$ 55	$ 70
Machine hours to produce 1 unit	0.2 hours	0.5 hours
Maximum unit sales per month	1,100 units	350 units

The company presently operates the machine for a single eight-hour shift for 22 working days each month. Management is thinking about operating the machine for two shifts, which will increase its productivity by another eight hours per day for 22 days per month. This change would require $30,000 additional fixed costs per month.

Required

1. Determine the contribution margin per machine hour that each product generates.

2. How many units of Product R and Product T should the company produce if it continues to operate with only one shift? How much total contribution margin does this mix produce each month?

Check Units of Product R: (2) 880, (3) 1,100, (4) 1,350

3. If the company adds another shift, how many units of Product R and Product T should it produce? How much total contribution margin would this mix produce each month? Should the company add the new shift? Explain.

4. Suppose that the company determines that it can increase Product R's maximum sales to 1,350 units per month by spending $9,000 per month in marketing efforts. Should the company pursue this strategy and the double shift? Explain.

Problem 10-6B

Analysis of possible elimination of a department

C1 A1 

Kumar Company's management is trying to decide whether to eliminate Department Z, which has produced low profits or losses for several years. The company's 2009 departmental income statement shows the following.

KUMAR COMPANY
Departmental Income Statements
For Year Ended December 31, 2009

	Dept. A	Dept. Z	Combined
Sales	$1,050,000	$262,500	$1,312,500
Cost of goods sold	691,950	187,650	879,600
Gross profit	358,050	74,850	432,900
Operating expenses			
Direct expenses			
Advertising	40,500	4,500	45,000
Store supplies used	8,400	2,100	10,500
Depreciation—Store equipment	21,000	10,500	31,500
Total direct expenses	69,900	17,100	87,000
Allocated expenses			
Sales salaries	105,300	35,100	140,400
Rent expense	33,120	8,280	41,400
Bad debts expense	31,500	6,000	37,500
Office salary	31,200	7,800	39,000
Insurance expense	6,300	2,100	8,400
Miscellaneous office expenses	2,550	3,750	6,300
Total allocated expenses	209,970	63,030	273,000
Total expenses	279,870	80,130	360,000
Net income (loss)	$ 78,180	$ (5,280)	$ 72,900

In analyzing whether to eliminate Department Z, management considers the following items:

a. The company has one office worker who earns $750 per week or $39,000 per year and four salesclerks who each earn $675 per week or $35,100 per year.

b. The full salaries of three salesclerks are charged to Department A. The full salary of one salesclerk is charged to Department Z.

c. Eliminating Department Z would avoid the sales salaries and the office salary currently allocated to it. However, management prefers another plan. Two salesclerks have indicated that they will be quitting soon. Management believes that their work can be done by the two remaining clerks if the one office worker works in sales half time. Eliminating Department Z will allow this shift of duties. If this change is implemented, half the office worker's salary would be reported as sales salaries and half would be reported as office salary.

d. The store building is rented under a long-term lease that cannot be changed. Therefore, Department A will use the space and equipment currently used by Department Z.

e. Closing Department Z will eliminate its expenses for advertising, bad debts, and store supplies; 65% of the insurance expense allocated to it to cover its merchandise inventory; and 30% of the miscellaneous office expenses presently allocated to it.

Required

1. Prepare a three-column report that lists items and amounts for (a) the company's total expenses (including cost of goods sold)—in column 1, (b) the expenses that would be eliminated by closing Department Z—in column 2, and (c) the expenses that will continue—in column 3.

Check (1) Total expenses: (a) $1,239,600, (b) $272,940

2. Prepare a forecasted annual income statement for the company reflecting the elimination of Department Z assuming that it will not affect Department A's sales and gross profit. The statement should reflect the reassignment of the office worker to one-half time as a salesclerk.

(2) Forecasted net income without Department Z, $83,340

Analysis Component

3. Reconcile the company's combined net income with the forecasted net income assuming that Department Z is eliminated (list both items and amounts). Analyze the reconciliation and explain why you think the department should or should not be eliminated.

SERIAL PROBLEM

Success Systems

(This serial problem began in Chapter 1 and continues through most of the book. If previous chapter segments were not completed, the serial problem can begin at this point. It is helpful, but not necessary, to use the Working Papers that accompany the book.)

SP 10 Adriana Lopez has found that her line of computer desks and chairs has become very popular and she is finding it hard to keep up with demand. She knows that she cannot fill all of her orders for both items, so she decides she must determine the optimal sales mix given the resources she has available. Information about the desks and chairs follows.

	Desks	Chairs
Selling price per unit	$1,125	$375
Variable costs per unit	500	200
Contribution margin per unit	$ 625	$175
Direct labor hours per unit	5 hours	4 hours
Expected demand for next quarter	175 desks	50 chairs

Adriana has determined that she only has 1,015 direct labor hours available for the next quarter and wants to optimize her contribution margin given the limited number of direct labor hours available.

Required

Determine the optimal sales mix for Adriana and the contribution margin she will earn at that sales mix.

BEYOND THE NUMBERS

REPORTING IN ACTION

C1 A1 P1

BTN 10-1 During a recent fiscal year, Best Buy (BestBuy.com) sold off its interest in Musicland. Information about operations for Best Buy and Musicland for the fiscal year before the sale of Musicland follows.

$ millions	Best Buy*	Musicland	Total
Revenues	$20,943	$1,727	$22,670
Operating expenses†	20,321	1,971	22,292

* Does not include Musicland results.
† Includes cost of goods sold.

Required

1. Compute operating income for Best Buy and Musicland, separately, and the total operating income for both.

2. If the results in part 1 for Musicland are typical, why do you believe Best Buy decided to sell off its interest in Musicland?

COMPARATIVE ANALYSIS

C1 

BTN 10-2 Best Buy, Circuit City, and RadioShack sell several different products; most are profitable but some are not. Teams of employees in each company make advertising, investment, and product mix decisions. A certain portion of advertising for both companies is on a local basis to a target audience.

Required

1. Find one major advertisement of a product or group of products for each company in your local newspaper. Contact the newspaper and ask the approximate cost of this ad space (for example, cost of one page or one-half page of advertising).
2. Estimate how many products this advertisement must sell to justify its cost. Begin by taking the product's sales price advertised for each company and assume a 20% contribution margin.
3. Prepare a one-half page memorandum explaining the importance of effective advertising when making a product mix decision. Be prepared to present your ideas in class.

ETHICS CHALLENGE

P1 

BTN 10-3 Bert Asiago, a salesperson for Convertco, received an order from a potential new customer for 50,000 units of Convertco's single product at a price $25 below its regular selling price of $65. Asiago knows that Convertco has the capacity to produce this order without affecting regular sales. He has spoken to Convertco's controller, Bia Morgan, who has informed Asiago that at the $40 selling price, Convertco will not be covering its variable costs of $42 for the product, and she recommends the order not be accepted. Asiago knows that variable costs include his sales commission of $4 per unit. If he accepts a $2 per unit commission, the sale will produce a contribution margin of zero. Asiago is eager to get the new customer because he believes that this could lead to the new customer becoming a regular customer.

Required

1. Determine the contribution margin per unit on the order as determined by the controller.
2. Determine the contribution margin per unit on the order as determined by Asiago if he takes the lower commission.
3. Do you recommend Convertco accept the special order? What factors must management consider?

COMMUNICATING IN PRACTICE

P1

BTN 10-4 Assume that you work for Greeble's Department Store, and your manager requests that you outline the pros and cons of discontinuing its hardware department. That department appears to be generating losses, and your manager believes that discontinuing it will increase overall store profits.

Required

Prepare a memorandum to your manager outlining what Greeble's management should consider when trying to decide whether to discontinue its hardware department.

TAKING IT TO THE NET

A1  

BTN 10-5 Many companies must determine whether to internally produce their component parts or to outsource them. Further, some companies now outsource key components or business processes to international providers. Access the Website BizBrim.com and review the available information on outsourcing—especially as it relates to both the advantages and the negative effects of outsourcing.

Required

1. What does Bizbrim identify as the major advantages and the major disadvantages of outsourcing?
2. Does it seem that Bizbrim is generally in favor of or opposed to outsourcing? Explain.

TEAMWORK IN ACTION

P1 

BTN 10-6 Break into teams and identify costs that an airline such as Northwest would incur on a flight from Green Bay to Minneapolis. (1) Identify the individual costs as variable or fixed. (2) Assume that Northwest is trying to decide whether to drop this flight because it seems to be unprofitable. Determine which costs are likely to be saved if the flight is dropped. Set up your answer in the following format.

Cost	Variable or Fixed	Cost Saved if Flight Is Dropped	Rationale

BTN 10-7 Jared Greenberg and Dan Zinger of **Prairie Sticks Bat Company** make baseball bats. They must decide on the best sales mix. Assume their company has a capacity of 80 hours of lathe/processing time available each month and it makes two types of bats, Deluxe and Premium. Information on these bats follows.

ENTREPRENEURIAL DECISION

A1  

	Deluxe	Premium
Selling price per bat	$70	$90
Variable costs per bat	$40	$50
Lathe/processing minutes per bat	6 minutes	12 minutes

Required

1. Assume the markets for both models of bats are unlimited. How many Deluxe bats and how many Premium bats should the company make each month? Explain. How much total contribution margin does this mix produce each month?
2. Assume the market for Deluxe bats is limited to 600 bats per month, with no market limit for Premium bats. How many Deluxe bats and how many Premium bats should the company make each month? Explain. How much total contribution margin does this mix produce each month?

BTN 10-8 Restaurants are often adding and removing menu items. Visit a restaurant and identify a new food item. Make a list of costs that the restaurant must consider when deciding whether to add that new item. Also, make a list of nonfinancial factors that the restaurant must consider when adding that item.

HITTING THE ROAD

C1 P1

BTN 10-9 Access **DSG**'s 2006 annual report dated April 29, 2006, from its Website www.DSGiplc.com. Identify its report on corporate responsibility.

GLOBAL DECISION

C1

DSG

Required

DSG reports that it recycled 25,607 tons of waste. Efforts such as these can be costly to a company. Why would a company such as DSG pursue these costly efforts?

ANSWERS TO MULTIPLE CHOICE QUIZ

1. a; Reworking provides incremental revenue of $11 per unit ($19 − $8); and, it costs $10 to rework them. The company is better off by $1 per unit when it reworks these products and sells them at the regular price.
2. e; Product X has a $2 contribution margin per machine hour [($32 − $12)/10 MH]; Product Y has a $7 contribution margin per machine hour [($24 − $10)/2 MH]. It should produce as much of Product Y as possible.
3. a; Total revenue from the special order = 3,000 units × $15 per unit = $45,000; and, Total costs for the special order = (3,000 units × $9 per unit) + $5,000 = $32,000. Net income from the special order = $45,000 − $32,000 = $13,000. Thus, yes, it should accept the order.
4. c
5. d

A Look Back

Chapter 10 described several procedures useful for making and evaluating short-term managerial decisions. It also assessed the consequences of such decisions.

A Look at This Chapter

This chapter focuses on evaluating capital budgeting decisions. Several methods are described and illustrated that help managers identify projects with the greater return on investment.

A Look Ahead

Chapter 12 focuses on reporting and analyzing a company's cash flows. Special emphasis is directed at the statement of cash flows—reported under the indirect method.

Chapter

Capital Budgeting and Investment Analysis

Learning Objectives

Conceptual

C1 Explain the importance of capital budgeting. *(p. 392)*

C2 Describe the selection of a hurdle rate for an investment. *(p. 401)*

Analytical

A1 Analyze a capital investment project using break-even time. *(p. 402)*

LP11

Procedural

P1 Compute payback period and describe its use. *(p. 393)*

P2 Compute accounting rate of return and explain its use. *(p. 395)*

P3 Compute net present value and describe its use. *(p. 397)*

P4 Compute internal rate of return and explain its use. *(p. 399)*

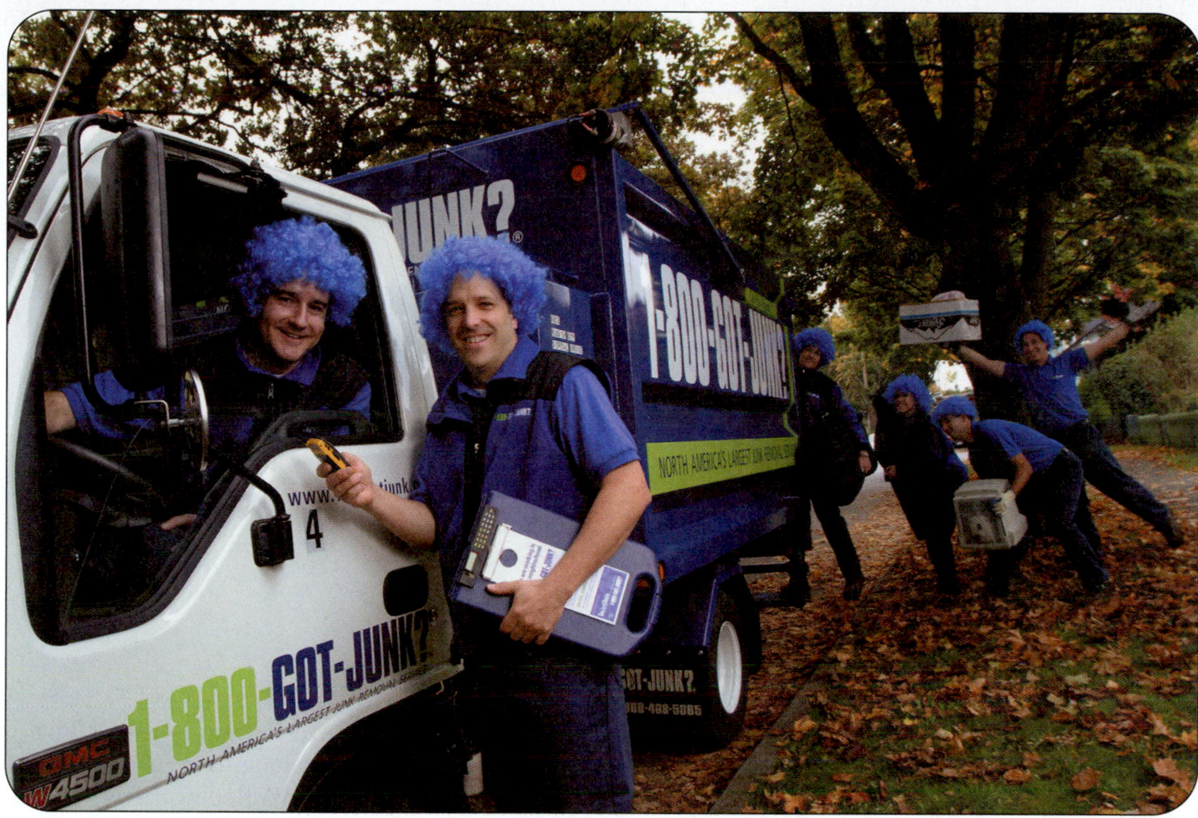

Decision Feature

One Man's Junk

"*1-800-GOT-JUNK brings together great people*"
—Brian Scudamore

VANCOUVER, CANADA—Brian Scudamore was waiting in a McDonald's drive-thru when he realized his future was junk. With his last $700, Brian bought a used pickup truck and began hauling junk—old couches, appliances, household clutter—any non-hazardous material that two people can lift. "With a vision of creating the 'FedEx' of junk removal, I became a full-time JUNKMAN," says Brian. "My father was not impressed in the least."

He is now. Brian's vision resulted in him starting **1-800-GOT-JUNK (1800gotjunk.com),** the world's largest junk removal service. The company's approach is simple: Use clean, shiny trucks that serve as mobile billboards, and employ professional, courteous drivers who are always on time. Develop a culture that is young, fun, and focused on employee growth, and "build a business that we can be proud of."

Priced at about $400 per full truckload, Brian's payback period on his initial $700 investment was brief. As his company grew, Brian bought newer trucks, with more sophisticated technology. This required Brian to use better capital budgeting techniques, like net present value and internal rate of return. These techniques enabled Brian to expand his truck capacity into the markets expected to deliver the highest returns. The company buys only a few types of trucks, and one type of dump box, to ensure reliability; added maintenance and rework costs from unreliable equipment can quickly sabotage cash flow estimates. While customers see clean trucks with courteous drivers, a high-tech backbone underlies the operation. Brian invested $500,000 in a computer software system to book and schedule jobs. This investment too had to provide a positive return.

Unlike many entrepreneurs who attempt to minimize risk by outsourcing to independent contractors, Brian took a different approach. "I hired my first employee, a good friend of mine, a week after I started. I always believed in hiring people versus contract or consultants. I felt that if I wasn't willing to make the investment then I was questioning my own faith in the business." While qualitative factors like employee morale are difficult to factor into capital budgeting decisions, they must be considered. Brian's goal is $150 million in annual revenues. Not bad for his initial investment of $700.

[Sources: *1-800-GOT-JUNK Website,* January 2009; *About.com,* December 2006; *BCBusinessMagazine.com,* December 2004; *NPR.org Morning Edition,* March 2008; *Fortune,* October 2003; *Business 2.0,* February 2007]

Chapter Preview

Management must assess alternative long-term strategies and investments, and then decide which assets to acquire or sell to achieve company objectives. This analysis process is called capital budgeting, which is one of the more challenging, risky, and important tasks that management undertakes. This task requires predictions and estimates, and management's capital budgeting decisions impact the company for years. This chapter explains and illustrates several methods to aid management in the capital budgeting decisions.

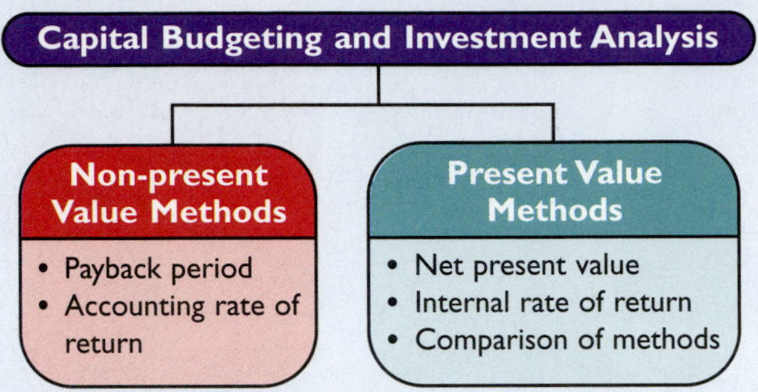

Introduction to Capital Budgeting

C1 Explain the importance of capital budgeting.

The capital expenditures budget is management's plan for acquiring and selling plant assets. **Capital budgeting** is the process of analyzing alternative long-term investments and deciding which assets to acquire or sell. These decisions can involve developing a new product or process, buying a new machine or a new building, or acquiring an entire company. An objective for these decisions is to earn a satisfactory return on investment.

Video11.2

Capital budgeting decisions require careful analysis because they are usually the most difficult and risky decisions that managers make. These decisions are difficult because they require predicting events that will not occur until well into the future. Many of these predictions are tentative and potentially unreliable. Specifically, a capital budgeting decision is risky because (1) the outcome is uncertain, (2) large amounts of money are usually involved, (3) the investment involves a long-term commitment, and (4) the decision could be difficult or impossible to reverse, no matter how poor it turns out to be. Risk is especially high for investments in technology due to innovations and uncertainty.

Point: The nature of capital spending has changed with the business environment. Budgets for information technology have increased from about 25% of corporate capital spending 20 years ago to an estimated 35% today.

Managers use several methods to evaluate capital budgeting decisions. Nearly all of these methods involve predicting cash inflows and cash outflows of proposed investments, assessing the risk of and returns on those flows, and then choosing the investments to make. Management often restates future cash flows in terms of their present value. This approach applies the time value of money: A dollar today is worth more than a dollar tomorrow. Similarly, a dollar tomorrow is worth less than a dollar today. The process of restating future cash flows in terms of their present value is called *discounting*. The time value of money is important when evaluating capital investments, but managers sometimes apply evaluation methods that ignore present value. This section describes four methods for comparing alternative investments.

Methods Not Using Time Value of Money

All investments, whether they involve the purchase of a machine or another long-term asset, are expected to produce net cash flows. *Net cash flow* is cash inflows minus cash outflows. Sometimes managers perform simple analyses of the financial feasibility of an investment's net cash flow without using the time value of money. This section explains two of the most common methods in this category: (1) payback period and (2) accounting rate of return.

Payback Period

An investment's **payback period (PBP)** is the expected time period to recover the initial investment amount. Managers prefer investing in assets with shorter payback periods to reduce the risk of an unprofitable investment over the long run. Acquiring assets with short payback periods reduces a company's risk from potentially inaccurate long-term predictions of future cash flows.

P1 Compute payback period and describe its use.

Computing Payback Period with Even Cash Flows To illustrate use of the payback period for an investment with even cash flows, we look at data from FasTrac, a manufacturer of exercise equipment and supplies. (*Even cash flows* are cash flows that are the same each and every year; *uneven cash flows* are cash flows that are not all equal in amount.) FasTrac is considering several different capital investments, one of which is to purchase a machine to use in manufacturing a new product. This machine costs $16,000 and is expected to have an eight-year life with no salvage value. Management predicts this machine will produce 1,000 units of product each year and that the new product will be sold for $30 per unit. Exhibit 11.1 shows the expected annual net cash flows for this asset over its life as well as the expected annual revenues and expenses (including depreciation and income taxes) from investing in the machine.

EXHIBIT 11.1

Cash Flow Analysis

FASTRAC
Cash Flow Analysis—Machinery Investment
January 15, 2009

	Expected Accrual Figures	Expected Net Cash Flows
Annual sales of new product	$30,000	$30,000
Deduct annual expenses		
Cost of materials, labor, and overhead (except depreciation)	15,500	15,500
Depreciation—Machinery	2,000	
Additional selling and administrative expenses	9,500	9,500
Annual pretax accrual income	3,000	
Income taxes (30%)	900	900
Annual net income	$ 2,100	
Annual net cash flow		**$ 4,100**

The amount of net cash flow from the machinery is computed by subtracting expected cash outflows from expected cash inflows. The cash flows column of Exhibit 11.1 excludes all noncash revenues and expenses. Depreciation is FasTrac's only noncash item. Alternatively, managers can adjust the projected net income for revenue and expense items that do not affect cash flows. For FasTrac, this means taking the $2,100 net income and adding back the $2,000 depreciation.

Point: Annual net cash flow in Exhibit 11.1 equals net income plus depreciation (a noncash expense).

The formula for computing the payback period of an investment that yields even net cash flows is in Exhibit 11.2.

EXHIBIT 11.2

Payback Period Formula with Even Cash Flows

$$\textbf{Payback period} = \frac{\textbf{Cost of investment}}{\textbf{Annual net cash flow}}$$

The payback period reflects the amount of time for the investment to generate enough net cash flow to return (or pay back) the cash initially invested to purchase it. FasTrac's payback period for this machine is just under four years:

$$\text{Payback period} = \frac{\$16,000}{\$4,100} = 3.9 \text{ years}$$

Example: If an alternative machine (with different technology) yields a payback period of 3.5 years, which one does a manager choose? Answer: The alternative (3.5 is less than 3.9).

The initial investment is fully recovered in 3.9 years, or just before reaching the halfway point of this machine's useful life of eight years.

Decision Insight

Payback Phones Profits of telecoms have declined as too much capital investment chased too little revenue. Telecom success depends on new technology, and communications gear is evolving at a dizzying rate. Consequently, managers of telecoms often demand short payback periods and large expected net cash flows to compensate for the investment risk.

Computing Payback Period with Uneven Cash Flows Computing the payback period in the prior section assumed even net cash flows. What happens if the net cash flows are uneven? In this case, the payback period is computed using the *cumulative total of net cash flows.* The word *cumulative* refers to the addition of each period's net cash flows as we progress through time. To illustrate, consider data for another investment that FasTrac is considering. This machine is predicted to generate uneven net cash flows over the next eight years. The relevant data and payback period computation are shown in Exhibit 11.3.

EXHIBIT 11.3

Payback Period Calculation with Uneven Cash Flows

Period*	Expected Net Cash Flows	Cumulative Net Cash Flows
Year 0	$(16,000)	$(16,000)
Year 1	3,000	(13,000)
Year 2	4,000	(9,000)
Year 3	4,000	(5,000)
Year 4	4,000	(1,000)
Year 5	5,000	4,000
Year 6	3,000	7,000
Year 7	2,000	9,000
Year 8	2,000	11,000
		Payback period = 4.2 years

* All cash inflows and outflows occur uniformly during the year.

Example: Find the payback period in Exhibit 11.3 if net cash flows for the first 4 years are:
Year 1 = $6,000; Year 2 = $5,000;
Year 3 = $4,000; Year 4 = $3,000.
Answer: 3.33 years

Year 0 refers to the period of initial investment in which the $16,000 cash outflow occurs at the end of year 0 to acquire the machinery. By the end of year 1, the cumulative net cash flow is reduced to $(13,000), computed as the $(16,000) initial cash outflow plus year 1's $3,000 cash inflow. This process continues throughout the asset's life. The cumulative net cash flow amount changes from negative to positive in year 5. Specifically, at the end of year 4, the cumulative net cash flow is $(1,000). As soon as FasTrac receives net cash inflow of $1,000 during the fifth year, it has fully recovered the investment. If we assume that cash flows are received uniformly *within* each year, receipt of the $1,000 occurs about one-fifth of the way through the year. This is computed as $1,000 divided by year 5's total net cash flow of $5,000, or 0.20. This yields a payback period of 4.2 years, computed as 4 years plus 0.20 of year 5.

"So what if I underestimated costs and overestimated revenues? It all averages out in the end."

Using the Payback Period Companies desire a short payback period to increase return and reduce risk. The more quickly a company receives cash, the sooner it is available for other uses and the less time it is at risk of loss. A shorter payback period also improves the company's ability to respond to unanticipated changes and lowers its risk of having to keep an unprofitable investment.

Payback period should never be the only consideration in evaluating investments. This is so because it ignores at least two important factors. First, it fails to reflect differences in the timing of net cash flows within the payback period. In Exhibit 11.3, FasTrac's net cash flows in the first five years were $3,000, $4,000, $4,000, $4,000, and $5,000. If another investment had predicted cash flows of $9,000, $3,000, $2,000, $1,800, and $1,000 in these five years, its payback period would also be 4.2 years, but this second alternative could be more desirable because it provides cash more quickly. The second important factor is that the payback period ignores *all* cash flows after the point where its costs are fully recovered. For example, one investment might pay back its cost in 3 years but stop producing cash after 4 years. A second investment might require 5 years to pay back its cost yet continue to produce net cash flows for another 15 years. A focus on only the payback period would mistakenly lead management to choose the first investment over the second.

Quick Check

Answers—p. 407

1. Capital budgeting is (*a*) concerned with analyzing alternative sources of capital, including debt and equity, (*b*) an important activity for companies when considering what assets to acquire or sell, or (*c*) best done by intuitive assessments of the value of assets and their usefulness.
2. Why are capital budgeting decisions often difficult?
3. A company is considering purchasing equipment costing $75,000. Future annual net cash flows from this equipment are $30,000, $25,000, $15,000, $10,000, and $5,000. The payback period is (*a*) 4 years, (*b*) 3.5 years, or (*c*) 3 years.
4. If depreciation is an expense, why is it added back to an investment's net income to compute the net cash flow from that investment?
5. If two investments have the same payback period, are they equally desirable? Explain.

Accounting Rate of Return

P2 Compute accounting rate of return and explain its use.

The **accounting rate of return,** also called *return on average investment,* is computed by dividing a project's after-tax net income by the average amount invested in it. To illustrate, we return to FasTrac's $16,000 machinery investment described in Exhibit 11.1. We first compute (1) the after-tax net income and (2) the average amount invested. The $2,100 after-tax net income is already available from Exhibit 11.1. To compute the average amount invested, we assume that net cash flows are received evenly throughout each year. Thus, the average investment for each year is computed as the average of its beginning and ending book values. If FasTrac's $16,000 machine is depreciated $2,000 each year, the average amount invested in the machine for each year is computed as shown in Exhibit 11.4. The average for any year is the average of the beginning and ending book values.

EXHIBIT 11.4

Computing Average Amount Invested

	Beginning Book Value	Annual Depreciation	Ending Book Value	Average Book Value
Year 1	$16,000	$2,000	$14,000	$15,000
Year 2	14,000	2,000	12,000	13,000
Year 3	12,000	2,000	10,000	11,000
Year 4	10,000	2,000	8,000	9,000
Year 5	8,000	2,000	6,000	7,000
Year 6	6,000	2,000	4,000	5,000
Year 7	4,000	2,000	2,000	3,000
Year 8	2,000	2,000	0	1,000
All years				**$ 8,000**

Next we need the average book value for the asset's entire life. This amount is computed by taking the average of the individual yearly averages. This average equals $8,000, computed as $64,000 (the sum of the individual years' averages) divided by eight years (see last column of Exhibit 11.4).

Point: General formula for *annual average investment* is the sum of individual years' average book values divided by the number of years of the planned investment.

If a company uses straight-line depreciation, we can find the average amount invested by using the formula in Exhibit 11.5. Because FasTrac uses straight-line depreciation, its average amount invested for the eight years equals the sum of the book value at the beginning of the asset's investment period and the book value at the end of its investment period, divided by 2, as shown in Exhibit 11.5.

EXHIBIT 11.5

Computing Average Amount Invested under Straight-Line Depreciation

$$\textbf{Annual average investment} = \frac{\textbf{Beginning book value + Ending book value}}{\textbf{2}}$$

(straight-line case only)

$$= \frac{\$16{,}000 + \$0}{2} = \$8{,}000$$

If an investment has a salvage value, the average amount invested when using straight-line depreciation is computed as (Beginning book value + Salvage value)/2.

Once we determine the after-tax net income and the average amount invested, the accounting rate of return on the investment can be computed from the annual after-tax net income divided by the average amount invested, as shown in Exhibit 11.6.

EXHIBIT 11.6

Accounting Rate of Return Formula

$$\textbf{Accounting rate of return} = \frac{\textbf{Annual after-tax net income}}{\textbf{Annual average investment}}$$

This yields an accounting rate of return of 26.25% ($2,100/$8,000). FasTrac management must decide whether a 26.25% accounting rate of return is satisfactory. To make this decision, we must factor in the investment's risk. For instance, we cannot say an investment with a 26.25% return is preferred over one with a lower return unless we recognize any differences in risk. Thus, an investment's return is satisfactory or unsatisfactory only when it is related to returns from other investments with similar lives and risk.

When accounting rate of return is used to choose among capital investments, the one with the least risk, the shortest payback period, and the highest return for the longest time period is often identified as the best. However, use of accounting rate of return to evaluate investment opportunities is limited because it bases the amount invested on book values (not predicted market values) in future periods. Accounting rate of return is also limited when an asset's net incomes are expected to vary from year to year. This requires computing the rate using *average* annual net incomes, yet this accounting rate of return fails to distinguish between two investments with the same average annual net income but different amounts of income in early years versus later years or different levels of income variability.

Quick Check Answers—p. 407

6. The following data relate to a company's decision on whether to purchase a machine:

Cost	$180,000
Salvage value	15,000
Annual after-tax net income	40,000

The machine's accounting rate of return, assuming the even receipt of its net cash flows during the year and use of straight-line depreciation, is (*a*) 22%, (*b*) 41%, or (*c*) 21%.

7. Is a 15% accounting rate of return for a machine a good rate?

Methods Using Time Value of Money

This section describes two methods that help managers with capital budgeting decisions and that use the time value of money: (1) net present value and (2) internal rate of return. *(To apply these methods, you need a basic understanding of the concept of present value. An expanded explanation of present value concepts is in Appendix B near the end of the book. You can use the present value tables at the end of Appendix B to solve many of this chapter's assignments that use the time value of money.)*

Net Present Value

P3 Compute net present value and describe its use.

Net present value analysis applies the time value of money to future cash inflows and cash outflows so management can evaluate a project's benefits and costs at one point in time. Specifically, **net present value (NPV)** is computed by discounting the future net cash flows from the investment at the project's required rate of return and then subtracting the initial amount invested. A company's required return, often called its hurdle rate, is typically its **cost of capital,** which is the rate the company must pay to its long-term creditors and shareholders.

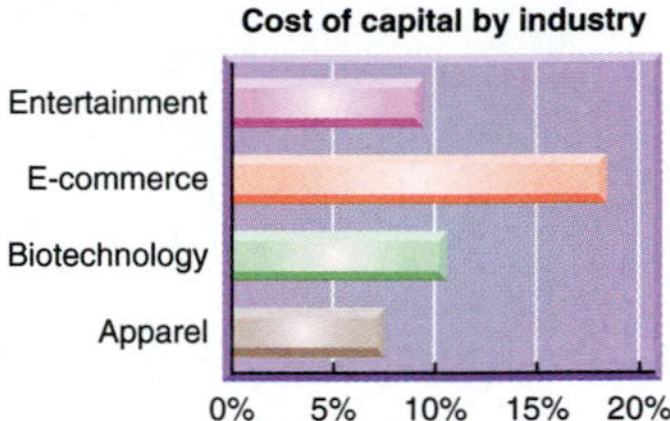

To illustrate, let's return to FasTrac's proposed machinery purchase described in Exhibit 11.1. Does this machine provide a satisfactory return while recovering the amount invested? Recall that the machine requires a $16,000 investment and is expected to provide $4,100 annual net cash inflows for the next eight years. If we assume that net cash flows from this machine are received at each year-end and that FasTrac requires a 12% annual return, net present value can be computed as in Exhibit 11.7.

EXHIBIT 11.7

Net Present Value Calculation with Equal Cash Flows

	Net Cash Flows*	Present Value of 1 at 12%†	Present Value of Net Cash Flows
Year 1	$ 4,100	0.8929	$ 3,661
Year 2	4,100	0.7972	3,269
Year 3	4,100	0.7118	2,918
Year 4	4,100	0.6355	2,606
Year 5	4,100	0.5674	2,326
Year 6	4,100	0.5066	2,077
Year 7	4,100	0.4523	1,854
Year 8	4,100	0.4039	1,656
Totals	$32,800		$20,367
Amount invested			(16,000)
Net present value			$ 4,367

* Cash flows occur at the end of each year.

† Present value of 1 factors are taken from Table B.1 in Appendix B.

The first number column of Exhibit 11.7 shows the annual net cash flows. Present value of 1 factors, also called *discount factors,* are shown in the second column. Taken from Table B.1 in Appendix B, they assume that net cash flows are received at each year-end. *(To simplify present value computations and for assignment material at the end of this chapter, we assume that net cash flows are received at each year-end.)* Annual net cash flows from the first column of Exhibit 11.7 are multiplied by the discount factors in the second column to give present values shown in the third column. The last three lines of this exhibit show the final NPV computations. The asset's $16,000 initial cost is deducted from the $20,367 total present value of all future net cash flows to give this asset's NPV of $4,367. The machine is thus expected to (1) recover its cost, (2) provide a 12% compounded return, and (3) generate $4,367 above cost. We summarize this analysis by saying the present value of this machine's future net cash flows to FasTrac exceeds the $16,000 investment by $4,367.

Point: The assumption of end-of-year cash flows simplifies computations and is common in practice.

Point: The amount invested includes all costs that must be incurred to get the asset in its proper location and ready for use.

Example: What is the net present value in Exhibit 11.7 if a 10% return is required? *Answer:* $5,873

Net Present Value Decision Rule The decision rule in applying NPV is as follows: When an asset's expected cash flows are discounted at the required rate and yield a *positive* net present value, the asset should be acquired. This decision rule is reflected in the graphic below. When comparing several investment opportunities of about the same cost and same risk, we prefer the one with the highest positive net present value.

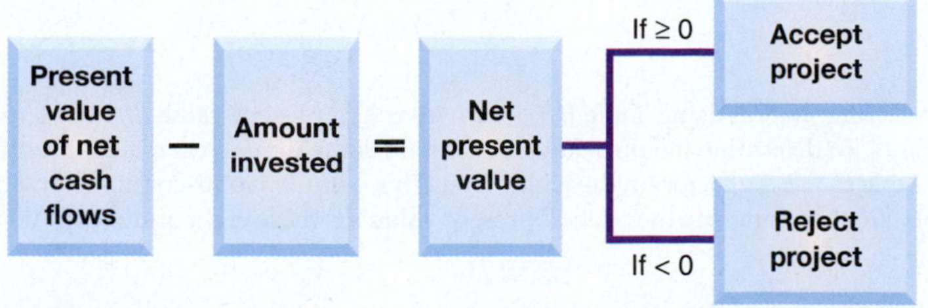

Example: Why does the net present value of an investment increase when a lower discount rate is used? *Answer:* The present value of net cash flows increases.

Simplifying Computations The computations in Exhibit 11.7 use separate present value of 1 factors for each of the eight years. Each year's net cash flow is multiplied by its present value of 1 factor to determine its present value. The individual present values for each of the eight net cash flows are added to give the asset's total present value. This computation can be simplified in two ways if annual net cash flows are equal in amount. One way is to add the eight annual present value of 1 factors for a total of 4.9676 and multiply this amount by the annual $4,100 net cash flow to get the $20,367 total present value of net cash flows.[1] A second simplification is to use a calculator with compound interest functions or a spreadsheet program. We show how to use Excel functions to compute net present value in this chapter's Appendix. Whatever procedure you use, it is important to understand the concepts behind these computations.

Decision Ethics

Systems Manager Top management adopts a policy requiring purchases in excess of $5,000 to be submitted with cash flow projections to the cost analyst for capital budget approval. As systems manager, you want to upgrade your computers at a $25,000 cost. You consider submitting several orders all under $5,000 to avoid the approval process. You believe the computers will increase profits and wish to avoid a delay. What do you do? [Answer—p. 406]

Uneven Cash Flows Net present value analysis can also be applied when net cash flows are uneven (unequal). To illustrate, assume that FasTrac can choose only one capital investment from among projects A, B, and C. Each project requires the same $12,000 initial investment. Future net cash flows for each project are shown in the first three number columns of Exhibit 11.8.

EXHIBIT 11.8

Net Present Value Calculation with Uneven Cash Flows

	Net Cash Flows			Present Value of 1 at 10%	Present Value of Net Cash Flows		
	A	B	C		A	B	C
Year 1	$ 5,000	$ 8,000	$ 1,000	0.9091	$ 4,546	$ 7,273	$ 909
Year 2	5,000	5,000	5,000	0.8264	4,132	4,132	4,132
Year 3	5,000	2,000	9,000	0.7513	3,757	1,503	6,762
Totals	$15,000	$15,000	$15,000		12,435	12,908	11,803
Amount invested					(12,000)	(12,000)	(12,000)
Net present value					**$ 435**	**$ 908**	**$ (197)**

Example: If 12% is the required return in Exhibit 11.8, which project is preferred? *Answer:* Project B. Net present values are: A = $10; B = $553; C = $(715).

Example: Will the rankings of Projects A, B, and C change with the use of different discount rates, assuming the same rate is used for all projects? *Answer:* No; only the NPV amounts will change.

The three projects in Exhibit 11.8 have the same expected total net cash flows of $15,000. Project A is expected to produce equal amounts of $5,000 each year. Project B is expected to produce a larger amount in the first year. Project C is expected to produce a larger amount in the third year. The fourth column of Exhibit 11.8 shows the present value of 1 factors from Table B.1 assuming 10% required return.

Computations in the right-most columns show that Project A has a $435 positive NPV. Project B has the largest NPV of $908 because it brings in cash more quickly. Project C has a $(197) *negative* NPV because its larger cash inflows are delayed. If FasTrac requires a 10% return, it should reject Project C because its NPV implies a return *under* 10%. If only one project can be accepted, project B appears best because it yields the highest NPV.

[1] We can simplify this computation using Table B.3, which gives the present value of 1 to be received periodically for a number of periods. To determine the present value of these eight annual receipts discounted at 12%, go down the 12% column of Table B.3 to the factor on the eighth line. This cumulative discount factor, also known as an *annuity* factor, is 4.9676. We then compute the $20,367 present value for these eight annual $4,100 receipts, computed as 4.9676 × $4,100.

Salvage Value and Accelerated Depreciation FasTrac predicted the $16,000 machine to have zero salvage value at the end of its useful life (recall Exhibit 11.1). In many cases, assets are expected to have salvage values. If so, this amount is an additional net cash inflow received at the end of the final year of the asset's life. All other computations remain the same.

Point: Projects with higher cash flows in earlier years generally yield higher net present values.

Depreciation computations also affect net present value analysis. FasTrac computes depreciation using the straight-line method. Accelerated depreciation is also commonly used, especially for income tax reports. Accelerated depreciation produces larger depreciation deductions in the early years of an asset's life and smaller deductions in later years. This pattern results in smaller income tax payments in early years and larger payments in later years. Accelerated depreciation does not change the basics of a present value analysis, but it can change the result. Using accelerated depreciation for tax reporting affects the NPV of an asset's cash flows because it produces larger net cash inflows in the early years of the asset's life and smaller ones in later years. Being able to use accelerated depreciation for tax reporting always makes an investment more desirable because early cash flows are more valuable than later ones.

Example: When is it appropriate to use different discount rates for different projects? *Answer:* When risk levels are different.

Point: Tax savings from depreciation is called: **depreciation tax shield.**

Use of Net Present Value In deciding whether to proceed with a capital investment project, we approve the proposal if the NPV is positive but reject it if the NPV is negative. When considering several projects of similar investment amounts and risk levels, we can compare the different projects' NPVs and rank them on the basis of their NPVs. However, if the amount invested differs substantially across projects, the NPV is of limited value for comparison purposes. One means to compare projects, especially when a company cannot fund all positive net present value projects, is to use the **profitability index,** which is computed as:

$$\textbf{Profitability index} = \frac{\textbf{Net present value of cash flows}}{\textbf{Investment}}$$

A higher profitability index suggests a more desirable project. To illustrate, suppose that Project X requires a $1 million investment and provides a $100,000 NPV. Project Y requires an investment of only $100,000 and returns a $75,000 NPV. Ranking on the basis of NPV puts Project X ahead of Y, yet X's profitability index is only 0.10 ($100,000/$1,000,000) whereas Y's profitability index is 0.75. We must also remember that when reviewing projects with different risks, we computed the NPV of individual projects using different discount rates. The higher the risk, the higher the discount rate.

Inflation Large price-level increases should be considered in NPV analyses. Hurdle rates already include investor's inflation forecasts. Net cash flows can be adjusted for inflation by using *future value* computations. For example, if the expected net cash inflow in year 1 is $4,100 and 5% inflation is expected, then the expected net cash inflow in year 2 is $4,305, computed as $4,100 × 1.05 (1.05 is the future value of $1 (Table B.2) for 1 period with a 5% rate).

Internal Rate of Return

P4 Compute internal rate of return and explain its use.

Another means to evaluate capital investments is to use the **internal rate of return (IRR),** which equals the rate that yields an NPV of zero for an investment. This means that if we compute the total present value of a project's net cash flows using the IRR as the discount rate and then subtract the initial investment from this total present value, we get a zero NPV.

To illustrate, we use the data for FasTrac's Project A from Exhibit 11.8 to compute its IRR. Exhibit 11.9 shows the two-step process in computing IRR.

EXHIBIT 11.9

Computing Internal Rate of Return (with even cash flows)

Step 1: Compute the present value factor for the investment project.

$$\textbf{Present value factor} = \frac{\textbf{Amount invested}}{\textbf{Net cash flows}} = \frac{\$12{,}000}{\$5{,}000} = 2.4000$$

Step 2: Identify the discount rate (IRR) yielding the present value factor

Search Table B.3 for a present value factor of 2.4000 in the three-year row (equaling the 3-year project duration). The 12% discount rate yields a present value factor of 2.4018. This implies that the IRR is approximately 12%.*

* Since the present value factor of 2.4000 is not exactly equal to the 12% factor of 2.4018, we can more precisely estimate the IRR as follows:

Discount rate	Present Value Factor from Table B.3
12%	2.4018
15%	2.2832
	0.1186 = difference

$$\text{Then, IRR} = 12\% + \left[(15\% - 12\%) \times \frac{2.4018 - 2.4000}{0.1186}\right] = \underline{\underline{12.05\%}}$$

When cash flows are equal, as with Project A, we compute the present value factor (as shown in Exhibit 11.9) by dividing the initial investment by its annual net cash flows. We then use an annuity table to determine the discount rate equal to this present value factor. For FasTrac's Project A, we look across the three-period row of Table B.3 and find that the discount rate corresponding to the present value factor of 2.4000 roughly equals the 2.4018 value for the 12% rate. This row is reproduced here:

Present Value of an Annuity of 1 for Three Periods

	Discount Rate				
Periods	1%	5%	10%	12%	15%
3	2.9410	2.7232	2.4869	2.4018	2.2832

The 12% rate is the Project's IRR. A more precise IRR estimate can be computed following the procedure shown in the note to Exhibit 11.9. Spreadsheet software and calculators can also compute this IRR. We show how to use an Excel function to compute IRR in this chapter's Appendix.

Uneven Cash Flows If net cash flows are uneven, we must use trial and error to compute the IRR. We do this by selecting any reasonable discount rate and computing the NPV. If the amount is positive (negative), we recompute the NPV using a higher (lower) discount rate. We continue these steps until we reach a point where two consecutive computations result in NPVs having different signs (positive and negative). Because the NPV is zero using IRR, we know that the IRR lies between these two discount rates. We can then estimate its value. Spreadsheet programs and calculators can do these computations for us.

Decision Insight

Fun-IRR Many theme parks use both financial and nonfinancial criteria to evaluate their investments in new rides and activities. The use of IRR is a major part of this evaluation. This requires good estimates of future cash inflows and outflows. It also requires risk assessments of the uncertainty of the future cash flows.

C2 Describe the selection of a hurdle rate for an investment.

Use of Internal Rate of Return When we use the IRR to evaluate a project, we compare it to a predetermined **hurdle rate,** which is a minimum acceptable rate of return and is applied as follows.

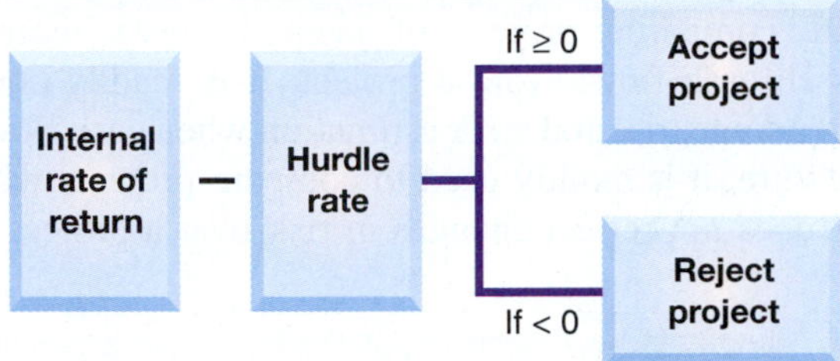

Top management selects the hurdle rate to use in evaluating capital investments. Financial formulas aid in this selection, but the choice of a minimum rate is subjective and left to management. For projects financed from borrowed funds, the hurdle rate must exceed the interest rate paid on these funds. The return on an investment must cover its interest and provide an additional profit to reward the company for its risk. For instance, if money is borrowed at 10%, an average risk investment often requires an after-tax return of 15% (or 5% above the borrowing rate). Remember that lower-risk investments require a lower rate of return compared with higher-risk investments.

If the project is internally financed, the hurdle rate is often based on actual returns from comparable projects. If the IRR is higher than the hurdle rate, the project is accepted. Multiple projects are often ranked by the extent to which their IRR exceeds the hurdle rate. The hurdle rate for individual projects is often different, depending on the risk involved. IRR is not subject to the limitations of NPV when comparing projects with different amounts invested because the IRR is expressed as a percent rather than as an absolute dollar value in NPV.

Example: How does management evaluate the risk of an investment? *Answer:* It must assess the uncertainty of future cash flows.

Point: A survey reports that 41% of top managers would reject a project with an internal rate of return *above* the cost of capital, *if* the project would cause the firm to miss its earnings forecast. The roles of benchmarks and manager compensation plans must be considered in capital budgeting decisions.

Decision Maker

Entrepreneur You are developing a new product and you use a 12% discount rate to compute its NPV. Your banker, from whom you hope to obtain a loan, expresses concern that your discount rate is too low. How do you respond? [Answer—p. 406]

Comparison of Capital Budgeting Methods

We explained four methods that managers use to evaluate capital investment projects. How do these methods compare with each other? Exhibit 11.10 addresses that question. Neither the payback period nor the accounting rate of return considers the time value of money. On the other hand, both the net present value and the internal rate of return do.

EXHIBIT 11.10
Comparing Capital Budgeting Methods

	Payback Period	Accounting Rate of Return	Net Present Value	Internal Rate of Return
Measurement basis	■ Cash flows	■ Accrual income	■ Cash flows ■ Profitability	■ Cash flows ■ Profitability
Measurement unit	■ Years	■ Percent	■ Dollars	■ Percent
Strengths	■ Easy to understand ■ Allows comparison of projects	■ Easy to understand ■ Allows comparison of projects	■ Reflects time value of money ■ Reflects varying risks over project's life	■ Reflects time value of money ■ Allows comparisons of dissimilar projects
Limitations	■ Ignores time value of money ■ Ignores cash flows after payback period	■ Ignores time value of money ■ Ignores annual rates over life of project	■ Difficult to compare dissimilar projects	■ Ignores varying risks over life of project

The payback period is probably the simplest method. It gives managers an estimate of how soon they will recover their initial investment. Managers sometimes use this method when they have limited cash to invest and a number of projects to choose from. The accounting rate of return yields a percent measure computed using accrual income instead of cash flows. The accounting rate of return is an average rate for the entire investment period. Net present value considers all estimated net cash flows for the project's expected life. It can be applied to even and uneven cash flows and can reflect changes in the level of risk over a project's life. Since it yields a dollar measure, comparing projects of unequal sizes is more difficult. The internal rate of return considers all cash flows from a project. It is readily computed when the cash flows are even but requires some trial and error estimation when cash flows are uneven. Because the IRR is a percent measure, it is readily used to compare projects with different investment amounts. However, IRR does not reflect changes in risk over a project's life.

Decision Insight

And the Winner Is . . . How do we choose among the methods for evaluating capital investments? Management surveys consistently show the internal rate of return (IRR) as the most popular method followed by the payback period and net present value (NPV). Few companies use the accounting rate of return (ARR), but nearly all use more than one method.

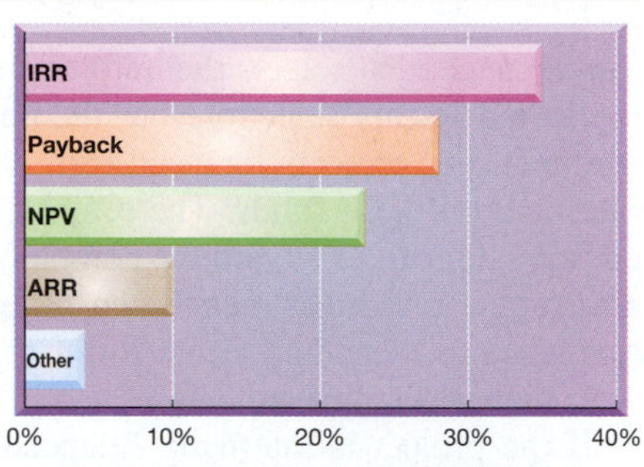

Company Usage for Capital Budgeting Methods

Quick Check

Answers—p. 407

8. A company can invest in only one of two projects, A or B. Each project requires a $20,000 investment and is expected to generate end-of-period, annual cash flows as follows:

	Year 1	Year 2	Year 3	Total
Project A	$12,000	$8,500	$4,000	$24,500
Project B	4,500	8,500	13,000	26,000

Assuming a discount rate of 10%, which project has the higher net present value?

9. Two investment alternatives are expected to generate annual cash flows with the same net present value (assuming the same discount rate applied to each). Using this information, can you conclude that the two alternatives are equally desirable?

10. When two investment alternatives have the same total expected cash flows but differ in the timing of those flows, which method of evaluating those investments is superior, (*a*) accounting rate of return or (*b*) net present value?

Decision Analysis — Break-Even Time

A1 Analyze a capital investment project using break-even time.

The first section of this chapter explained several methods to evaluate capital investments. Break-even time of an investment project is a variation of the payback period method that overcomes the limitation of not using the time value of money. **Break-even time (BET)** is a time-based measure used to evaluate a capital investment's acceptability. Its computation yields a measure of expected time, reflecting the time period until the *present value* of the net cash flows from an investment equals the initial cost of the investment. In basic terms, break-even time is computed by restating future cash flows in terms of present values and then determining the payback period using these present values.

To illustrate, we return to the FasTrac case described in Exhibit 11.1 involving a $16,000 investment in machinery. The annual net cash flows from this investment are projected at $4,100 for eight years. Exhibit 11.11 shows the computation of break-even time for this investment decision.

Year	Cash Flows	Present Value of 1 at 10%	Present Value of Cash Flows	Cumulative Present Value of Cash Flows
0	$(16,000)	1.0000	$(16,000)	$(16,000)
1	4,100	0.9091	3,727	(12,273)
2	4,100	0.8264	3,388	(8,885)
3	4,100	0.7513	3,080	(5,805)
4	4,100	0.6830	2,800	(3,005)
5	4,100	0.6209	2,546	(459)
6	4,100	0.5645	2,314	1,855
7	4,100	0.5132	2,104	3,959
8	4,100	0.4665	1,913	5,872

* The time of analysis is the start of year 1 (same as end of year 0). All cash flows occur at the end of each year.

EXHIBIT 11.11

Break-Even Time Analysis*

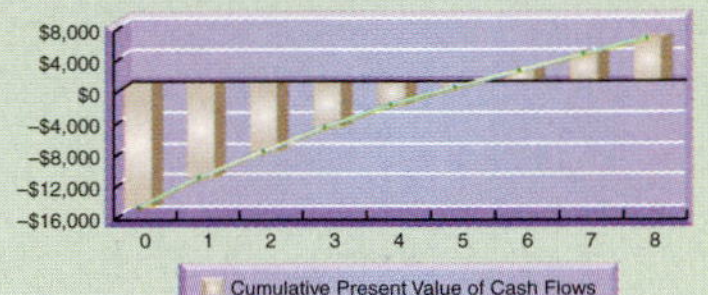

The right-most column of this exhibit shows that break-even time is between 5 and 6 years, or about 5.2 years—also see margin graph (where the line crosses the zero point). This is the time the project takes to break even after considering the time value of money (recall that the payback period computed without considering the time value of money was 3.9 years). We interpret this as cash flows earned after 5.2 years contribute to a positive net present value that, in this case, eventually amounts to $5,872.

Break-even time is a useful measure for managers because it identifies the point in time when they can expect the cash flows to begin to yield net positive returns. Managers expect a positive net present value from an investment if break-even time is less than the investment's estimated life. The method allows managers to compare and rank alternative investments, giving the project with the shortest break-even time the highest rank.

Decision Maker

Investment Manager Management asks you, the investment manager, to evaluate three alternative investments. Investment recovery time is crucial because cash is scarce. The time value of money is also important. Which capital budgeting method(s) do you use to assess the investments? [Answer—p. 406]

Demonstration Problem

White Company can invest in one of two projects, TD1 or TD2. Each project requires an initial investment of $101,250 and produces the year-end cash inflows shown in the following table.

	Net Cash Flows	
	TD1	TD2
Year 1	$ 20,000	$ 40,000
Year 2	30,000	40,000
Year 3	70,000	40,000
Totals	$120,000	$120,000

Required

1. Compute the payback period for both projects. Which project has the shortest payback period?
2. Assume that the company requires a 10% return from its investments. Compute the net present value of each project.
3. Drawing on your answers to parts 1 and 2, determine which project, if any, should be chosen.
4. Compute the internal rate of return for project TD2. Based on its internal rate of return, should project TD2 be chosen?

Planning the Solution

- Compute the payback period for the series of unequal cash flows (Project TD1) and for the series of equal cash flows (Project TD2).
- Compute White Company's net present value of each investment using a 10% discount rate.
- Use the payback and net present value rules to determine which project, if any, should be selected.
- Compute the internal rate of return for the series of equal cash flows (Project TD2) and determine whether that internal rate of return is greater than the company's 10% discount rate.

Solution to Demonstration Problem

1. The payback period for a project with a series of equal cash flows is computed as follows:

$$\text{Payback period} = \frac{\text{Cost of investment}}{\text{Annual net cash flow}}$$

For project TD2, the payback period equals 2.53 (rounded), computed as $101,250/$40,000. This means that the company expects to recover its investment in Project TD2 after approximately two and one-half years of its three-year life.

Next, determining the payback period for a series of unequal cash flows (as in Project TD1) requires us to compute the cumulative net cash flows from the project at the end of each year. Assuming the cash outflow for Project TD1 occurs at the end of year 0, and cash inflows occur continuously over years 1, 2, and 3, the payback period calculation follows.

TD1:

Period	Expected Net Cash Flows	Cumulative Net Cash Flows
0	$(101,250)	$(101,250)
1	20,000	(81,250)
2	30,000	(51,250)
3	70,000	18,750

The cumulative net cash flow for Project TD1 changes from negative to positive in year 3. As cash flows are received continuously, the point at which the company has recovered its investment into year 3 is 0.27 (rounded), computed as $18,750/$70,000. This means that the payback period for TD1 is 2.27 years, computed as 2 years plus 0.27 of year 3.

2. **TD1:**

	Net Cash Flows	Present Value of 1 at 10%	Present Value of Net Cash Flows
Year 1	$ 20,000	0.9091	$ 18,182
Year 2	30,000	0.8264	24,792
Year 3	70,000	0.7513	52,591
Totals	$120,000		95,565
Amount invested			(101,250)
Net present value			**$ (5,685)**

TD2:

	Net Cash Flows	Present Value of 1 at 10%	Present Value of Net Cash Flows
Year 1	$ 40,000	0.9091	$ 36,364
Year 2	40,000	0.8264	33,056
Year 3	40,000	0.7513	30,052
Totals	$120,000		99,472
Amount invested			(101,250)
Net present value			**$ (1,778)**

3. White Company should not invest in either project. Both are expected to yield a negative net present value, and it should invest only in positive net present value projects. Although the company expects to recover its investment from both projects before the end of these projects' useful lives, the projects are not acceptable after considering the time value of money.
4. To compute Project TD2's internal rate of return, we first compute a present value factor as follows:

$$\text{Present value factor} = \frac{\text{Amount invested}}{\text{Net cash flow}} = \$101{,}250/\$40{,}000 = 2.5313 \text{ (rounded)}$$

Then, we search Table B.3 for the discount rate that corresponds to the present value factor of 2.5313 for three periods. From Table B.3, this discount rate is 9%. Project TD2's internal rate of return of 9% is below this company's hurdle rate of 10%. Thus, Project TD2 should *not* be chosen.

APPENDIX

Using Excel to Compute Net Present Value and Internal Rate of Return

Computing present values and internal rates of return for projects with uneven cash flows is tedious and error prone. These calculations can be performed simply and accurately by using functions built into Excel. Many calculators and other types of spreadsheet software can perform them too. To illustrate, consider Fastrac, a company that is considering investing in a new machine with the expected cash flows shown in the following spreadsheet. Cash outflows are entered as negative numbers, and cash inflows are entered as positive numbers. Assume Fastrac requires a 12% annual return, entered as 0.12 in cell C1.

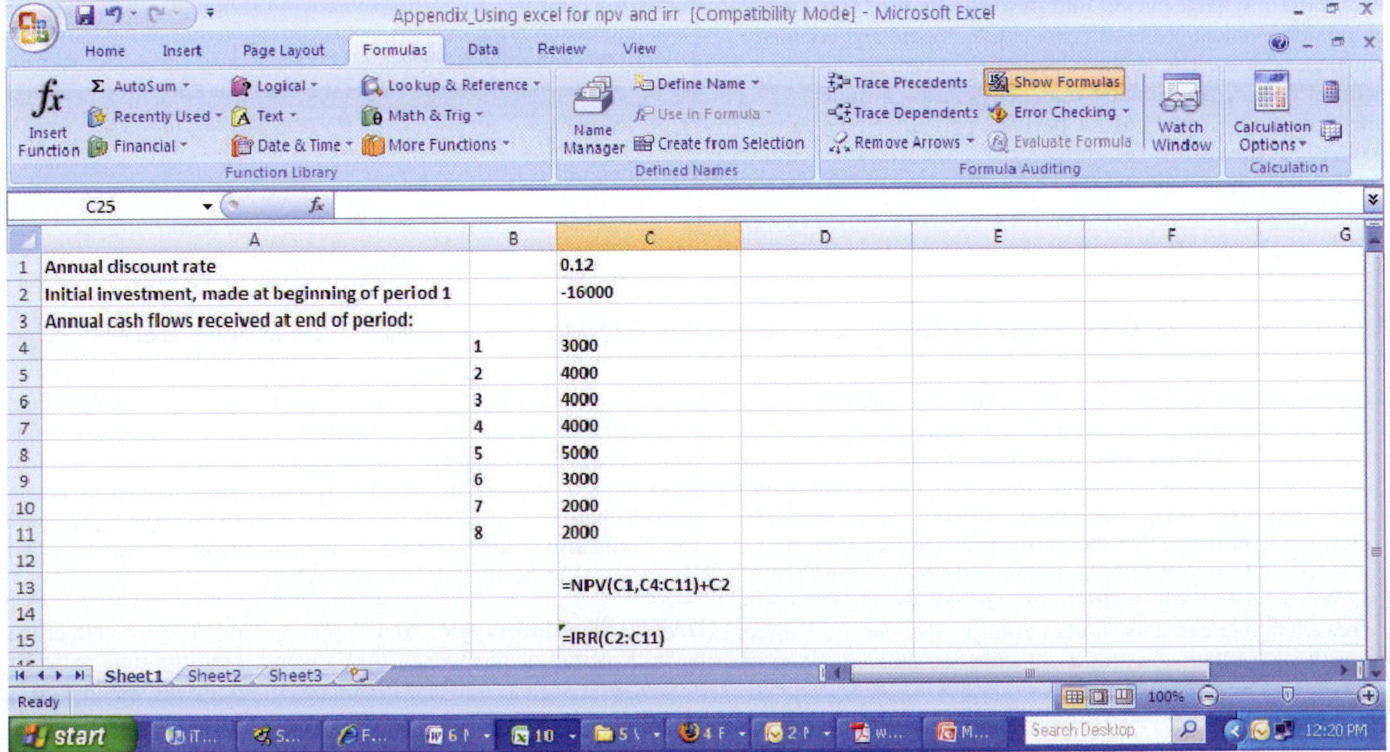

To compute the net present value of this project, the following is entered into cell C13:

=NPV(C1,C4:C11)+C2.

This instructs Excel to use its NPV function to compute the present value of the cash flows in cells C4 through C11, using the discount rate in cell C1, and then add the amount of the (negative) initial investment. For this stream of cash flows and a discount rate of 12%, the net present value is $1,326.03.

To compute the internal rate of return for this project, the following is entered into cell C15:

=IRR(C2:C11).

This instructs Excel to use its IRR function to compute the internal rate of return of the cash flows in cells C2 through C11. By default, Excel starts with a guess of 10%, and then uses trial and error to find the IRR. The IRR equals 14% for this project.

Summary

C1 Explain the importance of capital budgeting. Capital budgeting is the process of analyzing alternative investments and deciding which assets to acquire or sell. It involves predicting the cash flows to be received from the alternatives, evaluating their merits, and then choosing which ones to pursue.

C2 Describe the selection of a hurdle rate for an investment. Top management should select the hurdle (discount) rate to use in evaluating capital investments. The required hurdle rate should be at least higher than the interest rate on money borrowed because the return on an investment must cover the interest and provide an additional profit to reward the company for risk.

A1 Analyze a capital investment project using break-even time. Break-even time (BET) is a method for evaluating capital investments by restating future cash flows in terms of their present values (discounting the cash flows) and then calculating the payback period using these present values of cash flows.

P1 Compute payback period and describe its use. One way to compare potential investments is to compute and compare their payback periods. The payback period is an estimate of the expected time before the cumulative net cash inflow from the investment equals its initial cost. A payback period analysis fails to reflect risk of the cash flows, differences in the timing of cash flows within the payback period, and cash flows that occur after the payback period.

P2 Compute accounting rate of return and explain its use. A project's accounting rate of return is computed by dividing the expected annual after-tax net income by the average amount of investment in the project. When the net cash flows are received evenly throughout each period and straight-line depreciation is used, the average investment is computed as the average of the investment's initial book value and its salvage value.

P3 Compute net present value and describe its use. An investment's net present value is determined by predicting the future cash flows it is expected to generate, discounting them at a rate that represents an acceptable return, and then by subtracting the investment's initial cost from the sum of the present values. This technique can deal with any pattern of expected cash flows and applies a superior concept of return on investment.

P4 Compute internal rate of return and explain its use. The internal rate of return (IRR) is the discount rate that results in a zero net present value. When the cash flows are equal, we can compute the present value factor corresponding to the IRR by dividing the initial investment by the annual cash flows. We then use the annuity tables to determine the discount rate corresponding to this present value factor.

Guidance Answers to Decision Maker and Decision Ethics

Systems Manager Your dilemma is whether to abide by rules designed to prevent abuse or to bend them to acquire an investment that you believe will benefit the firm. You should not pursue the latter action because breaking up the order into small components is dishonest and there are consequences of being caught at a later stage. Develop a proposal for the entire package and then do all you can to expedite its processing, particularly by pointing out its benefits. When faced with controls that are not working, there is rarely a reason to overcome its shortcomings by dishonesty. A direct assault on those limitations is more sensible and ethical.

Entrepreneur The banker is probably concerned because new products are risky and should therefore be evaluated using a higher rate of return. You should conduct a thorough technical analysis and obtain detailed market data and information about any similar products available in the market. These factors might provide sufficient information to support the use of a lower return. You must convince yourself that the risk level is consistent with the discount rate used. You should also be confident that your company has the capacity and the resources to handle the new product.

Investment Manager You should probably focus on either the payback period or break-even time because both the time value of money and recovery time are important. Break-even time method is superior because it accounts for the time value of money, which is an important consideration in this decision.

Guidance Answers to **Quick Checks**

1. *b*

2. A capital budgeting decision is difficult because (1) the outcome is uncertain, (2) large amounts of money are usually involved, (3) a long-term commitment is required, and (4) the decision could be difficult or impossible to reverse.

3. *b*

4. Depreciation expense is subtracted from revenues in computing net income but does not use cash and should be added back to net income to compute net cash flows.

5. Not necessarily. One investment can continue to generate cash flows beyond the payback period for a longer time period than the other. The timing of their cash flows within the payback period also can differ.

6. *b*; Annual average investment = ($180,000 + $15,000)/2 = $97,500
Accounting rate of return = $40,000/$97,500 = 41%

7. For this determination, we need to compare it to the returns expected from alternative investments with similar risk.

8. Project A has the higher net present value as follows:

		Project A		Project B	
Year	Present Value of 1 at 10%	Net Cash Flows	Present Value of Net Cash Flows	Net Cash Flows	Present Value of Net Cash Flows
1	0.9091	$12,000	$10,909	$ 4,500	$ 4,091
2	0.8264	8,500	7,024	8,500	7,024
3	0.7513	4,000	3,005	13,000	9,767
Totals		$24,500	$20,938	$26,000	$20,882
Amount invested			(20,000)		(20,000)
Net present value			**$ 938**		**$ 882**

9. No, the information is too limited to draw that conclusion. For example, one investment could be riskier than the other, or one could require a substantially larger initial investment.

10. *b*

Key Terms

mhhe.com/wildMA2e

Key Terms are available at the book's Website for learning and testing in an online Flashcard Format.

Accounting rate of return (p. 395)
Break-even time (BET) (p. 402)
Capital budgeting (p. 392)
Cost of capital (p. 397)
Hurdle rate (p. 332)
Internal rate of return (IRR) (p. 399)
Net present value (NPV) (p. 397)
Payback period (PBP) (p. 393)
Profitability index (p. 399)

Multiple Choice Quiz

Answers on p. 420

mhhe.com/wildMA2e

Additional Quiz Questions are available at the book's Website.

Quiz11

1. The minimum acceptable rate of return for an investment decision is called the
a. Hurdle rate of return.
b. Payback rate of return.
c. Internal rate of return.
d. Average rate of return.
e. Maximum rate of return.

2. A corporation is considering the purchase of new equipment costing $90,000. The projected after-tax annual net income from the equipment is $3,600, after deducting $30,000 depreciation. Assume that revenue is to be received at each year-end, and the machine has a useful life of three years with zero salvage value. Management requires a 12% return on its investments. What is the net present value of this machine?
a. $ 60,444
b. $ 80,700
c. $(88,560)
d. $ 90,000
e. $ (9,300)

3. A disadvantage of using the payback period to compare investment alternatives is that it
a. Ignores cash flows beyond the payback period.
b. Cannot be used to compare alternatives with different initial investments.
c. Cannot be used when cash flows are not uniform.

d. Involves the time value of money.
e. Cannot be used if a company records depreciation.

4. A company is considering the purchase of equipment for $270,000. Projected annual cash inflow from this equipment is $61,200 per year. The payback period is:
a. 0.2 years
b. 5.0 years
c. 4.4 years
d. 2.3 years
e. 3.9 years

5. A company buys a machine for $180,000 that has an expected life of nine years and no salvage value. The company expects an annual net income (after taxes of 30%) of $8,550. What is the accounting rate of return?
a. 4.75%
b. 42.75%
c. 2.85%
d. 9.50%
e. 6.65%

Discussion Questions

1. What is capital budgeting?

2. Identify four reasons that capital budgeting decisions by managers are risky.

3. Capital budgeting decisions require careful analysis because they are generally the ________ ________ and ________ decisions that management faces.

4. Identify two disadvantages of using the payback period for comparing investments.

5. Why is an investment more attractive to management if it has a shorter payback period?

6. What is the average amount invested in a machine during its predicted five-year life if it costs $200,000 and has a $20,000 salvage value? Assume that net income is received evenly throughout each year and straight-line depreciation is used.

7. If the present value of the expected net cash flows from a machine, discounted at 10%, exceeds the amount to be invested, what can you say about the investment's expected rate of return? What can you say about the expected rate of return if the present value of the net cash flows, discounted at 10%, is less than the investment amount?

8. Why is the present value of $100 that you expect to receive one year from today worth less than $100 received today? What is the present value of $100 that you expect to receive one year from today, discounted at 12%?

9. Why should managers set the required rate of return higher than the rate at which money can be borrowed when making a typical capital budgeting decision?

10. Why does the use of the accelerated depreciation method (instead of straight line) for income tax reporting increase an investment's value?

11. The management of Best Buy is planning to invest in a new companywide computerized inventory tracking system. What makes this potential investment risky?

12. Circuit City is considering expanding a store. Identify three methods management can use to evaluate whether to expand.

13. The management of Apple is planning to acquire new equipment to manufacture some of its computer peripherals, and it intends to evaluate that investment decision using net present value. What are some of the costs and benefits that would be included in Apple's analysis?

Denotes Discussion Questions that involve decision making.

Most materials in this section are available in McGraw-Hill's Connect connect

QUICK STUDY

QS 11-1
Analyzing payback periods P1

Trek Company is considering two alternative investments. The payback period is 2.5 years for Investment A and 3 years for Investment B. (1) If management relies on the payback period, which investment is preferred? (2) Why might Trek's analysis of these two alternatives lead to the selection of B over A?

QS 11-2
Payback period P1

Foster Company is considering an investment that requires immediate payment of $360,000 and provides expected cash inflows of $120,000 annually for four years. What is the investment's payback period?

QS 11-3
Computation of net present value P3

If Kimball Company invests $100,000 today, it can expect to receive $20,000 at the end of each year for the next seven years plus an extra $12,000 at the end of the seventh year. What is the net present value of this investment assuming a required 8% return on investments?

QS 11-4
Net present value analysis
P3

Tinto Company is planning to invest in a project at a cost of $135,000. This project has the following expected cash flows over its three-year life: Year 1, $45,000; Year 2, $52,000; and Year 3, $78,000. Management requires a 10% rate of return on its investments. Compute the net present value of this investment.

QS 11-5
Computation of accounting rate of return
P2

Camino Company is considering an investment expected to generate an average net income after taxes of $3,825 for three years. The investment costs $90,000 and has an estimated $12,000 salvage value. Compute the accounting rate of return for this investment; assume the company uses straight-line depreciation. Hint: Use the formula in Exhibit 11.5 when computing the average annual investment.

QS 11-6
Computation of break-even time
A1

Fast Feet, a shoe manufacturer, is evaluating the costs and benefits of new equipment that would custom fit each pair of athletic shoes. The customer would have his or her foot scanned by digital computer equipment; this information would be used to cut the raw materials to provide the customer a perfect fit. The new equipment costs $300,000 and is expected to generate an additional $105,000 in cash flows for five years. A bank will make a $300,000 loan to the company at a 8% interest rate for this equipment's purchase. Use the following table to determine the break-even time for this equipment. (Round the present value of cash flows to the nearest dollar.)

Year	Cash Flows*	Present Value of 1 at 8%	Present Value of Cash Flows	Cumulative Present Value of Cash Flows
0	$(300,000)	1.0000		
1	105,000	0.9259		
2	105,000	0.8573		
3	105,000	0.7938		
4	105,000	0.7350		
5	105,000	0.6806		

* All cash flows occur at year-end.

QS 11-7
Profitability index
P3

Jemak Company is considering two alternative projects. Project 1 requires an initial investment of $800,000 and has a net present value of cash flows of $1,600,000. Project 2 requires an initial investment of $4,000,000 and has a net present value of cash flows of $2,000,000. Compute the profitability index for each project. Based on the profitability index, which project should the company prefer? Explain.

connect *Most materials in this section are available in McGraw-Hill's Connect*

EXERCISES

Exercise 11-1
Payback period computation; even cash flows
P1

Compute the payback period for each of these two separate investments (round the payback period to two decimals):

a. A new operating system for an existing machine is expected to cost $250,000 and have a useful life of four years. The system yields an incremental after-tax income of $72,000 each year after deducting its straight-line depreciation. The predicted salvage value of the system is $10,000.

b. A machine costs $180,000, has a $12,000 salvage value, is expected to last eight years, and will generate an after-tax income of $39,000 per year after straight-line depreciation.

Exercise 11-2
Payback period computation; uneven cash flows
P1

Walker Company is considering the purchase of an asset for $90,000. It is expected to produce the following net cash flows. The cash flows occur evenly throughout each year. Compute the payback period for this investment.

	Year 1	Year 2	Year 3	Year 4	Year 5	Total
Net cash flows	$40,000	$30,000	$40,000	$70,000	$29,000	$209,000

Check 2.5 years

Exercise 11-3
Payback period computation; declining-balance depreciation
P1

A machine can be purchased for $600,000 and used for 5 years, yielding the following net incomes. In projecting net incomes, double-declining balance depreciation is applied, using a 5-year life and a zero salvage value. Compute the machine's payback period (ignore taxes). (Round the payback period to two decimals.)

	Year 1	Year 2	Year 3	Year 4	Year 5
Net incomes	$40,000	$100,000	$200,000	$150,000	$400,000

Check 2.27 years

Exercise 11-4
Accounting rate of return
P2

A machine costs $200,000 and is expected to yield an after-tax net income of $5,040 each year. Management predicts this machine has a 12-year service life and a $40,000 salvage value, and it uses straight-line depreciation. Compute this machine's accounting rate of return.

Exercise 11-5
Payback period and accounting rate of return on investment
P1 P2

MLM Co. is considering the purchase of equipment that would allow the company to add a new product to its line. The equipment is expected to cost $324,000 with a 12-year life and no salvage value. It will be depreciated on a straight-line basis. The company expects to sell 128,000 units of the equipment's product each year. The expected annual income related to this equipment follows. Compute the (1) payback period and (2) accounting rate of return for this equipment.

Sales	$200,000
Costs	
Materials, labor, and overhead (except depreciation)	107,000
Depreciation on new equipment	27,000
Selling and administrative expenses	20,000
Total costs and expenses	154,000
Pretax income	46,000
Income taxes (30%)	13,800
Net income	$ 32,200

Check (1) 5.47 years (2) 19.88%

Exercise 11-6
Computing net present value
P3

After evaluating the risk of the investment described in Exercise 11-5, MLM Co. concludes that it must earn at least a 10% return on this investment. Compute the net present value of this investment. (Round the net present value to the nearest dollar.)

Exercise 11-7
Computation and interpretation of net present value and internal rate of return
P3 P4 

Cerritos Company can invest in each of three cheese-making projects: C1, C2, and C3. Each project requires an initial investment of $438,374 and would yield the following annual cash flows.

	C1	C2	C3
Year 1	$ 24,000	$192,000	$360,000
Year 2	216,000	192,000	120,000
Year 3	336,000	192,000	96,000
Totals	$576,000	$576,000	$576,000

(1) Assuming that the company requires a 12% return from its investments, use net present value to determine which projects, if any, should be acquired. (2) Using the answer from part 1, explain whether the internal rate of return is higher or lower than 12% for project C2. (3) Compute the internal rate of return for project C2.

Check (3) IRR = 15%

Exercise 11-8
NPV and profitability index
P3

Following is information on two alternative investments being considered by Jakem Company. The company requires a 10% return from its investments.

	Project A	Project B
Initial investment	$(180,325)	$(150,960)
Expected net cash flows in year:		
1	45,000	35,000
2	50,000	52,000
3	82,295	58,000
4	86,400	75,000
5	64,000	29,000

For each alternative project compute the (a) net present value, and (b) profitability index. If the company can only select one project, which should it choose? Explain.

Exercise 11-9^A
Using Excel to compute IRR
P4

Refer to the information in Exercise 11-8. Create an Excel spreadsheet to compute the internal rate of return for each of the projects. Round the percentage return to two decimals.

Exercise 11-10
Comparison of payback and BET
P1 A1

This chapter explained two methods to evaluate investments using recovery time, the payback period and break-even time (BET). Refer to QS 11-6 and (1) compute the recovery time for both the payback period and break-even time, (2) discuss the advantage(s) of break-even time over the payback period, and (3) list two conditions under which payback period and break-even time are similar.

connect *Most materials in this section are available in McGraw-Hill's Connect*

PROBLEM SET A

Problem 11-1A
Computation of payback period, accounting rate of return, and net present value
P1 P2 P3

mhhe.com/wildMA2e

Burtle Company is planning to add a new product to its line. To manufacture this product, the company needs to buy a new machine at a $488,000 cost with an expected four-year life and a $15,200 salvage value. All sales are for cash, and all costs are out of pocket except for depreciation on the new machine. Additional information includes the following.

Expected annual sales of new product	$1,870,000
Expected annual costs of new product	
Direct materials	465,000
Direct labor	680,000
Overhead excluding straight-line depreciation on new machine	335,000
Selling and administrative expenses	158,000
Income taxes	40%

Required

1. Compute straight-line depreciation for each year of this new machine's life. (Round depreciation amounts to the nearest dollar.)

2. Determine expected net income and net cash flow for each year of this machine's life. (Round answers to the nearest dollar.)

3. Compute this machine's payback period, assuming that cash flows occur evenly throughout each year. (Round the payback period to two decimals.)

4. Compute this machine's accounting rate of return, assuming that income is earned evenly throughout each year. (Round the percentage return to two decimals.)

5. Compute the net present value for this machine using a discount rate of 8% and assuming that cash flows occur at each year-end. (*Hint:* Salvage value is a cash inflow at the end of the asset's life. Round the net present value to the nearest dollar.)

Check (4) 27.14%

(5) $140,794

Problem 11-2A
Analysis and computation of payback period, accounting rate of return, and net present value
P1 P2 P3

Jackson Company has an opportunity to invest in one of two new projects. Project Y requires a $360,000 investment for new machinery with a four-year life and no salvage value. Project Z requires a $360,000 investment for new machinery with a three-year life and no salvage value. The two projects yield the following predicted annual results. The company uses straight-line depreciation, and cash flows occur evenly throughout each year.

	Project Y	Project Z
Sales	$355,000	$265,000
Expenses		
Direct materials	49,700	30,125
Direct labor	71,000	36,750
Overhead including depreciation	127,800	129,250
Selling and administrative expenses	25,000	20,000
Total expenses	273,500	216,125
Pretax income	81,500	48,875
Income taxes (30%)	24,450	14,663
Net income	$ 57,050	$ 34,212

Required

1. Compute each project's annual expected net cash flows. (Round the net cash flows to the nearest dollar.)
2. Determine each project's payback period. (Round the payback period to two decimals.)
3. Compute each project's accounting rate of return. (Round the percentage return to one decimal.)
4. Determine each project's net present value using 6% as the discount rate. For part 4 only, assume that cash flows occur at each year-end. (Round the net present value to the nearest dollar.)

Check For Project Y: (2) 2.45 years, (3) 31.7%, (4) $149,543

Analysis Component

5. Identify the project you would recommend to management and explain your choice.

Problem 11-3A
Computation of cash flows and net present values with alternative depreciation methods
P3 

Deandra Corporation is considering a new project requiring a $97,500 investment in test equipment with no salvage value. The project would produce $71,000 of pretax income before depreciation at the end of each of the next six years. The company's income tax rate is 32%. In compiling its tax return and computing its income tax payments, the company can choose between the two alternative depreciation schedules shown in the table.

	Straight-Line Depreciation	MACRS Depreciation
Year 1	$ 9,750	$19,500
Year 2	19,500	31,200
Year 3	19,500	18,720
Year 4	19,500	11,232
Year 5	19,500	11,232
Year 6	9,750	5,616
Totals	$97,500	$97,500

Required

1. Prepare a five-column table that reports amounts (assuming use of straight-line depreciation) for each of the following for each of the six years: (a) pretax income before depreciation, (b) straight-line depreciation expense, (c) taxable income, (d) income taxes, and (e) net cash flow. Net cash flow equals the amount of income before depreciation minus the income taxes. (Round answers to the nearest dollar.)
2. Prepare a five-column table that reports amounts (assuming use of MACRS depreciation) for each of the following for each of the six years: (a) pretax income before depreciation, (b) MACRS

depreciation expense, (c) taxable income, (d) income taxes, and (e) net cash flow. Net cash flow equals the income amount before depreciation minus the income taxes. (Round answers to the nearest dollar.)

3. Compute the net present value of the investment if straight-line depreciation is used. Use 10% as the discount rate. (Round the net present value to the nearest dollar.)

Check Net present value: (3) $135,347, (4) $136,893

4. Compute the net present value of the investment if MACRS depreciation is used. Use 10% as the discount rate. (Round the net present value to the nearest dollar.)

Analysis Component

5. Explain why the MACRS depreciation method increases this project's net present value.

Problem 11-4A

Computing net present value of alternate investments

P3

Interstate Manufacturing is considering either replacing one of its old machines with a new machine or having the old machine overhauled. Information about the two alternatives follows. Management requires a 10% rate of return on its investments.

Alternative 1: Keep the old machine and have it overhauled. If the old machine is overhauled, it will be kept for another five years and then sold for its salvage value.

Cost of old machine	$112,000
Cost of overhaul	150,000
Annual expected revenues generated	95,000
Annual cash operating costs after overhaul	42,000
Salvage value of old machine in 5 years	15,000

Alternative 2: Sell the old machine and buy a new one. The new machine is more efficient and will yield substantial operating cost savings with more product being produced and sold.

Cost of new machine	$300,000
Salvage value of old machine now	29,000
Annual expected revenues generated	100,000
Annual cash operating costs	32,000
Salvage value of new machine in 5 years	20,000

Required

1. Determine the net present value of alternative 1.

2. Determine the net present value of alternative 2.

3. Which alternative do you recommend that management select? Explain.

Check (1) Net present value of Alternative 1, $60,226

Problem 11-5A

Payback period, break-even time, and net present value

P1 A1

Sentinel Company is considering an investment in technology to improve its operations. The investment will require an initial outlay of $250,000 and will yield the following expected cash flows. Management requires investments to have a payback period of three years, and it requires a 10% return on investments.

Period	Cash Flow
1	$ 47,000
2	52,000
3	75,000
4	94,000
5	125,000

Required

1. Determine the payback period for this investment.

2. Determine the break-even time for this investment.

3. Determine the net present value for this investment.

Check (1) Payback period, 3.8 years

Analysis Component

4. Should management invest in this project? Explain.

Problem 11-6A
Payback period, break-even time, and net present value

P1 A1 

Lenitnes Company is considering an investment in technology to improve its operations. The investment will require an initial outlay of $250,000 and will yield the following expected cash flows. Management requires investments to have a payback period of three years, and it requires a 10% return on its investments.

Period	Cash Flow
1	$125,000
2	94,000
3	75,000
4	52,000
5	47,000

Required

Check (1) Payback period, 2.4 years

1. Determine the payback period for this investment.

2. Determine the break-even time for this investment.

3. Determine the net present value for this investment.

Analysis component

4. Should management invest in this project? Explain.

5. Compare your answers for parts 1 through 4 with those for Problem 11-5A. What are the causes of the differences in results and your conclusions?

PROBLEM SET B

Problem 11-1B
Computation of payback period, accounting rate of return, and net present value

P1 P2 P3

Sorbo Company is planning to add a new product to its line. To manufacture this product, the company needs to buy a new machine at a $600,000 cost with an expected four-year life and a $20,000 salvage value. All sales are for cash and all costs are out of pocket, except for depreciation on the new machine. Additional information includes the following.

Expected annual sales of new product	$2,300,000
Expected annual costs of new product	
Direct materials	600,000
Direct labor	840,000
Overhead excluding straight-line depreciation on new machine	420,000
Selling and administrative expenses	200,000
Income taxes	30%

Required

1. Compute straight-line depreciation for each year of this new machine's life. (Round depreciation amounts to the nearest dollar.)

2. Determine expected net income and net cash flow for each year of this machine's life. (Round answers to the nearest dollar.)

3. Compute this machine's payback period, assuming that cash flows occur evenly throughout each year. (Round the payback period to two decimals.)

Check (4) 21.45%

4. Compute this machine's accounting rate of return, assuming that income is earned evenly throughout each year. (Round the percentage return to two decimals.)

(5) $131,650

5. Compute the net present value for this machine using a discount rate of 7% and assuming that cash flows occur at each year-end. (*Hint:* Salvage value is a cash inflow at the end of the asset's life.)

Problem 11-2B
Analysis and computation of payback period, accounting rate of return, and net present value

P1 P2 P3 

Morris Company has an opportunity to invest in one of two projects. Project A requires a $480,000 investment for new machinery with a four-year life and no salvage value. Project B also requires a $480,000 investment for new machinery with a three-year life and no salvage value. The two projects yield the following predicted annual results. The company uses straight-line depreciation, and cash flows occur evenly throughout each year.

	Project A	Project B
Sales	$500,000	$400,000
Expenses		
Direct materials	70,000	50,000
Direct labor	100,000	60,000
Overhead including depreciation	180,000	180,000
Selling and administrative expenses	36,000	36,000
Total expenses	386,000	326,000
Pretax income	114,000	74,000
Income taxes (30%)	34,200	22,200
Net income	$ 79,800	$ 51,800

Required

1. Compute each project's annual expected net cash flows. (Round net cash flows to the nearest dollar.)

2. Determine each project's payback period. (Round the payback period to two decimals.)

3. Compute each project's accounting rate of return. (Round the percentage return to one decimal.)

4. Determine each project's net present value using 8% as the discount rate. For part 4 only, assume that cash flows occur at each year-end. (Round net present values to the nearest dollar.)

Check For Project A: (2) 2.4 years, (3) 33.3%, (4) $181,758

Analysis Component

5. Identify the project you would recommend to management and explain your choice.

Problem 11-3B
Computation of cash flows and net present values with alternative depreciation methods

P3

Lee Corporation is considering a new project requiring a $300,000 investment in an asset having no salvage value. The project would produce $125,000 of pretax income before depreciation at the end of each of the next six years. The company's income tax rate is 35%. In compiling its tax return and computing its income tax payments, the company can choose between two alternative depreciation schedules as shown in the table.

	Straight-Line Depreciation	MACRS Depreciation
Year 1	$ 30,000	$ 60,000
Year 2	60,000	96,000
Year 3	60,000	57,600
Year 4	60,000	34,560
Year 5	60,000	34,560
Year 6	30,000	17,280
Totals	$300,000	$300,000

Required

1. Prepare a five-column table that reports amounts (assuming use of straight-line depreciation) for each of the following items for each of the six years: (a) pretax income before depreciation, (b) straight-line depreciation expense, (c) taxable income, (d) income taxes, and (e) net cash flow. Net cash flow equals the amount of income before depreciation minus the income taxes. (Round answers to the nearest dollar.)

2. Prepare a five-column table that reports amounts (assuming use of MACRS depreciation) for each of the following items for each of the six years: (a) income before depreciation, (b) MACRS depreciation expense, (c) taxable income, (d) income taxes, and (e) net cash flow. Net cash flow equals the amount of income before depreciation minus the income taxes. (Round answers to the nearest dollar.)

Check Net present value: (3) $129,846, (4) $135,050

3. Compute the net present value of the investment if straight-line depreciation is used. Use 10% as the discount rate. (Round the net present value to the nearest dollar.)
4. Compute the net present value of the investment if MACRS depreciation is used. Use 10% as the discount rate. (Round the net present value to the nearest dollar.)

Analysis Component

5. Explain why the MACRS depreciation method increases the net present value of this project.

Problem 11-4B

Computing net present value of alternate investments

P3 

Archer Foods has a freezer that is in need of repair and is considering whether to replace the old freezer with a new freezer or have the old freezer extensively repaired. Information about the two alternatives follows. Management requires a 10% rate of return on its investments.

Alternative 1: Keep the old freezer and have it repaired. If the old freezer is repaired, it will be kept for another 8 years and then sold for its salvage value.

Cost of old freezer	$75,000
Cost of repair	50,000
Annual expected revenues generated	63,000
Annual cash operating costs after repair	55,000
Salvage value of old freezer in 8 years	3,000

Alternative 2: Sell the old freezer and buy a new one. The new freezer is larger than the old one and will allow the company to expand its product offerings, thereby generating more revenues. Also, it is more energy efficient and will yield substantial operating cost savings.

Cost of new freezer	$150,000
Salvage value of old freezer now	5,000
Annual expected revenues generated	68,000
Annual cash operating costs	30,000
Salvage value of new freezer in 8 years	8,000

Required

Check (1) Net present value of Alternative 1, $(5,921)

1. Determine the net present value of alternative 1.
2. Determine the net present value of alternative 2.
3. Which alternative do you recommend that management select? Explain.

Problem 11-5B

Payback period, break-even time, and net present value

P1 A1

Aster Company is considering an investment in technology to improve its operations. The investment will require an initial outlay of $800,000 and yield the following expected cash flows. Management requires investments to have a payback period of two years, and it requires a 10% return on its investments.

Period	Cash Flow
1	$300,000
2	350,000
3	400,000
4	450,000

Required

Check (1) Payback period, 2.4 years

1. Determine the payback period for this investment.
2. Determine the break-even time for this investment.
3. Determine the net present value for this investment.

Analysis Component

4. Should management invest in this project? Explain.

Problem 11-6B
Payback period, break-even time, and net present value
P1 A1 

Retsa Company is considering an investment in technology to improve its operations. The investment will require an initial outlay of $800,000 and will yield the following expected cash flows. Management requires investments to have a payback period of two years, and it requires a 10% return on its investments.

Period	Cash Flow
1	$450,000
2	400,000
3	350,000
4	300,000

Required

1. Determine the payback period for this investment.
2. Determine the break-even time for this investment.
3. Determine the net present value for this investment.

Check (1) Payback period, 1.9 years

Analysis Component

4. Should management invest in this project? Explain.
5. Compare your answers for parts 1 through 4 with those for Problem 11-5B. What are the causes of the differences in results and your conclusions?

SERIAL PROBLEM

Success Systems

(This serial problem began in Chapter 1 and continues through most of the book. If previous chapter segments were not completed, the serial problem can begin at this point. It is helpful, but not necessary, to use the Working Papers that accompany the book.)

SP 11 Adriana Lopez is considering the purchase of equipment for Success Systems that would allow the company to add a new product to its computer furniture line. The equipment is expected to cost $300,000 and to have a six-year life and no salvage value. It will be depreciated on a straight-line basis. Success Systems expects to sell 100 units of the equipment's product each year. The expected annual income related to this equipment follows.

Sales	$375,000
Costs	
Materials, labor, and overhead (except depreciation)	200,000
Depreciation on new equipment	50,000
Selling and administrative expenses	37,500
Total costs and expenses	287,500
Pretax income	87,500
Income taxes (30%)	26,250
Net income	$ 61,250

Required

Compute the (1) payback period and (2) accounting rate of return for this equipment.

BEYOND THE NUMBERS

REPORTING IN ACTION

C1 A1 P3

BTN 11-1 In fiscal 2007, **Best Buy** invested $251 million in store-related projects that included store remodels, relocations, expansions, and various merchandising projects. Assume that these projects have a seven-year life, and that Best Buy requires a 12% internal rate of return on these projects.

Required

1. What is the amount of annual cash flows that Best Buy must earn from these projects to have a 12% internal rate of return? (*Hint:* Identify the seven-period, 12% factor from the present value of an annuity table, and then divide $251 million by this factor to get the annual cash flows necessary.)

Fast Forward

2. Access Best Buy's financial statements for fiscal years ended after March 3, 2007, from its Website (BestBuy.com) or the SEC's Website (SEC.gov).

a. Determine the amount that Best Buy invested in similar store-related projects for the most recent year.

b. Assume a seven-year life and a 12% internal rate of return. What is the amount of cash flows that Best Buy must earn on these new projects?

COMPARATIVE ANALYSIS

P3 P4 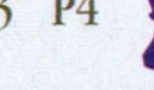

BTN 11-2 In fiscal 2007, Circuit City invested $242 million in capital expenditures, including $108 million related to store relocations, remodeling, and new store construction. Assume that these projects have a seven-year life and that management requires a 15% internal rate of return on those projects.

Required

1. What is the amount of annual cash flows that Circuit City must earn from those store-related projects to achieve a 15% internal rate of return? (*Hint:* Identify the 7-period, 15% factor from the present value of an annuity table and then divide $108 million by the factor to get the annual cash flows required.)

2. BTN 11-1 must be completed to answer part 2. How does your answer to part 1 compare to Best Buy's required cash flows determined in BTN 11-1? What does this imply about each company's cash flow requirements for these types of projects?

ETHICS CHALLENGE

P3

BTN 11-3 A consultant commented that "too often the numbers look good but feel bad." This comment often stems from estimation error common to capital budgeting proposals that relate to future cash flows. Three reasons for this error often exist. First, reliably predicting cash flows several years into the future is very difficult. Second, the present value of cash flows many years into the future (say, beyond 10 years) is often very small. Third, it is difficult for personal biases and expectations not to unduly influence present value computations.

Required

1. Compute the present value of $100 to be received in 10 years assuming a 12% discount rate.

2. Why is understanding the three reasons mentioned for estimation errors important when evaluating investment projects? Link this response to your answer for part 1.

COMMUNICATING IN PRACTICE

P1 P2 P3 P4

BTN 11-4 Payback period, accounting rate of return, net present value, and internal rate of return are common methods to evaluate capital investment opportunities. Assume that your manager asks you to identify the type of measurement basis and unit that each method offers and to list the advantages and disadvantages of each. Present your response in memorandum format of less than one page.

TAKING IT TO THE NET

BTN 11-5 Capital budgeting is an important topic and there are Websites designed to help people understand the methods available. Access TeachMeFinance.com's capital budgeting Webpage (teachmefinance.com/capitalbudgeting.html). This Webpage contains an example of a capital budgeting case involving a $15,000 initial cash outflow.

Required

Compute the payback period and the net present value (assuming a 10% required rate of return) of the following investment—assume that its cash flows occur at year-end. Compared to the example case at the Website, the larger cash inflows in the example below occur in the later years of the project's life. Is this investment acceptable based on the application of these two capital budgeting methods? Explain.

Year	Cash Flow
0	$(15,000)
1	1,000
2	2,000
3	3,000
4	6,000
5	7,000

TEAMWORK IN ACTION

P1 P3 

BTN 11-6 Break into teams and identify four reasons that an international airline such as **Southwest**, **Northwest**, or **American** would invest in a project when its direct analysis using both payback period and net present value indicate it to be a poor investment. (*Hint:* Think about qualitative factors.) Provide an example of an investment project supporting your answer.

ENTREPRENEURIAL DECISION

A1   

BTN 11-7 Read the chapter opener about Brian Scudamore and his company, **1-800-GOT-JUNK**. Brian is considering building a new, massive warehousing center to recycle the best of other people's junk. He expects that this recycling center could double company revenues.

Required

1. What are some of the management tools that Brian can use to evaluate whether the new warehousing center will be a good investment?
2. What information does Brian need to use the tools that you identified in your answer to part 1?
3. What are some of the advantages and disadvantages of each tool identified in your answer to part 1?

HITTING THE ROAD

C1 P3 

BTN 11-8 Visit or call a local auto dealership and inquire about leasing a car. Ask about the down payment and the required monthly payments. You will likely find the salesperson does not discuss the cost to purchase this car but focuses on the affordability of the monthly payments. This chapter gives you the tools to compute the cost of this car using the lease payment schedule in present dollars and to estimate the profit from leasing for an auto dealership.

Required

1. Compare the cost of leasing the car to buying it in present dollars using the information from the dealership you contact. (Assume you will make a final payment at the end of the lease and then own the car.)
2. Is it more costly to lease or buy the car? Support your answer with computations.

GLOBAL DECISION

C1

DSG

BTN 11-9 DSG's annual report includes information about its debt and interest rates. One statement in its annual report reveals that DSG has floating rate borrowings of more than £200 million at 6.125%.

Required

Explain how DSG would use that 6.125% rate to evaluate its investments in capital projects.

ANSWERS TO MULTIPLE CHOICE QUIZ

1. a

2. e;

	Net Cash Flow	Present Value of an Annuity of 1 at 12%	Present Value of Cash Flows
Years 1–3	$3,600 + $30,000	2.4018	$ 80,700
Amount invested			(90,000)
Net present value			$ (9,300)

3. a

4. c; Payback = $270,000/$61,200 per year = 4.4 years.

5. d; Accounting rate of return = $8,550/[($180,000 + $0)/2] = 9.5%.

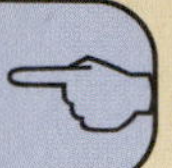

A Look Back

Chapter 11 focused on capital budgeting. It explained and illustrated several methods that help identify projects with the higher return on investment.

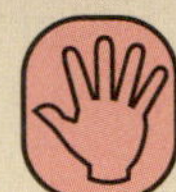

A Look at This Chapter

This chapter focuses on reporting and analyzing cash inflows and cash outflows. We emphasize how to prepare and interpret the statement of cash flows.

A Look Ahead

Chapter 13 focuses on tools to help us analyze financial statements. We also describe comparative analysis and the application of ratios for financial analysis.

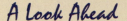

Reporting and Analyzing Cash Flows

Learning Objectives

CAP

Conceptual

C1 Explain the purpose and importance of cash flow information. *(p. 424)*

C2 Distinguish between operating, investing, and financing activities. *(p. 425)*

C3 Identify and disclose noncash investing and financing activities. *(p. 427)*

C4 Describe the format of the statement of cash flows. *(p. 427)*

Analytical

A1 Analyze the statement of cash flows. *(p. 441)*

A2 Compute and apply the cash flow on total assets ratio. *(p. 442)*

LP12

Procedural

P1 Prepare a statement of cash flows. *(p. 428)*

P2 Compute cash flows from operating activities using the indirect method. *(p. 431)*

P3 Determine cash flows from both investing and financing activities. *(p. 437)*

P4 *Appendix 12A*—Illustrate use of a spreadsheet to prepare a statement of cash flows. *(p. 445)*

P5 *Appendix 12B*—Compute cash flows from operating activities using the direct method. *(p. 448)*

Decision Feature

Wizard of Odd

"If you put enough energy into your dream, you can make anything happen" —Jim Bonaminio

FAIRFIELD, OH—Jim Bonaminio built his roadside produce stand while living in an abandoned gas station. "I would get up and leave at 4 in the morning to buy everything fresh [and] my wife opened the market at 8 a.m.," recalls Jim. "By 10 o'clock at night, we'd be sitting on the bed balancing the register receipts . . . we worked seven days a week." The fruit of those early efforts is **Jungle Jim's International Market (JungleJims.com).**

Jungle Jim's is no Wal-Mart wannabe, but it is arguably America's wackiest supermarket. Instead of trying to beat the big chains at the price-squeezing game, Jim's is a funhouse maze of a store. A seven-foot Elvis lion sings "Jailhouse Rock," an antique fire engine rests atop cases of hot sauce, port-a-potties lead to fancy restrooms, and Robin Hood greets customers with English food set within a 30-foot-tall Sherwood Forest. This is just a sampling.

"If you don't go out on a limb, then you're just like everybody else," insists Jim. "The stuff I've collected—all sorts of weird stuff—gets reused." Despite the wackiness, Jim is first and foremost a businessman. He learned firsthand about the importance of monitoring cash inflows and cash outflows. In the early days, recalls Jim, it was all about sales and profits. Then, inventory and asset growth yielded negative cash flows, and Jim was in a pinch. That's when he realized that tracking cash flows was important, explains Jim.

Jim eventually learned how to monitor and control cash flows for each of his operating, investing, and financing activities. Today, says Jim, "I hire professional people to [help me monitor cash] . . . and to look for ways to make money." Yet Jim explains that he always reviews the statement of cash flows and the individuals cash inflows and outflows.

Yet cash management has not curtailed Jim's fun-loving approach to business. "I'm trying to create something that has never been done," laughs Jim. "I just want to see if I can do it and have fun."

[Sources: *Jungle Jim's Website,* March 2009; *BusinessWeek,* April 2005; *Country Living,* November 2004; *Miamian,* Summer 2004; *Plain Dealer,* November 2004; *Supermarket News,* September 2006; *Cintas,* August 2007]

Chapter Preview

A company cannot achieve or maintain profits without carefully managing cash. Managers and other users of information pay attention to a company's cash position and the events and transactions affecting cash. This chapter explains how we prepare, analyze, and interpret a statement of cash flows. It also discusses the importance of cash flow information for predicting future performance and making managerial decisions. More generally, effectively using the statement of cash flows is crucial for managing and analyzing the operating, investing, and financing activities of businesses.

Reporting and Analyzing Cash Flows

Basics of Cash Flow Reporting
- Purpose
- Importance
- Measurement
- Classification
- Noncash activities
- Format and preparation

Cash Flows from Operating
- Indirect and direct methods of reporting
- Application of indirect method of reporting
- Summary of indirect method adjustments

Cash Flows from Investing
- Three-stage process of analysis
- Analysis of noncurrent assets
- Analysis of other assets

Cash Flows from Financing
- Three-stage process of analysis
- Analysis of noncurrent liabilities
- Analysis of equity

Basics of Cash Flow Reporting

This section describes the basics of cash flow reporting, including its purpose, measurement, classification, format, and preparation.

Purpose of the Statement of Cash Flows

C1 Explain the purpose and importance of cash flow information.

The purpose of the **statement of cash flows** is to report cash receipts (inflows) and cash payments (outflows) during a period. This includes separately identifying the cash flows related to operating, investing, and financing activities. The statement of cash flows does more than simply report changes in cash. It is the detailed disclosure of individual cash flows that makes this statement useful to users. Information in this statement helps users answer questions such as these:

- How does a company obtain its cash?
- Where does a company spend its cash?
- What explains the change in the cash balance?

Point: Internal users rely on the statement of cash flows to make investing and financing decisions. External users rely on this statement to assess the amount and timing of a company's cash flows.

The statement of cash flows addresses important questions such as these by summarizing, classifying, and reporting a company's cash inflows and cash outflows for each period.

Importance of Cash Flows

Information about cash flows can influence decision makers in important ways. For instance, we look more favorably at a company that is financing its expenditures with cash from operations than one that does it by selling its assets. Information about cash flows helps users decide whether a company has enough cash to pay its existing debts as they mature. It is also relied upon to evaluate a company's ability to meet unexpected obligations and pursue unexpected opportunities. External information users especially want to assess a company's ability to take advantage of new business opportunities. Internal users such as managers use cash flow information to plan day-to-day operating activities and make long-term investment decisions.

Macy's striking turnaround is an example of how analysis and management of cash flows can lead to improved financial stability. Several years ago Macy's obtained temporary protection from bankruptcy, at which time it desperately needed to improve its cash flows. It did so by engaging in aggressive cost-cutting measures. As a result, Macy's annual cash flow rose to $210 million, up from a negative cash flow of $38.9 million in the prior year. Macy's eventually met its financial obligations and then successfully merged with **Federated Department Stores**.

The case of W. T. Grant Co. is a classic example of the importance of cash flow information in predicting a company's future performance and financial strength. Grant reported net income of more than $40 million per year for three consecutive years. At that same time, it was experiencing an alarming decrease in cash provided by operations. For instance, net cash outflow was more than $90 million by the end of that three-year period. Grant soon went bankrupt. Users who relied solely on Grant's income numbers were unpleasantly surprised. This reminds us that cash flows as well as income statement and balance sheet information are crucial in making business decisions.

Video12.1

Decision Insight

Cash Savvy "A lender must have a complete understanding of a borrower's cash flows to assess both the borrowing needs and repayment sources. This requires information about the major types of cash inflows and outflows. I have seen many companies, whose financial statements indicate good profitability, experience severe financial problems because the owners or managers lacked a good understanding of cash flows."—Mary E. Garza, Bank of America.

Measurement of Cash Flows

Cash flows are defined to include both *cash* and *cash equivalents*. The statement of cash flows explains the difference between the beginning and ending balances of cash and cash equivalents. We continue to use the phrases *cash flows* and the *statement of cash flows,* but we must remember that both phrases refer to cash and cash equivalents. Recall that a cash equivalent must satisfy two criteria: (1) be readily convertible to a known amount of cash and (2) be sufficiently close to its maturity so its market value is unaffected by interest rate changes. In most cases, a debt security must be within three months of its maturity to satisfy these criteria. Companies must disclose and follow a clear policy for determining cash and cash equivalents and apply it consistently from period to period. American Express, for example, defines its cash equivalents as "time deposits and other highly liquid investments with original maturities of 90 days or less."

Classification of Cash Flows

C2 Distinguish between operating, investing, and financing activities.

Since cash and cash equivalents are combined, the statement of cash flows does not report transactions between cash and cash equivalents such as cash paid to purchase cash equivalents and cash received from selling cash equivalents. However, all other cash receipts and cash payments are classified and reported on the statement as operating, investing, or financing activities. Individual cash receipts and payments for each of these three categories are labeled to identify their originating transactions or events. A net cash inflow (source) occurs when the receipts in a category exceed the payments. A net cash outflow (use) occurs when the payments in a category exceed the receipts.

Operating Activities **Operating activities** include those transactions and events that determine net income. Examples are the production and purchase of merchandise, the sale of goods and services to customers, and the expenditures to administer the business. Not all items in income, such as unusual gains and losses, are operating activities (we discuss these exceptions later in the chapter). Exhibit 12.1 lists the more common cash inflows and outflows from operating activities. (Although cash receipts and cash payments from buying and selling trading

EXHIBIT 12.1

Cash Flows from Operating Activities

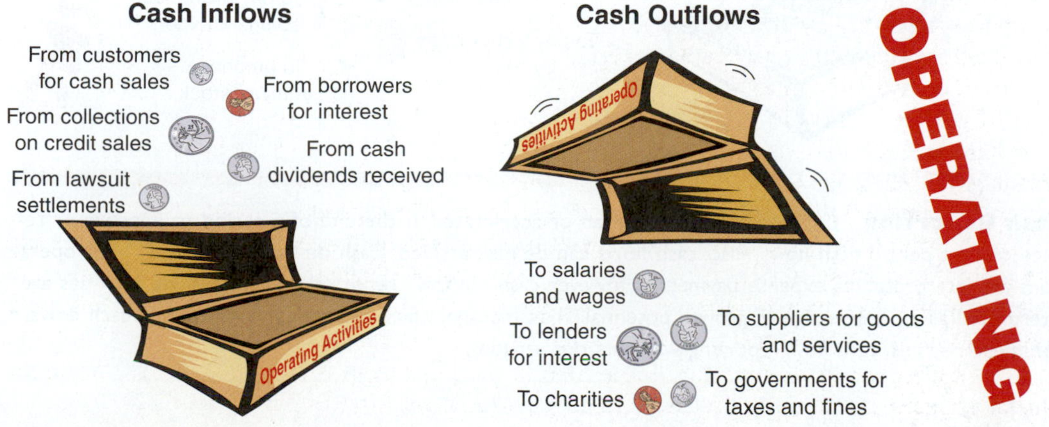

securities are often reported under operating activities, new standards require that these receipts and payments be classified based on the nature and purpose of those securities.)

Investing Activities **Investing activities** generally include those transactions and events that affect long-term assets, namely, the purchase and sale of long-term assets. They also include the (1) purchase and sale of short-term investments in the securities of other entities, other than cash equivalents and trading securities and (2) lending and collecting money for notes receivable. Exhibit 12.2 lists examples of cash flows from investing activities. Proceeds from collecting the principal amounts of notes deserve special mention. If the note results from sales to customers, its cash receipts are classed as operating activities whether short term or long term. If the note results from a loan to another party apart from sales, however, the cash receipts from collecting the note principal are classed as an investing activity. The FASB requires the collection of interest on loans be reported as an operating activity.

Point: The FASB requires that *cash dividends received* and *cash interest received* be reported as operating activities.

EXHIBIT 12.2

Cash Flows from Investing Activities

Cash Inflows

From selling investments in securities

From collecting principal on loans

From selling long-term productive assets

From selling (discounting) of notes

Investing Activities

Cash Outflows

Investing Activities

To make loans to others

To purchase long-term productive assets

To purchase investments in securities

INVESTING

Financing Activities **Financing activities** include those transactions and events that affect long-term liabilities and equity. Examples are (1) obtaining cash from issuing debt and repaying the amounts borrowed and (2) receiving cash from or distributing cash to owners. These activities involve transactions with a company's owners and creditors. They also often involve borrowing and repaying principal amounts relating to both short- and long-term debt. GAAP requires that payments of interest expense be classified as operating activities. Also, cash payments to settle credit purchases of merchandise, whether on account or by note, are operating activities. Exhibit 12.3 lists examples of cash flows from financing activities.

EXHIBIT 12.3

Cash Flows from Financing Activities

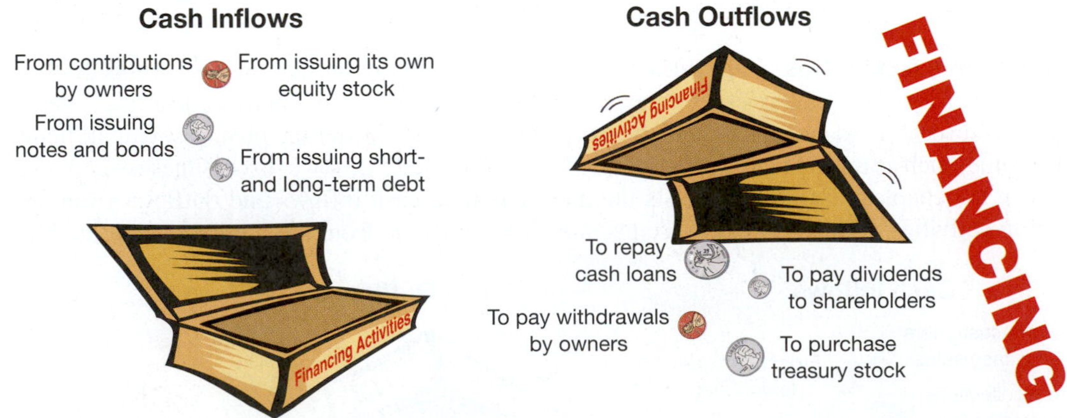

Point: Interest payments on a loan are classified as operating activities, but payments of loan principal are financing activities.

Decision Insight

Cash Reporting Cash flows can be delayed or accelerated at the end of a period to improve or reduce current period cash flows. Also, cash flows can be misclassified. Cash outflows reported under operations are interpreted as expense payments. However, cash outflows reported under investing activities are interpreted as a positive sign of growth potential. Thus, managers face incentives to misclassify cash flows. For these reasons, cash flow reporting warrants our scrutiny.

Noncash Investing and Financing

C3 Identify and disclose noncash investing and financing activities.

When important investing and financing activities do not affect cash receipts or payments, they are still disclosed at the bottom of the statement of cash flows or in a note to the statement because of their importance and the *full-disclosure principle*. One example of such a transaction is the purchase of long-term assets using a long-term note payable (loan). This transaction involves both investing and financing activities but does not affect any cash inflow or outflow and is not reported in any of the three sections of the statement of cash flows. This disclosure rule also extends to transactions with partial cash receipts or payments.

To illustrate, assume that Goorin purchases land for $12,000 by paying $5,000 cash and trading in used equipment worth $7,000. The investing section of the statement of cash flows reports only the $5,000 cash outflow for the land purchase. The $12,000 investing transaction is only partially described in the body of the statement of cash flows, yet this information is potentially important to users because it changes the makeup of assets. Goorin could either describe the transaction in a footnote or include information at the bottom of its statement that lists the $12,000 land purchase along with the cash financing of $5,000 and a $7,000 trade-in of equipment. As another example, Borg Co. acquired $900,000 of assets in exchange for $200,000 cash and a $700,000 long-term note, which should be reported as follows:

Point: A stock dividend transaction involving a transfer from retained earnings to common stock or a credit to contributed capital is *not* considered a noncash investing and financing activity because the company receives no consideration for shares issued.

Fair value of assets acquired	$900,000
Less cash paid	200,000
Liabilities incurred or assumed	$700,000

Exhibit 12.4 lists transactions commonly disclosed as noncash investing and financing activities.

EXHIBIT 12.4

Examples of Noncash Investing and Financing Activities

- Retirement of debt by issuing equity stock.
- Conversion of preferred stock to common stock.
- Lease of assets in a capital lease transaction.
- Purchase of long-term assets by issuing a note or bond.
- Exchange of noncash assets for other noncash assets.
- Purchase of noncash assets by issuing equity or debt.

Format of the Statement of Cash Flows

C4 Describe the format of the statement of cash flows.

Accounting standards require companies to include a statement of cash flows in a complete set of financial statements. This statement must report information about a company's cash receipts and cash payments during the period. Exhibit 12.5 shows the usual format. A company must report cash flows from three activities: operating, investing, and financing. The statement explains how transactions and events impact the prior period-end cash (and cash equivalents) balance to produce its current period-end balance.

EXHIBIT 12.5

Format of the Statement of Cash Flows

COMPANY NAME
Statement of Cash Flows
For *period* Ended *date*

Cash flows from operating activities		
[List of individual inflows and outflows]		
Net cash provided (used) by operating activities		$ #
Cash flows from investing activities		
[List of individual inflows and outflows]		
Net cash provided (used) by investing activities		#
Cash flows from financing activities		
[List of individual inflows and outflows]		
Net cash provided (used) by financing activities		#
Net increase (decrease) in cash		$ #
Cash (and equivalents) balance at prior period-end		#
Cash (and equivalents) balance at current period-end		$ #

Separate schedule or note disclosure of any "noncash investing and financing transactions" is required.

Decision Maker

Entrepreneur You are considering purchasing a start-up business that recently reported a $110,000 annual net loss and a $225,000 annual net cash inflow. How are these results possible? [Answer—p. 454]

Quick Check Answers—p. 454

1. Does a statement of cash flows report the cash payments to purchase cash equivalents? Does it report the cash receipts from selling cash equivalents?
2. Identify the three categories of cash flows reported separately on the statement of cash flows.
3. Identify the cash activity category for each transaction: (*a*) purchase equipment for cash, (*b*) cash payment of wages, (*c*) sale of common stock for cash, (*d*) receipt of cash dividends from stock investment, (e) cash collection from customers, (*f*) notes issued for cash.

Preparing the Statement of Cash Flows

P1 Prepare a statement of cash flows.

Preparing a statement of cash flows involves five steps: (1) compute the net increase or decrease in cash; (2) compute and report net cash provided or used by operating activities (using either the direct or indirect method; both are explained); (3) compute and report net cash provided or used by investing activities; (4) compute and report net cash provided or used by financing activities; and (5) compute the net cash flow by combining net cash provided or used by operating, investing, and financing activities and then *prove it* by adding it to the beginning cash balance to show that it equals the ending cash balance.

Step 1: Compute net increase or decrease in cash

Step 2: Compute net cash from operating activities

Step 3: Compute net cash from investing activities

Step 4: Compute net cash from financing activities

Step 5: Prove and report beginning and ending cash balances

Computing the net increase or net decrease in cash is a simple but crucial computation. It equals the current period's cash balance minus the prior period's cash balance. This is the *bottom-line* figure for the statement of cash flows and is a check on accuracy. The information we need to prepare a statement of cash flows comes from various sources including comparative balance sheets at the beginning and end of the period, and an income statement for the period. There are two alternative approaches to preparing the statement: (1) analyzing the Cash account and (2) analyzing noncash accounts.

Analyzing the Cash Account A company's cash receipts and cash payments are recorded in the Cash account in its general ledger. The Cash account is therefore a natural place to look for information about cash flows from operating, investing, and financing activities. To illustrate, review the summarized Cash T-account of Genesis, Inc., in Exhibit 12.6. Individual cash transactions are summarized in this Cash account according to the major types of cash receipts and cash payments. For instance, only the total of cash receipts from all customers is listed. Individual cash transactions underlying these totals can number in the thousands. Accounting software is available to provide summarized cash accounts.

Preparing a statement of cash flows from Exhibit 12.6 requires determining whether an individual cash inflow or outflow is an operating, investing, or financing activity, and then listing each by

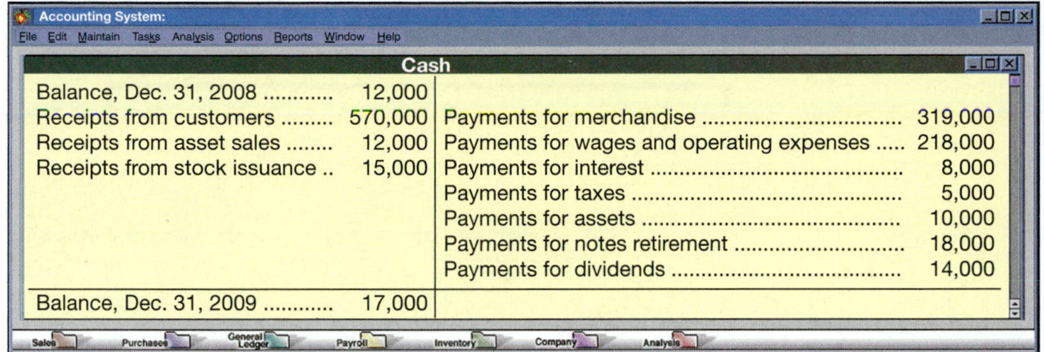

Cash			
Balance, Dec. 31, 2008	12,000		
Receipts from customers	570,000	Payments for merchandise	319,000
Receipts from asset sales	12,000	Payments for wages and operating expenses	218,000
Receipts from stock issuance	15,000	Payments for interest	8,000
		Payments for taxes	5,000
		Payments for assets	10,000
		Payments for notes retirement	18,000
		Payments for dividends	14,000
Balance, Dec. 31, 2009	17,000		

EXHIBIT 12.6

Summarized Cash Account

activity. This yields the statement shown in Exhibit 12.7. However, preparing the statement of cash flows from an analysis of the summarized Cash account has two limitations. First, most companies have many individual cash receipts and payments, making it difficult to review them all. Accounting software minimizes this burden, but it is still a task requiring professional judgment for many transactions. Second, the Cash account does not usually carry an adequate description of each cash transaction, making assignment of all cash transactions according to activity difficult.

Point: View the change in cash as a *target* number that we will fully explain and prove in the statement of cash flows.

EXHIBIT 12.7

Statement of Cash Flows—Direct Method

GENESIS
Statement of Cash Flows
For Year Ended December 31, 2009

Cash flows from operating activities		
Cash received from customers	$570,000	
Cash paid for merchandise	(319,000)	
Cash paid for wages and other operating expenses	(218,000)	
Cash paid for interest	(8,000)	
Cash paid for taxes	(5,000)	
Net cash provided by operating activities		$20,000
Cash flows from investing activities		
Cash received from sale of plant assets	12,000	
Cash paid for purchase of plant assets	(10,000)	
Net cash provided by investing activities		2,000
Cash flows from financing activities		
Cash received from issuing stock	15,000	
Cash paid to retire notes	(18,000)	
Cash paid for dividends	(14,000)	
Net cash used in financing activities		(17,000)
Net increase in cash		$ 5,000
Cash balance at prior year-end		12,000
Cash balance at current year-end		$17,000

Analyzing Noncash Accounts A second approach to preparing the statement of cash flows is analyzing noncash accounts. This approach uses the fact that when a company records cash inflows and outflows with debits and credits to the Cash account (see Exhibit 12.6), it also records credits and debits in noncash accounts (reflecting double-entry accounting). Many of these noncash accounts are balance sheet accounts, for instance, from the sale of land for cash. Others are revenue and expense accounts that are closed to equity. For instance, the sale of services for cash yields a credit to Services Revenue that is closed to Retained Earnings for a corporation. In sum, *all cash transactions eventually affect noncash balance sheet accounts*. Thus, we can determine cash inflows and outflows by analyzing changes in noncash balance sheet accounts.

Exhibit 12.8 uses the accounting equation to show the relation between the Cash account and the noncash balance sheet accounts. This exhibit starts with the accounting equation at the top. It is then expanded in line (2) to separate cash from noncash asset accounts. Line (3) moves noncash asset accounts to the right-hand side of the equality where they are subtracted. This shows that cash equals the sum of the liability and equity accounts *minus* the noncash asset accounts. Line (4) points

EXHIBIT 12.8

Relation between Cash and Noncash Accounts

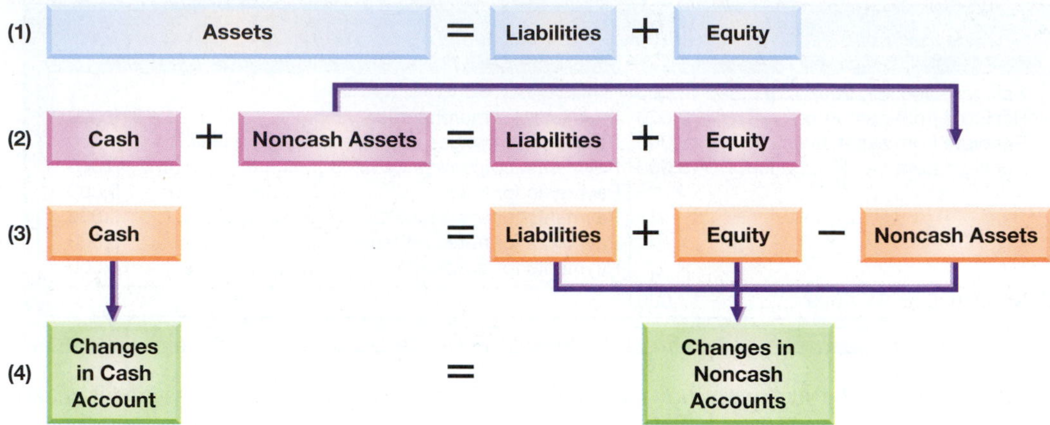

out that *changes* on one side of the accounting equation equal *changes* on the other side. It shows that we can explain changes in cash by analyzing changes in the noncash accounts consisting of liability accounts, equity accounts, and noncash asset accounts. By analyzing noncash balance sheet accounts and any related income statement accounts, we can prepare a statement of cash flows.

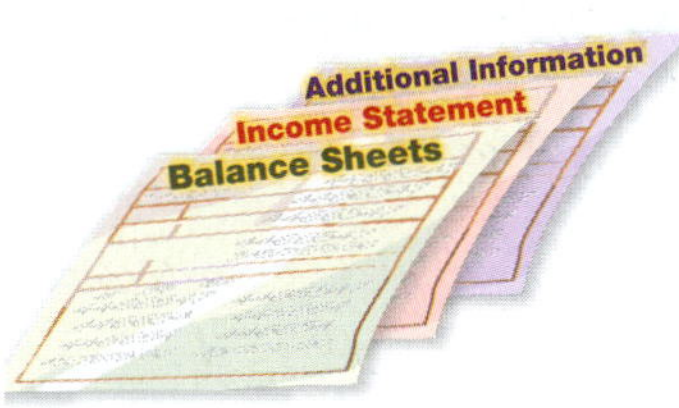

Information to Prepare the Statement Information to prepare the statement of cash flows usually comes from three sources: (1) comparative balance sheets, (2) current income statement, and (3) additional information. Comparative balance sheets are used to compute changes in noncash accounts from the beginning to the end of the period. The current income statement is used to help compute cash flows from operating activities. Additional information often includes details on transactions and events that help explain both the cash flows and noncash investing and financing activities.

Decision Insight

e-Cash Every credit transaction on the Net leaves a trail that a hacker or a marketer can pick up. Enter e-cash—or digital money. The encryption of e-cash protects your money from snoops and thieves and cannot be traced, even by the issuing bank.

Cash Flows from Operating

Indirect and Direct Methods of Reporting

Cash flows provided (used) by operating activities are reported in one of two ways: the *direct method* or the *indirect method.* **These two different methods apply only to the operating activities section.**

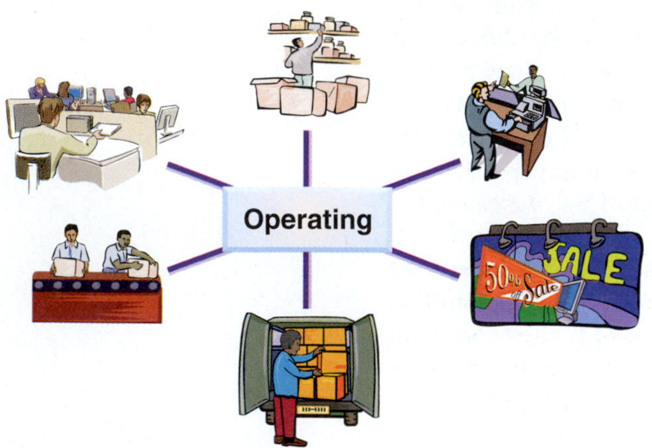

The **direct method** separately lists each major item of operating cash receipts (such as cash received from customers) and each major item of operating cash payments (such as cash paid for merchandise). The cash payments are subtracted from cash receipts to determine the net cash provided (used) by operating activities. The operating activities section of Exhibit 12.7 reflects the direct method of reporting operating cash flows.

The **indirect method** reports net income and then adjusts it for items necessary to obtain net cash provided or used by operating activities. It does *not* report individual items of cash inflows and cash outflows from operating activities. Instead, the indirect method reports the necessary adjustments to reconcile net income to net cash provided or used by operating activities. The operating activities section for Genesis prepared under the indirect method is shown in Exhibit 12.9.

EXHIBIT 12.9

Operating Activities Section—Indirect Method

Cash flows from operating activities		
Net income	$ 38,000	
Adjustments to reconcile net income to net cash provided by operating activities		
Increase in accounts receivable	(20,000)	
Increase in merchandise inventory	(14,000)	
Increase in prepaid expenses	(2,000)	
Decrease in accounts payable	(5,000)	
Decrease in interest payable	(1,000)	
Increase in income taxes payable	10,000	
Depreciation expense	24,000	
Loss on sale of plant assets	6,000	
Gain on retirement of notes	(16,000)	
Net cash provided by operating activities		**$20,000**

The net cash amount provided by operating activities is *identical* under both the direct and indirect methods. This equality always exists. The difference in these methods is with the computation and presentation of this amount. The FASB recommends the direct method, but because it is not required and the indirect method is arguably easier to compute, nearly all companies report operating cash flows using the indirect method.

Point: To better understand the direct and indirect methods of reporting operating cash flows, identify similarities and differences between Exhibits 12.7 and 12.11.

To illustrate, we prepare the operating activities section of the statement of cash flows for Genesis. Exhibit 12.10 shows the December 31, 2008 and 2009, balance sheets of Genesis along with its 2009 income statement. We use this information to prepare a statement of cash flows that explains the $5,000 increase in cash for 2009 as reflected in its balance sheets. This $5,000 is computed as Cash of $17,000 at the end of 2009 minus Cash of $12,000 at the end of 2008. Genesis discloses additional information on its 2009 transactions:

Video12.1

a. The accounts payable balances result from merchandise inventory purchases.

b. Purchased $70,000 in plant assets by paying $10,000 cash and issuing $60,000 of notes payable.

c. Sold plant assets with an original cost of $30,000 and accumulated depreciation of $12,000 for $12,000 cash, yielding a $6,000 loss.

d. Received $15,000 cash from issuing 3,000 shares of common stock.

e. Paid $18,000 cash to retire notes with a $34,000 book value, yielding a $16,000 gain.

f. Declared and paid cash dividends of $14,000.

The next section describes the indirect method. Appendix 12B describes the direct method. An instructor can choose to cover either one or both methods. Neither section depends on the other.

Application of the Indirect Method of Reporting

P2 Compute cash flows from operating activities using the indirect method.

Net income is computed using accrual accounting, which recognizes revenues when earned and expenses when incurred. Revenues and expenses do not necessarily reflect the receipt and payment of cash. The indirect method of computing and reporting net cash flows from operating activities involves adjusting the net income figure to obtain the net cash provided or used by operating activities. This includes subtracting noncash increases (credits) from net income and adding noncash charges (debits) back to net income.

To illustrate, the indirect method begins with Genesis's net income of $38,000 and adjusts it to obtain net cash provided by operating activities of $20,000. Exhibit 12.11 shows the results of the indirect method of reporting operating cash flows, which adjusts net income for three types of adjustments. There are adjustments ① to reflect changes in noncash current assets and current liabilities related to operating activities, ② to income statement items involving operating activities that do not affect cash inflows or outflows, and ③ to eliminate gains and losses resulting from investing and financing activities (not part of operating activities). This section describes each of these adjustments.

Point: *Noncash credits* refer to *revenue* amounts reported on the income statement that are *not collected in cash* this period. *Noncash charges* refer to *expense* amounts reported on the income statement that are *not paid* this period.

EXHIBIT 12.10

Financial Statements

GENESIS
Income Statement
For Year Ended December 31, 2009

Sales		$590,000
Cost of goods sold	$300,000	
Wages and other operating expenses	216,000	
Interest expense	7,000	
Depreciation expense	24,000	(547,000)
		43,000
Other gains (losses)		
Gain on retirement of notes	16,000	
Loss on sale of plant assets	(6,000)	10,000
Income before taxes		53,000
Income taxes expense		(15,000)
Net income		$ 38,000

GENESIS
Balance Sheets
December 31, 2009 and 2008

	2009	2008
Assets		
Current assets		
Cash	$ 17,000	$ 12,000
Accounts receivable	60,000	40,000
Merchandise inventory	84,000	70,000
Prepaid expenses	6,000	4,000
Total current assets	167,000	126,000
Long-term assets		
Plant assets	250,000	210,000
Accumulated depreciation	(60,000)	(48,000)
Total assets	$357,000	$288,000
Liabilities		
Current liabilities		
Accounts payable	$ 35,000	$ 40,000
Interest payable	3,000	4,000
Income taxes payable	22,000	12,000
Total current liabilities	60,000	56,000
Long-term notes payable	90,000	64,000
Total liabilities	150,000	120,000
Equity		
Common stock, $5 par	95,000	80,000
Retained earnings	112,000	88,000
Total equity	207,000	168,000
Total liabilities and equity	$357,000	$288,000

① **Adjustments for Changes in Current Assets and Current Liabilities** This section describes adjustments for changes in noncash current assets and current liabilities.

Point: Operating activities are typically those that determine income, which are often reflected in changes in current assets and current liabilities.

Adjustments for changes in noncash current assets. Changes in noncash current assets normally result from operating activities. Examples are sales affecting accounts receivable and building usage affecting prepaid rent. Decreases in noncash current assets yield the following adjustment:

Decreases in noncash current assets are added to net income.

To see the logic for this adjustment, consider that a decrease in a noncash current asset such as accounts receivable suggests more available cash at the end of the period compared to the beginning. This is so because a decrease in accounts receivable implies higher cash receipts than reflected in sales. We add these higher cash receipts (from decreases in noncash current assets) to net income when computing cash flow from operations.

In contrast, an increase in noncash current assets such as accounts receivable implies less cash receipts than reflected in sales. As another example, an increase in prepaid rent indicates that more cash is paid for rent than is deducted as rent expense. Increases in noncash current assets yield the following adjustment:

Increases in noncash current assets are subtracted from net income.

To illustrate, these adjustments are applied to the noncash current assets in Exhibit 12.10.

Accounts receivable. Accounts Receivable *increase* $20,000, from a beginning balance of $40,000 to an ending balance of $60,000. This increase implies that Genesis collects less cash than is reported in sales. That is, some of these sales were in the form of accounts receivable and that amount increased during the period. To see this it is helpful to use *account analysis.* This usually involves setting up a T-account and reconstructing its major entries to compute cash receipts or payments. The following reconstructed Accounts Receivable T-account reveals that cash receipts are less than sales:

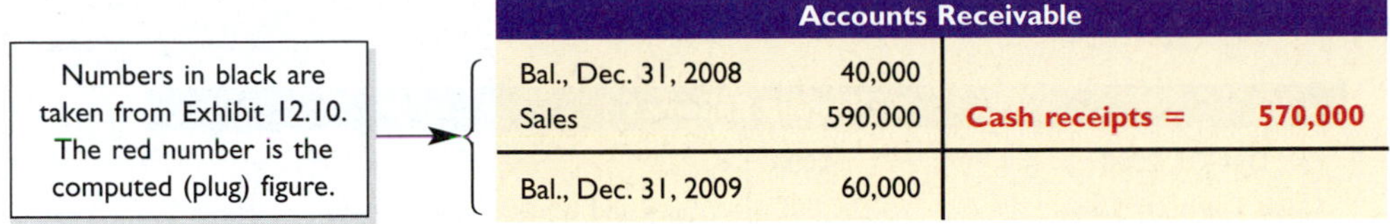

Numbers in black are taken from Exhibit 12.10. The red number is the computed (plug) figure.

Accounts Receivable			
Bal., Dec. 31, 2008	40,000		
Sales	590,000	**Cash receipts =**	**570,000**
Bal., Dec. 31, 2009	60,000		

We see that sales are $20,000 greater than cash receipts. This $20,000—as reflected in the $20,000 increase in Accounts Receivable—is subtracted from net income when computing cash provided by operating activities (see Exhibit 12.11).

Merchandise inventory. Merchandise inventory *increases* by $14,000, from a $70,000 beginning balance to an $84,000 ending balance. This increase implies that Genesis had greater cash purchases than cost of goods sold. This larger amount of cash purchases is in the form of inventory, as reflected in the following account analysis:

Merchandise Inventory			
Bal., Dec. 31, 2008	70,000		
Purchases =	**314,000**	Cost of goods sold	300,000
Bal., Dec. 31, 2009	84,000		

EXHIBIT 12.11

Statement of Cash Flows—Indirect Method

GENESIS Statement of Cash Flows For Year Ended December 31, 2009			
	Cash flows from operating activities		
	Net income	$ 38,000	
	Adjustments to reconcile net income to net cash provided by operating activities		
①	Increase in accounts receivable	(20,000)	
①	Increase in merchandise inventory	(14,000)	
①	Increase in prepaid expenses	(2,000)	
①	Decrease in accounts payable	(5,000)	
①	Decrease in interest payable	(1,000)	
①	Increase in income taxes payable	10,000	
②	Depreciation expense	24,000	
③	Loss on sale of plant assets	6,000	
③	Gain on retirement of notes	(16,000)	
	Net cash provided by operating activities		$20,000
	Cash flows from investing activities		
	Cash received from sale of plant assets	12,000	
	Cash paid for purchase of plant assets	(10,000)	
	Net cash provided by investing activities		2,000
	Cash flows from financing activities		
	Cash received from issuing stock	15,000	
	Cash paid to retire notes	(18,000)	
	Cash paid for dividends	(14,000)	
	Net cash used in financing activities		(17,000)
	Net increase in cash		$ 5,000
	Cash balance at prior year-end		12,000
	Cash balance at current year-end		$17,000

Point: Refer to Exhibit 12.10 and identify the $5,000 change in cash. This change is what the statement of cash flows explains; it serves as a check.

The amount by which purchases exceed cost of goods sold—as reflected in the $14,000 increase in inventory—is subtracted from net income when computing cash provided by operating activities (see Exhibit 12.11).

Prepaid expenses. Prepaid expenses *increase* $2,000, from a $4,000 beginning balance to a $6,000 ending balance, implying that Genesis's cash payments exceed its recorded prepaid expenses. These higher cash payments increase the amount of Prepaid Expenses, as reflected in its reconstructed T-account:

Prepaid Expenses			
Bal., Dec. 31, 2008	4,000		
Cash payments =	**218,000**	Wages and other operating exp.	216,000
Bal., Dec. 31, 2009	6,000		

The amount by which cash payments exceed the recorded operating expenses—as reflected in the $2,000 increase in Prepaid Expenses—is subtracted from net income when computing cash provided by operating activities (see Exhibit 12.11).

Adjustments for changes in current liabilities. Changes in current liabilities normally result from operating activities. An example is a purchase that affects accounts payable. Increases in current liabilities yield the following adjustment to net income when computing operating cash flows:

Increases in current liabilities are added to net income.

To see the logic for this adjustment, consider that an increase in the Accounts Payable account suggests that cash payments are less than the related (cost of goods sold) expense. As another example, an increase in wages payable implies that cash paid for wages is less than the recorded wages expense. Since the recorded expense is greater than the cash paid, we add the increase in wages payable to net income to compute net cash flow from operations.

Conversely, when current liabilities decrease, the following adjustment is required:

Decreases in current liabilities are subtracted from net income.

To illustrate, these adjustments are applied to the current liabilities in Exhibit 12.10.

Accounts payable. Accounts Payable *decrease* $5,000, from a beginning balance of $40,000 to an ending balance of $35,000. This decrease implies that cash payments to suppliers exceed purchases by $5,000 for the period, which is reflected in the reconstructed Accounts Payable T-account:

Accounts Payable			
		Bal., Dec. 31, 2008	40,000
Cash payments =	**319,000**	Purchases	314,000
		Bal., Dec. 31, 2009	35,000

The amount by which cash payments exceed purchases—as reflected in the $5,000 decrease in Accounts Payable—is subtracted from net income when computing cash provided by operating activities (see Exhibit 12.11).

Interest payable. Interest Payable *decreases* $1,000, from a $4,000 beginning balance to a $3,000 ending balance. This decrease indicates that cash paid for interest exceeds interest expense by $1,000, which is reflected in the Interest Payable T-account:

Interest Payable			
		Bal., Dec. 31, 2008	4,000
Cash paid for interest =	**8,000**	Interest expense	7,000
		Bal., Dec. 31, 2009	3,000

The amount by which cash paid exceeds recorded expense—as reflected in the $1,000 decrease in Interest Payable—is subtracted from net income (see Exhibit 12.11).

Income taxes payable. Income Taxes Payable *increase* $10,000, from a $12,000 beginning balance to a $22,000 ending balance. This increase implies that reported income taxes exceed the cash paid for taxes, which is reflected in the Income Taxes Payable T-account:

Income Taxes Payable			
		Bal., Dec. 31, 2008	12,000
Cash paid for taxes =	5,000	Income taxes expense	15,000
		Bal., Dec. 31, 2009	22,000

Summary Adjustments for Changes in Current Assets and Current Liabilities		
Account	Increases	Decreases
Noncash current assets	Deduct from NI	Add to NI
Current liabilities	Add to NI	Deduct from NI

The amount by which cash paid falls short of the reported taxes expense—as reflected in the $10,000 increase in Income Taxes Payable—is added to net income when computing cash provided by operating activities (see Exhibit 12.11).

② Adjustments for Operating Items Not Providing or Using Cash The income statement usually includes some expenses that do not reflect cash outflows in the period. Examples are depreciation, amortization, depletion, and bad debts expense. The indirect method for reporting operating cash flows requires that

Expenses with no cash outflows are added back to net income.

To see the logic of this adjustment, recall that items such as depreciation, amortization, depletion, and bad debts originate from debits to expense accounts and credits to noncash accounts. These entries have *no* cash effect, and we add them back to net income when computing net cash flows from operations. Adding them back cancels their deductions.

Similarly, when net income includes revenues that do not reflect cash inflows in the period, the indirect method for reporting operating cash flows requires that

Revenues with no cash inflows are subtracted from net income.

We apply these adjustments to the Genesis operating items that do not provide or use cash.

Depreciation. Depreciation expense is the only Genesis operating item that has no effect on cash flows in the period. We must add back the $24,000 depreciation expense to net income when computing cash provided by operating activities. (We later explain that any cash outflow to acquire a plant asset is reported as an investing activity.)

③ Adjustments for Nonoperating Items Net income often includes losses that are not part of operating activities but are part of either investing or financing activities. Examples are a loss from the sale of a plant asset and a loss from retirement of notes payable. The indirect method for reporting operating cash flows requires that

Nonoperating losses are added back to net income.

To see the logic, consider that items such as a plant asset sale and a notes retirement are normally recorded by recognizing the cash, removing all plant asset or notes accounts, and recognizing any loss or gain. The cash received or paid is not part of operating activities but is part of either investing or financing activities. *No* operating cash flow effect occurs. However, because the nonoperating loss is a deduction in computing net income, we need to add it back to net income when computing cash flow from operations. Adding it back cancels the deduction.

Point: An income statement reports revenues, gains, expenses, and losses on an accrual basis. The statement of cash flows reports cash received and cash paid for operating, financing, and investing activities.

Similarly, when net income includes gains not part of operating activities, the indirect method for reporting operating cash flows requires that

Nonoperating gains are subtracted from net income.

To illustrate these adjustments, we consider the nonoperating items of Genesis.

Loss on sale of plant assets. Genesis reports a $6,000 loss on sale of plant assets as part of net income. This loss is a proper deduction in computing income, but it is *not part of operating activities*. Instead, a sale of plant assets is part of investing activities. Thus, the $6,000 nonoperating loss is added back to net income (see Exhibit 12.11). Adding it back cancels the loss. We later explain how to report the cash inflow from the asset sale in investing activities.

Gain on retirement of debt. A $16,000 gain on retirement of debt is properly included in net income, but it is *not part of operating activities*. This means the $16,000 nonoperating gain must be subtracted from net income to obtain net cash provided by operating activities (see Exhibit 12.11). Subtracting it cancels the recorded gain. We later describe how to report the cash outflow to retire debt.

Summary of Adjustments for Indirect Method

Exhibit 12.12 summarizes the most common adjustments to net income when computing net cash provided or used by operating activities under the indirect method.

EXHIBIT 12.12

Summary of Selected Adjustments for Indirect Method

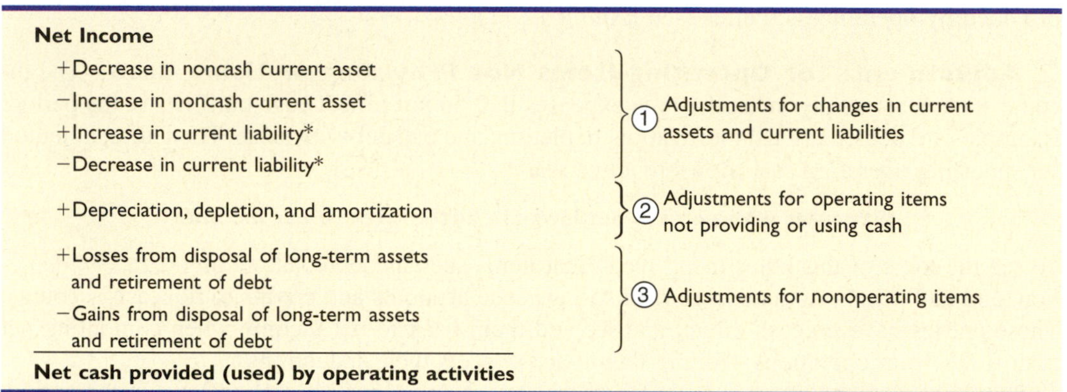

Net Income

+Decrease in noncash current asset
−Increase in noncash current asset
+Increase in current liability*
−Decrease in current liability*
} ① Adjustments for changes in current assets and current liabilities

+Depreciation, depletion, and amortization
} ② Adjustments for operating items not providing or using cash

+Losses from disposal of long-term assets and retirement of debt
−Gains from disposal of long-term assets and retirement of debt
} ③ Adjustments for nonoperating items

Net cash provided (used) by operating activities

* Excludes current portion of long-term debt and any (nonsales-related) short-term notes payable—both are financing activities.

The computations in determining cash provided or used by operating activities are different for the indirect and direct methods, but the result is identical. Both methods yield the same $20,000 figure for cash from operating activities for Genesis; see Exhibits 12.7 and 12.11.

Decision Insight

Cash or Income The difference between net income and operating cash flows can be large and sometimes reflects on the quality of earnings. This bar chart shows net income and operating cash flows of three companies. Operating cash flows can be either higher or lower than net income.

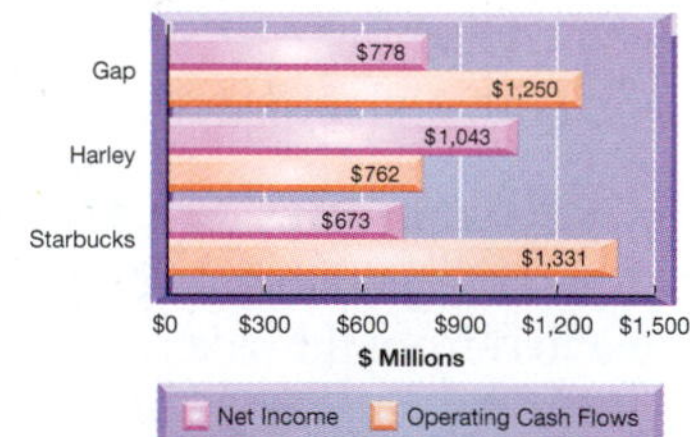

Quick Check

Answers—p. 454

4. Determine net cash provided or used by operating activities using the following data: net income, $74,900; decrease in accounts receivable, $4,600; increase in inventory, $11,700; decrease in accounts payable, $1,000; loss on sale of equipment, $3,400; payment of cash dividends, $21,500.
5. Why are expenses such as depreciation and amortization added to net income when cash flow from operating activities is computed by the indirect method?
6. A company reports net income of $15,000 that includes a $3,000 gain on the sale of plant assets. Why is this gain subtracted from net income in computing cash flow from operating activities using the indirect method?

Cash Flows from Investing

The third major step in preparing the statement of cash flows is to compute and report cash flows from investing activities. We normally do this by identifying changes in (1) all noncurrent asset accounts and (2) the current accounts for both notes receivable and investments in securities (excluding trading securities). We then analyze changes in these accounts to determine their effect, if any, on cash and report the cash flow effects in the investing activities section of the statement of cash flows. **Reporting of investing activities is identical under the direct method and indirect method.**

Three-Stage Process of Analysis

Video12.1

Information to compute cash flows from investing activities is usually taken from beginning and ending balance sheets and the income statement. We use a three-stage process to determine cash provided or used by investing activities: (1) identify changes in investing-related accounts, (2) explain these changes using reconstruction analysis, and (3) report their cash flow effects.

Analysis of Noncurrent Assets

P3 Determine cash flows from both investing and financing activities.

Information about the Genesis transactions provided earlier reveals that the company both purchased and sold plant assets during the period. Both transactions are investing activities and are analyzed for their cash flow effects in this section.

Point: Investing activities include (1) purchasing and selling long-term assets, (2) lending and collecting on notes receivable, and (3) purchasing and selling short-term investments other than cash equivalents and trading securities.

Plant Asset Transactions The first stage in analyzing the Plant Assets account and its related Accumulated Depreciation is to identify any changes in these accounts from comparative balance sheets in Exhibit 12.10. This analysis reveals a $40,000 increase in plant assets from $210,000 to $250,000 and a $12,000 increase in accumulated depreciation from $48,000 to $60,000.

The second stage is to explain these changes. Items *b* and *c* of the additional information for Genesis (page 431) are relevant in this case. Recall that the Plant Assets account is affected by both asset purchases and sales, while its Accumulated Depreciation account is normally increased from depreciation and decreased from the removal of accumulated depreciation in asset sales. To explain changes in these accounts and to identify their cash flow effects, we prepare *reconstructed entries* from prior transactions; *they are not the actual entries by the preparer*.

Point: Financing and investing info is available in ledger accounts to help explain changes in comparative balance sheets. Post references lead to relevant entries and explanations.

To illustrate, item *b* reports that Genesis purchased plant assets of $70,000 by issuing $60,000 in notes payable to the seller and paying $10,000 in cash. The reconstructed entry for analysis of item *b* follows:

Reconstruction	Plant Assets	70,000	
	Notes Payable		60,000
	Cash		**10,000**

This entry reveals a $10,000 cash outflow for plant assets and a $60,000 noncash investing and financing transaction involving notes exchanged for plant assets.

Next, item *c* reports that Genesis sold plant assets costing $30,000 (with $12,000 of accumulated depreciation) for $12,000 cash, resulting in a $6,000 loss. The reconstructed entry for analysis of item *c* follows:

Reconstruction	**Cash**	**12,000**	
	Accumulated Depreciation	12,000	
	Loss on Sale of Plant Assets	6,000	
	Plant Assets		30,000

This entry reveals a $12,000 cash inflow from assets sold. The $6,000 loss is computed by comparing the asset book value to the cash received and does not reflect any cash inflow or outflow. We also reconstruct the entry for Depreciation Expense using information from the income statement.

Reconstruction	Depreciation Expense	24,000	
	Accumulated Depreciation		24,000

This entry shows that Depreciation Expense results in no cash flow effect. These three reconstructed entries are reflected in the following plant asset and related T-accounts.

Plant Assets			
Bal., Dec. 31, 2008	210,000		
Purchase	**70,000**	**Sale**	**30,000**
Bal., Dec. 31, 2009	250,000		

Accumulated Depreciation—Plant Assets			
		Bal., Dec. 31, 2008	48,000
Sale	**12,000**	**Depr. expense**	**24,000**
		Bal., Dec. 31, 2009	60,000

Example: If a plant asset costing $40,000 with $37,000 of accumulated depreciation is sold at a $1,000 loss, what is the cash flow? What is the cash flow if this asset is sold at a gain of $3,000? *Answers:* +$2,000; +$6,000.

This reconstruction analysis is complete in that the change in plant assets from $210,000 to $250,000 is fully explained by the $70,000 purchase and the $30,000 sale. Also, the change in accumulated depreciation from $48,000 to $60,000 is fully explained by depreciation expense of $24,000 and the removal of $12,000 in accumulated depreciation from an asset sale. (Preparers of the statement of cash flows have the entire ledger and additional information at their disposal, but for brevity reasons only the information needed for reconstructing accounts is given.)

The third stage looks at the reconstructed entries for identification of cash flows. The two identified cash flow effects are reported in the investing section of the statement as follows (also see Exhibit 12.7 or 12.11):

Cash flows from investing activities	
Cash received from sale of plant assets	$12,000
Cash paid for purchase of plant assets	(10,000)

The $60,000 portion of the purchase described in item *b* and financed by issuing notes is a noncash investing and financing activity. It is reported in a note or in a separate schedule to the statement as follows:

Noncash investing and financing activity	
Purchased plant assets with issuance of notes	$60,000

Analysis of Other Assets

Many other asset transactions (including those involving current notes receivable and investments in certain securities) are considered investing activities and can affect a company's cash flows. Since Genesis did not enter into other investing activities impacting assets, we do not need to extend our analysis to these other assets. If such transactions did exist, we would analyze them using the same three-stage process illustrated for plant assets.

Quick Check

Answer—p. 454

7. Equipment costing $80,000 with accumulated depreciation of $30,000 is sold at a loss of $10,000. What is the cash receipt from this sale? In what section of the statement of cash flows is this transaction reported?

Cash Flows from Financing

The fourth major step in preparing the statement of cash flows is to compute and report cash flows from financing activities. We normally do this by identifying changes in all noncurrent liability accounts (including the current portion of any notes and bonds) and the equity accounts. These accounts include long-term debt, notes payable, bonds payable, common stock, and retained earnings. Changes in these accounts are then analyzed using available information to determine their effect, if any, on cash. Results are reported in the financing activities section of the statement. **Reporting of financing activities is identical under the direct method and indirect method.**

Three-Stage Process of Analysis

Video12.1

We again use a three-stage process to determine cash provided or used by financing activities: (1) identify changes in financing-related accounts, (2) explain these changes using reconstruction analysis, and (3) report their cash flow effects.

Analysis of Noncurrent Liabilities

Information about Genesis provided earlier reveals two transactions involving noncurrent liabilities. We analyzed one of those, the $60,000 issuance of notes payable to purchase plant assets. This transaction is reported as a significant noncash investing and financing activity in a footnote or a separate schedule to the statement of cash flows. The other remaining transaction involving noncurrent liabilities is the cash retirement of notes payable.

Point: Financing activities generally refer to changes in the noncurrent liability and the equity accounts. Examples are (1) receiving cash from issuing debt or repaying amounts borrowed and (2) receiving cash from or distributing cash to owners.

Notes Payable Transactions The first stage in analysis of notes is to review the comparative balance sheets from Exhibit 12.10. This analysis reveals an increase in notes payable from $64,000 to $90,000.

The second stage explains this change. Item *e* of the additional information for Genesis (page 431) reports that notes with a carrying value of $34,000 are retired for $18,000 cash, resulting in a $16,000 gain. The reconstructed entry for analysis of item *e* follows:

Reconstruction	Notes Payable	34,000	
	Gain on retirement of debt		16,000
	Cash		**18,000**

This entry reveals an $18,000 cash outflow for retirement of notes and a $16,000 gain from comparing the notes payable carrying value to the cash received. This gain does not reflect any cash inflow or outflow. Also, item *b* of the additional information reports that Genesis purchased plant assets costing $70,000 by issuing $60,000 in notes payable to the seller and paying $10,000 in cash. We reconstructed this entry when analyzing investing activities: It showed a $60,000 increase to notes payable that is reported as a noncash investing and financing transaction. The Notes Payable account reflects (and is fully explained by) these reconstructed entries as follows:

Notes Payable			
		Bal., Dec. 31, 2008	64,000
Retired notes	**34,000**	**Issued notes**	**60,000**
		Bal., Dec. 31, 2009	90,000

The third stage is to report the cash flow effect of the notes retirement in the financing section of the statement as follows (also see Exhibit 12.7 or 12.11):

Cash flows from financing activities	
Cash paid to retire notes	$(18,000)

Analysis of Equity

The Genesis information reveals two transactions involving equity accounts. The first is the issuance of common stock for cash. The second is the declaration and payment of cash dividends. We analyze both.

Common Stock Transactions The first stage in analyzing common stock is to review the comparative balance sheets from Exhibit 12.10, which reveals an increase in common stock from $80,000 to $95,000.

The second stage explains this change. Item *d* of the additional information (page 431) reports that 3,000 shares of common stock are issued at par for $5 per share. The reconstructed entry for analysis of item *d* follows:

Reconstruction	**Cash**	**15,000**	
	Common Stock		15,000

This entry reveals a $15,000 cash inflow from stock issuance and is reflected in (and explains) the Common Stock account as follows:

Common Stock			
		Bal., Dec. 31, 2008	80,000
		Issued stock	**15,000**
		Bal., Dec. 31, 2009	95,000

The third stage discloses the cash flow effect from stock issuance in the financing section of the statement as follows (also see Exhibit 12.7 or 12.11):

Cash flows from financing activities	
Cash received from issuing stock	$15,000

Retained Earnings Transactions The first stage in analyzing the Retained Earnings account is to review the comparative balance sheets from Exhibit 12.10. This reveals an increase in retained earnings from $88,000 to $112,000.

The second stage explains this change. Item *f* of the additional information (page 431) reports that cash dividends of $14,000 are paid. The reconstructed entry follows:

Reconstruction	Retained Earnings..........................	14,000	
	Cash.................................		**14,000**

This entry reveals a $14,000 cash outflow for cash dividends. Also see that the Retained Earnings account is impacted by net income of $38,000. (Net income was analyzed under the operating section of the statement of cash flows.) The reconstructed Retained Earnings account follows:

Retained Earnings			
		Bal., Dec. 31, 2008	88,000
Cash dividend	**14,000**	**Net income**	**38,000**
		Bal., Dec. 31, 2009	112,000

Point: Financing activities not affecting cash flow include *declaration* of a cash dividend, *declaration* of a stock dividend, payment of a stock dividend, and a stock split.

The third stage reports the cash flow effect from the cash dividend in the financing section of the statement as follows (also see Exhibit 12.7 or 12.11):

Cash flows from financing activities	
Cash paid for dividends	$(14,000)

Global: There are no requirements to separate domestic and international cash flows, leading some users to ask "Where in the world is cash flow?"

We now have identified and explained all of the Genesis cash inflows and cash outflows and one noncash investing and financing transaction. Specifically, our analysis has reconciled changes in all noncash balance sheet accounts.

Proving Cash Balances

The fifth and final step in preparing the statement is to report the beginning and ending cash balances and prove that the *net change in cash* is explained by operating, investing, and financing cash flows. This step is shown here for Genesis.

Net cash provided by operating activities	$20,000
Net cash provided by investing activities	2,000
Net cash used in financing activities	(17,000)
Net increase in cash	**$ 5,000**
Cash balance at 2008 year-end	12,000
Cash balance at 2009 year-end	$ 17,000

The preceding table shows that the $5,000 net increase in cash, from $12,000 at the beginning of the period to $17,000 at the end, is reconciled by net cash flows from operating ($20,000 inflow), investing ($2,000 inflow), and financing ($17,000 outflow) activities. This is formally reported at the bottom of the statement of cash flows as shown in both Exhibits 12.7 and 12.11.

Decision Maker

Reporter Management is in labor contract negotiations and grants you an interview. It highlights a recent $600,000 net loss that involves a $930,000 extraordinary loss and a total net cash outflow of $550,000 (which includes net cash outflows of $850,000 for investing activities and $350,000 for financing activities). What is your assessment of this company? [Answer—p. 454]

Cash Flow Analysis

Decision Analysis

Analyzing Cash Sources and Uses

A1 Analyze the statement of cash flows.

Most managers stress the importance of understanding and predicting cash flows for business decisions. Creditors evaluate a company's ability to generate cash before deciding whether to lend money. Investors also assess cash inflows and outflows before buying and selling stock. Information in the statement of cash flows helps address these and other questions such as (1) How much cash is generated from or used in operations? (2) What expenditures are made with cash from operations? (3) What is the source of cash for debt payments? (4) What is the source of cash for distributions to owners? (5) How is the increase in investing activities financed? (6) What is the source of cash for new plant assets? (7) Why is cash flow from operations different from income? (8) How is cash from financing used?

To effectively answer these questions, it is important to separately analyze investing, financing, and operating activities. To illustrate, consider data from three different companies in Exhibit 12.13. These companies operate in the same industry and have been in business for several years.

EXHIBIT 12.13

Cash Flows of Competing Companies

($ thousands)	BMX	ATV	Trex
Cash provided (used) by operating activities	$90,000	$40,000	$(24,000)
Cash provided (used) by investing activities			
Proceeds from sale of plant assets			26,000
Purchase of plant assets	(48,000)	(25,000)	
Cash provided (used) by financing activities			
Proceeds from issuance of debt			13,000
Repayment of debt	(27,000)		
Net increase (decrease) in cash	$15,000	$15,000	$ 15,000

Each company generates an identical $15,000 net increase in cash, but its sources and uses of cash flows are very different. BMX's operating activities provide net cash flows of $90,000, allowing it to purchase plant assets of $48,000 and repay $27,000 of its debt. ATV's operating activities provide $40,000 of cash flows, limiting its purchase of plant assets to $25,000. Trex's $15,000 net cash increase is due to selling plant assets and incurring additional debt. Its operating activities yield a net cash outflow of $24,000.

Overall, analysis of these cash flows reveals that BMX is more capable of generating future cash flows than is ATV or Trex.

Decision Insight

Free Cash Flows Many investors use cash flows to value company stock. However, cash-based valuation models often yield different stock values due to differences in measurement of cash flows. Most models require cash flows that are "free" for distribution to shareholders. These *free cash flows* are defined as cash flows available to shareholders after operating asset reinvestments and debt payments. Knowledge of the statement of cash flows is key to proper computation of free cash flows. A company's growth and financial flexibility depend on adequate free cash flows.

Cash Flow on Total Assets

A2 Compute and apply the cash flow on total assets ratio.

Cash flow information has limitations, but it can help measure a company's ability to meet its obligations, pay dividends, expand operations, and obtain financing. Users often compute and analyze a cash-based ratio similar to return on total assets except that its numerator is net cash flows from operating activities. The **cash flow on total assets** ratio is in Exhibit 12.14.

EXHIBIT 12.14

Cash Flow on Total Assets

$$\text{Cash flow on total assets} = \frac{\text{Cash flow from operations}}{\text{Average total assets}}$$

This ratio reflects actual cash flows and is not affected by accounting income recognition and measurement. It can help business decision makers estimate the amount and timing of cash flows when planning and analyzing operating activities.

To illustrate, the 2007 cash flow on total assets ratio for Nike is 18.3%—see Exhibit 12.15. Is an 18.3% ratio good or bad? To answer this question, we compare this ratio with the ratios of prior years (we could also compare its ratio with those of its competitors and the market). Nike's cash flow on total assets ratio for several prior years is in the second column of Exhibit 12.15. Results show that its 18.3% return is the median of the prior years' returns.

EXHIBIT 12.15

Nike's Cash Flow on Total Assets

Year	Cash Flow on Total Assets	Return on Total Assets
2007	18.3%	14.5%
2006	17.9	14.9
2005	18.8	14.5
2004	20.6	12.8
2003	13.9	7.1

As an indicator of *earnings quality,* some analysts compare the cash flow on total assets ratio to the return on total assets ratio. Nike's return on total assets is provided in the third column of Exhibit 12.15. Nike's cash flow on total assets ratio exceeds its return on total assets in each of the five years, leading some analysts to infer that Nike's earnings quality is high for that period because more earnings are realized in the form of cash.

Decision Insight

Cash Flow Ratios Analysts use various other cash-based ratios, including the following two:

(1) $$\text{Cash coverage of growth} = \frac{\text{Operating cash flow}}{\text{Cash outflow for plant assets}}$$

where a low ratio (less than 1) implies cash inadequacy to meet asset growth, whereas a high ratio implies cash adequacy for asset growth.

(2) $$\text{Operating cash flow to sales} = \frac{\text{Operating cash flow}}{\text{Net sales}}$$

when this ratio substantially and consistently differs from the operating income to net sales ratio, the risk of accounting improprieties increases.

Point: The following ratio helps assess whether operating cash flow is adequate to meet long-term obligations: **Cash coverage of debt** = Cash flow from operations ÷ Noncurrent liabilities. A low ratio suggests a higher risk of insolvency; a high ratio suggests a greater ability to meet long-term obligations.

Demonstration Problem

Umlauf's comparative balance sheets, income statement, and additional information follow.

UMLAUF COMPANY
Balance Sheets
December 31, 2009 and 2008

	2009	2008
Assets		
Cash	$ 43,050	$ 23,925
Accounts receivable	34,125	39,825
Merchandise inventory	156,000	146,475
Prepaid expenses	3,600	1,650
Equipment	135,825	146,700
Accum. depreciation—Equipment	(61,950)	(47,550)
Total assets	$310,650	$311,025
Liabilities and Equity		
Accounts payable	$ 28,800	$ 33,750
Income taxes payable	5,100	4,425
Dividends payable	0	4,500
Bonds payable	0	37,500
Common stock, $10 par	168,750	168,750
Retained earnings	108,000	62,100
Total liabilities and equity	$310,650	$311,025

UMLAUF COMPANY
Income Statement
For Year Ended December 31, 2009

Sales		$446,100
Cost of goods sold	$222,300	
Other operating expenses	120,300	
Depreciation expense	25,500	(368,100)
		78,000
Other gains (losses)		
Loss on sale of equipment	3,300	
Loss on retirement of bonds	825	(4,125)
Income before taxes		73,875
Income taxes expense		(13,725)
Net income		$ 60,150

Additional Information

a. Equipment costing $21,375 with accumulated depreciation of $11,100 is sold for cash.

b. Equipment purchases are for cash.

c. Accumulated Depreciation is affected by depreciation expense and the sale of equipment.

d. The balance of Retained Earnings is affected by dividend declarations and net income.

e. All sales are made on credit.

f. All merchandise inventory purchases are on credit.

g. Accounts Payable balances result from merchandise inventory purchases.

h. Prepaid expenses relate to "other operating expenses."

Required

1. Prepare a statement of cash flows using the indirect method for year 2009.

2.[B] Prepare a statement of cash flows using the direct method for year 2009.

Planning the Solution

- Prepare two blank statements of cash flows with sections for operating, investing, and financing activities using the (1) indirect method format and (2) direct method format.
- Compute the cash paid for equipment and the cash received from the sale of equipment using the additional information provided along with the amount for depreciation expense and the change in the balances of equipment and accumulated depreciation. Use T-accounts to help chart the effects of the sale and purchase of equipment on the balances of the Equipment account and the Accumulated Depreciation account.
- Compute the effect of net income on the change in the Retained Earnings account balance. Assign the difference between the change in retained earnings and the amount of net income to dividends declared. Adjust the dividends declared amount for the change in the Dividends Payable balance.
- Compute cash received from customers, cash paid for merchandise, cash paid for other operating expenses, and cash paid for taxes as illustrated in the chapter.
- Enter the cash effects of reconstruction entries to the appropriate section(s) of the statement.
- Total each section of the statement, determine the total net change in cash, and add it to the beginning balance to get the ending balance of cash.

Solution to Demonstration Problem

Supporting computations for cash receipts and cash payments.

(1)	*Cost of equipment sold	$ 21,375
	Accumulated depreciation of equipment sold	(11,100)
	Book value of equipment sold	10,275
	Loss on sale of equipment	(3,300)
	Cash received from sale of equipment	**$ 6,975**
	Cost of equipment sold	$ 21,375
	Less decrease in the equipment account balance	(10,875)
	Cash paid for new equipment	**$ 10,500**
(2)	Loss on retirement of bonds	$ 825
	Carrying value of bonds retired	37,500
	Cash paid to retire bonds	**$ 38,325**
(3)	Net income	$ 60,150
	Less increase in retained earnings	45,900
	Dividends declared	14,250
	Plus decrease in dividends payable	4,500
	Cash paid for dividends	**$ 18,750**
(4)[B]	Sales	$ 446,100
	Add decrease in accounts receivable	5,700
	Cash received from customers	**$451,800**
(5)[B]	Cost of goods sold	$ 222,300
	Plus increase in merchandise inventory	9,525
	Purchases	231,825
	Plus decrease in accounts payable	4,950
	Cash paid for merchandise	**$236,775**
(6)[B]	Other operating expenses	$ 120,300
	Plus increase in prepaid expenses	1,950
	Cash paid for other operating expenses	**$122,250**
(7)[B]	Income taxes expense	$ 13,725
	Less increase in income taxes payable	(675)
	Cash paid for income taxes	**$ 13,050**

* Supporting T-account analysis for part 1 follows:

Equipment			
Bal., Dec. 31, 2008	146,700		
Cash purchase	10,500	Sale	21,375
Bal., Dec. 31, 2009	135,825		

Accumulated Depreciation—Equipment			
		Bal., Dec. 31, 2008	47,550
Sale	11,100	Depr. expense	25,500
		Bal., Dec. 31, 2009	61,950

UMLAUF COMPANY
Statement of Cash Flows (Indirect Method)
For Year Ended December 31, 2009

Cash flows from operating activities		
Net income	$60,150	
Adjustments to reconcile net income to net cash provided by operating activities		
Decrease in accounts receivable	5,700	
Increase in merchandise inventory	(9,525)	
Increase in prepaid expenses	(1,950)	
Decrease in accounts payable	(4,950)	
Increase in income taxes payable	675	
Depreciation expense	25,500	
Loss on sale of plant assets	3,300	
Loss on retirement of bonds	825	
Net cash provided by operating activities		$79,725

[continued on next page]

[continued from previous page]

Cash flows from investing activities		
Cash received from sale of equipment	6,975	
Cash paid for equipment	(10,500)	
Net cash used in investing activities		(3,525)
Cash flows from financing activities		
Cash paid to retire bonds payable	(38,325)	
Cash paid for dividends	(18,750)	
Net cash used in financing activities		(57,075)
Net increase in cash		$19,125
Cash balance at prior year-end		23,925
Cash balance at current year-end		$43,050

UMLAUF COMPANY
Statement of Cash Flows (Direct Method)
For Year Ended December 31, 2009

Cash flows from operating activities		
Cash received from customers	$451,800	
Cash paid for merchandise	(236,775)	
Cash paid for other operating expenses	(122,250)	
Cash paid for income taxes	(13,050)	
Net cash provided by operating activities		$79,725
Cash flows from investing activities		
Cash received from sale of equipment	6,975	
Cash paid for equipment	(10,500)	
Net cash used in investing activities		(3,525)
Cash flows from financing activities		
Cash paid to retire bonds payable	(38,325)	
Cash paid for dividends	(18,750)	
Net cash used in financing activities		(57,075)
Net increase in cash		$19,125
Cash balance at prior year-end		23,925
Cash balance at current year-end		$43,050

APPENDIX

Spreadsheet Preparation of the Statement of Cash Flows 12A

This appendix explains how to use a spreadsheet to prepare the statement of cash flows under the indirect method.

Preparing the Indirect Method Spreadsheet

P4 Illustrate use of a spreadsheet to prepare a statement of cash flows.

Analyzing noncash accounts can be challenging when a company has a large number of accounts and many operating, investing, and financing transactions. A *spreadsheet,* also called *work sheet* or *working paper,* can help us organize the information needed to prepare a statement of cash flows. A spreadsheet also makes it easier to check the accuracy of our work. To illustrate, we return to the comparative balance sheets and income statement shown in Exhibit 12.10. We use the following identifying letters *a* through *g* to code changes in accounts, and letters *h* through *m* for additional information, to prepare the statement of cash flows:

a. Net income is $38,000.
b. Accounts receivable increase by $20,000.
c. Merchandise inventory increases by $14,000.
d. Prepaid expenses increase by $2,000.
e. Accounts payable decrease by $5,000.
f. Interest payable decreases by $1,000.
g. Income taxes payable increase by $10,000.
h. Depreciation expense is $24,000.
i. Plant assets costing $30,000 with accumulated depreciation of $12,000 are sold for $12,000 cash. This yields a loss on sale of assets of $6,000.
j. Notes with a book value of $34,000 are retired with a cash payment of $18,000, yielding a $16,000 gain on retirement.
k. Plant assets costing $70,000 are purchased with a cash payment of $10,000 and an issuance of notes payable for $60,000.
l. Issued 3,000 shares of common stock for $15,000 cash.
m. Paid cash dividends of $14,000.

Exhibit 12A.1 shows the indirect method spreadsheet for Genesis. We enter both beginning and ending balance sheet amounts on the spreadsheet. We also enter information in the Analysis of Changes columns (keyed to the additional information items *a* through *m*) to explain changes in the accounts and determine the cash flows for operating, investing, and financing activities. Information about noncash investing and financing activities is reported near the bottom.

Entering the Analysis of Changes on the Spreadsheet

The following sequence of procedures is used to complete the spreadsheet after the beginning and ending balances of the balance sheet accounts are entered:

① Enter net income as the first item in the Statement of Cash Flows section for computing operating cash inflow (debit) and as a credit to Retained Earnings.

② In the Statement of Cash Flows section, adjustments to net income are entered as debits if they increase cash flows and as credits if they decrease cash flows. Applying this same rule, adjust net income for the change in each noncash current asset and current liability account related to operating activities. For each adjustment to net income, the offsetting debit or credit must help reconcile the beginning and ending balances of a current asset or current liability account.

③ Enter adjustments to net income for income statement items not providing or using cash in the period. For each adjustment, the offsetting debit or credit must help reconcile a noncash balance sheet account.

④ Adjust net income to eliminate any gains or losses from investing and financing activities. Because the cash from a gain must be excluded from operating activities, the gain is entered as a credit in the operating activities section. Losses are entered as debits. For each adjustment, the related debit and/or credit must help reconcile balance sheet accounts and involve reconstructed entries to show the cash flow from investing or financing activities.

⑤ After reviewing any unreconciled balance sheet accounts and related information, enter the remaining reconciling entries for investing and financing activities. Examples are purchases of plant assets, issuances of long-term debt, stock issuances, and dividend payments. Some of these may require entries in the noncash investing and financing section of the spreadsheet (reconciled).

⑥ Check accuracy by totaling the Analysis of Changes columns and by determining that the change in each balance sheet account has been explained (reconciled).

Point: Analysis of the changes on the spreadsheet are summarized as:
1. Cash flows from operating activities generally affect net income, current assets, and current liabilities.
2. Cash flows from investing activities generally affect noncurrent asset accounts.
3. Cash flows from financing activities generally affect noncurrent liability and equity accounts.

We illustrate these steps in Exhibit 12A.1 for Genesis:

Step	Entries
①	(*a*)
②	(*b*) through (*g*)
③	(*h*)
④	(*i*) through (*j*)
⑤	(*k*) through (*m*)

EXHIBIT 12A.1

Spreadsheet for Preparing Statement of Cash Flows—Indirect Method

GENESIS Spreadsheet for Statement of Cash Flows—Indirect Method For Year Ended December 31, 2009						
	Dec. 31, 2008	Analysis of Changes				Dec. 31, 2009
			Debit		Credit	
Balance Sheet—Debits						
Cash	$ 12,000					$ 17,000
Accounts receivable	40,000	*(b)*	$ 20,000			60,000
Merchandise inventory	70,000	*(c)*	14,000			84,000
Prepaid expenses	4,000	*(d)*	2,000			6,000
Plant assets	210,000	*(k1)*	70,000	*(i)*	$ 30,000	250,000
	$336,000					$417,000
Balance Sheet—Credits						
Accumulated depreciation	$ 48,000	*(i)*	12,000	*(h)*	24,000	$ 60,000
Accounts payable	40,000	*(e)*	5,000			35,000
Interest payable	4,000	*(f)*	1,000			3,000
Income taxes payable	12,000			*(g)*	10,000	22,000
Notes payable	64,000	*(j)*	34,000	*(k2)*	60,000	90,000
Common stock, $5 par value	80,000			*(l)*	15,000	95,000
Retained earnings	88,000	*(m)*	14,000	*(a)*	38,000	112,000
	$336,000					$417,000
Statement of Cash Flows						
Operating activities						
Net income		*(a)*	38,000			
Increase in accounts receivable				*(b)*	20,000	
Increase in merchandise inventory				*(c)*	14,000	
Increase in prepaid expenses				*(d)*	2,000	
Decrease in accounts payable				*(e)*	5,000	
Decrease in interest payable				*(f)*	1,000	
Increase in income taxes payable		*(g)*	10,000			
Depreciation expense		*(h)*	24,000			
Loss on sale of plant assets		*(i)*	6,000			
Gain on retirement of notes				*(j)*	16,000	
Investing activities						
Receipts from sale of plant assets		*(i)*	12,000			
Payment for purchase of plant assets				*(k1)*	10,000	
Financing activities						
Payment to retire notes				*(j)*	18,000	
Receipts from issuing stock		*(l)*	15,000			
Payment of cash dividends				*(m)*	14,000	
Noncash Investing and Financing Activities						
Purchase of plant assets with notes		*(k2)*	60,000	*(k1)*	60,000	
			$337,000		$337,000	

Since adjustments *i, j,* and *k* are more challenging, we show them in the following debit and credit format. These entries are for purposes of our understanding; they are *not* the entries actually made in the journals. Changes in the Cash account are identified as sources or uses of cash.

i.	Loss from sale of plant assets	6,000	
	Accumulated depreciation	12,000	
	Receipt from sale of plant assets **(source of cash)**	12,000	
	Plant assets		30,000
	To describe sale of plant assets.		

[continued on next page]

[continued from previous page]

j.	Notes payable	34,000	
	Payments to retire notes **(use of cash)**		18,000
	Gain on retirement of notes		16,000
	To describe retirement of notes.		
k1.	Plant assets	70,000	
	Payment to purchase plant assets **(use of cash)**		10,000
	Purchase of plant assets financed by notes		60,000
	To describe purchase of plant assets.		
k2.	Purchase of plant assets financed by notes	60,000	
	Notes payable		60,000
	To issue notes for purchase of assets.		

APPENDIX

12B Direct Method of Reporting Operating Cash Flows

P5 Compute cash flows from operating activities using the direct method.

We compute cash flows from operating activities under the direct method by adjusting accrual-based income statement items to the cash basis. The usual approach is to adjust income statement accounts related to operating activities for changes in their related balance sheet accounts as follows:

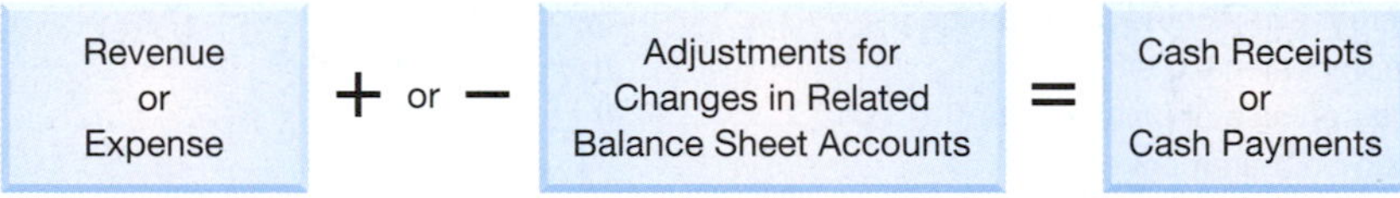

The framework for reporting cash receipts and cash payments for the operating section of the cash flow statement under the direct method is as in Exhibit 12B.1. We consider cash receipts first and then cash payments.

EXHIBIT 12B.1

Major Classes of Operating Cash Flows

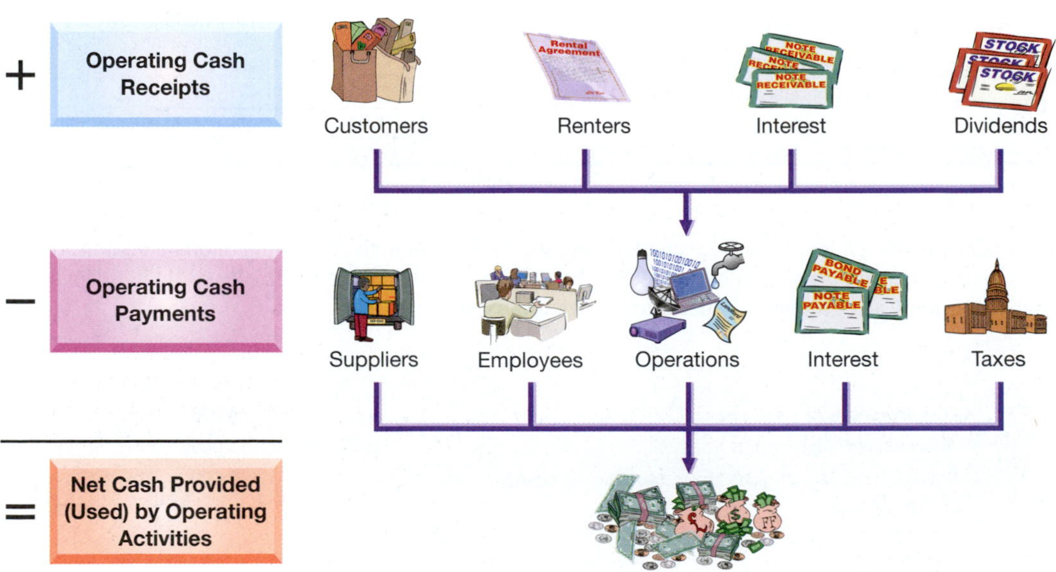

Operating Cash Receipts

A review of Exhibit 12.10 and the additional information reported by Genesis suggests only one potential cash receipt: sales to customers. This section, therefore, starts with sales to customers as reported on the income statement and then adjusts it as necessary to obtain cash received from customers to report on the statement of cash flows.

Cash Received from Customers If all sales are for cash, the amount received from customers equals the sales reported on the income statement. When some or all sales are on account, however, we must adjust the amount of sales for the change in Accounts Receivable. It is often helpful to use *account analysis* to do this. This usually involves setting up a T-account and reconstructing its major entries, with emphasis on cash receipts and payments. To illustrate, we use a T-account that includes accounts receivable balances for Genesis on December 31, 2008 and 2009. The beginning balance is $40,000 and the ending balance is $60,000. Next, the income statement shows sales of $590,000, which we enter on the debit side of this account. We now can reconstruct the Accounts Receivable account to determine the amount of cash received from customers as follows:

Point: An accounts receivable increase implies cash received from customers is less than sales (the converse is also true).

Accounts Receivable			
Bal., Dec. 31, 2008	40,000		
Sales	590,000	Cash receipts =	570,000
Bal., Dec. 31, 2009	60,000		

This T-account shows that the Accounts Receivable balance begins at $40,000 and increases to $630,000 from sales of $590,000, yet its ending balance is only $60,000. This implies that cash receipts from customers are $570,000, computed as $40,000 + $590,000 − [?] = $60,000. This computation can be rearranged to express cash received as equal to sales of $590,000 minus a $20,000 increase in accounts receivable. This computation is summarized as a general rule in Exhibit 12B.2. The statement of cash flows in Exhibit 12.7 reports the $570,000 cash received from customers as a cash inflow from operating activities.

Example: If the ending balance of accounts receivable is $20,000 (instead of $60,000), what is cash received from customers? *Answer:* $610,000

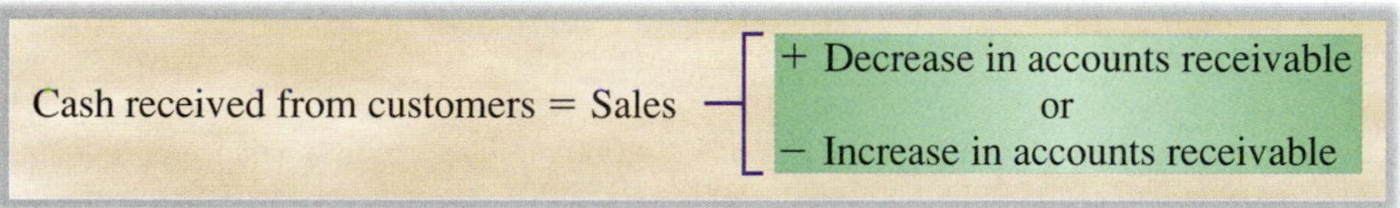

EXHIBIT 12B.2

Formula to Compute Cash Received from Customers—Direct Method

Other Cash Receipts While Genesis's cash receipts are limited to collections from customers, we often see other types of cash receipts, most commonly cash receipts involving rent, interest, and dividends. We compute cash received from these items by subtracting an increase in their respective receivable or adding a decrease. For instance, if rent receivable increases in the period, cash received from renters is less than rent revenue reported on the income statement. If rent receivable decreases, cash received is more than reported rent revenue. The same logic applies to interest and dividends. The formulas for these computations are summarized later in this appendix.

Point: Net income is measured using accrual accounting. Cash flows from operations are measured using cash basis accounting.

Operating Cash Payments

A review of Exhibit 12.10 and the additional Genesis information shows four operating expenses: cost of goods sold; wages and other operating expenses; interest expense; and taxes expense. We analyze each expense to compute its cash amounts for the statement of cash flows. (We then examine depreciation and the other losses and gains.)

Cash Paid for Merchandise We compute cash paid for merchandise by analyzing both cost of goods sold and merchandise inventory. If all merchandise purchases are for cash and the ending balance of Merchandise Inventory is unchanged from the beginning balance, the amount of cash paid for merchandise equals cost of goods sold—an uncommon situation. Instead, there normally is some change in the Merchandise Inventory balance. Also, some or all merchandise purchases are often made on credit, and this yields changes in the Accounts Payable balance. When the balances of both Merchandise Inventory and Accounts Payable change, we must adjust the cost of goods sold for changes in both accounts to compute cash paid for merchandise. This is a two-step adjustment.

First, we use the change in the account balance of Merchandise Inventory, along with the cost of goods sold amount, to compute cost of purchases for the period. An increase in merchandise inventory implies that we bought more than we sold, and we add this inventory increase to cost of goods sold to compute cost of purchases. A decrease in merchandise inventory implies that we bought less than we sold, and we subtract the inventory decrease from cost of goods sold to compute purchases. We illustrate the *first step* by reconstructing the Merchandise Inventory account of Genesis:

Merchandise Inventory			
Bal., Dec. 31, 2008	70,000		
Purchases =	**314,000**	Cost of goods sold	300,000
Bal., Dec. 31, 2009	84,000		

The beginning balance is $70,000, and the ending balance is $84,000. The income statement shows that cost of goods sold is $300,000, which we enter on the credit side of this account. With this information, we determine the amount for cost of purchases to be $314,000. This computation can be rearranged to express cost of purchases as equal to cost of goods sold of $300,000 plus the $14,000 increase in inventory.

The second step uses the change in the balance of Accounts Payable, and the amount of cost of purchases, to compute cash paid for merchandise. A decrease in accounts payable implies that we paid for more goods than we acquired this period, and we would then add the accounts payable decrease to cost of purchases to compute cash paid for merchandise. An increase in accounts payable implies that we paid for less than the amount of goods acquired, and we would subtract the accounts payable increase from purchases to compute cash paid for merchandise. The *second step* is applied to Genesis by reconstructing its Accounts Payable account:

Accounts Payable			
		Bal., Dec. 31, 2008	40,000
Cash payments =	**319,000**	Purchases	314,000
		Bal., Dec. 31, 2009	35,000

Example: If the ending balances of Inventory and Accounts Payable are $60,000 and $50,000, respectively (instead of $84,000 and $35,000), what is cash paid for merchandise? *Answer:* $280,000

Its beginning balance of $40,000 plus purchases of $314,000 minus an ending balance of $35,000 yields cash paid of $319,000 (or $40,000 + $314,000 − [?] = $35,000). Alternatively, we can express cash paid for merchandise as equal to purchases of $314,000 plus the $5,000 decrease in accounts payable. The $319,000 cash paid for merchandise is reported on the statement of cash flows in Exhibit 12.7 as a cash outflow under operating activities.

We summarize this two-step adjustment to cost of goods sold to compute cash paid for merchandise inventory in Exhibit 12B.3.

EXHIBIT 12B.3

Two Steps to Compute Cash Paid for Merchandise—Direct Method

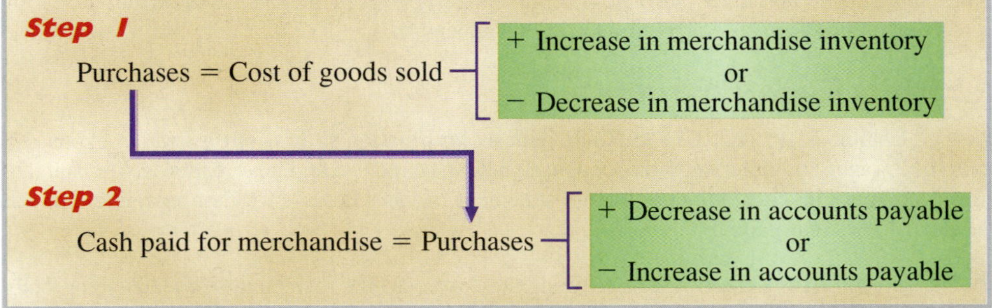

Cash Paid for Wages and Operating Expenses (excluding depreciation)

The income statement of Genesis shows wages and other operating expenses of $216,000 (see Exhibit 12.10). To compute cash paid for wages and other operating expenses, we adjust this amount for any changes in their related balance sheet accounts. We begin by looking for any prepaid expenses and accrued liabilities related to wages and other operating expenses in the balance sheets of Genesis in

Exhibit 12.10. The balance sheets show prepaid expenses but no accrued liabilities. Thus, the adjustment is limited to the change in prepaid expenses. The amount of adjustment is computed by assuming that all cash paid for wages and other operating expenses is initially debited to Prepaid Expenses. This assumption allows us to reconstruct the Prepaid Expenses account:

Prepaid Expenses			
Bal., Dec. 31, 2008	4,000		
Cash payments =	**218,000**	Wages and other operating exp.	216,000
Bal., Dec. 31, 2009	6,000		

Prepaid Expenses increase by $2,000 in the period, meaning that cash paid for wages and other operating expenses exceeds the reported expense by $2,000. Alternatively, we can express cash paid for wages and other operating expenses as equal to its reported expenses of $216,000 plus the $2,000 increase in prepaid expenses.[1]

Point: A decrease in prepaid expenses implies that reported expenses include an amount(s) that did not require a cash outflow in the period.

Exhibit 12B.4 summarizes the adjustments to wages (including salaries) and other operating expenses. The Genesis balance sheet did not report accrued liabilities, but we include them in the formula to explain the adjustment to cash when they do exist. A decrease in accrued liabilities implies that we paid cash for more goods or services than received this period, so we add the decrease in accrued liabilities to the expense amount to obtain cash paid for these goods or services. An increase in accrued liabilities implies that we paid cash for less than what was acquired, so we subtract this increase in accrued liabilities from the expense amount to get cash paid.

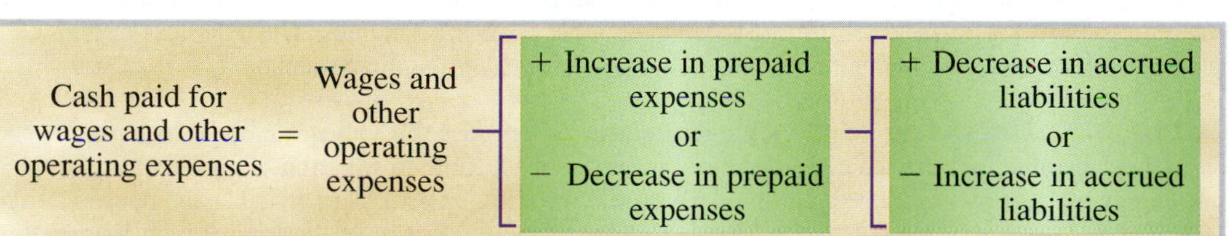

EXHIBIT 12B.4

Formula to Compute Cash Paid for Wages and Operating Expenses—Direct Method

Cash Paid for Interest and Income Taxes Computing operating cash flows for interest and taxes is similar to that for operating expenses. Both require adjustments to their amounts reported on the income statement for changes in their related balance sheet accounts. We begin with the Genesis income statement showing interest expense of $7,000 and income taxes expense of $15,000. To compute the cash paid, we adjust interest expense for the change in interest payable and then the income taxes expense for the change in income taxes payable. These computations involve reconstructing both liability accounts:

Interest Payable			
		Bal., Dec. 31, 2008	4,000
Cash paid for interest =	**8,000**	Interest expense	7,000
		Bal., Dec. 31, 2009	3,000

Income Taxes Payable			
		Bal., Dec. 31, 2008	12,000
Cash paid for taxes =	**5,000**	Income taxes expense	15,000
		Bal., Dec. 31, 2009	22,000

These accounts reveal cash paid for interest of $8,000 and cash paid for income taxes of $5,000. The formulas to compute these amounts are in Exhibit 12B.5. Both of these cash payments are reported as operating cash outflows on the statement of cash flows in Exhibit 12.7.

[1] The assumption that all cash payments for wages and operating expenses are initially debited to Prepaid Expenses is not necessary for our analysis to hold. If cash payments are debited directly to the expense account, the total amount of cash paid for wages and other operating expenses still equals the $216,000 expense plus the $2,000 increase in Prepaid Expenses (which arise from end-of-period adjusting entries).

EXHIBIT 12B.5

Formulas to Compute Cash Paid for Both Interest and Taxes—Direct Method

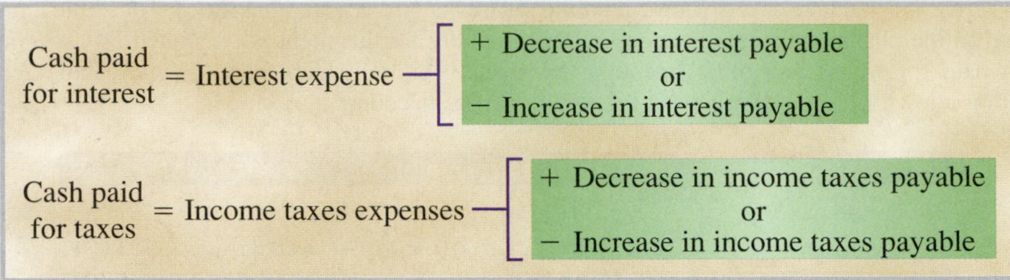

Analysis of Additional Expenses, Gains, and Losses Genesis has three additional items reported on its income statement: depreciation, loss on sale of assets, and gain on retirement of debt. We must consider each for its potential cash effects.

Depreciation Expense Depreciation expense is $24,000. It is often called a *noncash expense* because depreciation has no cash flows. Depreciation expense is an allocation of an asset's depreciable cost. The cash outflow with a plant asset is reported as part of investing activities when it is paid for. Thus, depreciation expense is *never* reported on a statement of cash flows using the direct method, nor is depletion or amortization expense.

Loss on Sale of Assets Sales of assets frequently result in gains and losses reported as part of net income, but the amount of recorded gain or loss does *not* reflect any cash flows in these transactions. Asset sales result in cash inflow equal to the cash amount received, regardless of whether the asset was sold at a gain or a loss. This cash inflow is reported under investing activities. Thus, the loss or gain on a sale of assets is *never* reported on a statement of cash flows using the direct method.

Gain on Retirement of Debt Retirement of debt usually yields a gain or loss reported as part of net income, but that gain or loss does *not* reflect cash flow in this transaction. Debt retirement results in cash outflow equal to the cash paid to settle the debt, regardless of whether the debt is retired at a gain or loss. This cash outflow is reported under financing activities; the loss or gain from retirement of debt is *never* reported on a statement of cash flows using the direct method.

Point: The direct method is usually viewed as *user friendly* because less accounting knowledge is required to understand and use it.

Summary of Adjustments for Direct Method

Exhibit 12B.6 summarizes common adjustments for net income to yield net cash provided (used) by operating activities under the direct method.

EXHIBIT 12B.6

Summary of Selected Adjustments for Direct Method

Item	From Income Statement	Adjustments to Obtain Cash Flow Numbers	
Receipts			
From sales	Sales Revenue	+Decrease in Accounts Receivable −Increase in Accounts Receivable	
From rent	Rent Revenue	+Decrease in Rent Receivable −Increase in Rent Receivable	
From interest	Interest Revenue	+Decrease in Interest Receivable −Increase in Interest Receivable	
From dividends	Dividend Revenue	+Decrease in Dividends Receivable −Increase in Dividends Receivable	
Payments			
To suppliers	Cost of Goods Sold	+Increase in Inventory −Decrease in Inventory	+Decrease in Accounts Payable −Increase in Accounts Payable
For operations	Operating Expense	+Increase in Prepaids −Decrease in Prepaids	+Decrease in Accrued Liabilities −Increase in Accrued Liabilities
To employees	Wages (Salaries) Expense	+Decrease in Wages (Salaries) Payable −Increase in Wages (Salaries) Payable	
For interest	Interest Expense	+Decrease in Interest Payable −Increase in Interest Payable	
For taxes	Income Tax Expense	+Decrease in Income Tax Payable −Increase in Income Tax Payable	

Direct Method Format of Operating Activities Section

Exhibit 12.7 shows the Genesis statement of cash flows using the direct method. Major items of cash inflows and cash outflows are listed separately in the operating activities section. The format requires that operating cash outflows be subtracted from operating cash inflows to get net cash provided (used) by operating activities. The FASB recommends that the operating activities section of the statement of cash flows be reported using the direct method, which is considered more useful to financial statement users. *However, the FASB requires a reconciliation of net income to net cash provided (used) by operating activities when the direct method is used* (which can be reported in the notes). This reconciliation is similar to preparation of the operating activities section of the statement of cash flows using the indirect method.

Point: Some preparers argue that it is easier to prepare a statement of cash flows using the indirect method. This likely explains its greater frequency in financial statements.

Decision Insight

IFRSs Like U.S. GAAP, IFRSs allow cash flows from operating activities to be reported using either the indirect method or the direct method.

Quick Check

Answers—p. 454

8. Net sales in a period are $590,000, beginning accounts receivable are $120,000, and ending accounts receivable are $90,000. What cash amount is collected from customers in the period?
9. The Merchandise Inventory account balance decreases in the period from a beginning balance of $32,000 to an ending balance of $28,000. Cost of goods sold for the period is $168,000. If the Accounts Payable balance increases $2,400 in the period, what is the cash amount paid for merchandise inventory?
10. This period's wages and other operating expenses total $112,000. Beginning-of-period prepaid expenses totaled $1,200, and its ending balance is $4,200. There were no beginning-of-period accrued liabilities, but end-of-period wages payable equal $5,600. How much cash is paid for wages and other operating expenses?

Summary

C1 Explain the purpose and importance of cash flow information. The main purpose of the statement of cash flows is to report the major cash receipts and cash payments for a period. This includes identifying cash flows as relating to either operating, investing, or financing activities. Most business decisions involve evaluating activities that provide or use cash.

C2 Distinguish between operating, investing, and financing activities. Operating activities include transactions and events that determine net income. Investing activities include transactions and events that mainly affect long-term assets. Financing activities include transactions and events that mainly affect long-term liabilities and equity.

C3 Identify and disclose noncash investing and financing activities. Noncash investing and financing activities must be disclosed either in a note or a separate schedule to the statement of cash flows. Examples are the retirement of debt by issuing equity and the exchange of a note payable for plant assets.

C4 Describe the format of the statement of cash flows. The statement of cash flows separates cash receipts and cash payments into operating, investing, or financing activities.

A1 Analyze the statement of cash flows. To understand and predict cash flows, users stress identification of the sources and uses of cash flows by operating, investing, and financing activities. Emphasis is on operating cash flows since they derive from continuing operations.

A2 Compute and apply the cash flow on total assets ratio. The cash flow on total assets ratio is defined as operating cash flows divided by average total assets. Analysis of current and past values for this ratio can reflect a company's ability to yield regular and positive cash flows. It is also viewed as a measure of earnings quality.

P1 Prepare a statement of cash flows. Preparation of a statement of cash flows involves five steps: (1) Compute the net increase or decrease in cash; (2) compute net cash provided or used by operating activities (*using either the direct or indirect method*); (3) compute net cash provided or used by investing activities; (4) compute net cash provided or used by financing activities; and (5) report the beginning and ending cash balance and prove that it is explained by net cash flows. Noncash investing and financing activities are also disclosed.

P2 Compute cash flows from operating activities using the indirect method. The indirect method for reporting net cash provided or used by operating activities starts with net income and then adjusts it for three items: (1) changes in noncash current assets and current liabilities related to operating activities, (2) revenues and expenses not providing or using cash, and (3) gains and losses from investing and financing activities.

P3 Determine cash flows from both investing and financing activities. Cash flows from both investing and financing activities are determined by identifying the cash flow effects of transactions and events affecting each balance sheet account related to these activities. All cash flows from these activities are identified when we can explain changes in these accounts from the beginning to the end of the period.

P4[A] **Illustrate use of a spreadsheet to prepare a statement of cash flows.** A spreadsheet is a useful tool in preparing a statement of cash flows. Six key steps (see appendix) are applied when using the spreadsheet to prepare the statement.

P5[B] **Compute cash flows from operating activities using the direct method.** The direct method for reporting net cash provided or used by operating activities lists major operating cash inflows less cash outflows to yield net cash inflow or outflow from operations.

Guidance Answers to **Decision Maker**

Entrepreneur Several factors might explain an increase in net cash flows when a net loss is reported, including (1) early recognition of expenses relative to revenues generated (such as research and development), (2) cash advances on long-term sales contracts not yet recognized in income, (3) issuances of debt or equity for cash to finance expansion, (4) cash sale of assets, (5) delay of cash payments, and (6) cash prepayment on sales. Analysis needs to focus on the components of both the net loss and the net cash flows and their implications for future performance.

Reporter Your initial reaction based on the company's $600,000 loss with a $550,000 decrease in net cash flows is not positive. However, closer scrutiny reveals a more positive picture of this company's performance. Cash flow from operating activities is $650,000, computed as [?] − $850,000 − $350,000 = $(550,000). You also note that net income *before* the extraordinary loss is $330,000, computed as [?] − $930,000 = $(600,000).

Guidance Answers to **Quick Checks**

1. No to both. The statement of cash flows reports changes in the sum of cash plus cash equivalents. It does not report transfers between cash and cash equivalents.
2. The three categories of cash inflows and outflows are operating activities, investing activities, and financing activities.
3. **a.** Investing **c.** Financing **e.** Operating
   b. Operating **d.** Operating **f.** Financing
4. $74,900 + $4,600 − $11,700 − $1,000 + $3,400 = $70,200
5. Expenses such as depreciation and amortization do not require current cash outflows. Therefore, adding these expenses back to net income eliminates these noncash items from the net income number, converting it to a cash basis.
6. A gain on the sale of plant assets is subtracted from net income because a sale of plant assets is not an operating activity; it is an investing activity for the amount of cash received from its sale. Also, such a gain yields no cash effects.
7. $80,000 − $30,000 − $10,000 = $40,000 cash receipt. The $40,000 cash receipt is reported as an investing activity.
8. $590,000 + ($120,000 − $90,000) = $620,000
9. $168,000 − ($32,000 − $28,000) − $2,400 = $161,600
10. $112,000 + ($4,200 − $1,200) − $5,600 = $109,400

Key Terms

mhhe.com/wildMA2e

Key Terms are available at the book's Website for learning and testing in an online Flashcard Format.

Cash flow on total assets (p. 442)
Direct method (p. 430)
Financing activities (p. 426)
Indirect method (p. 430)
Investing activities (p. 426)
Operating activities (p. 425)
Statement of cash flows (p. 424)

Multiple Choice Quiz

Answers on p. 473

mhhe.com/wildMA2e

Additional Quiz Questions are available at the book's Website.

Quiz12

1. A company uses the indirect method to determine its cash flows from operating activities. Use the following information to determine its net cash provided or used by operating activities.

Net income	$15,200
Depreciation expense	10,000
Cash payment on note payable	8,000
Gain on sale of land	3,000
Increase in inventory	1,500
Increase in accounts payable	2,850

a. $23,550 used by operating activities
b. $23,550 provided by operating activities
c. $15,550 provided by operating activities
d. $42,400 provided by operating activities
e. $20,850 provided by operating activities

2. A machine with a cost of $175,000 and accumulated depreciation of $94,000 is sold for $87,000 cash. The amount reported as a source of cash under cash flows from investing activities is:
a. $81,000.
b. $6,000.
c. $87,000.
d. Zero; this is a financing activity.
e. Zero; this is an operating activity.

3. A company settles a long-term note payable plus interest by paying $68,000 cash toward the principal amount and $5,440 cash for interest. The amount reported as a use of cash under cash flows from financing activities is:
a. Zero; this is an investing activity.
b. Zero; this is an operating activity.
c. $73,440.
d. $68,000.
e. $5,440.

4. The following information is available regarding a company's annual salaries and wages. What amount of cash is paid for salaries and wages?

Salaries and wages expense	$255,000
Salaries and wages payable, prior year-end	8,200
Salaries and wages payable, current year-end	10,900

a. $252,300
b. $257,700
c. $255,000
d. $274,100
e. $235,900

5. The following information is available for a company. What amount of cash is paid for merchandise for the current year?

Cost of goods sold	$545,000
Merchandise inventory, prior year-end	105,000
Merchandise inventory, current year-end	112,000
Accounts payable, prior year-end	98,500
Accounts payable, current year-end	101,300

a. $545,000
b. $554,800
c. $540,800
d. $535,200
e. $549,200

Superscript letter A (B) denotes assignments based on Appendix 12A (12B).

Discussion Questions

1. What is the reporting purpose of the statement of cash flows? Identify at least two questions that this statement can answer.

2. Describe the direct method of reporting cash flows from operating activities.

3. When a statement of cash flows is prepared using the direct method, what are some of the operating cash flows?

4. Describe the indirect method of reporting cash flows from operating activities.

5. What are some investing activities reported on the statement of cash flows?

6. What are some financing activities reported on the statement of cash flows?

7. Where on the statement of cash flows is the payment of cash dividends reported?

8. Assume that a company purchases land for $100,000, paying $20,000 cash and borrowing the remainder with a long-term note payable. How should this transaction be reported on a statement of cash flows?

9. On June 3, a company borrows $50,000 cash by giving its bank a 160-day, interest-bearing note. On the statement of cash flows, where should this be reported?

10. If a company reports positive net income for the year, can it also show a net cash outflow from operating activities? Explain.

11. Is depreciation a source of cash flow?

12. Refer to Best Buy's statement of cash flows in Appendix A. (*a*) Which method is used to compute its net cash provided by operating activities? (*b*) While its balance sheet shows an increase in receivables from fiscal years 2006 to 2007, why is this increase in receivables subtracted when computing net cash provided by operating activities for the year ended March 3, 2007?

13. Refer to Circuit City's statement of cash flows in Appendix A. What are its cash flows from financing activities for the year ended February 28, 2007? List items and amounts.

14. Refer to RadioShack's statement of cash flows in Appendix A. List its cash flows from operating activities, investing activities, and financing activities.

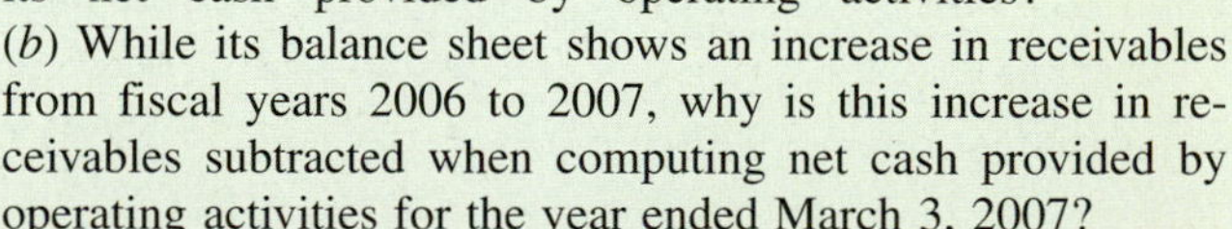

15. Refer to Apple's statement of cash flows in Appendix A. What investing activities result in cash outflows for the year ended September 30, 2006? List items and amounts.

Denotes Discussion Questions that involve decision making.

Most materials in this section are available in McGraw-Hill's Connect connect

QUICK STUDY

QS 12-1
Statement of cash flows
C1 C2 C3

The statement of cash flows is one of the four primary financial statements.

1. Describe the content and layout of a statement of cash flows, including its three sections.
2. List at least three transactions classified as investing activities in a statement of cash flows.
3. List at least three transactions classified as financing activities in a statement of cash flows.
4. List at least three transactions classified as significant noncash financing and investing activities in the statement of cash flows.

QS 12-2
Transaction classification by activity
C2

Classify the following cash flows as operating, investing, or financing activities.

1. Sold long-term investments for cash.
2. Received cash payments from customers.
3. Paid cash for wages and salaries.
4. Purchased inventories for cash.
5. Paid cash dividends.
6. Issued common stock for cash.
7. Received cash interest on a note.
8. Paid cash interest on outstanding notes.
9. Received cash from sale of land at a loss.
10. Paid cash for property taxes on building.

QS 12-3
Computing cash from operations (indirect)
P2

Use the following information to determine this company's cash flows from operating activities using the indirect method.

LOLLAND COMPANY
Selected Balance Sheet Information
December 31, 2009 and 2008

	2009	2008
Current assets		
Cash	$169,300	$ 53,600
Accounts receivable	50,000	64,000
Inventory	120,000	108,200
Current liabilities		
Accounts payable	60,800	51,400
Income taxes payable	4,100	4,400

LOLLAND COMPANY
Income Statement
For Year Ended December 31, 2009

Sales		$1,030,000
Cost of goods sold		663,200
Gross profit		366,800
Operating expenses		
Depreciation expense	$ 72,000	
Other expenses	243,000	315,000
Income before taxes		51,800
Income taxes expense		15,400
Net income		$ 36,400

QS 12-4
Computing cash from asset sales
P3

The following selected information is from Manning Company's comparative balance sheets.

At December 31	2009	2008
Furniture	$ 264,000	$ 369,000
Accumulated depreciation—Furniture	(174,400)	(221,400)

The income statement reports depreciation expense for the year of $36,000. Also, furniture costing $105,000 was sold for its book value. Compute the cash received from the sale of furniture.

QS 12-5
Computing financing cash flows
P3

The following selected information is from the Tanner Company's comparative balance sheets.

At December 31	2009	2008
Common stock, $10 par value	$ 210,000	$200,000
Paid-in capital in excess of par	1,134,000	684,000
Retained earnings	627,000	575,000

The company's net income for the year ended December 31, 2009, was $96,000.

1. Compute the cash received from the sale of its common stock during 2009.
2. Compute the cash paid for dividends during 2009.

Use the following balance sheets and income statement to answer QS 12-6 through QS 12-11.

QS 12-6
Computing cash from operations (indirect) P2 

Use the indirect method to prepare the cash provided or used from operating activities section only of the statement of cash flows for this company.

AMMONS, INC.
Comparative Balance Sheets
December 31, 2009

	2009	2008
Assets		
Cash	$189,600	$ 48,000
Accounts receivable, net	82,000	102,000
Inventory	171,600	191,600
Prepaid expenses	10,800	8,400
Furniture	218,000	238,000
Accum. depreciation—Furniture	(34,000)	(18,000)
Total assets	$638,000	$570,000
Liabilities and Equity		
Accounts payable	$ 30,000	$ 42,000
Wages payable	18,000	10,000
Income taxes payable	2,800	5,200
Notes payable (long-term)	58,000	138,000
Common stock, $5 par value	458,000	358,000
Retained earnings	71,200	16,800
Total liabilities and equity	$638,000	$570,000

AMMONS, INC.
Income Statement
For Year Ended December 31, 2009

Sales		$976,000
Cost of goods sold		628,000
Gross profit		348,000
Operating expenses		
Depreciation expense	$ 75,200	
Other expenses	178,200	253,400
Income before taxes		94,600
Income taxes expense		34,600
Net income		$ 60,000

QS 12-7
Computing cash from asset sales P3 

Refer to the data in QS 12-6.
Furniture costing $110,000 is sold at its book value in 2009. Acquisitions of furniture total $90,000 cash, on which no depreciation is necessary because it is acquired at year-end. What is the cash inflow related to the sale of furniture?

QS 12-8
Computing financing cash outflows P3

Refer to the data in QS 12-6.

1. Assume that all common stock is issued for cash. What amount of cash dividends is paid during 2009?
2. Assume that no additional notes payable are issued in 2009. What cash amount is paid to reduce the notes payable balance in 2009?

QS 12-9[B]
Computing cash received from customers P5

Refer to the data in QS 12-6.

1. How much cash is received from sales to customers for year 2009?
2. What is the net increase or decrease in cash for year 2009?

QS 12-10[B]
Computing operating cash outflows P5

Refer to the data in QS 12-6.

1. How much cash is paid to acquire merchandise inventory during year 2009?
2. How much cash is paid for operating expenses during year 2009?

QS 12-11[B]
Computing cash from operations (direct) P5 

Refer to the data in QS 12-6.
Use the direct method to prepare the cash provided or used from operating activities section only of the statement of cash flows for this company.

QS 12-12
Analyses of sources and uses of cash A1 A2 

Financial data from three competitors in the same industry follow.

1. Which of the three competitors is in the strongest position as shown by its statement of cash flows?
2. Analyze and discuss the strength of Peña's cash flow on total assets ratio to that of Garcia.

($ thousands)	Peña	Garcia	Piniella
Cash provided (used) by operating activities	$ 140,000	$ 120,000	$ (48,000)
Cash provided (used) by investing activities			
Proceeds from sale of operating assets			52,000
Purchase of operating assets	(56,000)	(68,000)	
Cash provided (used) by financing activities			
Proceeds from issuance of debt			46,000
Repayment of debt	(12,000)		
Net increase (decrease) in cash	$ 72,000	$ 52,000	$ 50,000
Average total assets	$ 1,580,000	$ 1,250,000	$ 600,000

QS 12-13[A]
Noncash accounts on a spreadsheet P4

When a spreadsheet for a statement of cash flows is prepared, all changes in noncash balance sheet accounts are fully explained on the spreadsheet. Explain how these noncash balance sheet accounts are used to fully account for cash flows on a spreadsheet.

QS 12-14
Computing cash flows from operations (indirect)
P2

For each of the following separate cases, compute cash flows from operations. The list includes all balance sheet accounts related to operating activities.

	Case A	Case B	Case C
Net income	$ 8,000	$200,000	$144,000
Depreciation expense	60,000	16,000	48,000
Accounts receivable increase (decrease)	80,000	40,000	(8,000)
Inventory increase (decrease)	(40,000)	(20,000)	21,000
Accounts payable increase (decrease)	48,000	(44,000)	28,000
Accrued liabilities increase (decrease)	(88,000)	24,000	(16,000)

QS 12-15
Computing cash flows from investing
P3

Compute cash flows from investing activities using the following company information.

Sale of short-term investments	$12,000
Cash collections from customers	32,000
Purchase of used equipment	10,000
Depreciation expense	4,000

QS 12-16
Computing cash flows from financing
P3

Compute cash flows from financing activities using the following company information.

Additional short-term borrowings	$40,000
Purchase of short-term investments	10,000
Cash dividends paid	32,000
Interest paid	16,000

Most materials in this section are available in McGraw-Hill's Connect connect

EXERCISES

Exercise 12-1
Cash flow from operations (indirect)
P2

Hehman Company reports net income of $530,000 for the year ended December 31, 2009. It also reports $95,400 depreciation expense and a $4,000 gain on the sale of machinery. Its comparative balance sheets reveal a $42,400 increase in accounts receivable, $21,730 increase in accounts payable, $11,660 decrease in prepaid expenses, and $16,430 decrease in wages payable.

Required

Prepare only the operating activities section of the statement of cash flows for 2009 using the *indirect method.*

Exercise 12-2
Cash flow classification (indirect) C2 C3 P2 

The following transactions and events occurred during the year. Assuming that this company uses the *indirect method* to report cash provided by operating activities, indicate where each item would appear on its statement of cash flows by placing an *x* in the appropriate column.

	Statement of Cash Flows			Noncash Investing and Financing Activities	Not Reported on Statement or in Notes
	Operating Activities	Investing Activities	Financing Activities		
a. Paid cash to purchase inventory.	____	____	____	____	____
b. Purchased land by issuing common stock.	____	____	____	____	____
c. Accounts receivable decreased in the year.	____	____	____	____	____
d. Sold equipment for cash, yielding a loss.	____	____	____	____	____
e. Recorded depreciation expense.	____	____	____	____	____
f. Income taxes payable increased in the year.	____	____	____	____	____
g. Declared and paid a cash dividend.	____	____	____	____	____
h. Accounts payable decreased in the year	____	____	____	____	____
i. Paid cash to settle notes payable	____	____	____	____	____
j. Prepaid expenses increased in the year	____	____	____	____	____

Exercise 12-3[B]
Cash flow classification (direct) C2 C3 P5

The following transactions and events occurred during the year. Assuming that this company uses the *direct method* to report cash provided by operating activities, indicate where each item would appear on the statement of cash flows by placing an *x* in the appropriate column.

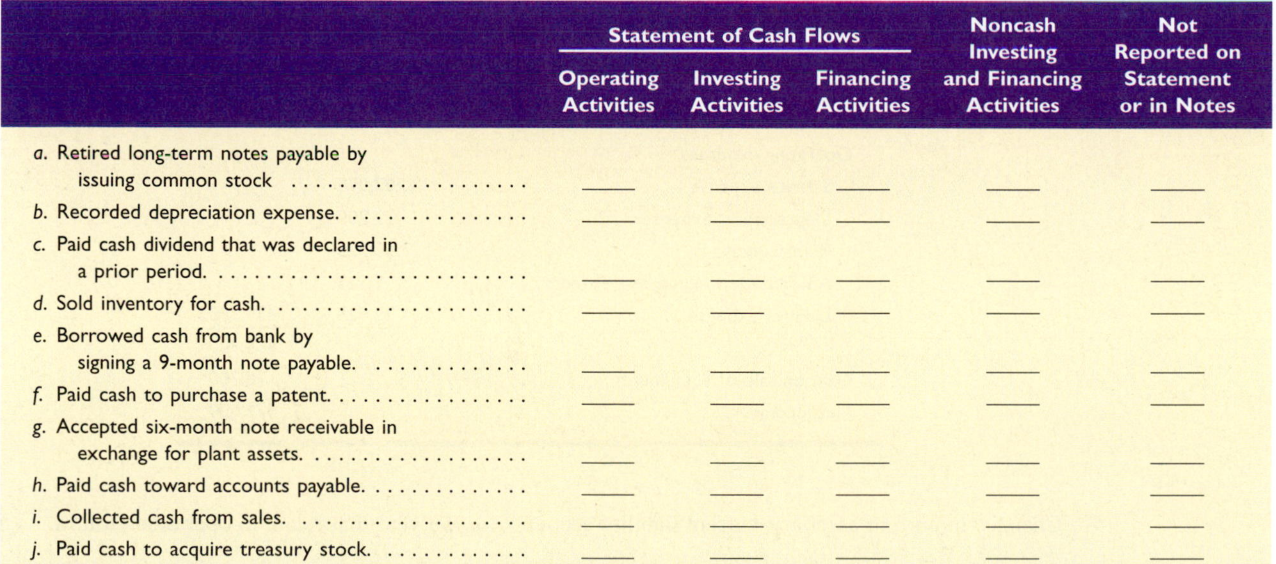

	Statement of Cash Flows			Noncash Investing and Financing Activities	Not Reported on Statement or in Notes
	Operating Activities	Investing Activities	Financing Activities		
a. Retired long-term notes payable by issuing common stock	____	____	____	____	____
b. Recorded depreciation expense.	____	____	____	____	____
c. Paid cash dividend that was declared in a prior period.	____	____	____	____	____
d. Sold inventory for cash.	____	____	____	____	____
e. Borrowed cash from bank by signing a 9-month note payable.	____	____	____	____	____
f. Paid cash to purchase a patent.	____	____	____	____	____
g. Accepted six-month note receivable in exchange for plant assets.	____	____	____	____	____
h. Paid cash toward accounts payable.	____	____	____	____	____
i. Collected cash from sales.	____	____	____	____	____
j. Paid cash to acquire treasury stock.	____	____	____	____	____

Exercise 12-4
Cash flows from operating activities (indirect)
P2

Zander Company's calendar-year 2009 income statement shows the following: Net Income, $395,000; Depreciation Expense, $48,980; Amortization Expense, $9,875; Gain on Sale of Plant Assets, $4,900. An examination of the company's current assets and current liabilities reveals the following changes (all from operating activities): Accounts Receivable decrease, $7,600; Merchandise Inventory decrease, $22,040; Prepaid Expenses increase, $2,000; Accounts Payable decrease, $5,000; Other Payables increase, $760. Use the *indirect method* to compute cash flow from operating activities.

Exercise 12-5B
Computation of cash flows (direct)
P5

For each of the following three separate cases, use the information provided about the calendar-year 2010 operations of Kowa Company to compute the required cash flow information.

Case A: Compute cash received from customers:	
Sales	$590,000
Accounts receivable, December 31, 2009	38,000
Accounts receivable, December 31, 2010	52,440
Case B: Compute cash paid for rent:	
Rent expense	$117,400
Rent payable, December 31, 2009	6,700
Rent payable, December 31, 2010	5,561
Case C: Compute cash paid for merchandise:	
Cost of goods sold	$651,000
Merchandise inventory, December 31, 2009	201,810
Accounts payable, December 31, 2009	84,760
Merchandise inventory, December 31, 2010	165,484
Accounts payable, December 31, 2010	105,102

Exercise 12-6
Cash flows from operating activities (indirect)
P2

Use the following income statement and information about changes in noncash current assets and current liabilities to prepare only the cash flows from operating activities section of the statement of cash flows using the *indirect* method.

SEYMOUR COMPANY
Income Statement
For Year Ended December 31, 2009

Sales		$2,175,000
Cost of goods sold		1,065,750
Gross profit		1,109,250
Operating expenses		
Salaries expense	$297,975	
Depreciation expense	52,200	
Rent expense	58,725	
Amortization expenses—Patents	6,525	
Utilities expense	23,925	439,350
		669,900
Gain on sale of equipment		8,700
Net income		$ 678,600

Changes in current asset and current liability accounts for the year that relate to operations follow.

Accounts receivable	$45,300 increase	Accounts payable	$10,075 decrease
Merchandise inventory	35,150 increase	Salaries payable	4,750 decrease

Exercise 12-7B
Cash flows from operating activities (direct)
P5

Refer to the information about Seymour Company in Exercise 12-6.
Use the *direct method* to prepare only the cash provided or used by operating activities section of the statement of cash flows for this company.

Exercise 12-8
Cash flows from investing activities
P3

Use the following information to determine this company's cash flows from investing activities.

a. Equipment with a book value of $72,500 and an original cost of $158,000 was sold at a loss of $22,000.
b. Paid $95,000 cash for a new truck.
c. Sold land costing $315,000 for $400,000 cash, yielding a gain of $15,000.
d. Long-term investments in stock were sold for $94,700 cash, yielding a gain of $5,750.

Exercise 12-9
Cash flows from financing activities
P3

Use the following information to determine this company's cash flows from financing activities.

a. Net income was $53,000.
b. Issued common stock for $75,000 cash.
c. Paid cash dividend of $13,000.
d. Paid $90,000 cash to settle a note payable at its $90,000 maturity value.
e. Paid $18,000 cash to acquire its treasury stock.
f. Purchased equipment for $67,000 cash.

Exercise 12-10
Preparation of statement of cash flows (indirect)
C2 A2 P1 P2 P3 

Use the following financial statements and additional information to (1) prepare a statement of cash flows for the year ended June 30, 2009, using the *indirect method,* and (2) compute the company's cash flow on total assets ratio for its fiscal year 2009.

BOULWARE INC.
Comparative Balance Sheets
June 30, 2009 and 2008

	2009	2008
Assets		
Cash	$ 84,663	$ 49,494
Accounts receivable, net	65,720	56,952
Inventory	62,620	106,107
Prepaid expenses	4,960	5,763
Equipment	118,387	131,532
Accum. depreciation—Equipment	(26,350)	(10,848)
Total assets	$310,000	$339,000
Liabilities and Equity		
Accounts payable	$ 24,490	$ 35,256
Wages payable	6,510	17,628
Income taxes payable	2,170	4,068
Notes payable (long term)	31,953	76,953
Common stock, $5 par value	208,000	158,000
Retained earnings	36,877	47,095
Total liabilities and equity	$310,000	$339,000

BOULWARE INC.
Income Statement
For Year Ended June 30, 2009

Sales		$976,600
Cost of goods sold		625,024
Gross profit		351,576
Operating expenses		
Depreciation expense	$ 88,753	
Other expenses	101,879	
Total operating expenses		190,632
		160,944
Other gains (losses)		
Gain on sale of equipment		3,125
Income before taxes		164,069
Income taxes expense		56,604
Net income		$107,465

Additional Information

a. A $45,000 note payable is retired at its carrying (book) value in exchange for cash.
b. The only changes affecting retained earnings are net income and cash dividends paid.
c. New equipment is acquired for $85,000 cash.
d. Received cash for the sale of equipment that had cost $98,145, yielding a $3,125 gain.
e. Prepaid Expenses and Wages Payable relate to Other Expenses on the income statement.
f. All purchases and sales of merchandise inventory are on credit.

Exercise 12-11[B]
Preparation of statement of cash flows (direct) C2 P1 P3 P5

Refer to the data in Exercise 12-10.
Using the *direct method,* prepare the statement of cash flows for the year ended June 30, 2009.

Exercise 12-12[B]
Preparation of statement of cash flows (direct) and supporting note
C2 C3 C4 P1

Use the following information about the cash flows of Valencia Company to prepare a complete statement of cash flows (*direct method*) for the year ended December 31, 2009. Use a note disclosure for any noncash investing and financing activities.

Cash and cash equivalents balance, December 31, 2008	$ 43,000
Cash and cash equivalents balance, December 31, 2009	120,916
Cash received as interest	4,300
Cash paid for salaries	124,700
Bonds payable retired by issuing common stock (no gain or loss on retirement)	180,000
Cash paid to retire long-term notes payable	215,000
Cash received from sale of equipment	105,350
Cash received in exchange for six-month note payable	43,000
Land purchased by issuing long-term note payable	104,400
Cash paid for store equipment	40,850
Cash dividends paid	25,800
Cash paid for other expenses	68,800
Cash received from customers	834,200
Cash paid for merchandise	433,784

Exercise 12-13[B]
Preparation of statement of cash flows (direct) from Cash T-account
C2 A1 P1 P3 P5 

The following summarized Cash T-account reflects the total debits and total credits to the Cash account of Clarett Corporation for calendar year 2009.

(1) Use this information to prepare a complete statement of cash flows for year 2009. The cash provided or used by operating activities should be reported using the *direct method.*

(2) Refer to the statement of cash flows prepared for part 1 to answer the following questions *a* through *d*: (*a*) Which section—operating, investing, or financing—shows the largest cash (i) inflow and (ii) outflow? (*b*) What is the largest individual item among the investing cash outflows? (*c*) Are the cash proceeds larger from issuing notes or issuing stock? (*d*) Does the company have a net cash inflow or outflow from borrowing activities?

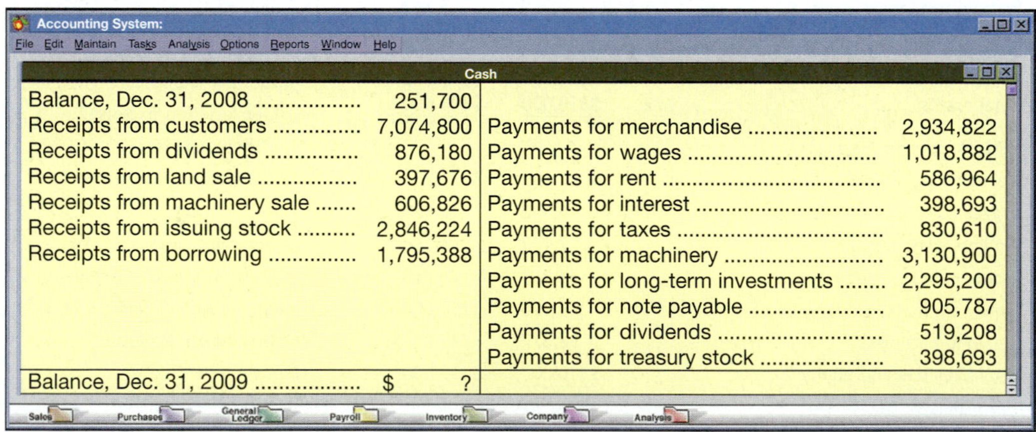
Accounting System:
File Edit Maintain Tasks Analysis Options Reports Window Help

Cash

Debits		Credits	
Balance, Dec. 31, 2008	251,700		
Receipts from customers	7,074,800	Payments for merchandise	2,934,822
Receipts from dividends	876,180	Payments for wages	1,018,882
Receipts from land sale	397,676	Payments for rent	586,964
Receipts from machinery sale	606,826	Payments for interest	398,693
Receipts from issuing stock	2,846,224	Payments for taxes	830,610
Receipts from borrowing	1,795,388	Payments for machinery	3,130,900
		Payments for long-term investments	2,295,200
		Payments for note payable	905,787
		Payments for dividends	519,208
		Payments for treasury stock	398,693
Balance, Dec. 31, 2009	$?		

Sales Purchases General Ledger Payroll Inventory Company Analysis

Exercise 12-14
Reporting cash flows from operations (indirect)
C4 P2

Woodlock Company reports the following information for its recent calendar year.

Sales	$80,000
Expenses	
Cost of goods sold	50,000
Salaries expense	12,000
Depreciation expense	6,000
Net income	$12,000
Accounts receivable increase	$ 5,000
Inventory decrease	8,000
Salaries payable increase	500

Required

Prepare the operating activities section of the statement of cash flows for Woodlock Company using the indirect method.

Exercise 12-15
Reporting and interpreting cash flows from operations (indirect)
C4 P2 

Portland Company disclosed the following information for its recent calendar year.

Revenues	$200,000
Expenses	
Salaries expense	168,000
Utilities expense	28,000
Depreciation expense	29,200
Other expenses	6,800
Net loss	$ (32,000)
Accounts receivable decrease	$ 48,000
Purchased a machine	20,000
Salaries payable increase	36,000
Other accrued liabilities decrease	16,000

Required

1. Prepare the operating activities section of the statement of cash flows using the indirect method.
2. What were the major reasons that this company was able to report a net loss but positive cash flow from operations?
3. Of the potential causes of differences between cash flow from operations and net income, which are the most important to investors?

connect *Most materials in this section are available in McGraw-Hill's Connect*

PROBLEM SET A

Problem 12-1A
Statement of cash flows (indirect method)
C2 C3 A1 P1 P2 P3

Georgia Company, a merchandiser, recently completed its calendar-year 2009 operations. For the year, (1) all sales are credit sales, (2) all credits to Accounts Receivable reflect cash receipts from customers, (3) all purchases of inventory are on credit, (4) all debits to Accounts Payable reflect cash payments for inventory, and (5) Other Expenses are paid in advance and are initially debited to Prepaid Expenses. The company's balance sheets and income statement follow.

GEORGIA COMPANY
Comparative Balance Sheets
December 31, 2009 and 2008

	2009	2008
Assets		
Cash	$ 49,800	$ 73,500
Accounts receivable	65,840	56,000
Merchandise inventory	277,000	252,000
Prepaid expenses	1,000	1,500
Equipment	158,500	107,500
Accum. depreciation—Equipment	(43,000)	(52,000)
Total assets	$509,140	$438,500
Liabilities and Equity		
Accounts payable	$ 42,965	$113,000
Short-term notes payable	10,000	7,000
Long-term notes payable	70,000	48,000
Common stock, $5 par value	162,750	151,000
Paid-in capital in excess of par, common stock	35,250	0
Retained earnings	188,175	119,500
Total liabilities and equity	$509,140	$438,500

GEORGIA COMPANY
Income Statement
For Year Ended December 31, 2009

Sales		$584,500
Cost of goods sold		281,000
Gross profit		303,500
Operating expenses		
Depreciation expense	$ 20,000	
Other expenses	132,800	152,800
Other gains (losses)		
Loss on sale of equipment		5,875
Income before taxes		144,825
Income taxes expense		24,250
Net income		$120,575

Additional Information on Year 2009 Transactions

a. The loss on the cash sale of equipment was $5,875 (details in *b*).

b. Sold equipment costing $46,500, with accumulated depreciation of $29,000, for $11,625 cash.

c. Purchased equipment costing $97,500 by paying $35,000 cash and signing a long-term note payable for the balance.

d. Borrowed $3,000 cash by signing a short-term note payable.

e. Paid $40,500 cash to reduce the long-term notes payable.

f. Issued 2,350 shares of common stock for $20 cash per share.

g. Declared and paid cash dividends of $51,900.

Required

Check Cash from operating activities, $42,075

1. Prepare a complete statement of cash flows; report its operating activities using the *indirect method.* Disclose any noncash investing and financing activities in a note.

Analysis Component

2. Analyze and discuss the statement of cash flows prepared in part 1, giving special attention to the wisdom of the cash dividend payment.

Problem 12-2A[A]
Cash flows spreadsheet (indirect method)
P1 P2 P3 P4

Refer to the information reported about Georgia Company in Problem 12-1A.

Required

Prepare a complete statement of cash flows using a spreadsheet as in Exhibit 12A.1; report its operating activities using the indirect method. Identify the debits and credits in the Analysis of Changes columns with letters that correspond to the following list of transactions and events.

a. Net income was $120,575.

b. Accounts receivable increased.

c. Merchandise inventory increased.

d. Prepaid expenses decreased.

e. Accounts payable decreased.

f. Depreciation expense was $20,000.

g. Sold equipment costing $46,500, with accumulated depreciation of $29,000, for $11,625 cash. This yielded a loss of $5,875.

h. Purchased equipment costing $97,500 by paying $35,000 cash and **(i.)** by signing a long-term note payable for the balance.

j. Borrowed $3,000 cash by signing a short-term note payable.

k. Paid $40,500 cash to reduce the long-term notes payable.

l. Issued 2,350 shares of common stock for $20 cash per share.

m. Declared and paid cash dividends of $51,900.

Check Analysis of Changes column totals, $594,850

Problem 12-3A[B]
Statement of cash flows (direct method) C3 P1 P3 P5

Check Cash used in financing activities, $(42,400)

Refer to Georgia Company's financial statements and related information in Problem 12-1A.

Required

Prepare a complete statement of cash flows; report its operating activities according to the *direct method.* Disclose any noncash investing and financing activities in a note.

Problem 12-4A
Statement of cash flows (indirect method) C3 P1 P2 P3

mhhe.com/wildMA2e

Memphis Corp., a merchandiser, recently completed its 2009 operations. For the year, (1) all sales are credit sales, (2) all credits to Accounts Receivable reflect cash receipts from customers, (3) all purchases of inventory are on credit, (4) all debits to Accounts Payable reflect cash payments for inventory, (5) Other Expenses are all cash expenses, and (6) any change in Income Taxes Payable reflects the accrual and cash payment of taxes. The company's balance sheets and income statement follow.

MEMPHIS CORPORATION
Comparative Balance Sheets
December 31, 2009 and 2008

	2009	2008
Assets		
Cash	$ 165,000	$137,000
Accounts receivable	82,000	74,000
Merchandise inventory	620,000	525,000
Equipment	345,000	240,000
Accum. depreciation—Equipment	(159,000)	(102,000)
Total assets	$1,053,000	$874,000
Liabilities and Equity		
Accounts payable	$ 160,000	$ 96,000
Income taxes payable	22,000	19,000
Common stock, $2 par value	588,000	560,000
Paid-in capital in excess of par value, common stock	201,000	159,000
Retained earnings	82,000	40,000
Total liabilities and equity	$1,053,000	$874,000

MEMPHIS CORPORATION
Income Statement
For Year Ended December 31, 2009

Sales		$1,794,000
Cost of goods sold		1,088,000
Gross profit		706,000
Operating expenses		
Depreciation expense	$ 57,000	
Other expenses	500,000	557,000
Income before taxes		149,000
Income taxes expense		22,000
Net income		$ 127,000

Additional Information on Year 2009 Transactions

a. Purchased equipment for $105,000 cash.
b. Issued 14,000 shares of common stock for $5 cash per share.
c. Declared and paid $85,000 in cash dividends.

Required

Prepare a complete statement of cash flows; report its cash inflows and cash outflows from operating activities according to the *indirect method*.

Check Cash from operating activities, $148,000

Problem 12-5A[A]
Cash flows spreadsheet (indirect method)
P1 P2 P3 P4

mhhe.com/wildMA2e

Refer to the information reported about Memphis Corporation in Problem 12-4A.

Required

Prepare a complete statement of cash flows using a spreadsheet as in Exhibit 12A.1; report operating activities under the indirect method. Identify the debits and credits in the Analysis of Changes columns with letters that correspond to the following list of transactions and events.

a. Net income was $127,000.
b. Accounts receivable increased.
c. Merchandise inventory increased.
d. Accounts payable increased.
e. Income taxes payable increased.
f. Depreciation expense was $57,000.
g. Purchased equipment for $105,000 cash.
h. Issued 14,000 shares at $5 cash per share.
i. Declared and paid $85,000 of cash dividends.

Check Analysis of Changes column totals, $614,000

Problem 12-6A[B]
Statement of cash flows (direct method) P1 P3 P5

mhhe.com/wildMA2e

Refer to Memphis Corporation's financial statements and related information in Problem 12-4A.

Required

Prepare a complete statement of cash flows; report its cash flows from operating activities according to the *direct method*.

Check Cash used in financing activities, $(15,000)

Problem 12-7A
Computing cash flows from operations (indirect)
C4 P2

Rawling Company's 2009 income statement and selected balance sheet data at December 31, 2008 and 2009, follow ($ thousands).

RAWLING COMPANY
Selected Balance Sheet Accounts

At Decmber 31	2009	2008
Accounts receivable	$280	$290
Inventory	99	77
Accounts payable	220	230
Salaries payable	44	35
Utilities payable	11	8
Prepaid insurance	13	14
Prepaid rent	11	9

RAWLING COMPANY
Income Statement

Sales revenue	$48,600
Expenses	
Cost of goods sold	21,000
Depreciation expense	6,000
Salaries expense	9,000
Rent expense	4,500
Insurance expense	1,900
Interest expense	1,800
Utilities expense	1,400
Net income	$ 3,000

Required

Prepare the cash flows from operating activities section only of the company's 2009 statement of cash flows using the indirect method.

Check Cash from operating activities, $8,989

Problem 12-8A[B]
Computing cash flows from operations (direct)
C4 P5

Refer to the information in Problem 12-7A.

Required

Prepare the cash flows from operating activities section only of the company's 2009 statement of cash flows using the direct method.

PROBLEM SET B

Problem 12-1B
Statement of cash flows (indirect method)
C2 C3 A1 P1 P2 P3

Wilson Corporation, a merchandiser, recently completed its calendar-year 2009 operations. For the year, (1) all sales are credit sales, (2) all credits to Accounts Receivable reflect cash receipts from customers, (3) all purchases of inventory are on credit, (4) all debits to Accounts Payable reflect cash payments for inventory, and (5) Other Expenses are paid in advance and are initially debited to Prepaid Expenses. The company's balance sheets and income statement follow.

WILSON CORPORATION
Comparative Balance Sheets
December 31, 2009 and 2008

	2009	2008
Assets		
Cash	$ 49,400	$ 74,000
Accounts receivable	65,830	55,000
Merchandise inventory	277,000	252,000
Prepaid expenses	1,250	1,600
Equipment	158,500	107,500
Accum. depreciation—Equipment	(36,625)	(46,000)
Total assets	$515,355	$444,100
Liabilities and Equity		
Accounts payable	$ 55,380	$112,000
Short-term notes payable	9,000	7,000
Long-term notes payable	70,000	48,250
Common stock, $5 par	162,500	150,750
Paid-in capital in excess of par, common stock	35,250	0
Retained earnings	183,225	126,100
Total liabilities and equity	$515,355	$444,100

WILSON CORPORATION
Income Statement
For Year Ended December 31, 2009

Sales		$585,000
Cost of goods sold		285,000
Gross profit		300,000
Operating expenses		
Depreciation expense	$ 20,000	
Other expenses	134,000	
Total operating expenses		154,000
		146,000
Other gains (losses)		
Loss on sale of equipment		5,625
Income before taxes		140,375
Income taxes expense		24,250
Net income		$116,125

Additional Information on Year 2009 Transactions

a. The loss on the cash sale of equipment was $5,625 (details in *b*).

b. Sold equipment costing $46,500, with accumulated depreciation of $29,375, for $11,500 cash.

c. Purchased equipment costing $97,500 by paying $25,000 cash and signing a long-term note payable for the balance.

d. Borrowed $2,000 cash by signing a short-term note payable.

e. Paid $50,750 cash to reduce the long-term notes payable.

f. Issued 2,350 shares of common stock for $20 cash per share.

g. Declared and paid cash dividends of $59,000.

Required

1. Prepare a complete statement of cash flows; report its operating activities using the *indirect method*. Disclose any noncash investing and financing activities in a note.

Check Cash from operating activities, $49,650

Analysis Component

2. Analyze and discuss the statement of cash flows prepared in part 1, giving special attention to the wisdom of the cash dividend payment.

Problem 12-2B[A]
Cash flows spreadsheet (indirect method)
P1 P2 P3 P4

Refer to the information reported about Wilson Corporation in Problem 12-1B.

Required

Prepare a complete statement of cash flows using a spreadsheet as in Exhibit 12A.1; report its operating activities using the *indirect method*. Identify the debits and credits in the Analysis of Changes columns with letters that correspond to the following list of transactions and events.

a. Net income was $116,125.

b. Accounts receivable increased.

c. Merchandise inventory increased.

d. Prepaid expenses decreased.

e. Accounts payable decreased.

f. Depreciation expense was $20,000.

g. Sold equipment costing $46,500, with accumulated depreciation of $29,375, for $11,500 cash. This yielded a loss of $5,625.

h. Purchased equipment costing $97,500 by paying $25,000 cash and **(i.)** by signing a long-term note payable for the balance.

j. Borrowed $2,000 cash by signing a short-term note payable.

k. Paid $50,750 cash to reduce the long-term notes payable.

l. Issued 2,350 shares of common stock for $20 cash per share.

m. Declared and paid cash dividends of $59,000.

Check Analysis of Changes column totals, $604,175

Problem 12-3B[B]
Statement of cash flows (direct method)
C3 P1 P3 P5

Refer to Wilson Corporation's financial statements and related information in Problem 12-1B.

Required

Prepare a complete statement of cash flows; report its operating activities according to the *direct method*. Disclose any noncash investing and financing activities in a note.

Check Cash used in financing activities, $(60,750)

Problem 12-4B
Statement of cash flows (indirect method)
C3 P1 P2 P3

Prius Company, a merchandiser, recently completed its 2009 operations. For the year, (1) all sales are credit sales, (2) all credits to Accounts Receivable reflect cash receipts from customers, (3) all purchases of inventory are on credit, (4) all debits to Accounts Payable reflect cash payments for inventory, (5) Other Expenses are cash expenses, and (6) any change in Income Taxes Payable reflects the accrual and cash payment of taxes. The company's balance sheets and income statement follow.

PRIUS COMPANY
Comparative Balance Sheets
December 31, 2009 and 2008

	2009	2008
Assets		
Cash	$ 164,000	$ 131,000
Accounts receivable	82,000	70,000
Merchandise inventory	605,000	515,000
Equipment	350,000	276,000
Accum. depreciation—Equipment	(157,000)	(102,000)
Total assets	$1,044,000	$ 890,000
Liabilities and Equity		
Accounts payable	$ 173,000	$ 119,000
Income taxes payable	20,000	17,000
Common stock, $2 par value	580,000	560,000
Paid-in capital in excess of par, common stock	193,000	163,000
Retained earnings	78,000	31,000
Total liabilities and equity	$1,044,000	$ 890,000

PRIUS COMPANY
Income Statement
For Year Ended December 31, 2009

Sales		$1,792,000
Cost of goods sold		1,087,000
Gross profit		705,000
Operating expenses		
Depreciation expense	$ 55,000	
Other expenses	494,000	549,000
Income before taxes		156,000
Income taxes expense		24,000
Net income		$ 132,000

Additional Information on Year 2009 Transactions

a. Purchased equipment for $74,000 cash.
b. Issued 10,000 shares of common stock for $5 cash per share.
c. Declared and paid $85,000 of cash dividends.

Required

Prepare a complete statement of cash flows; report its cash inflows and cash outflows from operating activities according to the *indirect method*.

Check Cash from operating activities, $142,000

Problem 12-5B[A]
Cash flows spreadsheet (indirect method)
P1 P2 P3 P4

Refer to the information reported about Prius Company in Problem 12-4B.

Required

Prepare a complete statement of cash flows using a spreadsheet as in Exhibit 12A.1; report operating activities under the *indirect method*. Identify the debits and credits in the Analysis of Changes columns with letters that correspond to the following list of transactions and events.

a. Net income was $132,000.
b. Accounts receivable increased.
c. Merchandise inventory increased.
d. Accounts payable increased.
e. Income taxes payable increased.
f. Depreciation expense was $55,000.
g. Purchased equipment for $74,000 cash.
h. Issued 10,000 shares at $5 cash per share.
i. Declared and paid $85,000 of cash dividends.

Check Analysis of Changes column totals, $555,000

Problem 12-6B[B]
Statement of cash flows (direct method) P1 P3 P5

Refer to Prius Company's financial statements and related information in Problem 12-4B.

Required

Prepare a complete statement of cash flows; report its cash flows from operating activities according to the *direct method.*

Check Cash used by financing activities, $(35,000)

Problem 12-7B
Computing cash flows from operations (indirect)
C4 P2

Kodak Company's 2009 income statement and selected balance sheet data at December 31, 2008 and 2009, follow ($ thousands).

KODAK COMPANY Income Statement	
Sales revenue	$312,000
Expenses	
Cost of goods sold	144,000
Depreciation expense	64,000
Salaries expense	40,000
Rent expense	10,000
Insurance expense	5,200
Interest expense	4,800
Utilities expense	4,000
Net income	$ 40,000

KODAK COMPANY Selected Balance Sheet Accounts		
At December 31	2009	2008
Accounts receivable	$720	$600
Inventory	172	196
Accounts payable	480	520
Salaries payable	180	120
Utilities payable	40	0
Prepaid insurance	28	36
Prepaid rent	20	40

Required

Prepare the cash flows from operating activities section only of the company's 2009 statement of cash flows using the indirect method.

Check Cash from operating activities, $103,992

Problem 12-8B[B]
Computing cash flows from operations (direct)
C4 P5

Refer to the information in Problem 12-7B.

Required

Prepare the cash flows from operating activities section only of the company's 2009 statement of cash flows using the direct method.

SERIAL PROBLEM

Success Systems

(This serial problem began in Chapter 1 and continues through most of the book. If previous chapter segments were not completed, the serial problem can begin at this point. It is helpful, but not necessary, to use the Working Papers that accompany the book.)

SP 12 Adriana Lopez, owner of Success Systems, decides to prepare a statement of cash flows for her business. (Although the serial problem allowed for various ownership changes in earlier chapters, we will prepare the statement of cash flows using the following financial data.)

SUCCESS SYSTEMS
Income Statement
For Three Months Ended March 31, 2010

Computer services revenue		$25,160
Net sales		18,693
Total revenue		43,853
Cost of goods sold	$14,052	
Depreciation expense—Office equipment	400	
Depreciation expense—Computer equipment	1,250	
Wages expense	3,250	
Insurance expense	555	
Rent expense	2,475	
Computer supplies expense	1,305	
Advertising expense	600	
Mileage expense	320	
Repairs expense—Computer	960	
Total expenses		25,167
Net income		$18,686

SUCCESS SYSTEMS
Comparative Balance Sheets
December 31, 2009, and March 31, 2010

	2010	2009
Assets		
Cash	$ 77,845	$58,160
Accounts receivable	22,720	5,668
Merchandise inventory	704	0
Computer supplies	2,005	580
Prepaid insurance	1,110	1,665
Prepaid rent	825	825
Office equipment	8,000	8,000
Accumulated depreciation—Office equipment	(800)	(400)
Computer equipment	20,000	20,000
Accumulated depreciation—Computer equipment	(2,500)	(1,250)
Total assets	$129,909	$93,248
Liabilities and Equity		
Accounts payable	$ 0	$ 1,100
Wages payable	875	500
Unearned computer service revenue	0	1,500
Common stock	108,000	83,000
Retained earnings	21,034	7,148
Total liabilities and equity	$129,909	$93,248

Required

Prepare a statement of cash flows for Success Systems using the *indirect method* for the three months ended March 31, 2010. Recall that the owner Adriana Lopez contributed $25,000 to the business in exchange for additional stock in the first quarter of 2010 and has received $4,800 in cash dividends.

Check Cash flows used by operations: $(515)

BEYOND THE NUMBERS

REPORTING IN ACTION

C4 A1

BTN 12-1 Refer to **Best Buy**'s financial statements in Appendix A to answer the following.

1. Is Best Buy's statement of cash flows prepared under the direct method or the indirect method? How do you know?
2. For each fiscal year 2007, 2006, and 2005, is the amount of cash provided by operating activities more or less than the cash paid for dividends?
3. What is the largest amount in reconciling the difference between net income and cash flow from operating activities in 2007? In 2006? In 2005?
4. Identify the largest cash flows for investing and for financing activities in 2007 and in 2006.

Fast Forward

5. Obtain Best Buy's financial statements for a fiscal year ending after March 3, 2007, from either its Website (BestBuy.com) or the SEC's EDGAR database (www.sec.gov). Since March 3, 2007, what are Best Buy's largest cash outflows and cash inflows in the investing and in the financing sections of its statement of cash flow?

BTN 12-2 Key figures for **Best Buy**, **Circuit City**, and **RadioShack** follow.

COMPARATIVE ANALYSIS

A1 A2

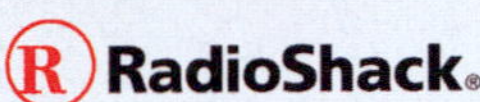

($ millions)	Best Buy			Circuit City			RadioShack		
	Current Year	1 Year Prior	2 Years Prior	Current Year	1 Year Prior	2 Years Prior	Current Year	1 Year Prior	2 Years Prior
Operating cash flows	$ 1,762	$ 1,740	$ 1,981	$ 316	$ 365	$ 389	$ 315	$ 363	$ 353
Total assets	13,570	11,864	10,294	4,007	4,069	3,840	2,070	2,205	2,517

Required

1. Compute the recent two years' cash flow on total assets ratios for Best Buy, Circuit City, and RadioShack.
2. What does the cash flow on total assets ratio measure?
3. Which company has the highest cash flow on total assets ratio for the periods shown?
4. Does the cash flow on total assets ratio reflect on the quality of earnings? Explain.

BTN 12-3 Kaelyn Gish is preparing for a meeting with her banker. Her business is finishing its fourth year of operations. In the first year, it had negative cash flows from operations. In the second and third years, cash flows from operations were positive. However, inventory costs rose significantly in year 4, and cash flows from operations will probably be down 25%. Gish wants to secure a line of credit from her banker as a financing buffer. From experience, she knows the banker will scrutinize operating cash flows for years 1 through 4 and will want a projected number for year 5. Gish knows that a steady progression upward in operating cash flows for years 1 through 4 will help her case. She decides to use her discretion as owner and considers several business actions that will turn her operating cash flow in year 4 from a decrease to an increase.

ETHICS CHALLENGE

C1 C2 A1

Required

1. Identify two business actions Gish might take to improve cash flows from operations.
2. Comment on the ethics and possible consequences of Gish's decision to pursue these actions.

BTN 12-4 Your friend, Hanna Willard, recently completed the second year of her business and just received annual financial statements from her accountant. Willard finds the income statement and balance sheet informative but does not understand the statement of cash flows. She says the first section is especially confusing because it contains a lot of additions and subtractions that do not make sense to her. Willard adds, "The income statement tells me the business is more profitable than last year and that's most important. If I want to know how cash changes, I can look at comparative balance sheets."

COMMUNICATING IN PRACTICE

C1 C4

Required

Write a half-page memorandum to your friend explaining the purpose of the statement of cash flows. Speculate as to why the first section is so confusing and how it might be rectified.

BTN 12-5 Access the April 19, 2007, filing of the 10-K report (for fiscal year ending February 3, 2007) of **J. Crew Group, Inc.**, at www.sec.gov.

TAKING IT TO THE NET

A1

Required

1. Does J. Crew use the direct or indirect method to construct its consolidated statement of cash flows?
2. For the fiscal year ended February 3, 2007, what is the largest item in reconciling the net income to net cash provided by operating activities?
3. In the recent three years, has the company been more successful in generating operating cash flows or in generating net income? Identify the figures to support the answer.
4. In the year ended February 3, 2007, what was the largest cash outflow for investing activities and for financing activities?
5. What item(s) does J. Crew report as supplementary cash flow information?
6. Does J. Crew report any noncash financing activities for fiscal year 2007? Identify them, if any.

TEAMWORK IN ACTION

C1 C4 A1 P2 P5

BTN 12-6 Team members are to coordinate and independently answer one question within each of the following three sections. Team members should then report to the team and confirm or correct teammates' answers.

1. Answer *one* of the following questions about the statement of cash flows.
   a. What are this statement's reporting objectives?
   b. What two methods are used to prepare it? Identify similarities and differences between them.
   c. What steps are followed to prepare the statement?
   d. What types of analyses are often made from this statement's information?
2. Identify and explain the adjustment from net income to obtain cash flows from operating activities using the indirect method for *one* of the following items.
   a. Noncash operating revenues and expenses.
   b. Nonoperating gains and losses.
   c. Increases and decreases in noncash current assets.
   d. Increases and decreases in current liabilities.
3. [B]Identify and explain the formula for computing cash flows from operating activities using the direct method for *one* of the following items.
   a. Cash receipts from sales to customers.
   b. Cash paid for merchandise inventory.
   c. Cash paid for wages and operating expenses.
   d. Cash paid for interest and taxes.

Note: For teams of more than four, some pairing within teams is necessary. Use as an in-class activity or as an assignment. If used in class, specify a time limit on each part. Conclude with reports to the entire class, using team rotation. Each team can prepare responses on a transparency.

ENTREPRENEURIAL DECISION

C1 A1

BTN 12-7 Review the chapter's opener involving **Jungle Jim's International Market**.

Required

1. In a business such as Jungle Jim's, monitoring cash flow is always a priority. Even though Jungle Jim's now has thousands in annual sales and earns a positive net income, explain how cash flow can lag behind earnings.
2. Jungle Jim's is a closely held corporation. What are potential sources of financing for its future expansion?

C2 A1

BTN 12-8 Jenna and Matt Wilder are completing their second year operating Mountain High, a downhill ski area and resort. Mountain High reports a net loss of $(10,000) for its second year, which includes an $85,000 extraordinary loss from fire. This past year also involved major purchases of plant assets for renovation and expansion, yielding a year-end total asset amount of $800,000. Mountain High's net cash outflow for its second year is $(5,000); a summarized version of its statement of cash flows follows:

Net cash flow provided by operating activities	$295,000
Net cash flow used by investing activities	(310,000)
Net cash flow provided by financing activities	10,000

Required

Write a one-page memorandum to the Wilders evaluating Mountain High's current performance and assessing its future. Give special emphasis to cash flow data and their interpretation.

HITTING THE ROAD

C1

BTN 12-9 Visit **The Motley Fool**'s Website (Fool.com). Click on the sidebar link titled *Fool's School* (or *Fool.com/School*). Identify and select the link *How to Value Stocks*.

Required

1. Click on *Introduction to Valuation,* and then *Cash-Flow-Based Valuations.* How does the Fool's school define cash flow? What is the School's reasoning for this definition?
2. Per the school's instruction, why do analysts focus on earnings before interest and taxes (EBIT)?
3. Visit other links at this Website that interest you such as "How to Read a Balance Sheet," or find out what the "Fool's Ratio" is. Write a half-page report on what you find.

BTN 12-10 Key comparative information for **DSG international plc** (DSGiplc.com) follows.

GLOBAL DECISION

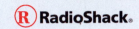

C1 C2 C4

RadioShack.

(£ millions)	Current Year	1 Year Prior	2 Years Prior
Operating cash flows	£ 207	£ 338	£ 375
Total assets	3,977	4,120	4,104

Required

1. Compute the recent two years' cash flow on total assets ratio for DSG.

2. How does DSG's ratio compare to Best Buy's, Circuit City's, and RadioShack's ratios from BTN 12-2?

ANSWERS TO MULTIPLE CHOICE QUIZ

1. b;

Net income	$15,200
Depreciation expense	10,000
Gain on sale of land	(3,000)
Increase in inventory	(1,500)
Increase in accounts payable	2,850
Net cash provided by operations	$23,550

2. c; cash received from sale of machine is reported as an investing activity.

3. d; FASB requires cash interest paid to be reported under operating.

4. a; Cash paid for salaries and wages = $255,000 + $8,200 − $10,900 = $252,300

5. e; Increase in inventory = $112,000 − $105,000 = $7,000
Increase in accounts payable = $101,300 − $98,500 = $2,800
Cash paid for merchandise = $545,000 + $7,000 − $2,800 = $549,200

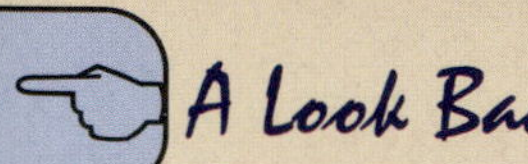

A Look Back

Chapter 12 focused on reporting and analyzing cash inflows and cash outflows. We explained how to prepare, analyze, and interpret the statement of cash flows.

A Look at This Chapter

This chapter emphasizes the analysis and interpretation of financial statement information. We learn to apply horizontal, vertical, and ratio analyses to better understand company performance and financial condition.

Chapter 13 Analyzing and Interpreting Financial Statements

Learning Objectives

CAP

Conceptual

C1 Explain the purpose of analysis. *(p. 476)*

C2 Identify the building blocks of analysis. *(p. 477)*

C3 Describe standards for comparisons in analysis. *(p. 478)*

C4 Identify the tools of analysis. *(p. 478)*

Analytical

A1 Summarize and report results of analysis. *(p. 496)*

A2 *Appendix 13A*—Explain the form and assess the content of a complete income statement. *(p. 499)*

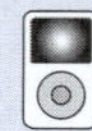

LP13

Procedural

P1 Explain and apply methods of horizontal analysis. *(p. 478)*

P2 Describe and apply methods of vertical analysis. *(p. 483)*

P3 Define and apply ratio analysis. *(p. 486)*

Decision Feature

Motley Fool

"What goes on at The Motley Fool . . . is similar to what goes on in a library"
—Tom Gardner (David Gardner on left)

ALEXANDRIA, VA—In Shakespeare's Elizabethan comedy *As You Like It,* only the fool could speak truthfully to the King without getting his head lopped off. Inspired by Shakespeare's stage character, Tom and David Gardner vowed to become modern-day fools who tell it like it is. With under $10,000 in start-up money, the brothers launched **The Motley Fool (Fool.com).** And befitting of a Shakespearean play, the two say they are "dedicated to educating, amusing, and enriching individuals in search of the truth."

The Gardners do not fear the wrath of any King, real or fictional. They are intent on exposing the truth, as they see it, "that the financial world preys on ignorance and fear." As Tom explains, "There is such a great need in the general populace for financial information." Who can argue, given their brilliant success through practically every medium; including their Website, radio shows, newspaper columns, online store, investment newsletters, and global expansion.

Despite the brothers' best efforts, however, ordinary people still do not fully use information contained in financial statements. For instance, discussions keep appearing on The Motley Fool's online bulletin board that can be easily resolved using reliable and available accounting data. So, it would seem that the Fools must continue their work of "educating and enriching" individuals.

Resembling The Motley Fools' objectives, this chapter introduces horizontal and vertical analyses—tools used to reveal crucial trends and insights from financial information. It also expands on ratio analysis, which gives insight into a company's financial condition and performance. By arming ourselves with the information contained in this chapter and the investment advice of The Motley Fool, *we* can be sure to not play the fool in today's financial world.

[Sources: *Motley Fool Website,* March 2009; *Entrepreneur,* July 1997; *What to Do with Your Money Now,* June 2002; *USA Weekend,* July 2004; *Washington Post,* November 2007; *Money after 40,* April 2007]

Chapter Preview

This chapter shows how we use financial statements to evaluate a company's financial performance and condition. We explain financial statement analysis, its basic building blocks, the information available, standards for comparisons, and tools of analysis. Three major analysis tools are presented: horizontal analysis, vertical analysis, and ratio analysis. We apply each of these tools using **Best Buy**'s financial statements, and we introduce comparative analysis using **Circuit City** and **RadioShack**. This chapter expands and organizes the ratio analyses introduced at the end of each chapter.

Analyzing and Interpreting Financial Statements

Basics of Analysis	Horizontal Analysis	Vertical Analysis	Ratio Analysis
• Purpose • Building blocks • Information • Standards for comparisons • Tools	• Comparative balance sheets • Comparative income statements • Trend analysis	• Common-size balance sheet • Common-size income statement • Common-size graphics	• Liquidity and efficiency • Solvency • Profitability • Market prospects • Ratio summary

Basics of Analysis

Video13.1

Financial statement analysis applies analytical tools to general-purpose financial statements and related data for making business decisions. It involves transforming accounting data into more useful information. Financial statement analysis reduces our reliance on hunches, guesses, and intuition as well as our uncertainty in decision making. It does not lessen the need for expert judgment; instead, it provides us an effective and systematic basis for making business decisions. This section describes the purpose of financial statement analysis, its information sources, the use of comparisons, and some issues in computations.

Purpose of Analysis

C1 Explain the purpose of analysis.

Internal users of accounting information are those involved in strategically managing and operating the company. They include managers, officers, internal auditors, consultants, budget directors, and market researchers. The purpose of financial statement analysis for these users is to provide strategic information to improve company efficiency and effectiveness in providing products and services.

External users of accounting information are *not* directly involved in running the company. They include shareholders, lenders, directors, customers, suppliers, regulators, lawyers, brokers, and the press. External users rely on financial statement analysis to make better and more informed decisions in pursuing their own goals.

Point: Financial statement analysis tools are also used for personal financial investment decisions.

We can identify other uses of financial statement analysis. Shareholders and creditors assess company prospects to make investing and lending decisions. A board of directors analyzes financial statements in monitoring management's decisions. Employees and unions use financial statements in labor negotiations. Suppliers use financial statement information in establishing credit terms. Customers analyze financial statements in deciding whether to establish supply relationships. Public utilities set customer rates by analyzing financial statements. Auditors use financial statements in assessing the "fair presentation" of their clients' financial results. Analyst services such as **Dun & Bradstreet**, **Moody's**, and **Standard & Poor's** use financial statements in making buy-sell recommendations and in setting credit ratings. The common goal of these users is to evaluate company performance and financial condition. This includes evaluating (1) past and current performance, (2) current financial position, and (3) future performance and risk.

Point: Financial statement analysis is a topic on the CPA, CMA, CIA, and CFA exams.

Building Blocks of Analysis

C2 Identify the building blocks of analysis.

Financial statement analysis focuses on one or more elements of a company's financial condition or performance. Our analysis emphasizes four areas of inquiry—with varying degrees of importance. These four areas are described and illustrated in this chapter and are considered the *building blocks* of financial statement analysis:

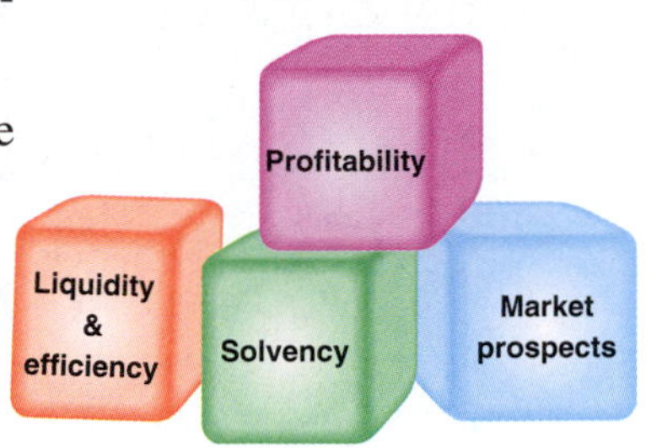

- **Liquidity** and **efficiency**—ability to meet short-term obligations and to efficiently generate revenues.
- **Solvency**—ability to generate future revenues and meet long-term obligations.
- **Profitability**—ability to provide financial rewards sufficient to attract and retain financing.
- **Market prospects**—ability to generate positive market expectations.

Applying the building blocks of financial statement analysis involves determining (1) the objectives of analysis and (2) the relative emphasis among the building blocks. We distinguish among these four building blocks to emphasize the different aspects of a company's financial condition or performance, yet we must remember that these areas of analysis are interrelated. For instance, a company's operating performance is affected by the availability of financing and short-term liquidity conditions. Similarly, a company's credit standing is not limited to satisfactory short-term liquidity but depends also on its profitability and efficiency in using assets. Early in our analysis, we need to determine the relative emphasis of each building block. Emphasis and analysis can later change as a result of evidence collected.

Decision Insight

Chips and Brokers The phrase *blue chips* refers to stock of big, profitable companies. The phrase comes from poker; where the most valuable chips are blue. The term *brokers* refers to those who execute orders to buy or sell stock. The term comes from wine retailers—individuals who broach (break) wine casks.

Information for Analysis

Some users, such as managers and regulatory authorities, are able to receive special financial reports prepared to meet their analysis needs. However, most users must rely on **general-purpose financial statements** that include the (1) income statement, (2) balance sheet, (3) statement of stockholders' equity (or statement of retained earnings), (4) statement of cash flows, and (5) notes to these statements.

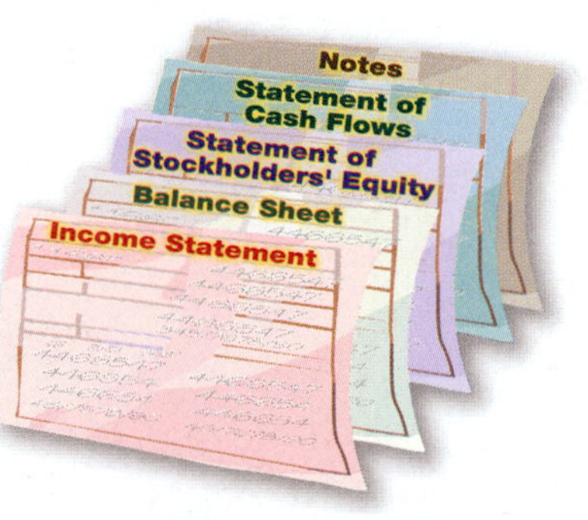

Financial reporting refers to the communication of financial information useful for making investment, credit, and other business decisions. Financial reporting includes not only general-purpose financial statements but also information from SEC 10-K or other filings, press releases, shareholders' meetings, forecasts, management letters, auditors' reports, and Webcasts.

Management's Discussion and Analysis (MD&A) is one example of useful information outside traditional financial statements. **Best Buy**'s MD&A (available at BestBuy.com), for example, begins with an overview and strategic initiatives. It then discusses operating results followed by liquidity and capital resources—roughly equivalent to investing and financing. The final few parts discuss special financing arrangements, key accounting policies, interim results, and the next year's outlook. The MD&A is an excellent starting point in understanding a company's business activities.

Decision Insight

Analysis Online Many Websites offer free access and screening of companies by key numbers such as earnings, sales, and book value. For instance, **Standard & Poor's** has information for more than 10,000 stocks (StandardPoor.com).

Standards for Comparisons

C3 Describe standards for comparisons in analysis.

When interpreting measures from financial statement analysis, we need to decide whether the measures indicate good, bad, or average performance. To make such judgments, we need standards (benchmarks) for comparisons that include the following:

- *Intracompany*—The company under analysis can provide standards for comparisons based on its own prior performance and relations between its financial items. **Best Buy**'s current net income, for instance, can be compared with its prior years' net income and in relation to its revenues or total assets.
- *Competitor*—One or more direct competitors of the company being analyzed can provide standards for comparisons. **Coca-Cola**'s profit margin, for instance, can be compared with **PepsiCo**'s profit margin.
- *Industry*—Industry statistics can provide standards of comparisons. Such statistics are available from services such as **Dun & Bradstreet**, **Standard & Poor's**, and **Moody's**.
- *Guidelines (rules of thumb)*—General standards of comparisons can develop from experience. Examples are the 2:1 level for the current ratio or 1:1 level for the acid-test ratio. Guidelines, or rules of thumb, must be carefully applied because context is crucial.

Point: Each chapter's *Reporting in Action* problems engage students in *intracompany* analysis, whereas *Comparative Analysis* problems require competitor analysis (Best Buy vs. Circuit City).

All of these comparison standards are useful when properly applied, yet measures taken from a selected competitor or group of competitors are often best. Intracompany and industry measures are also important. Guidelines or rules of thumb should be applied with care, and then only if they seem reasonable given past experience and industry norms.

Tools of Analysis

C4 Identify the tools of analysis.

Three of the most common tools of financial statement analysis are

1. **Horizontal analysis**—Comparison of a company's financial condition and performance across time.
2. **Vertical analysis**—Comparison of a company's financial condition and performance to a base amount.
3. **Ratio analysis**—Measurement of key relations between financial statement items.

The remainder of this chapter describes these analysis tools and how to apply them.

Quick Check

Answers—p. 502

1. Who are the intended users of general-purpose financial statements?
2. General-purpose financial statements consist of what information?
3. Which of the following is *least* useful as a basis for comparison when analyzing ratios? (*a*) Company results from a different economic setting. (*b*) Standards from past experience. (*c*) Rule-of-thumb standards. (*d*) Industry averages.
4. What is the preferred basis of comparison for ratio analysis?

Horizontal Analysis

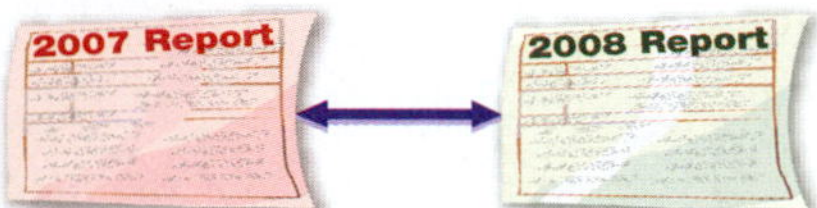

Analysis of any single financial number is of limited value. Instead, much of financial statement analysis involves identifying and describing relations between numbers, groups of numbers, and changes in those numbers. Horizontal analysis refers to examination of financial statement data *across time*. [The term *horizontal analysis* arises from the left-to-right (or right-to-left) movement of our eyes as we review comparative financial statements across time.]

Comparative Statements

P1 Explain and apply methods of horizontal analysis.

Comparing amounts for two or more successive periods often helps in analyzing financial statements. **Comparative financial statements** facilitate this comparison by showing financial amounts in side-by-side columns on a single statement, called a *comparative format*. Using figures from **Best Buy**'s financial statements, this section explains how to compute dollar changes and percent changes for comparative statements.

Video13.1

Computation of Dollar Changes and Percent Changes Comparing financial statements over relatively short time periods—two to three years—is often done by analyzing changes in line items. A change analysis usually includes analyzing absolute dollar amount changes and percent changes. Both analyses are relevant because dollar changes can yield large percent changes inconsistent with their importance. For instance, a 50% change from a base figure of $100 is less important than the same percent change from a base amount of $100,000 in the same statement. Reference to dollar amounts is necessary to retain a proper perspective and to assess the importance of changes. We compute the *dollar change* for a financial statement item as follows:

Example: What is a more significant change, a 70% increase on a $1,000 expense or a 30% increase on a $400,000 expense? *Answer:* The 30% increase.

$$\textbf{Dollar change} = \textbf{Analysis period amount} - \textbf{Base period amount}$$

Analysis period is the point or period of time for the financial statements under analysis, and *base period* is the point or period of time for the financial statements used for comparison purposes. The prior year is commonly used as a base period. We compute the *percent change* by dividing the dollar change by the base period amount and then multiplying this quantity by 100 as follows:

$$\textbf{Percent change (\%)} = \frac{\textbf{Analysis period amount} - \textbf{Base period amount}}{\textbf{Base period amount}} \times 100$$

We can always compute a dollar change, but we must be aware of a few rules in working with percent changes. To illustrate, look at four separate cases in this chart:

			Change Analysis	
Case	Analysis Period	Base Period	Dollar	Percent
A	$ 1,500	$(4,500)	$ 6,000	—
B	(1,000)	2,000	(3,000)	—
C	8,000	—	8,000	—
D	0	10,000	(10,000)	(100%)

When a negative amount appears in the base period and a positive amount in the analysis period (or vice versa), we cannot compute a meaningful percent change; see cases A and B. Also, when no value is in the base period, no percent change is computable; see case C. Finally, when an item has a value in the base period and zero in the analysis period, the decrease is 100 percent; see case D.

Example: When there is a value in the base period and zero in the analysis period, the decrease is 100%. Why isn't the reverse situation an increase of 100%? *Answer:* A 100% increase of zero is still zero.

It is common when using horizontal analysis to compare amounts to either average or median values from prior periods (average and median values smooth out erratic or unusual fluctuations).[1] We also commonly round percents and ratios to one or two decimal places, but practice on this matter is not uniform. Computations are as detailed as necessary, which is judged by whether rounding potentially affects users' decisions. Computations should not be excessively detailed so that important relations are lost among a mountain of decimal points and digits.

Comparative Balance Sheets Comparative balance sheets consist of balance sheet amounts from two or more balance sheet dates arranged side by side. Its usefulness is often improved by showing each item's dollar change and percent change to highlight large changes.

[1] *Median* is the middle value in a group of numbers. For instance, if five prior years' incomes are (in 000s) $15, $19, $18, $20, and $22, the median value is $19. When there are two middle numbers, we can take their average. For instance, if four prior years' sales are (in 000s) $84, $91, $96, and $93, the median is $92 (computed as the average of $91 and $93).

Point: Spreadsheet programs can help with horizontal, vertical, and ratio analyses, including graphical depictions of financial relations.

Point: Business consultants use comparative statement analysis to provide management advice.

Analysis of comparative financial statements begins by focusing on items that show large dollar or percent changes. We then try to identify the reasons for these changes and, if possible, determine whether they are favorable or unfavorable. We also follow up on items with small changes when we expected the changes to be large.

Exhibit 13.1 shows comparative balance sheets for **Best Buy**. A few items stand out. Many asset categories substantially increase, which is probably not surprising because Best Buy is a growth company. Much of the increase in current assets is from the 20.7% increase in merchandise inventories. The long-term assets of property, equipment, and goodwill also increased. Of course, its sizeable total asset growth of 14.4% must be accompanied by future income to validate Best Buy's growth strategy.

We likewise see substantial increases on the financing side, the most notable ones being accounts payable and long-term debt totaling about $1,112 million. The increase in payables is related to the increase in cash levels, and the increase in debt is partly explained by the increase in long-term assets. Best Buy also reinvested much of its income as reflected in the $1,203 million increase in retained earnings. Again, we must monitor these increases in

EXHIBIT 13.1

Comparative Balance Sheets

BEST BUY
Comparative Balance Sheets
March 3, 2007, and February 25, 2006

($ millions)	2007	2006	Dollar Change	Percent Change
Assets				
Cash and cash equivalents	$ 1,205	$ 748	$ 457	61.1%
Short-term investments	2,588	3,041	(453)	(14.9)
Receivables, net	548	449	99	22.0
Merchandise inventories	4,028	3,338	690	20.7
Other current assets	712	409	303	74.1
Total current assets	9,081	7,985	1,096	13.7
Property and equipment	4,904	4,836	68	1.4
Less accumulated depreciation	1,966	2,124	(158)	(7.4)
Net property and equipment	2,938	2,712	226	8.3
Goodwill	919	557	362	65.0
Tradenames	81	44	37	84.1
Long-term investments	318	218	100	45.9
Other long-term assets	233	348	(115)	(33.0)
Total assets	$13,570	$11,864	$1,706	14.4
Liabilities				
Accounts payable	$ 3,934	$ 3,234	$ 700	21.6%
Unredeemed gift card liabilities	496	469	27	5.8
Accrued compensation and related expenses	332	354	(22)	(6.2)
Accrued liabilities	990	878	112	12.8
Accrued income taxes	489	703	(214)	(30.4)
Short-term debt	41	0	41	—
Current portion of long-term debt	19	418	(399)	(95.5)
Total current liabilities	6,301	6,056	245	4.0
Long-term liabilities	443	373	70	18.8
Long-term debt	590	178	412	231.5
Minority interests	35	0	35	—
Stockholders' Equity				
Common stock	48	49	(1)	(2.0)
Additional paid-in capital	430	643	(213)	(33.1)
Retained earnings	5,507	4,304	1,203	28.0
Accumulated other comprehensive income	216	261	(45)	(17.2)
Total stockholders' equity	6,201	5,257	944	18.0
Total liabilities and stockholders' equity	$13,570	$11,864	$1,706	14.4

investing and financing activities to be sure they are reflected in increased operating performance.

Comparative Income Statements Comparative income statements are prepared similarly to comparative balance sheets. Amounts for two or more periods are placed side by side, with additional columns for dollar and percent changes. Exhibit 13.2 shows Best Buy's comparative income statements.

EXHIBIT 13.2

Comparative Income Statements

BEST BUY
Comparative Income Statements
For Years Ended March 3, 2007, and February 25, 2006

($ millions, except per share data)	2007	2006	Dollar Change	Percent Change
Revenues	$35,934	$30,848	$5,086	16.5%
Cost of goods sold	27,165	23,122	4,043	17.5
Gross profit	8,769	7,726	1,043	13.5
Selling, general, and administrative expenses	6,770	6,082	688	11.3
Operating income	1,999	1,644	355	21.6
Net interest income (expense)	111	77	34	44.2
Gain on investments	20	0	20	—
Earnings from continuing operations before income taxes	2,130	1,721	409	23.8
Income tax expense	752	581	171	29.4
Minority interest in earnings	1	0	1	—
Net earnings	$ 1,377	$ 1,140	$ 237	20.8
Basic earnings per share	$ 2.86	$ 2.33	$ 0.53	22.7
Diluted earnings per share	$ 2.79	$ 2.27	$ 0.52	22.9

Best Buy has substantial revenue growth of 16.5% in 2007. This finding helps support management's growth strategy as reflected in the comparative balance sheets. Best Buy also reveals some ability to control cost of sales and general and administrative expenses, which increased 17.5% and 11.3%, respectively. Best Buy's net income growth of 20.8% on revenue growth of 16.5% is impressive.

Point: Percent change can also be computed by dividing the current period by the prior period and subtracting 1.0. For example, the 16.5% revenue increase of Exhibit 13.2 is computed as: ($35,934/$30,848) − 1.

Trend Analysis

Trend analysis, also called *trend percent analysis* or *index number trend analysis,* is a form of horizontal analysis that can reveal patterns in data across successive periods. It involves computing trend percents for a series of financial numbers and is a variation on the use of percent changes. The difference is that trend analysis does not subtract the base period amount in the numerator. To compute trend percents, we do the following:

1. Select a *base period* and assign each item in the base period a weight of 100%.
2. Express financial numbers as a percent of their base period number.

Specifically, a *trend percent,* also called an *index number,* is computed as follows:

$$\text{Trend percent (\%)} = \frac{\text{Analysis period amount}}{\text{Base period amount}} \times 100$$

Point: *Index* refers to the comparison of the analysis period to the base period. Percents determined for each period are called *index numbers.*

To illustrate trend analysis, we use the **Best Buy** data shown in Exhibit 13.3.

EXHIBIT 13.3

Revenues and Expenses

($ millions)	2007	2006	2005	2004	2003
Revenues	$35,934	$30,848	$27,433	$24,548	$20,943
Cost of goods sold	27,165	23,122	20,938	18,677	15,998
Selling, general & administrative expenses	6,770	6,082	5,053	4,567	3,935

These data are from Best Buy's *Selected Financial Data* section. The base period is 2003 and the trend percent is computed in each subsequent year by dividing that year's amount by its 2003 amount. For instance, the revenue trend percent for 2007 is 171.6%, computed as $35,934/$20,943. The trend percents—using the data from Exhibit 13.3—are shown in Exhibit 13.4.

EXHIBIT 13.4

Trend Percents for Revenues and Expenses

	2007	2006	2005	2004	2003
Revenues	171.6%	147.3%	131.0%	117.2%	100.0%
Cost of goods sold	169.8	144.5	130.9	116.7	100.0
Selling, general & administrative expenses	172.0	154.6	128.4	116.1	100.0

Point: Trend analysis expresses a percent of base, not a percent of change.

Graphical depictions often aid analysis of trend percents. Exhibit 13.5 shows the trend percents from Exhibit 13.4 in a *line graph,* which can help us identify trends and detect changes in direction or magnitude. It reveals that the trend line for revenues consistently exceeds that for cost of goods sold. Moreover, the magnitude of that difference has slightly grown. This result bodes well for Best Buy because its cost of goods sold are by far its largest cost, and the company shows an ability to control these expenses as it expands. The line graph also reveals a consistent increase in each of these accounts, which is typical of growth companies. The trend line for selling, general and administrative expenses is less encouraging because it exceeds the revenue trend line in 2006–2007. The good news is that nearly all of that upward shift in costs occured in one year (2006). In other years, management appears to have limited those costs to not exceed revenue growth.

EXHIBIT 13.5

Trend Percent Lines for Revenues and Expenses of Best Buy

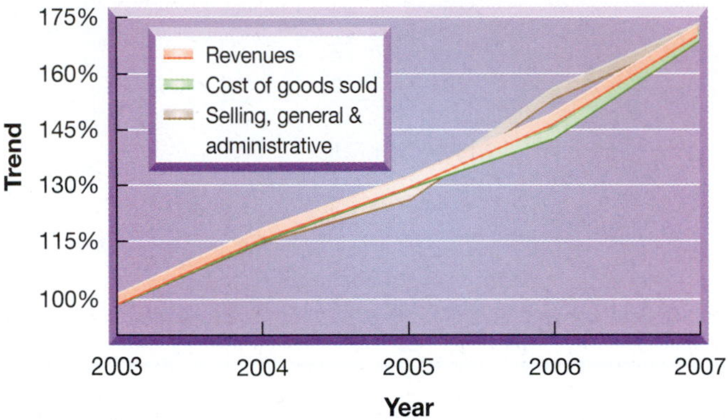

Exhibit 13.6 compares **Best Buy**'s revenue trend line to that of **Circuit City** and **RadioShack** for this same period. Best Buy's revenues sharply increased over this time period while those of Circuit City exhibited less growth, and those for RadioShack were flat. These data indicate that Best Buy's products and services have met with considerable consumer acceptance.

EXHIBIT 13.6

Trend Percent Lines—Best Buy, Circuit City, and RadioShack

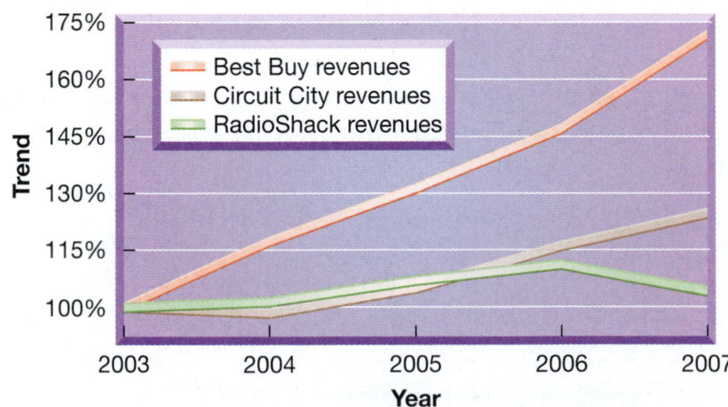

Trend analysis of financial statement items can include comparisons of relations between items on different financial statements. For instance, Exhibit 13.7 compares Best Buy's revenues and total assets. The rate of increase in total assets (176.4%) is greater than the increase in revenues (171.6%) since 2003. Is this result favorable or not? It suggests that Best Buy was slightly less efficient in using its assets in 2007. Management apparently is expecting future years' revenues to compensate for this asset growth.

Overall we must remember that an important role of financial statement analysis is identifying questions and areas of interest, which often direct us to important factors bearing

($ millions)	2007	2003	Trend Percent (2007 vs. 2003)
Revenues	$35,934	$20,943	171.6%
Total assets	13,570	7,694	176.4

EXHIBIT 13.7

Revenue and Asset Data for Best Buy

on a company's future. Accordingly, financial statement analysis should be seen as a continuous process of refining our understanding and expectations of company performance and financial condition.

Decision Maker

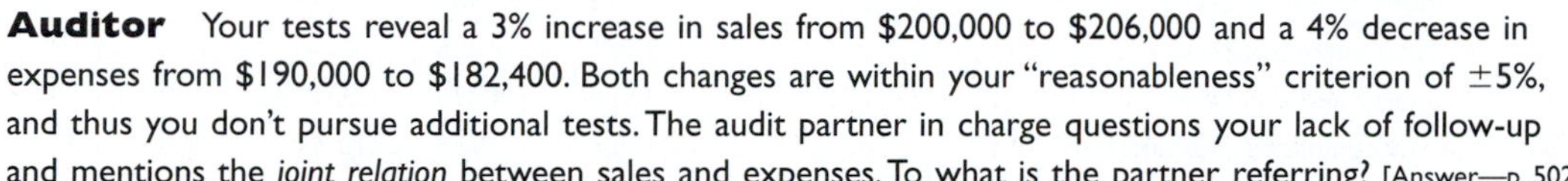

Auditor Your tests reveal a 3% increase in sales from $200,000 to $206,000 and a 4% decrease in expenses from $190,000 to $182,400. Both changes are within your "reasonableness" criterion of ±5%, and thus you don't pursue additional tests. The audit partner in charge questions your lack of follow-up and mentions the *joint relation* between sales and expenses. To what is the partner referring? [Answer—p. 502]

Vertical Analysis

Vertical analysis is a tool to evaluate individual financial statement items or a group of items in terms of a specific base amount. We usually define a key aggregate figure as the base, which for an income statement is usually revenue and for a balance sheet is usually total assets. This section explains vertical analysis and applies it to Best Buy. [The term *vertical analysis* arises from the up-down (or down-up) movement of our eyes as we review common-size financial statements. Vertical analysis is also called *common-size analysis.*]

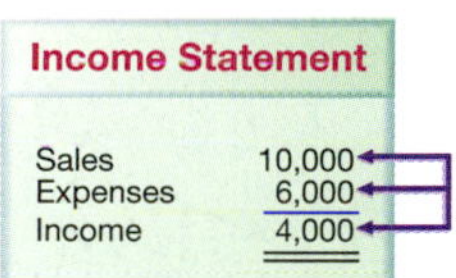

Common-Size Statements

P2 Describe and apply methods of vertical analysis.

The comparative statements in Exhibits 13.1 and 13.2 show the change in each item over time, but they do not emphasize the relative importance of each item. We use **common-size financial statements** to reveal changes in the relative importance of each financial statement item. All individual amounts in common-size statements are redefined in terms of common-size percents. A *common-size percent* is measured by dividing each individual financial statement amount under analysis by its base amount:

$$\textbf{Common-size percent (\%)} = \frac{\textbf{Analysis amount}}{\textbf{Base amount}} \times \textbf{100}$$

Common-Size Balance Sheets Common-size statements express each item as a percent of a *base amount,* which for a common-size balance sheet is usually total assets. The base amount is assigned a value of 100%. (This implies that the total amount of liabilities plus equity equals 100% since this amount equals total assets.) We then compute a common-size percent for each asset, liability, and equity item using total assets as the base amount. When we present a company's successive balance sheets in this way, changes in the mixture of assets, liabilities, and equity are apparent.

Point: The *base* amount in common-size analysis is an *aggregate* amount from that period's financial statement.

Exhibit 13.8 shows common-size comparative balance sheets for Best Buy. Some relations that stand out on both a magnitude and percentage basis include (1) a 41% increase in cash and equivalents, (2) a 6.5% decline in short-term investments as a percentage of assets, (3) a 1.2% decrease in net property and equipment as a percentage of assets, (4) a 1.7% increase in the percentage of accounts payable, (5) a 3.4% decline in the current portion of long-term debt, and (6) a marked increase in retained earnings. Most of these changes are characteristic of a successful growth/stable company. The concern, if any, is whether Best Buy can continue to generate sufficient revenues and income to support its asset buildup within a very competitive industry.

Point: Common-size statements often are used to compare two or more companies in the same industry.

Point: Common-size statements are also useful in comparing firms that report in different currencies.

EXHIBIT 13.8

Common-Size Comparative Balance Sheets

BEST BUY
Common-Size Comparative Balance Sheets
March 3, 2007, and February 25, 2006

($ millions)	2007	2006	Common-Size Percents* 2007	Common-Size Percents* 2006
Assets				
Cash and cash equivalents	$ 1,205	$ 748	8.9%	6.3%
Short-term investments	2,588	3,041	19.1	25.6
Receivables, net	548	449	4.0	3.8
Merchandise inventories	4,028	3,338	29.7	28.1
Other current assets	712	409	5.2	3.4
Total current assets	9,081	7,985	66.9	67.3
Property and equipment	4,904	4,836	36.1	40.8
Less accumulated depreciation	1,966	2,124	14.5	17.9
Net property and equipment	2,938	2,712	21.7	22.9
Goodwill	919	557	6.8	4.7
Tradenames	81	44	0.6	0.4
Long-term investments	318	218	2.3	1.8
Other long-term assets	233	348	1.7	2.9
Total assets	$13,570	$11,864	100.0%	100.0%
Liabilities				
Accounts payable	$ 3,934	$ 3,234	29.0%	27.3%
Unredeemed gift card liabilities	496	469	3.7	4.0
Accrued compensation and related expenses	332	354	2.4	3.0
Accrued liabilities	990	878	7.3	7.4
Accrued income taxes	489	703	3.6	5.9
Short-term debt	41	0	0.3	0.0
Current portion of long-term debt	19	418	0.1	3.5
Total current liabilities	6,301	6,056	46.4	51.0
Long-term liabilities	443	373	3.3	3.1
Long-term debt	590	178	4.3	1.5
Minority interests	35	0	0.3	0.0
Stockholders' Equity				
Common stock	48	49	0.4	0.4
Additional paid-in capital	430	643	3.2	5.4
Retained earnings	5,507	4,304	40.6	36.3
Accumulated other comprehensive income	216	261	1.6	2.2
Total stockholders' equity	6,201	5,257	45.7	44.3
Total liabilities and stockholders' equity	$13,570	$11,864	100.0%	100.0%

* Percents are rounded to one decimal and thus may not exactly sum to totals and subtotals.

Common-Size Income Statements Analysis also benefits from use of a common-size income statement. Revenues is usually the base amount, which is assigned a value of 100%. Each common-size income statement item appears as a percent of revenues. If we think of the 100% revenues amount as representing one sales dollar, the remaining items show how each revenue dollar is distributed among costs, expenses, and income.

Global: International companies sometimes disclose "convenience" financial statements, which are statements translated in other languages and currencies. However, these statements rarely adjust for differences in accounting principles across countries.

Exhibit 13.9 shows common-size comparative income statements for each dollar of Best Buy's revenues. The past two years' common-size numbers are similar. The good news is that Best Buy has been able to squeeze an extra 0.1 cent in earnings per revenue dollar—evidenced by the 3.7% to 3.8% rise in earnings as a percentage of revenues. This implies that management is effectively controlling costs and/or the company is reaping growth benefits, so-called *economies of scale*. The bad news is that gross profit lost 0.6 cent per revenue dollar—evidenced by the 25.0% to 24.4% decline in gross profit as a percentage of revenues. This is a concern given the price-competitive

EXHIBIT 13.9

Common-Size Comparative Income Statements

BEST BUY Common-Size Comparative Income Statements For Years Ended March 3, 2007, and February 25, 2006			Common-Size Percents*	
($ millions)	2007	2006	2007	2006
Revenues	$35,934	$30,848	100.0%	100.0%
Cost of goods sold	27,165	23,122	75.6	75.0
Gross profit	8,769	7,726	24.4	25.0
Selling, general, and administrative expenses	6,770	6,082	18.8	19.7
Operating income	1,999	1,644	5.6	5.3
Net interest income (expense)	111	77	0.3	0.2
Gain on investments	20	0	0.1	0.0
Earnings from continuing operations before income taxes	2,130	1,721	5.9	5.6
Income tax expense	752	581	2.1	1.9
Minority interest in earnings	1	0	0.0	0.0
Net earnings	$ 1,377	$ 1,140	3.8%	3.7%

* Percents are rounded to one decimal and thus may not exactly sum to totals and subtotals.

electronics market. Analysis here shows that common-size percents for successive income statements can uncover potentially important changes in a company's expenses. Evidence of no changes, especially when changes are expected, is also informative.

Common-Size Graphics

Two of the most common tools of common-size analysis are trend analysis of common-size statements and graphical analysis. The trend analysis of common-size statements is similar to that of comparative statements discussed under vertical analysis. It is not illustrated here because the only difference is the substitution of common-size percents for trend percents. Instead, this section discusses graphical analysis of common-size statements.

An income statement readily lends itself to common-size graphical analysis. This is so because revenues affect nearly every item in an income statement. Exhibit 13.10 shows **Best Buy**'s 2007 common-size income statement in graphical form. This pie chart highlights the contribution of each component of revenues for net earnings.

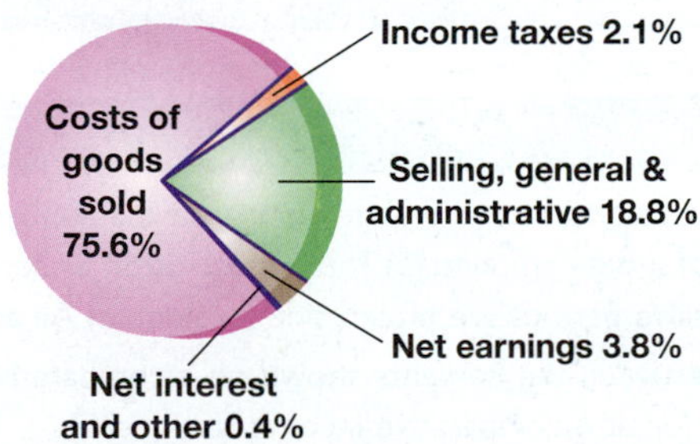

EXHIBIT 13.10

Common-Size Graphic of Income Statement

Exhibit 13.11 previews more complex graphical analyses available and the insights they provide. The data for this exhibit are taken from **Best Buy**'s *Segments* footnote. Best Buy has two reportable segments: domestic and international.

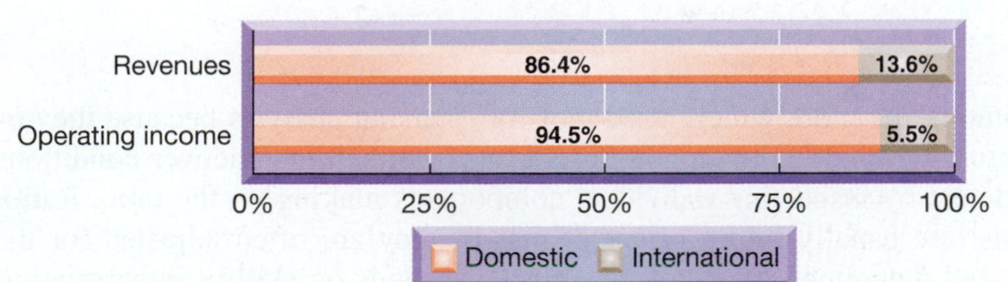

EXHIBIT 13.11

Revenue and Operating Income Breakdown by Segment

EXHIBIT 13.12

Common-Size Graphic of Asset Components

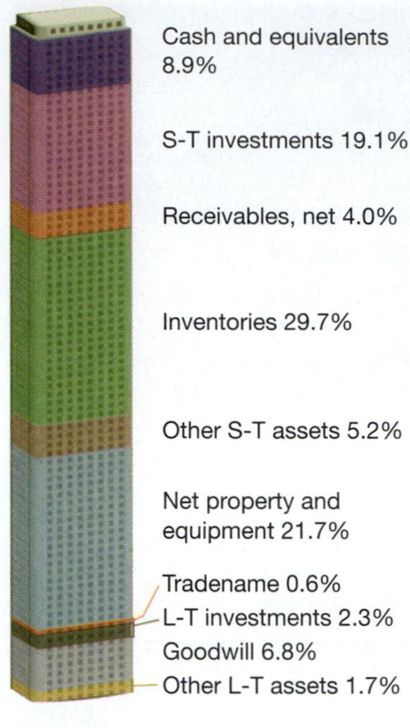

The upper bar in Exhibit 13.11 shows the percent of revenues from each segment. The major revenue source is Domestic (86.4%). The lower bar shows the percent of operating income from each segment. Although International provides 13.6% of revenues, it provides only 5.5% of operating income. This type of information can help users in determining strategic analyses and actions.

Graphical analysis is also useful in identifying (1) sources of financing including the distribution among current liabilities, noncurrent liabilities, and equity capital and (2) focuses of investing activities, including the distribution among current and noncurrent assets. As illustrative, Exhibit 13.12 shows a common-size graphical display of Best Buy's assets. Common-size balance sheet analysis can be extended to examine the composition of these subgroups. For instance, in assessing liquidity of current assets, knowing what proportion of current assets consists of inventories is usually important, and not simply what proportion inventories are of total assets.

Common-size financial statements are also useful in comparing different companies. Exhibit 13.13 shows common-size graphics of Best Buy, Circuit City, and RadioShack on financing sources. This graphic highlights the larger percent of equity financing for Best Buy and Circuit City than for RadioShack. It also highlights the much larger noncurrent (debt) financing of RadioShack. Comparison of a company's common-size statements with competitors' or industry common-size statistics alerts us to differences in the structure or distribution of its financial statements but not to their dollar magnitude.

EXHIBIT 13.13

Common-Size Graphic of Financing Sources—Competitor Analysis

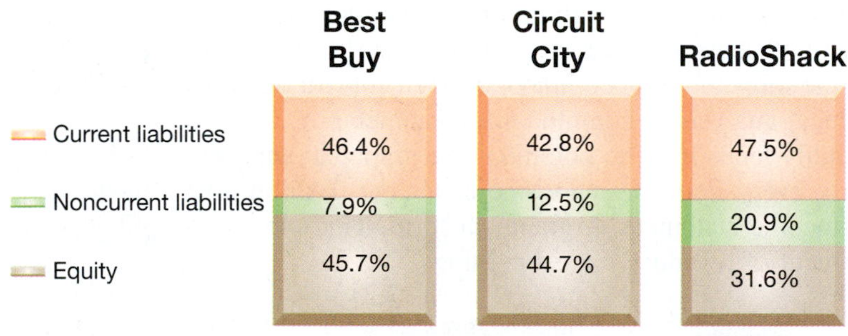

Quick Check

Answers—p. 502

5. Which of the following is true for common-size comparative statements? (*a*) Each item is expressed as a percent of a base amount. (*b*) Total assets often are assigned a value of 100%. (*c*) Amounts from successive periods are placed side by side. (*d*) All are true. (e) None is true.
6. What is the difference between the percents shown on a comparative income statement and those shown on a common-size comparative income statement?
7. Trend percents are (*a*) shown on comparative income statements and balance sheets, (*b*) shown on common-size comparative statements, or (*c*) also called *index numbers*.

Ratio Analysis

P3 Define and apply ratio analysis.

Ratios are among the more widely used tools of financial analysis because they provide clues to and symptoms of underlying conditions. A ratio can help us uncover conditions and trends difficult to detect by inspecting individual components making up the ratio. Ratios, like other analysis tools, are usually future oriented; that is, they are often adjusted for their probable future trend and magnitude, and their usefulness depends on skillful interpretation.

A ratio expresses a mathematical relation between two quantities. It can be expressed as a percent, rate, or proportion. For instance, a change in an account balance from $100 to $250 can be expressed as (1) 150%, (2) 2.5 times, or (3) 2.5 to 1 (or 2.5:1). Computation of a ratio is a simple arithmetic operation, but its interpretation is not. To be meaningful, a ratio must refer to an economically important relation. For example, a direct and crucial relation exists between an item's sales price and its cost. Accordingly, the ratio of cost of goods sold to sales is meaningful. In contrast, no obvious relation exists between freight costs and the balance of long-term investments.

This section describes an important set of financial ratios and its application. The selected ratios are organized into the four building blocks of financial statement analysis: (1) liquidity and efficiency, (2) solvency, (3) profitability, and (4) market prospects. We use four common standards, in varying degrees, for comparisons: intracompany, competitor, industry, and guidelines.

Point: Some sources for industry norms are *Annual Statement Studies* by Robert Morris Associates, *Industry Norms & Key Business Ratios* by Dun & Bradstreet, *Standard & Poor's Industry Surveys*, and Reuters.com/finance.

Liquidity and Efficiency

Liquidity refers to the availability of resources to meet short-term cash requirements. It is affected by the timing of cash inflows and outflows along with prospects for future performance. Analysis of liquidity is aimed at a company's funding requirements. *Efficiency* refers to how productive a company is in using its assets. Efficiency is usually measured relative to how much revenue is generated from a certain level of assets.

Both liquidity and efficiency are important and complementary. If a company fails to meet its current obligations, its continued existence is doubtful. Viewed in this light, all other measures of analysis are of secondary importance. Although accounting measurements assume the company's continued existence, our analysis must always assess the validity of this assumption using liquidity measures. Moreover, inefficient use of assets can cause liquidity problems. A lack of liquidity often precedes lower profitability and fewer opportunities. It can foretell a loss of owner control. To a company's creditors, lack of liquidity can yield delays in collecting interest and principal payments or the loss of amounts due them. A company's customers and suppliers of goods and services also are affected by short-term liquidity problems. Implications include a company's inability to execute contracts and potential damage to important customer and supplier relationships. This section describes and illustrates key ratios relevant to assessing liquidity and efficiency.

Working Capital and Current Ratio The amount of current assets less current liabilities is called **working capital,** or *net working capital.* A company needs adequate working capital to meet current debts, to carry sufficient inventories, and to take advantage of cash discounts. A company that runs low on working capital is less likely to meet current obligations or to continue operating. When evaluating a company's working capital, we must not only look at the dollar amount of current assets less current liabilities, but also at their ratio. The *current ratio* is defined as follows.

$$\textbf{Current ratio} = \frac{\textbf{Current assets}}{\textbf{Current liabilities}}$$

Drawing on information in Exhibit 13.1, **Best Buy**'s working capital and current ratio for both 2007 and 2006 are shown in Exhibit 13.14. **Circuit City** (1.68), **RadioShack** (1.63), and the Industry's current ratio of 1.6 is shown in the margin. Best Buy's 2007 ratio (1.44) is lower than any of the comparison ratios, but it does not appear in danger of defaulting on loan payments. A high current ratio suggests a strong liquidity position and an ability to meet current obligations. A company can, however, have a current ratio that is too high. An excessively high current ratio means that the company has invested too much in current assets compared to its current obligations. An

EXHIBIT 13.14

Best Buy's Working Capital and Current Ratio

($ millions)	2007	2006
Current assets	$ 9,081	$ 7,985
Current liabilities	6,301	6,056
Working capital	**$2,780**	**$1,929**
Current ratio		
$9,081/$6,301	**1.44 to 1**	
$7,985/$6,056		**1.32 to 1**

Current ratio
Circuit City = 1.68
RadioShack = 1.63
Industry = 1.6

excessive investment in current assets is not an efficient use of funds because current assets normally generate a low return on investment (compared with long-term assets).

Many users apply a guideline of 2:1 (or 1.5:1) for the current ratio in helping evaluate a company's debt-paying ability. A company with a 2:1 or higher current ratio is generally thought to be a good credit risk in the short run. Such a guideline or any analysis of the current ratio must recognize at least three additional factors: (1) type of business, (2) composition of current assets, and (3) turnover rate of current asset components.

Type of business. A service company that grants little or no credit and carries few inventories can probably operate on a current ratio of less than 1:1 if its revenues generate enough cash to pay its current liabilities. On the other hand, a company selling high-priced clothing or furniture requires a higher ratio because of difficulties in judging customer demand and cash receipts. For instance, if demand falls, inventory may not generate as much cash as expected. Accordingly, analysis of the current ratio should include a comparison with ratios from successful companies in the same industry and from prior periods. We must also recognize that a company's accounting methods, especially choice of inventory method, affect the current ratio. For instance, when costs are rising, a company using LIFO tends to report a smaller amount of current assets than when using FIFO.

Point: When a firm uses LIFO in a period of rising costs, the standard for an adequate current ratio usually is lower than if it used FIFO.

Composition of current assets. The composition of a company's current assets is important to an evaluation of short-term liquidity. For instance, cash, cash equivalents, and short-term investments are more liquid than accounts and notes receivable. Also, short-term receivables normally are more liquid than inventory. Cash, of course, can be used to immediately pay current debts. Items such as accounts receivable and inventory, however, normally must be converted into cash before payment is made. An excessive amount of receivables and inventory weakens a company's ability to pay current liabilities. The acid-test ratio (see below) can help with this assessment.

Turnover rate of assets. Asset turnover measures a company's efficiency in using its assets. One relevant measure of asset efficiency is the revenue generated. A measure of total asset turnover is revenues divided by total assets, but evaluation of turnover for individual assets is also first useful. We discuss both receivables turnover and inventory turnover on the next page.

Decision Maker

Banker A company requests a one-year, $200,000 loan for expansion. This company's current ratio is 4:1, with current assets of $160,000. Key competitors carry a current ratio of about 1.9:1. Using this information, do you approve the loan application? Does your decision change if the application is for a 10-year loan?
[Answer—p. 502]

Acid-Test Ratio Quick assets are cash, short-term investments, and current receivables. These are the most liquid types of current assets. The *acid-test ratio,* also called *quick ratio,* reflects on a company's short-term liquidity.

$$\text{Acid-test ratio} = \frac{\text{Cash + Short-term investments + Current receivables}}{\text{Current liabilities}}$$

Best Buy's acid-test ratio is computed in Exhibit 13.15. Best Buy's 2007 acid-test ratio (0.69) is between that for Circuit City (0.65) and RadioShack (0.73), and less than the 1:1 common

EXHIBIT 13.15

Acid-Test Ratio

($ millions)	2007	2006
Cash and equivalents	$1,205	$ 748
Short-term investments	2,588	3,041
Current receivables	548	449
Total quick assets	$4,341	$4,238
Current liabilities	$6,301	$6,056
Acid-test ratio		
$4,341/$6,301	**0.69 to 1**	
$4,238/$6,056		**0.70 to 1**

Acid-test ratio
Circuit City = 0.65
RadioShack = 0.73
Industry = 0.7

guideline for an acceptable acid-test ratio; each of these ratios is similar to the 0.7 industry ratio. As with analysis of the current ratio, we need to consider other factors. For instance, the frequency with which a company converts its current assets into cash affects its working capital requirements. This implies that analysis of short-term liquidity should also include an analysis of receivables and inventories, which we consider next.

Global: Ratio analysis helps overcome currency translation problems, but it does *not* overcome differences in accounting principles.

Accounts Receivable Turnover We can measure how frequently a company converts its receivables into cash by computing the *accounts receivable turnover*, which is defined as follows:

$$\text{Accounts receivable turnover} = \frac{\text{Net sales}}{\text{Average accounts receivable, net}}$$

Short-term receivables from customers are often included in the denominator along with accounts receivable. Also, accounts receivable turnover is more precise if credit sales are used for the numerator, but external users generally use net sales (or net revenues) because information about credit sales is typically not reported. Best Buy's 2007 accounts receivable turnover is computed as follows ($ millions).

Point: Some users prefer using gross accounts receivable (before subtracting the allowance for doubtful accounts) to avoid the influence of a manager's bad debts estimate.

$$\frac{\$35{,}934}{(\$548 + \$449)/2} = 72.1 \text{ times}$$

Accounts receivable turnover
Circuit City = 41.2
RadioShack = 17.1

Best Buy's value of 72.1 is larger than Circuit City's 41.2 and RadioShack's 17.1. Accounts receivable turnover is high when accounts receivable are quickly collected. A high turnover is favorable because it means the company need not commit large amounts of funds to accounts receivable. However, an accounts receivable turnover can be too high; this can occur when credit terms are so restrictive that they negatively affect sales volume.

Point: Ending accounts receivable can be substituted for the average balance in computing accounts receivable turnover if the difference between ending and average receivables is small.

Inventory Turnover How long a company holds inventory before selling it will affect working capital requirements. One measure of this effect is *inventory turnover,* also called *merchandise turnover* or *merchandise inventory turnover,* which is defined as follows.

$$\text{Inventory turnover} = \frac{\text{Cost of goods sold}}{\text{Average inventory}}$$

Using Best Buy's cost of goods sold and inventories information, we compute its inventory turnover for 2007 as follows (if the beginning and ending inventories for the year do not represent the usual inventory amount, an average of quarterly or monthly inventories can be used).

$$\frac{\$27{,}165}{(\$4{,}028 + \$3{,}338)/2} = 7.38 \text{ times}$$

Inventory turnover
Circuit City = 5.70
RadioShack = 2.96
Industry = 4.5

Best Buy's inventory turnover of 7.38 is higher than Circuit City's 5.70, RadioShack's 2.96, and the industry's 4.5. A company with a high turnover requires a smaller investment in inventory than one producing the same sales with a lower turnover. Inventory turnover can be too high, however, if the inventory a company keeps is so small that it restricts sales volume.

Days' Sales Uncollected Accounts receivable turnover provides insight into how frequently a company collects its accounts. Days' sales uncollected is one measure of this activity, which is defined as follows:

$$\text{Days' sales uncollected} = \frac{\text{Accounts receivable, net}}{\text{Net sales}} \times 365$$

Any short-term notes receivable from customers are normally included in the numerator.

Best Buy's 2007 days' sales uncollected follows.

Day's sales uncollected
Circuit City = 11.23
RadioShack = 18.94

$$\frac{\$548}{\$35{,}934} \times 365 = 5.57 \text{ days}$$

Both Circuit City's days' sales uncollected of 11.23 days and RadioShack's 18.94 days are longer than the 5.57 days for Best Buy. Days' sales uncollected is more meaningful if we know company credit terms. A rough guideline states that days' sales uncollected should not exceed $1\frac{1}{3}$ times the days in its (1) credit period, *if* discounts are not offered or (2) discount period, *if* favorable discounts are offered.

Days' Sales in Inventory *Days' sales in inventory* is a useful measure in evaluating inventory liquidity. Days' sales in inventory is linked to inventory in a way that days' sales uncollected is linked to receivables. We compute days' sales in inventory as follows.

$$\textbf{Days' sales in inventory} = \frac{\textbf{Ending inventory}}{\textbf{Cost of goods sold}} \times \textbf{365}$$

Best Buy's days' sales in inventory for 2007 follows.

Days' sales in inventory
Circuit City = 62.9
RadioShack = 107.9

$$\frac{\$4{,}028}{\$27{,}165} \times 365 = 54.1 \text{ days}$$

Point: *Average collection period* is estimated by dividing 365 by the accounts receivable turnover ratio. For example, 365 divided by an accounts receivable turnover of 6.1 indicates a 60-day average collection period.

If the products in Best Buy's inventory are in demand by customers, this formula estimates that its inventory will be converted into receivables (or cash) in 54.1 days. If all of Best Buy's sales were credit sales, the conversion of inventory to receivables in 54.1 days *plus* the conversion of receivables to cash in 5.57 days implies that inventory will be converted to cash in about 59.67 days (54.1 + 5.57).

Total Asset Turnover *Total asset turnover* reflects a company's ability to use its assets to generate sales and is an important indication of operating efficiency. The definition of this ratio follows.

$$\textbf{Total asset turnover} = \frac{\textbf{Net sales}}{\textbf{Average total assets}}$$

Best Buy's total asset turnover for 2007 follows and is less than Circuit City's, but greater than that for RadioShack.

Total asset turnover
Circuit City = 3.08
RadioShack = 2.24

$$\frac{\$35{,}934}{(\$13{,}570 + \$11{,}864)/2} = 2.83 \text{ times}$$

Quick Check

Answers—p. 502

8. Information from Paff Co. at Dec. 31, 2008, follows: cash, $820,000; accounts receivable, $240,000; inventories, $470,000; plant assets, $910,000; accounts payable, $350,000; and income taxes payable, $180,000. Compute its (*a*) current ratio and (*b*) acid-test ratio.
9. On Dec. 31, 2009, Paff Company (see question 8) had accounts receivable of $290,000 and inventories of $530,000. During 2009, net sales amounted to $2,500,000 and cost of goods sold was $750,000. Compute (*a*) accounts receivable turnover, (*b*) days' sales uncollected, (*c*) inventory turnover, and (*d*) days' sales in inventory.

Solvency

Solvency refers to a company's long-run financial viability and its ability to cover long-term obligations. All of a company's business activities—financing, investing, and operating—affect its solvency. Analysis of solvency is long term and uses less precise but more encompassing measures than liquidity. One of the most important components of solvency analysis is the composition of a company's capital structure. *Capital structure* refers to a company's financing sources. It ranges from relatively permanent equity financing to riskier or more temporary short-term financing. Assets represent security for financiers, ranging from loans secured by specific assets to the assets available as general security to unsecured creditors. This section describes the tools of solvency analysis. Our analysis focuses on a company's ability to both meet its obligations and provide security to its creditors *over the long run*. Indicators of this ability include *debt* and *equity* ratios, the relation between *pledged assets and secured liabilities,* and the company's capacity to earn sufficient income to *pay fixed interest charges*.

Debt and Equity Ratios One element of solvency analysis is to assess the portion of a company's assets contributed by its owners and the portion contributed by creditors. This relation is reflected in the debt ratio. The *debt ratio* expresses total liabilities as a percent of total assets. The **equity ratio** provides complementary information by expressing total equity as a percent of total assets. **Best Buy**'s debt and equity ratios follow.

($ millions)	2007	Ratios	
Total liabilities	$ 7,369	54.3%	[Debt ratio]
Total equity	6,201	45.7	[Equity ratio]
Total liabilities and equity	$13,570	100.0%	

Debt ratio :: Equity ratio
Circuit City = 55.3% :: 44.7%
RadioShack = 68.4% :: 31.6%

Best Buy's financial statements reveal more debt than equity. A company is considered less risky if its capital structure (equity and long-term debt) contains more equity. One risk factor is the required payment for interest and principal when debt is outstanding. Another factor is the greater the stockholder financing, the more losses a company can absorb through equity before the assets become inadequate to satisfy creditors' claims. From the stockholders' point of view, if a company earns a return on borrowed capital that is higher than the cost of borrowing, the difference represents increased income to stockholders. The inclusion of debt is described as *financial leverage* because debt can have the effect of increasing the return to stockholders. Companies are said to be highly leveraged if a large portion of their assets is financed by debt.

Point: Bank examiners from the FDIC and other regulatory agencies use debt and equity ratios to monitor compliance with regulatory capital requirements imposed on banks and S&Ls.

Debt-to-Equity Ratio The ratio of total liabilities to equity is another measure of solvency. We compute the ratio as follows.

$$\textbf{Debt-to-equity ratio} = \frac{\textbf{Total liabilities}}{\textbf{Total equity}}$$

Best Buy's debt-to-equity ratio for 2007 is

$$\$7,369/\$6,201 = 1.19$$

Debt-to-equity
Circuit City = 1.24
RadioShack = 2.17
Industry = 0.99

Best Buy's 1.19 debt-to-equity ratio is less than the 1.24 ratio for Circuit City and the 2.17 for RadioShack, but greater than the industry ratio of 0.99. Consistent with our inferences from the debt ratio, Best Buy's capital structure has more debt than equity, which increases risk. Recall that debt must be repaid with interest, while equity does not. These debt requirements can be burdensome when the industry and/or the economy experience a downturn. A larger debt-to-equity ratio also implies less opportunity to expand through use of debt financing.

Point: For analysis purposes, Minority Interest is usually included in equity.

Times Interest Earned The amount of income before deductions for interest expense and income taxes is the amount available to pay interest expense. The following *times interest*

Point: The times interest earned ratio and the debt and equity ratios are of special interest to bank lending officers.

earned ratio reflects the creditors' risk of loan repayments with interest.

$$\textbf{Times interest earned} = \frac{\textbf{Income before interest expense and income taxes}}{\textbf{Interest expense}}$$

The larger this ratio, the less risky is the company for creditors. One guideline says that creditors are reasonably safe if the company earns its fixed interest expense two or more times each year. Best Buy's times interest earned ratio follows; its value suggests that its creditors have little risk of nonrepayment.

Times interest earned
Circuit City = 12.5
RadioShack = 3.5

$$\frac{\$1{,}377 + \$31 \text{ (see Best Buy note \#7)} + \$752}{\$31} = 69.7$$

Decision Insight

Bears and Bulls A *bear market* is a declining market. The phrase comes from bear-skin jobbers who often sold the skins before the bears were caught. The term *bear* was then used to describe investors who sold shares they did not own in anticipation of a price decline. A *bull market* is a rising market. This phrase comes from the once popular sport of bear and bull baiting. The term *bull* came to mean the opposite of *bear.*

Profitability

We are especially interested in a company's ability to use its assets efficiently to produce profits (and positive cash flows). *Profitability* refers to a company's ability to generate an adequate return on invested capital. Return is judged by assessing earnings relative to the level and sources of financing. Profitability is also relevant to solvency. This section describes key profitability measures and their importance to financial statement analysis.

Profit Margin A company's operating efficiency and profitability can be expressed by two components. The first is *profit margin,* which reflects a company's ability to earn net income from sales. It is measured by expressing net income as a percent of sales (*sales* and *revenues* are similar terms). **Best Buy**'s profit margin follows.

Profit margin
Circuit City = −0.1%
RadioShack = 1.5%

$$\textbf{Profit margin} = \frac{\textbf{Net income}}{\textbf{Net sales}} = \frac{\$1{,}377}{\$35{,}934} = 3.8\%$$

To evaluate profit margin, we must consider the industry. For instance, an appliance company might require a profit margin between 10% and 15%; whereas a retail supermarket might require a profit margin of 1% or 2%. Both profit margin and *total asset turnover* make up the two basic components of operating efficiency. These ratios reflect on management because managers are ultimately responsible for operating efficiency. The next section explains how we use both measures to analyze return on total assets.

Return on Total Assets *Return on total assets* is defined as follows.

$$\textbf{Return on total assets} = \frac{\textbf{Net income}}{\textbf{Average total assets}}$$

Best Buy's 2007 return on total assets is

Return on total assets
Circuit City = −0.2%
RadioShack = 3.4%
Industry = 3.0

$$\frac{\$1{,}377}{(\$13{,}570 + \$11{,}864)/2} = 10.8\%$$

Best Buy's 10.8% return on total assets is lower than that for many businesses but is higher than RadioShack's return of 3.4% and the industry's 3.0% return. We also should evaluate any trend in the rate of return.

Point: Many analysts add back *Interest expense* × *(1 − Tax rate)* to net income in computing return on total assets.

The following equation shows the important relation between profit margin, total asset turnover, and return on total assets.

$$\textbf{Profit margin} \times \textbf{Total asset turnover} = \textbf{Return on total assets}$$

or

$$\frac{\text{Net income}}{\text{Net sales}} \times \frac{\text{Net sales}}{\text{Average total assets}} = \frac{\text{Net income}}{\text{Average total assets}}$$

Both profit margin and total asset turnover contribute to overall operating efficiency, as measured by return on total assets. If we apply this formula to Best Buy, we get

$$3.8\% \times 2.83 = 10.8\%$$

Circuit City: −0.1% × 3.08 = −0.2%
RadioShack: 1.5% × 2.24 = 3.4%
(with rounding)

This analysis shows that Best Buy's superior return on assets versus that of Circuit City and RadioShack is driven mainly by its higher profit margin.

Return on Common Stockholders' Equity Perhaps the most important goal in operating a company is to earn net income for its owner(s). *Return on common stockholders' equity* measures a company's success in reaching this goal and is defined as follows.

$$\text{Return on common stockholders' equity} = \frac{\text{Net income} - \text{Preferred dividends}}{\text{Average common stockholders' equity}}$$

Best Buy's 2007 return on common stockholders' equity is computed as follows:

$$\frac{\$1{,}377 - \$0}{(\$6{,}236 + \$5{,}257)/2} = 24.0\%$$

Return on common equity
Circuit City = −0.4%
RadioShack = 11.8%

The denominator in this computation is the book value of common equity (including minority interest). In the numerator, the dividends on cumulative preferred stock are subtracted whether they are declared or are in arrears. If preferred stock is noncumulative, its dividends are subtracted only if declared.

Decision Insight

Wall Street *Wall Street* is synonymous with financial markets, but its name comes from the street location of the original New York Stock Exchange. The street's name derives from stockades built by early settlers to protect New York from pirate attacks.

Market Prospects

Market measures are useful for analyzing corporations with publicly traded stock. These market measures use stock price, which reflects the market's (public's) expectations for the company. This includes expectations of both company return and risk—as the market perceives it.

Price-Earnings Ratio Computation of the *price-earnings ratio* follows.

$$\text{Price-earnings ratio} = \frac{\text{Market price per common share}}{\text{Earnings per share}}$$

Point: PE ratio can be viewed as an indicator of the market's expected growth and risk for a stock. High expected risk suggests a low PE ratio. High expected growth suggests a high PE ratio.

Predicted earnings per share for the next period is often used in the denominator of this computation. Reported earnings per share for the most recent period is also commonly used. In both cases, the ratio is used as an indicator of the future growth and risk of a company's earnings as perceived by the stock's buyers and sellers.

The market price of Best Buy's common stock at the start of fiscal year 2008 was $46.35. Using Best Buy's $2.86 basic earnings per share, we compute its price-earnings ratio as follows (some analysts compute this ratio using the median of the low and high stock price).

PE (year-end)
Circuit City = −380.0
RadioShack = 31.1

$$\frac{\$46.35}{\$2.86} = 16.2$$

Point: Some investors avoid stocks with high PE ratios under the belief they are "overpriced." Alternatively, some investors *sell these stocks short*—hoping for price declines.

Best Buy's price-earnings ratio is less than that for RadioShack, but is slightly higher than the norm. (Circuit City's ratio is negative due to its abnormally low earnings.) Best Buy's middle-of-the-pack ratio likely reflects investors' expectations of continued growth but normal earnings.

Dividend Yield *Dividend yield* is used to compare the dividend-paying performance of different investment alternatives. We compute dividend yield as follows.

$$\textbf{Dividend yield} = \frac{\textbf{Annual cash dividends per share}}{\textbf{Market price per share}}$$

Best Buy's dividend yield, based on its fiscal year-end market price per share of $46.35 and its policy of $0.36 cash dividends per share, is computed as follows.

Dividend yield
Circuit City = 0.6%
RadioShack = 1.5%

$$\frac{\$0.36}{\$46.35} = 0.8\%$$

Some companies do not declare and pay dividends because they wish to reinvest the cash.

Point: Corporate PE ratios and dividend yields are found in daily stock market quotations listed in *The Wall Street Journal*, *Investor's Business Daily*, or other publications and Web services.

Summary of Ratios

Exhibit 13.16 summarizes the major financial statement analysis ratios illustrated in this chapter. This summary includes each ratio's title, its formula, and the purpose for which it is commonly used.

Decision Insight

Ticker Prices *Ticker prices* refer to a band of moving data on a monitor carrying up-to-the-minute stock prices. The phrase comes from *ticker tape*, a 1-inch-wide strip of paper spewing stock prices from a printer that ticked as it ran. Most of today's investors have never seen actual ticker tape, but the phrase survives.

Quick Check

Answers—p. 502

10. Which ratio best reflects a company's ability to meet immediate interest payments? (*a*) Debt ratio. (*b*) Equity ratio. (*c*) Times interest earned.

11. Which ratio best measures a company's success in earning net income for its owner(s)? (*a*) Profit margin. (*b*) Return on common stockholders' equity. (*c*) Price-earnings ratio. (*d*) Dividend yield.

12. If a company has net sales of $8,500,000, net income of $945,000, and total asset turnover of 1.8 times, what is its return on total assets?

EXHIBIT 13.16

Financial Statement Analysis Ratios

Ratio	Formula	Measure of
Liquidity and Efficiency		
Current ratio	$= \frac{\text{Current assets}}{\text{Current liabilities}}$	Short-term debt-paying ability
Acid-test ratio	$= \frac{\text{Cash + Short-term investments + Current receivables}}{\text{Current liabilities}}$	Immediate short-term debt-paying ability
Accounts receivable turnover	$= \frac{\text{Net sales}}{\text{Average accounts receivable, net}}$	Efficiency of collection
Inventory turnover	$= \frac{\text{Cost of goods sold}}{\text{Average inventory}}$	Efficiency of inventory management
Days' sales uncollected	$= \frac{\text{Accounts receivable, net}}{\text{Net sales}} \times 365$	Liquidity of receivables
Days' sales in inventory	$= \frac{\text{Ending inventory}}{\text{Cost of goods sold}} \times 365$	Liquidity of inventory
Total asset turnover	$= \frac{\text{Net sales}}{\text{Average total assets}}$	Efficiency of assets in producing sales
Solvency		
Debt ratio	$= \frac{\text{Total liabilities}}{\text{Total assets}}$	Creditor financing and leverage
Equity ratio	$= \frac{\text{Total equity}}{\text{Total assets}}$	Owner financing
Debt-to-equity ratio	$= \frac{\text{Total liabilities}}{\text{Total equity}}$	Debt versus equity financing
Times interest earned	$= \frac{\text{Income before interest expense and income taxes}}{\text{Interest expense}}$	Protection in meeting interest payments
Profitability		
Profit margin ratio	$= \frac{\text{Net income}}{\text{Net sales}}$	Net income in each sales dollar
Gross margin ratio	$= \frac{\text{Net sales} - \text{Cost of goods sold}}{\text{Net sales}}$	Gross margin in each sales dollar
Return on total assets	$= \frac{\text{Net income}}{\text{Average total assets}}$	Overall profitability of assets
Return on common stockholders' equity	$= \frac{\text{Net income} - \text{Preferred dividends}}{\text{Average common stockholders' equity}}$	Profitability of owner investment
Book value per common share	$= \frac{\text{Shareholders' equity applicable to common shares}}{\text{Number of common shares outstanding}}$	Liquidation at reported amounts
Basic earnings per share	$= \frac{\text{Net income} - \text{Preferred dividends}}{\text{Weighted-average common shares outstanding}}$	Net income per common share
Market Prospects		
Price-earnings ratio	$= \frac{\text{Market price per common share}}{\text{Earnings per share}}$	Market value relative to earnings
Dividend yield	$= \frac{\text{Annual cash dividends per share}}{\text{Market price per share}}$	Cash return per common share

Decision Analysis — Analysis Reporting

A1 Summarize and report results of analysis.

Understanding the purpose of financial statement analysis is crucial to the usefulness of any analysis. This understanding leads to efficiency of effort, effectiveness in application, and relevance in focus. The purpose of most financial statement analyses is to reduce uncertainty in business decisions through a rigorous and sound evaluation. A *financial statement analysis report* helps by directly addressing the building blocks of analysis and by identifying weaknesses in inference by requiring explanation: It forces us to organize our reasoning and to verify its flow and logic. A report also serves as a communication link with readers, and the writing process reinforces our judgments and vice versa. Finally, the report helps us (re)evaluate evidence and refine conclusions on key building blocks. A good analysis report usually consists of six sections:

1. **Executive summary**—brief focus on important analysis results and conclusions.
2. **Analysis overview**—background on the company, its industry, and its economic setting.
3. **Evidential matter**—financial statements and information used in the analysis, including ratios, trends, comparisons, statistics, and all analytical measures assembled; often organized under the building blocks of analysis.
4. **Assumptions**—identification of important assumptions regarding a company's industry and economic environment, and other important assumptions for estimates.
5. **Key factors**—list of important favorable and unfavorable factors, both quantitative and qualitative, for company performance; usually organized by areas of analysis.
6. **Inferences**—forecasts, estimates, interpretations, and conclusions drawing on all sections of the report.

We must remember that the user dictates relevance, meaning that the analysis report should include a brief table of contents to help readers focus on those areas most relevant to their decisions. All irrelevant matter must be eliminated. For example, decades-old details of obscure transactions and detailed miscues of the analysis are irrelevant. Ambiguities and qualifications to avoid responsibility or hedging inferences must be eliminated. Finally, writing is important. Mistakes in grammar and errors of fact compromise the report's credibility.

Decision Insight

Short Selling *Short selling* refers to selling stock before you buy it. Here's an example: You borrow 100 shares of Nike stock, sell them at $40 each, and receive money from their sale. You then wait. You hope that Nike's stock price falls to, say, $35 each and you can replace the borrowed stock for less than you sold it for, reaping a profit of $5 each less any transaction costs.

Demonstration Problem

Use the following financial statements of Precision Co. to complete these requirements.

1. Prepare comparative income statements showing the percent increase or decrease for year 2009 in comparison to year 2008.

2. Prepare common-size comparative balance sheets for years 2009 and 2008.

3. Compute the following ratios as of December 31, 2009, or for the year ended December 31, 2009, and identify its building block category for financial statement analysis.

- **a.** Current ratio
- **b.** Acid-test ratio
- **c.** Accounts receivable turnover
- **d.** Days' sales uncollected
- **e.** Inventory turnover
- **f.** Debt ratio
- **g.** Debt-to-equity ratio
- **h.** Times interest earned
- **i.** Profit margin ratio
- **j.** Total asset turnover
- **k.** Return on total assets
- **l.** Return on common stockholders' equity

PRECISION COMPANY
Comparative Balance Sheets
December 31, 2009 and 2008

	2009	2008
Assets		
Current assets		
Cash	$ 79,000	$ 42,000
Short-term investments	65,000	96,000
Accounts receivable, net	120,000	100,000
Merchandise inventory	250,000	265,000
Total current assets	514,000	503,000
Plant assets		
Store equipment, net	400,000	350,000
Office equipment, net	45,000	50,000
Buildings, net	625,000	675,000
Land	100,000	100,000
Total plant assets	1,170,000	1,175,000
Total assets	$1,684,000	$1,678,000
Liabilities		
Current liabilities		
Accounts payable	$ 164,000	$ 190,000
Short-term notes payable	75,000	90,000
Taxes payable	26,000	12,000
Total current liabilities	265,000	292,000
Long-term liabilities		
Notes payable (secured by mortgage on buildings)	400,000	420,000
Total liabilities	665,000	712,000
Stockholders' Equity		
Common stock, $5 par value	475,000	475,000
Retained earnings	544,000	491,000
Total stockholders' equity	1,019,000	966,000
Total liabilities and equity	$1,684,000	$1,678,000

PRECISION COMPANY
Comparative Income Statements
For Years Ended December 31, 2009 and 2008

	2009	2008
Sales	$2,486,000	$2,075,000
Cost of goods sold	1,523,000	1,222,000
Gross profit	963,000	853,000
Operating expenses		
Advertising expense	145,000	100,000
Sales salaries expense	240,000	280,000
Office salaries expense	165,000	200,000
Insurance expense	100,000	45,000
Supplies expense	26,000	35,000
Depreciation expense	85,000	75,000
Miscellaneous expenses	17,000	15,000
Total operating expenses	778,000	750,000
Operating income	185,000	103,000
Interest expense	44,000	46,000
Income before taxes	141,000	57,000
Income taxes	47,000	19,000
Net income	$ 94,000	$ 38,000
Earnings per share	$ 0.99	$ 0.40

Planning the Solution

- Set up a four-column income statement; enter the 2009 and 2008 amounts in the first two columns and then enter the dollar change in the third column and the percent change from 2008 in the fourth column.
- Set up a four-column balance sheet; enter the 2009 and 2008 year-end amounts in the first two columns and then compute and enter the amount of each item as a percent of total assets.
- Compute the required ratios using the data provided. Use the average of beginning and ending amounts when appropriate (see Exhibit 13.16 for definitions).

Solution to Demonstration Problem

1.

PRECISION COMPANY
Comparative Income Statements
For Years Ended December 31, 2009 and 2008

			Increase (Decrease) in 2009	
	2009	2008	Amount	Percent
Sales	$2,486,000	$2,075,000	$411,000	19.8%
Cost of goods sold	1,523,000	1,222,000	301,000	24.6
Gross profit	963,000	853,000	110,000	12.9
Operating expenses				
Advertising expense	145,000	100,000	45,000	45.0
Sales salaries expense	240,000	280,000	(40,000)	(14.3)
Office salaries expense	165,000	200,000	(35,000)	(17.5)

[continued on next page]

[continued from previous page]

Insurance expense	100,000	45,000	55,000	122.2
Supplies expense	26,000	35,000	(9,000)	(25.7)
Depreciation expense	85,000	75,000	10,000	13.3
Miscellaneous expenses	17,000	15,000	2,000	13.3
Total operating expenses	778,000	750,000	28,000	3.7
Operating income	185,000	103,000	82,000	79.6
Interest expense	44,000	46,000	(2,000)	(4.3)
Income before taxes	141,000	57,000	84,000	147.4
Income taxes	47,000	19,000	28,000	147.4
Net income	$ 94,000	$ 38,000	$ 56,000	147.4
Earnings per share	$ 0.99	$ 0.40	$ 0.59	147.5

2.

PRECISION COMPANY
Common-Size Comparative Balance Sheets
December 31, 2009 and 2008

	December 31		Common-Size Percents	
	2009	2008	2009*	2008*
Assets				
Current assets				
Cash	$ 79,000	$ 42,000	4.7%	2.5%
Short-term investments	65,000	96,000	3.9	5.7
Accounts receivable, net	120,000	100,000	7.1	6.0
Merchandise inventory	250,000	265,000	14.8	15.8
Total current assets	514,000	503,000	30.5	30.0
Plant Assets				
Store equipment, net	400,000	350,000	23.8	20.9
Office equipment, net	45,000	50,000	2.7	3.0
Buildings, net	625,000	675,000	37.1	40.2
Land	100,000	100,000	5.9	6.0
Total plant assets	1,170,000	1,175,000	69.5	70.0
Total assets	$1,684,000	$1,678,000	100.0	100.0
Liabilities				
Current liabilities				
Accounts payable	$ 164,000	$ 190,000	9.7%	11.3%
Short-term notes payable	75,000	90,000	4.5	5.4
Taxes payable	26,000	12,000	1.5	0.7
Total current liabilities	265,000	292,000	15.7	17.4
Long-term liabilities				
Notes payable (secured by mortgage on buildings)	400,000	420,000	23.8	25.0
Total liabilities	665,000	712,000	39.5	42.4
Stockholders' Equity				
Common stock, $5 par value	475,000	475,000	28.2	28.3
Retained earnings	544,000	491,000	32.3	29.3
Total stockholders' equity	1,019,000	966,000	60.5	57.6
Total liabilities and equity	$1,684,000	$1,678,000	100.0	100.0

* Columns do not always add to 100 due to rounding.

3. Ratios for 2009:

a. Current ratio: $514,000/$265,000 = 1.9:1 (liquidity and efficiency)

b. Acid-test ratio: ($79,000 + $65,000 + $120,000)/$265,000 = 1.0:1 (liquidity and efficiency)

c. Average receivables: ($120,000 + $100,000)/2 = $110,000
Accounts receivable turnover: $2,486,000/$110,000 = 22.6 times (liquidity and efficiency)

d. Days' sales uncollected: ($120,000/$2,486,000) × 365 = 17.6 days (liquidity and efficiency)

e. Average inventory: ($250,000 + $265,000)/2 = $257,500
Inventory turnover: $1,523,000/$257,500 = 5.9 times (liquidity and efficiency)

f. Debt ratio: $665,000/$1,684,000 = 39.5% (solvency)

g. Debt-to-equity ratio: $665,000/$1,019,000 = 0.65 (solvency)

h. Times interest earned: $185,000/$44,000 = 4.2 times (solvency)

i. Profit margin ratio: $94,000/$2,486,000 = 3.8% (profitability)

j. Average total assets: ($1,684,000 + $1,678,000)/2 = $1,681,000
Total asset turnover: $2,486,000/$1,681,000 = 1.48 times (liquidity and efficiency)

k. Return on total assets: $94,000/$1,681,000 = 5.6% or 3.8% × 1.48 = 5.6% (profitability)

l. Average total common equity: ($1,019,000 + $966,000)/2 = $992,500
Return on common stockholders' equity: $94,000/$992,500 = 9.5% (profitability)

APPENDIX

13A Sustainable Income

A2 Explain the form and assess the content of a complete income statement.

When a company's revenue and expense transactions are from normal, continuing operations, a simple income statement is usually adequate. When a company's activities include income-related events not part of its normal, continuing operations, it must disclose information to help users understand these events and predict future performance. To meet these objectives, companies separate the income statement into continuing operations, discontinued segments, extraordinary items, comprehensive income, and earnings per share. For illustration, Exhibit 13A.1 shows such an income statement for ComUS. These separate distinctions help us measure *sustainable income,* which is the income level most likely to continue into the future. Sustainable income is commonly used in PE ratios and other market-based measures of performance.

Continuing Operations

The first major section (①) shows the revenues, expenses, and income from continuing operations. Users especially rely on this information to predict future operations. Many users view this section as the most important.

Discontinued Segments

A **business segment** is a part of a company's operations that serves a particular line of business or class of customers. A segment has assets, liabilities, and financial results of operations that can be distinguished from those of other parts of the company. A company's gain or loss from selling or closing down a segment is separately reported. Section ② of Exhibit 13A.1 reports both (1) income from operating the discontinued segment for the current period prior to its disposal and (2) the loss from disposing of the segment's net assets. The income tax effects of each are reported separately from the income taxes expense in section ①.

Extraordinary Items

Section ③ reports **extraordinary gains and losses,** which are those that are *both unusual* and *infrequent*. An **unusual gain or loss** is abnormal or otherwise unrelated to the company's regular activities and environment. An **infrequent gain or loss** is not expected to recur given the company's operating environment. Reporting extraordinary items in a separate category helps users predict future performance, absent the effects of extraordinary items. Items usually considered extraordinary include (1) expropriation (taking away) of property by a foreign government, (2) condemning of property by a domestic government body, (3) prohibition against using an asset by a newly enacted law, and (4) losses and gains from an unusual and infrequent calamity ("act of God"). Items *not* considered extraordinary include (1) write-downs

EXHIBIT 13A.1

Income Statement (all-inclusive) for a Corporation

ComUS
Income Statement
For Year Ended December 31, 2009

①	Net sales		$8,478,000
	Operating expenses		
	Cost of goods sold	$5,950,000	
	Depreciation expense	35,000	
	Other selling, general, and administrative expenses	515,000	
	Interest expense	20,000	
	Total operating expenses		(6,520,000)
	Other gains (losses)		
	Loss on plant relocation		(45,000)
	Gain on sale of surplus land		72,000
	Income from continuing operations before taxes		1,985,000
	Income taxes expense		(595,500)
	Income from continuing operations		1,389,500
②	**Discontinued segment**		
	Income from operating Division A (net of $180,000 taxes)	420,000	
	Loss on disposal of Division A (net of $66,000 tax benefit)	(154,000)	266,000
	Income before extraordinary items		1,655,500
③	**Extraordinary items**		
	Gain on land expropriated by state (net of $85,200 taxes)	198,800	
	Loss from earthquake damage (net of $270,000 tax benefit)	(630,000)	(431,200)
	Net income		$1,224,300
④	**Earnings per common share (200,000 outstanding shares)**		
	Income from continuing operations		$ 6.95
	Discontinued operations		1.33
	Income before extraordinary items		8.28
	Extraordinary items		(2.16)
	Net income (basic earnings per share)		$ 6.12

of inventories and write-offs of receivables, (2) gains and losses from disposing of segments, and (3) financial effects of labor strikes.

Gains and losses that are neither unusual nor infrequent are reported as part of continuing operations. Gains and losses that are *either* unusual *or* infrequent, but *not* both, are reported as part of continuing operations *but* after the normal revenues and expenses.

Decision Maker

Small Business Owner You own an orange grove near Jacksonville, Florida. A bad frost destroys about one-half of your oranges. You are currently preparing an income statement for a bank loan. Can you claim the loss of oranges as extraordinary? [Answer—p. 502]

Earnings per Share

The final section ④ of the income statement in Exhibit 13A.1 reports earnings per share for each of the three subcategories of income (continuing operations, discontinued segments, and extraordinary items) when they exist.

Changes in Accounting Principles

Point: Changes in principles are sometimes required when new accounting standards are issued.

The *consistency concept* directs a company to apply the same accounting principles across periods. Yet a company can change from one acceptable accounting principle (such as FIFO, LIFO, or weighted-average) to another as long as the change improves the usefulness of information in its financial statements. A footnote would describe the accounting change and why it is an improvement.

Changes in accounting principles require retrospective application to prior periods' financial statements. *Retrospective application* involves applying a different accounting principle to prior periods as if that principle had always been used. Retrospective application enhances the consistency of financial information between periods, which improves the usefulness of information, especially with comparative analyses. (Prior to 2005, the cumulative effect of changes in accounting principles was recognized in net income in the period of the change.) Accounting standards also require that *a change in depreciation, amortization, or depletion method for long-term operating assets is accounted for as a change in accounting estimate*—that is, prospectively over current and future periods. This reflects the notion that an entity should change its depreciation, amortization, or depletion method only with changes in estimated asset benefits, the pattern of benefit usage, or information about those benefits.

Comprehensive Income

Comprehensive income is net income plus certain gains and losses that bypass the income statement. These items are recorded directly to equity. Specifically, comprehensive income equals the change in equity for the period, excluding investments from and distributions (dividends) to its stockholders. For **Best Buy**, it is computed as follows ($ millions):

Net income	$1,377
Accumulated other comprehensive income (loss)	(45)
Comprehensive income	$1,332

The most common items included in *accumulated other comprehensive income,* or *AOCI,* are unrealized gains and losses on available-for-sale securities and foreign currency translation adjustments. (Detailed computations for these items are in advanced courses.) Analysts disagree on how to treat these items. Some analysts believe that AOCI items should not be considered when predicting future performance, and some others believe AOCI items should be considered as they reflect on company and managerial performance. Whatever our position, we must be familiar with what AOCI items are as they are commonly reported in financial statements. Best Buy reports its comprehensive income in its statement of shareholders' equity (see Appendix A).

Quick Check

Answers—p. 502

13. Which of the following is an extraordinary item? (*a*) a settlement paid to a customer injured while using the company's product, (*b*) a loss to a plant from damages caused by a meteorite, or (*c*) a loss from selling old equipment.

14. Identify the four major sections of an income statement that are potentially reportable.

15. A company using FIFO for the past 15 years decides to switch to LIFO. The effect of this event on prior years' net income is (*a*) reported as if the new method had always been used; (*b*) ignored because it is a change in an accounting estimate; or (*c*) reported on the current year income statement.

Summary

C1 Explain the purpose of analysis. The purpose of financial statement analysis is to help users make better business decisions. Internal users want information to improve company efficiency and effectiveness in providing products and services. External users want information to make better and more informed decisions in pursuing their goals. The common goals of all users are to evaluate a company's (1) past and current performance, (2) current financial position, and (3) future performance and risk.

C2 Identify the building blocks of analysis. Financial statement analysis focuses on four "building blocks" of analysis: (1) liquidity and efficiency—ability to meet short-term obligations and efficiently generate revenues; (2) solvency—ability to generate future revenues and meet long-term obligations; (3) profitability—ability to provide financial rewards sufficient to attract and retain financing; and (4) market prospects—ability to generate positive market expectations.

C3 Describe standards for comparisons in analysis. Standards for comparisons include (1) intracompany—prior performance and relations between financial items for the company under analysis; (2) competitor—one or more direct competitors of the company; (3) industry—industry statistics; and (4) guidelines (rules of thumb)—general standards developed from past experiences and personal judgments.

C4 Identify the tools of analysis. The three most common tools of financial statement analysis are (1) horizontal analysis—comparing a company's financial condition and performance across time; (2) vertical analysis—comparing a company's financial condition and performance to a base amount such as revenues or total assets; and (3) ratio analysis—using and quantifying key relations among financial statement items.

A1 Summarize and report results of analysis. A financial statement analysis report is often organized around the building blocks of analysis. A good report separates interpretations and conclusions of analysis from the information underlying them. An analysis report often consists of six sections: (1) executive summary, (2) analysis overview, (3) evidential matter, (4) assumptions, (5) key factors, and (6) inferences.

A2^A Explain the form and assess the content of a complete income statement. An income statement has four *potential* sections: (1) continuing operations, (2) discontinued segments, (3) extraordinary items, and (4) earnings per share.

P1 Explain and apply methods of horizontal analysis. Horizontal analysis is a tool to evaluate changes in data across time. Two important tools of horizontal analysis are comparative statements and trend analysis. Comparative statements show amounts for two or more successive periods, often with changes disclosed in both absolute and percent terms. Trend analysis is used to reveal important changes occurring from one period to the next.

P2 Describe and apply methods of vertical analysis. Vertical analysis is a tool to evaluate each financial statement item or group of items in terms of a base amount. Two tools of vertical analysis are common-size statements and graphical analyses. Each item in common-size statements is expressed as a percent of a base amount. For the balance sheet, the base amount is usually total assets, and for the income statement, it is usually sales.

P3 Define and apply ratio analysis. Ratio analysis provides clues to and symptoms of underlying conditions. Ratios, properly interpreted, identify areas requiring further investigation. A ratio expresses a mathematical relation between two quantities such as a percent, rate, or proportion. Ratios can be organized into the building blocks of analysis: (1) liquidity and efficiency, (2) solvency, (3) profitability, and (4) market prospects.

Guidance Answers to **Decision Maker**

Auditor The *joint relation* referred to is the combined increase in sales and the decrease in expenses yielding more than a 5% increase in income. Both *individual* accounts (sales and expenses) yield percent changes within the ±5% acceptable range. However, a joint analysis suggests a different picture. For example, consider a joint analysis using the profit margin ratio. The client's profit margin is 11.46% ($206,000 − $182,400/$206,000) for the current year compared with 5.0% ($200,000 − $190,000/$200,000) for the prior year—yielding a 129% increase in profit margin! This is what concerns the partner, and it suggests expanding audit tests to verify or refute the client's figures.

Banker Your decision on the loan application is positive for at least two reasons. First, the current ratio suggests a strong ability to meet short-term obligations. Second, current assets of $160,000 and a current ratio of 4:1 imply current liabilities of $40,000 (one-fourth of current assets) and a working capital excess of $120,000. This working capital excess is 60% of the loan amount. However, if the application is for a 10-year loan, our decision is less optimistic. The current ratio and working capital suggest a good safety margin, but indications of inefficiency in operations exist. In particular, a 4:1 current ratio is more than double its key competitors' ratio. This is characteristic of inefficient asset use.

Small Business Owner The frost loss is probably not extraordinary. Jacksonville experiences enough recurring frost damage to make it difficult to argue this event is both unusual and infrequent. Still, you want to highlight the frost loss and hope the bank views this uncommon event separately from continuing operations.

Guidance Answers to **Quick Checks**

1. General-purpose financial statements are intended for a variety of users interested in a company's financial condition and performance—users without the power to require specialized financial reports to meet their specific needs.

2. General-purpose financial statements include the income statement, balance sheet, statement of stockholders' (owner's) equity, and statement of cash flows plus the notes related to these statements.

3. *a*

4. Data from one or more direct competitors are usually preferred for comparative purposes.

5. *d*

6. Percents on comparative income statements show the increase or decrease in each item from one period to the next. On common-size comparative income statements, each item is shown as a percent of net sales for that period.

7. *c*

8. (*a*) ($820,000 + $240,000 + $470,000)/($350,000 + $180,000) = 2.9 to 1.
(*b*) ($820,000 + $240,000)/($350,000 + $180,000) = 2:1.

9. (*a*) $2,500,000/[($290,000 + $240,000)/2] = 9.43 times.
(*b*) ($290,000/$2,500,000) × 365 = 42 days.
(*c*) $750,000/[($530,000 + $470,000)/2] = 1.5 times.
(*d*) ($530,000/$750,000) × 365 = 258 days.

10. *c*

11. *b*

12. $$\text{Profit margin} \times \frac{\text{Total asset}}{\text{turnover}} = \frac{\text{Return on}}{\text{total assets}}$$

$$\frac{\$945{,}000}{\$8{,}500{,}000} \times 1.8 = 20\%$$

13. (*b*)

14. The four (potentially reportable) major sections are income from continuing operations, discontinued segments, extraordinary items, and earnings per share.

15. (*a*); known as retrospective application.

Key Terms

mhhe.com/wildMA2e

Key Terms are available at the book's Website for learning and testing in an online Flashcard Format.

Business segment (p. 499)
Common-size financial statement (p. 483)
Comparative financial statements (p. 478)
Efficiency (p. 477)
Equity ratio (p. 491)
Extraordinary gains and losses (p. 499)
Financial reporting (p. 477)
Financial statement analysis (p. 476)
General-purpose financial statements (p. 477)
Horizontal analysis (p. 478)
Infrequent gain or loss (p. 499)
Liquidity (p. 477)
Market prospects (p. 477)
Profitability (p. 477)
Ratio analysis (p. 478)
Solvency (p. 477)
Unusual gain or loss (p. 499)
Vertical analysis (p. 478)
Working capital (p. 487)

Multiple Choice Quiz

Answers on p. 518

mhhe.com/wildMA2e

Additional Quiz Questions are available at the book's Website.

Quiz13

1. A company's sales in 2008 were \$300,000 and in 2009 were \$351,000. Using 2008 as the base year, the sales trend percent for 2009 is:
   a. 17%
   b. 85%
   c. 100%
   d. 117%
   e. 48%

Use the following information for questions 2 through 5.

GALLOWAY COMPANY Balance Sheet December 31, 2009	
Assets	
Cash	\$ 86,000
Accounts receivable	76,000
Merchandise inventory	122,000
Prepaid insurance	12,000
Long-term investments	98,000
Plant assets, net	436,000
Total assets	\$830,000
Liabilities and Equity	
Current liabilities	\$124,000
Long-term liabilities	90,000
Common stock	300,000
Retained earnings	316,000
Total liabilities and equity	\$830,000

2. What is Galloway Company's current ratio?
   a. 0.69
   b. 1.31
   c. 3.88
   d. 6.69
   e. 2.39
3. What is Galloway Company's acid-test ratio?
   a. 2.39
   b. 0.69
   c. 1.31
   d. 6.69
   e. 3.88
4. What is Galloway Company's debt ratio?
   a. 25.78%
   b. 100.00%
   c. 74.22%
   d. 137.78%
   e. 34.74%
5. What is Galloway Company's equity ratio?
   a. 25.78%
   b. 100.00%
   c. 34.74%
   d. 74.22%
   e. 137.78%

Superscript letter A denotes assignments based on Appendix 13A.

Discussion Questions

1. What is the difference between comparative financial statements and common-size comparative statements?
2. Which items are usually assigned a 100% value on (*a*) a common-size balance sheet and (*b*) a common-size income statement?
3. Explain the difference between financial reporting and financial statements.
4. What three factors would influence your evaluation as to whether a company's current ratio is good or bad?

5. Suggest several reasons why a 2:1 current ratio might not be adequate for a particular company.

6. Why is working capital given special attention in the process of analyzing balance sheets?

7. What does the number of days' sales uncollected indicate?

8. What does a relatively high accounts receivable turnover indicate about a company's short-term liquidity?

9. Why is a company's capital structure, as measured by debt and equity ratios, important to financial statement analysts?

10. How does inventory turnover provide information about a company's short-term liquidity?

11. What ratios would you compute to evaluate management performance?

12. Why would a company's return on total assets be different from its return on common stockholders' equity?

13. Where on the income statement does a company report an unusual gain not expected to occur more often than once every two years or so?

14. Use **Best Buy**'s financial statements in Appendix A to compute its return on total assets for the years ended March 3, 2007, and February 25, 2006. Total assets at February 26, 2005, were $10,294 (in millions).

15. Refer to **Circuit City**'s financial statements in Appendix A to compute its equity ratio as of February 28, 2007, and February 28, 2006.

16. Refer to **RadioShack**'s financial statements in Appendix A. Compute its debt ratio as of December 31, 2006, and December 31, 2005.

(R) RadioShack.

17. Refer to **Apple**'s financial statements in Appendix A. Compute its profit margin for the fiscal year ended September 30, 2006.

Denotes Discussion Questions that involve decision making.

Most materials in this section are available in McGraw-Hill's Connect connect

QUICK STUDY

QS 13-1
Financial reporting C1

Which of the following items (1) through (9) are part of financial reporting but are *not* included as part of general-purpose financial statements? (1) stock price information and analysis, (2) statement of cash flows, (3) management discussion and analysis of financial performance, (4) income statement, (5) company news releases, (6) balance sheet, (7) financial statement notes, (8) statement of shareholders' equity, (9) prospectus.

QS 13-2
Standard of comparison C3

What are four possible standards of comparison used to analyze financial statement ratios? Which of these is generally considered to be the most useful? Which one is least likely to provide a good basis for comparison?

QS 13-3
Common-size and trend percents
P1 P2

Use the following information for Owens Corporation to determine (1) the 2008 and 2009 common-size percents for cost of goods sold using net sales as the base and (2) the 2008 and 2009 trend percents for net sales using 2008 as the base year.

($ thousands)	2009	2008
Net sales	$101,400	$58,100
Cost of goods sold	55,300	30,700

QS 13-4
Horizontal analysis
P1

Compute the annual dollar changes and percent changes for each of the following accounts.

	2009	2008
Short-term investments	$110,000	$80,000
Accounts receivable	22,000	25,000
Notes payable	30,000	0

QS 13-5
Building blocks of analysis
C2 C4 P3

Match the ratio to the building block of financial statement analysis to which it best relates.

A. Liquidity and efficiency **C.** Profitability
B. Solvency **D.** Market prospects

1. _____ Gross margin ratio
2. _____ Acid-test ratio
3. _____ Equity ratio
4. _____ Return on total assets
5. _____ Dividend yield
6. _____ Book value per common share
7. _____ Days' sales in inventory
8. _____ Accounts receivable turnover
9. _____ Debt-to-equity
10. _____ Times interest earned

QS 13-6
Identifying financial ratios
C4 P3 

1. Which two short-term liquidity ratios measure how frequently a company collects its accounts?
2. What measure reflects the difference between current assets and current liabilities?
3. Which two ratios are key components in measuring a company's operating efficiency? Which ratio summarizes these two components?

QS 13-7
Ratio interpretation
P3 

For each ratio listed, identify whether the change in ratio value from 2008 to 2009 is usually regarded as favorable or unfavorable.

Ratio	2009	2008	Ratio	2009	2008
1. Profit margin	10%	9%	5. Accounts receivable turnover	6.7	5.5
2. Debt ratio	43%	39%	6. Basic earnings per share	$1.25	$1.10
3. Gross margin	32%	44%	7. Inventory turnover	3.4	3.6
4. Acid-test ratio	1.20	1.05	8. Dividend yield	4%	3.2%

QS 13-8[A]
Error adjustments
A2 

A review of the notes payable files discovers that three years ago the company reported the entire amount of a payment (principal and interest) on an installment note payable as interest expense. This mistake had a material effect on the amount of income in that year. How should the correction be reported in the current year financial statements?

connect *Most materials in this section are available in McGraw-Hill's Connect*

EXERCISES

Exercise 13-1
Computation and analysis of trend percents
P1

Compute trend percents for the following accounts, using 2007 as the base year. State whether the situation as revealed by the trends appears to be favorable or unfavorable for each account.

	2011	2010	2009	2008	2007
Sales	$282,700	$270,700	$252,500	$234,460	$150,000
Cost of goods sold	128,100	121,980	115,180	106,340	67,000
Accounts receivable	18,000	17,200	16,300	15,100	9,000

Exercise 13-2
Determination of income effects from common-size and trend percents
P1 P2

Common-size and trend percents for Danian Company's sales, cost of goods sold, and expenses follow. Determine whether net income increased, decreased, or remained unchanged in this three-year period.

	Common-Size Percents			Trend Percents		
	2010	2009	2008	2010	2009	2008
Sales	100.0%	100.0%	100.0%	104.9%	103.7%	100.0%
Cost of goods sold	67.7	61.2	58.4	102.5	108.6	100.0
Total expenses	14.4	13.9	14.2	106.5	101.5	100.0

Exercise 13-3
Common-size percent computation and interpretation
P2 

Express the following comparative income statements in common-size percents and assess whether or not this company's situation has improved in the most recent year.

MULAN CORPORATION
Comparative Income Statements
For Years Ended December 31, 2009 and 2008

	2009	2008
Sales	$657,386	$488,400
Cost of goods sold	427,301	286,202
Gross profit	230,085	202,198
Operating expenses	138,051	94,750
Net income	$ 92,034	$107,448

Exercise 13-4
Analysis of short-term financial condition
A1 P3 

The following information is available for Orkay Company and Lowes Company, similar firms operating in the same industry. Write a half-page report comparing Orkay and Lowes using the available information. Your discussion should include their ability to meet current obligations and to use current assets efficiently.

Team Project: Assume that the two companies apply for a one-year loan from the team. Identify additional information the companies must provide before the team can make a loan decision.

	Orkay			Lowes		
	2010	2009	2008	2010	2009	2008
Current ratio	1.6	1.7	2.0	3.1	2.6	1.8
Acid-test ratio	0.9	1.0	1.1	2.7	2.4	1.5
Accounts receivable turnover	29.5	24.2	28.2	15.4	14.2	15.0
Merchandise inventory turnover	23.2	20.9	16.1	13.5	12.0	11.6
Working capital	$60,000	$48,000	$42,000	$121,000	$93,000	$68,000

Exercise 13-5
Analysis of efficiency and financial leverage
A1 P3 

Caren Company and Revlon Company are similar firms that operate in the same industry. Revlon began operations in 2009 and Caren in 2006. In 2011, both companies pay 7% interest on their debt to creditors. The following additional information is available.

	Caren Company			Revlon Company		
	2011	2010	2009	2011	2010	2009
Total asset turnover	3.0	2.7	2.9	1.6	1.4	1.1
Return on total assets	6.9%	6.5%	6.4%	4.3%	4.1%	3.1%
Profit margin ratio	2.3%	2.4%	2.2%	2.7%	2.9%	2.8%
Sales	$400,000	$370,000	$386,000	$200,000	$160,000	$100,000

Write a half-page report comparing Caren and Revlon using the available information. Your analysis should include their ability to use assets efficiently to produce profits. Also comment on their success in employing financial leverage in 2011.

Exercise 13-6
Common-size percents
P2

Nabisco Company's year-end balance sheets follow. Express the balance sheets in common-size percents. Round amounts to the nearest one-tenth of a percent. Analyze and comment on the results.

At December 31	2010	2009	2008
Assets			
Cash	$ 36,229	$ 42,780	$ 44,562
Accounts receivable, net	106,073	76,377	57,087
Merchandise inventory	137,408	98,929	62,038
Prepaid expenses	11,548	11,003	4,903
Plant assets, net	335,317	311,062	272,710
Total assets	$626,575	$540,151	$441,300
Liabilities and Equity			
Accounts payable	$157,577	$ 94,024	$ 57,087
Long-term notes payable secured by mortgages on plant assets	116,618	127,962	99,478
Common stock, $10 par value	163,500	163,500	163,500
Retained earnings	188,880	154,665	121,235
Total liabilities and equity	$626,575	$540,151	$441,300

Exercise 13-7
Liquidity analysis
P3 

Refer to Nabisco Company's balance sheets in Exercise 13-6. Analyze its year-end short-term liquidity position at the end of 2010, 2009, and 2008 by computing (1) the current ratio and (2) the acid-test ratio. Comment on the ratio results. (Round ratio amounts to two decimals.)

Exercise 13-8
Liquidity analysis and interpretation
P3 

Refer to the Nabisco Company information in Exercise 13-6. The company's income statements for the years ended December 31, 2010 and 2009, follow. Assume that all sales are on credit and then compute: (1) days' sales uncollected, (2) accounts receivable turnover, (3) inventory turnover, and (4) days' sales in inventory. Comment on the changes in the ratios from 2009 to 2010. (Round amounts to one decimal.)

For Year Ended December 31	2010		2009	
Sales		$685,000		$557,000
Cost of goods sold	$417,850		$356,265	
Other operating expenses	207,282		141,971	
Interest expense	8,175		8,960	
Income taxes	12,900		12,450	
Total costs and expenses		646,207		519,646
Net income		$ 38,793		$ 37,354
Earnings per share		$ 2.37		$ 2.28

Exercise 13-9
Risk and capital structure analysis
P3 

Refer to the Nabisco Company information in Exercises 13-6 and 13-8. Compare the company's long-term risk and capital structure positions at the end of 2010 and 2009 by computing these ratios: (1) debt and equity ratios, (2) debt-to-equity ratio, and (3) times interest earned. Comment on these ratio results.

Exercise 13-10
Efficiency and profitability analysis
P3 

Refer to Nabisco Company's financial information in Exercises 13-6 and 13-8. Evaluate the company's efficiency and profitability by computing the following for 2010 and 2009: (1) profit margin ratio, (2) total asset turnover, and (3) return on total assets. Comment on these ratio results.

Exercise 13-11
Profitability analysis
P3 

Refer to Nabisco Company's financial information in Exercises 13-6 and 13-8. Additional information about the company follows. To help evaluate the company's profitability, compute and interpret the following ratios for 2010 and 2009: (1) return on common stockholders' equity, (2) price-earnings ratio on December 31, and (3) dividend yield.

Common stock market price, December 31, 2010	$30.00
Common stock market price, December 31, 2009	28.00
Annual cash dividends per share in 2010	0.28
Annual cash dividends per share in 2009	0.24

Exercise 13-12[A]
Income statement categories
A2

In 2009, Simplon Merchandising, Inc., sold its interest in a chain of wholesale outlets, taking the company completely out of the wholesaling business. The company still operates its retail outlets. A listing of the major sections of an income statement follows:

A. Income (loss) from continuing operations
B. Income (loss) from operating, or gain (loss) from disposing, a discontinued segment
C. Extraordinary gain (loss)

Indicate where each of the following income-related items for this company appears on its 2009 income statement by writing the letter of the appropriate section in the blank beside each item.

Section	Item	Debit	Credit
______	1. Net sales		$3,000,000
______	2. Gain on state's condemnation of company property (net of tax)		330,000
______	3. Cost of goods sold	$1,580,000	
______	4. Income taxes expense	117,000	
______	5. Depreciation expense	332,500	
______	6. Gain on sale of wholesale business segment (net of tax)		875,000
______	7. Loss from operating wholesale business segment (net of tax)	544,000	
______	8. Salaries expense	740,000	

Exercise 13-13A
Income statement presentation
A2

Use the financial data for Simplon Merchandising, Inc., in Exercise 13-12 to prepare its income statement for calendar year 2009. (Ignore the earnings per share section.)

Most materials in this section are available in McGraw-Hill's Connect connect

PROBLEM SET A

Problem 13-1A
Ratios, common-size statements, and trend percents
P1 P2 P3 

mhhe.com/wildMA2e

Selected comparative financial statements of Astalon Company follow.

ASTALON COMPANY
Comparative Income Statements
For Years Ended December 31, 2010, 2009, and 2008

	2010	2009	2008
Sales	$526,304	$403,192	$279,800
Cost of goods sold	316,835	255,624	179,072
Gross profit	209,469	147,568	100,728
Selling expenses	74,735	55,640	36,934
Administrative expenses	47,367	35,481	23,223
Total expenses	122,102	91,121	60,157
Income before taxes	87,367	56,447	40,571
Income taxes	16,250	11,572	8,236
Net income	$ 71,117	$ 44,875	$ 32,335

ASTALON COMPANY
Comparative Balance Sheets
December 31, 2010, 2009, and 2008

	2010	2009	2008
Assets			
Current assets	$ 48,242	$ 38,514	$ 51,484
Long-term investments	0	800	3,620
Plant assets, net	92,405	97,259	58,047
Total assets	$140,647	$136,573	$113,151
Liabilities and Equity			
Current liabilities	$ 20,534	$ 20,349	$ 19,801
Common stock	69,000	69,000	51,000
Other paid-in capital	8,625	8,625	5,667
Retained earnings	42,488	38,599	36,683
Total liabilities and equity	$140,647	$136,573	$113,151

Required

1. Compute each year's current ratio. (Round ratio amounts to one decimal.)
2. Express the income statement data in common-size percents. (Round percents to two decimals.)
3. Express the balance sheet data in trend percents with 2008 as the base year. (Round percents to two decimals.)

Check (3) 2010, Total assets trend, 124.30%

Analysis Component

4. Comment on any significant relations revealed by the ratios and percents computed.

Problem 13-2A
Calculation and analysis of trend percents
A1 P1

Selected comparative financial statements of Adobe Company follow.

ADOBE COMPANY
Comparative Income Statements
For Years Ended December 31, 2010–2004

($ thousands)	2010	2009	2008	2007	2006	2005	2004
Sales	$2,431	$2,129	$1,937	$1,776	$1,657	$1,541	$1,263
Cost of goods sold	1,747	1,421	1,223	1,070	994	930	741
Gross profit	684	708	714	706	663	611	522
Operating expenses	521	407	374	276	239	236	196
Net income	$ 163	$ 301	$ 340	$ 430	$ 424	$ 375	$ 326

ADOBE COMPANY
Comparative Balance Sheets
December 31, 2010–2004

($ thousands)	2010	2009	2008	2007	2006	2005	2004
Assets							
Cash	$ 163	$ 216	$ 224	$ 229	$ 238	$ 235	$ 242
Accounts receivable, net	1,173	1,232	1,115	855	753	714	503
Merchandise inventory	4,244	3,090	2,699	2,275	2,043	1,735	1,258
Other current assets	109	98	60	108	91	93	48
Long-term investments	0	0	0	334	334	334	334
Plant assets, net	5,192	5,172	4,526	2,553	2,639	2,345	2,015
Total assets	$10,881	$9,808	$8,624	$6,354	$6,098	$5,456	$4,400
Liabilities and Equity							
Current liabilities	$ 2,734	$2,299	$1,509	$1,255	$1,089	$1,030	$ 664
Long-term liabilities	2,924	2,547	2,478	1,151	1,176	1,273	955
Common stock	1,980	1,980	1,980	1,760	1,760	1,540	1,540
Other paid-in capital	495	495	495	440	440	385	385
Retained earnings	2,748	2,487	2,162	1,748	1,633	1,228	856
Total liabilities and equity	$10,881	$9,808	$8,624	$6,354	$6,098	$5,456	$4,400

Required

1. Compute trend percents for all components of both statements using 2004 as the base year. (Round percents to one decimal.)

Check (1) 2010, Total assets trend, 247.3%

Analysis Component

2. Analyze and comment on the financial statements and trend percents from part 1.

Problem 13-3A
Transactions, working capital, and liquidity ratios
P3

mhhe.com/wildMA2e

Page Corporation began the month of May with $884,000 of current assets, a current ratio of 2.6:1, and an acid-test ratio of 1.5:1. During the month, it completed the following transactions (the company uses a perpetual inventory system).

May 2 Purchased $70,000 of merchandise inventory on credit.
8 Sold merchandise inventory that cost $60,000 for $130,000 cash.
10 Collected $30,000 cash on an account receivable.
15 Paid $31,000 cash to settle an account payable.

Check May 22: Current ratio, 2.23; Acid-test ratio, 1.37

May 29: Current ratio, 2.00; Working capital, $462,000

17 Wrote off a $5,000 bad debt against the Allowance for Doubtful Accounts account.
22 Declared a $1 per share cash dividend on its 67,000 shares of outstanding common stock.
26 Paid the dividend declared on May 22.
27 Borrowed $85,000 cash by giving the bank a 30-day, 10% note.
28 Borrowed $100,000 cash by signing a long-term secured note.
29 Used the $185,000 cash proceeds from the notes to buy new machinery.

Required

Prepare a table showing Page's (1) current ratio, (2) acid-test ratio, and (3) working capital, after each transaction. Round ratios to two decimals.

Problem 13-4A

Calculation of financial statement ratios

P3

mhhe.com/wildMA2e

Selected year-end financial statements of Cadet Corporation follow. (All sales were on credit; selected balance sheet amounts at December 31, 2008, were inventory, $56,900; total assets, $219,400; common stock, $85,000; and retained earnings, $52,348.)

CADET CORPORATION
Income Statement
For Year Ended December 31, 2009

Sales	$456,600
Cost of goods sold	297,450
Gross profit	159,150
Operating expenses	99,400
Interest expense	3,900
Income before taxes	55,850
Income taxes	22,499
Net income	$ 33,351

CADET CORPORATION
Balance Sheet
December 31, 2009

Assets		Liabilities and Equity	
Cash	$ 20,000	Accounts payable	$ 21,500
Short-term investments	8,200	Accrued wages payable	4,400
Accounts receivable, net	29,400	Income taxes payable	3,700
Notes receivable (trade)*	7,000	Long-term note payable, secured by mortgage on plant assets	67,400
Merchandise inventory	34,150	Common stock	85,000
Prepaid expenses	2,700	Retained earnings	66,750
Plant assets, net	147,300		
Total assets	$248,750	Total liabilities and equity	$248,750

* These are short-term notes receivable arising from customer (trade) sales.

Required

Check Acid-test ratio, 2.2 to 1; Inventory turnover, 6.5

Compute the following: (1) current ratio, (2) acid-test ratio, (3) days' sales uncollected, (4) inventory turnover, (5) days' sales in inventory, (6) debt-to-equity ratio, (7) times interest earned, (8) profit margin ratio, (9) total asset turnover, (10) return on total assets, and (11) return on common stockholders' equity.

Problem 13-5A

Comparative ratio analysis A1 P3

Summary information from the financial statements of two companies competing in the same industry follows.

	Karto Company	Bryan Company
Data from the current year-end balance sheets		
Assets		
Cash	$ 19,500	$ 36,000
Accounts receivable, net	36,400	53,400
Current notes receivable (trade)	9,400	7,600
Merchandise inventory	84,740	134,500
Prepaid expenses	6,200	7,250
Plant assets, net	350,000	307,400
Total assets	$506,240	$546,150
Liabilities and Equity		
Current liabilities	$ 63,340	$ 73,819
Long-term notes payable	82,485	99,000
Common stock, $5 par value	190,000	196,000
Retained earnings	170,415	177,331
Total liabilities and equity	$506,240	$546,150

	Karto Company	Bryan Company
Data from the current year's income statement		
Sales	$790,000	$897,200
Cost of goods sold	588,100	634,500
Interest expense	7,600	19,000
Income tax expense	15,185	24,769
Net income	$179,115	$218,931
Basic earnings per share	$ 4.71	$ 5.58
Beginning-of-year balance sheet data		
Accounts receivable, net	$ 26,800	$ 51,200
Current notes receivable (trade)	0	0
Merchandise inventory	55,600	107,400
Total assets	408,000	422,500
Common stock, $5 par value	190,000	196,000
Retained earnings	124,300	95,600

Required

1. For both companies compute the (*a*) current ratio, (*b*) acid-test ratio, (*c*) accounts (including notes) receivable turnover, (*d*) inventory turnover, (*e*) days' sales in inventory, and (*f*) days' sales uncollected. Identify the company you consider to be the better short-term credit risk and explain why.

Check (1) Bryan: Accounts receivable turnover, 16.0; Inventory turnover, 5.2

2. For both companies compute the (*a*) profit margin ratio, (*b*) total asset turnover, (*c*) return on total assets, and (*d*) return on common stockholders' equity. Assuming that each company paid cash dividends of $3.50 per share and each company's stock can be purchased at $85 per share, compute their (*e*) price-earnings ratios and (*f*) dividend yields. Identify which company's stock you would recommend as the better investment and explain why.

(2) Karto: Profit margin, 22.7%; PE, 18.0

Problem 13-6A[A]
Income statement computations and format
A2 

Selected account balances from the adjusted trial balance for Lindo Corporation as of its calendar year-end December 31, 2009, follow.

	Debit	Credit
a. Interest revenue		$ 15,000
b. Depreciation expense—Equipment	$ 35,000	
c. Loss on sale of equipment	26,850	
d. Accounts payable		45,000
e. Other operating expenses	107,400	
f. Accumulated depreciation—Equipment		72,600
g. Gain from settlement of lawsuit		45,000
h. Accumulated depreciation—Buildings		175,500
i. Loss from operating a discontinued segment (pretax)	19,250	
j. Gain on insurance recovery of tornado damage (pretax and extraordinary)		30,120
k. Net sales		999,500
l. Depreciation expense—Buildings	53,000	
m. Correction of overstatement of prior year's sales (pretax)	17,000	
n. Gain on sale of discontinued segment's assets (pretax)		35,000
o. Loss from settlement of lawsuit	24,750	
p. Income taxes expense	?	
q. Cost of goods sold	483,500	

Required

Answer each of the following questions by providing supporting computations.

1. Assume that the company's income tax rate is 30% for all items. Identify the tax effects and after-tax amounts of the four items labeled pretax.

2. What is the amount of income from continuing operations before income taxes? What is the amount of the income taxes expense? What is the amount of income from continuing operations?

3. What is the total amount of after-tax income (loss) associated with the discontinued segment?

4. What is the amount of income (loss) before the extraordinary items?

5. What is the amount of net income for the year?

Check (3) $11,025
(4) $241,325
(5) $262,409

PROBLEM SET B

Problem 13-1B

Ratios, common-size statements, and trend percents

P1 P2 P3 

Selected comparative financial statement information of Danno Corporation follows.

DANNO CORPORATION
Comparative Income Statements
For Years Ended December 31, 2010, 2009, and 2008

	2010	2009	2008
Sales	$392,000	$300,304	$208,400
Cost of goods sold	235,984	190,092	133,376
Gross profit	156,016	110,212	75,024
Selling expenses	55,664	41,442	27,509
Administrative expenses	35,280	26,427	17,297
Total expenses	90,944	67,869	44,806
Income before taxes	65,072	42,343	30,218
Income taxes	12,103	8,680	6,134
Net income	$ 52,969	$ 33,663	$ 24,084

DANNO CORPORATION
Comparative Balance Sheets
December 31, 2010, 2009, and 2008

	2010	2009	2008
Assets			
Current assets	$ 53,776	$ 42,494	$ 55,118
Long-term investments	0	400	4,110
Plant assets, net	99,871	106,303	64,382
Total assets	$153,647	$149,197	$123,610
Liabilities and Equity			
Current liabilities	$ 22,432	$ 22,230	$ 21,632
Common stock	70,000	70,000	52,000
Other paid-in capital	8,750	8,750	5,778
Retained earnings	52,465	48,217	44,200
Total liabilities and equity	$153,647	$149,197	$123,610

Required

1. Compute each year's current ratio. (Round ratio amounts to one decimal.)

2. Express the income statement data in common-size percents. (Round percents to two decimals.)

3. Express the balance sheet data in trend percents with 2008 as the base year. (Round percents to two decimals.)

Check (3) 2010, Total assets trend, 124.30%

Analysis Component

4. Comment on any significant relations revealed by the ratios and percents computed.

Problem 13-2B
Calculation and analysis of trend percents
A1 P1 

Selected comparative financial statements of Park Company follow.

PARK COMPANY Comparative Income Statements For Years Ended December 31, 2010–2004 ($ thousands)	2010	2009	2008	2007	2006	2005	2004
Sales	$570	$620	$640	$690	$750	$780	$870
Cost of goods sold	286	300	304	324	350	360	390
Gross profit	284	320	336	366	400	420	480
Operating expenses	94	114	122	136	150	154	160
Net income	$190	$206	$214	$230	$250	$266	$320

PARK COMPANY Comparative Balance Sheets December 31, 2010–2004 ($ thousands)	2010	2009	2008	2007	2006	2005	2004
Assets							
Cash	$ 54	$ 56	$ 62	$ 64	$ 70	$ 72	$ 78
Accounts receivable, net	140	146	150	154	160	164	170
Merchandise inventory	176	182	188	190	196	200	218
Other current assets	44	44	46	48	48	50	50
Long-term investments	46	40	36	120	120	120	120
Plant assets, net	520	524	530	422	430	438	464
Total assets	$980	$992	$1,012	$998	$1,024	$1,044	$1,100
Liabilities and Equity							
Current liabilities	$158	$166	$ 196	$200	$ 220	$ 270	$ 290
Long-term liabilities	102	130	152	158	204	224	270
Common stock	180	180	180	180	180	180	180
Other paid-in capital	80	80	80	80	80	80	80
Retained earnings	460	436	404	380	340	290	280
Total liabilities and equity	$980	$992	$1,012	$998	$1,024	$1,044	$1,100

Required

1. Compute trend percents for all components of both statements using 2004 as the base year. (Round percents to one decimal.)

Check (1) 2010, Total assets trend, 89.1%

Analysis Component

2. Analyze and comment on the financial statements and trend percents from part 1.

Problem 13-3B
Transactions, working capital, and liquidity ratios
P3

Check June 3: Current ratio, 2.88; Acid-test ratio, 2.40

June 30: Working capital, $(20,000); Current ratio, 0.97

Menardo Corporation began the month of June with $600,000 of current assets, a current ratio of 2.5:1, and an acid-test ratio of 1.4:1. During the month, it completed the following transactions (the company uses a perpetual inventory system).

June	1	Sold merchandise inventory that cost $150,000 for $240,000 cash.
	3	Collected $176,000 cash on an account receivable.
	5	Purchased $300,000 of merchandise inventory on credit.
	7	Borrowed $200,000 cash by giving the bank a 60-day, 8% note.
	10	Borrowed $240,000 cash by signing a long-term secured note.
	12	Purchased machinery for $550,000 cash.
	15	Declared a $1 per share cash dividend on its 160,000 shares of outstanding common stock.
	19	Wrote off a $10,000 bad debt against the Allowance for Doubtful Accounts account.
	22	Paid $24,000 cash to settle an account payable.
	30	Paid the dividend declared on June 15.

Required

Prepare a table showing the company's (1) current ratio, (2) acid-test ratio, and (3) working capital after each transaction. Round ratios to two decimals.

Problem 13-4B

Calculation of financial statement ratios

P3

Selected year-end financial statements of Steele Corporation follow. (All sales were on credit; selected balance sheet amounts at December 31, 2008, were inventory, $55,900; total assets, $249,400; common stock, $105,000; and retained earnings, $17,748.)

STEELE CORPORATION Income Statement For Year Ended December 31, 2009	
Sales	$447,600
Cost of goods sold	298,150
Gross profit	149,450
Operating expenses	98,500
Interest expense	4,600
Income before taxes	46,350
Income taxes	18,672
Net income	$ 27,678

STEELE CORPORATION Balance Sheet December 31, 2009			
Assets		**Liabilities and Equity**	
Cash	$ 8,000	Accounts payable	$ 25,500
Short-term investments	8,000	Accrued wages payable	3,000
Accounts receivable, net	28,800	Income taxes payable	4,000
Notes receivable (trade)*	8,000	Long-term note payable, secured by mortgage on plant assets	63,400
Merchandise inventory	34,150	Common stock, $5 par value	105,000
Prepaid expenses	2,750	Retained earnings	39,100
Plant assets, net	150,300		
Total assets	$240,000	Total liabilities and equity	$240,000

* These are short-term notes receivable arising from customer (trade) sales.

Required

Compute the following: (1) current ratio, (2) acid-test ratio, (3) days' sales uncollected, (4) inventory turnover, (5) days' sales in inventory, (6) debt-to-equity ratio, (7) times interest earned, (8) profit margin ratio, (9) total asset turnover, (10) return on total assets, and (11) return on common stockholders' equity.

Check Acid-test ratio, 1.6 to 1; Inventory turnover, 6.6

Problem 13-5B

Comparative ratio analysis A1 P3

Summary information from the financial statements of two companies competing in the same industry follows.

	Crisco Company	Silas Company
Data from the current year-end balance sheets		
Assets		
Cash	$ 21,000	$ 37,500
Accounts receivable, net	78,100	71,500
Current notes receivable (trade)	12,600	10,000
Merchandise inventory	87,800	83,000
Prepaid expenses	10,700	11,100
Plant assets, net	177,900	253,300
Total assets	$388,100	$466,400
Liabilities and Equity		
Current liabilities	$100,500	$ 98,000
Long-term notes payable	85,650	62,400
Common stock, $5 par value	150,000	170,000
Retained earnings	51,950	136,000
Total liabilities and equity	$388,100	$466,400

	Crisco Company	Silas Company
Data from the current year's income statement		
Sales	$394,600	$668,500
Cost of goods sold	291,600	481,000
Interest expense	6,900	13,300
Income tax expense	6,700	14,300
Net income	34,850	62,700
Basic earnings per share	1.16	1.84
Beginning-of-year balance sheet data		
Accounts receivable, net	$ 73,200	$ 74,300
Current notes receivable (trade)	0	0
Merchandise inventory	106,100	81,500
Total assets	384,400	444,000
Common stock, $5 par value	150,000	170,000
Retained earnings	50,100	110,700

Required

1. For both companies compute the (*a*) current ratio, (*b*) acid-test ratio, (*c*) accounts (including notes) receivable turnover, (*d*) inventory turnover, (*e*) days' sales in inventory, and (*f*) days' sales uncollected. Identify the company you consider to be the better short-term credit risk and explain why.

2. For both companies compute the (*a*) profit margin ratio, (*b*) total asset turnover, (*c*) return on total assets, and (*d*) return on common stockholders' equity. Assuming that each company paid cash dividends of $1.10 per share and each company's stock can be purchased at $25 per share, compute their (*e*) price-earnings ratios and (*f*) dividend yields. Identify which company's stock you would recommend as the better investment and explain why.

Check (1) Crisco: Accounts receivable turnover, 4.8; Inventory turnover, 3.0

(2) Silas: Profit margin, 9.4%; PE, 13.6

Problem 13-6B[A]
Income statement computations and format
A2

Selected account balances from the adjusted trial balance for Harton Corp. as of its calendar year-end December 31, 2009, follow.

	Debit	Credit
a. Accumulated depreciation—Buildings		$ 410,000
b. Interest revenue		30,000
c. Net sales		2,650,000
d. Income taxes expense	$?	
e. Loss on hurricane damage (pretax and extraordinary)	74,000	
f. Accumulated depreciation—Equipment		230,000
g. Other operating expenses	338,000	
h. Depreciation expense—Equipment	110,000	
i. Loss from settlement of lawsuit	46,000	
j. Gain from settlement of lawsuit		78,000
k. Loss on sale of equipment	34,000	
l. Loss from operating a discontinued segment (pretax)	130,000	
m. Depreciation expense—Buildings	166,000	
n. Correction of overstatement of prior year's expense (pretax)		58,000
o. Cost of goods sold	1,050,000	
p. Loss on sale of discontinued segment's assets (pretax)	190,000	
q. Accounts payable		142,000

Required

Answer each of the following questions by providing supporting computations.

1. Assume that the company's income tax rate is 25% for all items. Identify the tax effects and after-tax amounts of the four items labeled pretax.

2. What is the amount of income from continuing operations before income taxes? What is the amount of income taxes expense? What is the amount of income from continuing operations?

3. What is the total amount of after-tax income (loss) associated with the discontinued segment?

4. What is the amount of income (loss) before the extraordinary items?

5. What is the amount of net income for the year?

Check (3) $(240,000)
(4) $520,500
(5) $465,000

SERIAL PROBLEM

Success Systems

(This serial problem began in Chapter 1 and continues through most of the book. If previous chapter segments were not completed, the serial problem can begin at this point. It is helpful, but not necessary, to use the Working Papers that accompany the book.)

SP 13 Use the following selected data from Success Systems' income statement for the three months ended March 31, 2010, and from its March 31, 2010, balance sheet to complete the requirements below: computer services revenue, $25,160; net sales (of goods), $18,693; total sales and revenue, $43,853; cost of goods sold, $14,052; net income, $18,686; quick assets, $100,205; current assets, $105,209; total assets, $129,909; current liabilities, $875; total liabilities, $875; and total equity, $129,034.

Required

1. Compute the gross margin ratio (both with and without services revenue) and net profit margin ratio.

2. Compute the current ratio and acid-test ratio.

3. Compute the debt ratio and equity ratio.

4. What percent of its assets are current? What percent are long term?

BEYOND THE NUMBERS

REPORTING IN ACTION

A1 P1 P2 

BTN 13-1 Refer to Best Buy's financial statements in Appendix A to answer the following.

1. Using fiscal 2005 as the base year, compute trend percents for fiscal years 2005, 2006, and 2007 for revenues, cost of sales, selling general and administrative expenses, income taxes, and net income. (Round to the nearest whole percent.)

2. Compute common-size percents for fiscal years 2007 and 2006 for the following categories of assets: (*a*) total current assets, (*b*) property and equipment, net, and (*c*) intangible assets. (Round to the nearest tenth of a percent.)

3. Comment on any significant changes across the years for the income statement trends computed in part 1 and the balance sheet percents computed in part 2.

Fast Forward

4. Access Best Buy's financial statements for fiscal years ending after March 3, 2007, from Best Buy's Website (BestBuy.com) or the SEC database (www.SEC.gov). Update your work for parts 1, 2, and 3 using the new information accessed.

COMPARATIVE ANALYSIS

C3 P2

BTN 13-2 Key figures for Best Buy, Circuit City, and RadioShack follow.

($ millions)	Best Buy	Circuit City	RadioShack
Cash and equivalents	$ 1,205	$ 141	$ 472
Accounts receivable, net	548	383	248
Inventories	4,028	1,637	752
Retained earnings	5,507	1,336	1,781
Cost of sales	27,165	9,501	2,544
Revenues	35,934	12,430	4,778
Total assets	13,570	4,007	2,070

Required

1. Compute common-size percents for each of the companies using the data provided. (Round percents to one decimal.)

2. Which company retains a higher portion of cumulative net income in the company?

3. Which company has a higher gross margin ratio on sales?

4. Which company holds a higher percent of its total assets as inventory?

ETHICS CHALLENGE

A1

BTN 13-3 As Beacon Company controller, you are responsible for informing the board of directors about its financial activities. At the board meeting, you present the following information.

	2009	2008	2007
Sales trend percent	147.0%	135.0%	100.0%
Selling expenses to sales	10.1%	14.0%	15.6%
Sales to plant assets ratio	3.8 to 1	3.6 to 1	3.3 to 1
Current ratio	2.9 to 1	2.7 to 1	2.4 to 1
Acid-test ratio	1.1 to 1	1.4 to 1	1.5 to 1
Inventory turnover	7.8 times	9.0 times	10.2 times
Accounts receivable turnover	7.0 times	7.7 times	8.5 times
Total asset turnover	2.9 times	2.9 times	3.3 times
Return on total assets	10.4%	11.0%	13.2%
Return on stockholders' equity	10.7%	11.5%	14.1%
Profit margin ratio	3.6%	3.8%	4.0%

After the meeting, the company's CEO holds a press conference with analysts in which she mentions the following ratios.

	2009	2008	2007
Sales trend percent	147.0%	135.0%	100.0%
Selling expenses to sales	10.1%	14.0%	15.6%
Sales to plant assets ratio	3.8 to 1	3.6 to 1	3.3 to 1
Current ratio	2.9 to 1	2.7 to 1	2.4 to 1

Required

1. Why do you think the CEO decided to report 4 ratios instead of the 11 prepared?

2. Comment on the possible consequences of the CEO's reporting of the ratios selected.

COMMUNICATING IN PRACTICE

C2 A1 P3

BTN 13-4 Each team is to select a different industry, and each team member is to select a different company in that industry and acquire its financial statements. Use those statements to analyze the company, including at least one ratio from each of the four building blocks of analysis. When necessary, use the financial press to determine the market price of its stock. Communicate with teammates via a meeting, e-mail, or telephone to discuss how different companies compare to each other and to industry norms. The team is to prepare a single one-page memorandum reporting on its analysis and the conclusions reached.

TAKING IT TO THE NET

C4 P3 

BTN 13-5 Access the February 23, 2007, filing of the 2006 10-K report of the **Hershey Foods Corporation** (ticker HSY) at www.sec.gov and complete the following requirements.

Required

Compute or identify the following profitability ratios of Hershey for its years ending December 31, 2006, *and* December 31, 2005. Interpret its profitability using the results obtained for these two years.

1. Profit margin ratio.

2. Gross profit ratio.

3. Return on total assets. (Total assets in 2004 were $3,794,750,000.)

4. Return on common stockholders' equity. (Total shareholders' equity in 2004 was $1,137,103,000.)

5. Basic earnings per common share.

TEAMWORK IN ACTION

C2 P1 P2 P3

BTN 13-6 A team approach to learning financial statement analysis is often useful.

Required

1. Each team should write a description of horizontal and vertical analysis that all team members agree with and understand. Illustrate each description with an example.

2. *Each* member of the team is to select *one* of the following categories of ratio analysis. Explain what the ratios in that category measure. Choose one ratio from the category selected, present its formula, and explain what it measures.

a. Liquidity and efficiency **c.** Profitability

b. Solvency **d.** Market prospects

3. Each team member is to present his or her notes from part 2 to teammates. Team members are to confirm or correct other teammates' presentation.

Hint: Pairing within teams may be necessary for part 2. Use as an in-class activity or as an assignment. Consider presentations to the entire class using team rotation with transparencies.

ENTREPRENEURIAL DECISION

A1 P1 P2 P3 

BTN 13-7 Assume that David and Tom Gardner of **The Motley Fool** (Fool.com) have impressed you since you first heard of their rather improbable rise to prominence in financial circles. You learn of a staff opening at The Motley Fool and decide to apply for it. Your resume is successfully screened from the thousands received and you advance to the interview process. You learn that the interview consists of analyzing the following financial facts and answering analysis questions. (*Note:* The data are taken from a small merchandiser in outdoor recreational equipment.)

	2008	2007	2006
Sales trend percents	137.0%	125.0%	100.0%
Selling expenses to sales	9.8%	13.7%	15.3%
Sales to plant assets ratio	3.5 to 1	3.3 to 1	3.0 to 1
Current ratio	2.6 to 1	2.4 to 1	2.1 to 1
Acid-test ratio	0.8 to 1	1.1 to 1	1.2 to 1
Merchandise inventory turnover	7.5 times	8.7 times	9.9 times
Accounts receivable turnover	6.7 times	7.4 times	8.2 times
Total asset turnover	2.6 times	2.6 times	3.0 times
Return on total assets	8.8%	9.4%	11.1%
Return on equity	9.75%	11.50%	12.25%
Profit margin ratio	3.3%	3.5%	3.7%

Required

Use these data to answer each of the following questions with explanations.

1. Is it becoming easier for the company to meet its current liabilities on time and to take advantage of any available cash discounts? Explain.
2. Is the company collecting its accounts receivable more rapidly? Explain.
3. Is the company's investment in accounts receivable decreasing? Explain.
4. Is the company's investment in plant assets increasing? Explain.
5. Is the owner's investment becoming more profitable? Explain.
6. Did the dollar amount of selling expenses decrease during the three-year period? Explain.

HITTING THE ROAD

C1 P3

BTN 13-8 You are to devise an investment strategy to enable you to accumulate $1,000,000 by age 65. Start by making some assumptions about your salary. Next compute the percent of your salary that you will be able to save each year. If you will receive any lump-sum monies, include those amounts in your calculations. Historically, stocks have delivered average annual returns of 10–11%. Given this history, you should probably not assume that you will earn above 10% on the money you invest. It is not necessary to specify exactly what types of assets you will buy for your investments; just assume a rate you expect to earn. Use the future value tables in Appendix B to calculate how your savings will grow. Experiment a bit with your figures to see how much less you have to save if you start at, for example, age 25 versus age 35 or 40. (For this assignment, do not include inflation in your calculations.)

GLOBAL DECISION

A1

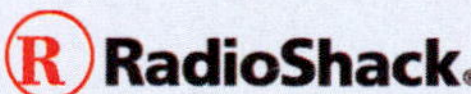

BTN 13-9 DSG international plc (www.DSGiplc.com), Best Buy, Circuit City, and RadioShack are competitors in the global marketplace. Key figures for DSG follow (in millions).

Cash and equivalents	£ 441
Accounts receivable, net	393
Inventories	1,031
Retained earnings	1,490
Cost of sales	7,285
Revenues	7,930
Total assets	3,977

Required

1. Compute common-sized percents for DSG using the data provided. (Round percents to one decimal.)
2. Compare the results with Best Buy, Circuit City, and RadioShack from BTN 13-2.

ANSWERS TO MULTIPLE CHOICE QUIZ

1. d; ($351,000/$300,000) × 100 = 117%
2. e; ($86,000 + $76,000 + $122,000 + $12,000)/$124,000 = 2.39
3. c; ($86,000 + $76,000)/$124,000 = 1.31
4. a; ($124,000 + $90,000)/$830,000 = 25.78%
5. d; ($300,000 + $316,000)/$830,000 = 74.22%

A Financial Statement Information

This appendix includes financial information for (1) **Best Buy**, (2) **Circuit City**, (3) **RadioShack**, and (4) **Apple**. This information is taken from their annual 10-K reports filed with the SEC. An **annual report** is a summary of a company's financial results for the year along with its current financial condition and future plans. This report is directed to external users of financial information, but it also affects the actions and decisions of internal users.

A company uses an annual report to showcase itself and its products. Many annual reports include attractive photos, diagrams, and illustrations related to the company. The primary objective of annual reports, however, is the *financial section,* which communicates much information about a company, with most data drawn from the accounting information system. The layout of an annual report's financial section is fairly established and typically includes the following:

- Letter to Shareholders
- Financial History and Highlights
- Management Discussion and Analysis
- Management's Report on Financial Statements and on Internal Controls
- Report of Independent Accountants (Auditor's Report) and on Internal Controls
- Financial Statements
- Notes to Financial Statements
- List of Directors and Officers

This appendix provides the financial statements for Best Buy (plus selected notes), Circuit City, RadioShack, and Apple. The appendix is organized as follows:

Many assignments at the end of each chapter refer to information in this appendix. We encourage readers to spend time with these assignments; they are especially useful in showing the relevance and diversity of financial accounting and reporting.

Special note: The SEC maintains the EDGAR (**E**lectronic **D**ata **G**athering, **A**nalysis, and **R**etrieval) database at www.sec.gov. The **Form 10-K** is the annual report form for most companies. It provides electronically accessible information. The **Form 10-KSB** is the annual report form filed by small businesses. It requires slightly less information than the Form 10-K. One of these forms must be filed within 90 days after the company's fiscal year-end. (Forms 10-K405, 10-KT, 10-KT405, and 10-KSB405 are slight variations of the usual form due to certain regulations or rules.)

BEST BUY

Financial Report

Selected Financial Data

The following table presents our selected financial data. In fiscal 2004, we sold our interest in Musicland. All fiscal years presented reflect the classification of Musicland's financial results as discontinued operations.

Five-Year Financial Highlights

$ in millions, except per share amounts

Fiscal Year	2007[1]	2006	2005	2004	2003
Consolidated Statements of Earnings Data					
Revenue	$35,934	$30,848	$27,433	$24,548	$20,943
Operating income	1,999	1,644	1,442	1,304	1,010
Earnings from continuing operations	1,377	1,140	934	800	622
Loss from discontinued operations, net of tax	—	—	—	(29)	(441)
Gain (loss) on disposal of discontinued operations, net of tax	—	—	50	(66)	—
Cumulative effect of change in accounting principles, net of tax	—	—	—	—	(82)
Net earnings	1,377	1,140	984	705	99
Per Share Data					
Continuing operations	$ 2.79	$ 2.27	$ 1.86	$ 1.61	$ 1.27
Discontinued operations	—	—	—	(0.06)	(0.89)
Gain (loss) on disposal of discontinued operations	—	—	0.10	(0.13)	—
Cumulative effect of accounting changes	—	—	—	—	(0.16)
Net earnings	2.79	2.27	1.96	1.42	0.20
Cash dividends declared and paid	0.36	0.31	0.28	0.27	—
Common stock price:					
High	59.50	56.00	41.47	41.80	35.83
Low	43.51	31.93	29.25	17.03	11.33
Operating Statistics					
Comparable store sales gain	5.0%	4.9%	4.3%	7.1%	2.4%
Gross profit rate	24.4%	25.0%	23.7%	23.9%	23.6%
Selling, general and administrative expenses rate	18.8%	19.7%	18.4%	18.6%	18.8%
Operating income rate	5.6%	5.3%	5.3%	5.3%	4.8%
Year-End Data					
Current ratio	1.4	1.3	1.4	1.3	1.3
Total assets	$13,570	$11,864	$10,294	$ 8,652	$ 7,694
Debt, including current portion	650	596	600	850	834
Total shareholders' equity	6,201	5,257	4,449	3,422	2,730
Number of stores					
Domestic	868	774	694	631	567
International	304	167	144	127	112
Total	1,172	941	838	758	679
Retail square footage (000s)					
Domestic	33,959	30,826	28,465	26,640	24,432
International	7,926	3,564	3,139	2,800	2,375
Total	41,885	34,390	31,604	29,440	26,807

[1] Fiscal 2007 included 53 weeks. All other periods presented included 52 weeks.

Consolidated Balance Sheets
$ in millions, except per share amounts

	March 3, 2007	February 25, 2006
Assets		
Current Assets		
Cash and cash equivalents	$ 1,205	$ 748
Short-term investments	2,588	3,041
Receivables	548	449
Merchandise inventories	4,028	3,338
Other current assets	712	409
Total current assets	9,081	7,985
Property and Equipment		
Land and buildings	705	580
Leasehold improvements	1,540	1,325
Fixtures and equipment	2,627	2,898
Property under capital lease	32	33
	4,904	4,836
Less accumulated depreciation	1,966	2,124
Net property and equipment	2,938	2,712
Goodwill	919	557
Tradenames	81	44
Long-Term Investments	318	218
Other Assets	233	348
Total Assets	$13,570	$11,864
Liabilities and Shareholders' Equity		
Current Liabilities		
Accounts payable	$ 3,934	$ 3,234
Unredeemed gift card liabilities	496	469
Accrued compensation and related expenses	332	354
Accrued liabilities	990	878
Accrued income taxes	489	703
Short-term debt	41	—
Current portion of long-term debt	19	418
Total current liabilities	6,301	6,056
Long-Term Liabilities	443	373
Long-Term Debt	590	178
Minority Interests	35	—
Shareholders' Equity		
Preferred stock, $1.00 par value: Authorized — 400,000 shares; Issued and outstanding — none	—	—
Common stock, $.10 par value: Authorized — 1 billion shares; Issued and outstanding — 480,655,000 and 485,098,000 shares, respectively	48	49
Additional paid-in capital	430	643
Retained earnings	5,507	4,304
Accumulated other comprehensive income	216	261
Total shareholders' equity	6,201	5,257
Total Liabilities and Shareholders' Equity	$13,570	$11,864

Consolidated Statements of Earnings
$ in millions, except per share amounts

Fiscal Years Ended	March 3, 2007	February 25, 2006	February 26, 2005
Revenue	$35,934	$30,848	$27,433
Cost of goods sold	27,165	23,122	20,938
Gross profit	8,769	7,726	6,495
Selling, general and administrative expenses	6,770	6,082	5,053
Operating income	1,999	1,644	1,442
Net interest income	111	77	1
Gain on investments	20	—	—
Earnings from continuing operations before income tax expense	2,130	1,721	1,443
Income tax expense	752	581	509
Minority interest in earnings	1	—	—
Earnings from continuing operations	1,377	1,140	934
Gain on disposal of discontinued operations, net of tax	—	—	50
Net earnings	$ 1,377	$ 1,140	$ 984
Basic earnings per share:			
Continuing operations	$ 2.86	$ 2.33	$ 1.91
Gain on disposal of discontinued operations	—	—	0.10
Basic earnings per share	$ 2.86	$ 2.33	$ 2.01
Diluted earnings per share:			
Continuing operations	$ 2.79	$ 2.27	$ 1.86
Gain on disposal of discontinued operations	—	—	0.10
Diluted earnings per share	$ 2.79	$ 2.27	$ 1.96
Basic weighted-average common shares outstanding (in millions)	482.1	490.3	488.9
Diluted weighted-average common shares outstanding (in millions)	496.2	504.8	505.0

BEST BUY

Consolidated Statements of Changes in Shareholders' Equity
$ and shares in millions

	Common Shares	Common Stock	Additional Paid-In Capital	Retained Earnings	Accumulated Other Comprehensive Income	Total
Balances at February 28, 2004	**487**	**$49**	**$819**	**$ 2,468**	**$ 86**	**$3,422**
Net earnings	—	—	—	984	—	984
Other comprehensive income, net of tax:						
Foreign currency translation adjustments	—	—	—	—	59	59
Other	—	—	—	—	4	4
Total comprehensive income						1,047
Stock options exercised	10	1	219	—	—	220
Tax benefit from stock options exercised and employee stock purchase plan	—	—	60	—	—	60
Issuance of common stock under employee stock purchase plan	2	—	36	—	—	36
Vesting of restricted stock awards	—	—	1	—	—	1
Common stock dividends, $0.28 per share	—	—	—	(137)	—	(137)
Repurchase of common stock	(6)	(1)	(199)	—	—	(200)
Balances at February 26, 2005	**493**	**49**	**936**	**3,315**	**149**	**4,449**
Net earnings	—	—	—	1,140	—	1,140
Other comprehensive income, net of tax:						
Foreign currency translation adjustments	—	—	—	—	101	101
Other	—	—	—	—	11	11
Total comprehensive income						1,252
Stock options exercised	9	1	256	—	—	257
Tax benefit from stock options exercised and employee stock purchase plan	—	—	55	—	—	55
Issuance of common stock under employee stock purchase plan	1	—	35	—	—	35
Stock-based compensation	—	—	132	—	—	132
Common stock dividends, $0.31 per share	—	—	—	(151)	—	(151)
Repurchase of common stock	(18)	(1)	(771)	—	—	(772)
Balances at February 25, 2006	**485**	**49**	**643**	**4,304**	**261**	**5,257**
Net earnings	—	—	—	1,377	—	1,377
Other comprehensive loss, net of tax:						
Foreign currency translation adjustments	—	—	—	—	(33)	(33)
Other	—	—	—	—	(12)	(12)
Total comprehensive income						1,332
Stock options exercised	7	1	167	—	—	168
Tax benefit from stock options exercised and employee stock purchase plan	—	—	47	—	—	47
Issuance of common stock under employee stock purchase plan	1	—	49	—	—	49
Stock-based compensation	—	—	121	—	—	121
Common stock dividends, $0.36 per share	—	—	—	(174)	—	(174)
Repurchase of common stock	(12)	(2)	(597)	—	—	(599)
Balances at March 3, 2007	**481**	**$48**	**$430**	**$5,507**	**$216**	**$6,201**

Consolidated Statements of Cash Flows
$ in millions

Fiscal Years Ended	March 3, 2007	February 25, 2006	February 26, 2005
Operating Activities			
Net earnings	$1,377	$1,140	$ 984
Gain from disposal of discontinued operations, net of tax	—	—	(50)
Earnings from continuing operations	1,377	1,140	934
Adjustments to reconcile earnings from continuing operations to total cash provided by operating activities from continuing operations:			
Depreciation	509	456	459
Asset impairment charges	32	4	22
Stock-based compensation	121	132	(1)
Deferred income taxes	82	(151)	(28)
Excess tax benefits from stock-based compensation	(50)	(55)	—
Other, net	(11)	(3)	24
Changes in operating assets and liabilities, net of acquired assets and liabilities:			
Receivables	(70)	(43)	(30)
Merchandise inventories	(550)	(457)	(240)
Other assets	(47)	(11)	(50)
Accounts payable	320	385	347
Other liabilities	185	165	243
Accrued income taxes	(136)	178	301
Total cash provided by operating activities from continuing operations	1,762	1,740	1,981
Investing Activities			
Additions to property and equipment, net of $75 and $117 noncash capital expenditures in fiscal 2006 and 2005, respectively	(733)	(648)	(502)
Purchases of available-for-sale securities	(4,541)	(4,319)	(8,517)
Sales of available-for-sale securities	4,886	4,187	7,730
Acquisitions of businesses, net of cash acquired	(421)	—	—
Proceeds from disposition of investments	24	—	—
Change in restricted assets	—	(20)	(140)
Other, net	5	46	7
Total cash used in investing activities from continuing operations	(780)	(754)	(1,422)
Financing Activities			
Repurchase of common stock	(599)	(772)	(200)
Issuance of common stock under employee stock purchase plan and for the exercise of stock options	217	292	256
Dividends paid	(174)	(151)	(137)
Repayments of debt	(84)	(69)	(371)
Proceeds from issuance of debt	96	36	—
Excess tax benefits from stock-based compensation	50	55	—
Other, net	(19)	(10)	(7)
Total cash used in financing activities from continuing operations	(513)	(619)	(459)
Effect of Exchange Rate Changes on Cash	(12)	27	9
Increase in Cash and Cash Equivalents	457	394	109
Cash and Cash Equivalents at Beginning of Year	748	354	245
Cash and Cash Equivalents at End of Year	$1,205	$ 748	$ 354
Supplemental Disclosure of Cash Flow Information			
Income taxes paid	$ 804	$ 547	$ 241
Interest paid	14	16	35

SELECTED Notes to Consolidated Financial Statements

$ in millions, except per share amounts

1. Summary of Significant Accounting Policies

Description of Business

Best Buy Co., Inc. is a specialty retailer of consumer electronics, home-office products, entertainment software, appliances and related services, with fiscal 2007 revenue from continuing operations of $35.9 billion.

We operate two reportable segments: Domestic and International. The Domestic segment is comprised of all U.S. store and online operations of Best Buy, Geek Squad, Magnolia Audio Video and Pacific Sales Kitchen and Bath Centers, Inc. ("Pacific Sales"). We acquired Pacific Sales on March 7, 2006. U.S. Best Buy stores offer a wide variety of consumer electronics, home-office products, entertainment software, appliances and related services through 822 stores at the end of fiscal 2007. Geek Squad provides residential and commercial computer repair, support and installation services in all U.S. Best Buy stores and at 12 stand-alone stores at the end of fiscal 2007. Magnolia Audio Video stores offer high-end audio and video products and related services through 20 stores at the end of fiscal 2007. Pacific Sales stores offer high-end home-improvement products, appliances and related services through 14 stores at the end of fiscal 2007.

Fiscal Year

Our fiscal year ends on the Saturday nearest the end of February. Fiscal 2007 included 53 weeks and fiscal 2006 and 2005 each included 52 weeks.

Cash and Cash Equivalents

Cash primarily consists of cash on hand and bank deposits. Cash equivalents primarily consist of money market accounts and other highly liquid investments with an original maturity of three months or less when purchased. We carry these investments at cost, which approximates market value. The amounts of cash equivalents at March 3, 2007, and February 25, 2006, were $695 and $350, respectively, and the weighted-average interest rates were 4.8% and 3.3%, respectively.

Outstanding checks in excess of funds on deposit ("book overdrafts") totaled $183 and $230 at March 3, 2007, and February 25, 2006, respectively, and are reflected as current liabilities in our consolidated balance sheets.

Merchandise Inventories

Merchandise inventories are recorded at the lower of average cost or market. In-bound freight-related costs from our vendors are included as part of the net cost of merchandise inventories. Also included in the cost of inventory are certain vendor allowances that are not a reimbursement of specific, incremental and identifiable costs to promote a vendor's products. Other costs associated with acquiring, storing and transporting merchandise inventories to our retail stores are expensed as incurred and included in cost of goods sold.

Our inventory loss reserve represents anticipated physical inventory losses (e.g., theft) that have occurred since the last physical inventory date. Independent physical inventory counts are taken on a regular basis to ensure that the inventory reported in our consolidated financial statements is properly stated. During the interim period between physical inventory counts, we reserve for anticipated physical inventory losses on a location-by-location basis.

Property and Equipment

Property and equipment are recorded at cost. We compute depreciation using the straight-line method over the estimated useful lives of the assets. Leasehold improvements are depreciated over the shorter of their estimated useful lives or the period from the date the assets are placed in service to the end of the initial lease term. Leasehold improvements made significantly after the initial lease term are depreciated over the shorter of their estimated useful lives or the remaining lease term, including renewal periods, if reasonably assured.

$ in millions, except per share amounts

Accelerated depreciation methods are generally used for income tax purposes.

When property is fully depreciated, retired or otherwise disposed of, the cost and accumulated depreciation are removed from the accounts and any resulting gain or loss is reflected in the consolidated statement of earnings.

Repairs and maintenance costs are charged directly to expense as incurred. Major renewals or replacements that substantially extend the useful life of an asset are capitalized and depreciated.

Estimated useful lives by major asset category are as follows:

Asset	Life (in years)
Buildings	30–40
Leasehold improvements	3–25
Fixtures and equipment	3–20
Property under capital lease	3–20

Impairment of Long-Lived Assets

We account for the impairment or disposal of long-lived assets in accordance with SFAS No. 144, *Accounting for the Impairment* or *Disposal of Long-Lived Assets,* which requires long-lived assets, such as property and equipment, to be evaluated for impairment whenever events or changes in circumstances indicate the carrying value of an asset may not be recoverable. Factors considered important that could result in an impairment review include, but are not limited to, significant underperformance relative to historical or planned operating results, significant changes in the manner of use of the assets or significant changes in our business strategies. An impairment loss is recognized when the estimated undiscounted cash flows expected to result from the use of the asset plus net proceeds expected from disposition of the asset (if any) are less than the carrying value of the asset. When an impairment loss is recognized, the carrying amount of the asset is reduced to its estimated fair value based on quoted market prices or other valuation techniques.

Leases

We conduct the majority of our retail and distribution operations from leased locations. The leases require payment of real estate taxes, insurance and common area maintenance, in addition to rent. The terms of our lease agreements generally range from 10 to 20 years. Most of the leases contain renewal options and escalation clauses, and certain store leases require contingent rents based on factors such as specified percentages of revenue or the consumer price index. Other leases contain covenants related to the maintenance of financial ratios.

Goodwill and Intangible Assets

Goodwill

Goodwill is the excess of the purchase price over the fair value of identifiable net assets acquired in business combinations accounted for under the purchase method. We do not amortize goodwill but test it for impairment annually, or when indications of potential impairment exist, utilizing a fair value approach at the reporting unit level. A reporting unit is the operating segment, or a business unit one level below that operating segment, for which discrete financial information is prepared and regularly reviewed by segment management.

Tradenames

We have an indefinite-lived intangible asset related to our Pacific Sales tradename which is included in the Domestic segment. We also have indefinite-lived intangible assets related to our Future Shop and Five Star tradenames which are included in the International segment.

We determine fair values utilizing widely accepted valuation techniques, including discounted cash flows and market multiple analyses. During the fourth quarter of fiscal 2007, we completed our annual impairment testing of our goodwill and tradenames, using the valuation techniques as described above, and determined there was no impairment.

Lease Rights

Lease rights represent costs incurred to acquire the lease of a specific commercial property. Lease rights are recorded at cost and are amortized to rent expense over the remaining lease term, including renewal periods, if reasonably assured. Amortization periods range up to 16 years, beginning with the date we take possession of the property.

$ in millions, except per share amounts

Investments

Short-term and long-term investments are comprised of municipal and United States government debt securities as well as auction-rate securities and variable-rate demand notes. In accordance with SFAS No. 115, *Accounting for Certain Investments in Debt and Equity Securities,* and based on our ability to market and sell these instruments, we classify auction-rate securities, variable-rate demand notes and other investments in debt securities as available-for-sale and carry them at amortized cost, which approximates fair value. Auction-rate securities and variable-rate demand notes are similar to short-term debt instruments because their interest rates are reset periodically. Investments in these securities can be sold for cash on the auction date. We classify auction-rate securities and variable-rate demand notes as short-term or long-term investments based on the reset dates.

We also hold investments in marketable equity securities and classify them as available-for-sale. Investments in marketable equity securities are included in other assets in our consolidated balance sheets. Investments in marketable equity securities are reported at fair value, based on quoted market prices when available. All unrealized holding gains or losses are reflected net of tax in accumulated other comprehensive income in shareholders' equity.

We review the key characteristics of our debt and marketable equity securities portfolio and their classification in accordance with GAAP on an annual basis, or when indications of potential impairment exist. If a decline in the fair value of a security is deemed by management to be other than temporary, the cost basis of the investment is written down to fair value, and the amount of the write-down is included in the determination of net earnings.

Income Taxes

We account for income taxes under the liability method. Under this method, deferred tax assets and liabilities are recognized for the estimated future tax consequences attributable to differences between the financial statement carrying amounts of existing assets and liabilities and their respective tax bases, and operating loss and tax credit carryforwards. Deferred tax assets and liabilities are measured using enacted income tax rates in effect for the year in which those temporary differences are expected to be recovered or settled. The effect on deferred tax assets and liabilities of a change in income tax rates is recognized in our consolidated statement of earnings in the period that includes the enactment date. A valuation allowance is recorded to reduce the carrying amounts of deferred tax assets if it is more likely than not that such assets will not be realized.

Long-Term Liabilities

The major components of long-term liabilities at March 3, 2007, and February 25, 2006, included long-term rent-related liabilities, deferred compensation plan liabilities, self-insurance reserves and advances received under vendor alliance programs.

Foreign Currency

Foreign currency denominated assets and liabilities are translated into U.S. dollars using the exchange rates in effect at our consolidated balance sheet date. Results of operations and cash flows are translated using the average exchange rates throughout the period. The effect of exchange rate fluctuations on translation of assets and liabilities is included as a component of shareholders' equity in accumulated other comprehensive income. Gains and losses from foreign currency transactions, which are included in SG&A, have not been significant.

Revenue Recognition

We recognize revenue when the sales price is fixed or determinable, collectibility is reasonably assured and the customer takes possession of the merchandise, or in the case of services, at the time the service is provided.

$ in millions, except per share amounts

Amounts billed to customers for shipping and handling are included in revenue. Revenue is reported net of estimated sales returns and excludes sales taxes.

We estimate our sales returns reserve based on historical return rates. We initially established our sales returns reserve in the fourth quarter of fiscal 2005. Our sales returns reserve was $104 and $78, at March 3, 2007, and February 25, 2006, respectively.

We sell extended service contracts on behalf of an unrelated third party. In jurisdictions where we are not deemed to be the obligor on the contract, commissions are recognized in revenue at the time of sale. In jurisdictions where we are deemed to be the obligor on the contract, commissions are recognized in revenue ratably over the term of the service contract. Commissions represented 2.2%, 2.5% and 2.6% of revenues in fiscal 2007, 2006 and 2005, respectively.

For revenue transactions that involve multiple deliverables, we defer the revenue associated with any undelivered elements. The amount of revenue deferred in connection with the undelivered elements is determined using the relative fair value of each element, which is generally based on each element's relative retail price. See additional information regarding our customer loyalty program in *Sales Incentives* below.

Gift Cards

We sell gift cards to our customers in our retail stores, through our Web sites, and through selected third parties. We do not charge administrative fees on unused gift cards and our gift cards do not have an expiration date. We recognize income from gift cards when: (i) the gift card is redeemed by the customer; or (ii) the likelihood of the gift card being redeemed by the customer is remote ("gift card breakage") and we determine that we do not have a legal obligation to remit the value of unredeemed gift cards to the relevant jurisdictions. We determine our gift card breakage rate based upon historical redemption patterns. Based on our historical information, the likelihood of a gift card remaining unredeemed can be determined 24 months after the gift card is issued. At that time, we recognize breakage income for those cards for which the likelihood of redemption is deemed remote and we do not have a legal obligation to remit the value of such unredeemed gift cards to the relevant jurisdictions. Gift card breakage income is included in revenue in our consolidated statements of earnings.

We began recognizing gift card breakage income during the third quarter of fiscal 2006. Gift card breakage income was as follows in fiscal 2007, 2006 and 2005:

	2007[1]	2006[1]	2005
Gift card breakage income	$46	$43	$ —

[1] Due to the resolution of certain legal matters associated with gift card liabilities, we recognized $19 and $27 of gift card breakage income in fiscal 2007 and 2006, respectively, that related to prior fiscal years.

Sales Incentives

We frequently offer sales incentives that entitle our customers to receive a reduction in the price of a product or service. Sales incentives include discounts, coupons and other offers that entitle a customer to receive a reduction in the price of a product or service by submitting a claim for a refund or rebate. For sales incentives issued to a customer in conjunction with a sale of merchandise or services, for which we are the obligor, the reduction in revenue is recognized at the time of sale, based on the retail value of the incentive expected to be redeemed.

Customer Loyalty Program

We have a customer loyalty program which allows members to earn points for each qualifying purchase. Points earned enable members to receive a certificate that may be redeemed on future purchases at U.S. Best Buy stores.

$ in millions, except per share amounts

Cost of Goods Sold and Selling, General and Administrative Expenses

The following table illustrates the primary costs classified in each major expense category:

Cost of Goods Sold	SG&A
• Total cost of products sold including: —Freight expenses associated with moving merchandise inventories from our vendors to our distribution centers; —Vendor allowances that are not a reimbursement of specific, incremental and identifiable costs to promote a vendor's products; and —Cash discounts on payments to vendors; • Cost of services provided including: —Payroll and benefits costs for services employees; and —Cost of replacement parts and related freight expenses; • Physical inventory losses; • Markdowns; • Customer shipping and handling expenses; • Costs associated with operating our distribution network, including payroll and benefit costs, occupancy costs, and depreciation; • Freight expenses associated with moving merchandise inventories from our distribution centers to our retail stores; and • Promotional financing costs.	• Payroll and benefit costs for retail and corporate employees; • Occupancy costs of retail, services and corporate facilities; • Depreciation related to retail, services and corporate assets; • Advertising; • Vendor allowances that are a reimbursement of specific, incremental and identifiable costs to promote a vendor's products; • Charitable contributions; • Outside service fees; • Long-lived asset impairment charges; and • Other administrative costs, such as credit card service fees, supplies, and travel and lodging.

Advertising Costs

Advertising costs, which are included in SG&A, are expensed the first time the advertisement runs. Advertising costs consist primarily of print and television advertisements as well as promotional events. Net advertising expenses were $692, $644 and $597 in fiscal 2007, 2006 and 2005, respectively. Allowances received from vendors for advertising of $140, $123 and $115, in fiscal 2007, 2006 and 2005, respectively, were classified as reductions of advertising expenses.

$ in millions, except per share amounts

4. Investments

Short-Term and Long-Term Investments

The following table presents the amortized principal amounts, related weighted-average interest rates, maturities and major security types for our investments:

	March 3, 2007		Feb. 25, 2006	
	Amortized Principal Amount	Weighted-Average Interest Rate	Amortized Principal Amount	Weighted-Average Interest Rate
Short-term investments (less than one year)	$2,588	5.68%	$3,041	4.76%
Long-term investments (one to three years)	318	5.68%	218	4.95%
Total	$2,906		$3,259	
Municipal debt securities	$2,840		$3,155	
Auction-rate and asset-backed securities	66		97	
Debt securities issued by U.S. Treasury and other U.S. government entities	—		7	
Total	$2,906		$3,259	

The carrying value of our investments approximated fair value at March 3, 2007, and February 25, 2006, due to the rapid turnover of our portfolio and the highly liquid nature of these investments. Therefore, there were no significant realized or unrealized gains or losses.

Marketable Equity Securities

The carrying values of our investments in marketable equity securities at March 3, 2007, and February 25, 2006, were $4 and $28, respectively. Net unrealized (loss)/gain, net of tax, included in accumulated other comprehensive income was ($1) and $12 at March 3, 2007, and February 25, 2006, respectively.

$ in millions, except per share amounts

5. Debt

Short-term debt consisted of the following:

	March 3, 2007	Feb. 25, 2006
Notes payable to banks, secured, interest rates ranging from 3.5% to 6.7%	$ 21	$ —
Revolving credit facility, secured, variable interest rate of 5.6% at March 3, 2007	20	—
Total short-term debt	$ 41	$ —
Weighted-average interest rate	5.3%	—

Long-term debt consisted of the following:

	March 3, 2007	Feb. 25, 2006
Convertible subordinated debentures, unsecured, due 2022, interest rate 2.25%	$402	$ 402
Financing lease obligations, due 2009 to 2023, interest rates ranging from 3.0% to 6.5%	171	157
Capital lease obligations, due 2008 to 2026, interest rates ranging from 1.8% to 8.0%	24	27
Other debt, due 2010, interest rate 8.8%	12	10
Total debt	609	596
Less: current portion[1]	(19)	(418)
Total long-term debt	$590	$ 178

[1] Since holders of our debentures due in 2022 could have required us to purchase all or a portion of their debentures on January 15, 2007, we classified our debentures in the current portion of long-term debt at February 25, 2006. However, no holders of our debentures exercised this put option on January 15, 2007. The next time the holders of our debentures could require us to purchase all or a portion of their debentures is January 15, 2012. Therefore, we classified our debentures as long-term debt at March 3, 2007.

Certain debt is secured by property and equipment with a net book value of $80 and $41 at March 3, 2007, and February 25, 2006, respectively.

Convertible Debentures

In January 2002, we sold convertible subordinated debentures having an aggregate principal amount of $402. The proceeds from the offering, net of $6 in offering expenses, were $396. The debentures mature in 2022 and are callable at par, at our option, for cash on or after January 15, 2007.

Holders may require us to purchase all or a portion of their debentures on January 15, 2012, and January 15, 2017, at a purchase price equal to 100% of the principal amount of the debentures plus accrued and unpaid interest up to but not including the date of purchase. We have the option to settle the purchase price in cash, stock, or a combination of cash and stock.

$ in millions, except per share amounts

Other

The fair value of debt approximated $683 and $693 at March 3, 2007, and February 25, 2006, respectively, based on the ask prices quoted from external sources, compared with carrying values of $650 and $596, respectively.

At March 3, 2007, the future maturities of long-term debt, including capitalized leases, consisted of the following:

Fiscal Year	
2008	$ 19
2009	18
2010	27
2011	18
2012	420
Thereafter	107
	$609

Earnings per Share

Our basic earnings per share calculation is computed based on the weighted-average number of common shares outstanding. Our diluted earnings per share calculation is computed based on the weighted-average number of common shares outstanding adjusted by the number of additional shares that would have been outstanding had the potentially dilutive common shares been issued. Potentially dilutive shares of common stock include stock options, nonvested share awards and shares issuable under our ESPP, as well as common shares that would have resulted from the assumed conversion of our convertible debentures. Since the potentially dilutive shares related to the convertible debentures are included in the calculation, the related interest expense, net of tax, is added back to earnings from continuing operations, as the interest would not have been paid if the convertible debentures had been converted to common stock. Nonvested market-based share awards and nonvested performance-based share awards are included in the average diluted shares outstanding each period if established market or performance criteria have been met at the end of the respective periods.

The following table presents a reconciliation of the numerators and denominators of basic and diluted earnings per share from continuing operations in fiscal 2007, 2006 and 2005:

	2007	2006	2005
Numerator:			
Earnings from continuing operations, basic	$1,377	$1,140	$ 934
Adjustment for assumed dilution:			
Interest on convertible debentures due in 2022, net of tax	7	7	7
Earnings from continuing operations, diluted	$1,384	$1,147	$ 941
Denominator (in millions):			
Weighted-average common shares outstanding	482.1	490.3	488.9
Effect of potentially dilutive securities:			
Shares from assumed conversion of convertible debentures	8.8	8.8	8.8
Stock options and other	5.3	5.7	7.3
Weighted-average common shares outstanding, assuming dilution	496.2	504.8	505.0
Basic earnings per share — continuing operations	$ 2.86	$ 2.33	$ 1.91
Diluted earnings per share — continuing operations	$ 2.79	$ 2.27	$ 1.86

$ in millions, except per share amounts

Comprehensive Income

Comprehensive income is computed as net earnings plus certain other items that are recorded directly to shareholders' equity. In addition to net earnings, the significant components of comprehensive income include foreign currency translation adjustments and unrealized gains and losses, net of tax, on available-for-sale marketable equity securities. Foreign currency translation adjustments do not include a provision for income tax expense when earnings from foreign operations are considered to be indefinitely reinvested outside the United States. Comprehensive income was $1,332, $1,252 and $1,047 in fiscal 2007, 2006 and 2005, respectively.

7. Net Interest Income

Net interest income was comprised of the following in fiscal 2007, 2006 and 2005:

	2007	2006	2005
Interest income	$142	$103	$ 45
Interest expense	(31)	(30)	(44)
Dividend income	—	4	—
Net interest income	$111	$ 77	$ 1

8. Leases

The composition of net rent expense for all operating leases, including leases of property and equipment, was as follows in fiscal 2007, 2006 and 2005:

	2007	2006	2005
Minimum rentals	$679	$569	$516
Contingent rentals	1	1	1
Total rent expense	680	570	517
Less: sublease income	(20)	(18)	(16)
Net rent expense	$660	$552	$501

$ in millions, except per share amounts

The future minimum lease payments under our capital, financing and operating leases by fiscal year (not including contingent rentals) at March 3, 2007, were as follows:

Fiscal Year	Capital Leases	Financing Leases	Operating Leases
2008	$ 6	$ 23	$ 741
2009	4	23	715
2010	4	23	672
2011	3	23	632
2012	1	23	592
Thereafter	17	112	3,316
Subtotal	35	227	$6,668
Less: imputed interest	(11)	(56)	
Present value of lease obligations	$24	$171	

Total minimum lease payments have not been reduced by minimum sublease rent income of approximately $119 due under future noncancelable subleases.

10. Income Taxes

The following is a reconciliation of the federal statutory income tax rate to income tax expense from continuing operations in fiscal 2007, 2006 and 2005:

	2007	2006	2005
Federal income tax at the statutory rate	$ 747	$ 603	$ 505
State income taxes, net of federal benefit	38	34	29
Benefit from foreign operations	(36)	(37)	(7)
Non-taxable interest income	(34)	(28)	(22)
Other	37	9	4
Income tax expense	$ 752	$ 581	$ 509
Effective income tax rate	35.3%	33.7%	35.3%

Income tax expense was comprised of the following in fiscal 2007, 2006 and 2005:

	2007	2006	2005
Current:			
Federal	$609	$640	$502
State	45	78	36
Foreign	16	14	(1)
	670	732	537
Deferred:			
Federal	51	(131)	(4)
State	19	(14)	(20)
Foreign	12	(6)	(4)
	82	(151)	(28)
Income tax expense	$752	$581	$509

Deferred taxes are the result of differences between the bases of assets and liabilities for financial reporting and income tax purposes.

BEST BUY

$ in millions, except per share amounts

11. Segment and Geographic Information

Segment Information

We operate two reportable segments: Domestic and International. The Domestic segment is comprised of U.S. store and online operations, including Best Buy, Geek Squad, Magnolia Audio Video and Pacific Sales. The International segment is comprised of all Canada store and online operations, including Best Buy, Future Shop and Geek Squad, as well as our Five Star and Best Buy retail and online operations in China.

The following tables present our business segment information for continuing operations in fiscal 2007, 2006 and 2005:

	2007	2006	2005
Revenue			
Domestic	$31,031	$27,380	$24,616
International	4,903	3,468	2,817
Total revenue	$35,934	$30,848	$27,433
Operating Income			
Domestic	$ 1,889	$ 1,588	$ 1,393
International	110	56	49
Total operating income	1,999	1,644	1,442
Net interest income	111	77	1
Gain on investments	20	—	—
Earnings from continuing operations before income tax expense	$ 2,130	$ 1,721	$ 1,443
Assets			
Domestic	$10,614	$ 9,722	$ 8,372
International	2,956	2,142	1,922
Total assets	$13,570	$11,864	$10,294

12. Contingencies and Commitments

Contingencies

On December 8, 2005, a purported class action lawsuit captioned, *Jasmen Holloway, et cl. v. Best Buy Co., Inc.*, was filed in the U.S. District Court for the Northern District of California alleging we discriminate against women and minority individuals on the basis of gender, race, color and/or national origin with respect to our employment policies and practices. The action seeks an end to discriminatory policies and practices, an award of back and front pay, punitive damages and injunctive relief, including rightful place relief for all class members. As of March 3, 2007, no accrual had been established as it was not possible to estimate the possible loss or range of loss because this matter had not advanced to a stage where we could make any such estimate. We believe the allegations are without merit and intend to defend this action vigorously.

We are involved in various other legal proceedings arising in the normal course of conducting business. We believe the amounts provided in our consolidated financial statements, as prescribed by GAAP, are adequate in light of the probable and estimable liabilities. The resolution of those other proceedings is not expected to have a material impact on our results of operations or financial condition.

Commitments

We engage Accenture LLP ("Accenture") to assist us with improving our operational capabilities and reducing our costs in the information systems, procurement and human resources areas. Our future contractual obligations to Accenture are expected to range from $76 to $334 per year through 2012, the end of the contract period. Prior to our engagement of Accenture, a significant portion of these costs were incurred as part of normal operations.

We had outstanding letters of credit for purchase obligations with a fair value of $85 at March 3, 2007.

At March 3, 2007, we had commitments for the purchase and construction of facilities valued at approximately $69. Also, at March 3, 2007, we had entered into lease commitments for land and buildings for 115 future locations. These lease commitments with real estate developers provide for minimum rentals ranging from seven to 20 years, which if consummated based on current cost estimates, will approximate $84 annually over the initial lease terms. These minimum rentals have been included in the future minimum lease payments included in Note 8, Leases.

Financial Reports

CIRCUIT CITY STORES, INC.

Circuit City Stores, Inc.
CONSOLIDATED BALANCE SHEETS

(Amounts in thousands except share data)	At February 28 2007	2006
ASSETS		
CURRENT ASSETS:		
Cash and cash equivalents	**$ 141,141**	$ 315,970
Short-term investments	**598,341**	521,992
Accounts receivable, net of allowance for doubtful accounts	**382,555**	220,869
Merchandise inventory	**1,636,507**	1,698,026
Deferred income taxes	**34,868**	29,598
Income tax receivable	**42,722**	5,571
Prepaid expenses and other current assets	**47,378**	41,315
TOTAL CURRENT ASSETS	**2,883,512**	2,833,341
Property and equipment, net of accumulated depreciation	**921,027**	839,356
Deferred income taxes	**31,910**	97,889
Goodwill	**121,774**	223,999
Other intangible assets, net of accumulated amortization	**19,285**	30,372
Other assets	**29,775**	44,087
TOTAL ASSETS	**$4,007,283**	$4,069,044
LIABILITIES AND STOCKHOLDERS' EQUITY		
CURRENT LIABILITIES:		
Merchandise payable	**$ 922,205**	$ 850,359
Expenses payable	**281,709**	202,300
Accrued expenses and other current liabilities	**404,444**	379,768
Accrued compensation	**98,509**	84,743
Accrued income taxes	**–**	75,909
Short-term debt	**–**	22,003
Current installments of long-term debt	**7,162**	7,248
TOTAL CURRENT LIABILITIES	**1,714,029**	1,622,330
Long-term debt, excluding current installments	**50,487**	51,985
Accrued straight-line rent and deferred rent credits	**277,636**	256,120
Accrued lease termination costs	**76,326**	79,091
Other liabilities	**97,561**	104,885
TOTAL LIABILITIES	**2,216,039**	2,114,411
Commitments and contingent liabilities		
STOCKHOLDERS' EQUITY:		
Common stock, $0.50 par value; 525,000,000 shares authorized; 170,689,406 shares issued and outstanding (174,789,390 in 2006)	**85,345**	87,395
Additional paid-in capital	**344,144**	458,211
Retained earnings	**1,336,317**	1,364,740
Accumulated other comprehensive income	**25,438**	44,287
TOTAL STOCKHOLDERS' EQUITY	**1,791,244**	1,954,633
TOTAL LIABILITIES AND STOCKHOLDERS' EQUITY	**$4,007,283**	$4,069,044

Circuit City Stores, Inc.
CONSOLIDATED STATEMENTS OF OPERATIONS

	Years Ended February 28					
(Amounts in thousands except per share data)	**2007**	%	2006	%	2005	%
NET SALES	**$12,429,754**	100.0	$11,514,151	100.0	$10,413,524	100.0
Cost of sales, buying and warehousing	**9,501,438**	76.4	8,703,683	75.6	7,861,364	75.5
GROSS PROFIT	**2,928,316**	23.6	2,810,468	24.4	2,552,160	24.5
Selling, general and administrative expenses	**2,841,619**	22.9	2,595,706	22.5	2,470,712	23.7
Impairment of goodwill	**92,000**	0.7	–	–	–	–
Finance income	**–**	–	–	–	5,564	0.1
OPERATING (LOSS) INCOME	**(5,303)**	–	214,762	1.9	87,012	0.8
Interest income	**27,150**	0.2	21,826	0.2	14,404	0.1
Interest expense	**1,519**	–	3,143	–	4,451	–
Earnings from continuing operations before income taxes	**20,328**	0.2	233,445	2.0	96,965	0.9
Income tax expense	**30,510**	0.2	85,996	0.7	36,396	0.3
NET (LOSS) EARNINGS FROM CONTINUING OPERATIONS	**(10,182)**	(0.1)	147,449	1.3	60,569	0.6
EARNINGS (LOSS) FROM DISCONTINUED OPERATIONS, NET OF TAX	**128**	–	(5,350)	–	1,089	–
CUMULATIVE EFFECT OF CHANGE IN ACCOUNTING PRINCIPLES, NET OF TAX	**1,773**	–	(2,353)	–	–	–
NET (LOSS) EARNINGS	**$ (8,281)**	(0.1)	$ 139,746	1.2	$ 61,658	0.6

	2007	2006	2005
Weighted average common shares:			
Basic	**170,448**	177,456	193,466
Diluted	**170,448**	180,653	196,227

	2007	2006	2005
(LOSS) EARNINGS PER SHARE:			
Basic:			
Continuing operations	**$ (0.06)**	$ 0.83	$ 0.31
Discontinued operations	**$ –**	$ (0.03)	$ 0.01
Cumulative effect of change in accounting principles	**$ 0.01**	$ (0.01)	$ –
Basic (loss) earnings per share	**$ (0.05)**	$ 0.79	$ 0.32
Diluted:			
Continuing operations	**$ (0.06)**	$ 0.82	$ 0.31
Discontinued operations	**$ –**	$ (0.03)	$ 0.01
Cumulative effect of change in accounting principles	**$ 0.01**	$ (0.01)	$ –
Diluted (loss) earnings per share	**$ (0.05)**	$ 0.77	$ 0.31

CIRCUIT CITY

Circuit City Stores, Inc.

CONSOLIDATED STATEMENTS OF STOCKHOLDERS' EQUITY AND COMPREHENSIVE INCOME

(Amounts in thousands except per share data)	Common Stock Shares	Common Stock Amount	Additional Paid-in Capital	Retained Earnings	Accumulated Other Comprehensive Income	Total
BALANCE AT FEBRUARY 29, 2004	203,899	$101,950	$922,600	$1,191,904	$ –	$2,216,454
Comprehensive income:						
Net earnings	–	–	–	61,658	–	61,658
Other comprehensive income, net of taxes:						
Foreign currency translation adjustment (net of deferred taxes of $13,707)	–	–	–	–	25,100	25,100
Comprehensive income						86,758
Repurchases of common stock	(19,163)	(9,582)	(250,250)	–	–	(259,832)
Compensation for stock awards	–	–	18,305	–	–	18,305
Exercise of common stock options	3,489	1,745	26,761	–	–	28,506
Shares issued under stock-based incentive plans, net of cancellations, and other	(75)	(38)	(1,312)	–	–	(1,350)
Tax effect from stock issued	–	–	(1,564)	–	–	(1,564)
Shares issued in acquisition of InterTAN, Inc.	–	–	6,498	–	–	6,498
Dividends – common stock ($0.07 per share)	–	–	–	(13,848)	–	(13,848)
BALANCE AT FEBRUARY 28, 2005	188,150	94,075	721,038	1,239,714	25,100	2,079,927
Comprehensive income:						
Net earnings	–	–	–	139,746	–	139,746
Other comprehensive income (loss), net of taxes:						
Foreign currency translation adjustment (net of deferred taxes of $11,316)	–	–	–	–	19,500	19,500
Minimum pension liability adjustment (net of deferred taxes of $182)	–	–	–	–	(313)	(313)
Comprehensive income						158,933
Repurchases of common stock	(19,396)	(9,698)	(328,778)	–	–	(338,476)
Compensation for stock awards	–	–	24,386	–	–	24,386
Exercise of common stock options	3,830	1,915	36,752	–	–	38,667
Shares issued under stock-based incentive plans, net of cancellations, and other	2,205	1,103	(2,160)	–	–	(1,057)
Tax effect from stock issued	–	–	6,973	–	–	6,973
Redemption of preferred share purchase rights	–	–	–	(1,876)	–	(1,876)
Dividends – common stock ($0.07 per share)	–	–	–	(12,844)	–	(12,844)
BALANCE AT FEBRUARY 28, 2006	174,789	87,395	458,211	1,364,740	44,287	1,954,633
Comprehensive loss:						
Net loss	–	–	–	(8,281)	–	(8,281)
Other comprehensive (loss) income, net of taxes:						
Foreign currency translation adjustment (net of deferred taxes of $3,630)	–	–	–	–	(7,793)	(7,793)
Unrealized gain on available-for-sale securities (net of deferred taxes of $219)	–	–	–	–	377	377
Minimum pension liability adjustment (net of deferred taxes of $136)	–	–	–	–	(229)	(229)
Comprehensive loss						(15,926)
Adjustment to initially apply SFAS No. 158 (net of deferred taxes of $6,628)	–	–	–	–	(11,204)	(11,204)
Repurchases of common stock	(10,032)	(5,016)	(232,187)	–	–	(237,203)
Compensation for stock awards	–	–	26,727	–	–	26,727
Adjustment to initially apply SFAS No. 123(R)	–	–	(2,370)	–	–	(2,370)
Exercise of common stock options, net	5,767	2,883	86,228	–	–	89,111
Shares issued under stock-based incentive plans, net of cancellations, and other	165	83	(1,027)	–	–	(944)
Tax effect from stock issued	–	–	8,562	–	–	8,562
Dividends – common stock ($0.115 per share)	–	–	–	(20,142)	–	(20,142)
BALANCE AT FEBRUARY 28, 2007	170,689	$85,345	$344,144	$1,336,317	$25,438	$1,791,244

Circuit City Stores, Inc.

CONSOLIDATED STATEMENTS OF CASH FLOWS

(Amounts in thousands)	Years Ended February 28 **2007**	2006	2005[a]
OPERATING ACTIVITIES:			
Net (loss) earnings	$ **(8,281)**	$ 139,746	$ 61,658
Adjustments to reconcile net (loss) earnings to net cash provided by operating activities of continuing operations:			
Net (earnings) loss from discontinued operations	**(128)**	5,350	(1,089)
Depreciation expense	**177,828**	160,608	151,597
Amortization expense	**3,645**	2,618	1,851
Impairment of goodwill	**92,000**	–	–
Stock-based compensation expense	**26,727**	24,386	18,305
(Gain) loss on dispositions of property and equipment	**(1,439)**	2,370	(206)
Provision for deferred income taxes	**72,717**	(14,252)	(116,300)
Cumulative effect of change in accounting principles	**(1,773)**	2,353	–
Other	**1,689**	(1,726)	–
Changes in operating assets and liabilities:			
Accounts receivable, net	**(133,152)**	16,552	(58,738)
Retained interests in securitized receivables	**–**	–	32,867
Merchandise inventory	**49,352**	(231,114)	160,037
Prepaid expenses and other current assets	**(9,580)**	(17,341)	7,207
Other assets	**535**	(3,061)	3,816
Merchandise payable	**73,317**	211,362	28,199
Expenses payable	**55,722**	40,921	(17,372)
Accrued expenses and other current liabilities, and accrued income taxes	**(81,364)**	43,202	54,021
Other long-term liabilities	**(1,474)**	(17,032)	63,494
NET CASH PROVIDED BY OPERATING ACTIVITIES OF CONTINUING OPERATIONS	**316,341**	364,942	389,347
INVESTING ACTIVITIES:			
Purchases of property and equipment	**(285,725)**	(254,451)	(261,461)
Proceeds from sales of property and equipment	**38,620**	55,421	106,369
Purchases of investment securities	**(2,002,123)**	(1,409,760)	(125,325)
Sales and maturities of investment securities	**1,926,086**	1,014,910	–
Other investing activities	**(11,567)**	–	–
Proceeds from the sale of the private-label finance operation	**–**	–	475,857
Acquisitions, net of cash acquired of $30,615	**–**	–	(262,320)
NET CASH USED IN INVESTING ACTIVITIES OF CONTINUING OPERATIONS	**(334,709)**	(593,880)	(66,880)
FINANCING ACTIVITIES:			
Proceeds from short-term borrowings	**35,657**	73,954	12,329
Principal payments on short-term borrowings	**(56,912)**	(53,893)	(13,458)
Proceeds from long-term debt	**1,216**	1,032	–
Principal payments on long-term debt	**(6,724)**	(1,829)	(28,008)
Changes in overdraft balances	**19,347**	(22,540)	36,329
Repurchases of common stock	**(237,203)**	(338,476)	(259,832)
Issuances of common stock	**89,662**	38,038	27,156
Dividends paid	**(20,126)**	(12,844)	(13,848)
Excess tax benefit from stock-based payments	**15,729**	–	–
Redemption of preferred share purchase rights	**–**	(1,876)	–
Other financing activities	**(1,424)**	–	–
NET CASH USED IN FINANCING ACTIVITIES OF CONTINUING OPERATIONS	**(160,778)**	(318,434)	(239,332)
DISCONTINUED OPERATIONS:			
Operating cash flows	**3,310**	(9,884)	(7,193)
Investing cash flows	**2,958**	(8,089)	(6,615)
Financing cash flows	**(592)**	–	(724)
NET CASH PROVIDED BY (USED IN) DISCONTINUED OPERATIONS	**5,676**	(17,973)	(14,532)
EFFECT OF EXCHANGE RATE CHANGES ON CASH	**(1,359)**	1,655	2,016
(Decrease) increase in cash and cash equivalents	**(174,829)**	(563,690)	70,619
Cash and cash equivalents at beginning of year	**315,970**	879,660	809,041
CASH AND CASH EQUIVALENTS AT END OF YEAR	$ **141,141**	$ 315,970	$879,660

CIRCUIT CITY

RADIOSHACK

RadioShack.

RadioShack Corporation | Financial Reports

CONSOLIDATED BALANCE SHEETS
RadioShack Corporation and Subsidiaries

(In millions, except for share amounts)	December 31, 2006	December 31, 2005
Assets		
Current assets:		
Cash and cash equivalents	$ 472.0	$ 224.0
Accounts and notes receivable, net	247.9	309.4
Inventories	752.1	964.9
Other current assets	127.6	129.0
Total current assets	1,599.6	1,627.3
Property, plant and equipment, net	386.3	476.2
Other assets, net	84.1	101.6
Total assets	$ 2,070.0	$ 2,205.1
Liabilities and Stockholders' Equity		
Current liabilities:		
Short-term debt, including current maturities of long-term debt	$ 194.9	$ 40.9
Accounts payable	254.5	490.9
Accrued expenses and other current liabilities	442.2	379.5
Income taxes payable	92.6	75.0
Total current liabilities	984.2	986.3
Long-term debt, excluding current maturities	345.8	494.9
Other non-current liabilities	86.2	135.1
Total liabilities	1,416.2	1,616.3
Commitments and contingent liabilities		
Stockholders' equity:		
Preferred stock, no par value, 1,000,000 shares authorized:		
Series A junior participating, 300,000 shares designated and none issued	—	—
Common stock, $1 par value, 650,000,000 shares authorized; 191,033,000 shares issued	191.0	191.0
Additional paid-in capital	92.6	87.7
Retained earnings	1,780.9	1,741.4
Treasury stock, at cost; 55,196,000 and 56,071,000 shares, respectively	(1,409.1)	(1,431.6)
Accumulated other comprehensive (loss) income	(1.6)	0.3
Total stockholders' equity	653.8	588.8
Total liabilities and stockholders' equity	$ 2,070.0	$ 2,205.1

RADIOSHACK

CONSOLIDATED STATEMENTS OF INCOME
RadioShack Corporation and Subsidiaries

	Year Ended December 31,					
	2006		2005		2004	
(In millions, except per share amounts)	Dollars	% of Revenues	Dollars	% of Revenues	Dollars	% of Revenues
Net sales and operating revenues	$ 4,777.5	100.0%	$ 5,081.7	100.0%	$ 4,841.2	100.0%
Cost of products sold	2,544.4	53.3	2,706.3	53.3	2,406.7	49.7
Gross profit	2,233.1	46.7	2,375.4	46.7	2,434.5	50.3
Operating expenses:						
Selling, general and administrative	1,903.7	39.8	1,901.7	37.4	1,774.8	36.7
Depreciation and amortization	128.2	2.7	123.8	2.4	101.4	2.1
Impairment of long-lived assets and other charges	44.3	0.9	—	—	—	—
Total operating expenses	2,076.2	43.4	2,025.5	39.8	1,876.2	38.8
Operating income	156.9	3.3	349.9	6.9	558.3	11.5
Interest income	7.4	0.1	5.9	0.1	11.4	0.2
Interest expense	(44.3)	(0.9)	(44.5)	(0.8)	(29.6)	(0.5)
Other (loss) income	(8.6)	(0.2)	10.2	0.2	2.0	—
Income before income taxes	111.4	2.3	321.5	6.4	542.1	11.2
Income tax provision	38.0	0.8	51.6	1.0	204.9	4.2
Income before cumulative effect of change in accounting principle	73.4	1.5	269.9	5.4	337.2	7.0
Cumulative effect of change in accounting principle, net of $1.8 million tax benefit in 2005	—	—	(2.9)	(0.1)	—	—
Net income	$ 73.4	1.5%	$ 267.0	5.3%	$ 337.2	7.0%
Net income per share						
Basic:						
Income before cumulative effect of change in accounting principle	$ 0.54		$ 1.82		$ 2.09	
Cumulative effect of change in accounting principle, net of taxes	—		(0.02)		—	
Basic income per share	$ 0.54		$ 1.80		$ 2.09	
Assuming dilution:						
Income before cumulative effect of change in accounting principle	$ 0.54		$ 1.81		$ 2.08	
Cumulative effect of change in accounting principle, net of taxes	—		(0.02)		—	
Diluted income per share	$ 0.54		$ 1.79		$ 2.08	
Shares used in computing income per share:						
Basic	136.2		148.1		161.0	
Diluted	136.2		148.8		162.5	

CONSOLIDATED STATEMENTS OF STOCKHOLDERS' EQUITY AND COMPREHENSIVE INCOME
RadioShack Corporation and Subsidiaries

	Shares at December 31,			Dollars at December 31,		
(In millions)	2006	2005	2004	2006	2005	2004
Common stock						
Beginning and end of year	191.0	191.0	191.0	$ 191.0	$ 191.0	$ 191.0
Treasury stock						
Beginning of year	(56.0)	(32.8)	(28.5)	$ (1,431.6)	$ (859.4)	$ (707.2)
Purchase of treasury stock	—	(25.3)	(8.0)	—	(625.8)	(246.9)
Issuance of common stock	0.6	1.2	1.3	18.6	31.8	33.8
Exercise of stock options and grant of stock awards	0.2	0.9	2.4	3.9	21.8	60.9
End of year	(55.2)	(56.0)	(32.8)	$ (1,409.1)	$ (1,431.6)	$ (859.4)
Additional paid-in capital						
Beginning of year				$ 87.7	$ 82.7	$ 75.2
Issuance of common stock				(5.7)	3.5	5.7
Exercise of stock options and grant of stock awards				(1.7)	(5.0)	(9.5)
Stock option compensation				12.0	—	—
Stock option income tax benefits				0.3	6.5	11.3
End of year				$ 92.6	$ 87.7	$ 82.7
Retained earnings						
Beginning of year				$ 1,741.4	$ 1,508.1	$ 1,210.6
Net income				73.4	267.0	337.2
Common stock cash dividends declared				(33.9)	(33.7)	(39.7)
End of year				$ 1,780.9	$ 1,741.4	$ 1,508.1
Accumulated other comprehensive (loss) income						
Beginning of year				$ 0.3	$ (0.3)	$ (0.3)
Pension adjustments, net of tax				(1.0)	—	—
Other comprehensive (loss) income				(0.9)	0.6	—
End of year				$ (1.6)	$ 0.3	$ (0.3)
Total stockholders' equity				$ 653.8	$ 588.8	$ 922.1
Comprehensive income						
Net income				$ 73.4	$ 267.0	$ 337.2
Other comprehensive income, net of tax:						
Foreign currency translation adjustments				0.3	(0.4)	0.1
Amortization of gain on cash flow hedge				(0.1)	(0.1)	(0.1)
Unrealized (loss) gain on securities				(1.1)	1.1	—
Other comprehensive (loss) income				(0.9)	0.6	—
Comprehensive income				$ 72.5	$ 267.6	$ 337.2

RADIOSHACK

CONSOLIDATED STATEMENTS OF CASH FLOWS
RadioShack Corporation and Subsidiaries

(In millions)	2006	2005	2004
	Year Ended December 31,		
Cash flows from operating activities:			
Net income	$ 73.4	$ 267.0	$ 337.2
Adjustments to reconcile net income to net cash provided by operating activities:			
Depreciation and amortization	128.2	123.8	101.4
Cumulative effect of change in accounting principle	—	4.7	—
Impairment of long-lived assets and other charges	44.3	—	—
Stock option compensation	12.0	—	—
Deferred income taxes and other items	(27.6)	(76.9)	50.2
Provision for credit losses and bad debts	0.4	0.1	(0.3)
Changes in operating assets and liabilities, excluding acquisitions:			
Accounts and notes receivable	61.8	(68.2)	(53.0)
Inventories	212.8	38.8	(234.2)
Other current assets	2.5	28.5	(7.5)
Accounts payable, accrued expenses, income taxes payable and other	(193.0)	45.1	158.7
Net cash provided by operating activities	314.8	362.9	352.5
Cash flows from investing activities:			
Additions to property, plant and equipment	(91.0)	(170.7)	(229.4)
Proceeds from sale of property, plant and equipment	11.1	226.0	2.5
Purchase of kiosk business	—	—	(59.1)
Other investing activities	0.6	(16.0)	(4.2)
Net cash (used in) provided by investing activities	(79.3)	39.3	(290.2)
Cash flows from financing activities:			
Purchases of treasury stock	—	(625.8)	(251.1)
Sale of treasury stock to employee benefit plans	10.5	30.1	35.4
Proceeds from exercise of stock options	1.7	17.4	50.4
Payments of dividends	(33.9)	(33.7)	(39.7)
Changes in short-term borrowings and outstanding checks in excess of cash balances, net	42.2	(4.0)	(14.0)
Reductions of long-term borrowings	(8.0)	(0.1)	(40.1)
Net cash provided by (used in) financing activities	12.5	(616.1)	(259.1)
Net increase (decrease) in cash and cash equivalents	248.0	(213.9)	(196.8)
Cash and cash equivalents, beginning of period	224.0	437.9	634.7
Cash and cash equivalents, end of period	$ 472.0	$ 224.0	$ 437.9
Supplemental cash flow information:			
Interest paid	$ 44.0	$ 43.4	$ 29.3
Income taxes paid	52.9	158.5	182.7

Apple Financial Report

CONSOLIDATED BALANCE SHEETS
(In millions, except share amounts)

	September 30, 2006	September 24, 2005
ASSETS		
Current assets:		
Cash and cash equivalents	$ 6,392	$ 3,491
Short-term investments	3,718	4,770
Accounts receivable, less allowances of $52 and $46, respectively	1,252	895
Inventories	270	165
Deferred tax assets	607	331
Other current assets	2,270	648
Total current assets	14,509	10,300
Property, plant, and equipment, net	1,281	817
Goodwill	38	69
Acquired intangible assets, net	139	27
Other assets	1,238	303
Total assets	$17,205	$11,516
LIABILITIES AND SHAREHOLDERS' EQUITY		
Current liabilities:		
Accounts payable	$ 3,390	$ 1,779
Accrued expenses	3,081	1,708
Total current liabilities	6,471	3,487
Noncurrent liabilities	750	601
Total liabilities	7,221	4,088
Commitments and contingencies		
Shareholders' equity:		
Common stock, no par value; 1,800,000,000 shares authorized; 855,262,568 and 835,019,364 shares issued and outstanding, respectively	4,355	3,564
Deferred stock compensation	—	(61)
Retained earnings	5,607	3,925
Accumulated other comprehensive income	22	—
Total shareholders' equity	9,984	7,428
Total liabilities and shareholders' equity	$17,205	$11,516

APPLE

CONSOLIDATED STATEMENTS OF OPERATIONS
(In millions, except share and per share amounts)

Three fiscal years ended September 30, 2006	2006	2005	2004
Net sales	$ 19,315	$ 13,931	$ 8,279
Cost of sales	13,717	9,889	6,022
Gross margin	5,598	4,042	2,257
Operating expenses:			
Research and development	712	535	491
Selling, general, and administrative	2,433	1,864	1,430
Restructuring costs	—	—	23
Total operating expenses	3,145	2,399	1,944
Operating income	2,453	1,643	313
Other income and expense	365	165	57
Income before provision for income taxes	2,818	1,808	370
Provision for income taxes	829	480	104
Net income	$ 1,989	$ 1,328	$ 266
Earnings per common share:			
Basic	$ 2.36	$ 1.64	$ 0.36
Diluted	$ 2.27	$ 1.55	$ 0.34
Shares used in computing earnings per share (in thousands):			
Basic	844,058	808,439	743,180
Diluted	877,526	856,878	774,776

CONSOLIDATED STATEMENTS OF SHAREHOLDERS' EQUITY
(In millions, except share amounts which are in thousands)

	Common Stock Shares	Common Stock Amount	Deferred Stock Compensation	Retained Earnings	Accumulated Other Comprehensive Income (Loss)	Total Shareholders' Equity
Balances as of September 27, 2003 as previously reported	733,454	$1,926	$ (62)	$2,394	$(35)	$4,223
Adjustments to opening shareholders' equity	—	85	(22)	(63)	—	—
Balance as of September 27, 2003 as restated	733,454	$2,011	$ (84)	$2,331	$(35)	$4,223
Components of comprehensive income:						
Net income	—	—	—	266	—	266
Change in foreign currency translation	—	—	—	—	13	13
Change in unrealized gain on available-for-sale securities, net of tax	—	—	—	—	(5)	(5)
Change in unrealized loss on derivative investments, net of tax	—	—	—	—	12	12
Total comprehensive income						286
Issuance of stock-based compensation awards	—	63	(63)	—	—	—
Adjustment to common stock related to a prior year acquisition	(159)	(2)	—	—	—	(2)
Stock-based compensation	—	—	46	—	—	46
Common stock issued under stock plans	49,592	427	—	—	—	427
Tax benefit related to stock options	—	83	—	—	—	83
Balances as of September 25, 2004	782,887	$2,582	$(101)	$2,597	$(15)	$5,063
Components of comprehensive income:						
Net income	—	—	—	1,328	—	1,328
Change in foreign currency translation	—	—	—	—	7	7
Change in unrealized gain on derivative investments, net of tax	—	—	—	—	8	8
Total comprehensive income						1,343
Issuance of stock-based compensation awards	—	7	(7)	—	—	—
Stock-based compensation	—	—	47	—	—	47
Common stock issued under stock plans	52,132	547	—	—	—	547
Tax benefit related to stock options	—	428	—	—	—	428
Balances as of September 24, 2005	835,019	$3,564	$ (61)	$3,925	$ —	$7,428
Components of comprehensive income:						
Net income	—	—	—	1,989	—	1,989
Change in foreign currency translation	—	—	—	—	19	19
Change in unrealized gain on available-for-sale securities, net of tax	—	—	—	—	4	4
Change in unrealized loss on derivative investments, net of tax	—	—	—	—	(1)	(1)
Total comprehensive income						2,011
Common stock repurchased	(4,574)	(48)	—	(307)	—	(355)
Stock-based compensation	—	163	—	—	—	163
Deferred compensation	—	(61)	61	—	—	—
Common stock issued under stock plans	24,818	318	—	—	—	318
Tax benefit related to stock-based compensation	—	419	—	—	—	419
Balances as of September 30, 2006	855,263	$4,355	$ —	$5,607	$ 22	$9,984

APPLE

CONSOLIDATED STATEMENTS OF CASH FLOWS
(In millions)

Three fiscal years ended September 30, 2006	2006	2005	2004
Cash and cash equivalents, beginning of the year	$ 3,491	$ 2,969	$ 3,396
Operating Activities:			
Net income	1,989	1,328	266
Adjustments to reconcile net income to cash generated by operating activities:			
Depreciation, amortization and accretion	225	179	150
Stock-based compensation expense	163	49	46
Provision for deferred income taxes	53	50	19
Excess tax benefits from stock options	—	428	83
Gain on sale of PowerSchool net assets	(4)	—	—
Loss on disposition of property, plant, and equipment	15	9	7
Gains on sales of investments, net	—	—	(5)
Changes in operating assets and liabilities:			
Accounts receivable	(357)	(121)	(8)
Inventories	(105)	(64)	(45)
Other current assets	(1,626)	(150)	(176)
Other assets	(1,040)	(35)	(25)
Accounts payable	1,611	328	297
Other liabilities	1,296	534	325
Cash generated by operating activities	2,220	2,535	934
Investing Activities:			
Purchases of short-term investments	(7,255)	(11,470)	(3,270)
Proceeds from maturities of short-term investments	7,226	8,609	1,141
Proceeds from sales of investments	1,086	586	806
Purchases of long-term investments	(25)	—	—
Proceeds from sale of PowerSchool net assets	40	—	—
Purchases of property, plant, and equipment	(657)	(260)	(176)
Other	(58)	(21)	11
Cash generated by (used for) investing activities	357	(2,556)	(1,488)
Financing Activities:			
Payment of long-term debt	—	—	(300)
Proceeds from issuance of common stock	318	543	427
Excess tax benefits from stock-based compensation	361	—	—
Repurchases of common stock	(355)	—	—
Cash generated by financing activities	324	543	127
Increase (decrease) in cash and cash equivalents	2,901	522	(427)
Cash and cash equivalents, end of the year	$ 6,392	$ 3,491	$ 2,969
Supplemental cash flow disclosures:			
Cash paid during the year for interest	$ —	$ —	$ 10
Cash paid (received) for income taxes, net	$ 194	$ 17	$ (7)

B Time Value of Money

Learning Objectives

CAP

Conceptual

C1 Describe the earning of interest and the concepts of present and future values. *(p. B-1)*

Procedural

P1 Apply present value concepts to a single amount by using interest tables. *(p. B-3)*

P2 Apply future value concepts to a single amount by using interest tables. *(p. B-4)*

P3 Apply present value concepts to an annuity by using interest tables. *(p. B-5)*

P4 Apply future value concepts to an annuity by using interest tables. *(p. B-6)*

Appendix Preview

The concepts of present and future values are important to modern business, including the preparation and analysis of financial statements. The purpose of this appendix is to explain, illustrate, and compute present and future values. This appendix applies these concepts with reference to both business and everyday activities.

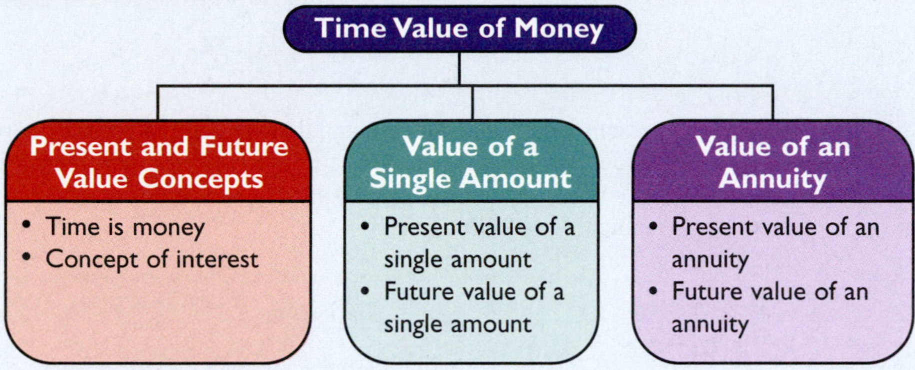

Present and Future Value Concepts

C1 Describe the earning of interest and the concepts of present and future values.

The old saying "Time is money" reflects the notion that as time passes, the values of our assets and liabilities change. This change is due to *interest,* which is a borrower's payment to the owner of an asset for its use. The most common example of interest is a savings account asset. As we keep a balance of cash in the account, it earns interest that the financial institution pays us. An example of a liability is a car loan. As we carry the balance of the loan, we accumulate interest costs on it. We must ultimately repay this loan with interest.

Present and future value computations enable us to measure or estimate the interest component of holding assets or liabilities over time. The present value computation is important when we want to know the value of future-day assets *today.* The future value computation is important when we want to know the value of present-day assets *at a future date.* The first section focuses on the present value of a single amount. The second section focuses on the future value of a single amount. Then both the present and future values of a series of amounts (called an *annuity*) are defined and explained.

Decision Insight

Keep That Job Lottery winners often never work again. Kenny Dukes, a recent Georgia lottery winner, doesn't have that option. He is serving parole for burglary charges, and Georgia requires its parolees to be employed (or in school). For his lottery winnings, Dukes had to choose between $31 million in 30 annual payments or $16 million in one lump sum ($10.6 million after-tax); he chose the latter.

Present Value of a Single Amount

We graphically express the present value, called p, of a single future amount, called f, that is received or paid at a future date in Exhibit B.1.

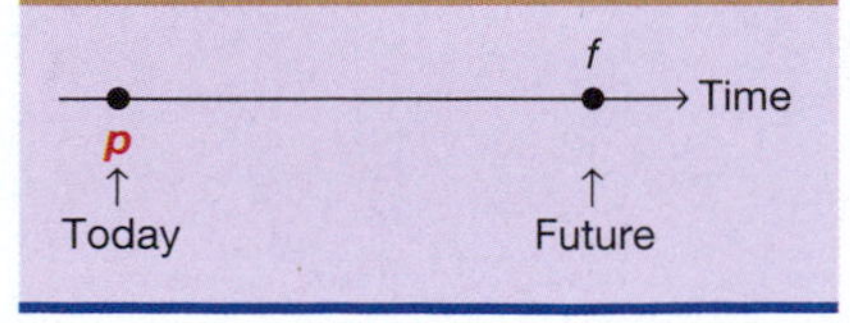

EXHIBIT B.1

Present Value of a Single Amount Diagram

The formula to compute the present value of a single amount is shown in Exhibit B.2, where p = present value; f = future value; i = rate of interest per period; and n = number of periods. (Interest is also called the *discount,* and an interest rate is also called the *discount rate.*)

EXHIBIT B.2

Present Value of a Single Amount Formula

$$p = \frac{f}{(1 + i)^n}$$

To illustrate present value concepts, assume that we need \$220 one period from today. We want to know how much we must invest now, for one period, at an interest rate of 10% to provide for this \$220. For this illustration, the p, or present value, is the unknown amount—the specifics are shown graphically as follows:

(i = 0.10) f = \$220

p = ?

Conceptually, we know p must be less than \$220. This is obvious from the answer to this question: Would we rather have \$220 today or \$220 at some future date? If we had \$220 today, we could invest it and see it grow to something more than \$220 in the future. Therefore, we would prefer the \$220 today. This means that if we were promised \$220 in the future, we would take less than \$220 today. But how much less? To answer that question, we compute an estimate of the present value of the \$220 to be received one period from now using the formula in Exhibit B.2 as follows:

$$p = \frac{f}{(1 + i)^n} = \frac{\$220}{(1 + 0.10)^1} = \$200$$

We interpret this result to say that given an interest rate of 10%, we are indifferent between \$200 today or \$220 at the end of one period.

We can also use this formula to compute the present value for *any number of periods.* To illustrate, consider a payment of \$242 at the end of two periods at 10% interest. The present value of this \$242 to be received two periods from now is computed as follows:

$$p = \frac{f}{(1 + i)^n} = \frac{\$242}{(1 + 0.10)^2} = \$200$$

I will pay your allowance at the end of the month. Do you want to wait or receive its present value today?

Together, these results tell us we are indifferent between \$200 today, or \$220 one period from today, or \$242 two periods from today given a 10% interest rate per period.

The number of periods (n) in the present value formula does not have to be expressed in years. Any period of time such as a day, a month, a quarter, or a year can be used. Whatever period is used, the interest rate (i) must be compounded for the same period. This means that if a situation expresses n in months and i equals 12% per year, then i is transformed into interest earned per month (or 1%). In this case, interest is said to be *compounded monthly.*

A present value table helps us with present value computations. It gives us present values (factors) for a variety of both interest rates (i) and periods (n). Each present value in a present value table assumes that the future value (f) equals 1. When the future value (f) is different from 1, we simply multiply the present value (p) from the table by that future value to give us the estimate. The formula used to construct a table of present values for a single future amount of 1 is shown in Exhibit B.3.

EXHIBIT B.3

Present Value of 1 Formula

$$p = \frac{1}{(1 + i)^n}$$

This formula is identical to that in Exhibit B.2 except that f equals 1. Table B.1 at the end of this appendix is such a present value table. It is often called a **present value of 1 table**. A present value table involves three factors: p, i, and n. Knowing two of these three factors allows us to compute the third. (A fourth is f, but as already explained, we need only multiply the 1 used in the formula by f.) To illustrate the use of a present value table, consider three cases.

P1 Apply present value concepts to a single amount by using interest tables.

Case 1 (solve for p when knowing i and n). To show how we use a present value table, let's look again at how we estimate the present value of \$220 (the f value) at the end of one period ($n = 1$) where the interest rate (i) is 10%. To solve this case, we go to the present value table (Table B.1) and look in the row for 1 period and in the column for 10% interest. Here we find a present value (p) of 0.9091 based on a future value of 1. This means, for instance, that \$1 to be received one period from today at 10% interest is worth \$0.9091 today. Since the future value in this case is not \$1 but \$220, we multiply the 0.9091 by \$220 to get an answer of \$200.

Case 2 (solve for n when knowing p and i). To illustrate, assume a \$100,000 future value (f) that is worth \$13,000 today (p) using an interest rate of 12% (i) but where n is unknown. In particular, we want to know how many periods (n) there are between the present value and the future value. To put this in context, it would fit a situation in which we want to retire with \$100,000 but currently have only \$13,000 that is earning a 12% return and we will be unable to save any additional money. How long will it be before we can retire? To answer this, we go to Table B.1 and look in the 12% interest column. Here we find a column of present values (p) based on a future value of 1. To use the present value table for this solution, we must divide \$13,000 (p) by \$100,000 (f), which equals 0.1300. This is necessary because *a present value table defines* f *equal to 1, and* p *as a fraction of 1.* We look for a value nearest to 0.1300 (p), which we find in the row for 18 periods (n). This means that the present value of \$100,000 at the end of 18 periods at 12% interest is \$13,000; alternatively stated, we must work 18 more years.

Case 3 (solve for i when knowing p and n). In this case, we have, say, a \$120,000 future value (f) worth \$60,000 today (p) when there are nine periods (n) between the present and future values, but the interest rate is unknown. As an example, suppose we want to retire with \$120,000, but we have only \$60,000 and we will be unable to save any additional money, yet we hope to retire in nine years. What interest rate must we earn to retire with \$120,000 in nine years? To answer this, we go to the present value table (Table B.1) and look in the row for nine periods. To use the present value table, we must divide \$60,000 (p) by \$120,000 (f), which equals 0.5000. Recall that this step is necessary because a present value table defines f equal to 1 and p as a fraction of 1. We look for a value in the row for nine periods that is nearest to 0.5000 (p), which we find in the column for 8% interest (i). This means that the present value of \$120,000 at the end of nine periods at 8% interest is \$60,000 or, in our example, we must earn 8% annual interest to retire in nine years.

Quick Check Answer—p. B-7

1. A company is considering an investment expected to yield \$70,000 after six years. If this company demands an 8% return, how much is it willing to pay for this investment?

Future Value of a Single Amount

We must modify the formula for the present value of a single amount to obtain the formula for the future value of a single amount. In particular, we multiply both sides of the equation in Exhibit B.2 by $(1 + i)^n$ to get the result shown in Exhibit B.4.

EXHIBIT B.4

Future Value of a Single Amount Formula

$$f = p \times (1 + i)^n$$

The future value (f) is defined in terms of p, i, and n. We can use this formula to determine that \$200 (p) invested for 1 (n) period at an interest rate of 10% (i) yields a future value of

$220 as follows:

$$\begin{aligned} f &= p \times (1 + i)^n \\ &= \$200 \times (1 + 0.10)^1 \\ &= \$220 \end{aligned}$$

P2 Apply future value concepts to a single amount by using interest tables.

This formula can also be used to compute the future value of an amount for *any number of periods* into the future. To illustrate, assume that $200 is invested for three periods at 10%. The future value of this $200 is $266.20, computed as follows:

$$\begin{aligned} f &= p \times (1 + i)^n \\ &= \$200 \times (1 + 0.10)^3 \\ &= \$266.20 \end{aligned}$$

A future value table makes it easier for us to compute future values (f) for many different combinations of interest rates (i) and time periods (n). Each future value in a future value table assumes the present value (p) is 1. As with a present value table, if the future amount is something other than 1, we simply multiply our answer by that amount. The formula used to construct a table of future values (factors) for a single amount of 1 is in Exhibit B.5.

EXHIBIT B.5

Future Value of 1 Formula

$$f = (1 + i)^n$$

Table B.2 at the end of this appendix shows a table of future values for a current amount of 1. This type of table is called a **future value of 1 table**.

There are some important relations between Tables B.1 and B.2. In Table B.2, for the row where $n = 0$, the future value is 1 for each interest rate. This is so because no interest is earned when time does not pass. We also see that Tables B.1 and B.2 report the same information but in a different manner. In particular, one table is simply the *inverse* of the other. To illustrate this inverse relation, let's say we invest $100 for a period of five years at 12% per year. How much do we expect to have after five years? We can answer this question using Table B.2 by finding the future value (f) of 1, for five periods from now, compounded at 12%. From that table we find $f = 1.7623$. If we start with $100, the amount it accumulates to after five years is $176.23 ($100 × 1.7623). We can alternatively use Table B.1. Here we find that the present value (p) of 1, discounted five periods at 12%, is 0.5674. Recall the inverse relation between present value and future value. This means that $p = 1/f$ (or equivalently, $f = 1/p$). We can compute the future value of $100 invested for five periods at 12% as follows: $f = \$100 \times (1/0.5674) = \$176.24$ (which equals the $176.23 just computed, except for a 1 cent rounding difference).

A future value table involves three factors: f, i, and n. Knowing two of these three factors allows us to compute the third. To illustrate, consider these three possible cases.

Case 1 (solve for f when knowing i and n). Our preceding example fits this case. We found that $100 invested for five periods at 12% interest accumulates to $176.24.

Case 2 (solve for n when knowing f and i). In this case, we have, say, $2,000 ($p$) and we want to know how many periods (n) it will take to accumulate to $3,000 ($f$) at 7% ($i$) interest. To answer this, we go to the future value table (Table B.2) and look in the 7% interest column. Here we find a column of future values (f) based on a present value of 1. To use a future value table, we must divide $3,000 ($f$) by $2,000 ($p$), which equals 1.500. This is necessary because *a future value table defines* p *equal to 1, and* f *as a multiple of 1.* We look for a value nearest to 1.50 (f), which we find in the row for six periods (n). This means that $2,000 invested for six periods at 7% interest accumulates to $3,000.

Case 3 (solve for i when knowing f and n). In this case, we have, say, $2,001 ($p$), and in nine years ($n$) we want to have $4,000 ($f$). What rate of interest must we earn to accomplish this? To answer that, we go to Table B.2 and search in the row for nine periods. To use a future value table, we must divide $4,000 ($f$) by $2,001 ($p$), which equals 1.9990. Recall that this is necessary because a future value table defines p equal to 1 and f as a multiple of 1. We look for a value nearest to 1.9990 (f), which we find in the column for 8% interest (i). This means that $2,001 invested for nine periods at 8% interest accumulates to $4,000.

Quick Check Answer—p. B-7

2. Assume that you win a $150,000 cash sweepstakes. You decide to deposit this cash in an account earning 8% annual interest, and you plan to quit your job when the account equals $555,000. How many years will it be before you can quit working?

Present Value of an Annuity

P3 Apply present value concepts to an annuity by using interest tables.

An *annuity* is a series of equal payments occurring at equal intervals. One example is a series of three annual payments of $100 each. An *ordinary annuity* is defined as equal end-of-period payments at equal intervals. An ordinary annuity of $100 for three periods and its present value (p) are illustrated in Exhibit B.6.

EXHIBIT B.6

Present Value of an Ordinary Annuity Diagram

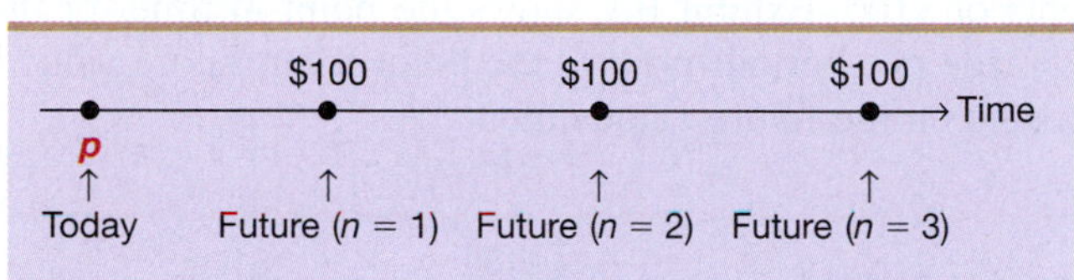

One way to compute the present value of an ordinary annuity is to find the present value of each payment using our present value formula from Exhibit B.3. We then add each of the three present values. To illustrate, let's look at three $100 payments at the end of each of the next three periods with an interest rate of 15%. Our present value computations are

$$p = \frac{\$100}{(1 + 0.15)^1} + \frac{\$100}{(1 + 0.15)^2} + \frac{\$100}{(1 + 0.15)^3} = \$228.32$$

This computation is identical to computing the present value of each payment (from Table B.1) and taking their sum or, alternatively, adding the values from Table B.1 for each of the three payments and multiplying their sum by the $100 annuity payment.

A more direct way is to use a present value of annuity table. Table B.3 at the end of this appendix is one such table. This table is called a **present value of an annuity of 1 table**. If we look at Table B.3 where $n = 3$ and $i = 15\%$, we see the present value is 2.2832. This means that the present value of an annuity of 1 for three periods, with a 15% interest rate, equals 2.2832.

A present value of an annuity formula is used to construct Table B.3. It can also be constructed by adding the amounts in a present value of 1 table. To illustrate, we use Tables B.1 and B.3 to confirm this relation for the prior example:

From Table B.1		From Table B.3	
$i = 15\%, n = 1$	0.8696		
$i = 15\%, n = 2$	0.7561		
$i = 15\%, n = 3$	0.6575		
Total	2.2832	$i = 15\%, n = 3$	2.2832

We can also use business calculators or spreadsheet programs to find the present value of an annuity.

Decision Insight

Better Lucky Than Good "I don't have good luck—I'm blessed," proclaimed Andrew "Jack" Whittaker, 55, a sewage treatment contractor, after winning the largest ever undivided jackpot in a U.S. lottery. Whittaker had to choose between $315 million in 30 annual installments or $170 million in one lump sum ($112 million after-tax).

Quick Check Answer—p. B-7

3. A company is considering an investment paying $10,000 every six months for three years. The first payment would be received in six months. If this company requires an 8% annual return, what is the maximum amount it is willing to pay for this investment?

Future Value of an Annuity

P4 Apply future value concepts to an annuity by using interest tables.

The future value of an *ordinary annuity* is the accumulated value of each annuity payment with interest as of the date of the final payment. To illustrate, let's consider the earlier annuity of three annual payments of $100. Exhibit B.7 shows the point in time for the future value (f). The first payment is made two periods prior to the point when future value is determined, and the final payment occurs on the future value date.

EXHIBIT B.7

Future Value of an Ordinary Annuity Diagram

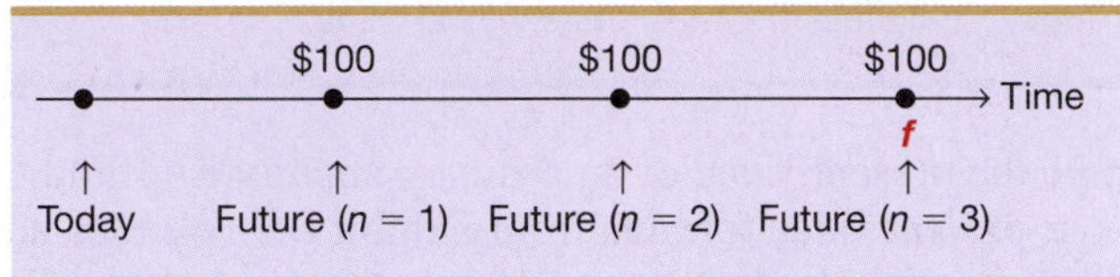

One way to compute the future value of an annuity is to use the formula to find the future value of *each* payment and add them. If we assume an interest rate of 15%, our calculation is

$$f = \$100 \times (1 + 0.15)^2 + \$100 \times (1 + 0.15)^1 + \$100 \times (1 + 0.15)^0 = \$347.25$$

This is identical to using Table B.2 and summing the future values of each payment, or adding the future values of the three payments of 1 and multiplying the sum by $100.

A more direct way is to use a table showing future values of annuities. Such a table is called a **future value of an annuity of 1 table**. Table B.4 at the end of this appendix is one such table. Note that in Table B.4 when $n = 1$, the future values equal 1 ($f = 1$) for all rates of interest. This is so because such an annuity consists of only one payment and the future value is determined on the date of that payment—no time passes between the payment and its future value. The future value of an annuity formula is used to construct Table B.4. We can also construct it by adding the amounts from a future value of 1 table. To illustrate, we use Tables B.2 and B.4 to confirm this relation for the prior example:

From Table B.2		From Table B.4	
i = 15%, n = 0	1.0000		
i = 15%, n = 1	1.1500		
i = 15%, n = 2	1.3225		
Total	3.4725	i = 15%, n = 3	3.4725

Note that the future value in Table B.2 is 1.0000 when $n = 0$, but the future value in Table B.4 is 1.0000 when $n = 1$. Is this a contradiction? No. When $n = 0$ in Table B.2, the future value is determined on the date when a single payment occurs. This means that no interest is earned because no time has passed, and the future value equals the payment. Table B.4 describes annuities with equal payments occurring at the end of each period. When $n = 1$, the annuity has one payment, and its future value equals 1 on the date of its final and only payment. Again, no time passes between the payment and its future value date.

Quick Check

Answer—p. B-7

4. A company invests $45,000 per year for five years at 12% annual interest. Compute the value of this annuity investment at the end of five years.

Summary

C1 Describe the earning of interest and the concepts of present and future values. Interest is payment by a borrower to the owner of an asset for its use. Present and future value computations are a way for us to estimate the interest component of holding assets or liabilities over a period of time.

P1 Apply present value concepts to a single amount by using interest tables. The present value of a single amount received at a future date is the amount that can be invested now at the specified interest rate to yield that future value.

P2 Apply future value concepts to a single amount by using interest tables. The future value of a single amount invested at a specified rate of interest is the amount that would accumulate by the future date.

P3 Apply present value concepts to an annuity by using interest tables. The present value of an annuity is the amount that can be invested now at the specified interest rate to yield that series of equal periodic payments.

P4 Apply future value concepts to an annuity by using interest tables. The future value of an annuity invested at a specific rate of interest is the amount that would accumulate by the date of the final payment.

Guidance Answers to Quick Checks

1. $70,000 × 0.6302 = $44,114 (use Table B.1, $i = 8\%$, $n = 6$).
2. $555,000/$150,000 = 3.7000; Table B.2 shows this value is not achieved until after 17 years at 8% interest.
3. $10,000 × 5.2421 = $52,421 (use Table B.3, $i = 4\%$, $n = 6$).
4. $45,000 × 6.3528 = $285,876 (use Table B.4, $i = 12\%$, $n = 5$).

connect *Most materials in this section are available in McGraw-Hill's Connect*

QUICK STUDY

QS B-1 Identifying interest rates in tables C1

Assume that you must make future value estimates using the *future value of 1 table* (Table B.2). Which interest rate column do you use when working with the following rates?

1. 8% compounded quarterly
2. 12% compounded annually
3. 6% compounded semiannually
4. 12% compounded monthly

QS B-2 Interest rate on an investment P1

Ken Francis is offered the possibility of investing $2,745 today and in return to receive $10,000 after 15 years. What is the annual rate of interest for this investment? (Use Table B.1.)

QS B-3 Number of periods of an investment P1

Megan Brink is offered the possibility of investing $6,651 today at 6% interest per year in a desire to accumulate $10,000. How many years must Brink wait to accumulate $10,000? (Use Table B.1.)

QS B-4 Present value of an amount P1

Flaherty is considering an investment that, if paid for immediately, is expected to return $140,000 five years from now. If Flaherty demands a 9% return, how much is she willing to pay for this investment?

QS B-5 Future value of an amount P2

CII, Inc., invests $630,000 in a project expected to earn a 12% annual rate of return. The earnings will be reinvested in the project each year until the entire investment is liquidated 10 years later. What will the cash proceeds be when the project is liquidated?

QS B-6
Present value of an annuity P3

Beene Distributing is considering a project that will return $150,000 annually at the end of each year for six years. If Beene demands an annual return of 7% and pays for the project immediately, how much is it willing to pay for the project?

QS B-7
Future value of an annuity P4

Claire Fitch is planning to begin an individual retirement program in which she will invest $1,500 at the end of each year. Fitch plans to retire after making 30 annual investments in the program earning a return of 10%. What is the value of the program on the date of the last payment?

Most materials in this section are available in McGraw-Hill's Connect connect

EXERCISES

Exercise B-1
Number of periods of an investment P2

Bill Thompson expects to invest $10,000 at 12% and, at the end of a certain period, receive $96,463. How many years will it be before Thompson receives the payment? (Use Table B.2.)

Exercise B-2
Interest rate on an investment P2

Ed Summers expects to invest $10,000 for 25 years, after which he wants to receive $108,347. What rate of interest must Summers earn? (Use Table B.2.)

Exercise B-3
Interest rate on an investment P3

Jones expects an immediate investment of $57,466 to return $10,000 annually for eight years, with the first payment to be received one year from now. What rate of interest must Jones earn? (Use Table B.3.)

Exercise B-4
Number of periods of an investment P3

Keith Riggins expects an investment of $82,014 to return $10,000 annually for several years. If Riggins earns a return of 10%, how many annual payments will he receive? (Use Table B.3.)

Exercise B-5
Interest rate on an investment P4

Algoe expects to invest $1,000 annually for 40 years to yield an accumulated value of $154,762 on the date of the last investment. For this to occur, what rate of interest must Algoe earn? (Use Table B.4.)

Exercise B-6
Number of periods of an investment P4

Kate Beckwith expects to invest $10,000 annually that will earn 8%. How many annual investments must Beckwith make to accumulate $303,243 on the date of the last investment? (Use Table B.4.)

Exercise B-7
Present value of an annuity P3

Sam Weber finances a new automobile by paying $6,500 cash and agreeing to make 40 monthly payments of $500 each, the first payment to be made one month after the purchase. The loan bears interest at an annual rate of 12%. What is the cost of the automobile?

Exercise B-8
Present value of bonds P1 P3

Spiller Corp. plans to issue 10%, 15-year, $500,000 par value bonds payable that pay interest semiannually on June 30 and December 31. The bonds are dated December 31, 2008, and are issued on that date. If the market rate of interest for the bonds is 8% on the date of issue, what will be the total cash proceeds from the bond issue?

Exercise B-9
Present value of an amount P1

McAdams Company expects to earn 10% per year on an investment that will pay $606,773 six years from now. Use Table B.1 to compute the present value of this investment. (Round the amount to the nearest dollar.)

Exercise B-10
Present value of an amount and of an annuity P1 P3

Compute the amount that can be borrowed under each of the following circumstances:

1. A promise to repay $90,000 seven years from now at an interest rate of 6%.
2. An agreement made on February 1, 2008, to make three separate payments of $20,000 on February 1 of 2009, 2010, and 2011. The annual interest rate is 10%.

Exercise B-11
Present value of an amount P1

On January 1, 2008, a company agrees to pay $20,000 in three years. If the annual interest rate is 10%, determine how much cash the company can borrow with this agreement.

Find the amount of money that can be borrowed today with each of the following separate debt agreements *a* through *f*. (Round amounts to the nearest dollar.)

Exercise B-12
Present value of an amount P1

Case	Single Future Payment	Number of Periods	Interest Rate
a.	$40,000	3	4%
b.	75,000	7	8
c.	52,000	9	10
d.	18,000	2	4
e.	63,000	8	6
f.	89,000	5	2

C&H Ski Club recently borrowed money and agrees to pay it back with a series of six annual payments of $5,000 each. C&H subsequently borrows more money and agrees to pay it back with a series of four annual payments of $7,500 each. The annual interest rate for both loans is 6%.

1. Use Table B.1 to find the present value of these two separate annuities. (Round amounts to the nearest dollar.)

2. Use Table B.3 to find the present value of these two separate annuities. (Round amounts to the nearest dollar.)

Exercise B-13
Present values of annuities
P3

Otto Co. borrows money on April 30, 2008, by promising to make four payments of $13,000 each on November 1, 2008; May 1, 2009; November 1, 2009; and May 1, 2010.

1. How much money is Otto able to borrow if the interest rate is 8%, compounded semiannually?

2. How much money is Otto able to borrow if the interest rate is 12%, compounded semiannually?

3. How much money is Otto able to borrow if the interest rate is 16%, compounded semiannually?

Exercise B-14
Present value with semiannual compounding
C1 P3

Mark Welsch deposits $7,200 in an account that earns interest at an annual rate of 8%, compounded quarterly. The $7,200 plus earned interest must remain in the account 10 years before it can be withdrawn. How much money will be in the account at the end of 10 years?

Exercise B-15
Future value of an amount P2

Kelly Malone plans to have $50 withheld from her monthly paycheck and deposited in a savings account that earns 12% annually, compounded monthly. If Malone continues with her plan for two and one-half years, how much will be accumulated in the account on the date of the last deposit?

Exercise B-16
Future value of an annuity P4

Starr Company decides to establish a fund that it will use 10 years from now to replace an aging production facility. The company will make a $100,000 initial contribution to the fund and plans to make quarterly contributions of $50,000 beginning in three months. The fund earns 12%, compounded quarterly. What will be the value of the fund 10 years from now?

Exercise B-17
Future value of an amount plus an annuity P2 P4

Catten, Inc., invests $163,170 today earning 7% per year for nine years. Use Table B.2 to compute the future value of the investment nine years from now. (Round the amount to the nearest dollar.)

Exercise B-18
Future value of an amount P2

For each of the following situations, identify (1) the case as either (*a*) a present or a future value and (*b*) a single amount or an annuity, (2) the table you would use in your computations (but do not solve the problem), and (3) the interest rate and time periods you would use.

a. You need to accumulate $10,000 for a trip you wish to take in four years. You are able to earn 8% compounded semiannually on your savings. You plan to make only one deposit and let the money accumulate for four years. How would you determine the amount of the one-time deposit?

b. Assume the same facts as in part (*a*) except that you will make semiannual deposits to your savings account.

c. You want to retire after working 40 years with savings in excess of $1,000,000. You expect to save $4,000 a year for 40 years and earn an annual rate of interest of 8%. Will you be able to retire with more than $1,000,000 in 40 years? Explain.

d. A sweepstakes agency names you a grand prize winner. You can take $225,000 immediately or elect to receive annual installments of $30,000 for 20 years. You can earn 10% annually on any investments you make. Which prize do you choose to receive?

Exercise B-19
Using present and future value tables
C1 P1 P2 P3 P4

TABLE B.1

Present Value of 1

$p = 1/(1 + i)^n$

Periods	Rate 1%	2%	3%	4%	5%	6%	7%	8%	9%	10%	12%	15%
1	0.9901	0.9804	0.9709	0.9615	0.9524	0.9434	0.9346	0.9259	0.9174	0.9091	0.8929	0.8696
2	0.9803	0.9612	0.9426	0.9246	0.9070	0.8900	0.8734	0.8573	0.8417	0.8264	0.7972	0.7561
3	0.9706	0.9423	0.9151	0.8890	0.8638	0.8396	0.8163	0.7938	0.7722	0.7513	0.7118	0.6575
4	0.9610	0.9238	0.8885	0.8548	0.8227	0.7921	0.7629	0.7350	0.7084	0.6830	0.6355	0.5718
5	0.9515	0.9057	0.8626	0.8219	0.7835	0.7473	0.7130	0.6806	0.6499	0.6209	0.5674	0.4972
6	0.9420	0.8880	0.8375	0.7903	0.7462	0.7050	0.6663	0.6302	0.5963	0.5645	0.5066	0.4323
7	0.9327	0.8706	0.8131	0.7599	0.7107	0.6651	0.6227	0.5835	0.5470	0.5132	0.4523	0.3759
8	0.9235	0.8535	0.7894	0.7307	0.6768	0.6274	0.5820	0.5403	0.5019	0.4665	0.4039	0.3269
9	0.9143	0.8368	0.7664	0.7026	0.6446	0.5919	0.5439	0.5002	0.4604	0.4241	0.3606	0.2843
10	0.9053	0.8203	0.7441	0.6756	0.6139	0.5584	0.5083	0.4632	0.4224	0.3855	0.3220	0.2472
11	0.8963	0.8043	0.7224	0.6496	0.5847	0.5268	0.4751	0.4289	0.3875	0.3505	0.2875	0.2149
12	0.8874	0.7885	0.7014	0.6246	0.5568	0.4970	0.4440	0.3971	0.3555	0.3186	0.2567	0.1869
13	0.8787	0.7730	0.6810	0.6006	0.5303	0.4688	0.4150	0.3677	0.3262	0.2897	0.2292	0.1625
14	0.8700	0.7579	0.6611	0.5775	0.5051	0.4423	0.3878	0.3405	0.2992	0.2633	0.2046	0.1413
15	0.8613	0.7430	0.6419	0.5553	0.4810	0.4173	0.3624	0.3152	0.2745	0.2394	0.1827	0.1229
16	0.8528	0.7284	0.6232	0.5339	0.4581	0.3936	0.3387	0.2919	0.2519	0.2176	0.1631	0.1069
17	0.8444	0.7142	0.6050	0.5134	0.4363	0.3714	0.3166	0.2703	0.2311	0.1978	0.1456	0.0929
18	0.8360	0.7002	0.5874	0.4936	0.4155	0.3503	0.2959	0.2502	0.2120	0.1799	0.1300	0.0808
19	0.8277	0.6864	0.5703	0.4746	0.3957	0.3305	0.2765	0.2317	0.1945	0.1635	0.1161	0.0703
20	0.8195	0.6730	0.5537	0.4564	0.3769	0.3118	0.2584	0.2145	0.1784	0.1486	0.1037	0.0611
25	0.7798	0.6095	0.4776	0.3751	0.2953	0.2330	0.1842	0.1460	0.1160	0.0923	0.0588	0.0304
30	0.7419	0.5521	0.4120	0.3083	0.2314	0.1741	0.1314	0.0994	0.0754	0.0573	0.0334	0.0151
35	0.7059	0.5000	0.3554	0.2534	0.1813	0.1301	0.0937	0.0676	0.0490	0.0356	0.0189	0.0075
40	0.6717	0.4529	0.3066	0.2083	0.1420	0.0972	0.0668	0.0460	0.0318	0.0221	0.0107	0.0037

TABLE B.2

Future Value of 1

$f = (1 + i)^n$

Periods	Rate 1%	2%	3%	4%	5%	6%	7%	8%	9%	10%	12%	15%
0	1.0000	1.0000	1.0000	1.0000	1.0000	1.0000	1.0000	1.0000	1.0000	1.0000	1.0000	1.0000
1	1.0100	1.0200	1.0300	1.0400	1.0500	1.0600	1.0700	1.0800	1.0900	1.1000	1.1200	1.1500
2	1.0201	1.0404	1.0609	1.0816	1.1025	1.1236	1.1449	1.1664	1.1881	1.2100	1.2544	1.3225
3	1.0303	1.0612	1.0927	1.1249	1.1576	1.1910	1.2250	1.2597	1.2950	1.3310	1.4049	1.5209
4	1.0406	1.0824	1.1255	1.1699	1.2155	1.2625	1.3108	1.3605	1.4116	1.4641	1.5735	1.7490
5	1.0510	1.1041	1.1593	1.2167	1.2763	1.3382	1.4026	1.4693	1.5386	1.6105	1.7623	2.0114
6	1.0615	1.1262	1.1941	1.2653	1.3401	1.4185	1.5007	1.5869	1.6771	1.7716	1.9738	2.3131
7	1.0721	1.1487	1.2299	1.3159	1.4071	1.5036	1.6058	1.7138	1.8280	1.9487	2.2107	2.6600
8	1.0829	1.1717	1.2668	1.3686	1.4775	1.5938	1.7182	1.8509	1.9926	2.1436	2.4760	3.0590
9	1.0937	1.1951	1.3048	1.4233	1.5513	1.6895	1.8385	1.9990	2.1719	2.3579	2.7731	3.5179
10	1.1046	1.2190	1.3439	1.4802	1.6289	1.7908	1.9672	2.1589	2.3674	2.5937	3.1058	4.0456
11	1.1157	1.2434	1.3842	1.5395	1.7103	1.8983	2.1049	2.3316	2.5804	2.8531	3.4785	4.6524
12	1.1268	1.2682	1.4258	1.6010	1.7959	2.0122	2.2522	2.5182	2.8127	3.1384	3.8960	5.3503
13	1.1381	1.2936	1.4685	1.6651	1.8856	2.1329	2.4098	2.7196	3.0658	3.4523	4.3635	6.1528
14	1.1495	1.3195	1.5126	1.7317	1.9799	2.2609	2.5785	2.9372	3.3417	3.7975	4.8871	7.0757
15	1.1610	1.3459	1.5580	1.8009	2.0789	2.3966	2.7590	3.1722	3.6425	4.1772	5.4736	8.1371
16	1.1726	1.3728	1.6047	1.8730	2.1829	2.5404	2.9522	3.4259	3.9703	4.5950	6.1304	9.3576
17	1.1843	1.4002	1.6528	1.9479	2.2920	2.6928	3.1588	3.7000	4.3276	5.0545	6.8660	10.7613
18	1.1961	1.4282	1.7024	2.0258	2.4066	2.8543	3.3799	3.9960	4.7171	5.5599	7.6900	12.3755
19	1.2081	1.4568	1.7535	2.1068	2.5270	3.0256	3.6165	4.3157	5.1417	6.1159	8.6128	14.2318
20	1.2202	1.4859	1.8061	2.1911	2.6533	3.2071	3.8697	4.6610	5.6044	6.7275	9.6463	16.3665
25	1.2824	1.6406	2.0938	2.6658	3.3864	4.2919	5.4274	6.8485	8.6231	10.8347	17.0001	32.9190
30	1.3478	1.8114	2.4273	3.2434	4.3219	5.7435	7.6123	10.0627	13.2677	17.4494	29.9599	66.2118
35	1.4166	1.9999	2.8139	3.9461	5.5160	7.6861	10.6766	14.7853	20.4140	28.1024	52.7996	133.1755
40	1.4889	2.2080	3.2620	4.8010	7.0400	10.2857	14.9745	21.7245	31.4094	45.2593	93.0510	267.8635

$$p = \left[1 - \frac{1}{(1+i)^n}\right] / i$$

TABLE B.3

Present Value of an Annuity of 1

Periods	Rate 1%	2%	3%	4%	5%	6%	7%	8%	9%	10%	12%	15%
1	0.9901	0.9804	0.9709	0.9615	0.9524	0.9434	0.9346	0.9259	0.9174	0.9091	0.8929	0.8696
2	1.9704	1.9416	1.9135	1.8861	1.8594	1.8334	1.8080	1.7833	1.7591	1.7355	1.6901	1.6257
3	2.9410	2.8839	2.8286	2.7751	2.7232	2.6730	2.6243	2.5771	2.5313	2.4869	2.4018	2.2832
4	3.9020	3.8077	3.7171	3.6299	3.5460	3.4651	3.3872	3.3121	3.2397	3.1699	3.0373	2.8550
5	4.8534	4.7135	4.5797	4.4518	4.3295	4.2124	4.1002	3.9927	3.8897	3.7908	3.6048	3.3522
6	5.7955	5.6014	5.4172	5.2421	5.0757	4.9173	4.7665	4.6229	4.4859	4.3553	4.1114	3.7845
7	6.7282	6.4720	6.2303	6.0021	5.7864	5.5824	5.3893	5.2064	5.0330	4.8684	4.5638	4.1604
8	7.6517	7.3255	7.0197	6.7327	6.4632	6.2098	5.9713	5.7466	5.5348	5.3349	4.9676	4.4873
9	8.5660	8.1622	7.7861	7.4353	7.1078	6.8017	6.5152	6.2469	5.9952	5.7590	5.3282	4.7716
10	9.4713	8.9826	8.5302	8.1109	7.7217	7.3601	7.0236	6.7101	6.4177	6.1446	5.6502	5.0188
11	10.3676	9.7868	9.2526	8.7605	8.3064	7.8869	7.4987	7.1390	6.8052	6.4951	5.9377	5.2337
12	11.2551	10.5753	9.9540	9.3851	8.8633	8.3838	7.9427	7.5361	7.1607	6.8137	6.1944	5.4206
13	12.1337	11.3484	10.6350	9.9856	9.3936	8.8527	8.3577	7.9038	7.4869	7.1034	6.4235	5.5831
14	13.0037	12.1062	11.2961	10.5631	9.8986	9.2950	8.7455	8.2442	7.7862	7.3667	6.6282	5.7245
15	13.8651	12.8493	11.9379	11.1184	10.3797	9.7122	9.1079	8.5595	8.0607	7.6061	6.8109	5.8474
16	14.7179	13.5777	12.5611	11.6523	10.8378	10.1059	9.4466	8.8514	8.3126	7.8237	6.9740	5.9542
17	15.5623	14.2919	13.1661	12.1657	11.2741	10.4773	9.7632	9.1216	8.5436	8.0216	7.1196	6.0472
18	16.3983	14.9920	13.7535	12.6593	11.6896	10.8276	10.0591	9.3719	8.7556	8.2014	7.2497	6.1280
19	17.2260	15.6785	14.3238	13.1339	12.0853	11.1581	10.3356	9.6036	8.9501	8.3649	7.3658	6.1982
20	18.0456	16.3514	14.8775	13.5903	12.4622	11.4699	10.5940	9.8181	9.1285	8.5136	7.4694	6.2593
25	22.0232	19.5235	17.4131	15.6221	14.0939	12.7834	11.6536	10.6748	9.8226	9.0770	7.8431	6.4641
30	25.8077	22.3965	19.6004	17.2920	15.3725	13.7648	12.4090	11.2578	10.2737	9.4269	8.0552	6.5660
35	29.4086	24.9986	21.4872	18.6646	16.3742	14.4982	12.9477	11.6546	10.5668	9.6442	8.1755	6.6166
40	32.8347	27.3555	23.1148	19.7928	17.1591	15.0463	13.3317	11.9246	10.7574	9.7791	8.2438	6.6418

$$f = [(1+i)^n - 1] / i$$

TABLE B.4

Future Value of an Annuity of 1

Periods	Rate 1%	2%	3%	4%	5%	6%	7%	8%	9%	10%	12%	15%
1	1.0000	1.0000	1.0000	1.0000	1.0000	1.0000	1.0000	1.0000	1.0000	1.0000	1.0000	1.0000
2	2.0100	2.0200	2.0300	2.0400	2.0500	2.0600	2.0700	2.0800	2.0900	2.1000	2.1200	2.1500
3	3.0301	3.0604	3.0909	3.1216	3.1525	3.1836	3.2149	3.2464	3.2781	3.3100	3.3744	3.4725
4	4.0604	4.1216	4.1836	4.2465	4.3101	4.3746	4.4399	4.5061	4.5731	4.6410	4.7793	4.9934
5	5.1010	5.2040	5.3091	5.4163	5.5256	5.6371	5.7507	5.8666	5.9847	6.1051	6.3528	6.7424
6	6.1520	6.3081	6.4684	6.6330	6.8019	6.9753	7.1533	7.3359	7.5233	7.7156	8.1152	8.7537
7	7.2135	7.4343	7.6625	7.8983	8.1420	8.3938	8.6540	8.9228	9.2004	9.4872	10.0890	11.0668
8	8.2857	8.5830	8.8923	9.2142	9.5491	9.8975	10.2598	10.6366	11.0285	11.4359	12.2997	13.7268
9	9.3685	9.7546	10.1591	10.5828	11.0266	11.4913	11.9780	12.4876	13.0210	13.5795	14.7757	16.7858
10	10.4622	10.9497	11.4639	12.0061	12.5779	13.1808	13.8164	14.4866	15.1929	15.9374	17.5487	20.3037
11	11.5668	12.1687	12.8078	13.4864	14.2068	14.9716	15.7836	16.6455	17.5603	18.5312	20.6546	24.3493
12	12.6825	13.4121	14.1920	15.0258	15.9171	16.8699	17.8885	18.9771	20.1407	21.3843	24.1331	29.0017
13	13.8093	14.6803	15.6178	16.6268	17.7130	18.8821	20.1406	21.4953	22.9534	24.5227	28.0291	34.3519
14	14.9474	15.9739	17.0863	18.2919	19.5986	21.0151	22.5505	24.2149	26.0192	27.9750	32.3926	40.5047
15	16.0969	17.2934	18.5989	20.0236	21.5786	23.2760	25.1290	27.1521	29.3609	31.7725	37.2797	47.5804
16	17.2579	18.6393	20.1569	21.8245	23.6575	25.6725	27.8881	30.3243	33.0034	35.9497	42.7533	55.7175
17	18.4304	20.0121	21.7616	23.6975	25.8404	28.2129	30.8402	33.7502	36.9737	40.5447	48.8837	65.0751
18	19.6147	21.4123	23.4144	25.6454	28.1324	30.9057	33.9990	37.4502	41.3013	45.5992	55.7497	75.8364
19	20.8109	22.8406	25.1169	27.6712	30.5390	33.7600	37.3790	41.4463	46.0185	51.1591	63.4397	88.2118
20	22.0190	24.2974	26.8704	29.7781	33.0660	36.7856	40.9955	45.7620	51.1601	57.2750	72.0524	102.4436
25	28.2432	32.0303	36.4593	41.6459	47.7271	54.8645	63.2490	73.1059	84.7009	98.3471	133.3339	212.7930
30	34.7849	40.5681	47.5754	56.0849	66.4388	79.0582	94.4608	113.2832	136.3075	164.4940	241.3327	434.7451
35	41.6603	49.9945	60.4621	73.6522	90.3203	111.4348	138.2369	172.3168	215.7108	271.0244	431.6635	881.1702
40	48.8864	60.4020	75.4013	95.0255	120.7998	154.7620	199.6351	259.0565	337.8824	442.5926	767.0914	1,779.0903

Glossary

Absorption costing A costing method that includes all manufacturing costs—direct materials, direct labor, and both variable and fixed manufacturing overhead—in unit product costs. Absorption costing is also referred to as the full cost method; also called *full costing. (p. 206)*

Account Record within an accounting system in which increases and decreases are entered and stored in a specific asset, liability, equity, revenue, or expense. *(p. C-3)*

Account balance Difference between total debits and total credits (including the beginning balance) for an account. *(p. C-3)*

Accounting rate of return Rate used to evaluate the acceptability of an investment; equals the after-tax periodic income from a project divided by the average investment in the asset; also called *rate of return on average investment. (p. 395)*

Activity An event that causes the consumption of overhead resources in an entity. *(p. 135)*

Activity-based budgeting (ABB) Budget system based on expected activities. *(p. 251)*

Activity-based costing (ABC) A two-stage costing method in which overhead costs are assigned to products on the basis of the activities required. *(p. 135)*

Activity-based management A management approach that focuses on managing activities as a way of eliminating waste and reducing delays and defects. *(p. 135)*

Activity cost driver An allocation base in an activity-based costing system; a measure of what caused the costs in an activity cost pool. *(p. 139)*

Activity cost pool A grouping of costs that are accumulated and relate to a single activity measure in the activity-based costing system. *(p. 135)*

Activity driver (See *activity cost driver.*) *(p. 139)*

Activity overhead (pool) rate A predetermined overhead rate in activity-based costing; each activity cost pool has its own activity rate that is used to apply overhead to products and services. *(p. 135)*

Annual report Summary of a company's financial results for the year with its current financial condition and future plans; directed to external users of financial information. *(p. A-1)*

Avoidable expense Expense (or cost) that is relevant for decision making; expense that is not incurred if a department, product, or service is eliminated. *(p. 371)*

Balance column account Account with debit and credit columns for recording entries and another column for showing the balance of the account after each entry. *(p. C-10)*

Balanced scorecard A set of performance evaluation measures on four perspectives of a company's strategy: financial, customer, internal process, and learning. *(pp. 323, 332)*

Batch level activities Activities that are performed each time a batch of goods is handled or processed, regardless of how many units are in a batch; the amount of resources used depends on the number of batches run rather than on the number of units in the batch. *(p. 137)*

Break-even point Output level at which sales equals fixed plus variable costs; where income equals zero. *(p. 175)*

Break-even time (BET) Time-based measurement used to evaluate the acceptability of an investment; equals the time expected to pass before the present value of the net cash flows from an investment equals its initial cost. *(p. 402)*

Budget Formal statement of future plans, usually expressed in monetary terms. *(p. 238)*

Budget report Report comparing actual results to planned objectives; sometimes used as a progress report. *(p. 278)*

Budgetary control Management use of budgets to monitor and control company operations. *(p. 278)*

Budgeted balance sheet Accounting report that presents predicted amounts of the company's assets, liabilities, and equity balances as of the end of the budget period. *(p. 250)*

Budgeted income statement Accounting report that presents predicted amounts of the company's revenues and expenses for the budget period. *(p. 250)*

Budgeting Process of planning future business actions and expressing them as formal plans. *(p. 238)*

Business segment Part of a company that can be separately identified by the products or services that it provides or by the geographic markets that it serves; also called *segment. (p. 499)*

Capital budgeting Process of analyzing alternative investments and deciding which assets to acquire or sell. *(p. 392)*

Capital expenditures budget Plan that lists dollar amounts to be both received from disposal of plant assets and spent to purchase plant assets. *(p. 247)*

Cash budget Plan that shows expected cash inflows and outflows during the budget period, including receipts from loans needed to maintain a minimum cash balance and repayments of such loans. *(p. 248)*

Cash flow on total assets Ratio of operating cash flows to average total assets; not sensitive to income recognition and measurement; partly reflects earnings quality. *(p. 442)*

Chart of accounts List of accounts used by a company; includes an identification number for each account. *(p. C-6)*

Clock card Source document used to record the number of hours an employee works and to determine the total labor cost for each pay period. *(p. 54)*

Common stock Corporation's basic ownership share; also generically called *capital stock. (p. C-5)*

Common-size financial statement Statement that expresses each amount as a percent of a base amount. In the balance sheet, total assets is usually the base and is expressed as 100%. In the income statement, net sales is usually the base. *(p. 483)*

Comparative financial statement Statement with data for two or more successive periods placed in side-by-side columns, often with changes shown in dollar amounts and percents. *(p. 478)*

Composite unit Generic unit consisting of a specific number of units of each product; unit comprised in proportion to the expected sales mix of its products. *(p. 182)*

Compound journal entry Journal entry that affects at least three accounts. *(p. C-13)*

Continuous budgeting Practice of preparing budgets for a selected number of future periods and revising those budgets as each period is completed. *(p. 240)*

Continuous improvement Concept requiring every manager and employee continually to look to improve operations. *(p. 8)*

Contribution format An income statement format that is geared to cost behavior in that costs are separated into variable and fixed categories rather than being separated according to the functions of production, sales, and administration. *(p. 216)*

Contribution margin income statement Income statement that separates variable and fixed costs; highlights the contribution margin, which is sales less variable expenses. *(p. 209)*

Contribution margin per unit Amount that the sale of one unit contributes toward recovering fixed costs and earning profit; defined as sales price per unit minus variable expense per unit. *(p. 174)*

Contribution margin ratio Product's contribution margin divided by its sale price. *(p. 174)*

Contribution margin report A managerial statement listing sales less variable expenses, which are the components of contribution margin. *(p. 209)*

Control Process of monitoring planning decisions and evaluating the organization's activities and employees. *(p. 5)*

Controllable costs Costs that a manager has the power to control or at least strongly influence. *(pp. 11, 216, 334)*

Controllable variance Combination of both overhead spending variances (variable and fixed) and the variable overhead efficiency variance. *(p. 291)*

Conversion costs Expenditures incurred in converting raw materials to finished goods; includes direct labor costs and overhead costs. *(p. 16)*

Cost accounting system Accounting system for manufacturing activities based on the perpetual inventory system. *(p. 48)*

Cost-based transfer pricing A method of assigning prices on transfers between divisions within a company based on the cost of the item being transferred. *(p. 340)*

Cost center Department that incurs costs but generates no revenues; common example is the accounting or legal department. *(p. 323)*

Cost driver Variable that causes an activity's cost to go up or down; a causal factor. *(p. 139)*

Cost object Product, process, department, or customer to which costs are assigned. *(pp. 11 & 131)*

Cost of capital The minimum desired rate of return on an investment. *(p. 397)*

Cost of goods manufactured Total manufacturing costs (direct materials, direct labor, and factory overhead) for the period plus beginning goods in process less ending goods in process; also called *net cost of goods manufactured* and *cost of goods completed. (p. 99)*

Cost variance Difference between the actual incurred cost and the standard cost. *(p. 284)*

Cost-volume-profit (CVP) analysis Planning method that includes predicting the volume of activity, the costs incurred, sales earned, and profits received. *(p. 168)*

Cost-volume-profit (CVP) chart Graphic representation of cost-volume-profit relations. *(p. 176)*

Credit Recorded on the right side; an entry that decreases asset and expense accounts, and increases liability, revenue, and most equity accounts; abbreviated Cr. *(p. C-7)*

Creditors Individuals or organizations entitled to receive payments. *(p. C-4)*

Curvilinear cost Cost that changes with volume but not at a constant rate. *(p. 170)*

Customer orientation Company position that its managers and employees be in tune with the changing wants and needs of consumers. *(p. 7)*

CVP chart Graphic representation of cost-volume-profit relations. *(p. 170)*

Cycle efficiency (CE) A measure of production efficiency, which is defined as value-added (process) time divided by total cycle time. *(p. 2)*

Cycle time (CT) A measure of the time to produce a product or service, which is the sum of process time, inspection time, move time, and wait time; also called *throughput time. (p. 21)*

Debit Recorded on the left side; an entry that increases asset and expense accounts, and decreases liability, revenue, and most equity accounts; abbreviated Dr. *(p. C-7)*

Debt ratio Ratio of total liabilities to total assets; used to reflect risk associated with a company's debts. *(p. C-21)*

Debtors Individuals or organizations that owe money. *(pp. 49, C-3)*

Degree of operating leverage (DOL) Ratio of contribution margin divided by pretax income; used to assess the effect on income of changes in sales. *(p. 184)*

Departmental accounting system Accounting system that provides information useful in evaluating the profitability or cost effectiveness of a department. *(p. 322)*

Departmental contribution to overhead Amount by which a department's revenues exceed its direct expenses. *(p. 329)*

Direct costs Costs incurred for the benefit of one specific cost object. *(p. 10)*

Direct expenses Expenses traced to a specific department (object) that are incurred for the sole benefit of that department. *(p. 324)*

Direct labor Efforts of employees who physically convert materials to finished product. *(p. 16)*

Direct labor costs Wages and salaries for direct labor that are separately and readily traced through the production process to finished goods. *(p. 16)*

Direct material Raw material that physically becomes part of the product and is clearly identified with specific products or batches of product. *(p. 16)*

Direct material costs Expenditures for direct material that are separately and readily traced through the production process to finished goods. *(p. 16)*

Direct method Presentation of net cash from operating activities for the statement of cash flows that lists major operating cash receipts less major operating cash payments. *(p. 430)*

Discount rate Expected rate of return on investments; also called *cost of capital, hurdle rate,* or *required rate of return. (p. B-2)*

Dividends Corporation's distributions of assets to its owners. *(p. C-5)*

Double-entry accounting Accounting system in which each transaction affects at least two accounts and has at least one debit and one credit. *(p. C-7)*

Efficiency Company's productivity in using its assets; usually measured relative to how much revenue a certain level of assets generates. *(p. 477)*

Efficiency variance Difference between the actual quantity of an input and the standard quantity of that input. *(p. 291)*

Equity ratio Portion of total assets provided by equity, computed as total equity divided by total assets. *(p. 491)*

Equivalent units of production (EUP) Number of units that would be completed if all effort during a period had been applied to units that were started and finished. *(p. 93)*

Estimated line of cost behavior Line drawn on a graph to visually fit the relation between cost and sales. *(p. 172)*

Ethics Codes of conduct by which actions are judged as right or wrong, fair or unfair, honest or dishonest. *(p. 9)*

Extraordinary gains or losses Gains or losses reported separately from continuing operations because they are both unusual and infrequent. *(p. 499)*

Facility level activities Activities that relate to overall production and cannot be traced to specific products; costs associated with these activities pertain to a plant's general manufacturing process. *(p. 137)*

Factory overhead Factory activities supporting the production process that are not direct material or direct labor; also called *overhead* and *manufacturing overhead. (p. 16)*

Factory overhead costs Expenditures for factory overhead that cannot be separately or readily traced to finished goods; also called *overhead costs. (p. 16)*

Favorable variance Difference in actual revenues or expenses from the budgeted amount that contributes to a higher income. *(p. 279)*

Financing activities Transactions with owners and creditors that include obtaining cash from issuing long-term debt, repaying amounts borrowed, and obtaining cash from or distributing cash to owners. *(p. 426)*

Financial reporting Process of communicating information relevant to investors, creditors, and others in making investment, credit, and business decisions. *(p. 477)*

Financial statement analysis Application of analytical tools to general-purpose financial statements and related data for making business decisions. *(p. 476)*

Finished goods inventory Account that controls the finished goods files, which acts as a subsidiary ledger (of the Inventory account) in which the costs of finished goods that are ready for sale are recorded. *(pp. 14 & 50)*

First-in, first-out (FIFO) Method to assign cost to inventory that assumes items are sold in the order acquired; earliest items purchased are the first sold. *(p. 105)*

Fixed budget Planning budget based on a single predicted amount of volume; unsuitable for evaluations if the actual volume differs from predicted volume. *(p. 279)*

Fixed budget performance report Report that compares actual revenues and costs with fixed budgeted amounts and identifies the differences as favorable or unfavorable variances. *(p. 279)*

Fixed cost Cost that does not change with changes in the volume of activity. *(p. 10)*

Fixed overhead cost deferred in inventory The portion of the fixed manufacturing overhead cost of a period that goes into inventory under the absorption costing method as a result of production exceeding sales. *(p. 213)*

Fixed overhead cost recognized from inventory The portion of the fixed manufacturing overhead cost of a prior period that becomes an expense of the current period under the absorption costing method as a result of sales exceeding production. *(p. 213)*

Flexible budget Budget prepared (using actual volume) once a period is complete that helps managers evaluate past performance; uses fixed and variable costs in determining total costs. *(p. 280)*

Flexible budget performance report Report that compares actual revenues and costs with their variable budgeted amounts based on actual sales volume (or other level of activity) and identifies the differences as variances. *(p. 282)*

Form 10-K (or 10-KSB) Annual report form filed with SEC by businesses (small businesses) with publicly-traded securities. *(p. A-1)*

General accounting system Accounting system for manufacturing activities based on the *periodic* inventory system. *(p. 48)*

General and administrative expense budget Plan that shows predicted operating expenses not included in the selling expenses budget. *(p. 246)*

General journal All-purpose journal for recording the debits and credits of transactions and events. *(p. C-8)*

General ledger (See *ledger.*) *(p. C-3)*

General partner Partner who assumes unlimited liability for the debts of the partnership; responsible for partnership management. *(p. D-3)*

General partnership Partnership in which all partners have mutual agency and unlimited liability for partnership debts. *(p. D-3)*

General-purpose financial statements Statements published periodically for use by a variety of interested parties; includes the income statement, balance sheet, statement of stockholders' equity (or statement of retained earnings), statement of cash flows, and notes to these statements. *(p. 477)*

Goods in process inventory Account in which costs are accumulated for products that are in the process of being produced but are not yet complete; also called *work in process inventory. (pp. 14 & 50)*

High-low method Procedure that yields an estimated line of cost behavior by graphically connecting costs associated with the highest and lowest sales volume. *(p. 172)*

Horizontal analysis Comparison of a company's financial condition and performance across time. *(p. 478)*

Hurdle rate Minimum acceptable rate of return (set by management) for an investment. *(p. 332)*

Incremental cost Additional cost incurred only if a company pursues a specific course of action. *(p. 366)*

Indirect costs Costs incurred for the benefit of more than one cost object. *(p. 10)*

Indirect expenses Expenses incurred for the joint benefit of more than one department (or cost object). *(p. 324)*

Indirect labor Efforts of production employees who do not work specifically on converting direct materials into finished products and who are not clearly identified with specific units or batches of product. *(p. 16)*

Indirect labor costs Labor costs that cannot be physically traced to production of a product or service; included as part of overhead. *(p. 16)*

Indirect material Material used to support the production process but not clearly identified with products or batches of product. *(p. 13)*

Indirect method Presentation that reports net income and then adjusts it by adding and subtracting items to yield net cash from operating activities on the statement of cash flows. *(p. 430)*

Infrequent gain or loss Gain or loss not expected to recur given the operating environment of the business. *(p. 499)*

Institute of management accountants (IMA) A professional association of management accountants. *(p. 9)*

Internal controls or **Internal control system** All policies and procedures used to protect assets, ensure reliable accounting, promote efficient operations, and urge adherence to company policies. *(p. 9)*

Internal rate of return (IRR) Rate used to evaluate the acceptability of an investment; equals the rate that yields a net present value of zero for an investment. *(p. 399)*

Investing activities Transactions that involve purchasing and selling of long-term assets, includes making and collecting notes receivable and investments in other than cash equivalents. *(p. 426)*

Investment center Center of which a manager is responsible for revenues, costs, and asset investments. *(p. 323)*

Investment center residual income The net income an investment center earns above a target return on average invested assets. *(p. 331)*

Investment center return on total assets Center net income divided by average total assets for the center. *(p. 331)*

Investment turnover The efficiency with which a company generates sales from its available assets; computed as sales divided by average invested assets. *(p. 336)*

Job Production of a customized product or service. *(p. 48)*

Job cost sheet Separate record maintained for each job. *(p. 50)*

Job lot Production of more than one unit of a customized product or service. *(p. 49)*

Job order cost accounting system Cost accounting system to determine the cost of producing each job or job lot. *(pp. 50 & 89)*

Job order production Production of special-order products; also called *customized production*. *(p. 48)*

Joint cost Cost incurred to produce or purchase two or more products at the same time. *(p. 341)*

Journal Record in which transactions are entered before they are posted to ledger accounts; also called *book of original entry*. *(p. C-8)*

Journalizing Process of recording transactions in a journal. *(p. C-8)*

Just-in-time (JIT) manufacturing Process of acquiring or producing inventory only when needed. *(p. 8)*

Lean business model Practice of eliminating waste while meeting customer needs and yielding positive company returns. *(p. 8)*

Least-squares regression Statistical method for deriving an estimated line of cost behavior that is more precise than the high-low method and the scatter diagram. *(p. 173)*

Ledger Record containing all accounts (with amounts) for a business; also called *general ledger*. *(p. C-3)*

Limited liability company Organization form that combines select features of a corporation and a limited partnership; provides limited liability to its members (owners), is free of business tax, and allows members to actively participate in management. *(p. D-4)*

Limited liability partnership Partnership in which a partner is not personally liable for malpractice or negligence unless that partner is responsible for providing the service that resulted in the claim. *(p. D-3)*

Limited partners Partners who have no personal liability for partnership debts beyond the amounts they invested in the partnership. *(p. D-3)*

Limited partnership Partnership that has two classes of partners, limited partners and general partners. *(p. D-3)*

Liquidation Process of going out of business; involves selling assets, paying liabilities, and distributing remainder to owners. *(p. D-11)*

Liquidity Availability of resources to meet short-term cash requirements. *(p. 477)*

Management by exception Management process to focus on significant variances and give less attention to areas where performance is close to the standard. *(p. 294)*

Managerial accounting Area of accounting mainly aimed at serving the decision-making needs of internal users; also called *management accounting*. *(p. 4)*

Manufacturing budget Plan that shows the predicted costs for direct materials, direct labor, and overhead to be incurred in manufacturing units in the production budget. *(p. 257)*

Manufacturing statement Report that summarizes the types and amounts of costs incurred in a company's production process for a period; also called *cost of goods manufacturing statement*. *(p. 18)*

Margin of safety Excess of expected sales over the level of break-even sales. *(p. 180)*

Marginal costing (See *variable costing*.) *(p. 206)*

Market-based transfers price A method of assigning prices on transfers between divisions within a company based on the market price of the item being transferred. *(p. 340)*

Market prospects Expectations (both good and bad) about a company's future performance as assessed by users and other interested parties. *(p. 477)*

Markup The difference between selling price and cost; often expressed as a percentage of cost. *(p. 372)*

Master budget Comprehensive business plan that includes specific plans for expected sales, product units to be produced, merchandise (or materials) to be purchased, expenses to be incurred, plant assets to be purchased, and amounts of cash to be borrowed or loans to be repaid, as well as a budgeted income statement and balance sheet. *(p. 242)*

Materials consumption report Document that summarizes the materials a department uses during a reporting period; replaces materials requisitions. *(p. 90)*

Materials ledger card Perpetual record updated each time units are purchased or issued for production use. *(p. 51)*

Materials requisition Source document production managers use to request materials for production; used to assign materials costs to specific jobs or overhead. *(p. 52)*

Merchandise purchases budget Plan that shows the units or costs of merchandise to be purchased by a merchandising company during the budget period. *(p. 245)*

Mixed cost Cost that behaves like a combination of fixed and variable costs. *(p. 169)*

Mutual agency Legal relationship among partners whereby each partner is an agent of the partnership and is able to bind the partnership to contracts within the scope of the partnership's business. *(p. D-3)*

Negotiated transfer price A method of determining prices on transfers between divisions within a company based on negotiations between division managers. *(p. 341)*

Net present value (NPV) Dollar estimate of an asset's value that is used to evaluate the acceptability of an investment; computed by discounting future cash flows from the investment at a satisfactory rate and then subtracting the initial cost of the investment. *(p. 397)*

Non-value-added time The portion of cycle time that is not directed at producing a product or service; equals the sum of inspection time, move time, and wait time. *(p. 21)*

Not controllable costs Costs that a manager does not have the power to control or strongly influence. *(p. 11)*

Operating activities Activities that involve the production or purchase of merchandise and the sale of goods or services to customers, including expenditures related to administering the business. *(p. 425)*

Operating leverage Extent, or relative size, of fixed costs in the total cost structure. *(p. 184)*

Opportunity cost Potential benefit lost by choosing a specific action from two or more alternatives. *(p. 11)*

Out-of-pocket cost Cost incurred or avoided as a result of management's decisions. *(p. 11)*

Overapplied overhead Amount by which the overhead applied to production in a period using the predetermined overhead rate exceeds the actual overhead incurred in a period. *(p. 60)*

Overhead cost variance Difference between the total overhead cost applied to products and the total overhead cost actually incurred. *(p. 290)*

Partner return on equity Partner net income divided by average partner equity for the period. *(p. D-14)*

Partnership Unincorporated association of two or more persons to pursue a business for profit as co-owners. *(p. D-2)*

Partnership contract Agreement among partners that sets terms under which the affairs of the partnership are conducted; also called *articles of partnership*. *(p. D-2)*

Partnership liquidation Dissolution of a partnership by (1) selling noncash assets and allocating any gain or loss according to partners' income-and-loss ratio, (2) paying liabilities, and (3) distributing any remaining cash according to partners' capital balances. *(p. D-12)*

Payback period (PBP) Time-based measurement used to evaluate the acceptability of an investment; equals the time expected to pass before an investment's net cash flows equal its initial cost. *(p. 393)*

Period costs Expenditures identified more with a time period than with finished products costs; includes selling and general administrative expenses. *(p. 11)*

Planning Process of setting goals and preparing to achieve them. *(p. 4)*

Posting Process of transferring journal entry information to the ledger; computerized systems automate this process. *(p. C-8)*

Posting reference (PR) column A column in journals in which individual ledger account numbers are entered when entries are posted to those ledger accounts. *(p. C-10)*

Predetermined overhead rate Rate established prior to the beginning of a period that relates estimated overhead to another variable, such as estimated direct labor, and is used to assign overhead cost to production. *(p. 56)*

Price variance Difference between actual and budgeted revenue or cost caused by the difference between the actual price per unit and the budgeted price per unit. *(p. 282)*

Prime costs Expenditures directly identified with the production of finished goods; include direct materials costs and direct labor costs. *(p. 16)*

Process cost accounting system System of assigning direct materials, direct labor, and overhead to specific processes; total costs associated with each process are then divided by the number of units passing through that process to determine the cost per equivalent unit. *(p. 89)*

Process cost summary Report of costs charged to a department, its equivalent units of production achieved, and the costs assigned to its output. *(p. 98)*

Process operations Processing of products in a continuous (sequential) flow of steps; also called *process operations* or *process production*. *(p. 86)*

Product costs Costs that are capitalized as inventory because they produce benefits expected to have future value; include direct materials, direct labor, and overhead. *(p. 11)*

Production budget Plan that shows the units to be produced each period. *(p. 257)*

Product level activities Activities that relate to specific products that must be carried out regardless of how many units are produced and sold or batches run. *(p. 137)*

Profit center Business unit that incurs costs and generates revenues. *(p. 323)*

Profit margin Ratio of a company's net income to its net sales; the percent of income in each dollar of revenue; also called *net profit margin*. *(p. 336)*

Profitability Company's ability to generate an adequate return on invested capital. *(p. 477)*

Profitability index A measure of the relation between the expected benefits of a project and its investment, computed as the present value of expected future cash flows from the investment divided by the cost of the investment; a higher value indicates a more desirable investment, and a value below 1 indicates an unacceptable project. *(p. 399)*

Quantity variance Difference between actual and budgeted revenue or cost caused by the difference between the actual number of units and the budgeted number of units. *(p. 282)*

Ratio analysis Determination of key relations between financial statement items as reflected in numerical measures. *(p. 478)*

Raw materials inventory Goods a company acquires to use in making products. *(p. 13)*

Relevant benefits Additional or incremental revenue generated by selecting a particular course of action over another. *(p. 365)*

Relevant range of operations Company's normal operating range; excludes extremely high and low volumes not likely to occur. *(p. 177)*

Responsibility accounting budget Report of expected costs and expenses under a manager's control. *(p. 334)*

Responsibility accounting performance report Responsibility report that compares actual costs and expenses for a department with budgeted amounts. *(p. 334)*

Responsibility accounting system System that provides information that management can use to evaluate the performance of a department's manager. *(p. 322)*

Rolling budget New set of budgets a firm adds for the next period (with revisions) to replace the ones that have lapsed. *(p. 240)*

S corporation Corporation that meets special tax qualifications so as to be treated like a partnership for income tax purposes. *(p. D-4)*

Safety stock Quantity of inventory or materials over the minimum needed to satisfy budgeted demand. *(p. 245)*

Sales budget Plan showing the units of goods to be sold or services to be provided; the starting point in the budgeting process for most departments. *(p. 244)*

Sales mix Ratio of sales volumes for the various products sold by a company. *(p. 181)*

Scatter diagram Graph used to display data about past cost behavior and sales as points on a diagram. *(p. 171)*

Selling expense budget Plan that lists the types and amounts of selling expenses expected in the budget period. *(p. 246)*

Solvency Company's long-run financial viability and its ability to cover long-term obligations. *(p. 477)*

Source documents Source of information for accounting entries that can be in either paper or electronic form; also called *business papers. (p. C-2)*

Spending variance Difference between the actual price of an item and its standard price. *(p. 291)*

Standard costs Costs that should be incurred under normal conditions to produce a product or component or to perform a service. *(p. 283)*

Statement of cash flows A financial statement that lists cash inflows (receipts) and cash outflows (payments) during a period; arranged by operating, investing, and financing. *(p. 424)*

Statement of partners' equity Financial statement that shows total capital balances at the beginning of the period, any additional investment by partners, the income or loss of the period, the partners' withdrawals, and the partners' ending capital balances; also called *statement of partners' capital. (p. D-7)*

Step-wise cost Cost that remains fixed over limited ranges of volumes but changes by a lump sum when volume changes occur outside these limited ranges. *(p. 170)*

Sunk cost Cost already incurred and cannot be avoided or changed. *(p. 11)*

T-account Tool used to show sthe effects of transactions and events on individual accounts. *(p. C-7)*

Target cost Maximum allowable cost for a product or service; defined as expected selling price less the desired profit. *(p. 49)*

Time ticket Source document used to report the time an employee spent working on a job or on overhead activities and then to determine the amount of direct labor to charge to the job or the amount of indirect labor to charge to overhead. *(p. 54)*

Total cost method Procedure to establish selling price, where price is set equal to the product's total cost plus a desired profit on that product. *(p. 372)*

Total quality management (TQM) Concept calling for all managers and employees at all stages of operations to strive toward higher standards and reduce number of defects. *(p. 8)*

Transfer price A price on a transfer of goods or services across divisions within a company. *(p. 339)*

Trial balance List of accounts and their balances at a point in time; total debit balances equal total credit balances. *(p. C-17)*

Unavoidable expense Expense (or cost) that is not relevant for business decisions; an expense that would continue even if a department, product, or service is eliminated. *(p. 371)*

Uncontrollable costs Costs that a manager does not have the power to determine or strongly influence. *(pp. 216 & 334)*

Underapplied overhead Amount by which overhead incurred in a period exceeds the overhead applied to that period's production using the predetermined overhead rate. *(p. 59)*

Unearned revenue Liability created when customers pay in advance for products or services; earned when the products or services are later delivered. *(p. C-4)*

Unfavorable variance Difference in revenues or costs, when the actual amount is compared to the budgeted amount, that contributes to a lower income. *(p. 279)*

Unit level activities Activities that arise as a result of the total vloume of goods and services that are produced, and that are performed each time a unit is produced. *(p. 137)*

Unlimited liability Legal relationship among general partners that makes each of them responsible for partnership debts if the other partners are unable to pay their shares. *(p. D-3)*

Unusual gain or loss Gain or loss that is abnormal or unrelated to the company's ordinary activities and environment. *(p. 499)*

Value-added time The portion of cycle time that is directed at producing a product or service; equals process time. *(p. 21)*

Value chain Sequential activities that add value to an entity's products or services; includes design, production, marketing, distribution, and service. *(p. 18)*

Variable cost Cost that changes in proportion to changes in the activity output volume. *(p. 10)*

Variance analysis Process of examining differences between actual and budgeted revenues or costs and describing them in terms of price and quantity differences. *(p. 282)*

Vertical analysis Evaluation of each financial statement item or group of items in terms of a specific base amount. *(p. 478)*

Volume variance Difference between two dollar amounts of fixed overhead cost; one amount is the total budgeted overhead cost, and the other is the overhead cost allocated to products using the predetermined fixed overhead rate. *(p. 291)*

Weighted average contribution margin For multi-product firms, the sum of each product's unit contribution margin multiplied by that product's sales mix percentage. *(p. 182)*

Weighted average method Method to assign inventory cost to sales; the cost of available-for-sale units is divided by the number of units available to determine per unit cost prior to each sale that is then multiplied by the units sold to yield the cost of that sale. *(p. 96)*

Working capital Current assets minus current liabilities at a point in time. *(p. 487)*

Photo Credits

Chapter 1
Page 3 Courtesy of Kernel Seasons
Page 7 AP Images/KEYSTONE/Alessandro Della Bella
Page 13 © Jeff Greenberg/The Image Works
Page 14 © Darrell Ingham/Getty Images
Page 20 GABRIEL BOUYS/AFP/Getty Images

Chapter 2
Page 47 Courtesy of Specialty Surfaces International, Inc. d/b/a Sprinturf
Page 48 Peter Newcomb/Bloomberg News/Landov
Page 55 © Photodisc/Alamy
Page 60 image100/Punchstock

Chapter 3
Page 85 Courtesy of Hood River Juice Company
Page 85 © Grant V. Faint/Getty Images/Iconica
Page 86 © INGO WAGNER/dpa/Landov
Page 90 © Tom Tracy Photography/Alamy
Page 96 © Lester Lefkowitz /Getty Images/Stone
Page 101 © Frederic Pitchal/Sygma/Corbis

Chapter 4
Page 129 Courtesy of Oregon Ice Cream
Page 132 © Philippe Eranian/Corbis
Page 135 © Stock4B/Jupiterimages
Page 137 AP Images/Maurilio Cheli
Page 139 AP Images/Christof Stache
Page 142 © Jan Greune/Getty Images/LOOK

Chapter 5
Page 167 Courtesy of Moe's Southwest Grill
Page 169 © Royalty Free/Corbis
Page 174 © Rob Tringali/Sportschrome/Getty Images
Page 181 © Jonathan Fickies/Getty Images
Page 182 © Nick Onken/Getty Images/UpperCut Images

Chapter 6
Page 205 Warwick Saint/Courtesy of Bonobos
Page 207 © TOSHIFUMI KITAMURA/AFP/Getty Images
Page 210 © Steve Mason/Getty Images
Page 215 © David Young-Wolff/PhotoEdit

Chapter 7
Page 237 AP Images/David Zalubowski
Page 244 © Royalty Free/Corbis
Page 247 Courtesy © BP p.l.c.
Page 248 Jeff Vinnick/Getty Images
Page 249 Jim McIsaac/Getty Images
Page 250 Teo Lannie/Getty Images/PhotoAlto Agency RF Collections

Chapter 8
Page 277 Courtesy of Martin Guitar Co.
Page 280 Ken Samuelsen/PhotoDisc/Getty Images
Page 284 AP Images/David Vincent
Page 286 © Kristjan Maack/Getty Images/Nordic Photos
Page 287 © ColorBlind Images/Corbis
Page 289 © Patrik Giardino/Photolibrary
Page 290 © Nick Daly/Getty Images/Digital Vision
Page 295 © Photodisc/Alamy

Chapter 9
Page 321 Courtesy of RockBottomGolf.com
Page 326 © Christian Hoehn/Getty Images/Stone

Chapter 10
Page 363 Courtesy of Danielle Greenberg/
Prairie Sticks Bat Company
Page 365 © JOHN SOMMERS/Reuters/Corbis
Page 371 © Dimas Ardian/Getty Images
Page 372 © Louie Psihoyos/CORBIS

Chapter 11
Page 391 Courtesy of 1-800-GOT-JUNK?
Page 394 AP Images/Katsumi Kasahara
Page 400 © Philip Lee Harvey/Getty Images/Taxi

Chapter 12
Page 423 Courtesy of Jungle Jim's International Market
Page 424 AP Images/Brian Kersey
Page 430 © Corbis Super RF/Alamy

Chapter 13
Page 475 © Dirck Halstead/Liaison/Getty Images
Page 489 AP Images/Ben Margot
Page 494 AP Images/Chuck Burton

Web Appendix C
Page C-2 Courtesy of Spanx
Page C-5 Courtesy of Spanx
Page C-6 © Jonathan Daniel/Getty Images
Page C-7 Copyright 2007 NBAE.Photo by Joe Murphy/
NBAE via Getty Images

Web Appendix D
Page D-3 © David R. Frazier Photolibrary, Inc./Alamy
Page D-5 © Erik Freeland/Corbis
Page D-8 © Bill Bachmann/Alamy
Page D-11 © James Doberman/Getty Images/Iconica

Index

Note: Page numbers followed by *n* indicate material in footnotes.

Chart of Accounts

Following is a typical chart of accounts. Each company has its own unique accounts and numbering system.

Assets

Current Assets

101 Cash
102 Petty cash
103 Cash equivalents
104 Short-term investments
105 Market adjustment, _______ securities (S-T)
106 Accounts receivable
107 Allowance for doubtful accounts
108 Legal fees receivable
109 Interest receivable
110 Rent receivable
111 Notes receivable
119 Merchandise inventory
120 __________ inventory
121 __________ inventory
124 Office supplies
125 Store supplies
126 _______ supplies
128 Prepaid insurance
129 Prepaid interest
131 Prepaid rent
132 Raw materials inventory
133 Goods in process inventory, _______
134 Goods in process inventory, _______
135 Finished goods inventory

Long-Term Investments

141 Long-term investments
142 Market adjustment, _______ securities (L-T)
144 Investment in _______
145 Bond sinking fund

Plant Assets

151 Automobiles
152 Accumulated depreciation—Automobiles
153 Trucks
154 Accumulated depreciation—Trucks
155 Boats
156 Accumulated depreciation—Boats
157 Professional library
158 Accumulated depreciation—Professional library
159 Law library
160 Accumulated depreciation—Law library
161 Furniture
162 Accumulated depreciation—Furniture
163 Office equipment
164 Accumulated depreciation—Office equipment
165 Store equipment
166 Accumulated depreciation—Store equipment
167 _______ equipment
168 Accumulated depreciation—_______ equipment
169 Machinery
170 Accumulated depreciation—Machinery
173 Building _______
174 Accumulated depreciation—Building _______
175 Building _______
176 Accumulated depreciation—Building _______
179 Land improvements _______
180 Accumulated depreciation—Land improvements _______
181 Land improvements _______
182 Accumulated depreciation—Land improvements _______
183 Land

Natural Resources

185 Mineral deposit
186 Accumulated depletion—Mineral deposit

Intangible Assets

191 Patents
192 Leasehold
193 Franchise
194 Copyrights
195 Leasehold improvements
196 Licenses
197 Accumulated amortization—_______

Liabilities

Current Liabilities

201 Accounts payable
202 Insurance payable
203 Interest payable
204 Legal fees payable
207 Office salaries payable
208 Rent payable
209 Salaries payable
210 Wages payable
211 Accrued payroll payable
214 Estimated warranty liability
215 Income taxes payable
216 Common dividend payable
217 Preferred dividend payable
218 State unemployment taxes payable
219 Employee federal income taxes payable
221 Employee medical insurance payable
222 Employee retirement program payable
223 Employee union dues payable
224 Federal unemployment taxes payable
225 FICA taxes payable
226 Estimated vacation pay liability

Unearned Revenues

230 Unearned consulting fees
231 Unearned legal fees
232 Unearned property management fees
233 Unearned _______ fees
234 Unearned _______ fees
235 Unearned janitorial revenue
236 Unearned _______ revenue
238 Unearned rent

Notes Payable

240 Short-term notes payable
241 Discount on short-term notes payable
245 Notes payable
251 Long-term notes payable
252 Discount on long-term notes payable

Long-Term Liabilities

253 Long-term lease liability
255 Bonds payable
256 Discount on bonds payable
257 Premium on bonds payable
258 Deferred income tax liability

Equity

Owner's Equity

301 _______________, Capital
302 _______________, Withdrawals
303 _______________, Capital
304 _______________, Withdrawals
305 _______________, Capital
306 _______________, Withdrawals

Paid-In Capital

307 Common stock, $ _______ par value
308 Common stock, no-par value
309 Common stock, $ _______ stated value
310 Common stock dividend distributable
311 Paid-in capital in excess of par value, Common stock
312 Paid-in capital in excess of stated value, No-par common stock
313 Paid-in capital from retirement of common stock
314 Paid-in capital, Treasury stock
315 Preferred stock
316 Paid-in capital in excess of par value, Preferred stock

Retained Earnings

318 Retained earnings
319 Cash dividends (or Dividends)
320 Stock dividends

Other Equity Accounts

321 Treasury stock, Common
322 Unrealized gain—Equity
323 Unrealized loss—Equity

Revenues

401 ______________ fees earned
402 ______________ fees earned
403 ______________ services revenue
404 ______________ services revenue
405 Commissions earned
406 Rent revenue (or Rent earned)
407 Dividends revenue (or Dividend earned)
408 Earnings from investment in _______
409 Interest revenue (or Interest earned)
410 Sinking fund earnings
413 Sales
414 Sales returns and allowances
415 Sales discounts

Cost of Sales

Cost of Goods Sold

502 Cost of goods sold
505 Purchases
506 Purchases returns and allowances
507 Purchases discounts
508 Transportation-in

Manufacturing

520 Raw materials purchases
521 Freight-in on raw materials
530 Factory payroll
531 Direct labor
540 Factory overhead
541 Indirect materials
542 Indirect labor
543 Factory insurance expired
544 Factory supervision
545 Factory supplies used
546 Factory utilities
547 Miscellaneous production costs
548 Property taxes on factory building
549 Property taxes on factory equipment
550 Rent on factory building
551 Repairs, factory equipment
552 Small tools written off
560 Depreciation of factory equipment
561 Depreciation of factory building

Standard Cost Variance

580 Direct material quantity variance
581 Direct material price variance
582 Direct labor quantity variance
583 Direct labor price variance
584 Factory overhead volume variance
585 Factory overhead controllable variance

Expenses

Amortization, Depletion, and Depreciation

601 Amortization expense—_______
602 Amortization expense—_______
603 Depletion expense—_______
604 Depreciation expense—Boats
605 Depreciation expense—Automobiles
606 Depreciation expense—Building _______
607 Depreciation expense—Building _______
608 Depreciation expense—Land improvements _______
609 Depreciation expense—Land improvements _______
610 Depreciation expense—Law library
611 Depreciation expense—Trucks
612 Depreciation expense—_______ equipment
613 Depreciation expense—_______ equipment
614 Depreciation expense—_______
615 Depreciation expense—_______

Employee-Related Expenses

620 Office salaries expense
621 Sales salaries expense
622 Salaries expense
623 _______ wages expense
624 Employees' benefits expense
625 Payroll taxes expense

Financial Expenses

630 Cash over and short
631 Discounts lost
632 Factoring fee expense
633 Interest expense

Insurance Expenses

635 Insurance expense—Delivery equipment
636 Insurance expense—Office equipment
637 Insurance expense—_______

Rental Expenses

640 Rent expense
641 Rent expense—Office space
642 Rent expense—Selling space
643 Press rental expense
644 Truck rental expense
645 _______ rental expense

Supplies Expenses

650 Office supplies expense
651 Store supplies expense
652 _______ supplies expense
653 _______ supplies expense

Miscellaneous Expenses

655 Advertising expense
656 Bad debts expense
657 Blueprinting expense
658 Boat expense
659 Collection expense
661 Concessions expense
662 Credit card expense
663 Delivery expense
664 Dumping expense
667 Equipment expense
668 Food and drinks expense
671 Gas and oil expense
672 General and administrative expense
673 Janitorial expense
674 Legal fees expense
676 Mileage expense
677 Miscellaneous expenses
678 Mower and tools expense
679 Operating expense
680 Organization expense
681 Permits expense
682 Postage expense
683 Property taxes expense
684 Repairs expense—_______
685 Repairs expense—_______
687 Selling expense
688 Telephone expense
689 Travel and entertainment expense
690 Utilities expense
691 Warranty expense
695 Income taxes expense

Gains and Losses

701 Gain on retirement of bonds
702 Gain on sale of machinery
703 Gain on sale of investments
704 Gain on sale of trucks
705 Gain on _______
706 Foreign exchange gain or loss
801 Loss on disposal of machinery
802 Loss on exchange of equipment
803 Loss on exchange of _______
804 Loss on sale of notes
805 Loss on retirement of bonds
806 Loss on sale of investments
807 Loss on sale of machinery
808 Loss on _______
809 Unrealized gain—Income
810 Unrealized loss—Income

Clearing Accounts

901 Income summary
902 Manufacturing summary

MANAGERIAL ANALYSES AND REPORTS

① Cost Types

Variable costs:	Total cost changes in proportion to volume of activity
Fixed costs:	Total cost does not change in proportion to volume of activity
Mixed costs:	Cost consists of both a variable and a fixed element

② Cost Sources

Direct materials:	Raw materials costs directly linked to finished product
Direct labor:	Employee costs directly linked to finished product
Overhead:	Costs indirectly linked to finished product

③ Costing Systems

Job order costing:	Costs assigned to each unique unit or batch of units
Process costing:	Costs assigned to similar products that are mass-produced in a continuous manner

④ Costing Ratios

Contribution margin ratio = (Net sales − Variable costs)/Net sales

Predetermined overhead rate = Estimated overhead costs/Estimated activity base

Break-even point in units = Total fixed costs/Contribution margin per unit

⑤ Planning and Control Metrics

Cost variance = Actual cost − Standard (budgeted) cost

Sales (revenue) variance = Actual sales − Standard (budgeted) sales

⑥ Capital Budgeting

Payback period = Time expected to recover investment cost

Accounting rate of return = Expected annual net income/Average annual investment

Net present value (NPV) = Present value of future cash flows − Investment cost

NPV rule:
1. Compute net present value (NPV in $)
2. If NPV $\geq$ 0, then accept project; If NPV $<$ 0, then reject project

Internal rate of return rule:
1. Compute internal rate of return (IRR in %)
2. If IRR $\geq$ hurdle rate, accept project; If IRR $<$ hurdle rate, reject project

⑦ Costing Terminology

Relevant range:	Organization's normal range of operating activity.
Direct cost:	Cost incurred for the benefit of one cost object.
Indirect cost:	Cost incurred for the benefit of more than one cost object.
Product cost:	Cost that is necessary and integral to finished products.
Period cost:	Cost identified more with a time period than with finished products.
Overhead cost:	Cost not separately or directly traceable to a cost object.
Relevant cost:	Cost that is pertinent to a decision.
Opportunity cost:	Benefit lost by choosing an action from two or more alternatives.
Sunk cost:	Cost already incurred that cannot be avoided or changed.
Standard cost:	Cost computed using standard price and standard quantity.
Budget:	Formal statement of an organization's future plans.
Break-even point:	Sales level at which an organization earns zero profit.
Incremental cost:	Cost incurred only if the organization undertakes a certain action.
Transfer price:	Price on transactions between divisions within a company.

⑧ Standard Cost Variances

Total materials variance = Materials price variance + Materials quantity variance

Total labor variance = Labor (rate) variance + Labor efficiency (quantity) variance

Total overhead variance = Overhead controllable variance + Fixed overhead volume variance

Variable overhead variance = Variable overhead spending variance + Variable overhead efficiency variance

Fixed overhead variance = Fixed overhead spending variance + Fixed overhead volume variance

(Variable overhead variance + Fixed overhead variance) = Total overhead variance

Overhead controllable variance = Variable overhead spending variance + Variable overhead efficiency variance + Fixed overhead spending variance

Materials price variance	$= [AQ \times AP] - [AQ \times SP]$
Materials quantity variance	$= [AQ \times SP] - [SQ \times SP]$
Labor (rate) variance	$= [AH \times AR] - [AH \times SR]$
Labor efficiency (quantity) variance	$= [AH \times SR] - [SH \times SR]$
Variable overhead spending variance	$= [AH \times AVR] - [AH \times SVR]$
Variable overhead efficiency variance	$= [AH \times SVR] - [SH \times SVR]$
Fixed overhead spending variance	= Actual overhead − Budgeted overhead
Fixed overhead volume variance	= Budgeted overhead − Applied overhead

where AQ is actual quantity of materials; AP is actual price of materials; AH is actual hours of labor; AR is actual rate of wages; AVR is actual variable rate of overhead; SQ is standard quantity of materials; SP is standard price of materials; SH is standard hours of labor; SR is standard rate of wages; SVR is standard variable rate of overhead.

⑨ Sales Variances

Sales price variance	$= [AS \times AP] - [AS \times BP]$
Sales volume variance	$= [AS \times BP] - [BS \times BP]$

where AS = actual sales units; AP = actual sales price; BP = budgeted sales price; BS = budgeted sales units (fixed budget)

Manufacturing Statement
For _period_ Ended _date_

Direct materials	
Raw materials inventory, Beginning	$ #
Raw materials purchases	#
Raw materials available for use	#
Raw materials inventory, Ending	(#)
Direct materials used	#
Direct labor	#
Overhead costs	
Total overhead costs	#
Total manufacturing costs	#
Add goods in process inventory, Beginning	#
Total cost of goods in process	#
Deduct goods in process inventory, Ending	(#)
Cost of goods manufactured	$ #

Contribution Margin Income Statement
For _period_ Ended _date_

Net sales (revenues)	$ #
Total variable costs	#
Contribution margin	#
Total fixed costs	#
Net income	$ #

Flexible Budget
For _period_ Ended _date_

	Flexible Budget: Variable Amount per Unit	Flexible Budget: Fixed Cost	Flexible Budget for Unit Sales of #
Sales (revenues)	$ #		$ #
Variable costs			
Examples: Direct materials, Direct labor,			
Other variable costs	#		#
Total variable costs	#		#
Contribution margin	$ #		#
Fixed costs			
Examples: Depreciation, Manager		$ #	#
salaries, Administrative salaries		#	#
Total fixed costs		$ #	#
Income from operations			$ #

Fixed Budget Performance Report
For _period_ Ended _date_

	Fixed Budget	Actual Performance	Variances†
Sales: In units	#	#	
In dollars	$ #	$ #	$ # F or U
Cost of sales			
Direct costs	#	#	# F or U
Indirect costs	#	#	# F or U
Selling expenses			
Examples: Commissions,	#	#	# F or U
Shipping expenses	#	#	# F or U
General and administrative expenses			
Examples: Administrative salaries	#	#	# F or U
Total expenses	$ #	$ #	$ # F or U
Income from operations	$ #	$ #	$ # F or U

†*F = Favorable variance; U = Unfavorable variance.*

Master Budget Sequence

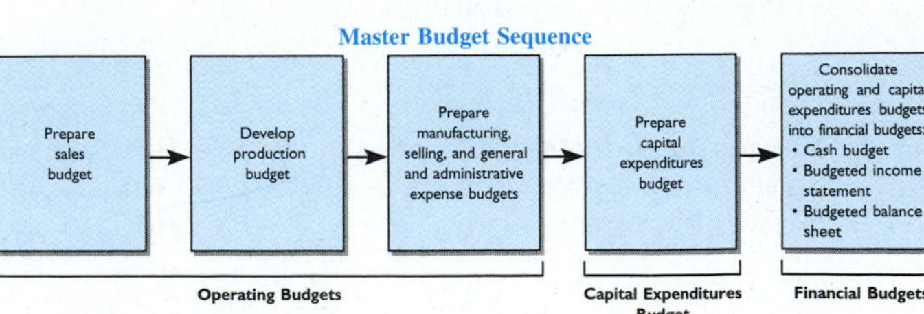